KEY TO WORLD MAP PAGES

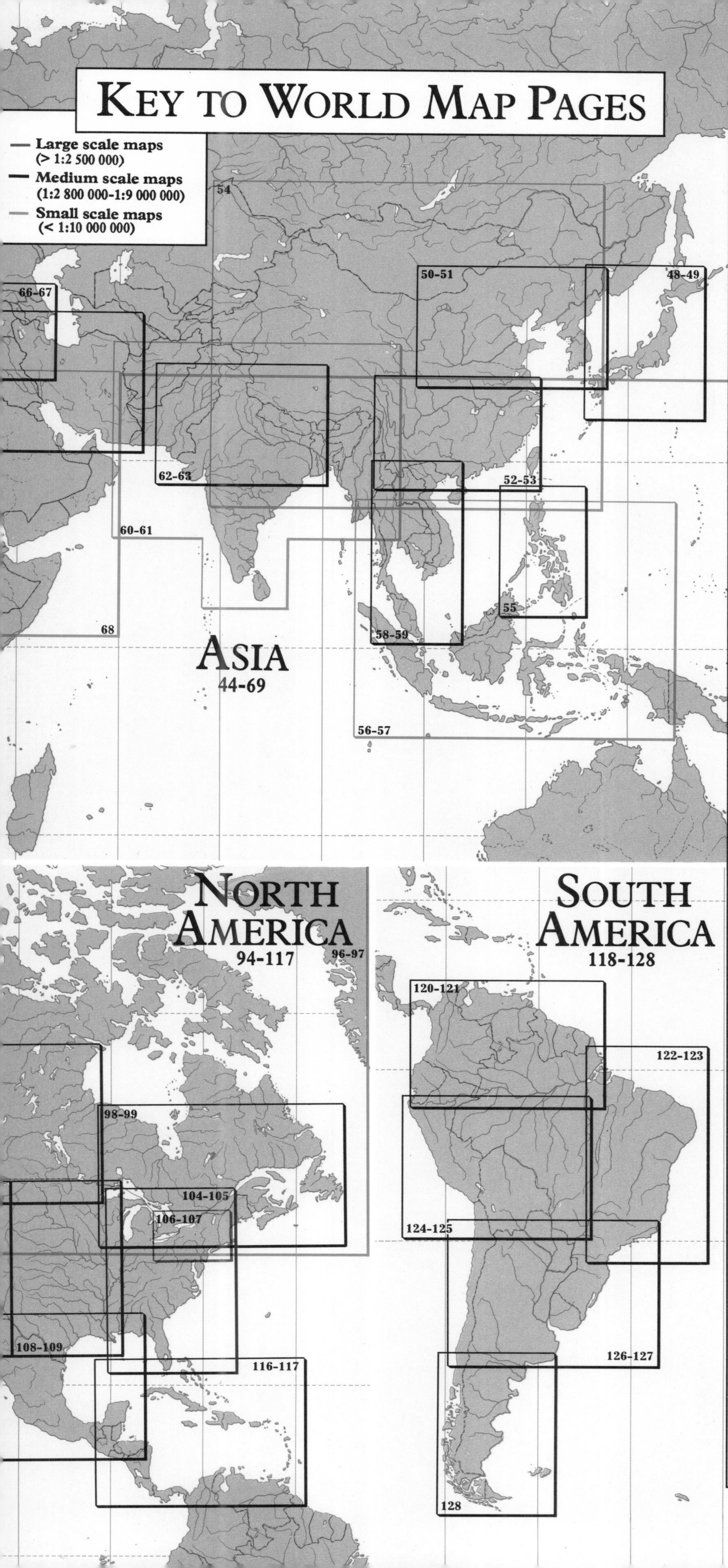

— **Large scale maps**
(> 1:2 500 000)

— **Medium scale maps**
(1:2 800 000–1:9 000 000)

— **Small scale maps**
(< 1:10 000 000)

54

66–67

50–51

48–49

62–63

52–53

60–61

55

58–59

56–57

68

ASIA
44–69

NORTH AMERICA
94–117

96–97

98–99

104–105

106–107

108–109

116–117

SOUTH AMERICA
118–128

120–121

122–123

124–125

126–127

128

COUNTRY INDEX

Afghanistan	60	Kyrgyzstan	44
Albania	38–39		
Algeria	74–75	Laos	58
Angola	80–81	Latvia	40
Argentina	126, 128	Lebanon	69
Armenia	67	Lesotho	85
Australia	88–91	Liberia	78
Austria	19, 20–21	Libya	73
Azerbaijan	67	Lithuania	40
		Luxembourg	17
Bahamas	116–117		
Bahrain	65	Macedonia	38–39
Bangladesh	61	Madagascar	85
Barbados	117	Malawi	83
Belarus	40	Malaysia	55–56
Belgium	17	Mali	78–79
Belize	116	Malta	37
Benin	79	Mauritania	78
Bhutan	61	Mauritius	71
Bolivia	124–125	Mexico	114–115
Bosnia-		Moldova	41
Herzegovina	21	Mongolia	54
Botswana	84–85	Morocco	74
Brazil	120–127	Mozambique	83
Brunei	56		
Bulgaria	38–39	Namibia	84
Burkina Faso	78–79	Nepal	63
Burma	61	Netherlands	16–17
Burundi	82	New Zealand	87
		Nicaragua	116
Cambodia	58–59	Niger	79
Cameroon	82	Nigeria	79
Canada	96–101	Northern Ireland	15
Central African		Norway	8–9
Republic	82		
Chad	73	Oman	68
Chile	126, 128		
China	50–54	Pakistan	62
Colombia	120	Panama	116
Congo	80	Papua New Guinea	86
Costa Rica	116	Paraguay	126–127
Croatia	21	Peru	124
Cuba	116–117	Philippines	55
Cyprus	37	Poland	20
Czech Republic	20–21	Portugal	30–31
		Puerto Rico	117
Denmark	11		
Djibouti	68	Qatar	65
Dominican			
Republic	117	Romania	38
		Russia	40–45
Ecuador	120	Rwanda	82
Egypt	76		
El Salvador	116	Saudi Arabia	68
England	12–13	Scotland	14
Equatorial Guinea	80	Senegal	78
Eritrea	76–77	Sierra Leone	78
Estonia	40	Singapore	59
Ethiopia	68, 77	Slovak Republic	20–21
		Slovenia	33
Fiji	87	Somali Republic	68
Finland	8–9	South Africa	84–85
France	24–27	Spain	28–31
French Guiana	121	Sri Lanka	60
		Sudan	77
Gabon	80	Surinam	121
Gambia	78	Swaziland	85
Georgia	43	Sweden	8–9
Germany	18–19	Switzerland	22–23
Ghana	78–79	Syria	67
Greece	39		
Greenland	4	Taiwan	53
Guatemala	116	Tajikistan	44
Guinea	78	Tanzania	82–83
Guinea-Bissau	78	Thailand	58–59
Guyana	121	Togo	79
		Trinidad and	
Haiti	117	Tobago	117
Honduras	116	Tunisia	75
Hong Kong	53	Turkey	66–67
Hungary	21	Turkmenistan	44
Iceland	8	Uganda	82
India	60–63	Ukraine	41
Indonesia	56–57	United Arab Emirates	65
Iran	64–65	United Kingdom	12–15
Iraq	64–65	USA	102–113
Irish Republic	15	Uruguay	126–127
Israel	69	Uzbekistan	44
Italy	32–35		
Ivory Coast	78	Venezuela	120–121
		Vietnam	58–59
Jamaica	116		
Japan	48–49	Wales	12–13
Jordan	69		
		Yemen	68
Kazakhstan	44	Yugoslavia	38–39
Kenya	82		
Korea, North	51	Zaïre	80–81
Korea, South	51	Zambia	83
Kuwait	64–65	Zimbabwe	83

PHILIP'S

CONCISE WORLD ATLAS

This edition published 1995
by BCA by arrangement with
George Philip Limited,
an imprint of Reed Books

Cartography by Philip's

Copyright © 1995 Reed International Books Limited

CN 2379

Produced by Mandarin Offset
Printed and bound in China

PHILIP'S
CONCISE WORLD ATLAS

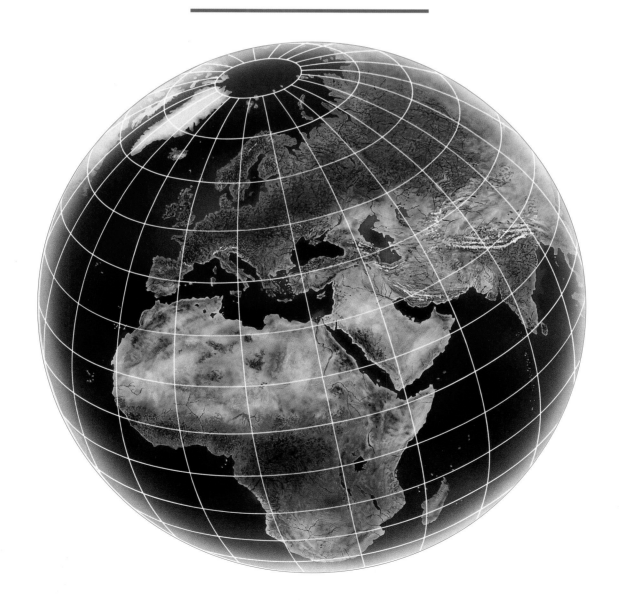

BCA

LONDON NEW YORK SYDNEY TORONTO

CONTENTS

WORLD STATISTICS

Countries vi
Physical
Dimensions vii
Philip's World Maps viii

WORLD MAPS

1–128

Map Symbols
1

The World: Political
1:71 100 000
2–3

Arctic Ocean 1:31 100 000
4

Antarctica 1:31 100 000
5

EUROPE

Europe: Physical
1:17 800 000
6

Europe: Political
1:17 800 000
7

Scandinavia 1:4 400 000

8–9

Denmark and Southern Sweden 1:2 200 000

10–11

England and Wales
1:1 800 000

12–13

Scotland 1:1 800 000

14

Ireland 1:1 800 000

15

Netherlands, Belgium and Luxembourg 1:1 100 000

16–17

Germany 1:2 200 000

18–19

Middle Europe 1:3 100 000

20–21

Switzerland 1:900 000

22–23

Northern France 1:2 200 000

24–25

Southern France 1:2 200 000

26–27

Eastern Spain 1:2 200 000

28–29

Western Spain and Portugal 1:2 200 000

30–31

Northern Italy, Slovenia and Croatia
1:2 200 000

32–33

Southern Italy 1:2 200 000

34–35

Balearics, Canaries and Madeira 1:900 000 / 1:1 800 000

36

Malta, Crete, Corfu, Rhodes and Cyprus
1:900 000 / 1:1 200 000

37

The Balkans 1:3 100 000

38–39

Baltic States, Belarus and Ukraine 1:4 400 000

40–41

Volga Basin and the Caucasus 1:4 400 000

42–43

ASIA

Russia and Central Asia
1:17 800 000

44–45

Asia: Physical
1:44 400 000
46

Asia: Political
1:44 400 000
47

Japan 1:4 400 000

48–49

Northern China and Korea
1:5 300 000

50–51

Southern China 1:5 300 000

52–53

China 1:17 800 000

54

Philippines 1:6 700 000

55

Indonesia 1:11 100 000

56–57

Mainland South-East Asia
1:5 300 000

58–59

South Asia 1:8 900 000

60–61

The Indo-Gangetic Plain
1:5 300 000

62–63

The Middle East 1:6 200 000

64–65

Turkey and Transcaucasia 1:4 400 000

66–67

Arabia and the Horn of Africa 1:13 300 000

68

The Near East 1:2 200 000

69

AFRICA

Africa: Physical
1:37 300 000
70

Africa: Political
1:37 300 000
71

Northern Africa 1:13 300 000

72–73

North-West Africa
1:7 100 000

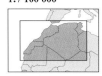

74–75

The Nile Valley 1:7 100 000
The Nile Delta 1:3 600 000

76–77

West Africa 1:7 100 000

78–79

Central and Southern Africa 1:13 300 000

80–81

East Africa 1:7 100 000

82–83

Southern Africa 1:7 100 000
Madagascar 1:7 100 000

84–85

AUSTRALIA AND OCEANIA

Australia and Oceania: Physical and Political
1:44 400 000
86

New Zealand 1:5 300 000

87

Western Australia
1:7 100 000

88–89

Eastern Australia 1:7 100 000

90–91

Pacific Ocean 1:48 000 000
92–93

NORTH AMERICA

North America: Physical
1:31 100 000
94

North America: Political
1:31 100 000
95

Canada 1:13 300 000
Alaska 1:26 700 000

96–97

Eastern Canada 1:6 200 000

98–99

Western Canada 1:6 200 000

100–101

United States 1:10 700 000
Hawaii 1:8 900 000

102–103

Eastern United States
1:5 300 000

104–105

North-Eastern United States 1:2 200 000

106–107

Middle United States
1:5 300 000

108–109

Western United States
1:5 300 000

110–111

Central and Southern California and Washington 1:2 200 000

112–113

Mexico 1:7 100 000

114–115

Central America and the West Indies 1:7 100 000

116–117

SOUTH AMERICA

South America: Physical
1:31 100 000
118

South America: Political
1:31 100 000
119

South America – North-West 1:7 100 000

120–121

Eastern Brazil 1:7 100 000

122–123

South America – West
1:7 100 000

124–125

Central South America
1:7 100 000

126–127

Southern Chile and Argentina 1:7 100 000

128

INDEX TO WORLD MAPS
129–224

World: Regions in the News 225

WORLD STATISTICS: COUNTRIES

This alphabetical list includes all the countries and territories of the world. If a territory is not completely independent, then the country it is associated with is named. The area figures give the total area of land, inland water and ice. Units for areas and populations are thousands. The annual income is the Gross National Product per capita in US dollars. The figures are the latest available, usually 1994.

Country/Territory	Area km² Thousands	Area miles² Thousands	Population Thousands	Capital	Annual Income US $
Adélie Land (Fr.)	432	167	0.03	–	–
Afghanistan	652	252	18,879	Kabul	450
Albania	28.8	11.1	3,414	Tirana	820
Algeria	2,382	920	27,325	Algiers	1,840
American Samoa (US)	0.20	0.08	53	Pago Pago	6,000
Amsterdam Is. (Fr.)	0.05	0.02	0.03	–	–
Andorra	0.45	0.17	65	Andorra la Vella	14,000
Angola	1,247	481	10,674	Luanda	620
Anguilla (UK)	0.1	0.04	8	The Valley	6,800
Antigua & Barbuda	0.44	0.17	65	St John's	4,770
Argentina	2,767	1,068	34,182	Buenos Aires	2,780
Armenia	29.8	11.5	3,548	Yerevan	780
Aruba (Neths)	0.19	0.07	69	Oranjestad	6,000
Ascension Is. (UK)	0.09	0.03	1.5	Georgetown	–
Australia	7,687	2,968	17,847	Canberra	17,260
Australian Antarctic Territory	6,120	2,363	0	–	–
Austria	83.9	32.4	7,918	Vienna	22,380
Azerbaijan	86.6	33.4	7,472	Baku	740
Azores (Port.)	2.2	0.87	238	Ponta Delgada	–
Bahamas	13.9	5.4	272	Nassau	12,070
Bahrain	0.68	0.26	549	Manama	6,910
Bangladesh	144	56	117,787	Dhaka	220
Barbados	0.43	0.17	261	Bridgetown	6,540
Belarus	207.6	80.1	10,163	Minsk	2,930
Belgium	30.5	11.8	10,080	Brussels	20,880
Belize	23	8.9	210	Belmopan	2,220
Benin	113	43	5,246	Porto-Novo	410
Bermuda (UK)	0.05	0.02	63	Hamilton	27,800
Bhutan	47	18.1	1,614	Thimphu	180
Bolivia	1,099	424	7,237	La Paz/Sucre	680
Bosnia-Herzegovina	51	20	3,527	Sarajevo	2,454
Botswana	582	225	1,443	Gaborone	2,790
Bouvet Is. (Nor.)	0.05	0.02	0.02	–	–
Brazil	8,512	3,286	159,143	Brasilia	2,770
British Antarctic Terr. (UK)	1,709	660	0.3	Stanley	–
British Indian Ocean Terr. (UK)	0.08	0.03	0	–	–
Brunei	5.8	2.2	280	Bandar Seri Begawan	14,120
Bulgaria	111	43	8,818	Sofia	1,330
Burkina Faso	274	106	10,046	Ouagadougou	300
Burma (Myanmar)	677	261	45,555	Rangoon	500
Burundi	27.8	10.7	6,209	Bujumbura	210
Cambodia	181	70	9,968	Phnom Penh	202
Cameroon	475	184	12,871	Yaoundé	820
Canada	9,976	3,852	29,141	Ottawa	20,710
Canary Is. (Spain)	7.3	2.8	1,494	Las Palmas/Santa Cruz	–
Cape Verde Is.	4	1.6	381	Praia	850
Cayman Is. (UK)	0.26	0.10	30	George Town	20,000
Central African Republic	623	241	3,235	Bangui	410
Chad	1,284	496	6,183	Ndjamena	222
Chatham Is. (NZ)	0.96	0.37	0.05	Waitangi	–
Chile	757	292	14,044	Santiago	2,730
China	9,597	3,705	1,208,841	Beijing (Peking)	470
Christmas Is. (Aus.)	0.14	0.05	2	The Settlement	–
Cocos (Keeling) Is. (Aus.)	0.01	0.005	0.6	West Island	–
Colombia	1,139	440	34,545	Bogotá	1,330
Comoros	2.2	0.86	630	Moroni	500
Congo	342	132	2,516	Brazzaville	1,030
Cook Is. (NZ)	0.24	0.09	19	Avarua	900
Costa Rica	51.1	19.7	3,347	San José	1,960
Croatia	56.5	21.8	4,504	Zagreb	1,800
Crozet Is. (Fr.)	0.51	0.19	35	–	–
Cuba	111	43	10,960	Havana	1,580
Cyprus	9.3	3.6	734	Nicosia	9,820
Czech Republic	78.9	30.4	10,295	Prague	2,450
Denmark	43.1	16.6	5,173	Copenhagen	26,000
Djibouti	23.2	9	566	Djibouti	1,000
Dominica	0.75	0.29	71	Roseau	2,520
Dominican Republic	48.7	18.8	7,684	Santo Domingo	1,050
Ecuador	284	109	11,220	Quito	1,070
Egypt	1,001	387	61,636	Cairo	640
El Salvador	21	8.1	5,641	San Salvador	1,170
Equatorial Guinea	28.1	10.8	389	Malabo	330
Eritrea	94	36	3,437	Asmara	150
Estonia	44.7	17.3	1,541	Tallinn	2,760
Ethiopia	1,128	436	53,435	Addis Ababa	110
Falkland Is. (UK)	12.2	4.7	2	Stanley	–
Faroe Is. (Den.)	1.4	0.54	47	Tórshavn	23,660
Fiji	18.3	7.1	771	Suva	2,010
Finland	338	131	5,083	Helsinki	21,970
France	552	213	57,747	Paris	22,260
French Guiana (Fr.)	90	34.7	141	Cayenne	2,500
French Polynesia (Fr.)	4	1.5	215	Papeete	6,000
Gabon	268	103	1,283	Libreville	4,450
Gambia, The	11.3	4.4	1,081	Banjul	370
Georgia	69.7	26.9	5,450	Tbilisi	850
Germany	357	138	80,278	Berlin/Bonn	23,030
Ghana	239	92	16,944	Accra	450
Gibraltar (UK)	0.007	0.003	28	Gibraltar Town	15,080
Greece	132	51	10,416	Athens	7,290
Greenland (Den.)	2,176	840	58	Godthåb (Nuuk)	9,000
Grenada	0.34	0.13	92	St George's	2,310
Guadeloupe (Fr.)	1.7	0.66	421	Basse-Terre	7,000
Guam (US)	0.55	0.21	147	Agana	6,000
Guatemala	109	42	10,322	Guatemala City	980
Guinea	246	95	6,501	Conakry	570
Guinea-Bissau	36.1	13.9	1,050	Bissau	220
Guyana	215	83	825	Georgetown	330
Haiti	27.8	10.7	7,035	Port-au-Prince	380
Honduras	112	43	5,493	Tegucigalpa	580
Hong Kong (UK)	1.1	0.40	5,838	Victoria	15,360
Hungary	93	35.9	10,161	Budapest	2,970
Iceland	103	40	266	Reykjavik	23,880
India	3,288	1,269	918,570	New Delhi	310
Indonesia	1,905	735	194,615	Jakarta	670
Iran	1,648	636	65,758	Tehran	2,200
Iraq	438	169	19,925	Baghdad	2,000
Ireland	70.3	27.1	3,539	Dublin	12,210
Israel	27	10.3	5,458	Jerusalem	13,220
Italy	301	116	57,157	Rome	20,460
Ivory Coast	322	125	13,780	Yamoussoukro	670
Jamaica	11	4.2	2,429	Kingston	1,340
Jan Mayen Is. (Nor.)	0.38	0.15	0.06	–	–
Japan	378	146	124,815	Tokyo	28,190
Johnston Is. (US)	0.002	0.0009	1	–	–
Jordan	89.2	34.4	5,198	Amman	1,120
Kazakhstan	2,717	1,049	17,027	Alma-Ata	1,680
Kenya	580	224	27,343	Nairobi	310
Kerguelen Is. (Fr.)	7.2	2.8	0.7	–	–
Kermadec Is. (NZ)	0.03	0.01	0.1	–	–
Kiribati	0.72	0.28	77	Tarawa	750
Korea, North	121	47	23,483	Pyongyang	1,040
Korea, South	99	38.2	44,563	Seoul	6,790
Kuwait	17.8	6.9	1,633	Kuwait City	16,150
Kyrgyzstan	198.5	76.6	4,667	Bishkek	820
Laos	237	91	4,742	Vientiane	250
Latvia	65	25	2,583	Riga	1,930
Lebanon	10.4	4	2,915	Beirut	1,400
Lesotho	30.4	11.7	1,996	Maseru	590

Country/Territory	Area km² Thousands	Area miles² Thousands	Population Thousands	Capital	Annual Income US $
Liberia	111	43	2,941	Monrovia	400
Libya	1,760	679	5,225	Tripoli	5,800
Liechtenstein	0.16	0.06	30	Vaduz	33,000
Lithuania	65.2	25.2	3,706	Vilnius	1,310
Luxembourg	2.6	1	401	Luxembourg	35,160
Macau (Port.)	0.02	0.006	398	Macau	2,000
Macedonia	25.3	9.8	2,142	Skopje	1,812
Madagascar	587	227	14,303	Antananarivo	230
Madeira (Port.)	0.81	0.31	253	Funchal	–
Malawi	118	46	10,843	Lilongwe	210
Malaysia	330	127	19,695	Kuala Lumpur	2,790
Maldives	0.30	0.12	246	Malé	460
Mali	1,240	479	10,462	Bamako	254
Malta	0.32	0.12	364	Valletta	7,300
Marshall Is.	0.18	0.07	52	Dalap-Uliga-Darrit	1,500
Martinique (Fr.)	1.1	0.42	375	Fort-de-France	4,000
Mauritania	1,025	396	2,217	Nouakchott	530
Mauritius	2.0	0.72	1,104	Port Louis	2,700
Mayotte (Fr.)	0.37	0.14	101	Mamoundzou	–
Mexico	1,958	756	91,858	Mexico City	3,470
Micronesia, Fed. States	0.70	0.27	121	Palikir	1,500
Midway Is. (US)	0.005	0.002	2	–	–
Moldova	33.7	13	4,420	Kishinev	1,300
Monaco	0.002	0.0001	31	Monaco	16,000
Mongolia	1,567	605	2,363	Ulan Bator	112
Montserrat (UK)	0.10	0.04	11	Plymouth	5,800
Morocco	447	172	26,488	Rabat	1,030
Mozambique	802	309	15,527	Maputo	60
Namibia	825	318	1,500	Windhoek	1,610
Nauru	0.02	0.008	11	Yaren District	–
Nepal	141	54	21,360	Katmandu	170
Netherlands	41.5	16	15,397	Amsterdam/The Hague	20,480
Neths Antilles (Neths)	0.99	0.38	197	Willemstad	6,000
New Caledonia (Fr.)	19	7.3	178	Nouméa	4,000
New Zealand	269	104	3,531	Wellington	12,300
Nicaragua	130	50	4,275	Managua	340
Niger	1,267	489	8,846	Niamey	284
Nigeria	924	357	88,515	Abuja	320
Niue (NZ)	0.26	0.10	2	Alofi	–
Norfolk Is. (Aus.)	0.03	0.01	2	Kingston	–
Northern Mariana Is. (US)	0.48	0.18	47	Saipan	11,500
Norway	324	125	4,318	Oslo	25,820
Oman	212	82	2,077	Muscat	6,480
Pakistan	796	307	136,645	Islamabad	420
Palau	0.46	0.18	17	Koror	2,260
Panama	77.1	29.8	2,585	Panama City	2,420
Papua New Guinea	463	179	4,205	Port Moresby	950
Paraguay	407	157	4,830	Asunción	1,380
Peru	1,285	496	23,331	Lima	950
Peter 1st Is. (Nor.)	0.18	0.07	0	–	–
Philippines	300	116	66,188	Manila	770
Pitcairn Is. (UK)	0.03	0.01	0.07	Adamstown	–
Poland	313	121	38,341	Warsaw	1,910
Portugal	92.4	35.7	9,830	Lisbon	7,450
Puerto Rico (US)	9	3.5	3,646	San Juan	6,330
Qatar	11	4.2	540	Doha	15,860
Queen Maud Land (Nor.)	2,800	1,081	0	–	–
Réunion (Fr.)	2.5	0.97	644	Saint-Denis	4,000
Romania	238	92	22,922	Bucharest	1,130
Ross Dependency (NZ)	435	168	0	–	–
Russia	17,075	6,592	147,370	Moscow	2,510
Rwanda	26.3	10.2	7,750	Kigali	250
St Christopher & Nevis	0.36	0.14	41	Basseterre	3,960
St Helena (UK)	0.12	0.05	6	Jamestown	–
St Lucia	0.62	0.24	141	Castries	2,500
St Paul Is. (Fr.)	0.007	0.003	0	–	–
St Pierre & Miquelon (Fr.)	0.24	0.09	6	Saint Pierre	–
St Vincent & Grenadines	0.39	0.15	111	Kingstown	1,730
San Marino	0.06	0.02	25	San Marino	20,000
São Tomé & Príncipe	0.96	0.37	130	São Tomé	350
Saudi Arabia	2,150	830	17,451	Riyadh	7,510
Senegal	197	76	8,102	Dakar	780
Seychelles	0.46	0.18	73	Victoria	5,110
Sierra Leone	71.7	27.7	4,402	Freetown	160
Singapore	0.62	0.24	2,821	Singapore	15,730
Slovak Republic	49	18.9	5,333	Bratislava	1,930
Slovenia	20.3	7.8	1,942	Ljubljana	7,150
Solomon Is.	28.9	11.2	366	Honiara	690
Somalia	638	246	9,077	Mogadishu	150
South Africa	1,220	471	40,555	Pretoria/Cape Town	2,670
South Georgia (UK)	3.8	1.4	0.05	–	–
South Sandwich Is. (UK)	0.38	0.15	0	–	–
Spain	505	195	39,568	Madrid	13,970
Sri Lanka	65.6	25.3	18,125	Colombo	540
Sudan	2,506	967	27,361	Khartoum	277
Surinam	163	63	418	Paramaribo	4,280
Svalbard (Nor.)	62.9	24.3	4	Longyearbyen	–
Swaziland	17.4	6.7	832	Mbabane	1,090
Sweden	450	174	8,738	Stockholm	27,010
Switzerland	41.3	15.9	7,131	Bern	36,080
Syria	185	71	14,171	Damascus	1,170
Taiwan	36	13.9	20,659	Taipei	8,780
Tajikistan	143.1	55.2	5,933	Dushanbe	490
Tanzania	945	365	28,846	Dodoma	110
Thailand	513	198	58,183	Bangkok	1,840
Togo	56.8	21.9	4,010	Lomé	390
Tokelau (NZ)	0.01	0.005	2	Nukunonu	–
Tonga	0.75	0.29	98	Nuku'alofa	1,100
Trinidad & Tobago	5.1	2	1,292	Port of Spain	3,940
Tristan da Cunha (UK)	0.11	0.04	0.33	Edinburgh	–
Tunisia	164	63	8,733	Tunis	1,720
Turkey	779	301	60,771	Ankara	1,980
Turkmenistan	488.1	188.5	4,010	Ashkhabad	1,230
Turks & Caicos Is. (UK)	0.43	0.17	14	Cockburn Town	5,000
Tuvalu	0.03	0.01	9	Fongafale	600
Uganda	236	91	20,621	Kampala	170
Ukraine	603.7	233.1	51,465	Kiev	1,820
United Arab Emirates	83.6	32.3	1,861	Abu Dhabi	20,020
United Kingdom	243.3	94	58,091	London	17,790
United States of America	9,373	3,619	260,631	Washington, DC	23,240
Uruguay	177	68	3,167	Montevideo	3,340
Uzbekistan	447.4	172.7	22,349	Tashkent	850
Vanuatu	12.2	4.7	165	Port-Vila	1,120
Vatican City	0.0004	0.0002	1	–	–
Venezuela	912	352	21,378	Caracas	2,910
Vietnam	332	127	72,931	Hanoi	220
Virgin Is. (UK)	0.15	0.06	18	Road Town	–
Virgin Is. (US)	0.34	0.13	104	Charlotte Amalie	12,000
Wake Is.	0.008	0.003	0.30	–	–
Wallis & Futuna Is. (Fr.)	0.20	0.08	19	Mata-Utu	–
Western Sahara	266	103	272	El Aaiún	–
Western Samoa	2.8	1.1	169	Apia	940
Yemen	528	204	13,873	Sana	520
Yugoslavia	102.3	39.5	10,763	Belgrade	3,000
Zaire	2,345	905	42,552	Kinshasa	220
Zambia	753	291	9,196	Lusaka	460
Zimbabwe	391	151	11,002	Harare	570

World Statistics: Physical Dimensions

Each topic list is divided into continents and within a continent the items are listed in size order. The order of the continents is as in the atlas, Europe through to South America. Certain lists down to this mark > are complete; below they are selective. The world top ten are shown in square brackets; in the case of mountains this has not been done because the world top 30 are all in Asia. The figures are rounded as appropriate.

World, Continents, Oceans

	km²	miles²	%
The World	509,450,000	196,672,000	–
Land	149,450,000	57,688,000	29.3
Water	360,000,000	138,984,000	70.7
Asia	44,500,000	17,177,000	29.8
Africa	30,302,000	11,697,000	20.3
North America	24,241,000	9,357,000	16.2
South America	17,793,000	6,868,000	11.9
Antarctica	14,100,000	5,443,000	9.4
Europe	9,957,000	3,843,000	6.7
Australia & Oceania	8,557,000	3,303,000	5.7
Pacific Ocean	179,679,000	69,356,000	49.9
Atlantic Ocean	92,373,000	35,657,000	25.7
Indian Ocean	73,917,000	28,532,000	20.5
Arctic Ocean	14,090,000	5,439,000	3.9

Mountains

Europe		m	ft
Mont Blanc	*France/Italy*	4,807	15,771
Monte Rosa	*Italy/Switz.*	4,634	15,203
Dom	*Switzerland*	4,545	14,911
Weisshorn	*Switzerland*	4,505	14,780
Matterhorn/Cervino	*Italy/Switz.*	4,478	14,691
Mt Maudit	*France/Italy*	4,465	14,649
Finsteraarhorn	*Switzerland*	4,274	14,022
Aletschhorn	*Switzerland*	4,182	13,720
Jungfrau	*Switzerland*	4,158	13,642
Barre des Ecrins	*France*	4,103	13,461
Schreckhorn	*Switzerland*	4,078	13,380
Gran Paradiso	*Italy*	4,061	13,323
Piz Bernina	*Italy/Switz.*	4,049	13,284
Ortles	*Italy*	3,899	12,792
Monte Viso	*Italy*	3,841	12,602
Grossglockner	*Austria*	3,797	12,457
Wildspitze	*Austria*	3,774	12,382
Weisskügel	*Austria/Italy*	3,736	12,257
Balmhorn	*Switzerland*	3,709	12,169
Dammastock	*Switzerland*	3,630	11,909
Tödi	*Switzerland*	3,620	11,877
Presanella	*Italy*	3,556	11,667
Monte Adamello	*Italy*	3,554	11,660
Mulhacén	*Spain*	3,478	11,411
Pico de Aneto	*Spain*	3,404	11,168
Posets	*Spain*	3,375	11,073
Marmolada	*Italy*	3,342	10,964
Etna	*Italy*	3,340	10,958
> Olympus	*Greece*	2,917	9,570
Galdhöpiggen	*Norway*	2,469	8,100
Pietrosul	*Romania*	2,305	7,562
Hvannadalshnúkur	*Iceland*	2,119	6,952
Narodnaya	*Russia*	1,894	6,214
Ben Nevis	*UK*	1,343	4,406

Asia		m	ft
Everest	*China/Nepal*	8,848	29,029
Godwin Austen (K2)	*China/Kashmir*	8,611	28,251
Kanchenjunga	*India/Nepal*	8,598	28,208
Lhotse	*China/Nepal*	8,516	27,939
Makalu	*China/Nepal*	8,481	27,824
Cho Oyu	*China/Nepal*	8,201	26,906
Dhaulagiri	*Nepal*	8,172	26,811
Manaslu	*Nepal*	8,156	26,758
Nanga Parbat	*Kashmir*	8,126	26,660
Annapurna	*Nepal*	8,078	26,502
Gasherbrum	*China/Kashmir*	8,068	26,469
Broad Peak	*China/Kashmir*	8,051	26,414
Gosainthan	*China*	8,012	26,286
Disteghil Sar	*Kashmir*	7,885	25,869
Nuptse	*Nepal*	7,879	25,849
Masherbrum	*Kashmir*	7,821	25,659
Nanda Devi	*India*	7,817	25,646
Rakaposhi	*Kashmir*	7,788	25,551
Kanjut Sar	*India*	7,760	25,459
Kamet	*India*	7,756	25,446
Namcha Barwa	*China*	7,756	25,446
Gurla Mandhata	*China*	7,728	25,354
Muztag	*China*	7,723	25,338
Kongur Shan	*China*	7,719	25,324
Tirich Mir	*Pakistan*	7,690	25,229
Saser	*Kashmir*	7,672	25,170
> K'ula Shan	*Bhutan/China*	7,543	24,747
Pik Kommunizma	*Tajikistan*	7,495	24,590
Aling Gangri	*China*	7,314	23,996
Elbrus	*Russia*	5,642	18,510
Demavend	*Iran*	5,604	18,386
Ararat	*Turkey*	5,165	16,945
Gunong Kinabalu	*Borneo*	4,101	13,455
Yu Shan	*Taiwan*	3,997	13,113
Fuji-san	*Japan*	3,776	12,388
Rinjani	*Indonesia*	3,726	12,224
Mt Rajang	*Philippines*	3,364	11,037
Pidurutalagala	*Sri Lanka*	2,524	8,281

Africa		m	ft
Kilimanjaro	*Tanzania*	5,895	19,340
Mt Kenya	*Kenya*	5,199	17,057
Ruwenzori	*Uganda/Zaire*	5,109	16,762
Ras Dashan	*Ethiopia*	4,620	15,157
Meru	*Tanzania*	4,565	14,977
Karisimbi	*Rwanda/Zaire*	4,507	14,787
Mt Elgon	*Kenya/Uganda*	4,321	14,176
Batu	*Ethiopia*	4,307	14,130
Guna	*Ethiopia*	4,231	13,882
Toubkal	*Morocco*	4,165	13,665
Irhil Mgoun	*Morocco*	4,071	13,356
Mt Cameroon	*Cameroon*	4,070	13,353
Amba Ferit	*Ethiopia*	3,875	13,042
Teide	*Spain (Tenerife)*	3,718	12,198
Thabana Ntlenyana	*Lesotho*	3,482	11,424
Emi Koussi	*Chad*	3,415	11,204

Oceania		m	ft
Puncak Jaya	*Indonesia*	5,029	16,499
Puncak Trikora	*Indonesia*	4,750	15,584
Puncak Mandala	*Indonesia*	4,702	15,427
Mt Wilhelm	*Papua N. Guinea*	4,508	14,790
> Mauna Kea	*USA (Hawaii)*	4,205	13,796
Mauna Loa	*USA (Hawaii)*	4,170	13,681
Mt Cook	*New Zealand*	3,753	12,313
Mt Balbi	*Solomon Is.*	2,439	8,002
Mt Kosciusko	*Australia*	2,237	7,339

North America		m	ft
Mt McKinley	*USA (Alaska)*	6,194	20,321
Mt Logan	*Canada*	6,050	19,849
Citlaltepetl	*Mexico*	5,959	19,551
Mt St Elias	*USA/Canada*	5,489	18,008
Popocatepetl	*Mexico*	5,452	17,887
Mt Foraker	*USA (Alaska)*	5,304	17,401
Ixtaccihuatl	*Mexico*	5,286	17,342
Lucania	*Canada*	5,227	17,149
Mt Steele	*Canada*	5,073	16,644
Mt Bona	*USA (Alaska)*	5,005	16,420
Mt Blackburn	*USA (Alaska)*	4,996	16,391
Mt Sanford	*USA (Alaska)*	4,940	16,207
Mt Wood	*Canada*	4,848	15,905
Nevado de Toluca	*Mexico*	4,670	15,321
Mt Fairweather	*USA (Alaska)*	4,663	15,298
Mt Whitney	*USA*	4,418	14,495
Mt Elbert	*USA*	4,399	14,432
Mt Harvard	*USA*	4,395	14,419
Mt Rainier	*USA*	4,392	14,409
Blanca Peak	*USA*	4,372	14,344
Long's Peak	*USA*	4,345	14,255
Nevado de Colima	*Mexico*	4,339	14,235
Mt Shasta	*USA*	4,317	14,163
Tajumulco	*Guatemala*	4,220	13,845
> Gannett Peak	*USA*	4,202	13,786
Mt Waddington	*Canada*	3,994	13,104
Mt Robson	*Canada*	3,954	12,972
Chirripó Grande	*Costa Rica*	3,837	12,589
Pico Duarte	*Dominican Rep.*	3,175	10,417

South America		m	ft
Aconcagua	*Argentina*	6,960	22,834
Illimani	*Bolivia*	6,882	22,578
Bonete	*Argentina*	6,872	22,546
Ojos del Salado	*Argentina/Chile*	6,863	22,516
Tupungato	*Argentina/Chile*	6,800	22,309
Pissis	*Argentina*	6,779	22,241
Mercedario	*Argentina/Chile*	6,770	22,211
Huascaran	*Peru*	6,768	22,204
Llullaillaco	*Argentina/Chile*	6,723	22,057
Nudo de Cachi	*Argentina*	6,720	22,047
Yerupaja	*Peru*	6,632	21,758
N. de Tres Cruces	*Argentina/Chile*	6,620	21,719
Incahuasi	*Argentina/Chile*	6,600	21,654
Ancohuma	*Bolivia*	6,550	21,489
Sajama	*Bolivia*	6,542	21,463
Coropuna	*Peru*	6,425	21,079
Ausangate	*Peru*	6,384	20,945
Cerro del Toro	*Argentina*	6,380	20,932
Ampato	*Peru*	6,310	20,702
Chimborasso	*Ecuador*	6,267	20,561
> Cotopaxi	*Ecuador*	5,896	19,344
S. Nev. de S. Marta	*Colombia*	5,800	19,029
Cayambe	*Ecuador*	5,796	19,016
Pico Bolivar	*Venezuela*	5,007	16,427

Antarctica		m	ft
Vinson Massif		4,897	16,066
Mt Kirkpatrick		4,528	14,855

Ocean Depths

Atlantic Ocean	m	ft
Puerto Rico (Milwaukee) Deep [7]	9,220	30,249
Cayman Trench [10]	7,680	25,197
Gulf of Mexico	5,203	17,070
Mediterranean Sea	5,121	16,801
Black Sea	2,211	7,254
North Sea	660	2,165
Baltic Sea	463	1,519
Hudson Bay	258	846

Indian Ocean	m	ft
Java Trench	7,450	24,442
Red Sea	2,635	8,454
Persian Gulf	73	239

Pacific Ocean	m	ft
Mariana Trench [1]	11,022	36,161
Tonga Trench [2]	10,882	35,702
Japan Trench [3]	10,554	34,626
Kuril Trench [4]	10,542	34,587
Mindanao Trench [5]	10,497	34,439
Kermadec Trench [6]	10,047	32,962
Peru-Chile Trench [8]	8,050	26,410
Aleutian Trench [9]	7,822	25,662
Middle American Trench	6,662	21,857

Arctic Ocean	m	ft
Molloy Deep	5,608	18,399

Land Lows

		m	ft
Caspian Sea	*Europe*	–28	–92
Dead Sea	*Asia*	–403	–1,322
Lake Assal	*Africa*	–156	–512
Lake Eyre North	*Oceania*	–16	–52
Death Valley	*N. America*	–86	–282
Valdés Peninsula	*S. America*	–40	–131

Rivers

Europe		km	miles
Volga	*Caspian Sea*	3,700	2,300
Danube	*Black Sea*	2,850	1,770
Ural	*Caspian Sea*	2,535	1,575
Dnepr (Dnipro)	*Volga*	2,285	1,420
Kama	*Volga*	2,030	1,260
Don	*Volga*	1,990	1,240
Petchora	*Arctic Ocean*	1,790	1,110
Oka	*Volga*	1,480	920
Belaya	*Kama*	1,420	880
Dnestr (Dnister)	*Black Sea*	1,400	870
Vyatka	*Kama*	1,370	850
Rhine	*North Sea*	1,320	820
N. Dvina	*Arctic Ocean*	1,290	800
Desna	*Dnepr*	1,190	740
Elbe	*North Sea*	1,145	710
> Vistula	*Baltic Sea*	1,090	675
Loire	*Atlantic Ocean*	1,020	635
W. Dvina	*Baltic Sea*	1,019	633

Asia		km	miles
Yangtze [3]	*Pacific Ocean*	6,380	3,960
Yenisey-Angara [5]	*Arctic Ocean*	5,550	3,445
Huang He [6]	*Pacific Ocean*	5,464	3,395
Ob-Irtysh [7]	*Arctic Ocean*	5,410	3,360
Mekong [9]	*Pacific Ocean*	4,500	2,795
Amur [10]	*Pacific Ocean*	4,400	2,730
Lena	*Arctic Ocean*	4,400	2,730
Irtysh	*Ob*	4,250	2,640
Yenisey	*Arctic Ocean*	4,090	2,540
Ob	*Arctic Ocean*	3,680	2,285
Indus	*Indian Ocean*	3,100	1,925
Brahmaputra	*Indian Ocean*	2,900	1,800
Syrdarya	*Aral Sea*	2,860	1,775
Salween	*Indian Ocean*	2,800	1,740
Euphrates	*Indian Ocean*	2,700	1,675
Vilyuy	*Lena*	2,650	1,645
Kolyma	*Arctic Ocean*	2,600	1,615
Amudarya	*Aral Sea*	2,540	1,575
Ural	*Caspian Sea*	2,535	1,575
Ganges	*Indian Ocean*	2,510	1,560
> Si Kiang	*Pacific Ocean*	2,100	1,305
Irrawaddy	*Indian Ocean*	2,010	1,250
Tigris	*Indian Ocean*	1,900	1,180
Angara	*Yenisey*	1,830	1,135
Yamuna	*Indian Ocean*	1,400	870

Africa		km	miles
Nile [1]	*Mediterranean*	6,670	4,140
Zaïre/Congo [8]	*Atlantic Ocean*	4,670	2,900
Niger	*Atlantic Ocean*	4,180	2,595
Zambezi	*Indian Ocean*	3,540	2,200
Oubangi/Uele	*Zaïre*	2,250	1,400
Kasai	*Zaïre*	1,950	1,210
Shaballe	*Indian Ocean*	1,930	1,200
Orange	*Atlantic Ocean*	1,860	1,155
Cubango	*Okavango*	1,800	1,120
Limpopo	*Indian Ocean*	1,600	995
> Senegal	*Atlantic Ocean*	1,600	995
Volta	*Atlantic Ocean*	1,500	930
Benue	*Niger*	1,350	840

Australia		km	miles
Murray-Darling	*Indian Ocean*	3,750	2,330
Darling	*Murray*	3,070	1,905
Murray	*Indian Ocean*	2,575	1,600
Murrumbidgee	*Murray*	1,690	1,050

North America		km	miles
Mississ.-Missouri [4]	*Gulf of Mexico*	6,020	3,740
Mackenzie	*Arctic Ocean*	4,240	2,630
Mississippi	*Gulf of Mexico*	3,780	2,350
Missouri	*Mississippi*	3,780	2,350
Yukon	*Pacific Ocean*	3,185	1,980
Rio Grande	*Gulf of Mexico*	3,030	1,880
Arkansas	*Mississippi*	2,340	1,450
Colorado	*Pacific Ocean*	2,330	1,445
Red	*Mississippi*	2,040	1,270
Columbia	*Pacific Ocean*	1,950	1,210
Saskatchewan	*Lake Winnipeg*	1,940	1,205
Snake	*Columbia*	1,670	1,040
Churchill	*Hudson Bay*	1,600	990
Ohio	*Mississippi*	1,580	980
Brazos	*Gulf of Mexico*	1,400	870
> St Lawrence	*Atlantic Ocean*	1,170	730

South America		km	miles
Amazon [2]	*Atlantic Ocean*	6,450	4,010
Paraná-Plate	*Atlantic Ocean*	4,500	2,800
Purus	*Amazon*	3,350	2,080
Madeira	*Amazon*	3,200	1,990
São Francisco	*Atlantic Ocean*	2,900	1,800
Paraná	*Plate*	2,800	1,740
Tocantins	*Atlantic Ocean*	2,750	1,710
Paraguay	*Paraná*	2,550	1,580
Orinoco	*Atlantic Ocean*	2,500	1,550
Pilcomayo	*Paraná*	2,500	1,550
Araguaia	*Tocantins*	2,250	1,400
Juruá	*Amazon*	2,000	1,240
Xingu	*Amazon*	1,980	1,230
Ucayali	*Amazon*	1,900	1,180
Maranón	*Amazon*	1,600	990
> Uruguay	*Plate*	1,600	990
Magdalena	*Caribbean Sea*	1,540	960

Lakes

Europe		km²	miles²
Lake Ladoga	*Russia*	17,700	6,800
Lake Onega	*Russia*	9,700	3,700
Saimaa system	*Finland*	8,000	3,100
Vänern	*Sweden*	5,500	2,100
Rybinsk Res.	*Russia*	4,700	1,800

Asia		km²	miles²
Caspian Sea [1]	*Asia*	371,800	143,550
Aral Sea [6]	*Kazakh./Uzbek.*	33,640	13,000
Lake Baykal [9]	*Russia*	30,500	11,780
Tonlé Sap	*Cambodia*	20,000	7,700
Lake Balkhash	*Kazakhstan*	18,500	7,100
> Dongting Hu	*China*	12,000	4,600
Ysyk Köl	*Kyrgyzstan*	6,200	2,400
Lake Urmia	*Iran*	5,900	2,300
Koko Nur	*China*	5,700	2,200
Poyang Hu	*China*	5,000	1,900
Lake Khanka	*China/Russia*	4,400	1,700
Lake Van	*Turkey*	3,500	1,400
Ubsa Nur	*China*	3,400	1,300

Africa		km²	miles²
Lake Victoria [3]	*E. Africa*	68,000	26,000
Lake Tanganyika [7]	*C. Africa*	33,000	13,000
Lake Malawi [10]	*E. Africa*	29,600	11,430
Lake Chad	*C. Africa*	25,000	9,700
Lake Turkana	*Ethiop./Kenya*	8,500	3,300
Lake Volta	*Ghana*	8,500	3,300
Lake Bangweulu	*Zambia*	8,000	3,100
Lake Rukwa	*Tanzania*	7,000	2,700
Lake Mai-Ndombe	*Zaïre*	6,500	2,500
> Lake Kariba	*Zamb./Zimbab.*	5,300	2,000
Lake Albert	*Uganda/Zaïre*	5,300	2,000
Lake Nasser	*Egypt/Sudan*	5,200	2,000
Lake Mweru	*Zambia/Zaïre*	4,900	1,900
Lake Kyoga	*Uganda*	4,400	1,700
Lake Tana	*Ethiopia*	3,630	1,400

Australia		km²	miles²
Lake Eyre	*Australia*	8,900	3,400
Lake Torrens	*Australia*	5,800	2,200

North America		km²	miles²
Lake Superior [2]	*Canada/USA*	82,350	31,800
Lake Huron [4]	*Canada/USA*	59,600	23,010
Lake Michigan [5]	*USA*	58,000	22,400
Great Bear Lake [8]	*Canada*	31,800	12,280
Great Slave Lake	*Canada*	28,500	11,000
Lake Erie	*Canada/USA*	25,700	9,900
Lake Winnipeg	*Canada*	24,400	9,400
Lake Ontario	*Canada/USA*	19,500	7,500
Lake Nicaragua	*Nicaragua*	8,200	3,200
Lake Athabasca	*Canada*	8,100	3,100
> Smallwood Res.	*Canada*	6,530	2,520
Reindeer Lake	*Canada*	6,400	2,500
Lake Winnipegosis	*Canada*	5,400	2,100
Nettilling Lake	*Canada*	5,500	2,100

South America		km²	miles²
Lake Titicaca	*Bolivia/Peru*	8,300	3,200
Lake Poopo	*Peru*	2,800	1,100

Islands

Europe		km²	miles²
Great Britain [8]	*UK*	229,880	88,700
Iceland	*Atlantic Ocean*	103,000	39,800
Ireland	*Ireland/UK*	84,400	32,600
Novaya Zemlya (N.)	*Russia*	48,200	18,600
W. Spitzbergen	*Norway*	39,000	15,100
Novaya Zemlya (S.)	*Russia*	33,200	12,800
Sicily	*Italy*	25,500	9,800
Sardinia	*Italy*	24,000	9,300
N. E. Spitzbergen	*Norway*	15,000	5,600
Corsica	*France*	8,700	3,400
Crete	*Greece*	8,350	3,200
Zealand	*Denmark*	6,850	2,600

Asia		km²	miles²
Borneo [3]	*S. E. Asia*	744,360	287,400
Sumatra [6]	*Indonesia*	473,600	182,860
Honshu [7]	*Japan*	230,500	88,980
Celebes	*Indonesia*	189,000	73,000
Java	*Indonesia*	126,700	48,900
Luzon	*Philippines*	104,700	40,400
Mindanao	*Philippines*	101,500	39,200
Hokkaido	*Japan*	78,400	30,300
Sakhalin	*Russia*	74,060	28,600
Sri Lanka	*Indian Ocean*	65,600	25,300
Taiwan	*Pacific Ocean*	36,000	13,900
Kyushu	*Japan*	35,700	13,800
Hainan	*China*	34,000	13,100
Timor	*Indonesia*	33,600	13,000
Shikoku	*Japan*	18,800	7,300
Halmahera	*Indonesia*	18,000	6,900
Ceram	*Indonesia*	17,150	6,600
Sumbawa	*Indonesia*	15,450	6,000
Flores	*Indonesia*	15,200	5,900
Samar	*Philippines*	13,100	5,100
> Negros	*Philippines*	12,700	4,900
Bangka	*Indonesia*	12,000	4,600
Panay	*Philippines*	11,500	4,400
Sumba	*Indonesia*	11,100	4,300
Mindoro	*Philippines*	9,750	3,800
Bali	*Indonesia*	5,600	2,200
Cyprus	*Mediterranean*	3,570	1,400
Wrangel Is.	*Russia*	2,800	1,000

Africa		km²	miles²
Madagascar [4]	*Indian Ocean*	587,040	226,660
Socotra	*Indian Ocean*	3,600	1,400
Réunion	*Indian Ocean*	2,500	965
Tenerife	*Atlantic Ocean*	2,350	900
Mauritius	*Indian Ocean*	1,865	720

Oceania		km²	miles²
New Guinea [2]	*Indon./Pap.NG*	821,030	317,000
New Zealand (S.)	*Pacific Ocean*	150,500	58,100
New Zealand (N.)	*Pacific Ocean*	114,700	44,300
Tasmania	*Australia*	67,800	26,200
New Britain	*Papua NG*	37,800	14,600
New Caledonia	*Pacific Ocean*	19,100	7,400
Viti Levu	*Fiji*	10,500	4,100
Hawaii	*Pacific Ocean*	10,450	4,000
Bougainville	*Papua NG*	9,600	3,700
Guadalcanal	*Solomon Is.*	6,500	2,500
> Vanua Levu	*Fiji*	5,550	2,100
New Ireland	*Papua NG*	3,200	1,200

North America		km²	miles²
Greenland [1]	*Atlantic Oc.*	2,175,600	839,800
Baffin Is. [5]	*Canada*	508,000	196,100
Victoria Is. [9]	*Canada*	212,200	81,900
Ellesmere Is. [10]	*Canada*	212,000	81,800
Cuba	*Caribbean Sea*	110,860	42,800
Newfoundland	*Canada*	110,680	42,700
Hispaniola	*Dom.Rep./Haiti*	76,200	29,400
Banks Is.	*Canada*	67,000	25,900
Devon Is.	*Canada*	54,500	21,000
Melville Is.	*Canada*	42,400	16,400
> Vancouver Is.	*Canada*	32,150	12,400
Somerset Is.	*Canada*	24,300	9,400
Jamaica	*Caribbean Sea*	11,400	4,400
Puerto Rico	*Atlantic Ocean*	8,900	3,400
Cape Breton Is.	*Canada*	4,000	1,500

South America		km²	miles²
Tierra del Fuego	*Argent./Chile*	47,000	18,100
Falkland Is. (E.)	*Atlantic Ocean*	6,800	2,600
South Georgia	*Atlantic Ocean*	4,200	1,600
Galapagos (Isabela)	*Pacific Ocean*	2,250	870

PHILIP'S WORLD MAPS

The reference maps which form the main body of this atlas have been prepared in accordance with the highest standards of international cartography to provide an accurate and detailed representation of the Earth. The scales and projections used have been carefully chosen to give balanced coverage of the world, while emphasizing the most densely populated and economically significant regions. A hallmark of Philip's mapping is the use of hill shading and relief colouring to create a graphic impression of landforms: this makes the maps exceptionally easy to read. However, knowledge of the key features employed in the construction and presentation of the maps will enable the reader to derive the fullest benefit from the atlas.

Map sequence

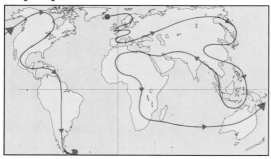

The atlas covers the Earth continent by continent: first Europe; then its land neighbour Asia (mapped north before south, in a clockwise sequence), then Africa, Australia and Oceania, North America and South America. This is the classic arrangement adopted by most cartographers since the 16th century. For each continent, there are maps at a variety of scales. First, physical relief and political maps of the whole continent; then a series of larger-scale maps of the regions within the continent, each followed, where required, by still larger-scale maps of the most important or densely populated areas. The governing principle is that by turning the pages of the atlas, the reader moves steadily from north to south through each continent, with each map overlapping its neighbours. A key map showing this sequence, and the area covered by each map, can be found on the endpapers of the atlas.

Map presentation

With very few exceptions (e.g. for the Arctic and Antarctic), the maps are drawn with north at the top, regardless of whether they are presented upright or sideways on the page. In the borders will be found the map title; a locator diagram showing the area covered and the page numbers for maps of adjacent areas; the scale; the projection used; the degrees of latitude and longitude; and the letters and figures used in the index for locating place names and geographical features. Physical relief maps also have a height reference panel identifying the colours used for each layer of contouring.

Map symbols

Each map contains a vast amount of detail which can only be conveyed clearly and accurately by the use of symbols. Points and circles of varying sizes locate and identify the relative importance of towns and cities; different styles of type are employed for administrative, geographical and regional place names. A variety of pictorial symbols denote landscape features such as glaciers, marshes and reefs, and man-made structures including roads, railways, airports, canals and dams. International borders are shown by red lines. Where neighbouring countries are in dispute, for example in the Middle East, the maps show the *de facto* boundary between nations, regardless of the legal or historical situation. The symbols are explained on the first page of the World Maps section of the atlas.

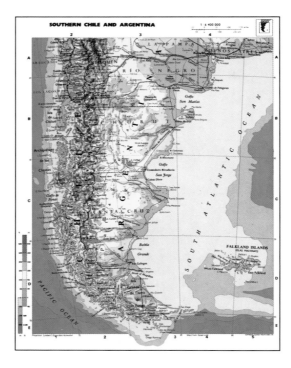

Map scales

1: 16 000 000
1 inch = 252 statute miles

The scale of each map is given in the numerical form known as the 'representative fraction'. The first figure is always one, signifying one unit of distance on the map; the second figure, usually in millions, is the number by which the map unit must be multiplied to give the equivalent distance on the Earth's surface. Calculations can easily be made in centimetres and kilometres, by dividing the Earth units figure by 100 000 (i.e. deleting the last five 0s). Thus 1:1 000 000 means 1 cm = 10 km. The calculation for inches and miles is more laborious, but 1 000 000 divided by 63 360 (the number of inches in a mile) shows that 1:1 000 000 means approximately 1 inch = 16 miles. The table below provides distance equivalents for scales down to 1:50 000 000.

LARGE SCALE		
1: 1 000 000	1 cm = 10 km	1 inch = 16 miles
1: 2 500 000	1 cm = 25 km	1 inch = 39.5 miles
1: 5 000 000	1 cm = 50 km	1 inch = 79 miles
1: 6 000 000	1 cm = 60 km	1 inch = 95 miles
1: 8 000 000	1 cm = 80 km	1 inch = 126 miles
1: 10 000 000	1 cm = 100 km	1 inch = 158 miles
1: 15 000 000	1 cm = 150 km	1 inch = 237 miles
1: 20 000 000	1 cm = 200 km	1 inch = 316 miles
1: 50 000 000	1 cm = 500 km	1 inch = 790 miles
SMALL SCALE		

Measuring distances

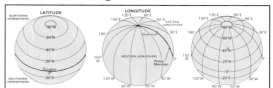

Although each map is accompanied by a scale bar, distances cannot always be measured with confidence because of the distortions involved in portraying the curved surface of the Earth on a flat page. As a general rule, the larger the map scale (i.e. the lower the number of Earth units in the representative fraction), the more accurate and reliable will be the distance measured. On small-scale maps such as those of the world and of entire continents, measurement may only be accurate along the 'standard parallels', or central axes, and should not be attempted without considering the map projection.

Map projections

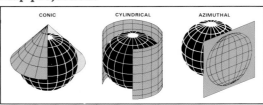

Unlike a globe, no flat map can give a true scale representation of the world in terms of area, shape and position of every region. Each of the numerous systems that have been devised for projecting the curved surface of the Earth on to a flat page involves the sacrifice of accuracy in one or more of these elements. The variations in shape and position of landmasses such as Alaska, Greenland and Australia, for example, can be quite dramatic when different projections are compared.

For this atlas, the guiding principle has been to select projections that involve the least distortion of size and distance. The projection used for each map is noted in the border. Most fall into one of three categories – conic, cylindrical or azimuthal – whose basic concepts are shown above. Each involves plotting the forms of the Earth's surface on a grid of latitude and longitude lines, which may be shown as parallels, curves or radiating spokes.

Latitude and longitude

Accurate positioning of individual points on the Earth's surface is made possible by reference to the geometrical system of latitude and longitude. Latitude *parallels* are drawn west–east around the Earth and numbered by degrees north and south of the Equator, which is designated 0° of latitude. Longitude *meridians* are drawn north–south and numbered by degrees east and west of the *prime meridian*, 0° of longitude, which passes through Greenwich in England. By referring to these co-ordinates and their subdivisions of minutes (1/60th of a degree) and seconds (1/60th of a minute), any place on Earth can be located to within a few hundred yards. Latitude and longitude are indicated by blue lines on the maps; they are straight or curved according to the projection employed. Reference to these lines is the easiest way of determining the relative positions of places on different maps, and for plotting compass directions.

Name forms

For ease of reference, both English and local name forms appear in the atlas. Oceans, seas and countries are shown in English throughout the atlas; country names may be abbreviated to their commonly accepted form (e.g. Germany, not The Federal Republic of Germany). Conventional English forms are also used for place names on the smaller-scale maps of the continents. However, local name forms are used on all large-scale and regional maps, with the English form given in brackets only for important cities – the large-scale map of Russia and Central Asia thus shows Moskva (Moscow). For countries which do not use a Roman script, place names have been transcribed according to the systems adopted by the British and US Geographic Names Authorities. For China, the Pin Yin system has been used, with some more widely known forms appearing in brackets, as with Beijing (Peking). Both English and local names appear in the index, the English form being cross-referenced to the local form.

WORLD MAPS

MAP SYMBOLS

SETTLEMENTS

⬡ PARIS   ▣ Berne   ◉ Livorno   ◉ Brugge   ◎ Algeciras   ⊙ Fréjus   ○ Oberammergau   ○ Thira

Settlement symbols and type styles vary according to the scale of each map and indicate the importance
of towns on the map rather than specific population figures

∴   Ruins or Archæological Sites   ˘   Wells in Desert

ADMINISTRATION

—————— International Boundaries

— — — International Boundaries
(Undefined or Disputed)

·············· Internal Boundaries

National Parks

Country Names

NICARAGUA

Administrative
Area Names

KENT

CALABRIA

International boundaries show the *de facto* situation where there are rival claims to territory

COMMUNICATIONS

—————— Principal Roads

⌒ Other Roads

‿‿ Trails and Seasonal Roads

≍ Passes

✧ Airfields

⌒ Principal Railways

······· Railways
Under Construction

⌒ Other Railways

⊐---⊏ Railway Tunnels

············ Principal Canals

PHYSICAL FEATURES

⌇ Perennial Streams

········ Intermittent Streams

⬭ Perennial Lakes

⬭ Intermittent Lakes

Swamps and Marshes

Permanent Ice
and Glaciers

▲ 8848   Elevations in metres

▾ 8050   Sea Depths in metres

1134   Height of Lake Surface
Above Sea Level
in metres

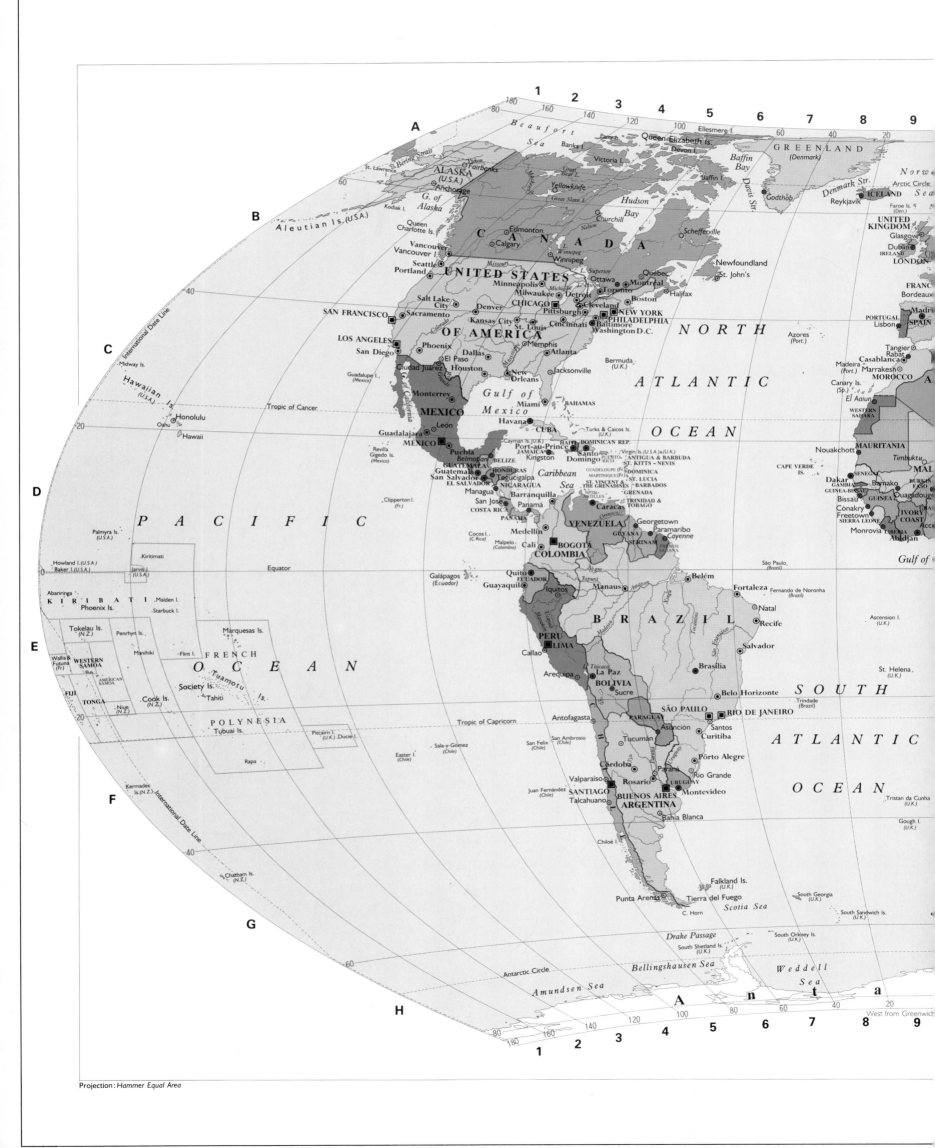

Projection: Hammer Equal Area

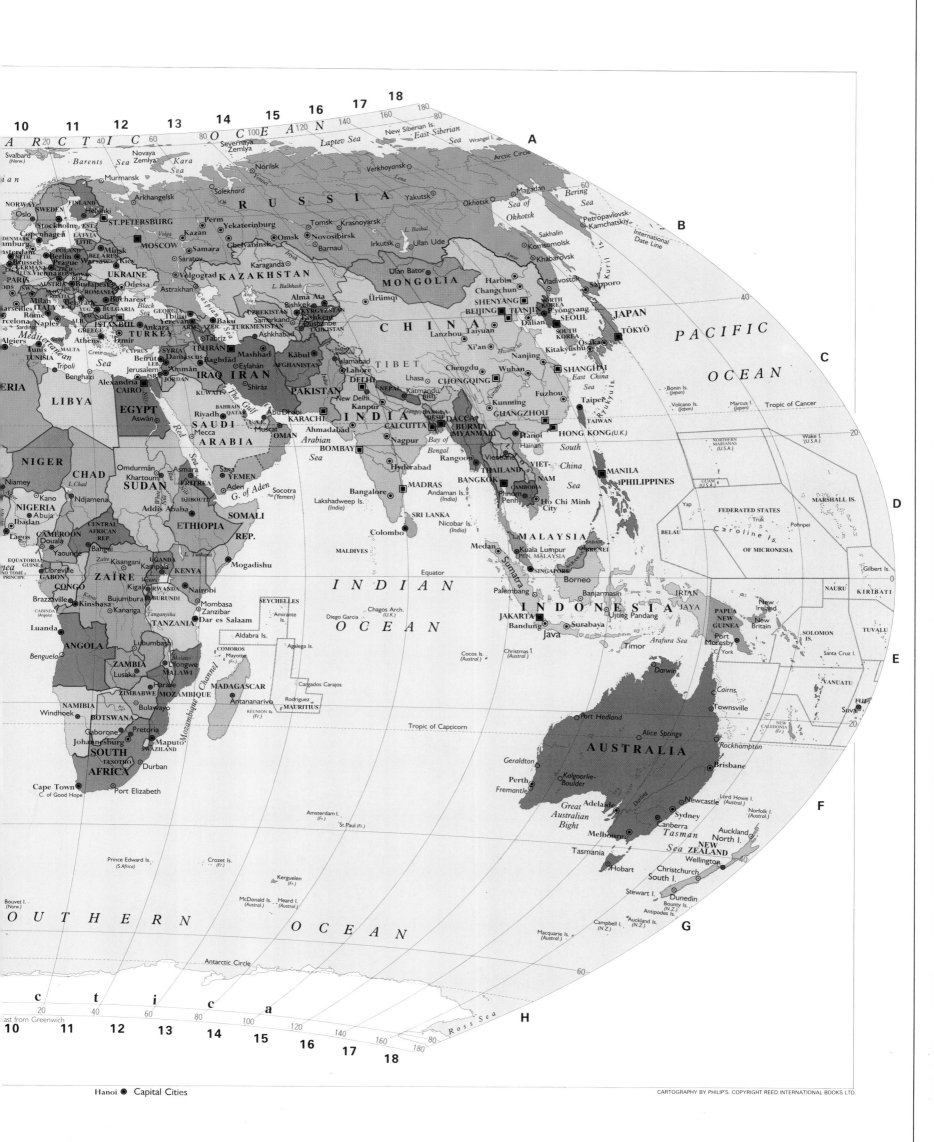

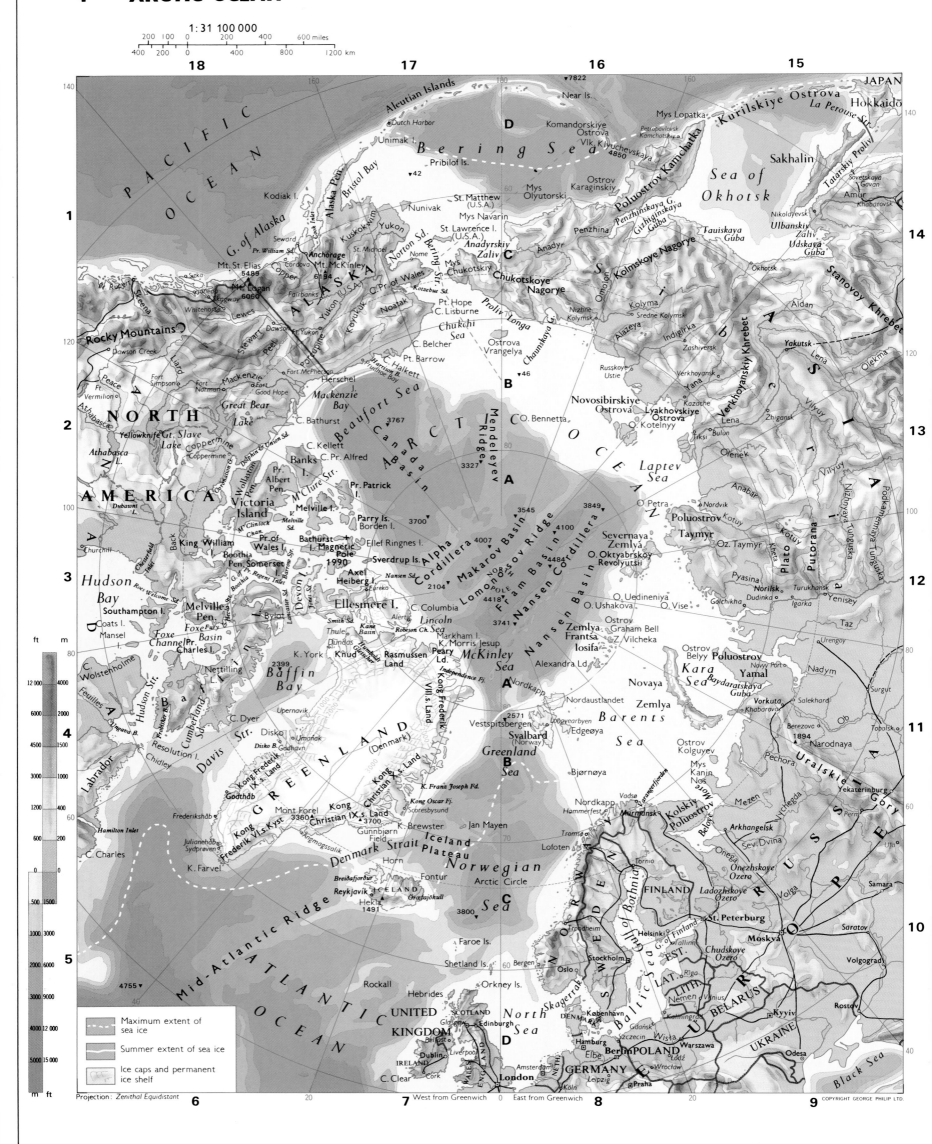

1:31 100 000

Projection: Zenithal Equidistant

West from Greenwich   East from Greenwich

Maximum extent of sea ice

Summer extent of sea ice

Ice caps and permanent ice shelf

COPYRIGHT GEORGE PHILIP LTD.

1 : 31 100 000

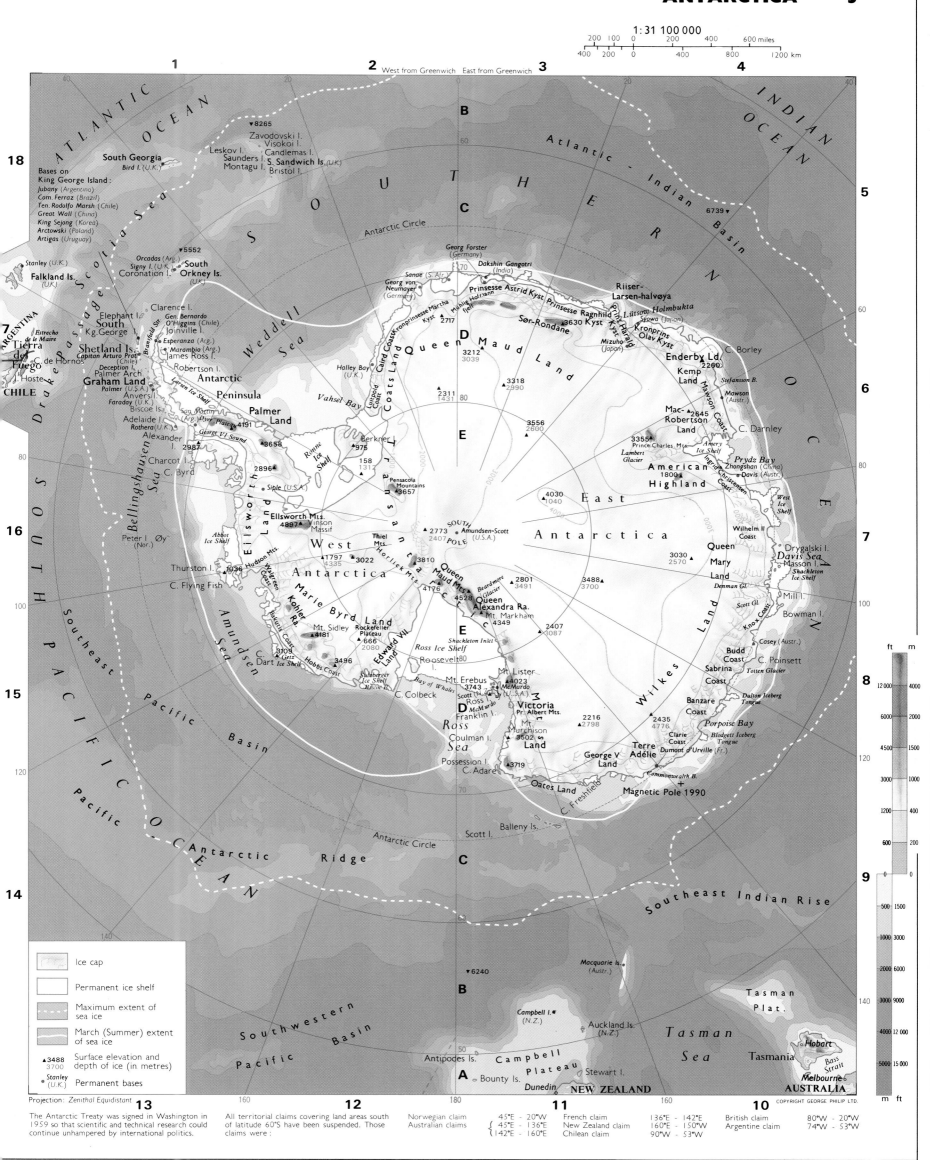

ATLANTIC OCEAN

SOUTHERN

Atlantic – Indian Basin

INDIAN OCEAN

Scotia Sea

Weddell Sea

▼8265
Zavodovski I.
Visokoi I.
Leskov I.   Candlemas I.
Saunders I.   S. Sandwich Is. (U.K.)
Montagu I.   Bristol I.

Bases on
King George Island:
Jubany (Argentina)
Com. Ferraz (Brazil)
Ten. Rodolfo Marsh (Chile)
Great Wall (China)
King Sejong (Korea)
Arctowski (Poland)
Artigas (Uruguay)

South Georgia
Bird I. (U.K.)

Stanley (U.K.)
Falkland Is.
(U.K.)

ARGENTINA
Estrecho
de la Maire
Tierra
del
Fuego
I. Hoste C. de Hornos
CHILE

▼5552
Orcadas (Arg.)
Signy I. (U.K.)   South
Coronation I.   Orkney Is.
(U.K.)

Clarence I.
Elephant I.
Gen. Bernardo
O'Higgins (Chile)
Joinville I.
South   Kg.George I.
Shetland Is. Brabant Str.
Capitan Arturo Prat (Chile)
Deception I.   Esperanza (Arg.)
Marambio (Arg.)
James Ross I.
Robertson I.
Graham Land
Palmer (U.S.A.)
Anvers I.
Faraday (U.K.)
Biscoe Is.
Adelaide I.   Dyer Plateau 4191
Rothera (U.K.)
Alexander
I.   2987
Charcot I.
C. Byrd

Antarctic
Peninsula

Palmer
Land

Bellingshausen
Sea

Peter I. Øy
(Nor.)

Thurston I.
C. Flying Fish

Southeast
PACIFIC

Pacific
Basin

Antarctic
Ridge

Pacific
OCEAN

Southwestern
Basin

Pacific

Antarctic Circle

Halley Bay
(U.K.)

Vahsel Bay

Ronne
Ice
Shelf

2896▲
3658▲
158
975
4335
1797
3022
1036
Hudson Mts.
Walgreen
Coast
Kohler
Ra.
Mt. Sidley
4181
Bakutis Coast
3109
Dart
Getz Ice Shelf
Hobbs Coast
3496

Marie Byrd
Land

Amundsen
Sea

West
Antarctica

Ellsworth Mts.
4897▲ Vinson
Massif

Siple (U.S.A.)
▲3657

Pensacola
Mountains

Thiel
Mts.
3810

Horlick Mts.

Queen
Maud Mts.
4176 C.
4528

Rockefeller
Plateau
666
2080
Edward VII
Land
Roosevelt I.
Sulzberger
Ice Shelf
Bay of Whales
Prince I.
C. Colbeck

Ross Ice Shelf

Shackleton Inlet

Beardmore
Glacier
2801
3491
Queen
Alexandra Ra.
Mt. Markham
4349

2407
3087

Georg Forster
(Germany)
Dakshin Gangotri
(India)
Sanae (S. Afr.)
Georg von
Neumayer
(Germany)

Prinsesse Astrid Kyst Prinsesse Ragnhild

Caird Coast Kronprinsesse Martha
Kyst   2717

Mühlig
Hofmann
fjell

Riiser-
Larsen-halvøya

Sør-Rondane
3630 Kyst

Prins Harald Kyst

Prins Olav Kyst
Lützow Holmbukta
Syowa (Japan)
Mizuho (Japan)
Kronprins
Olav Kyst

Queen Maud Land

3212
3039
3318
2990

2311
1431

3556
2600

SOUTH
POLE
2773
2407
Amundsen-Scott
(U.S.A.)

East
Antarctica

4030
1040

3355▲
Prince Charles Mts.
1800
3030
2570

3488▲
3700

Enderby Ld.
2260
Kemp
Land
Mac-
Robertson
Land
2645

Amery
Ice Shelf
Lambert
Glacier
American
Highland

C. Borley

Stefansson B.
Mawson
(Austr.)

C. Darnley

Prydz Bay
Zhongshan (China)
Davis (Austr.)

West
Ice Shelf

Wilhelm II
Coast
Queen
Mary
Land

Drygalski I.
Davis Sea
Masson I.
Shackleton
Ice Shelf
Mill I.
Bowman I.

Scott Gl.
Denman Gl.
Knox Coast
Casey (Austr.)

Budd
Coast
Sabrina
Coast

Banzare
Coast

C. Poinsett
Totten Glacier
Dalton Iceberg
Tongue

Wilkes
Land

Porpoise Bay
Blodgett Iceberg
Tongue
Clarie
Coast
2435
4776

2216
2798

Terre
Adélie
Dumont d'Urville (Fr.)

Commonwealth B.
+
Magnetic Pole 1990

Victoria
Land

Mt. Lister
4023
McMurdo
(U.S.A.)
Scott (N.Z.)
Ross (N.Z.)
Franklin I.
Mt. Erebus
3743

Mt.
Murchison
3502

Ross
Sea

Coulman I.
Possession I.
C. Adare
3719

Oates Land

C. Freshfield

George V
Land

Balleny Is.

Scott I.

Antarctic Circle

Southeast Indian Rise

Macquarie Is.
(Austr.)

Campbell I.
(N.Z.)

Auckland Is.
(N.Z.)

Tasman
Plat.

Tasman
Sea

Hobart
Bass
Strait
Tasmania
Melbourne
AUSTRALIA

Antipodes Is.   Campbell
Plateau
Bounty Is.   Stewart I.
Dunedin   NEW ZEALAND

▼6240

Projection: Zenithal Equidistant

COPYRIGHT GEORGE PHILIP LTD.

Legend:

- Ice cap
- Permanent ice shelf
- Maximum extent of sea ice
- March (Summer) extent of sea ice
- ▲3488 / 3700 Surface elevation and depth of ice (in metres)
- Stanley (U.K.) Permanent bases

West from Greenwich   East from Greenwich

The Antarctic Treaty was signed in Washington in 1959 so that scientific and technical research could continue unhampered by international politics.

All territorial claims covering land areas south of latitude 60°S have been suspended. Those claims were:

Norwegian claim	45°E – 20°W
Australian claims	45°E – 136°E / 142°E – 160°E
French claim	136°E – 142°E
New Zealand claim	160°E – 150°W
Chilean claim	90°W – 53°W
British claim	80°W – 20°W
Argentine claim	74°W – 53°W

ft m
12 000 / 4000
6000 / 2000
4500 / 1500
3000 / 1000
1200 / 400
600 / 200
0 / 0
500 / 1500
1000 / 3000
2000 / 6000
3000 / 9000
4000 / 12 000
5000 / 15 000
m ft

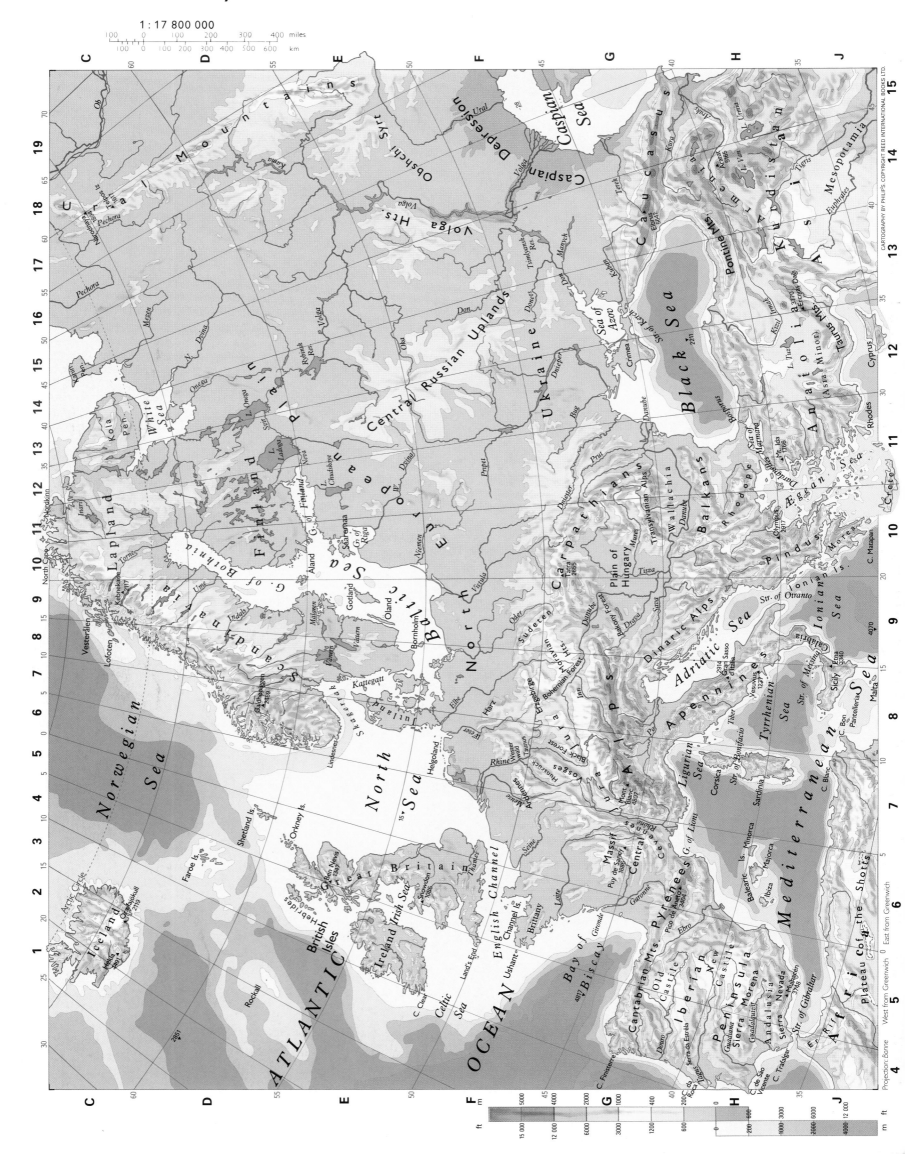

1 : 17 800 000

CARTOGRAPHY BY PHILIP'S COPYRIGHT REED INTERNATIONAL BOOKS LTD.

Projection: Bonne

1 : 17 800 000

100   0   100   200   300   400 miles

100 0 100 200 300 400 500 600 km

ICELAND
Reykjavik

NORWEGIAN Sea

ATLANTIC OCEAN

Arctic Circle

Faroe Is. (Den.)

Shetland Is.

Orkney Is.

Hebrides

UNITED KINGDOM

SCOTLAND
Glasgow Edinburgh Dundee Aberdeen
Newcastle-upon-Tyne
IRELAND Belfast
Dublin Cork
WALES ENGLAND
Manchester Leeds Sheffield Liverpool
Birmingham Cardiff Bristol
LONDON
Plymouth Southampton Brighton
English Channel Channel Is.

NORWAY
Oslo Stavanger Bergen Trondheim Narvik Tromsø Hammerfest

SWEDEN
Stockholm Göteborg Malmö Uppsala Örebro Kiruna Luleå

FINLAND
Helsinki Turku Tampere Vaasa

Gulf of Bothnia

North Sea

Baltic Sea

Skagerrak Kattegat

DENMARK
Copenhagen Aarhus Ålborg Odense

NETHER. Amsterdam The Hague Rotterdam
BELGIUM Brussels Antwerp
LUX. Luxembourg

FRANCE
PARIS Lille Rouen Le Havre Brest Nantes Tours Orléans Dijon Lyons St-Étienne Limoges Bordeaux Toulouse Grenoble Nice Marseilles Toulon Strasbourg

GERMANY
Berlin Hamburg Hanover Cologne Frankfurt Munich Stuttgart Bremen Dortmund Essen Dresden Leipzig Halle Chemnitz Nuremberg Bonn Kiel Magdeburg Wiesbaden

Rhine Elbe Oder

POLAND
Warsaw Gdańsk Kraków Łódź Poznań Wrocław Szczecin Bydgoszcz Katowice Białystok Lublin
Vistula

CZECH REP.
Prague
SLOVAK REP.
Bratislava
AUSTRIA
Vienna Linz Salzburg Graz Innsbruck
SWITZERLAND Bern Zürich Geneva Basle
LIECH.

HUNGARY
Budapest Miskolc Debrecen
Danube

SLOVENIA Ljubljana
CROATIA Zagreb
BOSNIA-HERZ. Sarajevo
YUGOSLAVIA SERBIA Belgrade Niš
MONTENEGRO
MACEDONIA Skopje
ALBANIA Tirana

ROMANIA
Bucharest Cluj-Napoca Timișoara Galați Ploiești Constanța
MOLDOVA Kishinev

BULGARIA
Sofia Plovdiv Varna

ITALY
Rome Naples Milan Turin Genoa Florence Bologna Venice Bari Taranto Palermo Catania Messina Cagliari
SAN MARINO MONACO
Tiber
Sardinia Corsica Sicily
Adriatic Sea Tyrrhenian Sea Ionian Sea Aegean Sea
MALTA Valletta

GREECE
Athens Thessaloníki Patras Corfu
Crete

SPAIN
Madrid Barcelona Valencia Seville Zaragoza Málaga Murcia Bilbao Valladolid Córdoba Granada Alicante La Coruña Vigo
Balearic Is. Majorca Minorca Ibiza
PORTUGAL Lisbon Porto
ANDORRA Andorra-la-Vella
Ebro Tagus Duero Guadiana Guadalquivir
Str. of Gibraltar Gibraltar (U.K.)
Ceuta (Sp.)

Mediterranean Sea
Bay of Biscay

MOROCCO Tangier Tetuán Melilla
ALGERIA Algiers Oran Constantine Annaba
TUNISIA Tunis
Africa

RUSSIA
MOSCOW ST. PETERSBURG Samara Kazan Perm Ufa Saratov Volgograd Voronezh Tula Orel Kursk Penza Tambov Ryazan Kaluga Yaroslavl Ivanovo Kostroma Vologda Nizhny Tagil Yekaterinburg Chelyabinsk Magnitogorsk Orenburg Ulyanovsk Simbirsk Novgorod Pskov Smolensk Bryansk Murmansk Arkhangelsk Syktyvkar Kirov Vyatka Kotlas Nizhny Novgorod
White Sea L. Onega L. Ladoga
Volga N. Dvina Ob Kama Ural

ESTONIA Tallinn
LATVIA Riga
LITHUANIA Vilnius Kaunas Kaliningrad
BELARUS Minsk Mogilev Vitebsk Gomel Brest
W. Dvina Pripet

UKRAINE
Kiev Kharkov Dnepropetrovsk Donetsk Odessa Zaporozhye Krivoy Rog Nikolayev Lvov Zhitomir Chernigov Mariupol
Dnestr Dnepr Bug Crimea Sevastopol

KAZAKHSTAN
Astrakhan Uralsk

Caspian Sea Black Sea
Rostov Krasnodar Stavropol

GEORGIA Tbilisi
ARMENIA
AZERBAIJAN Baku

TURKEY
Ankara Istanbul Izmir Bursa Adana Konya Antalya Kayseri Samsun Erzurum Diyarbakır Trabzon
Bosphorus
CYPRUS Nicosia
Rhodes

SYRIA Aleppo
IRAQ Baghdad
IRAN Tabriz
Tigris Euphrates

■ LONDON Capital Cities

Projection: Bonne   West from Greenwich 0 East from Greenwich

CARTOGRAPHY BY PHILIP'S. COPYRIGHT REED INTERNATIONAL BOOKS LTD.

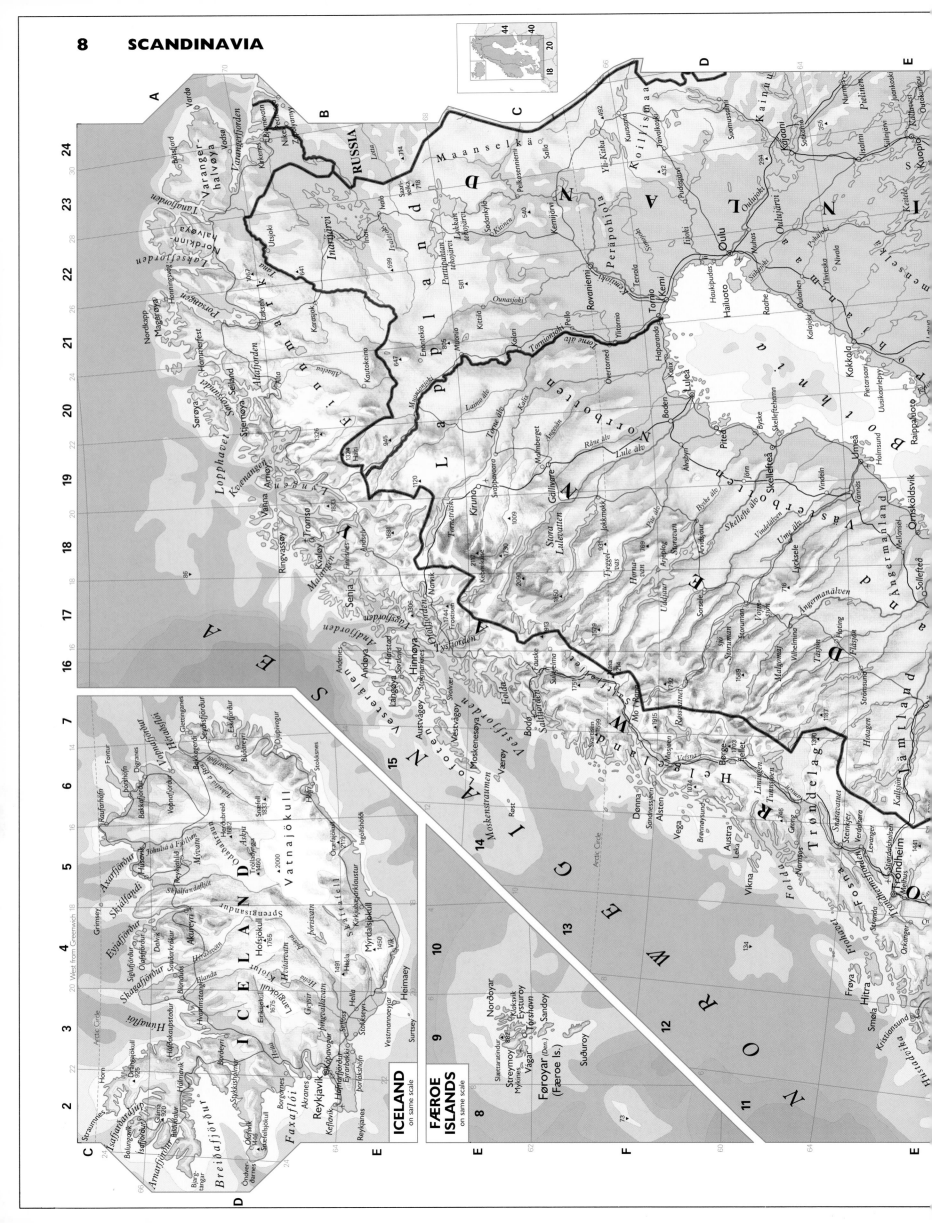

1 : 4 400 000

50 0 50 100 miles
50 0 50 100 150 km

CARTOGRAPHY BY PHILIP'S. COPYRIGHT REED INTERNATIONAL BOOKS LTD

East from Greenwich

Projection: Conical with two standard parallels

FINLAND · **ESTONIA** · **LATVIA** · **LITHUANIA** · **RUSSIA** · **BELARUS**

SWEDEN · **NORWAY** · **DENMARK** · **GERMANY** · **POLAND**

Helsinki (Helsingfors) · Tallinn · Riga · Vilnius · Kaunas · Klaipėda

STOCKHOLM · Uppsala · Göteborg (Gothenburg) · KØBENHAVN (Copenhagen) · Malmö · Oslo

Gulf of Finland · Gulf of Riga · Ålands hav · Kattegat · Skagerrak · BALTIC SEA

Gotland · Öland · Bornholm · Rügen · Usedom · Gdańsk · Gdynia · Elbląg

Daugava · Neman · Göta älv · Vänern · Vättern

ft m
6000 2000
3000 1000
1500 500
600 200
0 0
−50 −100
−100 −200
−200 −500
−500 −1000
−1000 −2000
m ft

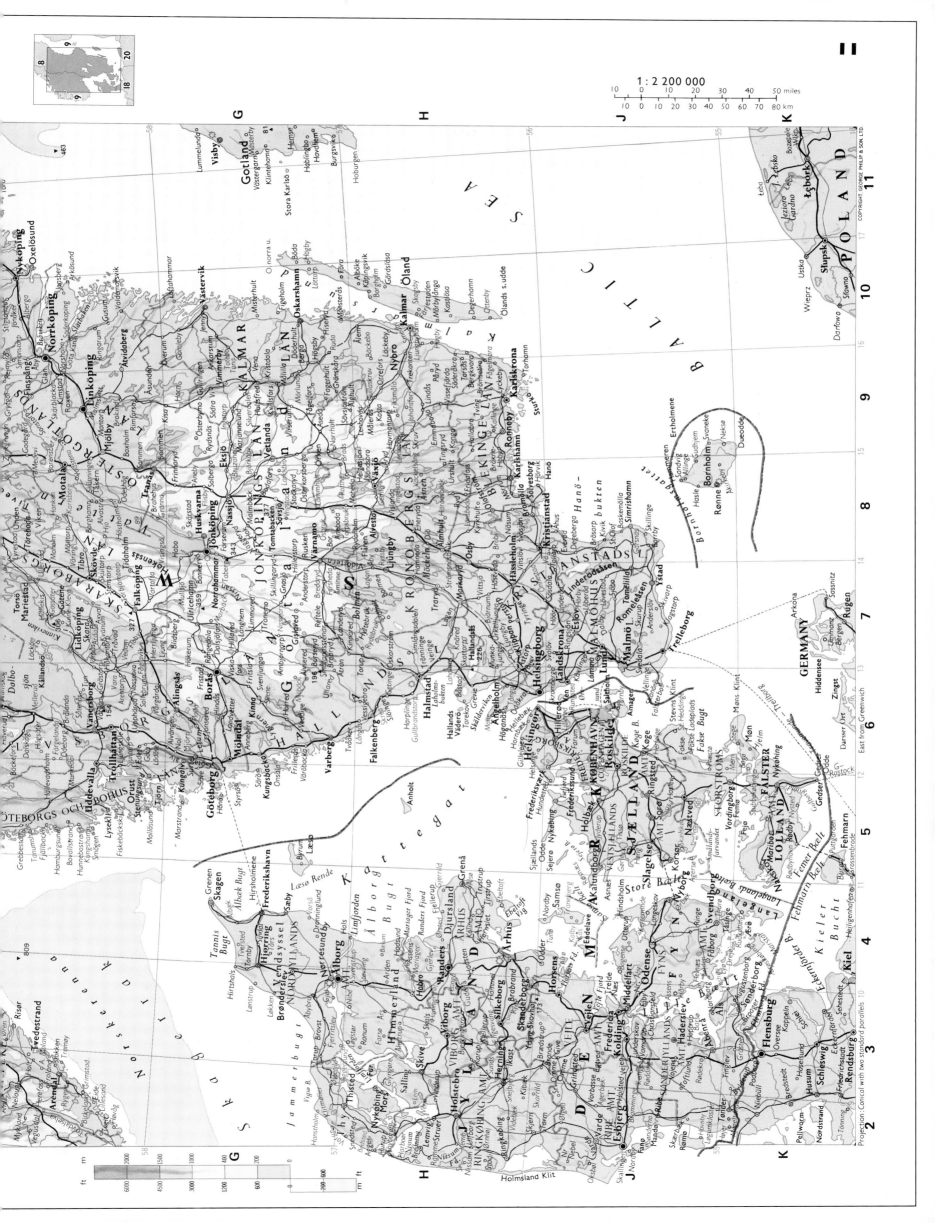

NORTH SEA

IRISH SEA

North Channel

SCOTLAND

ENGLAND

PENNINES

SOUTHERN UPLANDS

NORTHUMBERLAND

DURHAM

TYNE & WEAR

CLEVELAND

N. YORK MOORS

NORTH YORKSHIRE

W. YORKSHIRE

SOUTH YORKSHIRE

HUMBERSIDE

LINCOLN

NOTTS

DERBY

CHESHIRE

MERSEYSIDE

LANCASHIRE

CUMBRIA

Cumbrian Mts.

GWYNEDD

CLWYD

Anglesey

ISLE OF MAN

Fife Ness
Anstruther
Kirkcaldy
Firth of Forth
North Berwick
Bass Rock
Dunbar
Dunfermline
Kinross
Loch Leven
Alloa
Stirling
Ochil Hills
Forth
Helensburgh
Dumbarton
Clydebank
Glasgow
Greenock
Port Glasgow
Paisley
Rutherglen
Hamilton
Motherwell
Wishaw
Airdrie
Coatbridge
Falkirk
Lanark
Carstairs
Lomond
L. Katrine
Trossachs
Inveraray
Loch Fyne
Lochgilphead
Jura
Sound of Jura
Gigha I.
Campbeltown
Mull of Kintyre
Kintyre
Arran
Goat Fell 874
Ailsa Craig
Firth of Clyde
Saltcoats
Irvine
Kilmarnock
Ayr
Girvan
Stranraer
Portpatrick
Newton Stewart
Wigtown
Wigtown Bay
Whithorn
Luce Bay
Mull of Galloway
Port Erin
Calf of Man
Castletown
Peel
Douglas
Ramsey
Pt. of Ayre
Snaefell 620

Belfast
Belfast Lough
Bangor
Newtownards
Strangford L.
Downpatrick
Ardglass
Donaghadee
Larne
Magee
Carrickfergus
Lough

Holyhead
Holy I.
Caernarfon
Caernarfon Bay
Menai Strait
Beaumaris
Amlwch
Skerries
Bardsey I.
Pwllheli
Nefyn
Barmouth
Braich-y-Pwll
Snowdon 1085
Betws-y-Coed
Ffestiniog
Bala
L. Bala
Llangollen
Wrexham
Ruabon
Llanrwst
Conwy
Colwyn Bay
Llandudno
Gt. Ormes Hd.
Rhyl
Prestatyn
Flint
Mold
Denbigh
Ruthin

Berwick-upon-Tweed
Tweed
Holy I.
Farne Is.
Eyemouth
St. Abb's Hd.
Coldstream
Flodden
Cheviot Hills
The Cheviot 816
Kelso
Jedburgh
Hawick
Selkirk
Galashiels
Peebles
Moorfoot Hills
Lammermuir Hills
Pentland Hills
Edinburgh
Leith
Musselburgh
Haddington
Broad Law 840
Lanark
Carstairs
Langholm
Annan
Dumfries
Nithsdale
Sanquhar
Dalmellington
Doon
Leadhills
Nith
Merrick 843
Galloway
Dalbeattie
Castle Douglas
Kirkcudbright
Solway Firth
Maryport
Workington
Whitehaven
St. Bees Hd.
Seascale
Silloth
Carlisle
Annan
HADRIAN'S WALL
Brampton
Penrith
Keswick
Skiddaw 931
Derwentwater
Ullswater
Helvellyn
Ambleside
Windermere
Scafell Pike 978
Kendal
Morecambe Bay
Barrow
Walney I.
Ulverston
Heysham
Morecambe
Lancaster
Fleetwood
Cleveleys
Blackpool
Lytham St. Annes
Fylde
Preston
Southport
Formby Pt.
Ormskirk
Bootle
Wallasey
Birkenhead
Liverpool
St. Helens
Wigan
Bolton
Bury
Rochdale
Oldham
Manchester
Stockport
Chorley
Blackburn
Burnley
Nelson
Colne
Skipton
Settle
Forest of Bowland
Clitheroe
Ingleborough 723
Whernside
Pen-y-Ghent 693
Wensleydale
Swaledale
Richmond
Northallerton
Thirsk
Ripon
Harrogate
Knaresborough
Keighley
Bradford
Leeds
Halifax
Huddersfield
Dewsbury
Wakefield
Barnsley
Rotherham
Sheffield
Doncaster
Goole
Selby
York
Tadcaster
Pontefract
Chesterfield
Buxton
Macclesfield
Crewe
Chester
Nantwich
Stoke-on-Trent
Newcastle-under-Lyme
Leek
Stafford
Uttoxeter
Ashbourne
Matlock
Belper
Derby
Burton upon Trent
Nottingham
Mansfield
Sutton in Ashfield
Worksop
Newark
Sherwood Forest
Retford
Gainsborough
Lincoln
Lincoln Wolds
Louth
Market Rasen
Horncastle
Alford
Mablethorpe
Skegness
Boston
The Fens
Spalding
Bourne
Grantham
Sleaford
Witham
Trent
Grimsby
Cleethorpes
Immingham
Barton-upon-Humber
Humber
Kingston upon Hull
Hessle
Beverley
Market Weighton
Goole
Withernsea
Hornsea
Holderness
Bridlington
Flamborough Hd.
Filey
Scarborough
Whitby
Robin Hood's Bay
Pickering
Malton
Helmsley
Rye
Esk
Middlesbrough
Redcar
Hartlepool
Stockton
Billingham
Darlington
Bishop Auckland
Durham
Consett
Chester-le-Street
Houghton-le-Spring
Sunderland
South Shields
Tynemouth
Newcastle
Gateshead
Blyth
Ashington
Morpeth
N. Tyne
S. Tyne
Hexham
Prudhoe
St. John's Chapel
Cross Fell 893
Alston
Appleby
Brough
Kirkby Stephen
Sedbergh
Ullswater

Cromer
Hunstanton
Sandringham
Fakenham
King's Lynn
The Wash
The Broads

1 : 1 800 000

10   0   10   20   30   40   50 miles
10   0   10   20 30 40 50 60 70 80 km

E Lowestoft
Beccles
Southwold
Sizewell
Aldeburgh
Orford Ness
SUFFOLK
Ipswich
Felixstowe
Harwich
Walton on the Naze
The Naze
Clacton

F Margate
North Foreland
Ramsgate
Deal
Canterbury
South Foreland
Dover
Folkestone
Hythe
New Romney
Dungeness

ESSEX
Colchester
Southend
Shoeburyness
Maldon
Basildon
Chelmsford
Gravesend
Gillingham
Chatham
Rochester
Maidstone
Ashford
Rye
Romney Marsh
Hastings
KENT

Cambridge
CAMBRIDGE
Bedford
BEDFORD
Luton
Hertford
HERTS
St. Albans
Enfield
Barnet
Harrow
LONDON
Croydon
Bromley
Sevenoaks
Tonbridge
Tunbridge Wells
Eastbourne
Beachy Hd.
Bexhill
EAST SUSSEX
Lewes
Brighton
Hove
Newhaven

NORTHAMPTON
Northampton
Milton Keynes
BUCKS
Aylesbury
OXFORD
Oxford
BERKS
Reading
Windsor
Maidenhead
Guildford
SURREY
WEST SUSSEX
Worthing
Littlehampton
Bognor Regis
Chichester
Selsey Bill

WARWICK
Leamington
Redditch
Worcester
WORCESTER
Cheltenham
GLOUCESTER
Gloucester
Cirencester
Stroud
Swindon
WILTS
Marlborough
Newbury
Basingstoke
HANTS
Winchester
Southampton
Portsmouth
Gosport
Fareham
Havant
ISLE OF WIGHT
Newport
Ryde
Ventnor
St. Catherine's Point

Birmingham
WEST Bromwich
Dudley
Stourbridge
Kidderminster
HEREFORD & WORCESTER
Hereford
Malvern
Ross
Forest of Dean
Monmouth
GWENT
Pontypool
Cwmbran
Newport
Avonmouth
Bristol
AVON
Bath
Trowbridge
Frome
Mendip Hills
Polden Hills
SOMERSET
Bridgwater
Taunton
Chard
Yeovil
DORSET
Dorchester
Weymouth
Portland I.
Portland Bill
Poole
Bournemouth
Christchurch
Swanage
I. of Purbeck
St. Alban's Hd.

Cardiff
MID GLAMORGAN
SOUTH GLAMORGAN
Barry
Porthcawl
Port Talbot
Swansea
WEST GLAMORGAN
Neath
Aberdare
Merthyr Tydfil
Brecon Beacons
Black Mt.

Aberystwyth
Cardigan Bay
Aberdovey
DYFED
Carmarthen
Llanelli
Tenby
Pembroke
Milford Haven
St. David's Hd.
St. Bride's Bay
Fishguard

Bristol Channel
Ilfracombe
Minehead
Lynton
Exmoor
Barnstaple
Bideford
Hartland Point
Lundy
Bude
Boscastle
CORNWALL
Padstow
Bodmin Moor
Bodmin
Newquay
St. Austell
Truro
Redruth
Camborne
St. Ives
Penzance
St. Michael's Mount
Helston
Falmouth
Lizard
Land's End

DEVON
Exeter
Exmouth
Teignmouth
Dawlish
Torquay (Torbay)
Paignton
Dartmouth
Start Pt.
Salcombe
Kingsbridge
Plymouth
Devonport
Dartmoor
Okehampton
Tavistock
Launceston
Eddystone

ENGLISH CHANNEL

Guernsey
St. Peter Port
Sark
Alderney
C. de la Hague
Cherbourg
Barfleur
Channel Islands
Jersey
St. Helier
Barneville
Carentan
Périers
Coutances
Valognes
Quinéville

FRANCE
Dieppe
le Tréport
St. Valéry
Fécamp
Étretat
C. d' Antifer
C. de la Hève
Le Havre
Honfleur
Trouville
Deauville
Rouen
Elbeuf
Yvetot
Caudebec
Yerville
Louviers
Bernay
Lisieux
Pont l' Évêque
Caen
Bayeux
Arromanches
Vierville
Isigny
St. Lô
Aromanches

SCILLY ISLES
On same Scale
St. Ives
Penzance
Land's End
Isles of Scilly
St. Mary's

COPYRIGHT GEORGE PHILIP & SON, LTD.
Projection: Conical with two standard parallels.

East from Greenwich
West from Greenwich

ft
m 3000
1200
600
400
200
100
0
50
100
300
ft
m

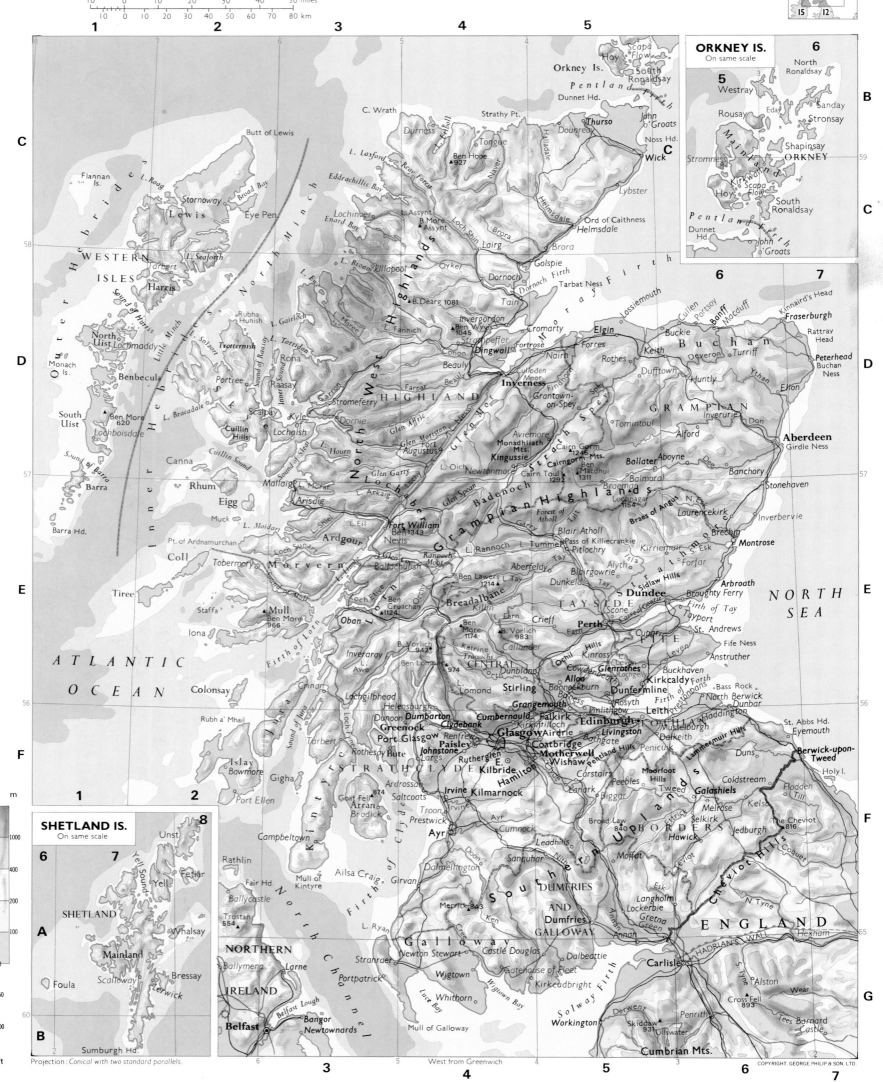

1 : 1 800 000

ORKNEY IS.
On same scale

SHETLAND IS.
On same scale

Projection : Conical with two standard parallels.

West from Greenwich

COPYRIGHT. GEORGE PHILIP & SON. LTD.

1 : 1 800 000

10   0   10   20   30   40   50 miles
10   0   10 20 30 40 50 60 70 80 km

I2
I3

1 2 3 4 5 6

Projection: Conical with two standard parallels.

8 West from Greenwich

COPYRIGHT. GEORGE PHILIP & SON. LTD.

Towns underlined in Northern Ireland give their
names to the Districts in which they stand

The remaining Districts are:—
1 Fermanagh   5 Castlereagh
2 Moyle   6 Ards
3 Newtownabbey   7 Down
4 North Down   8 Newry & Mourne

A T L A N T I C   O C E A N

NORTH CHANNEL

I R I S H   S E A

St. George's Channel

ft   m
3000 1000
1200 400
600   200
300   100
0   0
100   300
200   600
m   ft

Kintyre
Arran
Campbeltown
Mull of Kintyre
Ailsa Craig
Stranraer
Portpatrick
I. Magee
Aras Pen.

Malin Hd.
Tory I.   Horn Hd.
Sheep Haven
Lough Swilly
Carndonagh
Moville
Inishowen Pen.
Bloody Foreland
Bunbeg
Buncrana
Giant's Causeway
Rathlin I.
Fair Hd.
Ballycastle
2
Portrush
Rathlin I.
Portstewart
Gweedore
Errigal 752
Derryveagh Mts.
Letterkenny
Londonderry
Limavady
Coleraine
Ballymoney
Mt. Trostan 554
Aran I.
Gweebarra B.
Glenties
DONEGAL
Sperrin Mts.
Strabane
Sawel 683
Magherafelt
Ballymena
Larne
Antrim
Carrickfergus
Belfast L.
Donaghadee
Bangor
Newtownards
Loughros More B.
Bluestack 676
Finn
Lifford
Deele
Cookstown
Antrim
Lough
Neagh
Belfast
5
6
Rossan Pt.
Killybegs
Donegal
Rathlin O Birne I.
NORTHERN IRELAND
Dungannon
Portadown
Lurgan (Craigavon)
Lisburn
7
Donegal Bay
Ballyshannon
Erne
Bundoran
Omagh
1
Enniskillen
Irvinestown
Blackwater
Upper L. Erne
Lower L. Erne
Armagh
Banbridge
Downpatrick
Slieve Donard 852
Newcastle
Dundrum
Sligo B.
Killala B.
Downpatrick Hd.
Killala Hd.
Sligo
Colloney
L. Allen
Arrow
Belturbet
Clones
Upper L. Erne
Monaghan
MONAGHAN
Newry
St. Gullion 577
8
Mourne Mts.
Warrenpoint
Carlingford L.
Dundrum Bay
Broad Haven
Erris Hd.
Belmullet
Mullet Peninsula
Ballina
Killala
SLIGO
Ox Mts.
Moy
L. Conn
Collooney
L. Gill
LEITRIM
CAVAN
Annalee
Cootehill
Carrickmacross
Castleblayney
Carlingford L.
Greenore
Dundalk
Dundalk Bay
Blacksod Bay
Achill Hd.
Achill I.
Achill
Nephin 806
Castlebar
MAYO
Boyle
Carrick-on-Shannon
Cavan
Kingscourt
Gowna
L. Sheelin
Ardee
LOUTH
Clare I.
Clew Bay
Croagh Patrick 765
Westport
CONNACHT
Claremorris
ROSCOMMON
Castlerea
Leitrim
L. Ramor
An Uaimh (Navan)
Ceananas Mor (Kells)
Drogheda
Balbriggan
Inishbofin
Killary Harbour
Mweelrea 819
L. Mask
Robe
Ballinrobe
Roscommon
Longford
LONGFORD
Granard
Oldcastle
Blackwater
Athboy
Trim
Boyne
MEATH
Slane
Clifden
Twelve Pins
Connemara
L. Corrib
Tuam
Suck
L. Ree
Inn
Mullingar
WESTMEATH
Swords
Lambay I.
Slyne Hd.
Clare
Athenry
Ballinasloe
I R E L A N D
Athlone
Clara
Edenderry
Maynooth
Celbridge
DUBLIN
Ireland's Eye
Howth Head
Galway
GALWAY
Galway Bay
Loughrea
Brosna
Tullamore
OFFALY
Daingean
Bog
Droichead Nua
Naas
Dun Laoghaire
Dublin (Baile Atha Cliath)
Dublin Bay
Aran Is.
Inishmore
Kilkieran B.
Gort
Slieve Aughty
Portumna
Shannon
Birr
Sl. Bloom
Portarlington
Mountmellick
Port Laoise
KILDARE
Kildare
Kippure 754
Poulaphouca Res.
Bray
Hags Hd.
Ennistymon
L. Derg
Roscrea
LEINSTER
LAOIS
Athy
Barrow
Nore
WICKLOW
Lugnaquilla 923
Wicklow
Wicklow Hd.
Liscannor Bay
Mal Bay
Miltown Malbay
Ennis
CLARE
Killaloe
Ballina
Nenagh
Keeper 694
Ardnacrusha
Templemore
Thurles
Carlow
Tullow
Muine Bheag
Mt. Leinster 796
Shillelagh
Gorey
Rathdrum
Avoca
Mizen Hd.
Arklow
Kilkee
Kilrush
Rineanna
Foynes
Limerick
TIPPERARY
Golden Vale
Suir
Kilkenny
KILKENNY
Callan
Slaney
CARLOW
Enniscorthy
Cahore Pt.
Loop Hd.
R. Shannon
Rathkeale
LIMERICK
Newcastle
Tipperary
Cashel
Slievenamon
Carrick-on-Suir
WEXFORD
Listowel
Feale
Rath Luirc (Charleville)
Galtymore 920
Galty Mts.
Caher
Clonmel
722
New Ross
Wexford Harbour
Kerry Hd.
Brandon Hd.
Tralee Bay
Maine
Newmarket
Mitchelstown
Knockmealdown Mts.
Comeragh Mts.
Stradbally
Wexford
Rosslare
Brandon Mt. 953
Dingle
Sl. Mish
Laune
KERRY
Kanturk
Mallow
Blackwater
Fermoy
Lismore
Dungarvan
Waterford
Tramore
Greenore Pt.
Tuscar Rock
Carnsore Pt.
Gt. Blasket
Dunmore Hd.
Dingle Bay
Killarney
Lakes of Killarney
Macgillycuddy's Reeks
Boggeragh Mts.
Blackwater
WATERFORD
Dungarvan Bay
Hook Hd.
Saltee Is.
Waterford Harbour
St. David's Hd.
Valencia Harbour
Valencia I.
Carrauntuohill 1040
CORK
Blarney
Lee
Cork
Midleton
Youghal
Youghal Harbour
Skellig Rocks
Cahirciveen
Kenmare
Macroom
Passage West
Cobh
Crosshaven
Kinsale
Cork Harbour
Ballinskelligs B.
Kenmare River
Caha Mts.
Glengarriff
Bandon
Bandon
Old Head of Kinsale
Castletown Bearhaven
Bantry
Clonakilty
Bear I.
Bantry Bay
Crow Hd.
Dunmanus Bay
Skull
Clonakilty Bay
Galley Hd.
Mizen Hd.
Baltimore
Clear I.
C. Clear
Fastnet Rock
Skibbereen

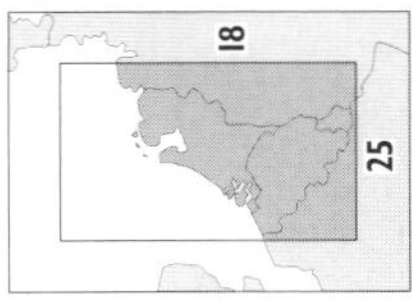

NORTH SEA
WADDENEILANDEN
OSTFRIESISCHE INSELN
WADDENZEE
IJSSELMEER
Markermeer
Texel
Vlieland
Terschelling
Ameland
Schiermonnikoog
Noordoostpolder
Oostelijk-Flevoland
Zuidelijk-Flevoland
AMSTERDAM
ROTTERDAM
'S GRAVENHAGE (DEN HAAG) (THE HAGUE)
Utrecht
Haarlem
Leiden
Den Helder
Alkmaar
Leeuwarden
Groningen
Assen
Emmen
Zwolle
Kampen
Deventer
Apeldoorn
Arnhem
Nijmegen
Hilversum
Amersfoort
Lelystad
Hengelo
Enschede
Almelo
Zutphen
Dordrecht
Emden
Borkum
Norden
Harlingen
Hoogeveen
Meppel
Sneek
Heerenveen
Drachten

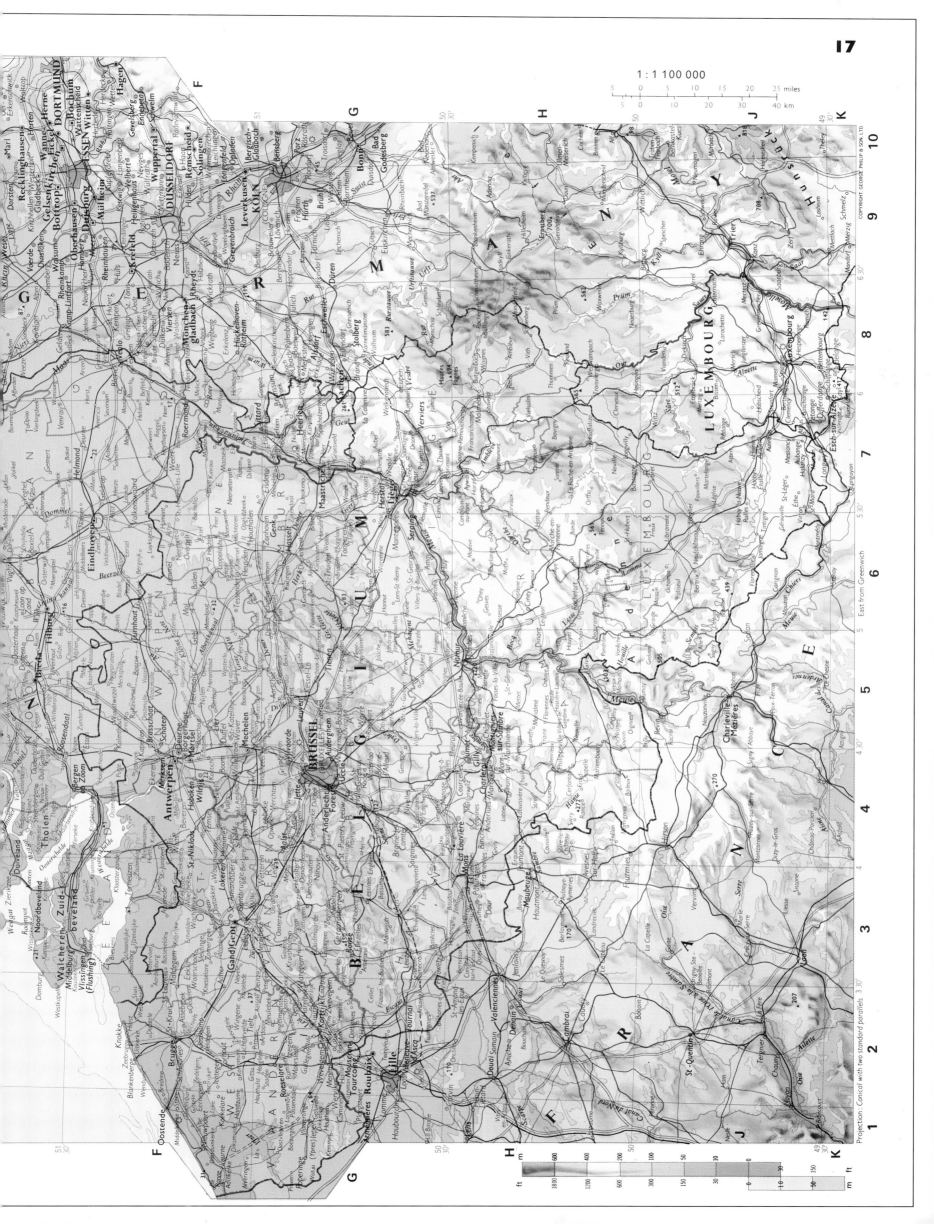

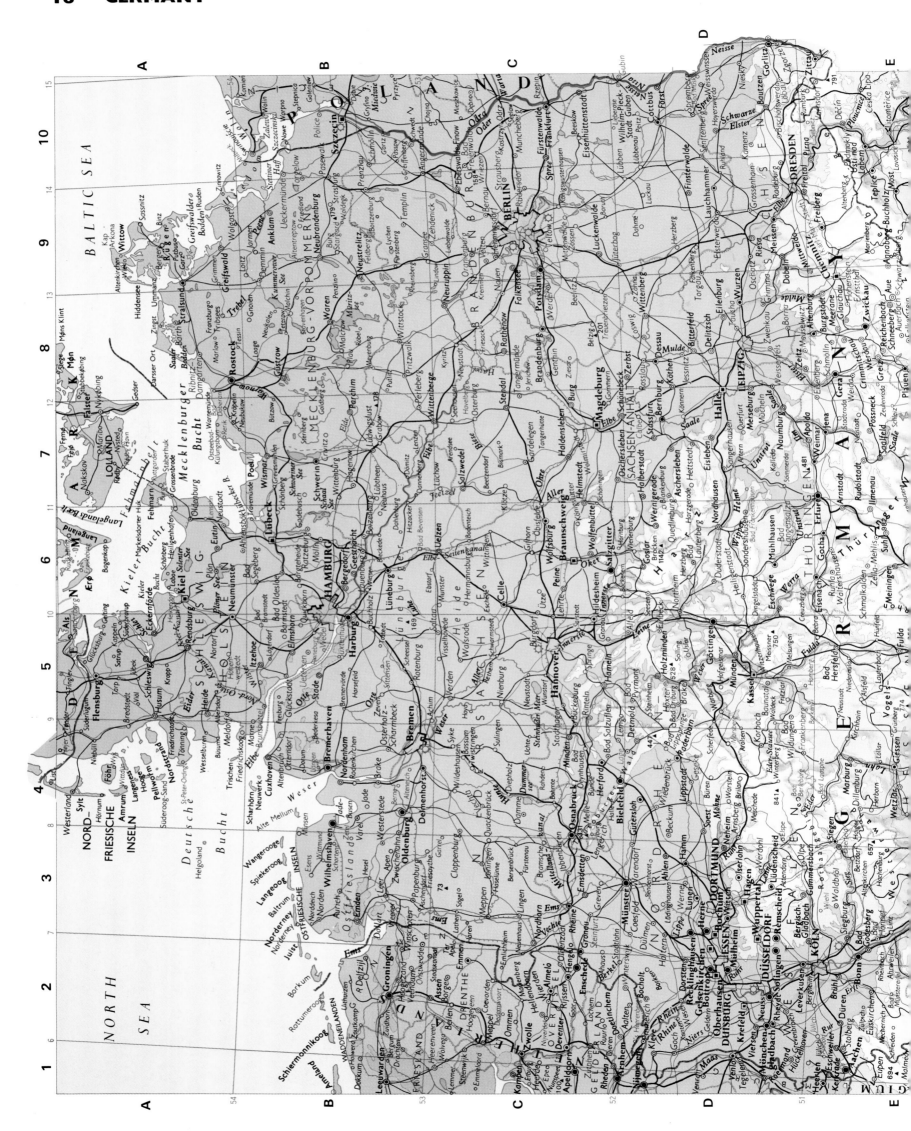

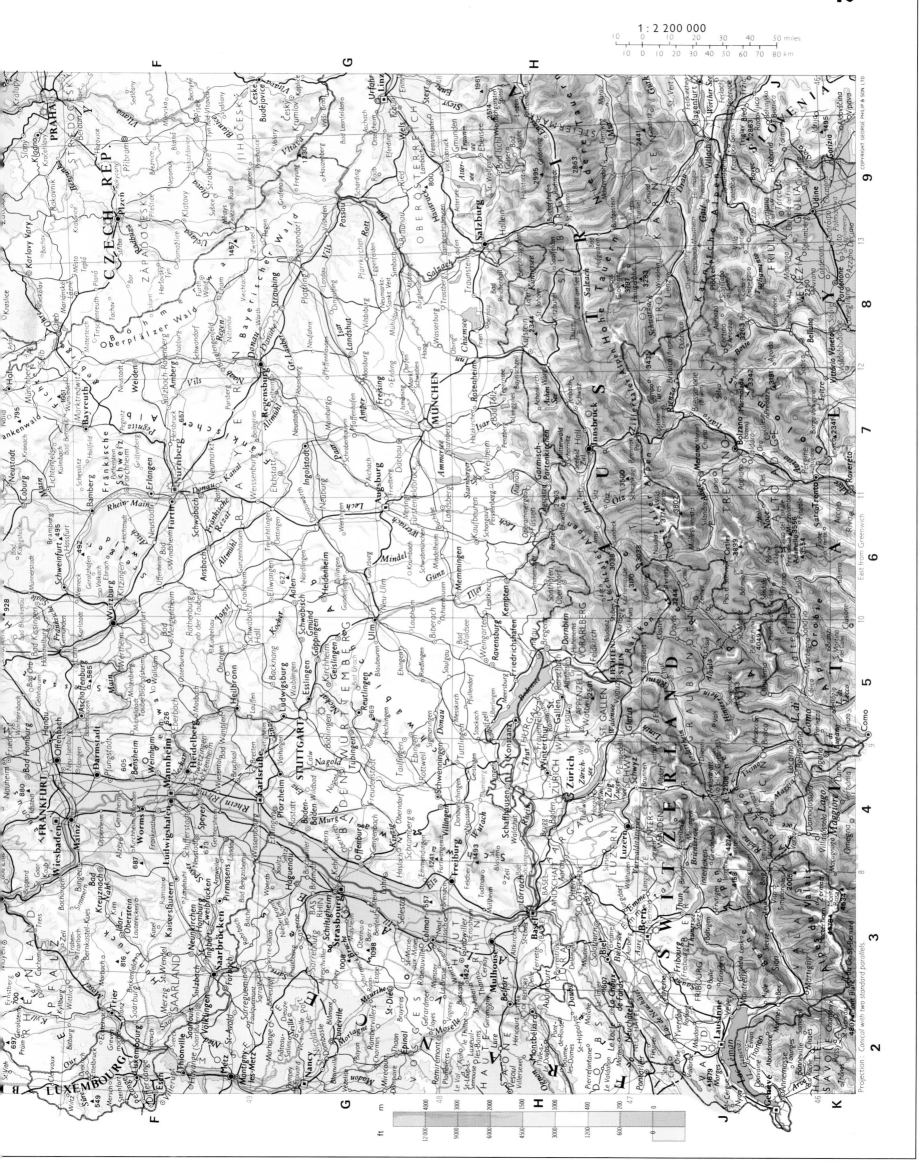

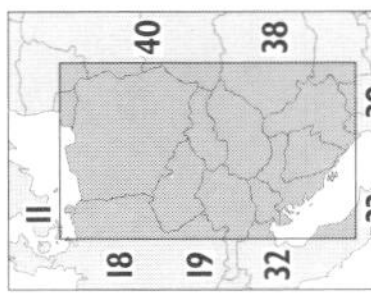

BALTIC SEA

DENMARK

LITHUANIA

BELARUS

UKRAINE

GERMANY

POLAND

CZECH REP.

SLOVAKIA

WARSZAWA (Warsaw)

BERLIN

PRAHA

KRAKÓW

WROCŁAW

POZNAŃ

ŁÓDŹ

GDAŃSK

Gdynia

Szczecin (Stettin)

Lublin

Białystok

Kalingrad

Brest

Lviv

DRESDEN

LEIPZIG

Rostock

Hrodna

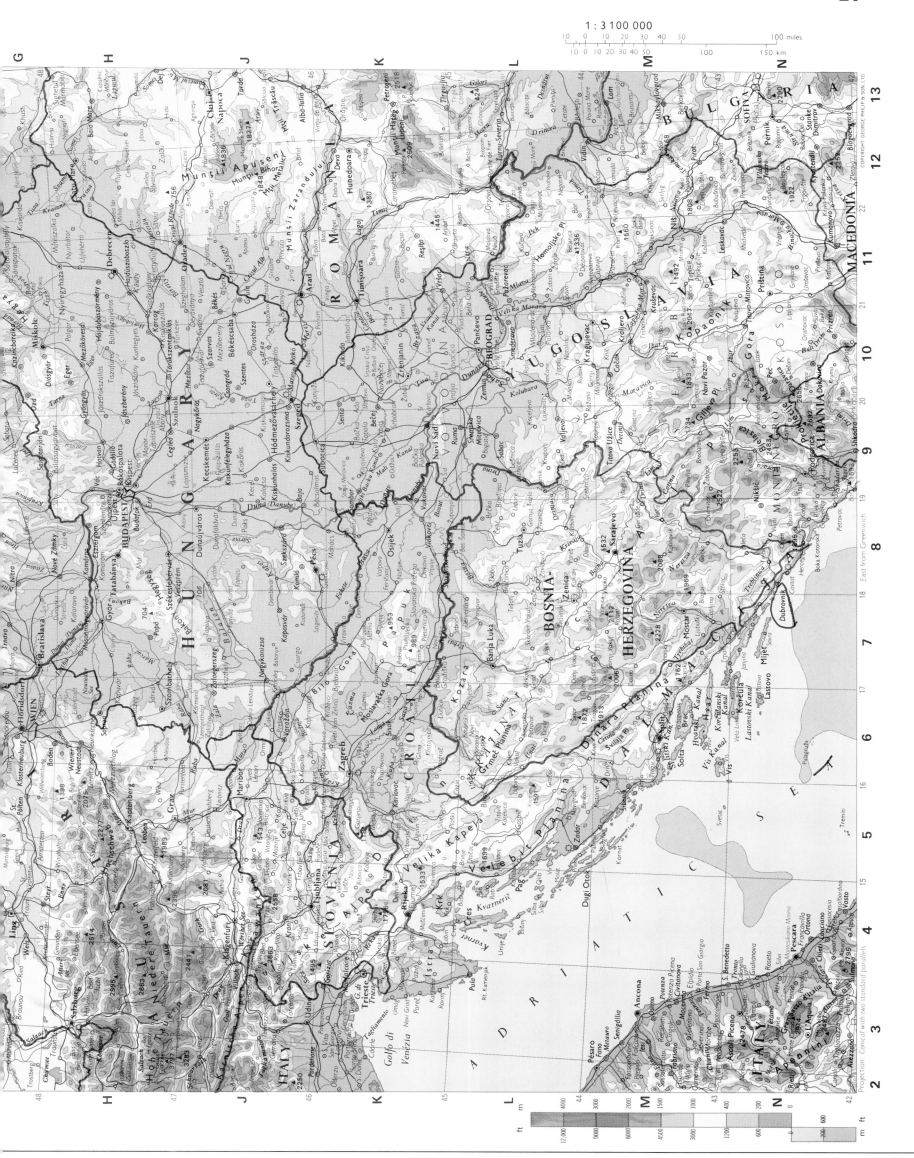

25 19
25
27   32
32

1   2   3   4   5   6

Fayl-Billot
Vitrey-sur-Mance
Jussey
Amance
Lanterne
Mélisey
St-Sauveur
Luxeuil-les-Bains
Servance
Plancher-les-Mines
Ballon d'Alsace
St-Maurice-s.-M.
Moosch
Thann
Cernay
Wittelsheim
Wittenheim
Heitersheim
Belchen Todtnau
Mülheim
Lörrach
Brombach a
Genevrières
Combeaufontaine
Faverney
Meurcourt
Giromagny
Masevaux
MULHOUSE
Lutterbach
Badenweiler 1415
Schönau im Schwarzwald

Lavoncourt
Échenoz-la-Méline
Vesoul
Noroy-le-Bourg
Port-s.-Saône
Saulx
Lure
Champagney
HAUT
RHIN
Brunstatt
Oberwil
Steinen
Schopfheim
Wehr
Waldshut

Valte
Dampierre-sur-Salon
Fresne-St.-Mames
Athesans
Héricourt
BELFORT
Belfort
SUNDGAU
Porte de Bourgogne
Dannemarie
Altkirch
Blotzheim
BASEL (BASLE)
B. Rheinfelden
Albbruck
Säckingen

Gray
Marnay
Rioz
Roche-les-Beaupré
Montbéliard
Audincourt
Valentigney
Delle
Pfetterhouse
Ferrette
Oberwil
Arlesheim
Reinach
Prattein
Liestal
BASEL-LANDSCHAFT
Frick

FRANCE
L'Isle s. le Doubs
Mandeure
Hérimoncourt
AJOIE
JURA
Delémont
Birs
Laufen
Passwang 1204
Waldenburg
Balsthal
Schönenwerd
AARGAU
Aarau
Lenzburg

BESANÇON
Mamirolle
Roulans
Baume-les-Dames
Montagnes du Lomont 839
Pont-de-Roide
Bassecourt
Moutier
SOLOTHURN
Niederbipp
Oberbipp
Rothrist
Zofingen
Olten
Oberentfelden
Suhr

St.-Vit
Dampierre
Quingey
Valdahon
Maîche
Le Russey
Franches Montagnes
Tramelan
Tavannes
Grenchen
Solothurn
Biberist
Herzogenbuchsee
Langenthal
Lotzwil
Reiden
Reinach

Mouchard
Ornans
Lods
St-Imier
Chasseral
1607
Biel (Bienne)
Nidau
Brügg
Kirchberg
Schüpfen
Burgdorf
Huttwil
Willisau
Ruswil
LUZERN

Mont-sous-Vaudrey
DOUBS
Morteau
Le Locle
La Chaux-de-Fonds
La Neuveville
429
Bielersee
Lyss
Aarberg
Sumiswald
Eriswil
Wolhusen

Arc-et-Senans
Loue
Amancey
Levier
NEUCHÂTEL
St-Blaise
Ins
Karzers
BERN (BERNE)
Zollikofen
Napf 1408
Langnau i. E.
Schüpfheim
Entlebuch

Poligny
Salins-les-Bains
Pontarlier
Les Verrières
Couvet
Boudry
Peseux
Colombier
Neuchâtel
429
Ostermundigen
Worb
Signau
Eggiwil
Escholzmatt

Arbois
Andelot-en-Montagne
Frasne
Fleurier
Chasseron 1607
St-Aubin
Estavayer-le-Lac
Payerne
Avenches
Murten
Neuenegg
Köniz
Münsingen
Konolfingen
Schangnau
OBWALDEN
Giswil

Champagnole
Marigny
Mouthe
Ste-Croix
Grandson
Yvonand
Yverdon
Lucens
Moudon
FRIBOURG (Freiburg)
Marly-le-Grand
Düdingen
Schwarzenburg
Wattenwil
Uetendorf
Thun
Steffisburg
Brienz

Pont-du-Navoy
Conliège
Labergement Ste-Marie
Le Mt. d'Or 1461
Vallorbe
Orbe
Bruye
Romont
La Roche
BERN
Stockhorn 2190
Thunersee 558
Spiez
Brienzersee 564
Interlaken
Meiringen

Le Sentier
Mt. Tendre 1679
Le Brassus
La Sarraz
Echallens
FRIBOURG
Gruyère
Vaulruz
Bulle
Gruyères
Bofligen
Simme 2362
Niesen
Reichenbach
Frutigen
Lauterbrunnen
Wengen
Grindelwald
Schreckhorn 4078
Finsteraarhorn 4274

St-Laurent-en-Grandvaux
Morbier
Morez
VAUD
Bussigny
LAUSANNE
Oron
Châtel-St-Denis
Mont 2002
Moléson
Zweisimmen
Gstaad
Berner Oberland
Adelboden
Kandersteg
Blümlisalphorn 3664
Jungfrau 4158
Lötschental

Les Rousses
La Côte
Morges
Lutry
Lavaux
Vevey
Château d'Oex
Col des Mosses 1445
Wildstrubel 3243
Balmhorn 3709
Lötschberg tunnel

Moirans-en-Montagne
St-Cergue
Rolle
Léman (L. Geneva) 372
Montreux
Villeneuve
Wildhorn 3248
Leukerbad
Naters
Simplon tunnel

St-Claude
Divonne-les-Bains
Gex
Nyon
Thonon-les-Bains
310
Evian-les-Bains
St-Gingolph
Aigle
Leysin
Les Diablerets
Leuk
Sierre
Visp
Brig
Simplonpass 2005
Pte Leone 3553
3194

Dortan
St-Lupicin
Crêt de la Neige 1718
Versoix
Chêne-Bourg
Dranse
Chablais
Vouvry
Monthey
Bex
3051
Conthey
Sion
Stalden
Simplon

Oyonnax
Chézery-Forens
St-Germain-de-Joux
GENÈVE (GENEVA)
Vernier
Annemasse
2244
2432
Champéry
Dents du Midi 3257
St-Maurice
Vétroz
Riddes
Saxon
St-Niklaus
Weisshorn 4506
Dom 4545
Weissmies 4023
Saas Fee

Bellegarde-s.-V.
Chancy
Veyrier
HAUTE-SAVOIE
Bonneville
La Roche
Martigny
1527
Barr. de la Grande Dixence
Arolla
Zermatt
Matterhorn (Mte Cervino) 4634
Monte Rosa 4637
Villadòssola

Chailland-de-Michaille
Frangy
Cruseilles
Thorens-Glières
Cluses
Faucigny
Le Châtelard
Orsières
Bourg St-Pierre
PENNINE
Dufourspitze

PAYS DE GEX
Seyssel
Genevois
Pte Percée 2752
Sallanches
St-Gervais-les-B.
Aig. d'Argentière 3898
Col du Gt-St-Bernard 2469
Champoluc
3320
Gressoney
Macugnaga

Artemare
Rumilly
Annecy
Mégève
Chamonix-Mont-Blanc
Aosta
VALLE D'AOSTA
Alagna Valsesia

Chazey-Bons
Belley
Lac du Bourget
Lac d'Annecy
Thônes
Tournette 2351
Flumet
Mt Blanc 4807
Pre S. Didier
Courmayeur
Châtillon
Scopello

Yenne
Lescheraines
Le Châtelard
Ugine
Beaufort
3120
La Thuile
Villeneuve
3559
Verrès
Mte Barl 2044
Trivero
PIE

SAVOIE
Aix-les-Bains
Le Bourget-du-...
Albertville
SAVOIE
2188
Col du Petit St-Bernard
Dora Baltea
Piedicavallo

Projection: Conical with two standard parallels

ft   m
9000 3000
6000 2000
4500 1500
3000 1000
1200   500
600   200

1   2   6 30'   3   7   4   7 30'   5   8

1 : 900 000

5 0 5 10 15 20 25 miles
5 0 10 20 30 40 km

COPYRIGHT. GEORGE PHILIP & SON. LTD.

East from Greenwich

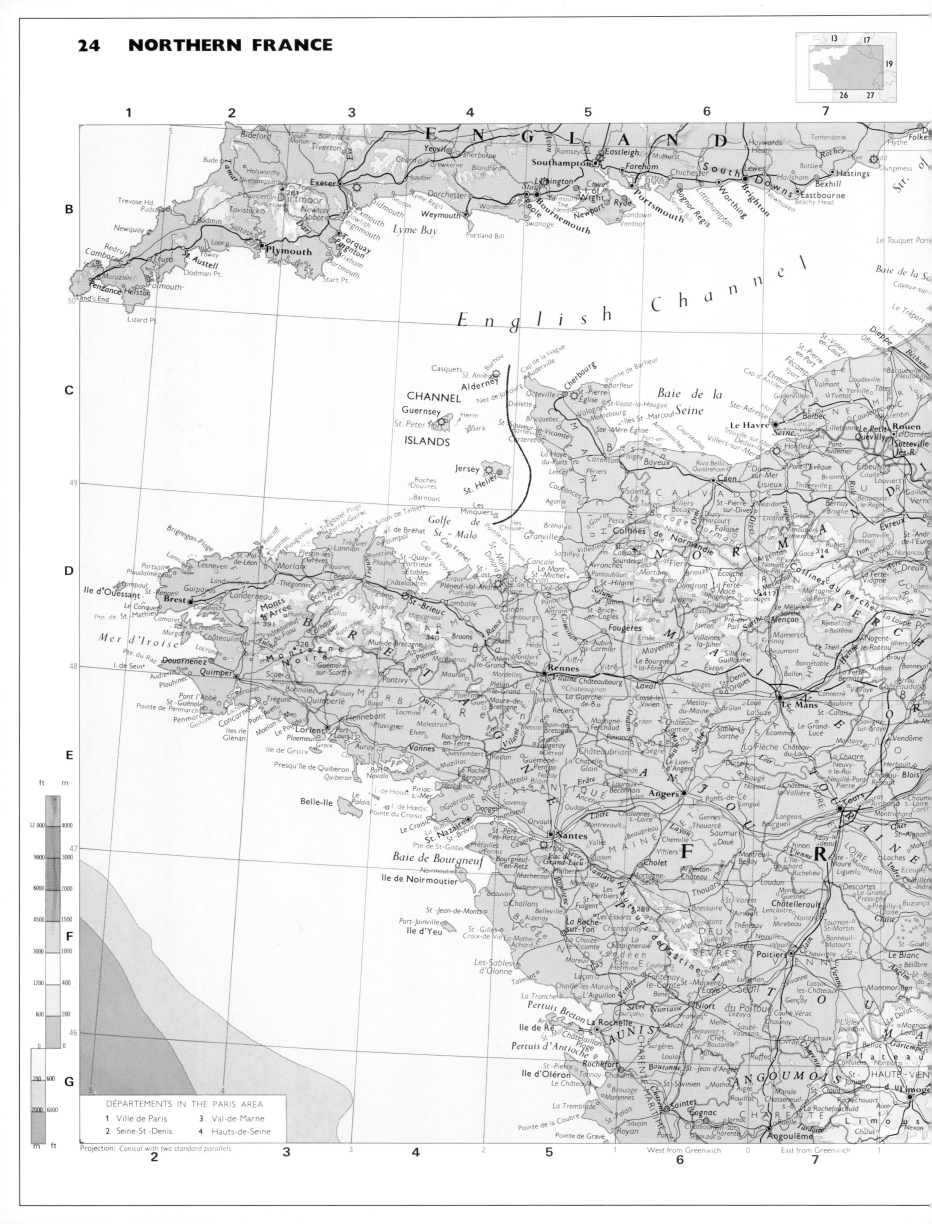

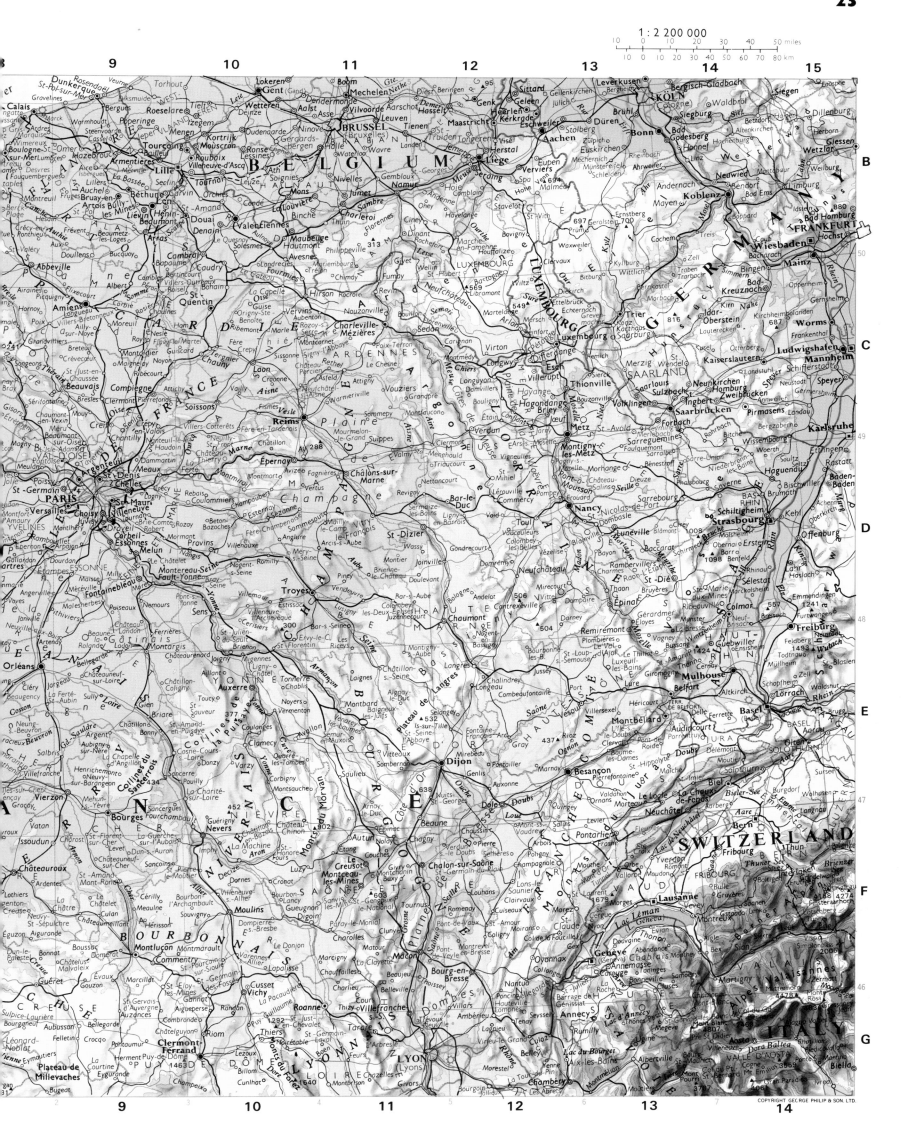

1 : 2 200 000

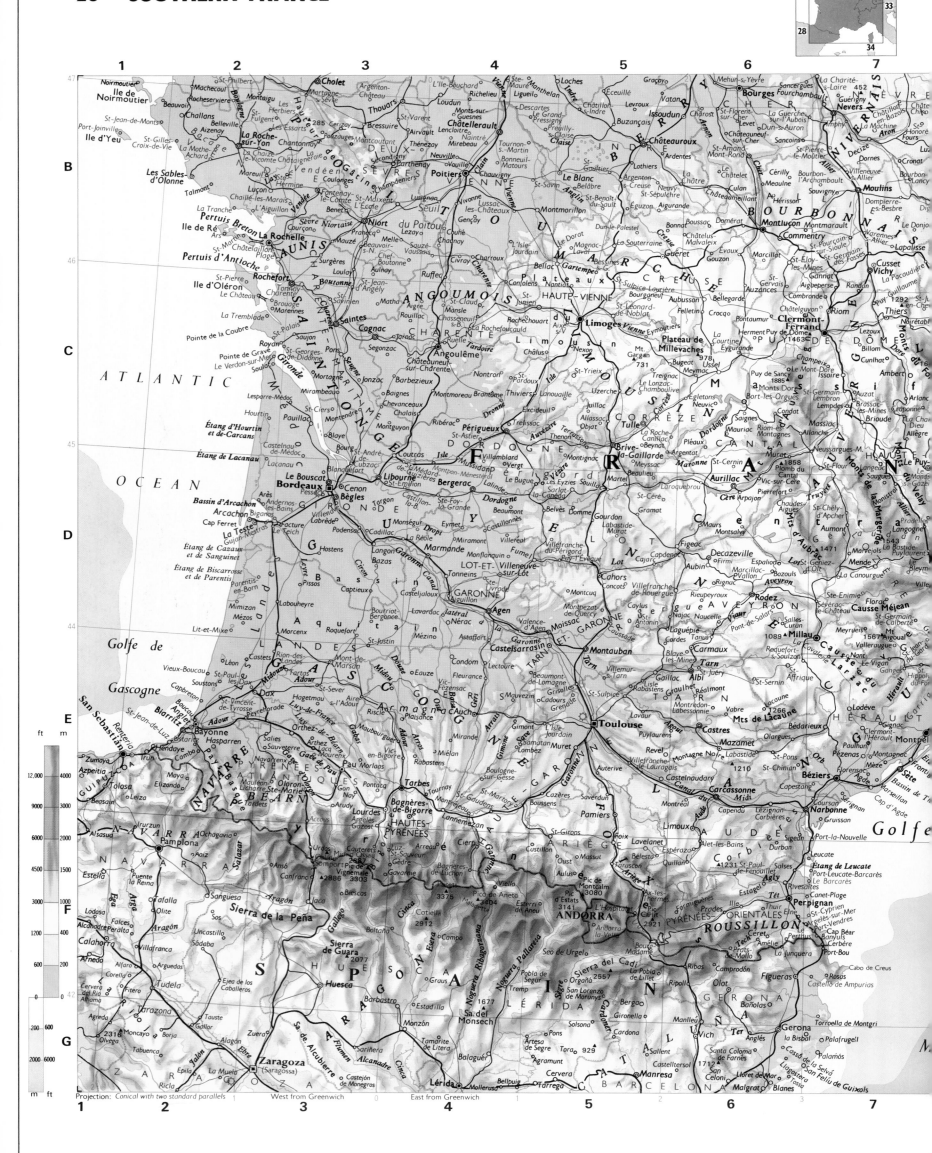

1 : 2 200 000

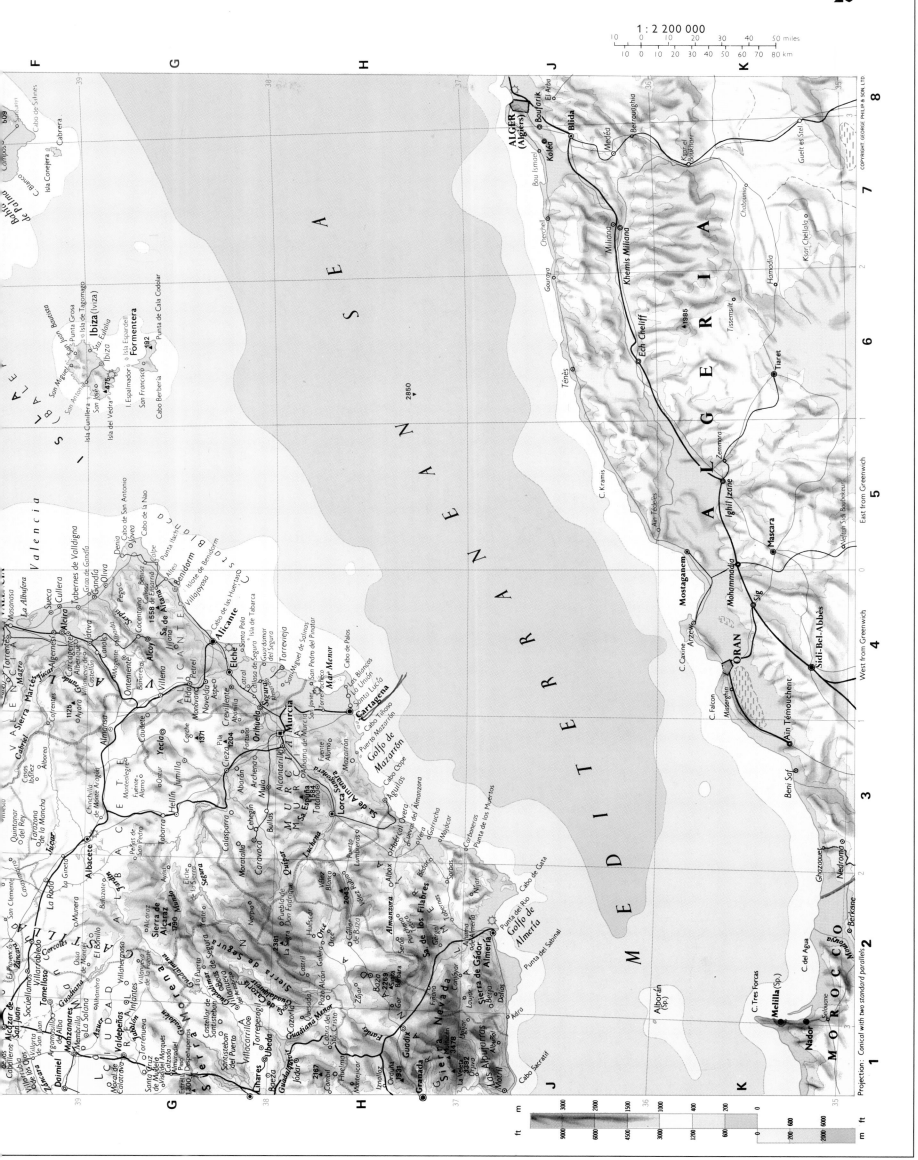

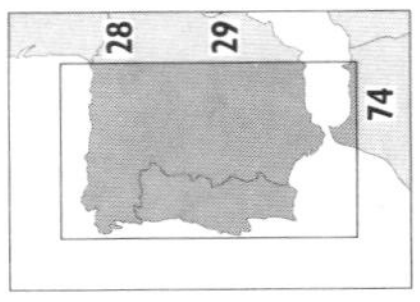
28
29
74

BAY OF BISCAY
ATLANTIC OCEAN
San Sebastián
Bilbao
Santander
Gijón
Oviedo
León
Burgos
Valladolid
Palencia
Salamanca
Zamora
Segovia
Avila
MADRID
Vitoria
Logroño
Lugo
Orense
La Coruña (Corunna)
El Ferrol
Santiago de Compostela
Pontevedra
Vigo
Braga
Porto (Oporto)
Vila Nova de Gaia
Coimbra
Aveiro
Viseu
Guadalajara
Picos de Europa
Sierra de Guadarrama
Sierra de Gredos
Sierra de Gata
Serra da Estrela
Duero
Douro
Miño
A
B
C
D
E
F
1
2
3
4
5
6
7
8

1 : 2 200 000

Projection: Conical with two standard parallels

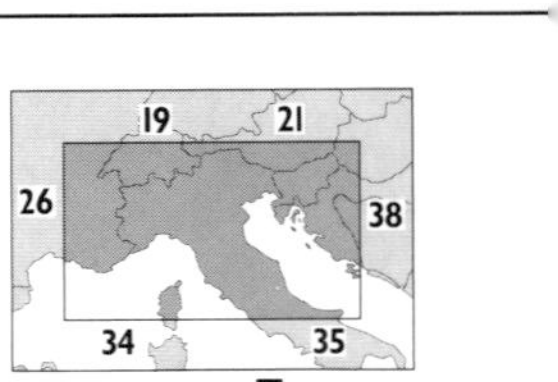

Grid references (top): 1 2 3 4 5 6 7

Row labels: A B C D E F G

SWITZERLAND

VORARLBERG
Feldkirch
LIECHTEN-STEIN
Vaduz
ST. GALLEN
GRAUBÜNDEN
LUZERN
Luzern
Zürich-see
Zug
Schwyz
Glarus
Bern (Berne)
Fribourg
FRIBOURG
VAUD
Lausanne
Neuchâtel
La Chaux-de-Fonds
Biel
VALAIS
TICINO
BERNER ALPEN
Interlaken
Thun
Thunersee
Brienzersee
Jungfrau 4274
Finsteraarhorn
Matterhorn 4478
Monte Rosa 4634
Simplonpass 2005
St. Gottardo Passo del
Passo dello Stelvio 2757
Ortles 3899
Bormio

FRANCHE-COMTÉ
Dole
Besançon
Pontarlier
Ornans

BOURGOGNE
Beaune
Chalon-sur-Saône
Mâcon
SAÔNE-ET-LOIRE
Lons-le-Saunier
JURA
St-Claude
AIN
Bourg-en-Bresse
Nantua
Bellegarde

Lyon (Lyons)
Vienne
RHÔNE
ISÈRE
Grenoble
Chambéry
SAVOIE
Annecy
HAUTE-SAVOIE
Genève (GENEVA)
Annemasse
Thonon
Évian
Lac Léman
Aix-les-Bains
Lac du Bourget
Albertville
Moûtiers
Mont Blanc 4807
TARENTAISE
VANOISE
Modane

HAUTES-ALPES
Gap
Briançon
Embrun
Lac de Serre-Ponçon
Massif du Pelvoux 4103
Mont Pelat 3052
Barcelonnette

DRÔME
Valence
Romans
Montélimar
Die
Crest

VAUCLUSE
Avignon
Orange
Carpentras
Ventoux
Cavaillon
Apt

ALPES-DE-HAUTE-PROVENCE
Digne-les-Bains
Sisteron
Forcalquier
Manosque

ALPES-MARITIMES
Nice
Antibes
Cannes
Grasse
Vence
Menton
MONACO
Monte-Carlo

BOUCHES-DU-RHÔNE
MARSEILLE (Marseilles)
Aix-en-Provence
Arles
Salon
Martigues
Étang de Berre

VAR
Toulon
Hyères
ILES D'HYÈRES
Fréjus
St-Raphaël
Draguignan
Brignoles
Ste-Maxime
St-Tropez
Cap Camarat
Côte d'Azur

PIEMONTE
TORINO (Turin)
Moncalieri
Chieri
Asti
Alessandria
Tortona
Casale Monferrato
Vercelli
Novara
Ivrea
Biella
Cúneo
Mondovì
Saluzzo
Fossano
Savigliano
Alba
Bra
Pinerolo
Carmagnola
Gran Paradiso 4061
Monte Viso 3841

VALLE D'AOSTA
Aosta
Dora Baltea

LOMBARDIA
MILANO (Milan)
Monza
Bérgamo
Bréscia
Como
L. di Como
Lago Maggiore
Varese
Lecco
Pavia
Lodi
Crema
Cremona
Busto Arsizio
Legnano
Saronno
Sondrio
Valtellina
Adda
Lago d'Iseo
Garda (Lago di)
Desenzano
Mántova

EMILIA ROMAGNA
Parma
Piacenza
Réggio nell'Emilia
Módena
Fidenza
Salsomaggiore
Borgo Val di Taro
Bóbbio

LIGURIA
GÉNOVA (Genoa)
Savona
La Spézia
Imperia (Maurizio-Oneglia)
San Remo
Ventimíglia
Albenga
Rapallo
Sta. Margherita
Chiávari
Sestri
Levanto
Finale Ligure
Vado
Varazze
Golfo di Génova
Riviera di Ponente
Riviera di Levante
Portovénere

TOSCANA
Livorno (Leghorn)
Pisa
Lucca
Pistóia
Carrara
Massa
Viareggio
Camaiore
Pietrasanta
San Giuliano
Fucécchio
Empoli
Cécina
Volterra
Piombino
Portoferráio
ELBA
Rosignano
Castagneto Carducci
San Vincenzo
Follónica
Colline Metallífere
Arcipelago Toscano
Pianosa
Montecristo
Giglio
Golfo di Follónica

CORSE (CORSICA)
HAUTE-CORSE
CORSE-DU-SUD
Ajaccio
Bastia
St-Florent
G. de St-Florent
L'Île Rousse
Calvi
Corte
Sagone
G. de Sagone
G. d'Ajaccio
Bonifacio
Porto-Vecchio
Monte Cinto 2710
Monte Rotondo 2625
Aléria
Ghisonaccia
Sartène
Propriano
Iles Sanguinaires
C. Corse

LIGURIAN SEA

Golfo di Génova

Gorgona
Capraia 447
C. Corse

Projection: Conical with two standard parallels
East from Greenwich

Elevation scale (left margin):
ft / m
12 000 / 4000
9000 / 3000
6000 / 2000
4500 / 1500
3000 / 1000
1200 / 400
600 / 200
0 / 0
600 / 200
6000 / 2000

1 : 2 200 000

CORSE / CORSICA

Iles Sanguinaires
G. d'Ajaccio
C. di Muro
Petreto
Zonza
Levie
Favone
Solenzara
Taravo
2136
Propriano
Porto-Vecchio
Sartène
CORSE-DU-SUD
Iles Cerbicales
G. de Valinco
Bonifacio
I. de Cavallo
Bouches de Bonifacio
Santa Teresa Gallura
Maddalena
La Maddalena
Caprera
Punta dello Scorno
Asinara
Golfo dell' Asinara
Liscia
Pto. Cervo
Costa Smeralda
Arzachena
Coghinas
Àggius
Calangiánus
Golfo Aranci
G. di Ólbia
Porto Tórres
Témpio Pausania
1362
Tavolara
Ólbia
Sorso
Sennori
M. Limbara
C. dell'Argentiera
Sássari
Osilo
Oschiri
Tanaúnella
Fertília
Íttiri
Ozieri
L. di Coghinas
Álghero
Pattada
Buddusò
Posada
Villanova
Monteleone
1259
Bórrova
Bitti
Siniscóla
C. Comino
Temo
Tirso
Orune
Bosa
Macomer
Núoro
Dórgali
Oliena
Golfo di Orosei
SARDEGNA
Ghilarza
L. del Tirso
Fonni
Cedrino
Cábras
Oristano
Sórgono
Monti del Gennargentu
Baunei
C. di Monte Santu
M. Arci
SARDEGNA
1834
Golfo di Oristano
Laconia
Árbatax
Arborea
Terralba
Nurri
Lanusei
Jerzu
SARDINIA
C. Pécora
Gúspini
S. Gavino
Mónreale
Mandas
Senorbi
Flumendosa
Fluminimaggiore
Arbus
Villacidro
1236
M. Línas
Gonnosfanadiga
Serramanna
S. Vitao
Villaputzu
Muravera
Iglésias
Dolianova
Cíxerri
Assémini
Sestu
Sínnai
1069
C. Ferrato
Portoscuso
Gonnesa
Síliqua
Selárgius
Quartu Sant'Elena
Carloforte
Carbonia
1116
Serpentara
San Pietro
Santadi
Cágliari
Golfo di Cágliari
Sant'Antíoco
Porto Botte
Teulada
Pula
C. Carbonara
Sant' Antíoco
Porto Botte
G. di Pálmas
C. Spartivento

TYRRHENIAN SEA

3719
3589
Ustica

East from Greenwich

Scale bar (left)

ft	m
9000	3000
6000	2000
4500	1500
3000	1000
1200	400
600	200
0	0
	200
	600
2000	6000
4000	12,000
m	ft

ROMA (Rome)
Vatican City
Tívoli
Subiaco
Trosacco
Conca del Fúcino
Fregene
Palestrina
Valmontone
Lido di Óstia (Lido di Roma)
Tévere (Tiber)
Frascati
Anagni
Alatri
Véroli
Sora
Ísola del Lir
Arpino
Pomézia
Albano Laziale
Aprília
Velletri
Cori
Ferentino
Monte S. Giova
Latina
Cisterna di Latina
Ceccano
Ceprano
Cassino
Anzio
Nettuno
Priverno
Sonnino
Pontecor
Pontínia
Fondi
Liri
Sabáudia
1533
Monte Circeo
Terracina
Gaeta
541
Aur
Palmarola
Zannone
Golfo di
Gaeta
Garigliano
Ísole Ponziane
Ponza
283
Mondragone
Voltur
Ventotene
Casal
Giugli
788
Pro
Íschia
(Nap

SICILIA / SICILY

C. San Vito
Golfo di Castellammare
Castellammare
Favarotta
C. Gallo
Carini
Mondeglo
PALERMO
Bagheria
Levanto
Trápani
1110
Érice
G. di Carini
Partinico
Misilmeri
Términi Im
Ísole Égadi
Alcamo
S. Giuseppe
Maréttimo
Poceco
Calatafimi
Iato
Camporeale
Marineo
Favignana
Salemi
Corleone
1613
Belsia
Stagnone
Gibellina
Lercara
Le Ma
Marsala
Partanna
Bisacquino
Prizzi
Friddle
Alía
Castelvetrano
Sambuca di Sicilia
Menfi
Mussomeli
Cate
Mazara del Vallo
Bùrgio
San Catal
Belice
Campobello di Mazara
Castelterm
Calta
Sciacca
Caltabellotta
Platani
Racalmuto
Canic
Sicilian Channel
Ribera
Siculiano
Aragona
Negro
Cattólica Eraclea
Raffadali
Favara
Porto Empédocle
Agrigento
Palma di Montechiaro
Campobello
Lic
Pantelleria
Pantelleria (It.)
836
1319
Palma di Montechiaro

TUNISIA

Iles de la Galite
Bizerte (Binzert)
C. Blanc
Cani
Plane
C. Serrat
Menzel-Bourguiba
Zembra
C. Bon
El Kala
Mateur
Golfe de Tunis
Tabarka
Téboursba
TUNIS
Halq el Oued
Kelibia
ALGERIA
Béja
Medjerda
Menzel-Temime
Bou Salem
Medjerda
Soliman
Nabeul
Téboursouk
Zaghouan
Hammamet

MEDITE... (MEDITERRANEAN)

1 : 2 200 000

10 0 10 20 30 40 50 miles
10 0 10 20 30 40 50 60 70 80 km

ADRIATIC

SEA

A B R U Z Z I

MOLISE

A D R I A T I C

S E A

G. di Manfredónia

Strait of Otranto

ALBANIA

Tirana (Tiranë)

Durrësi (Durazzo)

Vlora (Valona)

BERATI

Golfo di Táranto

Bari

Brindisi

Lecce

Táranto

NAPOLI

BASILICATA

Potenza

G. di Salerno

G. di Policastro

Kérkira (Corfu)

Kérkira

CALABRIA

Cosenza

Catanzaro

Crotone

Golfo di Sant'Eufémia

Golfo di Squillace

Isole Eólie o Lípari (Æolian Is.)

Strómboli

I O N I A N

Reggio

Messina

Str. di Messina

Mt. Peloritani

Monti Nebrodi

Taormina

Catánia

Etna 3340

Golfo di Catánia

S E A

Siracusa

Noto

S I C I L I A

Golfo di Gela

C. Passero

Channel

M E D I T E R R A N E A N   S E A

COPYRIGHT, GEORGE PHILIP & SON, LTD

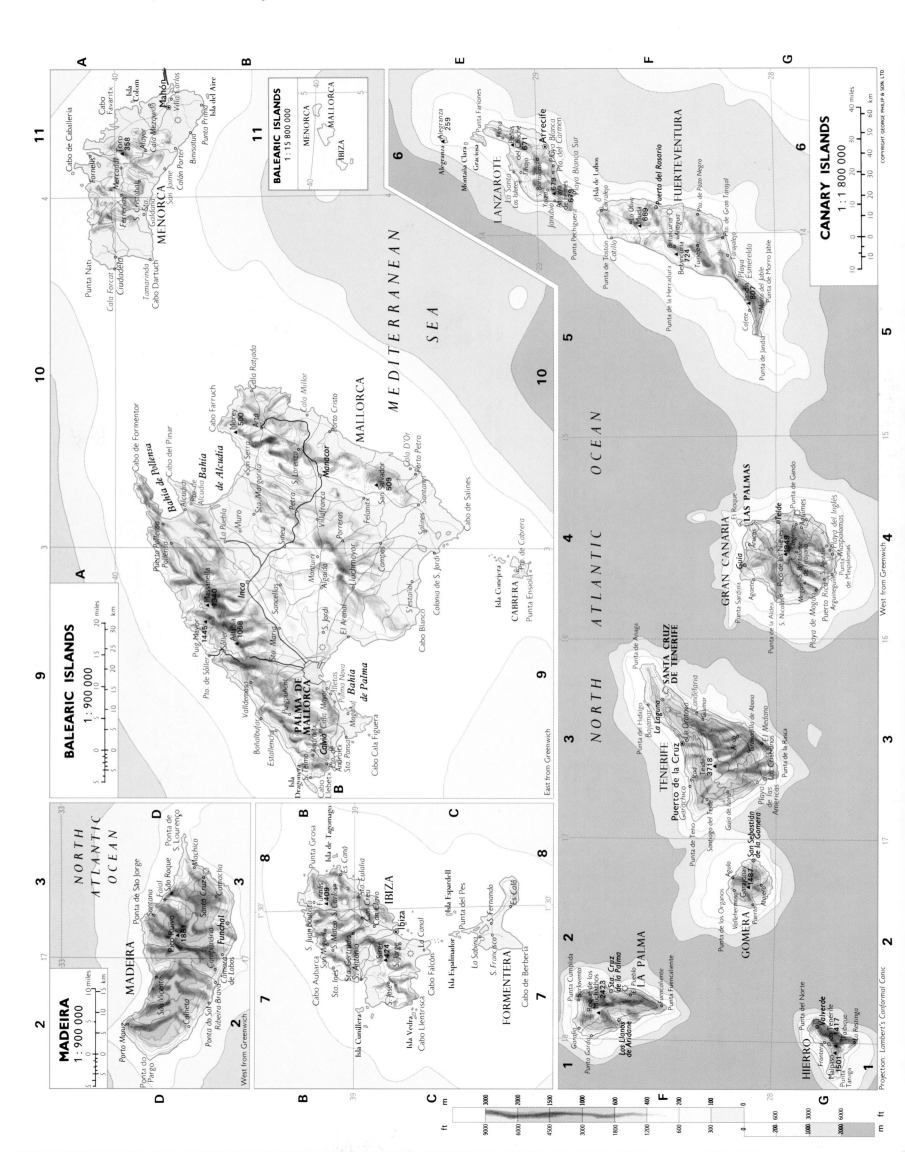

BALEARIC ISLANDS
1 : 900 000

BALEARIC ISLANDS
1 : 15 800 000

MENORCA

MALLORCA

IBIZA

MADEIRA
1 : 900 000

CANARY ISLANDS
1 : 1 800 000

COPYRIGHT GEORGE PHILIP & SON LTD.

Projection: Lambert's Conformal Conic

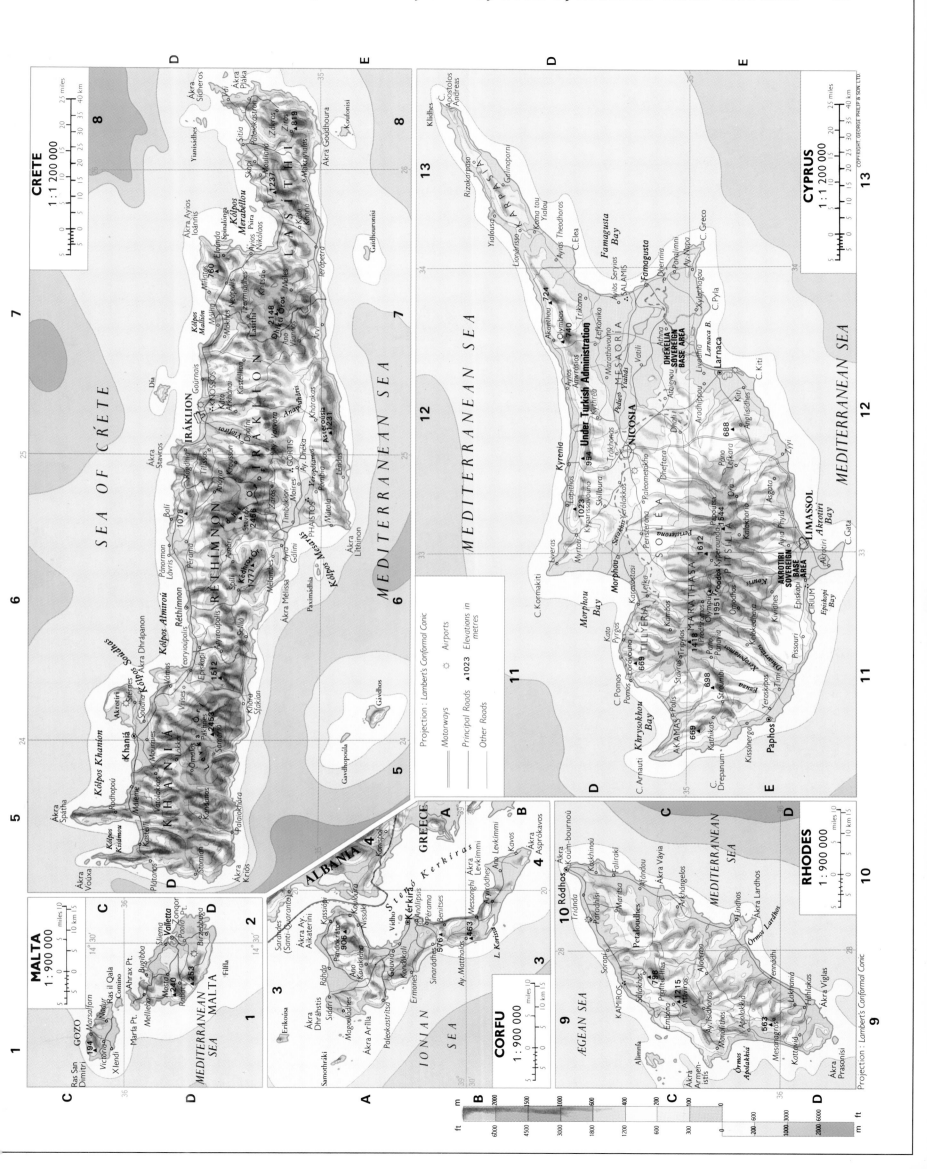

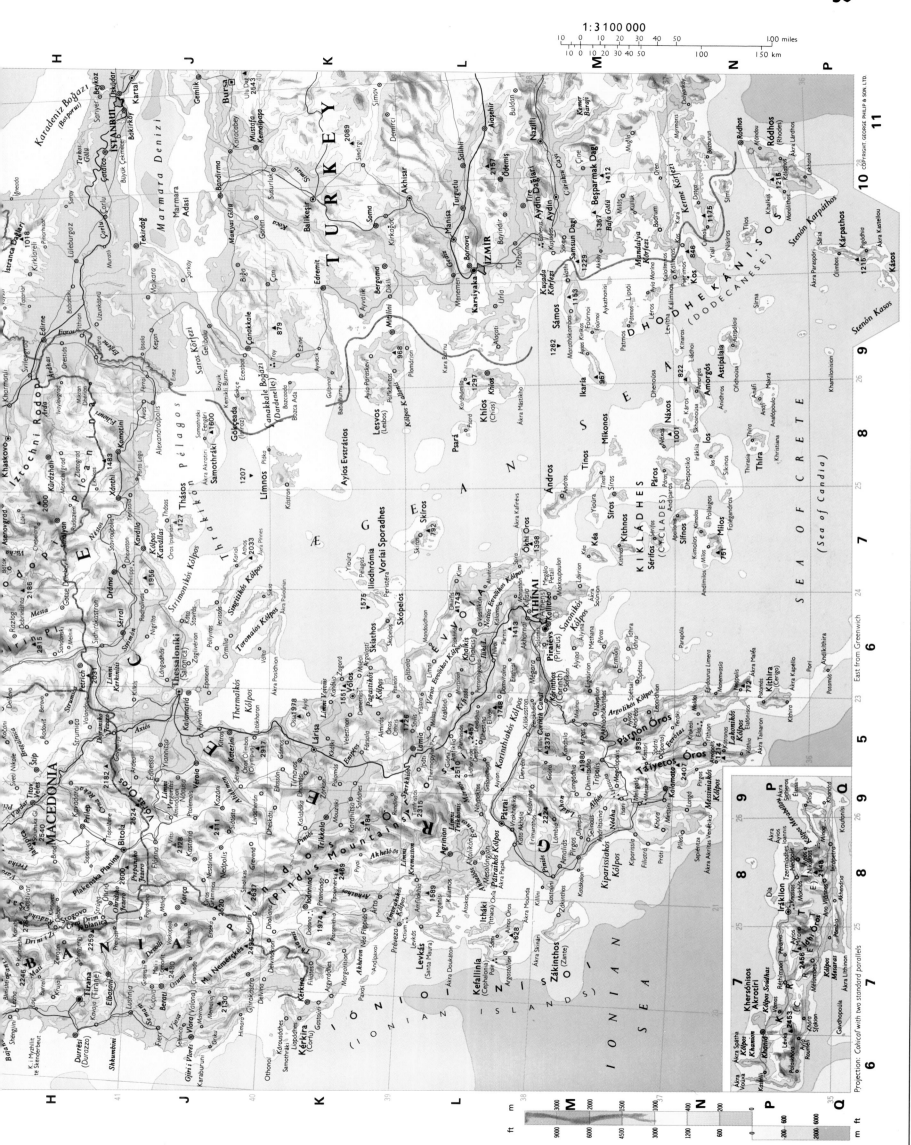

1 : 3 100 000

10   0   10 20 30 40   50   100 miles
10   0   10 20 30 40 50   100   150 km

Projection: Conical with two standard parallels

East from Greenwich

TURKEY

Karadeniz Boğazı (Bosporus)

İSTANBUL
Üsküdar
Beykoz
Kartal

Marmara Denizi

Marmara Adası

Edirne

Bursa
Ulu Dağ 2543

Gemlik
Mustafa Kemalpaşa

Bandırma
Balıkesir

Çanakkale Boğazı (Dardanelles)

İZMİR
Karşıyaka
Bornova

Manisa
Turgutlu

Aydın Dağları
Aydın 1367
Beşparmak Dağı 1412

Nazilli

Kuşada Körfezi
Sámos 1153
1262

Sakin Dağı
Samsun Dağı 1229

Mandalya Körfezi

Kerme Körfezi
Kos 846
1175

DHODEKANISOS (DODECANESE)

Ródhos
Rhodes 1215

Stenón Kárpathos
Kárpathos 1215

Stenón Kásos
Kásos

Lesvos (Lesbos)
Mitilíni 968

Khíos (Chios) 1297

Psará

Ikaría 1037
Sámos 957

Amorgós 822

Náxos 1001

Astipálaia

Páros

KIKLÁDHES (CYCLADES)

Andros
Tínos
Míkonos
Síros
Kéa
Kíthnos
Sérifos
Sífnos
Mílos 751

SEA OF CRETE
(Sea of Candia)

Æ G E A N   S E A

Thásos
Kaválla

Samothráki 1600

Límnos 1207

Ayios Evstrátios

Skíros 792

Iliódhrómia
Vórial Sporádhes
Skópelos
Skíathos 1575

Vólos

Pagasitikós Kólpos

EVVOIA
Khalkís 1743
1398 Ókhi Oros

ATHÍNAI
Piraiévs (Piraeus)

Saronikós Kólpos

Korinthos (Corinth)
Korinthiakós Kólpos

Pátrai
Pátraikós Kólpos

MACEDONIA

Thessaloniki (Salonica)

Drama
Serrai

Strimonikós Kólpos
Singitikós Kólpos
Toronaios Kólpos
Thermaïkós Kólpos

Olimbos (Olympus) 2917

Kateríni

Lárisa

Tríkkala
Pindus Mountains 2184

ALBANIA

Tirana (Tiranë)

Durrёs (Durazzo)

Elbasan

Berat

Vlorë (Valona)

Kérkira (Corfu)

Kefallínía (Cephalonia)

Zákinthos (Zante)

Levkás (Santa Maura)

Ithaki (Ithaca)

I O N I A N   S E A

(I O N I A N   I S L A N D S)

Agrínion
Aitolikón Kólpos

Mesolongi

Pirgos

Kalamata
Messiniakós Kólpos
Taïyetos Oros 2407

Párnon Oros 1935
Lakonikós Kólpos

Akra Maléa

Kíthira (Cérigo)

Argolikós Kólpos

Nauplia
Argos
Trípolis

KRITI

Khersónisos Akrotíri

Khaniá
Iráklion
Levká Óri 2453

Kólpos Mesarás

Ídhi Oros 2456

Dhíkti Oros 2148

1 : 4 400 000

50 0 50 100 miles
50 0 50 100 150 km

FINLAND

Gulf of Bothnia

Gulf of Finland

BALTIC SEA

Gulf of Riga

ESTONIA

LATVIA

LITHUANIA

BELARUS

RUSSIA

Onezhskoye Ozero (L. Onega)

Ladozhskoye Ozero (L. Ladoga)

SANKT-PETERBURG (Leningrad)

MOSKVA (Moscow)

Tallinn

Riga

Vilnius

MINSK

Smolensk

Vologda

Yaroslavl

Kostroma

Rybinsk

Ivanovo

Vladimir

Tula

Ryazan

Kaluga

Tver

Novgorod

Pskov

Vitsyebsk

Mahilyow

Orsha

Polatsk

Daugavpils

Kaunas

Klaipeda

Panevezys

Siauliai

Tartu

Parnu

Petrozavodsk

Rybinskoye Vdkhr.

Valdayskaya Vozvyshennost

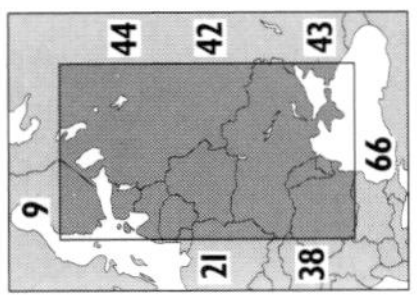

Ozero Chudskoye

Ozero Pskovskoye

Ozero Ilmen

Volga

Dnepr (Dnieper)

Daugava

(Russia)

Åland (Ahvenanmaa)

Hiiumaa (Dagö)

Saaremaa (Ösel)

Muhu

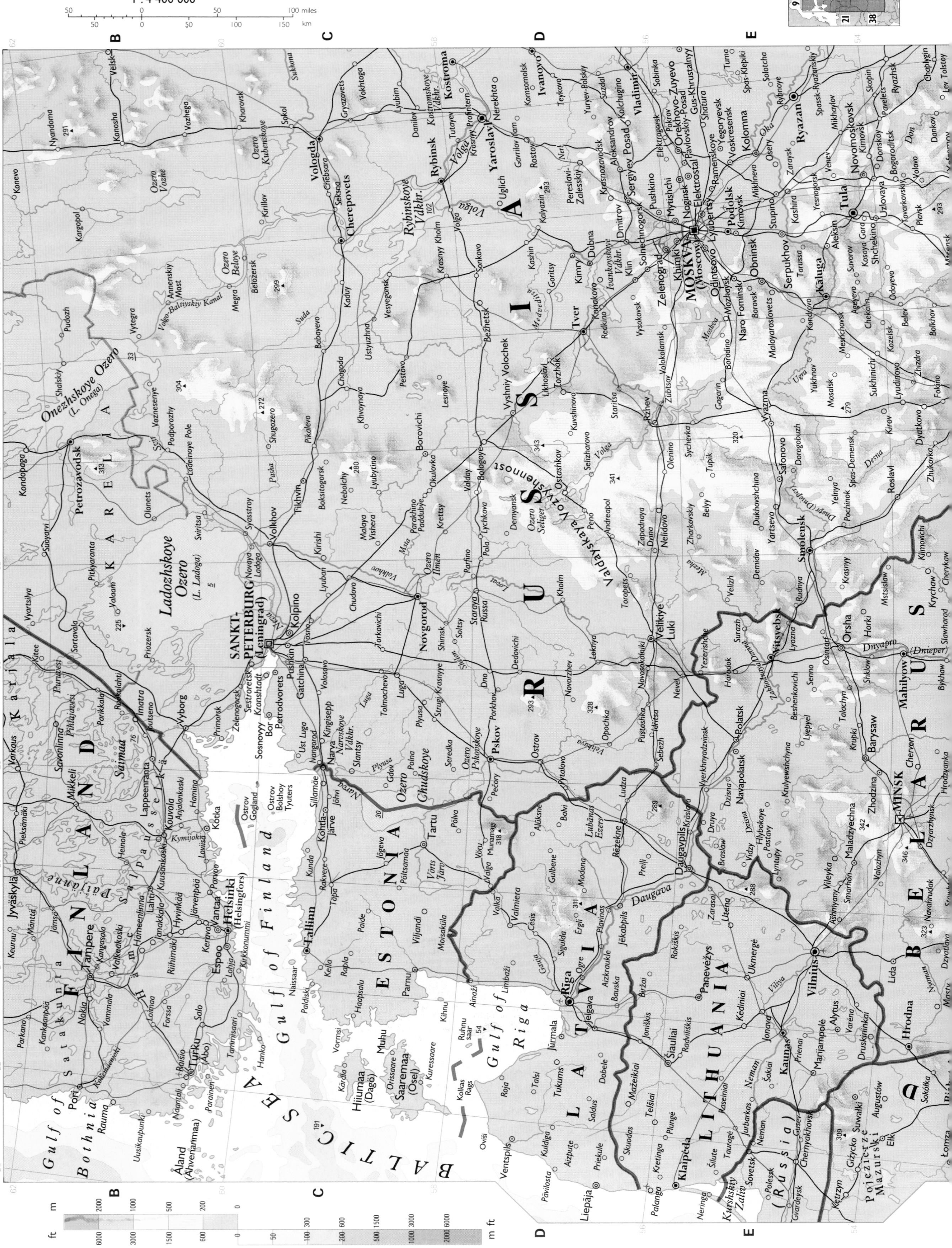

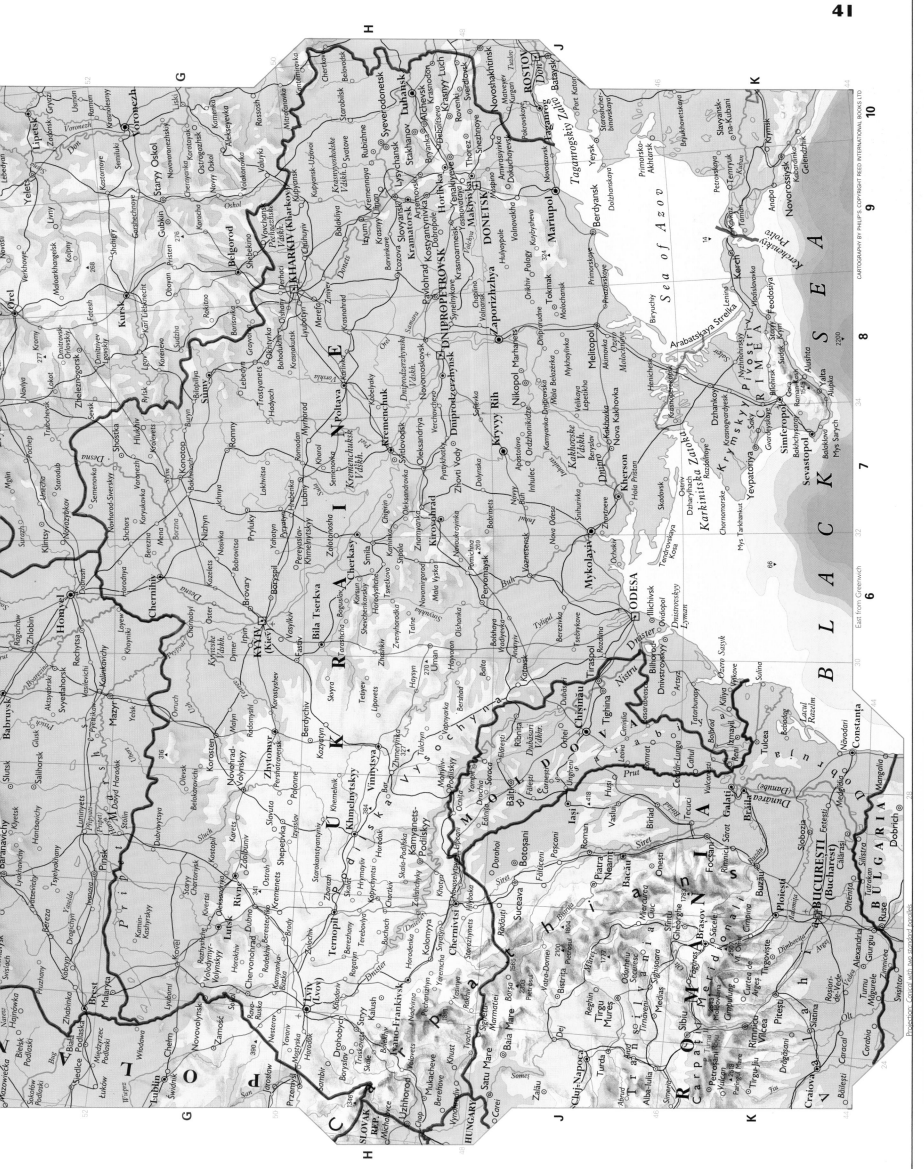

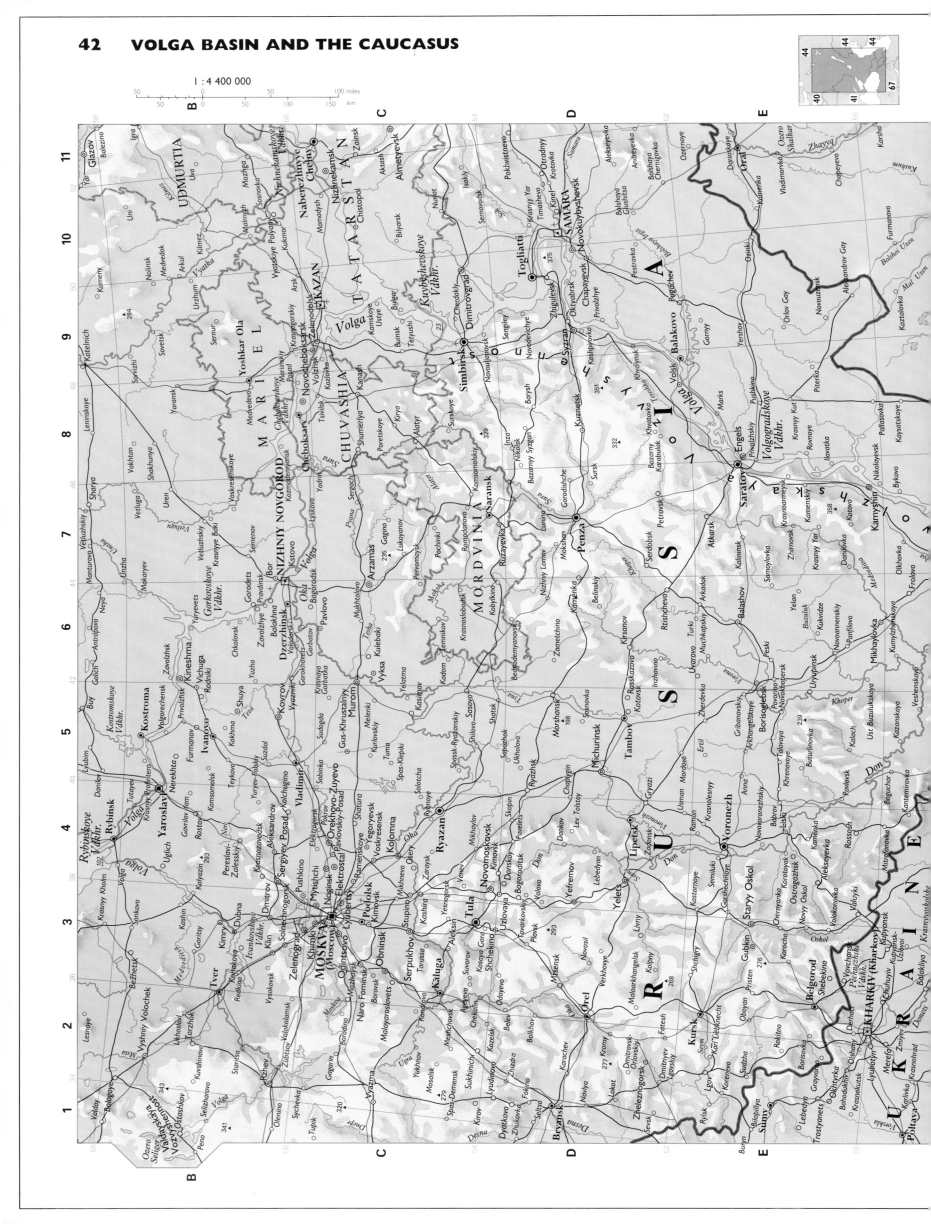

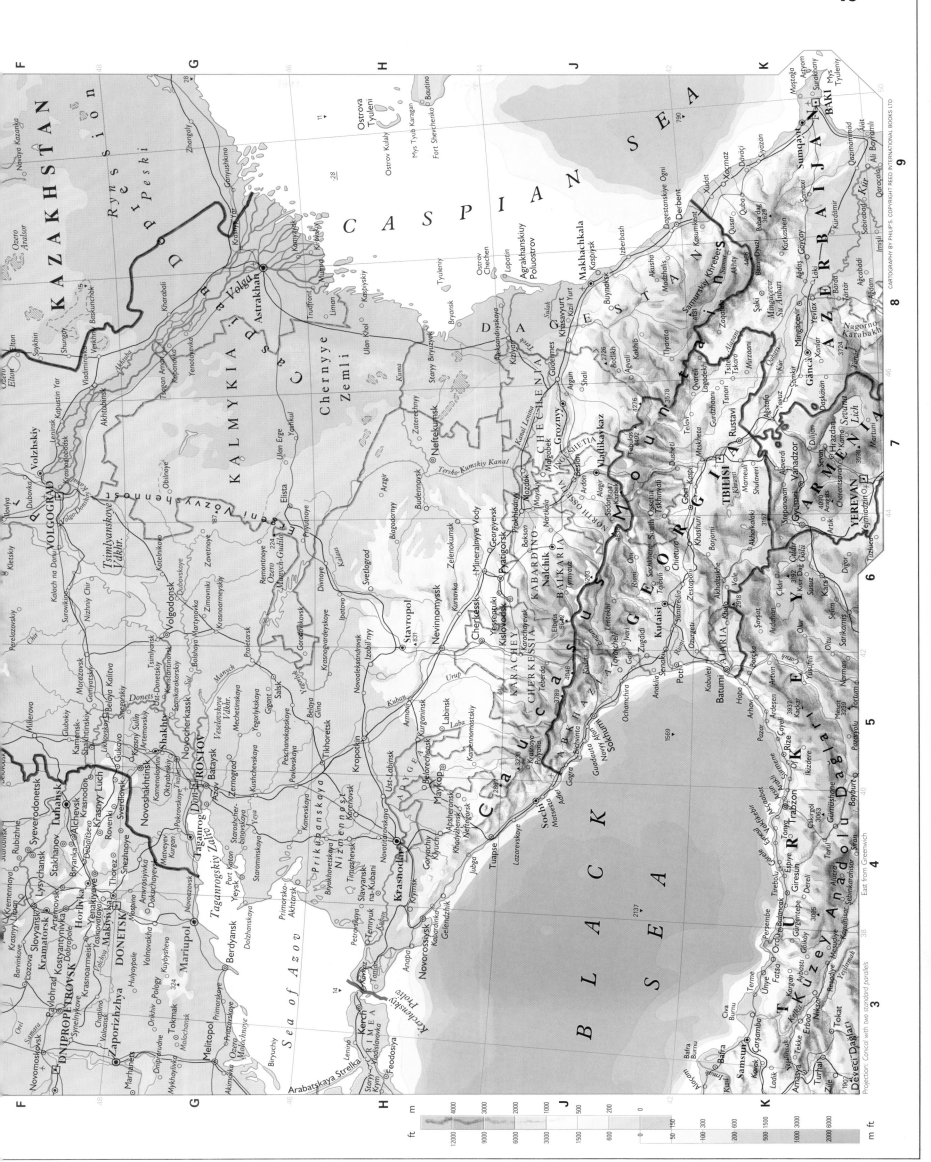

CARTOGRAPHY BY PHILIP'S. COPYRIGHT REED INTERNATIONAL BOOKS LTD

CASPIAN SEA

BLACK SEA

Sea of Azov

KAZAKHSTAN

KALMYKIA

Chernyye Zemli

DAGESTAN

CHECHENYA

INGUSHETIA

NORTH OSSETIA

South Ossetia

KABARDINO-BALKARIA

KARACHEY-CHERKESSIA

ABKHAZIA

ADYGEA

Caucasus Mountains

GEORGIA

ADJARIA

ARMENIA

AZERBAIJAN

Nagorno-Karabakh

Küzey Anadolu Dağları

T U R K E Y

Projection: Conical with two standard parallels

East from Greenwich

Astrakhan
Volgograd
Volzhskiy
Rostov
Donetsk
Makhachkala
Groznyy
Vladikavkaz
Nalchik
Stavropol
Krasnodar
Sochi
Novorossiysk
TBILISI
YEREVAN
BAKI
Batumi
Trabzon
Samsun

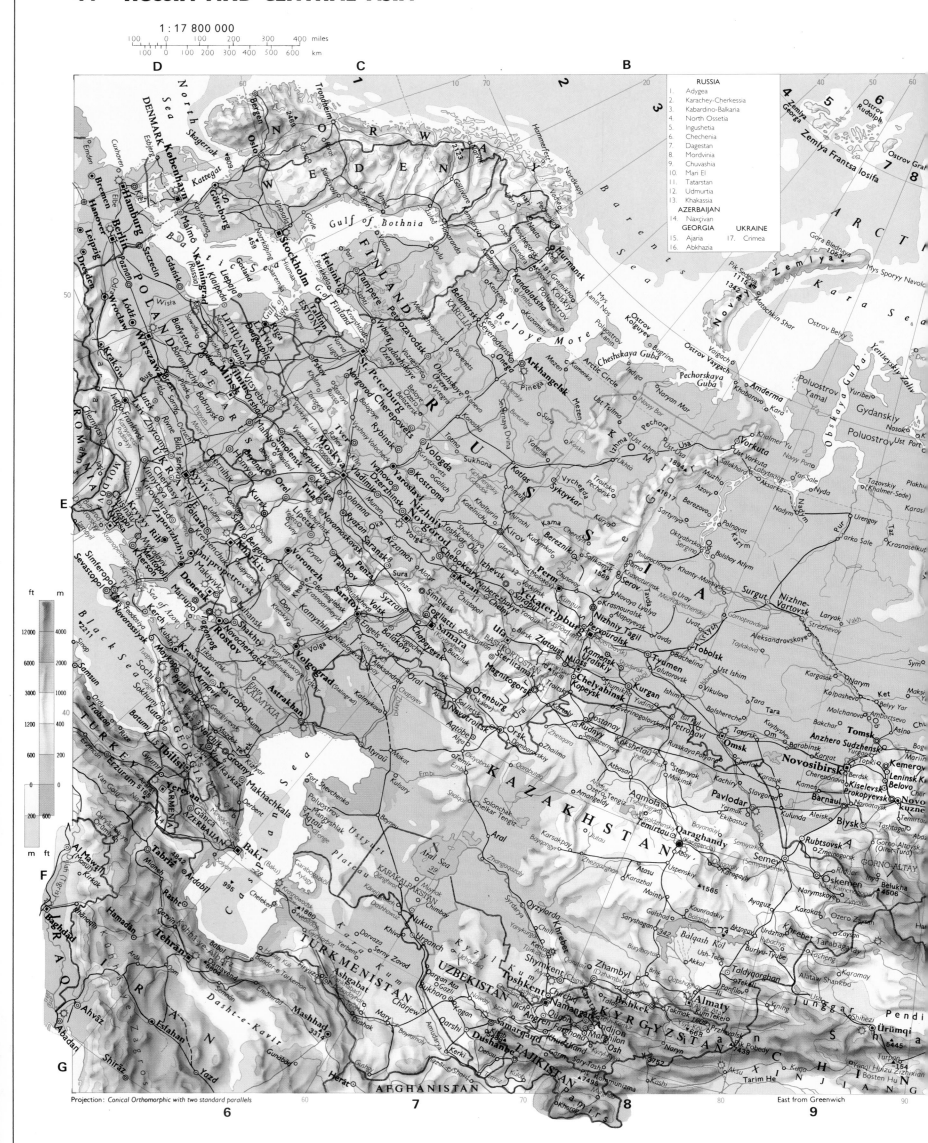

1 : 44 400 000

250   0   250   500   750   1000 miles
250   0   500   1000   1500   km

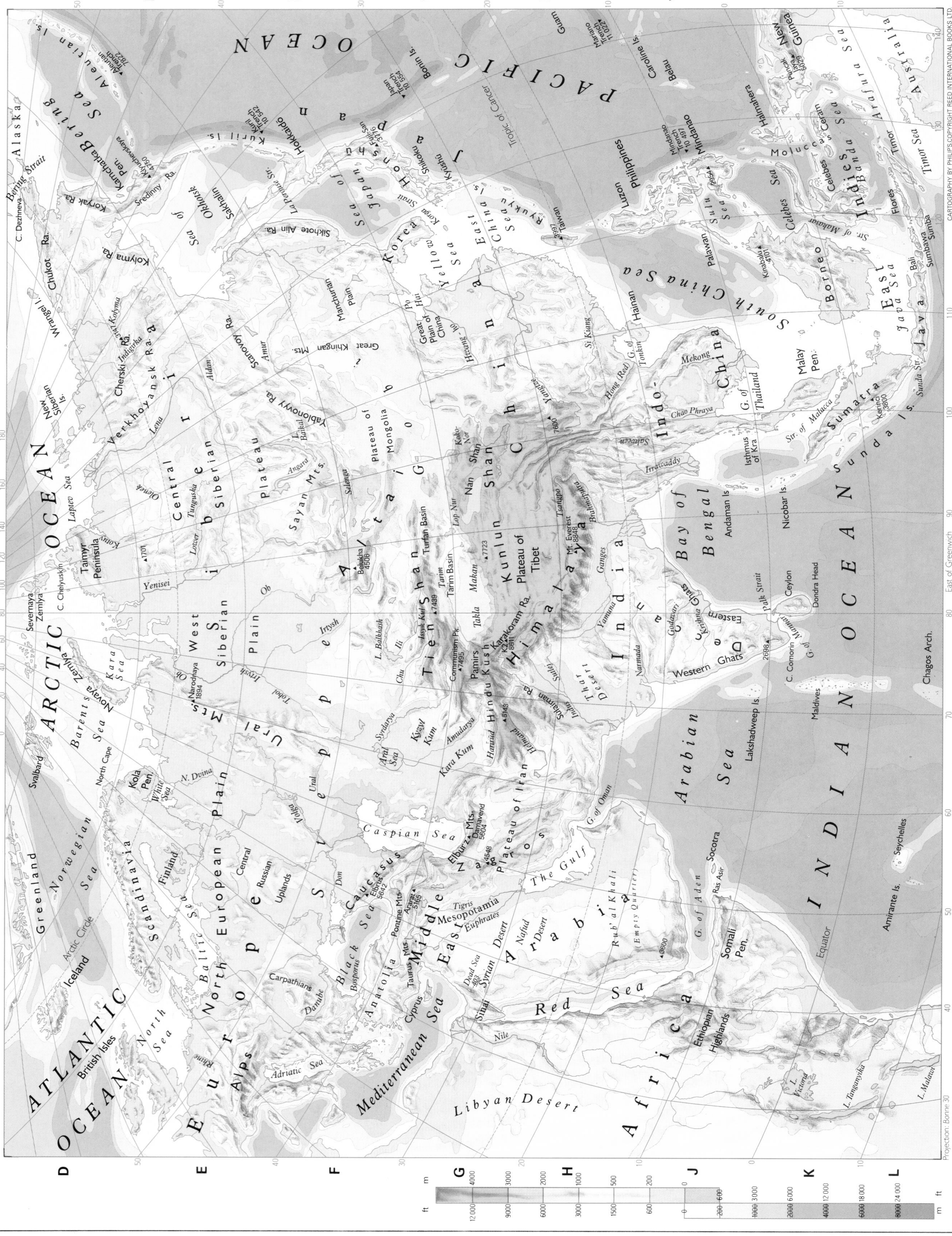

PACIFIC OCEAN

ARCTIC OCEAN

ATLANTIC OCEAN

INDIAN OCEAN

Bering Sea
Alaska
C. Dezhneva
Chukot Ra.
Wrangel I.
Kamchatka Pen.
Koryak Ra.
Sredinny Ra.
Kolyma Ra.
Aleutian Is.
Bering Strait
Sea of Okhotsk
Sakhalin
Cherski Ra.
Verkhoyansk Ra.
Stanovoy Ra.
Aldan
Lena
Amur
Kuril Is.
Hokkaido
Honshu
Sea of Japan
Japan
Shikoku
Kyushu
Korea
Korea Str.
La Pérouse Str.
Sikhote Alin Ra.
Manchurian Plain
Great Khingan Mts.
Yellow Sea
East China Sea
Ryukyu
Taiwan
Hainan
Si Kiang
Luzon
Philippines
Mindanao
Mindanao Trench
Caroline Is.
Belau
Guam
Bonin Is.
Tropic of Cancer
New Guinea
Halmahera
Molucca Sea
Ceram
Banda Sea
Arafura Sea
Timor Sea
Australia
Flores
Sumbawa
Sumba
Bali
Java Sea
Java
Sunda Str.
Borneo
Celebes
Celebes Sea
Sulu Sea
Palawan
Str. of Malacca
Malay Pen.
Sumatra
Sunda Is.
Bay of Bengal
Andaman Is.
Nicobar Is.
Irrawaddy
Isthmus of Kra
G. of Thailand
Chao Phraya
Mekong
Indo-China
Hong (Red)
G. of Tonkin
Salween
Nan Shan
Altai
Plateau of Mongolia
Selenga
Sayan Mts.
Baikal
Angara
Yablonovyy Ra.
Plateau of Tibet
Kunlun Shan
Tsaidam
Koko Nor
Lop Nur
Tarim Basin
Turfan Basin
Tien Shan
Communism Pk.
Pamirs
Hindu Kush
Karakoram Ra.
Himalaya
Mt. Everest
Ganges
Brahmaputra
Tsangpo
Makan
Takla
Irtysh
L. Balkhash
Ili
Chu
Aral Sea
Syrdarya
Kyzyl Kum
Amudarya
Kara Kum
West Siberian Plain
Central Siberian Plateau
Yenisei
Ob
Tobol
Ural Mts.
Ural
Taimyr Peninsula
C. Chelyuskin
Severnaya Zemlya
New Siberian Is.
Laptev Sea
Kara Sea
Novaya Zemlya
Barents Sea
Svalbard
Greenland
Norwegian Sea
Iceland
British Isles
North Sea
Scandinavia
Finland
White Sea
Kola Pen.
North Cape
N. Dvina
North European Plain
Central Russian Uplands
Volga
Don
Caspian Sea
Caucasus
Elbrus
Black Sea
Bosporus
Danube
Carpathians
Alps
Adriatic Sea
Rhine
Mediterranean Sea
Cyprus
Anatolia
Taurus Mts.
Pontine Mts.
Middle East
Tigris
Euphrates
Mesopotamia
Dead Sea
Syrian Desert
Sinai
Nile
Red Sea
Libyan Desert
Africa
Ethiopian Highlands
Somali Pen.
Ras Asir
G. of Aden
Socotra
Gulf of Oman
The Gulf
Zagros Mts.
Plateau of Iran
Elburz Mts.
Damavend
Arabia
Nafud Desert
Rub' al Khali
Empty Quarter
Arabian Sea
Amirante Is.
Seychelles
Maldives
Lakshadweep Is.
Western Ghats
Eastern Ghats
Deccan
India
Narmada
Indus
Thar Desert
Sulaiman Ra.
Helmand
Plateau of Iran
Hamud
C. Comorin
Ceylon
Dondra Head
Palk Strait
Krishna
Godavari
Yamuna
Chagos Arch.
Equator
Projection Bonne 30
Cartography by Philip's, Copyright Reed International Books Ltd.
East of Greenwich

m 4000 3000 2000 1000 500 200 0 -200 -600
ft 12000 9000 6000 3000 1500 600 0 -600 -1800
2000 6000 12000 18000 24000
ft

1 : 44 400 000

250   0   250   500   750   1000 miles
250   0   500   1000   1500   km

CARTOGRAPHY BY PHILIP'S. COPYRIGHT REED INTERNATIONAL BOOKS LTD.

East from Greenwich

Hanoi ● Capital Cities

Projection: Bonne

Oceans and Seas

PACIFIC OCEAN
ARCTIC OCEAN
ATLANTIC OCEAN
INDIAN OCEAN
Bering Sea
Sea of Okhotsk
Sea of Japan
Yellow Sea
East China Sea
South China Sea
Philippine Sea
Celebes Sea
Sulu Sea
Banda Sea
Arafura Sea
Timor Sea
Flores Sea
Java Sea
Bay of Bengal
Arabian Sea
Str. of Malacca
G. of Thailand
G. of Oman
The Gulf
Red Sea
G. of Aden
Caspian Sea
Black Sea
Mediterranean Sea
Aral Sea
Barents Sea
Kara Sea
Laptev Sea
White Sea
North Sea
L. Baikal
L. Balkhash
L. Victoria

Countries and Regions

RUSSIA
CHINA
MONGOLIA
KAZAKHSTAN
INDIA
IRAN
IRAQ
SAUDI ARABIA
TURKEY
PAKISTAN
AFGHANISTAN
UZBEKISTAN
TURKMENISTAN
TAJIKISTAN
KYRGYZSTAN
TIBET
SINKIANG
UIGHUR
JAMMU & KASHMIR
NEPAL
BHUTAN
BANGLADESH
BURMA (MYANMAR)
THAILAND
LAOS
VIETNAM
CAMBODIA
MALAYSIA
PEN. MALAYSIA
INDONESIA
PHILIPPINES
TAIWAN
JAPAN
NORTH KOREA
SOUTH KOREA
SRI LANKA
MALDIVES
SEYCHELLES
OMAN
YEMEN
UNITED ARAB EMIRATES
QATAR
BAHRAIN
KUWAIT
SYRIA
LEBANON
ISRAEL
JORDAN
CYPRUS
GEORGIA
ARMENIA
AZERBAIJAN
EGYPT
LIBYA
SUDAN
ERITREA
ETHIOPIA
DJIBOUTI
SOMALI REP.
KENYA
UGANDA
TANZANIA
ZAIRE
ZAMBIA
MALAWI
Africa
Europe
FINLAND
SWEDEN
NORWAY
ICELAND
GREENLAND
UNITED KINGDOM
FRANCE
GERMANY
ITALY
UKRAINE
AUSTRALIA
FED. STATES OF MICRONESIA
GUAM (USA)
PALAU
ALASKA (USA)
Aleutian Is. (USA)

Cities and Capitals

TOKYO
Yokohama
Osaka
Kyoto
Sapporo
SEOUL
PYONGYANG
BEIJING
TIANJIN
SHANGHAI
SHENYANG
Harbin
Changchun
Jilin
Dalian
Jinzhou
Taiyuan
Jinan
Qingdao
Zhengzhou
HANGZHOU
Nanjing
Wuhan
Nanchang
Fuzhou
GUANGZHOU
HONG KONG (U.K.)
Macau (Port.)
CHONGQING
Chengdu
Kunming
Lanzhou
Xi'an
Baotou
Yumen
Hami
Ürümqi
Hotan
Kashi
Lhasa
Changsha
MANILA
TAIPEI
JAKARTA
Bandung
Surabaya
Semarang
Banjarmasin
Ujung Pandang
Medan
Palembang
SINGAPORE
Kuala Lumpur
BANGKOK
Rangoon
Vientiane
Hanoi
Ho Chi Minh City
Phnom Penh
Haiphong
Chittagong
DACCA
CALCUTTA
DELHI
New Delhi
Lucknow
Kanpur
Varanasi
Patna
Jaipur
Bhopal
Indore
BOMBAY
Pune
Surat
Ahmadabad
Vadodara
Nagpur
Hyderabad
Bangalore
MADRAS
Madurai
Colombo
Male
Kathmandu
Thimphu
Islamabad
Lahore
Faisalabad
KARACHI
Multan
Kabul
Qandahar
Herat
Mashhad
TEHRAN
Esfahan
Shiraz
Tabriz
Ashkhabad
Zahedan
Muscat
Abu Dhabi
Dubai
Doha
Manamah
Riyadh
Kuwait
Basra
BAGHDAD
Mosul
Medina
Mecca
Jedda
Sana
Aden
Aswan
CAIRO
Alexandria
Suez
Port Sudan
Khartoum
Asmara
Addis Ababa
Mogadishu
Nairobi
Mombasa
Dar es Salaam
Damascus
Beirut
Amman
Jerusalem
Aleppo
Adana
Konya
Izmir
Bursa
ISTANBUL
Ankara
Nicosia
Tbilisi
Yerevan
Baku
Tashkent
Samarkand
Dushanbe
Bishkek
Alma Ata
Semey
Pavlodar
Karaganda
Astrakhan
Volgograd
Rostov
Samara
Kazan
Nizhniy Novgorod
Ufa
Perm
Yekaterinburg
Chelyabinsk
Omsk
Novosibirsk
Novokuznetsk
Tomsk
Krasnoyarsk
Bratsk
Irkutsk
Ulan Bator
Ulan Ude
Chita
Yakutsk
Verkhoyansk
Norilsk
Khatanga
Vorkuta
Salekhard
Murmansk
Arkhangelsk
MOSCOW
ST. PETERSBURG
Kaliningrad
Warsaw
Prague
Vienna
Belgrade
Rome
Berlin
PARIS
LONDON
Athens
Odessa
Kiev
Don
Volga
Yenisei
Lena
Amur
Irtysh
Ob
Syrdarya
Danube
Nile
Euphrates
Tigris
Indus
Ganges
Brahmaputra
Mekong
Yangtze
Si Kiang
Irrawaddy
Salween
Vladivostok
Khabarovsk
Komsomolsk
Blagoveshchensk
Hailar
Qiqihar
Petropavlovsk
Magadan
Okhotsk
Yuzhno-Sakhalinsk
Kamchatsky
Wrangel I.
New Siberian Is.
Novaya Zemlya
Svalbard
Franz Josef Ld.
Hokkaido
Honshu
Kyushu
Shikoku
Kuril Is.
Sakhalin
Ryukyu Is.
Hainan
Luzon
Mindanao
Palawan
Borneo
Sumatra
Java
Sumba
Ceram
Halmahera
Amboina
Manado
Zamboanga
Bandar Seri Begawan
BRUNEI
SABAH
SARAWAK
Andaman Is. (India)
Nicobar Is. (India)
Lakshadweep Is. (India)
Chagos Arch. (U.K.)
Aldabra Is. (Seychelles)
Amirante Is. (Seychelles)
Socotra (Yemen)
Victoria
Volcano Is. (Japan)
Tropic of Cancer
Arctic Circle
Equator

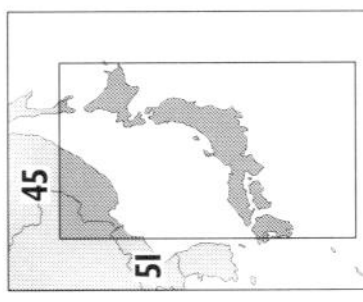

Grid references (top)

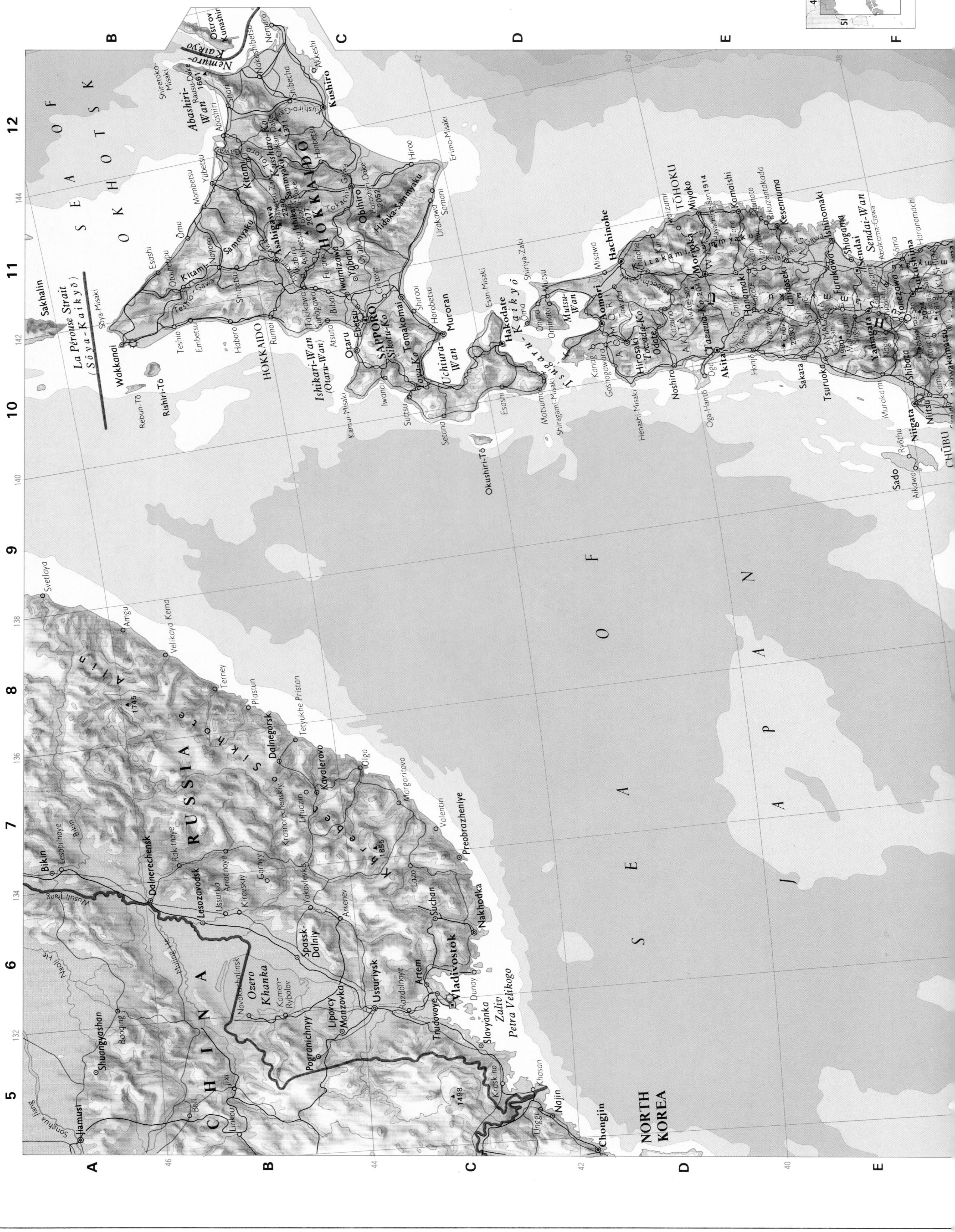

B C D E F

12 11 10 9 8 7 6 5

Grid references (left/bottom)

A B C D E

Map labels

S E A O F O K H O T S K

Sakhalin

La Pérouse Strait
(Sōya-Kaikyō)

Nemuro-Kaikyō

Ostrov Kunashir

Wakkanai

Rebun-Tō
Rishiri-Tō
Sōya-Misaki

Shiretoko-Misaki
Rausu-Dake 1661
Abashiri-Wan
Abashiri
Nakashibetsu
Nemuro
Akkeshi
Shari
Kushiro-Gawa
Shibecha
Kushiro

Ōmu
Mombetsu
Yūbetsu
Esashi
Otoineppu
HOKKAIDO
Kitami
Asahigawa
Sammyaku
Kushiro-Kō
Kitami-Zaki
Sammyaku 2290
Teshikaga-Zan 1321
Horobetsu
Hiroo
Erimo-Misaki
Somami

Teshio
Ōmu
Embetsu
Haboro
Rumoi
Ishikari
Ishikari-Gawa
Furano
Bibai
Iwamizawa
Obihiro
Yoshino-Dake 2052
Hidaka-Sammyaku
Tokachi-Gawa
Urakawa
Urozawa

HOKKAIDO
Otaru
Ishikari-Wan
(Otaru-Wan)
SAPPORO
Ebetsu
Yūbari
Chitose
Shikotsu-Ko
Tomakomai
Shiraoi
Horobetsu
Muroran
Uchiura-Wan

Kamui-Misaki
Iwanai
Suttsu
Setana
Okushiri-Tō
Esashi

Hakodate
Tsugaru-Kaikyō
Esan-Misaki
Matsumae-Misaki
Shiragami-Misaki
Ōma
Shinrya-Zaki
Ominato
Mutsu
Misawa

Shiokubi-Misaki
Shinya-Zaki
Mutsu-Wan
Ōhata
Mutsu

TŌHOKU
Iwaizumi
Miyoko
Iwate-San 1914

Hachinohe
Aomori
AOMORI
Kitakami
Kitakami-Sammyaku
Morioka
Kamaishi
Miyako
Ōfunato
Kesennuma

Kanagi
Goshogawara
Hirosaki
Towada-Ko
Towada
Odate
AKITA
Kazuno
Hachimantai

Noshiro
Oga-Hantō
Oga
Akita
Ōmagari
Honjō
Yokote
Naruko
Furukawa
Ishinomaki
Shiogama
Sendai
Sendai-Wan

Tazawa-Kō
Komaga-Take 204
Yamagata
YAMAGATA
Murakami
Sakata
Ōmono-Gawa
Mogami-Gawa
Tsuruoka
Chōkai-San 1980
Gassan
Yonezawa 2024
Shibata
Abukuma-Gawa
Haranomachi

Niigata
Nitsu
CHŪBU
Sado
Ryōtsu
Akkowa

S E A O F J A P A N

Svetlaya
Amgu
Velikaya Kema
Terney
Pilostun
Tetyukhe Pristan

RUSSIA
Sikhote Alin
1745
1855
Dalnegorsk
Kavalerovo
Olga
Margaritovo
Valentin

Bikin
Lesopilnoye
Bikin
Dalnerechensk
Rakitnoye
Krasnorechenskiy
Lifudzin
Olga
Lazo
Suchan
Preobrazheniye
Nakhodka

CHINA
Wusuli Jiang
Ussuri
Lesozavodsk
Ussurka
Arsenev
Gornyy
Yakovlevka

Shuangyashan
Baoqing
Linkou
Jixi

Ussuri Jiang
Songhua Jiang
Jiamusi
Ozero Khanka
Novoselishche
Kamen-Rybolov
Spassk-Dalniy
Lipovcy
Arseadnoye
Kirovskiy

Pogranichny
Manzovka
Trudovoye
Ussuriysk
Artem
Vladivostok
Razdolnoye
Dunay

Slavyanka
Zaliv Petra Velikogo

Kraskino
Khasan
Najin
1498
Unggi
Chongjin

NORTH KOREA

Neoli He

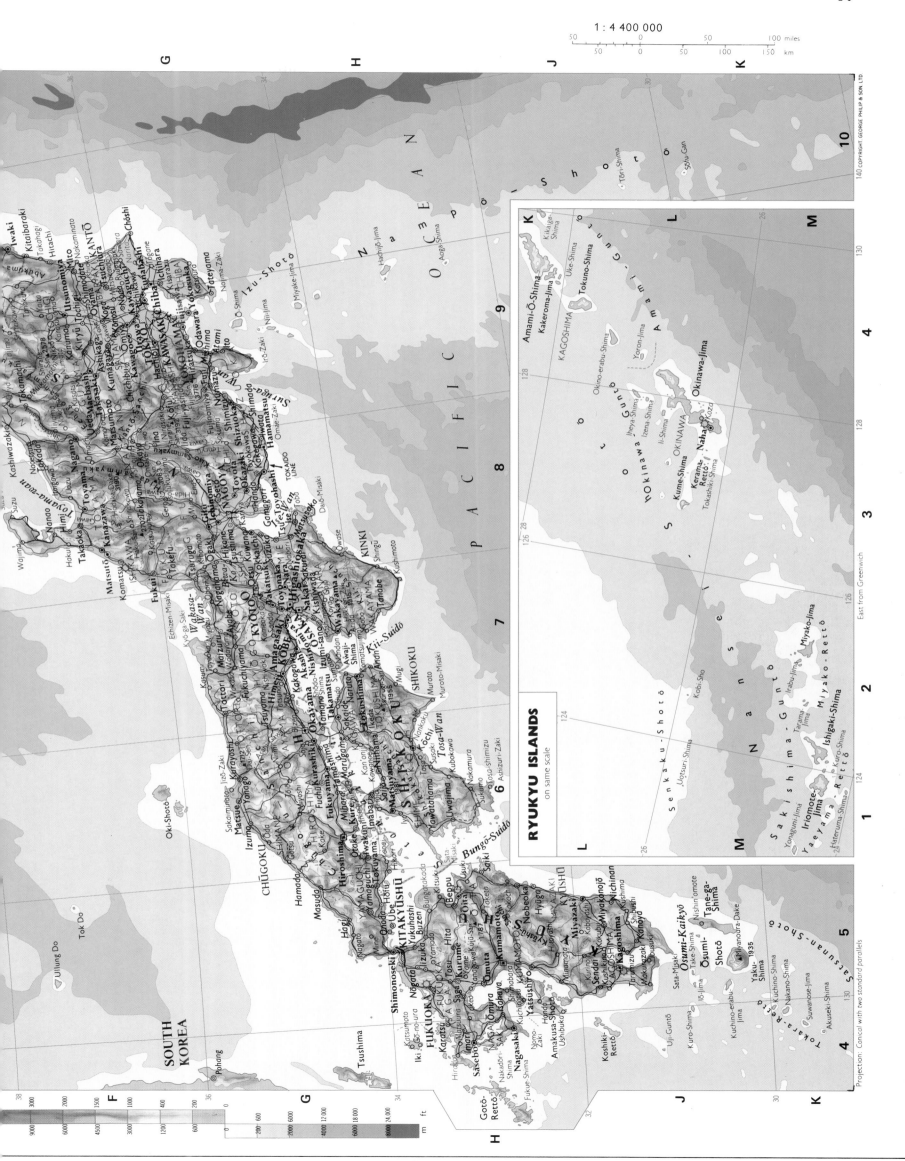

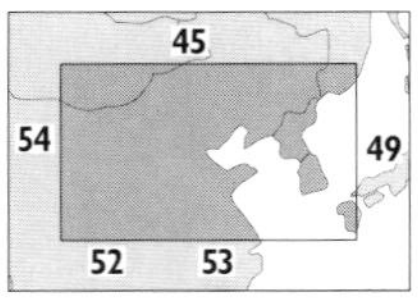

45
54 · 49
52 · 53

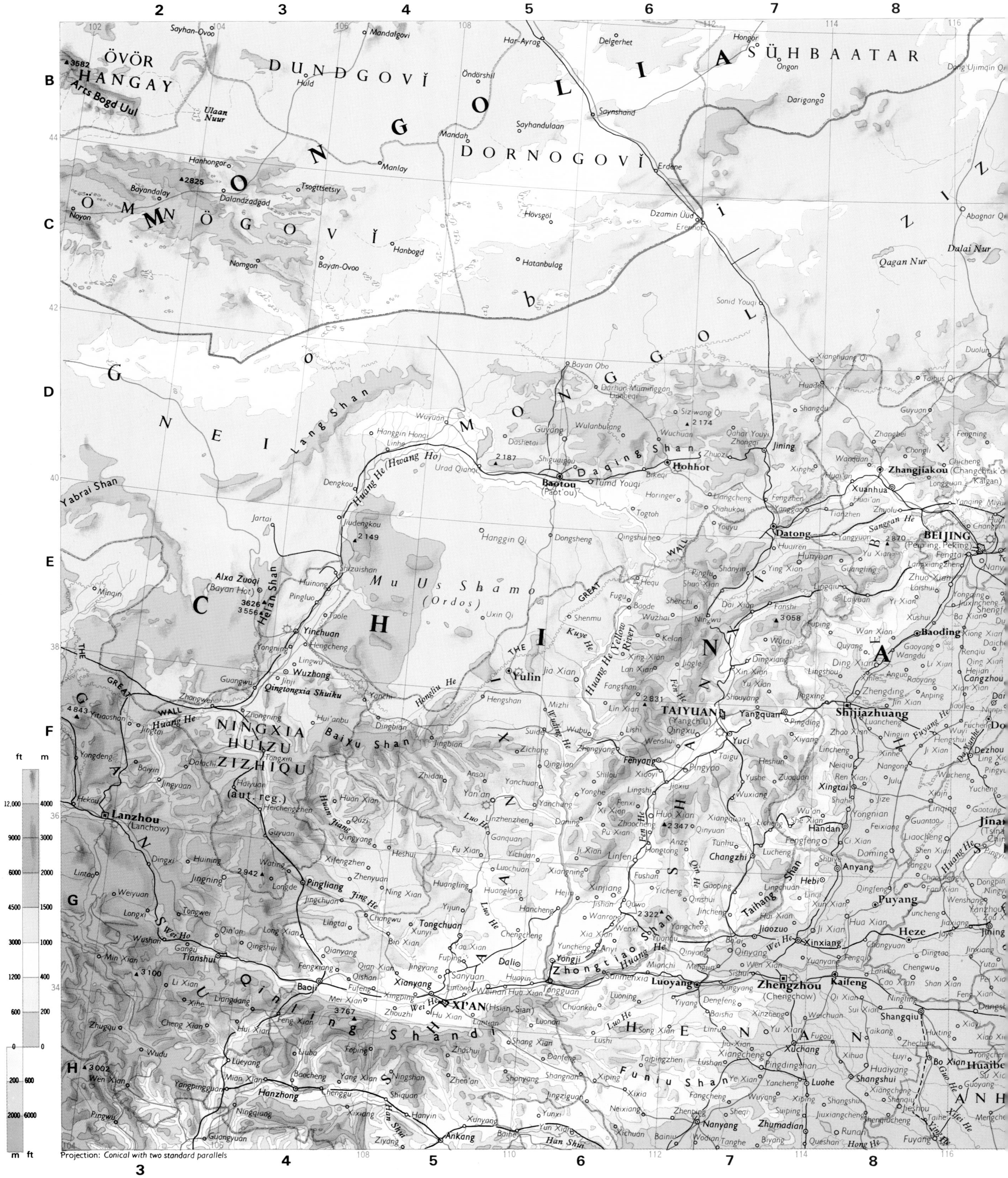

ÖVÖR
HANGAY
Arts Bogd Uul
▲3582

Sayhan-Ovoo
Mandalgovi
D U N D G O V I
Hüld
Ulaan Nuur
Hongor
Har-Ayrag
Delgerhet
Ongon
Ö N D O R S H I L
S Ü H B A A T A R
Dariganga
Dong Ujimqin Qi

M O N G O L I A
Hanhongor
▲2825
Tsogttsetsiy
Manlay
Sayhandulaan
Saynshand
Erdene

Bayandalay
Dalandzadgad
Mandah
Z I Z
Abagnar Qi

Noyon
Ö M N Ö G O V Ï
Hanbogd
Nomgon
Bayan-Ovoo
Hövsgöl
Hatanbulag
Dzamin Üüd
Ereen
Qagan Nur
Dalai Nur

G O B I
N E I
Bayan Obo
Darhan-Muminggan Lianheqi
Siziwang Qi
▲2174
Shangdu
Xianghuang Qi
Taihus Qi
Duolun
Guyuan

M O N G O L
Wuyuan
Hanggin Houqi
Linhe
Guyang
Wulanbulang
Qahar Youyi Zhongqi
Zhuozi
Jining
Xinghe
Wanquan
Zhabei
Chongli
Qicheng
Fengning

Langshan
Dengkou
Huang He (Hwang Ho)
Urad Qianqi
▲2187
Shiguaigou
Daqing Shan
Baotou (Paot'ou)
Bikeqi
Hohhot
Liangcheng
Fengzhen
Hua'an
Xuanhua
Zhangjiakou (Changchiak)
Longguan
Yanqing Miyu

Yabrai Shan
Jartai
Tumd Youqi
Horinger
Shahukou
Youyu
Datong
Huairen
Yangyuan
Tianzhen
Zhuolu
BEIJING (Peip'ing, Peking)

Jiudengkou
▲2149
Hanggin Qi
Dongsheng
Qingshuihe
Togtoh
Shuo Xian
Hunyuan
Ying Xian
Guangling
Lanxiangzhen
Fengtai

Alxa Zuoqi (Bayan Hot)
Huinong
▲3626
3556▲
Shizuishan
M u U s S h a m o (Ordos)
Uxin Qi
Fugu
Hequ
Baode
Wuzhai
Shenchi
Ninglu
Dai Xian
Fanshi
Yi Xian
Wutai
▲3058
Baoding

Yinchuan
Taole
Pingluo
Hengcheng
Yongning
Lingwu
Shenmu
Kuye He
Huang He (Yellow River)
Xing Xian
Lan Xian
Jiogle
Dingxiang
Lingshou
Ding Xian
Qing Xian

Wuzhong
Guangwu
Jinji
Qingtongxia Shuiku
Zhongning
Yanchi
Hongliu He
Yulin
Jia Xian
Fangshan
Linxian
Xin Xian
Yu Xian
Shouyang
Jingxing
Zhengding
Jin Xian
Anping

NINGXIA HUIZU ZIZHIQU (aut. reg.)
Hui'anbu
Dingbian
Hengshan
Mizhi
Lin Xian
▲2831
TAIYUAN (Yangch'u)
Yangquan
Pingding
Shijiazhuang
Luancheng

Zhongwei
Zhongning
Haiyuan
Baixu Shan
Suide
Wubu
Zhongyang
Fenyang
Qingxu
Taigu
Zhao Xian
Ningjin

THE GREAT WALL
▲4843 Yitiaoshan
Jingtai
Dalachi
Zhidan
Ansai
Qingjian
Shilou
Xidoyi
Pingyao
Yuci
Yusbe
Zuoquan
Lincheng

Lanzhou (Lanchow)
Baiyin
Jingyuan
Heichengzhen
Yan'an
Yanchuan
Yanchang
Daning
Fenxi
Huo Xian
▲2347 Zhaocheng
Wuxiang
Xingtai
Julu

Hekou
Yongdeng
Dingxi
Huining
Guyuan
Huan Xian
Huan Jiang
Quzi
Qingyang
Luo He
Unzhenzhen
Ganquan
Yichuan
Lingshi
Xi Xian
Fen He
Hongtong
Qinyuan
Tunliu
Changzhi
Lucheng
Shexian
Handan
Feixiang
Qiu Xian

Weiyuan
Longxi
Tongwei
Jingning
▲2942
Wating
Longde
Pingliang
Heshui
Zhenyuan
Fu Xian
Yichuan
Huangling
Hejin
Jishan
Quwo
▲2322
Yangcheng
Jincheng
Taihang Shan
Hui Xian
Anyang
Qingfeng
Fan Xian

Lintao
Longxi
Qin'an
Tianshui
Jingchuan
Xifengzhen
Ning Xian
Huangling
Huanglong
Xinjiang
Yicheng
Qushou
Lingchuan
Jiaozuo
Puyang
Wenshang

Gangu
Wushan
Qingshui
Changwu
Bin Xian
Yijun
Luo He
Hancheng
Wanrong
Wenxi
Yangcheng
Qinyang
Wen Xian
Wei He
Xinxiang
Heze
Jining

▲3100
Li Xian
Lingtai
Qianyang
Jingchuan
Tongchuan
Chengcheng
Dali
Yuncheng
Anyi
Yongji
Mengjin
Luoyang
Zhengzhou (Chengchow)
Kaifeng
Shangqiu

Liangdang
Xihe
Qishan
Fengxiang
Qianyang
Jingyang
Sanyuan
Lintong
Huayin
Huiyin
Sanmenxia
Mianchi
Luoning
Yiyang
Dengfeng
Xuchang
Shangshui

Zhugou
Cheng Xian
Hui Xian
Baoji
Mei Xian
Fufeng
Xianyang
Weinan Hua Xian
Tongguan
Chuankou
Luo He
Song Xian
Linru
Yu Xian
Fugou
Taikang

▲3767
Zhouzhi
XI'AN (Hsian, Sian)
Wei He
Lantian
Zhashui
Shang Xian
Lushi
Jia Xian
Xiangcheng
Linying
Luohe
Shangshui

▲3002
Wen Xian
Lüeyang
Yangpingguan
Mian Xian
Liuba
Qinling Shandi
Foping
Zhen'an
Shangnan
Xiping
Funiu Shan
Ye Xian
Xiangcheng
Shangshui
Huaiyang
ANHU

Pingwu
Zhugou
Guangyuan
Ningqiang
Hanzhong
Chenggu
Shiquan
Hanyin
Xunyang
Yunxi
Neixiang
Nanyang
Zhumadian
Biyang
Hong He
Fuyang

Hanzhong
Xixiang
Han Shui
Shangnan
Ziyang
Ankang
Baihe
Yun Xian
Bainiu
Wodian Tanghe
Suiping
Jiuxiangcheng

Projection: Conical with two standard parallels

ft m
12,000 4000
9000 3000
6000 2000
4500 1500
3000 1000
1200 400
600 200
0 0
200 600
2000 6000
m ft

1 : 5 300 000

50   50   100   150 miles

50   0   50   100 150 200 km

B

9   10   11   12   13   14   15   16

Horqin Youyi Qianqi

HARBIN (Haerhpin)

HEILONGJIANG

Zhenlai   Acheng   Yanshou

Taoer He   Maoxing   Zhaoyuan   Shuangcheng   Shangzhi

Hulin He   Tuquan   Nen   Songhua Jiang   Lalin He   Shanhetun   Midan Jiang   Jixi

Balcheng   Dajan   Fuyu   Changchunling   Wuchang   Muling   Turiy Rog-o

Tuquan   Tao'an   Songhua   Shulan   Mudanjiang   Hailin   Suifenhe   Ozero Khanka

Jarud Qi   Tongyu   Qian Gorlos   Nong'an   Dehui   Gongzhuling   Ning'an   Dongning   Pogranichnyy

1949   Bairin Zuoqi   Zhangwu   Changling   Fulongquan   Wutaijie   Dongjingcheng   Golenki   44

Linxi   Kailu   Maolin   Huaidezhen   Fangzheng   Emu   Daxinggou   Jingho   Suiyang   Ussuriysk (Voroshilov)

2 029   Hexigten Qi   Shuangliao   Siping   Yitong   Chili   Songhua Hu   Huangsongdian   Dunhua   Wangqing   Shixian   Razdolnoye   Artem

Xar Moron He   Jargalang   Bamianchneg   Xifeng   Panshi   Huadian   Helong   Antu   Mingyuegue   Yanji   Tumen   Hunchun   Krasknoe   Stvanka   C

Ongniud Qi   2 020   Wutonghaolai   Hure Qi   Kangping   Zhongwei   Hailong   Huinan   Jingyu   Fusong   1 677   Changbai Shan   Helong   Musan   Hoeamdong   Unggi   Sosura   42

Chifeng   Kailu   Kaiyuan   Shanchengzhen   Linjiang   Changbai   Paektu-san   Puryong   Najin

Xiawa   Qingyuan   Tonghua   Chunggang-up   2 541   Kyongsong   Pugdong

Weichang   1 885   Beipiao   Qinghemen   Fuxin   Faku   Tieling   Xinbin   Paekam   Hyesan   Kapsan   Kilju   Kimchaek (Songjin)

Ningcheng   Chaoyang   Heishan   SHENYANG (Mukden)   Fushun   Huajianzi 845   J'an   Manpojin   Kanggye   Pungsan   Simpungdong   Tanchon

Chengde   Jianchang   Xingcheng   Liaozhong   Benxi   Qinghecheng   Hun Jiang   Kuup-tong   2 522   Pujon-chosuji   Kwongdong   Pukchong   D

Luanping   Shangbanchheng   Jinzhou   Panshan   Anping   Hun Jiang   Supung Sk.   Chosan   Changjin-chosuji   Kwangyang   Pukchong   40

Longhua   Lingyuan   Jianchang   Jinxi   Tianzhuangti   Nuzhuang   Haicheng   Lianshanguan   Kuandian   Pyoktong   Kojin-dong   Changjin   Sinhung   Sohori

Chengde   Dugou Pingquan   Anshan   Yingkou   Fengcheng   Taegwan   Pukchin   Hamhung   Iwon

Xinglong   Kuancheng   Yingkou   Yingkou   Dandong   Sinuiju   Chongju   Kujang   NORTH   Hungnam   Tongjoson   SEA   OF

Fuming   Qinhuangdao   Changli   Liaodong   Xiuyan   Zhuanghe   Yalu Jiang   Sonchon   KOREA   Yonghung   Man   Kosong

TANGSHAN   Leting   Wan   Fu Xian   Gushan   Donggou   Yongampo   Sukchon   Anju   Simcheon-ni   Tokchon-ni   JAPAN

TIANJIN (Tientsin, Tienching)   Jin Xian   Lushun   Sinanju   Unsan   Yonghung   E

Tanggu   Dagu   Lushan   DALIAN (Luda)   Korea   P'YONGYANG   Chunghwa   Songchon   Tongyang   Anbyon   Kojo

Oikou   Bo Hai   Bay   Chinnampo   Suan   Singnam   Wonsan   38

(Gulf of Chihli)   Cho-do   Sariwon   Pyonggang   Hoeyang   1 638

Huang He   Longkou   Penglai   Xian   Yantai   Chaeryong   Sinmak   Namchon   Kumhwa   Hwachon-chosuji   Yongyang   Ullung-do

Zhanhua   Huang He   Daxinglong   Sinmak   Haeju   Kumchon   Hwachon   1 578   Chumunjin

Huimin   Laizhou   Zhaoyuan   Fushan   Ongjin   Kaesong   Uijongbu   Chunchon   Kangnung   F

Binzhou   Beizhen   Wan   Muping   Weihai   Paengnyong-do   Cease Fire Line   Yongdungpo   SOUL   Hoengsong   Samchok

Shanghe   Ye Xian   923   Wendeng   INCH'ON   Suwon   Wonju   Yongwol

Shandong Banda   Rushan   Pyongtaek   Chungju   Chechon   Uichin

Guangrao   Changyi   Pingdu   Laixi   Haiyang   Shidao   Osan   Chonan   SOUTH   Yongju

Huantai   Laiyang   Nanhuang   Chochiwon   Chongju   Andong   Yongdok

ZIBO   Yidu   Fangzi   Jiao Xian   Chongju   KOREA   Uisong   Chongha   36

Zhoucun   Linzi   Anqiu   Jimo   Yesan   Kanggyong   Taejon   Yongchon   Pohang

Xintai   Laiwu   Zhucheng   Shengyang   Nonsan   Kimchon   Hadong

4   Shan   1 108   Zhuchang   Kunsan   Kangyong-do   Taechon   Waegwan   Ulsan

ANDONG   Jiao Xian   QINGDAO (Ch'ingtao)   Iri   Chonju   TAEGU   Chongdo

Xintai   Yishui   Wulian   Jiaozhou Wan   Puan   Kimje   Kyongju

Pingyi   Mengyin   Changcheng   Kimhae   Masan   Langnae

Linyi   Ganyu   Haizhou Wan   HUANG HAI   Chongup   Namwon   1 915   Chinju   Chinhae   PUSAN   G

Zaozhuang   Tancheng   Lianyungang   (Yellow Sea)   Kochang   Hoyang   Samchonpo   Chungmu   Korea   Sosuna

Hanzhuang   Haizhou   Lianyungang (Hsinhailien)   Kwangju   Hadong   Strait   Tsushima   Saka

Feng Xian   Teng Xian   Guanyun   Naju   Posong   Polgyo-ri   Yosu   Tsushima   Izuhara   Iki

Zhangqiu   Guannan   Chindo   Changheung   Haenam   34

Suining   Shuyang   Da Yunhe   Changle   Mokpo   Cheju   Cheju-do   Sogwi-po   TSushima-kaikyo   JAPAN   Karatsu   Imori

Lingbi   Sugian   Binhai   Hallim   1 950   Onpyong-ni   Nakadori-jima   Kashima

Bengbu   Qingjiang   Funing   Mosulpo   Sogwi-po   Omura   Isahaya

Guzhen   Hongze Hu   Lianshui   Fukue-jima   Nagasaki   Kuchinotsu   H

Wuhe   Huai'an   Baoying   YANCHENG

Guoyang   Huai He   Luzhuang   Xinghua

9   10   11   12   13   14   15

East from Greenwich

COPYRIGHT. GEORGE PHILIP & SON. LTD.

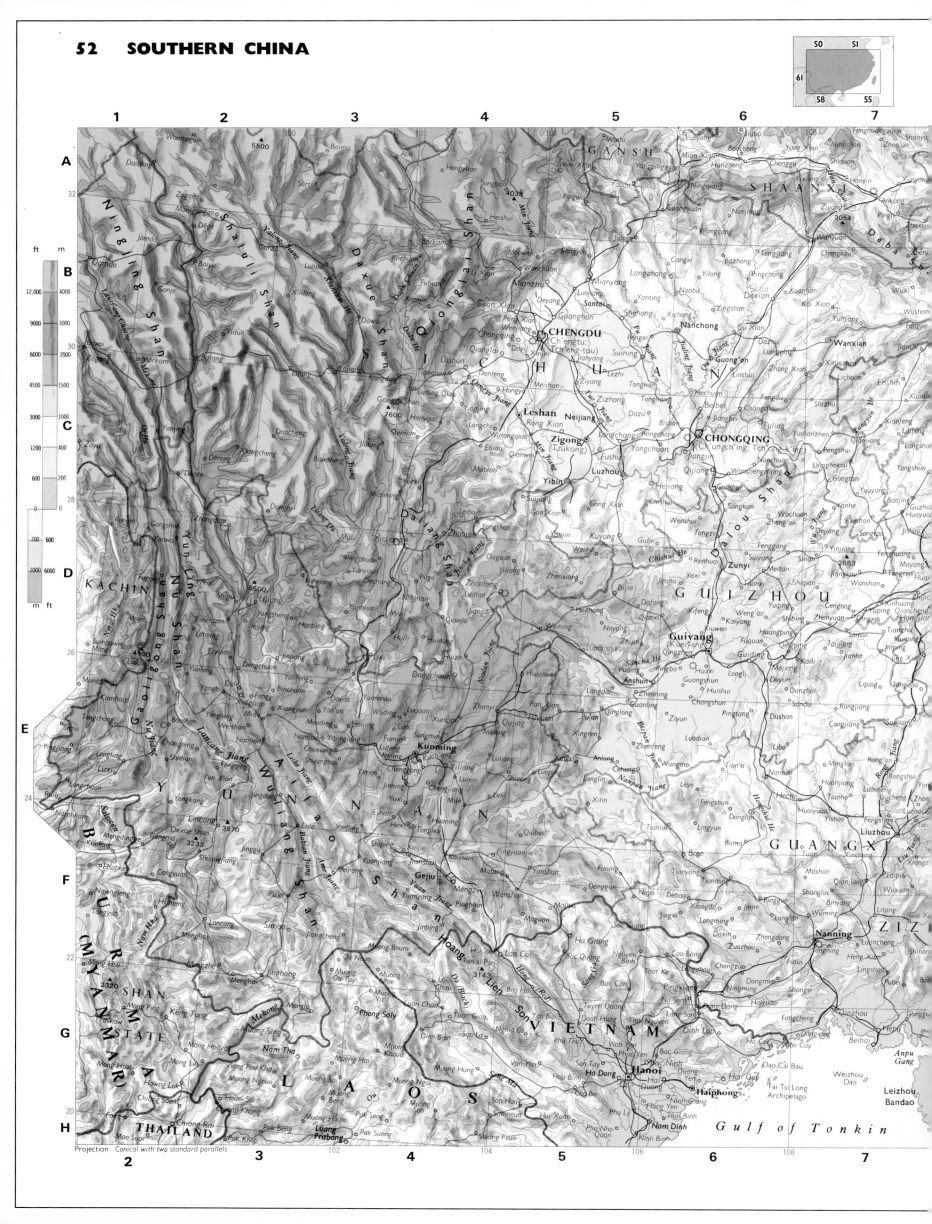

1 : 5 300 000

50   0   50   100   150 miles

50 0 50 100 150 200

km

East from Greenwich

120 COPYRIGHT. GEORGE PHILIP & SON. LTD.

1 : 17 800 000

100 0 100 200 300 400 miles

100 0 100 200 300 400 500 600 km

RUSSIA
MONGOLIA
KAZAKHSTAN
KYRGYZSTAN
XIZANG (TIBET)
NEPAL
BHUTAN
INDIA
BURMA (MYANMAR)
THAILAND
LAOS
PHILIPPINES
JAPAN
NORTH KOREA
SOUTH KOREA
TAIWAN
YELLOW SEA
EAST CHINA SEA
SOUTH CHINA SEA
BAY OF BENGAL
BEIJING
SHANGHAI
Hong Kong
Tarim Pendi
Kunlun Shan
Projection: Bonne
East from Greenwich

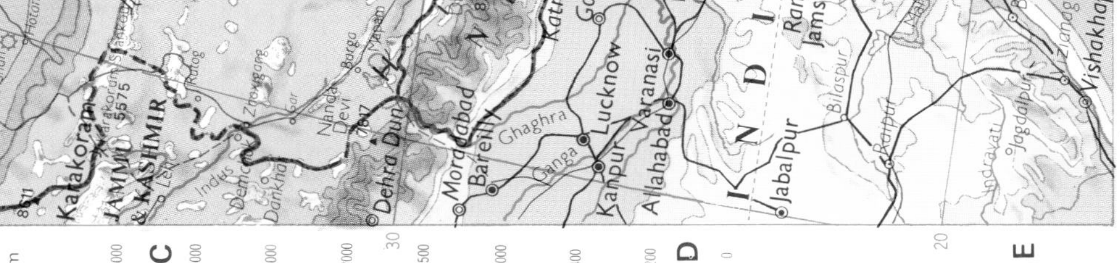
m
ft
6000 18 000
4000 12 000
3000 9000
2000 6000
1500 4500
1000 3000
400 1200
200 600
0 0
200 600
2000 6000
4000 12 000
6000 18 000

53

56 57

1 : 6 700 000

50   100   150   200 miles
50   0   50   100   200   300 km

A

20

Ibtayat
Batanes Is.
Batan

Balintang Channel

B
Calayan   *Babuyan*
Dalupiri   Babuyan   *Camiguin*
Islands
18   *Fuga*
Mayraira Pt.   Babuyan Channel
Bacarra   *Bangui*   *Claveria*   *Ballesteros*   Aparri   *Port San Vicente*
San Nicolas   Laoag   *Kabugao*   *Gonzaga*
Batac   *Gattaran*
Cabagan   ▲2360   *Tuao*   *Chico*   Tuguegarao
Vigan   *Banna*   Bangued   *Lubuagan*   *Ilagan*
Santa   *Cordillera Central*   *Cresta*
Maria   ▲1672
Candon   *Bontoc*   *San Mateo*   *Palanan Pt.*

C   *Tagudin*   *Luna*   *Palanan*
San Fernando   Pulog   *Cordon*   *Santiago*
Bolinao   Lingayen Gulf   ▲2929   Solano   *Casiguran*
Baguio   Bayombong
Alaminos   *Anacuao*
16   *Rosario*   Dagupan   ▲1850   *C. San Ildefonso*
Lingayen   *San Manuel*
San Carlos   Bayambang   San Jose   *Baler Bay*
Santa Cruz   *Moncada*   *Cuyapo*   *Baler*
Camiling   Victoria
Palauig   Tarlac   LUZON
▲2038   *La*   *Cabanatuan*
Iba   *Capas*   *Paz*   *Gapan*   *Dingalan*

D   *San Narciso*   *Concepcion*   Angeles   *San Fernando*   *Polillo Is.*
San Antonio   *Malabon*   *Patnanongan*
Olongapo   *Caloocan*   *Jomalig*
Bataan   *Quezon City*   *Lamon Bay*
Manila Bay   MANILA   *Larap*   *Paracale*
14   Cavite   Pasay   *Santa Cruz*   *Alabat*   Daet
Trece Martires   *Lucban*   *Atimonan*   *Pandan*
Nasugbu   San Pablo   *Lopez*   *Calabanga*   Catanduanes
Balayan   *Tagaytay*   Lucena   *Calauag*   *Virac*
Lipa   *Catanauan*   *Calolbon*
Lemery   Batangas   *Lobo*   *Tabas Bay*   Naga   Iriga   Lagonoy Gulf   *Rapu Rapu*
Verde I.   *Pass.*   *Marinduque*   Nabua   Tabaco
C. Calavite   *Tablas Str.*   *Boac*   Legazpi   Sorsogon

E   *Mamburao*   MINDORO   Baco   *Pinamalayan*   *Donsol*   *Gubat*
▲2488   *Burias*   Bulan   *Casiguran*
Sablayan   *Irosin*
12   *Bongabong*   *Romblon*   *Sibuyan*   *C. San Bernardino Str.*
Busuanga   *Roxas*   *Tablas*   *Laoang*
Calamian   *San Jose*   *Ilin*   *Odiongan*   *Catarman*   *Mondragon*
Group   *Sibuyan*   *Pt.*   *Lavezares*   *Gamay*
Culion   SEA   *Milagros*   Calbayog   *Asteche*   *Oras*
Semirara Is.   Mandaon   Masbate   *Catbalogan*   Wright   SAMAR

F   *Libra Pt.*   *Cuyo West Pass*   *Kalibo*   Roxas   *Placer*   *Bantayan*   *Gutusan*   *Villa Real*   *Maydolong*
Taytay   *Pandan*   VISAYAN   *Carigara*   *San Antonio*   General MacArthur
Bugasong   *Sigma*   *Estancia*   SEA   *Palompon*   LEYTE   Tacloban   *Guiuan*
▲2117   *Ajuy*   *Sara*   *Bogo*   Ormoc   *Dulag*
10   PANAY   *Pototan*   *Camotes Is.*   *Leyte Gulf*
Cuyo Is.   *San Jose*   *Pototan*   Cadiz   Sagay   *Tabuelan*   *Abuyog*   *Homonhon*
de Buenavista   Iloilo   Silay   Victorias   *Camotes*   Baybay   *Sogod*
PALAWAN   *Dumaran*   *Guimaras*   Bacolod   San Carlos   Cebu   Sea   *Matalom*
▲1593   *Jordan*   ▲2465   *Mandaue*   *Cabalian*   *Dinagat*
Irahuan   *Cagayan*   *Hinigaran*   *La*   Calamba   Carcar   *Maasin*   *Siargao*
Honda B.   *Binalbagan*   Carlota   *Argao*   *Panaon*   *Surigao Str.*
Puerto Princesa   *Himamaylan*   *Caliling*   Bohol   Surigao

G   *Kabankalan*   *Baiso*   *Oslob*   Tagbilaran   BOHOL   *Bucas Grande*   10 497
Sipalay   Tanjay   *Bais*   *Malimono*   *Carrascal*
SULU   NEGROS   Dumaguete   *Siquijor*   *Butuan*   *Lanuza*
Bayawan   *Camiguin*   *Cabadbaran*   *Tandag*   *Tago*
Bonawan   *Zamboanguita*   *Talisayan*   *Hilonghilong*   L.   *Esperanza*   *Marihatag*
Mantalingajan   *Dapitan*   *Nasipit*   Maimit   *Lianga*
▲2085   Dipolog   *Alubijid*   *Balingasag*   ▲1837   *San Juan*
SEA   *Manucan*   Oroquieta   *Balingasag*   *Talacogon*   *Mangagoy*
C. Buliluyan   *Bugsuk*   *Sindangan*   Iligan   Opol   Cagayan de Oro   *Malaybalay*   *Bunawan*   *Baganga*
8   *Balabac*   *Liloy*   Ozamiz   Iligan   *Malaybalay*   *Cateel*
Labason   *Tubod*   ▲2896   *Tagum*
Kabasalan   *Pagadian*   MINDANAO   *Panabo*

H   *Balabac*   *Balambangan*   *Siocon*   *Margosatubig*   *Marawi*   L. Lanao   *Manay*
Bangsi   *Kudat*   *Sibuco*   ▲2915   *Midsayap*   Apo   Davao
Balabac Strait   *Marudu B.*   *Jambongan*   *Parang*   *Cotabato*   Bunawan   ▲2954   Davao
Langkon   *Sibuco*   Moro Gulf   *Datu Piang*   *Pikit*   *Digos*   Gulf   *Batobato*
Kota Belud   *Kinabalu*   Zamboanga   *Talayan*   *Koronadal*   *Malita*
6   *Tuaran*   Kinabalu   *Salaman*   *Lebak*
▲4101   *Linbawan*   Isabela   *Milbuk*   ▲2346   General   *C. San Agustin*
Penampang   Basilan   *Kiamba*   Santos
Tuaran   SABAH   *Sandakan*   *Samales*   *Sarangani Bay*
Beaufort   *Meliau*   *Beluran*   *Pangutaran*   Group   Jolo   Jolo   *Tinaca Pt.*
Kimanis   *Belud*   *Tampias*   Group
Kota   *Keningau*   *Sukau*   *Laparan*   *Parang*   *Lahiang Lahiang*
Kinabalu   *Tamoi*   *Pintasan*   *Sukau*   *Tapul*   *Pata*

J   *Papar*   Crocker Range   *Labuk*   *Litang*   *Tapul*   *Sarangani Is.*
Melalap   *Penungah*   *Kuamut*   Group   *Siasi*   CELEBES
Tenom   *Lahad Datu*   *Silam*   *Hog Pt.*   *Tawitawi*
Kemabong   Brassey Range   *Baturong*   *Darvel Bay*   *Group*   SEA
Sopulut   *Semporna*   *Sibutu*   *Kawio Is.*   *Talaud Is.*

PACIFIC

OCEAN

SOUTH

CHINA

SEA

SULU

SEA

Mindoro Strait

Tablas Str.

Sierra Madre

BOHOL
SEA

Mindanao Trench

SULU ARCHIPELAGO

ft   m
9000   3000
6000   2000
4500   1500
3000   1000
1200   400
600   200
0   0
200   600
4000   12 000
8000   24 000
m   ft

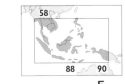

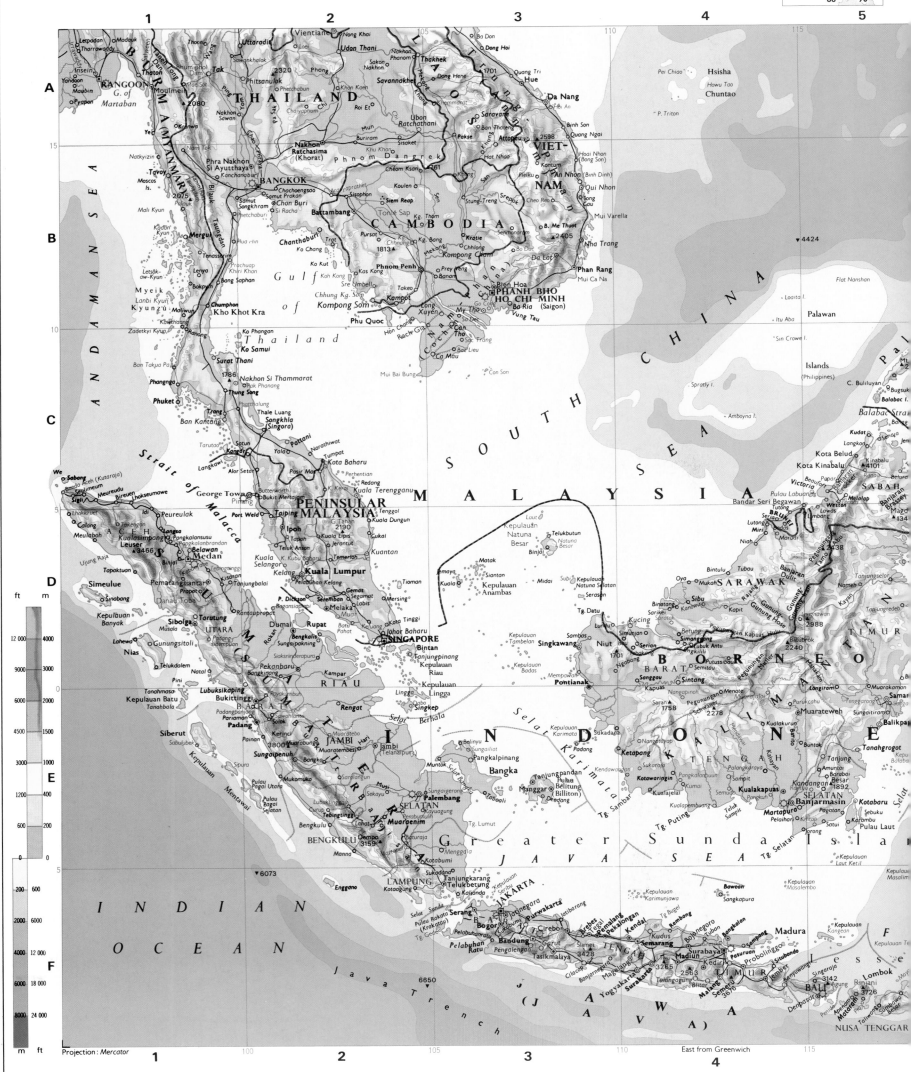

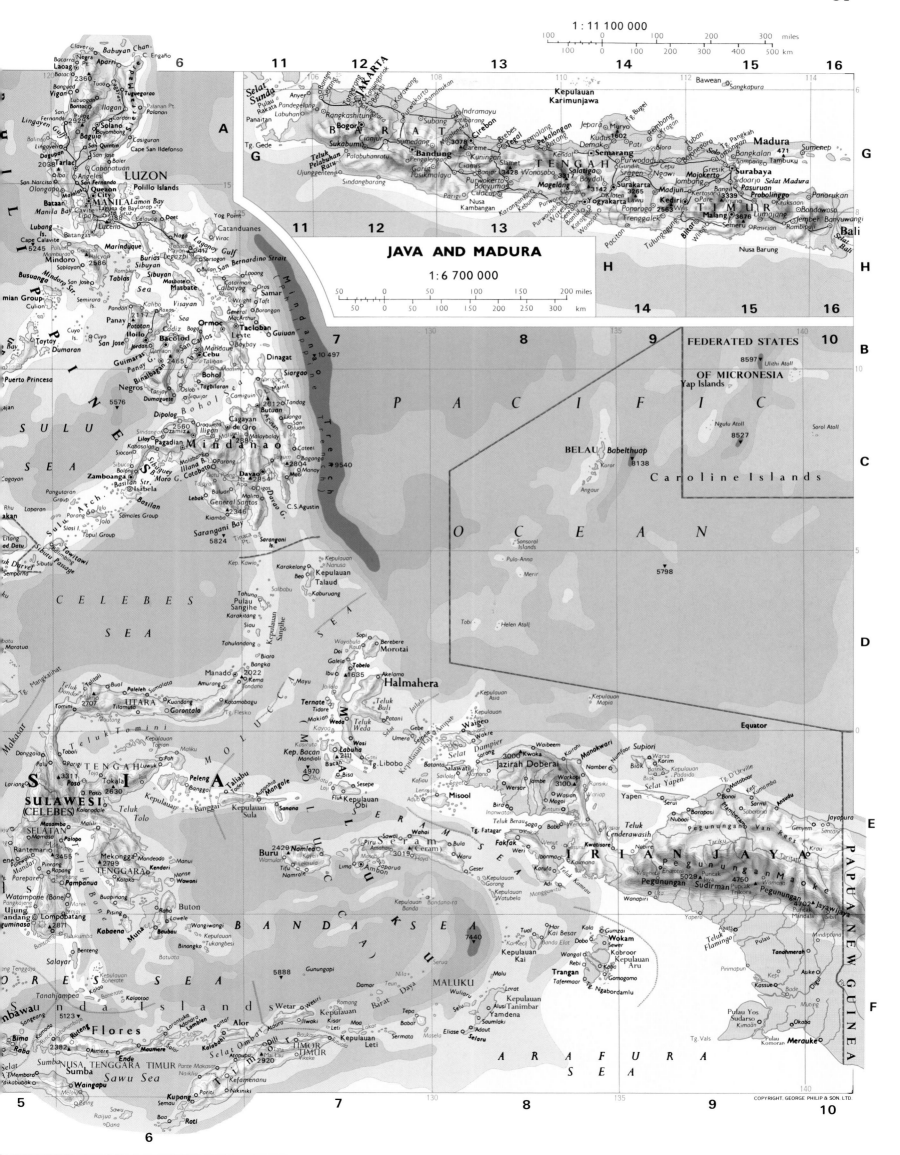

Gulf of Tonkin

HAINAN

GUANGXI ZHUANGZU ZIZHIQU AUTONOMOUS REGION

Nanning

Qiongzhou Haixia (Hainan Str.)

Red River Delta

Hanoi

Haiphong

YUNNAN

TONKIN

BAC

ANNAM

LAOS

Vientiane

Luang Prabang

Cao Nguyen Tran Ninh

Plaine des Jarres

Plateau Cao Nguyen

Central Highlands

Da Nang

Hue

THAILAND

Khorat

Cao Nguyen Khorat

Thiu Khao Phetchabun

Phnom Dangrek

CAMBODIA

BANGKOK

Thon Buri

Nakhon Ratchasima (Khorat)

Ubon Ratchathani

Udon Thani

Khon Kaen

Mekong

BURMA (MYANMAR)

SHAN STATE

KAYAH

KAWTHULE

TENASSERIM

Mandalay

Rangoon

Chiang Mai

Lampang

Phitsanulok

Dawna Range

Bilauktaung

Gulf of Martaban

Mergui Arch.

Tonle Sap (Great Lake)

Battambang

Phnom Penh

Mekong

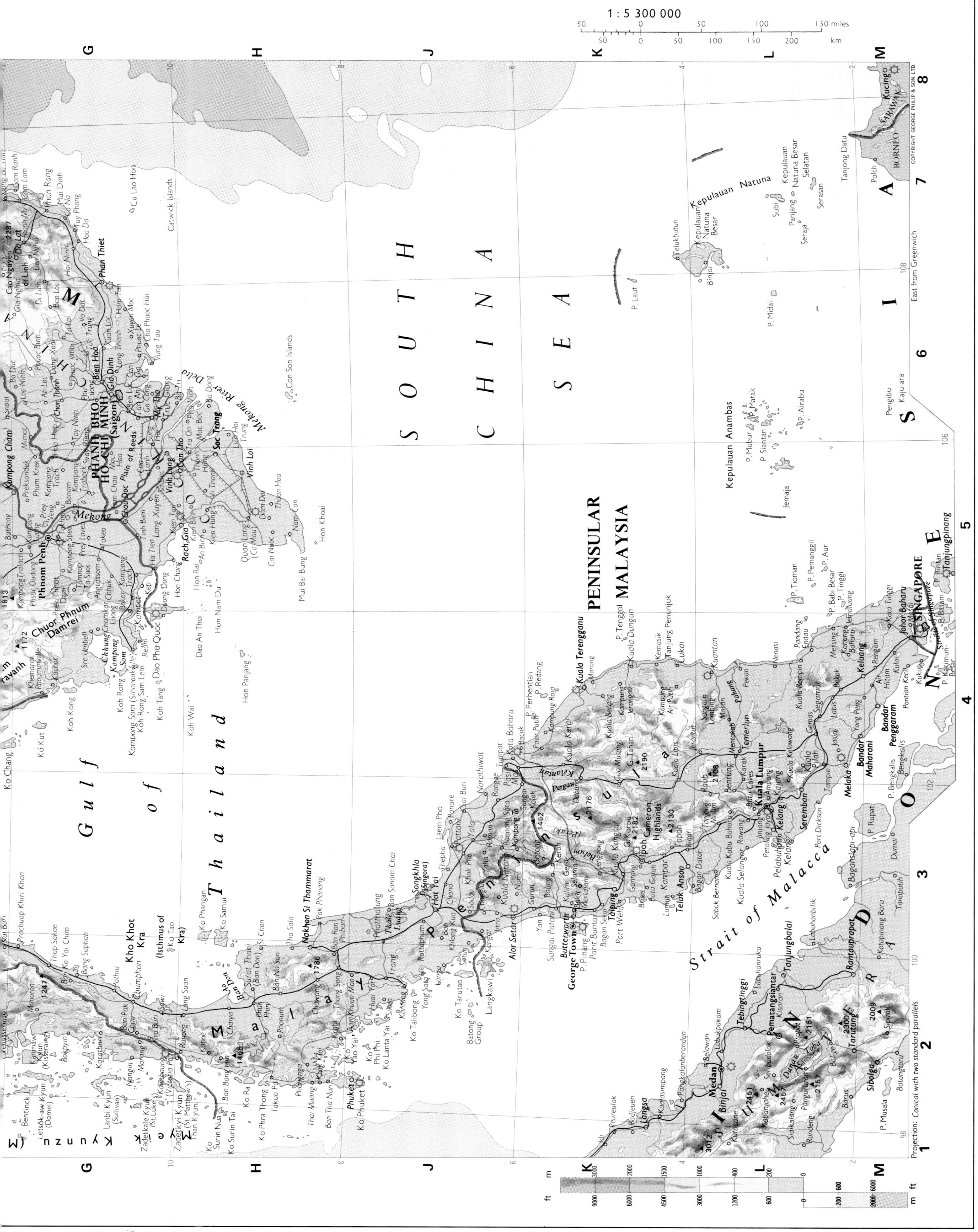

1 : 5 300 000

50   0   50   100   150 miles
50   0   50   100   150   200   km

Projection: Conical with two standard parallels

SOUTH CHINA SEA

Gulf of Thailand

Strait of Malacca

PENINSULAR MALAYSIA

SINGAPORE

BORNEO
SARAWAK
Kuching

Kepulauan Natuna
Kepulauan Natuna Besar
Natuna Besar
Subi
Panjang
Seraja
Serasan
Binjai
Tanjung Datu
Polch

Kepulauan Anambas
Jemaja
P. Mubur
Matak
P. Siantan
Np. Airabu
Pengibu
Kaju-ara

P. Laut
P. Midai

East from Greenwich

Kho Khot Kra
(Isthmus of Kra)

HO CHI MINH
Saigon
PHANH BHO
Bien Hoa
Gio Dinh
Phan Thiet
Phan Rang
Cao Nguyen 2287

Phnom Penh
Kompong Cham
Kompong Som (Sihanoukville)

Mekong River Delta
Mekong
Plain of Reeds
Con Son Islands

Soc Trang
Vinh Long
Can Tho
Rach Gia

Chuor Phnum Damrei

Koh Kong
Koh Kut
Ko Chang

Nakhon Si Thammarat
Songkhla (Singora)
Hat Yai
Narathiwat

George Town
Butterworth
Alor Setar
Langkawi

Taiping
Ipoh
Cameron Highlands
Kuala Lumpur
Kelang
Seremban
Melaka

Kuala Terengganu
Kota Baharu
Kuala Dungun
Kuantan
Pekan

Johor Baharu
Kluang
Bandar Penggaram
Bandar Maharani

Medan
Binjai
Pematangsiantar
Tebingtinggi
Tanjungbalai
Rantauprapat
Sibolga
Tarutung

T H A I L A N D

M A L A Y A

I N D O N E S I A

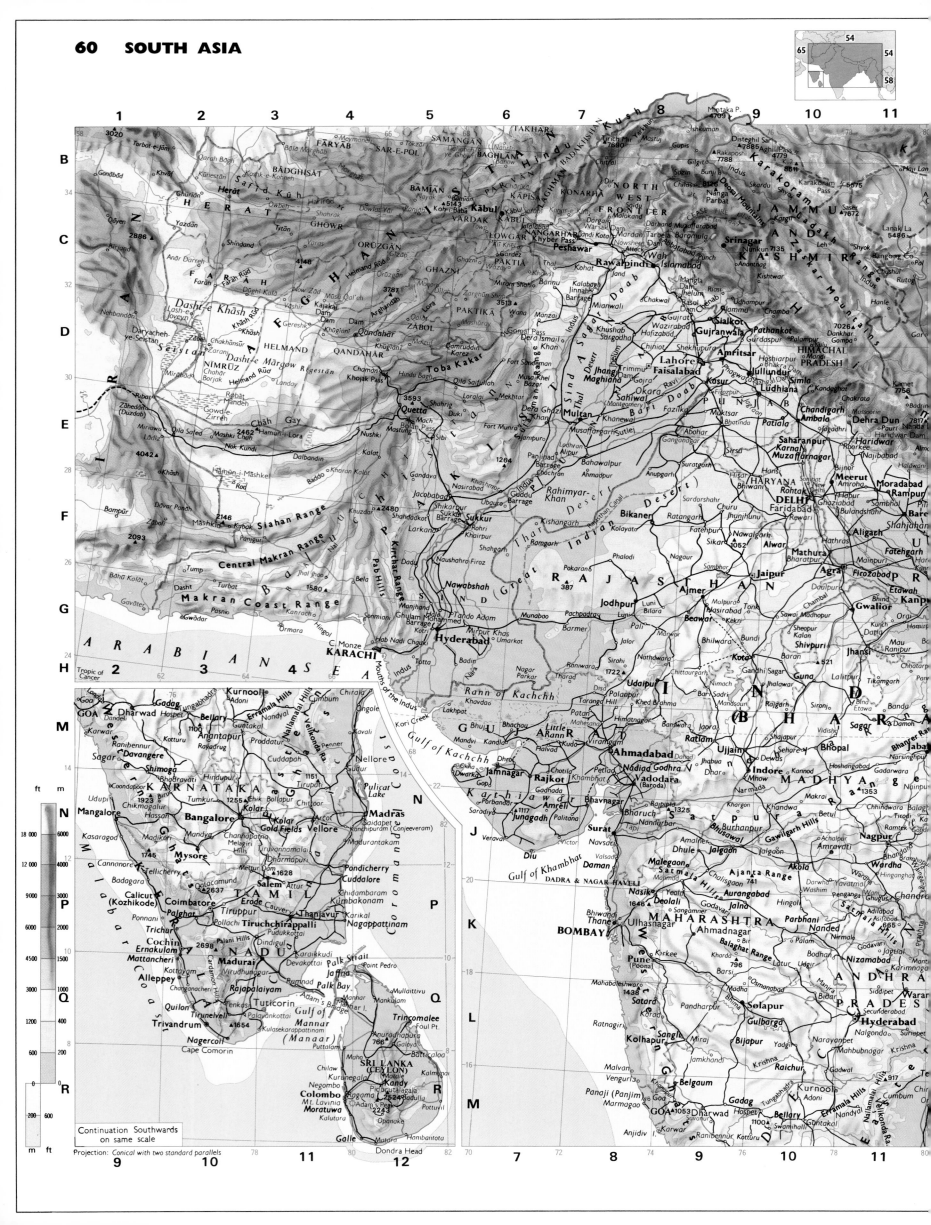

1 : 8 900 000

100   50   0   50   100   150   200 miles
100   0   100   200   300 km

B

C

D

E

F

G

H

AJ

K

L

M

CHINA

QINGHAI

XIZANG
(TIBET)

SICHUAN

YUNNAN

NEPAL

BHUTAN

SIKKIM

ASSAM

ARUNACHAL PRADESH

KACHIN

NAGALAND

MEGHALAYA

MANIPUR

BANGLADESH

WEST BENGAL

BIHAR

TRIPURA

MIZORAM

CHIN

Lhasa

Katmandu

Gorakhpur

Lucknow

Faizabad

Patna

Allahabad

Varanasi

Mirzapur

Gaya

Bhagalpur

Munger

Darbhanga

Muzaffarpur

Shillong

Tezpur

Nowgong

Jorhat

Myitkyina

Mandalay

Dhaka

CALCUTTA

Haora

Kharagpur

Jamshedpur

Ranchi

Raurkela

Asansol

Durgapur

Barddhaman

Khulna

Barisal

Chittagong

Comilla

Agartala

Raipur

Bilaspur

Sambalpur

Cuttack

Bhubaneshwar

ORISSA

BERHAMPUR

Vishakhapatnam

Vizianagaram

Kakinada (Cocanada)

Rajahmundry

BURMA
(MYANMAR)

Rangoon

Maulamyaing
Moulmein

SHAN

KAYAH

KAREN

THAILAND

Chiengmai

Tropic of Cancer

BAY OF BENGAL

INDIAN OCEAN

Gulf of Martaban

Preparis North Channel

Preparis South Channel

Pariparit Kyun
(Burma)

Koko Kyunzu
(Burma)

Heinze Is.
Moscos
Maungmagan
Islands
Launglon Bok Is.

Tavoy

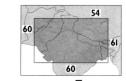

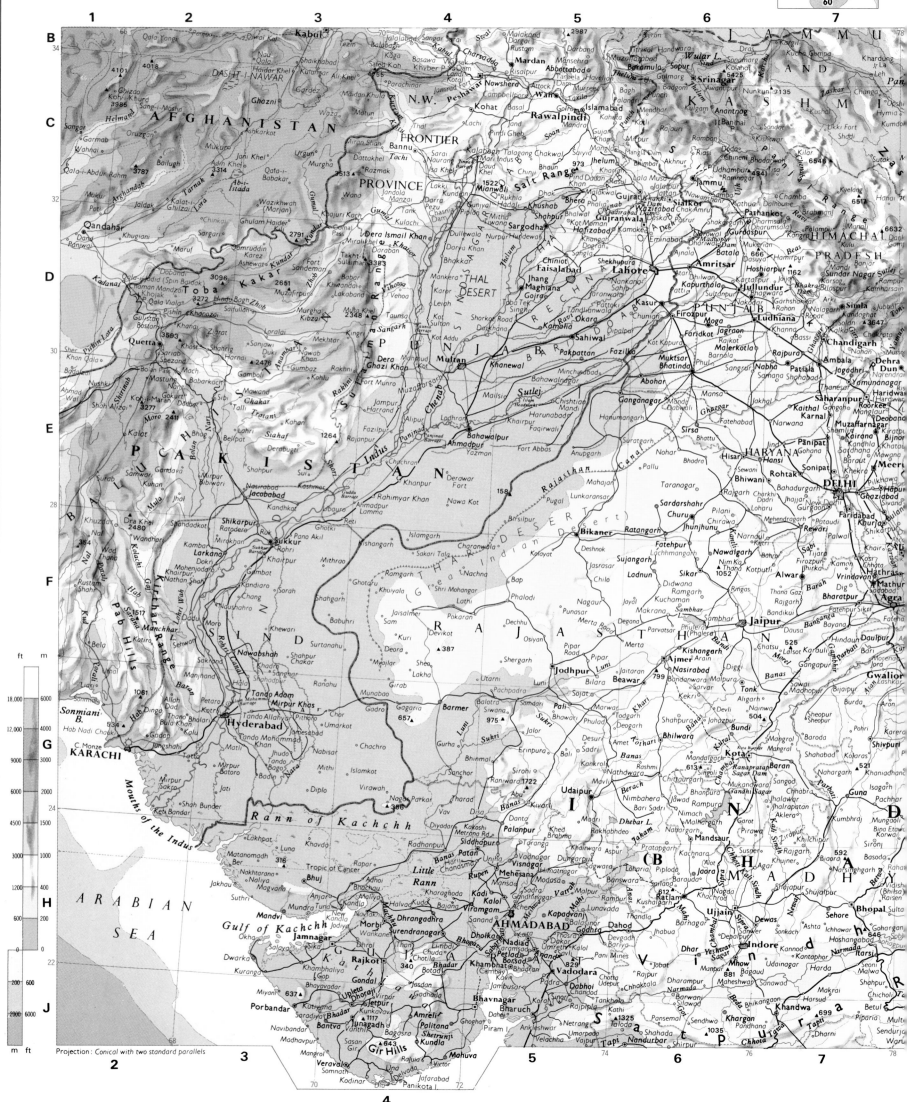

1 : 5 300 000

50   0   50   100 miles
50 0 50 100 150 km

JAMMU AND KASHMIR
On same scale as Main Map

A
B
C
D
E
F
G
H
J

8   9   10   5   6   7

East from Greenwich

8   9   10   11   12   13

COPYRIGHT. GEORGE PHILIP & SON. LTD.

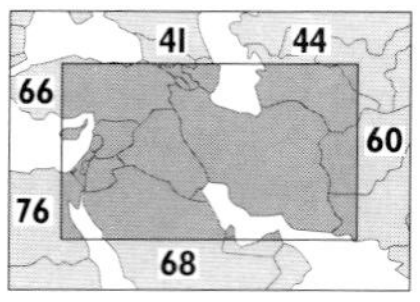

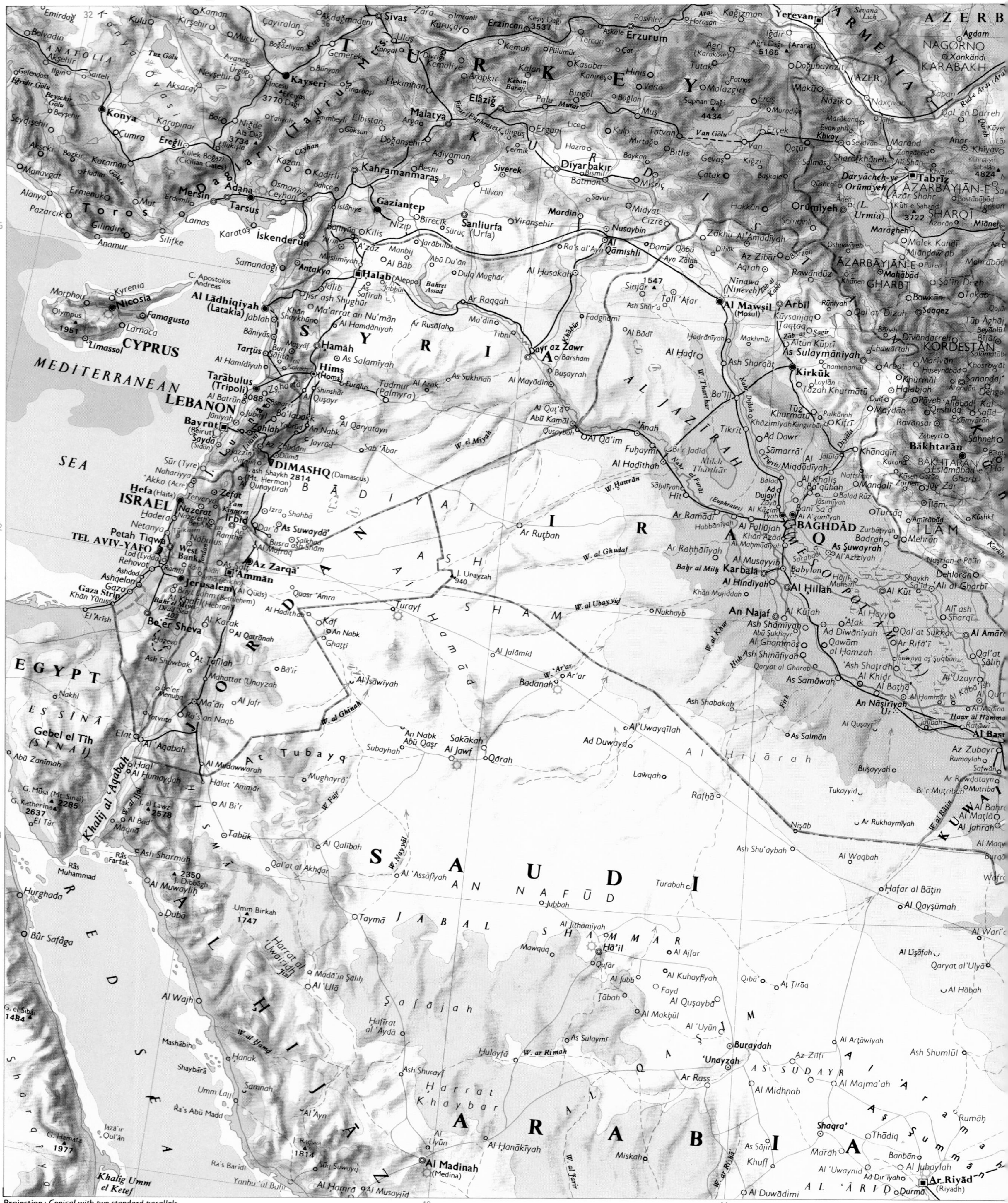

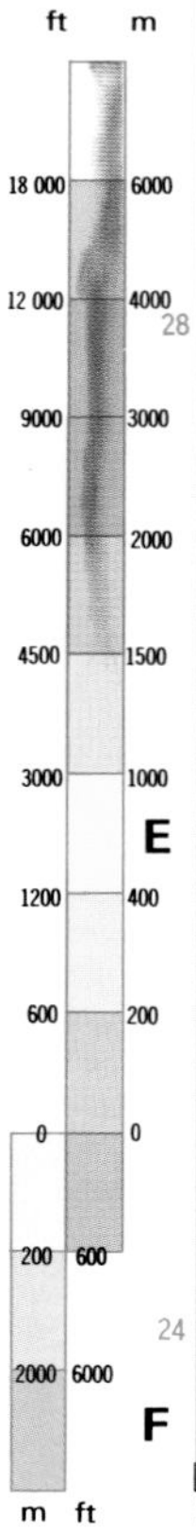

1   2   3   4   5

TURKEY

ANATOLIA

Emirdağ · Bolvadin · Kulu · Kırşehir · Kaman · Akdağmadeni · Sivas · Zara · İmranlı · Erzincan 3537 · Keşiş Dağı · Pasinler · Aras · Kağızman · Yerevan · ARMENIA · AZERB

Konya · Kayseri 3770 Dağı · Malatya · Elazığ · Erzurum · Ağrı (Karaköse) · 5165 · Iğdir · Nахçıvan · NAGORNO-KARABAKH (AZER.)

Ereğli · Niğde 3734 Aladağ · Kahramanmaraş · Besni · Adıyaman · Diyarbakır · Van Gölü · Van · Tabriz · AZARBĀYJĀN-E SHARQĪ

Toros · Adana · Mersin · Tarsus · Gaziantep · Şanlıurfa (Urfa) · Mardin · Nusaybin · Al Qāmishlī · ĀZARBĀYJĀN-E GHARBĪ

CYPRUS · Nicosia · Famagusta · Limassol

MEDITERRANEAN SEA

Al Lādhiqiyah (Latakia) · **SYRIA** · Ar Raqqah · Dayr az Zawr · Al Mawşil (Mosul) · Arbīl · KORDESTĀN

Ţarţūs · Ḩamāh · Hims (Homs) · Tudmur (Palmyra) · **AL JAZĪRAH** · Kirkūk · Ash Shaqāţ · As Sulaymānīyah

Tarābulus (Tripoli) · **LEBANON** · Bayrūt (Beirut) · Tikrīt · BĀKHTARĀN · ĪLĀM

DIMASHQ (Damascus) · Abū Kamāl · 'Ānah · Al Ḩadīthah · Sāmarrā' · Khānaqīn

Ḩefa (Haifa) · **ISRAEL** · Nazeret · Irbid · Ar Ramādī · **BAGHDĀD**

TEL AVIV-YAFO · West Bank · **Ammān** · Az Zarqā' · Karbalā' · Babylon · Al Ḩillah

Ashqelon · Gaza Strip · **Jerusalem** (Al Quds) · **JORDAN** · An Najaf · Ad Dīwānīyah

Be'er Sheva · **IRAQ** · As Samāwah · An Nāşirīyah

EGYPT · ES SINĀ' (SINAI) · Gebel el Tih · Ma'ān · **SAUDI** · Al Jawf · Sakākah · Ḩafar al Bāţin

Gebel Katherînā 2637 · Khalīj al 'Aqabah · Tabūk · **AN NAFŪD** · **KUWAIT**

RED SEA · Al Wajh · Umm Lajj · **HIJĀZ** · JABAL SHAMMAR · Ḩā'il · Buraydah

Hurghada · Bûr Safâga · **AL HIJĀZ** · Taymā' · 'Unayzah

ARABIA · Harrat Khaybar · Al Madīnah (Medina) · **AL ʿĀRIḌ** · **Ar Riyāḍ** (Riyadh)

ft m
18 000 6000
12 000 4000
9000 3000
6000 2000
4500 1500
3000 1000
1200 400
600 200
0 0
200 600
2000 6000
m ft

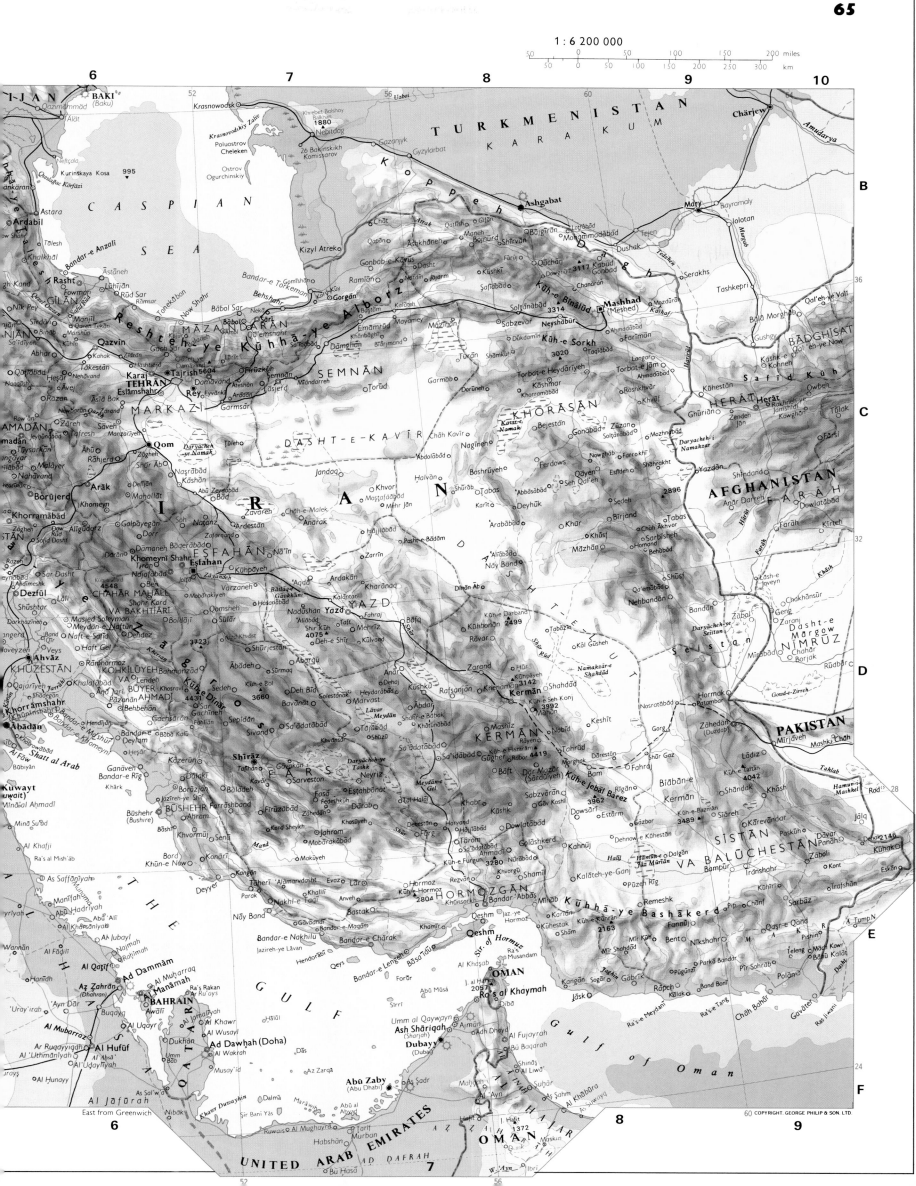

1 : 6 200 000

50 0 50 100 150 200 miles
50 0 50 100 150 200 250 300 km

6   7   8   9   10

I-JAN   BAKI (Baku)
Qazimämmäd
Älät

Krasnowodsk
Krasnovodskiy Zaliv   Uzboi
Khrebet Bolshoy   1880   Nebitdag
26 Bakinskikh   Gyzylarbat
Komissarov

T U R K M E N I S T A N

K A R A   K U M

Chärjew

Amudarya

B

Ostrov Ogurchinskiy
Poluostrov Cheleken

CASPIAN

995

Kizyl Atrek

Gazanjyk

Chät

Arrak

Qatlysh

Gifan

Ashgabat

Mary   Bayramaly

Jolotan

Murgab

Ardabil
Astara
Neftçala
Kurinskaya Kosa

SEA

Bandar-e Anzali

Bandar-e Torkeman

Bojnurd

Shirvan

Bügiran

Mohammadäbad

Dushak

Tejen

Serakhs

Tashkepri

Qal'eh-ye Vali

36

'e-ye
Tälesh
Rasht
GILAN
Nik Pey
njäno
Sirdan
Binäb

Bandar-e Gomishan
Gonbad-e Kavus
Dasht

Gorgän

Nardin

Jäjarm

Farüj

Qüchän

Dowghä-i   3117

Chanärän

Kabud Gonbad

Mashhad (Meshed)

Mozdurän

Kashaf

Balä Morghäb

Gushgy

Kashke-ye Kohneh

BADGHISAT

Qal'eh-ye Now

Ärdabil

Qare Tekän
Qazvin
Abhar
Kahak

Tonekäbon
Now Shahr
Babol Sar
Neka
Sari
MAZANDARAN
Amol
Babol
Behshahr
Kaläteh

Soltänäbad

Neyshabur

3314
Kuh-e Binälüd
Ahmadäbad

Färiman

Kühestän

Safid Küh

Owben

Roshkhvär

Khväf

HERAT
Herät

Rakhneh-ye Jamshidi
Kowghan

Tülak

C

njän
Sa'idiyeh
kühlo
Tajrish 5604
Karaj
TEHRÄN
Rey
Eslämshahr
Garmsär

Zanjän
Hashtrud
Firüzküh
Semnän
SEMNAN
Lasjerd
Mändarreh

Emämrüd
Damghän
Biärjand

Shämkuh
Türän
Garmäb

Mäzinän
Sabzevär
Dükdamin
Küh-e Sorkh
3020
Taqäbäd

Torbat-e Heydäriyeh
Käshmar
Khorramäbad

Torbat-e Jäm
Langar

KHORÄSAN
Bejestän
Zuzan
Gonäbäd
Soltänäbäd
Mozhnäbäd

Ghürian
Zendeh
Jän

Daryächeh-i
Namakzar

FÄRSI

AMADÄN
madän
HAMADÄN
Tüysarkän
ibad
ngoväri
ribäd
Nahävand

Kabak
Nehävand
Zefreh
Ähü
Räjherd
Säveh
Manzariyeh
Qom
Daryächeh-ye Namak

Nägräbäd
Käshän
Jandaq

Khvor
Moştäfäbäd
Mehr Jän

Häjjäbäd

Halvän

Shüräb
Tabas

Nagineh

Boshrüyeh

Abdoläbäd

Qäyen
Seh Qal'eh

Shahrakht
Yazdän

Nowghäb
Farrokhi
Esfideh

Ferdows

Shindand

AFGHANISTAN

F A R A H

C

Borüjerd
Khorramäbad
Zägheh

Arāk
MARKAZI
Khomeyn
Mahalllät

Golpäyegän
Dorr
Bäqeräbäd

Abü Zeydäbäd
Bäd

Zavärih
Chäh-e Malek

Anärak

Zarrin

Naginebäd

Sedeh
Karit
'Aräbäbäd

Deyhük

Khür
Khüsf
Homand
Mäzhän
Behbäd

Nehbandän

Birjand
Tabas
Chäh Akhvor
Sarbisheh
Qa'emäbäd

Anär Darreh
Härüt
Farah
Farah

Kirteh
Dowlatäbäd

32

STÄN
Sofid Dasht
Dezfül

Sar Dasht
R256

Dämaneh
Khomeyni Shahr
Tirän

I R A N

ESFAHÄN
Esfahan
Najafäbäd
Jolfä
Zavändeh

Kühpäyeh

Nä'in
'Äqdä

Ardistän

Ardakän

Dinän Äb

Äliäbäd
Näy Band

Shüst

Gowd-e-Zirreh

Rüdbär

Khüshäb

Shüshtar
Dorkhäzineh
Masjed Soleymän
Lälı

Izeh
CHAHÄR MAHÄLL
VA BAKHTIÄRI
4548
Shahr Kord
Ben

Mobärakiyeh
Varzaneh
Rattäq
Gävkhüni

Hosänäbäd

Nadushan
Aliäbäd
Yazd

Taft
Mehriz
Bäfq

Deh-e Shir

Khür

Kühbonän 2499

Rävar

Küh-e Darband

Ravar

Seistän
Daryächeh-ye
Seistän

Miräbäd

Zäbol

Zaranj
Dasht-e
Märgow
NIMRÜZ
Chähär
Borjak

ngera
Ahväz
Rämhormoz

KHÜZESTÄN
Qäjäriyeh
Khalafäbäd
Jarräh

KOHKILÜYEH
BÜYER
AHMADI

Z   3723
Semirom
4431
Pazänän

Küh-e Dinär
3660

Sedeh
Khänsät
Khosrovi
Äqä Järi

Ä Jari

Behbahän
Gachsärän
Bäbä Kalü

Deh Bid
Bavänät
Golestänak

Äbädeh
Sürmaq

Anär

Shahr-e Bäbak

Khätünäbäd
Rafsanjän
Kushkü

Dehaj
Heydaräbäd

Zarand
Küpäyeh

Kermän 3142
Shahdäd

Käl Shür

Namakzär-e
Shahdäd

Küh-e
Seh Konj

Nosratäbäd

Hormak
Patämbär

Zähedän
(Duzdäb)

PAKISTAN

Mirjäveh
Mashki Chäh

D

Khorramshahr
Khuniinshahr
Äbädän
Al Fäw
Bübiyän

Bandar-e Mäshür
Hendijän
Shädegän
Borazjän

Bandar-e Khomeyni

Deylam

Bandar-e Rig

Küh-e Bäl
Ganäveh
Dälaki
Büshehr
(Bushire)

Sepidän
Sivand

Sa'ädatäbäd
Marvast

Shulär
Sa'ädatäbäd

Shiräz
Tafihän
Gaväkän
Sarvestän

F A R S
Daryächeh-ye
Tashk
Neyriz

Qotrüyeh

 Shul

KERMÄN
Mashiz
Gügher
4419

Baft
Dar Mazär
(Särdüyeh)
Mahän

Küh-e Hazärän
3992

Nobäd

Tahrüd
Däreston

Morghak
Gorg

Fahraj
Shür Gaz

Rigän
Bam

Küh-e Jebäl Bärez
3962

Zähedän

Dösträn
Estärm

Gäzbor
Küh-e-Bazmän
3489

Siäreh

Biäbän-e
Kermän

Tädiz
4042

Khäsh

Shändak

Kärevändar

Jälq

Hämun-i
Mashkel

Röd

28

Kuwayt
uwait
Minä al Ahmadi
Minä Su'üd
Al Khafji
Ra's al Mish'äb

As Saffäniyah
Al Fädili
Manifah
Abü 'Ali
Al Jubayl
Al Hadriyah
Al Khawr

Al Khärk

Hesär

Bandar-e Deylam

Kangän
Farräshband
Ahram
Bäshi
Khvormüj
Senä

Bord
Khün-e Now

Mand

Konäri

Jazireh-ye Shif

Firüzäbäd
Zähedän
Fasä
Fedeshküh
Däräb

Makuyeh

Deyyer
Tähéri 'Älamarvdasht
Evaz
Lär

Parak
Nakhl-e Taqi
Khalili
Anveh
Bastak

Kangän
Näy Band
Gävbandi
Bandar-e Maqäm

Bandar-e Nakhilu
Bandar-e Chärak

Küh-e Furgän
3280

Eshtabänät
Jahrom
Khosüyeh
Fürg

Khabr
Käshk

Dehbäkri
Dowlatäbäd

Tärom
Sa'ädatäbäd
Ahmadi
Khvorgü
Shämil

Küh-e Bämän

Goläshgerd
Nürüäbäd

Dehnow-e Kühestän
Kahnüj
Halil
Hämun-e
Jäz Müriän
Dolgän

Kälätéh-ye-Ganj

Püzeh Rig

Dävar
Panäh

Küh
2146

Kühak

Kont

Bampür
Iränshahr
Trätshan

SISTÄN
VA BALÜCHESTÄN

Sarbäz

Qasr-e Qand
Pishin

Al Tumpt N

E

Al Qatif
Az Zahrän
(Dhahran)
Al Manämah
BAHRAIN
Awäli

Najmah
Rahimah
Ra's Rakan
Ra's Ru'ays

Ad Dammäm
Al Muharraq
Al Jumaylah

Al Wusayl

Dukhän
QATAR

Al Uqayr

Al Khawr
Al Mafjar

Bastak
Bandar-e Lengeh
Qeys

THE

Hendoräbi
Jazireh-ye Läväh

Küh-e Kürän
Kühestän
Shäm

2163

Fannüj
Bent

Mir Küh

Geläk

Ntkshahr

Teleng
Mäch Kowr
Bähü Kalät

Sogar
Gäbrik

Polän

Räpch

Band Bont

Küh-e Meydäni

Chäh Bahär

Ra's Tang

Gaväter

Ras Jiväni

24

Hanidh
Uray'irah
'Ayn Där
Al Fädili

Buqayq
Al Hufüf
Al Ahsä'
Al 'Uthmäniyah

Ar Ruqayyiqah
Al Mubarraz

Al Hunayy

Al Ghäwar
Al 'Uqayr

As Sal'w

Musay'id
Az Zakhnüniyah

Umm
Said

Däs
Az Zarqä
Dalmä

Marawwah
Abü al
Abyad

Sirri

Abü Müsä

Umm al Qaywayn
Ash Shäriqah
(Sharjah)
Ajmän
Adh Dhayd
Al Fujayrah
Bü Baqarah

Dubayy
(Dubai)

Shinäs
Al Liwä

Dibä

Ra's al Khaymah

OMAN

J. al Harim
2057
Ra's al
Musandam

Str. of Hormuz
Ra's
Musandam

Al Khasab

GULF

Abü Zaby
(Abu Dhabi)

Bü Hasä

Jabal
Hafit
1372

Khäwr Duwayhin
Sir Bani Yäs

UNITED ARAB

Tarif
Ruwais
Murban

AD DAFRAH

Bada'
Al Mughayrä

W. 'Ayn
Hili

EMIRATES

Al Wasit
Al 'Ayn
Al Khäbürä

Mahadah
As Sadr

Süfär
Al Sahm

Masfah
Ibri

O M A N

AL HAJAR

Gulf of
Oman

F

East from Greenwich

60 COPYRIGHT. GEORGE PHILIP & SON. LTD.

6   7   8   9

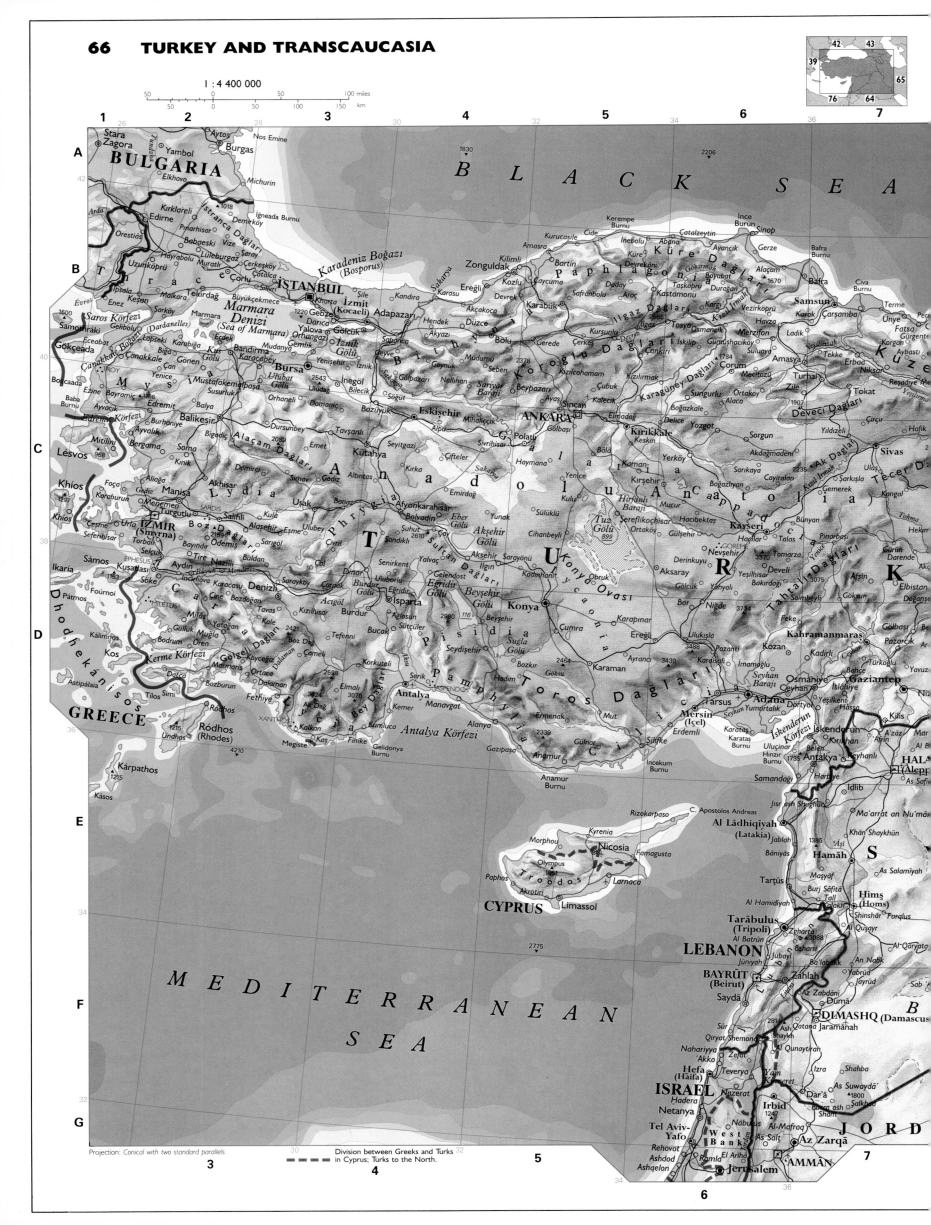

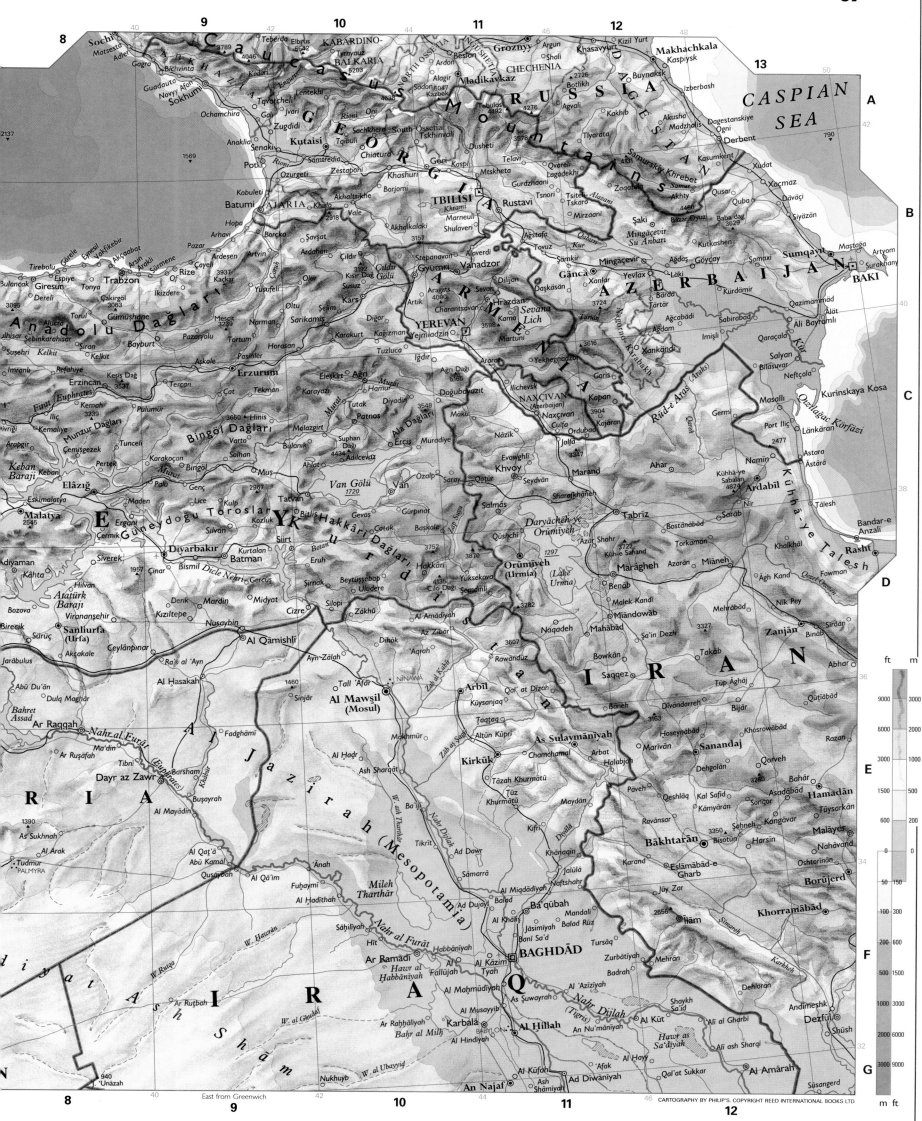

CASPIAN SEA

RUSSIA

GEORGIA

ARMENIA

AZERBAIJAN

TURKEY

IRAN

IRAQ

SYRIA

Caucasus Mountains

Anadolu Dağları

Güneydoğu Toroslar

Kurdistan

Al Jazirah (Mesopotamia)

Ash Shām

TBILISI

YEREVAN

BAGHDĀD

BAKİ

Makhachkala

Grozny

Vladikavkaz

Sochi

Trabzon

Erzurum

Malatya

Elâzığ

Diyarbakır

Tabrīz

Ardabīl

Rasht

Tehrān

Al Mawşil (Mosul)

Kirkūk

As Sulaymānīyah

Sanandaj

Hamadān

Bākhtarān

Khorramābād

Borūjerd

Zanjān

Karbalā'

An Najaf

Al Ḥillah

Ar Ramādī

Dayr az Zawr

Ar Raqqah

Al Ḥasakah

Şanlıurfa (Urfa)

Al Qāmishlī

PALMYRA

Batumi

Kutaisi

Poti

Sumqayıt

Gäncä

Gyumri

Vanadzor

Naxçıvan (Azerbaijan)

Kars

Van

Hakkâri

Orūmīyeh (Urmia)

Marāgheh

Saqqez

Mahābād

Nāqadeh

Rawāndūz

Arbīl

CARTOGRAPHY BY PHILIP'S. COPYRIGHT REED INTERNATIONAL BOOKS LTD

East from Greenwich

ft   m
9000 3000
6000 2000
3000 1000
1500   500
600   200
200   0
0   0
50   150
100   300
200   600
500 1500
1000 3000
2000 6000
3000 9000
m   ft

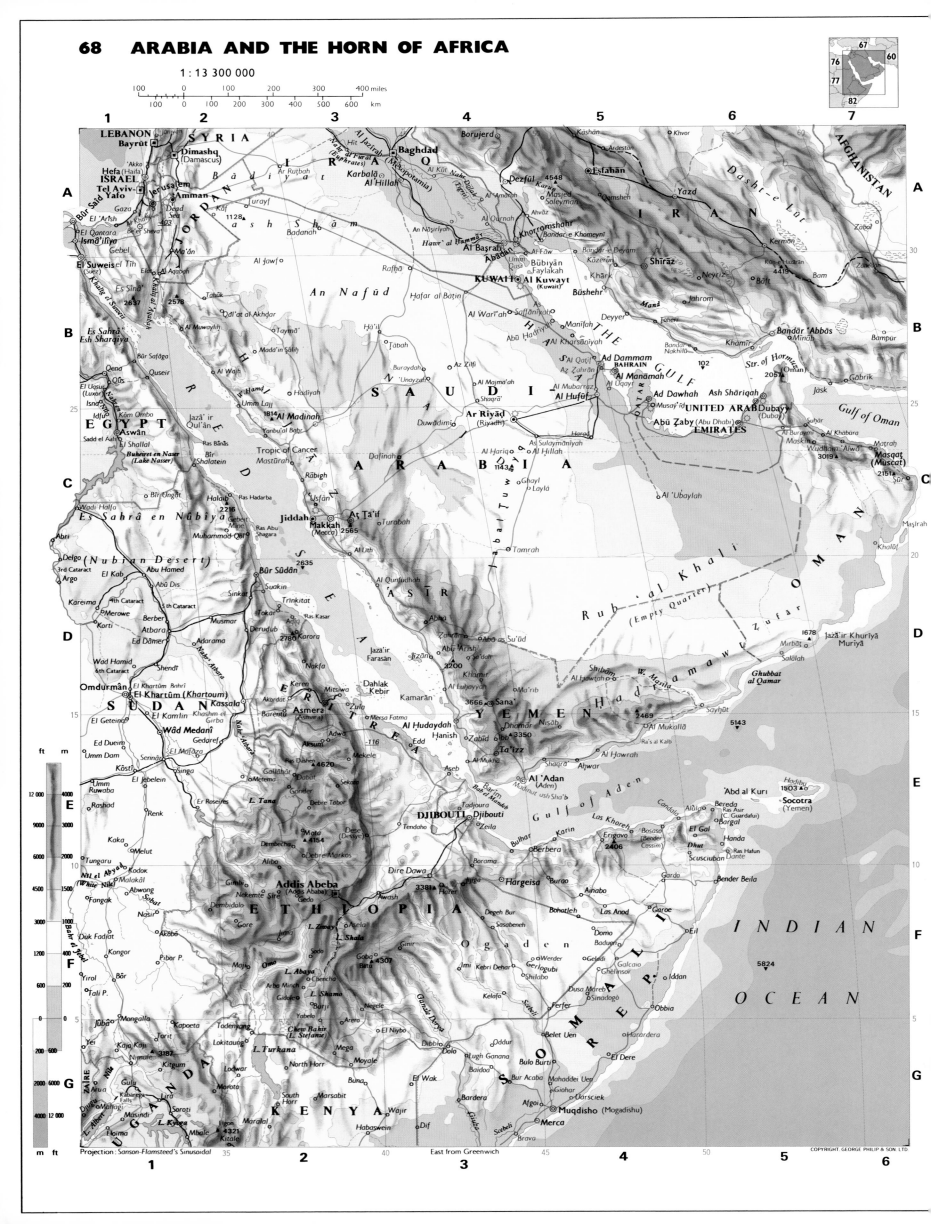

1 : 13 300 000

100   0   100   200   300   400 miles
100   0   100   200   300   400   500   600 km

1   2   3   4   5   6   7

LEBANON   Jūniyah   SYRIA
Bayrūt
Hefa (Haifa)   Dimashq (Damascus)
ISRAEL   Baghdād
Tel Aviv-Yafo   Jerusalem   Amman   JORDAN   Al Jazīrah   Nahr al Furāt   Al Hillah   Karbalā'   Borujerd   Khvor   Kāshān   Ardeston   AFGHANISTAN
Gaza   Dead Sea   Turayf   IRAQ   Hit   Tigris   Esfahān   Yazd   Dasht-e Lūt   Zābol
El 'Arīsh   Bādiyat   ash Shām   Badanah   Rafḥā   Al 'Amārah   Ahvāz   Qomsheh
Bûr Saïd   Ismā'īlīya   Ma'ān   Al Jawf   Al Qurnah   Dezfūl 4548   Masjed Soleymān   Bandar-e Khomeynī   Kermān   Bam   Zāhedān

EGYPT   An Nafūd   Hafar al Bātin   KUWAIT   Al Kuwayt (Kuwait)   Būshehr   Shīrāz   Neyrīz   Kūh-e Ḥazārān 4419   Būft

SAUDI   ARABIA

Rub' al Khali (Empty Quarter)

OMAN

YEMEN

ETHIOPIA

SOMALI REP.

KENYA

UGANDA

SUDAN

INDIAN OCEAN

Projection : Sanson-Flamsteed's Sinusoidal   East from Greenwich   COPYRIGHT. GEORGE PHILIP & SON. LTD

64
64
76
76

1 : 2 200 000

10 0 10 20 30 40 50 miles
10 0 10 20 30 40 50 60 70 80 km

CYPRUS

Paphos
Episkopi
Limassol
Episkopi Bay
Akrotiri Bay
C. Gata

M E D I T E R R A N E A N

S E A

Al Hamidiyah
Tall Kalakh
Ḥimṣ (Homs)
1075
Furqlus

Halbā
ASH
Al Mīnā'
Ṭarābulus (Tripoli) **SHAMĀL**
Al Hirmil
Al Quşayr **ḤIMŞ**
Al Qaryatayn
Gharta
Al Batrūn
Qurnat as Sawdā' ▲3088
Al Buray j
Dūmā
Bsharri
Jubayl
Qartaba
2464▲ Al Labwah
Bi'r Ghadīr
Ibrāhīm
2616▲
An Nabk
Jūniyah
Biktayyā
2628▲ Ba'labakk
Yabrūd
SYRIA
BAYRŪT (Beirut)
Zaḥlah
J. az Zubaydīyah ▲1406
Ash Shuwayfāt
2420▲ **ASH**
Al Qutaylī
Alayh
LEBANON
Khirbat Qanāfār
Az Zabdānī
Khān Abū Shāmāt
Sayda (Sidon)
al Bārūk 1942
Al Kiswah **DIMASHQ**
Jazzīn
DIMASHQ (Damascus)
Qaṭanā Darayyā
A'waj
An Nabaṭīyah at Taḥta
Ash Shaykh (Mt. Hermon) 2814▲
Al Ḥījānah
AL
Al Khiyām
Būraq
Şūr (Tyre) **JANŪB**
1197▲ Al Qunayṭirah
As Sanamayn
Qiryat Shemona
Ḥ
W. al Ḥarīr
Nahariyya Me'ona **HAZOR** Ḥijollan (Golan Heights)
Izra
'Akko (Acre) Zefat Rafīd
Dar'ā Shahba
Hagalil Sakhnīn **DAR'Ā**
AS SUWAYDĀ'
Mifraz Hefa Qiryat Yam Migdal Tiberias
Şaḥam al Jawlān As Suwaydā' ▲1800
Hefa (Haifa) Qiryat Ata Teverya (Tiberias) **Yam Kinneret**
Dar'ā Salah
Ṭīrat Karmel Naẕerat (Nazareth) Yarmūk Buşrā ash Shām Salkhad
Dāliyat el Karmel **HAZAFON** Afula Ṭayyiba Ar Ramthā
HEFA Tayyiba
TEL MEGIDDO Bet She'an
Caesarea Umm el Fahm
Irbid Al Mafraq
CAESAREA **Shōmrōn** Jānīn
Ajlūn Umm al Qiṭṭayn
Ḥadera Burqīn
Hadera Pardes Ḥanna 'ad Darah 1247
Umm al Qiṭṭayn
ISRAEL Ṭūbās **IRBID**
Jarash
Netanya Ṭulkarm **SAMARIA** Jordan
Anabta **Zarqā'**
HAMERKAZ Nābulus
Herzliyya Azzūn Al Balqā'
Benē Beraq **WEST** As Salṭ **Az Zarqā'**
Tel Aviv-Yafo Petaḥ Tiqwa SHILO
Ramat Gan **Bank** **AMMĀN**
Bat Yam Tall 'Āşūr ▲1016
Rishon le Ziyyon 289 Wādi as Sīr **AL ĀŞIMAH**
N. Soreq Ramla El Arīḥā (Jericho) Na'ūr
Reḥovot Rām Allāh At Tunayb
Ashdod Yavne **Jerusalem** (Yerushalayim) (Al Quds) Ma'dabā
Qiryat Malakhi Bet Shemesh
Ashqelon Qiryat Gat Bayt Laḥm (Bethlehem)
TEL LAKHISH Al Khalīl (Hebron)
Gaza N. Shiqma W. al Ḥaydān Dhībān
Sederot Al Mūjib
Gaza Az Zāhirīya
Strip 1065
Khān Yūnis **Be'er Sheva** 'Arad
Rafaḥ Al Karak
Bûr Sa'îd (Port Said) Al Qaṭrānah
Rās Burūn El Daheir 981
Khalīg el Tîna Sabkhet el Bardawīl Bor Mashash W. al Ghadaf
Rās el 'Abd Dimona 1305 Al Mazār W. al Makhruq
Romāni Bīr el Garārāt 682 **JORDAN**
El 'Arīsh Bīr Laḥfān –333 At Ṭafīlah W. Bā'ir
El Qanṭara Bīr Qaṭia **HADAROM** **AL KARAK**
Ismâ'îliya Bīr el Duweidar Bā'ir
Wāḥid –121
Bīr el Jafir Qeẕi'ot Bīr ad Dabbāghāt J. ash Shawmari
Khamsa Bīr Madkūr Birein Ruim Tal'at 1072
El Buheirat al Jamā'ah ▲1736
el Murrat Muweilih Nijil W. Abu Şafāt
el Kubra 892 **Hanegev** Mahattat Unayza
(Gt. Bitter L.) El Quşaimā (Negev Desert) Qa' el Jafr
G. Yi 'Allaq Bīr Beida Al Jafr
Gineifa 1094 W. Qiraiya El Agrūp N. Paran
EL Bīr el Thamāda **PETRA** Ma'ān
SUWEIS N. Ḥiyyon Ma'ān
Nakhl Yotvata
El Suweis (Suez) W. el Brūk El Kuntilla Ra's an Naqb **MA'ĀN**
875 Bīr Gebel Ḥişn Mahattat ash Shidīya
Būr Taufiq W. el Tamad Bīr el Mārī
Uyūn Mūsa 'En Avrona **SAUDI**
Ghubbet 948▲ Ra's an Naqb ▲1435
1272▲ el Bûs G. el Kabrit Bīr el Qaṭṭār
Gebel el Tîh El Thamad **ARABIA**
Bīr Abu Şanāfa
Rās Matarma W. Warqa 952▲
Sinâi Peninsula 1592
EGYPT Ekot Al 'Aqabah **Aṭ Ṭubāyq**
W. Abu Ga'da Bīr el Ḥesi
W. Abu el Gattī
Bīr Wuseit 1165 Haql

ft m
9000 3000
6000 2000
4500 1500
3000 1000
1200 400
600 200
0 0
200 600
2000 6000
m ft

Projection: Polyconic
East from Greenwich
COPYRIGHT GEORGE PHILIP & SON LTD.
– – – 1974 Cease Fire Lines

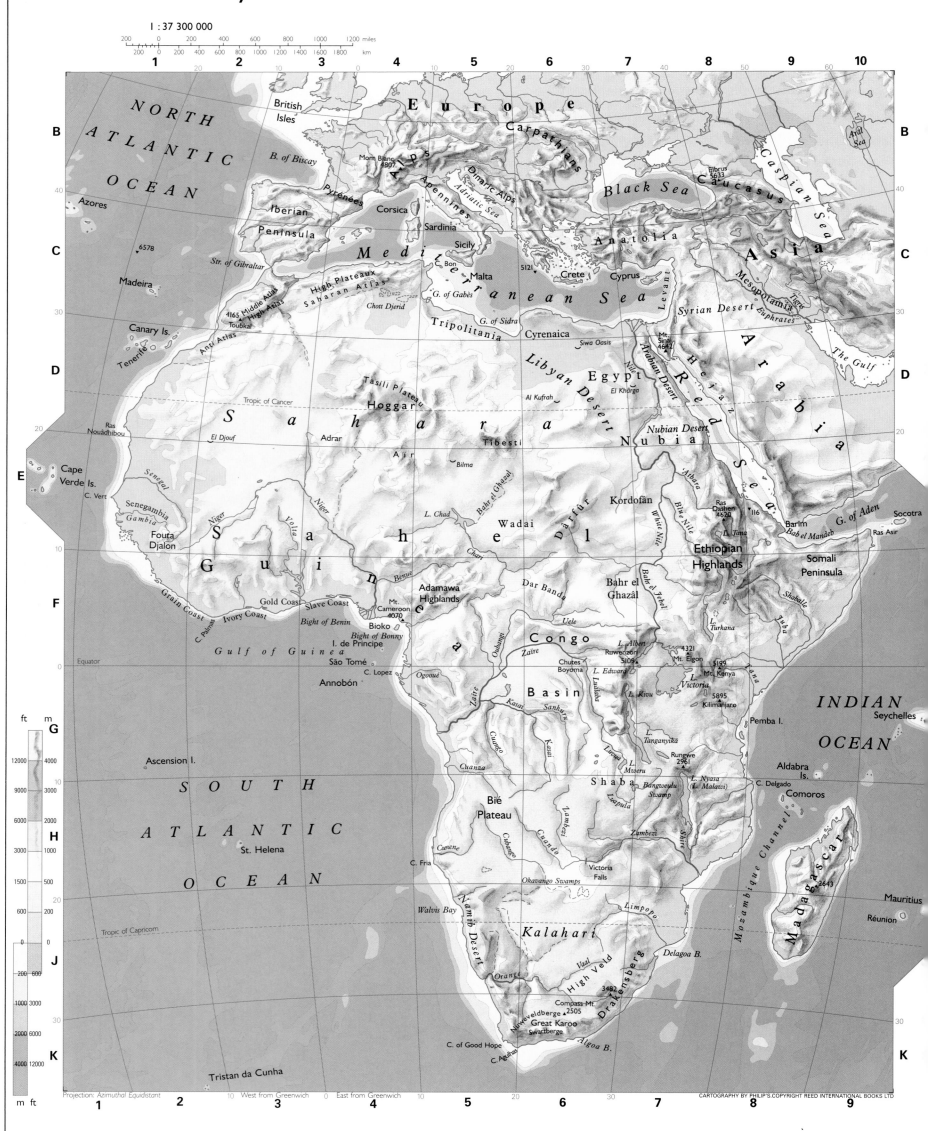

1 : 37 300 000

CARTOGRAPHY BY PHILIP'S.COPYRIGHT REED INTERNATIONAL BOOKS LTD

1 : 37 300 000

200 0 200 400 600 800 1000 1200 miles
200 0 200 400 600 800 1000 1200 1400 1600 1800 km

NORTH ATLANTIC OCEAN

SOUTH ATLANTIC OCEAN

INDIAN OCEAN

Mediterranean Sea

Black Sea

Caspian Sea

Red Sea

Gulf of Guinea

Bight of Benin

Mozambique Channel

G. of Aden

The Gulf

Adriatic Sea

B. of Biscay

Syrian Desert

Sahara

UNITED KINGDOM · London
NETH. · BELG.
GERMANY · POLAND · Warsaw
PARIS · FRANCE · Prague · CZECH REP.
SWITZ. · Vienna · SLOVAK REP. · Kiev
AUSTRIA · HUNGARY · UKRAINE · Volgograd · KAZAKHSTAN
CROATIA · BOS.-HERZ. · YUG. · ROMANIA · Odessa
ITALY · BULGARIA · Aral Sea
Corsica · Rome · Sardinia
Madrid · SPAIN · Sicily · GREECE · Athens · TURKEY · Ankara · GEORGIA · AZER. · Baku · TURKMEN.
Lisbon · PORTUGAL · MALTA · Crete · CYPRUS · ARM. · Mosul · Eşfahān
Azores (Port.)
Algiers · Annaba · Constantine · Tunis · Tripoli · Misrātah · Benghazi · Aleppo · SYRIA · Tigris · Baghdād · IRAN
Rabat · Tétouan · Tunis · Sfax · Tel Aviv-Jaffa · Damascus · Euphrates · IRAQ
Casablanca · Fès · Chott Djérid · LEB. · Jerusalem · Basra · KUWAIT
MOROCCO · Marrakesh · ISRAEL · JORDAN · Suez
Madeira (Port.) · Alexandria · Port Said · CAIRO · SAUDI · BAHRAIN
Canary Is. (Sp.) · El Faiyûm · QATAR
El Aaiún · ALGERIA · LIBYA · EGYPT · Asyût · Aswān · ARABIA · Medina · Riyadh
Dakhla · In Salah · Marzûq · Al Jawf · Wadi Halfa · Jedda · Mecca
Fdérik · Tropic of Cancer · Port Sudan · YEMEN · Socotra (Yemen)
Ras Nouâdhibou
MAURITANIA · Nouakchott · NIGER · Agadès · CHAD · Atbara · Omdurmân · Khartoum · ERITREA · Mesewa · Ras Asir
VERDE IS. · Tombouctou · Abéché · Wâd Medani · Asmera
St-Louis · Senegal · L. Chad · Ndjamena · El Fâsher · SUDAN · El Obeid · L. Tana · DJIBOUTI · Berbera
C. Vert · Dakar · SENEGAL · MALI · NIGER · Niamey · Kano · Maiduguri · Djibouti
GAMBIA · Banjul · BURKINA · Ouagadougou · NIGERIA · Malakâl · Addis Ababa · Harer
GUINEA BISSAU · Bissau · FASO · Abuja · Wau · ETHIOPIA · Shabalê
Conakry · GUINEA · Bobo-Dioulasso · BENIN · Benue · Bahr el Jebel · Juba
Freetown · SIERRA LEONE · IVORY COAST · GHANA · Ibadan · Enugu · CENTRAL AFRICAN REP. · L. Turkana · SOMALI REP. · Mogadishu
Monrovia · LIBERIA · Bouaké · Kumasi · Lomé · Lagos · CAMEROON · Bangui · Oubangui · L. Albert · KENYA
Abidjan · Yamoussoukro · TOGO · Porto Novo · Douala · Yaoundé · Zaïre · Mbandaka · Kisangani · UGANDA · Kampala · Kisumu · Nairobi · Kismayu
Sekondi-Takoradi · Accra · Port Harcourt · Malabo · EQUATORIAL GUINEA · CONGO · ZAÏRE · L. Edward · RWANDA · Kigali · L. Victoria · Mombasa
SÃO TOMÉ & PRINCIPE · Libreville · GABON · Brazzaville · Kasai · Lualaba · L. Kivu · BURUNDI · Bujumbura · SEYCHELLES
Equator · C. Lopez · Pointe Noire · Kinshasa · Kananga · TANZANIA · Dodoma · Zanzibar · Dar es Salaam
Annobón · CABINDA (Angola) · Matadi · Cuango · L. Tanganyika
Ascension I. (U.K.) · Luanda · L. Mweru · Likasi · Lubumbashi · L. Malawi · C. Delgado · COMOROS · Antsiranana
ANGOLA · Huambo · Ndola · MALAWI · Lilongwe · Moçambique · Mayotte (Fr.)
St. Helena (U.K.) · Namibe · ZAMBIA · Lusaka · Zambezi · Blantyre · Mahajanga
Lobito · Kariba · MOZAMBIQUE · Toamasina
Cunene · Livingstone · Harare · Beira · Antananarivo
C. Fria · NAMIBIA · Cubango · ZIMBABWE · Bulawayo · MADAGASCAR · MAURITIUS
Tropic of Capricorn · Windhoek · BOTSWANA · Limpopo · Fianarantsoa · Réunion (Fr.)
Gaborone · Pretoria · Maputo
Johannesburg · Vaal · Mbabane · SWAZ.
Orange · Kimberley · Maseru · LESOTHO · Durban
SOUTH AFRICA · East London
Cape Town · Port Elizabeth
C. of Good Hope · C. Agulhas
Tristan da Cunha (U.K.)

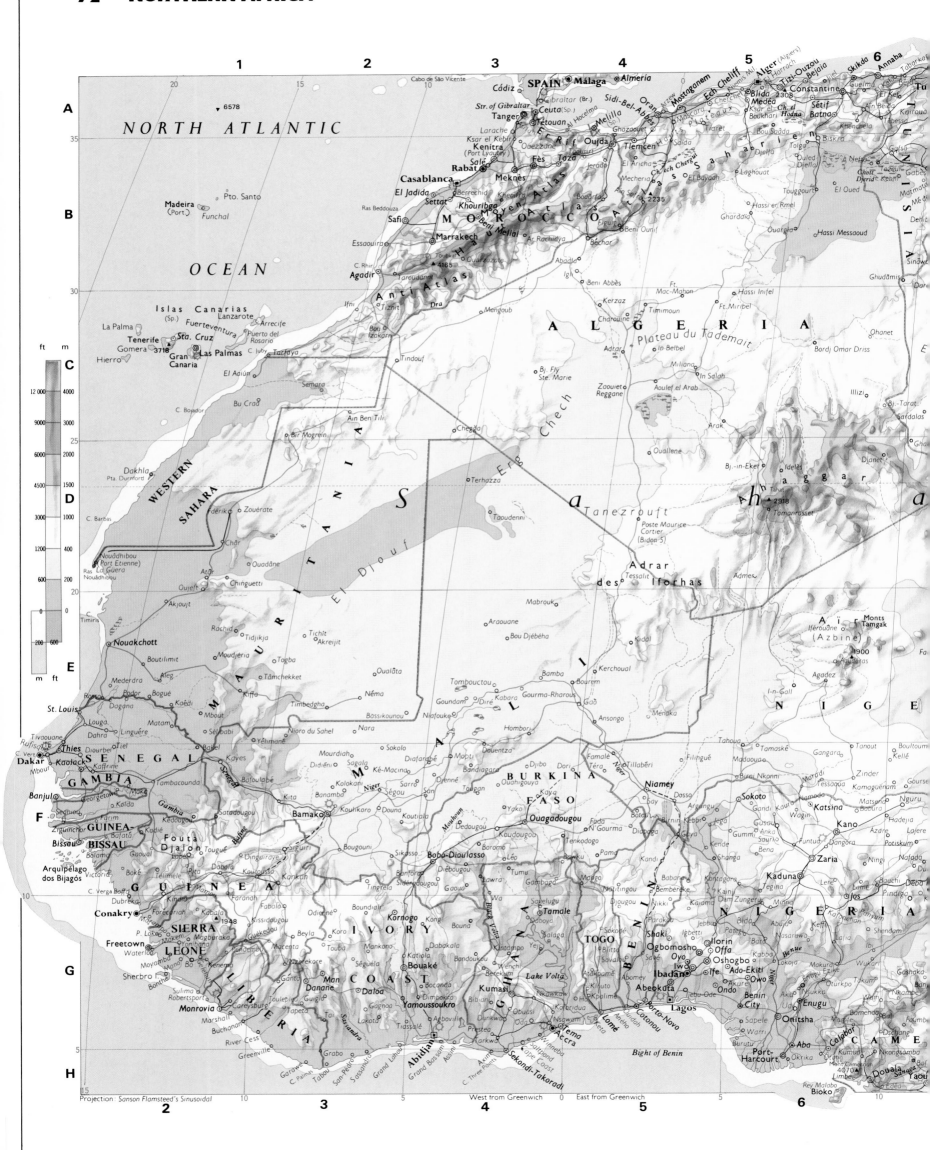

NORTH ATLANTIC

OCEAN

NORTH ATLANTIC

Cabo de São Vicente

SPAIN
Cádiz
Málaga
Almería

Gibraltar (Br.)
Str. of Gibraltar
Ceuta (Sp.)
Tanger
Tétouan
Melilla

Madeira (Port.)
Funchal

Pto. Santo

6578

Larache (Port Lyautey)
Kenitra
Salé
Rabat
Casablanca
El Jadida
Settat
Berrechid
Khouribga
Safi

Essaouira
Marrakech
C. Rhir
Agadir

Islas Canarias (Sp.)
Lanzarote
Arrecife
Fuerteventura
Puerto del Rosario
La Palma
Tenerife
Sta. Cruz
Gomera 3718
Gran Canaria
Las Palmas
Hierro

Ifni
Tiznit

Anti Atlas

Bou Izakarn
C. Juby
Tarfaya

El Aiún
Semara

C. Bojador
Bu Craa

Ain Ben Tili

Dakhla
Pta. Durnford

WESTERN SAHARA

C. Barbas

Fdérik
Zouérate

Nouâdhibou (Port Étienne)
Ras La Güera
Nouâdhibou

Chār

Ouadâne

Atâr
Chinguetti

Oujeft

Akjoujt

MAURITANIA

Timiris

Nouakchott

Boutilimit

Rachid
Tidjikja
Tichit
Akreijit

Moudjéria
Togba

Mederdra
Aleg
Tâmchekket
Oualâta

St. Louis
Rosso
Podor
Dagana
Louga
Linguère
Dahra
Tivaouane
Thiès
Diourbel
Kaolack
Kaffrine

Matam
Sélibabi
Bogué
Kaédi
Mbout
Kiffa

Nioro du Sahel
Nara

Bássikounou
Néma

SENEGAL
Dakar
C. Verga
Rufisque
Mbour

GAMBIA
Banjul
Georgetown
Ziguinchor

GUINEA-BISSAU
Bissau
Bolama
Arquipélago dos Bijagós
C. Verga

GUINEA
Conakry
Dubréka
Kindia

SIERRA LEONE
Freetown
Waterloo

Monrovia
Marshall
Buchanan
River Cess
Greenville

LIBERIA

ALGERIA

Plateau du Tademait

Chech

Erg Chech

Sahara

El Djouf

Tanezrouft

Adrar des Iforhas
Tessalit

Aïr (Azbine)
Monts Tamgak

Agadez

NIGER

MALI

Tombouctou
Goundam
Diré
Kabara
Gourma-Rharous
Gao
Bamba
Ansongo
Ménaka

Kidal

Kerchoual
Bourem

Araouane
Bou Djébéha

Mabrouk

Timbedgha
Niafunké

Mourdiah
Sokolo
Diafarabé
Mopti
Douentza

Bamako
Koulikoro
Banamba
Ségou
Djenné
Bandiagara

BURKINA FASO
Ouagadougou
Ouahigouya
Djibo
Dori
Téra
Tillabéri
Filingué

Niamey
Dosso
Say

Bobo-Dioulasso
Sikasso
Koutiala
San

SIERRA LEONE

IVORY COAST

GHANA

Kumasi
Accra
Tema
Sekondi-Takoradi

TOGO
Lomé

BENIN
Cotonou
Porto-Novo

Lagos
Ibadan
Abeokuta
Benin City
Onitsha

NIGERIA
Kano
Katsina
Zaria
Kaduna
Sokoto

Lake Volta

Bight of Benin

Bioko

CAME...

Port-Harcourt

Projection: Sanson Flamsteed's Sinusoidal

West from Greenwich   East from Greenwich

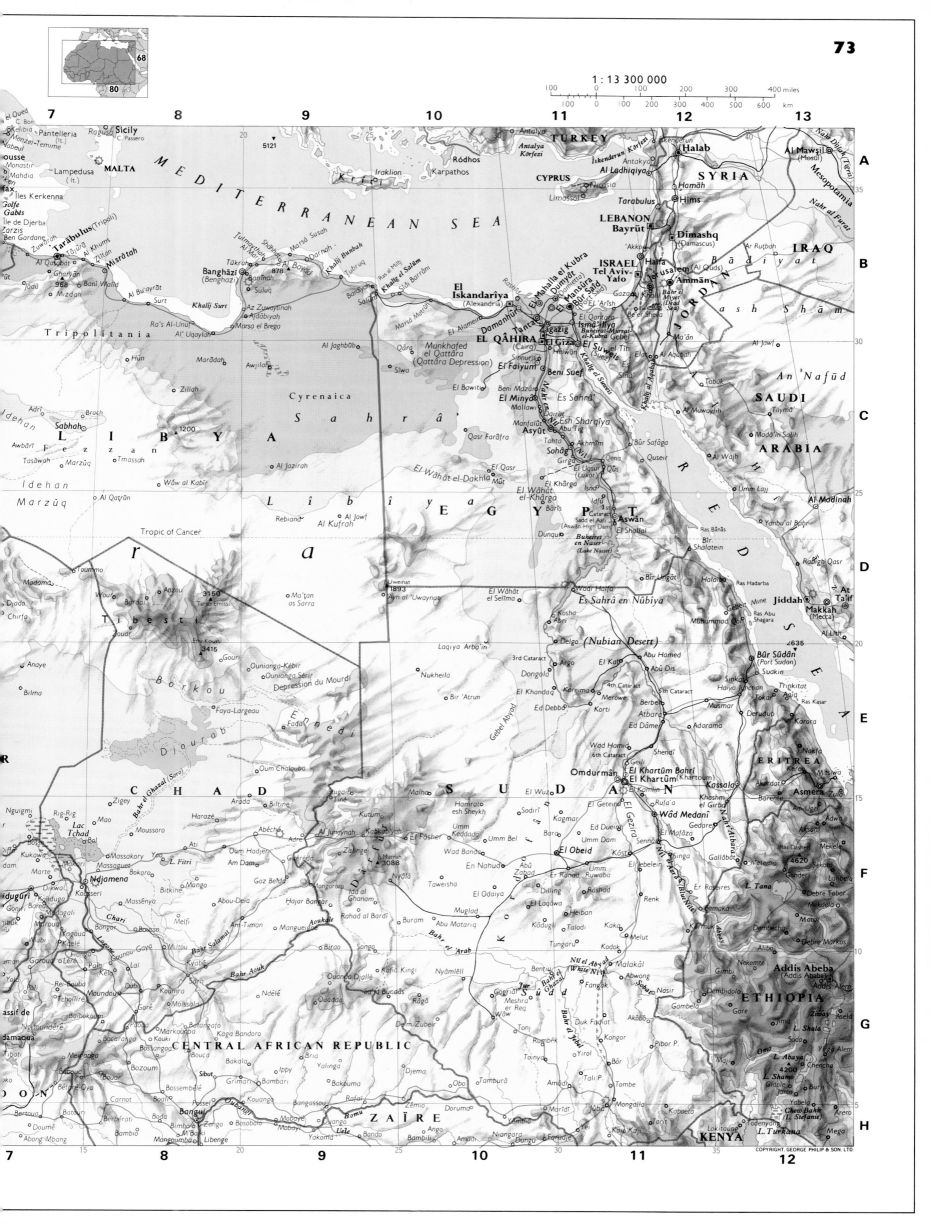

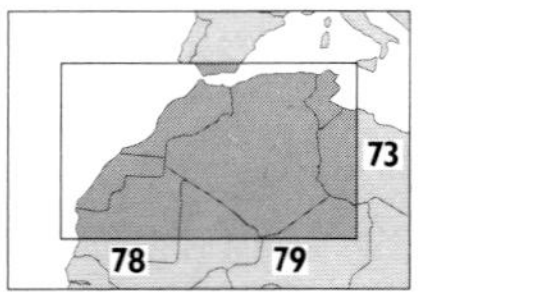

NORTH

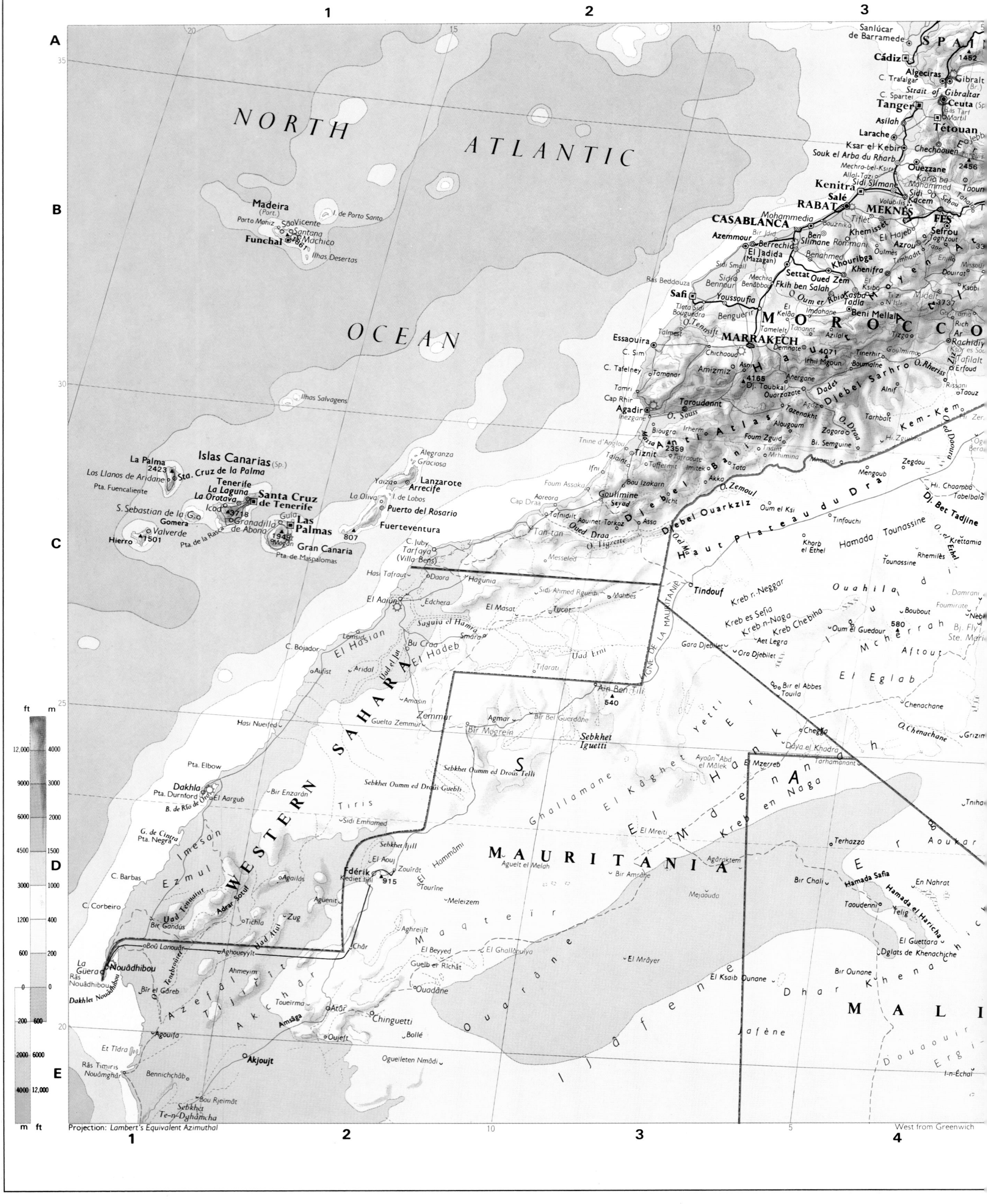

ATLANTIC

OCEAN

SPAIN
Sanlúcar de Barramede
Cádiz
Algeciras
Gibralt. (Br.)
C. Trafalgar
C. Spartel
Strait of Gibraltar
Tanger
Ceuta
Ras Tarf
Asilah
Martil
Larache
Tétouan
Ksar el Kebir
Chechaouen
Souk el Arba du Rharb
Ouezzane
Mechra-bel-Ksiri
Allal-Tazi
Sidi Slimane
Karia ba Mohammed
Taoun
Kenitra
Sidi Kacem
Sebou
Salé
Volubilis
RABAT
MEKNES
FES
Sefrou
CASABLANCA
Mohammedia
Taghzout
Azemmour
Ben Slimane
Rommani
El Hajeb
Azrou
Berrechid
Benahmed
Oulmès
Ksiba
El Jadida (Mazagan)
Khouribga
Kasbá
Settat Oued Zem
Khenifra
Sidi Small
Sidi Bennour
Fkih ben Salah
Tadla
Beni Mellal
Safi
Youssoufia
Tleta de Bouguedra
Benguerir
MARRAKECH
Azilal
Rich
Essaouira
Chichaoua
Demnate
Tinerhir
Goulimima
C. Sim
C. Tafelney
Tamanar
Amizmiz
Asni
Irhil M'Goun
Boumalne
Tafilalt
Erfoud
Tamri
Dj. Toubkal 4165
Ouarzazate
Tazenakht
Alnif
Rissani
Cap Rhir
Taroudannt
Inezgane
O. Souss
Zagora
O. Draa
Tarhbalt
Agadir
Irherm
Djebel Sarhro
Kem-Kem
Anti Atlas
Biougra
Tissint
Hi. Zguilma
Tiznit
Tafraoute
Tata
Hamid
Zegdou
Ifni
Toffermit
Imitek
Mrhimina
Bou Izakarn
O. Zemoul
Mengoub
Goulimine
Seyad
Djebel Bani
Haut Plateau du Dra
Foum Assaka
Aounet Torkoz
Djebel Ouarkziz
Tan-tan
Oued Draa
O. Tigzerte
Messeled
Tinfouchi
Hamada Tounassine
C. Juby
Tarfaya (Villa Bens)
Hagunia
Sidi Ahmed Rgueibet
Mahbes
Tindouf
Khorb el Ethel
Tounassine
Rhemilès
Hasi Tafrauit
Daora
Edchera
El Aaiún
Saguia el Hamra
Smara
Uad Erni
Ora Djebilet
Boubout
Lemsid
Bu Craa
El Hadeb
Tifariti
Gara Djebilet
Aftout
El Hasian
Aridal
WESTERN SAHARA
Amasin
Ain Ben Tili 540
El Eglab
Aufist
Zemmur
Agmar
Bir Bel Guerdâne
Bir el Abbes
Touila
Chenachane
Chega
Hasi Nueifed
Guelta Zemmur
Bir Moghrein
Sebkhet Iguetti
O. Chenachane
Grizim
Ayoûn Abd el Mâlek
Dâya el Khadra
Mzerreb
Tarhamanant
Pta. Elbow
Ghallamane
El Kâghet
Naga
Dakhla
Pta. Durnford
El Aargub
Bir Enzaran
Sebkhet Oumm ed Drous Telli
Sebkhet Oumm ed Drous Guebli
B. de Río de Oro
Sidi Emhamed
Tiris
El Mreiti
Terhazza
C. Barbas
Hamada Safia
G. de Cintra
Pta. Negra
Sebkhet Ijill
El Mreyer
El Aouj
Zouirât
En Nahrat
Imesain
Fdérik
Kediet Ijill 915
Hammâmi
Bir Chali
Taoudenni
C. Corbeiro
El Tourine
MAURITANIA
Telig
Adrar Souttuf
Tichla
Meleizem
El Guettara
Aguenit
Aguelt el Melah
Bir Amrâne
Mejaouda
Dglats de Khenachiche
Ezmul
Zug
Bou Lanouar
Aghoueyyit
Châr
El Beyyed
Guelb er Richât
El Ksaib Ounane
Bir Ounane
La Güera
Nouâdhibou
Ras Nouâdhibou
Bir el Gâreb
Aghreijit
El Ghallaouiya
Dhar Khenachich
Dakhlet Nouâdhibou
Ahmeyim
Toueirma
Ouadâne
MALI
Et Tidra
Agouifa
Akchar
Amsaga
Chinguetti
Bollé
Râs Timiris
Nouâmghâr
Bennichchâb
Atâr
Oujeft
Oguelleten Nmâdi
Ijâfène
Douaouir
Ergli
Bou Rjeimât
Akjoujt
I-n-Échar
Sebkhet Te-n-Dghâmcha

Islas Canarias (Sp.)
La Palma 2423
Los Llanos de Aridane
Sta. Cruz de la Palma
Pta. Fuencaliente
Alegranza
Graciosa
Tenerife
La Laguna
Lanzarote
Arrecife
Yaizo
La Orotava
Santa Cruz de Tenerife
La Oliva
I. de Lobos
S. Sebastian de la G.a
Icod 3718
Puerto del Rosario
Gomera
Granadilla de Abona
Guia
Valverde
1949
Mogán
Las Palmas
807
Hierro 1501
Pta. de la Rasca
Gran Canaria
Fuerteventura
Pta. de Maspalomas

Madeira (Port.)
Porto Moniz
I. de Porto Santo
SãoVicente
Santana
Machico
Funchal
Ilhas Desertas

Ilhas Salvagens

Ligne de la Mauritanie

Projection: Lambert's Equivalent Azimuthal

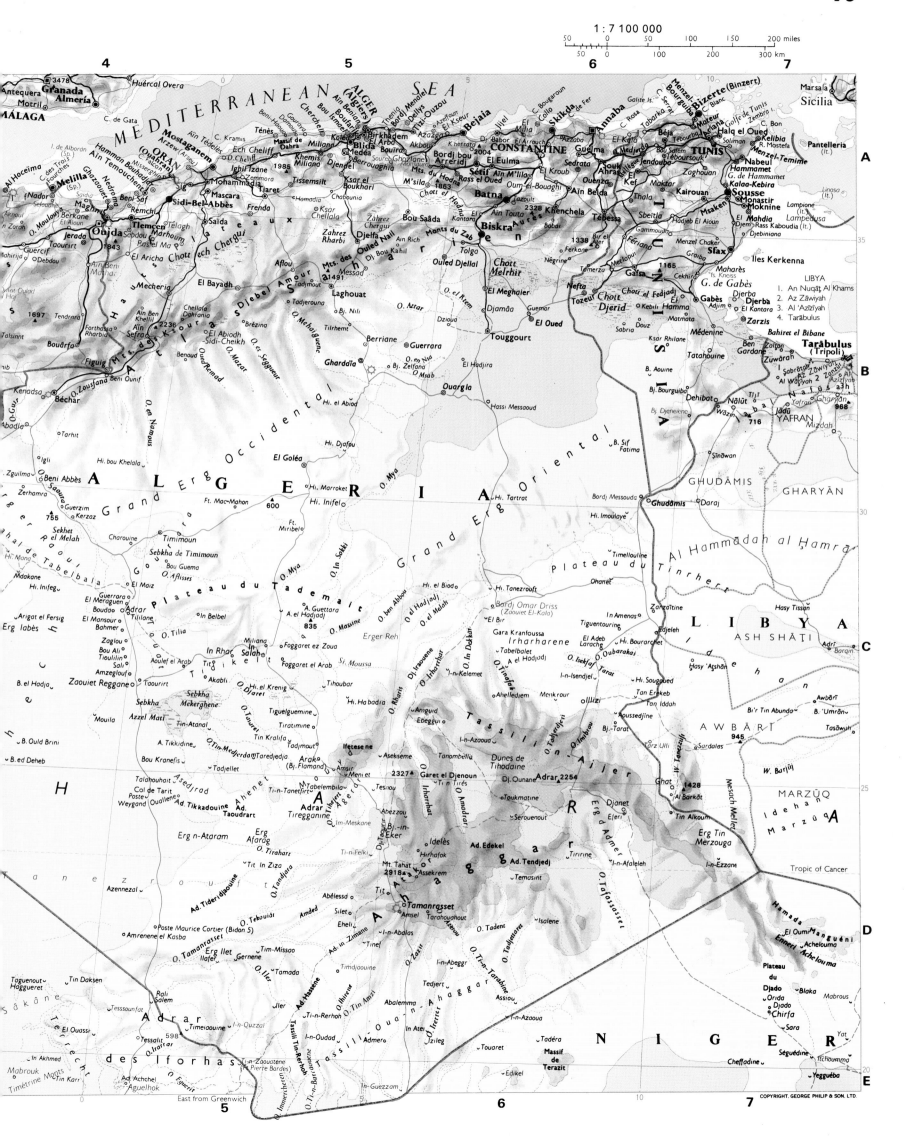

75

1 : 7 100 000

50   0   50   100   150   200 miles
50   0   100   200   300 km

4   5   6   7

MEDITERRANEAN SEA

MÁLAGA

Granada 3478
Almería
Antequera
Motril
Huércal Overa

C. de Gata

Al Hoceima
Melilla (Sp.)
Nador

ALGER (Algiers)
ORAN (Ouhran)
Mostaganem
Arzew (Arzeu)

Bejaia
Jijel
Collo
Skikda
CONSTANTINE
Annaba

Bizerte (Binzert)
TUNIS
Nabeul
Sfax
Sousse
Monastir

Marsala
Sicilia
Pantelleria (It.)

A

Sidi-Bel-Abbès
Tlemcen
Oujda
Mascara
Saïda

Batna
Biskra
Tébessa
Kairouan

LIBYA
1. An Nuqāṭ Al Khams
2. Az Zāwiyah
3. Al 'Azīzīyah
4. Tarābulus

35

Béchar

Ghardaïa
Ouargla
Touggourt
El Oued
Gabès
Zarzis

Tarābulus (Tripoli)

B

ALGERIA

Grand Erg Occidental

Grand Erg Oriental

El Goléa

Ghudāmis

Al Hammādah al Ḥamrā

GHARYĀN

30

Plateau du Tademaït

Plateau du Tinrhert

In Salah

LIBYA
ASH SHĀṬI

C

H

Adrar

Tassili-n-Ajjer

AWBĀRI

MARZŪQ

25

Tamanrasset
Mt. Tahat 2918

Ahaggar

Ghat
Djanet

Tropic of Cancer

Plateau du Djado

D

Adrar des Iforhas

NIGER

Massif de Terazit

E

East from Greenwich

5   6   7

COPYRIGHT. GEORGE PHILIP & SON, LTD.

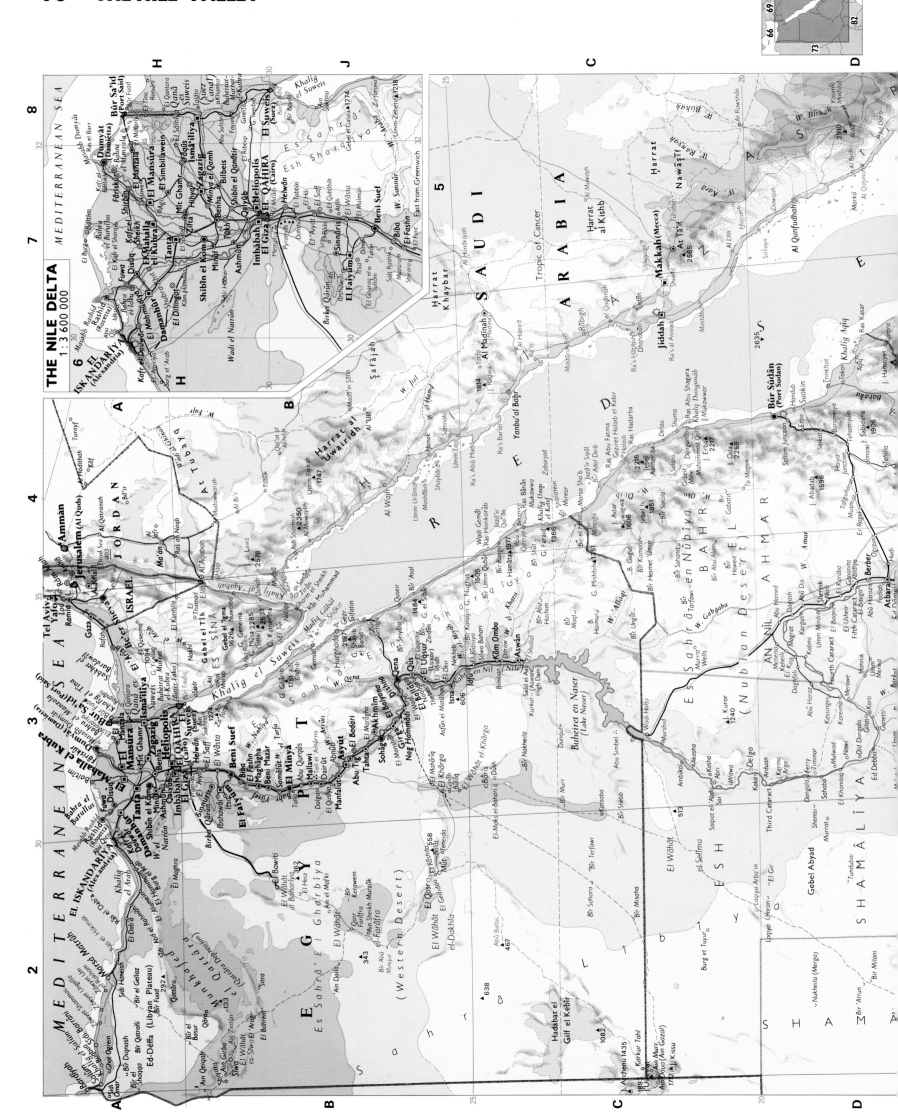

THE NILE DELTA
1:3 600 000

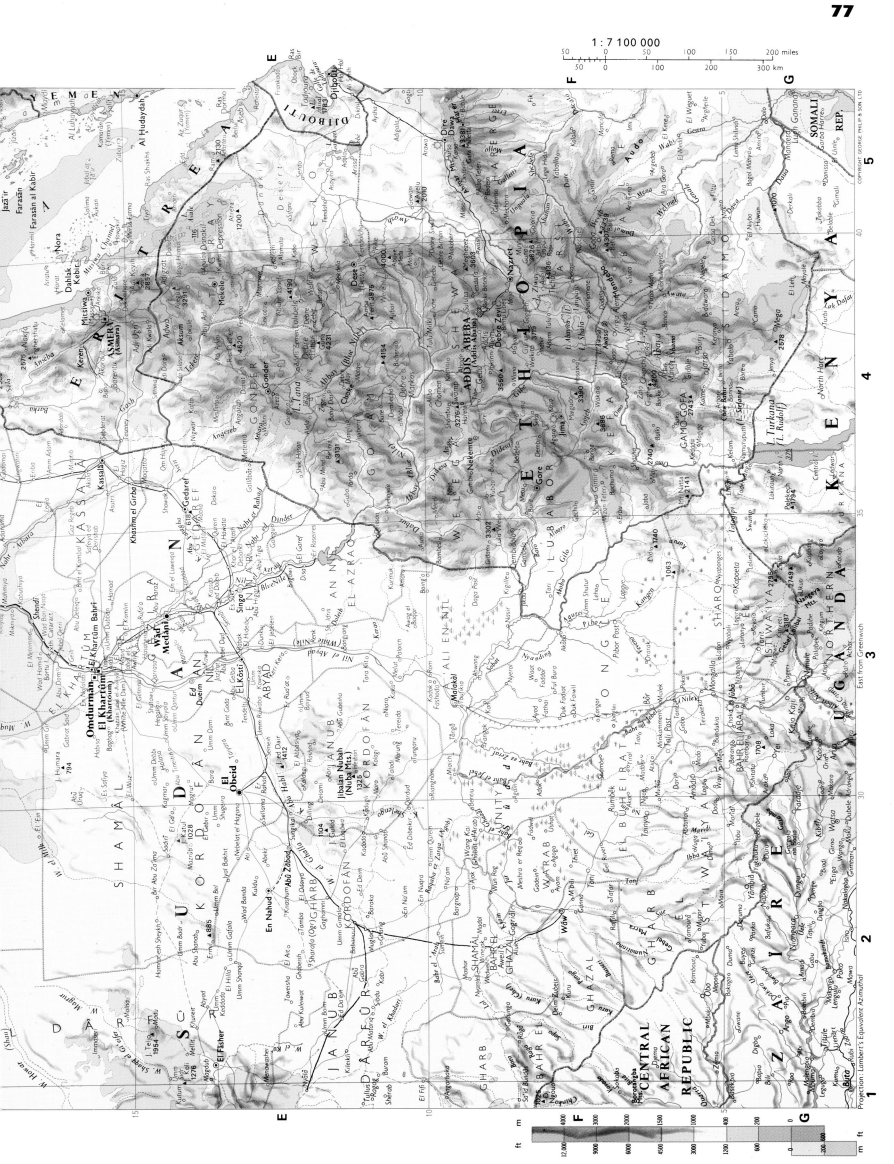

1 : 7 100 000

Projection : Lambert's Equivalent Azimuthal

COPYRIGHT GEORGE PHILIP & SON LTD

72
72
80

M A U R I T A N I A

Et Tidra
Râs Timirist
Nouâmghâr
Akjoujt
Oujeft
Oguelet en Nmâdi
Bennichâb
Bourâa
Araouane
Sebkhet Te-n-Dghâmcha
Rachid
Tidjikja
Gâneb
Tichît
Aratâne
Akreijit
Sidi Moktâr
420
Akortâl
Nouakchott
Idîni
Moudjéria
Letfotar
522
Toueirat
Boutilimit
Boûmdeïd
Togba
In-Ahmer
Tagourâret
Ouâlâta
Néma
I. Faguibine
Tombouctou (Timbuktu)
Dayet en Naharat
Tintehoun
In-Del
Mederdra
Aleg
Mâl
El Ghabré
Kiffa
'Ayoûn el 'Atroûs
Râs el Mâ
Goundam
Diré
Harib
Massène
Dagana
Rosso
Podor
Bogué
Mbagne
Kaédi
Mbout
H ô d
Timbedgha
Kobenni
Djiguéni
Niyoût
Bassikounou
L. Tanda
Niafounke
Goun
Ngorkou
Ore Vendou
L. Korarou
Sénégal
St. Louis
Richard-Toll
Thillé-Boubacar
N'Dioum
Cascas
Matam
Magtama
Ould Yéngé
409
Sêlibabi
Amourj
Akka
Korienze
L. Déba
Douentz
Louga
Mbeté
Linguère
Ranérou
Séme
Kandi
Bouli
Sêtibabi
El Guelete
Kirané
Ballé
Sampaka
Karounga
Bare
M.L. Korarou
791
Koki
Dahra
Barkédi
Fété Bowé
Yélimané
Nioro du Sahel
Boulal
Tanganga Ba
Nara
Akor
Toguere-Koumbe
Ténenkou
Mopti
C. Vert
Thiès
Khombole
Touba
Taltal
Vélingara
Logué Tékodé
Gani
Ambidédi
Koussané
Sandaré
Diéma
Digna
Dilly
Goumbou
Dioura
M a c i n a
Sürédina
Gondo-Gina
DAKAR
Rufisque
Pout
Diourbel
Gossas
Kaolack
Nhar
Kidira
Goudiri
Kayes
Dinguiraye
Diamou
Lakamané
584
Séfeto
Diala
Didiéni
Maréna
Mourdiah
Dampha
Diongoi
Fallou
Sagala
Sokolo
Niono
Canal du Sahel
Manimpé
Diafarabé
Ke-Macina
Say
Sofara
Bandiagara
Gangefani
Diougani
Bambey
Fatick
Mbour
Joal
Saloum
Foundiougne
Passi
Nioro du Rip
Goudomp
Tambacounda
Maka
Bala
Koussanar
Bafoulabé
Badoumbé
Kita
Sébékoro
Négala
Koulikoro
Fana
Ségou
Douna
San
Tominian
Bénéna
Tougan
Gassan
Gourci
Diallassagou
Bankas
Koro
Ouahigouya
GAMBIA
Banjul
Brikama
Georgetown
Santa
Velingara
Medina Gonasse
Kolda
Patine Kouka
Kédougou
Satadougou
Kourouto
Sirakoro
Kati
Bamako
Dialakoro
Dioïla
Kléla
Koutiala
Yorosso
Koumankou
Ziguéna
Sanaba
Dédougou
Réo
Ouaga
Koudougou
SENEGAL
GUINEA-BISSAU
Arquipélago dos Bijagós
Bissau
Ziguinchor
São Domingos
Cacheu
Nova Lamego
Farim
Mansoa
Bafatá
Gabú
Koundara
Mali
1537
M. Tinguê
Gadaoundou
Kambali
Niagassola
Kourouba
Kangare
Sido
Massigui
Doro
Sikasso
820
Sifarasso
Sotuba
Boromo
Houndé
Boura
Tenado
Faramana
BURKINA FASO
Bolama
Caravela
Buba
Medina Boé
Koumbia
Yambéring
Labé
Dinguiraye
Siguiri
Yanfolila
Kolondiéba
Orodara
Bobo-Dioulasso
Diébougou
Ouessa
Bula
Catió
Gaoual
Pita
952
Timbo
Dalaba
Télimélé
Koundara
Mamou
Dabola
Kouroussa
Ténétou
Bougouni
Tiékoungoba
Dioïla
Dalakoro
Dran
Koumbia
Banfora
Sidéradougou
Zéguoua
Kabala
GUINEA
Kankan
Tintioulé
Manankoro
Foulalaba
Kadiolo
Tingréla
Niellé
Mbingué
Wandérama
C. Verga
Boffa
Dubréka
Kindia
Faranah
Saro
Kalankalan
Manianko
Mamnian
Sanhala
Niaragoloko
Gaoua
Busié
Sangareya B.
Conakry
Îles de Los
Forécariah
Kamakwie
Balia
Doyako
Moribaya
Fabala
Guéléban
Sirana
Koutou
Kolia
Korhogo
Ferkessédougou
Téhini
Varalé
Kaloum Peninsula
Kambia
Pendembu
Mambolo
Bambaya
Kissidougou
Kérouane
Kimbirila
Madinani
Dikodougou
Niofé
Ouangolo
Kong
Bouna
Kampti
Wa
Port Loko
Makeni
Sefadu
Yende Millimou
Konsankoro
1504
Pic de Tibé
Nzebéla
Borotou
Mórondo
Kati
Tafiré
Bromonou
Dédi
Farako
Lawra
Busie
SIERRA LEONE
Freetown
Waterloo
WESTERN
Banana Is.
Rokel
Loma Mansa
1948
Kayima
Guékédou
Macenta
Beyla
Touba
Biankouma
Séguéla
Mankono
Katiola
Tabagné
Bondoukou
741
Wenchi
Marampa
Magburaka
Bo
Kenema
Gelahun
Kailahun
Irié
Woninou
Sifié
Tiénigbé
Botro
Satama-Soukoura
Tanda
Sampa
Yawri Bay
Shenge
Mano
Segbwema
Pendembu
Lola
Fouénon
Worofla
Katiala
Beumé
Bouaké
Prikro
Berekum
Moyamba
Matru
Gbangbama
Kpo Ra
Belle Yella
Zorzor
Nzerekore
752
Danané
Man
Fakobli
Zuénoula
Vavoua
Tiébissou
M'Bahiakro
Koun
Jiminini
Sunyani
Sherbro
Turtle Is.
West B.
Bonthe
Zimmi
Bomi Hills
Ganta (Gompa)
Sanniquellie
Kouibli
Bangolo
Daloa
Bouaflé
Yamoussoukro
Dimbokro
Bongouanou
Abengourou
Goaso
Kum
IVORY COAST
Robertsport
Arthington
Whiteplains
Kakata
Saglepie
Zouan-Hounien
Toulepleu
Guiglo
Duékoué
Issia
Oumé
Gagnoa
Divo
Lakota
Tiassalé
Agboville
Adzopé
Bibiani
LIBERIA
Monrovia
Paynesville
Marshall
Edina
St. Buchanan
Trade Town
Kakata
Careysburg
645
Gbarnga
Tapeta
Tchien
914
Gray
Sidibo
Youkou
Tai
Buyo
Guibéroua
Morronou
Mbatto
Anoumaba
Rubino
Akoupé
Agnibilékrou
Ahenkro
Asafo
Wigwso
Soubré
Gagnoa
Guéyo
Dabou
Abidjan
Bingerville
Ayamé
Aboisso
Maféré
Prestea
Tarkwa
Paynesville
St. John
Hartford
No. 3 Compound
Timbo
River Cess
Cestos
Grabo
Sassandra
Soubré
Bakayo
Fresco
Grand Lahou
Lagune Ébrié
Grand Bassam
Assini
Newtown
Half Assini
Esiama
Axim
Cape Three Points
Greenville
Sino Bay
Nyaake (Webo)
Barclayville
San-Pédro
Sassandra
Grand Béreby
Tabou
Nyaake
Sino
Kanu Krou
Sastown
Grand Cess
Garawe
Cape Palmas
Harper
6363

Grain Coast
Ivory Coast
GUL...
West from Greenw...

ft m
12 000 4000
9000 3000
6000 2000
4500 1500
3000 1000
1200 400
600 200
0 0
200 600
2000 6000
4000 12 000
6000 18 000
m ft

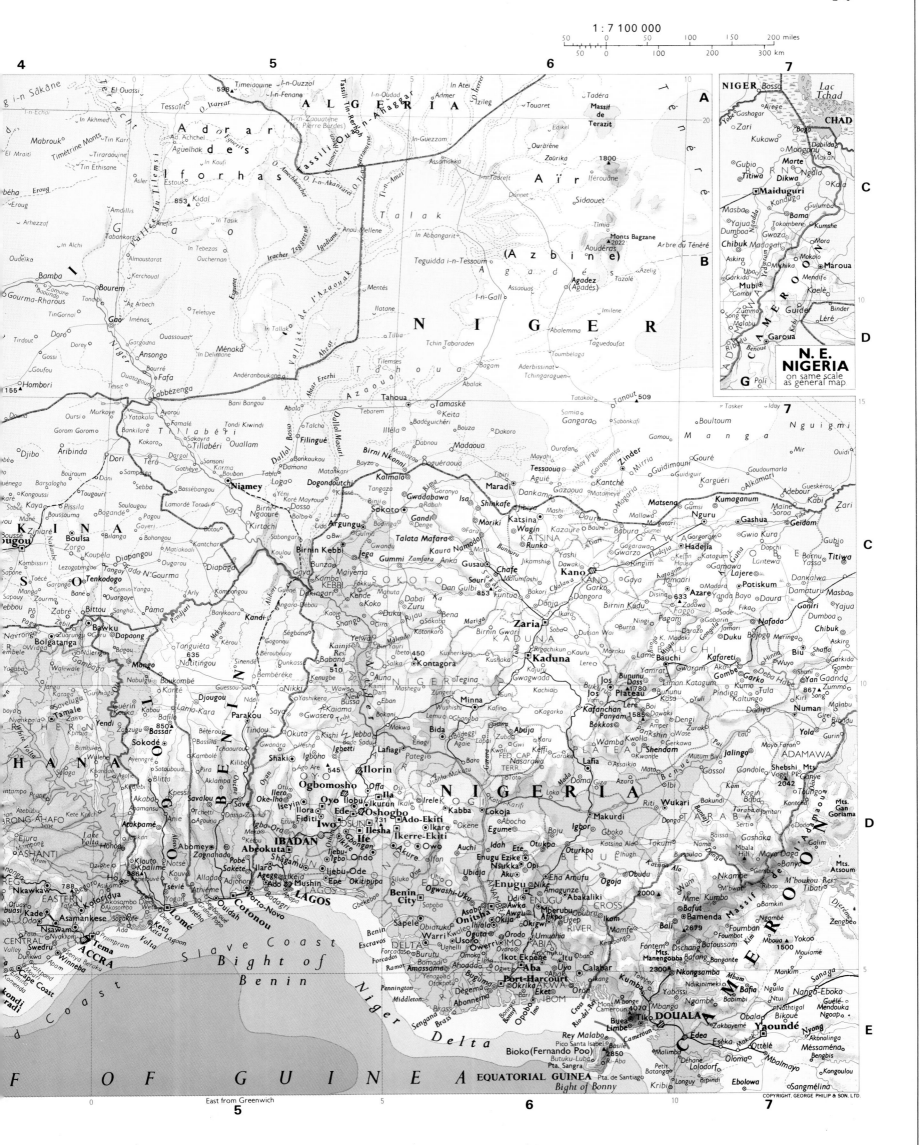

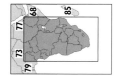

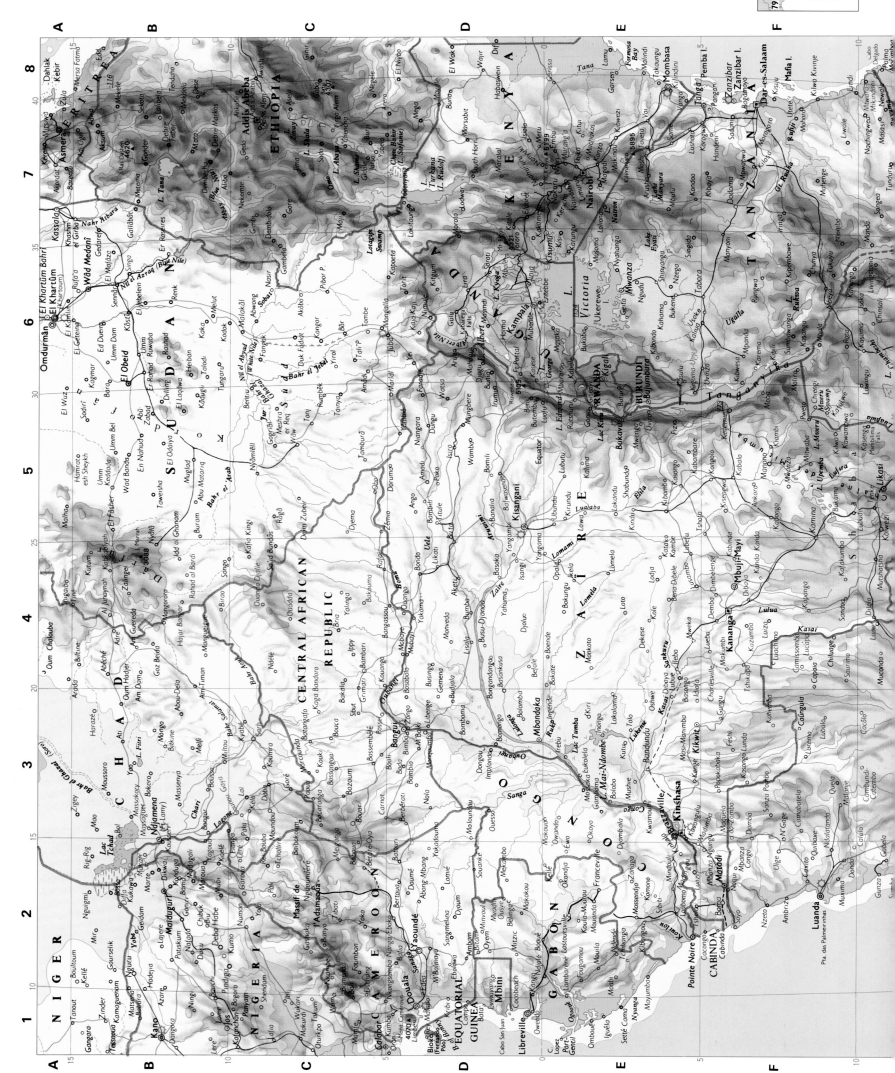

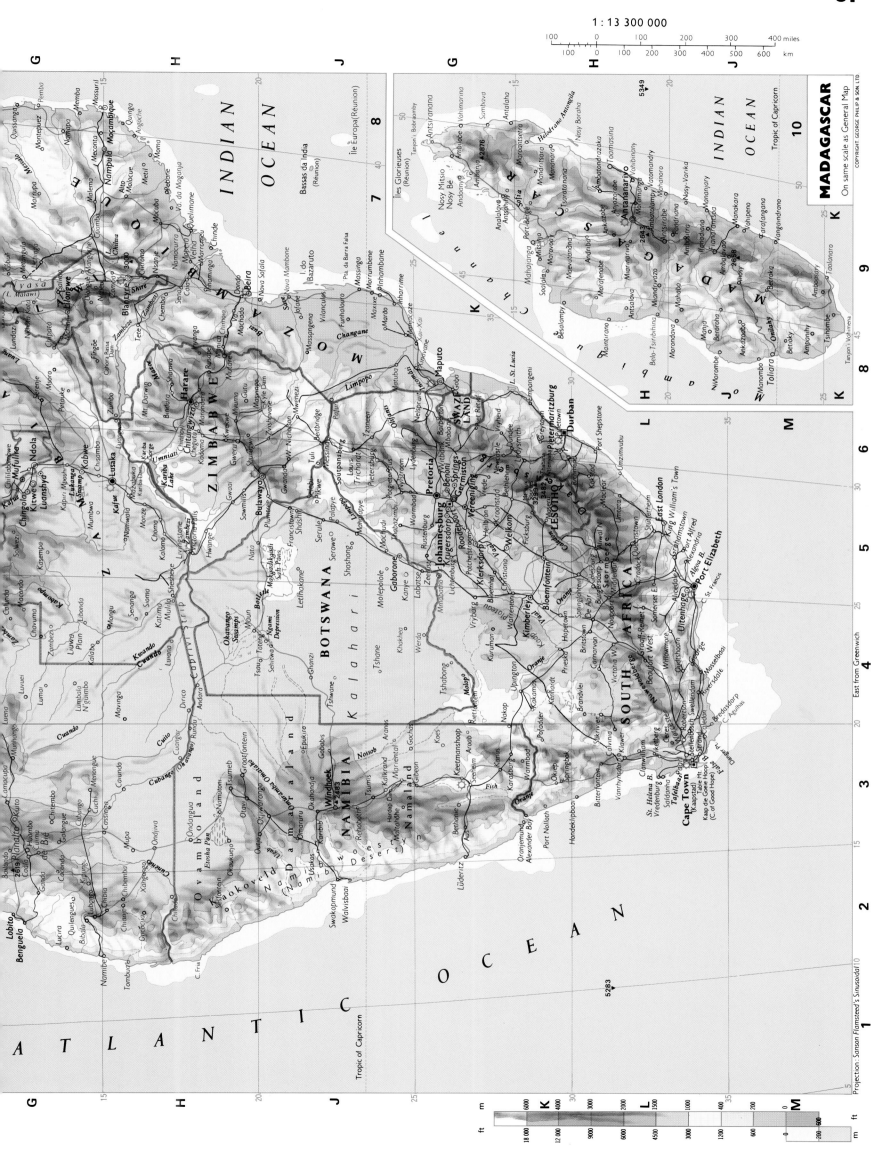

1 : 13 300 000

| 100 | 0 | 100 | 200 | 300 | 400 miles |

| 100 | 0 | 100 | 200 | 300 | 400 | 500 | 600 | km |

MADAGASCAR
On same scale as General Map

COPYRIGHT GEORGE PHILIP & SON LTD

INDIAN OCEAN

ATLANTIC OCEAN

INDIAN OCEAN

Tropic of Capricorn

East from Greenwich

Projection: Sanson Flamsteed's Sinusoidal

Tropic of Capricorn

SOMALI REP.

ETHIOPIA

SUDAN

KENYA

UGANDA

TANZANIA

RWANDA

BURUNDI

CENTRAL AFRICAN REPUBLIC

HAUT-ZAIRE

Lake Victoria

L. Turkana (L. Rudolf)

L. Albert

L. Kivu

L. Tanganyika

NAIROBI

MOMBASA

DAR ES SALAAM

Zanzibar

Kampala

Kisangani

Juba

Pemba I.

Mafia I.

EQUATOR

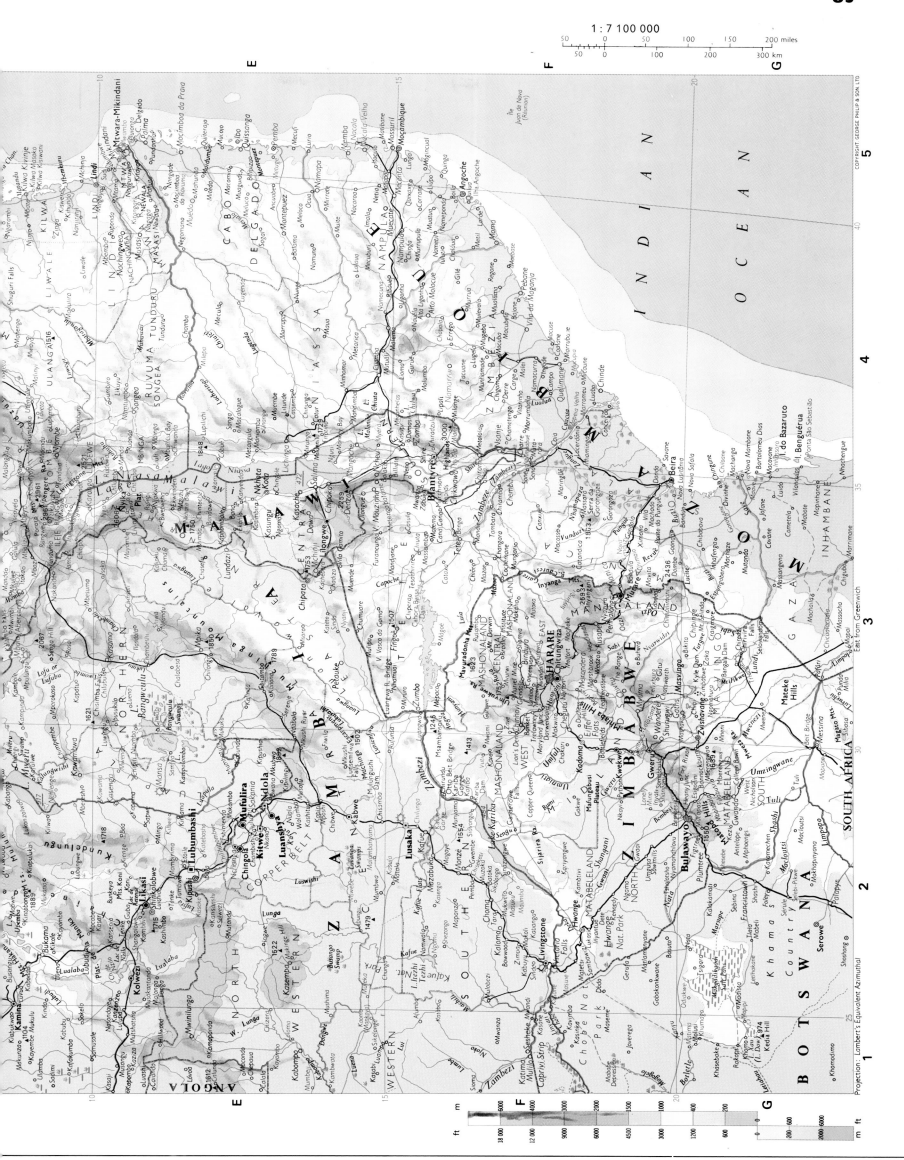

1 : 7 100 000

INDIAN OCEAN

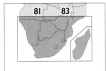

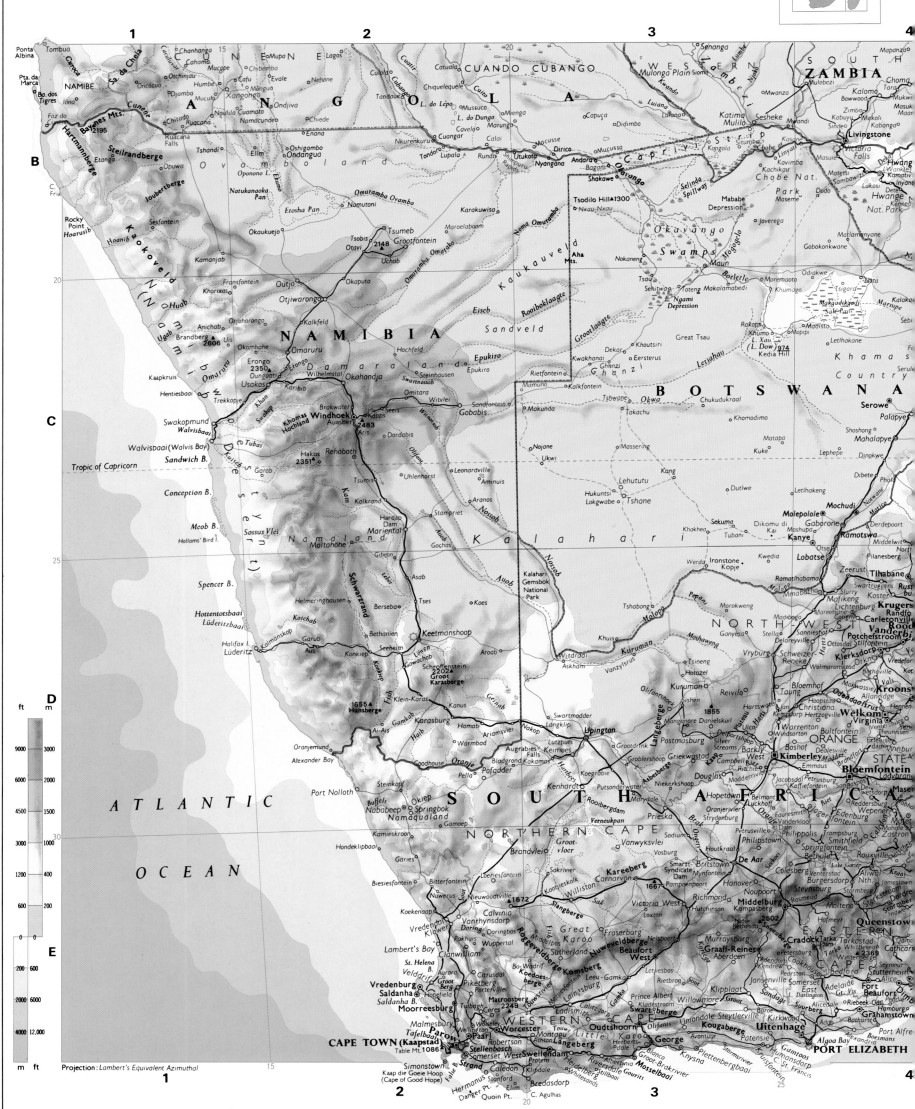

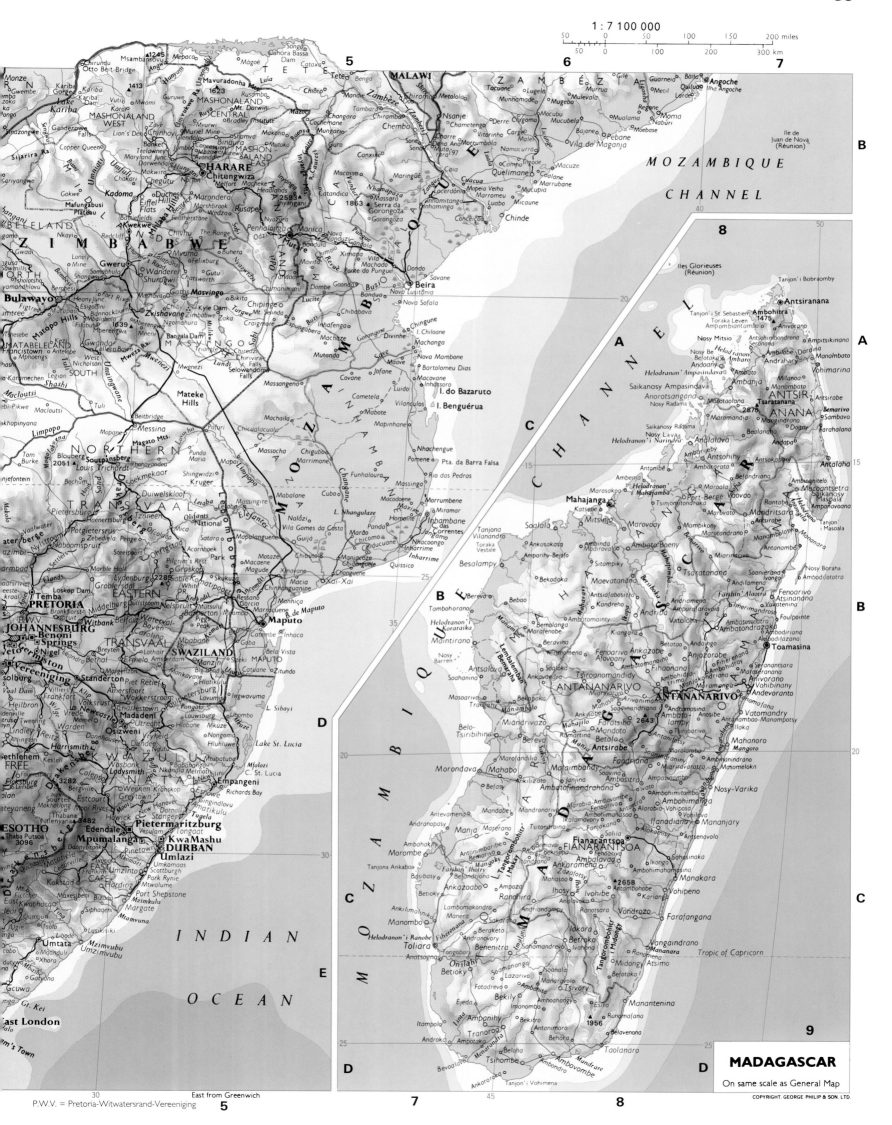

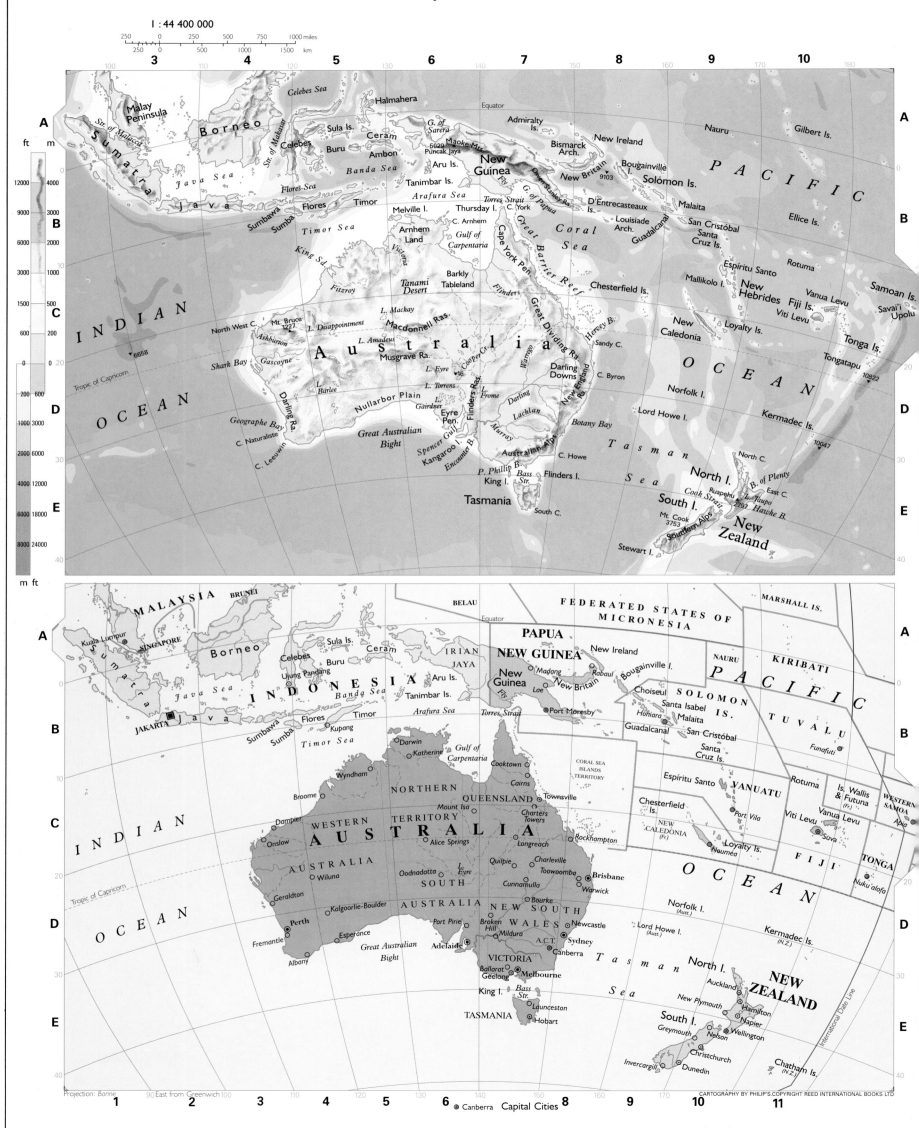

1 : 44 400 000

Projection: Bonne

CARTOGRAPHY BY PHILIP'S.COPYRIGHT REED INTERNATIONAL BOOKS LTD

● Canberra Capital Cities

1 : 5 300 000

20 0 20 40 60 80 100 miles
20 0 40 80 120 160 km

92
92 92
92

KIRIBATI

TUVALU
(Ellice Is.)

Tokelau Is.(N.Z.)

Tongareva
(Penrhyn) I.
Rakahanga
Pukapuka Manihiki
WESTERN Nassau
SAMOA Suwarrow Northern Group
Savai'i Upolu Tutuila
Wallis & AMER. Cook Is.(N.Z.)
Futuna SAMOA
(Fr.) (U.S.) Palmerston
Atoll Aitutaki
Rotuma Lau or TONGA Niue Mitiaro
Eastern (Friendly (N.Z.) Atiu Mauke
FIJI Group Is.) Lower Group
Viti Rarotonga
Levu Mangaia Îles de la Société

VAN-
UATU Tropic of Capricorn FRENCH
POLYNESIA

P A C I F I C   O C E A N

Macauley
Raoul (Sunday) I.
Kermadec Is. Curtis
(N.Z.)

Three Kings Is. **Auckland**
NORTH I.
NEW Cook Strait
ZEALAND **Wellington** Chatham I.
SOUTH I. **Christchurch** Chatham Is.
Tasman Pitt I.
Sea **Dunedin** Bounty Is.
Stewart I. Antipodes Is.
Snares Campbell I.
Auckland Is.
Macquarie I. (Austr.) SOUTHERN OCEAN

**NEW ZEALAND &
S.W. PACIFIC**

1 : 53 000 000

200 0 200 400 600 800 miles
200 0 400 800 1200 km

NORTH ISLAND

Three Kings Is. North C.
C. Reinga
C. Maria Rangaunu Bay
van Diemen Mongonui Doubtless Bay
Houhora Whangaroa Bay
Ahipara B. B. of Islands
Kaitaia Opua C. Brett
Tauroa Pt. Rawene Hikurangi
Hokianga Harb. Kaikohe
Donnelly's Crossing **Whangarei** Whangarei Harb.
Bream Hd.
Dargaville Waipu Bream Bay
Lit. Barrier I.
C. Rodney Gt. Barrier I.
Kaipara Harb. Warkworth C. Colville Cuvier I.
Helensville Hauraki
Takapuna **Devonport** Gulf Coromandel
Onehunga **AUCKLAND** Whitianga
Manukau Papakura Thames
Waiuku Pukekohe Mayor I. Tauranga Harb.
Waikato Mercer Waihi
Huntly Te Tauranga
Morrinsville Aroha Mt. Maunganui White I. Runaway
Raglan Hamilton Cambridge Puke Bay of Plenty
Kawhia Harb. Te Awamutu Putaruru Whakatane East
Otorohanga Kinleith Opotiki C.
Te Kuiti Rotorua Kawerau Raukumara Ra. Hikurangi
Mokau Mokai Murupara Waipiro
North Taranaki L. Taupo KAINGAROA Tolaga
Bight Taupo FOREST Bay
Waitara Taumarunui Ongarue Kaimanawa Mts. Waikaremoana Ormond **Gisborne**
New Plymouth Tutira Poverty Bay
Inglewood Whangamomona Tarawera Wairoa Waikokopu
Mt. Egmont (Taranaki) **Stratford** Ruahine Waiouru Mahia
C. Egmont Eltham Ohakune Peninsula
Opunake Kaponga Raetihi Waipukurau Bay Hawke Bay
South Taranaki Hawera Taihape View **Napier**
Bight Patea Mangaweka C. Kidnappers
Waverley **Hastings**
Wanganui Marton Hunterville Waipawa
Foxton Feilding Dannevirke
Palmerston Woodville
N. Shannon Pahiatua
Levin Eketahuna C. Turnagain
Paraparaumu Otaki
Kapiti I. Carterton
Up. Hutt Masterton
Petone Lr. Hutt Featherston
Eastbourne **WELLINGTON** Martinborough
Cook Strait

SOUTH ISLAND

C. Farewell
Golden D'Urville I.
Collingwood Bay
Takaka Tasman
Tasman Mts. Bay Pelorus Sd.
Karamea Motueka Picton
Bight Tadmor **Nelson**
Seddonville Wakefield Richmond Havelock
Granity Motupiko Renwick Seddon
Westport Lyell Wairau **Blenheim**
Inangahua Murchison Ward
Junction Mt. Travers 2038
Reefton Spenser Kaikoura
Blackball Mts. Hanmer Kaikoura
Runanga Amuri B. Springs
Greymouth Kumara Waiau
Kumara Stillwater Waiau
Hokitika Jacksons L. Brunner Culverden
Ross Otira Waikari Waipara
Arthur's Pass Hurunui
Abut Hd. Amberley
Okarito Coleridge Oxford Pegasus Bay
Springfield Rangiora Kaiapoi
Whitecliffs New Brighton
Mt. Cook **Christchurch**
3753 Methven Riccarton Lyttelton
Staveley Lincoln Banks Peninsula
Mt. Aspiring Fairlie Akaroa
3027 Little River Southern Alps
Jackson B. L. Tekapo Rakaia
Okuru Rakaia L. Ellesmere
Pukaki Southbridge Ashburton
Haast Ohau Ashburton Bight
Hawea Canterbury Bight
Milford Sd. Wanaka Canterbury Plains
Bligh Sd. Mt. Earnslaw St. Andrews
George Sd. 2819 Arrowtown Waitaki **Temuka** **Timaru**
Secretary I. Queenstown Cromwell Kurow **Waimate**
Doubtful Sd. Clyde Tokarahi Ngapara
Breaksea Sd. Te Anau Alexandra Kakanui **Oamaru**
Resolution Kingston Roxburgh Mts. Maheno
I. Manapouri Waikouaiti Hampden
Dusky Sd. Mossburn   Edievale Palmerston
Preservation Lumsden Kelso Port Chalmers
Inlet Ohai Lawrence Otago Harbour
Chalky Tuatapere Winton Milton **Dunedin** C. Saunders
Inlet Nightcaps Kaitangata Mosgiel
Te Waewae B. Orepuki Edendale **Gore** Balclutha St. Kilda
Riverton Wyndham Mataura Fairfield
Invercargill Owaka Nugget Pt.
Bluff Ruapuke I. Tokanui Kahakopa
Invercargill Foveaux Str.
Halfmoon B.
Stewart I. Port Pegasus
S.W. Cape

T A S M A N   S E A

P A C I F I C   O C E A N

SAMOA ISLANDS

1 : 10 700 000

WESTERN AMERICAN
SAMOA SAMOA
Savai'i **Apia**
Upolu Pago Pago Manua Is.
Tutuila Rose I.

**FIJI AND TONGA
ISLANDS**

1 : 10 700 000

50 0 50 100 150 miles
50 0 50 100 150 200 250 km

Wallis & Futuna (Fr.) WESTERN SAMOA

Niuafo'ou
(Tonga)

Thikombia

Lambasa Yasawa Group
Vanua Levu Taveuni
Lautoka Koro Vanua Balavu
Nandi Levuka Lau or Eastern Group
1323 Ovalau
Viti Levu Koro Sea Lakemba
Suva Ngau
Moala TONGA
(Friendly Is.)
Kandavu Vatoa Vava'u
Tofua I.
Tongatapu Nuku'alofa

ft m
12 000 4000
9000 3000
6000 2000
3000 1000
1200 400
600 200
0
200 600
m ft

Projection: Conical with two standard parallels

NORTHERN TERRITORY

TIMOR SEA

INDIAN OCEAN

INDONESIA

Timor

Sumba

Sumbawa

Lombok

Joseph Bonaparte Gulf

Cambridge Gulf

Queens Channel

Admiralty Gulf

Bonaparte Archipelago

Buccaneer Archipelago

King Sound

King Leopold Ranges

Durack Range

Chamberlain Ra.

Carr Boyd Ra.

Stokes Ra.

Pine Creek

Wingate Mts.

Mt. Greenwood 152

Great Sandy Desert

Tanami Desert

Gibson Desert

Hamersley Range

Chichester Ra.

Macdonnell Ranges

Darwin
Melville I.
Bathurst I.
C. Van Diemen
Cobourg Pen.
Van Diemen Gulf

Katherine
Victoria River Downs
Wave Hill
Hooker Creek
Top Springs
Montejinni

Wyndham
Windham
Ord
L. Argyle
Turkey Creek
Halls Creek
Gordon Downs
Sturt Creek

Derby
Fitzroy
Fitzroy Crossing
Noonkanbah
Myroodah
Kimberley Downs
Napier Downs

Broome
Roebuck B.
Roebuck Plains
La Grange B.
Anna Plains
Frazier Downs
Wallal Downs
Eighty Mile Beach

Port Hedland
De Grey
Marble Bar
Nullagine
Roy Hill
Newman
Marillana
Roebourne
Karratha
Dampier Archipelago

Tropic of Capricorn

Lake Mackay
L. White
L. Wills
L. Hazlett
Lake Disappointment
L. Auld
L. George
L. Dora
L. Tobin
Gregory Lake
L. Bennett
L. Neale

Mt. Liebig 1524
Mt. Leisler 901
Mt. Ziel 1510
Mt. Bruce 1235

Reynolds Ra.
Stansmore Ra.
McKay Ra.
Paterson Ra.
Broadhurst Ra.
Lewis Ra.
Stuart Bluff Ra.
James Ranges
Hopkins
Kintore Ra.
Baron Ra.
Angas Hills
Horden Hills

1 : 7 100 000

50   0   50   100   150   200 miles

50   0   100   200   300 km

COPYRIGHT GEORGE PHILIP & SON, LTD.

Projection: Bonne

East from Greenwich

WESTERN AUSTRALIA

SOUTH AUSTRALIA

Great Victoria Desert

Great Australian Bight

SOUTHERN OCEAN

Nullarbor Plain

Hampton Tableland

PERTH

Fremantle
New Town
Kwinana
Rockingham

Bunbury

Geraldton

Albany

Esperance

Norseman

Kalgoorlie-Boulder

Ayers Rock 868

Mt. Olga 1069 ▲

Mann Ra, Mt. Morris 1387 ▲

Mt. Woodroffe 1549 ▲

Musgrave Ranges

The Officer

Everard Park

Everard Ranges

L. Meramangye

Wilkinson Lakes

Nurrari Lakes

Serpentine Lakes

L. Dey-Dey
L. Maurice

Mt. Blackstone 1058

Mt. Aloysius 1126

Cavenagh Ra.

Mt. Buttfield

Rawlinson Ra.

Christopher
Mt. Forrest

Barrow Ra.

Warburton

Mt. Squires 705

Warburton Ra.

Pt. Lilian 466

Macintosh Ra.

Saunders Pt. 466

L. Ell

L. Minigwal

L. Throssell

L. Yeo

L. Breaden

L. Baker

L. Gillen

Ernest Giles Ra. 712

L. Wells

L. Carnegie

L. Eureka 499

Brassey Ra.

Mt. Normanhurst

L. Burnside

L. Buchanan

Granite Peak

Earaheedy

Wongawol

Bondya

Cosmo Newbery

L. Darlot

L. Carey

Laverton

Mt. Redcliffe 576

Melrose

L. Rebecca

L. Minigwal

Rason L.

Jubilee L.

Stoll Lakes

Kirgella Rocks

Cundeelee

Zanthus

Balladonia

Mt. Ragged 585

C. Arid

Middle I.

Archipelago of the Recherche

Eastern Group

Pt. Malcolm

Sandy Bight

South East Is.

Pt. Culver

Pt. Dover

Cocklebiddy Motel

Madura Motel

Mundrabilla

Eucla Motel

Wilson Bluff

Low Pt.

Red Rocks Pt.

Eyre

Forrest

Deakin

Reid

Loongana

Nurina

Haig

Rawlinna

Naretha

Kitchener

Zanthus

Cook

Fisher

Watson

Ooldea

Barton

Bates

C. Adieu

Coorabie

Coorabie

C. Nuyts

Head of Bight

Hughes

Murunna

L. Ifould

Golea

Nullarbor

L. Carey

Leonora

Leinster

Agnew

Murrin Murrin

Mt. Margaret

Mt. Malcolm

Yundamindera

Edjudina

Kookynie

Menzies

Niagara

Broad Arrow

Ora Banda

Bardoc

Credo

Coolgardie

Widgiemooltha

Norseman

Mt. Burges 554

Bulong

Kanowna

Kalgoorlie-Boulder

Bonnie Rock

Southern Cross

Marvel Loch

Coolgardie

Yellowdine

Mt. Jackson

Bullfinch

Koolyanobbing

Bodallin

Merredin

Kellerberrin

Quairading

Corrigin

Narembeen

Bruce Rock

Wyalkatchem

Dowerin

Goomalling

Toodyay

Northam

York

Beverley

Brookton

Pingelly

Cuballing

Narrogin

Wagin

Katanning

Broomehill

Tambellup

Cranbrook

Mt. Barker

Mt. Manypeaks

Stirling Ra. 1073

Bluff Knoll

Gnowangerup

Borden

Ongerup

Jerramungup

Ravensthorpe

Hopetoun

Hood Pt.

k.knob

L. King

Lake King

Newdegate

Lake Grace

Lake Magenta

Dumbleyung

Wickepin

Kukerin

Kulin

Kondinin

Hyden

Kulja

Wialki

Mukinbudin

Nungarin

Trayning

Kununoppin

Wyalkatchem

Mt. Magnet

Paynes Find

Sandstone

Barlee Ra.

Wynyangoo 543

L. Barlee

L. Marmion

Riverina

Rowles Lagoon

Davyhurst

Bullabulling

Yilgarn

Mt. Jackson

Diemals

L. Deborah

Mt. Alexander

L. Ballard

Bullabulling

Mt. Keith

Mt. Eureka

Yandal

Lawlers

Darlot

Depot Springs

Montague Ra.

Bates Ra.

Barr Smith Ra.

Wiluna

L. Nabberu

Mt. Essendon 906

Carnarvon Ra.

Mt. Fraser 799

New Springs

Three Rivers

L. Gregory

Robinson Ra.

Milgun

Mt. Augustus 1105

Waldburg Ra.

Mt. Vernon

Godrey Ra.

Errabiddy

Mt. Phillip

Mt. Gould

Peak Hill

Cue

Mt. Magnet

L. Austin

Meekatharra

Nannine

Wandinna

Mt. Singleton 677

Yalgoo

L. Moore

Morawa

Perenjori

Mullewa

Yuna

Northampton

Geraldton

Greenough

Dongara

Eneabba

Carnamah

Three Springs

Coorow

Moora

New Norcia

Gingin

Bindoon

Wongan Hills

Dalwallinu

Wubin

Calingiri

Dandaragan

Jurien B.

Lancelin I.

North Hd.

Fremantle

Rockingham

Mandurah

Pinjarra

Waroona

Harvey

Collie

Bunbury

Busselton

Dunsborough

Yallingup

C. Naturaliste

Margaret River

Augusta

C. Leeuwin

Pt. D'Entrecasteaux

Nannup

Bridgetown

Manjimup

Pemberton

Northcliffe

Walpole

Denmark

Albany

Bald Hd.

West Cape Howe

Frankland

Mt. Frankland

Cranbrook

Kojonup

Boyup Brook

Darkan

Williams

Quindanning

Boddington

Wandering

Brookton

Corrigin

Wickepin

Donnybrook

Boyanup

Capel

Carnarvon

Shark Bay

Denham

Dirk Hartog I.

Steep Pt.

Hamelin Pool

Peron Pen.

Geographe Channel

C. Farquhar

Bernier I.

Dorre I.

C. Cuvier

C. St. Cric

Inscription

Edel Ld.

Kennedy Ra.

Lyons

Gascoyne

Minnie Creek

Mininya

Williambury

Mt. Lucas

C. Ronsard

Houtman Abrolhos

Gantheaume B.

Bluff Pt.

Greenough Ch.

Gregory

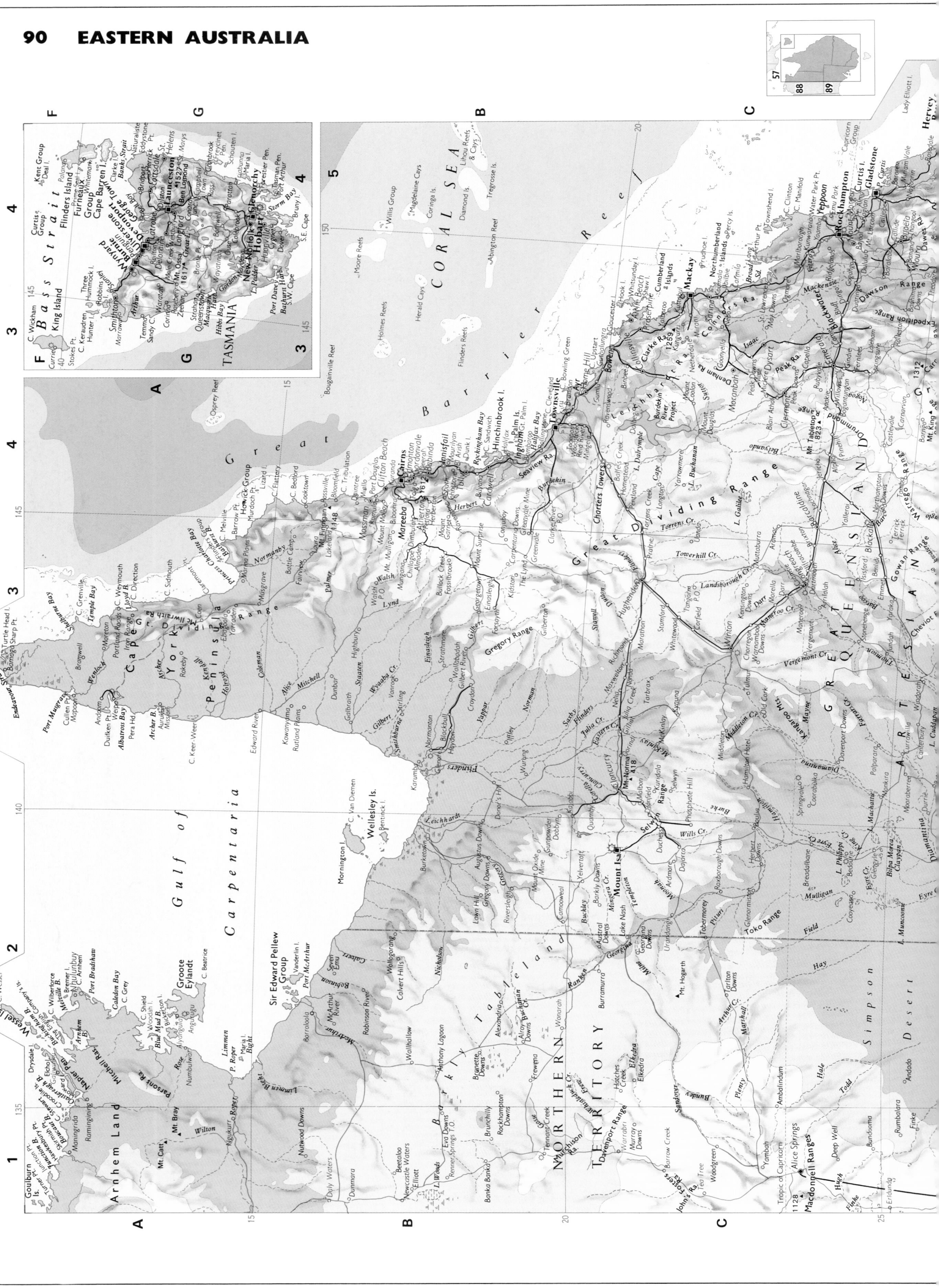

CORAL SEA

Great Barrier Reef

Gulf of Carpentaria

Cape York Peninsula

Great Dividing Range

QUEENSLAND

NORTHERN TERRITORY

GREAT ARTESIAN BASIN

Arnhem Land

Barkly Tableland

Simpson Desert

TASMANIA

Bass Strait

Rockhampton
Gladstone
Mackay
Townsville
Cairns
Mareeba
Mount Isa
Cloncurry
Winton
Alice Springs

Macdonnell Ranges

Hobart
Launceston
Burnie
King Island
Flinders Island

1 : 7 100 000

50　　0　　50　　100　　150　　200 miles
50　0　　100　　　200　　　300 km

COPYRIGHT GEORGE PHILIP & SON LTD

TASMAN SEA

SOUTH AUSTRALIA

NEW SOUTH WALES

Great Dividing Range

Darling Downs

BRISBANE
Gold Coast
Ipswich
Toowoomba
Maryborough
Gympie
Dalby
Kingaroy
Charleville
Roma
Mitchell

SYDNEY
Newcastle
Wollongong
Port Kembla
CANBERRA
Coffs Harbour
Port Macquarie
Kempsey
Tamworth
Armidale
Inverell
Moree
Narrabri
Dubbo
Orange
Bathurst
Parkes
Forbes
Cowra
Goulburn
Wagga Wagga
Albury
Griffith
Broken Hill
Bourke

MELBOURNE
Geelong
Ballarat
Bendigo
Shepparton
Wangaratta
Warrnambool
Mount Gambier
Colac
Sale
Bairnsdale
Traralgon
Morwell

ADELAIDE
Port Augusta
Port Pirie
Whyalla
Port Lincoln
Kangaroo I.

Lake Eyre
Lake Torrens
Lake Gairdner
Lake Frome

Eyre Peninsula
Yorke Peninsula
Spencer Gulf
Flinders Ra.

King Island
Flinders Island
Furneaux Group
Cape Barren I.
Bass Strait

Murray R.
Darling R.
Cooper Cr.

Fraser Island

East from Greenwich

Projection: Bonne

m ft
4500
3000
1500
1000
600
400
200
0
-200
-600
-2000
-4000
12000
6000

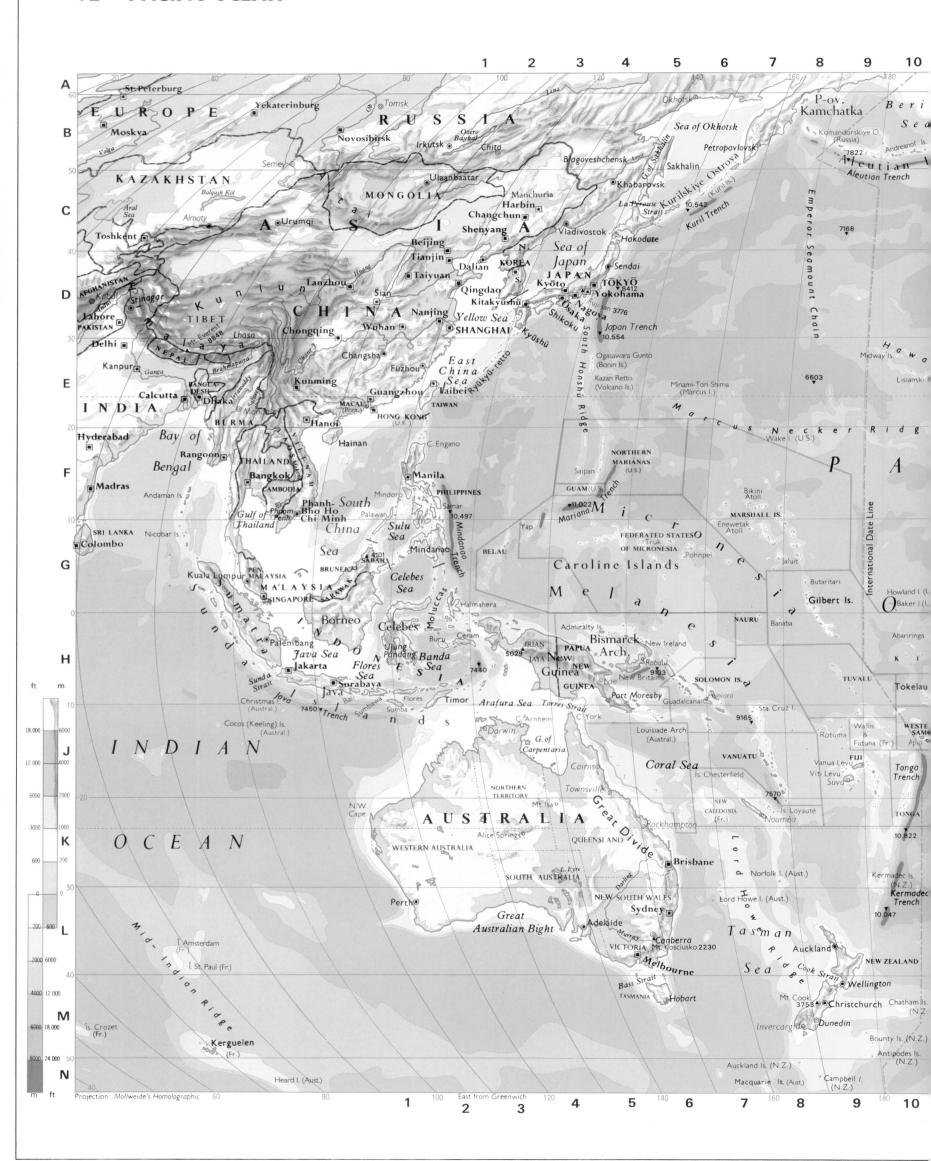

1 2 3 4 5 6 7 8 9 10

A

B

C

D

E

F

G

H

J

K

L

M

N

EUROPE
St. Peterburg
Yekaterinburg
Volga
Moskva
KAZAKHSTAN
Balqash Köl
Aral Sea
Toshkent
Almaty
Urumqi
AFGHANISTAN
Kabul
Srinagar
Lahore
PAKISTAN
Delhi
Kanpur
Ganga
Kunlun
TIBET
Mt. Everest 8848
Lhasa
NEPAL
BANGLA-DESH
Brahmaputra
Calcutta
Dhaka
INDIA
Hyderabad
Bay of Bengal
Rangoon
BURMA
Madras
Andaman Is.
SRI LANKA
Colombo
Nicobar Is.
Mandalay
THAILAND
Bangkok
CAMBODIA
Phanh-Bho Ho
Chi Minh
Gulf of Thailand
Kuala Lumpur
PEN. MALAYSIA
MALAYSIA
SINGAPORE
SARAWAK
Sumatra
Sunda Strait
Palembang
Java Sea
Jakarta
Surabaya
Java
Christmas (Austral.)
Cocos (Keeling) Is. (Austral.)

RUSSIA
Tomsk
Novosibirsk
Irkutsk
Ozero Baykal
Chita
Ob
Lena
Semey
Ulaanbaatar
MONGOLIA
Altai
ASIA
Manchuria
Harbin
Changchun
Shenyang
Beijing
Tianjin
Taiyuan
Lanzhou
Huang
Sian
CHINA
Chongqing
Chang J.
Wuhan
Changsha
Kunming
Guangzhou
MACAU (Port.)
HONG KONG (U.K.)
Hainan
Mindoro
South China Sea
Palawan
Sabah
4101
BRUNEI
Borneo
Celebes
INDONESIA
Ujung Pandang
Flores Sea
Bali
Sumbawa
Sumba
Flores
Timor

Sea of Okhotsk
Blagoveshchensk
Amur
Khabarovsk
G. of Sakhalin
Sakhalin
Vladivostok
Hakodate
KOREA
N
S
Dalian
Qingdao
Kyōto
JAPAN
Sendai
Nagoya
Kitakyūshū
Osaka
Shikoku
Kyūshū
Nanjing
Fuzhou
Yellow Sea
SHANGHAI
East China Sea
Taibei
Ryukyu-retto
TAIWAN
Hanoi
VIETNAM
C. Engano
Manila
PHILIPPINES
Samar
10,497
Sulu Sea
Mindanao
Mindanao Trench
Celebes Sea
Moluccas
Halmahera
Buru
Ceram
Banda Sea
7440
IRIAN JAYA
5029
PAPUA NEW GUINEA
Arafura Sea
Torres Strait
Java Trench
7450

Okhotsk
P-ov. Kamchatka
Komandorskiye O. (Russia)
Petropavlovsk
Kurilskiye Ostrova
La Perouse Strait
Kuril Is.
10,542
Kuril Trench
TOKYO
8412
Yokohama
Fujisan 3776
South Honshu Ridge
Japan Trench
10,554
Ogasawara Gunto (Bonin Is.)
Kazan Retto (Volcano Is.)
Minami-Tori-Shima (Marcus I.)
6603
Emperor Seamount Chain
7168
Midway Is.
Hawa
Lisianski
Marcus Necker Ridge
Wake I. (U.S.)
NORTHERN MARIANAS (U.S.)
Saipan
GUAM (U.S.)
11,022
Mariana Trench
Yap
BELAU
FEDERATED STATES OF MICRONESIA
Truk
Pohnpei
Caroline Islands
Melanesia
Admiralty Is.
New Ireland
Bismarck Arch.
Rabaul
New Britain
9103
SOLOMON IS.
Port Moresby
Guadalcanal
Honiara
9165

Beri
Sea
Aleutian
Andreanof Is.
Aleutian Trench
P
A
Micronesia
MARSHALL IS.
Enewetak Atoll
Jaluit
Bikini Atoll
O
International Date Line
Butaritari
Gilbert Is.
Howland I. (U.
Baker I. (U.
Abariringa
K
I
NAURU
Banaba
TUVALU
Tokelau
Sta. Cruz I.
Rotuma
Wallis & Futuna (Fr.)
WESTE SAM
Apia
FIJI
Vanua Levu
Viti Levu
Suva
Tonga Trench
TONGA
10,822

INDIAN

OCEAN
I. Amsterdam (Fr.)
I. St. Paul (Fr.)
Mid-Indian Ridge
Is. Crozet (Fr.)
Kerguelen (Fr.)
Heard I. (Aust.)

AUSTRALIA
N.W. Cape
Darwin
Arnhem
G. of Carpentaria
NORTHERN TERRITORY
Cairns
Townsville
WESTERN AUSTRALIA
Alice Springs
QUEENSLAND
Perth
SOUTH AUSTRALIA
L. Eyre
Great Australian Bight
Adelaide
NEW SOUTH WALES
Sydney
VICTORIA
Mt. Kosciusko 2230
Canberra
Melbourne
Murray
Darling
C. York
Louisiade Arch. (Austral.)
Mt. Isa
Rockhampton
Brisbane
Great Divide
Coral Sea
Is. Chesterfield
NEW CALEDONIA (Fr.)
7570
Nouméa
Norfolk I. (Aust.)
Lord Howe I. (Aust.)
Lord Howe Ridge
Kermadec Is. (N.Z.)
Kermadec Trench
10,047
Is. Loyauté
Tasman Sea
Cook Strait
Auckland
NEW ZEALAND
Wellington
Mt. Cook 3753
Christchurch
Chatham Is. (N.Z.)
Invercargill
Dunedin
Bounty Is. (N.Z.)
Antipodes Is. (N.Z.)
Bass Strait
TASMANIA
Hobart
Auckland Is. (N.Z.)
Macquarie Is. (Aust.)
Campbell I. (N.Z.)

ft m
18,000 6000
12 000 4000
6000 2000
3000 1000
600 200
0 0
200 600
2000 6000
4000 12 000
6000 18 000
8000 24,000
m ft

Projection: Mollweide's Homolographic

40   60   80   100   East from Greenwich   120   140   160   180

1 2 3 4 5 6 7 8 9 10

1 : 48 000 000

11   12   13   14   15   16   17   18   19   20

A L A S K A
(U.S.)

Bristol Bay

Gulf of Alaska

Juneau

Prince of Wales I.

Queen Charlotte Is.

Prince Rupert

Kitimat

GREENLAND

C. Farewell

Hudson Bay

C A N A D A

Edmonton

L. Winnipeg

Labrador

NORTH AMERICA

NORTH

Vancouver
Vancouver I.
Victoria
Seattle

Calgary

Regina

Winnipeg

Missouri

L. Superior

Montréal

Quebec

St. Lawrence

Pr. Edward I.

Saint John

Newfoundland

Portland

Boise

Minneapolis

L. Huron

Ottawa

Toronto

L. Ontario

Buffalo

Pittsburgh

Saint Sable

Detroit

NEW YORK
Philadelphia

ATLANTIC

C. Mendocino

Salt Lake
City

Denver

Colorado

Snake

CHICAGO

Kansas
City

St. Louis

Cincinnati

Baltimore
Washington

San Francisco

4418

UNITED STATES

Oklahoma

Memphis

Appalachian Mts.

C. Hatteras

6741

Los Angeles
San Diego

Dallas

Mississippi

Atlanta

Jacksonville

Bermuda (U.K.)

OCEAN

Ciudad
Juárez

San Antonio

Houston

New
Orleans

Gulf of Mexico

Miami

Florida Strait

I. Guadalupe
(Mexico)

6225

Sierra Madre

Gulf of California

Monterrey

BAHAMAS

Tropic of Cancer

Hawaiian Is.
(U.S.)

Oahu

Honolulu

4205

Hawaii

Is. Revilla Gigedo
(Mexico)

M E X I C O

México

Guadalajara

Puebla

5700

Acapulco

Mérida

Yucatan Channel

CUBA

La Habana

West Indies

Hispaniola

DOM.
REP.

9200

7680

JAMAICA

HAITI

Kingston

PUERTO
RICO
(U.S.)

Leeward
Is.

C I F I C

Christmas Island Ridge

Palmyra Is. (U.S.)

Teraina
Tabuaeran

Kiritimati

Jarvis I.
(U.S.)

I. Clipperton (Fr.)

GUATEMALA
Guatemala

6852

San Salvador

EL SALVADOR

BELIZE

HONDURAS

Caribbean Sea

NICARAGUA

Managua

San José

CENTRAL
AMERICA

COSTA RICA

PANAMA

Panamá

Colón

Canal

Barranquilla

Maracaibo

Windward
Is.

BARBADOS

TRINIDAD &
TOBAGO

Caracas

VENEZUELA

Orinoco

E A N

Canterbury I.

Phoenix Is.

KIRIBATI

Malden I.

Starbuck I.

Equator

I. del Coco
(Costa Rica)

I. de Malpelo
(Colombia)

Medellín

Bogotá

Cali

COLOMBIA

Galápagos
(Ecuador)

Quito

ECUADOR

Guayaquil

Iquitos

Amazonas

Manaus

BRAZIL

Tongareva
Penrhyn Is.

Manihiki
Pukapuka

Suwarrow Is.

SAMOA (U.S.)

Niue
(N.Z.)

Cook
Islands
(N.Z.)

Vostok
I.

Flint I.

Îs. Marquises

Caroline I.

C. Pariñas

SOUTH

Trujillo

PERU

6369

Lima

AMERICA

Rarotonga

Austral

Îs. de la
Société

Tahiti

Manuae

FRENCH POLYNESIA

Îs. Tuamotu

Tuamotu Ridge

Rapa

Seamount Chain

Îs. Tubuai
(Îs. Australes)

Pitcairn I. (U.K.)

Ducie I.
(U.K.)

East Pacific Ridge

I. de Pascua
(Easter I.)
(Chile)

Sala-y-Gomez
(Chile)

San Félix (Chile)

San Ambrosio (Chile)

Cuzco

Arequipa

L. Titicaca

Illampu & Ancohuma
6550

La Paz

6866

BOLIVIA

Peru-

Iquique

Chile

Tropic of Capricorn

8050

Antofagasta

Trench

PARAGUAY

Asunción

Arch. de Juan Fernández
(Chile)

6960

Valparaíso

Santiago

Córdoba

Rosario

URUGUAY

Tucumán

Pto. Alegre

Concepción

Buenos Aires

Montevideo

Río de la Plata

ARGENTINA

Chile Rise

Pacific - Antarctic Ridge

Patagonia

Andes

SOUTH

ATLANTIC

OCEAN

6212

Punta Arenas

Str. of Magellan

Tierra del Fuego

C. Horn

Falkland Is. (U.K.)

South Georgia (U.K.)

A
B
C
D
E
F
G
H
J
K
L
M
N

11   12   13   14   15   16   17   18   19   20

160   140   120   100   West from Greenwich   80   60   40

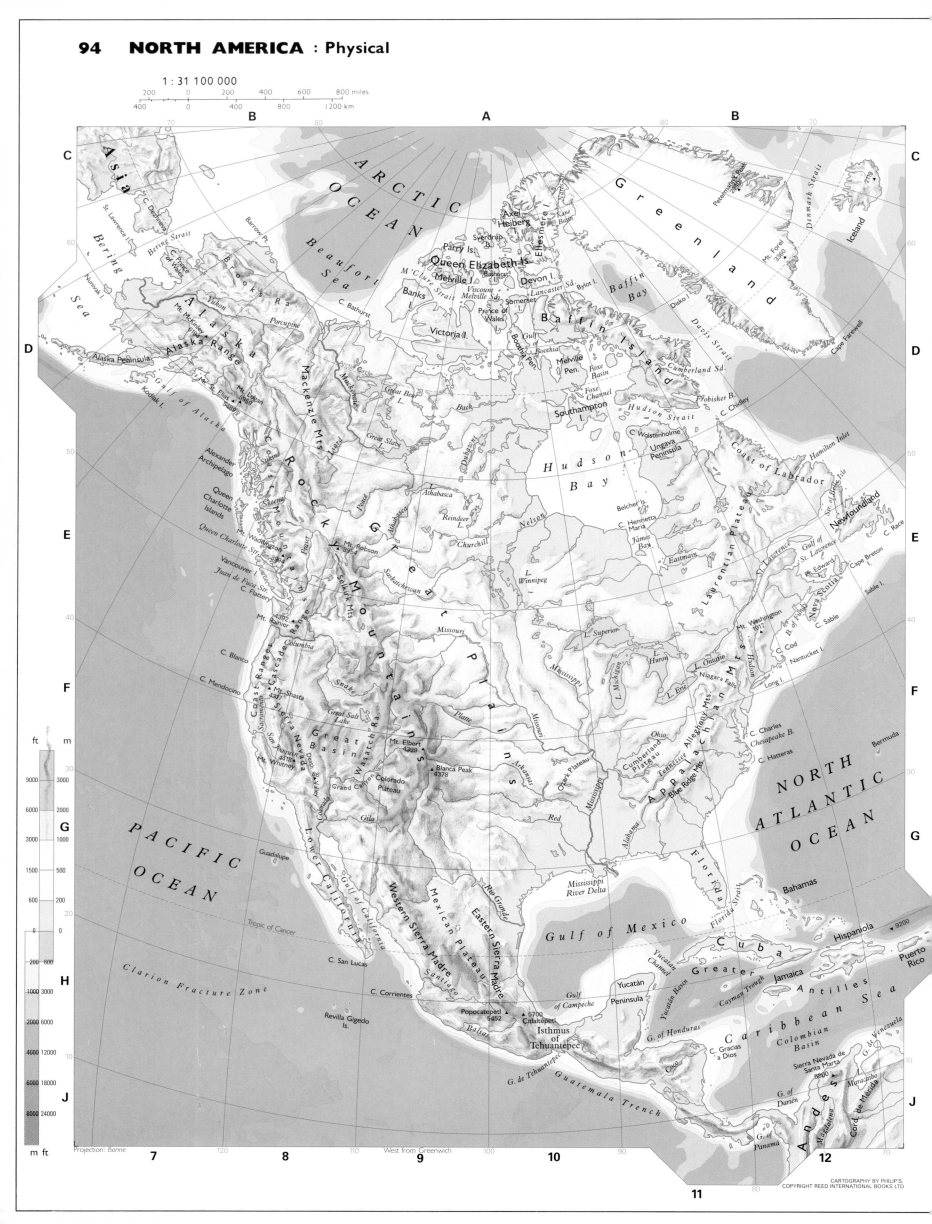

1 : 31 100 000

200   0   200   400   600   800 miles
400   0   400   800   1200 km

A   **B**   **C**

Asia

ARCTIC OCEAN

Greenland

St. Lawrence I.
C. Dezhneva
Bering Strait
Barrow Pt.
Peary Peak 2119
Denmark Strait
Iceland
Mt. Forel 3360

Nunivak I.
Bering Sea
C. Prince of Wales
Brooks Ra.
Beaufort Sea
Axel Heiberg I.
Ellesmere I.
Kane Basin

Alaska
Yukon
Porcupine
Parry Is.
Sverdrup Is.
Queen Elizabeth Is.
Melville I.
Bathurst
Devon I.
Baffin Bay

Alaska Peninsula
Kodiak I.
Mt. McKinley 6194
Alaska Range
Gulf of Alaska
Mackenzie Mts.
C. Bathurst
M'Clure Strait
Banks
Viscount Melville Sd.
Victoria I.
Prince of Wales
Lancaster Sd.
Bylot I.
Somerset
Disko I.

Mt. St. Elias 5489
Mt. Logan 6050
Mackenzie
Great Bear L.
Arctic Circle
Gulf of Boothia
Boothia Pen.
Melville Pen.
Foxe Basin
Baffin Island
Cumberland Sd.
Cape Farewell

Alexander Archipelago
Coast Mountains
Liard
Great Slave L.
Back
Dubawnt
Foxe Channel
Southampton I.
Frobisher B.
C. Chidley

Queen Charlotte Islands
Skeena
Rocky Mountains
Peace
Athabasca
Reindeer L.
Nelson
Hudson Strait
C. Wolstenholme
Ungava Peninsula
Coast of Labrador
Hamilton Inlet

Queen Charlotte Str.
Mt. Waddington 3994
Selkirk Mts.
Mt. Robson 3954
Athabasca
Saskatchewan
Churchill
Hudson Bay
Belcher Is.
C. Henrietta Maria
James Bay
Eastmain
Laurentian Plateau
Str. of Belle Isle
Newfoundland
C. Race

Vancouver I.
Juan de C. Flattery
Juan de Fuca Str.
L. Winnipeg
St. Lawrence
Gulf of St. Lawrence
Cape Breton I.

Mt. Rainier 4392
Cascade Range
Columbia
Great Plains
Missouri
L. Superior
L. Huron
Nova Scotia
Sable I.
Pt. Edward

C. Blanco
Snake
L. Michigan
L. Ontario
Hudson
Mt. Washington 1917
B. of Fundy
C. Sable

C. Mendocino
Sacramento
Sierra Nevada
Great Salt Lake
Mississippi
Platte
Niagara Falls
L. Erie
Appalachian Mts.
Long I.
Nantucket I.
C. Cod

Coast Range
Mt. Shasta 4317
San Joaquin
Wasatch Ra.
Mt. Elbert 4399
Missouri
Arkansas
Ohio
Cumberland Plateau
Allegheny Mts.
Tennessee
C. Charles
Chesapeake B.
Bermuda

Mt. Whitney 4418
Death Valley 86
Great Basin
Blanca Peak 4378
Colorado Plateau
Grand Canyon
Ozark Plateau
Blue Ridge Mts.
C. Hatteras

NORTH ATLANTIC OCEAN

PACIFIC OCEAN

Guadalupe
Gila
Colorado
Red
Alabama
Florida

Lower California
Mississippi River Delta
Bahamas

Tropic of Cancer
Gulf of California
Rio Grande
Gulf of Mexico
Florida Strait

C. San Lucas
Western Sierra Madre
Eastern Sierra Madre
Mexican Plateau
Cuba
Hispaniola 9200
Puerto Rico

Clarion Fracture Zone
Santiago
Yucatán Channel
Greater Antilles
Jamaica
Cayman Trough
Yucatán Basin

Revilla Gigedo Is.
C. Corrientes
Popocatepetl 5452
Citlaltepetl 5700
Gulf of Campeche
Yucatán Peninsula
Colombian Basin
Caribbean Sea

Balsas
Isthmus of Tehuantepec
G. of Honduras
G. de Tehuantepec
C. Gracias a Dios
Sierra Nevada de Santa Marta 5800

Guatemala Trench
Coco
G. of Darién
Andes
Magdalena
Cord. de Mérida
Maracaibo
G. de Venezuela

G. of Panama

ft   m

9000   3000
6000   2000
3000   1000
1500   500
600   200
0   0
200   600
1000   3000
2000   6000
4000   12000
6000   18000
8000   24000
m ft

Projection: Bonne

7   120   **8**   110   **9**   West from Greenwich   100   **10**   90   80   **12**

11

CARTOGRAPHY BY PHILIP'S.
COPYRIGHT REED INTERNATIONAL BOOKS LTD

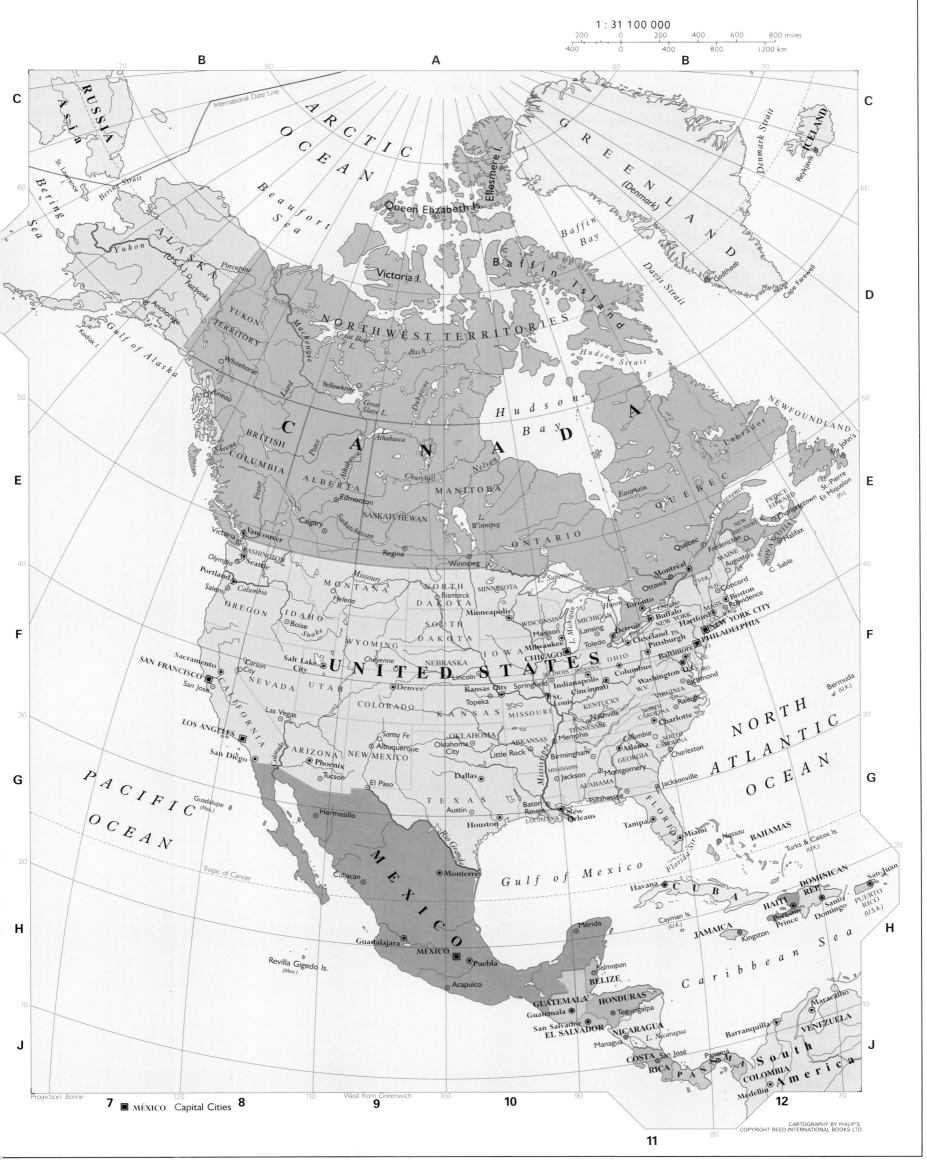

1 : 31 100 000

200   0   200   400   600   800 miles
400   0   400   800   1200 km

RUSSIA
Asia

ICELAND
Reykjavik

ARCTIC   OCEAN

GREENLAND
(Denmark)

Denmark Strait

Beaufort Sea

Bering Strait

Bering Sea

St. Lawrence I.

ALASKA
(U.S.A.)
Yukon
Fairbanks
Anchorage
Kodiak I.

Gulf of Alaska

Porcupine

Queen Elizabeth Is.

Ellesmere I.

Baffin Bay

Victoria I.

Baffin Island

Davis Strait

Godthaab

Cape Farewell

NORTHWEST TERRITORIES

Great Bear L.

Mackenzie

Back

Hudson Strait

Whitehorse

Juneau

YUKON TERRITORY

Arctic Circle

Liard

Yellowknife

Great Slave L.

Dubawnt

C A N A D A

Hudson Bay

NEWFOUNDLAND

Labrador

St. John's

St-Pierre Et Miquelon (Fr.)

Athabasca

Peace

BRITISH COLUMBIA

Skeena

Fraser

Churchill

Nelson

Eastmain

QUÉBEC

ALBERTA

Athabasca

SASKATCHEWAN

MANITOBA

L. Winnipeg

St. Lawrence

PRINCE EDWARD I.

Charlottetown

NOVA SCOTIA

Halifax

Edmonton

Calgary

Saskatchewan

Regina

ONTARIO

Québec

NEW BRUNSWICK

Fredericton

C. Sable

Victoria

Vancouver

Winnipeg

Montréal

MAINE

Augusta

VT.

N.H. Concord

Olympia

WASHINGTON

Seattle

Ottawa

L. Superior

Toronto

Ontario

Boston

MASS.

Providence

Portland

MONTANA

Missouri

NORTH DAKOTA

Bismarck

MINNESOTA

Huron

L. Michigan

Buffalo

NEW YORK

Hartford

NEW YORK CITY

Salem

Columbia

OREGON

Helena

Minneapolis

WISCONSIN

MICHIGAN

Lansing

Detroit

Erie

Cleveland

PA.

Pittsburgh

PHILADELPHIA

IDAHO

Boise

Snake

WYOMING

SOUTH DAKOTA

IOWA

Madison

Milwaukee

CHICAGO

Toledo

OHIO

Columbus

Baltimore

Washington D.C.

DE.

MD.

Sacramento

Carson City

Salt Lake City

Cheyenne

NEBRASKA

ILLINOIS

INDIANA

Indianapolis

Cincinnati

W.V.

Richmond

SAN FRANCISCO

San Jose

NEVADA

UTAH

Denver

Lincoln

Kansas City

Springfield

St. Louis

KENTUCKY

VIRGINIA

Raleigh

Bermuda (U.K.)

CALIFORNIA

Las Vegas

U N I T E D   S T A T E S

COLORADO

Topeka

K A N S A S

MISSOURI

Nashville

TENNESSEE

NORTH CAROLINA

Charlotte

LOS ANGELES

San Diego

Colorado

ARIZONA

NEW MEXICO

Santa Fe

Albuquerque

OKLAHOMA

Oklahoma City

ARKANSAS

Little Rock

Memphis

Birmingham

Atlanta

SOUTH CAROLINA

Columbia

Charleston

Phoenix

Tucson

El Paso

Dallas

MISSISSIPPI

Jackson

ALABAMA

Montgomery

GEORGIA

Jacksonville

NORTH

PACIFIC

OCEAN

Guadalupe (Mex.)

Rio Grande

T E X A S

Austin

Houston

Baton Rouge

LOUISIANA

New Orleans

Tallahassee

FLORIDA

Tampa

Miami

ATLANTIC

OCEAN

Tropic of Cancer

Hermosillo

M E X I C O

Monterrey

Gulf of Mexico

Havana

C U B A

Nassau

BAHAMAS

Turks & Caicos Is. (U.K.)

Florida Str.

Cayman Is. (U.K.)

DOMINICAN REP.

San Juan

PUERTO RICO (U.S.A.)

Culiacan

Guadalajara

MÉXICO

Puebla

Mérida

HAITI

Port-au-Prince

Santo Domingo

JAMAICA

Kingston

Caribbean Sea

Revilla Gigedo Is. (Mex.)

Acapulco

Belmopan

BELIZE

GUATEMALA

Guatemala

San Salvador

EL SALVADOR

HONDURAS

Tegucigalpa

Managua

NICARAGUA

L. Nicaragua

Barranquilla

Maracaibo

VENEZUELA

COSTA RICA

San José

Panama

PANAMA

COLOMBIA

Medellín

South America

International Date Line

West from Greenwich

Projection: Bonne

7 ■ MÉXICO Capital Cities 8

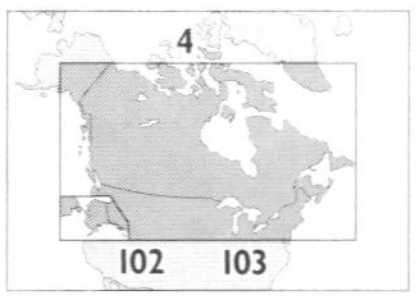

102 103

CANADA

B A

N U V A K
NORTHWEST TERRITORIES
KITIKMEOT
KEEW

YUKON TERRITORY
Whitehorse
Dawson

BRITISH COLUMBIA

ALBERTA
Edmonton
Calgary

SASKATCHEWAN
Saskatoon
Prince Albert
Regina
Moose Jaw

MANITOBA
Winnipeg

PACIFIC OCEAN

Vancouver
Victoria
Seattle
Tacoma
Spokane

WASHINGTON

Queen Charlotte Is.
Vancouver I.

Great Slave L.
Yellowknife
Great Bear Lake
Coronation Gulf
Amundsen Gulf
Victoria Island
Banks Island
Prince Albert Pen.
Wales Island
Somerset Island
Prince of Wales Island
Queen Maud Gulf
Lake Athabasca

Projection: Bonne

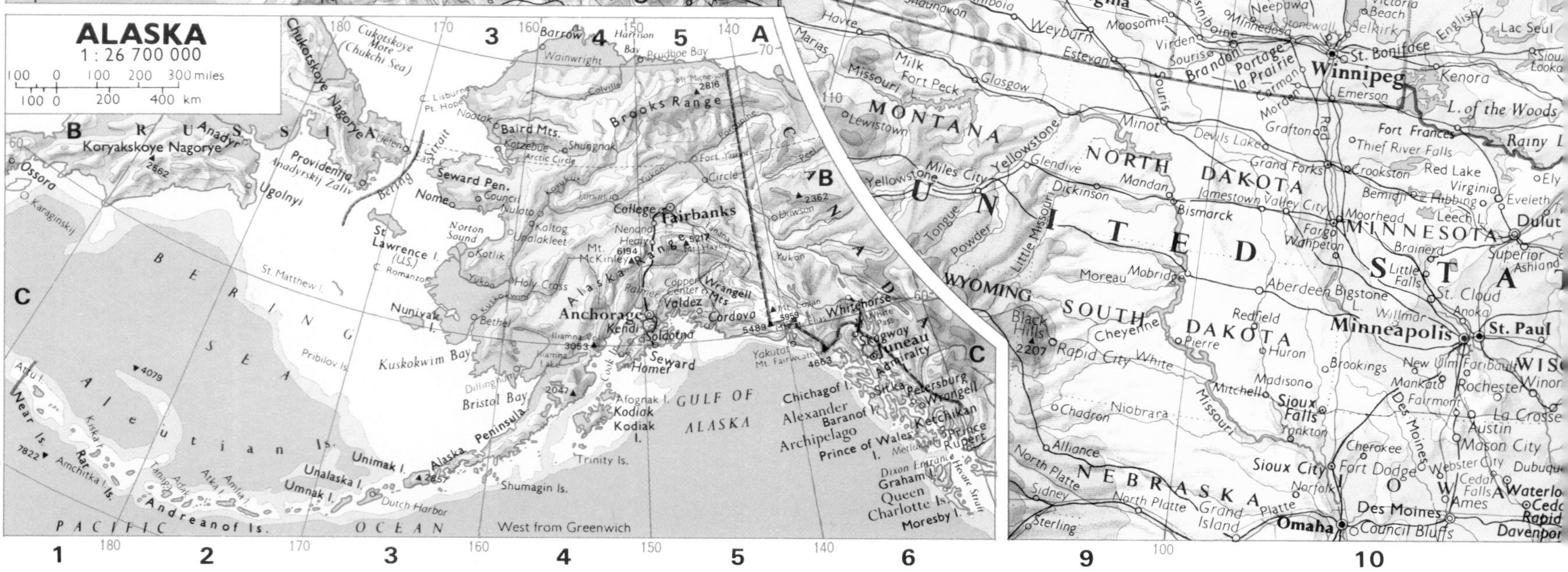

ALASKA
1 : 26 700 000
100 0 100 200 300 miles
100 0 200 400 km

A
B
C

R U S S I A
Koryakskoye Nagorye
BERING SEA
Aleutian Is.
Anchorage
Fairbanks
Brooks Range
Seward Pen.
Nome
Mt. McKinley 6194
Kodiak
GULF OF ALASKA
Juneau
Skagway
Whitehorse
Valdez
Cordova
Bristol Bay
Kuskokwim Bay
St. Lawrence I.
Nunivak I.
Norton Sound
Unalaska I.
Dutch Harbor
PACIFIC OCEAN
West from Greenwich

MONTANA
WYOMING
NORTH DAKOTA
SOUTH DAKOTA
NEBRASKA
MINNESOTA
WISC
IOWA

Bismarck
Pierre
Rapid City
Cheyenne
Minneapolis
St. Paul
Sioux Falls
Sioux City
Omaha
Des Moines
Council Bluffs

UNITED STATES

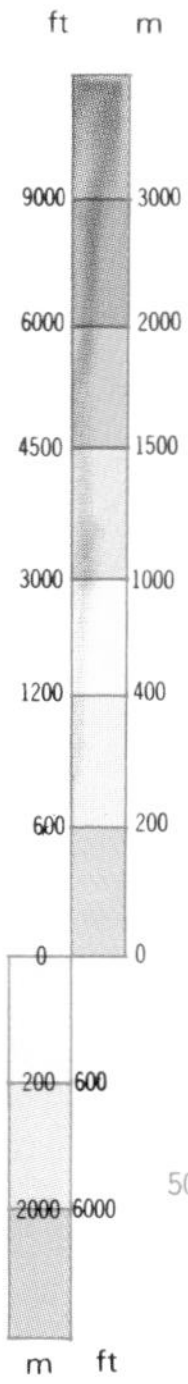

ft m
9000 3000
6000 2000
4500 1500
3000 1000
1200 400
600 200
0 0
200 600
2000 6000
m ft

1 2 3 4 5 6 9 10

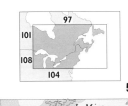

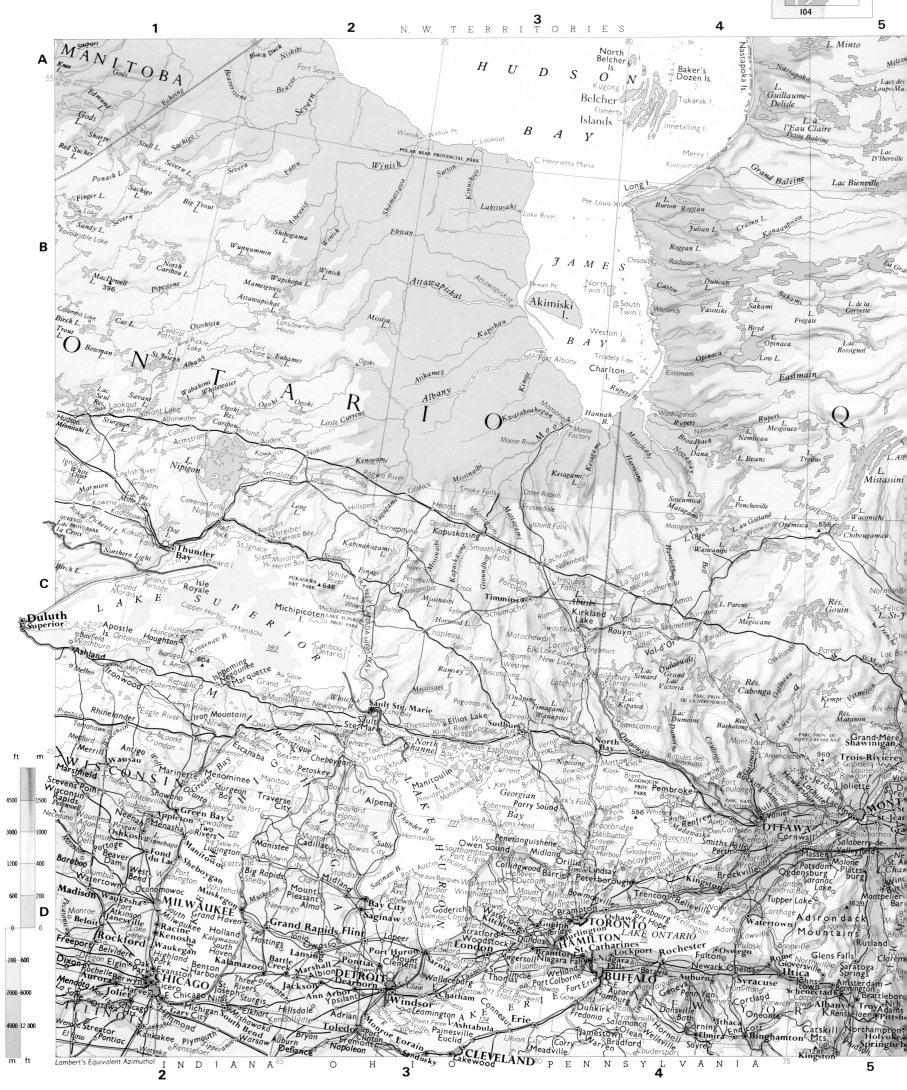

MANITOBA

N. W. TERRITORIES

HUDSON BAY

ONTARIO

QUEBEC

LAKE SUPERIOR

LAKE HURON

LAKE MICHIGAN

WISCONSIN

MICHIGAN

LAKE ERIE

LAKE ONTARIO

NEW YORK

ILLINOIS

INDIANA   OHIO   PENNSYLVANIA

Duluth
Superior
Ashland
Thunder Bay
Timmins
Sudbury
North Bay
Ottawa
MONTREAL
Trois-Rivières
Shawinigan
Milwaukee
CHICAGO
Madison
Rockford
Green Bay
DETROIT
TORONTO
Hamilton
London
BUFFALO
CLEVELAND
Toledo
Windsor
Rochester
Syracuse
Albany
Kingston

Lambert's Equivalent Azimuthal

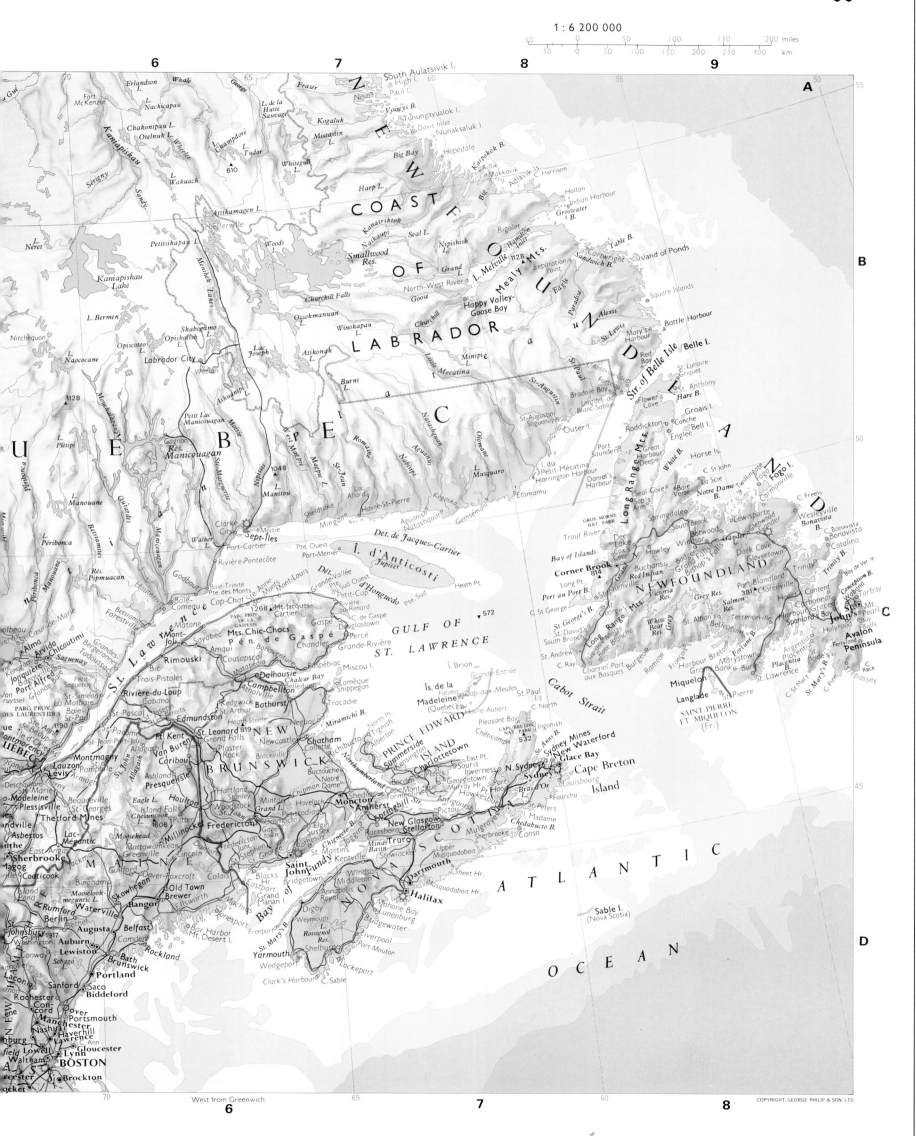

1 : 6 200 000

50   100   150   200 miles
50   0   50   100   150   200   250   300 km

6 **7** **8** **9**

A

COAST OF NEWFOUNDLAND

B

LABRADOR

QUEBEC

50

South Aulatsivik I.
High I.
St. Paul I.
Voisey's B.
Tunungayualok I.
Davis Inlet
Nunaksaluk I.
Hopedale
Kaipokok B.
Adlavik Is.
C. Harrison
Mokkovik
Aillik
Holton
Indian Harbour
Grosswater
B.
Cartwright
Table B.
Sandwich B.
Island of Ponds
Square Islands

Erlandson
Whale
Fraser
Nain
Nachicapau L.
Chakonipau L.
Otelnuk L.
de la Hutte Sauvage
Kogaluk
L. de
Champdoré
L. Tudor
Whitegull L.
Big Bay
Harp L.
Kanairiktok
Naskaupi
Seal L.
Nipishish
Rigolet
Mistastin L.

Fort McKenzie
Sérigny
Kaniapiskau
610
Smallwood Res.
Wheeler
Mealy Mts.
1128
Separation Point
Eagle
Paradise
St. Lewis
Alexis

Shefferville
Woods L.
Churchill Falls
North-West River
Goose
Happy Valley-Goose Bay
L. Melville
Mary's Harbour
Battle Harbour

Petitsikapau L.
Kamapiskau Lake
Ossokmanuan L.
Churchill
Minipi
Red Bay
St. Lunaire-Griquet
Belle I.

Nitchequon
L. Bermen
Shabogamo L.
Opiskatish
Opisconeau L.
Winokapau L.
Lac Joseph
Atikonak L.
Burnt L.
Little Mecatina
St. Paul
Str. of Belle Isle
St. Anthony
Hare B.

L. Néret
Naococane
Opisteo
Labrador City
Wabush
Natashquan
St-Augustin
Bradore Bay
Lourdes-de-Blanc-Sablon
Flower's Cove
Groais I.
Conche
Engle
Bell I.

1128
L. Plétipi
Gagnon
Rés. Manicouagan
Ashuanipi
West Maire
Romaine
St-Augustin-(Saguenay)
Outer I.
Roddickton
White B.
Horse Is.

Péribonca
L. Manouane
Opiscoteo
L. Manitou
L. Musquaro
I. du Petit-Mécatina
Harrington Harbour
Daniel's Harbour
Port Saunders
Long Range Mts.
Seal Cove
Baie Verte
Notre Dame B.
C. St. John
Fogo I.

L. Péribonca
Bessisarbis
Manicouagan
1048
Sheldrake
Aguanish
Natashquan
Kegaska
Etamamu
GROS MORNE NAT. PARK
Deer Lake
South Brook
Botwood
Lewisporte
Twillingate
Carmanville
C. Freels

Quiards
Clarke City
Sept-Îles
Moisie
Mingan
Gethsemani
Trout River
Cox's Cove
Howley
Buchans
Windsor
Gander
Dark Cove
Glovertown
Wesleyville
Bonavista

Rés. Pipmuacan
Godbout
Baie-Trinité
Port-Cartier
Pte. Ouest
Port-Menier
Bay of Islands
Corner Brook
814
Red Indian L.
Grand Falls
Bishop's Falls
NEWFOUNDLAND
C. Bonavista
Catalina

Manouane
Forestville
Betsiamites
Pointe-des-Monts
Cap-Chat
Î. d'Anticosti
Jupiter
Heath Pt.
Long Pt.
Stephenville
Victoria L.
Grey Res.
Salmon Res.
381
Trinity
Trinity B.
Bay de Verde

Baie-Comeau
Ste-Anne
Mont-Louis
Dét. Vallée
Grande-Rivière
GULF OF
572
Port au Port B.
Port au Port
St. George's B.
White Bear Res.
Grey L.
Terrenceville
Clarenville
Content
Carbonear
Harbour Grace
Conception B.
Wabana
Torbay

1268
Mt. Jacques-Cartier
Mts. Chic-Chocs
Gaspé
ST. LAWRENCE
C. de Gaspé
Douglastown
C. St. George
St. David's
Long Range Mts.
St. Alban's
Belleoram
Marystown
Placentia
St. John's
Spaniard's Bay
Holyrood

Matane
Pén. de Gaspé
Percé
Grande-Grève
Chandler
St. Andrew's
Rose Blanche
Harbour Breton
Fortune B.
Argentia
Placentia B.
C. Race

Alma
Arvida
Chicoutimi
Amqui
Causapscal
Bonaventure
Chaleur Bay
Miscou I.
Î. Brion
C. Ray
Channel-Port aux Basques
Burgeo
Ramea
François
Hermitage
Fortune
Burin
Avalon Peninsula
C. Pine

Jonquière
Port Alfred
Saguenay
Rimouski
Matapédia
Gaspébiac
Lamèque
Shippegan
Tracadie
Îs. de la Madeleine (Quebec)
Cap-aux-Meules
St. Paul
Miquelon
Langlade
St-Pierre

La Malbaie
Bic
Trois-Pistoles
Rivière-du-Loup
Belledune
Miramichi B.
North Pt.
Tignish
Havre-Aubert
St. Lawrence
SAINT-PIERRE ET MIQUELON (Fr.)

1190
PARC PROV. DES LAURENTIDES
St-Siméon
Campbellton
Atholville
Bathurst
Neguac
Alberton
PRINCE EDWARD
Pleasant Bay
CAPE BRETON NAT. PARK
Ingonish
45

QUÉBEC
Lauzon
Lévis
Kedgwick
Edmundston
St. Leonard 819
Grand Falls
Newcastle
Chatham
Kouchibouguac
Summerside
Kensington
ISLAND
Chéticamp
532
Inverness
Sydney Mines
New Waterford
Glace Bay

Montmagny
Van Buren
Caribou
Plaster Rock
Chipman
Dame
Shediac
Borden
Charlottetown
East Pt.
Souris
Cape Breton
Louisbourg

St-Jean-Port-Joli
Ashland
Fort Kent
Allagash
Presque Isle
Hartland
Stanley
Minto
Grand L.
Havelock
Moncton
Amherst
Georgetown
Cape George
Murray Hr.
N. Sydney
Sydney
Island

Montreal
Beauceville
St-Georges
Eagle L.
Houlton
Woodstock
Fredericton
NEW BRUNSWICK
Petitcodiac
Dorchester
Springhill
Pictou
New Glasgow
Stellarton
Hawkesbury
Bras d'Or
L.
St. Peters
Fourchu

Plessisville
Thetford Mines
Island Falls
Patten
1606
Chesuncook L.
Minturn
Fredericton Junc.
Gagetown
Sussex
Elgin
Rothesay
Chignecto B.
Joggins
Truro
Antigonish
St. Madame
Chedabucto B.
Canso

Asbestos
Lac-Mégantic
Moosehead L.
Millinocket
Lincoln
Stanley
St. John
Sackville
Minas Basin
Stewiacke
Mulgrave
Sherbrooke

East Angus
Greenville
Mattawamkeag
MAINE
Fredericton
Gagetown
St. Stephen
St. George
St. Martins
FUNDY
Windsor
Upper Musquodoboit
Sheet Hr.
ATLANTIC

Sherbrooke
Magog
Coaticook
Binghamyam
Skowhegan
Old Town
Brewer
Calais
Eastport
Grand Manan I.
Saint John
Bay of
Bridgetown
Middleton
Annapolis Royal
NOVA SCOTIA
Dartmouth
Musquodoboit Hr.
OCEAN

1917
Berlin
Mooselookmeguntic L.
Waterville
Bangor
Ellsworth
Machias
Jonesport
Weymouth
Digby
Mahone Bay
Halifax
Sable I. (Nova Scotia)

Rumford
Bethel
Belfast
Bar Harbor
Mt. Desert I.
St. Mary's B.
Freeport
Lunenburg
Bridgewater

St. Johnsbury
Washington
Augusta
Camden
Rockland
Yarmouth
Rossignol Res.
Liverpool
Port Mouton

Auburn
Lewiston
Bath
Brunswick
Wedgeport
Shelburne
C. Sable

Conway
Sebago L.
Portland
Sanford
Saco
Biddeford
Clark's Harbour
Lockeport

Laconia
Rochester
Concord
Dover
Portsmouth
Manchester
Nashua
Haverhill
Lawrence
Lowell
Gloucester
Lynn
BOSTON
Brockton

C

D

GULF OF ST. LAWRENCE

Cabot Strait

Northumberland Str.

Bay of Fundy

ATLANTIC OCEAN

Dét. de Jacques-Cartier

Str. of Belle Isle

St. Lawrence R.

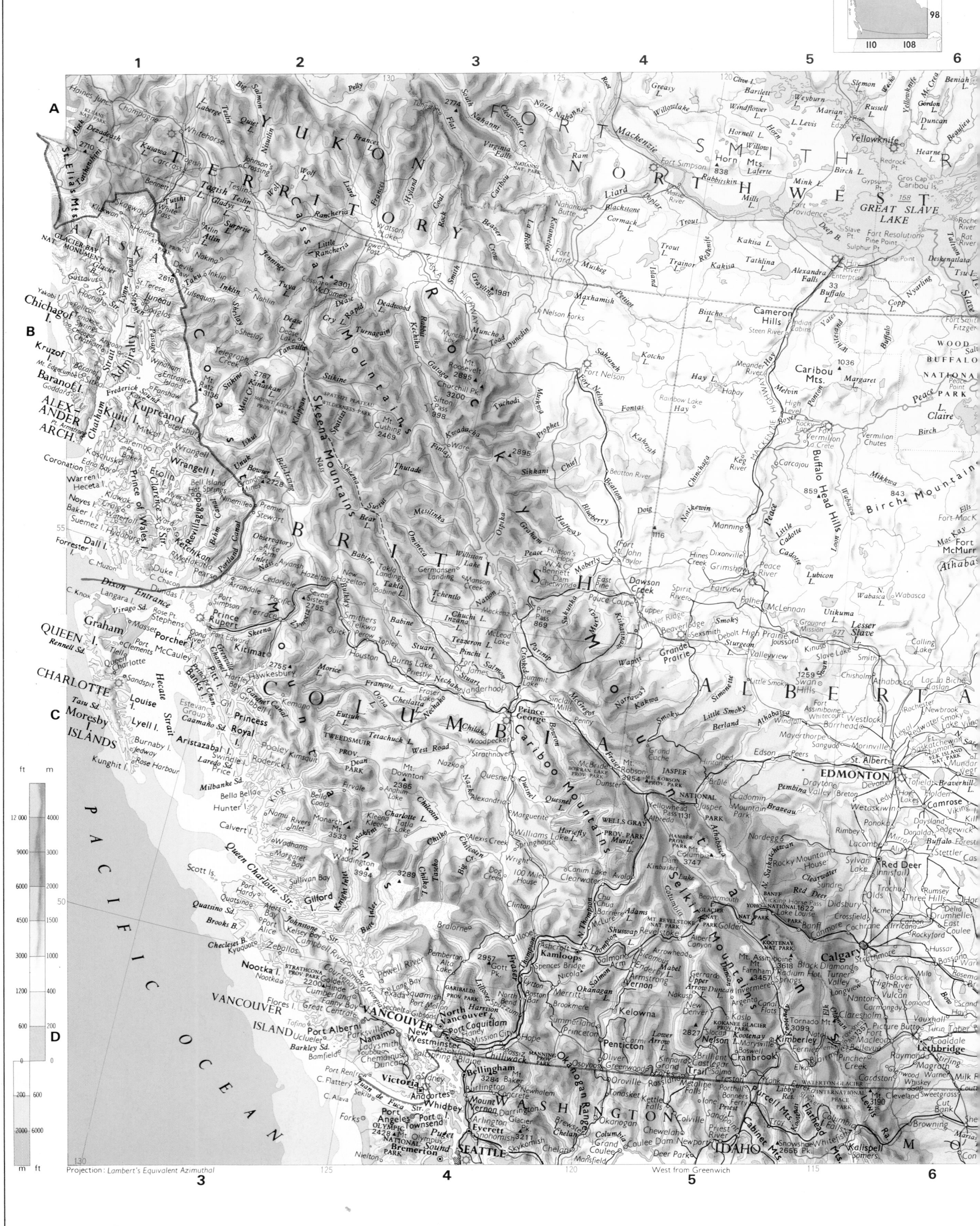

PACIFIC OCEAN

YUKON TERRITORY

NORTHWEST

GREAT SLAVE LAKE

BRITISH COLUMBIA

ALBERTA

ALASKA

ALEXANDER ARCH

QUEEN CHARLOTTE ISLANDS

CHARLOTTE

VANCOUVER ISLAND

WASHINGTON

IDAHO

EDMONTON

Calgary

Red Deer

Lethbridge

VANCOUVER

Victoria

SEATTLE

Whitehorse

Prince Rupert

Prince George

Dawson Creek

Grande Prairie

Kelowna

Penticton

Projection: Lambert's Equivalent Azimuthal

West from Greenwich

ft m

12 000 4000

9000 3000

6000 2000

4500 1500

3000 1000

1200 400

600 200

0 0

200 600

2000 6000

m ft

96 97
114 116

1   2   3   4   5   6

A   B   C   D   E

CANADA

BRITISH COLUMBIA   ALBERTA   SASKATCHEWAN   MANITOBA

Vancouver I   Vancouver   New Westminster   Calgary   Saskatoon   Lake Winnipegosis   Reindeer L.
Georgia Str.   Victoria   Bellingham   Lethbridge   Last Mountain Lake   L. Manitoba   Baldy Mtn 831
Barkley Sd.   C. Flattery   Juan de Luca Str.   Vernon   Lytton   Mt. Assiniboine 3618   Medicine Hat   Regina   Moose Jaw   Minnedosa   Neepawa
Olympic Mtns   Puget   Upper Arrow Lake   Kootenay Lake   Raymond   Milk   Swift Current   Maple Creek   Virden   Brandon   La Prairie   Carman   Morden   Boissevain

WASHINGTON
Seattle   Tacoma   Everett   Spokane   Wenatchee   Moses Lake   Coeur d'Alene   Great Falls   Havre   Shelby   Fort Peck Reservoir   Williston   Minot   Devils Lake
Olympia   Aberdeen   Hoquiam   Centralia   Ellensburg   Kellogg   Wallace   Kalispell   Glacier Nat. Park   Lewistown   Lake Sakakawea   Bismarck   Jamestown
Cape Disappointment   Chehalis   Yakima   Pullman   Moscow   Bitterroot   Anaconda   Butte   Musselshell   Miles City   Dickinson   Mandan

OREGON
Portland   Salem   Albany   Eugene   Springfield   Bend   Pendleton   La Grande   Baker   Boise   Weiser   Payette   Caldwell   Nampa   Ontario   Burns
Astoria   McMinnville   Corvallis   Roseburg   Medford   Grants Pass   Klamath Falls   Blue Mountains   John Day   Deschutes   Harney Basin   Summer L.   Malheur L.
Mt. Hood 3427   Mt. Rainier 4392   Mt. St. Helens   Mt. Baker 3285

NORTH DAKOTA
SOUTH DAKOTA
Pierre   Rapid City   Black Hills 2207   Bad Lands   Cheyenne   Moreau   Oahe Reservoir   Mitchell   Aberdeen   Randall Res.

MONTANA
Missoula   Helena   Bozeman   Billings   Livingston   Yellowstone National Park   Absaroka Range   Bighorn Mts   Sheridan   Buffalo   Powder   Tongue
Teton   Clark Fork   Salmon   Salmon River Mts   Hyndman Pk. 3681   Sun Valley   Idaho Falls   St. Anthony   Rexburg   Teton Pk. 4196   Gannett Pk. 4202

IDAHO
Boise   Twin Falls   Pocatello   Blackfoot   Shoshone   Rupert   Burley   Malad City

WYOMING
Casper   Rawlins   Rock Springs   Green River   Laramie   Cheyenne   Laramie Mts   Wind River   South Pass   Pathfinder Res.   Thermopolis   Hot Springs
Wind River Range 4207

NEVADA
Reno   Sparks   Carson City   Winnemucca   Elko   Ely   Tonopah   Las Vegas   Humboldt   Walker Lake   Carson Sink   Pyramid L.   Ruby L.   Franklin L.
Great Basin   Wheeler Pk. 3882   3710

UTAH
Salt Lake City   Ogden   Provo   Murray   Bountiful   Nephi   Price   Springville   Payson   Spanish Fork   Logan   Brigham   Great Salt Lake 1282   Great Salt Lake Desert
Wasatch Range   Uinta Mts   Sevier L.   Cedar City   St. George   Zion Nat. Park   Lake Powell

CALIFORNIA
San Francisco   Oakland   Berkeley   San Jose   Santa Clara   Stockton   Sacramento   Modesto   Merced   Fresno   Visalia   Bakersfield   Los Angeles   Long Beach   San Diego
Santa Rosa   Napa   Vallejo   Roseville   Santa Cruz   Monterey   Salinas   San Luis Obispo   Santa Maria   Santa Barbara   Glendale   Pasadena   Anaheim   San Bernardino   Riverside
Eureka   Redding   Red Bluff   Chico   Yuba City   Golden Gate   San Mateo   Humboldt Bay   Arena Pt.   C. Mendocino   Pt. Conception
Mt. Shasta 4317   Lassen Pk. 3187   Mt. Whitney 4418   Yosemite National Park   Sequoia Nat. Park   Death Valley −86   Owens Lake   Mojave Desert   Salton Sea   Tehachapi Pass
Sierra Nevada   Coast Range   San Joaquin   Klamath   Goose L.   Honey L.   Tulare   Sta. Catalina   S. Clemente I.   S. Nicolas I.   Santa Rosa I.   Santa Barbara Is.

Hollywood   Santa Monica   Santa Ana   Redlands   Brawley   El Centro   Yuma   Tijuana   Mexicali   Ensenada

COLORADO
Denver   Colorado Springs   Pueblo   Fort Collins   Greeley   Longmont   Boulder   Grand Junction   Montrose   Durango   Alamosa   Trinidad   Leadville   Gunnison
Pikes Peak 4301   Mt. Elbert 4399   Sawatch Range   Sangre de Cristo Mts   Park Range   Front Range   Blanca 4372   Yampa   White   San Juan Mts   Cortez
Roof Butte 2919

ARIZONA
Phoenix   Tucson   Flagstaff   Prescott   Kingman   Winslow   Mesa   Globe   Nogales   Douglas   Gila   Grand Canyon Nat. Park   Painted Desert   Mogollon Mesa   Humphreys Pk. 3851
Havasu Lake   Lake Mead   Painted Desert   Baldy Pk. 3532   Mt. Taylor 3471

NEW MEXICO
Albuquerque   Santa Fe   Las Cruces   Roswell   Carlsbad   Clovis   Hobbs   Artesia   Socorro   Gallup   Los Alamos   Las Vegas   Raton   Tucumcari   Alamogordo   Deming   Silver City   Lordsburg
Rio Grande   Pecos   Sacramento Mts   San Andres Mts   Sierra Blanca 3658   Elephant Butte Res.   Black Range   Llano Estacado

KANSAS
Hays   Garden City   Dodge City   Liberal   Pratt   Hutchinson   McPherson   Gt. Bend   Concordia   Smoky Hill   Arkansas   Cimarron   Lamar   Rocky Ford   La Junta   Walsenburg

NEBRASKA
North Platte   Scottsbluff   Sidney   McCook   Holdrege   Hastings   Grand Island   Republican   Superior   Platte   South Platte   Chadron   Alliance   Niobrara   Sterling

OKLAHOMA
Enid   Woodward   Boise City   Clinton   Chickasha   Lawton   Duncan   Altus   El Reno   Perryton   Guymon   Borger   Pampa   Canadian   North Canadian   Salt Fork
Childress

TEXAS
Amarillo   Lubbock   Midland   Odessa   San Angelo   Abilene   Fort Worth   Wichita Falls   Austin   San Antonio   Del Rio   Eagle Pass   Laredo   Brownsville   McAllen   Harlingen
Plainview   Levelland   Big Spring   Sweetwater   Mineral Wells   Brazos   Pecos   Colorado   Edwards Plateau   New Braunfels   San Marcos   Kingsville   Matamoros   Alpine   Presidio

MEXICO
BAJA CALIFORNIA   BAJA CALIFORNIA SUR   SONORA   CHIHUAHUA   COAHUILA   DURANGO   SINALOA
Tijuana   Mexicali   Ensenada   Hermosillo   Guaymas   Ciudad Obregón   Los Mochis   Chihuahua   Ciudad Juárez   Nuevo Laredo   Monterrey   Torreón   Gómez Palacio   Monclova
Golfo de California   Sierra Madre   Guadalupe (Mex.)   I. de Cedros   Punta Eugenia   I. Ángel de la Guarda   Tiburón   Bahía Sebastián Vizcaíno   B. de Todos Santos
Magdalena   Cananea   Ures   Moctezuma   Sahuaripa   Santa Ana   Nogales   Sta. Rosalía   Mulegé   La Paz   La Purísima   Santa Rosalía   3200   3078   3150
Nacozari   Batopilas   Parral   Hidalgo del Parral   San Pedro   Camargo   Jiménez   Ciudad Camargo   Llano de los Cristianos   Bolsón de Mapimí   Nueva Rosita   Piedras Negras   Salado
Presidio   Conchos   Rio Grande   Uvalde   Del Rio   Zaragoza   Lampazos   Sabinas

PACIFIC OCEAN

West from Greenwich   110   105   100

Projection: Albers' Equal Area with two standard parallels

HAWAII
1 : 8 900 000

G   H   J
15   16   17

Kauai   Niihau   Kaula   Oahu   Honolulu   Pearl City   Wahiawa   Kahana   Kahuku   Molokai   Lanai   Maui   Kahoolawe   Hawaii
Lihue   Mana   Kalaupapa   Lahaina   Paia   Hana   Makena   Hilo   Keaau   Pahala   Kailua   Kawaihae   Kaunakakai
Kauai Channel   Kaiwi Channel   Kalohi Channel   Alenuihaha Channel   Hawaiian Islands
Haleakala 3056   Mauna Kea 4205   Mauna Loa 4170   Kilauea Crater 1247
Pearl Harbor

ft   m
12 000   4000
9000   3000
6000   2000
4500   1500
3000   1000
1200   400
600   200
0   0
200   600
2000   6000
m   ft

20   0   20   40   60   80 miles
20   0   40   80   120 km

130   120   115   160   158   156
45   40   35   30   25   22   20

1 : 10 700 000

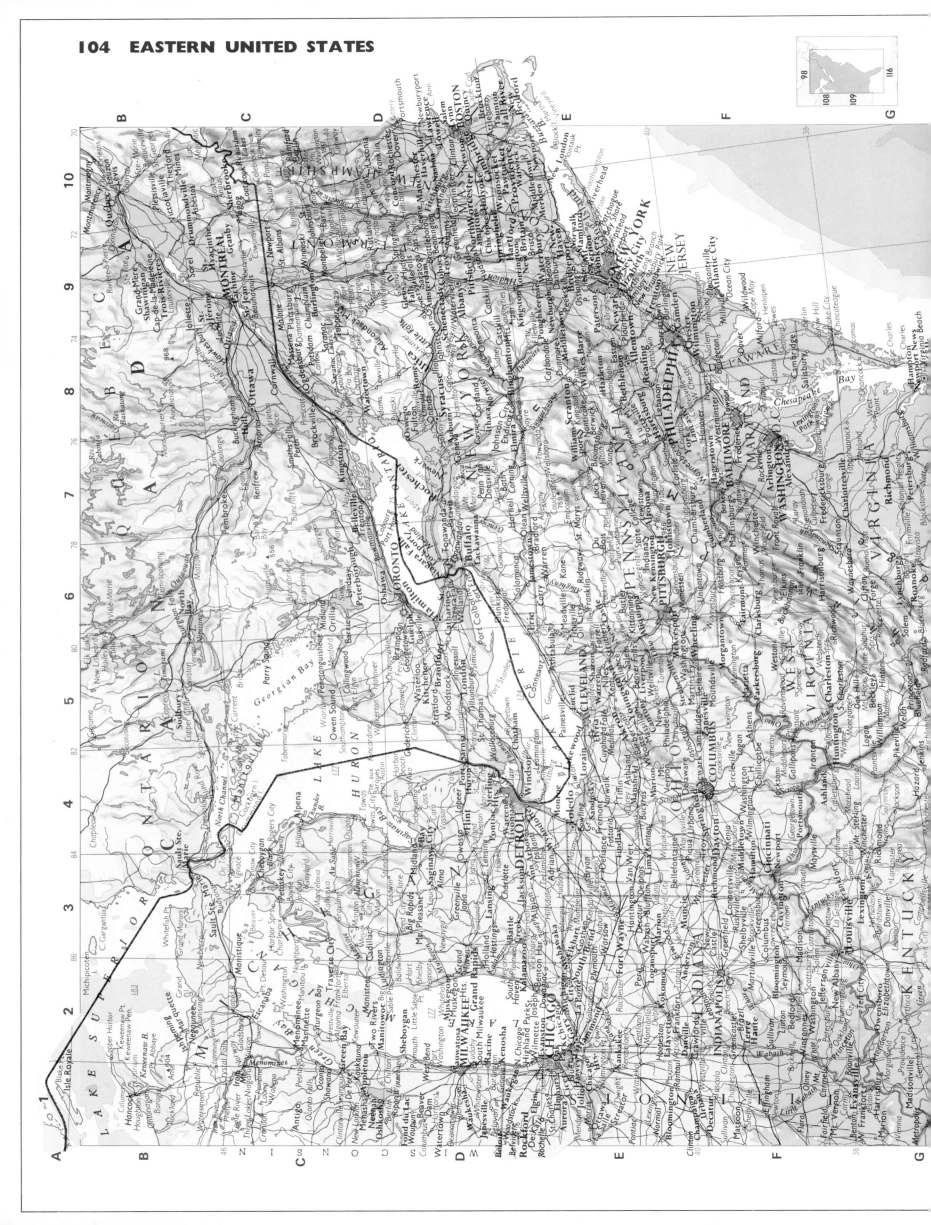

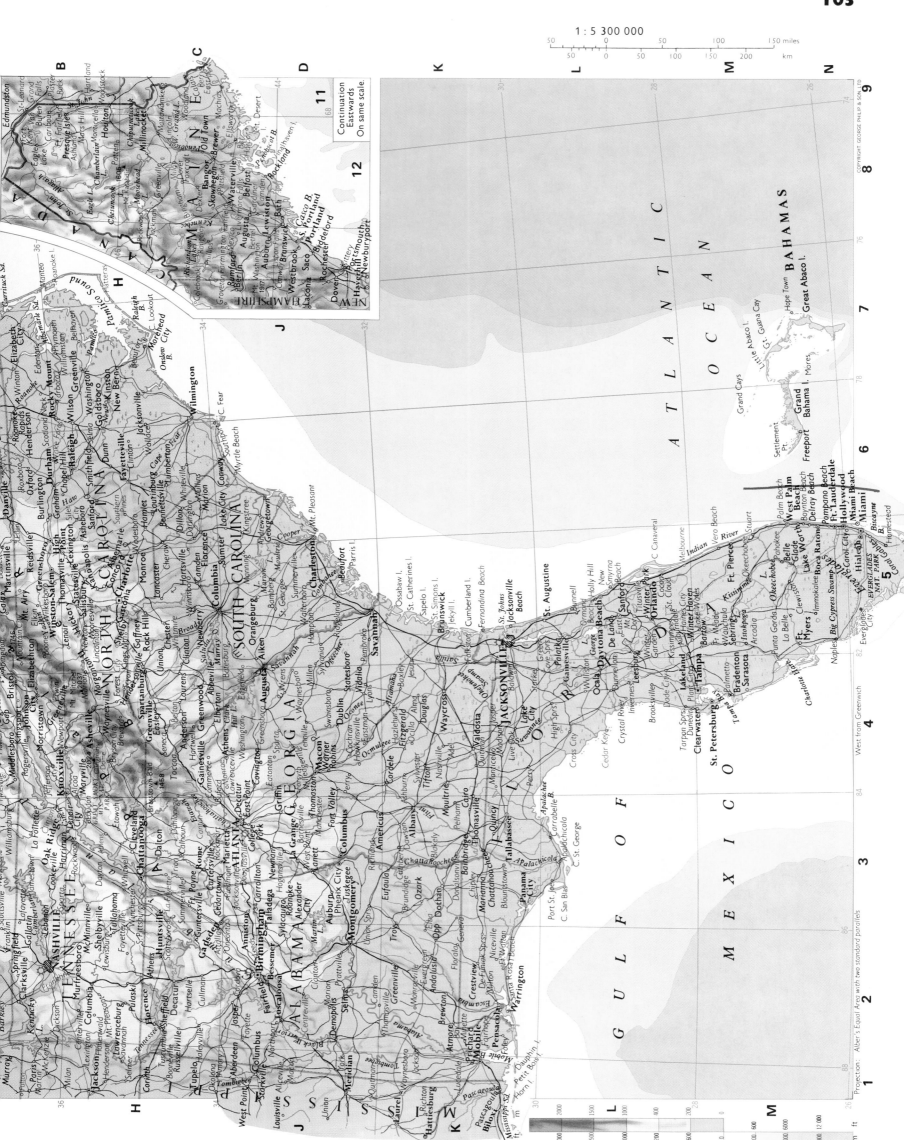

1 2 3 4 5 6 7

A B C D E F G

LAKE HURON

LAKE ERIE

LAKE ONTARIO

Georgian Bay

Bruce Peninsula

MICHIGAN

OHIO

PENNSYLVANIA

ONTARIO

NEW

W. VA.

DETROIT **CLEVELAND** **TORONTO** **BUFFALO** **Rochester**

PITTSBURGH **Akron** **Youngstown** **Hamilton** **Niagara Falls**

Windsor **Sarnia** **London** **Guelph** **Kitchener**

Thunder Bay · North Pt. · South Pt. · Blackriver · Harrisville · Greenbush · Oscoda · Au Sable · Au Sable Pt. · Port Austin · Pte Aux Barques · Kinde · Port Hope · Harbor Beach · Bad Axe · Elkton · Ruth · Cass · Deckerville · Carsonville · Sandusky · Port Sanilac · Croswell · Lexington · Brown City · Yale · Imlay City · Capac · Almont · Memphis · Richmond · New Haven · Mt. Clemens · E. Detroit · Roseville · Tecumseh · Essex · Kingsville · Leamington · Wheatley · Comber · Tilbury · Blenheim · Chatham · Erieau · Pelee I.

Projection: Bonne

ft m — 6000 2000 · 4500 1500 · 3000 1000 · 1200 400 · 600 200 · 0 · 200 600 · m ft

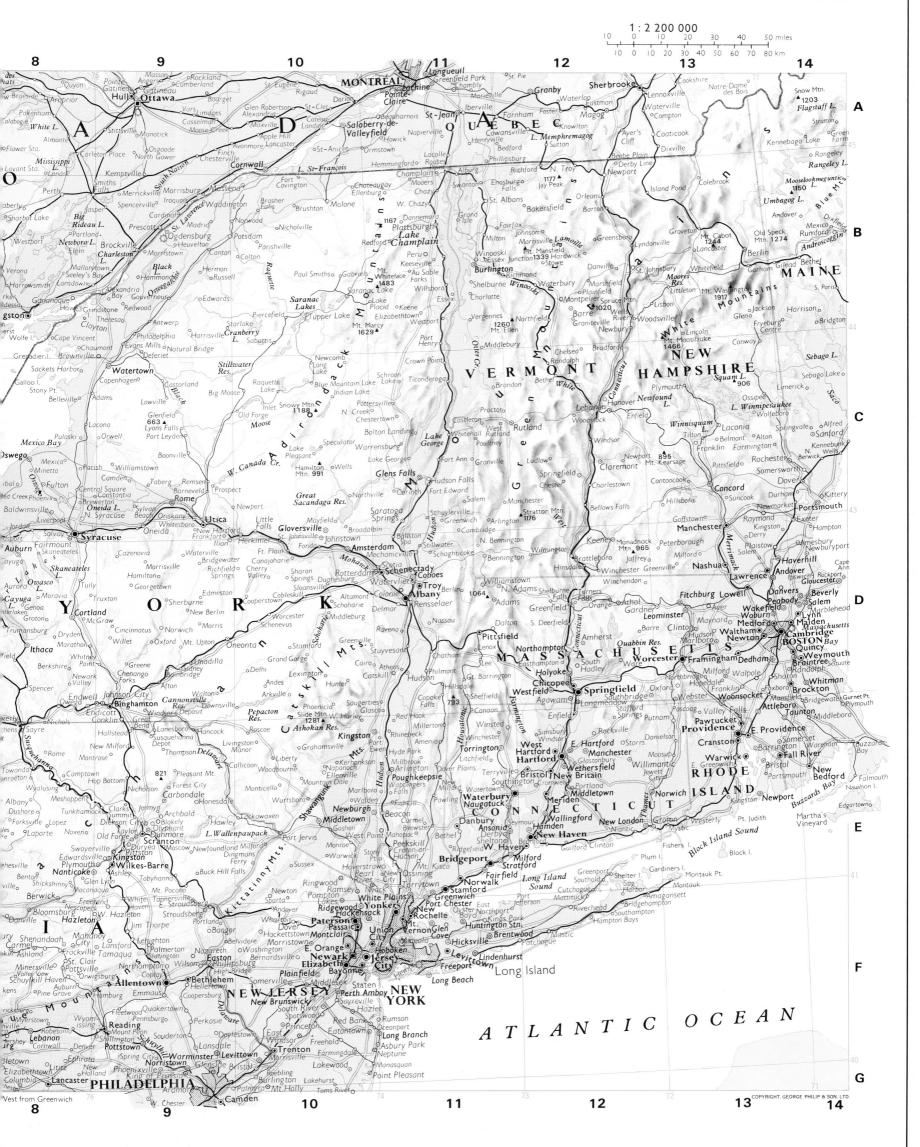

1 : 2 200 000

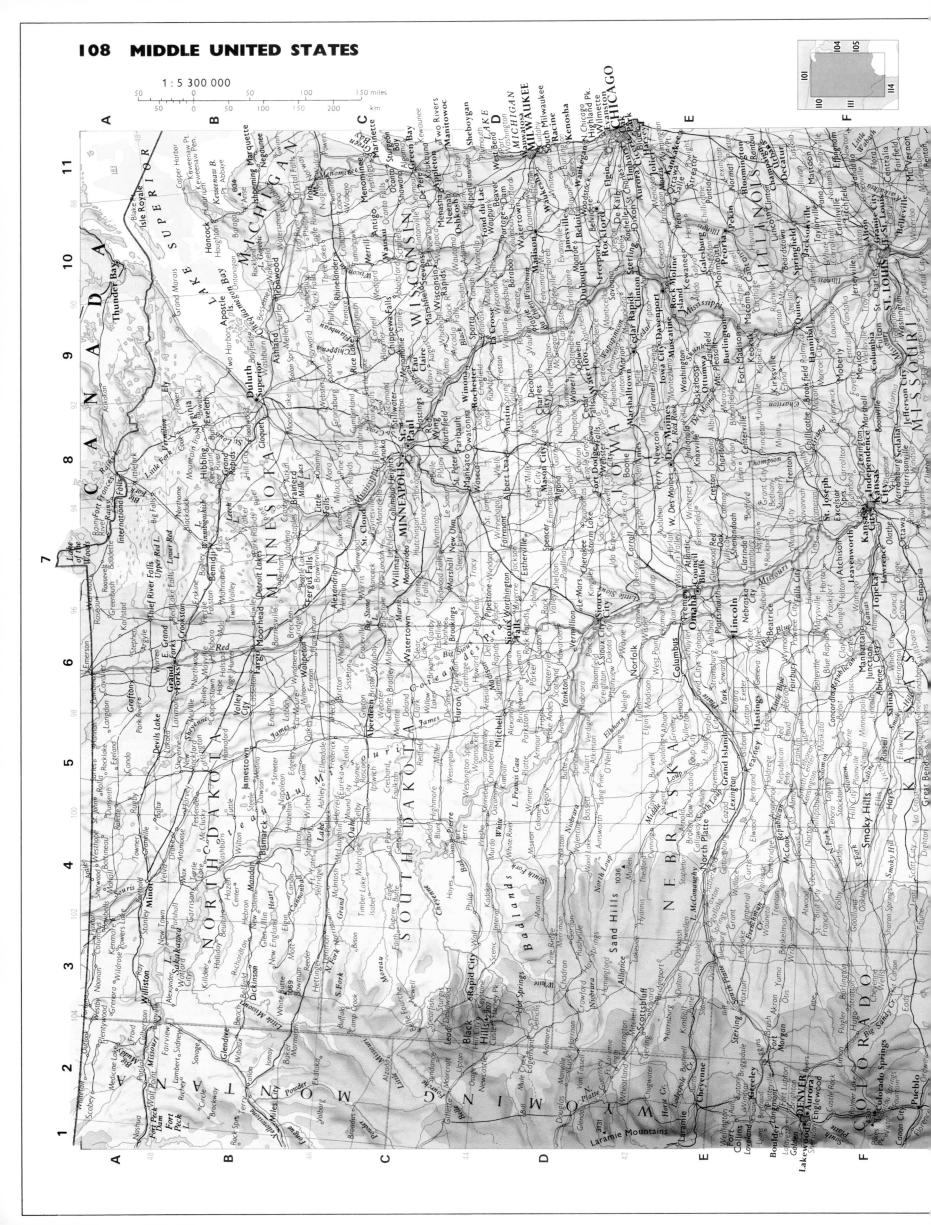

MISSISSIPPI
LOUISIANA
ARKANSAS
OKLAHOMA
TEXAS
NEW MEXICO
TENNESSEE
MEXICO
COAHUILA
CHIHUAHUA

GULF OF MEXICO

Laguna Madre

Continuation Southwards on same scale

Projection: Albers' Equal Area with two standard parallels

West from Greenwich

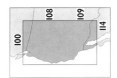

1 : 5 300 000

50   0   50   100   miles
50   0   50   100   150   km

Projection: Albers' Equal Area with two standard parallels

West from Greenwich

COLORADO

NEW MEXICO

TEXAS

ARIZONA

CALIFORNIA

NEVADA

UTAH

SONORA

CHIHUAHUA

BAJA CALIFORNIA

M E X I C O

PACIFIC OCEAN

Golfo de California

San Juan Mts.

Sangre de Cristo Mts.

Colorado Plateau

Painted Desert

Mogollon Rim

Sonora Desert

Desierto de Altar

Gran Desierto

Santa Lucia Range

Grand Canyon

Lake Mead

Death Valley

Sierra de Juarez

Bahia Sebastián Vizcaíno

LOS ANGELES

SAN DIEGO

PHOENIX

Tucson

Albuquerque

Santa Fe

Las Vegas

Ciudad Juárez

El Paso

Hermosillo

Fresno

Bakersfield

Mexicali

Tijuana

Flagstaff

I. de Guadalupe (Mexico)

ft   m
12,000
9000
6000
4500
3000
1500
1200
600
400
200
0
200 600
2000 6000
4000 12,000
m   ft

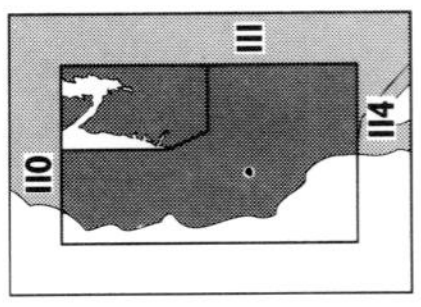

SEATTLE-PORTLAND REGION
On same scale

CANADA

WASHINGTON

OREGON

Vancouver Island

Olympic Mountains

NATIONAL PARK

Juan de Fuca Strait

Strait of Georgia

SEATTLE
Tacoma
Bremerton
Olympia
Everett
Bellingham
Victoria
Vancouver
Portland

PACIFIC OCEAN

NEVADA

CALIFORNIA

Sierra Nevada

SAN FRANCISCO
Oakland
San Jose
Sacramento
Stockton
Modesto
Fresno
Merced
Reno
Sparks
Santa Rosa
Napa
Vallejo
Concord
Monterey
Santa Cruz
Salinas
San Mateo
Palo Alto
Fremont

San Joaquin Valley

Santa Lucia Range

Inyo Mts.

White Mts.

Owens
Mono L.

YOSEMITE NATIONAL PARK

SEQUOIA NAT. PARK

Pahute Mesa

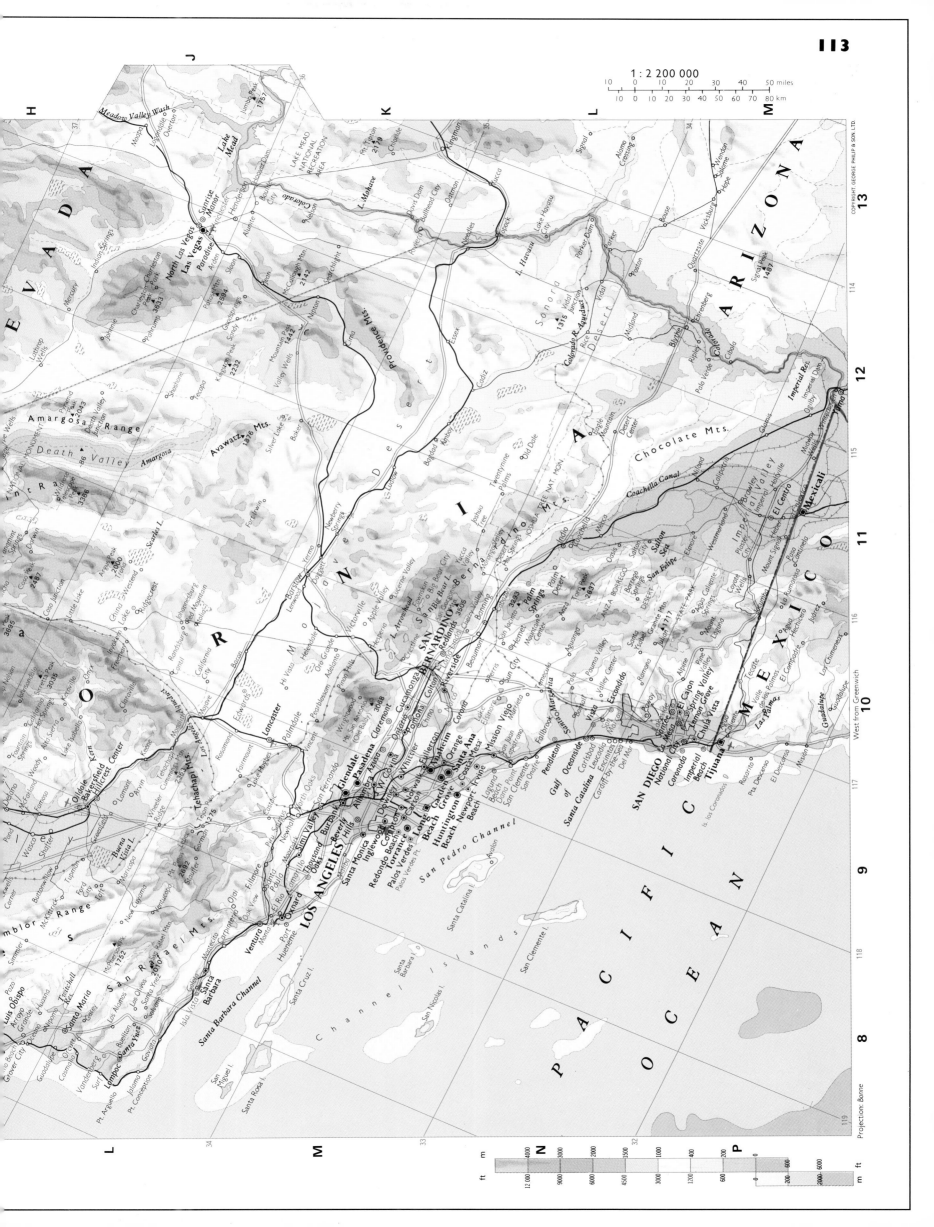

1 : 2 200 000

10   0   10   20   30   40   50 miles
10   0   10   20   30   40   50   60   70   80 km

NEVADA
H
J
Meadow Valley Wash
Jumbo Peak 1757
Overton
Logandale
Moapa
Indian Springs
Lake Mead
LAKE MEAD NATIONAL RECREATION AREA
Las Vegas
North Las Vegas
Sunrise Manor
Henderson
Paradise
Whitney
Arden
Mt Charleston
Charleston Peak 3633
Lee Canyon
Potosi 2594
Sloan
Boulder City
Hoover Dam
Davis Dam
Bullhead City
Kingman
Mt Tipton 2179
Chloride
Oatman
Yucca
Mt Callaghan 2142
Searchlight
Nipton
L. Mohave
Needles
Topock
L. Havasu
Lake Havasu City
Parker Dam
Bouse
Vidal
Parker
Poston
Mercury
Johnnie
Pahrump
Stewart
Mountain Pass 1442
Goodsprings
K
L
M
13
114
12
ARIZONA
Signal Peak 1487
Ehrenberg
Quartzsite
Vicksburg
Salome
Hope
Wendon
Aguila
Bouse
Blythe
Ripley
Palo Verde
Cibola
Colorado R. Aqueduct
Rice
Vidal Junction
Sonora
1315
Desert
Providence Mts.
Pt Tipton

Death Valley
Amargosa Range
NATIONAL MONUMENT
2043
Furnace Creek
Death Valley
3366
Panamint Range
Wildrose Peak
Telescope Peak 86
Amargosa
Shoshone
Tecopa
Silurian L.
Baker
Silver Lake
Avawatz Mts. 1876
Valley Wells
2232
Cima
Kelso
Sonora
Desert
Chocolate Mts.
Coachella Canal
Imperial Res.
Imperial Dam
Yuma

Ballarat
Darwin
Keeler
Owens L.
Coso Peak 2487
Coso Junction
China Lake
Little Lake
Ridgecrest
Inyokern
Red Mountain
Trona
Argus Peak 2040
Searles L.
Randsburg
Johannesburg
Atolia
Kramer Junction
Boron
Hinkley
Barstow
Lenwood
Daggett
Yermo
Newberry Springs
Ludlow
Bagdad
Amboy
Cadiz
Essex
Twentynine Palms
Joshua
Yucca Valley
JOSHUA TREE NAT. MON.
Old Dale
Desert Center
Eagle Mountain
Niland
Calipatria
Brawley
Westmorland
Imperial Valley
Holtville
El Centro
Seeley
Heber
Calexico
Mexicali
MEXICO
Salton Sea
Mecca
Coachella
Indio
Thermal
Salton City

MOJAVE
DESERT
3895
a
Walker Pass
Freeman
Cantil
Mojave
Rosamond
Edwards
California City
Kramer Junction
Hi Vista
Helendale
Oro Grande
Adelanto
Victorville
Hesperia
Apple Valley
Lucerne Valley
Big Bear City
Big Bear L.
L. Arrowhead
Running Springs
3068
Wrightwood
Mt San Antonio (Old Baldy) 3068
Cucamonga
Pomona
Chino
Corona
Riverside
Colton
Redlands
SAN BERNARDINO
San Jacinto
Beaumont
Banning
3505
Palm Springs
Desert Hot Springs
Palm Desert
Indian Wells
3293
Mt San Jacinto
Hemet
Perris
Sun City
Lake Elsinore
Temecula
Murrieta
San Bernardino Mts.
Berdoo
San Gorgonio Mtn.
Santa Ana
Mountain Center
Aguanga

Inyokern
Kernville
Isabella
Lake Isabella
Wofford Heights
Woody
Glennville
Caliente
Bodfish
Weldon
3035
Piute Peak
Mt Pinos 2692
Frazier Park
Lebec
Gorman
Lancaster
Palmdale
Vincent
Lake Hughes
Fairmont
Littlerock
Pearblossom
Valyermo

Bakersfield
Oildale
Hillcrest Center
Lamont
Arvin
Tehachapi
Tehachapi Mts.
2256
Keene
Mojave
Rosamond
Willow Springs
Neenach
Quail L.
Gorman
Castaic
Newhall
San Fernando
Pacoima
Sylmar
North Hills
Burbank
Glendale
Pasadena
Azusa
Glendora
Claremont
Ontario
W. Covina
El Monte
Alhambra
Pomona
Whittier
Fullerton
Anaheim
Orange
Santa Ana
Costa Mesa
Norwalk
Downey
Compton
Garden Grove
Westminster
Huntington Beach
Newport Beach
Irvine
Mission Viejo
Laguna Beach
San Juan Capistrano
Dana Point
San Clemente
San Onofre
Pendleton
Oceanside
Carlsbad
Leucadia
Encinitas
Cardiff-by-the-Sea
Del Mar
Escondido
San Marcos
Vista
Poway
Ramona
Santa Ysabel
Julian
Pine Valley
Alpine
El Cajon
La Mesa
SAN DIEGO
National City
Coronado
Imperial Beach
Chula Vista
Tijuana
Rosarito
Pta. Descanso
El Descanso
Tecate
Jacumba
El Centro

McKittrick
Taft
Maricopa
Cuyama
New Cuyama
Ventucopa
Ozena
Frazier Mtn 2692
Mt Pinos
Ojai
Ventura
Oak View
Fillmore
Santa Paula
Piru
Moorpark
Simi Valley
Thousand Oaks
Camarillo
Oxnard
Port Hueneme
El Rio
Montalvo
Saticoy
Carpinteria
Santa Barbara
Goleta
Santa Ynez
Los Olivos
Ballard
Buellton
Solvang
Lompoc
Surf
Vandenberg
Guadalupe
Santa Maria
Orcutt
Casmalia
Sisquoc
Garey
San Rafael Mts.
1752
Mt Abel
San Luis Obispo
Los Osos
Grover City
Arroyo Grande
Nipomo
Oceano
Pt Sal
Pismo Beach
Los Alamos

LOS ANGELES
Beverly Hills
Santa Monica
Inglewood
Culver City
El Segundo
Manhattan Beach
Hermosa Beach
Redondo Beach
Torrance
Palos Verdes Pt.
Long Beach
San Pedro
Avalon
Santa Catalina I.
San Pedro Channel
Is los Coronados
Gulf of Santa Catalina

Channel Islands
Santa Cruz I.
Santa Rosa I.
San Miguel I.
Santa Barbara I.
San Nicolas I.
San Clemente I.

PACIFIC
OCEAN

Pt Conception
Pt Arguello

C A L I F O R N I A
San Bernardino Mts.

Isla Vista
Santa Barbara Channel

West from Greenwich

9
10
11
12
115
116
117
118
119
8

L
M
N
P

Projection Bonne

m
ft
4000   12 000
3000   9000
2000   6000
1500   4500
1000   3000
600   1800
400   1200
200   600
0   0
0
200   600
2000   6000
m   ft

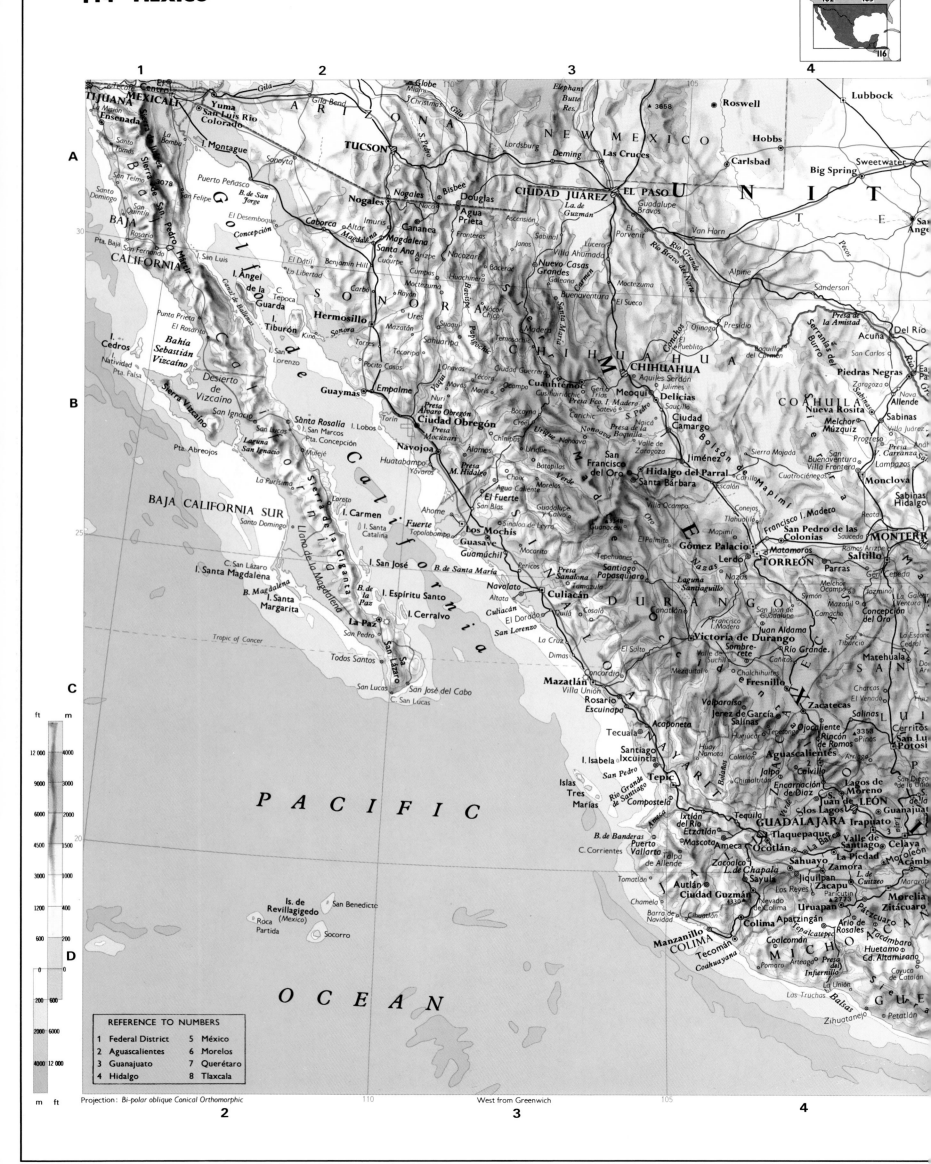

102 103
116
4

1   2   3   4

A

B

30

C

25

D

PACIFIC

OCEAN

Tropic of Cancer

ft   m
12 000   4000
9000   3000
6000   2000
4500   1500
3000   1000
1200   400
600   200
0   0
200   600
2000   6000
4000   12 000
m   ft

REFERENCE TO NUMBERS

1	Federal District	5	México
2	Aguascalientes	6	Morelos
3	Guanajuato	7	Querétaro
4	Hidalgo	8	Tlaxcala

Projection: *Bi-polar oblique Conical Orthomorphic*

110   West from Greenwich   105

2   3   4

Tijuana, Tecate, Mexicali, Ensenada, Yuma, San Luis Rio Colorado, San Felipe, ARIZONA, TUCSON, Nogales, Douglas, Agua Prieta, CIUDAD JUAREZ, EL PASO, NEW MEXICO, Las Cruces, Carlsbad, Hobbs, Big Spring, Sweetwater, Lubbock, Roswell

BAJA CALIFORNIA, Hermosillo, SONORA, Guaymas, Empalme, Ciudad Obregón, Navojoa, CHIHUAHUA, Delicias, Ciudad Camargo, Jiménez, COAHUILA, Nueva Rosita, Sabinas, Monclova, Piedras Negras, MONTERREY, Saltillo, Parras

BAJA CALIFORNIA SUR, La Paz, San José del Cabo, DURANGO, Victoria de Durango, Gómez Palacio, Lerdo, TORREÓN, Matehuala, Fresnillo, Zacatecas

PACIFIC OCEAN, Mazatlán, Rosario, Acaponeta, Tepic, NAYARIT, Aguascalientes, San Luis Potosí, GUADALAJARA, Irapuato, Celaya, Colima, COLIMA, Manzanillo, MICHOACÁN, Morelia, Uruapan

Is. de Revillagigedo (Mexico), Socorro, Roca Partida, San Benedicto

1 : 7 100 000

50   0   50   100   150   200 miles
50   0   100   200   300 km

5   **6**   **7**   **8**

Wichita
Falls
Denison Paris Hope
Sherman Texarkana Camden
Denton Greenville Texarkana El Dorado ARKANSAS Greenville MISSISSIPPI Tuscaloosa Opelika McRae
FORT WORTH DALLAS Marshall Monroe Vicksburg Meridian Montgomery Phenix City Columbus Ogmulgee
Ranger Longview Shreveport Tallulah Jackson Selma Troy Americus Cordele
bilene Cleburne Tyler Natchez Laurel Alabama Dothan Albany GEORGIA Tifton Waycross
Hillsboro Corsicana Toledo Alexandria Hattiesburg Jim Woodruff Valdosta
Brownwood Palestine Bend Nacogdoches McComb Bogalusa Res. Tallahassee
Waco Res. Lufkin Baton Biloxi Pensacola FLORIDA Lake
Temple Sam Rouge Hammond MOBILE Panama City City
Huntsville Rayburn Res. Gulfport C. San Blas Apalachee
Austin Bryan Lake Charles L. Pontchartrain Bay Suwannee
Beaumont Lafayette NEW Breton Sound
HOUSTON Port ORLEANS Mobile Bay
Rosenberg Arthur Atchafalaya Mississippi
SAN Galveston Bay Delta Clearwater
ANTONIO Victoria Terrebonne B.

GULF   OF

Alice Corpus Christi
Laredo Kingsville
Nuevo Laredo
Zapata
Laguna Madre
Camargo Mc Allen Harlingen
Presa Reynosa Brownsville
M.R. Gomez Matamoros
China Valle Hermoso
Montemorelos Santa Teresa
Mendez Laguna Madre
Linares San Fernando

M E X I C O

Tropic of Cancer

C

CUBA
Guane
La Fé
La Esperanza
Ciudad La Pesca Corrientes
Victoria Soto la Marina
Sierra de Isla
Tamaulipas Desterrada C. San Antonio
Ciudad Mante Isla Pérez
Pta. Jerez
Ciudad Madero Canal de Yucatán
Aldama Pta. Rio Lagartos C. Catoche
Ciudad de Tampico Yalkubul El Cuyo Cancún
Valles Altamira Dzilam Pto. Juárez
Pánuco de Bravo Temax Tizimín
Laguna de Tamiahua Progreso Motul Izamal Espita Puerto Morelos
Tempoal Mérida Sotuta Valladolid
Tantoyuca C. Rojo YUCATÁN Isla
Tamazunchale Macanú Ticul Cozumel
Tuxpan Uxmal Tekax Peto Cozumel
Chicontepec Tenabo Bolonchenticul Vigía Chico
Poza Rica Campeche B. de la Ascensión
Papantla Hopelchen
Juan del Rio Nautla Champotón Felipe Carrillo B. del Espíritu Santo
Pachuca Huauchinango Chenkán Puerto QUINTANA
Tula Tulancingo ROO Banco
Teziutlán Jalapa Golfo Chinchorro
MÉXICO Enríquez de Bacalar
Tlaxcala Zempoala Campeche Chetumal B. de
PUEBLA Coatepec Veracruz Ciudad del Corozo Chetumal
luca Orizaba Llave Carmen Laguna de Términos Matamoros
Citlaltépetl Alvarado CAMPECHE Orange Walk Ambergris Cay
Córdoba Tlacotalpan Frontera
Cuernavaca Tehuacán San Andrés Coatzacoalcos Palizada Concepción Hondo Turneffe Is.
Cosamaloapan Tuxtla Paraiso Belize
Iguala La Venta Comalcalco City
Chilapa Acatlán Miguel TABASCO Villahermosa BELIZE
Chilpancingo Huajuapan Alemán Cárdenas Uaxactún Belmopan Dangriga
de León San Juan Acayucan Tikal San Ignacio
Oaxaca Asunción Bautista Minatitlán Benque Islas de
Monte Nochixtlán Jesús Carranza L. Petén Itza Viejo la Bahía
Acapulco Albán Valle Nacional La Libertad Flores Roatán Puerto
Tlaxiaco Copanalá Palenque Monkey River Castilla
Ometepec Trinidad Presa Simojovel San Luis Maya Mts. San Pedro Sula
Ocotlán Netzahualcóyotl Ocosingo San Antonio Puerto Cortés La Ceiba
Chilpa Ixtepec Matías Romero San Cristóbal de Tela
Ejutla Tehuantepec las Casas Usumacinta Punta Gorda Puerto Barrios
Tututepec Juchitán Tuxtla CHIAPA Livingston
Miahuatlán Istmo Gutiérrez La Independencia Sa. de las Minas
Salina Cruz de Comitán Sebol HONDURAS
Pochutla Tehuantepec GUATEMALA Cobán Zacapa Santa Bárbara
Puerto Golfo de Mar Muerto La Concordia Cuchumatanes El Jaral Santa Rosa Juticalpa
Escondido Tehuantepec Pijijiapan Motozintla Huehuetenango de Copán
Puerto Ángel Mapastepec Huixtla Totonicapán Jalapa Chiquimula Tegucigalpa
Tapachula San Marcos Quez. Antigua La Paz Danlí
Coatepeque Mazate- GUATEMALA Yuscarán
Ocós Retalhuleu nango Amatitlán

COPYRIGHT. GEORGE PHILIP & SON. LTD.

5   **6**   **7**

1 2 3 4

A

25

GULF OF MEXICO

U.S.A.

L. Okeechobee
West Palm Beach
Fort Myers
Fort Lauderdale
Boca Raton
Naples
C. Romano
Everglades
Hialeah
MIAMI
Little Abaco I.
Grand Bahama I.
Freeport
Great Abaco I.
Northwest Providence Channel
Bimini Is.
Berry Is.
Nassau
New Providence
Eleuthera
Great Exuma I.
Jumentos Cays

Isla Desterrada
Isla Pérez

B

C. Sable
Florida Bay
Key West
Dry Tortugas
Florida City
Florida Keys
Straits of Florida
Santaren Channel
Cay Sal Bank

(Havana) LA HABANA
San Antonio de los Baños
MARIANAO
Guanabacoa
Guanajay
Bahía Honda
La Esperanza
Matanzas
Colón
Cárdenas
Sagua la Grande
Santa Clara
Caibarién
Canal Nicolás
Canal Viejo de Bahama

Pinar del Río
Los Palacios
Güines
Batabanó
Jagüey Grande
Jovellanos
Placetas
Morón
Cayo Romano
Duncan Town

Guane
La Fé
San Luis
Nueva Gerona
Cienfuegos
Trinidad
Sancti-Spíritus
Ciego de Ávila
Florida
Camagüey
Nuevitas
Puerto Manati
Puerto Padre
Gibara
Holguín

Corrientes
Isla de la Juventud
Archipiélago de los Canarreos
Júcaro
Tunas de Zaza
Arch. de los Jardines de la Reina
Santa Cruz del Sur
Golfo de Guacanayabo
Victoria de las Tunas
Bayamo
Manzanillo
Palma Soriano
C. Cruz
Sierra Maestra 2000
SANTIAGO DE CUBA

GREATER

C U B A

20

Cayman Islands (Br.)
Georgetown
Grand Cayman
7680
Cayman Brac
Little Cayman

Montego Bay
Lucea
Falmouth
St. Ann's Bay
Savanna la Mar
South Negril Pt.
Black River
Mandeville
May Pen
Spanish Town
KINGSTON
Port Antonio
Port Maria
JAMAICA
Pedro Cays (Jamaica)

Progreso
Pta. Yalkubul
Río Lagartos
C. Catoche
Dzilam de Bravo
Cancún
Pta. Juárez
Mérida
Motul
Izamal
Temax
Tizimín
Valladolid
El Diaz
Cozumel
Isla Cozumel
Puerto Morelos

Campeche
Ticul
Tekax
Peto
Vigía Chico
Champotón
Hopelchén
B. de la Ascensión

Ciudad del Carmen
CAMPECHE
Laguna de Términos
QUINTANA ROO
Chetumal
B. de Chetumal
Banco Chinchorro
B. del Espíritu Santo

YUCATÁN
Chichén Itzá
Mayapán

Palizada
Balancán
Chenkán

C

Ambergris Cay

Palenque
L. Petén Itzá
La Libertad
Flores
BELIZE
Belize City
Middlesex
Benque Viejo
Dangriga
Turneffe Is.

Ocosingo
Tikal
Uaxactún
Belmopan
San Ignacio
Maya Mts.
Swan Islands (U.S.A. & Honduras)

Comitán
La Independencia
San Luis
San Antonio
Monkey River
Punta Gorda
Golfo de Honduras
Islas de la Bahía

3993
GUATEMALA
Cobán
Huehuetenango
Puerto Barrios
Livingston
L. de Izabal
Puerto Cortés
Tela
La Ceiba
Roatán
Puerto Castilla
Trujillo
C. Camarón
Balfate
Iriona
Pta. Patuca
Brus Laguna
Laguna Caratasca

San Marcos
Totonicapán
Sololá
Zacapa
HONDURAS
San Pedro Sula
El Progreso
Santa Bárbara
Sa. de las Minas
Catacamas
Mosquitia
C. Falso
Bajo Nuevo (Colombia)

Antigua
GUATEMALA
Chiquimula
Santa Rosa de Copán
Yoro
Comayagua
Juticalpa
Patuca
C. Gracias á Dios
Puerto Cabo Gracias á Dios

Quezaltenango
Amatitlán
Escuintla
Tegucigalpa
Danlí
Coco (Segovia)
Kisalaya

CARIB

Ahuachapán
Santa Ana
Suchitoto
Cojutepeque
La Paz
Cayos Miskitos (Nicaragua)
Pta. Gorda
I. de Providencia (Colombia)

D

SAN SALVADOR
Usulután
Zacatecoluca
San Miguel
EL SALVADOR
Choluteca
Estelí
Cord. Isabelia
Tuma
San Pedro del Norte
Tungla
Bonanza
Siuna
Prinzapolca

Chinandega
NICARAGUA
Matagalpa
Muy Muy
Río Grande
I. de San Andrés (Colombia)
Cayos de Albuquerque (Colombia)

Corinto
León
Boaco
Siquia
Santo Domingo
Rama
Pta. de Perlas
Cayos Roncador (U.S.A. & Colombia)

La Paz Centro
MANAGUA
Masaya
Juigalpa
Bluefields
Diriamba
Granada
Lago de Nicaragua
Cord. de Yolaina
El Bluff
Islas del Maíz (Nicaragua, U.S.A.)
Pta. Mico

San Juan del Sur
B. de Salinas
Rivas
San Carlos
Bahía de San Juan del Norte
C. Sta. Elena
San Juan
San Juan del Norte

Golfo de Papagayo
Liberia
COSTA
10
Santa Cruz
Nicoya
Cord. de Guanacaste
Cord. Central
Guápiles
Siquirres
Limón

C. Velas
Puntarenas
Alajuela
San José
Pta. Mona

Pen. de Nicoya
Golfo de Nicoya
Cartago
Esparza
RICA
Cord. de Talamanca
Is. de San Bernardo

C. Blanco
3837
Puerto Quepos
3374
Golfo de los Mosquitos
Colón
Archipiélago de San Blas
Golfo del Darién

E

Bahía de Coronado
Puerto Cortés
Buenos Aires
Boquete
David
Serranía de Tabasará
La Chorrera
PANAMÁ
Serranía del Darién

Pen. de Osa
Golfito
Puerto Armuelles
Pta. Burica
Golfo Dulce
Santiago
Chitré
Golfo de Panamá
Las Tablas
El Real

I. de Coiba
I. de Cébaco
I. Jicarón
Pen. de Azuero
Pocrí
Pta. Mala
Jaqué

CARTAG

CARIBBEAN

90 85 80

1 2 3 4

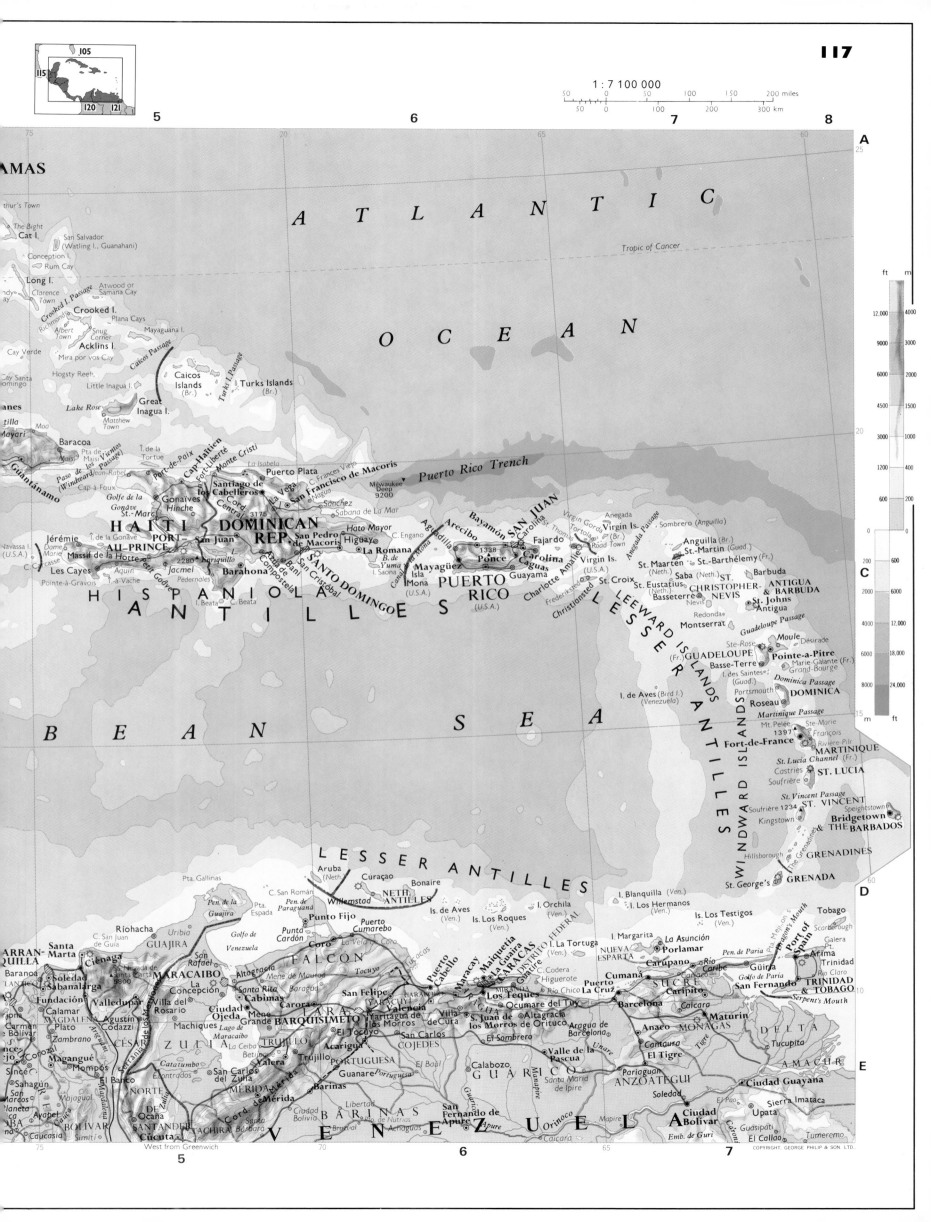

1 : 7 100 000

50   0   50   100   150   200 miles
50   0   100   200   300 km

5   **6**   **7**   **8**

75   70   65   60

A

AMAS

ar's Town
The Bight
Cat I.
San Salvador
(Watling I., Guanahani)
Conception I.
Rum Cay
Long I.
Clarence Town
Cay Verde
Crooked I. Passage
Richmond
Albert Town
Snug Corner
Acklins I.
Mira por vos Cay
Hogsty Reefs
Plana Cays
Mayaguana I.
Crooked I.
ndy
Cay Santa
omingo
Little Inagua I.
Caicos Passage
Turks I. Passage
Caicos Islands (Br.)
Turks Islands (Br.)
Lake Rose
Great Inagua I.
Matthew Town
Cay Verde
tilla
Mayari
Moa
Baracoa
Pta. de Maisí
Paso de los Vientos (Windward Passage)
Port-de-Paix
Î. de la Tortue
Cap-Haïtien
Fort-Liberté
Monte Cristi
La Isabela
Puerto Plata
C. Frances Viejo
San Francisco de Macorís
Nagua
Guantánamo
Cap-à-Foux
Jean-Rabel
Santiago de los Cabelleros
La Vega
1338
Sánchez
Sabana de la Mar
Milwaukee Deep 9200
Puerto Rico Trench
A T L A N T I C

O C E A N

Tropic of Cancer

Guantánamo
Golfe de la Gonâve
St.-Marc
Gonaïves
Hinche
Cord. Central
3175
Hato Mayor
C. Engano
Aguadilla
Arecibo
Bayamón
San Juan
Carolina
St. Thomas
Virgin Gorda
Virgin Is. (Br.)
Anegada
Anegada Passage
Sombrero (Anguilla)
Jérémie
Î. de la Gonâve
Dame Marie
Navassa I. (U.S.A.)
HAITI
PORT-AU-PRINCE
San Juan
DOMINICAN REP.
San Pedro de Macorís
Higüey
La Romana
B. de Yuma
Mayagüez
Isla Mona (U.S.A.)
Ponce
Fajardo
Carolina
Caguas
Guayama
Virgin Is. (U.S.A.)
Charlotte Amalie
St. Croix
Christiansted
Frederiksted
Road Town
Tortola
Anguilla (Br.)
St.-Martin (Guad.)
St.-Barthélemy (Fr.)
St. Maarten (Neth.)
Saba (Neth.)
St. Eustatius (Neth.)
Basseterre
Nevis
ST. CHRISTOPHER-NEVIS
Barbuda
ANTIGUA & BARBUDA
St. Johns
Antigua
Redonda
Montserrat

Les Cayes
Massif de la Hotte
Pointe-à-Gravois
I.-à-Vache
C. C.
Aquin
Barton Godève
Jacmel
2280
Enriquillo
Azua
Bani
San Cristóbal
Compostela
Pedernales
Barahona
SANTO DOMINGO
Canal de la Mona
Isla Saona
I. Beata
C. Beata
PUERTO RICO
L E S S E R
LEEWARD ISLANDS
Guadeloupe Passage
Ste-Rose
Moule
Désirade
GUADELOUPE (Fr.)
Basse-Terre
Pointe-à-Pitre
Marie-Galante (Fr.)
Grand-Bourg
I. des Saintes (Guad.)
Dominica Passage
Portsmouth
DOMINICA
Roseau

H I S P A N I O L A
A N T I L L E S

I. de Aves (Bird I.) (Venezuela)

B E A N   S E A

A N T I L L E S

Martinique Passage
Mt. Pelée 1397
Ste-Marie
François
Rivière-Pil.
Fort-de-France
MARTINIQUE
St. Lucia Channel (Fr.)
Castries
ST. LUCIA
Soufrière
St. Vincent Passage
Soufrière 1234
ST. VINCENT
Speightstown
Kingstown
Bridgetown
THE BARBADOS
Hillsborough
The Grenadines
GRENADINES
St. George's
GRENADA

C

D

WINDWARD ISLANDS

L E S S E R   A N T I L L E S

Aruba (Neth)
Curaçao
Bonaire
Willemstad
NETH. ANTILLES
Is. de Aves (Ven.)
I. Orchila (Ven.)
Is. Los Roques (Ven.)
I. Blanquilla (Ven.)
I. Los Hermanos (Ven.)
I. Los Testigos (Ven.)
Tobago
Scarborough
Galera Pt.

Pta. Gallinas
Pen. de la Guajira
Pta. Espada
C. San Román
Pen. de Paraguaná
Punto Fijo
Puerto Cumarebo
Coro
La Vela de Coro
I. La Tortuga (Ven.)
I. Margarita
La Asunción
NUEVA ESPARTA
Porlamar
Pen. de Paria
Pta. Mejdpo S
Dragon's Mouth
Port of Spain
Arima
Trinidad

ARRAN-
QUILLA
Ríohacha
Uribia
GUAJIRA
C. San Juan de Guía
Golfo de Venezuela
Punta Cardón
La Concepción
FALCÓN
Tucacas
Puerto Cabello
Maiquetía
La Guaira
CARACAS
DISTRITO FEDERAL
Guatire
C. Codera
Higuerote
Carúpano
Río Caribe
Cariaco
Güiria
SUCRE
Cumaná
Carúpano
Serpent's Mouth
San Fernando
TRINIDAD & TOBAGO

Santa Marta
Cienaga
San Rafael
Altagracia
Mene de Mauroa
Baragua
MARACAIBO
Cabimas
Carora
San Felipe
Yaracuy
YARACUY
Valencia
Maracay
Villa de Cura
MIRANDA
Los Teques
Ocumare del Tuy
Río Chico
Puerto La Cruz
Barcelona
Calcara
Anaco
MONAGAS
Maturín
DELTA AMACUR
Tucupita

Baranoa
Soledad
Sabanalarga
Fundación
Calamar
 Agustín
MAGDALENA
Plato
Zambrano
Valledupar
Villa del Rosario
CÉSAR
Machiques
Ciudad Ojeda
Grande
BARQUISIMETO
El Tocuyo
LARA
San Carlos
S. Juan de los Morros
Villa de Altagracia
Valle de la Pascua
Calabozo
GUÁRICO
Valle de la Pascua
El Sombrero
Aragua de Barcelona
El Tigre
Cantaura
Pariaguan
ANZOÁTEGUI
Soledad
El Pao
Ciudad Guayana
Upata
Sierra Imataca
El Callao
Tumeremo

Magangué
Mompós
Banco
BOLÍVAR
SANTANDER
Ocaña
NORTE
Pamplona
TÁCHIRA
San Carlos del Zulia
MÉRIDA
Mérida
Trujillo
TRUJILLO
Valera
Betijoque
PORTUGUESA
Guanare
Acarigua
COJEDES
San Carlos
El Baúl
Ciudad Bolivia
BARINAS
Barinas
Libertad
San Fernando de Apure
Achaguas
V E N E Z U E L A
Apure
Río de Nutrias
Embalse de Guri
Ciudad Bolívar
Caicara
Caura
Guasipati
Tumeremo

E

West from Greenwich

5   **6**   **7**

75   70   65

COPYRIGHT. GEORGE PHILIP & SON. LTD.

105
115   120   121

1 : 31 100 000

200   0   200   400   600   800 miles
400   0   200   400   600   800   1200 km

Projection: Lambert's Azimuthal Equal Area

30 CARTOGRAPHY BY PHILIP'S
COPYRIGHT REED INTERNATIONAL BOOKS LTD

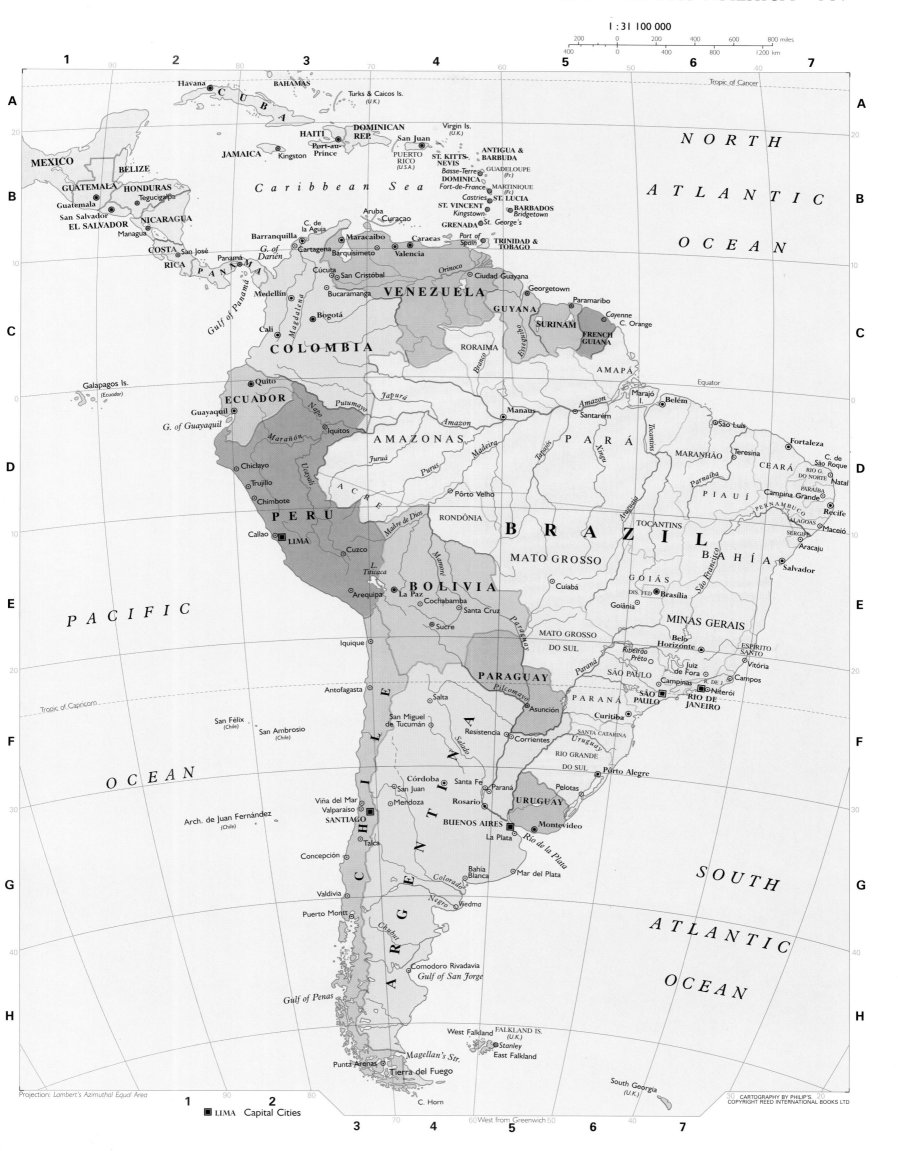

1 : 31 100 000

200   0   400   600   800 miles
400   0   400   800   1200 km

1   90   **2**   80   **3**   70   **4**   **5**   50   **6**   40   **7**

Tropic of Cancer

A

Havana   BAHAMAS   Turks & Caicos Is. (U.K.)
CUBA

N O R T H

HAITI   DOMINICAN REP.   Virgin Is. (U.K.)
Port-au-Prince   San Juan
JAMAICA   Kingston   PUERTO RICO (U.S.A.)   ST. KITTS-NEVIS   ANTIGUA & BARBUDA
Basse-Terre   GUADELOUPE (Fr.)
DOMINICA
A T L A N T I C

MEXICO   BELIZE
GUATEMALA   HONDURAS   *Caribbean Sea*   Fort-de-France   MARTINIQUE (Fr.)
Guatemala   Castries   ST. LUCIA
San Salvador   Tegucigalpa   ST. VINCENT   BARBADOS
EL SALVADOR   NICARAGUA   Kingstown   Bridgetown
Managua   GRENADA   St. George's
COSTA   San José   Aruba   Curaçao   *O C E A N*
RICA   Panamá   Barranquilla   Maracaibo   Caracas   Port of Spain   TRINIDAD & TOBAGO
C. de la Aguja   Valencia
G. of Darién   Cartagena   Barquisimeto
Medellín   Cúcuta   San Cristóbal   *Orinoco*   Ciudad Guayana
Bucaramanga   VENEZUELA   Georgetown   Paramaribo
Bogotá   GUYANA   SURINAM   Cayenne
Cali   RORAIMA   FRENCH GUIANA   C. Orange

C

COLOMBIA   *Branco*   AMAPÁ

Galapagos Is. (Ecuador)   Quito   Equator
ECUADOR   *Napo*   *Putumayo*   *Japurá*   Marajó I.   Belém
Guayaquil   *Amazon*   Manaus   Santarém   São Luís
G. of Guayaquil   *Marañón*   Iquitos   AMAZONAS   *Amazon*   Fortaleza
Chiclayo   *Juruá*   *Purus*   *Madeira*   PARÁ   MARANHÃO   Teresina   C. de São Roque
Trujillo   *Ucayali*   ACRE   *Xingu*   *Tocantins*   CEARÁ   Natal
Chimbote   Pôrto Velho   *Iriri*   PIAUÍ   PARAÍBA   Campina Grande
PERU   RONDÔNIA   *Araguaia*   PERNAMBUCO   Recife
Callao   LIMA   Madre de Dios   B R A Z I L   TOCANTINS   ALAGOAS   Maceió
Cuzco   MATO GROSSO   SERGIPE   Aracaju
L. Titicaca   *Mamoré*   *São Francisco*   BAHÍA   Salvador
Arequipa   BOLIVIA   Cuiabá   GOIÁS   DIS. FED.   Brasília
La Paz   Cochabamba   Goiânia   MINAS GERAIS
Sucre   Santa Cruz   Belo Horizonte   ESPÍRITO SANTO
Iquique   MATO GROSSO DO SUL   Ribeirão Prêto   Juiz de Fora   Vitória
Paraguay   SÃO PAULO   Campos
PACIFIC   *Paraná*   PARANÁ   SÃO PAULO   Campinas   R. DE J.   Niterói
Antofagasta   PARAGUAY   *Pilcomayo*   RIO DE JANEIRO
Tropic of Capricorn   Salta   Asunción   Curitiba
San Félix (Chile)   San Miguel de Tucumán   SANTA CATARINA
San Ambrosio (Chile)   Resistencia   Corrientes   *Uruguay*
O C E A N   RIO GRANDE DO SUL
Saladillo   Pôrto Alegre
Córdoba   Santa Fe   Paraná   Pelotas
Arch. de Juan Fernández (Chile)   San Juan   Rosario   URUGUAY
Viña del Mar   Mendoza   Montevideo
Valparaíso   SANTIAGO   BUENOS AIRES   *Rio de la Plata*
Talca   La Plata
Concepción   *Colorado*   Bahía Blanca   Mar del Plata   *S O U T H*

Negro   Valdivia   Viedma
Puerto Montt   *Chubut*   A R G E N T I N A   *A T L A N T I C*

Comodoro Rivadavia
Gulf of San Jorge   *O C E A N*

Gulf of Penas

H

West Falkland   FALKLAND IS. (U.K.)
Stanley
Magellan's Str.   East Falkland
Punta Arenas
Tierra del Fuego   South Georgia (U.K.)

C. Horn

Projection: *Lambert's Azimuthal Equal Area*

1   90   **2**

■ LIMA   Capital Cities

3   70   **4**   60 West from Greenwich   **5**   50   **6**   40   **7**

CARTOGRAPHY BY PHILIP'S
COPYRIGHT REED INTERNATIONAL BOOKS LTD

Projection: Lambert's Equivalent Azimuthal

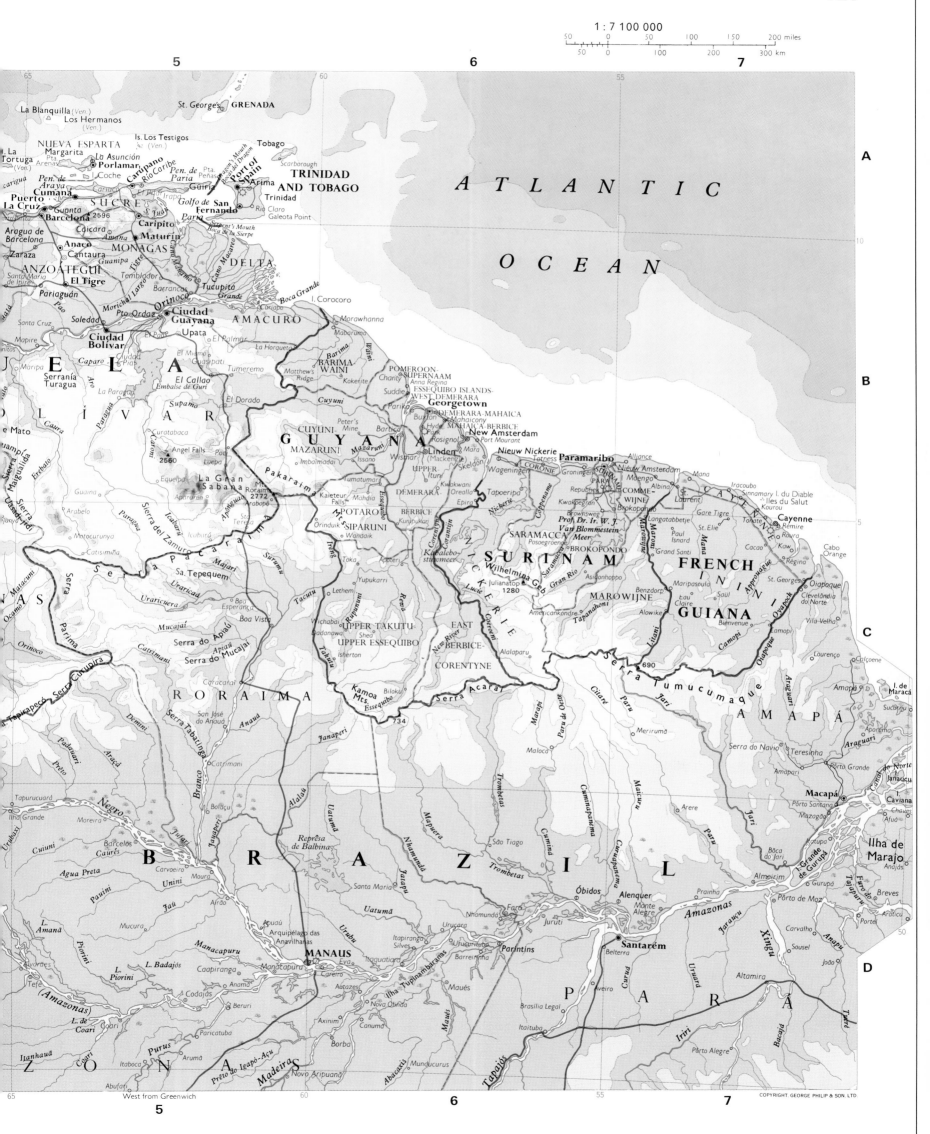

1 : 7 100 000

| | 50 | | 0 | 50 | | 100 | 150 | 200 miles |

| | 50 | 0 | | 100 | 200 | 300 km |

5   6   7

La Blanquilla (Ven.)
Los Hermanos (Ven.)   St. George's GRENADA

La Tortuga (Ven.)
NUEVA ESPARTA   Margarita   Is. Los Testigos (Ven.)   Tobago
Pta. Arenas   La Asunción   Scarborough

Porlamar   Coche
Cumaná   Carúpano   Pen. de Paria   Pta. Peñas   Port of Spain   TRINIDAD
Pen. de Araya   Rio Caribe   Güiria   Arima   AND TOBAGO
Puerto La Cruz   SUCRE   Trinidad
Barcelona   2596   Golfo de San   San Fernando   Claro
Caicara   Amana   Maturín   Pari   Galeota Point

A T L A N T I C

Aragua de Barcelona   Anaco   Cantaura   MONAGAS   DELTA
ANZOÁTEGUI   Guanipa   Tigre   Temblador
Santa Maria de Ipire   El Tigre   Barrancas   Caño Mariusa
Pariaguán   Pao   Morichal Largo   Orinoco   Tucupita   Boca Grande

O C E A N

Zaraza   Soledad   Pto. Ordaz   Ciudad Guayana   AMACURO   I. Corocoro
Mapire   Santa Cruz   Ciudad Bolívar   Coriapa   Morawhanna
Caparo   Ciudad Piar   Upata   El Palmar   La Horqueta   Mabaruma

M100 y   Maripa   Serranía Turagua   El Miamo   BARIMA   Waini
Arú   Guasipati   Tumeremo   WAINI   Pomeroon   Morawhanna
e Mato   Caura   BOLÍVAR   Matthew's Ridge   SUPERNAAM
Sierra Magualida   La Paragua   El Callao   Kokerite   Anna Regina   B
Erebato   Embalse de Guri   El Dorado   Charity   Suddie   ESSEQUIBO ISLANDS-
Sierra   Supamo   Cuyuni   WEST DEMERARA
Curutabaca   Paragua   Pariko   Georgetown
Caroní   Angel Falls   Peter's Mine   Bartica   Buxton   DEMERARA-MAHAICA
2560   GUYANA   Hyde Park   Mahaicony   New Amsterdam
Guaina   Imbaimadai   CUYUNI-   Issano   MAHAICA-BERBICE
Arabelo   La Gran Sabana   MAZARUNI   Wismar   Rosignol   Port Mourant
        Equelpa   Mt. Roraima   Mazaruni   Linden   Mara   CORONIE   Paramaribo
        Aparurén   2772   Kaieteur Falls   (Mackenzie)   Skeldon   Totness   Nieuw Nickerie   Nieuw Amsterdam
Matacurunya   Pakaraima   Tumatumari   UPPER-   Wageningen   Groningen   PARA   Moengo   Mana
Icabaru   Sta. Teresa   Arabopó   Mahdia   ITUNI   Kwakwani   Orealla   Republiek   COMME-   Albina   Iracoubo
Catisimiña   Icubutú   POTARO-   Orinduik   DEMERARA-   Tapoeripa   Nickerie   Brownsweg   WIJNE   Laurent   Iles du Salut
Sierra del Zamuro   Sa. Tepequem   SIPARUNI   Wandaik   BERBICE   Kwakoegron   Brokopondo   Gare Tigre   Kourou
Arabopó   Majari   Surumu   Kunjpukuari   Kubalebo-   Z   Asídonhopo   Paul Isnard   St. Elie   Cayenne
Mucajaí   Urancaá   Urarícoara   Boa Esperança   Toka   Apoteri   stinnmeer   SARAMACCA   Wilhelmina Geb   Grand Santi   Rémire
Serra do Apiaú   Surumu   Lethem   Yupukarri   Reru   I   Van Blommestein   BROKOPONDO   FRENCH   Roura   Cacao
Serra   Boa Vista   Wichabai   Isherton   UPPER TAKUTU-   C   Meer   Posoegroene   GUIANA   Regina
Partima   Catrimani   Serra do Mucajaí   Shea   UPPER ESSEQUIBO   New River   K   SURINAM   MAROWIJNE   Benzdorp   St. Georges
Serra   Caracaraí   Majari   Takutu   EAST   E   Americankondre   Tapanahoni   Maripasoula   Bienvenue   I. de Maracá
Serra Cucupira   San José do Anaud   Anaud   BERBICE-   R   Alalaparu   690   Saul   Approuague   Cleveländia do Norte
Tapirapecó   Demini   ESSEQUIBO   CORENTYNE   I   MAROWIJNE   Alowiki   Camopi   Vila-Velha
Orinoco   Serra Tabatinga   Catrimani   Kamoa Mts.   Biloku   E   Ciiaré   Litani   Oyapock
Padauari   Branco   Janapari   734   Serra Acarai   Marapi   Serra Tumucumaque   Camopi   Lourenço
Preto   Bolaçu   RORAIMA   Essequibo   Maloca   Paru de Oeste   Paru   Jari   Amapá   Calçoene   C
Araçá   Jufari   Alalaú   Uatumã   Meriruma   Serra do Navio   Aporema   Araguari   I. de Maracá

Negro   Uatumã   Mapuera   São Tiago   Trombetas   Camutapanema   Teresinha   Pôrto Grande   Canal do Norte
Barcelos   Moura   Represa de Balbinas   Nhamundá   Maloca   Cuminá   Carapapori   Macapá   I. Janaucu
B   R   A   Z   I   L
Agua Preta   Carvoeiro   Jaú   Uini   Japurá   Uatumã   Santa Maria   Nhamundá   Maicuru   Amapari   Jari   I. Caviana
Cuiuni   Apuaú   Urubu   Silves   Faro   Óbidos   Alenquer   Monte Alegre   Pôrto Santana   Mazagão   I. Grande de Gurupá
L. Amana   Mucura   Afuá   Arquipélago das Anavilhanas   Uruca   Nhamundá   Juruti   Faro   Belterra   Amazonas   Pôrto de Moz   Ilha de Marajó
Manacapuru   Manacapura   Nova Obidas   Itapiranga   Uruçurituba   Parintins   Santarém   Prainha   Almeirim   Gurupá   Breves
L. Badajós   Caapiranga   Anamã   MANAUS   Eva   Itacoatiara   Barreirinha   Maués   Canal do Norte   Sousel   João   Araticu
Piorini   Careiro   Autazes   D
L. Piorini   (Amazonas)   Codajás   Canumá   Axinim   Aveiro   Brasília Legal   Cuiabá   Altamira   Anapu   Portel
Beruri   Nova Aripuana   Maués   Itaituba   PARÁ   Xingu   Faro do Jari
Tefé   L. de Coari   Borba   Canumã   Mundurucus   Tapajós   Pôrto Alegre   Bacajá
Z   O   N   A   P   A   R   Á
Itanhauã   Coari   Purus   Itacoa   Abacaxis   Iriri   50
L. de Coari   Paricatuba   Preto do Igapó-Açu   Madeiras
Abufari

West from Greenwich   60   6   55   7

5   6   7

COPYRIGHT. GEORGE PHILIP & SON, LTD.

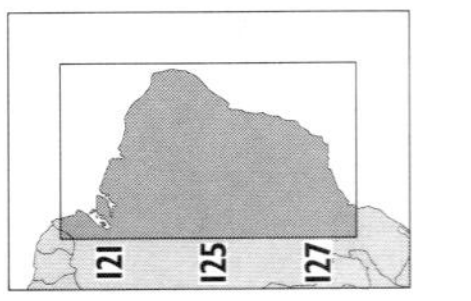

A T L A N T I C   O C E A N

FORTALEZA (Ceará)

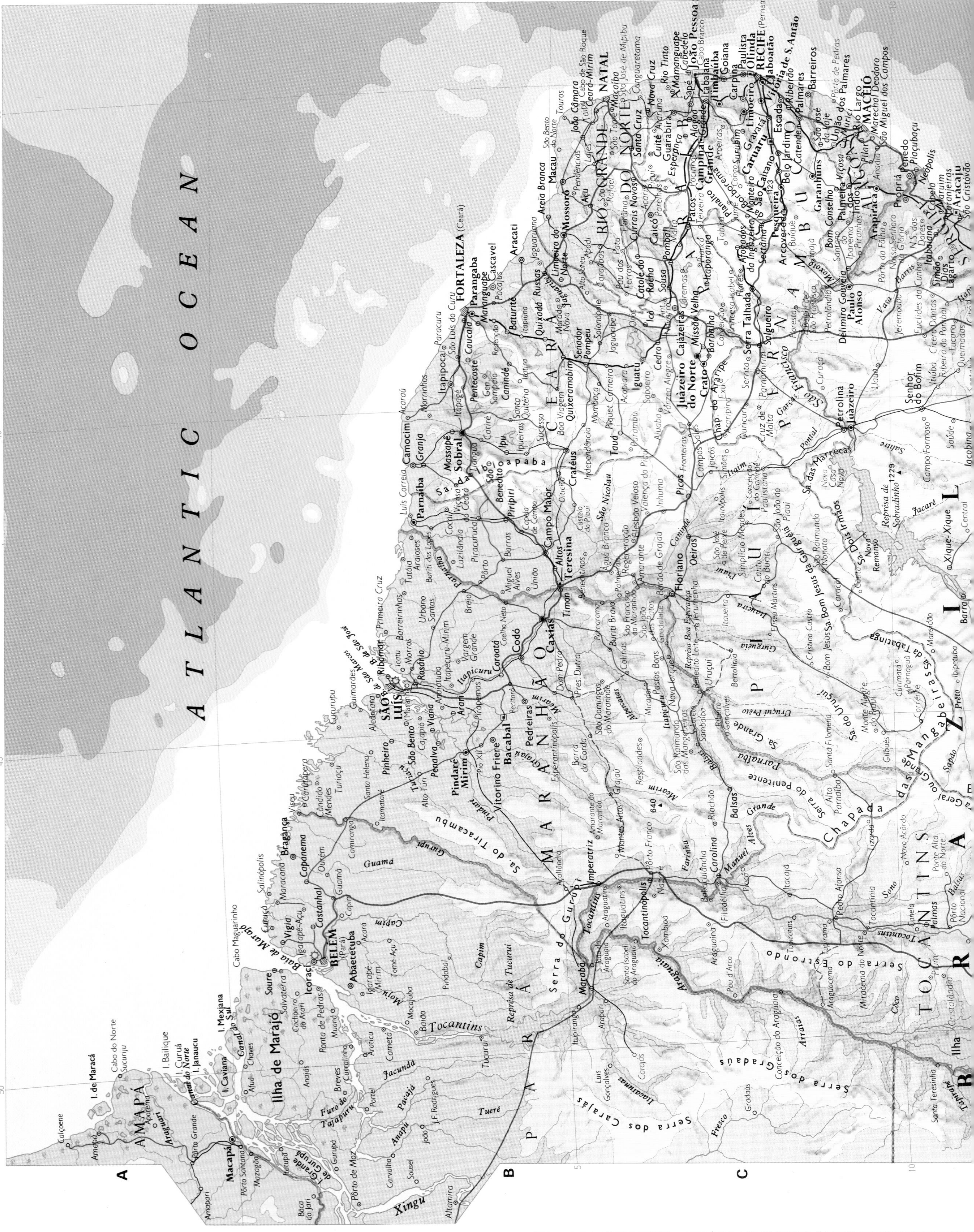

NATAL

RECIFE (Pernambuco)

MACEIÓ

João Pessoa (Paraíba)

Olinda

SÃO LUÍS

BELÉM (Pará)

Macapá

A M A P Á

Ilha de Marajó

Baía de Marajó

P A R Á

M A R A N H Ã O

C E A R Á

RIO GRANDE DO NORTE

P A R A Í B A

P E R N A M B U C O

A L A G Ô A S

P I A U Í

T O C A N T I N S

B A H I A

Teresina

Timon

Caxias

Codó

Sobral

Parnaíba

Camocim

Granja

Mossoró

Macau

Aracati

Cascavel

Baturité

Quixadá

Russas

Iguatu

Crato

Juàzeiro do Norte

Patos

Campina Grande

Garanhuns

Petrolina

Juàzeiro

Floriano

Oeiras

Imperatriz

Tocantinópolis

Marabá

Bragança

Capanema

Castanhal

Vigia

Abaetetuba

Tucuruí

Represa de Tucuruí

Xingu

Tocantins

Araguaia

Serra dos Carajás

São Francisco

Represa de Sobradinho

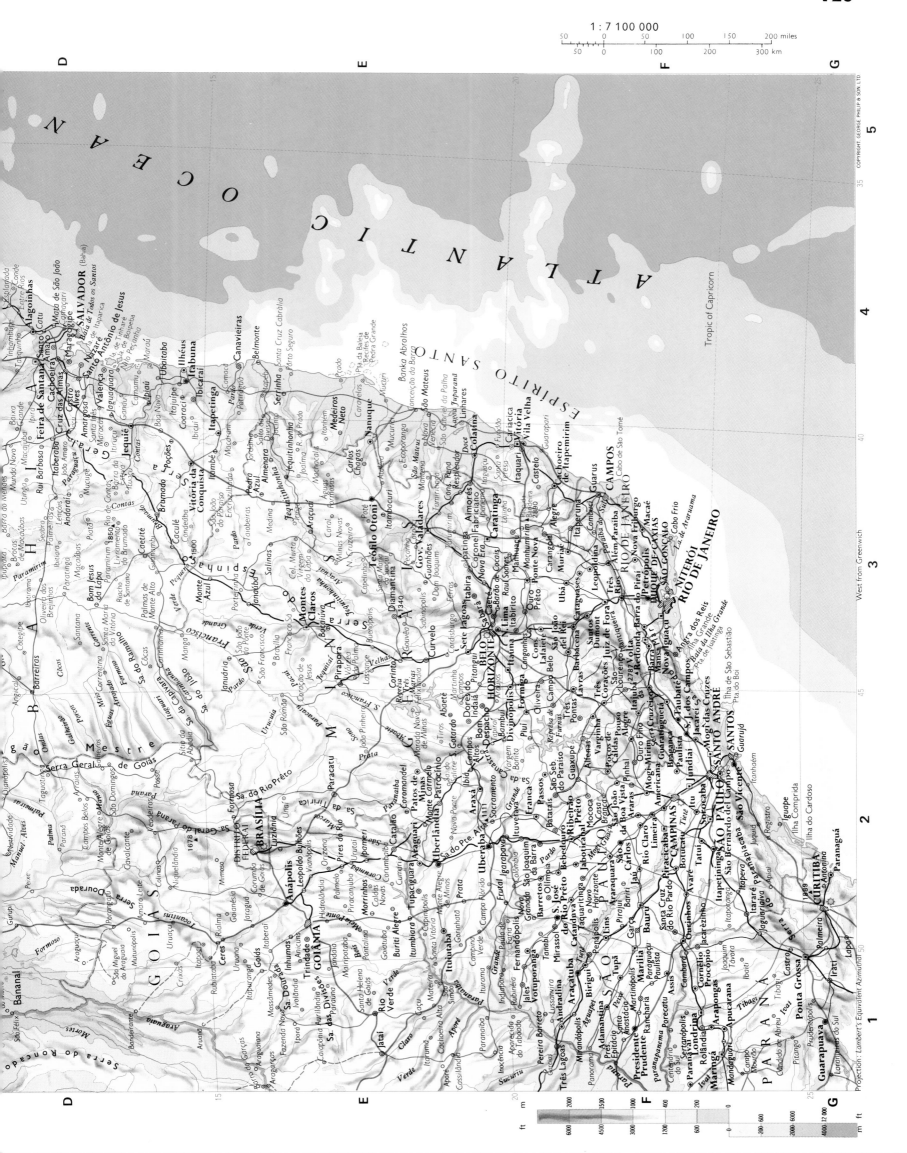

123

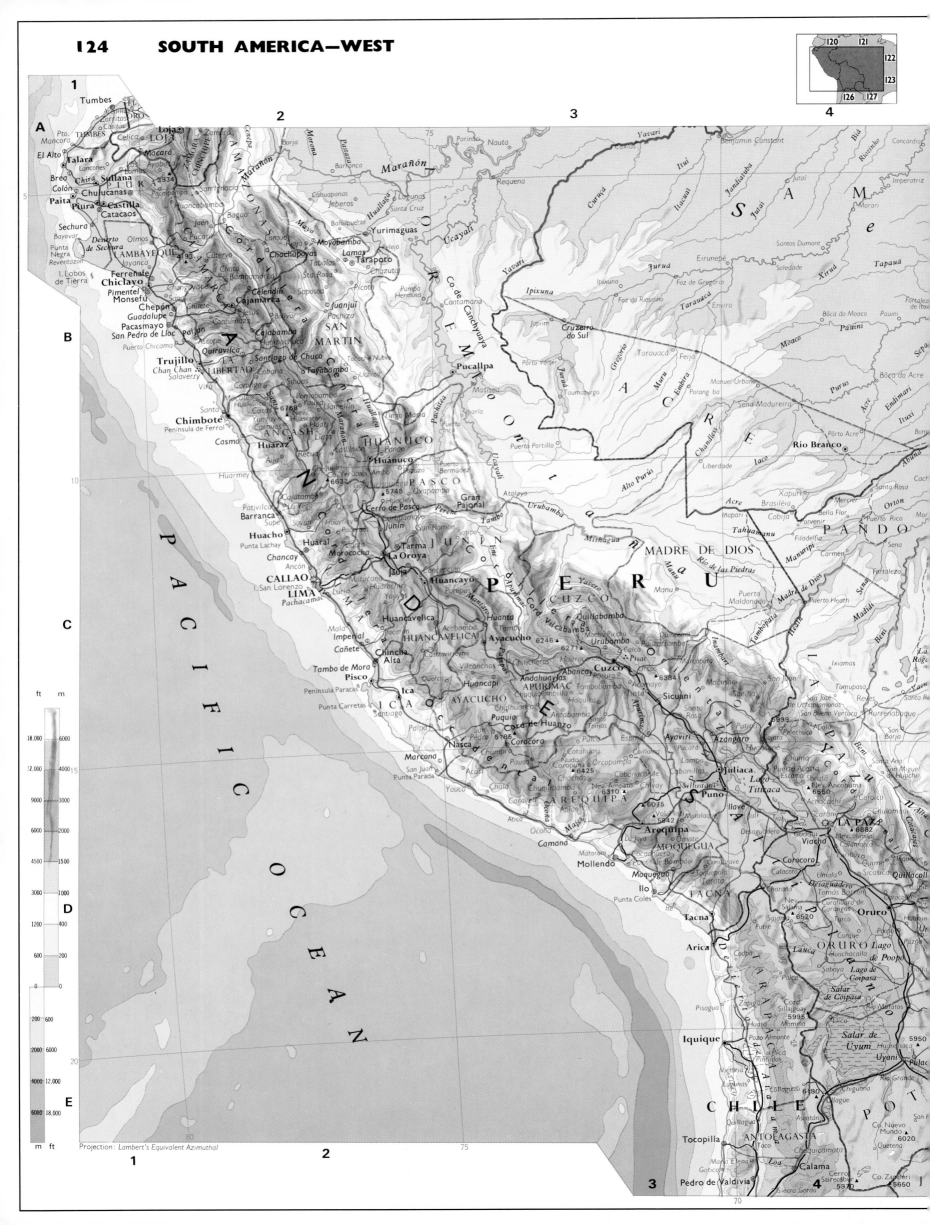

PACIFIC OCEAN

PERU

Projection: Lambert's Equivalent Azimuthal

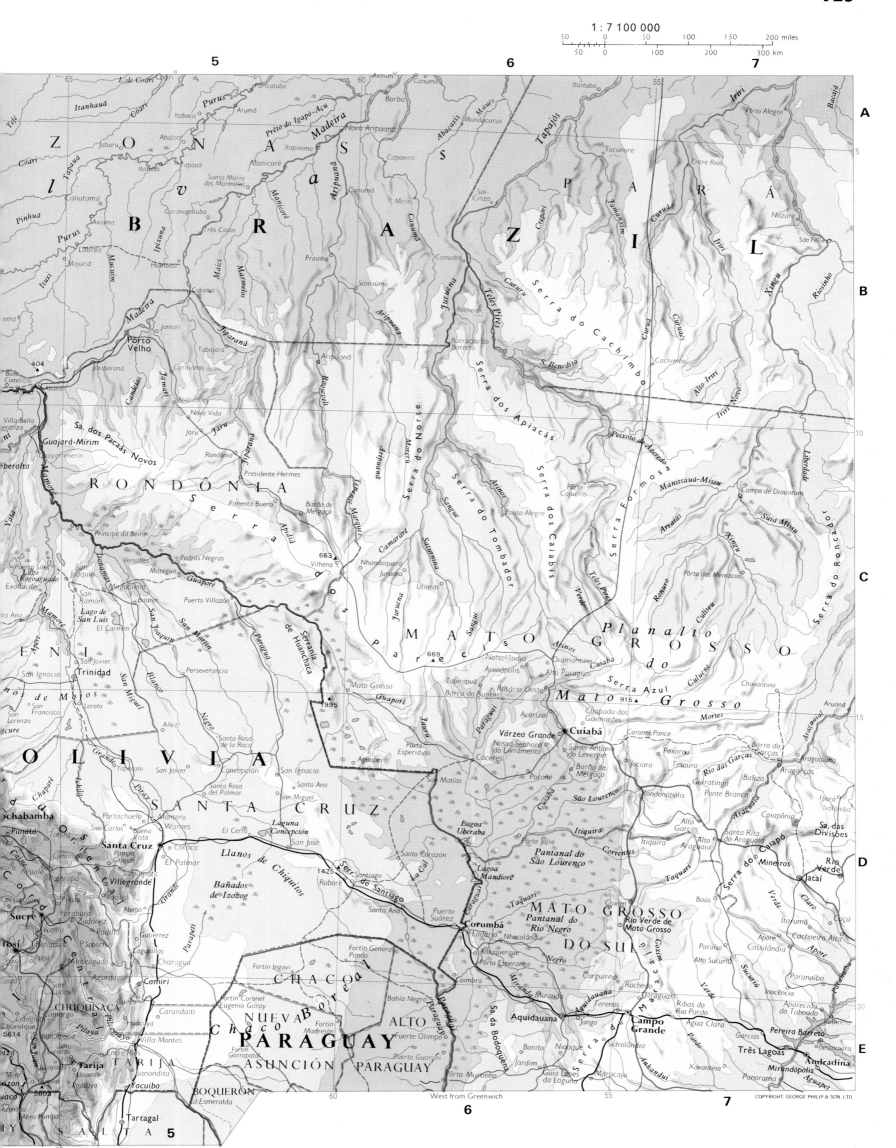

1 : 7 100 000

50   0   50   100   150   200 miles

50   0   100   200   300 km

West from Greenwich

COPYRIGHT. GEORGE PHILIP & SON. LTD.

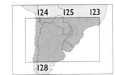

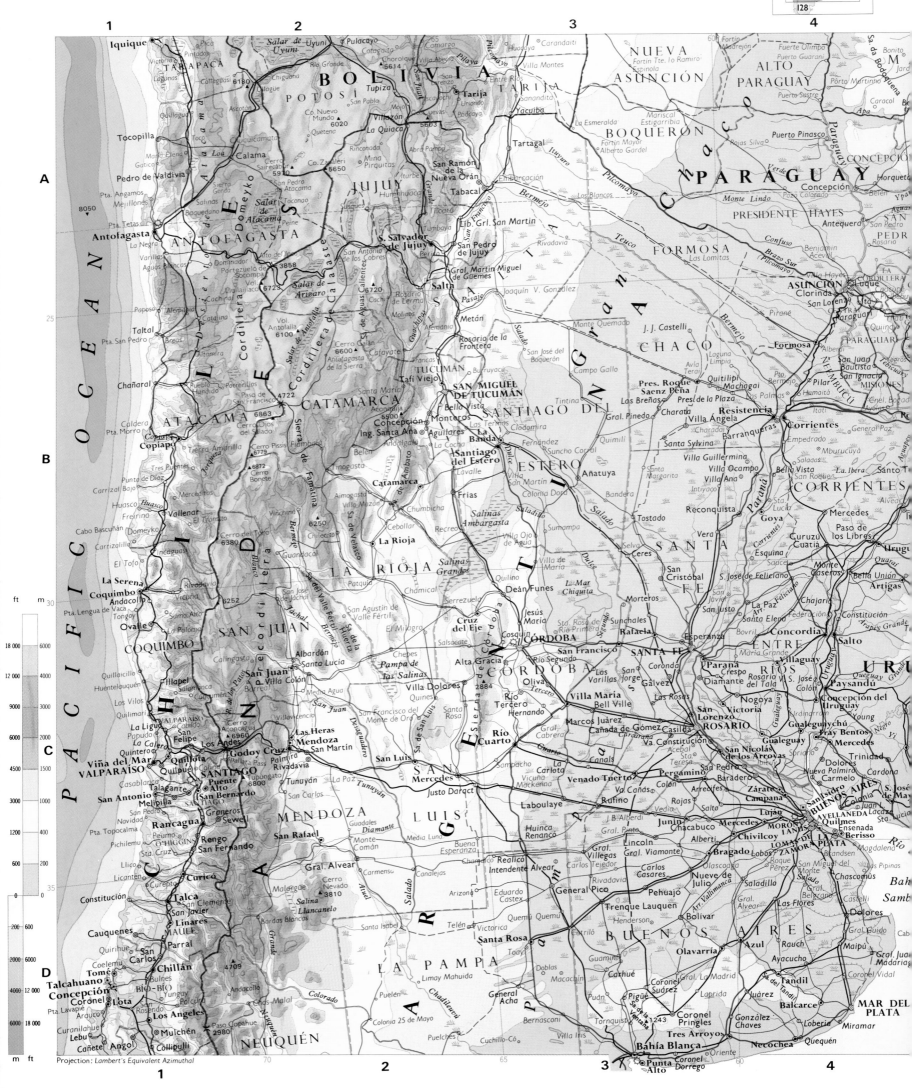

1 : 7 100 000

50   100   150   200 miles

50   0   100   200   300 km

BELO HORIZONTE

ATLANTIC

OCEAN

5304

1 : 7 100 000

50   0   50   100   150   200 miles
50   0   100   200   300 km

126 127

2   **3**   **4**   **5**

A

ARAUCO
Cañete · Angol
Capitán Pastene
I. Mocha · Cautín
Carahue
Temuco · Lautaro
Puerto Saavedra
Nueva Imperial
Pitrufquén
ARAUCANIA
Tolten

Mulchén
Collipulli · Victoria
Curacautín · 3124
Loncoche
Cunco
Freire
Lanco

Paso Copahue 2980
Loncopué
Las Lajas
Paso de los Indios
Zapala · Cutral-Có
Chos Malal
Paso Pino Hachado 1824

Colonia 25 de Mayo
Bernasconi
Puelches
LA PAMPA
Tornquist 1243
Villa Iris
Coronel Pringles
Tres Arroyos
Juárez
Balcarce
González Chaves
Loberia
Necochea · Quequén

Neuquén · Cipolletti
Gral. Roca · Negro
Allen · Río Colorado
Choele Choel
Colorado
Fortín Uno
Médanos
Bahía Blanca
BUENOS AIRES
Punta Alta
Coronel Dorrego
Oriente
B. Blanca
I. Trinidad

NEUQUÉN
Paso Mamuil Malal
Junín de los Andes
1253
3776
San Martín de los Andes
Las Coloradas
Picún Leufú
Limay
Piedra del Aguila

RÍO NEGRO
Barda del Medio
El Cuy
La Esperanza
Gral. Conesa
Sa. Colorada 1314
Los Menucos
Valcheta
Aguada Cecilio
San Antonio Oeste
Pta. Rasa
Viedma
Carmen de Patagones
Stroeder
B. Anegada
Gen. Lorenzo Vintter
Mayor Buratovich

B

Valdivia · Corral
Pta. Galera
La Unión
Ranco · Lago Ranco
Osorno
Río Bueno
Riñihue
LOS LAGOS
Río Negro
L. Llanquihue
Puerto Varas
Maullín
Tronador 3554
Puerto Montt 2680
La Ensenada
2185

Loncoche
Los Panguipulli
Villarica
Lanín
San Carlos de Bariloche
El Bolsón
2185
El Maitén
Ingeniero Jacobacci
El Caín 1879
Norquinco
Leleque
Gastre

Maquinchao
Meseta de Somuncurá
Cona Niyeu
Salado
Sierra Grande
Verde
Telsen
Puerto Lobos
G. San José
Pta. Norte
Golfo San Matías
Pen. Valdés
Puerto Pirámides
G. Nuevo
Punta Delgada
Puerto Madryn
Rawson
Trelew
Gaimán

G. de los Coronados
Pta. Huechucuicui
Ancud
Isla de Chiloé
Castro 820
Achao
G. de Ancud
Puerto Quellón
C. Quilán
Boca del Guafo
I. Guafo
Islas Guaitecas

2470
2440
Chaitén
2300
2075
Velcho
El Corcovado
Tecka
Esquel
CHUBUT
Gualjaina
Pampa de Agnia
Perdido
Las Plumas
Chubut
Meseta de Montemayor

C

Archipiélago de los Chonos
I. Guamblin
C. Taitao
1372
Península de Taitao
C. Tres Montes
I. Javier
Golfo de Penas
Archipiélago Guayaneco
I. Campana
I. Patricio Lynch
I. Esmeralda
I. Mornington
G. Ladrillero
G. Trinidad
I. Madre de Dios
I. Duque de York
I. Santiago
B. Salvación
I. Hanover

Palena
Palena
La Plata 2020
L. Gral. Vintter
Río Pico
José de San Martín
1245
Gran Laguna Salada
Camarones
B. Camarones
C. Dos Bahías
C. Raso

Magdalena
Canal Moraleda
Fontana
Alto Río Senguerr
Coihaique
Puerto Aisén
Balmaceda
L. Buenos Aires
Perito Moreno
Los Antiguos
Mayo
Río Mayo
Holdich
L. Musters
L. Colhué Huapi
Sarmiento
Facundo
L. Pueyrredón
Lago Posadas
Las Horquetas
San Lorenzo 3700
Cochrane
3437
Arenales
Mte. San Valentín 4058
Chile Chico
L. Gral. Carrera
2726
1335
Fitz Roy
Jaramillo
Mazarredo
Pico Truncado
Deseado
Puerto Deseado
Pta. Medanosa
C. Tres Puntas
C. Blanco

Golfo San Jorge
Comodoro Rivadavia
Colonia Las Heras
Caleta Olivia
B. Bustamante

PATAGONIA

D

I. Patricio Lynch
I. Campana
C. Tres Montes
3050
Melizo Sur
L. San Martín
L. Cardiel
Gran Altiplanicie Central
Mt. Inés 1120
Gob. Gregores
San Julián
SANTA CRUZ
L. Viedma
Mte. Fitzroy 3375
Murallón 3600
Lago Argentino
Calafate
Tres Lagos
Shehuen
Chico
Cmte. Luis Piedrabuena
Santa Cruz
Bahía Grande
Bahía Laura

I. Wellington
Canal Baker
Canal Messier
MAGALLANES
L. Viedma
2280
San Martín
2469

E

I. Madre de Dios
I. Duque de York
I. Santiago
B. Salvación
I. Hanover
Arch. Reina Adelaida
C. Jorge
Estrecho Nelson
I. Desolación
I. Stewart
I. Londonderry
B. Cook
Pen. Hardy
Is. Hermite

C. Deseado
Estrecho de Magallanes
Puerto Natales
El Turbio
Gallegos
Río Gallegos
Monte Dinero
C. Virgenes
Strait of Magellan
Cerro Sombrero
Porvenir
San Sebastián
Río Grande
Misión Fagnano
C. San Diego
I. de los Estados (Staten I.)

Pen. Muñoz
Gamero
Seno Skyring
Seno Otway
Punta Arenas
Pen. Brunswick
Santa Inés
Pen. Córdova
Isla Riesco
B. Inútil
Dawson
Whiteside
Isla Grande de Tierra del Fuego
TIERRA DEL FUEGO
L. Fagnano
Ushuaia
Picton
Lennox
Nueva
Canal Beagle
Navarino
B. Nassau
Islas Wollaston
Cabo de Hornos (Cape Horn)

PACIFIC OCEAN

SOUTH ATLANTIC OCEAN

Golfo de Penas

Islas Diego Ramírez

Beauchêne I.

FALKLAND ISLANDS (ISLAS MALVINAS)
Jason Is.
Pebble I.
King George B.
Queen Charlotte B.
Mt. Adam 700
C. Dolphin
Weddell I.
Falkland Sound
Port Darwin
Mt. Usborne 705
Stanley
West Falkland
C. Meredith
East Falkland

ft   m
9000   3000
6000   2000
4500   1500
3000   1000
1200   400
600   200
0   0
200   600
2000   6000
4000   12,000
m   ft

Projection: Lambert's Equivalent Azimuthal

West from Greenwich

COPYRIGHT GEORGE PHILIP & SON LTD.

1   **2**   **3**   **4**   **5**

INDEX

The index contains the names of all the principal places and features shown on the World Maps. Each name is followed by an additional entry in italics giving the country or region within which it is located. The alphabetical order of names composed of two or more words is governed primarily by the first word and then by the second. This is an example of the rule:

Mīr Kūh, *Iran* **65** **E8**
Mīr Shahdād, *Iran* **65** **E8**
Miraj, *India* **60** **L9**
Miram Shah, *Pakistan* **62** **C4**
Miramar, *Mozam.* **85** **C6**

Physical features composed of a proper name (Erie) and a description (Lake) are positioned alphabetically by the proper name. The description is positioned after the proper name and is usually abbreviated:

Erie, L., *N. Amer.* **106** **D3**

Where a description forms part of a settlement or administrative name however, it is always written in full and put in its true alphabetic position:

Mount Morris, *U.S.A.* **106** **D7**

Names beginning with M' and Mc are indexed as if they were spelt Mac. Names beginning St. are alphabetised under Saint, but Sankt, Sint, Sant', Santa and San are all spelt in full and are alphabetised accordingly. If the same place name occurs two or more times in the index and all are in the same country, each is followed by the name of the administrative subdivision in which it is located. The names are placed in the alphabetical order of the subdivisions. For example:

Jackson, *Ky., U.S.A.* **104** **G4**
Jackson, *Mich., U.S.A.* **104** **D3**
Jackson, *Minn., U.S.A.* **108** **D7**

The number in bold type which follows each name in the index refers to the number of the map page where that feature or place will be found. This is usually the largest scale at which the place or feature appears. The letter and figure which are in bold type immediately after the page number give the grid square on the map page, within which the feature is situated. The letter represents the latitude and the figure the longitude.

In some cases the feature itself may fall within the specified square, while the name is outside. This is usually the case only with features which are larger than a grid square. Rivers are indexed to their mouths or confluences, and carry the symbol ➝ after their names. A solid square ■ follows the name of a country while, an open square □ refers to a first order administrative area.

ABBREVIATIONS USED IN THE INDEX

A.C.T. — Australian Capital Territory
Afghan. — Afghanistan
Ala. — Alabama
Alta. — Alberta
Amer. — America(n)
Arch. — Archipelago
Ariz. — Arizona
Ark. — Arkansas
Atl. Oc. — Atlantic Ocean
B. — Baie, Bahía, Bay, Bucht, Bugt
B.C. — British Columbia
Bangla. — Bangladesh
Barr. — Barrage
Bos.-H. — Bosnia-Herzegovina
C. — Cabo, Cap, Cape, Coast
C.A.R. — Central African Republic
C. Prov. — Cape Province
Calif. — California
Cent. — Central
Chan. — Channel
Colo. — Colorado
Conn. — Connecticut
Cord. — Cordillera
Cr. — Creek
Czech. — Czech Republic
D.C. — District of Columbia
Del. — Delaware
Dep. — Dependency
Des. — Desert
Dist. — District
Dj. — Djebel
Domin. — Dominica
Dom. Rep. — Dominican Republic
E. — East
El Salv. — El Salvador

Eq. Guin. — Equatorial Guinea
Fla. — Florida
Falk. Is. — Falkland Is.
G. — Golfe, Golfo, Gulf, Guba, Gebel
Ga. — Georgia
Gt. — Great, Greater
Guinea-Biss. — Guinea-Bissau
H.K. — Hong Kong
H.P. — Himachal Pradesh
Hants. — Hampshire
Harb. — Harbor, Harbour
Hd. — Head
Hts. — Heights
I.(s). — Île, Ilha, Insel, Isla, Island, Isle
Ill. — Illinois
Ind. — Indiana
Ind. Oc. — Indian Ocean
Ivory C. — Ivory Coast
J. — Jabal, Jebel, Jazira
Junc. — Junction
K. — Kap, Kapp
Kans. — Kansas
Kep. — Kepulauan
Ky. — Kentucky
L. — Lac, Lacul, Lago, Lagoa, Lake, Limni, Loch, Lough
La. — Louisiana
Liech. — Liechtenstein
Lux. — Luxembourg
Mad. P. — Madhya Pradesh
Madag. — Madagascar
Man. — Manitoba
Mass. — Massachusetts
Md. — Maryland

Me. — Maine
Medit. S. — Mediterranean Sea
Mich. — Michigan
Minn. — Minnesota
Miss. — Mississippi
Mo. — Missouri
Mont. — Montana
Moza. — Mozambique
Mt.(e). — Mont, Monte, Monti, Montaña, Mountain
N. — Nord, Norte, North, Northern, Nouveau
N.B. — New Brunswick
N.C. — North Carolina
N. Cal. — New Caledonia
N. Dak. — North Dakota
N.H. — New Hampshire
N.I. — North Island
N.J. — New Jersey
N. Mex. — New Mexico
N.S. — Nova Scotia
N.S.W. — New South Wales
N.W.T. — North West Territory
N.Y. — New York
N.Z. — New Zealand
Nebr. — Nebraska
Neths. — Netherlands
Nev. — Nevada
Nfld. — Newfoundland
Nic. — Nicaragua
O. — Oued, Ouadi
Occ. — Occidentale
O.F.S. — Orange Free State
Okla. — Oklahoma
Ont. — Ontario
Or. — Orientale

Oreg. — Oregon
Os. — Ostrov
Oz. — Ozero
P. — Pass, Passo, Pasul, Pulau
P.E.I. — Prince Edward Island
Pa. — Pennsylvania
Pac. Oc. — Pacific Ocean
Papua N.G. — Papua New Guinea
Pass. — Passage
Pen. — Peninsula, Péninsule
Phil. — Philippines
Pk. — Park, Peak
Plat. — Plateau
P-ov. — Poluostrov
Prov. — Province, Provincial
Pt. — Point
Pta. — Ponta, Punta
Pte. — Pointe
Qué. — Québec
Queens. — Queensland
R. — Rio, River
R.I. — Rhode Island
Ra.(s). — Range(s)
Raj. — Rajasthan
Reg. — Region
Rep. — Republic
Res. — Reserve, Reservoir
S. — San, South, Sea
Si. Arabia — Saudi Arabia
S.C. — South Carolina
S. Dak. — South Dakota
S.I. — South Island
S. Leone — Sierra Leone
Sa. — Serra, Sierra
Sask. — Saskatchewan
Scot. — Scotland

Sd. — Sound
Sev. — Severnaya
Sib. — Siberia
Sprs. — Springs
St. — Saint, Sankt, Sint
Sta. — Santa, Station
Ste. — Sainte
Sto. — Santo
Str. — Strait, Stretto
Switz. — Switzerland
Tas. — Tasmania
Tenn. — Tennessee
Tex. — Texas
Tg. — Tanjung
Trin. & Tob. — Trinidad & Tobago
U.A.E. — United Arab Emirates
U.K. — United Kingdom
U.S.A. — United States of America
Ut. P. — Uttar Pradesh
Va. — Virginia
Vdkhr. — Vodokhranilishche
Vf. — Vîrful
Vic. — Victoria
Vol. — Volcano
Vt. — Vermont
W. — Wadi, West
W. Va. — West Virginia
Wash. — Washington
Wis. — Wisconsin
Wlkp. — Wielkopolski
Wyo. — Wyoming
Yorks. — Yorkshire
Yug. — Yugoslavia

A

A Coruña = La Coruña,
  Spain 30   B2
Aachen, Germany 18   E2
Aadorf, Switz. 23   B7
Aalborg = Ålborg,
  Denmark 11   G3
Aalen, Germany 19   G6
A'âli en Nîl □, Sudan .. 77   F3
Aalsmeer, Neths. 16   D5
Aalst, Belgium 17   G4
Aalst, Neths. 17   F6
Aalten, Neths. 16   E9
Aalter, Belgium 17   F2
Äänekoski, Finland 9   E21
Aarau, Switz. 22   B5
Aarberg, Switz. 22   B4
Aardenburg, Belgium ... 17   F2
Aare →, Switz. 22   A6
Aargau □, Switz. 22   B5
Aarhus = Århus, Denmark 11   H4
Aarle, Neths. 17   E7
Aarschot, Belgium 17   G5
Aarsele, Belgium 17   G2
Aartrijke, Belgium ... 17   F2
Aarwangen, Switz. 22   B5
Aba, China 52   A3
Aba, Nigeria 79   D6
Aba, Zaïre 82   B3
Âbâ, Jazîrat, Sudan ... 77   E3
Abacaxis →, Brazil ... 121   D6
Ābādān, Iran 65   D6
Abade, Ethiopia 77   F4
Ābādeh, Iran 65   D7
Abadin, Spain 30   B3
Abadla, Algeria 75   B4
Abaeté, Brazil 123   E2
Abaeté →, Brazil 123   E2
Abaetetuba, Brazil ... 122   B2
Abagnar Qi, China 50   C9
Abai, Paraguay 127   B4
Abak, Nigeria 79   E6
Abakaliki, Nigeria ... 79   D6
Abakan, Russia 45   D10
Abalemma, Niger 79   B6
Abana, Turkey 66   B6
Abancay, Peru 124   C3
Abanilla, Spain 29   G3
Abano Terme, Italy ... 33   C8
Abapó, Bolivia 125   D5
Abarán, Spain 29   G3
Abariringa, Kiribati .. 92   H10
Abarqû, Iran 65   D7
Abashiri, Japan 48   B12
Abashiri-Wan, Japan .. 48   B12
Abaújszántó, Hungary . 21   G11
Abay, Kazakhstan 44   E8
Abaya, L., Ethiopia .. 77   F4
Abaza, Russia 44   D10
Abbadia San Salvatore,
  Italy 33   F8
'Abbāsābād, Iran 65   C8
Abbay = Nîl el Azraq →,
  Sudan 77   D3
Abbaye, Pt., U.S.A. .. 104   B1
Abbé, L., Ethiopia ... 77   E5
Abbeville, France ... 25   B8
Abbeville, La., U.S.A. 109   K8
Abbeville, S.C., U.S.A. 105   H4
Abbiategrasso, Italy . 32   C5
Abbieglassie, Australia 91   D4
Abbot Ice Shelf, Antarctica 5   D16
Abbotsford, Canada .. 100   D4
Abbotsford, U.S.A. .. 108   C9
Abbottabad, Pakistan . 62   B5
Abcoude, Neths. 16   D5
Abd al Kūrī, Ind. Oc. . 68   E5
Ābdar, Iran 65   D7
'Abdolābād, Iran 65   C8
Abéché, Chad 73   F9
Abejar, Spain 28   D2
Abekr, Sudan 77   E2
Abêlessa, Algeria ... 75   D5
Abengourou, Ivory C. . 78   D4
Åbenrå, Denmark 11   J3
Abensberg, Germany . 19   G7
Abeokuta, Nigeria ... 79   D5
Aber, Uganda 82   B3
Aberaeron, U.K. 13   E3
Aberayron = Aberaeron,
  U.K. 13   E3
Abercorn = Mbala,
  Zambia 83   D3
Abercorn, Australia . 91   D5
Aberdare, U.K. 13   F4
Aberdare Ra., Kenya . 82   C4
Aberdeen, Australia . 91   E5
Aberdeen, Canada ... 101   C7
Aberdeen, S. Africa . 84   E3
Aberdeen, U.K. 14   D6
Aberdeen, Ala., U.S.A. 105   J1
Aberdeen, Idaho, U.S.A. 110   E7
Aberdeen, S. Dak., U.S.A. 108   C5
Aberdeen, Wash., U.S.A. 112   D3
Aberdovey = Aberdyfi,
  U.K. 13   E3
Aberdyfi, U.K. 13   E3
Aberfeldy, U.K. 14   E5
Abergaria-a-Velha,
  Portugal 30   E2
Abergavenny, U.K. ... 13   F4
Abernathy, U.S.A. ... 109   J4
Abert, L., U.S.A. ... 110   E3
Aberystwyth, U.K. ... 13   E3
Abha, Si. Arabia 76   D5

Abhar, Iran 67   D13
Abhayapuri, India ... 63   F14
Abia □, Nigeria 79   D6
Abidiya, Sudan 76   D3
Abidjan, Ivory C. ... 78   D4
Abilene, Kans., U.S.A. 108   F6
Abilene, Tex., U.S.A. 109   J5
Abingdon, U.K. 13   F6
Abingdon, Ill., U.S.A. 108   E9
Abingdon, Va., U.S.A. 105   G5
Abington Reef, Australia 90   B4
Abitau →, Canada ... 101   B7
Abitau L., Canada ... 101   A7
Abitibi L., Canada ... 98   C4
Abiy Adi, Ethiopia .. 77   E4
Abkhaz Republic =
  Abkhazia □, Georgia . 43   J5
Abkhazia □, Georgia . 43   J5
Abkit, Russia 45   C16
Abminga, Australia .. 91   D1
Abnûb, Egypt 76   B3
Åbo = Turku, Finland .. 9   F20
Abocho, Nigeria 79   D6
Abohar, India 62   D6
Aboisso, Ivory C. ... 78   D4
Aboméy, Benin 79   D5
Abondance, France .. 27   B10
Abong-Mbang, Cameroon 80   D2
Abonnema, Nigeria .. 79   E6
Abony, Hungary 21   H10
Aboso, Ghana 78   D4
Abou-Deïa, Chad 73   F8
Aboyne, U.K. 14   D6
Abra Pampa, Argentina . 126   A2
Abrantes, Portugal .. 31   F2
Abraveses, Portugal . 30   E3
Abreojos, Pta., Mexico 114   B2
Abreschviller, France 25   D14
Abri, Esh Shamâliya,
  Sudan 76   C3
Abri, Janub Kordofân,
  Sudan 77   E3
Abrolhos, Banka, Brazil . 123   E4
Abruzzi □, Italy 33   F10
Absaroka Range, U.S.A. 110   D9
Abū al Khaşīb, Iraq . 65   D6
Abū 'Alī, Si. Arabia . 65   E6
Abū 'Alī →, Lebanon . 69   A4
Abū 'Arīsh, Si. Arabia 68   D3
Abū Ballas, Egypt ... 76   C2
Abu Deleiq, Sudan .. 77   D3
Abu Dhabi = Abū Ząby,
  U.A.E. 65   E7
Abū Dis, Sudan 76   D3
Abū Dom, Sudan 77   D3
Abū Du'ān, Syria ... 67   D8
Abu el Gairi, W. →,
  Egypt 69   F2
Abū Gabra, Sudan ... 77   E2
Abu Ga'da, W. →, Egypt 69   F1
Abu Gubeiha, Sudan . 77   E3
Abu Habl, Khawr →,
  Sudan 77   E3
Abū Ḩadrīyah, Si. Arabia 65   E6
Abu Hamed, Sudan .. 76   D3
Abu Haraz,
  An Nîl el Azraq, Sudan . 77   E3
Abū Haraz, Esh Shamâliya,
  Sudan 76   D3
Abū Higar, Sudan ... 77   E3
Abū Kamāl, Syria ... 67   E9
Abū Madd, Ra's,
  Si. Arabia 64   E3
Abu Matariq, Sudan . 77   E2
Abu Qir, Egypt 76   H7
Abu Qireiya, Egypt .. 76   C4
Abu Qurqâs, Egypt .. 76   J7
Abū Şafāt, W. →, Jordan 69   E5
Abū Simbel, Egypt .. 76   C3
Abū Ţig, Egypt 76   B3
Abu Tiga, Sudan 77   E3
Abū Zabad, Sudan ... 77   E2
Abū Ząby, U.A.E. ... 65   E7
Abū Zeydābād, Iran . 65   C6
Abufari, Brazil 125   B5
Abuja, Nigeria 79   D6
Abukuma-Gawa →, Japan 48   E10
Abukuma-Sammyaku,
  Japan 48   F10
Abunã, Brazil 125   B4
Abunã →, Brazil 125   B4
Aburo, Zaïre 82   B3
Abut Hd., N.Z. 87   K3
Abwong, Sudan 77   F3
Åby, Sweden 11   F10
Aby, Lagune, Ivory C. . 78   D4
Acacías, Colombia ... 120   C3
Acajutla, El Salv. ... 116   D2
Açallândia, Brazil ... 122   C2
Acámbaro, Mexico ... 114   C4
Acaponeta, Mexico ... 114   C3
Acapulco, Mexico ... 115   D5
Acarai, Serra, Brazil . 121   C6
Acaraú, Brazil 122   B3
Acari, Brazil 122   C4
Acarí, Peru 124   D3
Acarigua, Venezuela . 120   B4
Acatlán, Mexico 115   D5
Acayucan, Mexico ... 115   D6
Accéglio, Italy 32   D3
Accomac, U.S.A. 104   G8
Accous, France 26   E3
Accra, Ghana 79   D4
Accrington, U.K. 12   D5
Acebal, Argentina ... 126   C3
Acebo, Spain 30   E2
Aceguá, Brazil 127   C5
Acerenza, Italy 35   B8
Acerra, Italy 35   B7
Aceuchal, Spain 31   G4
Achacachi, Bolivia .. 124   D4
Achaguas, Venezuela . 120   B4
Achalpur, India 60   J10
Achao, Chile 128   B2
Achel, Belgium 17   F6
Acheng, China 51   B14
Achenkirch, Austria . 19   H7
Achensee, Austria ... 19   H7
Acher, India 62   H5
Achern, Germany ... 19   G4
Achill, Ireland 15   C2
Achill Hd., Ireland .. 15   C1
Achill I., Ireland ... 15   C1
Achill Sd., Ireland .. 15   C2
Achim, Germany 18   B5
Achinsk, Russia 45   D10
Achol, Sudan 77   F3
Acıgöl, Turkey 66   D3
Acireale, Italy 35   E8
Ackerman, U.S.A. ... 109   J10
Acklins I., Bahamas . 117   B5
Acme, Canada 100   C6
Acobamba, Peru 124   C3
Acomayo, Peru 124   C3
Aconcagua, Cerro,
  Argentina 126   C2
Aconquija, Mt., Argentina 126   B2
Acopiara, Brazil 122   C4
Açores, Is. dos = Azores,
  Atl. Oc. 2   C8
Acorizal, Brazil 125   D6
Acquapendente, Italy . 33   F8
Acquasanta Terme, Italy 33   F10
Acquaviva delle Fonti, Italy 35   B9
Acqui Terme, Italy .. 32   D5
Acraman, L., Australia 91   E2
Acre □, Brazil 124   B3
Acre →, Brazil 124   B4
Acri, Italy 35   C9
Acs, Hungary 21   H8
Acton, Canada 106   C4
Açu, Brazil 122   C4
Ad Dammām, Si. Arabia 65   E6
Ad Dawhah, Qatar ... 65   E6
Ad Dawr, Iraq 67   E10
Ad Dir'īyah, Si. Arabia 64   E5
Ad Dīwānīyah, Iraq . 67   F11
Ad Dujayl, Iraq 67   F11
Ad Durūz, J., Jordan . 69   C5
Ada, Ghana 79   D5
Ada, Serbia, Yug. ... 21   K10
Ada, Minn., U.S.A. .. 108   B6
Ada, Okla., U.S.A. .. 109   H6
Adaja →, Spain 30   D6
Ådalsliden, Sweden .. 10   A10
Adam, Mt., Falk. Is. . 128   D4
Adamantina, Brazil .. 123   F1
Adamaoua, Massif de l',
  Cameroon 79   D7
Adamawa □, Nigeria . 79   D7
Adamawa Highlands =
  Adamaoua, Massif de l',
  Cameroon 79   D7
Adamello, Mte., Italy . 32   B7
Adami Tulu, Ethiopia . 77   F4
Adaminaby, Australia . 91   F4
Adams, Mass., U.S.A. . 107   D11
Adams, N.Y., U.S.A. . 107   C8
Adams, Wis., U.S.A. . 108   D10
Adam's Bridge, Sri Lanka 60   Q11
Adams L., Canada ... 100   C5
Adams Mt., U.S.A. .. 112   D5
Adam's Peak, Sri Lanka 60   R12
Adamuz, Spain 31   G6
Adana, Turkey 66   D6
Adanero, Spain 30   E6
Adapazarı, Turkey .. 66   B4
Adarama, Sudan 77   D3
Adare, C., Antarctica . 5   D11
Adaut, Indonesia ... 57   F8
Adavale, Australia .. 91   D3
Adda →, Italy 32   C6
Addis Ababa = Addis
  Abeba, Ethiopia ... 77   F4
Addis Abeba, Ethiopia . 77   F4
Addis Alem, Ethiopia . 77   F4
Addison, U.S.A. 106   D7
Addo, S. Africa 84   E4
Adebour, Niger 79   C7
Ādeh, Iran 64   B5
Adel, U.S.A. 105   K4
Adelaide, Australia . 91   E2
Adelaide, Bahamas .. 116   A4
Adelaide, S. Africa .. 84   E4
Adelaide I., Antarctica 5   C17
Adelaide Pen., Canada 96   B10
Adelaide River, Australia 88   B5
Adelanto, U.S.A. 113   L9
Adelboden, Switz. ... 22   D5
Adele I., Australia .. 88   C3
Adélie, Terre, Antarctica 5   C10
Adélie Land = Adélie,
  Terre, Antarctica .. 5   C10
Ademuz, Spain 28   E3
Aden = Al 'Adan, Yemen 68   E4
Aden, G. of, Asia 68   E4
Adendorp, S. Africa . 84   E3
Adh Dhayd, U.A.E. .. 65   E7
Adhoi, India 62   H4
Adi, Indonesia 57   E8
Adi Daro, Ethiopia .. 77   E4
Adi Keyih, Eritrea .. 77   E4
Adi Kwala, Eritrea .. 77   E4

Adi Ugri, Eritrea 77   E4
Adieu, C., Australia . 89   F5
Adieu Pt., Australia . 88   C3
Adigala, Ethiopia ... 77   E5
Adige →, Italy 33   C9
Adigrat, Ethiopia ... 77   E4
Adilabad, India 60   K11
Adilcevaz, Turkey .. 67   C10
Adin, U.S.A. 110   F3
Adin Khel, Afghan. .. 60   C6
Adinkerke, Belgium . 17   F1
Adirondack Mts., U.S.A. 107   C10
Adıyaman, Turkey .. 67   D8
Adjim, Tunisia 75   B7
Adjohon, Benin 79   D5
Adjud, Romania 38   C10
Adjumani, Uganda .. 82   B3
Adlavik Is., Canada . 99   B8
Adler, Russia 43   J4
Adliswil, Switz. 23   B7
Admer, Algeria 75   D6
Admer, Erg d', Algeria . 75   D6
Admiralty G., Australia 88   B4
Admiralty I., U.S.A. . 96   C6
Admiralty Inlet, U.S.A. 112   C4
Admiralty Is., Papua N. G. 92   H6
Ado, Nigeria 79   D5
Ado-Ekiti, Nigeria .. 79   D6
Adok, Sudan 77   F3
Adola, Ethiopia 77   E5
Adonara, Indonesia . 57   F6
Adoni, India 60   M10
Adony, Hungary 21   H8
Adour →, France ... 26   E2
Adra, India 63   H12
Adra, Spain 29   J1
Adrano, Italy 35   E7
Adrar, Algeria 75   C4
Adré, Chad 73   F9
Adri, Libya 75   C7
Ádria, Italy 33   C9
Adrian, Mich., U.S.A. 104   E3
Adrian, Tex., U.S.A. . 109   H3
Adriatic Sea, Medit. S. 6   G9
Adua, Indonesia 57   E7
Adula, Switz. 23   D8
Adwa, Ethiopia 77   E4
Adygea □, Russia ... 43   H5
Adzhar Republic =
  Ajaria □, Georgia .. 43   K6
Adzopé, Ivory C. ... 78   D4
Ægean Sea, Medit. S. 39   L8
Æolian Is. = Eólie, Ís.,
  Italy 35   D7
Aerhtai Shan, Mongolia 54   B4
Ærø, Denmark 11   K4
Ærøskøbing, Denmark . 11   K4
Aesch, Switz. 22   B5
'Afak, Iraq 67   F11
Afándou, Greece 37   C10
Afarag, Erg, Algeria . 75   D5
Afars & Issas, Terr. of =
  Djibouti ■, Africa .. 68   E3
Affreville = Khemis
  Miliana, Algeria ... 75   A5
Afghanistan ■, Asia . 60   C4
Afgoi, Somali Rep. .. 68   G3
Afikpo, Nigeria 79   D6
Aflou, Algeria 75   B5
Afogados da Ingàzeira,
  Brazil 122   C4
Afognak I., U.S.A. .. 96   C4
Afragola, Italy 35   B7
Afrera, Ethiopia 77   E5
'Afrīn, Syria 66   D7
Afşin, Turkey 66   C7
Afton, U.S.A. 107   D9
Aftout, Algeria 74   C4
Afuá, Brazil 121   D7
Afula, Israel 69   C4
Afyonkarahisar, Turkey 66   C4
Aga, Egypt 76   H7
Agadès = Agadez, Niger . 79   B6
Agadez, Niger 79   B6
Agadir, Morocco 74   B3
Agaete, Canary Is. .. 36   F4
Agailás, Mauritania . 74   D2
Agapa, Russia 45   B9
Agar, India 62   H7
Agaro, Ethiopia 77   F4
Agartala, India 61   H17
Agassiz, Canada 100   D4
Agats, Indonesia 57   F9
Agbélouvé, Togo 79   D5
Agboville, Ivory C. . 78   D4
Ağcabädi, Azerbaijan . 43   K8
Ağdam, Azerbaijan .. 43   L8
Ağdaş, Azerbaijan .. 43   K8
Agde, France 26   E7
Agde, C. d', France . 26   E7
Agdz, Morocco 74   B3
Agdzhabedi = Ağcabädi,
  Azerbaijan 43   K8
Agen, France 26   D4
Agersø, Denmark ... 11   J5
Ageyevo, Russia 42   C3
Agger, Denmark 11   H2
Ággius, Italy 34   B2
Agh Kand, Iran 67   D13
Aghoueyyît, Mauritania 74   D1
Aginskoye, Russia .. 45   D12
Agira, Italy 35   E7
Agly →, France 26   F7
Agnibilékrou, Ivory C. 78   D4
Agnita, Romania 38   D7
Agnone, Italy 35   A7

Agofie, Ghana 79   D5
Agogna →, Italy ... 32   C5
Agogo, Sudan 77   F2
Agon, France 24   C5
Ågordo, Italy 33   B9
Agout →, France ... 26   E5
Agra, India 62   F7
Agrakhanskiy Poluostrov,
  Russia 43   J8
Agramunt, Spain ... 28   D6
Agreda, Spain 28   D3
Ağrı, Turkey 67   C10
Agri →, Italy 35   B9
Ağrı Dağı, Turkey .. 67   C11
Agrigento, Italy 34   E6
Agrinion, Greece ... 39   L4
Agrópoli, Italy 35   B7
Ağstafa, Azerbaijan . 43   K7
Água Branca, Brazil . 122   C3
Agua Caliente, Baja Calif.,
  Mexico 113   N10
Agua Caliente, Sinaloa,
  Mexico 114   B3
Agua Caliente Springs,
  U.S.A. 113   N10
Água Clara, Brazil .. 125   E7
Agua Hechicero, Mexico 113   N10
Agua Preta →, Brazil 121   D5
Agua Prieta, Mexico . 114   A3
Aguachica, Colombia . 120   B3
Aguada Cecilio, Argentina 128   E3
Aguadas, Colombia .. 120   B2
Aguadilla, Puerto Rico . 117   C6
Aguadulce, Panama .. 116   E3
Aguanga, U.S.A. 113   M10
Aguanish, Canada ... 99   B7
Aguanus →, Canada . 99   B7
Aguapeí, Brazil 125   D6
Aguapeí →, Brazil .. 123   F1
Aguapey →, Argentina 126   B4
Aguaray Guazú →,
  Paraguay 126   A4
Aguarico →, Ecuador . 120   D2
Aguas →, Spain 28   D4
Aguas Blancas, Chile . 126   A2
Aguas Calientes, Sierra de,
  Argentina 126   B2
Águas Formosas, Brazil 123   E3
Aguascalientes, Mexico 114   C4
Aguascalientes □, Mexico 114   C4
Agudo, Spain 31   G6
Águeda, Portugal ... 30   E2
Agueda →, Spain ... 30   D4
Aguié, Niger 79   C6
Aguilafuente, Spain . 30   D6
Aguilar, Spain 31   H6
Aguilar de Campóo, Spain 30   C6
Aguilares, Argentina . 126   B2
Aguilas, Spain 29   H3
Agüimes, Canary Is. . 36   G4
Aguja, C. de la, Colombia 120   A3
Agulaa, Ethiopia 77   E4
Agulhas, C., S. Africa . 84   E3
Agulo, Canary Is. ... 36   F2
Agung, Indonesia ... 56   F5
Agusan →, Phil. 55   G6
Agustín Codazzi, Colombia 120   A3
Agvali, Russia 43   J8
Aha Mts., Botswana . 84   B3
Ahaggar, Algeria 75   D6
Ahamansu, Ghana ... 79   D5
Ahar, Iran 67   C12
Ahaus, Germany 18   C3
Ahelledjem, Algeria . 75   C6
Ahipara B., N.Z. 87   F4
Ahiri, India 60   K12
Ahlat, Turkey 67   C10
Ahlen, Germany 18   D3
Ahmad Wal, Pakistan . 62   E1
Ahmadabad, India .. 62   H5
Ahmadābād, Khorāsān,
  Iran 65   C9
Ahmadābād, Khorāsān,
  Iran 65   C8
Aḥmadī, Iran 65   E8
Ahmadnagar, India .. 60   K9
Ahmadpur, Pakistan . 62   E4
Ahmar, Ethiopia 77   F5
Ahmedabad =
  Ahmadabad, India .. 62   H5
Ahmednagar =
  Ahmadnagar, India .. 60   K9
Ahoada, Nigeria 79   D6
Ahome, Mexico 114   B3
Ahr →, Germany ... 18   E3
Ahram, Iran 65   D6
Ahrax Pt., Malta 37   D1
Ahrensbök, Germany . 18   A6
Ahrweiler, Germany . 18   E3
Āhū, Iran 65   C6
Ahuachapán, El Salv. . 116   D2
Ahväz, Iran 65   D6
Ahvenanmaa = Åland,
  Finland 9   F19
Ahzar, Yemen 68   E4
Aiari →, Brazil 120   C4
Aichach, Germany .. 19   G7
Aichi □, Japan 49   G8
Aidone, Italy 35   E7
Aiello Cálabro, Italy . 35   C9
Aigle, Switz. 22   D3
Aignay-le-Duc, France . 25   E11
Aigoual, Mt., France . 26   D7
Aigre, France 26   C4

130

Aleksandrov

Aigua, *Uruguay* 127 C5
Aigueperse, *France* 26 B7
Aigues →, *France* 27 D8
Aigues-Mortes, *France* 27 E8
Aigues-Mortes, G. d', *France* 27 E8
Aiguilles, *France* 27 D10
Aiguillon, *France* 26 D4
Aigurande, *France* 26 B5
Aihui, *China* 54 A7
Aija, *Peru* 124 B2
Aikawa, *Japan* 48 E9
Aiken, *U.S.A.* 105 J5
Ailao Shan, *China* 52 F3
Aillant-sur-Tholon, *France* 25 E10
Aillik, *Canada* 99 A8
Ailly-sur-Noye, *France* 25 C9
Ailsa Craig, *U.K.* 14 F3
'Ailūn, *Jordan* 69 C4
Aim, *Russia* 45 D14
Aimere, *Indonesia* 57 F6
Aimogasta, *Argentina* 126 B2
Aimorés, *Brazil* 123 E3
Ain □, *France* 27 B9
Ain →, *France* 27 C9
Aïn Beïda, *Algeria* 75 A6
Aïn Ben Khellil, *Algeria* 75 B4
Aïn Ben Tili, *Mauritania* 74 C3
Aïn Beni Mathar, *Morocco* 75 B4
Aïn Benian, *Algeria* 75 A5
Ain Dalla, *Egypt* 76 B2
Ain el Mafki, *Egypt* 76 B2
Ain Girba, *Egypt* 76 B2
Aïn M'lila, *Algeria* 75 A6
Ain Qeiqab, *Egypt* 76 B1
Aïn-Sefra, *Algeria* 75 B4
Ain Sheikh Murzûk, *Egypt* 76 B2
'Ain Sudr, *Egypt* 69 F2
Ain Sukhna, *Egypt* 76 J8
Aïn Tédelès, *Algeria* 75 A5
Aïn-Témouchent, *Algeria* 75 A4
Aïn Touta, *Algeria* 75 A6
Ain Zeitûn, *Egypt* 76 B2
Aïn Zorah, *Morocco* 75 B4
Ainabo, *Somali Rep.* 68 F4
Ainaži, *Latvia* 9 H21
Aínos Óros, *Greece* 39 L3
Ainsworth, *U.S.A.* 108 D5
Aipe, *Colombia* 120 C2
Aiquile, *Bolivia* 125 D4
Aïr, *Niger* 79 B6
Air Hitam, *Malaysia* 59 M4
Airaines, *France* 25 C8
Airão, *Brazil* 121 D5
Airdrie, *U.K.* 14 F5
Aire →, *France* 25 C11
Aire →, *U.K.* 12 D7
Aire, I. del, *Spain* 36 B11
Aire-sur-la-Lys, *France* 25 B9
Aire-sur-l'Adour, *France* 26 E3
Airlie Beach, *Australia* 90 C4
Airolo, *Switz.* 23 C7
Airvault, *France* 24 F6
Aisch →, *Germany* 19 F7
Aisen □, *Chile* 128 C2
Aisne □, *France* 25 C10
Aisne →, *France* 25 C9
Aitana, Sierra de, *Spain* 29 G4
Aitkin, *U.S.A.* 108 B8
Aitolikón, *Greece* 39 L4
Aiuaba, *Brazil* 122 C3
Aiud, *Romania* 38 C6
Aix-en-Provence, *France* 27 E9
Aix-la-Chapelle = Aachen, *Germany* 18 E2
Aix-les-Bains, *France* 27 C9
Aixe-sur-Vienne, *France* 26 C5
Aiyansh, *Canada* 100 B3
Aíyina, *Greece* 39 M6
Aiyínion, *Greece* 39 J5
Aiyion, *Greece* 39 L5
Aizawl, *India* 61 H18
Aizenay, *France* 24 F5
Aizkraukle, *Latvia* 9 H21
Aizpute, *Latvia* 9 H19
Aizuwakamatsu, *Japan* 48 F9
Ajaccio, *France* 27 G12
Ajaccio, G. d', *France* 27 G12
Ajaju →, *Colombia* 120 C3
Ajalpan, *Mexico* 115 D5
Ajanta Ra., *India* 60 J9
Ajari Rep. = Ajaria □, *Georgia* 43 K6
Ajaria □, *Georgia* 43 K6
Ajax, *Canada* 106 C5
Ajdâbiyah, *Libya* 73 B9
Ajdovščina, *Slovenia* 33 C10
Ajibar, *Ethiopia* 77 E4
Ajka, *Hungary* 21 H7
'Ajmān, *U.A.E.* 65 E7
Ajmer, *India* 62 F6
Ajo, *U.S.A.* 111 K7
Ajoie, *Switz.* 22 B4
Ajok, *Sudan* 77 F2
Ajuy, *Phil.* 55 F5
Ak Dağ, *Turkey* 66 D3
Ak Daglař, *Turkey* 66 C7
Akaba, *Togo* 79 D5
Akabira, *Japan* 48 C11
Akabli, *Algeria* 75 C5
Akaki Beseka, *Ethiopia* 77 F4
Akala, *Sudan* 77 D4
Akamas □, *Cyprus* 37 D11
Akanthou, *Cyprus* 37 D12
Akaroa, *N.Z.* 87 K4
Akasha, *Sudan* 76 C3
Akashi, *Japan* 49 G7
Akbou, *Algeria* 75 A5
Akçaabat, *Turkey* 67 B8
Akçadağ, *Turkey* 66 C7
Akçakale, *Turkey* 67 D8
Akçakoca, *Turkey* 66 B4
Akchâr, *Mauritania* 74 D2
Akdağmadeni, *Turkey* 66 C6
Akelamo, *Indonesia* 57 D7
Akershus fylke □, *Norway* 10 E5
Aketi, *Zaïre* 80 D4
Akhalkalaki, *Georgia* 43 K6
Akhaltsikhe, *Georgia* 43 K6
Akharnaí, *Greece* 39 L6
Akhelóös →, *Greece* 39 L4
Akhendria, *Greece* 39 Q8
Akhéron →, *Greece* 39 K3
Akhisar, *Turkey* 66 C2
Akhladhókambos, *Greece* 39 M5
Akhmîm, *Egypt* 76 B3
Akhnur, *India* 63 C6
Akhtuba →, *Russia* 43 G8
Akhtubinsk, *Russia* 43 F8
Akhty, *Russia* 43 K8
Akhtyrka = Okhtyrka, *Ukraine* 41 G8
Aki, *Japan* 49 H6
Akimiski I., *Canada* 98 B3
Akimovka, *Ukraine* 41 J8
Akita, *Japan* 48 E10
Akita □, *Japan* 48 E10
Akjoujt, *Mauritania* 78 B2
Akka, *Morocco* 74 C3
Akkeshi, *Japan* 48 C12
'Akko, *Israel* 69 C4
Akkol, *Kazakhstan* 44 E8
Akkrum, *Neths.* 16 B7
Aklampa, *Benin* 79 D5
Aklavik, *Canada* 96 B6
Akmolinsk = Aqmola, *Kazakhstan* 44 D8
Akmonte, *Spain* 31 H4
Aknoul, *Morocco* 75 B4
Akō, *Japan* 49 G7
Ako, *Nigeria* 79 C7
Akobo →, *Ethiopia* 77 F3
Akola, *India* 60 J10
Akonolinga, *Cameroon* 79 E7
Akordat, *Eritrea* 77 D4
Akosombo Dam, *Ghana* 79 D5
Akot, *Sudan* 77 F3
Akpatok I., *Canada* 97 B13
Åkrahamn, *Norway* 9 G11
Akranes, *Iceland* 8 D2
Akreïjit, *Mauritania* 78 B3
Akrítas Venétiko, Ákra, *Greece* 39 N4
Akron, *Colo., U.S.A.* 108 E3
Akron, *Ohio, U.S.A.* 106 E3
Akrotiri, *Cyprus* 66 E5
Akrotíri, Ákra, *Greece* 39 J8
Akrotiri Bay, *Cyprus* 37 E12
Aksai Chin, *India* 63 B8
Aksaray, *Turkey* 66 C6
Aksarka, *Russia* 44 C7
Aksay, *Kazakhstan* 44 D6
Akşehir, *Turkey* 66 C4
Akşehir Gölü, *Turkey* 66 C4
Aksenovo Zilovskoye, *Russia* 45 D12
Akstafa = Ağstafa, *Azerbaijan* 43 K7
Aksu, *China* 54 B3
Aksu →, *Turkey* 66 D4
Aksum, *Ethiopia* 77 E4
Aktash, *Russia* 42 C11
Aktogay, *Kazakhstan* 44 E8
Aktsyabrski, *Belarus* 41 F5
Aktyubinsk = Aqtöbe, *Kazakhstan* 44 D6
Aku, *Nigeria* 79 D6
Akure, *Nigeria* 79 D6
Akureyri, *Iceland* 8 D4
Akuseki-Shima, *Japan* 49 K4
Akusha, *Russia* 43 J8
Akwa-Ibom □, *Nigeria* 79 E6
Akyab = Sittwe, *Burma* 61 J18
Akyazı, *Turkey* 66 B4
Al 'Adan, *Yemen* 68 E4
Al Aḩsā, *Si. Arabia* 65 E6
Al Ajfar, *Si. Arabia* 64 E4
Al Amādīyah, *Iraq* 67 D10
Al Amārah, *Iraq* 67 G12
Al 'Aqabah, *Jordan* 69 F4
Al Arak, *Syria* 67 E8
Al 'Aramah, *Si. Arabia* 64 E5
Al Arṭāwīyah, *Si. Arabia* 64 E5
Al 'Āşimah □, *Jordan* 69 D5
Al' Assāfīyah, *Si. Arabia* 64 D3
Al 'Ayn, *Oman* 65 E7
Al 'Ayn, *Si. Arabia* 64 E3
Al A'ẓamīyah, *Iraq* 64 C5
Al 'Azīzīyah, *Iraq* 67 F11
Al 'Azīzīyah, *Libya* 75 B7
Al Bāb, *Syria* 66 D7
Al Bad', *Si. Arabia* 64 D2
Al Bādī, *Iraq* 64 C4
Al Baḩrah, *Kuwait* 64 D5
Al Balqā' □, *Jordan* 69 C4
Al Barkāt, *Libya* 75 D7
Al Bārūk, J., *Lebanon* 69 B4
Al Başrah, *Iraq* 64 D5
Al Baṭḩā, *Iraq* 64 D5
Al Batrūn, *Lebanon* 69 A4
Al Bayḍā, *Libya* 73 B9
Al Biqā □, *Lebanon* 69 A5
Al Bi'r, *Si. Arabia* 64 D3
Al Bu'ayrāt al Ḩasūn, *Libya* 73 B8
Al Burayj, *Syria* 69 A5
Al Fallūjah, *Iraq* 67 F10
Al Fāw, *Iraq* 65 D6
Al Fujayrah, *U.A.E.* 65 E8
Al Ghadaf, W. →, *Jordan* 69 D5
Al Ghammās, *Iraq* 64 D5
Al Hābah, *Si. Arabia* 64 E5
Al Ḩadīthah, *Iraq* 67 E10
Al Ḩadīthah, *Si. Arabia* 64 D3
Al Ḩaḍr, *Iraq* 67 E10
Al Ḩājānah, *Syria* 69 B5
Al Ḩāmad, *Si. Arabia* 64 D3
Al Hamdāniyah, *Syria* 64 C3
Al Ḩamidīyah, *Syria* 69 A4
Al Ḩammādah al Ḩamrā', *Libya* 75 C7
Al Ḩammār, *Iraq* 64 D5
Al Ḩarīr, W. →, *Syria* 69 C4
Al Ḩasā, W. →, *Jordan* 69 D4
Al Ḩasakah, *Syria* 67 D9
Al Ḩawrah, *Yemen* 68 E4
Al Ḩaydān, W. →, *Jordan* 69 D4
Al Ḩayy, *Iraq* 67 F12
Al Ḩijāz, *Si. Arabia* 68 B2
Al Ḩillah, *Iraq* 67 F11
Al Ḩillah, *Si. Arabia* 68 C4
Al Hindīyah, *Iraq* 67 F11
Al Hirmil, *Lebanon* 69 A5
Al Hoceïma, *Morocco* 74 A4
Al Ḩudaydah, *Yemen* 68 E3
Al Ḩufūf, *Si. Arabia* 65 E6
Al Ḩumaydah, *Si. Arabia* 64 D2
Al Ḩunayy, *Si. Arabia* 65 E6
Al Īsāwīyah, *Si. Arabia* 64 D3
Al Ittihad = Madīnat ash Sha'b, *Yemen* 68 E3
Al Jafr, *Jordan* 69 E5
Al Jaghbūb, *Libya* 73 C9
Al Jahrah, *Kuwait* 64 D5
Al Jalāmīd, *Si. Arabia* 64 D3
Al Jamalīyah, *Qatar* 65 E6
Al Janūb □, *Lebanon* 69 B4
Al Jawf, *Libya* 73 D9
Al Jawf, *Si. Arabia* 64 D3
Al Jazirah, *Iraq* 67 E10
Al Jazirah, *Libya* 73 C9
Al Jithāmīyah, *Si. Arabia* 64 E4
Al Jubayl, *Si. Arabia* 65 E6
Al Jubaylah, *Si. Arabia* 64 E5
Al Jubb, *Si. Arabia* 64 E4
Al Junaynah, *Sudan* 73 F9
Al Kabā'ish, *Iraq* 64 D5
Al Karak, *Jordan* 69 D4
Al Karak □, *Jordan* 69 E5
Al Kāẓim Tyah, *Iraq* 67 F11
Al Khalīl, *West Bank* 69 D4
Al Khāliş, *Iraq* 67 F11
Al Khawr, *Qatar* 65 E6
Al Khiḍr, *Iraq* 64 D5
Al Khiyām, *Lebanon* 69 B4
Al Kiswah, *Syria* 69 B5
Al Kūfah, *Iraq* 67 F11
Al Kufrah, *Libya* 73 D9
Al Kuhayfīyah, *Si. Arabia* 64 E4
Al Kūt, *Iraq* 67 F11
Al Kuwayt, *Kuwait* 64 D5
Al Labwah, *Lebanon* 69 A5
Al Lādhiqīyah, *Syria* 66 E6
Al Līth, *Si. Arabia* 76 C5
Al Liwā', *Oman* 65 E8
Al Luḩayyah, *Yemen* 68 D3
Al Madīnah, *Iraq* 64 D5
Al Madīnah, *Si. Arabia* 64 E3
Al-Mafraq, *Jordan* 69 C5
Al Maḩmūdīyah, *Iraq* 67 F11
Al Majma'ah, *Si. Arabia* 64 E5
Al Makhruq, W. →, *Jordan* 69 D6
Al Makḩūl, *Si. Arabia* 64 E4
Al Manāmah, *Bahrain* 65 E6
Al Maqwa', *Kuwait* 64 D5
Al Marj, *Libya* 73 B9
Al Maţlā, *Kuwait* 64 D5
Al Mawjib, W. →, *Jordan* 69 D4
Al Mawşil, *Iraq* 67 D10
Al Mayādin, *Syria* 67 E9
Al Mazār, *Jordan* 69 D4
Al Midhnab, *Si. Arabia* 64 E5
Al Minā', *Lebanon* 69 A4
Al Miqdādīyah, *Iraq* 67 E11
Al Mubarraz, *Si. Arabia* 65 E6
Al Mughayrā', *U.A.E.* 65 E7
Al Muḩarraq, *Bahrain* 65 E6
Al Mukallā, *Yemen* 68 E4
Al Mukhā, *Yemen* 68 E3
Al Musayjīd, *Si. Arabia* 64 E3
Al Musayyib, *Iraq* 67 F11
Al Muwayliḩ, *Si. Arabia* 64 E2
Al Owuho = Otukpa, *Nigeria* 79 D6
Al Qā'im, *Iraq* 67 E9
Al Qalībah, *Si. Arabia* 64 D3
Al Qāmishlī, *Syria* 67 D9
Al Qaryatayn, *Syria* 69 A6
Al Qaşabát, *Libya* 73 B7
Al Qaţ'ā, *Syria* 67 E9
Al Qaţīf, *Si. Arabia* 65 E6
Al Qatrānah, *Jordan* 69 D5
Al Qaţrūn, *Libya* 73 D8
Al Qayşūmah, *Si. Arabia* 64 D5
Al Quds = Jerusalem, *Israel* 69 D4
Al Qunaytirah, *Syria* 69 C4
Al Qunfudhah, *Si. Arabia* 76 D5
Al Qurnah, *Iraq* 64 D5
Al Quşayr, *Iraq* 64 D5
Al Quşayr, *Syria* 69 A5
Al Qutayfah, *Syria* 69 B5
Al' Uḑaylīyah, *Si. Arabia* 65 E6
Al 'Ulā, *Si. Arabia* 64 E3
Al Uqaylah ash Sharqīgah, *Libya* 73 B8
Al Uqayr, *Si. Arabia* 65 E6
Al 'Uwaynid, *Si. Arabia* 64 E5
Al 'Uwayqīlah, *Si. Arabia* 64 D4
Al 'Uyūn, *Si. Arabia* 64 E4
Al 'Uyūn, *Si. Arabia* 64 E3
Al Wajh, *Si. Arabia* 64 E3
Al Wakrah, *Qatar* 65 E6
Al Wannān, *Si. Arabia* 65 E6
Al Waqbah, *Si. Arabia* 64 D5
Al Wari'āh, *Si. Arabia* 64 E5
Al Wātīyah, *Libya* 75 B7
Al Wusayl, *Qatar* 65 E6
Ala, *Italy* 32 C8
Ala Dağları, *Turkey* 67 C10
Alabama □, *U.S.A.* 105 J2
Alabama →, *U.S.A.* 105 K2
Alaca, *Turkey* 66 B6
Alaçam, *Turkey* 66 B6
Alaçam Dağları, *Turkey* 66 C3
Alaejos, *Spain* 30 D5
Alaérma, *Greece* 37 C9
Alagir, *Russia* 43 J7
Alagna Valsésia, *Italy* 32 C4
Alagoa Grande, *Brazil* 122 C4
Alagoas □, *Brazil* 122 C4
Alagoinhas, *Brazil* 123 D4
Alagón, *Spain* 28 D3
Alagón →, *Spain* 31 F4
Alajero, *Canary Is.* 36 F2
Alajuela, *Costa Rica* 116 D3
Alakamisy, *Madag.* 85 C8
Alalapura, *Surinam* 121 C6
Alalaú →, *Brazil* 121 D5
Alameda, *Spain* 31 H6
Alameda, *Calif., U.S.A.* 112 H4
Alameda, *N. Mex., U.S.A.* 111 J10
Alaminos, *Phil.* 55 C3
Alamo, *U.S.A.* 113 J11
Alamo Crossing, *U.S.A.* 113 L13
Alamogordo, *U.S.A.* 111 K11
Alamos, *Mexico* 114 B3
Alamosa, *U.S.A.* 111 H11
Åland, *Finland* 9 F19
Alandroal, *Portugal* 31 G3
Ålands hav, *Sweden* 9 F18
Alandur, *India* 60 N12
Alange, Presa de, *Spain* 31 G4
Alania = North Ossetia □, *Russia* 43 J7
Alanis, *Spain* 31 G5
Alanya, *Turkey* 66 D5
Alaotra, Farihin', *Madag.* 85 B8
Alapayevsk, *Russia* 44 D7
Alar del Rey, *Spain* 30 C6
Alaraz, *Spain* 30 E5
Alaşehir, *Turkey* 66 C3
Alaska □, *U.S.A.* 96 B5
Alaska, G. of, *Pac. Oc.* 96 C5
Alaska Highway, *Canada* 100 B3
Alaska Peninsula, *U.S.A.* 96 C4
Alaska Range, *U.S.A.* 96 B4
Alássio, *Italy* 32 D5
Älät, *Azerbaijan* 43 L9
Alataw Shankou, *China* 54 B3
Alatri, *Italy* 34 A6
Alatyr, *Russia* 42 C8
Alatyr →, *Russia* 42 C8
Alausi, *Ecuador* 120 D2
Álava □, *Spain* 28 C2
Alava, C., *U.S.A.* 110 B1
Alaverdi, *Armenia* 43 K7
Alavus, *Finland* 9 E20
Alawoona, *Australia* 91 E3
'Alayh, *Lebanon* 69 B4
Alayor, *Spain* 36 B11
Alazani →, *Azerbaijan* 43 K8
Alba, *Italy* 32 D5
Alba de Tormes, *Spain* 30 E5
Alba-Iulia, *Romania* 38 C6
Albac, *Romania* 38 C6
Albacete, *Spain* 29 G3
Albacete □, *Spain* 29 G3
Albacutya, L., *Australia* 91 F3
Ålbæk, *Denmark* 11 G4
Ålbæk Bugt, *Denmark* 11 G4
Albaida, *Spain* 29 G4
Albalate de las Nogueras, *Spain* 28 E2
Albalate del Arzobispo, *Spain* 28 D4
Albania ■, *Europe* 39 J3
Albano Laziale, *Italy* 34 A5
Albany, *Australia* 89 G2
Albany, *Ga., U.S.A.* 105 K3
Albany, *Minn., U.S.A.* 108 C7
Albany, *N.Y., U.S.A.* 107 D11
Albany, *Oreg., U.S.A.* 110 D2
Albany, *Tex., U.S.A.* 109 J5
Albany →, *Canada* 98 B3
Albardón, *Argentina* 126 C2
Albarracín, *Spain* 28 E3
Albarracín, Sierra de, *Spain* 28 E3
Albatross B., *Australia* 90 A3
Albegna →, *Italy* 33 F8
Albemarle, *U.S.A.* 105 H5
Albemarle Sd., *U.S.A.* 105 H7
Albenga, *Italy* 32 D5
Alberche →, *Spain* 30 F6
Alberdi, *Paraguay* 126 B4
Alberes, Mts., *Spain* 28 C7
Alberique, *Spain* 29 F4
Albersdorf, *Germany* 18 A5
Albert, *France* 25 B9
Albert, L., *Australia* 91 F2
Albert Canyon, *Canada* 100 C5
Albert Edward Ra., *Australia* 88 C4
Albert L., *Africa* 82 B3
Albert Lea, *U.S.A.* 108 D8
Albert Nile →, *Uganda* 82 B3
Albert Town, *Bahamas* 117 B5
Alberta □, *Canada* 100 C6
Alberti, *Argentina* 126 D3
Albertinia, *S. Africa* 84 E3
Albertkanaal →, *Belgium* 17 F4
Alberton, *Canada* 99 C7
Albertville = Kalemie, *Zaïre* 82 D2
Albertville, *France* 27 C10
Albi, *France* 26 E6
Albia, *U.S.A.* 108 E8
Albina, *Surinam* 121 B7
Albina, Ponta, *Angola* 84 B1
Albino, *Italy* 32 C6
Albion, *Idaho, U.S.A.* 110 E7
Albion, *Mich., U.S.A.* 104 D3
Albion, *Nebr., U.S.A.* 108 E5
Albion, *Pa., U.S.A.* 106 E4
Alblasserdam, *Neths.* 16 E5
Albocácer, *Spain* 28 E5
Alborán, *Medit. S.* 31 K7
Alborea, *Spain* 29 F3
Ålborg, *Denmark* 11 G3
Ålborg Bugt, *Denmark* 11 H4
Alborz, Reshteh-ye Kūhhā-ye, *Iran* 65 C7
Albox, *Spain* 29 H2
Albreda, *Canada* 100 C5
Albufeira, *Portugal* 31 H2
Albula →, *Switz.* 23 C8
Albuñol, *Spain* 29 J1
Albuquerque, *Brazil* 125 D6
Albuquerque, *U.S.A.* 111 J10
Albuquerque, Cayos de, *Caribbean* 116 D3
Alburg, *U.S.A.* 107 B11
Alburno, Mte., *Italy* 35 B8
Alburquerque, *Spain* 31 F4
Albury, *Australia* 91 F4
Alby, *Sweden* 10 B9
Alcácer do Sal, *Portugal* 31 G2
Alcaçovas, *Portugal* 31 G2
Alcalá de Chisvert, *Spain* 28 E5
Alcalá de Guadaira, *Spain* 31 H5
Alcalá de Henares, *Spain* 28 E1
Alcalá de los Gazules, *Spain* 31 J5
Alcalá la Real, *Spain* 31 H7
Alcamo, *Italy* 34 E5
Alcanadre, *Spain* 28 C2
Alcanadre →, *Spain* 28 D4
Alcanar, *Spain* 28 E5
Alcanede, *Portugal* 31 F2
Alcanena, *Portugal* 31 F2
Alcañices, *Spain* 30 D4
Alcañiz, *Spain* 28 D4
Alcântara, *Brazil* 122 B3
Alcántara, *Spain* 31 F4
Alcantara L., *Canada* 101 A7
Alcantarilla, *Spain* 29 H3
Alcaracejos, *Spain* 31 G6
Alcaraz, *Spain* 29 G2
Alcaraz, Sierra de, *Spain* 29 G2
Alcaudete, *Spain* 31 H6
Alcázar de San Juan, *Spain* 29 F1
Alchevsk, *Ukraine* 41 H10
Alcira, *Spain* 29 F4
Alcoa, *U.S.A.* 105 H4
Alcobaça, *Portugal* 31 F2
Alcobendas, *Spain* 28 E1
Alcolea del Pinar, *Spain* 28 D2
Alcora, *Spain* 28 E4
Alcorcón, *Spain* 30 E7
Alcoutim, *Portugal* 31 H3
Alcova, *U.S.A.* 110 E10
Alcoy, *Spain* 29 G4
Alcubierre, Sierra de, *Spain* 28 D4
Alcublas, *Spain* 28 F4
Alcudia, *Spain* 36 B10
Alcudia, B. de, *Spain* 36 B10
Alcudia, Sierra de la, *Spain* 31 G6
Aldabra Is., *Seychelles* 71 G8
Aldama, *Mexico* 115 C5
Aldan, *Russia* 45 D13
Aldan →, *Russia* 45 C13
Aldea, Pta. de la, *Canary Is.* 36 G4
Aldeburgh, *U.K.* 13 E9
Aldeia Nova, *Portugal* 31 H3
Alder, *U.S.A.* 110 D7
Alder Pk., *U.S.A.* 112 K5
Alderney, *U.K.* 13 H5
Aldershot, *U.K.* 13 F7
Aledo, *U.S.A.* 108 E9
Alefa, *Ethiopia* 77 E4
Aleg, *Mauritania* 78 B2
Alegranza, *Canary Is.* 36 E6
Alegranza, I., *Canary Is.* 36 E6
Alegre, *Brazil* 123 F3
Alegrete, *Brazil* 127 B4
Aleisk, *Russia* 44 D9
Aleksandriya = Oleksandriya, *Ukraine* 41 H7
Aleksandriya = Oleksandriya, *Ukraine* 41 G4
Aleksandriyskaya, *Russia* 43 J8
Aleksandrov, *Russia* 42 B4

Aleksandrov Gay, *Russia* . 42 E9
Aleksandrovac,
  Serbia, Yug. 21 L11
Aleksandrovka =
  Oleksandrovka, *Ukraine* 41 H7
Aleksandrovo, *Bulgaria* .. 38 F7
Aleksandrovsk-
  Sakhalinskiy, *Russia* .. 45 D15
Aleksandrovskiy Zavod,
  Russia 45 D12
Aleksandrovskoye, *Russia* 44 C8
Aleksandrów Kujawski,
  Poland 20 C8
Aleksandrów Łódźki,
  Poland 20 D9
Alekseyevka, *Russia* 42 D10
Alekseyevka, *Russia* 42 E4
Aleksin, *Russia* 42 C3
Aleksinac, *Serbia, Yug.* .. 21 M11
Além Paraíba, *Brazil* 123 F3
Alemania, *Argentina* 126 B2
Alemania, *Chile* 126 B2
Ålen, *Norway* 10 B5
Alençon, *France* 24 D7
Alenuihaha Channel,
  U.S.A. 102 H17
Aleppo = Ḩalab, *Syria* .. 66 D7
Aléria, *France* 27 F13
Alert Bay, *Canada* 100 C3
Alès, *France* 27 D8
Aleşd, *Romania* 38 B5
Alessándria, *Italy* 32 D5
Ålestrup, *Denmark* 11 H3
Ålesund, *Norway* 9 E12
Alet-les-Bains, *France* ... 26 F6
Aletschhorn, *Switz.* 22 D6
Aleutian Is., *Pac. Oc.* ... 96 C2
Aleutian Trench, *Pac. Oc.* 92 B10
Alexander, *U.S.A.* 108 B3
Alexander, Mt., *Australia* . 89 E3
Alexander Arch., *U.S.A.* . 100 B2
Alexander Bay, *S. Africa* . 84 D2
Alexander City, *U.S.A.* .. 105 J3
Alexander I., *Antarctica* .. 5 C17
Alexandra, *Australia* 91 F4
Alexandra, *N.Z.* 87 L2
Alexandra Falls, *Canada* . 100 A5
Alexandretta =
  Iskenderun, *Turkey* .. 66 D7
Alexandria = El
  Iskandarîya, *Egypt* 76 H6
Alexandria, *Australia* 90 B2
Alexandria, *B.C., Canada* 100 C4
Alexandria, *Ont., Canada* 98 C5
Alexandria, *Romania* 38 F8
Alexandria, *S. Africa* 84 E4
Alexandria, *Ind., U.S.A.* . 104 E3
Alexandria, *La., U.S.A.* .. 109 K8
Alexandria, *Minn., U.S.A.* 108 C7
Alexandria, *S. Dak.,
  U.S.A.* 108 D6
Alexandria, *Va., U.S.A.* .. 104 F7
Alexandria Bay, *U.S.A.* .. 107 B9
Alexandrina, L., *Australia* 91 F2
Alexandroúpolis, *Greece* . 39 J8
Alexis →, *Canada* 99 B8
Alexis Creek, *Canada* 100 C4
Alfabia, *Spain* 36 B9
Alfambra, *Spain* 28 E3
Alfândega da Fé, *Portugal* 30 D4
Alfaro, *Spain* 28 C3
Alfenas, *Brazil* 127 A6
Alfiós →, *Greece* 39 M4
Alfonsine, *Italy* 33 D9
Alford, *U.K.* 14 D6
Alfred, *Maine, U.S.A.* ... 107 C14
Alfred, *N.Y., U.S.A.* 106 D7
Alfreton, *U.K.* 12 D6
Alga, *Kazakhstan* 44 E6
Algaida, *Spain* 36 B9
Algar, *Spain* 31 J5
Algård, *Norway* 9 G11
Algarinejo, *Spain* 31 H6
Algarve, *Portugal* 31 J2
Algeciras, *Spain* 31 J5
Algemesí, *Spain* 29 F4
Alger, *Algeria* 75 A5
Algeria ■, *Africa* 75 C5
Alghero, *Italy* 34 B1
Algiers = Alger, *Algeria* . 75 A5
Algoa B., *S. Africa* 84 E4
Algodonales, *Spain* 31 J5
Algodor →, *Spain* 30 F7
Algoma, *U.S.A.* 104 C2
Algona, *U.S.A.* 108 D7
Algonac, *U.S.A.* 106 D2
Alhama de Almería, *Spain* 29 J2
Alhama de Aragón, *Spain* 28 D3
Alhama de Granada, *Spain* 31 J7
Alhama de Murcia, *Spain* . 29 H3
Alhambra, *Spain* 29 G1
Alhambra, *U.S.A.* 113 L8
Alhaurín el Grande, *Spain* 31 J6
Alhucemas = Al Hoceïma,
  Morocco 74 A4
'Alī al Gharbī, *Iraq* 67 F12
'Alī ash Sharqī, *Iraq* 67 F12
Äli Bayramlı, *Azerbaijan* . 43 L9
'Alī Khēl, *Afghan.* 62 C3
Ali Sahîh, *Djibouti* 77 E5
Alī Shāh, *Iran* 64 B5
Ália, *Italy* 34 E6
'Alīābād, *Khorāsān, Iran* . 65 C8
'Alīābād, *Kordestān, Iran* . 64 C5
'Alīābād, *Yazd, Iran* 65 D7
Aliaga, *Spain* 28 E4

Aliağa, *Turkey* 66 C2
Aliákmon →, *Greece* ... 39 J5
Alibo, *Ethiopia* 77 F4
Alibunar, *Serbia, Yug.* ... 21 K10
Alicante, *Spain* 29 G4
Alicante □, *Spain* 29 G4
Alice, *S. Africa* 84 E4
Alice, *U.S.A.* 109 M5
Alice →, *Queens.,
  Australia* 90 C3
Alice →, *Queens.,
  Australia* 90 B3
Alice, Punta dell', *Italy* .. 35 C10
Alice Arm, *Canada* 100 B3
Alice Downs, *Australia* .. 88 C4
Alice Springs, *Australia* .. 90 C1
Alicedale, *S. Africa* 84 E4
Aliceville, *U.S.A.* 105 J1
Alick Cr. →, *Australia* .. 90 C3
Alicudi, I., *Italy* 35 D7
Alida, *Canada* 101 D8
Aligarh, *Raj., India* 62 G7
Aligarh, *Ut. P., India* ... 62 F8
Alīgūdarz, *Iran* 65 C6
Alijó, *Portugal* 30 D3
Alimena, *Italy* 35 E7
Alimnía, *Greece* 37 C9
Alingsås, *Sweden* 11 G6
Alipur, *Pakistan* 62 E4
Alipur Duar, *India* 61 F16
Aliquippa, *U.S.A.* 106 F4
Aliste →, *Spain* 30 D5
Alivérion, *Greece* 39 L7
Aliwal North, *S. Africa* .. 84 E4
Alix, *Canada* 100 C6
Aljezur, *Portugal* 31 H2
Aljustrel, *Portugal* 31 H2
Alkamari, *Niger* 79 C7
Alken, *Belgium* 17 G6
Alkmaar, *Neths.* 16 C5
All American Canal,
  U.S.A. 111 K6
Allada, *Benin* 79 D5
Allah Dad, *Pakistan* 62 G2
Allahabad, *India* 63 G9
Allakh-Yun, *Russia* 45 C14
Allal Tazi, *Morocco* 74 B3
Allan, *Canada* 101 C7
Allanmyo, *Burma* 61 K19
Allanche, *France* 26 C6
Allanridge, *S. Africa* 84 D4
Allanwater, *Canada* 98 B1
Allaqi, Wadi →, *Egypt* . 76 C3
Allariz, *Spain* 30 C3
Allassac, *France* 26 C5
Alle, *Belgium* 17 J5
Allegan, *U.S.A.* 104 D3
Allegany, *U.S.A.* 106 D6
Allegheny →, *U.S.A.* .. 106 F5
Allegheny Plateau, *U.S.A.* 104 G6
Allegheny Reservoir,
  U.S.A. 106 E6
Allègre, *France* 26 C7
Allen, *Argentina* 128 A3
Allen, Bog of, *Ireland* ... 15 C4
Allen, L., *Ireland* 15 B3
Allende, *Mexico* 114 B4
Allentown, *U.S.A.* 107 F9
Alleppey, *India* 60 Q10
Aller →, *Germany* 18 C5
Alleur, *Belgium* 17 G7
Allevard, *France* 27 C10
Alliance, *Surinam* 121 B7
Alliance, *Nebr., U.S.A.* . 108 D3
Alliance, *Ohio, U.S.A.* .. 106 F3
Allier □, *France* 26 B6
Allier →, *France* 25 F10
Allingåbro, *Denmark* ... 11 H4
Alliston, *Canada* 98 D4
Alloa, *U.K.* 14 E5
Allora, *Australia* 91 D5
Allos, *France* 27 D10
Alluitsup Paa = Sydprøven,
  Greenland 4 C5
Alma, *Canada* 99 C5
Alma, *Ga., U.S.A.* 105 K4
Alma, *Kans., U.S.A.* ... 108 F6
Alma, *Mich., U.S.A.* ... 104 D3
Alma, *Nebr., U.S.A.* ... 108 E5
Alma, *Wis., U.S.A.* 108 C9
Alma Ata = Almaty,
  Kazakhstan 44 E8
Almada, *Portugal* 31 G1
Almadén, *Australia* 90 B3
Almadén, *Spain* 31 G6
Almagro, *Spain* 31 G7
Almansa, *Spain* 29 G3
Almanza, *Spain* 30 C5
Almanzor, Pico del Moro,
  Spain 30 E5
Almanzora →, *Spain* ... 29 H3
Almas, *Brazil* 123 D2
Almaty, *Kazakhstan* 44 E8
Almazán, *Spain* 28 D2
Almazora, *Spain* 28 F4
Almeirim, *Brazil* 121 D7
Almeirim, *Portugal* 31 F2
Almelo, *Neths.* 16 D9
Almenar, *Spain* 28 D2
Almenara, *Brazil* 123 E3
Almenara, *Spain* 28 F4
Almenara, Sierra de, *Spain* 29 H3
Almendralejo, *Spain* ... 31 G4
Almería, *Spain* 29 J2
Almería □, *Spain* 29 H2

Almería, G. de, *Spain* ... 29 J2
Almetyevsk, *Russia* 42 C11
Almirante, *Panama* 116 E3
Almirante Montt, G., *Chile* 128 D2
Almirós, *Greece* 39 K5
Almirou, Kólpos, *Greece* . 37 D6
Almodôvar, *Portugal* 31 H2
Almodóvar del Campo,
  Spain 31 G6
Almogia, *Spain* 31 J6
Almonaster la Real, *Spain* 31 H4
Almont, *U.S.A.* 106 D1
Almonte, *Canada* 107 A8
Almonte →, *Spain* 31 F4
Almora, *India* 63 E8
Almoradí, *Spain* 29 G4
Almorox, *Spain* 30 E6
Almoustarat, *Mali* 79 B5
Almuñécar, *Spain* 31 J7
Alnif, *Morocco* 74 B3
Alnwick, *U.K.* 12 B6
Aloi, *Uganda* 82 B3
Alon, *Burma* 61 H19
Alor, *Indonesia* 57 F6
Alor Setar, *Malaysia* 59 J3
Alora, *Spain* 31 J6
Alosno, *Spain* 31 H3
Alougoum, *Morocco* 74 B3
Aloysius, Mt., *Australia* . 89 E4
Alpaugh, *U.S.A.* 112 K7
Alpedrinha, *Portugal* ... 30 E3
Alpena, *U.S.A.* 104 C4
Alpercatas →, *Brazil* ... 122 C3
Alpes-de-Haute-
  Provence □, *France* ... 27 D10
Alpes-Maritimes □, *France* 27 E11
Alpha, *Australia* 90 C4
Alphen, *Neths.* 17 F5
Alphen aan den Rijn,
  Neths. 16 D5
Alpiarça, *Portugal* 31 F2
Alpine, *Ariz., U.S.A.* ... 111 K9
Alpine, *Calif., U.S.A.* ... 113 N10
Alpine, *Tex., U.S.A.* 109 K3
Alpnach, *Switz.* 23 C6
Alps, *Europe* 6 F7
Alpu, *Turkey* 66 C4
Alrø, *Denmark* 11 J4
Alroy Downs, *Australia* . 90 B2
Alsace, *France* 25 D14
Alsask, *Canada* 101 C7
Alsásua, *Spain* 28 C2
Alsdorf, *Germany* 18 E2
Alsen, *Sweden* 10 A7
Alsfeld, *Germany* 18 E5
Alsten, *Norway* 8 D15
Alta, *Norway* 8 B20
Alta Gracia, *Argentina* .. 126 C3
Alta Lake, *Canada* 100 C4
Alta Sierra, *U.S.A.* 113 K8
Altaelva →, *Norway* ... 8 B20
Altafjorden, *Norway* ... 8 A20
Altagracia, *Venezuela* .. 120 A3
Altagracia de Orituco,
  Venezuela 120 B4
Altai = Aerhtai Shan,
  Mongolia 54 B4
Altamachi →, *Bolivia* .. 124 D4
Altamaha →, *U.S.A.* .. 105 K5
Altamira, *Brazil* 121 D7
Altamira, *Chile* 126 B2
Altamira, *Colombia* 120 C2
Altamira, *Mexico* 115 C5
Altamira, Cuevas de, *Spain* 30 B6
Altamont, *U.S.A.* 107 D10
Altamura, *Italy* 35 B9
Altanbulag, *Mongolia* .. 54 A5
Altar, *Mexico* 114 A2
Altata, *Mexico* 114 C3
Altavista, *U.S.A.* 104 G6
Altay, *China* 54 B3
Alte Mellum, *Germany* . 18 B4
Altea, *Spain* 29 G4
Altenberg, *Germany* ... 18 E9
Altenbruch, *Germany* .. 18 B4
Altenburg, *Germany* ... 18 E8
Altenkirchen,
  *Mecklenburg-Vorpommern,
  Germany* 18 A9
Altenkirchen, *Rhld.-Pfz.,
  Germany* 18 E3
Altentreptow, *Germany* . 18 B9
Alter do Chão, *Portugal* . 31 F3
Altıntaş, *Turkey* 66 C4
Altiplano, *Bolivia* 124 D4
Altkirch, *France* 25 E14
Altmühl →, *Germany* . 19 G7
Alto Adige = Trentino-
  Alto Adige □, *Italy* ... 32 B8
Alto Araguaia, *Brazil* .. 125 D7
Alto Cuchumatanes =
  Cuchumatanes, Sierra de
  los, *Guatemala* 116 C1
Alto del Inca, *Chile* 126 A2
Alto Garças, *Brazil* 125 D7
Alto Iriri →, *Brazil* 125 B7
Alto Ligonha, *Mozam.* .. 83 F4
Alto Molocue, *Mozam.* .. 83 F4
Alto Paraguai, *Brazil* ... 125 C6
Alto Paraguay □, *Paraguay* 126 A4
Alto Paraná □, *Paraguay* 127 B5
Alto Parnaíba, *Brazil* ... 122 C2
Alto Purús →, *Peru* ... 124 B3
Alto Río Senguerr,
  Argentina 128 C2

Alto Santo, *Brazil* 122 C4
Alto Sucuriú, *Brazil* 125 D7
Alto Turi, *Brazil* 122 B2
Alton, *Canada* 106 C4
Alton, *U.S.A.* 108 F9
Alton Downs, *Australia* . 91 D2
Altoona, *U.S.A.* 106 F6
Altópascio, *Italy* 32 E7
Altos, *Brazil* 122 C3
Altötting, *Germany* 19 G8
Altstätten, *Switz.* 23 B9
Altūn Kūprī, *Iraq* 67 E11
Altun Shan, *China* 54 C3
Alturas, *U.S.A.* 110 F3
Altus, *U.S.A.* 109 H5
Alubijid, *Phil.* 55 G6
Alucra, *Turkey* 67 B8
Alùla, *Somali Rep.* 68 E5
Alunite, *U.S.A.* 113 K12
Alupka, *Ukraine* 41 K8
Alushta, *Ukraine* 41 K8
Alusi, *Indonesia* 57 F8
Alustante, *Spain* 28 E3
Al'Uzayr, *Iraq* 64 D5
Alva, *U.S.A.* 109 G5
Alvaiázere, *Portugal* ... 30 F2
Älvängen, *Sweden* 11 G6
Alvarado, *Mexico* 115 D5
Alvarado, *U.S.A.* 109 J6
Alvarães, *Brazil* 121 D5
Alvaro Obregón, Presa,
  Mexico 114 B3
Alvdal, *Norway* 10 B4
Alvear, *Argentina* 126 B4
Alverca, *Portugal* 31 G1
Alveringem, *Belgium* ... 17 F1
Alvesta, *Sweden* 9 H16
Alvie, *Australia* 91 F3
Alvin, *U.S.A.* 109 L7
Alvinston, *Canada* 106 D3
Alvito, *Portugal* 31 G3
Älvkarleby, *Sweden* ... 9 F17
Älvros, *Sweden* 10 B8
Älvsbyn, *Sweden* 8 D19
Älvsborgs län □, *Sweden* 11 F6
Älvsered, *Sweden* 11 G6
Alwar, *India* 62 F7
Alxa Zuoqi, *China* 50 E3
Alyangula, *Australia* ... 90 A2
Alyata = Älät, *Azerbaijan* 43 L9
Alyth, *U.K.* 14 E5
Alytus, *Lithuania* 9 J21
Alzada, *U.S.A.* 108 C2
Alzano Lombardo, *Italy* . 32 C6
Alzette →, *Lux.* 17 J8
Alzey, *Germany* 19 F4
Am Dam, *Chad* 73 F9
Am-Timan, *Chad* 73 F9
Amacuro □, *Venezuela* . 121 B5
Amadeus, L., *Australia* . 89 D5
Amâdi, *Sudan* 77 F3
Amadi, *Zaïre* 82 B2
Amadjuak, *Canada* 97 B12
Amadjuak L., *Canada* .. 97 B12
Amadora, *Portugal* 31 G1
Amagasaki, *Japan* 49 G7
Amager, *Denmark* 11 J6
Amakusa-Shotō, *Japan* . 49 H5
Åmål, *Sweden* 9 G15
Amalfi, *Colombia* 120 B2
Amalfi, *Italy* 35 B7
Amaliás, *Greece* 39 M4
Amalner, *India* 60 J9
Amambaí, *Brazil* 127 A4
Amambaí →, *Brazil* ... 127 A5
Amambay □, *Paraguay* . 127 A4
Amambay, Cordillera de,
  S. Amer. 127 A4
Amami-Guntō, *Japan* .. 49 L4
Amami-Ō-Shima, *Japan* . 49 L4
Amana →, *Venezuela* .. 121 B5
Amaná, L., *Brazil* 121 D5
Amanda Park, *U.S.A.* .. 112 C3
Amándola, *Italy* 33 F10
Amangeldy, *Kazakhstan* . 44 D7
Amantea, *Italy* 35 C9
Amapá, *Brazil* 121 C7
Amapá □, *Brazil* 121 C7
Amapari, *Brazil* 121 C7
Amara, *Sudan* 77 E3
Amarante, *Brazil* 122 C3
Amarante, *Portugal* ... 30 D2
Amarante do Maranhão,
  Brazil 122 C2
Amaranth, *Canada* 101 C9
Amareleja, *Portugal* ... 31 G3
Amargosa, *Brazil* 123 D4
Amargosa →, *U.S.A.* .. 113 J10
Amargosa Range, *U.S.A.* 113 J10
Amári, *Greece* 37 D6
Amarillo, *U.S.A.* 109 H4
Amaro, Mte., *Italy* 33 F11
Amaro Leite, *Brazil* ... 123 D2
Amarpur, *India* 63 G12
Amasra, *Turkey* 66 B5
Amassama, *Nigeria* 79 D6
Amasya, *Turkey* 66 B6
Amataurá, *Brazil* 120 D4
Amatikulu, *S. Africa* ... 85 D5
Amatitlán, *Guatemala* .. 116 D1
Amatrice, *Italy* 33 F10
Amay, *Belgium* 17 G6
Amazon = Amazonas →,
  S. Amer. 121 D7
Amazonas □, *Brazil* ... 125 B5
Amazonas □, *Peru* 124 B2

Amazonas □, *Venezuela* . 120 C4
Amazonas →, *S. Amer.* . 121 D7
Ambahakily, *Madag.* ... 85 C7
Ambala, *India* 62 D7
Ambalavao, *Madag.* ... 85 C8
Ambalindum, *Australia* . 90 C2
Ambam, *Cameroon* 80 D2
Ambanja, *Madag.* 85 A8
Ambarchik, *Russia* 45 C17
Ambarijeby, *Madag.* ... 85 A8
Ambaro, Helodranon',
  Madag. 85 A8
Ambartsevo, *Russia* ... 44 D9
Ambato, *Ecuador* 120 D2
Ambato, Sierra de,
  Argentina 126 B2
Ambato Boeny, *Madag.* . 85 B8
Ambatofinandrahana,
  Madag. 85 C8
Ambatolampy, *Madag.* . 85 B8
Ambatondrazaka, *Madag.* 85 B8
Ambatosoratra, *Madag.* . 85 B8
Ambenja, *Madag.* 85 B8
Amberg, *Germany* 19 F7
Ambergris Cay, *Belize* .. 115 D7
Ambérieu-en-Bugey,
  France 27 C9
Amberley, *N.Z.* 87 K4
Ambert, *France* 26 C7
Ambidédi, *Mali* 78 C2
Ambikapur, *India* 63 H10
Ambikol, *Sudan* 76 C3
Ambilobé, *Madag.* 85 A8
Ambinanindrano, *Madag.* 85 C8
Ambjörnarp, *Sweden* .. 11 G7
Ambleside, *U.K.* 12 C5
Ambler →, *Belgium* ... 17 H8
Amblève →, *Belgium* .. 17 H7
Ambo, *Ethiopia* 77 F4
Ambo, *Peru* 124 C2
Ambodifototra, *Madag.* . 85 B8
Ambodilazana, *Madag.* . 85 B8
Ambohimahasoa, *Madag.* 85 C8
Ambohimanga, *Madag.* . 85 C8
Ambohitra, *Madag.* 85 A8
Amboise, *France* 24 E8
Ambon, *Indonesia* 57 E7
Amboseli L., *Kenya* 82 C4
Ambositra, *Madag.* 85 C8
Ambovombé, *Madag.* .. 85 D8
Amboy, *U.S.A.* 113 L11
Amboyna I., *S. China Sea* 56 C4
Ambridge, *U.S.A.* 106 F4
Ambriz, *Angola* 80 F2
Amby, *Australia* 91 D4
Amchitka I., *U.S.A.* ... 96 C1
Amderma, *Russia* 44 C7
Ameca, *Mexico* 114 C4
Ameca →, *Mexico* 114 C3
Amecameca, *Mexico* ... 115 D5
Ameland, *Neths.* 16 B7
Amélia, *Italy* 33 F9
Amélie-les-Bains-Palalda,
  France 26 F6
Amen, *Russia* 45 C18
Amendolara, *Italy* 35 C9
America, *Neths.* 17 F7
American Falls, *U.S.A.* . 110 E7
American Falls Reservoir,
  U.S.A. 110 E7
American Highland,
  Antarctica 5 D6
American Samoa ■,
  Pac. Oc. 87 B13
Americana, *Brazil* 127 A6
Americus, *U.S.A.* 105 J3
Amersfoort, *Neths.* 16 D6
Amersfoort, *S. Africa* ... 85 D4
Amery, *Australia* 89 F2
Amery, *Canada* 101 B10
Amery Ice Shelf, *Antarctica* 5 C6
Ames, *U.S.A.* 108 E8
Amesbury, *U.S.A.* 107 D14
Amfíklia, *Greece* 39 L5
Amfilokhía, *Greece* 39 L4
Amga, *Russia* 45 C14
Amga →, *Russia* 45 C14
Amgu, *Russia* 45 E14
Amgun →, *Russia* 45 D14
Amherst, *Burma* 61 L20
Amherst, *Canada* 99 C7
Amherst, *Mass., U.S.A.* . 107 D12
Amherst, *N.Y., U.S.A.* .. 106 D6
Amherst, *Ohio, U.S.A.* . 106 E2
Amherst, *Tex., U.S.A.* .. 109 H3
Amherst I., *Canada* 107 B8
Amherstburg, *Canada* .. 98 D3
Amiata, Mte., *Italy* 33 F8
Amiens, *France* 25 C9
Amindaion, *Greece* 39 J4
Amīrābād, *Iran* 64 C5
Amirante Is., *Seychelles* . 3 E12
Amisk L., *Canada* 101 C8
Amistad, Presa de la,
  Mexico 114 B4
Amite, *U.S.A.* 109 K9
Amizmiz, *Morocco* 74 B3
Åmli, *Norway* 11 F2
Amlwch, *U.K.* 12 D3
Amm Adam, *Sudan* 77 D4
'Ammān, *Jordan* 69 D4
Ammanford, *U.K.* 13 F3
Ammassalik =
  Angmagssalik, *Greenland* 4 C6
Ammerån, *Sweden* 10 A10
Ammerån →, *Sweden* .. 10 A10
Ammersee, *Germany* .. 19 G7

Ammerzoden, *Neths.* 16 E6
Amnat Charoen, *Thailand* . 58 E5
Amo Jiang →, *China* 52 F3
Åmol, *Iran* 65 B7
Amorebieta, *Spain* 28 B2
Amorgós, *Greece* 39 N8
Amory, *U.S.A.* 105 J1
Amos, *Canada* 98 C4
Åmot, *Buskerud, Norway* . . 10 E3
Åmot, *Telemark, Norway* . 10 E2
Åmotsdal, *Norway* 10 E2
Amour, Djebel, *Algeria* . . 75 B5
Amoy = Xiamen, *China* . . 53 E12
Ampang, *Malaysia* 59 L3
Ampanihy, *Madag.* 85 C7
Ampasindava,
  Helodranon', *Madag.* . . 85 A8
Ampasindava, Saikanosy,
  Madag. 85 A8
Ampato, Nevado, *Peru* . . 124 D3
Ampenan, *Indonesia* 56 F5
Amper, *Nigeria* 79 D6
Amper →, *Germany* 19 G7
Ampezzo, *Italy* 33 B9
Amposta, *Spain* 28 E5
Ampotaka, *Madag.* 85 D7
Ampoza, *Madag.* 85 C7
Amqui, *Canada* 99 C6
Amravati, *India* 60 J10
Amreli, *India* 62 J4
Amrenene el Kasba,
  Algeria 75 D5
Amriswil, *Switz.* 23 A8
Amritsar, *India* 62 D6
Amroha, *India* 63 E8
Amrum, *Germany* 18 A4
Amsel, *Algeria* 75 D6
Amsterdam, *Neths.* 16 D5
Amsterdam, *U.S.A.* 107 D10
Amsterdam, I., *Ind. Oc.* . . 3 F13
Amstetten, *Austria* 21 G4
Amudarya →, *Uzbekistan* . 44 E6
Amundsen Gulf, *Canada* . 96 A7
Amundsen Sea, *Antarctica* . 5 D15
Amuntai, *Indonesia* 56 E5
Amur →, *Russia* 45 D15
Amurang, *Indonesia* 57 D6
Amuri Pass, *N.Z.* 87 K4
Amurrio, *Spain* 28 B1
Amursk, *Russia* 45 D14
Amurzet, *Russia* 45 E14
Amusco, *Spain* 30 C6
Amvrakikós Kólpos, *Greece* . 39 L4
Amvrosiyivka, *Ukraine* . . . 41 J10
Amyderya =
  Amudarya →,
  Uzbekistan 44 E6
Amzeglouf, *Algeria* 75 C5
An Bien, *Vietnam* 59 H5
An Hoa, *Vietnam* 58 E7
An Khe, *Vietnam* 58 F7
An Nabatīyah at Tahta,
  Lebanon 69 B4
An Nabk, *Si. Arabia* 64 D3
An Nabk, *Syria* 69 A5
An Nabk Abū Qaşr,
  Si. Arabia 64 D3
An Nafūd, *Si. Arabia* . . . 64 D4
An Najaf, *Iraq* 67 G11
An Nāşirīyah, *Iraq* 64 D5
An Nhon, *Vietnam* 58 F7
An Nîl □, *Sudan* 76 D3
An Nîl el Abyad □, *Sudan* . 77 E3
An Nîl el Azraq □, *Sudan* . 77 E3
An Nu'ayrīyah, *Si. Arabia* . 65 E6
An Nu'mānīyah, *Iraq* . . . 67 F11
An Nuwayb'ī, W. →,
  Si. Arabia 69 F3
An Thoi, Dao, *Vietnam* . . 59 H4
An Uaimh, *Ireland* 15 C5
Anabar →, *Russia* 45 B12
'Anabtā, *West Bank* 69 C4
Anaco, *Venezuela* 121 B5
Anaconda, *U.S.A.* 110 C7
Anacortes, *U.S.A.* 112 B4
Anacuao, Mt., *Phil.* 55 C4
Anadarko, *U.S.A.* 109 H5
Anadia, *Brazil* 122 C4
Anadia, *Portugal* 30 E2
Anadolu, *Turkey* 66 C5
Anadyr, *Russia* 45 C18
Anadyr →, *Russia* 45 C18
Anadyrskiy Zaliv, *Russia* . 45 C19
Anáfi, *Greece* 39 N8
Anafópoulo, *Greece* 39 N8
Anaga, Pta. de, *Canary Is.* . 36 F3
Anagni, *Italy* 34 A6
'Ānah, *Iraq* 67 E10
Anaheim, *U.S.A.* 113 M9
Anahim Lake, *Canada* . . 100 C3
Anáhuac, *Mexico* 114 B4
Anajás, *Brazil* 122 B2
Anajatuba, *Brazil* 122 B3
Anakapalle, *India* 61 L13
Anakie, *Australia* 90 C4
Anaklia, *Georgia* 43 J5
Analalava, *Madag.* 85 A8
Análipsis, *Greece* 37 A3
Anamã, *Brazil* 121 D6
Anambar →, *Pakistan* . . 62 D3
Anambas, Kepulauan,
  Indonesia 56 D3
Anambas Is. = Anambas,
  Kepulauan, *Indonesia* . . 56 D3
Anambra □, *Nigeria* 79 D6
Anamoose, *U.S.A.* 108 B4
Anamosa, *U.S.A.* 108 D9

Anamur, *Turkey* 66 D5
Anamur Burnu, *Turkey* . . 66 D5
Anan, *Japan* 49 H7
Anand, *India* 62 H5
Anantnag, *India* 63 C6
Ananyiv, *Ukraine* 41 J5
Anapa, *Russia* 43 H3
Anapodháris →, *Greece* . . 37 E7
Anápolis, *Brazil* 123 E2
Anapu →, *Brazil* 121 D7
Anār, *Iran* 65 D7
Anārak, *Iran* 65 C7
Anatolia = Anadolu,
  Turkey 66 C5
Anatone, *U.S.A.* 110 C5
Anatsogno, *Madag.* 85 C7
Añatuya, *Argentina* 126 B3
Anauá →, *Brazil* 121 C5
Anaunethad L., *Canada* . 101 A8
Anavilhanas, Arquipélago
  das, *Brazil* 121 D5
Anaye, *Niger* 73 E7
Anbyŏn, *N. Korea* 51 E14
Ancash □, *Peru* 124 B2
Ancenis, *France* 24 E5
Ancho, Canal, *Chile* 128 D2
Anchor Bay, *U.S.A.* 112 G3
Anchorage, *U.S.A.* 96 B5
Anci, *China* 50 E9
Ancohuma, Nevada,
  Bolivia 124 D4
Ancón, *Peru* 124 C2
Ancona, *Italy* 33 E10
Ancud, *Chile* 128 B2
Ancud, G. de, *Chile* 128 B2
Andacollo, *Argentina* . . . 126 D1
Andacollo, *Chile* 126 C1
Andado, *Australia* 90 D2
Andahuaylas, *Peru* 124 C3
Andalgalá, *Argentina* . . . 126 B2
Åndalsnes, *Norway* 10 B1
Andalucía □, *Spain* 31 H6
Andalusia, *U.S.A.* 105 K2
Andalusia = Andalucía □,
  Spain 31 H6
Andaman Is., *Ind. Oc.* . . 46 H13
Andaman Sea, *Ind. Oc.* . . 56 B1
Andara, *Namibia* 84 B3
Andaraí, *Brazil* 123 D3
Andeer, *Switz.* 23 C8
Andelfingen, *Switz.* 23 A7
Andelot, *France* 25 D12
Andenes, *Norway* 8 B17
Andenne, *Belgium* 17 H6
Andéranboukane, *Mali* . . 79 B5
Anderlecht, *Belgium* 17 G4
Anderlues, *Belgium* 17 H4
Andermatt, *Switz.* 23 C7
Andernach, *Germany* 18 E3
Andernos-les-Bains, *France* 26 D2
Anderslöv, *Sweden* 11 J7
Anderson, *Calif., U.S.A.* . 110 F2
Anderson, *Ind., U.S.A.* . . 104 E3
Anderson, *Mo., U.S.A.* . . 109 G7
Anderson, *S.C., U.S.A.* . . 105 H4
Anderson →, *Canada* . . . 96 B7
Andes = Andes, Cord. de
  los, *S. Amer.* 124 C3
Andes, *S. Amer.* 124 C2
Andes, Cord. de los,
  S. Amer. 124 C3
Andfjorden, *Norway* 8 B17
Andhra Pradesh □, *India* . 60 L11
Andijon, *Uzbekistan* 44 E8
Andikíthira, *Greece* 39 P6
Andīmeshk, *Iran* 67 F13
Andímilos, *Greece* 39 N7
Andípaxoi, *Greece* 39 K3
Andizhan = Andijon,
  Uzbekistan 44 E8
Andoany, *Madag.* 85 A8
Andoas, *Peru* 120 D2
Andong, *S. Korea* 51 F15
Andongwei, *China* 51 G10
Andorra ■, *Europe* 28 C6
Andorra La Vella, *Andorra* . 28 C6
Andover, *U.K.* 13 F6
Andover, *Mass., U.S.A.* . 107 D13
Andover, *N.Y., U.S.A.* . . 106 D7
Andover, *Ohio, U.S.A.* . . 106 E4
Andøya, *Norway* 8 B16
Andradina, *Brazil* 123 F1
Andrahary, Mt., *Madag.* . . 85 A8
Andraitx, *Spain* 36 B9
Andramasina, *Madag.* . . . 85 B8
Andranopasy, *Madag.* . . . 85 C7
Andreanof Is., *U.S.A.* . . . 96 C2
Andreapol, *Russia* 40 D7
Andrespol, *Poland* 20 D9
Andrewilla, *Australia* 91 D2
Andrews, *S.C., U.S.A.* . . 105 J6
Andrews, *Tex., U.S.A.* . . 109 J3
Andreyevka, *Russia* 42 D10
Ándria, *Italy* 35 A9
Andriba, *Madag.* 85 B8
Andrijevica,
  Montenegro, Yug. 21 N9
Andrítsaina, *Greece* 39 M4
Androka, *Madag.* 85 C7
Andropov = Rybinsk,
  Russia 42 A4
Ándros, *Greece* 39 M7
Andros I., *Bahamas* 116 B4
Andros Town, *Bahamas* . 116 B4
Andselv, *Norway* 8 B18
Andújar, *Spain* 31 G6
Andulo, *Angola* 80 G3

Anegada, B., *Argentina* . 128 B4
Anegada I., *Virgin Is.* . . 117 C7
Anegada Passage,
  W. Indies 117 C7
Aného, *Togo* 79 D5
Añelo, *Argentina* 128 A3
Anergane, *Morocco* 74 B3
Aneto, Pico de, *Spain* . . . 28 C5
Añez, *Bolivia* 125 D5
Anfu, *China* 53 D10
Ang Thong, *Thailand* . . . 58 E3
Angamos, Punta, *Chile* . . 126 A1
Ang'angxi, *China* 54 B7
Angara →, *Russia* 45 D10
Angarab, *Ethiopia* 77 E4
Angarsk, *Russia* 45 D11
Angas Downs, *Australia* . 89 E5
Angas Hills, *Australia* . . . 88 D4
Angaston, *Australia* 91 E2
Ånge, *Sweden* 10 B9
Ángel, Salto = Angel Falls,
  Venezuela 121 B5
Ángel de la Guarda, I.,
  Mexico 114 B2
Angel Falls, *Venezuela* . . 121 B5
Ángeles, *Phil.* 55 D4
Angels Camp, *U.S.A.* . . . 111 G3
Ängelholm, *Sweden* 11 H6
Angellala, *Australia* 91 D4
Angels Camp, *U.S.A.* . . . 111 G3
Anger →, *Ethiopia* 77 F4
Angereb →, *Ethiopia* . . . 77 E4
Ångermanälven →,
  Sweden 10 B12
Ångermanland, *Sweden* . . 8 E18
Angermünde, *Germany* . . 18 B10
Angers, *Canada* 107 A9
Angers, *France* 24 E6
Angerville, *France* 25 D8
Ångesån →, *Sweden* 8 C20
Anghiari, *Italy* 33 E9
Angical, *Brazil* 123 D3
Angikuni L., *Canada* . . . 101 A9
Angkor, *Cambodia* 58 F4
Anglés, *Spain* 28 D7
Anglesey, *U.K.* 12 D3
Anglet, *France* 26 E2
Angleton, *U.S.A.* 109 L7
Angleur, *Belgium* 17 G7
Anglin →, *France* 26 B4
Anglisidhes, *Cyprus* 37 E12
Anglure, *France* 25 D10
Angmagssalik, *Greenland* . 4 C6
Ango, *Zaïre* 82 B2
Angoche, *Mozam.* 83 F4
Angoche, I., *Mozam.* 83 F4
Angol, *Chile* 126 D1
Angola, *Ind., U.S.A.* . . . 104 E3
Angola, *N.Y., U.S.A.* . . . 106 D5
Angola ■, *Africa* 81 G3
Angoon, *U.S.A.* 100 B2
Angoulême, *France* 26 C4
Angoumois, *France* 26 C4
Angra dos Reis, *Brazil* . . 127 A7
Angren, *Uzbekistan* 44 E8
Angtassom, *Cambodia* . . . 59 G5
Angu, *Zaïre* 82 B1
Anguang, *China* 51 B12
Anguilla ■, *W. Indies* . . . 117 C7
Anguo, *China* 50 E8
Angurugu, *Australia* 90 A2
Angus, Braes of, *U.K.* . . . 14 E5
Anhanduí →, *Brazil* 127 A5
Anhée, *Belgium* 17 H5
Anholt, *Denmark* 11 H5
Anhua, *China* 53 C8
Anhui □, *China* 53 B11
Anhwei = Anhui □, *China* . 53 B11
Anichab, *Namibia* 84 C1
Anicuns, *Brazil* 123 E2
Anidhros, *Greece* 39 N8
Anie, *Togo* 79 D5
Animas, *U.S.A.* 111 L9
Ånimskog, *Sweden* 11 F6
Anina, *Romania* 38 D4
Anivorano, *Madag.* 85 B8
Anjalankoski, *Finland* . . . 9 F22
Anjar, *India* 62 H4
Anjidiv I., *India* 60 M9
Anjou, *France* 24 E6
Anjozorobe, *Madag.* 85 B8
Anju, *N. Korea* 51 E13
Anka, *Nigeria* 79 C6
Ankaboa, Tanjona, *Madag.* . 85 C7
Ankang, *China* 50 H5
Ankara, *Turkey* 66 C5
Ankaramena, *Madag.* . . . 85 C8
Ankazoabo, *Madag.* 85 C7
Ankazobe, *Madag.* 85 B8
Ankisabe, *Madag.* 85 B8
Anklam, *Germany* 18 B9
Ankober, *Ethiopia* 77 F4
Ankoro, *Zaïre* 82 D2
Anlong, *China* 52 E5
Anlu, *China* 53 B9
Anmyŏn-do, *S. Korea* . . . 51 F14
Ånn, *Sweden* 10 A6
Ann, C., *U.S.A.* 107 D14
Ann Arbor, *U.S.A.* 104 D4
Anna, *Russia* 42 E5
Anna, *U.S.A.* 109 G10
Anna Plains, *Australia* . . 88 C3
Anna Regina, *Guyana* . . 121 B6
Annaba, *Algeria* 75 A6
Annaberg-Buchholz,
  Germany 18 E8
Annalee →, *Ireland* 15 B4

Annam = Trung-Phan,
  Vietnam 58 E7
Annamitique, Chaîne, *Asia* 58 D6
Annan, *U.K.* 14 G5
Annan →, *U.K.* 14 G5
Annapolis, *U.S.A.* 104 F7
Annapolis Royal, *Canada* . 99 D6
Annapurna, *Nepal* 63 E10
Annean, L., *Australia* . . . 89 E2
Anneberg, *Sweden* 11 G6
Annecy, *France* 27 C10
Annecy, L. d', *France* . . . 27 C10
Annemasse, *France* 27 B10
Annenskiy Most, *Russia* . 40 B9
Anning, *China* 52 E4
Anningie, *Australia* 88 D5
Anniston, *U.S.A.* 105 J3
Annobón, *Atl. Oc.* 71 G4
Annonay, *France* 27 C8
Annot, *France* 27 E10
Annotto Bay, *Jamaica* . . 116 C4
Annuello, *Australia* 91 E3
Annville, *U.S.A.* 107 F8
Annweiler, *Germany* 19 F3
Áno Viánnos, *Greece* . . . 37 D7
Anoka, *U.S.A.* 108 C8
Anorotsangana, *Madag.* . . 85 A8
Anóyia, *Greece* 37 D6
Anping, *Hebei, China* . . . 50 E8
Anping, *Liaoning, China* . 51 D12
Anpu Gang, *China* 52 G7
Anqing, *China* 53 B11
Anqiu, *China* 51 F10
Anren, *China* 53 D9
Ans, *Belgium* 17 G7
Ansai, *China* 50 F5
Ansbach, *Germany* 19 F6
Anseba →, *Eritrea* 77 D4
Anserma, *Colombia* 120 B2
Anseroeul, *Belgium* 17 G3
Anshan, *China* 51 D12
Anshun, *China* 52 D5
Ansião, *Portugal* 30 F2
Ansirabe, *Madag.* 85 B8
Ansley, *U.S.A.* 108 E5
Ansó, *Spain* 28 C4
Anson, *U.S.A.* 109 J5
Anson B., *Australia* 88 B5
Ansongo, *Mali* 79 B5
Ansonia, *U.S.A.* 107 E11
Anstruther, *U.K.* 14 E6
Ansudu, *Indonesia* 57 E9
Antabamba, *Peru* 124 C3
Antakya, *Turkey* 66 D7
Antalaha, *Madag.* 85 A9
Antalya, *Turkey* 66 D4
Antalya Körfezi, *Turkey* . . 66 D4
Antananarivo, *Madag.* . . . 85 B8
Antananarivo □, *Madag.* . 85 B8
Antanimbaribe, *Madag.* . . 85 C7
Antarctic Pen., *Antarctica* . 5 C18
Antarctica 5 E3
Antelope, *Zimbabwe* 83 G2
Antenor Navarro, *Brazil* . 122 C4
Antequera, *Paraguay* . . . 126 A4
Antequera, *Spain* 31 H6
Antero, Mt., *U.S.A.* 111 G10
Anthony, *Kans., U.S.A.* . . 109 G5
Anthony, *N. Mex., U.S.A.* . 111 K10
Anthony Lagoon, *Australia* . 90 B2
Anti Atlas, *Morocco* 74 C2
Anti-Lebanon = Ash
  Sharqi, Al Jabal,
  Lebanon 69 B5
Antibes, *France* 27 E11
Antibes, C. d', *France* . . . 27 E11
Anticosti, I. d', *Canada* . . 99 C7
Antifer, C. d', *France* . . . 24 C7
Antigo, *U.S.A.* 108 C10
Antigonish, *Canada* 99 C7
Antigua, *Canary Is.* 36 F5
Antigua, *Guatemala* 116 D1
Antigua, *W. Indies* 117 C7
Antigua & Barbuda ■,
  W. Indies 117 C7
Antilla, *Cuba* 116 B4
Antimony, *U.S.A.* 111 G8
Antioch, *U.S.A.* 112 G5
Antioche, Pertuis d',
  France 26 B2
Antioquia, *Colombia* 120 B2
Antioquia □, *Colombia* . . 120 B2
Antipodes Is., *Pac. Oc.* . . 92 M9
Antler, *U.S.A.* 108 A4
Antler →, *Canada* 101 D8
Antlers, *U.S.A.* 109 H7
Antofagasta, *Chile* 126 A1
Antofagasta □, *Chile* . . . 126 A2
Antofagasta de la Sierra,
  Argentina 126 B2
Antofalla, *Argentina* 126 B2
Antofalla, Salar de,
  Argentina 126 B2
Antoing, *Belgium* 17 G2
Anton, *U.S.A.* 109 J3
Anton Chico, *U.S.A.* 111 J11
Antongila, Helodrano,
  Madag. 85 B8
Antonibé, *Madag.* 85 B8
Antonibé, Presqu'île d',
  Madag. 85 A8
Antonina, *Brazil* 127 B6
Antonito, *U.S.A.* 111 H10
Antrain, *France* 24 D5
Antrim, *U.K.* 15 B5
Antrim □, *U.K.* 15 B5
Antrim, Mts. of, *U.K.* . . . 15 B5

Antrim Plateau, *Australia* . 88 C4
Antrodoco, *Italy* 33 F10
Antropovo, *Russia* 42 A6
Antsalova, *Madag.* 85 B7
Antsiranana, *Madag.* 85 A8
Antsohihy, *Madag.* 85 A8
Antsohimbondrona
  Seranana, *Madag.* 85 A8
Antu, *China* 51 C15
Antwerp = Antwerpen,
  Belgium 17 F4
Antwerp, *U.S.A.* 107 B9
Antwerpen, *Belgium* 17 F4
Antwerpen □, *Belgium* . . . 17 F5
Anupgarh, *India* 62 E5
Anuradhapura, *Sri Lanka* . 60 Q12
Anveh, *Iran* 65 E7
Anvers = Antwerpen,
  Belgium 17 F4
Anvers I., *Antarctica* 5 C17
Anxi, *Fujian, China* 53 E12
Anxi, *Gansu, China* 54 B4
Anxiang, *China* 53 C9
Anxious B., *Australia* . . . 91 E1
Anyama, *Ivory C.* 78 D4
Anyang, *China* 50 F8
Anyi, *Jiangxi, China* 53 C10
Anyi, *Shanxi, China* 50 G6
Anyuan, *China* 53 E10
Anza, *U.S.A.* 113 M10
Anze, *China* 50 F7
Anzhero-Sudzhensk, *Russia* 44 D9
Ánzio, *Italy* 34 A5
Anzoátegui □, *Venezuela* . 121 B5
Aoga-Shima, *Japan* 49 H9
Aoiz, *Spain* 28 C3
Aomori, *Japan* 48 D10
Aomori □, *Japan* 48 D10
Aonla, *India* 63 E8
Aosta, *Italy* 32 C4
Aoudéras, *Niger* 79 B6
Aouinet Torkoz, *Morocco* . 74 C3
Aoukar, *Mali* 74 D4
Aouker, *Mauritania* 78 B3
Aoulef el Arab, *Algeria* . . 75 C5
Apa →, *S. Amer.* 126 A4
Apache, *U.S.A.* 109 H5
Apalachee B., *U.S.A.* . . . 105 L3
Apalachicola, *U.S.A.* . . . 105 L3
Apalachicola →, *U.S.A.* . 105 L3
Apapa, *Nigeria* 79 D5
Apaporis →, *Colombia* . . 120 D4
Aparecida do Taboado,
  Brazil 123 F1
Aparri, *Phil.* 55 B4
Aparurén, *Venezuela* . . . 121 B5
Apateu, *Romania* 38 C4
Apatin, *Serbia, Yug.* 21 K8
Apatzingán, *Mexico* 114 D4
Apeldoorn, *Neths.* 16 D7
Apeldoornsch Kanaal →,
  Neths. 16 D8
Apen, *Germany* 18 B3
Apennines = Appennini,
  Italy 32 D7
Apere →, *Bolivia* 125 C4
Apia, *W. Samoa* 87 A13
Apiacás, Serra dos, *Brazil* . 125 B6
Apiaú →, *Brazil* 121 C5
Apiaú, Serra do, *Brazil* . . 121 C5
Apidiá →, *Brazil* 125 C5
Apinajé, *Brazil* 123 D2
Apizaco, *Mexico* 115 D5
Aplao, *Peru* 124 D3
Apo, Mt., *Phil.* 57 C7
Apodi, *Brazil* 122 C4
Apolakkiá, *Greece* 37 C9
Apolakkiá, Órmos, *Greece* . 37 C9
Apolda, *Germany* 18 D7
Apollonia = Marsá Susah,
  Libya 73 B9
Apollonia, *Greece* 39 N7
Apolo, *Bolivia* 124 C4
Apónguao →, *Venezuela* . 121 C5
Aporé →, *Brazil* 123 E1
Aporé →, *Brazil* 123 E1
Aporema, *Brazil* 122 A1
Apostle Is., *U.S.A.* 108 B9
Apóstoles, *Argentina* . . . 127 B4
Apostolos Andreas, C.,
  Cyprus 66 E6
Apostolovo, *Ukraine* 41 J7
Appalachian Mts., *U.S.A.* . 104 G6
Appelscha, *Neths.* 16 C8
Appennini, *Italy* 32 D7
Appennino Ligure, *Italy* . . 32 D5
Appenzell, *Switz.* 23 B8
Appenzell-Ausser
  Rhoden □, *Switz.* 23 B8
Appenzell-Inner
  Rhoden □, *Switz.* 23 B8
Appiano, *Italy* 33 B8
Appingedam, *Neths.* 16 B9
Apple Hill, *Canada* 107 A10
Apple Valley, *U.S.A.* . . . 113 L9
Appleby-in-Westmorland,
  U.K. 12 C5
Appleton, *U.S.A.* 104 C1
Approuague, *Fr. Guiana* . 121 C7
Approuague →,
  Fr. Guiana 121 C7
Apricena, *Italy* 35 A8
Aprigliano, *Italy* 35 C9
Aprília, *Italy* 34 A5
Apsheronsk, *Russia* 43 H4
Apt, *France* 27 E9

133

Apuane, Alpi, *Italy* 32 D7
Apuaú, *Brazil* 121 D5
Apucarana, *Brazil* 127 A5
Apulia = Púglia, *Italy* .. 35 B9
Apure □, *Venezuela* 120 B4
Apure →, *Venezuela* 120 B4
Apurímac □, *Peru* 124 C3
Apurimac →, *Peru* 124 C3
Apuseni, Munții, *Romania* 38 C5
Aqabah = Al 'Aqabah, *Jordan* 69 F4
'Aqabah, Khalīj al, *Red Sea* 64 D2
'Aqdā, *Iran* 65 C7
Aqīq, *Sudan* 76 D4
Aqīq, Khalīg, *Sudan* 76 D4
Aqmola, *Kazakhstan* 44 D8
Aqrah, *Iraq* 67 D10
Aqtöbe, *Kazakhstan* 44 D6
Aquidauana, *Brazil* 125 E6
Aquidauana →, *Brazil* .. 125 D6
Aquiles Serdán, *Mexico* .. 114 B4
Aquin, *Haiti* 117 C5
Ar Rachidiya, *Morocco* .. 74 B4
Ar Rafīd, *Syria* 69 C4
Ar Raḩḩālīyah, *Iraq* 67 F10
Ar Ramādī, *Iraq* 67 F10
Ar Ramthā, *Jordan* 69 C5
Ar Raqqah, *Syria* 67 E8
Ar Rass, *Si. Arabia* 64 E4
Ar Rifā'ī, *Iraq* 64 D5
Ar Riyāḍ, *Si. Arabia* 64 E5
Ar Ru'ays, *Qatar* 65 E6
Ar Rukhaymīyah, *Iraq* .. 64 D5
Ar Ruqayyidah, *Si. Arabia* 65 E6
Ar Ruṣāfah, *Syria* 67 E8
Ar Ruṭbah, *Iraq* 67 F9
Ara, *India* 63 G11
'Arab, Bahr el →, *Sudan* 77 F2
Arab, Khalīg el, *Egypt* .. 76 H6
'Arabābād, *Iran* 65 C8
Araban, *Turkey* 66 D7
Arabatskaya Strelka, *Ukraine* 41 K8
Arabba, *Italy* 33 B8
Arabelo, *Venezuela* 121 C5
Arabia, *Asia* 68 C4
Arabian Desert = Es Sahrâ' Esh Sharqîya, *Egypt* 76 B3
Arabian Gulf = Gulf, The, *Asia* 65 E6
Arabian Sea, *Ind. Oc.* ... 47 H10
Araç, *Turkey* 66 B5
Aracaju, *Brazil* 122 D4
Aracataca, *Colombia* 120 A3
Aracati, *Brazil* 122 B4
Araçatuba, *Brazil* 127 A5
Aracena, *Spain* 31 H4
Aracena, Sierra de, *Spain* . 31 H4
Araçuaí, *Brazil* 123 E3
Araçuaí →, *Brazil* 123 E3
'Arad, *Israel* 69 D4
Arad, *Romania* 38 C4
Arada, *Chad* 73 F9
Aradhippou, *Cyprus* 37 E12
Arafura Sea, *E. Indies* ... 57 F8
Aragarças, *Brazil* 125 D7
Aragats, *Armenia* 43 K7
Aragón □, *Spain* 28 D4
Aragón →, *Spain* 28 C3
Aragona, *Italy* 34 E6
Aragua □, *Venezuela* 120 B4
Aragua de Barcelona, *Venezuela* 121 B5
Araguacema, *Brazil* 122 C2
Araguaçu, *Brazil* 123 D2
Araguaia →, *Brazil* 122 C2
Araguaiana, *Brazil* 125 D7
Araguaína, *Brazil* 122 C2
Araguari, *Brazil* 123 E2
Araguari →, *Brazil* 121 C8
Araioses, *Brazil* 122 B3
Arak, *Algeria* 75 C5
Arāk, *Iran* 65 C6
Arakan Coast, *Burma* 61 K19
Arakan Yoma, *Burma* 61 K19
Arakli, *Turkey* 67 B8
Araks = Aras, Rūd-e →, *Azerbaijan* 43 K9
Aral, *Kazakhstan* 44 E7
Aral Sea, *Asia* 44 E7
Aral Tengizi = Aral Sea, *Asia* 44 E7
Aralsk = Aral, *Kazakhstan* 44 E7
Aralskoye More = Aral Sea, *Asia* 44 E7
Aralsor, Ozero, *Kazakhstan* 43 F9
Aramac, *Australia* 90 C4
Arambag, *India* 63 H12
Aran I., *Ireland* 15 B3
Aran Is., *Ireland* 15 C2
Aranda de Duero, *Spain* . 28 D1
Arandān, *Iran* 64 C5
Aranjuez, *Spain* 30 E7
Aranos, *Namibia* 84 C2
Aransas Pass, *U.S.A.* 109 M6
Aranzazu, *Colombia* 120 B2
Araouane, *Mali* 78 B4
Arapahoe, *U.S.A.* 108 E5
Arapey Grande →, *Uruguay* 126 C4
Arapgir, *Turkey* 67 C8
Arapiraca, *Brazil* 122 C4
Arapongas, *Brazil* 127 A5
Ar'ar, *Si. Arabia* 64 D4

Araracuara, *Colombia* 120 D3
Araranguá, *Brazil* 127 B6
Araraquara, *Brazil* 123 F2
Ararás, Serra das, *Brazil* . 127 B5
Ararat, *Armenia* 67 C11
Ararat, *Australia* 91 F3
Ararat, Mt. = Ağrı Dağı, *Turkey* 67 C11
Arari, *Brazil* 122 B3
Araria, *India* 63 F12
Araripe, Chapada do, *Brazil* 122 C3
Araripina, *Brazil* 122 C3
Araruama, L. de, *Brazil* .. 123 F3
Araruna, *Brazil* 122 C4
Aras, Rūd-e →, *Azerbaijan* 43 K9
Araticu, *Brazil* 122 B2
Arauca, *Colombia* 120 B3
Arauca □, *Colombia* 120 B3
Arauca →, *Venezuela* 120 B4
Arauco, *Chile* 126 D1
Arauco □, *Chile* 126 D1
Araújos, *Brazil* 123 E2
Arauquita, *Colombia* 120 B3
Araure, *Venezuela* 120 B4
Arawa, *Ethiopia* 77 F5
Araxá, *Brazil* 123 E2
Araya, Pen. de, *Venezuela* 121 A5
Arba Minch, *Ethiopia* ... 77 F4
Arbat, *Iraq* 67 E11
Arbatax, *Italy* 34 C2
Arbedo, *Switz.* 23 D8
Arbīl, *Iraq* 67 D11
Arbois, *France* 25 F12
Arbon, *Switz.* 23 A8
Arbore, *Ethiopia* 77 F4
Arborea, *Italy* 34 C1
Arborfield, *Canada* 101 C8
Arborg, *Canada* 101 C9
Arbrå, *Sweden* 10 C10
Arbroath, *U.K.* 14 E6
Arbuckle, *U.S.A.* 112 F4
Arbus, *Italy* 34 C1
Arc, *France* 25 E12
Arc →, *France* 27 C10
Arcachon, *France* 26 D2
Arcachon, Bassin d', *France* 26 D2
Arcade, *U.S.A.* 106 D6
Arcadia, *Fla., U.S.A.* 105 M5
Arcadia, *La., U.S.A.* 109 J8
Arcadia, *Nebr., U.S.A.* ... 108 E5
Arcadia, *Pa., U.S.A.* 106 F6
Arcadia, *Wis., U.S.A.* ... 108 C9
Arcata, *U.S.A.* 110 F1
Arcévia, *Italy* 33 E9
Archangel = Arkhangelsk, *Russia* 44 C5
Archar, *Bulgaria* 38 F5
Archbald, *U.S.A.* 107 E9
Archena, *Spain* 29 G3
Archer →, *Australia* 90 A3
Archer B., *Australia* 90 A3
Archers Post, *Kenya* 82 B4
Archidona, *Spain* 31 H6
Arci, Mte., *Italy* 34 C1
Arcidosso, *Italy* 33 F8
Arcila = Asilah, *Morocco* . 74 A3
Arcis-sur-Aube, *France* .. 25 D11
Arckaringa, *Australia* ... 91 D1
Arckaringa Cr. →, *Australia* 91 D2
Arco, *Italy* 32 C7
Arco, *U.S.A.* 110 E7
Arcola, *Canada* 101 D8
Arcos, *Spain* 28 D2
Arcos de la Frontera, *Spain* 31 J5
Arcos de Valdevez, *Portugal* 30 D2
Arcot, *India* 60 N11
Arcoverde, *Brazil* 122 C4
Arctic Bay, *Canada* 97 A11
Arctic Ocean, *Arctic* 4 B18
Arctic Red River, *Canada* . 96 B6
Arda →, *Bulgaria* 39 H9
Arda →, *Italy* 32 D6
Ardabīl, *Iran* 67 C13
Ardahan, *Turkey* 67 B10
Ardakān = Sepīdān, *Iran* . 65 D7
Ardales, *Spain* 31 J6
Ardalstangen, *Norway* ... 10 C1
Ardea, *Greece* 39 J5
Ardèche □, *France* 27 D8
Ardèche →, *France* 27 D8
Arden, *Ireland* 15 C5
Arden, *Canada* 106 B8
Arden, *Denmark* 11 H3
Arden, *Calif., U.S.A.* 112 G5
Arden, *Nev., U.S.A.* 113 J11
Ardennes = Ardenne, *Belgium* 25 C12
Ardennes □, *France* 25 C11
Ardentes, *France* 25 F8
Ardeşen, *Turkey* 67 B9
Ardestān, *Iran* 65 C7
Ardgour, *U.K.* 14 E3
Árdhas →, *Greece* 39 H9
Ardila →, *Portugal* 31 G3
Ardlethan, *Australia* 91 E4
Ardmore, *Australia* 90 C2
Ardmore, *Okla., U.S.A.* .. 109 H6
Ardmore, *Pa., U.S.A.* ... 107 G9
Ardmore, *S. Dak., U.S.A.* 108 D3
Ardnacrusha, *Ireland* ... 15 D3

Ardnamurchan, Pt. of, *U.K.* 14 E2
Ardon, *Russia* 43 J7
Ardooie, *Belgium* 17 G2
Ardore, *Italy* 35 D9
Ardres, *France* 25 B8
Ardrossan, *Australia* 91 E2
Ardrossan, *U.K.* 14 F4
Ards □, *U.K.* 15 B6
Ards Pen., *U.K.* 15 B6
Ardud, *Romania* 38 B5
Åre, *Sweden* 10 A7
Arecibo, *Puerto Rico* 117 C6
Areia Branca, *Brazil* 122 B4
Arena, Pt., *U.S.A.* 112 G3
Arena de San Pedro, *Spain* 30 E5
Arenales, Cerro, *Chile* ... 128 C2
Arenápolis, *Brazil* 125 C6
Arenas, *Spain* 30 B6
Arenas de San Pedro, *Spain* 30 E5
Arendal, *Norway* 11 F2
Arendonk, *Belgium* 17 F6
Arendsee, *Germany* 18 C7
Arenillas, *Ecuador* 120 D1
Arenys de Mar, *Spain* ... 28 D7
Arenzano, *Italy* 32 D5
Areópolis, *Greece* 39 N5
Arequipa, *Peru* 124 D3
Arequipa □, *Peru* 124 D3
Arere, *Brazil* 121 D7
Arero, *Ethiopia* 77 G4
Arès, *France* 26 D2
Arévalo, *Spain* 30 D6
Arezzo, *Italy* 33 E8
Arga →, *Spain* 28 C3
Argalastí, *Greece* 39 K6
Argamakmur, *Indonesia* .. 56 E2
Argamasilla de Alba, *Spain* 29 F1
Arganda, *Spain* 28 E1
Arganil, *Portugal* 30 E2
Argelès-Gazost, *France* .. 26 F3
Argelès-sur-Mer, *France* . 26 F7
Argens →, *France* 27 E10
Argent-sur-Sauldre, *France* 25 E9
Argenta, *Italy* 33 D8
Argentan, *France* 24 D6
Argentário, Mte., *Italy* ... 33 F8
Argentat, *France* 26 C5
Argentera, *Italy* 32 D3
Argentera, Monte del, *Italy* 32 D4
Argenteuil, *France* 25 D9
Argentia, *Canada* 99 C9
Argentiera, C. dell', *Italy* . 34 B1
Argentière, Aiguilles d', *Switz.* 22 E4
Argentina ■, *S. Amer.* ... 128 B3
Argentina Is., *Antarctica* . 5 C17
Argentino, L., *Argentina* . 128 D2
Argenton-Château, *France* 24 F6
Argenton-sur-Creuse, *France* 26 B5
Argeş →, *Romania* 38 E9
Arghandab →, *Afghan.* .. 62 D1
Argo, *Sudan* 76 D3
Argolikós Kólpos, *Greece* . 39 M5
Argonne, *France* 25 C12
Árgos, *Greece* 39 M5
Argostólion, *Greece* 39 L3
Arguedas, *Spain* 28 C3
Arguello, Pt., *U.S.A.* 113 L6
Arguineguín, *Canary Is.* . 36 G4
Argun →, *Russia* 43 J7
Argun →, *Russia* 45 D13
Argungu, *Nigeria* 79 C5
Argus Pk., *U.S.A.* 113 K9
Argyle, *U.S.A.* 108 A6
Argyle, L., *Australia* 88 C4
Arhavi, *Turkey* 67 B9
Århus, *Denmark* 11 H4
Århus Amtskommune □, *Denmark* 11 H4
Ariadnoye, *Russia* 48 B7
Ariamsvlei, *Namibia* 84 D2
Ariana, *Tunisia* 75 A7
Ariano Irpino, *Italy* 35 A8
Ariano nel Polèsine, *Italy* . 33 D9
Ariari →, *Colombia* 120 C3
Aribinda, *Burkina Faso* .. 79 C4
Arica, *Chile* 124 D3
Arica, *Colombia* 120 D3
Arico, *Canary Is.* 36 F3
Arid, C., *Australia* 89 F3
Arida, *Japan* 49 G7
Ariège □, *France* 26 F5
Ariège →, *France* 26 E5
Arieş →, *Romania* 38 C6
Arīḩā, *Syria* 64 C3
Arílla, Ákra, *Greece* 37 A3
Arímismendi, *Venezuela* .. 120 B4
Arinos →, *Brazil* 125 C6
Ario de Rosales, *Mexico* . 114 D4
Aripuanã, *Brazil* 125 B5
Aripuanã →, *Brazil* 125 B5
Ariquemes, *Brazil* 125 B5
Arisaig, *U.K.* 14 E3
Arîsh, W. el →, *Egypt* .. 76 H8
Arismendi, *Venezuela* ... 120 B4
Arissa, *Ethiopia* 77 E5
Aristazabal I., *Canada* ... 100 C3
Arivaca, *U.S.A.* 111 L8
Arivonimamo, *Madag.* ... 85 B8
Ariza, *Spain* 28 D2
Arizaro, Salar de, *Argentina* 126 A2
Arizona, *Argentina* 126 D2
Arizona □, *U.S.A.* 111 J8
Arizpe, *Mexico* 114 A2

Arjeplog, *Sweden* 8 D18
Arjona, *Colombia* 120 A2
Arjona, *Spain* 31 H6
Arjuno, *Indonesia* 57 G15
Arka, *Russia* 45 C15
Arkadak, *Russia* 42 E6
Arkadelphia, *U.S.A.* 109 H8
Arkaig, L., *U.K.* 14 E3
Arkalyk = Arqalyq, *Kazakhstan* 44 D7
Arkansas □, *U.S.A.* 109 H8
Arkansas →, *U.S.A.* 109 J9
Arkansas City, *U.S.A.* ... 109 G6
Árkathos →, *Greece* 39 K4
Arkhángelos, *Greece* 37 C10
Arkhangelsk, *Russia* 44 C5
Arkhangelskoye, *Russia* .. 42 E5
Arkiko, *Eritrea* 77 D4
Arklow, *Ireland* 15 D5
Arkona, Kap, *Germany* .. 18 A9
Arkösund, *Sweden* 11 F10
Arkticheskiy, Mys, *Russia* 45 A10
Arkul, *Russia* 42 B10
Arlanc, *France* 26 C7
Arlanza →, *Spain* 30 C6
Arlanzón →, *Spain* 30 C6
Arlberg P., *Austria* 19 H6
Arlee, *U.S.A.* 110 C6
Arles, *France* 27 E8
Arlesheim, *Switz.* 22 B5
Arlington, *S. Africa* 85 D4
Arlington, *Oreg., U.S.A.* . 110 D3
Arlington, *S. Dak., U.S.A.* 108 C6
Arlington, *Va., U.S.A.* ... 104 F7
Arlington, *Wash., U.S.A.* . 112 B4
Arlon, *Belgium* 17 J7
Arlöv, *Sweden* 11 J7
Arly, *Burkina Faso* 79 C5
Arman, *France* 26 E4
Armação, *France* 25 E10
Armavir, *Russia* 43 H5
Armenia, *Colombia* 120 C2
Armenia ■, *Asia* 43 K7
Armenistís, Ákra, *Greece* . 37 C9
Armentières, *France* 25 B9
Armidale, *Australia* 91 E5
Armour, *U.S.A.* 108 D5
Armstrong, *B.C., Canada* . 100 C5
Armstrong, *Ont., Canada* . 98 B2
Armstrong, *U.S.A.* 109 M6
Armstrong →, *Australia* .. 88 C5
Arnarfjörður, *Iceland* ... 8 D2
Arnaud →, *Canada* 97 B12
Arnauti, C., *Cyprus* 37 D11
Arnay-le-Duc, *France* ... 25 E11
Arnedillo, *Spain* 28 C2
Arnedo, *Spain* 28 C2
Arnemuiden, *Neths.* 17 F3
Årnes, *Norway* 10 D5
Arnett, *U.S.A.* 109 G5
Arnhem, *Neths.* 17 E7
Arnhem, C., *Australia* ... 90 A2
Arnhem B., *Australia* 90 A2
Arnhem Land, *Australia* . 90 A1
Arno →, *Italy* 32 E7
Arno Bay, *Australia* 91 E2
Arnold, *Calif., U.S.A.* ... 112 G6
Arnold, *Nebr., U.S.A.* ... 108 E4
Arnoldstein, *Austria* 21 J3
Arnon →, *France* 25 E9
Arnot, *Canada* 101 B9
Arnøy, *Norway* 8 A19
Arnprior, *Canada* 98 C4
Arnsberg, *Germany* 18 D4
Arnstadt, *Germany* 18 E6
Aro →, *Venezuela* 121 B5
Aroab, *Namibia* 84 D2
Aroeiras, *Brazil* 122 C4
Arolla, *Switz.* 22 D4
Arolsen, *Germany* 18 D5
Aron →, *France* 26 B7
Arona, *Italy* 32 C5
Aroroy, *Phil.* 55 E5
Arosa, *Switz.* 23 C9
Arosa, Ria de, *Spain* 30 C2
Arpajon, *France* 25 D9
Arpajon-sur-Cère, *France* 26 D6
Arpino, *Italy* 34 A6
Arqalyq, *Kazakhstan* 44 D7
Arque, *Bolivia* 124 D4
Arrabury, *Australia* 91 D3
Arrah = Ara, *India* 63 G11
Arraias, *Brazil* 123 D2
Arraias →, *Mato Grosso, Brazil* 125 C7
Arraias →, *Pará, Brazil* .. 122 C2
Arraiolos, *Portugal* 31 G3
Arran, *U.K.* 14 F3
Arrandale, *Canada* 100 C3
Arras, *France* 25 B9
Arrats →, *France* 26 D4
Arreau, *France* 26 F4
Arrecife, *Canary Is.* 36 F6
Arrecifes, *Argentina* 126 C3
Arrée, Mts. d', *France* ... 24 D3
Arriaga, *Chiapas, Mexico* . 115 D6
Arriaga, *San Luis Potosí, Mexico* 114 C4
Arrilalah P.O., *Australia* . 90 C3
Arrino, *Australia* 89 E2
Arrojado →, *Brazil* 123 D3
Arromanches-les-Bains, *France* 24 C6
Arronches, *Portugal* 31 F3

Arros →, *France* 26 E3
Arrou, *France* 24 D8
Arrow, L., *Ireland* 15 B3
Arrow Rock Res., *U.S.A.* . 110 E6
Arrowhead, *Canada* 100 C5
Arrowhead, L., *U.S.A.* ... 113 L9
Arrowtown, *N.Z.* 87 L2
Arroyo de la Luz, *Spain* . 31 F4
Arroyo Grande, *U.S.A.* .. 113 K6
Ârs, *Denmark* 11 H3
Ars, *Iran* 64 B5
Ars-en-Ré, *France* 26 B2
Ars-sur-Moselle, *France* . 25 C13
Arsenault L., *Canada* ... 101 B7
Arsenev, *Russia* 48 B6
Arsi □, *Ethiopia* 77 F4
Arsiero, *Italy* 33 C8
Arsin, *Turkey* 67 B8
Arsk, *Russia* 42 B9
Árta, *Greece* 39 K4
Artá, *Spain* 36 B10
Arteaga, *Mexico* 114 D4
Arteche, *Phil.* 55 E6
Arteijo, *Spain* 30 B2
Artem, *Russia* 48 C6
Artem, Ostrov = Artyom, *Azerbaijan* 43 K10
Artemovsk, *Russia* 45 D10
Artemovsk, *Ukraine* 41 H9
Artemovskiy, *Russia* 43 G5
Artenay, *France* 25 D8
Artern, *Germany* 18 D7
Artesa de Segre, *Spain* .. 28 D6
Artesia = Mosomane, *Botswana* 84 C4
Artesia, *U.S.A.* 109 J2
Artesia Wells, *U.S.A.* ... 109 L5
Artesian, *U.S.A.* 108 C6
Arth, *Switz.* 23 B7
Arthez-de-Béarn, *France* . 26 E3
Arthington, *Liberia* 78 D2
Arthur →, *Australia* 90 G3
Arthur Cr. →, *Australia* . 90 C2
Arthur Pt., *Australia* 90 C5
Arthur's Pass, *N.Z.* 87 K3
Arthur's Town, *Bahamas* . 117 B4
Artigas, *Uruguay* 126 C4
Artik, *Armenia* 43 K6
Artillery L., *Canada* 101 A7
Artois, *France* 25 B9
Artsyz, *Ukraine* 41 J5
Artvin, *Turkey* 67 B9
Artyom, *Azerbaijan* 43 K10
Aru, Kepulauan, *Indonesia* 57 F8
Aru Is. = Aru, Kepulauan, *Indonesia* 57 F8
Aru Meru □, *Tanzania* .. 82 C4
Arua, *Uganda* 82 B3
Aruanã, *Brazil* 123 D1
Aruba ■, *W. Indies* 117 D6
Arucas, *Canary Is.* 36 F4
Arudy, *France* 26 E3
Arumã, *Brazil* 121 D5
Arumpo, *Australia* 91 E3
Arun →, *Nepal* 63 F12
Arunachal Pradesh □, *India* 61 E19
Arusha, *Tanzania* 82 C4
Arusha □, *Tanzania* 82 C4
Arusha Chini, *Tanzania* .. 82 C4
Aruwimi →, *Zaïre* 82 B1
Arvada, *U.S.A.* 110 D10
Arvayheer, *Mongolia* 54 B5
Arve →, *France* 27 B10
Árvi, *Greece* 37 E7
Arvida, *Canada* 99 C5
Arvidsjaur, *Sweden* 8 D18
Arvika, *Sweden* 9 G15
Arvin, *U.S.A.* 113 K8
Arxan, *China* 54 B6
Aryirádhes, *Greece* 37 B3
Aryiroúpolis, *Greece* 37 D6
Arys, *Kazakhstan* 44 E7
Arzachena, *Italy* 34 A2
Arzamas, *Russia* 42 C6
Arzew, *Algeria* 75 A4
Arzgir, *Russia* 43 H7
Arzignano, *Italy* 33 C8
As, *Belgium* 17 F7
Aş Şadr, *U.A.E.* 65 E7
Aş Şafā, *Syria* 69 B6
'Aş Şaffānīyah, *Si. Arabia* 65 D6
Aş Şafīrah, *Syria* 66 B4
Aş Saḩm, *Oman* 65 E8
Aş Sājir, *Si. Arabia* 64 E5
Aş Salamīyah, *Syria* 66 C4
Aş Salṭ, *Jordan* 69 C4
Aş Samāwah, *Iraq* 64 D5
Aş Sanamayn, *Syria* 69 B5
Aş Sukhnah, *Syria* 67 E8
Aş Sulaymānīyah, *Iraq* .. 67 E11
Aş Sulaymī, *Si. Arabia* .. 64 E4
Aş Summān, *Si. Arabia* .. 64 E5
Aş Suwaydā, *Syria* 69 C5
Aş Suwaydā □, *Syria* 69 C5
Aş Şuwayrah, *Iraq* 67 F11
Asab, *Namibia* 84 D2
Asaba, *Nigeria* 79 D6
Asadābād, *Iran* 67 E13
Asafo, *Ghana* 78 D4
Asahi-Gawa →, *Japan* .. 49 G6
Asahigawa, *Japan* 48 C11
Asale, L., *Ethiopia* 77 E5
Asamankese, *Ghana* 79 D4
Åsansol, *India* 63 H12
Åsarna, *Sweden* 10 B8

Asbe Teferi, Ethiopia 77 F5
Asbesberge, S. Africa 84 D3
Asbestos, Canada 99 C5
Asbury Park, U.S.A. 107 F10
Ascensión, Mexico 114 A3
Ascensión, B. de la, Mexico 115 D7
Ascension I., Atl. Oc. 2 E9
Aschaffenburg, Germany . 19 F5
Aschendorf, Germany 18 B3
Aschersleben, Germany .. 18 D7
Asciano, Italy 33 E8
Áscoli Piceno, Italy 33 F10
Áscoli Satriano, Italy 35 A8
Ascona, Switz. 23 D7
Ascope, Peru 124 B2
Ascotán, Chile 126 A2
Aseb, Eritrea 68 E3
Asedjrad, Algeria 75 D5
Asela, Ethiopia 77 F4
Asenovgrad, Bulgaria ... 39 G7
Asfeld, France 25 C11
Asfûn el Matâ'na, Egypt . 76 B3
Åsgårdstrand, Norway 10 E4
Asgata, Cyprus 37 E12
Ash Fork, U.S.A. 111 J7
Ash Grove, U.S.A. 109 G8
Ash Shamâl □, Lebanon . 69 A5
Ash Shāmīyah, Iraq 67 G11
Ash Shārīqah, U.A.E. ... 65 E7
Ash Sharmah, Si. Arabia . 64 D2
Ash Sharqāt, Iraq 67 E10
Ash Sharqi, Al Jabal, Lebanon 69 B5
Ash Shaṭrah, Iraq 64 D5
Ash Shawbak, Jordan 64 D2
Ash Shawmari, J., Jordan 69 E5
Ash Shaykh, J., Lebanon . 69 B4
Ash Shināfīyah, Iraq 64 D5
Ash Shu'aybah, Si. Arabia 64 E5
Ash Shumlūl, Si. Arabia . 64 E5
Ash Shūr'a, Iraq 64 C4
Ash Shurayf, Si. Arabia . 64 E3
Ash Shuwayfāt, Lebanon . 69 B4
Ashanti □, Ghana 79 D4
Ashau, Vietnam 58 D6
Ashburn, U.S.A. 105 K4
Ashburton, N.Z. 87 K3
Ashburton →, Australia . 88 D1
Ashburton Downs, Australia 88 D2
Ashby de la Zouch, U.K. . 12 E6
Ashcroft, Canada 100 C4
Ashdod, Israel 69 D3
Asheboro, U.S.A. 105 H6
Asherton, U.S.A. 109 L5
Asheville, U.S.A. 105 H4
Asheweig →, Canada ... 98 B2
Ashford, Australia 91 D5
Ashford, U.K. 13 F8
Ashford, U.S.A. 110 C2
Ashgabat, Turkmenistan . 44 F6
Ashibetsu, Japan 48 C11
Ashikaga, Japan 49 F9
Ashizuri-Zaki, Japan 49 H6
Ashkarkot, Afghan. 62 C2
Ashkhabad = Ashgabat, Turkmenistan 44 F6
Ashland, Kans., U.S.A. . 109 G5
Ashland, Ky., U.S.A. ... 104 F4
Ashland, Maine, U.S.A. . 99 C6
Ashland, Mont., U.S.A. . 110 D10
Ashland, Nebr., U.S.A. . 108 E6
Ashland, Ohio, U.S.A. .. 106 F2
Ashland, Oreg., U.S.A. .. 110 E2
Ashland, Pa., U.S.A. 107 F8
Ashland, Va., U.S.A. 104 G7
Ashland, Wis., U.S.A. ... 108 B9
Ashley, N. Dak., U.S.A. . 108 B5
Ashley, Pa., U.S.A. 107 E9
Ashmont, Canada 100 C6
Ashmore Reef, Australia . 88 B3
Ashmûn, Egypt 76 H7
Ashmyany, Belarus 9 J21
Ashqelon, Israel 69 D3
Ashtabula, U.S.A. 106 E4
Ashton, S. Africa 84 E3
Ashton, U.S.A. 110 D8
Ashton under Lyne, U.K. 12 D5
Ashuanipi, L., Canada .. 99 B6
'Aṣī →, Asia 66 D6
Asia, Kepulauan, Indonesia 57 D8
Asia Bak, Iran 65 C6
Asiago, Italy 33 C8
Asidonhoppo, Surinam .. 121 C6
Asifabad, India 60 K11
Asike, Indonesia 57 F10
Asilah, Morocco 74 A3
Asinara, Italy 34 A1
Asinara, G. dell', Italy ... 34 B1
Asino, Russia 44 D9
Asipovichy, Belarus 40 F5
'Asīr □, Si. Arabia 68 D3
Asir, Ras, Somali Rep. .. 68 E5
Aşkale, Turkey 67 C9
Asker, Norway 10 E4
Askersund, Sweden 11 F8
Askham, S. Africa 84 D3
Askim, Norway 10 E5
Askja, Iceland 8 D5
Askøy, Norway 9 F11
Asl, Egypt 76 J8
Asmara = Asmera, Eritrea 77 D4
Asmera, Eritrea 77 D4
Asnæs, Denmark 11 J5
Åsnen, Sweden 9 H16
Asni, Morocco 74 B3

Ásola, Italy 32 C7
Asoteriba, Jebel, Sudan .. 76 C4
Asotin, U.S.A. 110 C5
Aspe, Spain 29 G4
Aspen, U.S.A. 111 G10
Aspendos, Turkey 66 D4
Aspermont, U.S.A. 109 J4
Aspiring, Mt., N.Z. 87 L2
Aspres-sur-Buëch, France . 27 D9
Aspromonte, Italy 35 D8
Aspur, India 62 H6
Asquith, Canada 101 C7
Assa, Morocco 74 C3
Assâba, Mauritania 78 B2
Assad, Bahret, Syria 67 D8
Assam □, India 61 F18
Assamakka, Niger 79 B6
Asse, Belgium 17 H4
Assebroek, Belgium 17 F2
Assekrem, Algeria 75 D6
Assémini, Italy 34 C2
Assen, Neths. 16 C9
Assendelft, Neths. 16 D5
Assenede, Belgium 17 F3
Assens, Århus, Denmark . 11 H4
Assens, Fyn, Denmark ... 11 J3
Assesse, Belgium 17 H6
Assini, Ivory C. 78 D4
Assiniboia, Canada 101 D7
Assiniboine →, Canada . 101 D9
Assis, Brazil 127 A5
Assisi, Italy 33 E9
Assynt, L., U.K. 14 C3
Astaffort, France 26 D4
Astara, Azerbaijan 67 C13
Āstārā, Iran 67 C13
Asten, Neths. 17 F7
Asterousia, Greece 37 E7
Asti, Italy 32 D5
Astipálaia, Greece 39 N9
Astorga, Spain 30 C4
Astoria, U.S.A. 112 D3
Åstorp, Sweden 11 H6
Astrakhan, Russia 43 G9
Astudillo, Spain 30 C6
Asturias □, Spain 30 B5
Asunción, Paraguay 126 B4
Asunción Nochixtlán, Mexico 115 D5
Asutri, Sudan 77 D4
Aswa →, Uganda 82 B3
Aswad, Ras al, Si. Arabia 76 C4
Aswân, Egypt 76 C3
Aswân High Dam = Sadd el Aali, Egypt 76 C3
Asyût, Egypt 76 B3
Asyûti, Wadi →, Egypt . 76 B3
Aszód, Hungary 21 H9
At Ṭafīlah, Jordan 69 E4
At Ṭā'if, Si. Arabia 68 C3
Aṭ Ṭiraq, Si. Arabia 64 E5
Atacama □, Chile 126 B2
Atacama, Desierto de, Chile 126 A2
Atacama, Salar de, Chile . 126 A2
Ataco, Colombia 120 C2
Atakor, Algeria 75 D6
Atakpamé, Togo 79 D5
Atalándi, Greece 39 L5
Atalaya, Peru 124 C3
Atalaya de Femes, Canary Is. 36 F6
Ataléia, Brazil 123 E3
Atami, Japan 49 G9
Atapupu, Indonesia 57 F6
Atâr, Mauritania 74 D2
Ataram, Erg n-, Algeria . 75 D5
Atarfe, Spain 31 H7
Atascadero, U.S.A. 111 J3
Atasu, Kazakhstan 44 E8
Atatürk Baraji, Turkey .. 67 D8
Atauro, Indonesia 57 F7
Atbara, Sudan 76 D3
'Atbara →, Sudan 76 D3
Atbasar, Kazakhstan 44 D7
Atchafalaya B., U.S.A. .. 109 L9
Atchison, U.S.A. 108 F7
Atebubu, Ghana 79 D4
Ateca, Spain 28 D3
Aterno →, Italy 33 F10
Atesine, Alpi, Italy 32 B8
Atessa, Italy 33 F11
Ath, Belgium 17 G3
Athabasca, Canada 100 C6
Athabasca →, Canada .. 101 B6
Athabasca, L., Canada .. 101 B7
Athboy, Ireland 15 C5
Athenry, Ireland 15 C3
Athens = Athínai, Greece 39 M6
Athens, Ala., U.S.A. 105 H2
Athens, Ga., U.S.A. 105 J4
Athens, N.Y., U.S.A. ... 107 D11
Athens, Ohio, U.S.A. ... 104 F4
Athens, Pa., U.S.A. 107 E8
Athens, Tenn., U.S.A. .. 105 H3
Athens, Tex., U.S.A. ... 109 J7
Atherley, Canada 106 B5
Atherton, Australia 90 B4
Athiéme, Benin 79 D5
Athienou, Cyprus 37 D12
Athínai, Greece 39 M6
Athlone, Ireland 15 C4
Athna, Cyprus 37 D12
Atholl, Forest of, U.K. .. 14 E5
Atholville, Canada 99 C6
Áthos, Greece 39 J7

Athus, Belgium 17 J7
Athy, Ireland 15 D5
Ati, Chad 73 F8
Ati, Sudan 77 E2
Atiak, Uganda 82 B3
Atico, Peru 124 D3
Atienza, Spain 28 D2
Atikokan, Canada 98 C1
Atikonak L., Canada 99 B7
Atimonan, Phil. 55 E4
Atka, Russia 45 C16
Atkarsk, Russia 42 E7
Atkinson, U.S.A. 108 D5
Atlanta, Ga., U.S.A. ... 105 J3
Atlanta, Tex., U.S.A. ... 109 J7
Atlantic, U.S.A. 108 E7
Atlantic City, U.S.A. ... 104 F8
Atlantic Ocean 2 E9
Atlántico □, Colombia .. 120 A2
Atlas Mts. = Haut Atlas, Morocco 74 B3
Atlin, Canada 100 B2
Atlin, L., Canada 100 B2
Atmore, U.S.A. 105 K2
Atoka, U.S.A. 109 H6
Átokos, Greece 39 L3
Atolia, U.S.A. 113 K9
Atouguia, Portugal 31 F1
Atoyac →, Mexico 115 D5
Atrak = Atrek →, Turkmenistan 65 B8
Ātran →, Sweden 11 G6
Atrato →, Colombia ... 120 B2
Atrauli, India 62 E8
Atrek →, Turkmenistan . 65 B8
Atri, Italy 33 F10
Atsbi, Ethiopia 77 E4
Atsoum, Mts., Cameroon 79 D7
Atsuta, Japan 48 C10
Attalla, U.S.A. 105 H2
Attáviros, Greece 37 C9
Attawapiskat, Canada .. 98 B3
Attawapiskat →, Canada 98 B3
Attawapiskat L., Canada 98 B2
Attendorn, Germany 18 D3
Attert, Belgium 17 J7
Attica, U.S.A. 104 E2
Attichy, France 25 C10
Attigny, France 25 C11
Attikamagen L., Canada . 99 A6
Attleboro, U.S.A. 107 E13
Attock, Pakistan 62 C5
Attopeu, Laos 58 E6
Attur, India 60 P11
Atuel →, Argentina 126 D2
Åtvidaberg, Sweden 11 F10
Atwater, U.S.A. 111 H3
Atwood, Canada 106 C3
Atwood, U.S.A. 108 F4
Atyraū, Kazakhstan 44 E6
Au Sable →, U.S.A. ... 104 C4
Au Sable Pt., U.S.A. ... 98 C2
Aubagne, France 27 E9
Aubange, Belgium 17 J7
Aubarca, C., Spain 36 B7
Aube □, France 25 D11
Aube →, France 25 D10
Aubel, Belgium 17 G7
Aubenas, France 27 D8
Aubenton, France 25 C11
Auberry, U.S.A. 112 H7
Aubigny-sur-Nère, France 25 E9
Aubin, France 26 D6
Aubrac, Mts. d', France . 26 D7
Auburn, Ala., U.S.A. ... 105 J3
Auburn, Calif., U.S.A. .. 112 G5
Auburn, Ind., U.S.A. ... 104 E3
Auburn, N.Y., U.S.A. .. 107 D8
Auburn, Nebr., U.S.A. . 108 E7
Auburn, Wash., U.S.A. . 112 C4
Auburn Ra., Australia .. 91 D5
Auburndale, U.S.A. 105 L5
Aubusson, France 26 C6
Auch, France 26 E4
Auchel, France 25 B9
Auchi, Nigeria 79 D6
Auckland, N.Z. 87 G5
Auckland Is., Pac. Oc. .. 92 N8
Aude □, France 26 E6
Aude →, France 26 E7
Auden, Canada 98 B2
Auderghem, Belgium ... 17 G4
Auderville, France 24 C5
Audierne, France 24 D2
Audincourt, France 25 E13
Audo, Ethiopia 77 F5
Audubon, U.S.A. 108 E7
Aue, Germany 18 E8
Auer = Ora, Italy 33 B8
Auerbach, Germany 18 E8
Aueti Paraná →, Brazil . 120 D4
Aufist, W. Sahara 74 C2
Augathella, Australia ... 91 D4
Augrabies Falls, S. Africa 84 D3
Augsburg, Germany 19 G6
Augusta, Italy 35 E8
Augusta, Ark., U.S.A. .. 109 H9
Augusta, Ga., U.S.A. ... 105 J5
Augusta, Kans., U.S.A. . 109 G6
Augusta, Maine, U.S.A. . 99 D6
Augusta, Mont., U.S.A. . 110 C7
Augusta, Wis., U.S.A. .. 108 C9
Augustenborg, Denmark . 11 K3
Augustów, Poland 20 B12
Augustus, Mt., Australia 88 D2
Augustus Downs, Australia 90 B2
Augustus I., Australia .. 88 C3

Aukan, Eritrea 77 D5
Aukum, U.S.A. 112 G6
Auld, L., Australia 88 D3
Aulla, Italy 32 D6
Aulnay, France 26 B3
Aulne →, France 24 D2
Aulnoye-Aymeries, France 25 B10
Ault, France 24 B8
Ault, U.S.A. 108 E2
Aulus-les-Bains, France . 26 F5
Aumale, France 25 C8
Aumont-Aubrac, France . 26 D7
Auna, Nigeria 79 C5
Auponhia, Indonesia ... 57 E7
Aups, France 27 E10
Aur, P., Malaysia 59 L5
Auraiya, India 63 F8
Auray, France 24 E4
Aurangabad, Bihar, India . 63 G11
Aurangabad, Maharashtra, India 60 K9
Auronzo di Cadore, Italy . 33 B9
Aurich, Germany 18 B3
Aurilândia, Brazil 123 E1
Aurillac, France 26 D6
Aurora, Canada 106 C5
Aurora, S. Africa 84 E2
Aurora, Colo., U.S.A. .. 108 F2
Aurora, Ill., U.S.A. 104 E1
Aurora, Mo., U.S.A. ... 109 G8
Aurora, Nebr., U.S.A. .. 108 E6
Aurora, Ohio, U.S.A. ... 106 E3
Aurukun Mission, Australia 90 A3
Aursmoen, Norway 10 E5
Aus, Namibia 84 D2
Austin, Minn., U.S.A. .. 108 D8
Austin, Nev., U.S.A. ... 110 G5
Austin, Pa., U.S.A. 106 E6
Austin, Tex., U.S.A. ... 109 K6
Austin, L., Australia ... 89 E2
Austra, Norway 8 D14
Austral Downs, Australia . 90 C2
Austral Is. = Tubuai Is., Pac. Oc. 93 K12
Austral Seamount Chain, Pac. Oc. 93 K13
Australia ■, Oceania ... 92 K5
Australian Alps, Australia 91 F4
Australian Capital Territory □, Australia .. 91 F4
Austria ■, Europe 21 H4
Austvågøy, Norway 8 B16
Autazes, Brazil 121 D6
Autelbas, Belgium 17 J7
Auterive, France 26 E5
Authie →, France 25 B8
Authon-du-Perche, France 24 D7
Autlán, Mexico 114 D4
Autun, France 25 F11
Auvelais, Belgium 17 H5
Auvergne, Australia 88 C5
Auvergne, France 26 C7
Auvergne, Mts. d', France 26 C6
Auvézère →, France ... 26 C4
Auxerre, France 25 E10
Auxi-le-Château, France . 25 B9
Auxonne, France 25 E12
Auzances, France 26 B6
Auzat-sur-Allier, France . 26 C7
Avallon, France 25 E10
Avalon, U.S.A. 113 M8
Avaré, Brazil 127 A6
Ávas, Greece 39 J8
Avawatz Mts., U.S.A. .. 113 K10
Aveiro, Brazil 121 D6
Aveiro, Portugal 30 E2
Aveiro □, Portugal 30 E2
Āvej, Iran 65 C6
Avellaneda, Argentina .. 126 C4
Avellino, Italy 35 B7
Avenal, U.S.A. 112 K6
Avenches, Switz. 22 C4
Averøya, Norway 10 A1
Aversa, Italy 35 B7
Avery, U.S.A. 110 C6
Aves, I. de, W. Indies ... 117 C7
Aves, Is. de, Venezuela . 117 D6
Avesnes-sur-Helpe, France 25 B10
Avesta, Sweden 9 F17
Aveyron □, France 26 D6
Aveyron →, France 26 D5
Avezzano, Italy 33 F10
Aviá Terai, Argentina ... 126 B3
Aviano, Italy 33 B9
Avigliana, Italy 32 C4
Avigliano, Italy 35 B8
Avignon, France 27 E8
Ávila, Spain 30 E6
Ávila □, Spain 30 E6
Ávila, Sierra de, Spain .. 30 E5
Avila Beach, U.S.A. 113 K6
Avilés, Spain 30 B5
Avis, Portugal 31 F3
Avize, France 25 D11
Avoca, Ireland 15 D5
Avoca →, Australia 91 F3
Avoca →, Ireland 15 D5
Avola, Canada 100 C5
Avola, Italy 35 F8
Avon, N.Y., U.S.A. 106 D7

Avon, S. Dak., U.S.A. ... 108 D5
Avon □, U.K. 13 F5
Avon →, Australia 89 F2
Avon →, Avon, U.K. .. 13 F5
Avon →, Hants., U.K. . 13 G6
Avon →, Warks., U.K. . 13 F5
Avondale, Zimbabwe 83 F3
Avonlea, Canada 101 D7
Avonmore, Canada 107 A10
Avonmouth, U.K. 13 F5
Avranches, France 24 D5
Avre →, France 24 D8
Awag el Baqar, Sudan .. 77 E3
A'waj →, Syria 69 B5
Awaji-Shima, Japan 49 G7
'Awālī, Bahrain 65 E6
Awantipur, India 63 C6
Awasa, Ethiopia 77 F4
Awash, Ethiopia 68 F3
Awash →, Ethiopia 77 E5
Awaso, Ghana 78 D4
Awatere →, N.Z. 87 J5
Awbārī, Libya 75 C7
Awbārī □, Libya 75 C7
Awe, L., U.K. 14 E3
Aweil, Sudan 77 F2
Awgu, Nigeria 79 D6
Awjilah, Libya 73 C9
Ax-les-Thermes, France . 26 F5
Axarfjörður, Iceland 8 C5
Axel, Neths. 17 F3
Axel Heiberg I., Canada . 4 B3
Axim, Ghana 78 E4
Axinim, Brazil 121 D6
Axintele, Romania 38 E9
Axioma, Brazil 125 B5
Axiós →, Greece 39 J5
Axminster, U.K. 13 G4
Axvall, Sweden 11 F7
Aÿ, France 25 C11
Ayabaca, Peru 124 A2
Ayabe, Japan 49 G7
Ayacucho, Argentina ... 126 D4
Ayacucho, Peru 124 C3
Ayaguz, Kazakhstan 44 E9
Ayamonte, Spain 31 H3
Ayan, Russia 45 D14
Ayancık, Turkey 66 B6
Ayapel, Colombia 120 B2
Ayas, Turkey 66 B5
Ayaviri, Peru 124 C3
Aybastı, Turkey 66 B7
Aydın, Turkey 66 D2
Aye, Belgium 17 H6
Ayenngré, Togo 79 D5
Ayer's Cliff, Canada ... 107 A12
Ayers Rock, Australia .. 89 E5
Ayiá, Greece 39 K5
Ayia Aikateríni, Ákra, Greece 37 A3
Ayía Dhéka, Greece 37 D6
Ayía Gálini, Greece 37 D6
Ayía Marína, Greece ... 39 M9
Ayia Napa, Cyprus 37 E13
Ayía Paraskeví, Greece .. 39 K9
Ayía Phyla, Cyprus 39 E12
Ayía Rouméli, Greece ... 39 P6
Ayia Varvára, Greece ... 37 D7
Áyios Amvrósios, Cyprus . 37 D12
Áyios Andréas, Greece .. 39 M5
Áyios Evstrátios, Greece . 39 K7
Áyios Ioánnis, Ákra, Greece 37 D7
Áyios Isídhoros, Greece . 37 C9
Áyios Kiríkos, Greece ... 39 M9
Áyios Matthaíos, Greece . 37 B3
Áyios Mírono, Greece ... 39 P8
Áyios Nikólaos, Greece .. 37 D7
Áyios Seryios, Cyprus ... 37 D12
Áyios Theodhoros, Cyprus 37 D13
Aykathonísi, Greece 39 M9
Aylesbury, U.K. 13 F7
Aylmer, Canada 106 D4
Aylmer, L., Canada 96 B8
Ayn Zālah, Iraq 67 D10
Ayna, Spain 29 G2
Ayolas, Paraguay 126 B4
Ayom, Sudan 77 F2
Ayon, Ostrov, Russia ... 45 C17
Ayora, Spain 29 F3
Ayr, Australia 90 B4
Ayr, U.K. 14 F4
Ayr →, U.K. 14 F4
Ayrancı, Turkey 66 D5
Ayre, Pt. of, U.K. 12 C3
Aysha, Ethiopia 77 E5
Aytos, Bulgaria 38 G10
Ayu, Kepulauan, Indonesia 57 D8
Ayutla, Guatemala 116 D1
Ayutla, Mexico 115 D5
Ayvacık, Turkey 66 C2
Ayvalık, Turkey 66 C2
Aywaille, Belgium 17 H7
Az Zāhirīyah, West Bank . 69 D3
Az Zahrān, Si. Arabia .. 65 E6
Az Zarqā, Jordan 69 C5
Az Zāwiyah, Libya 75 B7
Az Zubayr, Iraq 67 D11
Az-Zilfī, Si. Arabia 64 E5
Az Zuwaytīnah, Libya .. 73 B9
Azambuja, Portugal 31 F2
Azamgarh, India 63 F10
Azangaro, Peru 124 C3
Azaouak, Vallée de l', Mali 79 B5
Āzār Shahr, Iran 67 D11

Azarān, *Iran* 67 D12
Azärbayjan =
  Azerbaijan ■, *Asia* ... 43 K9
Äzarbāyjān-e Gharbī □,
  Iran 64 B5
Āzarbāyjān-e Sharqī □,
  Iran 64 B5
Azare, *Nigeria* 79 C7
Azay-le-Rideau, *France* .. 24 E7
A'zāz, *Syria* 66 D7
Azazga, *Algeria* 75 A5
Azbine = Aïr, *Niger* 79 B6
Azefal, *Mauritania* 74 D2
Azeffoun, *Algeria* 75 A5
Azemmour, *Morocco* ... 74 B3
Azerbaijan ■, *Asia* 43 K9
Azerbaijchan =
  Azerbaijan ■, *Asia* ... 43 K9
Azezo, *Ethiopia* 77 E4
Azimganj, *India* 63 G13
Aznalcóllar, *Spain* 31 H4
Azogues, *Ecuador* 120 D2
Azores, *Atl. Oc.* 2 C8
Azov, *Russia* 43 G4
Azov, Sea of, *Europe* ... 43 H3
Azovskoye More = Azov,
  Sea of, *Europe* 43 H3
Azovy, *Russia* 44 C7
Azpeitia, *Spain* 28 B2
Azrou, *Morocco* 74 B3
Azuaga, *Spain* 31 G5
Azuara, *Spain* 28 D4
Azuay □, *Ecuador* 120 D2
Azuer →, *Spain* 31 F7
Azuero, Pen. de, *Panama* 116 E3
Azul, *Argentina* 126 D4
Azul, Serra, *Brazil* 125 C7
Azurduy, *Bolivia* 125 D5
Azusa, *U.S.A.* 113 L9
Azzaba, *Algeria* 75 A6
Azzano Décimo, *Italy* ... 33 C9
'Azzūn, *West Bank* 69 C4

B

Ba Don, *Vietnam* 58 D6
Ba Dong, *Vietnam* 59 H6
Ba Ngoi = Cam Lam,
  Vietnam 59 G7
Ba Ria, *Vietnam* 59 G6
Ba Tri, *Vietnam* 59 G6
Ba Xian, *China* 50 E9
Baa, *Indonesia* 57 F6
Baamonde, *Spain* 30 B3
Baar, *Switz.* 23 B7
Baarle Nassau, *Belgium* . 17 F5
Baarlo, *Neths.* 17 F8
Baarn, *Neths.* 16 D6
Bab el Mandeb, *Red Sea* . 68 E3
Baba Burnu, *Turkey* 66 C2
Baba dag, *Azerbaijan* ... 43 K9
Bābā Kalū, *Iran* 65 D6
Babaçulândia, *Brazil* ... 122 C2
Babadag, *Romania* 38 E11
Babadayhan, *Turkmenistan* 44 F7
Babaeski, *Turkey* 66 B2
Babahoyo, *Ecuador* 120 D2
Babakin, *Australia* 89 F2
Babana, *Nigeria* 79 C5
Babar, *Algeria* 75 A6
Babar, *Indonesia* 57 F7
Babar, *Pakistan* 62 D3
Babarkach, *Pakistan* 62 E2
Babayevo, *Russia* 40 C8
Babb, *U.S.A.* 110 B7
Babenhausen, *Germany* . 19 F4
Babi Besar, P., *Malaysia* . 59 L4
Babian Jiang →, *China* . 52 F3
Babile, *Ethiopia* 77 F5
Babinda, *Australia* 90 B4
Babine, *Canada* 100 B3
Babine →, *Canada* 100 B3
Babine L., *Canada* 100 C3
Babo, *Indonesia* 57 E8
Bābol, *Iran* 65 B7
Bābol Sar, *Iran* 65 B7
Baboua, *C.A.R.* 80 C2
Babruysk, *Belarus* 41 F5
Babura, *Nigeria* 79 C6
Babusar Pass, *Pakistan* . 63 B5
Babušnica, *Serbia, Yug.* . 21 M12
Babuyan Chan., *Phil.* ... 55 B4
Babuyan Is., *Phil.* 55 B4
Babylon, *Iraq* 67 F11
Bac Can, *Vietnam* 58 A5
Bac Giang, *Vietnam* 58 B6
Bac Ninh, *Vietnam* 58 B6
Bac Phan, *Vietnam* 58 B5
Bac Quang, *Vietnam* 58 A5
Bacabal, *Brazil* 122 B3
Bacajá →, *Brazil* 121 D7
Bacalar, *Mexico* 115 D7
Bacan, Kepulauan,
  Indonesia 57 E7
Bacan, Pulau, *Indonesia* . 57 E7
Bacarra, *Phil.* 55 B4
Bacău, *Romania* 38 C9
Baccarat, *France* 25 D13
Bacerac, *Mexico* 114 A3
Băcești, *Romania* 38 C10
Bach Long Vi, Dao,
  Vietnam 58 B6

Bachaquero, *Venezuela* .. 120 B3
Bacharach, *Germany* 19 E3
Bachelina, *Russia* 44 D7
Bachuma, *Ethiopia* 77 F4
Bačina, *Serbia, Yug.* 21 M11
Back →, *Canada* 96 B9
Bačka Palanka,
  Serbia, Yug. 21 K9
Bačka Topola, *Serbia, Yug.* 21 K9
Bäckefors, *Sweden* 11 F6
Backnang, *Germany* 19 G5
Backstairs Passage,
  Australia 91 F2
Baco, Mt., *Phil.* 55 E4
Bacolod, *Phil.* 55 F5
Bacqueville-en-Caux,
  France 24 C8
Bácsalmás, *Hungary* 21 J9
Bacuag, *Phil.* 55 G6
Bacuk, *Malaysia* 59 J4
Bād, *Iran* 65 C7
Bad →, *U.S.A.* 108 C4
Bad Axe, *U.S.A.* 106 C2
Bad Bergzabern, *Germany* 19 F4
Bad Berleburg, *Germany* . 18 D4
Bad Bevensen, *Germany* . 18 B6
Bad Bramstedt, *Germany* . 18 B5
Bad Brückenau, *Germany* 19 E5
Bad Doberan, *Germany* . 18 A7
Bad Ems, *Germany* 19 E3
Bad Frankenhausen,
  Germany 18 D7
Bad Freienwalde, *Germany* 18 C10
Bad Godesberg, *Germany* 18 E3
Bad Hersfeld, *Germany* . 18 E5
Bad Hofgastein, *Austria* . 21 H3
Bad Homburg, *Germany* . 19 E4
Bad Honnef, *Germany* .. 18 E3
Bad Ischl, *Austria* 21 H3
Bad Kissingen, *Germany* . 19 E6
Bad Königshofen, *Germany* 19 E6
Bad Kreuznach, *Germany* 19 F3
Bad Laasphe, *Germany* .. 18 E4
Bad Lands, *U.S.A.* 108 D3
Bad Langensalza, *Germany* 18 D6
Bad Lauterberg, *Germany* 18 D6
Bad Lippspringe, *Germany* 18 D4
Bad Mergentheim,
  Germany 19 F5
Bad Münstereifel, *Germany* 18 E2
Bad Muskau, *Germany* .. 18 D10
Bad Nauheim, *Germany* . 19 E4
Bad Oeynhausen, *Germany* 18 C4
Bad Oldesloe, *Germany* . 18 B6
Bad Orb, *Germany* 19 E5
Bad Pyrmont, *Germany* . 18 D5
Bad Ragaz, *Switz.* 23 B9
Bad Reichenhall, *Germany* 19 H8
Bad Säckingen, *Germany* . 19 H3
Bad Salzuflen, *Germany* . 18 C4
Bad Segeberg, *Germany* . 18 B6
Bad Tölz, *Germany* 19 H7
Bad Urach, *Germany* 19 G5
Bad Waldsee, *Germany* . 19 H5
Bad Wildungen, *Germany* 18 D5
Bad Wimpfen, *Germany* . 19 F5
Bad Windsheim, *Germany* 19 F6
Badagara, *India* 60 P9
Badagri, *Nigeria* 79 D5
Badajós, L., *Brazil* 121 D5
Badajoz, *Spain* 31 G4
Badajoz □, *Spain* 31 G4
Badalona, *Spain* 28 D7
Badalzai, *Afghan.* 62 E1
Badampahar, *India* 61 H15
Badanah, *Si. Arabia* 64 D4
Badas, *Brunei* 56 D4
Badas, Kepulauan,
  Indonesia 56 D3
Baddo →, *Pakistan* 60 F4
Bade, *Indonesia* 57 F9
Baden, *Austria* 21 G6
Baden, *Switz.* 23 B6
Baden-Baden, *Germany* . 19 G4
Baden-Württemberg □,
  Germany 19 G5
Badenoch, *U.K.* 14 E4
Badger, *Canada* 99 C8
Badger, *U.S.A.* 112 J7
Bādghīsāt □, *Afghan.* ... 60 B3
Badgom, *India* 63 B6
Badhoevedorp, *Neths.* .. 16 D5
Badia Polésine, *Italy* 33 C8
Badin, *Pakistan* 62 G3
Badogo, *Mali* 78 C3
Badong, *China* 53 B8
Badrah, *Iraq* 67 F11
Baduen, *Somali Rep.* 68 F4
Badulla, *Sri Lanka* 60 R12
Baena, *Spain* 31 H6
Baexem, *Neths.* 17 F7
Baeza, *Ecuador* 120 D2
Baeza, *Spain* 29 H1
Bafang, *Cameroon* 79 D7
Bafatá, *Guinea-Biss.* 78 C2
Baffin B., *Canada* 4 B4
Baffin I., *Canada* 97 B12
Bafia, *Cameroon* 79 E7
Bafilyūn, *Syria* 64 B3
Baflo, *Neths.* 16 B9
Bafoulabé, *Mali* 78 C2
Bafoussam, *Cameroon* ... 79 D7
Bāfq, *Iran* 65 D7

Bafra, *Turkey* 66 B6
Bafra Burnu, *Turkey* 66 B7
Bāft, *Iran* 65 D8
Bafut, *Cameroon* 79 D7
Bafwasende, *Zaïre* 82 B2
Bagamoyo, *Tanzania* 82 D4
Bagamoyo □, *Tanzania* . 82 D4
Bagan Datoh, *Malaysia* .. 59 L3
Bagan Serai, *Malaysia* ... 59 K3
Baganga, *Phil.* 55 H7
Bagani, *Namibia* 84 B3
Bagansiapiapi, *Indonesia* . 56 D2
Bagasra, *India* 62 J4
Bagawi, *Sudan* 77 E3
Bagdad, *U.S.A.* 113 L11
Bagdarin, *Russia* 45 D12
Bagé, *Brazil* 127 C5
Bagenalstown = Muine
  Bheag, *Ireland* 15 D5
Baggs, *U.S.A.* 110 F10
Baghdād, *Iraq* 67 F11
Bagheria, *Italy* 34 D6
Baghlān, *Afghan.* 60 A6
Bagley, *U.S.A.* 108 B7
Bagnacavallo, *Italy* 33 D8
Bagnara Cálabra, *Italy* ... 35 D8
Bagnères-de-Bigorre,
  France 26 E4
Bagnères-de-Luchon,
  France 26 F4
Bagni di Lucca, *Italy* 32 D7
Bagno di Romagna, *Italy* . 33 E8
Bagnoles-de-l'Orne, *France* 24 D6
Bagnoli di Sopra, *Italy* ... 33 C8
Bagnolo Mella, *Italy* 32 C7
Bagnols-sur-Cèze, *France* . 27 D8
Bagnorégio, *Italy* 33 F9
Bagolino, *Italy* 32 C7
Bagotville, *Canada* 99 C5
Bagrationovsk, *Russia* ... 9 J19
Bagua, *Peru* 124 B2
Baguio, *Phil.* 55 C4
Bahābón de Esgueva, *Spain* 28 D1
Bahadurgarh, *India* 62 E7
Bahama, Canal Viejo de,
  W. Indies 116 B4
Bahamas ■, *N. Amer.* ... 117 B5
Bahār, *Iran* 67 E13
Baharampur, *India* 63 G13
Baharîya, El Wâhât al,
  Egypt 76 J6
Bahau, *Malaysia* 59 L4
Bahawalnagar, *Pakistan* . 62 D5
Bahawalpur, *Pakistan* ... 62 E4
Bahçe, *Turkey* 66 D7
Baheri, *India* 63 E8
Bahi, *Tanzania* 82 D4
Bahi Swamp, *Tanzania* .. 82 D4
Bahía = Salvador, *Brazil* . 123 D4
Bahia □, *Brazil* 123 D3
Bahía, Is. de la, *Honduras* 116 C2
Bahía Blanca, *Argentina* . 126 D3
Bahía de Caráquez,
  Ecuador 120 D1
Bahia Honda, *Cuba* 116 B3
Bahía Laura, *Argentina* .. 128 C3
Bahía Negra, *Paraguay* .. 125 E6
Bahir Dar, *Ethiopia* 77 E4
Bahmanzād, *Iran* 65 D6
Bahmer, *Algeria* 75 C4
Bahönye, *Hungary* 21 J7
Bahr Aouk →, *C.A.R.* ... 80 C3
Bahr el Ahmar □, *Sudan* . 76 C3
Bahr el Ghazâl □, *Sudan* . 77 F2
Bahr Salamat →, *Chad* . 73 G8
Bahr Yûsef →, *Egypt* ... 76 J7
Bahra el Burullus, *Egypt* . 76 H7
Bahraich, *India* 63 F9
Bahrain ■, *Asia* 65 E6
Bahror, *India* 62 F7
Bāhū Kalāt, *Iran* 65 E9
Bai, *Mali* 78 C4
Bai Bung, Mui, *Vietnam* . 59 H5
Bai Duc, *Vietnam* 58 C5
Bai Thuong, *Vietnam* ... 58 C5
Baia Mare, *Romania* 38 B6
Baia-Sprie, *Romania* 38 B6
Baião, *Brazil* 122 B2
Baïbokoum, *Chad* 73 G8
Baicheng, *China* 51 B12
Baidoa, *Somali Rep.* 68 G3
Baie Comeau, *Canada* ... 99 C6
Baie-St-Paul, *Canada* 99 C5
Baie Trinité, *Canada* 99 C6
Baie Verte, *Canada* 99 C8
Baignes-Ste.-Radegonde,
  France 26 C3
Baigneux-les-Juifs, *France* 25 E11
Baihe, *China* 50 H6
Baihe, *Taiwan* 53 F13
Ba'ījī, *Iraq* 67 E10
Baikal, L. = Baykal, Oz.,
  Russia 45 D11
Baile Atha Cliath =
  Dublin, *Ireland* 15 C5
Bailei, *Ethiopia* 77 F5
Bailén, *Spain* 31 G7
Băilești, *Romania* 38 E6
Baileux, *Belgium* 17 H4
Bailique, Ilha, *Brazil* 122 A2
Bailleul, *France* 25 B9
Bailundo, *Angola* 81 G3
Baima, *China* 52 A3
Bain-de-Bretagne, *France* 24 E5
Bainbridge, *Ga., U.S.A.* . 105 K3
Bainbridge, *N.Y., U.S.A.* 107 D9

Baing, *Indonesia* 57 F6
Bainiu, *China* 50 H7
Bainville, *U.S.A.* 108 A2
Ba'ir, *Jordan* 69 E5
Baird, *U.S.A.* 109 J5
Baird Mts., *U.S.A.* 96 B3
Bairin Youqi, *China* 51 C10
Bairin Zuoqi, *China* 51 C10
Bairnsdale, *Australia* 91 F4
Bais, *Phil.* 55 G5
Baisha, *China* 50 G7
Baïsole →, *France* 26 E4
Baissa, *Nigeria* 79 D7
Baitadi, *Nepal* 63 E9
Baixa Grande, *Brazil* 123 D3
Baiyin, *China* 50 F3
Baiyu, *China* 52 B2
Baiyu Shan, *China* 50 F4
Baiyuda, *Sudan* 76 D3
Baj Baj, *India* 63 H13
Baja, *Hungary* 21 J8
Baja, Pta., *Mexico* 114 B1
Baja California, *Mexico* .. 114 A1
Baja California □, *Mexico* 114 A2
Baja California Sur □,
  Mexico 114 B2
Bajamar, *Canary Is.* 36 F3
Bajana, *India* 62 H4
Bájgīrān, *Iran* 65 B8
Bajimba, Mt., *Australia* . 91 D5
Bajo Nuevo, *Caribbean* .. 116 C4
Bajoga, *Nigeria* 79 C7
Bajool, *Australia* 90 C5
Bakala, *C.A.R.* 73 G9
Bakar, *Croatia* 33 C11
Bakchar, *Russia* 44 D9
Bakel, *Neths.* 17 E7
Bakel, *Senegal* 78 C2
Baker, *Calif., U.S.A.* 113 K10
Baker, *Mont., U.S.A.* ... 108 B2
Baker, *Oreg., U.S.A.* 110 D5
Baker, Canal, *Chile* 128 C2
Baker, L., *Canada* 96 B10
Baker I., *Pac. Oc.* 92 G10
Baker Lake, *Canada* 96 B10
Baker Mt., *U.S.A.* 110 B3
Bakers Creek, *Australia* .. 90 C4
Baker's Dozen Is., *Canada* 98 A4
Bakersfield, *Calif., U.S.A.* 113 K7
Bakersfield, *Vt., U.S.A.* .. 107 B12
Bakhchysaray, *Ukraine* .. 41 K7
Bakhmach, *Ukraine* 41 G7
Bākhtarān, *Iran* 67 E12
Bākhtarān □, *Iran* 64 C5
Bakı, *Azerbaijan* 43 K9
Bakırdaği, *Turkey* 66 C6
Bakırköy, *Turkey* 39 H11
Bakkafjörður, *Iceland* ... 8 C6
Bakkagerði, *Iceland* 8 D7
Bakony □, *Hungary* 21 H7
Bakony Forest = Bakony
  Hegyseg, *Hungary* ... 21 H7
Bakony Hegyseg, *Hungary* 21 H7
Bakori, *Nigeria* 79 C6
Bakouma, *C.A.R.* 73 G9
Baksan, *Russia* 43 J6
Baku = Bakı, *Azerbaijan* 43 K9
Bakutis Coast, *Antarctica* 5 D15
Baky = Bakı, *Azerbaijan* . 43 K9
Bala, *Canada* 106 A5
Bâlâ, *Turkey* 66 C5
Bala, L., *U.K.* 12 E4
Balabac I., *Phil.* 55 H2
Balabac Str., *E. Indies* ... 56 C5
Balabagh, *Afghan.* 62 B4
Ba'labakk, *Lebanon* 69 A5
Balabalangan, Kepulauan,
  Indonesia 56 E5
Bălăcița, *Romania* 38 E6
Balad, *Iraq* 67 F11
Balad Rūz, *Iraq* 67 F11
Bālādeh, *Fārs, Iran* 65 D6
Bālādeh, *Māzandaran, Iran* 65 B6
Balaghat, *India* 60 J12
Balaghat Ra., *India* 60 K10
Balaguer, *Spain* 28 D5
Balakhna, *Russia* 42 B7
Balaklava, *Australia* 91 E2
Balaklava, *Ukraine* 41 K7
Balakliya, *Ukraine* 41 H9
Balakovo, *Russia* 42 D8
Balancán, *Mexico* 115 D6
Balashov, *Russia* 42 E6
Balasinor, *India* 62 H5
Balasore = Baleshwar,
  India 61 J15
Balassagyarmat, *Hungary* 21 G9
Balāt, *Egypt* 76 B2
Balaton, *Hungary* 21 J7
Balayan, *Phil.* 55 E4
Balazote, *Spain* 29 G2
Balbina, Reprêsa de, *Brazil* 121 D6
Balboa, *Panama* 116 E4
Balbriggan, *Ireland* 15 C5
Balcarce, *Argentina* 126 D4
Balcarres, *Canada* 101 C8
Balchik, *Bulgaria* 38 F11
Bald Hd., *Australia* 89 G2
Bald I., *Australia* 89 F2
Bald Knob, *U.S.A.* 109 H9
Baldock L., *Canada* 101 B9
Baldwin, *Mich., U.S.A.* .. 104 D3
Baldwinsville, *U.S.A.* 107 C8
Baldy Peak, *U.S.A.* 111 K9

Bale, *Croatia* 33 C10
Bale □, *Ethiopia* 77 F5
Baleares □, *Spain* 28 F7
Balearic Is. = Baleares, Is.,
  Spain 36 B10
Baleia, Pta. da, *Brazil* ... 123 E4
Balen, *Belgium* 17 F6
Baler, *Phil.* 55 D4
Baler Bay, *Phil.* 55 D4
Balerna, *Switz.* 23 E8
Baleshwar, *India* 61 J15
Balezino, *Russia* 42 B11
Balfate, *Honduras* 116 C2
Balfe's Creek, *Australia* .. 90 C4
Bali, *Cameroon* 79 D6
Balí, *Greece* 37 D6
Bali, *Indonesia* 56 F5
Bali □, *Indonesia* 56 F5
Bali, Selat, *Indonesia* 57 H16
Baligród, *Poland* 20 F12
Balikeşir, *Turkey* 66 C2
Balikpapan, *Indonesia* ... 56 E5
Balimbing, *Phil.* 57 C5
Baling, *Malaysia* 59 K3
Balintang Channel, *Phil.* . 55 B4
Balipara, *India* 61 F18
Baliza, *Brazil* 125 D7
Balk, *Neths.* 16 C7
Balkan Mts. = Stara
  Planina, *Bulgaria* 38 F6
Balkhash = Balqash,
  Kazakhstan 44 E8
Balkhash, Ozero = Balqash
  Köl, *Kazakhstan* 44 E8
Balla, *Bangla.* 61 G17
Ballachulish, *U.K.* 14 E3
Balladonia, *Australia* 89 F3
Ballarat, *Australia* 91 F3
Ballard, L., *Australia* 89 E3
Ballater, *U.K.* 14 D5
Ballenas, Canal de, *Mexico* 114 B2
Balleny Is., *Antarctica* ... 5 C11
Ballesteros, *Phil.* 55 B4
Ballia, *India* 63 G11
Ballidu, *Australia* 89 F2
Ballina, *Australia* 91 D5
Ballina, *Mayo, Ireland* ... 15 B2
Ballina, *Tipp., Ireland* ... 15 D3
Ballinasloe, *Ireland* 15 C3
Ballinger, *U.S.A.* 109 K5
Ballinrobe, *Ireland* 15 C2
Ballinskelligs B., *Ireland* . 15 E1
Ballon, *France* 24 D7
Ballycastle, *U.K.* 15 A5
Ballymena, *U.K.* 15 B5
Ballymena □, *U.K.* 15 B5
Ballymoney, *U.K.* 15 A5
Ballymoney □, *U.K.* 15 A5
Ballyshannon, *Ireland* ... 15 B3
Balmaceda, *Chile* 128 C2
Balmazújváros, *Hungary* . 21 H11
Balmhorn, *Switz.* 22 D5
Balmoral, *Australia* 91 F3
Balmoral, *U.K.* 14 D5
Balmorhea, *U.S.A.* 109 K3
Balonne →, *Australia* ... 91 D4
Balqash, *Kazakhstan* 44 E8
Balqash Köl, *Kazakhstan* . 44 E8
Balrampur, *India* 63 F10
Balranald, *Australia* 91 E3
Balş, *Romania* 38 E7
Balsapuerto, *Peru* 124 B2
Balsas, *Mexico* 115 D5
Balsas →, *Maranhão,
  Brazil* 122 C3
Balsas →, *Tocantins,
  Brazil* 122 C2
Balsas →, *Mexico* 114 D4
Bålsta, *Sweden* 10 E11
Balsthal, *Switz.* 22 B5
Balston Spa, *U.S.A.* 107 D11
Balta, *Romania* 38 E5
Balta, *Ukraine* 41 H5
Balta, *U.S.A.* 108 A4
Baltanás, *Spain* 30 D6
Bălți, *Moldova* 41 J4
Baltic Sea, *Europe* 9 H18
Baltîm, *Egypt* 76 H7
Baltimore, *Ireland* 15 E2
Baltimore, *U.S.A.* 104 F7
Baltit, *Pakistan* 63 A6
Baltiysk, *Russia* 9 J18
Baltrum, *Germany* 18 B3
Baluchistan □, *Pakistan* . 60 F4
Balurghat, *India* 63 G13
Balvi, *Latvia* 9 H22
Balya, *Turkey* 66 C2
Balygychan, *Russia* 45 C16
Balzar, *Ecuador* 120 D2
Bam, *Iran* 65 D8
Bama, *China* 52 E6
Bama, *Nigeria* 79 C7
Bamako, *Mali* 78 C3
Bamba, *Mali* 79 B4
Bambamarca, *Peru* 124 B2
Bambari, *C.A.R.* 73 G9
Bambaroo, *Australia* 90 B4
Bamberg, *Germany* 19 F6
Bamberg, *U.S.A.* 105 J5
Bambesi, *Ethiopia* 77 F3
Bambey, *Senegal* 78 C1
Bambili, *Zaïre* 82 B2
Bambuí, *Brazil* 123 F2
Bamenda, *Cameroon* 79 D7
Bamfield, *Canada* 100 D3
Bāmīān □, *Afghan.* 60 B5

Båstad

Bamiancheng, *China* 51 C13
Bamkin, *Cameroon* 79 D7
Bampūr, *Iran* 65 E9
Ban Aranyaprathet, *Thailand* 58 F4
Ban Ban, *Laos* 58 C4
Ban Bang Hin, *Thailand* 59 H2
Ban Chiang Klang, *Thailand* 58 C3
Ban Chik, *Laos* 58 D4
Ban Choho, *Thailand* 58 E4
Ban Dan Lan Hoi, *Thailand* 58 D2
Ban Don = Surat Thani, *Thailand* 59 H2
Ban Don, *Vietnam* 58 F6
Ban Don, Ao, *Thailand* 59 H2
Ban Dong, *Thailand* 58 C3
Ban Hong, *Thailand* 58 C2
Ban Kaeng, *Thailand* 58 D3
Ban Keun, *Laos* 58 C4
Ban Khai, *Thailand* 58 F3
Ban Kheun, *Laos* 58 B3
Ban Khlong Kua, *Thailand* 59 J3
Ban Khuan Mao, *Thailand* 59 J2
Ban Khun Yuam, *Thailand* 58 C1
Ban Ko Yai Chim, *Thailand* 59 G2
Ban Kok, *Thailand* 58 D4
Ban Laem, *Thailand* 58 F2
Ban Lao Ngam, *Laos* 58 E6
Ban Le Kathe, *Thailand* 58 E2
Ban Mae Chedi, *Thailand* 58 C2
Ban Mae Laeng, *Thailand* 58 B2
Ban Mae Sariang, *Thailand* 58 C1
Ban Mê Thuôt = Buon Me Thuot, *Vietnam* 58 F7
Ban Mi, *Thailand* 58 E3
Ban Muong Mo, *Laos* 58 C4
Ban Na Mo, *Laos* 58 D5
Ban Na San, *Thailand* 59 H2
Ban Na Tong, *Laos* 58 B3
Ban Nam Bac, *Laos* 58 B4
Ban Nam Ma, *Laos* 58 A3
Ban Ngang, *Laos* 58 E6
Ban Nong Bok, *Laos* 58 D5
Ban Nong Boua, *Laos* 58 E6
Ban Nong Pling, *Thailand* 58 E3
Ban Pak Chan, *Thailand* 59 G2
Ban Phai, *Thailand* 58 D4
Ban Pong, *Thailand* 58 F2
Ban Ron Phibun, *Thailand* 59 H2
Ban Sanam Chai, *Thailand* 59 J3
Ban Sangkha, *Thailand* 58 E4
Ban Tak, *Thailand* 58 D2
Ban Tako, *Thailand* 58 E4
Ban Tha Dua, *Thailand* 58 D2
Ban Tha Li, *Thailand* 58 D3
Ban Tha Nun, *Thailand* 59 H2
Ban Thahine, *Laos* 58 E5
Ban Xien Kok, *Laos* 58 B3
Ban Yen Nhan, *Vietnam* 58 B6
Baña, Punta de la, *Spain* 28 E5
Banaba, *Kiribati* 92 H8
Bañalbufar, *Spain* 36 B9
Banalia, *Zaïre* 82 B2
Banam, *Cambodia* 59 G5
Banamba, *Mali* 78 C3
Banana, *Australia* 90 C5
Bananal, I. do, *Brazil* 123 D1
Banaras = Varanasi, *India* 63 G10
Banas →, *Gujarat, India* 62 H4
Banas →, *Mad. P., India* 63 G9
Bânâs, Ras, *Egypt* 76 C4
Banaz, *Turkey* 66 C3
Banbān, *Si. Arabia* 64 E5
Banbridge, *U.K.* 15 B5
Banbridge □, *U.K.* 15 B5
Banbury, *U.K.* 13 E6
Banchory, *U.K.* 14 D6
Bancroft, *Canada* 98 C4
Band Bonī, *Iran* 65 E8
Band Qīr, *Iran* 65 D6
Banda, *India* 63 G9
Banda, Kepulauan, *Indonesia* 57 E7
Banda Aceh, *Indonesia* 56 C1
Banda Banda, Mt., *Australia* 91 E5
Banda Elat, *Indonesia* 57 F8
Banda Is. = Banda, Kepulauan, *Indonesia* 57 E7
Banda Sea, *Indonesia* 57 F7
Bandai-San, *Japan* 48 F10
Bandama →, *Ivory C.* 78 D3
Bandān, *Iran* 65 D9
Bandanaira, *Indonesia* 57 E7
Bandanwara, *India* 62 F6
Bandar = Machilipatnam, *India* 61 L12
Bandār 'Abbās, *Iran* 65 E8
Bandar-e Anzalī, *Iran* 67 D13
Bandar-e Bushehr = Būshehr, *Iran* 65 D6
Bandar-e Chārak, *Iran* 65 E7
Bandar-e Deylam, *Iran* 65 D6
Bandar-e Khomeynı, *Iran* 65 D6
Bandar-e Lengeh, *Iran* 65 E7
Bandar-e Maqām, *Iran* 65 E7
Bandar-e Ma'shur, *Iran* 65 D6
Bandar-e Nakhīlū, *Iran* 65 E7
Bandar-e Rīg, *Iran* 65 D6
Bandar-e Torkeman, *Iran* 65 B7
Bandar Maharani = Muar, *Malaysia* 59 L4
Bandar Penggaram = Batu Pahat, *Malaysia* 59 M4
Bandar Seri Begawan, *Brunei* 56 C4
Bandawe, *Malawi* 83 E3
Bande, *Belgium* 17 H6
Bande, *Spain* 30 C3
Bandeira, Pico da, *Brazil* 123 F3
Bandeirante, *Brazil* 123 D1
Bandera, *Argentina* 126 B3
Bandera, *U.S.A.* 109 L5
Banderas, B. de, *Mexico* 114 C3
Bandiagara, *Mali* 78 C4
Bandırma, *Turkey* 66 B3
Bandon, *Ireland* 15 E3
Bandon →, *Ireland* 15 E3
Bandula, *Mozam.* 83 F3
Bandundu, *Zaïre* 80 E3
Bandung, *Indonesia* 57 G12
Bandya, *Australia* 89 E3
Bāneh, *Iran* 67 E11
Bañeres, *Spain* 29 G4
Banes, *Cuba* 117 B4
Banff, *Canada* 100 C5
Banff, *U.K.* 14 D6
Banff Nat. Park, *Canada* 100 C5
Banfora, *Burkina Faso* 78 C4
Bang Fai →, *Laos* 58 D5
Bang Hieng →, *Laos* 58 D5
Bang Krathum, *Thailand* 58 D3
Bang Lamung, *Thailand* 58 F3
Bang Mun Nak, *Thailand* 58 D3
Bang Pa In, *Thailand* 58 E3
Bang Rakam, *Thailand* 58 D3
Bang Saphan, *Thailand* 59 G2
Bangala Dam, *Zimbabwe* 83 G3
Bangalore, *India* 60 N10
Bangante, *Cameroon* 79 D7
Bangaon, *India* 63 H13
Bangassou, *C.A.R.* 80 D4
Banggai, Kepulauan, *Indonesia* 57 E6
Banggi, P., *Malaysia* 56 C5
Banghāzī, *Libya* 73 B9
Bangil, *Indonesia* 57 G15
Bangjang, *Sudan* 77 E3
Bangka, P., *Sulawesi, Indonesia* 57 D7
Bangka, P., *Sumatera, Indonesia* 56 E3
Bangka, Selat, *Indonesia* 56 E3
Bangkalan, *Indonesia* 57 G15
Bangkinang, *Indonesia* 56 D2
Bangko, *Indonesia* 56 E2
Bangkok, *Thailand* 58 F3
Bangladesh ■, *Asia* 61 H17
Bangolo, *Ivory C.* 78 D3
Bangong Co, *India* 63 B8
Bangor, *Down, U.K.* 15 B6
Bangor, *Gwynedd, U.K.* 12 D3
Bangor, *Maine, U.S.A.* 99 D6
Bangor, *Pa., U.S.A.* 107 F9
Bangued, *Phil.* 55 C4
Bangui, *C.A.R.* 80 D3
Bangui, *Phil.* 55 B4
Banguru, *Zaïre* 82 B2
Bangweulu, L., *Zambia* 83 E3
Bangweulu Swamp, *Zambia* 83 E3
Bani, *Dom. Rep.* 117 C5
Bani →, *Mali* 78 C4
Bani, Djebel, *Morocco* 74 C3
Bani Bangou, *Niger* 79 B5
Banī Sa'd, *Iraq* 67 F11
Banī Walīd, *Libya* 73 B7
Bania, *Ivory C.* 78 D4
Banihal Pass, *India* 63 C6
Banīnah, *Libya* 73 B9
Bāniyās, *Syria* 66 E6
Banja Luka, *Bos.-H.* 21 L7
Banjar, *Indonesia* 57 G13
Banjarmasin, *Indonesia* 56 E4
Banjarnegara, *Indonesia* 57 G13
Banjul, *Gambia* 78 C1
Banka Banka, *Australia* 90 B1
Banket, *Zimbabwe* 83 F3
Bankilaré, *Niger* 79 C5
Bankipore, *India* 63 G11
Banks I., *B.C., Canada* 100 C3
Banks I., *N.W.T., Canada* 96 A7
Banks Pen., *N.Z.* 87 K4
Banks Str., *Australia* 90 G4
Bankura, *India* 63 H12
Bann →, *L'derry., U.K.* 15 A5
Bann →, *Tyrone, U.K.* 15 B5
Banna, *Phil.* 55 C4
Bannalec, *France* 24 E3
Bannang Sata, *Thailand* 59 J3
Banning, *U.S.A.* 113 M10
Banningville = Bandundu, *Zaïre* 80 E3
Bannockburn, *Canada* 106 B7
Bannockburn, *U.K.* 14 E5
Bannockburn, *Zimbabwe* 83 G2
Bannu, *Pakistan* 60 C7
Bañolas, *Spain* 28 C7
Banon, *France* 27 D9
Baños de la Encina, *Spain* 31 G7
Baños de Molgas, *Spain* 30 C3
Banská Bystrica, *Slovak Rep.* 20 G9
Banská Štiavnica, *Slovak Rep.* 21 G8
Banswara, *India* 62 H6
Bantayan, *Phil.* 55 F5
Banten, *Indonesia* 57 G12
Bantry, *Ireland* 15 E2
Bantry B., *Ireland* 15 E2
Bantul, *Indonesia* 57 G14
Bantva, *India* 62 J4
Banu, *Afghan.* 60 B6
Banyak, Kepulauan, *Indonesia* 56 D1
Banyo, *Cameroon* 79 D7
Banyuls-sur-Mer, *France* 26 F7
Banyumas, *Indonesia* 57 G13
Banyuwangi, *Indonesia* 57 H16
Banzare Coast, *Antarctica* 5 C9
Banzyville = Mobayi, *Zaïre* 80 D4
Bao Ha, *Vietnam* 58 A5
Bao Lac, *Vietnam* 58 A5
Bao Loc, *Vietnam* 59 G6
Bao'an = Shenzhen, *China* 53 F10
Baocheng, *China* 50 H4
Baode, *China* 50 E6
Baodi, *China* 51 E9
Baoding, *China* 50 E8
Baoji, *China* 50 G4
Baojing, *China* 52 C7
Baokang, *China* 53 B8
Baoshan, *Shanghai, China* 53 B13
Baoshan, *Yunnan, China* 52 E2
Baotou, *China* 50 D6
Baoying, *China* 51 H10
Bap, *India* 62 F5
Bapatla, *India* 61 M12
Bapaume, *France* 25 B9
Bāqerābād, *Iran* 65 C6
Ba'qūbah, *Iraq* 67 F11
Baquedano, *Chile* 126 A2
Bar, *Montenegro, Yug.* 21 N9
Bar, *Ukraine* 41 H4
Bar Bigha, *India* 63 G11
Bar Harbor, *U.S.A.* 99 D6
Bar-le-Duc, *France* 25 D12
Bar-sur-Aube, *France* 25 D11
Bar-sur-Seine, *France* 25 D11
Barabai, *Indonesia* 56 E5
Barabinsk, *Russia* 44 D8
Baraboo, *U.S.A.* 108 D10
Baracaldo, *Spain* 28 B2
Baracoa, *Cuba* 117 B5
Baradero, *Argentina* 126 C4
Baraga, *U.S.A.* 108 B10
Barahona, *Dom. Rep.* 117 C5
Barahona, *Spain* 28 D2
Barail Range, *India* 61 G18
Baraka →, *Sudan* 76 D4
Barakhola, *India* 61 G18
Barakot, *India* 63 J11
Barakpur, *India* 63 H13
Barakula, *Australia* 91 D5
Baralaba, *Australia* 90 C4
Baralzon L., *Canada* 101 B9
Barameiya, *Sudan* 76 D4
Baramula, *India* 63 B6
Baran, *India* 62 G7
Baranavichy, *Belarus* 41 F4
Baranoa, *Colombia* 120 A3
Baranof I., *U.S.A.* 100 B1
Barão de Cocais, *Brazil* 123 E3
Barão de Grajaú, *Brazil* 122 C3
Barão de Melgaço, *Mato Grosso, Brazil* 125 D6
Barão de Melgaço, *Rondônia, Brazil* 125 C5
Baraolt, *Romania* 38 C8
Barapasi, *Indonesia* 57 E9
Barasat, *India* 63 H13
Barat Daya, Kepulauan, *Indonesia* 57 F7
Barataria B., *U.S.A.* 109 L10
Baraut, *India* 62 E7
Baraya, *Colombia* 120 C2
Barbacena, *Brazil* 123 F3
Barbacoas, *Colombia* 120 C2
Barbacoas, *Venezuela* 120 B4
Barbados ■, *W. Indies* 117 D8
Barbalha, *Brazil* 122 C4
Barban, *Croatia* 33 C11
Barbastro, *Spain* 28 C5
Barbate, *Spain* 31 J5
Barberino di Mugello, *Italy* 33 D8
Barberton, *S. Africa* 85 D5
Barberton, *U.S.A.* 106 E3
Barbezieux, *France* 26 C3
Barbosa, *Colombia* 120 B3
Barbourville, *U.S.A.* 105 G4
Barbuda, *W. Indies* 117 C7
Barcaldine, *Australia* 90 C4
Barcarrota, *Spain* 31 G4
Barcellona Pozzo di Gotto, *Italy* 35 D8
Barcelona, *Spain* 28 D7
Barcelona, *Venezuela* 121 A5
Barcelona □, *Spain* 28 D7
Barcelonette, *France* 27 D10
Barcelos, *Brazil* 121 D5
Barcoo →, *Australia* 90 D3
Barcs, *Hungary* 21 K7
Bärdä, *Azerbaijan* 43 K8
Barda del Medio, *Argentina* 128 A3
Bardai, *Chad* 73 D8
Bardas Blancas, *Argentina* 126 D2
Barddhaman, *India* 63 H12
Bardejov, *Slovak Rep.* 20 F11
Bardera, *Somali Rep.* 68 G3
Bardi, *Italy* 32 D6
Bardīyah, *Libya* 73 B9
Bardolino, *Italy* 32 C7
Bardsey I., *U.K.* 12 E3
Bardstown, *U.S.A.* 104 G3
Bareilly, *India* 63 E8
Barentin, *France* 24 C7
Barenton, *France* 24 D6
Barents Sea, *Arctic* 4 B9
Barentu, *Eritrea* 77 D4
Barfleur, *France* 24 C5
Barfleur, Pte. de, *France* 24 C5
Barga, *China* 54 C3
Barga, *Italy* 32 D7
Bargal, *Somali Rep.* 68 E5
Bargara, *Australia* 90 C5
Barge, *Italy* 32 D4
Bargnop, *Sudan* 77 F2
Bargteheide, *Germany* 18 B6
Barguzin, *Russia* 45 D11
Barh, *India* 63 G11
Barhaj, *India* 63 F10
Barhi, *India* 63 G11
Bari, *India* 62 F7
Bari, *Italy* 35 A9
Bari Doab, *Pakistan* 62 D5
Bariadi □, *Tanzania* 82 C3
Barīm, *Yemen* 68 E3
Barima →, *Guyana* 121 B5
Barinas, *Venezuela* 120 B3
Barinas □, *Venezuela* 120 B4
Baring, C., *Canada* 96 B8
Baringo, *Kenya* 82 B4
Baringo □, *Kenya* 82 B4
Baringo, L., *Kenya* 82 B4
Barinitas, *Venezuela* 120 B3
Bariri, *Brazil* 123 F2
Bârîs, *Egypt* 76 C3
Barisal, *Bangla.* 61 H17
Barisan, Bukit, *Indonesia* 56 E2
Barito →, *Indonesia* 56 E4
Barjac, *France* 27 D8
Barjols, *France* 27 E10
Barjūj, Wadi →, *Libya* 75 C7
Bark L., *Canada* 106 A7
Barka = Baraka →, *Sudan* 76 D4
Barkam, *China* 52 B4
Barker, *U.S.A.* 106 C6
Barkley Sound, *Canada* 100 D3
Barkly Downs, *Australia* 90 C2
Barkly East, *S. Africa* 84 E4
Barkly Tableland, *Australia* 90 B2
Barkly West, *S. Africa* 84 D3
Barkol, Wadi →, *Sudan* 76 D3
Barksdale, *U.S.A.* 109 L4
Barlee, L., *Australia* 89 E2
Barlee, Mt., *Australia* 89 D4
Barletta, *Italy* 35 A9
Barlinek, *Poland* 20 C5
Barlovento, *Canary Is.* 36 F2
Barlow L., *Canada* 101 A8
Barmedman, *Australia* 91 E4
Barmer, *India* 62 G4
Barmera, *Australia* 91 E3
Barmouth, *U.K.* 12 E3
Barmstedt, *Germany* 18 B5
Barnagar, *India* 62 H6
Barnard Castle, *U.K.* 12 C6
Barnato, *Australia* 91 E3
Barnaul, *Russia* 44 D9
Barnesville, *U.S.A.* 105 J3
Barnet, *U.K.* 13 F7
Barneveld, *Neths.* 16 D7
Barneveld, *U.S.A.* 107 C9
Barneville-Cartevert, *France* 24 C5
Barngo, *Australia* 90 D4
Barnhart, *U.S.A.* 109 K4
Barnsley, *U.K.* 12 D6
Barnstaple, *U.K.* 13 F3
Barnsville, *U.S.A.* 108 B6
Baro, *Nigeria* 79 D6
Baro →, *Ethiopia* 77 F3
Baroda = Vadodara, *India* 62 H5
Baroda, *India* 62 G7
Baroe, *S. Africa* 84 E3
Baron Ra., *Australia* 88 D4
Barpeta, *India* 61 F17
Barques, Pt. Aux, *U.S.A.* 104 C4
Barquinha, *Portugal* 31 F2
Barquísimeto, *Venezuela* 120 A4
Barr, *France* 25 D14
Barra, *Brazil* 122 D3
Barra, *U.K.* 14 E1
Barra, Sd. of, *U.K.* 14 D1
Barra da Estiva, *Brazil* 123 D3
Barra de Navidad, *Mexico* 114 D4
Barra do Corda, *Brazil* 122 C2
Barra do Mendes, *Brazil* 123 D3
Barra do Piraí, *Brazil* 123 F3
Barra Falsa, Pta. da, *Mozam.* 85 C6
Barra Hd., *U.K.* 14 E1
Barra Mansa, *Brazil* 123 F3
Barraba, *Australia* 91 E5
Barracão do Barreto, *Brazil* 125 B6
Barrackpur = Barakpur, *India* 63 H13
Barrafranca, *Italy* 35 E7
Barraigh = Barra, *U.K.* 14 E1
Barranca, *Lima, Peru* 124 C2
Barranca, *Loreto, Peru* 120 D2
Barrancabermeja, *Colombia* 120 B3
Barrancas, *Colombia* 120 A3
Barrancas, *Venezuela* 121 B5
Barrancos, *Portugal* 31 G4
Barranqueras, *Argentina* 126 B4
Barranquilla, *Colombia* 120 A3
Barras, *Brazil* 122 B3
Barras, *Colombia* 120 D3
Barraute, *Canada* 98 C4
Barre, *Mass., U.S.A.* 107 D12
Barre, *Vt., U.S.A.* 107 B12
Barre do Bugres, *Brazil* 125 C6
Barreal, *Argentina* 126 C2
Barreiras, *Brazil* 123 D3
Barreirinha, *Brazil* 121 D6
Barreirinhas, *Brazil* 122 B3
Barreiro, *Portugal* 31 G1
Barreiros, *Brazil* 122 C4
Barrême, *France* 27 E10
Barren, Nosy, *Madag.* 85 B7
Barretos, *Brazil* 123 F2
Barrhead, *Canada* 100 C6
Barrie, *Canada* 98 D4
Barrier Ra., *Australia* 91 E3
Barrière, *Canada* 100 C4
Barrington, *U.S.A.* 107 E13
Barrington L., *Canada* 101 B8
Barrington Tops, *Australia* 91 E5
Barringun, *Australia* 91 D4
Barro do Garças, *Brazil* 125 D7
Barrow, *U.S.A.* 96 A4
Barrow →, *Ireland* 15 D4
Barrow Creek, *Australia* 90 C1
Barrow I., *Australia* 88 D2
Barrow-in-Furness, *U.K.* 12 C4
Barrow Pt., *Australia* 90 A3
Barrow Ra., *Australia* 89 E4
Barrow Str., *Canada* 4 B3
Barruecopardo, *Spain* 30 D4
Barruelo, *Spain* 30 C6
Barry, *U.K.* 13 F4
Barry's Bay, *Canada* 98 C4
Barsalogho, *Burkina Faso* 79 C4
Barsat, *Pakistan* 63 A5
Barsham, *Syria* 67 E9
Barsi, *India* 60 K9
Barsø, *Denmark* 11 J3
Barsoi, *India* 61 G15
Barstow, *Calif., U.S.A.* 113 L9
Barstow, *Tex., U.S.A.* 109 K3
Barth, *Germany* 18 A8
Barthélemy, Col, *Vietnam* 58 C5
Bartica, *Guyana* 121 B6
Bartin, *Turkey* 66 B5
Bartlesville, *U.S.A.* 109 G7
Bartlett, *Calif., U.S.A.* 112 J8
Bartlett, *Tex., U.S.A.* 109 K6
Bartlett, L., *Canada* 100 A5
Bartolomeu Dias, *Mozam.* 83 G4
Barton, *Australia* 89 F5
Barton upon Humber, *U.K.* 12 D7
Bartoszyce, *Poland* 20 A10
Bartow, *U.S.A.* 105 M5
Barú, I. de, *Colombia* 120 A2
Barú, Volcan, *Panama* 116 E3
Barumba, *Zaïre* 82 B1
Baruth, *Germany* 18 C9
Barvaux, *Belgium* 17 H6
Barvinkove, *Ukraine* 41 H9
Barwani, *India* 62 H6
Barysaw, *Belarus* 40 E5
Barysh, *Russia* 42 D8
Barzān, *Iraq* 64 B5
Bas-Rhin □, *France* 25 D14
Bašaid, *Serbia, Yug.* 21 K10
Bāsa'idū, *Iran* 65 E7
Basal, *Pakistan* 62 C5
Basankusa, *Zaïre* 80 D3
Basarabeasca, *Moldova* 41 J5
Basawa, *Afghan.* 62 B4
Bascharage, *Lux.* 17 J7
Bascuñán, C., *Chile* 126 B1
Basècles, *Belgium* 17 G3
Basel, *Switz.* 22 A5
Basel-Stadt □, *Switz.* 22 A5
Baselland □, *Switz.* 22 B5
Basento →, *Italy* 35 B9
Bāshī, *Iran* 65 D6
Bashi Channel, *Phil.* 54 D7
Bashkir Republic = Bashkortostan □, *Russia* 44 D6
Bashkortostan □, *Russia* 44 D6
Basilan, *Phil.* 55 H5
Basilan Str., *Phil.* 55 H5
Basildon, *U.K.* 13 F8
Basilicata □, *Italy* 35 B9
Basim = Washim, *India* 60 J10
Basin, *U.S.A.* 110 D9
Basingstoke, *U.K.* 13 F6
Baška, *Croatia* 33 D11
Başkale, *Turkey* 67 C10
Baskatong, Rés., *Canada* 98 C4
Basle = Basel, *Switz.* 22 A5
Basoda, *India* 62 H7
Basodino, *Switz.* 23 D6
Basoka, *Zaïre* 82 B1
Basongo, *Zaïre* 80 E4
Basque, Pays, *France* 26 E2
Basque Provinces = País Vasco □, *Spain* 28 C2
Basra = Al Başrah, *Iraq* 64 D5
Bass Rock, *U.K.* 14 E6
Bass Str., *Australia* 90 F4
Bassano, *Canada* 100 C6
Bassano del Grappa, *Italy* 33 C8
Bassar, *Togo* 79 D5
Bassas da India, *Ind. Oc.* 81 J7
Basse Santa-Su, *Gambia* 78 C2
Basse-Terre, *Guadeloupe* 117 C7
Bassecourt, *Switz.* 22 B4
Bassein, *Burma* 61 L19
Basseterre, *St. Christopher-Nevis* 117 C7
Bassett, *Nebr., U.S.A.* 108 D5
Bassett, *Va., U.S.A.* 105 G6
Bassevelde, *Belgium* 17 F3
Bassi, *India* 62 D7
Bassigny, *France* 25 E12
Bassikounou, *Mauritania* 78 B3
Bassilly, *Belgium* 17 G3
Bassum, *Germany* 18 C4
Båstad, *Sweden* 11 H6

Bastak

Bastak, Iran 65 E7
Baştām, Iran 65 B7
Bastar, India 61 K12
Bastelica, France 27 F13
Basti, India 63 F10
Bastia, France 27 F13
Bastia Umbra, Italy 33 E9
Bastogne, Belgium 17 H7
Bastrop, U.S.A. 109 K6
Bat Yam, Israel 69 C3
Bata, Eq. Guin. 80 D1
Bata, Romania 38 C5
Bataan, Phil. 55 D4
Batabanó, Cuba 116 B3
Batabanó, G. de, Cuba 116 B3
Batac, Phil. 55 B4
Batagoy, Russia 45 C14
Batak, Bulgaria 39 H7
Batalha, Portugal 31 F2
Batama, Zaïre 82 B2
Batamay, Russia 45 C13
Batan I., Phil. 55 A4
Batanes Is., Phil. 55 A4
Batang, China 52 B2
Batang, Indonesia 57 G13
Batangafo, C.A.R. 73 G8
Batangas, Phil. 55 E4
Batanta, Indonesia 57 E8
Batatais, Brazil 127 A6
Batavia, U.S.A. 106 D6
Bataysk, Russia 43 G4
Batchelor, Australia 88 B5
Bateman's B., Australia 91 F5
Batemans Bay, Australia 91 F5
Bates Ra., Australia 89 E3
Batesburg, U.S.A. 105 J5
Batesville, Ark., U.S.A. 109 H9
Batesville, Miss., U.S.A. 109 H10
Batesville, Tex., U.S.A. 109 L5
Bath, U.K. 13 F5
Bath, Maine, U.S.A. 99 D6
Bath, N.Y., U.S.A. 106 D7
Batheay, Cambodia 59 G5
Bathgate, U.K. 14 F5
Bathmen, Neths. 16 D8
Bathurst = Banjul, Gambia 78 C1
Bathurst, Australia 91 E4
Bathurst, Canada 99 C6
Bathurst, S. Africa 84 E4
Bathurst, C., Canada 96 A7
Bathurst B., Australia 90 A3
Bathurst Harb., Australia 90 G4
Bathurst I., Australia 88 B5
Bathurst I., Canada 4 B2
Bathurst Inlet, Canada 96 B9
Batie, Burkina Faso 78 D4
Batlow, Australia 91 F4
Batman, Turkey 67 D9
Batna, Algeria 75 A6
Batobato, Phil. 55 H7
Batoka, Zambia 83 F2
Baton Rouge, U.S.A. 109 K9
Batong, Ko, Thailand 59 J2
Batopilas, Mexico 114 B3
Batouri, Cameroon 80 D2
Båtsfjord, Norway 8 A23
Battambang, Cambodia 58 F4
Batticaloa, Sri Lanka 60 R12
Battice, Belgium 17 G7
Battipáglia, Italy 35 B7
Battle, U.K. 13 G8
Battle →, Canada 101 C7
Battle Camp, Australia 90 B3
Battle Creek, U.S.A. 104 D3
Battle Ground, U.S.A. 112 E4
Battle Harbour, Canada 99 B8
Battle Lake, U.S.A. 108 B7
Battle Mountain, U.S.A. 110 F5
Battlefields, Zimbabwe 83 F2
Battleford, Canada 101 C7
Battonya, Hungary 21 J11
Batu, Ethiopia 68 F2
Batu, Kepulauan, Indonesia 56 E1
Batu Caves, Malaysia 59 L3
Batu Gajah, Malaysia 59 K3
Batu Is. = Batu, Kepulauan, Indonesia 56 E1
Batu Pahat, Malaysia 59 M4
Batuata, Indonesia 57 F6
Batumi, Georgia 43 K5
Baturaja, Indonesia 56 E2
Baturité, Brazil 122 B4
Bau, Malaysia 56 D4
Baubau, Indonesia 57 F6
Bauchi, Nigeria 79 C6
Bauchi □, Nigeria 79 C6
Baud, France 24 E3
Baudette, U.S.A. 108 A7
Baudour, Belgium 17 H3
Bauer, C., Australia 91 E1
Baugé, France 24 E6
Bauhinia Downs, Australia 90 C4
Baukau, Indonesia 57 F7
Bauma, Switz. 23 B7
Baume-les-Dames, France 25 E13
Baunatal, Germany 18 D5
Baunei, Italy 34 B2
Baures, Bolivia 125 C5
Bauru, Brazil 127 A6
Baús, Brazil 125 D7
Bauska, Latvia 9 H21
Bautino, Kazakhstan 43 H10
Bautzen, Germany 18 D10
Bavānāt, Iran 65 D7
Bavaria = Bayern □, Germany 19 F7
Båven, Sweden 10 F10
Bavi Sadri, India 62 G6
Bavispe →, Mexico 114 B3
Bawdwin, Burma 61 H20
Bawean, Indonesia 56 F4
Bawku, Ghana 79 C4
Bawlake, Burma 61 K20
Bawolung, China 52 C3
Baxley, U.S.A. 105 K4
Baxoi, China 52 B1
Baxter Springs, U.S.A. 109 G7
Bay, L. de, Phil. 57 B6
Bay Bulls, Canada 99 C9
Bay City, Mich., U.S.A. 104 D4
Bay City, Oreg., U.S.A. 110 D2
Bay City, Tex., U.S.A. 109 L7
Bay de Verde, Canada 99 C9
Bay Minette, U.S.A. 105 K2
Bay St. Louis, U.S.A. 109 K10
Bay Springs, U.S.A. 109 K10
Bay View, N.Z. 87 H6
Baya, Zaïre 83 E2
Bayamo, Cuba 116 B4
Bayamón, Puerto Rico 117 C6
Bayan Har Shan, China 54 C4
Bayan Hot = Alxa Zuoqi, China 50 E3
Bayan Obo, China 50 D5
Bayan-Ovoo, Mongolia 50 C4
Bayana, India 62 F7
Bayanaūyl, Kazakhstan 44 D8
Bayandalay, Mongolia 50 C2
Bayanhongor, Mongolia 54 B5
Bayard, U.S.A. 108 E3
Bayawan, Phil. 55 G5
Baybay, Phil. 55 F6
Bayburt, Turkey 67 B9
Bayerischer Wald, Germany 19 F8
Bayern □, Germany 19 F7
Bayeux, France 24 C6
Bayfield, Canada 106 C3
Bayfield, U.S.A. 108 B9
Bayındır, Turkey 66 C2
Baykal, Oz., Russia 45 D11
Baykit, Russia 45 C10
Baykonur = Bayqongyr, Kazakhstan 44 E7
Baynes Mts., Namibia 84 B1
Bayombong, Phil. 55 C4
Bayon, France 25 D13
Bayona, Spain 30 C2
Bayonne, France 26 E2
Bayonne, U.S.A. 107 F10
Bayovar, Peru 124 B1
Bayqongyr, Kazakhstan 44 E7
Bayram-Ali = Bayramaly, Turkmenistan 44 F7
Bayramaly, Turkmenistan 44 F7
Bayramiç, Turkey 66 C2
Bayreuth, Germany 19 F7
Bayrischzell, Germany 19 H8
Bayrūt, Lebanon 69 B4
Bayt Lahm, West Bank 69 D4
Baytown, U.S.A. 109 L7
Bayzo, Niger 79 C5
Baza, Spain 29 H2
Bazar Dyuzi, Russia 43 K8
Bazardüzü = Bazar Dyuzi, Russia 43 K8
Bazarny Karabulak, Russia 42 D8
Bazarnyy Syzgan, Russia 42 D8
Bazaruto, I. do, Mozam. 85 C6
Bazas, France 26 D3
Bazhong, China 52 B6
Bazmān, Kūh-e, Iran 65 D9
Beach, U.S.A. 108 B3
Beach City, U.S.A. 106 F3
Beachport, Australia 91 F2
Beachy Hd., U.K. 13 G8
Beacon, Australia 89 F2
Beacon, U.S.A. 107 E11
Beaconia, Canada 101 C9
Beagle, Canal, S. Amer. 128 E3
Beagle Bay, Australia 88 C3
Bealanana, Madag. 85 A8
Beamsville, Canada 106 C5
Bear →, U.S.A. 112 G5
Béar, C., France 26 F7
Bear I., Ireland 15 E2
Bear L., B.C., Canada 100 B3
Bear L., Man., Canada 101 B9
Bear L., U.S.A. 110 E8
Bearcreek, U.S.A. 110 D9
Beardmore, Canada 98 C2
Beardmore Glacier, Antarctica 5 E11
Beardstown, U.S.A. 108 F9
Béarn, France 26 E3
Bearpaw Mts., U.S.A. 110 B9
Bearskin Lake, Canada 98 B1
Beas de Segura, Spain 29 G2
Beasain, Spain 28 B2
Beata, C., Dom. Rep. 117 C5
Beata, I., Dom. Rep. 117 C5
Beatrice, U.S.A. 108 E6
Beatrice, Zimbabwe 83 F3
Beatrice, C., Australia 90 A2
Beatton →, Canada 100 B4
Beatton River, Canada 100 B4
Beatty, U.S.A. 111 H5
Beaucaire, France 27 E8
Beauce, Plaine de la, France 25 D8
Beauceville, Canada 99 C5
Beauchêne, I., Falk. Is. 128 D5
Beaudesert, Australia 91 D5
Beaufort, Malaysia 56 C5
Beaufort, N.C., U.S.A. 105 H7
Beaufort, S.C., U.S.A. 105 J5
Beaufort Sea, Arctic 4 B1
Beaufort West, S. Africa 84 E3
Beaugency, France 25 E8
Beauharnois, Canada 98 C5
Beaujeu, France 27 B8
Beaulieu →, Canada 100 A6
Beaulieu-sur-Dordogne, France 26 D5
Beaulieu-sur-Mer, France 27 E11
Beauly, U.K. 14 D4
Beauly →, U.K. 14 D4
Beaumaris, U.K. 12 D3
Beaumetz-lès-Loges, France 25 B9
Beaumont, Belgium 17 H4
Beaumont, France 26 D4
Beaumont, Calif., U.S.A. 113 M10
Beaumont, Tex., U.S.A. 109 K7
Beaumont-de-Lomagne, France 26 E4
Beaumont-le-Roger, France 24 C7
Beaumont-sur-Oise, France 25 C9
Beaumont-sur-Sarthe, France 24 D7
Beaune, France 25 E11
Beaune-la-Rolande, France 25 D9
Beaupréau, France 24 E6
Beauraing, Belgium 17 H5
Beauséjour, Canada 101 C9
Beauvais, France 25 C9
Beauval, Canada 101 B7
Beauvoir-sur-Mer, France 24 F4
Beauvoir-sur-Niort, France 26 B3
Beaver, Alaska, U.S.A. 96 B5
Beaver, Okla., U.S.A. 109 G4
Beaver, Pa., U.S.A. 106 F4
Beaver, Utah, U.S.A. 111 G7
Beaver →, B.C., Canada 100 B4
Beaver →, Ont., Canada 98 A2
Beaver →, Sask., Canada 101 B7
Beaver City, U.S.A. 108 E5
Beaver Dam, U.S.A. 108 D10
Beaver Falls, U.S.A. 106 F4
Beaver Hill L., Canada 101 C10
Beaver I., U.S.A. 104 C3
Beaverhill L., Alta., Canada 100 C6
Beaverhill L., N.W.T., Canada 101 A8
Beaverlodge, Canada 100 B5
Beavermouth, Canada 100 C5
Beaverstone →, Canada 98 B2
Beaverton, Canada 106 B5
Beaverton, U.S.A. 112 E4
Beawar, India 62 F6
Bebedouro, Brazil 127 A6
Beboa, Madag. 85 B7
Bebra, Germany 18 E5
Beccles, U.K. 13 E9
Bečej, Serbia, Yug. 21 K10
Becerreá, Spain 30 C3
Béchar, Algeria 75 B4
Beckley, U.S.A. 104 G5
Beckum, Germany 18 D4
Bečva →, Czech. 20 F7
Bédar, Spain 29 H3
Bédarieux, France 26 E7
Bédarrides, France 27 D8
Beddouza, Ras, Morocco 74 B3
Bedele, Ethiopia 77 F4
Bederkesa, Germany 18 B4
Bedeso, Ethiopia 77 F5
Bedford, Canada 98 C5
Bedford, S. Africa 84 E4
Bedford, U.K. 13 E7
Bedford, Ind., U.S.A. 104 F2
Bedford, Iowa, U.S.A. 108 E7
Bedford, Ohio, U.S.A. 106 E3
Bedford, Pa., U.S.A. 106 F6
Bedford, Va., U.S.A. 104 G6
Bedford, C., Australia 90 B4
Bedford Downs, Australia 88 C4
Bedfordshire □, U.K. 13 E7
Będków, Poland 20 D9
Bednja →, Croatia 33 B13
Bednodemyanovsk, Russia 42 D6
Bedónia, Italy 32 D6
Bedourie, Australia 90 C2
Bedretto, Switz. 23 C7
Bedum, Neths. 16 B9
Będzin, Poland 20 E9
Beech Grove, U.S.A. 104 F2
Beechy, Canada 101 C7
Beek, Gelderland, Neths. 16 E8
Beek, Limburg, Neths. 17 G7
Beek, Noord-Brabant, Neths. 17 E7
Beekbergen, Neths. 16 D7
Beelitz, Germany 18 C8
Beenleigh, Australia 91 D5
Be'er Menuha, Israel 64 D2
Be'er Sheva, Israel 69 D3
Beersheba = Be'er Sheva, Israel 69 D3
Beerta, Neths. 16 B10
Beerze →, Neths. 16 E6
Beesd, Neths. 16 E6
Beeskow, Germany 18 C10
Beeston, U.K. 12 E6
Beetaloo, Australia 90 B1
Beetsterzwaag, Neths. 16 B8
Beetzendorf, Germany 18 C7
Beeville, U.S.A. 109 L6
Befale, Zaïre 80 D4
Befandriana, Madag. 85 C7
Befotaka, Madag. 85 C8
Bega, Australia 91 F4
Bega, Canalul, Romania 38 D3
Bégard, France 24 D3
Bègles, France 26 D3
Begna →, Norway 10 D4
Begonte, Spain 30 B3
Begusarai, India 63 G12
Behābād, Iran 65 C8
Behara, Madag. 85 C8
Behbehān, Iran 65 D6
Behshahr, Iran 65 B7
Bei Jiang →, China 53 F9
Bei'an, China 54 B7
Beibei, China 54 D5
Beigang, Taiwan 53 F13
Beihai, China 52 G7
Beijing, China 50 E9
Beijing □, China 50 E9
Beilen, Neths. 16 C8
Beiliu, China 53 F8
Beilngries, Germany 19 F7
Beilpajah, Australia 91 E3
Beilul, Eritrea 77 E5
Beinn na Faoghla = Benbecula, U.K. 14 D1
Beipiao, China 51 D11
Beira, Mozam. 83 F3
Beirut = Bayrūt, Lebanon 69 B4
Beitaolaizhao, China 51 B13
Beitbridge, Zimbabwe 83 G3
Beiuş, Romania 38 C5
Beizhen, Liaoning, China 51 D11
Beizhen, Shandong, China 51 F10
Beizhengzhen, China 51 B12
Beja, Portugal 31 G3
Béja, Tunisia 75 A6
Beja □, Portugal 31 H3
Bejaia, Algeria 75 A6
Béjar, Spain 30 E5
Bejestān, Iran 65 C8
Bekaa Valley = Al Biqā □, Lebanon 69 A5
Bekasi, Indonesia 57 G12
Békés, Hungary 21 J11
Békéscsaba, Hungary 21 J11
Bekily, Madag. 85 C8
Bekkevoort, Belgium 17 G5
Bekoji, Ethiopia 77 F4
Bekok, Malaysia 59 L4
Bekwai, Ghana 79 D4
Bela, India 63 G9
Bela, Pakistan 62 F2
Bela Crkva, Serbia, Yug. 21 L11
Bela Palanka, Serbia, Yug. 21 M12
Bela Vista, Brazil 126 A4
Bela Vista, Mozam. 85 D5
Bélâbre, France 26 B5
Belalcázar, Spain 31 G5
Belarus ■, Europe 40 F4
Belau ■, Pac. Oc. 92 G5
Belavenona, Madag. 85 C8
Belawan, Indonesia 56 D1
Belaya, Ethiopia 77 E4
Belaya Glina, Russia 43 G5
Belaya Kalitva, Russia 43 F5
Belaya Tserkov = Bila Tserkva, Ukraine 41 H6
Belcher Is., Canada 97 C12
Belchite, Spain 28 D4
Belden, U.S.A. 112 E5
Belém, Brazil 122 B2
Belém de São Francisco, Brazil 122 C4
Belén, Argentina 126 B2
Belén, Colombia 120 C2
Belén, Paraguay 126 A4
Belen, U.S.A. 111 J10
Beleni, Turkey 66 D7
Bélesta, France 26 F5
Belet Uen, Somali Rep. 68 G4
Belev, Russia 42 D3
Belfair, U.S.A. 112 C4
Belfast, S. Africa 85 D5
Belfast, U.K. 15 B6
Belfast, Maine, U.S.A. 99 D6
Belfast, N.Y., U.S.A. 106 D6
Belfast □, U.K. 15 B6
Belfast L., U.K. 15 B6
Belfeld, Neths. 17 F8
Belfield, U.S.A. 108 B3
Belfort, France 25 E13
Belfort, Territoire de □, France 25 E13
Belfry, U.S.A. 110 D9
Belgaum, India 60 M9
Belgioioso, Italy 32 C6
Belgium ■, Europe 17 G5
Belgorod, Russia 42 E3
Belgorod-Dnestrovskiy = Bilhorod-Dnivstrovskyy, Ukraine 41 J6
Belgrade = Beograd, Serbia, Yug. 21 L10
Belgrade, U.S.A. 110 D8
Belhaven, U.S.A. 105 H7
Beli Drim →, Europe 21 N10
Beli Manastir, Croatia 21 K8
Belice →, Italy 34 E5
Belin-Béliet, France 26 D3
Belinga, Gabon 80 D2
Belinskiy, Russia 42 D6
Belinyu, Indonesia 56 E3
Beliton Is. = Belitung, Indonesia 56 E3
Belitung, Indonesia 56 E3
Beliu, Romania 38 C5
Belize ■, Cent. Amer. 115 D7
Belize City, Belize 115 D7
Beljanica, Serbia, Yug. 21 L11
Belkovskiy, Ostrov, Russia 45 B14
Bell →, Canada 98 C4
Bell Bay, Australia 90 G4
Bell I., Canada 99 B8
Bell-Irving →, Canada 100 B3
Bell Peninsula, Canada 97 B11
Bell Ville, Argentina 126 C3
Bella Bella, Canada 100 C3
Bella Coola, Canada 100 C3
Bella Flor, Bolivia 124 C4
Bella Unión, Uruguay 126 C4
Bella Vista, Corrientes, Argentina 126 B4
Bella Vista, Tucuman, Argentina 126 B2
Bellac, France 26 B5
Bellágio, Italy 32 C6
Bellaire, U.S.A. 106 F4
Bellary, India 60 M10
Bellata, Australia 91 D4
Belle Fourche, U.S.A. 108 C3
Belle Fourche →, U.S.A. 108 C3
Belle Glade, U.S.A. 105 M5
Belle-Ile, France 24 E3
Belle Isle, Canada 99 B8
Belle Isle, Str. of, Canada 99 B8
Belle-Isle-en-Terre, France 24 D3
Belle Plaine, Iowa, U.S.A. 108 E8
Belle Plaine, Minn., U.S.A. 108 C8
Belle Yella, Liberia 78 D3
Belledonne, Chaîne de, France 27 C10
Belledune, Canada 99 C6
Bellefontaine, U.S.A. 104 E4
Bellefonte, U.S.A. 106 F7
Bellegarde, France 25 E9
Bellegarde-en-Marche, France 26 C6
Bellegarde-sur-Valserine, France 27 B9
Bellême, France 24 D7
Belleoram, Canada 99 C8
Belleville, Canada 98 D4
Belleville, France 27 B8
Belleville, Ill., U.S.A. 108 F10
Belleville, Kans., U.S.A. 108 F6
Belleville, N.Y., U.S.A. 107 C8
Belleville-sur-Vie, France 24 F5
Bellevue, Canada 100 D6
Bellevue, Idaho, U.S.A. 110 E6
Bellevue, Ohio, U.S.A. 106 E2
Bellevue, Wash., U.S.A. 112 C4
Belley, France 27 C9
Bellin = Kangirsuk, Canada 97 B13
Bellingen, Australia 91 E5
Bellingham, U.S.A. 112 B4
Bellingshausen Sea, Antarctica 5 C17
Bellinzona, Switz. 23 D8
Bello, Colombia 120 B2
Bellows Falls, U.S.A. 107 C12
Bellpat, Pakistan 62 E3
Bellpuig, Spain 28 D6
Belluno, Italy 33 B9
Bellville, U.S.A. 109 L6
Bellwood, U.S.A. 106 F6
Bélmez, Spain 31 G5
Belmont, Australia 91 E5
Belmont, Canada 106 D3
Belmont, S. Africa 84 D3
Belmont, U.S.A. 106 D6
Belmonte, Brazil 123 E4
Belmonte, Portugal 30 E3
Belmonte, Spain 28 F2
Belmopan, Belize 115 D7
Belmullet, Ireland 15 B2
Belo Horizonte, Brazil 123 E3
Belo Jardim, Brazil 122 C4
Belo-sur-Mer, Madag. 85 C7
Belo-Tsiribihina, Madag. 85 B7
Belogorsk = Bilohirsk, Ukraine 41 K8
Belogorsk, Russia 45 D13
Belogradchik, Bulgaria 38 F5
Beloha, Madag. 85 D8
Beloit, Kans., U.S.A. 108 F5
Beloit, Wis., U.S.A. 108 D10
Belokorovichi, Ukraine 41 G5
Belomorsk, Russia 44 C4
Belonia, India 61 H17
Belopolye = Bilopillya, Ukraine 41 G8
Belorechensk, Russia 43 H4
Belorussia = Belarus ■, Europe 40 F4
Belovo, Russia 44 D9
Belovodsk, Ukraine 41 H10
Beloye, Ozero, Russia 40 B9
Beloye More, Russia 44 C4
Belozersk, Russia 40 B9
Belpasso, Italy 35 E7
Belsele, Belgium 17 F4
Belsito, Italy 34 E6
Beltana, Australia 91 E2
Belterra, Brazil 121 D7
Beltinci, Slovenia 33 B13
Belton, S.C., U.S.A. 105 H4
Belton, Tex., U.S.A. 109 K6
Belton Res., U.S.A. 109 K6
Beltsy = Bălţi, Moldova 41 J4
Belturbet, Ireland 15 B4
Belukha, Russia 44 E9
Beluran, Malaysia 56 C5
Belvedere Marittimo, Italy 35 C8

Bilaspur

Belvès, France 26 D5
Belvidere, Ill., U.S.A. 108 D10
Belvidere, N.J., U.S.A. 107 F9
Belvis de la Jara, Spain 31 F6
Belyando →, Australia 90 C4
Belyy, Russia 40 E7
Belyy, Ostrov, Russia 44 B8
Belyy Yar, Russia 44 D9
Belzig, Germany 18 C8
Belzoni, U.S.A. 109 J9
Bemaraha, Lembalemban' i, Madag. 85 B7
Bemarivo, Madag. 85 C7
Bemarivo →, Madag. 85 B8
Bemavo, Madag. 85 C8
Bembéréke, Benin 79 C5
Bembesi, Zimbabwe 83 F2
Bembesi →, Zimbabwe 83 F2
Bembézar →, Spain 31 H5
Bemidji, U.S.A. 108 B7
Bemmel, Neths. 16 E7
Ben, Iran 65 C6
Ben Cruachan, U.K. 14 E3
Ben Dearg, U.K. 14 D4
Ben Gardane, Tunisia 75 B7
Ben Hope, U.K. 14 C4
Ben Lawers, U.K. 14 E4
Ben Lomond, N.S.W., Australia 91 E5
Ben Lomond, Tas., Australia 90 G4
Ben Lomond, U.K. 14 E4
Ben Luc, Vietnam 59 G6
Ben Macdhui, U.K. 14 D5
Ben Mhor, U.K. 14 D1
Ben More, Central, U.K. 14 E4
Ben More, Strath., U.K. 14 E2
Ben More Assynt, U.K. 14 C4
Ben Nevis, U.K. 14 E4
Ben Quang, Vietnam 58 D6
Ben Slimane, Morocco 74 B3
Ben Tre, Vietnam 59 G6
Ben Vorlich, U.K. 14 E4
Ben Wyvis, U.K. 14 D4
Bena, Nigeria 79 C6
Bena Dibele, Zaïre 80 E4
Benāb, Iran 67 D12
Benagalbón, Spain 31 J6
Benagerie, Australia 91 E3
Benahmed, Morocco 74 B3
Benalla, Australia 91 F4
Benambra, Mt., Australia 91 F4
Benamejí, Spain 31 H6
Benares = Varanasi, India 63 G10
Bénat, C., France 27 E10
Benavente, Portugal 31 G2
Benavente, Spain 30 C5
Benavides, Spain 30 C5
Benavides, U.S.A. 109 M5
Benbecula, U.K. 14 D1
Benbonyathe, Australia 91 E2
Bencubbin, Australia 89 F2
Bend, U.S.A. 110 D3
Bender Beila, Somali Rep. 68 F5
Bendering, Australia 89 F2
Bendery = Tighina, Moldova 41 J5
Bendigo, Australia 91 F3
Bendorf, Germany 18 E3
Benē Beraq, Israel 69 C3
Beneden Knijpe, Neths. 16 C7
Beneditinos, Brazil 122 C3
Benedito Leite, Brazil 122 C3
Bénéna, Mali 78 C4
Benenitra, Madag. 85 C8
Benešov, Czech. 20 F4
Bénestroff, France 25 D13
Benet, France 26 B3
Benevento, Italy 35 A7
Benfeld, France 25 D14
Benga, Mozam. 83 F3
Bengal, Bay of, Ind. Oc. 61 K16
Bengbu, China 51 H9
Benghazi = Banghāzī, Libya 73 B9
Bengkalis, Indonesia 56 D2
Bengkulu, Indonesia 56 E2
Bengkulu □, Indonesia 56 E2
Bengough, Canada 101 D7
Benguela, Angola 81 G2
Benguerir, Morocco 74 B3
Benguérua, I., Mozam. 85 C6
Benha, Egypt 76 H7
Beni, Zaïre 82 B2
Beni □, Bolivia 125 C4
Beni →, Bolivia 125 C4
Beni Abbès, Algeria 75 B4
Beni-Haoua, Algeria 75 A5
Beni Mazâr, Egypt 76 J7
Beni Mellal, Morocco 74 B3
Beni Ounif, Algeria 75 B4
Beni Saf, Algeria 75 A4
Beni Suef, Egypt 76 J7
Beniah L., Canada 100 A6
Benicarló, Spain 28 E5
Benicia, U.S.A. 112 G4
Benidorm, Spain 29 G4
Benidorm, Islote de, Spain 29 G4
Benin ■, Africa 79 D5
Benin, Bight of, W. Afr. 79 D5
Benin City, Nigeria 79 D6
Benisa, Spain 29 G5
Benitses, Greece 37 A3
Benjamin Aceval, Paraguay 126 A4
Benjamin Constant, Brazil 120 D3
Benjamin Hill, Mexico 114 A2
Benkelman, U.S.A. 108 E4
Benkovac, Croatia 33 D12
Benlidi, Australia 90 C3
Bennebroek, Neths. 16 D5
Bennekom, Neths. 16 D7
Bennett, Canada 100 B2
Bennett, L., Australia 88 D5
Bennett, Ostrov, Russia 45 B15
Bennettsville, U.S.A. 105 H6
Bennington, U.S.A. 107 D11
Bénodet, France 24 E2
Benoni, S. Africa 85 D4
Benoud, Algeria 75 B5
Benque Viejo, Belize 115 D7
Bensheim, Germany 19 F4
Benson, U.S.A. 111 L8
Bent, Iran 65 E8
Benteng, Indonesia 57 F6
Bentinck I., Australia 90 B2
Bentiu, Sudan 77 F2
Bento Gonçalves, Brazil 127 B5
Benton, Ark., U.S.A. 109 H8
Benton, Calif., U.S.A. 112 H8
Benton, Ill., U.S.A. 108 F10
Benton Harbor, U.S.A. 104 D2
Bentu Liben, Ethiopia 77 F4
Bentung, Malaysia 59 L3
Benue □, Nigeria 79 D6
Benue →, Nigeria 79 D6
Benxi, China 51 D12
Benzdorp, Surinam 121 C7
Beo, Indonesia 57 D7
Beograd, Serbia, Yug. 21 L10
Beowawe, U.S.A. 110 F5
Bepan Jiang →, China 52 E6
Beppu, Japan 49 H5
Beqaa Valley = Al Biqā □, Lebanon 69 A5
Berati, Albania 39 J2
Berau, Teluk, Indonesia 57 E8
Berber, Sudan 76 D3
Berbera, Somali Rep. 68 E4
Berbérati, C.A.R. 80 D3
Berberia, C. del, Spain 36 C7
Berbice →, Guyana 121 B6
Berceto, Italy 32 D7
Berchtesgaden, Germany 19 H8
Berck-Plage, France 25 B8
Berdichev = Berdychiv, Ukraine 41 H5
Berdsk, Russia 44 D9
Berdyansk, Ukraine 41 J9
Berdychiv, Ukraine 41 H5
Berea, U.S.A. 104 G3
Berebere, Indonesia 57 D7
Bereda, Somali Rep. 68 E5
Berehove, Ukraine 41 H2
Berekum, Ghana 78 D4
Berenice, Egypt 76 C4
Berens →, Canada 101 C9
Berens I., Canada 101 C9
Berens River, Canada 101 C9
Berestechko, Ukraine 41 G3
Bereşti, Romania 38 C10
Beretău →, Romania 38 B4
Berettyo →, Hungary 21 J11
Berettyóújfalu, Hungary 21 H11
Berevo, Mahajanga, Madag. 85 B7
Berevo, Toliara, Madag. 85 B7
Bereza, Belarus 41 F3
Berezhany, Ukraine 41 H3
Berezina = Byarezina →, Belarus 41 F6
Berezivka, Ukraine 41 J6
Berezna, Ukraine 41 G6
Berezniki, Russia 44 D6
Berezovo, Russia 44 C7
Berga, Spain 28 C6
Bergama, Turkey 66 C2
Bergambacht, Neths. 16 E5
Bérgamo, Italy 32 C6
Bergantiños, Spain 30 B2
Bergara, Spain 28 B2
Bergedorf, Germany 18 B6
Bergeijk, Neths. 17 F6
Bergen, Germany 18 A9
Bergen, Neths. 16 C5
Bergen, Norway 9 F11
Bergen, U.S.A. 106 C7
Bergen-op-Zoom, Neths. 17 F4
Bergerac, France 26 D4
Bergheim, Germany 18 E2
Berghem, Neths. 16 E7
Bergisch Gladbach, Germany 18 E3
Bergschenhoek, Neths. 16 E5
Bergsjö, Sweden 10 C11
Bergues, France 25 B9
Bergum, Neths. 16 B7
Bergville, S. Africa 85 D4
Berhala, Selat, Indonesia 56 E2
Berhampore = Baharampur, India 63 G13
Berhampur, India 61 K14
Berheci →, Romania 38 C10
Bering Sea, Pac. Oc. 96 C1
Bering Strait, U.S.A. 96 B3
Beringen, Belgium 17 F6
Beringen, Switz. 23 A7
Beringovskiy, Russia 45 C18
Berisso, Argentina 126 C4
Berja, Spain 29 J2
Berkane, Morocco 75 B4
Berkel →, Neths. 16 D8
Berkeley, U.K. 13 F5
Berkeley, U.S.A. 112 H4
Berkeley Springs, U.S.A. 104 F6
Berkhout, Neths. 16 C5
Berkner I., Antarctica 5 D18
Berkovitsa, Bulgaria 38 F6
Berkshire □, U.K. 13 F6
Berlaar, Belgium 17 F5
Berland →, Canada 100 C5
Berlanga, Spain 31 G5
Berlare, Belgium 17 F4
Berlenga, I., Portugal 31 F1
Berlin, Germany 18 C9
Berlin, Md., U.S.A. 104 F8
Berlin, N.H., U.S.A. 107 B13
Berlin, Wis., U.S.A. 104 D1
Bermeja, Sierra, Spain 31 J5
Bermejo →, Formosa, Argentina 126 B4
Bermejo →, San Juan, Argentina 126 C2
Bermeo, Spain 28 B2
Bermillo de Sayago, Spain 30 D4
Bermuda ■, Atl. Oc. 2 C6
Bern, Switz. 22 C4
Bern □, Switz. 22 C5
Bernado, U.S.A. 111 J10
Bernalda, Italy 35 B9
Bernalillo, U.S.A. 111 J10
Bernardo de Irigoyen, Argentina 127 B5
Bernardo O'Higgins □, Chile 126 C1
Bernasconi, Argentina 126 D3
Bernau, Bayern, Germany 19 H8
Bernau, Brandenburg, Germany 18 C9
Bernay, France 24 C7
Bernburg, Germany 18 D7
Berne = Bern, Switz. 22 C4
Berne = Bern □, Switz. 22 C5
Berner Alpen, Switz. 22 D5
Bernese Oberland = Oberland, Switz. 22 C5
Bernier I., Australia 89 D1
Bernina, Piz, Switz. 23 D9
Bernina, Pizzo, Switz. 23 D9
Bernissart, Belgium 17 H3
Bernkastel-Kues, Germany 19 F3
Beroroha, Madag. 85 C8
Béroubouay, Benin 79 C5
Beroun, Czech. 20 F4
Berounka →, Czech. 20 F4
Berovo, Macedonia 39 H5
Berrahal, Algeria 75 A6
Berre, Étang de, France 27 E9
Berrechid, Morocco 74 B3
Berri, Australia 91 E3
Berriane, Algeria 75 B5
Berrouaghia, Algeria 75 A5
Berry, Australia 91 E5
Berry, France 25 F8
Berry Is., Bahamas 116 A4
Berryessa L., U.S.A. 112 G4
Berryville, U.S.A. 109 G8
Bersenbrück, Germany 18 C3
Bershad, Ukraine 41 H5
Berthold, U.S.A. 108 A4
Berthoud, U.S.A. 108 E2
Bertincourt, France 25 B9
Bertoua, Cameroon 80 D2
Bertrand, U.S.A. 108 E5
Bertrange, Lux. 17 J8
Bertrix, Belgium 17 J6
Beruri, Brazil 121 D5
Berwick, U.S.A. 107 E8
Berwick-upon-Tweed, U.K. 12 B5
Berwyn Mts., U.K. 12 E4
Beryslav, Ukraine 41 J7
Berzasca, Romania 38 E4
Besal, Pakistan 63 B5
Besalampy, Madag. 85 B7
Besançon, France 25 E13
Besar, Indonesia 56 E5
Beshenkovichi, Belarus 40 E5
Beslan, Russia 43 J7
Besnard L., Canada 101 B7
Besni, Turkey 66 D7
Besor, N. →, Egypt 69 D3
Bessarabiya, Moldova 41 J5
Bessarabka = Basarabeasca, Moldova 41 J5
Bessèges, France 27 D8
Bessemer, Ala., U.S.A. 105 J2
Bessemer, Mich., U.S.A. 108 B9
Bessin, France 24 C5
Bessines-sur-Gartempe, France 26 B5
Best, Neths. 17 E6
Bet She'an, Israel 69 C4
Bet Shemesh, Israel 69 D3
Bet Tadjine, Djebel, Algeria 74 C4
Betafo, Madag. 85 B8
Betancuria, Canary Is. 36 F5
Betanzos, Bolivia 125 D4
Betanzos, Spain 30 B2
Bétaré Oya, Cameroon 80 C2
Bétera, Spain 28 F4
Bethal, S. Africa 85 D4
Bethanien, Namibia 84 D2
Bethany, U.S.A. 108 E7
Bethel, Alaska, U.S.A. 96 B3
Bethel, Vt., U.S.A. 107 C12
Bethel Park, U.S.A. 106 F4
Bethlehem = Bayt Lahm, West Bank 69 D4
Bethlehem, S. Africa 85 D4
Bethlehem, U.S.A. 107 F9
Bethulie, S. Africa 84 E4
Béthune, France 25 B9
Béthune →, France 24 C8
Bethungra, Australia 91 E4
Betijoque, Venezuela 120 B3
Betim, Brazil 123 E3
Betioky, Madag. 85 C7
Beton-Bazoches, France 25 D10
Betong, Thailand 59 K3
Betoota, Australia 90 D3
Betroka, Madag. 85 C8
Betsiamites, Canada 99 C6
Betsiamites →, Canada 99 C6
Betsiboka →, Madag. 85 B8
Bettembourg, Lux. 17 J8
Bettiah, India 63 F11
Bèttola, Italy 32 D6
Betul, India 60 J10
Betung, Malaysia 56 D4
Betzdorf, Germany 18 E3
Beuca, Romania 38 E7
Beuil, France 27 D10
Beulah, U.S.A. 108 B4
Beuvron →, France 24 E8
Beveren, Belgium 17 F4
Beverley, Australia 89 F2
Beverley, U.K. 12 D7
Beverlo, Belgium 17 F6
Beverly, Mass., U.S.A. 107 D14
Beverly, Wash., U.S.A. 110 C4
Beverly Hills, U.S.A. 113 L8
Beverwijk, Neths. 16 D5
Bex, Switz. 22 D4
Bey Dağları, Turkey 66 D4
Beya, Russia 45 D10
Beyānlū, Iran 64 C5
Beyin, Ghana 78 D4
Beyla, Guinea 78 D3
Beynat, France 26 C5
Beyneu, Kazakhstan 44 E6
Beypazarı, Turkey 66 B4
Beyşehir, Turkey 66 D4
Beyşehir Gölü, Turkey 66 D4
Beytüşşebap, Turkey 67 D10
Bezhetsk, Russia 42 B3
Bezhitsa, Russia 44 D4
Béziers, France 26 E7
Bezwada = Vijayawada, India 61 L12
Bhachau, India 60 H7
Bhadarwah, India 63 C6
Bhadrakh, India 61 J15
Bhadravati, India 60 N9
Bhagalpur, India 63 G12
Bhakkar, Pakistan 62 D4
Bhakra Dam, India 62 D7
Bhamo, Burma 61 G20
Bhandara, India 60 J11
Bhanrer Ra., India 62 H8
Bharat = India ■, Asia 60 K11
Bharatpur, India 62 F7
Bhatinda, India 62 D6
Bhatpara, India 63 H13
Bhaun, Pakistan 62 C5
Bhaunagar = Bhavnagar, India 62 J5
Bhavnagar, India 62 J5
Bhawanipatna, India 61 K12
Bhera, Pakistan 62 C5
Bhilsa = Vidisha, India 62 H7
Bhilwara, India 62 G6
Bhima →, India 60 L10
Bhimavaram, India 61 L12
Bhimbar, Pakistan 63 C6
Bhind, India 63 F8
Bhiwandi, India 60 K8
Bhiwani, India 62 E7
Bhola, Bangla. 61 H17
Bhopal, India 62 H7
Bhubaneshwar, India 61 J14
Bhuj, India 62 H3
Bhumiphol Dam = Phumiphon, Khuan, Thailand 58 D2
Bhusaval, India 60 J9
Bhutan ■, Asia 61 F17
Biá →, Brazil 120 D4
Biafra, B. of = Bonny, Bight of, Africa 79 E6
Biak, Indonesia 57 E9
Biała →, Poland 20 E10
Biała Podlaska, Poland 20 C13
Białogard, Poland 20 A5
Białystok, Poland 20 B13
Biancavilla, Italy 35 E7
Bīārjmand, Iran 65 B7
Biaro, Indonesia 57 D7
Biarritz, France 26 E2
Biasca, Switz. 23 D7
Biba, Egypt 76 J7
Bibai, Japan 48 C10
Bibala, Angola 81 G2
Bibane, Bahiret el, Tunisia 75 B7
Bibbiena, Italy 33 E8
Bibby I., Canada 101 A10
Biberach, Germany 19 G5
Biberist, Switz. 22 B5
Bibey →, Spain 30 C3
Bibiani, Ghana 78 D4
Biboohra, Australia 90 B4
Bibungwa, Zaïre 82 C2
Bic, Canada 99 C6
Bicaz, Romania 38 C9
Biccari, Italy 35 A8
Bichena, Ethiopia 77 E4
Bichvinta, Georgia 43 J5
Bickerton I., Australia 90 A2
Bicknell, Ind., U.S.A. 104 F2
Bicknell, Utah, U.S.A. 111 G8
Bida, Nigeria 79 D6
Bidar, India 60 L10
Biddeford, U.S.A. 99 D5
Biddwara, Ethiopia 77 F4
Bideford, U.K. 13 F3
Bidon 5 = Poste Maurice Cortier, Algeria 75 D5
Bidor, Malaysia 59 K3
Bié, Planalto de, Angola 81 G3
Bieber, U.S.A. 110 F3
Biel, Switz. 22 B4
Bielawa, Poland 20 E6
Bielé Karpaty, Europe 20 F7
Bielefeld, Germany 18 C4
Bielersee, Switz. 22 B4
Biella, Italy 32 C5
Bielsk Podlaski, Poland 20 C13
Bielsko-Biała, Poland 20 F9
Bien Hoa, Vietnam 59 G6
Bienfait, Canada 101 D8
Bienne = Biel, Switz. 22 B4
Bienvenida, Spain 31 G4
Bienvenue, Fr. Guiana 121 C7
Bienville, L., Canada 98 A5
Biescas, Spain 28 C4
Biese →, Germany 18 C7
Biesiesfontein, S. Africa 84 E2
Bietigheim, Germany 19 G5
Bievre, Belgium 17 J6
Biferno →, Italy 35 A8
Big →, Canada 99 B8
Big B., Canada 99 A7
Big Bear City, U.S.A. 113 L10
Big Bear Lake, U.S.A. 113 L10
Big Beaver, Canada 101 D7
Big Belt Mts., U.S.A. 110 C8
Big Bend, Swaziland 85 D5
Big Bend National Park, U.S.A. 109 L3
Big Black →, U.S.A. 109 J9
Big Blue →, U.S.A. 108 F6
Big Cr. →, Canada 100 C4
Big Creek, U.S.A. 112 H7
Big Cypress Swamp, U.S.A. 105 M5
Big Falls, U.S.A. 108 A8
Big Fork →, U.S.A. 108 A8
Big Horn Mts. = Bighorn Mts., U.S.A. 110 D10
Big Lake, U.S.A. 109 K4
Big Moose, U.S.A. 107 C10
Big Muddy Cr. →, U.S.A. 108 A2
Big Pine, U.S.A. 111 H4
Big Piney, U.S.A. 110 E8
Big Quill L., Canada 101 C8
Big Rapids, U.S.A. 104 D3
Big River, Canada 101 C7
Big Run, U.S.A. 106 F6
Big Sable Pt., U.S.A. 104 C2
Big Sand L., Canada 101 B9
Big Sandy, U.S.A. 110 B8
Big Sandy Cr. →, U.S.A. 108 F3
Big Sioux →, U.S.A. 108 D6
Big Spring, U.S.A. 109 J4
Big Springs, U.S.A. 108 E3
Big Stone City, U.S.A. 108 C6
Big Stone Gap, U.S.A. 105 G4
Big Stone L., U.S.A. 108 C6
Big Sur, U.S.A. 112 J5
Big Timber, U.S.A. 110 D9
Big Trout L., Canada 98 B1
Biğa, Turkey 66 B2
Bigadiç, Turkey 66 C3
Biganos, France 26 D3
Bigfork, U.S.A. 110 B6
Biggar, Canada 101 C7
Biggar, U.K. 14 F5
Bigge I., Australia 88 B4
Biggenden, Australia 91 D5
Biggs, U.S.A. 112 F5
Bighorn, U.S.A. 110 C10
Bighorn →, U.S.A. 110 C10
Bighorn Mts., U.S.A. 110 D10
Bignona, Senegal 78 C1
Bigorre, France 26 E4
Bigstone L., Canada 101 C9
Biguglia, Étang de, France 27 F13
Bigwa, Tanzania 82 D4
Bihać, Bos.-H. 33 D12
Bihar, India 63 G11
Bihar □, India 63 G11
Biharamulo, Tanzania 82 C3
Biharamulo □, Tanzania 82 C3
Bihor, Munţii, Romania 38 C5
Bijagós, Arquipélago dos, Guinea-Biss. 78 C1
Bijaipur, India 62 F7
Bijapur, Karnataka, India 60 L9
Bijapur, Mad. P., India 61 K12
Bījār, Iran 67 E12
Bijeljina, Bos.-H. 21 L9
Bijelo Polje, Montenegro, Yug. 21 M9
Bijie, China 52 D5
Bijnor, India 62 E8
Bikaner, India 62 E5
Bikapur, India 63 F10
Bikeqi, China 50 D6
Bikfayyā, Lebanon 69 B4
Bikin, Russia 45 E14
Bikin →, Russia 48 A7
Bikini Atoll, Pac. Oc. 92 F8
Bikoué, Cameroon 79 E7
Bila Tserkva, Ukraine 41 H6
Bilara, India 62 F5
Bilaspur, Mad. P., India 63 H10

Bilaspur, *Punjab, India* ... 62 D7
Biläsuvar, *Azerbaijan* 67 C13
Bilauk Taungdan, *Thailand* 58 F2
Bilbao, *Spain* 28 B2
Bilbo = Bilbao, *Spain* 28 B2
Bilbor, *Romania* 38 B8
Bíldudalur, *Iceland* 8 D2
Bileća, *Bos.-H.* 21 N8
Bilecik, *Turkey* 66 B4
Bilgoraj, *Poland* 20 E12
Bilhorod-Dnivstrovskyy,
　Ukraine 41 J6
Bilibino, *Russia* 45 C17
Bilibiza, *Mozam.* 83 E5
Bilir, *Russia* 45 C14
Biliran I., *Phil.* 55 F6
Bill, *U.S.A.* 108 D2
Billabalong, *Australia* 89 E2
Billiluna, *Australia* 88 C4
Billingham, *U.K.* 12 C6
Billings, *U.S.A.* 110 D9
Billiton Is. = Belitung,
　Indonesia 56 E3
Billom, *France* 26 C7
Bilma, *Niger* 73 E7
Bilo Gora, *Croatia* 21 K7
Biloela, *Australia* 90 C5
Bilohirsk, *Ukraine* 41 K8
Biloku, *Guyana* 121 C6
Bilopillya, *Ukraine* 41 G8
Biloxi, *U.S.A.* 109 K10
Bilpa Morea Claypan,
　Australia 90 D2
Bilthoven, *Neths.* 16 D6
Biltine, *Chad* 73 F9
Bilyana, *Australia* 90 B4
Bilyarsk, *Russia* 42 C10
Bilyarsk, *Russia* 42 C10
Bilzen, *Belgium* 17 G7
Bima, *Indonesia* 57 F5
Bimban, *Egypt* 76 C3
Bimbila, *Ghana* 79 D5
Bimbo, *C.A.R.* 80 D3
Bimini Is., *Bahamas* 116 A4
Bin Xian, *Heilongjiang,*
　China 51 B14
Bin Xian, *Shaanxi, China* . 50 G5
Bina-Etawah, *India* 62 G8
Bināb, *Iran* 67 D13
Binalbagan, *Phil.* 55 F5
Bīnālūd, Kūh-e, *Iran* 65 B8
Binatang, *Malaysia* 56 D4
Binbee, *Australia* 90 C4
Binche, *Belgium* 17 H4
Binchuan, *China* 52 E3
Binda, *Australia* 91 D4
Bindle, *Australia* 91 D4
Bindura, *Zimbabwe* 83 F3
Bingara, *N.S.W., Australia* 91 D5
Bingara, *Queens., Australia* 91 D3
Bingen, *Germany* 19 F3
Bingerville, *Ivory C.* 78 D4
Bingham, *U.S.A.* 99 C6
Bingham Canyon, *U.S.A.* . 110 F7
Binghamton, *U.S.A.* 107 D9
Bingöl, *Turkey* 67 C9
Bingöl Dağları, *Turkey* ... 67 C9
Binh Dinh = An Nhon,
　Vietnam 58 F7
Binh Khe, *Vietnam* 58 F7
Binh Son, *Vietnam* 58 E7
Binhai, *China* 51 G10
Binisatua, *Spain* 36 B11
Binjai, *Indonesia* 56 D1
Binnaway, *Australia* 91 E4
Binongko, *Indonesia* 57 F6
Binscarth, *Canada* 101 C8
Bintan, *Indonesia* 56 D2
Bintulu, *Malaysia* 56 D4
Bintuni, *Indonesia* 57 E8
Binyang, *China* 52 F7
Binz, *Germany* 18 A9
Binzert = Bizerte, *Tunisia* 75 A6
Bío Bío □, *Chile* 126 D1
Biograd, *Croatia* 33 E12
Bioko, *Eq. Guin.* 79 E6
Biougra, *Morocco* 74 B3
Bir, *India* 60 K9
Bir, Ras, *Djibouti* 77 E5
Bîr Abu Hashim, *Egypt* .. 76 C3
Bîr Abu M'nqar, *Egypt* .. 76 B2
Bîr Abu Muḥammad, *Egypt* 69 F3
Bi'r ad Dabbāghāt, *Jordan* 69 E4
Bir Adal Deib, *Sudan* 76 C4
Bi'r al Butayyiḥāt, *Jordan* 69 F4
Bi'r al Mārī, *Jordan* 69 E4
Bi'r al Qattār, *Jordan* 69 F4
Bir Aouine, *Tunisia* 75 B6
Bîr 'Asal, *Egypt* 76 B3
Bir Autrun, *Sudan* 76 D2
Bîr Beiḍa, *Egypt* 69 E3
Bîr Diqnash, *Egypt* 76 A2
Bir el Abbes, *Algeria* 74 C3
Bîr el 'Abd, *Egypt* 69 D2
Bir el Ater, *Algeria* 75 B6
Bîr el Basur, *Egypt* 76 B2
Bîr el Biarât, *Egypt* 69 F3
Bîr el Duweidar, *Egypt* ... 69 E1
Bîr el Garârât, *Egypt* 69 D2
Bîr el Gellaz, *Egypt* 76 A2
Bîr el Heisi, *Egypt* 69 F3
Bîr el Jafir, *Egypt* 69 E1
Bîr el Mâlḥi, *Egypt* 69 E2
Bîr el Shaqqa, *Egypt* 76 A2
Bîr el Thamâda, *Egypt* ... 69 E2
Bîr Fuad, *Egypt* 76 A2

Bîr Gebeil Ḥiṣn, *Egypt* ... 69 E2
Bi'r Ghadīr, *Syria* 69 A6
Bîr Haimur, *Egypt* 76 C3
Bîr Ḥasana, *Egypt* 69 E2
Bi'r Jadīd, *Iraq* 64 C4
Bir Jdid, *Morocco* 74 B3
Bîr Kanayis, *Egypt* 76 C3
Bîr Kaseiba, *Egypt* 69 E2
Bîr Kerawein, *Egypt* 76 B2
Bîr Lahfân, *Egypt* 69 D2
Bir Lahrache, *Algeria* 75 B6
Bîr Madkûr, *Egypt* 69 E1
Bîr Maql, *Egypt* 76 C3
Bîr Misaha, *Egypt* 76 C2
Bir Mogrein, *Mauritania* . 74 C2
Bîr Murr, *Egypt* 76 C3
Bi'r Muṭribah, *Kuwait* 64 D5
Bîr Nakheila, *Egypt* 76 C3
Bîr Qaṭia, *Egypt* 69 E1
Bîr Qatrani, *Egypt* 76 A2
Bîr Ranga, *Egypt* 76 C4
Bîr Sahara, *Egypt* 76 C2
Bîr Seiyâla, *Egypt* 76 B3
Bir Semguine, *Morocco* .. 74 B3
Bîr Shalatein, *Egypt* 76 C4
Bîr Shebb, *Egypt* 76 C2
Bîr Shût, *Egypt* 76 C4
Bîr Terfawi, *Egypt* 76 C2
Bîr Umm Qubûr, *Egypt* .. 76 C3
Bîr Ungât, *Egypt* 76 C3
Bîr Za'farâna, *Egypt* 76 J8
Bîr Zeidûn, *Egypt* 76 B3
Bira, *Indonesia* 57 E8
Bîra, *Romania* 38 B10
Biramféro, *Guinea* 78 C3
Birao, *C.A.R.* 73 F9
Birawa, *Zaïre* 82 C2
Bîrca, *Romania* 38 F6
Birch Hills, *Canada* 101 C7
Birch I., *Canada* 101 C9
Birch L., *N.W.T., Canada* . 100 A5
Birch L., *Ont., Canada* ... 98 B1
Birch Mts., *Canada* 100 B6
Birch River, *Canada* 101 C8
Birchip, *Australia* 91 F3
Bird, *Canada* 101 B10
Bird City, *U.S.A.* 108 F4
Bird I. = Aves, I. de,
　W. Indies 117 C7
Birdaard, *Neths.* 16 B7
Birdlip, *U.K.* 13 F5
Birdsville, *Australia* 90 D2
Birdum, *Australia* 88 C5
Birecik, *Turkey* 67 D8
Birein, *Israel* 69 E3
Bireuen, *Indonesia* 56 C1
Birifo, *Gambia* 78 C2
Birigui, *Brazil* 127 A5
Birkenfeld, *Germany* 19 F3
Birkenhead, *U.K.* 12 D4
Birket Qârûn, *Egypt* 76 J7
Birkhadem, *Algeria* 75 A5
Bîrlad, *Romania* 38 C10
Birmingham, *U.K.* 13 E6
Birmingham, *U.S.A.* 105 J2
Birmitrapur, *India* 61 H14
Birni Ngaouré, *Niger* 79 C5
Birni Nkonni, *Niger* 79 C6
Birnin Gwari, *Nigeria* 79 C6
Birnin Kebbi, *Nigeria* 79 C5
Birnin Kudu, *Nigeria* 79 C6
Birobidzhan, *Russia* 45 E14
Birr, *Ireland* 15 C4
Birrie →, *Australia* 91 D4
Birs →, *Switz.* 22 B5
Birsilpur, *India* 62 E5
Birsk, *Russia* 44 D6
Birtin, *Romania* 38 C5
Birtle, *Canada* 101 C8
Birur, *India* 60 N9
Biryuchiy, *Ukraine* 41 J8
Biržai, *Lithuania* 9 H21
Birzava, *Romania* 38 C4
Birzebugga, *Malta* 37 D2
Bisa, *Indonesia* 57 E7
Bisáccia, *Italy* 35 A8
Bisacquino, *Italy* 34 E6
Bisalpur, *India* 63 E8
Bisbee, *U.S.A.* 111 L9
Biscarrosse et de Parentis,
　Étang de, *France* 26 D2
Biscay, B. of, *Atl. Oc.* 6 F5
Biscayne B., *U.S.A.* 105 N5
Biscéglie, *Italy* 35 A9
Bischofshofen, *Austria* ... 21 H3
Bischofswerda, *Germany* . 18 D10
Bischofszell, *Switz.* 23 B8
Bischwiller, *France* 25 D14
Biscoe Bay, *Antarctica* ... 5 D13
Biscoe Is., *Antarctica* 5 C17
Biscostasing, *Canada* 98 C3
Biscucuy, *Venezuela* 120 B4
Biševo, *Croatia* 33 F13
Bisha, *Eritrea* 77 D4
Bishah, W., *Si. Arabia* ... 76 C5
Bishan, *China* 52 C6
Bishkek, *Kyrgyzstan* 44 E8
Bishnupur, *India* 63 H12
Bisho, *S. Africa* 85 E4
Bishop, *Calif., U.S.A.* 111 H4
Bishop, *Tex., U.S.A.* 109 M6
Bishop Auckland, *U.K.* ... 12 C6
Bishop's Falls, *Canada* ... 99 C8
Bishop's Stortford, *U.K.* . 13 F8
Bisignano, *Italy* 35 C9
Bisina, L., *Uganda* 82 B3

Biskra, *Algeria* 75 B6
Bislig, *Phil.* 57 C7
Bismarck, *U.S.A.* 108 B4
Bismarck Arch.,
　Papua N. G. 92 H6
Bismark, *Germany* 18 C7
Bismil, *Turkey* 67 D9
Biso, *Uganda* 82 B3
Bison, *U.S.A.* 108 C3
Bīsotūn, *Iran* 67 E12
Bispgården, *Sweden* 10 A10
Bissagos = Bijagós,
　Arquipélago dos,
　Guinea-Biss. 78 C1
Bissau, *Guinea-Biss.* 78 C1
Bissett, *Canada* 101 C9
Bissikrima, *Guinea* 78 C2
Bistcho L., *Canada* 100 B5
Bistreţu, *Romania* 38 F6
Bistrica = Ilirska-Bistrica,
　Slovenia 33 C11
Bistriţa, *Romania* 38 B7
Bistriţa →, *Romania* 38 C9
Bistriţei, Munţii, *Romania* 38 B8
Biswan, *India* 63 F9
Bitam, *Gabon* 80 D2
Bitburg, *Germany* 19 F2
Bitche, *France* 25 C14
Bithynia, *Turkey* 66 B4
Bitkine, *Chad* 73 F8
Bitlis, *Turkey* 67 C10
Bitola, *Macedonia* 39 H4
Bitolj = Bitola, *Macedonia* 39 H4
Bitonto, *Italy* 35 A9
Bitter Creek, *U.S.A.* 110 F9
Bitter L. = Buheirat-
　Murrat-el-Kubra, *Egypt* 76 H8
Bitterfeld, *Germany* 18 D8
Bitterfontein, *S. Africa* ... 84 E2
Bitterroot →, *U.S.A.* 110 C6
Bitterroot Range, *U.S.A.* . 110 D6
Bitterwater, *U.S.A.* 112 J5
Bitti, *Italy* 34 B2
Bittou, *Burkina Faso* 79 C4
Biu, *Nigeria* 79 C7
Bivolari, *Romania* 38 B10
Biwa-Ko, *Japan* 49 G8
Biwabik, *U.S.A.* 108 B8
Bixad, *Romania* 38 B6
Biyang, *China* 50 H7
Biysk, *Russia* 44 D9
Bizana, *S. Africa* 85 E4
Bizen, *Japan* 49 G7
Bizerte, *Tunisia* 75 A6
Bjargtangar, *Iceland* 8 D1
Bjelasica,
　Montenegro, Yug. 21 N9
Bjelovar, *Croatia* 21 K6
Bjerringbro, *Denmark* 11 H3
Bjervamoen, *Norway* 10 E3
Bjørnevatn, *Norway* 8 B23
Bjørnøya, *Arctic* 4 B8
Bjuv, *Sweden* 11 H6
Blace, *Serbia, Yug.* 21 M11
Black = Da →, *Vietnam* . 58 B5
Black →, *Canada* 106 B5
Black →, *Ark., U.S.A.* ... 109 H9
Black →, *N.Y., U.S.A.* .. 107 C8
Black →, *Wis., U.S.A.* .. 108 D9
Black Diamond, *Canada* . 100 C6
Black Forest =
　Schwarzwald, *Germany* . 19 H4
Black Hills, *U.S.A.* 108 C3
Black I., *Canada* 101 C9
Black L., *Canada* 101 B7
Black L., *U.S.A.* 104 C3
Black Mesa, *U.S.A.* 109 G3
Black Mt. = Mynydd Du,
　U.K. 13 F4
Black Mts., *U.K.* 13 F4
Black Range, *U.S.A.* 111 K10
Black River, *Jamaica* 116 C4
Black River Falls, *U.S.A.* . 108 C9
Black Sea, *Eurasia* 46 E7
Black Volta →, *Africa* ... 78 D4
Black Warrior →, *U.S.A.* 105 J2
Blackall, *Australia* 90 C4
Blackball, *N.Z.* 87 K3
Blackbull, *Australia* 90 B3
Blackburn, *U.K.* 12 D5
Blackduck, *U.S.A.* 108 B7
Blackfoot, *U.S.A.* 110 E7
Blackfoot →, *U.S.A.* 110 C7
Blackfoot River Reservoir,
　U.S.A. 110 E8
Blackie, *Canada* 100 C6
Blackpool, *U.K.* 12 D4
Blackriver, *U.S.A.* 106 B1
Blacks Harbour, *Canada* . 99 C6
Blacksburg, *U.S.A.* 104 G5
Blacksod B., *Ireland* 15 B2
Blackstone, *U.S.A.* 104 G6
Blackstone →, *Canada* ... 100 A4
Blackstone Ra., *Australia* . 89 E4
Blackville, *Canada* 99 C6
Blackwater, *Australia* 90 C4
Blackwater →, *Ireland* ... 15 D4
Blackwater →, *U.K.* 15 B5
Blackwater Cr. →,
　Australia 91 D3
Blackwell, *U.S.A.* 109 G6
Blackwells Corner, *U.S.A.* 113 K7
Bladel, *Neths.* 17 F6
Blaenau Ffestiniog, *U.K.* . 12 E4
Blagodarnoye =
　Blagodarnyy, *Russia* ... 43 H6
Blagodarnyy, *Russia* 43 H6

Blagoevgrad, *Bulgaria* 39 G6
Blagoveshchensk, *Russia* . 45 D13
Blain, *France* 24 E5
Blaine, *U.S.A.* 112 B4
Blaine Lake, *Canada* 101 C7
Blainville-sur-l'Eau, *France* 25 D13
Blair, *U.S.A.* 108 E6
Blair Athol, *Australia* 90 C4
Blair Atholl, *U.K.* 14 E5
Blairgowrie, *U.K.* 14 E5
Blairmore, *Canada* 100 D6
Blairsden, *U.S.A.* 112 F6
Blairsville, *U.S.A.* 106 F5
Blaj, *Romania* 38 C6
Blake Pt., *U.S.A.* 108 A10
Blakely, *U.S.A.* 105 K3
Blâmont, *France* 25 D13
Blanc, *France* 75 A6
Blanc, Mont, *Alps* 27 C10
Blanca, B., *Argentina* 128 A4
Blanca Peak, *U.S.A.* 111 H11
Blanche, C., *Australia* 91 E1
Blanche, L., *S. Austral.,*
　Australia 91 D2
Blanche, L., *W. Austral.,*
　Australia 88 D3
Blanco, *S. Africa* 84 E3
Blanco, *U.S.A.* 109 K5
Blanco →, *Argentina* 126 C2
Blanco, C., *Costa Rica* ... 116 E2
Blanco, C., *Spain* 36 B9
Blanco, C., *U.S.A.* 110 E1
Blanda →, *Iceland* 8 D3
Blandford Forum, *U.K.* .. 13 G5
Blanding, *U.S.A.* 111 H9
Blanes, *Spain* 28 D7
Blangy-sur-Bresle, *France* 25 C8
Blankenberge, *Belgium* ... 17 F2
Blankenburg, *Germany* ... 18 D6
Blanquefort, *France* 26 D3
Blanquillo, *Uruguay* 127 C4
Blansko, *Czech.* 20 F6
Blantyre, *Malawi* 83 F4
Blaricum, *Neths.* 16 D6
Blarney, *Ireland* 15 E3
Blato, *Croatia* 33 F13
Blatten, *Switz.* 22 D5
Blaubeuren, *Germany* 19 G5
Blåvands Huk, *Denmark* . 9 J13
Blaydon, *U.K.* 12 C6
Blaye, *France* 26 C3
Blaye-les-Mines, *France* .. 26 D6
Blayney, *Australia* 91 E4
Blaze, Pt., *Australia* 88 B5
Błażowa, *Poland* .... 20 F12 (?)
Bleckede, *Germany* 18 B6
Bled, *Slovenia* 33 B11
Blednaya, Gora, *Russia* .. 44 B7
Bléharis, *Belgium* 17 G2
Bleiburg, ...
Blejeşti, *Romania* 38 E8
Blekinge, *Sweden* 9 H16
Blenheim, *Canada* 106 D2
Blenheim, *N.Z.* 87 J4
Bléone →, *France* 27 D10
Blerick, *Neths.* 17 F8
Bletchley, *U.K.* 13 F7
Blida, *Algeria* 75 A5
Blidet Amor, *Algeria* 75 B6
Blidö, *Sweden* 10 E12
Bligh Sound, *N.Z.* 87 L1
Blind River, *Canada* 98 C3
Blinnenhorn, *Switz.* 23 D6
Blitar, *Indonesia* 57 H15
Blitta, *Togo* 79 D5
Block I., *U.S.A.* 107 E13
Block Island Sd., *U.S.A.* . 107 E13
Blodgett Iceberg Tongue,
　Antarctica 5 C9
Bloemendaal, *Neths.* 16 D5
Bloemfontein, *S. Africa* .. 84 D4
Bloemhof, *S. Africa* 84 D4
Blois, *France* 24 E8
Blokziji, *Neths.* 16 C7
Blöndós, *Iceland* 8 D3
Bloodvein →, *Canada* ... 101 C9
Bloody Foreland, *Ireland* . 15 A3
Bloomer, *U.S.A.* 108 C9
Bloomfield, *Australia* 90 B4
Bloomfield, *Canada* 106 C7
Bloomfield, *Iowa, U.S.A.* 108 E8
Bloomfield, *N. Mex.,*
　U.S.A. 111 H10
Bloomington, *Ill., U.S.A.* 108 E10
Bloomington, *Ind., U.S.A.* 104 F2
Bloomsburg, *U.S.A.* 107 F8
Blora, *Indonesia* 57 G14
Blossburg, *U.S.A.* 106 E7
Blouberg, *S. Africa* 85 C4
Blountstown, *U.S.A.* 105 K3
Bludenz, *Austria* 19 H5
Blue Island, *U.S.A.* 104 E2
Blue Lake, *U.S.A.* 110 F2
Blue Mesa Reservoir,
　U.S.A. 111 G10
Blue Mts., *Oreg., U.S.A.* . 110 D4
Blue Mts., *Pa., U.S.A.* ... 107 F8
Blue Mud B., *Australia* ... 90 A2
Blue Nile = Nîl el
　Azraq →, *Sudan* 77 D3
Blue Rapids, *U.S.A.* 108 F6
Blue Ridge Mts., *U.S.A.* . 105 G5
Blue Stack Mts., *Ireland* . 15 B3
Blueberry →, *Canada* 100 B4
Bluefield, *U.S.A.* 104 G5
Bluefields, *Nic.* 116 D3

Bluff, *Australia* 90 C4
Bluff, *N.Z.* 87 M2
Bluff, *U.S.A.* 111 H9
Bluff Knoll, *Australia* 89 F2
Bluff Pt., *Australia* 89 E1
Bluffton, *U.S.A.* 104 E3
Blumenau, *Brazil* 127 B6
Blümisalphorn, *Switz.* 22 D5
Blunt, *U.S.A.* 108 C4
Bly, *U.S.A.* 110 E3
Blyth, *Canada* 106 C3
Blyth, *U.K.* 12 B6
Blyth Bridge, *U.K.* 12 E5
Blythe, *U.S.A.* 113 M12
Bø, *Norway* 10 E3
Bo, *S. Leone* 78 D2
Bo Duc, *Vietnam* 59 G6
Bo Hai, *China* 51 E10
Bo Xian, *China* 50 H8
Boa Esperança, *Brazil* ... 121 C5
Boa Esperança, Reprêsa,
　Brazil 122 C3
Boa Nova, *Brazil* 123 D3
Boa Viagem, *Brazil* 122 C4
Boa Vista, *Brazil* 121 C5
Boac, *Phil.* 55 E4
Boaco, *Nic.* 116 D2
Bo'ai, *China* 50 G7
Boal, *Spain* 30 A4
Boardman, *U.S.A.* 106 E4
Boatman, *Australia* 91 D4
Bobadah, *Australia* 91 E4
Bobai, *China* 52 F7
Bobbili, *India* 61 K13
Bóbbio, *Italy* 32 D6
Bobcaygeon, *Canada* 98 D4
Böblingen, *Germany* 19 G5
Bobo-Dioulasso,
　Burkina Faso 78 C4
Boboc, *Romania* 38 D9
Bobonaza →, *Ecuador* .. 120 D2
Bobov Dol, *Bulgaria* 38 G5
Bóbr →, *Poland* 20 C5
Bobraomby, Tanjon' i,
　Madag. 85 A8
Bobrinets, *Ukraine* 41 H7
Bobrov, *Russia* 42 E5
Bobrovitsa, *Ukraine* 41 G6
Bobruysk = Babruysk,
　Belarus 41 F5
Bobures, *Venezuela* 120 B3
Boca de Drago, *Venezuela* 121 A5
Bôca do Acre, *Brazil* 124 B4
Bôca do Jari, *Brazil* 121 D7
Bôca do Moaco, *Brazil* .. 124 B4
Boca Grande, *Venezuela* . 121 B5
Boca Raton, *U.S.A.* 105 M5
Bocaiúva, *Brazil* 123 E3
Bocanda, *Ivory C.* 78 D4
Bocaranga, *C.A.R.* 73 G8
Bocas del Toro, *Panama* . 116 E3
Boceguillas, *Spain* 28 D1
Bochnia, *Poland* 20 F10
Bocholt, *Belgium* 17 F7
Bocholt, *Germany* 18 D2
Bochum, *Germany* 18 D3
Bockenem, *Germany* 18 C6
Bocognano, *France* 27 F13
Boconó, *Venezuela* 120 B3
Boconó →, *Venezuela* ... 120 B4
Bocoyna, *Mexico* 114 B3
Bocq →, *Belgium* 17 H5
Boda, *C.A.R.* 80 D3
Bodaybo, *Russia* 45 D12
Boddington, *Australia* 89 F2
Bodega Bay, *U.S.A.* 112 G3
Bodegraven, *Neths.* 16 D5
Boden, *Sweden* 8 D19
Bodensee, *Europe* 23 A8
Bodenteich, *Germany* 18 C6
Bodhan, *India* 60 K10
Bodinga, *Nigeria* 79 C6
Bodio, *Switz.* 23 D7
Bodmin, *U.K.* 13 G3
Bodmin Moor, *U.K.* 13 G3
Bodø, *Norway* 8 C16
Bodoquena, Serra da,
　Brazil 125 E6
Bodrog →, *Hungary* 21 G11
Bodrum, *Turkey* 66 D2
Boechout, *Belgium* 17 F5
Boekelo, *Neths.* 16 D9
Boelenslaan, *Neths.* 16 B8
Boën, *France* 27 C8
Boende, *Zaïre* 80 E4
Boerne, *U.S.A.* 109 L5
Boertange, *Neths.* 16 B10
Boezinge, *Belgium* 17 G1
Boffa, *Guinea* 78 C2
Bogalusa, *U.S.A.* 109 K10
Bogan Gate, *Australia* ... 91 E4
Bogantungan, *Australia* .. 90 C4
Bogata, *U.S.A.* 109 J7
Bogatić, *Serbia, Yug.* 21 L9
Boğazkale, *Turkey* 66 B6
Boğazlıyan, *Turkey* 66 C6
Bogense, *Denmark* 11 J4
Boggabilla, *Australia* 91 D5
Boggabri, *Australia* 91 E5
Boggeragh Mts., *Ireland* . 15 D3
Bognor Regis, *U.K.* 13 G7
Bogø, *Denmark* 11 K6
Bogo, *Phil.* 55 F6
Bogodukhiv =
　Bohoduhiv, *Ukraine* ... 41 G8
Bogong, Mt., *Australia* ... 91 F4
Bogor, *Indonesia* 57 G12

Bogoroditsk, *Russia* 42 D4
Bogorodsk, *Russia* 42 B6
Bogorodskoye, *Russia* ... 45 D15
Bogoso, *Ghana* 78 D4
Bogotá, *Colombia* 120 C3
Bogotol, *Russia* 44 D9
Bogra, *Bangla.* 61 G16
Boguchany, *Russia* 45 D10
Boguchar, *Russia* 42 F5
Bogué, *Mauritania* 78 B2
Boguslav, *Ukraine* 41 H6
Bohain-en-Vermandois,
  France 25 C10
Bohemia Downs, *Australia* 88 C4
Bohemian Forest =
  Böhmerwald, *Germany* . 19 F8
Bohena Cr. →, *Australia* . 91 E4
Bohinjska Bistrica, *Slovenia* 33 B11
Böhmerwald, *Germany* .. 19 F8
Bohmte, *Germany* 18 C4
Bohol, *Phil.* 55 G6
Bohol Sea, *Phil.* 57 C6
Bohotleh, *Somali Rep.* .. 68 F4
Bohuslän, *Sweden* 9 G14
Boi, *Nigeria* 79 D6
Boi, Pta. de, *Brazil* 127 A6
Boiaçu, *Brazil* 121 D5
Boiano, *Italy* 35 A7
Boileau, C., *Australia* ... 88 C3
Boipeba, I. de, *Brazil* ... 123 D4
Bois →, *Brazil* 123 E1
Boischot, *Belgium* 17 F5
Boise, *U.S.A.* 110 E5
Boise City, *U.S.A.* 109 G3
Boissevain, *Canada* 101 D8
Boite →, *Italy* 33 B9
Boitzenburg, *Germany* ... 18 B9
Boizenburg, *Germany* ... 18 B6
Bojador C., *W. Sahara* ... 74 C2
Bojnūrd, *Iran* 65 B8
Bojonegoro, *Indonesia* .. 57 G14
Boju, *Nigeria* 79 D6
Boka Kotorska,
  Montenegro, Yug. 21 N8
Bokala, *Ivory C.* 78 D4
Boké, *Guinea* 78 C2
Bokhara →, *Australia* ... 91 D4
Bokkos, *Nigeria* 79 D6
Boknafjorden, *Norway* .. 9 G11
Bokoro, *Chad* 73 F8
Bokote, *Zaïre* 80 E4
Boksitogorsk, *Russia* 40 C7
Bokungu, *Zaïre* 80 E4
Bol, *Chad* 73 F7
Bol, *Croatia* 33 E13
Bolama, *Guinea-Biss.* ... 78 C1
Bolan Pass, *Pakistan* ... 60 E5
Bolaños →, *Mexico* 114 C4
Bolbec, *France* 24 C7
Boldājī, *Iran* 65 D6
Boldeşti, *Romania* 38 D9
Bole, *China* 54 B3
Bole, *Ethiopia* 77 F4
Bolekhiv, *Ukraine* 41 H2
Bolekhov = Bolekhiv,
  Ukraine 41 H2
Bolesławiec, *Poland* 20 D5
Bolgatanga, *Ghana* 79 C4
Bolgrad = Bolhrad,
  Ukraine 41 K5
Bolhrad, *Ukraine* 41 K5
Boli, *Sudan* 77 F2
Bolinao, *Phil.* 55 C3
Bolinao C., *Phil.* 57 A5
Bolívar, *Argentina* 126 D3
Bolívar, *Antioquía,
  Colombia* 120 B2
Bolívar, *Cauca, Colombia* 120 C2
Bolívar, *Peru* 124 B2
Bolivar, *Mo., U.S.A.* 109 G8
Bolivar, *Tenn., U.S.A.* .. 109 H10
Bolívar □, *Colombia* 120 B3
Bolívar □, *Ecuador* 120 D2
Bolívar □, *Venezuela* ... 121 B5
Bolivia ■, *S. Amer.* 125 D5
Bolivian Plateau, *S. Amer.* 118 D4
Bolkhov, *Russia* 42 D3
Bollène, *France* 27 D8
Bollnäs, *Sweden* 10 C10
Bollon, *Australia* 91 D4
Bollstabruk, *Sweden* 10 A11
Bollullos, *Spain* 31 H4
Bolmen, *Sweden* 9 H15
Bolobo, *Zaïre* 80 E3
Bologna, *Italy* 33 D8
Bologne, *France* 25 D12
Bologoye, *Russia* 42 B2
Bolomba, *Zaïre* 80 D3
Bolonchenticul, *Mexico* . 115 D7
Bolong, *Phil.* 57 C6
Boloven, Cao Nguyen,
  Laos 58 E6
Bolpur, *India* 63 H12
Bolsena, *Italy* 33 F8
Bolsena, L. di, *Italy* 33 F8
Bolshaya Chernigovka,
  Russia 42 D10
Bolshaya Glushitsa, *Russia* 42 D10
Bolshaya Martynovka,
  Russia 43 G5
Bolshaya Vradiyevka,
  Ukraine 41 J6
Bolshereche, *Russia* 44 D8
Bolshevik, Ostrov, *Russia* 45 B11
Bolshoi Kavkas = Caucasus
  Mountains, *Eurasia* .. 43 J7

Bolshoy Anyuy →, *Russia* 45 C17
Bolshoy Atlym, *Russia* ... 44 C7
Bolshoy Begichev, Ostrov,
  Russia 45 B12
Bolshoy Lyakhovskiy,
  Ostrov, *Russia* 45 B15
Bolshoy Tokmak =
  Tokmak, *Ukraine* 41 J8
Bolshoy Tyuters, Ostrov,
  Russia 9 G22
Bolsward, *Neths.* 16 B7
Boltaña, *Spain* 28 C5
Boltigen, *Switz.* 22 C4
Bolton, *Canada* 106 C5
Bolton, *U.K.* 12 D5
Bolu, *Turkey* 66 B4
Bolungavík, *Iceland* 8 C2
Boluo, *China* 53 F10
Bolvadin, *Turkey* 66 C4
Bolzano, *Italy* 33 B8
Bom Comércio, *Brazil* .. 125 B4
Bom Conselho, *Brazil* ... 122 C4
Bom Despacho, *Brazil* ... 123 E2
Bom Jesus, *Brazil* 122 C3
Bom Jesus da Gurguéia,
  Serra, *Brazil* 122 C3
Bom Jesus da Lapa, *Brazil* 123 D3
Boma, *Zaïre* 80 F2
Bomaderry, *Australia* ... 91 E5
Bombala, *Australia* 91 F4
Bombarral, *Portugal* 31 F1
Bombay, *India* 60 K8
Bomboma, *Zaïre* 80 D3
Bombombwa, *Zaïre* 82 B2
Bomi Hills, *Liberia* 78 D2
Bomili, *Zaïre* 82 B2
Bømlo, *Norway* 9 G11
Bommel, *Neths.* 16 E4
Bomokandi →, *Zaïre* ... 82 B2
Bomongo, *Zaïre* 80 D3
Bomu →, *C.A.R.* 80 D4
Bon, C., *Tunisia* 75 A7
Bon Sar Pa, *Vietnam* ... 58 F6
Bonaduz, *Switz.* 23 C8
Bonaire, *Neth. Ant.* 117 D6
Bonang, *Australia* 91 F4
Bonanza, *Nic.* 116 D3
Bonaparte Arch., *Australia* 88 B3
Boñar, *Spain* 30 C5
Bonaventure, *Canada* ... 99 C6
Bonavista, *Canada* 99 C9
Bonavista, C., *Canada* .. 99 C9
Bonawan, *Phil.* 55 G5
Bondeno, *Italy* 33 D8
Bondo, *Zaïre* 82 B1
Bondoukou, *Ivory C.* ... 78 D4
Bondowoso, *Indonesia* .. 57 G15
Bone, Teluk, *Indonesia* .. 57 E6
Bonefro, *Italy* 35 A7
Bonerate, *Indonesia* 57 F6
Bonerate, Kepulauan,
  Indonesia 57 F6
Bo'ness, *U.K.* 14 E5
Bonete, Cerro, *Argentina* 126 B2
Bong Son = Hoai Nhon,
  Vietnam 58 E7
Bongabong, *Phil.* 55 E4
Bongandanga, *Zaïre* 80 D4
Bongor, *Chad* 73 F8
Bongouanou, *Ivory C.* .. 78 D4
Bonham, *U.S.A.* 109 J6
Bonheiden, *Belgium* 17 F5
Bonifacio, *France* 27 G13
Bonifacio, Bouches de,
  Medit. S. 34 A2
Bonin Is. = Ogasawara
  Gunto, *Pac. Oc.* 92 E6
Bonke, *Ethiopia* 77 F4
Bonn, *Germany* 18 E3
Bonnat, *France* 26 B5
Bonne Terre, *U.S.A.* 109 G9
Bonners Ferry, *U.S.A.* .. 110 B5
Bonnétable, *France* 24 D7
Bonneuil-Matours, *France* 24 F7
Bonneval, *France* 24 D8
Bonneville, *France* 27 B10
Bonney, L., *Australia* ... 91 F3
Bonnie Downs, *Australia* 90 C3
Bonnie Rock, *Australia* .. 89 F2
Bonny, *Nigeria* 79 E6
Bonny →, *Nigeria* 79 E6
Bonny, Bight of, *Africa* .. 79 E6
Bonny-sur-Loire, *France* . 25 E9
Bonnyville, *Canada* 101 C6
Bonoi, *Indonesia* 57 E9
Bonorva, *Italy* 34 B1
Bonsall, *U.S.A.* 113 M9
Bontang, *Indonesia* 56 D5
Bonthain, *Indonesia* 57 F5
Bonthe, *S. Leone* 78 D2
Bontoc, *Phil.* 55 C4
Bonyeri, *Ghana* 78 D4
Bonython Ra., *Australia* . 88 D4
Bookabie, *Australia* 89 F5
Booker, *U.S.A.* 109 G4
Boolaboolka L., *Australia* 91 E3
Booligal, *Australia* 91 E3
Boom, *Belgium* 17 F4
Boonah, *Australia* 91 D5
Boone, *Iowa, U.S.A.* 108 D8
Boone, *N.C., U.S.A.* 105 G5
Booneville, *Ark., U.S.A.* . 109 H8
Booneville, *Miss., U.S.A.* 105 H1
Boonville, *Calif., U.S.A.* . 112 F3
Boonville, *Ind., U.S.A.* .. 104 F2
Boonville, *Mo., U.S.A.* .. 108 F8
Boonville, *N.Y., U.S.A.* .. 107 C9

Boorindal, *Australia* 91 E4
Boorowa, *Australia* 91 E4
Boothia, Gulf of, *Canada* . 97 A11
Boothia Pen., *Canada* ... 96 A10
Bootle, *U.K.* 12 D4
Booué, *Gabon* 80 E2
Boppard, *Germany* 19 E3
Boquerón □, *Paraguay* .. 125 E5
Boquete, *Panama* 116 E3
Boquilla, Presa de la,
  Mexico 114 B3
Boquillas del Carmen,
  Mexico 114 A4
Bor, *Czech.* 20 F2
Bor, *Russia* 42 B7
Bor, *Serbia, Yug.* 21 L12
Bôr, *Sudan* 77 F3
Bor, *Turkey* 66 D6
Bor Mashash, *Israel* 69 D3
Borāda →, *Syria* 69 B5
Borah Peak, *U.S.A.* 110 D7
Borama, *Somali Rep.* ... 68 F3
Borang, *Sudan* 77 G3
Borås, *Sweden* 11 G6
Borāzjān, *Iran* 65 D6
Borba, *Brazil* 121 D6
Borba, *Portugal* 31 G3
Borborema, Planalto da,
  Brazil 122 C4
Borça, *Turkey* 67 B9
Borculo, *Neths.* 16 D9
Bord Khūn-e Now, *Iran* . 65 D6
Borda, C., *Australia* 91 F2
Bordeaux, *France* 26 D3
Borden, *Australia* 89 F2
Borden, *Canada* 99 C7
Borden I., *Canada* 4 B2
Borders □, *U.K.* 14 F6
Bordertown, *Australia* .. 91 F3
Borðeyri, *Iceland* 8 D3
Bordighera, *Italy* 32 E4
Bordj bou Arreridj, *Algeria* 75 A5
Bordj Bourguiba, *Tunisia* 75 B7
Bordj Fly Ste. Marie,
  Algeria 74 C4
Bordj-in-Eker, *Algeria* ... 75 D6
Bordj Menaiel, *Algeria* .. 75 A5
Bordj Messouda, *Algeria* 75 B6
Bordj Nili, *Algeria* 75 B5
Bordj Omar Driss, *Algeria* 75 C6
Bordj Sif Fatima, *Algeria* 75 B6
Bordj-Tarat, *Algeria* 75 C6
Bordj Zelfana, *Algeria* ... 75 B5
Borensberg, *Sweden* 11 F9
Borgå = Porvoo, *Finland* . 9 F21
Borgarnes, *Iceland* 8 D3
Børgefjellet, *Norway* 8 D15
Borger, *Neths.* 16 C9
Borger, *U.S.A.* 109 H4
Borgerhout, *Belgium* ... 17 F4
Borghamn, *Sweden* 11 F8
Borgholm, *Sweden* 9 H17
Bórgia, *Italy* 35 D9
Borgloon, *Belgium* 17 G6
Borgo San Dalmazzo, *Italy* 32 D4
Borgo San Lorenzo, *Italy* . 33 E8
Borgo Valsugana, *Italy* .. 32 C5
Borgonovo Val Tidone,
  Italy 32 C6
Borgorose, *Italy* 33 F10
Borgosésia, *Italy* 32 C5
Borgvattnet, *Sweden* ... 10 A9
Borikhane, *Laos* 58 C4
Borisoglebsk, *Russia* 42 E6
Borisov = Barysaw,
  Belarus 40 E5
Borisovka, *Russia* 42 E3
Borja, *Peru* 120 D2
Borja, *Spain* 28 D3
Borjas Blancas, *Spain* ... 28 D5
Borjomi, *Georgia* 43 K6
Borken, *Germany* 18 D2
Borkou, *Chad* 73 E8
Borkum, *Germany* 18 B2
Borlänge, *Sweden* 9 F16
Borley, C., *Antarctica* ... 5 C5
Bormida →, *Italy* 32 D5
Bórmio, *Italy* 32 B7
Born, *Neths.* 17 F7
Borna, *Germany* 18 D8
Borndiep, *Neths.* 16 B7
Borne, *Neths.* 16 D9
Bornem, *Belgium* 17 F4
Borneo, *E. Indies* 56 D5
Bornholm, *Denmark* 9 J16
Borno □, *Nigeria* 79 C7
Bornos, *Spain* 31 J5
Bornu Yassa, *Nigeria* ... 79 C7
Borobudur, *Indonesia* ... 57 G14
Borodino, *Russia* 42 C2
Borogontsy, *Russia* 45 C14
Boromo, *Burkina Faso* .. 78 C4
Boron, *U.S.A.* 113 L9
Borongan, *Phil.* 55 F6
Bororen, *Australia* 90 C5
Borotangba Mts., *C.A.R.* 77 F1
Borovan, *Bulgaria* 38 F6
Borovichi, *Russia* 42 B7
Borovsk, *Russia* 42 C3
Borrego Springs, *U.S.A.* . 113 M10
Borriol, *Spain* 28 E4
Borroloola, *Australia* ... 90 B2
Borşa, *Romania* 38 B7
Borssele, *Neths.* 17 F3
Bort-les-Orgues, *France* . 26 C6
Borth, *U.K.* 13 E3

Borūjerd, *Iran* 67 F13
Boryslav, *Ukraine* 41 H2
Boryspil, *Ukraine* 41 G6
Borzhomi = Borjomi,
  Georgia 43 K6
Borzna, *Ukraine* 41 G7
Borzya, *Russia* 45 D12
Bosa, *Italy* 34 B1
Bosanska Dubica, *Bos.-H.* 33 C13
Bosanska Gradiška,
  Bos.-H. 21 K7
Bosanska Kostajnica,
  Bos.-H. 33 C13
Bosanska Krupa, *Bos.-H.* 33 D13
Bosanski Novi, *Bos.-H.* .. 33 C13
Bosanski Šamac, *Bos.-H.* 21 K8
Bosansko Grahovo,
  Bos.-H. 33 D13
Bosansko Petrovac,
  Bos.-H. 33 D13
Bosaso, *Somali Rep.* 68 E4
Boscastle, *U.K.* 13 G3
Boscotrecase, *Italy* 35 B7
Bose, *China* 52 F6
Boshan, *China* 51 F9
Boshof, *S. Africa* 84 D4
Boshrūyeh, *Iran* 65 C8
Bosilegrad, *Serbia, Yug.* . 21 N12
Boskoop, *Neths.* 16 D5
Bosna →, *Bos.-H.* 21 K8
Bosna i Hercegovina =
  Bosnia-Herzegovina ■,
  Europe 21 L7
Bosnia-Herzegovina ■,
  Europe 21 L7
Bosnik, *Indonesia* 57 E9
Bosobolo, *Zaïre* 80 D3
Bosporus = Karadeniz
  Boğazı, *Turkey* 66 B3
Bossangoa, *C.A.R.* 73 G8
Bossembélé, *C.A.R.* 73 G8
Bossier City, *U.S.A.* 109 J8
Bosso, *Niger* 79 C7
Bostānābād, *Iran* 67 D12
Bosten Hu, *China* 54 B3
Boston, *U.K.* 12 E7
Boston, *U.S.A.* 107 D13
Boston Bar, *Canada* 100 D4
Bosut →, *Croatia* 21 K8
Boswell, *Canada* 100 D5
Boswell, *Okla., U.S.A.* .. 109 H7
Boswell, *Pa., U.S.A.* 106 F5
Botad, *India* 62 H4
Botan →, *Turkey* 67 D10
Botany B., *Australia* 91 E5
Botene, *Laos* 58 D3
Botevgrad, *Bulgaria* 38 G6
Bothaville, *S. Africa* 84 D4
Bothnia, G. of, *Europe* .. 8 E19
Bothwell, *Australia* 90 G4
Bothwell, *Canada* 106 D3
Boticas, *Portugal* 30 D3
Botletle →, *Botswana* ... 84 C3
Botlikh, *Russia* 43 J8
Botoşani, *Romania* 38 B9
Botro, *Ivory C.* 78 D3
Botswana ■, *Africa* 84 C3
Bottineau, *U.S.A.* 108 A4
Bottrop, *Germany* 17 E9
Botucatu, *Brazil* 127 A6
Botwood, *Canada* 99 C8
Bou Alam, *Algeria* 75 B5
Bou Ali, *Algeria* 75 C4
Bou Djébéha, *Mali* 78 B4
Bou Guema, *Algeria* 75 C5
Bou Ismael, *Algeria* 75 A5
Bou Izakarn, *Morocco* .. 74 C3
Boû Lanouâr, *Mauritania* 74 D1
Bou Saâda, *Algeria* 75 A5
Bou Salem, *Tunisia* 75 A6
Bouaké, *Ivory C.* 78 D3
Bouar, *C.A.R.* 80 C3
Bouârfa, *Morocco* 75 B4
Bouca, *C.A.R.* 73 G8
Boucau, *France* 26 E2
Boucaut B., *Australia* ... 90 A1
Bouches-du-Rhône □,
  France 27 E9
Bouda, *Algeria* 75 C4
Boudenib, *Morocco* 74 B4
Boudry, *Switz.* 22 C3
Boufarik, *Algeria* 75 A5
Bougainville, C., *Australia* 88 B4
Bougainville Reef,
  Australia 90 B4
Bougaroun, C., *Algeria* .. 75 A6
Bougie = Bejaia, *Algeria* . 75 A6
Bougouni, *Mali* 78 C3
Bouillon, *Belgium* 17 J6
Bouïra, *Algeria* 75 A5
Boulder, *Colo., U.S.A.* .. 108 E2
Boulder, *Mont., U.S.A.* .. 110 C7
Boulder City, *U.S.A.* 113 K12
Boulder Creek, *U.S.A.* .. 112 H4
Boulder Dam = Hoover
  Dam, *U.S.A.* 113 K12
Bouli, *Mauritania* 78 B2
Boulia, *Australia* 90 C2
Bouligny, *France* 25 C12
Boulogne →, *France* 24 E5
Boulogne-sur-Gesse, *France* 26 E4
Boulogne-sur-Mer, *France* 25 B8
Bouloire, *France* 24 E7
Boulsa, *Burkina Faso* ... 79 C4
Boultoum, *Niger* 79 C7
Boumalne, *Morocco* 74 B3
Boun Neua, *Laos* 58 B3

Boun Tai, *Laos* 58 B3
Bouna, *Ivory C.* 78 D4
Boundary Peak, *U.S.A.* .. 112 H8
Boundiali, *Ivory C.* 78 D3
Bountiful, *U.S.A.* 110 F8
Bounty Is., *Pac. Oc.* 92 M9
Bourbon-Lancy, *France* .. 26 B7
Bourbon-l'Archambault,
  France 26 B7
Bourbonnais, *France* 26 B7
Bourbonne-les-Bains,
  France 25 E12
Bourem, *Mali* 79 B4
Bourg, *France* 26 C3
Bourg-Argental, *France* .. 27 C8
Bourg-de-Péage, *France* . 27 C9
Bourg-en-Bresse, *France* . 27 B9
Bourg-St.-Andéol, *France* 27 C8
Bourg-St.-Maurice, *France* 27 C10
Bourg-St.-Pierre, *Switz.* . 22 E4
Bourganeuf, *France* 26 C5
Bourget, *Canada* 107 A9
Bourget, L. du, *France* ... 27 C9
Bourgneuf, B. de, *France* . 24 E4
Bourgneuf-en-Retz, *France* 24 E5
Bourgogne, *France* 25 F11
Bourgoin-Jallieu, *France* . 27 C9
Bourgueil, *France* 24 E7
Bourke, *Australia* 91 E4
Bournemouth, *U.K.* 13 G6
Bourriot-Bergonce, *France* 26 D3
Bouse, *U.S.A.* 113 M13
Boussac, *France* 26 B6
Boussens, *France* 26 E4
Boussu, *Belgium* 17 H3
Boutilimit, *Mauritania* ... 78 B2
Boutonne →, *France* 26 C3
Bouvet I. = Bouvetøya,
  Antarctica 3 G10
Bouvetøya, *Antarctica* ... 3 G10
Bouznika, *Morocco* 74 B3
Bouzonville, *France* 25 C13
Bova Marina, *Italy* 35 E8
Bovalino Marina, *Italy* .. 35 D9
Bovec, *Slovenia* 33 B10
Bovenkarspel, *Neths.* ... 16 C6
Bovigny, *Belgium* 17 H7
Bovill, *U.S.A.* 110 C5
Bovino, *Italy* 35 A8
Bow Island, *Canada* 100 D6
Bowbells, *U.S.A.* 108 A3
Bowdle, *U.S.A.* 108 C5
Bowelling, *Australia* 89 F2
Bowen, *Australia* 90 C4
Bowen Mts., *Australia* ... 91 F4
Bowie, *Ariz., U.S.A.* 111 K9
Bowie, *Tex., U.S.A.* 109 J6
Bowkān, *Iran* 67 D12
Bowland, Forest of, *U.K.* . 12 D5
Bowling Green, *Ky.,
  U.S.A.* 104 G2
Bowling Green, *Ohio,
  U.S.A.* 104 E4
Bowling Green, C.,
  Australia 90 B4
Bowman, *U.S.A.* 108 B3
Bowman I., *Antarctica* .. 5 C8
Bowmans, *Australia* 91 E2
Bowmanville, *Canada* ... 98 D4
Bowmore, *U.K.* 14 F2
Bowral, *Australia* 91 E5
Bowraville, *Australia* ... 91 E5
Bowron →, *Canada* 100 C4
Bowser L., *Canada* 100 B3
Bowsman, *Canada* 101 C8
Bowwood, *Zambia* 83 F2
Boxholm, *Sweden* 11 F9
Boxmeer, *Neths.* 17 E7
Boxtel, *Neths.* 17 E6
Boyabat, *Turkey* 66 B6
Boyaca □ = Casanare □,
  Colombia 120 B3
Boyce, *U.S.A.* 109 K8
Boyer →, *Canada* 100 B5
Boyle, *Ireland* 15 C3
Boyne →, *Ireland* 15 C5
Boyne City, *U.S.A.* 104 C3
Boynton Beach, *U.S.A.* .. 105 M5
Boyoma, Chutes, *Zaïre* .. 82 B2
Boyup Brook, *Australia* .. 89 F2
Boz Dağ, *Turkey* 66 D3
Boz Dağları, *Turkey* 66 C3
Bozburun, *Turkey* 66 D3
Bozcaada, *Turkey* 66 C2
Bozdoğan, *Turkey* 66 D3
Bozeman, *U.S.A.* 110 D8
Bozen = Bolzano, *Italy* .. 33 B8
Bozkır, *Turkey* 66 D5
Bozouls, *France* 26 D6
Bozoum, *C.A.R.* 73 G8
Bozova, *Turkey* 67 D8
Bozovici, *Romania* 38 E5
Bozüyük, *Turkey* 66 C4
Bra, *Italy* 32 D4
Brabant □, *Belgium* 17 G5
Brabant L., *Canada* 101 B8
Brabrand, *Denmark* 11 H4
Brač, *Croatia* 33 E13
Bracadale, L., *U.K.* 14 D2
Bracciano, *Italy* 33 F9
Bracciano, L. di, *Italy* ... 33 F9
Bracebridge, *Canada* 98 C4
Brach, *Libya* 73 C7
Bracieux, *France* 25 E8
Bräcke, *Sweden* 10 B9

Brackettville

Brackettville, U.S.A. 109 L4
Brački Kanal, Croatia 33 E13
Brad, Romania 38 C5
Brádano →, Italy 35 B9
Bradenton, U.S.A. 105 M4
Bradford, Canada 106 B5
Bradford, U.K. 12 D6
Bradford, Pa., U.S.A. 106 E6
Bradford, Vt., U.S.A. 107 C12
Brădiceni, Romania 38 D6
Bradley, Ark., U.S.A. 109 J8
Bradley, Calif., U.S.A. 112 K6
Bradley, S. Dak., U.S.A. 108 C6
Bradley Institute, Zimbabwe 83 F3
Bradore Bay, Canada 99 B8
Bradshaw, Australia 88 C5
Brady, U.S.A. 109 K5
Brædstrup, Denmark 11 J3
Braemar, Australia 91 E2
Braeside, Canada 107 A8
Braga, Portugal 30 D2
Braga □, Portugal 30 D2
Bragado, Argentina 126 D3
Bragança, Brazil 122 B2
Bragança, Portugal 30 D4
Bragança □, Portugal 30 D4
Bragança Paulista, Brazil 127 A6
Brahmanbaria, Bangla. 61 H17
Brahmani →, India 61 J15
Brahmaputra →, India 63 G13
Braich-y-pwll, U.K. 12 E3
Braidwood, Australia 91 F4
Brăila, Romania 38 D10
Braine-l'Alleud, Belgium 17 G4
Braine-le-Comte, Belgium 17 G4
Brainerd, U.S.A. 108 B7
Braintree, U.K. 13 F8
Braintree, U.S.A. 107 D14
Brak →, S. Africa 84 D3
Brake, Germany 18 B4
Brakel, Germany 18 D5
Brakel, Neths. 16 E6
Brakwater, Namibia 84 C2
Brålanda, Sweden 11 F6
Bralorne, Canada 100 C4
Bramberg, Germany 19 E6
Bramminge, Denmark 11 J2
Brämön, Sweden 10 B11
Brampton, Canada 98 D4
Bramsche, Germany 18 C3
Bramwell, Australia 90 A3
Branco →, Brazil 121 D5
Branco, C., Brazil 122 C5
Brande, Denmark 11 J3
Brandenburg = Neubrandenburg, Germany 18 B9
Brandenburg, Germany 18 C8
Brandenburg □, Germany 18 C9
Brandfort, S. Africa 84 D4
Brandon, Canada 101 D9
Brandon, U.S.A. 107 C11
Brandon B., Ireland 15 D1
Brandon Mt., Ireland 15 D1
Brandsen, Argentina 126 D4
Brandval, Norway 10 D6
Brandvlei, S. Africa 84 E3
Branford, U.S.A. 107 E12
Braniewo, Poland 20 A9
Bransfield Str., Antarctica 5 C18
Branson, Colo., U.S.A. 109 G3
Branson, Mo., U.S.A. 109 G8
Brantford, Canada 98 D3
Brantôme, France 26 C4
Branxholme, Australia 91 F3
Branzi, Italy 32 B6
Bras d'Or, L., Canada 99 C7
Brasiléia, Brazil 124 C4
Brasília, Brazil 123 E2
Brasília Legal, Brazil 121 D6
Braslaw, Belarus 9 J22
Braslovce, Slovenia 33 B12
Braşov, Romania 38 D8
Brass, Nigeria 79 E6
Brass →, Nigeria 79 E6
Brassac-les-Mines, France 26 C7
Brasschaat, Belgium 17 F4
Brassey, Banjaran, Malaysia 56 D5
Brassey Ra., Australia 89 E3
Brasstown Bald, U.S.A. 105 H4
Brastad, Sweden 9 G14
Bratislava, Slovak Rep. 21 G7
Bratsk, Russia 45 D11
Brattleboro, U.S.A. 107 D12
Braunau, Austria 21 G3
Braunschweig, Germany 18 C6
Braunton, U.K. 13 F3
Brava, Somali Rep. 68 G3
Bråviken, Sweden 10 F10
Bravo del Norte →, Mexico 114 B5
Bravo del Norte, R. = Grande, Rio →, U.S.A. 109 N6
Brawley, U.S.A. 113 N11
Bray, Ireland 15 C5
Bray, Mt., Australia 90 A1
Bray, Pays de, France 25 C8
Bray-sur-Seine, France 25 D10
Brazeau →, Canada 100 C5
Brazil, U.S.A. 104 F2
Brazil ■, S. Amer. 123 D2
Brazo Sur →, S. Amer. 126 B4
Brazos →, U.S.A. 109 L7
Brazzaville, Congo 80 E3

Brčko, Bos.-H. 21 L8
Brea, Peru 124 A1
Breadalbane, Australia 90 C2
Breadalbane, U.K. 14 E4
Breaden, L., Australia 89 E4
Breaksea Sd., N.Z. 87 L1
Bream B., N.Z. 87 F5
Bream Hd., N.Z. 87 F5
Breas, Chile 126 B1
Brebes, Indonesia 57 G13
Brechin, Canada 106 B5
Brechin, U.K. 14 E6
Brecht, Belgium 17 F5
Breckenridge, Colo., U.S.A. 110 G10
Breckenridge, Minn., U.S.A. 108 B6
Breckenridge, Tex., U.S.A. 109 J5
Breckland, U.K. 13 E8
Brecknock, Pen., Chile 128 D2
Břeclav, Czech. 20 G6
Brecon, U.K. 13 F4
Brecon Beacons, U.K. 13 F4
Breda, Neths. 17 E5
Bredasdorp, S. Africa 84 E3
Bredbo, Australia 91 F4
Bredene, Belgium 17 F1
Bredstedt, Germany 18 A4
Bree, Belgium 17 F7
Breezand, Neths. 16 C5
Bregalnica →, Macedonia 39 H5
Bregenz, Austria 19 H5
Bréhal, France 24 D5
Bréhat, I. de, France 24 D4
Breiðafjörður, Iceland 8 D2
Breil-sur-Roya, France 27 E11
Breisach, Germany 19 G3
Brejinho de Nazaré, Brazil 122 D2
Brejo, Brazil 122 B3
Bremen, Germany 18 B4
Bremen □, Germany 18 B4
Bremer I., Australia 90 A2
Bremerton, U.S.A. 112 C4
Bremervörde, Germany 18 B5
Bremsnes, Norway 10 A1
Brenes, Spain 31 H5
Brenham, U.S.A. 109 K6
Brenner P., Austria 19 H7
Breno, Italy 32 C7
Brent, Canada 98 C4
Brent, U.K. 13 F7
Bréscia, Italy 32 C7
Breskens, Neths. 17 F3
Breslau = Wrocław, Poland 20 D7
Bresle →, France 24 B8
Bresles, France 25 C9
Bressanone, Italy 33 B8
Bressay, U.K. 14 A7
Bresse, France 25 F12
Bressuire, France 24 F6
Brest, Belarus 41 F2
Brest, France 24 D2
Brest-Litovsk = Brest, Belarus 41 F2
Bretagne, France 24 D4
Breţcu, Romania 38 C9
Breteuil, Eure, France 24 D7
Breteuil, Oise, France 25 C9
Breton, Canada 100 C6
Breton, Pertuis, France 26 B2
Breton Sd., U.S.A. 109 L10
Brett, C., N.Z. 87 F5
Bretten, Germany 19 F4
Breukelen, Neths. 16 D6
Brevard, U.S.A. 105 H4
Breves, Brazil 122 B1
Brevik, Norway 10 E3
Brewarrina, Australia 91 D4
Brewer, U.S.A. 99 D6
Brewer, Mt., U.S.A. 112 J8
Brewster, N.Y., U.S.A. 107 E11
Brewster, Wash., U.S.A. 110 B4
Brewster, Kap, Greenland 4 B6
Brewton, U.S.A. 105 K2
Breyten, S. Africa 85 D4
Brezhnev = Naberezhnyye Chelny, Russia 42 C11
Brežice, Slovenia 33 C12
Březina, Algeria 75 B5
Březnice, Czech. 20 F3
Breznik, Bulgaria 38 G5
Brezno, Slovak Rep. 20 G9
Bria, C.A.R. 73 G9
Briançon, France 27 D10
Briare, France 25 E9
Bribie I., Australia 91 D5
Bricquebec, France 24 C5
Bridgehampton, U.S.A. 107 F12
Bridgend, U.K. 13 F4
Bridgeport, Calif., U.S.A. 111 G4
Bridgeport, Conn., U.S.A. 107 E11
Bridgeport, Nebr., U.S.A. 108 E3
Bridgeport, Tex., U.S.A. 109 J6
Bridger, U.S.A. 110 D9
Bridgeton, U.S.A. 104 F8
Bridgetown, Australia 89 F2
Bridgetown, Barbados 117 D8
Bridgetown, Canada 99 D6
Bridgewater, Canada 99 D7
Bridgewater, Mass., U.S.A. 107 E14
Bridgewater, S. Dak., U.S.A. 108 D6
Bridgewater, C., Australia 91 F3

Bridgnorth, U.K. 13 E5
Bridgton, U.S.A. 107 B14
Bridgwater, U.K. 13 F4
Bridlington, U.K. 12 C7
Bridport, Australia 90 G4
Bridport, U.K. 13 G5
Brie, Plaine de la, France 25 D10
Brie-Comte-Robert, France 25 D9
Briec, France 24 D2
Brielle, Neths. 16 E4
Brienon-sur-Armançon, France 25 E10
Brienz, Switz. 22 C6
Brienzersee, Switz. 22 C6
Brig, Switz. 22 D5
Brigg, U.K. 12 D7
Briggsdale, U.S.A. 108 E2
Brigham City, U.S.A. 110 F7
Bright, Australia 91 F4
Brighton, Australia 91 F2
Brighton, Canada 98 D4
Brighton, U.K. 13 G7
Brighton, U.S.A. 108 F2
Brignogan-Plage, France 24 D2
Brignoles, France 27 E10
Brihuega, Spain 28 E2
Brikama, Gambia 78 C1
Brilliant, Canada 100 D5
Brilliant, U.S.A. 106 F4
Brilon, Germany 18 D4
Bríndisi, Italy 35 B10
Brinje, Croatia 33 D12
Brinkley, U.S.A. 109 H9
Brinkworth, Australia 91 E2
Brinnon, U.S.A. 112 C4
Brion, I., Canada 99 C7
Brionne, France 24 C7
Brionski, Croatia 33 D10
Brioude, France 26 C7
Briouze, France 24 D6
Brisbane, Australia 91 D5
Brisbane →, Australia 91 D5
Brisighella, Italy 33 D8
Bristol, U.K. 13 F5
Bristol, Conn., U.S.A. 107 E12
Bristol, Pa., U.S.A. 107 F10
Bristol, R.I., U.S.A. 107 E13
Bristol, S. Dak., U.S.A. 108 C6
Bristol, Tenn., U.S.A. 105 G4
Bristol B., U.S.A. 96 C4
Bristol Channel, U.K. 13 F3
Bristol I., Antarctica 5 B1
Bristol L., U.S.A. 111 J5
Bristow, U.S.A. 109 H6
British Columbia □, Canada 100 C3
British Isles, Europe 6 E5
Brits, S. Africa 85 D4
Britstown, S. Africa 84 E3
Britt, Canada 98 C3
Brittany = Bretagne, France 24 D4
Britton, U.S.A. 108 C6
Brive-la-Gaillarde, France 26 C5
Briviesca, Spain 28 C1
Brixen = Bressanone, Italy 33 B8
Brixton, Australia 90 C3
Brlik, Kazakhstan 44 E8
Brno, Czech. 20 F6
Bro, Sweden 10 E11
Broad →, U.S.A. 105 J5
Broad Arrow, Australia 89 F3
Broad B., U.K. 14 C2
Broad Haven, Ireland 15 B2
Broad Law, U.K. 14 F5
Broad Sd., Australia 90 C4
Broadhurst Ra., Australia 88 D3
Broads, The, U.K. 12 E9
Broadus, U.S.A. 108 C2
Broadview, Canada 101 C8
Broager, Denmark 11 K3
Broaryd, Sweden 11 G7
Brochet, Canada 101 B8
Brochet, L., Canada 101 B8
Brock, Canada 101 C7
Brocken, Germany 18 D6
Brockport, U.S.A. 106 C7
Brockton, U.S.A. 107 D13
Brockville, Canada 98 D4
Brockway, Mont., U.S.A. 108 B2
Brockway, Pa., U.S.A. 106 E6
Brocton, U.S.A. 106 D5
Brod, Macedonia 39 H4
Brodarevo, Serbia, Yug. 21 M9
Brodeur Pen., Canada 97 A11
Brodick, U.K. 14 F3
Brodnica, Poland 20 B9
Brody, Ukraine 41 G3
Broechem, Belgium 17 F5
Broek, Neths. 16 B6
Broek op Langedijk, Neths. 16 C5
Brogan, U.S.A. 110 D5
Broglie, France 24 C7
Broken Bow, Nebr., U.S.A. 108 E5
Broken Bow, Okla., U.S.A. 109 H7
Broken Hill = Kabwe, Zambia 83 E2
Broken Hill, Australia 91 E3
Brokind, Sweden 11 F9
Brokopondo, Surinam 121 B7
Brokopondo □, Surinam 121 C6
Bromfield, U.K. 13 E5
Bromley, U.K. 13 F8
Brønderslev, Denmark 11 G3

Brong-Ahafo □, Ghana 78 D4
Bronkhorstspruit, S. Africa 85 D4
Brønnøysund, Norway 8 D15
Bronte, Italy 35 E7
Bronte, U.S.A. 109 K4
Bronte Park, Australia 90 G4
Brook Park, U.S.A. 106 E4
Brookfield, U.S.A. 108 F8
Brookhaven, U.S.A. 109 K9
Brookings, Oreg., U.S.A. 110 E1
Brookings, S. Dak., U.S.A. 108 C6
Brooklin, Canada 106 C6
Brookmere, Canada 100 D4
Brooks, Canada 100 C6
Brooks B., Canada 100 C3
Brooks L., Canada 101 A7
Brooks Ra., U.S.A. 96 B5
Brooksville, U.S.A. 105 L4
Brookville, U.S.A. 104 F3
Brooloo, Australia 91 D5
Broom, L., U.K. 14 D3
Broome, Australia 88 C3
Broomehill, Australia 89 F2
Broons, France 24 D4
Brora, U.K. 14 C5
Brora →, U.K. 14 C5
Brosna →, Ireland 15 C4
Broşteni, Romania 38 B8
Brotas de Macaúbas, Brazil 123 D3
Brothers, U.S.A. 110 E3
Brøttum, Norway 10 C4
Brou, France 24 D8
Brouage, Ramparts de, France 26 C2
Brough, U.K. 12 C5
Broughton Island, Canada 97 B13
Broughty Ferry, U.K. 14 E6
Brouwershaven, Neths. 16 E3
Brouwershavensche Gat, Neths. 16 E3
Brovary, Ukraine 41 G6
Brovst, Denmark 11 G3
Browerville, U.S.A. 108 B7
Brown, Pt., Australia 91 E1
Brown Willy, U.K. 13 G3
Brownfield, U.S.A. 109 J3
Browning, U.S.A. 110 B7
Brownlee, Canada 101 C7
Brownsville, Oreg., U.S.A. 110 D2
Brownsville, Tenn., U.S.A. 109 H10
Brownsville, Tex., U.S.A. 109 N6
Brownsweg, Surinam 121 B6
Brownwood, U.S.A. 109 K5
Brownwood, L., U.S.A. 109 K5
Browse I., Australia 88 B3
Broye →, Switz. 22 C3
Brozas, Spain 31 F4
Bruas, Malaysia 59 K3
Bruay-en-Artois, France 25 B9
Bruce, Mt., Australia 88 D2
Bruce Pen., Canada 106 A3
Bruce Rock, Australia 89 F2
Bruche →, France 25 D14
Bruchsal, Germany 19 F4
Bruck an der Leitha, Austria 21 G6
Bruck an der Mur, Austria 21 H5
Brue →, U.K. 13 F5
Brugelette, Belgium 17 G3
Bruges = Brugge, Belgium 17 F2
Brugg, Switz. 22 B6
Brugge, Belgium 17 F2
Brühl, Germany 18 E2
Bruinisse, Neths. 17 E4
Brûlé, Canada 100 C5
Brûlon, France 24 E6
Brûly, Belgium 17 J5
Brumado, Brazil 123 D3
Brumado →, Brazil 123 D3
Brumath, France 25 D14
Brummen, Neths. 16 D8
Brumunddal, Norway 10 D4
Brunchilly, Australia 90 B1
Brundidge, U.S.A. 105 K3
Bruneau, U.S.A. 110 E6
Bruneau →, U.S.A. 110 E6
Bruneck = Brunico, Italy 33 B8
Brunei = Bandar Seri Begawan, Brunei 56 C4
Brunei ■, Asia 56 C4
Brunette Downs, Australia 90 B2
Brunflo, Sweden 10 A8
Brunico, Italy 33 B8
Brünig, P., Switz. 22 C6
Brunkeberg, Norway 10 E2
Brunna, Sweden 10 E11
Brunnen, Switz. 23 C7
Brunner, L., N.Z. 87 K3
Bruno, Canada 101 C7
Brunsbüttel, Germany 18 B5
Brunssum, Neths. 17 G7
Brunswick = Braunschweig, Germany 18 C6
Brunswick, Ga., U.S.A. 105 K5
Brunswick, Maine, U.S.A. 99 D6
Brunswick, Md., U.S.A. 104 F7
Brunswick, Mo., U.S.A. 108 F8
Brunswick, Ohio, U.S.A. 106 E3
Brunswick, Pen. de, Chile 128 D2
Brunswick B., Australia 88 C3
Brunswick Junction, Australia 89 F2
Bruntál, Czech. 20 F7
Bruny I., Australia 90 G4
Brus Laguna, Honduras 116 C3
Brusartsi, Bulgaria 38 F6
Brush, U.S.A. 108 E3

Brushton, U.S.A. 107 B10
Brusio, Switz. 23 D10
Brusque, Brazil 127 B6
Brussel, Belgium 17 G4
Brussels = Brussel, Belgium 17 G4
Brussels, Canada 106 C3
Brustem, Belgium 17 G6
Bruthen, Australia 91 F4
Bruxelles = Brussel, Belgium 17 G4
Bruyères, France 25 D13
Bryan, Ohio, U.S.A. 104 E3
Bryan, Tex., U.S.A. 109 K6
Bryan, Mt., Australia 91 E2
Bryanka, Ukraine 41 H10
Bryansk, Russia 42 D2
Bryansk, Russia 43 H8
Bryanskoye = Bryansk, Russia 43 H8
Bryant, U.S.A. 108 C6
Bryne, Norway 9 G11
Bryson City, U.S.A. 105 H4
Bryukhovetskaya, Russia 43 H4
Brza Palanka, Serbia, Yug. 21 L12
Brzeg, Poland 20 E7
Brzeg Din, Poland 20 D6
Brzava →, Serbia, Yug. 21 K10
Bsharri, Lebanon 69 A5
Bū Baqarah, U.A.E. 65 E8
Bu Craa, W. Sahara 74 C2
Bū Ḥasā, U.A.E. 65 F7
Bua Yai, Thailand 58 E4
Buapinang, Indonesia 57 E6
Buayan, Phil. 57 C7
Buba, Guinea-Biss. 78 C2
Bubanza, Burundi 82 C2
Būbiyān, Kuwait 65 D6
Bucak, Turkey 66 D4
Bucaramanga, Colombia 120 B3
Bucas Grande I., Phil. 55 G6
Buccaneer Arch., Australia 88 C3
Bucchiánico, Italy 33 F11
Bucecea, Romania 38 B9
Buchach, Ukraine 41 H3
Buchan, U.K. 14 D6
Buchan Ness, U.K. 14 D7
Buchanan, Canada 101 C8
Buchanan, Liberia 78 D2
Buchanan, L., Queens., Australia 90 C4
Buchanan, L., W. Austral., Australia 89 E3
Buchanan, L., U.S.A. 109 K5
Buchanan Cr. →, Australia 90 B2
Buchans, Canada 99 C8
Bucharest = Bucureşti, Romania 38 E9
Buchholz, Germany 18 B5
Buchloe, Germany 19 G6
Buchon, Pt., U.S.A. 112 K6
Buchs, Switz. 23 B8
Bückeburg, Germany 18 C5
Buckeye, U.S.A. 111 K7
Buckhannon, U.S.A. 104 F5
Buckhaven, U.K. 14 E5
Buckie, U.K. 14 D6
Buckingham, Canada 98 C4
Buckingham, U.K. 13 F7
Buckingham B., Australia 90 A2
Buckinghamshire □, U.K. 13 F7
Buckle Hd., Australia 88 B4
Buckleboo, Australia 91 E2
Buckley, U.S.A. 110 C2
Buckley →, Australia 90 C2
Bucklin, U.S.A. 109 G5
Bucks L., U.S.A. 112 F5
Bucquoy, France 25 B9
Buctouche, Canada 99 C7
Bucureşti, Romania 38 E9
Bucyrus, U.S.A. 104 E4
Budafok, Hungary 21 H9
Budalin, Burma 61 H19
Budapest, Hungary 21 H9
Budaun, India 63 E8
Budd Coast, Antarctica 5 C8
Buddusò, Italy 34 B2
Bude, U.K. 13 G3
Budel, Neths. 17 F7
Budennovsk, Russia 43 H7
Budeşti, Romania 38 E9
Budge Budge = Baj Baj, India 63 H13
Budgewoi, Australia 91 E5
Búðareyri, Iceland 8 D6
Budia, Spain 28 E2
Budjala, Zaïre 80 D3
Búdrio, Italy 33 D8
Buea, Cameroon 79 E6
Buellton, U.S.A. 113 L6
Buena Vista, Colo., U.S.A. 111 G10
Buena Vista, Va., U.S.A. 104 G6
Buena Vista L., U.S.A. 113 K7
Buenaventura, Colombia 120 C2
Buenaventura, Mexico 114 B3
Buenaventura, B. de, Colombia 120 C2
Buendía, Pantano de, Spain 28 E2
Buenópolis, Brazil 123 E3
Buenos Aires, Argentina 126 C4
Buenos Aires, Colombia 120 C3
Buenos Aires, Costa Rica 116 E3
Buenos Aires □, Argentina 126 D4
Buenos Aires, L., Chile 128 C2
Buesaco, Colombia 120 C2
Buffalo, Mo., U.S.A. 109 G8

Buffalo, N.Y., U.S.A. 106 D6
Buffalo, Okla., U.S.A. ... 109 G5
Buffalo, S. Dak., U.S.A. .. 108 C3
Buffalo, Wyo., U.S.A. 110 D10
Buffalo →, Canada 100 A5
Buffalo Head Hills, Canada 100 B5
Buffalo L., Canada 100 C6
Buffalo Narrows, Canada . 101 B7
Buffels →, S. Africa 84 D2
Buford, U.S.A. 105 H4
Bug = Buh →, Ukraine ... 41 J6
Bug →, Poland 20 C11
Buga, Colombia 120 C2
Buganda, Uganda 82 C3
Buganga, Uganda 82 C3
Bugasong, Phil. 55 F5
Bugeat, France 26 C5
Bugel, Tanjung, Indonesia 56 F4
Buggenhout, Belgium 17 F4
Bugibba, Malta 37 D1
Bugsuk, Phil. 55 G2
Buguma, Nigeria 79 E6
Bugun Shara, Mongolia .. 54 B5
Buguruslan, Russia 44 D6
Buh →, Ukraine 41 J6
Buhăești, Romania 38 C10
Buheirat-Murrat-el-Kubra,
  Egypt 76 H8
Buhl, Idaho, U.S.A. 110 E6
Buhl, Minn., U.S.A. 108 B8
Buick, U.S.A. 109 G9
Builth Wells, U.K. 13 E4
Buinsk, Russia 42 C9
Buíque, Brazil 122 C4
Buir Nur, Mongolia 54 B6
Buis-les-Baronnies, France 27 D9
Buitenpost, Neths. 16 B8
Buitrago, Spain 30 E7
Bujalance, Spain 31 H6
Bujaraloz, Spain 28 D4
Buján, Spain 30 C2
Buje, Croatia 33 C10
Bujumbura, Burundi 82 C2
Bukachacha, Russia 45 D12
Bukama, Zaïre 83 D2
Bukavu, Zaïre 82 C2
Bukene, Tanzania 82 C3
Bukhara = Bukhoro,
  Uzbekistan 44 F7
Bukhoro, Uzbekistan 44 F7
Bukima, Tanzania 82 C3
Bukit Mertajam, Malaysia 59 K3
Bukittinggi, Indonesia .. 56 E2
Bukoba, Tanzania 82 C3
Bukoba □, Tanzania 82 C3
Bukuru, Nigeria 79 D6
Bukuya, Uganda 82 B3
Bula, Guinea-Biss. 78 C1
Bula, Indonesia 57 E8
Bülach, Switz. 23 A7
Bulahdelah, Australia ... 91 E5
Bulan, Phil. 55 E5
Bulancak, Turkey 67 B8
Bulandshahr, India 62 E7
Bulanık, Turkey 67 C10
Bûlâq, Egypt 76 B3
Bulawayo, Zimbabwe ... 83 G2
Buldan, Turkey 66 C3
Bulgan, Mongolia 54 B5
Bulgar, Russia 42 C9
Bulgaria ■, Europe 38 G8
Bulgroo, Australia 91 D3
Bulgunnia, Australia ... 91 E1
Bulhar, Somali Rep. 68 E3
Buli, Teluk, Indonesia .. 57 D7
Buliluyan, C., Phil. 55 G2
Bulki, Ethiopia 77 F4
Bulkley →, Canada 100 B3
Bull Shoals L., U.S.A. .. 109 G8
Bullange, Belgium 17 H8
Bullaque →, Spain 31 G6
Bullara, Australia 88 D1
Bullaring, Australia 89 F2
Bullas, Spain 29 G3
Bulle, Switz. 22 C4
Bulli, Australia 91 E5
Bullock Creek, Australia 90 B3
Bulloo →, Australia ... 91 D3
Bulloo Downs, Queens.,
  Australia 91 D3
Bulloo Downs, W. Austral.,
  Australia 88 D2
Bulloo L., Australia 91 D3
Bulls, N.Z. 87 J5
Bully-les-Mines, France .. 25 B9
Bulnes, Chile 126 D1
Bulo Burti, Somali Rep. . 68 G4
Bulsar = Valsad, India .. 60 J8
Bultfontein, S. Africa ... 84 D4
Bulu Karakelong, Indonesia 57 D7
Bulukumba, Indonesia .. 57 F6
Bulun, Russia 45 B13
Bulus, Russia 45 C13
Bumba, Zaïre 80 D4
Bumbiri I., Tanzania 82 C3
Bumhpa Bum, Burma ... 61 F20
Bumi →, Zimbabwe 83 F2
Buna, Kenya 82 B4
Bunawan, Agusan del S.,
  Phil. 55 G6
Bunawan, Davao del S.,
  Phil. 55 H6
Bunazi, Tanzania 82 C3
Bunbah, Khalīj, Libya ... 73 B9
Bunbury, Australia 89 F2
Buncrana, Ireland 15 A4
Bundaberg, Australia ... 91 C5

Bünde, Germany 18 C4
Bundey →, Australia ... 90 C2
Bundi, India 62 G6
Bundooma, Australia ... 90 C1
Bundoran, Ireland 15 B3
Bundukia, Sudan 77 F3
Bung Kan, Thailand 58 C4
Bungatakada, Japan 49 H5
Bungil Cr. →, Australia 90 D4
Bungo-Suidō, Japan 49 H6
Bungoma, Kenya 82 B3
Bungu, Tanzania 82 D4
Bunia, Zaïre 82 B3
Bunji, Pakistan 63 B6
Bunkie, U.S.A. 109 K8
Bunnell, U.S.A. 105 L5
Bunnik, Neths. 16 D6
Buñol, Spain 29 F4
Bunsbeek, Belgium 17 G5
Bunschoten, Neths. 16 D6
Buntok, Indonesia 56 E4
Bununu, Nigeria 79 D6
Bununu Dass, Nigeria .. 79 C6
Bünyan, Turkey 66 C6
Bunyu, Indonesia 56 D5
Bunza, Nigeria 79 C5
Buol, Indonesia 57 D6
Buon Brieng, Vietnam .. 58 F7
Buon Me Thuot, Vietnam 58 F7
Buong Long, Cambodia . 58 F6
Buorkhaya, Mys, Russia . 45 B14
Buqayq, Si. Arabia 65 E6
Buqbua, Egypt 76 A2
Bur Acaba, Somali Rep. . 68 G3
Bûr Fuad, Egypt 76 H8
Bûr Safâga, Egypt 76 B3
Bûr Sa'îd, Egypt 76 H8
Bûr Sûdân, Sudan 76 D4
Bûr Taufiq, Egypt 76 J8
Bura, Kenya 82 C4
Burao, Somali Rep. 68 F4
Burãq, Syria 69 B5
Buras, U.S.A. 109 L10
Buraydah, Si. Arabia ... 64 E5
Burbank, U.S.A. 113 L8
Burcher, Australia 91 E4
Burdekin →, Australia . 90 B4
Burdett, Canada 100 D6
Burdur, Turkey 66 D4
Burdur Gölü, Turkey ... 66 D4
Burdwan = Barddhaman,
  India 63 H12
Bure, Ethiopia 77 E4
Bure →, U.K. 12 E9
Büren, Germany 18 D4
Buren, Neths. 16 E6
Bureya →, Russia 45 E13
Burford, Canada 106 C4
Burg, Germany 18 C7
Burg auf Fehmarn,
  Germany 18 A7
Burg el Arab, Egypt ... 76 H6
Burg et Tuyur, Sudan .. 76 C2
Burg Stargard, Germany 18 B9
Burgas, Bulgaria 38 G10
Burgdorf, Germany 18 C5
Burgdorf, Switz. 22 B5
Burgeo, Canada 99 C8
Burgersdorp, S. Africa .. 84 E4
Burges, Mt., Australia .. 89 F3
Burghausen, Germany .. 19 G8
Búrgio, Italy 34 E6
Bürglen, Switz. 23 C7
Burgo de Osma, Spain .. 28 D1
Burgohondo, Spain 30 E6
Burgos, Spain 28 C1
Burgos □, Spain 28 C1
Burgstädt, Germany ... 18 E8
Burgsvik, Sweden 9 H18
Burguillos del Cerro, Spain 31 G4
Burgundy = Bourgogne,
  France 25 F11
Burhaniye, Turkey 66 C2
Burhanpur, India 60 J10
Burhou, U.K. 24 C4
Buri Pen., Eritrea 77 D4
Burias, Phil. 55 E5
Burica, Pta., Costa Rica . 116 E3
Burigi, L., Tanzania ... 82 C3
Burin, Canada 99 C8
Buriram, Thailand 58 E4
Buriti Alegre, Brazil ... 123 E2
Buriti Bravo, Brazil ... 122 C3
Buriti dos Lopes, Brazil . 122 B3
Burj Sāfitā, Syria 66 E7
Burji, Ethiopia 77 F4
Burkburnett, U.S.A. ... 109 H5
Burke, U.S.A. 110 C6
Burke →, Australia ... 90 B2
Burketown, Australia .. 90 B2
Burkina Faso ■, Africa . 78 C4
Burk's Falls, Canada ... 98 C4
Burley, U.S.A. 110 E7
Burlingame, U.S.A. ... 112 H4
Burlington, Canada 106 C5
Burlington, Colo., U.S.A. 108 F3
Burlington, Iowa, U.S.A. 108 E9
Burlington, Kans., U.S.A. 108 F7
Burlington, N.C., U.S.A. 105 G6
Burlington, N.J., U.S.A. 107 F10
Burlington, Vt., U.S.A. . 107 B11
Burlington, Wash., U.S.A. 110 B2
Burlington, Wis., U.S.A. 104 D1
Burlyu-Tyube, Kazakhstan 44 E8
Burma ■, Asia 61 J20
Burnaby I., Canada 100 C2

Burnet, U.S.A. 109 K5
Burney, U.S.A. 110 F3
Burngup, Australia 89 F2
Burnham, U.S.A. 106 F7
Burnie, Australia 90 G4
Burnley, U.K. 12 D5
Burns, Oreg., U.S.A. .. 110 E4
Burns, Wyo., U.S.A. ... 108 E2
Burns Lake, Canada ... 100 C3
Burnside →, Canada .. 96 B9
Burnside, L., Australia . 89 E3
Burnt River, Canada ... 106 B6
Burntwood →, Canada . 101 B9
Burntwood L., Canada . 101 B8
Burqān, Kuwait 64 D5
Burqin, China 54 B3
Burra, Australia 91 E2
Burramurra, Australia . 90 C2
Burreli, Albania 39 H3
Burren Junction, Australia 91 E4
Burrendong Dam, Australia 91 E4
Burriana, Spain 28 F4
Burrinjuck Res., Australia 91 F4
Burro, Serranías del,
  Mexico 114 B4
Burruyacú, Argentina .. 126 B3
Burry Port, U.K. 13 F3
Bursa, Turkey 66 B3
Burseryd, Sweden 11 G7
Burstall, Canada 101 C7
Burton L., Canada 98 B4
Burton upon Trent, U.K. 12 E6
Burtundy, Australia ... 91 E3
Buru, Indonesia 57 E7
Burullus, Bahra el, Egypt 76 H7
Burûn, Râs, Egypt 69 D2
Bururi, Burundi 82 C2
Burutu, Nigeria 79 D6
Burwell, U.S.A. 108 E5
Bury, U.K. 12 D5
Bury St. Edmunds, U.K. 13 E8
Buryatia □, Russia 45 D11
Buryn, Ukraine 41 G7
Busalla, Italy 32 D5
Busango Swamp, Zambia 83 E2
Busãyrah, Syria 67 E9
Buşayyah, Iraq 64 D5
Busca, Italy 32 D4
Büshehr, Iran 65 D6
Büshehr □, Iran 65 D6
Bushell, Canada 101 B7
Bushenyi, Uganda 82 C3
Bushire = Büshehr, Iran 65 D6
Bushnell, Ill., U.S.A. .. 108 E9
Bushnell, Nebr., U.S.A. . 108 E3
Busia □, Kenya 82 B3
Busie, Ghana 78 C4
Businga, Zaïre 80 D4
Buskerud fylke □, Norway 10 D3
Busko Zdrój, Poland .. 20 E10
Busovača, Bos.-H. 21 L7
Busra ash Shãm, Syria . 69 C5
Bussang, France 25 E13
Busselton, Australia ... 89 F2
Busseto, Italy 32 D7
Bussigny, Switz. 22 C3
Bussum, Neths. 16 D6
Bustamante, B., Argentina 128 C3
Busto, C., Spain 30 B4
Busto Arsízio, Italy 32 C5
Busu-Djanoa, Zaïre ... 80 D4
Busuanga, Phil. 55 E3
Büsum, Germany 18 A4
Buta, Zaïre 82 B1
Butare, Rwanda 82 C2
Butaritari, Kiribati 92 G9
Bute, U.K. 14 F3
Bute Inlet, Canada 100 C4
Butemba, Uganda 82 B3
Butembo, Zaïre 82 B2
Butera, Italy 35 E7
Bütgenbach, Belgium .. 17 H8
Butha Qi, China 54 B7
Butiaba, Uganda 82 B3
Butler, Mo., U.S.A. ... 108 F7
Butler, Pa., U.S.A. 106 F5
Buton, Indonesia 57 E6
Butterworth = Gcuwa,
  S. Africa 85 E4
Butterworth, Malaysia . 59 K3
Buttfield, Mt., Australia 89 D4
Button B., Canada 101 B10
Buttonwillow, U.S.A. .. 113 K7
Butty Hd., Australia ... 89 F3
Butuan, Phil. 55 G6
Butuku-Luba, Eq. Guin. 79 E6
Butung = Buton, Indonesia 57 E6
Buturlinovka, Russia .. 42 E5
Butzbach, Germany ... 18 E4
Bützow, Germany 18 B7
Buxar, India 63 G10
Buxton, Guyana 121 B6
Buxton, U.K. 12 D6
Buxy, France 25 F11
Buy, Russia 42 A5
Buynaksk, Russia 43 J8
Büyük Menderes →,
  Turkey 66 D2
Büyükçekmece, Turkey 66 B3
Buzançais, France 24 F8
Buzău, Romania 38 D9
Buzău □, Romania 38 D10
Buzău →, Romania ... 38 D10

Buzău, Pasul, Romania . 38 D9
Buzen, Japan 49 H5
Buzet, Croatia 33 C10
Buzi →, Mozam. 83 F3
Buziaş, Romania 38 D4
Buzuluk, Russia 44 D6
Buzuluk →, Russia ... 42 E6
Buzzards Bay, U.S.A. .. 107 E14
Bwana Mkubwe, Zaïre . 83 E2
Byala, Bulgaria 38 F8
Byala Slatina, Bulgaria . 38 F6
Byarezina →, Belarus . 41 F6
Bychawa, Poland 20 D12
Bydgoszcz, Poland 20 B8
Byelarus = Belarus ■,
  Europe 40 F4
Byelorussia = Belarus ■,
  Europe 40 F4
Byers, U.S.A. 108 F2
Byesville, U.S.A. 106 G3
Byhalia, U.S.A. 109 H10
Bykhaw, Belarus 40 F6
Bykhov = Bykhaw, Belarus 40 F6
Bykovo, Russia 42 F7
Bylas, U.S.A. 111 K8
Bylderup, Denmark ... 11 K3
Bylot I., Canada 97 A12
Byrd, C., Antarctica ... 5 C17
Byro, Australia 89 E2
Byrock, Australia 91 E4
Byron Bay, Australia .. 91 D5
Byrranga, Gory, Russia . 45 B11
Byrranga Mts. = Byrranga,
  Gory, Russia 45 B11
Byrum, Denmark 11 G5
Byske, Sweden 8 D19
Byske älv →, Sweden . 8 D19
Bystrzyca Kłodzka, Poland 20 E6
Bytom, Poland 20 E8
Bytów, Poland 20 A7
Byumba, Rwanda 82 C3

C

Ca →, Vietnam 58 C5
Ca Mau = Quan Long,
  Vietnam 59 H5
Ca Mau, Mui = Bai Bung,
  Mui, Vietnam 59 H5
Ca Na, Vietnam 59 G7
Caacupé, Paraguay 126 B4
Caála, Angola 81 G3
Caamano Sd., Canada . 100 C3
Caapiranga, Brazil 121 D5
Caazapá, Paraguay 126 B4
Caazapá □, Paraguay .. 127 B4
Cabadbaran, Phil. 55 G6
Cabalian, Phil. 55 F6
Caballeria, C. de, Spain . 36 A11
Cabana, Peru 124 B2
Cabanaconde, Peru ... 124 D3
Cabañaquinta, Spain .. 30 B5
Cabanatuan, Phil. 55 D4
Cabanes, Spain 28 E5
Cabanillas, Peru 124 D3
Cabano, Canada 99 C6
Čabar, Croatia 33 C11
Cabazon, U.S.A. 113 M10
Cabedelo, Brazil 122 C5
Cabeza del Buey, Spain . 31 G5
Cabildo, Chile 126 C1
Cabimas, Venezuela ... 120 A3
Cabinda, Angola 80 F2
Cabinda □, Angola ... 80 F2
Cabinet Mts., U.S.A. .. 110 C6
Cabo Blanco, Argentina 128 C3
Cabo Frio, Brazil 123 F3
Cabo Pantoja, Peru ... 120 D2
Cabo Raso, Argentina .. 128 B3
Cabonga, Réservoir,
  Canada 98 C4
Cabool, U.S.A. 109 G8
Caboolture, Australia .. 91 D5
Cabora Bassa Dam =
  Cahora Bassa Dam,
  Mozam. 83 F3
Caborca, Mexico 114 A2
Cabot, Mt., U.S.A. 107 B13
Cabot Str., Canada ... 99 C8
Cabra, Spain 31 H6
Cabra del Santo Cristo,
  Spain 29 H1
Cábras, Italy 34 C1
Cabrera, Spain 36 B9
Cabrera, Sierra, Spain . 30 C4
Cabri, Canada 101 C7
Cabriel →, Spain 29 F3
Cabruta, Venezuela ... 120 B4
Cabugao, Phil. 55 C4
Cabuyaro, Colombia .. 120 C3
Cacabelos, Spain 30 C4
Cacador, Brazil 127 B5
Cacahuatepec, Mexico . 115 D5
Čačak, Serbia, Yug. ... 21 M10
Cacao, Fr. Guiana 121 C7
Cáceres, Brazil 125 D6
Cáceres, Colombia 120 B2
Cáceres, Spain 31 F4
Cáceres □, Spain 31 F4
Cache Bay, Canada ... 98 C4
Cache Cr. →, U.S.A. .. 112 G5
Cachepo, Portugal ... 31 H3
Cachéu, Guinea-Biss. .. 78 C1
Cachi, Argentina 126 B2
Cachimbo, Brazil 125 B7
Cachimbo, Serra do, Brazil 125 B6

Cachoeira, Brazil 123 D4
Cachoeira Alta, Brazil .. 123 E1
Cachoeira de Itapemirim,
  Brazil 123 F3
Cachoeira do Sul, Brazil . 127 C5
Cachoeiro do Arari, Brazil 122 B2
Cachopo, Portugal 31 H3
Cachuela Esperanza,
  Bolivia 125 C4
Cacólo, Angola 80 G3
Caconda, Angola 81 G3
Cacongo, Angola 80 F2
Caçu, Brazil 123 E1
Caculé, Brazil 123 D3
Cadarache, France 27 E9
Čadca, Slovak Rep. ... 20 F8
Caddo, U.S.A. 109 H6
Cadell Cr. →, Australia 90 C3
Cadenazzo, Switz. 23 D7
Cader Idris, U.K. 12 E4
Cadí, Sierra del, Spain . 28 C6
Cadibarrawirracanna, L.,
  Australia 91 D2
Cadillac, Canada 98 C4
Cadillac, France 26 D3
Cadillac, U.S.A. 104 C3
Cadiz, Phil. 55 F5
Cádiz, Spain 31 J4
Cadiz, U.S.A. 106 F4
Cádiz □, Spain 31 J5
Cádiz, G. de, Spain ... 31 J4
Cadney Park, Australia 91 D1
Cadomin, Canada 100 C5
Cadotte →, Canada .. 100 B5
Cadours, France 26 E5
Cadoux, Australia 89 F2
Caen, France 24 C6
Caernarfon, U.K. 12 D3
Caernarfon B., U.K. ... 12 D3
Caernarvon = Caernarfon,
  U.K. 12 D3
Caerphilly, U.K. 13 F4
Caesarea, Israel 69 C3
Caetá, Brazil 123 E3
Caetité, Brazil 123 D3
Cafayate, Argentina ... 126 B2
Cafifi, Colombia 120 B3
Cafu, Angola 84 B2
Cagayan →, Phil. 55 B4
Cagayan de Oro, Phil. . 55 G6
Cagayan Is., Phil. 55 G4
Cagayan Sulu I., Phil. . 55 H3
Cagli, Italy 33 E9
Cágliari, Italy 34 C2
Cágliari, G. di, Italy ... 34 C2
Cagnano Varano, Italy . 35 A8
Cagnes-sur-Mer, France 27 E11
Caguán →, Colombia . 120 D3
Caguas, Puerto Rico ... 117 C6
Caha Mts., Ireland 15 E2
Cahama, Angola 84 B1
Caher, Ireland 15 D4
Caherciveen, Ireland .. 15 E1
Cahora Bassa Dam,
  Mozam. 83 F3
Cahore Pt., Ireland ... 15 D5
Cahors, France 26 D5
Cahuapanas, Peru 124 B2
Cahuinari →, Colombia 120 D3
Cahul, Moldova 41 K5
Cai Bau, Dao, Vietnam . 58 B6
Cai Nuoc, Vietnam ... 59 H5
Caia, Mozam. 83 F4
Caiabis, Serra dos, Brazil 125 C6
Caianda, Angola 83 E1
Caiapó, Serra do, Brazil 125 D7
Caiapônia, Brazil 125 D7
Caibarién, Cuba 116 B4
Caibiran, Phil. 55 F6
Caicara, Bolívar, Venezuela 120 B4
Caicara, Monagas,
  Venezuela 121 B5
Caicó, Brazil 122 C4
Caicos Is., W. Indies ... 117 B5
Caicos Passage, W. Indies 117 B5
Cailloma, Peru 124 D3
Caine →, Bolivia 125 D4
Caird Coast, Antarctica . 5 D1
Cairn Gorm, U.K. 14 D5
Cairn Toul, U.K. 14 D5
Cairngorm Mts., U.K. . 14 D5
Cairns, Australia 90 B4
Cairo = El Qâhira, Egypt 76 H7
Cairo, Ga., U.S.A. 105 K3
Cairo, Ill., U.S.A. 109 G10
Cairo Montenotte, Italy . 32 D5
Caithness, Ord of, U.K. . 14 C5
Caiundo, Angola 81 H3
Caiza, Bolivia 125 E4
Cajabamba, Peru 124 B2
Cajamarca, Peru 124 B2
Cajamarca □, Peru 124 B2
Cajápio, Brazil 122 B3
Cajarc, France 26 D5
Cajatambo, Peru 124 C2
Cajàzeiras, Brazil 122 C4
Čajetina, Serbia, Yug. . 21 M9
Çakirgol, Turkey 67 B8
Čakovec, Croatia 33 B13
Çal, Turkey 66 C3
Cala, Spain 31 H4
Cala →, Spain 31 H4
Cala Cadolar, Punta de,
  Spain 29 G6
Cala d'Or, Spain 36 B10
Cala Figuera, C., Spain . 36 B9
Cala Forcat, Spain 36 A10

Cala Mayor, *Spain* 36 B9
Cala Mezquida, *Spain* 36 B11
Cala Millor, *Spain* 36 B10
Cala Ratjada, *Spain* 36 B10
Calabanga, *Phil.* 55 E5
Calabar, *Nigeria* 79 E6
Calabozo, *Venezuela* 120 B4
Calábria □, *Italy* 35 C9
Calaburras, Pta. de, *Spain* . 31 J6
Calaceite, *Spain* 28 D5
Calacota, *Bolivia* 124 D4
Calafate, *Argentina* 128 D2
Calahorra, *Spain* 28 C3
Calais, *France* 25 B8
Calais, *U.S.A.* 99 C6
Calais, Pas de, *France* 25 B8
Calalaste, Cord. de,
  Argentina 126 B2
Calama, *Brazil* 125 B5
Calama, *Chile* 126 A2
Calamar, *Bolívar,
  Colombia* 120 A3
Calamar, *Vaupés, Colombia* 120 C3
Calamarca, *Bolivia* 124 D4
Calamba, *Phil.* 55 F5
Calamian Group, *Phil.* 55 F3
Calamocha, *Spain* 28 E3
Calamocha, *Spain* 28 E3
Calán Porter, *Spain* 36 B11
Calañas, *Spain* 31 H4
Calanda, *Spain* 28 E4
Calang, *Indonesia* 56 D1
Calangiánus, *Italy* 34 B1
Calapan, *Phil.* 55 E4
Cǎlǎraşi, *Romania* 38 E10
Calasparra, *Spain* 29 G3
Calatafimi, *Italy* 34 E5
Calatayud, *Spain* 28 D3
Calato = Kálathos, *Greece* . 39 N11
Calauag, *Phil.* 55 E5
Calavà, C., *Italy* 35 D7
Calavite, C., *Phil.* 55 E4
Calayan, *Phil.* 55 B4
Calbayog, *Phil.* 55 E6
Calbe, *Germany* 18 D7
Calca, *Peru* 124 C3
Calcasieu L., *U.S.A.* 109 L8
Calci, *Italy* 32 E7
Calcutta, *India* 63 H13
Caldaro, *Italy* 33 B8
Caldas □, *Colombia* 120 B2
Caldas da Rainha, *Portugal* 31 F1
Caldas de Reyes, *Spain* ... 30 C2
Caldas Novas, *Brazil* 123 E2
Calder →, *U.K.* 12 D6
Caldera, *Chile* 126 B1
Caldwell, *Idaho, U.S.A.* ... 110 E5
Caldwell, *Kans., U.S.A.* .. 109 G6
Caldwell, *Tex., U.S.A.* ... 109 K6
Caledon, *S. Africa* 84 E2
Caledon →, *S. Africa* 84 E4
Caledon B., *Australia* 90 A2
Caledonia, *Canada* 106 C5
Caledonia, *U.S.A.* 106 D7
Calella, *Spain* 28 D7
Calemba, *Angola* 84 B2
Calenzana, *France* 27 F12
Caleta Olivia, *Argentina* . 128 C3
Calexico, *U.S.A.* 113 N11
Calf of Man, *U.K.* 12 C3
Calgary, *Canada* 100 C6
Calheta, *Madeira* 36 D2
Calhoun, *U.S.A.* 105 H3
Cali, *Colombia* 120 C2
Calicut, *India* 60 P9
Caliente, *U.S.A.* 111 H6
California, *Mo., U.S.A.* ... 108 F8
California, *Pa., U.S.A.* ... 106 F5
California □, *U.S.A.* 111 H4
California, Baja, *Mexico* . 114 A1
California, Baja, T.N. =
  Baja California □,
  Mexico 114 A2
California, Baja, T.S. =
  Baja California Sur □,
  Mexico 114 B2
California, G. de, *Mexico* . 114 B2
California City, *U.S.A.* ... 113 K9
California Hot Springs,
  U.S.A. 113 K8
Cǎlimǎneşti, *Romania* 38 D7
Cǎlimani, Munţii, *Romania* 38 B8
Cǎlineşti, *Romania* 38 D7
Calingasta, *Argentina* 126 C2
Calipatria, *U.S.A.* 113 M11
Calistoga, *U.S.A.* 112 G4
Calitri, *Italy* 35 B8
Calitzdorp, *S. Africa* 84 E3
Callabonna, L., *Australia* . 91 D3
Callac, *France* 24 D3
Callan, *Ireland* 15 D4
Callander, *U.K.* 14 E4
Callantsoog, *Neths.* 16 C5
Callao, *Peru* 124 C2
Callaway, *U.S.A.* 108 E5
Calles, *Mexico* 115 C5
Callide, *Australia* 90 C5
Calling Lake, *Canada* 100 B6
Calliope, *Australia* 90 C5
Callola, *Brazil* 84 B2
Callosa de Ensarriá, *Spain* 29 G4
Callosa de Segura, *Spain* . 29 G4
Calola, *Brazil* 122 B2
Calolbon, *Phil.* 55 E6
Caloocan, *Phil.* 55 D4
Calore →, *Italy* 35 A7
Caloundra, *Australia* 91 D5
Calpe, *Spain* 29 G5
Calpella, *U.S.A.* 112 F3

Calpine, *U.S.A.* 112 F6
Calstock, *Canada* 98 C3
Caltabellotta, *Italy* 34 E6
Caltagirone, *Italy* 35 E7
Caltanissetta, *Italy* 35 E7
Calulo, *Angola* 80 G2
Calumet, *U.S.A.* 104 B1
Calunda, *Angola* 81 G4
Caluso, *Italy* 32 C4
Calvados □, *France* 24 C6
Calvert, *U.S.A.* 109 K6
Calvert →, *Australia* 90 B2
Calvert Hills, *Australia* ... 90 B2
Calvert I., *Canada* 100 C3
Calvert Ra., *Australia* 88 D3
Calvi, *France* 27 F12
Calvillo, *Mexico* 114 C4
Calvinia, *S. Africa* 84 E2
Calw, *Germany* 19 G4
Calwa, *U.S.A.* 112 J7
Calzada Almuradiel, *Spain* 29 G1
Calzada de Calatrava,
  Spain 31 G7
Cam →, *U.K.* 13 E8
Cam Lam, *Vietnam* 59 G7
Cam Pha, *Vietnam* 58 B6
Cam Ranh, *Vietnam* 59 G7
Cam Xuyen, *Vietnam* 58 C6
Camabatela, *Angola* 80 F3
Camacã, *Brazil* 123 E4
Camaçari, *Brazil* 123 D4
Camacha, *Madeira* 36 D3
Camacho, *Mexico* 114 C4
Camacupã, *Angola* 81 G3
Camaguán, *Venezuela* 120 B4
Camagüey, *Cuba* 116 B4
Camaiore, *Italy* 32 E7
Camamu, *Brazil* 123 D4
Camaná, *Peru* 124 D3
Camanche Reservoir,
  U.S.A. 112 G6
Camaquã →, *Brazil* 127 C5
Câmara de Lobos, *Madeira* 36 D3
Camararé →, *Brazil* 125 C6
Camarat, C., *France* 27 E10
Camaret, *France* 24 D2
Camargo, *Bolivia* 125 E4
Camargue, *France* 27 E8
Camarillo, *U.S.A.* 113 L7
Camariñas, *Spain* 30 B1
Camarón, C., *Honduras* ... 116 C2
Camarones, *Argentina* 128 B3
Camarones, B., *Argentina* 128 B3
Camas, *U.S.A.* 112 E4
Camas Valley, *U.S.A.* 110 E2
Cambados, *Spain* 30 C2
Cambará, *Brazil* 127 A5
Cambay = Khambhat,
  India 62 H5
Cambay, G. of =
  Khambat, G. of, *India* . 62 J5
Cambil, *Spain* 29 H1
Cambo-les-Bains, *France* . 26 E2
Cambodia ■, *Asia* 58 F5
Camborne, *U.K.* 13 G2
Cambrai, *France* 25 B10
Cambria, *U.S.A.* 111 J3
Cambrian Mts., *U.K.* 13 E4
Cambridge, *Canada* 98 D3
Cambridge, *Jamaica* 116 C4
Cambridge, *N.Z.* 87 G5
Cambridge, *U.K.* 13 E8
Cambridge, *Idaho, U.S.A.* . 110 D5
Cambridge, *Mass., U.S.A.* . 107 D13
Cambridge, *Md., U.S.A.* .. 104 F7
Cambridge, *Minn., U.S.A.* 108 C8
Cambridge, *N.Y., U.S.A.* . 107 C11
Cambridge, *Nebr., U.S.A.* . 108 E4
Cambridge, *Ohio, U.S.A.* . 106 F3
Cambridge Bay, *Canada* .. 96 B9
Cambridge G., *Australia* .. 88 B4
Cambridge Springs, *U.S.A.* 106 E4
Cambridgeshire □, *U.K.* .. 13 E8
Cambrils, *Spain* 28 D6
Cambuci, *Brazil* 123 F3
Cambundi-Catembo,
  Angola 80 G3
Camden, *Ala., U.S.A.* 105 K2
Camden, *Ark., U.S.A.* 109 J8
Camden, *Maine, U.S.A.* .. 99 D11
Camden, *N.J., U.S.A.* 107 G9
Camden, *S.C., U.S.A.* 105 H5
Camden Sd., *Australia* ... 88 C3
Camdenton, *U.S.A.* 109 F8
Cameron, *Ariz., U.S.A.* ... 111 J8
Cameron, *La., U.S.A.* 109 L8
Cameron, *Mo., U.S.A.* ... 108 F7
Cameron, *Tex., U.S.A.* ... 109 K6
Cameron Falls, *Canada* ... 98 C2
Cameron Highlands,
  Malaysia 59 K3
Cameron Hills, *Canada* ... 100 B5
Camerota, *Italy* 35 B8
Cameroon ■, *Africa* 73 G7
Cameroun →, *Cameroon* . 79 E6
Cameroun, Mt., *Cameroon* 79 E6
Cametá, *Brazil* 122 B2
Camiguin □, *Phil.* 55 G6
Camiguin I., *Phil.* 55 B4
Camiling, *Phil.* 55 D4
Caminha, *Portugal* 30 D2
Camino, *U.S.A.* 112 G6
Camira Creek, *Australia* .. 91 D5

Camiranga, *Brazil* 122 B2
Camiri, *Bolivia* 125 E5
Camissombo, *Angola* 80 F4
Cammal, *U.S.A.* 106 E7
Camocim, *Brazil* 122 B3
Camogli, *Italy* 32 D6
Camooweal, *Australia* 90 B2
Camopi, *Fr. Guiana* 121 C7
Camopi →, *Fr. Guiana* .. 121 C7
Camotes Is., *Phil.* 55 F6
Camotes Sea, *Phil.* 55 F6
Camp Crook, *U.S.A.* 108 C3
Camp Nelson, *U.S.A.* 113 J8
Camp Wood, *U.S.A.* 109 L4
Campagna, *Italy* 35 B8
Campana, *Argentina* 126 C4
Campana, I., *Chile* 128 C1
Campanário, *Madeira* 36 D2
Campanario, *Spain* 31 G5
Campánia □, *Italy* 35 B7
Campbell, *S. Africa* 84 D3
Campbell, *Calif., U.S.A.* .. 112 H5
Campbell, *Ohio, U.S.A.* .. 106 E4
Campbell L., *Pac. Oc.* 92 N8
Campbell L., *Canada* 101 A7
Campbell River, *Canada* .. 100 C3
Campbell Town, *Australia* 90 G4
Campbellford, *Canada* ... 106 B7
Campbellpur, *Pakistan* ... 62 C5
Campbellsville, *U.S.A.* ... 104 G3
Campbellton, *Canada* 99 C6
Campbelltown, *Australia* . 91 E5
Campbeltown, *U.K.* 14 F3
Campeche, *Mexico* 115 D6
Campeche □, *Mexico* 115 D6
Campeche, B. de, *Mexico* 115 D6
Camperdown, *Australia* .. 91 F3
Camperville, *Canada* 101 C8
Campi Salentina, *Italy* ... 35 B11
Campidano, *Italy* 34 C1
Campíglia Maríttima, *Italy* 32 E7
Campillo de Altobuey,
  Spain 28 F3
Campillo de Llerena, *Spain* 31 G5
Campillos, *Spain* 31 H6
Campina Grande, *Brazil* .. 122 C4
Campina Verde, *Brazil* ... 123 E2
Campinas, *Brazil* 127 A6
Campine, *Belgium* 17 F6
Campli, *Italy* 33 F10
Campo, *Cameroon* 80 D1
Campo, *Spain* 28 C5
Campo Belo, *Brazil* 123 F2
Campo de Criptana, *Spain* 29 F1
Campo de Diauarum,
  Brazil 125 C7
Campo de Gibraltar, *Spain* 31 J5
Campo Flórido, *Brazil* ... 123 E2
Campo Formoso, *Brazil* .. 122 D3
Campo Grande, *Brazil* ... 125 E7
Campo Maíor, *Brazil* 122 B3
Campo Maior, *Portugal* .. 31 G3
Campo Mourão, *Brazil* ... 127 A5
Campo Tencia, *Switz.* 23 D7
Campo Túres, *Italy* 33 B8
Campoalegre, *Colombia* .. 120 C2
Campobasso, *Italy* 35 A7
Campobello di Licata, *Italy* 34 E6
Campobello di Mazara,
  Italy 34 E5
Campofelice di Roccella,
  Italy 34 E6
Camporeale, *Italy* 34 E6
Campos, *Brazil* 123 F3
Campos Altos, *Brazil* 123 E2
Campos Belos, *Brazil* 123 D2
Campos del Puerto, *Spain* 36 B10
Campos Novos, *Brazil* ... 127 B5
Campos Sales, *Brazil* 122 C3
Campródon, *Spain* 28 C7
Camptonville, *U.S.A.* 112 F5
Campuya →, *Peru* 120 D3
Camrose, *Canada* 100 C6
Camsell Portage, *Canada* . 101 B7
Çan, *Turkey* 66 B2
Can Clavo, *Spain* 36 C7
Can Creu, *Spain* 36 C7
Can Gio, *Vietnam* 59 G6
Can Tho, *Vietnam* 59 G5
Canaan, *U.S.A.* 107 D11
Canada ■, *N. Amer.* 96 C10
Cañada de Gómez,
  Argentina 126 C3
Canadian, *U.S.A.* 109 H4
Canadian →, *U.S.A.* 109 H7
Canadian Shield, *Canada* . 97 C10
Çanakkale, *Turkey* 66 B2
Çanakkale Boğazı, *Turkey* 66 B2
Canal Flats, *Canada* 100 C5
Canalejas, *Argentina* 126 C2
Canals, *Argentina* 126 C3
Canals, *Spain* 29 G4
Canandaigua, *U.S.A.* 106 D7
Cananea, *Mexico* 114 A2
Cañar, *Ecuador* 120 D2
Cañar □, *Ecuador* 120 D2
Canarias, Is., *Atl. Oc.* 36 F4
Canarreos, Arch. de los,
  Cuba 116 B3
Canary Is. = Canarias, Is.,
  Atl. Oc. 36 F4
Canastra, Serra da, *Brazil* 123 F2
Canatlán, *Mexico* 114 C4
Canaveral, C., *U.S.A.* 105 L5
Cañaveras, *Spain* 28 E2
Canavieiras, *Brazil* 123 E4
Canbelego, *Australia* 91 E4

Canberra, *Australia* 91 F4
Canby, *Calif., U.S.A.* 110 F3
Canby, *Minn., U.S.A.* 108 C6
Canby, *Oreg., U.S.A.* 112 E4
Cancale, *France* 24 D5
Canche →, *France* 25 B8
Canchyuaya, Cordillera de,
  Peru 124 B3
Cancún, *Mexico* 115 C7
Candala, *Somali Rep.* 68 E4
Candarave, *Peru* 124 D3
Candas, *Spain* 30 B5
Candé, *France* 24 E5
Candeias →, *Brazil* 125 B5
Candela, *Italy* 35 A8
Candelaria, *Argentina* 127 B4
Candelaria, *Canary Is.* ... 36 F3
Candelaria, Pta. de la,
  Spain 30 B2
Candeleda, *Spain* 30 E5
Candelo, *Australia* 91 F4
Candia = Iráklion, *Greece* 37 D7
Candia, Sea of = Crete,
  Sea of, *Greece* 39 N8
Cândido de Abreu, *Brazil* 123 F1
Cândido Mendes, *Brazil* . 122 B2
Candle L., *Canada* 101 C7
Candlemas I., *Antarctica* . 5 B1
Cando, *U.S.A.* 108 A5
Candon, *Phil.* 55 C4
Canea = Khaniá, *Greece* . 37 D6
Canela, *Brazil* 122 B2
Canelli, *Italy* 32 D5
Canelones, *Uruguay* 127 C4
Canet-Plage, *France* 26 F7
Cañete, *Chile* 126 D1
Cañete, *Peru* 124 C2
Cañete, *Spain* 28 E3
Cañete de las Torres, *Spain* 31 H6
Canfranc, *Spain* 28 C4
Cangas, *Spain* 30 C2
Cangas de Narcea, *Spain* . 30 B4
Cangas de Onís, *Spain* ... 30 B5
Canguaretama, *Brazil* 122 C4
Canguçu, *Brazil* 127 C5
Cangxi, *China* 52 B5
Cangyuan, *China* 52 F2
Cangzhou, *China* 50 E9
Canicattì, *Italy* 34 E6
Canicattini Bagni, *Italy* .. 35 E8
Canim Lake, *Canada* 100 C4
Canindé, *Brazil* 122 B4
Canindé →, *Brazil* 122 C3
Canindeyu □, *Paraguay* .. 127 A4
Canipaan, *Phil.* 56 C5
Canisteo, *U.S.A.* 106 D7
Canisteo →, *U.S.A.* 106 D7
Cañitas, *Mexico* 114 C4
Cañizal, *Spain* 30 D5
Canjáyar, *Spain* 29 H2
Çankırı, *Turkey* 66 B5
Çankuzo, *Burundi* 82 C3
Cann River, *Australia* 91 F4
Canna, *U.K.* 14 D2
Cannanore, *India* 60 P9
Cannes, *France* 27 E11
Canning Town = Port
  Canning, *India* 63 H13
Cannington, *Canada* 106 B5
Cannock, *U.K.* 12 E5
Cannon Ball →, *U.S.A.* . 108 B4
Cannondale Mt., *Australia* 90 D4
Cannonvale, *Australia* ... 90 C4
Caño Colorado, *Colombia* 120 C4
Canoas, *Brazil* 127 B5
Canoe L., *Canada* 101 B7
Canon City, *U.S.A.* 108 F2
Canora, *Canada* 101 C8
Canosa di Púglia, *Italy* ... 35 A9
Canowindra, *Australia* ... 91 E4
Canso, *Canada* 99 C7
Canta, *Peru* 124 C2
Cantabria □, *Spain* 30 B6
Cantabria, Sierra de, *Spain* 28 C2
Cantabrian Mts. =
  Cantábrica, Cordillera,
  Spain 30 C5
Cantábrica, Cordillera,
  Spain 30 C5
Cantal □, *France* 26 C6
Cantal, Plomb du, *France* 26 C6
Cantanhede, *Portugal* ... 30 E2
Cantaura, *Venezuela* 121 B5
Canterbury, *Australia* 90 D3
Canterbury, *U.K.* 13 F9
Canterbury □, *N.Z.* 87 K3
Canterbury Bight, *N.Z.* .. 87 L3
Canterbury Plains, *N.Z.* . 87 K3
Cantil, *U.S.A.* 113 K9
Cantillana, *Spain* 31 H5
Canto do Buriti, *Brazil* ... 122 C3
Canton = Guangzhou,
  China 53 F9
Canton, *Ga., U.S.A.* 105 H3
Canton, *Ill., U.S.A.* 108 E9
Canton, *Miss., U.S.A.* ... 109 J9
Canton, *Mo., U.S.A.* 108 E9
Canton, *N.Y., U.S.A.* 107 B9
Canton, *Ohio, U.S.A.* ... 106 F3
Canton, *Okla., U.S.A.* ... 109 G5
Canton, *S. Dak., U.S.A.* . 108 D6
Canton L., *U.S.A.* 109 G5
Cantù, *Italy* 32 C6
Canudos, *Brazil* 125 B6
Canumã, *Amazonas, Brazil* 121 D6
Canumã, *Amazonas, Brazil* 125 B5

Canumã →, *Brazil* 125 A6
Canutama, *Brazil* 125 B5
Canutillo, *U.S.A.* 111 L10
Canyon, *Tex., U.S.A.* 109 H4
Canyon, *Wyo., U.S.A.* ... 110 D8
Canyonlands National Park,
  U.S.A. 111 G9
Canyonville, *U.S.A.* 110 E2
Canzo, *Italy* 32 C6
Cao Bang, *Vietnam* 58 A6
Cao He →, *China* 51 D13
Cao Lanh, *Vietnam* 59 G5
Cao Xian, *China* 50 G8
Cáorle, *Italy* 33 C9
Cap-aux-Meules, *Canada* . 99 C7
Cap-Chat, *Canada* 99 C6
Cap-de-la-Madeleine,
  Canada 98 C5
Cap-Haïtien, *Haiti* 117 C5
Cap St.-Jacques = Vung
  Tau, *Vietnam* 59 G6
Capa, *Vietnam* 58 A4
Capa Stilo, *Italy* 35 D9
Capáccio, *Italy* 35 B8
Capaia, *Angola* 80 F4
Capanaparo →, *Venezuela* 120 B4
Capanema, *Brazil* 122 B2
Caparo →, *Barinas,
  Venezuela* 120 B3
Caparo →, *Bolívar,
  Venezuela* 121 B5
Capatárida, *Venezuela* ... 120 A3
Capbreton, *France* 26 E2
Capdenac, *France* 26 D6
Cape →, *Australia* 90 C4
Cape Barren I., *Australia* . 90 G4
Cape Breton Highlands
  Nat. Park, *Canada* 99 C7
Cape Breton I., *Canada* .. 99 C7
Cape Charles, *U.S.A.* 104 G8
Cape Coast, *Ghana* 79 D4
Cape Dorset, *Canada* 97 B12
Cape Dyer, *Canada* 97 B13
Cape Fear →, *U.S.A.* ... 105 H6
Cape Girardeau, *U.S.A.* . 109 G10
Cape Jervis, *Australia* 91 F2
Cape May, *U.S.A.* 104 F8
Cape May Point, *U.S.A.* . 103 C12
Cape Palmas, *Liberia* 78 E4
Cape Tormentine, *Canada* 99 C7
Cape Town, *S. Africa* 84 E2
Cape Verde Is. ■, *Atl. Oc.* 2 D8
Cape Vincent, *U.S.A.* 107 B8
Cape York Peninsula,
  Australia 90 A3
Capela, *Brazil* 122 D4
Capela de Campo, *Brazil* 122 B3
Capelinha, *Brazil* 123 E3
Capella, *Australia* 90 C4
Capendu, *France* 26 E6
Capestang, *France* 26 E7
Capim, *Brazil* 122 B2
Capim →, *Brazil* 122 B2
Capinópolis, *Brazil* 123 E2
Capinota, *Bolivia* 124 D4
Capitan, *U.S.A.* 111 K11
Capitán Aracena, I., *Chile* 128 D2
Capitán Pastene, *Chile* .. 128 A2
Capitola, *U.S.A.* 112 J5
Capivara, Serra da, *Brazil* 123 D3
Capizzi, *Italy* 35 E7
Čapljina, *Bos.-H.* 21 M7
Capoche →, *Mozam.* 83 F3
Capoeira, *Brazil* 125 B6
Cappadocia, *Turkey* 66 C6
Capraia, *Italy* 32 E6
Caprarola, *Italy* 33 F9
Capreol, *Canada* 98 C3
Caprera, *Italy* 34 A2
Capri, *Italy* 35 B7
Capricorn Group, *Australia* 90 C5
Capricorn Ra., *Australia* . 88 D2
Caprino Veronese, *Italy* .. 32 C7
Caprivi Strip, *Namibia* ... 84 B3
Captainganj, *India* 63 F10
Captain's Flat, *Australia* . 91 F4
Captieux, *France* 26 D3
Cápua, *Italy* 35 A7
Caquetá □, *Colombia* ... 120 C3
Caquetá →, *Colombia* ... 120 D4
Carabobo, *Venezuela* 120 A4
Carabobo □, *Venezuela* . 120 A4
Caracal, *Romania* 38 E7
Caracaraí, *Brazil* 121 C5
Caracas, *Venezuela* 120 A4
Caracol, *Brazil* 122 C3
Caracollo, *Bolivia* 124 D4
Caradoc, *Australia* 91 E3
Carádoc, *Italy* 32 E4
Carahue, *Chile* 128 A2
Caraí, *Brazil* 123 E3
Carajás, Serra dos, *Brazil* 122 C1
Caranapatuba, *Brazil* 125 B5
Carandaiti, *Bolivia* 125 E5
Carangola, *Brazil* 123 F3
Carani, *Australia* 89 F2
Caransebeş, *Romania* 38 D5
Carantec, *France* 24 D3
Caraparaná →, *Colombia* 120 D3
Carapelle →, *Italy* 35 A8
Caras, *Peru* 124 B2
Caratasca, L., *Honduras* . 116 C3
Caratinga, *Brazil* 123 E3
Caraúbas, *Brazil* 122 C4
Caravaca, *Spain* 29 G3
Caravággio, *Italy* 32 C6
Caravelas, *Brazil* 123 E4

Caraveli, Peru 124 D3
Caràzinho, Brazil 127 B5
Carballino, Spain 30 C2
Carballo, Spain 30 B2
Carberry, Canada 101 D9
Carbia, Spain 30 C2
Carbó, Mexico 114 B2
Carbon, Canada 100 C6
Carbonara, C., Italy 34 C2
Carbondale, Colo., U.S.A. 110 G10
Carbondale, Ill., U.S.A. 109 G10
Carbondale, Pa., U.S.A. 107 E9
Carbonear, Canada 99 C9
Carboneras, Spain 29 J3
Carboneras de Guadazón, Spain 28 F3
Carbonia, Italy 34 C1
Carcabuey, Spain 31 H6
Carcagente, Spain 29 F4
Carcajou, Canada 100 B5
Carcar, Phil. 55 F5
Carcasse, C., Haiti 117 C5
Carcassonne, France 26 E6
Carche, Spain 29 G3
Carchi □, Ecuador 120 C2
Carcross, Canada 96 B6
Cardabia, Australia 88 D1
Çardak, Turkey 66 D3
Cardamon Hills, India 60 Q10
Cárdenas, Cuba 116 B3
Cárdenas, San Luis Potosí, Mexico 115 C5
Cárdenas, Tabasco, Mexico 115 D6
Cardenete, Spain 28 F3
Cardiel, L., Argentina 128 C2
Cardiff, U.K. 13 F4
Cardiff-by-the-Sea, U.S.A. 113 M9
Cardigan, U.K. 13 E3
Cardigan B., U.K. 13 E3
Cardinal, Canada 107 B9
Cardón, Punta, Venezuela 120 A3
Cardona, Spain 28 D6
Cardona, Uruguay 126 C4
Cardoner →, Spain 28 D6
Cardross, Canada 101 D7
Cardston, Canada 100 D6
Cardwell, Australia 90 B4
Careen L., Canada 101 B7
Carei, Romania 38 B5
Careiro, Brazil 121 D6
Careme, Indonesia 57 G13
Carentan, France 24 C5
Carey, Idaho, U.S.A. 110 E7
Carey, Ohio, U.S.A. 104 E4
Carey, L., Australia 89 E3
Carey, L., Canada 101 A8
Careysburg, Liberia 78 D2
Cargèse, France 27 F12
Carhuamayo, Peru 124 C2
Carhuas, Peru 124 B2
Carhué, Argentina 126 D3
Caria, Turkey 66 D3
Cariacica, Brazil 123 F3
Caribbean Sea, W. Indies 117 C5
Cariboo Mts., Canada 100 C4
Caribou, U.S.A. 99 C6
Caribou →, Man., Canada 101 B10
Caribou →, N.W.T., Canada 100 A3
Caribou I., Canada 98 C2
Caribou Is., Canada 100 A6
Caribou L., Man., Canada 101 B9
Caribou L., Ont., Canada 98 B2
Caribou Mts., Canada 100 B5
Carichic, Mexico 114 B3
Carigara, Phil. 55 F6
Carignan, France 25 C12
Carignano, Italy 32 D4
Carillo, Mexico 114 B4
Carinda, Australia 91 E4
Cariñena, Spain 28 D3
Carinhanha, Brazil 123 D3
Carinhanha →, Brazil 123 D3
Carini, Italy 34 D6
Carinola, Italy 34 A6
Caripito, Venezuela 121 A5
Caritianas, Brazil 125 B5
Carlbrod = Dimitrovgrad, Serbia, Yug. 21 M12
Carleton Place, Canada 98 C4
Carletonville, S. Africa 84 D4
Carlin, U.S.A. 110 F5
Carlingford L., U.K. 15 B5
Carlinville, U.S.A. 108 F10
Carlisle, U.K. 12 C5
Carlisle, U.S.A. 106 F7
Carlit, Pic, France 26 F5
Carloforte, Italy 34 C1
Carlos Casares, Argentina 126 D3
Carlos Chagas, Brazil 123 E3
Carlos Tejedor, Argentina 126 D3
Carlow, Ireland 15 D4
Carlow □, Ireland 15 D5
Carlsbad, Calif., U.S.A. 113 M9
Carlsbad, N. Mex., U.S.A. 109 J2
Carlyle, Canada 101 D8
Carlyle, U.S.A. 108 F10
Carmacks, Canada 96 B6
Carmagnola, Italy 32 D4
Carman, Canada 101 D9
Carmanville, Canada 99 C9
Carmangay, Canada 100 C6
Carmarthen, U.K. 13 F3
Carmarthen B., U.K. 13 F3
Carmaux, France 26 D6

Carmel, U.S.A. 107 E11
Carmel-by-the-Sea, U.S.A. 111 H3
Carmel Valley, U.S.A. 112 J5
Carmelo, Uruguay 126 C4
Carmen, Bolivia 124 C4
Carmen, Colombia 120 B2
Carmen, Paraguay 127 B4
Carmen →, Mexico 114 A3
Carmen, I., Mexico 114 B2
Carmen de Patagones, Argentina 128 B4
Cármenes, Spain 30 C5
Carmensa, Argentina 126 D2
Carmi, U.S.A. 104 F1
Carmila, Australia 90 C4
Carmona, Spain 31 H5
Carnac, France 24 E3
Carnarvon, Queens., Australia 90 C4
Carnarvon, W. Austral., Australia 89 D1
Carnarvon, S. Africa 84 E3
Carnarvon Ra., Queens., Australia 90 D4
Carnarvon Ra., W. Austral., Australia 89 E3
Carnation, U.S.A. 112 C5
Carnaxide, Portugal 31 G1
Carndonagh, Ireland 15 A4
Carnduff, Canada 101 D8
Carnegie, U.S.A. 106 F4
Carnegie, L., Australia 89 E3
Carnic Alps = Karnische Alpen, Europe 21 J3
Carniche Alpi = Karnische Alpen, Europe 21 J3
Carnot, C.A.R. 80 D3
Carnot, C., Australia 91 E2
Carnot B., Australia 88 C3
Carnsore Pt., Ireland 15 D5
Caro, U.S.A. 104 D4
Carol City, U.S.A. 105 N5
Carolina, Brazil 122 C2
Carolina, Puerto Rico 117 C6
Carolina, S. Africa 85 D5
Caroline I., Kiribati 93 H12
Caroline Is., Pac. Oc. 92 G6
Caron, Canada 101 C7
Caroni →, Venezuela 121 B5
Caronie = Nébrodi, Monti, Italy 35 E7
Caroona, Australia 91 E5
Carora, Venezuela 120 A3
Carovigno, Italy 35 B10
Carpathians, Europe 20 F11
Carpații Meridionali, Romania 38 D8
Carpenédolo, Italy 32 C7
Carpentaria, G. of, Australia 90 A2
Carpentaria Downs, Australia 90 B3
Carpentras, France 27 D9
Carpi, Italy 32 D7
Carpina, Brazil 122 C4
Carpino, Italy 35 A8
Carpinteria, U.S.A. 113 L7
Carpio, Spain 30 D5
Carpolac = Morea, Australia 91 F3
Carr Boyd Ra., Australia 88 C4
Carrabelle, U.S.A. 105 L3
Carranya, Australia 88 C4
Carrara, Italy 32 D7
Carrascal, Phil. 55 G6
Carrascosa del Campo, Spain 28 E2
Carrauntoohill, Ireland 15 E2
Carretas, Punta, Peru 124 C2
Carrick-on-Shannon, Ireland 15 C3
Carrick-on-Suir, Ireland 15 D4
Carrickfergus, U.K. 15 B6
Carrickfergus □, U.K. 15 B6
Carrickmacross, Ireland 15 C5
Carrieton, Australia 91 E2
Carrington, U.S.A. 108 B5
Carrión →, Spain 30 D6
Carrión de los Condes, Spain 30 C6
Carrizal Bajo, Chile 126 B1
Carrizalillo, Chile 126 B1
Carrizo Cr. →, U.S.A. 109 G3
Carrizo Springs, U.S.A. 109 L5
Carrizozo, U.S.A. 111 K11
Carroll, U.S.A. 108 D7
Carrollton, Ga., U.S.A. 105 J3
Carrollton, Ill., U.S.A. 108 F9
Carrollton, Ky., U.S.A. 104 F3
Carrollton, Mo., U.S.A. 108 F8
Carrollton, Ohio, U.S.A. 106 F3
Carron →, U.K. 14 D3
Carron, L., U.K. 14 D3
Carrot →, Canada 101 C8
Carrot River, Canada 101 C8
Carrouges, France 24 D6
Carruthers, Canada 101 C7
Çarşamba, Turkey 66 B7
Carse of Gowrie, U.K. 14 E5
Carsóli, Italy 33 F10
Carson, Calif., U.S.A. 113 M8
Carson, N. Dak., U.S.A. 108 B4
Carson City, U.S.A. 112 F7
Carson Sink, U.S.A. 110 G4
Carstairs, U.K. 14 F5

Cartagena, Colombia 120 A2
Cartagena, Spain 29 H4
Cartago, Colombia 120 C2
Cartago, Costa Rica 116 E3
Cartaxo, Portugal 31 F2
Cartaya, Spain 31 H3
Carteret, France 24 C5
Cartersville, U.S.A. 105 H3
Carterton, N.Z. 87 J5
Carthage, Ark., U.S.A. 109 H8
Carthage, Ill., U.S.A. 108 E9
Carthage, Mo., U.S.A. 109 G7
Carthage, S. Dak., U.S.A. 108 C6
Carthage, Tex., U.S.A. 109 J7
Cartier I., Australia 88 B3
Cartwright, Canada 99 B8
Caruaru, Brazil 122 C4
Carúpano, Venezuela 121 A5
Carutapera, Brazil 122 B2
Caruthersville, U.S.A. 109 G10
Carvalho, Brazil 121 D7
Carvin, France 25 B9
Carvoeiro, Brazil 121 D5
Carvoeiro, C., Portugal 31 F1
Casa Branca, Brazil 123 F2
Casa Branca, Portugal 31 G2
Casa Grande, U.S.A. 111 K8
Casablanca, Chile 126 C1
Casablanca, Morocco 74 B3
Casacalenda, Italy 35 A7
Casal di Príncipe, Italy 35 B7
Casalbordino, Italy 33 F11
Casale Monferrato, Italy 32 C5
Casalmaggiore, Italy 32 D7
Casalpusterlengo, Italy 32 C6
Casamance →, Senegal 78 C1
Casamássima, Italy 35 B9
Casanare □, Colombia 120 B3
Casanare →, Colombia 120 B3
Casarano, Italy 35 B11
Casares, Spain 31 J5
Casas Grandes, Mexico 114 A3
Casas Ibáñez, Spain 29 F3
Casasimarro, Spain 29 F2
Casatejada, Spain 30 F5
Casavieja, Spain 30 E6
Cascade, Idaho, U.S.A. 110 D5
Cascade, Mont., U.S.A. 110 C8
Cascade Locks, U.S.A. 112 E5
Cascade Ra., U.S.A. 112 D5
Cascais, Portugal 31 G1
Cascavel, Brazil 127 A5
Cáscina, Italy 32 E7
Caselle Torinese, Italy 32 C4
Caserta, Italy 35 A7
Cashel, Ireland 15 D4
Cashmere, U.S.A. 110 C3
Cashmere Downs, Australia 89 E2
Casibare →, Colombia 120 C3
Casiguran, Phil. 55 C5
Casilda, Argentina 126 C3
Casino, Australia 91 D5
Casiquiare →, Venezuela 120 C4
Casitas, Peru 124 A1
Caslan, Canada 100 C6
Casma, Peru 124 B2
Casmalia, U.S.A. 113 L6
Casola Valsenio, Italy 33 D8
Cásoli, Italy 33 F11
Caspe, Spain 28 D4
Casper, U.S.A. 110 E10
Caspian Depression, Eurasia 43 G9
Caspian Sea, Eurasia 44 E6
Casquets, U.K. 24 C4
Cass City, U.S.A. 104 D4
Cass Lake, U.S.A. 108 B7
Cassá de la Selva, Spain 28 D7
Cassano Iónio, Italy 35 C9
Cassel, France 25 B9
Casselman, Canada 107 A9
Casselton, U.S.A. 108 B6
Cassiar, Canada 100 B3
Cassiar Mts., Canada 100 B2
Cassilândia, Brazil 125 D7
Cassinga, Angola 81 H3
Cassino, Italy 34 A6
Cassis, France 27 E9
Cassville, U.S.A. 109 G8
Cástagneto Carducci, Italy 32 E7
Castaic, U.S.A. 113 L8
Castanhal, Brazil 122 B2
Casteau, Belgium 17 G4
Castéggio, Italy 32 C6
Castejón de Monegros, Spain 28 D4
Castel di Sangro, Italy 33 G11
Castel San Giovanni, Italy 32 C6
Castel San Pietro Terme, Italy 33 D8
Castelbuono, Italy 35 E7
Casteldelfino, Italy 32 D4
Castelfiorentino, Italy 32 E7
Castelfranco Emília, Italy 32 D8
Castelfranco Véneto, Italy 33 C8
Casteljaloux, France 26 D4
Castellabate, Italy 35 B7
Castellammare, G. di, Italy 34 D5
Castellammare del Golfo, Italy 34 D5
Castellammare di Stábia, Italy 35 B7
Castellamonte, Italy 32 C4
Castellana Grotte, Italy 35 B10
Castellane, France 27 E10
Castellaneta, Italy 35 B9

Castellar de Santisteban, Spain 29 G1
Castelleone, Italy 32 C6
Castelli, Argentina 126 D4
Castelló de Ampurias, Spain 28 C8
Castellón □, Spain 28 E4
Castellón de la Plana, Spain 28 E4
Castellote, Spain 28 E4
Castelltérsol, Spain 28 D7
Castelmáuro, Italy 35 A7
Castelnau-de-Médoc, France 26 C3
Castelnaudary, France 26 E5
Castelnovo ne' Monti, Italy 32 D7
Castelnuovo di Val di Cécina, Italy 32 E7
Castelo, Brazil 123 F3
Castelo Branco, Portugal 30 F3
Castelo Branco □, Portugal 30 F3
Castelo de Paiva, Portugal 30 D2
Castelo de Vide, Portugal 31 F3
Castelo do Piauí, Brazil 122 C3
Castelsarrasin, France 26 D5
Casteltérmini, Italy 34 E6
Castelvetrano, Italy 34 E5
Casterton, Australia 91 F3
Castets, France 26 E2
Castiglione del Lago, Italy 33 E9
Castiglione della Pescáia, Italy 32 F7
Castiglione delle Stiviere, Italy 32 C7
Castiglione Fiorentino, Italy 33 E8
Castilblanco, Spain 31 F5
Castilla, Peru 124 B1
Castilla, Playa de, Spain 31 H4
Castilla La Mancha □, Spain 31 F7
Castilla y Leon □, Spain 30 D6
Castillon, Barr. de, France 27 E10
Castillon-en-Couserans, France 26 F5
Castillon-la-Bataille, France 26 D3
Castillonès, France 26 D4
Castillos, Uruguay 127 C5
Castle Dale, U.S.A. 110 G8
Castle Douglas, U.K. 14 G5
Castle Rock, Colo., U.S.A. 108 F2
Castle Rock, Wash., U.S.A. 112 D4
Castlebar, Ireland 15 C2
Castleblaney, Ireland 15 B5
Castlegar, Canada 100 D5
Castlemaine, Australia 91 F3
Castlerea, Ireland 15 C3
Castlereagh □, U.K. 15 B6
Castlereagh →, Australia 91 E4
Castlereagh B., Australia 90 A2
Castletown, I. of Man 12 C3
Castletown Bearhaven, Ireland 15 E2
Castlevale, Australia 90 C4
Castor, Canada 100 C6
Castres, France 26 E6
Castricum, Neths. 16 C5
Castril, Spain 29 H2
Castries, St. Lucia 117 D7
Castro, Brazil 127 A5
Castro, Chile 128 B2
Castro Alves, Brazil 123 D4
Castro del Río, Spain 31 H6
Castro Marim, Portugal 31 H3
Castro Urdiales, Spain 28 B1
Castro Verde, Portugal 31 H2
Castrojeriz, Spain 30 C6
Castropol, Spain 30 B3
Castroreale, Italy 35 D8
Castrovíllari, Italy 35 C9
Castroville, Calif., U.S.A. 112 J5
Castroville, Tex., U.S.A. 109 L5
Castrovirreyna, Peru 124 C2
Castuera, Spain 31 G5
Casummit Lake, Canada 98 B1
Çat, Turkey 67 C9
Cat Ba, Dao, Vietnam 58 B6
Cat I., Bahamas 117 B4
Cat I., U.S.A. 109 K10
Cat L., Canada 98 B1
Catacamas, Honduras 116 D2
Catacáos, Peru 124 B1
Cataguases, Brazil 123 F3
Catahoula L., U.S.A. 109 K8
Çatak, Turkey 67 C10
Catalão, Brazil 123 E2
Çatalca, Turkey 66 B3
Catalina, Canada 99 C9
Catalonia = Cataluña □, Spain 28 D6
Cataluña □, Spain 28 D6
Çatalzeytin, Turkey 66 B6
Catamarca, Argentina 126 B2
Catamarca □, Argentina 126 B2
Catanauan, Phil. 55 E5
Catanduanes, Phil. 55 E6
Catanduva, Brazil 127 A6
Catánia, Italy 35 E8
Catánia, G. di, Italy 35 E8
Catanzaro, Italy 35 D9
Catarman, Phil. 55 E6
Catbalogan, Phil. 55 F6
Cateel, Phil. 55 H7
Catende, Brazil 122 C4
Cathcart, S. Africa 84 E4
Cathlamet, U.S.A. 112 D3
Catio, Guinea-Biss. 78 C1
Catismiña, Venezuela 121 C5

Catita, Brazil 122 C3
Catlettsburg, U.S.A. 104 F4
Catoche, C., Mexico 115 C7
Catolé do Rocha, Brazil 122 C4
Catral, Spain 29 G4
Catria, Mt., Italy 33 E9
Catrimani, Brazil 121 C5
Catrimani →, Brazil 121 C5
Catskill, U.S.A. 107 D11
Catskill Mts., U.S.A. 107 D10
Catt, Mt., Australia 90 A1
Cattaraugus, U.S.A. 106 D6
Cáttolica, Italy 33 E9
Cáttolica Eraclea, Italy 34 E6
Catu, Brazil 123 D4
Catuala, Angola 84 B2
Catur, Mozam. 83 E4
Catwick Is., Vietnam 59 G7
Cauca □, Colombia 120 C2
Cauca →, Colombia 120 B3
Caucaia, Brazil 122 B4
Caucasia, Colombia 120 B2
Caucasus Mountains, Eurasia 43 J7
Caudebec-en-Caux, France 24 C7
Caudebec-lès-Elbeuf, France 24 C8
Caudry, France 25 B10
Caudete, Spain 29 G3
Caulnes, France 24 D4
Caulónia, Italy 35 D9
Caúngula, Angola 80 F3
Cauquenes, Chile 126 D1
Caura →, Venezuela 121 B5
Caurés →, Brazil 121 D5
Cauresi →, Mozam. 83 F3
Causapscal, Canada 99 C6
Caussade, France 26 D5
Causse-Méjean, France 26 D7
Cauterets, France 26 F3
Cautín □, Chile 128 A2
Cauvery →, India 60 P11
Caux, Pays de, France 24 C7
Cava dei Tirreni, Italy 35 B7
Cávado →, Portugal 30 D2
Cavaillon, France 27 E9
Cavalaire-sur-Mer, France 27 E10
Cavalcante, Brazil 123 D2
Cavalese, Italy 33 B8
Cavalier, U.S.A. 108 A6
Cavalla = Cavally →, Africa 78 E3
Cavallo, I. de, France 27 G13
Cavally →, Africa 78 E3
Cavan, Ireland 15 C4
Cavan □, Ireland 15 C4
Cavárzere, Italy 33 C9
Cave City, U.S.A. 104 G3
Cavenagh Ra., Australia 89 E4
Cavendish, Australia 91 F3
Caviana, I., Brazil 121 C7
Cavite, Phil. 55 D4
Cavour, Italy 32 D4
Cavtat, Croatia 21 N8
Cawndilla L., Australia 91 E3
Cawnpore = Kanpur, India 63 F9
Caxias, Brazil 122 B3
Caxias do Sul, Brazil 127 B5
Caxito, Angola 80 F2
Çay, Turkey 66 C4
Cay Sal Bank, Bahamas 116 B3
Cayambe, Napo, Ecuador 120 C2
Cayambe, Quito, Ecuador 120 C2
Çaycuma, Turkey 66 B5
Çayeli, Turkey 67 B9
Cayenne, Fr. Guiana 121 B7
Cayenne □, Fr. Guiana 121 C7
Cayeux-sur-Mer, France 25 B8
Çayırhan, Turkey 66 C5
Caylus, France 26 D5
Cayman Brac, Cayman Is. 116 C4
Cayman Is. ■, W. Indies 116 C3
Cayo Romano, Cuba 117 B4
Cayuga, Canada 106 D5
Cayuga, U.S.A. 107 D8
Cayuga L., U.S.A. 107 D8
Cazalla de la Sierra, Spain 31 H5
Căzănești, Romania 38 E10
Cazaux et de Sanguinet, Étang de, France 26 D2
Cazères, France 26 E5
Cazin, Bos.-H. 33 D12
Cazma, Croatia 33 C13
Cazma →, Croatia 33 C13
Cazombo, Angola 81 G4
Cazorla, Spain 29 H1
Cazorla, Venezuela 120 B4
Cazorla, Sierra de, Spain 29 G2
Cea →, Spain 30 C5
Ceadâr-Lunga, Moldova 41 J5
Ceanannus Mor, Ireland 15 C5
Ceará = Fortaleza, Brazil 122 B4
Ceará □, Brazil 122 C4
Ceará Mirim, Brazil 122 C4
Cebaco, I. de, Panama 116 E3
Cebollar, Argentina 126 B2
Cebollera, Sierra de, Spain 28 D2
Cebreros, Spain 30 E6
Cebu, Phil. 55 F5
Ceccano, Italy 34 A6
Cechi, Ivory C. 78 D4
Čechy, Czech. 19 F9
Cecil Plains, Australia 91 D5
Cécina, Italy 32 E7
Cécina →, Italy 32 E7
Ceclavín, Spain 30 F4
Cedar →, U.S.A. 108 E9

Cedar City, *U.S.A.* 111 H7
Cedar Creek Reservoir, *U.S.A.* 109 J6
Cedar Falls, *Iowa, U.S.A.* 108 D8
Cedar Falls, *Wash., U.S.A.* 112 C5
Cedar Key, *U.S.A.* 105 L4
Cedar L., *Canada* 101 C8
Cedar Rapids, *U.S.A.* ... 108 E9
Cedartown, *U.S.A.* 105 H3
Cedarvale, *Canada* 100 B3
Cedarville, *S. Africa* 85 E4
Cedarville, *U.S.A.* 110 F3
Cedeira, *Spain* 30 B2
Cedral, *Mexico* 114 C4
Cedro, *Brazil* 122 C4
Cedros, I. de, *Mexico* ... 114 B1
Ceduna, *Australia* 91 E1
Cefalù, *Italy* 35 D7
Cega →, *Spain* 30 D6
Cegléd, *Hungary* 21 H9
Céglie Messápico, *Italy* ... 35 B10
Cehegín, *Spain* 29 G3
Ceheng, *China* 52 E5
Cehu-Silvaniei, *Romania* .. 38 B6
Ceira →, *Portugal* 30 E2
Cekhira, *Tunisia* 75 B7
Celano, *Italy* 33 F10
Celanova, *Spain* 30 C3
Celaya, *Mexico* 114 C4
Celbridge, *Ireland* □ 15 C5
Celebes = Sulawesi □, *Indonesia* 57 E6
Celebes Sea, *Indonesia* ... 57 D6
Celendín, *Peru* 124 B2
Čelić, *Bos.-H.* 21 L8
Celica, *Ecuador* 120 D2
Celina, *U.S.A.* 104 E3
Celje, *Slovenia* 33 B12
Celle, *Germany* 18 C6
Celles, *Belgium* 17 G2
Celorico da Beira, *Portugal* 30 E3
Cement, *U.S.A.* 109 H5
Çemişgezek, *Turkey* 67 C8
Cenepa →, *Peru* 120 D2
Cengong, *China* 52 D7
Ceno →, *Italy* 32 D7
Cenon, *France* 26 D3
Centallo, *Italy* 32 D4
Centenário do Sul, *Brazil* . 123 F1
Center, *N. Dak., U.S.A.* .. 108 B4
Center, *Tex., U.S.A.* 109 K7
Centerfield, *U.S.A.* 111 G8
Centerville, *Calif., U.S.A.* . 112 J7
Centerville, *Iowa, U.S.A.* . 108 E8
Centerville, *Pa., U.S.A.* .. 106 F5
Centerville, *S. Dak., U.S.A.* 108 D6
Centerville, *Tenn., U.S.A.* . 105 H2
Centerville, *Tex., U.S.A.* . 109 K7
Cento, *Italy* 33 D8
Central, *Brazil* 122 D3
Central, *U.S.A.* 111 K9
Central □, *Kenya* 82 C4
Central □, *Malawi* 83 E3
Central □, *U.K.* 14 E4
Central □, *Zambia* 83 E2
Central, Cordillera, *Bolivia* 125 D5
Central, Cordillera, *Colombia* 120 C2
Central, Cordillera, *Costa Rica* 116 D3
Central, Cordillera, *Dom. Rep.* 117 C5
Central, Cordillera, *Peru* . 124 B2
Central, Cordillera, *Phil.* . 55 C4
Central, Sistema, *Spain* ... 30 E5
Central African Rep. ■, *Africa* 73 G9
Central City, *Ky., U.S.A.* . 104 G2
Central City, *Nebr., U.S.A.* 108 E5
Central I., *Kenya* 82 B4
Central Makran Range, *Pakistan* 60 F4
Central Patricia, *Canada* . 98 B1
Central Russian Uplands, *Europe* 6 E13
Central Siberian Plateau, *Russia* 46 C14
Centralia, *Ill., U.S.A.* ... 108 F10
Centralia, *Mo., U.S.A.* ... 108 F8
Centralia, *Wash., U.S.A.* . 112 D4
Centreville, *Ala., U.S.A.* . 105 J2
Centreville, *Miss., U.S.A.* 109 K9
Centúripe, *Italy* 35 E7
Cephalonia = Kefallinía, *Greece* 39 L3
Ceprano, *Italy* 34 A6
Cepu, *Indonesia* 57 G14
Ceram = Seram, *Indonesia* 57 E7
Ceram Sea = Seram Sea, *Indonesia* 57 E7
Cerbère, *France* 26 F7
Cerbicales, I., *France* ... 27 G13
Cercal, *Portugal* 31 H2
Cercemaggiore, *Italy* ... 35 A7
Cerdaña, *Spain* 28 C6
Cerdedo, *Spain* 30 C2
Cère →, *France* 26 D5
Cerea, *Italy* 33 C8
Ceres, *Argentina* 126 B3
Ceres, *Brazil* 123 E2
Ceres, *Italy* 32 C4
Ceres, *S. Africa* 84 E2
Ceres, *U.S.A.* 112 H6
Céret, *France* 26 F6
Cereté, *Colombia* 120 B2

Cerfontaine, *Belgium* 17 H4
Cerignola, *Italy* 35 A8
Cerigo = Kíthira, *Greece* . 39 N7
Cérilly, *France* 26 B6
Cerisiers, *France* 25 D10
Cerizay, *France* 24 F6
Çerkeş, *Turkey* 66 B5
Çerkezköy, *Turkey* 66 B2
Cerknica, *Slovenia* 33 C11
Çermik, *Turkey* 67 C8
Černa →, *Romania* 38 E7
Cernavodă, *Romania* ... 38 E11
Cernay, *France* 25 E14
Cernik, *Croatia* 21 K7
Cerralvo, I., *Mexico* ... 114 C3
Cerreto Sannita, *Italy* ... 35 A7
Cerritos, *Mexico* 114 C4
Cerro Sombrero, *Chile* ... 128 D3
Certaldo, *Italy* 32 E8
Cervaro →, *Italy* 35 A8
Cervera, *Spain* 28 D6
Cervera de Pisuerga, *Spain* 30 C6
Cervera del Río Alhama, *Spain* 28 C3
Cérvia, *Italy* 33 D9
Cervignano del Friuli, *Italy* 33 C10
Cervinara, *Italy* 35 A7
Cervione, *France* 27 F13
Cervo, *Spain* 30 B3
César □, *Colombia* 120 B3
Cesaro, *Italy* 35 E7
Cesena, *Italy* 33 D9
Cesenático, *Italy* 33 D9
Cēsis, *Latvia* 9 H21
Česká Lípa, *Czech.* 20 E4
Česka Republika = Czech Rep. ■, *Europe* 20 F4
České Budějovice, *Czech.* . 20 G4
Ceskomoravská Vrchovina, *Czech.* 20 F5
Český Brod, *Czech.* 20 E4
Český Krumlov, *Czech.* .. 20 G4
Český Těšín, *Czech.* ... 20 F8
Çeşme, *Turkey* 66 C2
Cessnock, *Australia* ... 91 E5
Cestos →, *Liberia* 78 D3
Cétin Grad, *Croatia* ... 33 C12
Cetina →, *Croatia* 33 E13
Cetraro, *Italy* 35 C8
Ceuta, *N. Afr.* 74 A3
Ceva, *Italy* 32 D5
Cévennes, *France* 26 D7
Ceyhan, *Turkey* 66 D6
Ceyhan →, *Turkey* ... 66 D6
Ceylânpınar, *Turkey* ... 67 D9
Ceylon = Sri Lanka ■, *Asia* 60 R12
Cèze →, *France* 27 D8
Cha-am, *Thailand* 58 F2
Chaam, *Neths.* 17 E5
Chabeuil, *France* 27 D9
Chablais, *France* 27 B10
Chablis, *France* 25 E10
Chabounia, *Algeria* ... 75 A5
Chacabuco, *Argentina* . 126 C3
Chachapoyas, *Peru* 124 B2
Chachasp, *Peru* 124 D3
Chachoengsao, *Thailand* . 58 F3
Chachran, *Pakistan* ... 60 E7
Chachro, *Pakistan* 62 G4
Chaco □, *Argentina* ... 126 B3
Chaco □, *Paraguay* ... 126 B3
Chad ■, *Africa* 73 E8
Chad, L. = Tchad, L., *Chad* 73 F7
Chadan, *Russia* 45 D10
Chadileuvú →, *Argentina* 126 D2
Chadiza, *Zambia* 83 E3
Chadron, *U.S.A.* 108 D3
Chadyr-Lunga = Ceadâr-Lunga, *Moldova* 41 J5
Chae Hom, *Thailand* .. 58 C2
Chaem →, *Thailand* .. 58 C2
Chaeryŏng, *N. Korea* .. 51 E13
Chagai Hills, *Afghan.* .. 60 E3
Chagda, *Russia* 45 D14
Chagny, *France* 25 F11
Chagoda, *Russia* 40 C8
Chagos Arch., *Ind. Oc.* . 46 K11
Chāh Ākhvor, *Iran* 65 C8
Chāh Bahār, *Iran* 65 E9
Chāh-e-Malek, *Iran* ... 65 D8
Chāh Kavīr, *Iran* 65 D7
Chahar Burjak, *Afghan.* . 60 D3
Chaibasa, *India* 61 H14
Chaillé-les-Marais, *France* 26 B2
Chainat, *Thailand* 58 E3
Chaitén, *Chile* 128 B2
Chaiya, *Thailand* 59 H2
Chaj Doab, *Pakistan* .. 62 C5
Chajari, *Argentina* 126 C4
Chake Chake, *Tanzania* . 82 D4
Chakhānsūr, *Afghan.* .. 60 D3
Chakonipau, L., *Canada* . 99 A6
Chakradharpur, *India* .. 63 H11
Chakwal, *Pakistan* 62 C5
Chala, *Peru* 124 D3
Chalais, *France* 26 C4
Chalchihuites, *Mexico* .. 114 C4
Chalcis = Khalkís, *Greece* . 39 L6
Chaleur B., *Canada* ... 99 C6
Chalfant, *U.S.A.* 112 H8
Chalhuanca, *Peru* 124 C3
Chalindrey, *France* ... 25 E12
Chaling, *China* 53 D9
Chalisgaon, *India* 60 J9
Chalky Inlet, *N.Z.* 87 M1

Challans, *France* 24 F5
Challapata, *Bolivia* 124 D4
Challis, *U.S.A.* 110 D6
Chalna, *India* 63 H13
Chalon-sur-Saône, *France* 25 F11
Chalonnes-sur-Loire, *France* 24 E6
Châlons-sur-Marne, *France* 25 D11
Châlus, *France* 26 C4
Chalyaphum, *Thailand* ... 58 E4
Cham, *Germany* 19 F8
Cham, *Switz.* 23 B6
Cham, Cu Lao, *Vietnam* . 58 E7
Chama, *U.S.A.* 111 H10
Chaman, *Pakistan* 60 D5
Chamba, *India* 62 C7
Chamba, *Tanzania* 83 E4
Chambal →, *India* ... 63 F8
Chamberlain, *U.S.A.* ... 108 D5
Chamberlain →, *Australia* 88 C4
Chambers, *U.S.A.* 111 J9
Chambersburg, *U.S.A.* . 104 F7
Chambéry, *France* 27 C9
Chambly, *Canada* 107 A11
Chambord, *Canada* ... 99 C5
Chamchamal, *Iraq* 67 E11
Chamela, *Mexico* 114 D3
Chamical, *Argentina* ... 126 C2
Chamkar Luong, *Cambodia* 59 G4
Chamonix-Mont Blanc, *France* 27 C10
Champa, *India* 63 H10
Champagne, *Canada* ... 100 A1
Champagne, *France* ... 25 D11
Champagne, Plaine de, *France* 25 D11
Champagnole, *France* .. 25 F12
Champaign, *U.S.A.* ... 104 E1
Champassak, *Laos* 58 E5
Champaubert, *France* .. 25 D10
Champdeniers, *France* . 26 B3
Champeix, *France* 26 C7
Champlain, *Canada* ... 104 B9
Champlain, *U.S.A.* ... 107 B11
Champlain, L., *U.S.A.* . 107 B11
Champotón, *Mexico* ... 115 D6
Chamusca, *Portugal* ... 31 F2
Chan Chan, *Peru* 124 B2
Chana, *Thailand* 59 J3
Chañaral, *Chile* 126 B1
Chanārān, *Iran* 65 B8
Chanasma, *India* 62 H5
Chancay, *Peru* 124 C2
Chancy, *Switz.* 22 D1
Chandannagar, *India* .. 63 H13
Chandausi, *India* 63 E8
Chandeleur Is., *U.S.A.* . 109 L10
Chandeleur Sd., *U.S.A.* . 109 L10
Chandigarh, *India* 62 D7
Chandler, *Australia* ... 91 D1
Chandler, *Canada* 99 C7
Chandler, *Ariz., U.S.A.* . 111 K8
Chandler, *Okla., U.S.A.* . 109 H6
Chandless →, *Brazil* .. 124 B4
Chandmani, *Mongolia* .. 54 B4
Chandpur, *Bangla.* 61 H17
Chandpur, *India* 62 E8
Chandrapur, *India* 60 K11
Chānf, *Iran* 65 E9
Chang, *Pakistan* 62 F3
Chang, Ko, *Thailand* .. 59 F4
Ch'ang Chiang = Chang Jiang →, *China* 53 B13
Chang Jiang →, *China* . 53 B13
Changa, *India* 63 C7
Changanacheri, *India* .. 60 Q10
Changane →, *Mozam.* . 85 C5
Changbai, *China* 51 D15
Changbai Shan, *China* .. 51 C15
Changchiak'ou = Zhangjiakou, *China* .. 50 D8
Ch'angchou = Changzhou, *China* 53 B12
Changchun, *China* 51 C13
Changchunling, *China* .. 51 B13
Changde, *China* 53 C8
Chango-ri, *N. Korea* .. 51 E14
Changfeng, *China* 53 A11
Changhai = Shanghai, *China* 53 B13
Changhua, *China* 53 B12
Changhŭng, *S. Korea* .. 51 G14
Changhŭngni, *N. Korea* . 51 D15
Changjiang, *China* 54 E5
Changjin, *N. Korea* ... 51 D14
Changjin-chŏsuji, *N. Korea* 51 D14
Changle, *China* 53 E12
Changli, *China* 51 E10
Changling, *China* 51 B12
Changlun, *Malaysia* ... 59 J3
Changning, *Hunan, China* 53 D9
Changning, *Yunnan, China* 52 E2
Changping, *China* 50 D9
Changsha, *China* 53 C9
Changshan, *China* 53 C12
Changshou, *China* 52 C6
Changshu, *China* 53 B13
Changshun, *China* 52 D6
Changtai, *China* 53 E11
Changting, *China* 53 E11
Changwu, *China* 50 G5
Changxing, *China* 53 B12
Changyang, *China* 53 B8
Changyi, *China* 51 F10
Changyŏn, *N. Korea* .. 51 E13
Changyuan, *China* 50 G8
Changzhi, *China* 50 F7

Changzhou, *China* 53 B12
Chanhanga, *Angola* ... 84 B1
Chanlar = Xanlar, *Azerbaijan* 43 K8
Channapatna, *India* ... 60 N10
Channel Is., *U.K.* 13 H5
Channel Is., *U.S.A.* ... 113 M7
Channel-Port aux Basques, *Canada* 99 C8
Channing, *Mich., U.S.A.* 104 B1
Channing, *Tex., U.S.A.* . 109 H3
Chantada, *Spain* 30 C3
Chanthaburi, *Thailand* . 58 F4
Chantilly, *France* 25 C9
Chantonnay, *France* ... 24 F5
Chantrey Inlet, *Canada* . 96 B10
Chanute, *U.S.A.* 109 G7
Chanza →, *Spain* 31 H3
Chao Hu, *China* 53 B11
Chao Phraya →, *Thailand* 58 F3
Chao Phraya Lowlands, *Thailand* 58 E3
Chao Xian, *China* 53 B11
Chao'an, *China* 53 F11
Chaocheng, *China* 50 F8
Chaoyang, *Guangdong, China* 53 F11
Chaoyang, *Liaoning, China* 51 D11
Chapada dos Guimarães, *Brazil* 125 D6
Chapala, *Mozam.* 83 F4
Chapala, L. de, *Mexico* . 114 C4
Chaparé →, *Bolivia* ... 125 D5
Chaparral, *Colombia* ... 120 C2
Chapayev, *Kazakhstan* . 42 E10
Chapayevsk, *Russia* ... 42 D9
Chapecó, *Brazil* 127 B5
Chapel Hill, *U.S.A.* ... 105 H6
Chapleau, *Canada* 98 C3
Chaplin, *Canada* 101 C7
Chaplino, *Ukraine* 41 H9
Chaplygin, *Russia* 42 D5
Chapra = Chhapra, *India* 63 G11
Châr, *Mauritania* 74 D2
Chara, *Russia* 45 D12
Charadai, *Argentina* ... 126 B4
Charagua, *Bolivia* 125 D5
Charalá, *Colombia* 120 B3
Charambirá, Punta, *Colombia* 120 C2
Charaña, *Bolivia* 124 D4
Charantsavan, *Armenia* . 43 K7
Charapita, *Colombia* ... 120 D3
Charata, *Argentina* ... 126 B3
Charcas, *Mexico* 114 C4
Charcoal L., *Canada* ... 101 B8
Chard, *U.K.* 13 G5
Chardara, *Kazakhstan* . 44 E7
Chardon, *U.S.A.* 106 E3
Chardzhou = Chärjew, *Turkmenistan* 44 F7
Charente □, *France* ... 26 C4
Charente →, *France* .. 26 C2
Charente-Maritime □, *France* 26 C3
Chari →, *Chad* 73 F7
Chārīkār, *Afghan.* 60 B6
Chariton →, *U.S.A.* .. 108 F8
Charity, *Guyana* 121 B6
Chärjew, *Turkmenistan* . 44 F7
Charkhari, *India* 63 G8
Charkhi Dadri, *India* .. 62 E7
Charleroi, *Belgium* 17 H4
Charleroi, *U.S.A.* 106 F5
Charles, C., *U.S.A.* ... 104 G8
Charles City, *U.S.A.* .. 108 D8
Charles L., *Canada* ... 101 B6
Charles Town, *U.S.A.* . 104 F7
Charleston, *Ill., U.S.A.* . 104 F1
Charleston, *Miss., U.S.A.* 109 H9
Charleston, *Mo., U.S.A.* 109 G10
Charleston, *S.C., U.S.A.* 105 J6
Charleston, *W. Va., U.S.A.* 104 F5
Charleston Peak, *U.S.A.* 113 J11
Charlestown, *S. Africa* .. 85 D4
Charlestown, *U.S.A.* ... 104 F3
Charleville = Rath Luirc, *Ireland* 15 D3
Charleville, *Australia* ... 91 D4
Charleville-Mézières, *France* 25 C11
Charlevoix, *U.S.A.* ... 104 C3
Charlieu, *France* 27 B8
Charlotte, *Mich., U.S.A.* 104 D3
Charlotte, *N.C., U.S.A.* 105 H5
Charlotte Amalie, *Virgin Is.* 117 C7
Charlotte Harbor, *U.S.A.* 105 M4
Charlottesville, *U.S.A.* . 104 F6
Charlottetown, *Canada* . 99 C7
Charlton, *Australia* ... 91 F3
Charlton, *U.S.A.* 108 E8
Charlton I., *Canada* ... 98 B4
Charmes, *France* 25 D13
Charny, *Canada* 99 C5
Charolles, *France* 27 B8
Chârost, *France* 25 F9
Charouine, *Algeria* ... 75 C4
Charre, *Mozam.* 83 F4
Charroux, *France* 26 B4
Charsadda, *Pakistan* .. 62 B4
Charters Towers, *Australia* 90 C4
Chartres, *France* 24 D8
Chascomús, *Argentina* . 126 D4
Chasefu, *Zambia* 83 E3

Chasovnya-Uchurskaya, *Russia* 45 D14
Chasseneuil-sur-Bonnieure, *France* 26 C4
Chāt, *Iran* 65 B7
Chatal Balkan = Udvoy Balkan, *Bulgaria* 38 G9
Château-Arnoux, *France* . 27 D10
Château-Chinon, *France* . 25 E10
Château d'Oex, *Switz.* ... 22 D4
Château-du-Loir, *France* . 24 E7
Château-Gontier, *France* . 24 E6
Château-la-Vallière, *France* 24 E7
Château-Landon, *France* . 25 D9
Château-Porcien, *France* . 25 C11
Château-Renault, *France* . 24 E7
Château-Salins, *France* . 25 D13
Château-Thierry, *France* . 25 C10
Châteaubourg, *France* .. 24 D5
Châteaubriant, *France* .. 24 E5
Châteaudun, *France* ... 24 D8
Châteaugiron, *France* .. 24 D5
Châteaulin, *France* ... 24 D2
Châteaumeillant, *France* . 26 B6
Châteauneuf-du-Faou, *France* 24 D3
Châteauneuf-en-Thymerais, *France* 24 D8
Châteauneuf-sur-Charente, *France* 26 C3
Châteauneuf-sur-Cher, *France* 25 F9
Châteauneuf-sur-Loire, *France* 25 E9
Châteaurenard, *Bouches-du-Rhône, France* 27 E8
Châteaurenard, *Loiret, France* 25 E9
Châteauroux, *France* ... 25 F8
Châtel-St.-Denis, *Switz.* . 22 C3
Châtelaillon-Plage, *France* 26 B2
Châtelaudren, *France* .. 24 D4
Châtelet, *Belgium* 17 H5
Châtelguyon, *France* ... 26 C7
Châtellerault, *France* .. 24 F7
Châtelus-Malvaleix, *France* 26 B6
Chatfield, *U.S.A.* 108 D8
Chatham, *N.B., Canada* . 99 C6
Chatham, *Ont., Canada* . 98 D3
Chatham, *U.K.* 13 F8
Chatham, *La., U.S.A.* . 109 J8
Chatham, *N.Y., U.S.A.* 107 D11
Chatham, I., *Chile* 128 D2
Chatham Is., *Pac. Oc.* . 92 M10
Chatham Str., *U.S.A.* . 100 B2
Châtillon, *Italy* 32 C4
Châtillon-Coligny, *France* . 25 E9
Châtillon-en-Bazois, *France* 25 E10
Châtillon-en-Diois, *France* 27 D9
Châtillon-sur-Indre, *France* 24 F8
Châtillon-sur-Loire, *France* 25 E9
Châtillon-sur-Marne, *France* 25 C10
Châtillon-sur-Seine, *France* 25 E11
Chatmohar, *Bangla.* ... 63 G13
Chatra, *India* 63 G11
Chatrapur, *India* 61 K14
Chats, L. des, *Canada* . 107 A8
Chatsworth, *Canada* .. 106 B4
Chatsworth, *Zimbabwe* . 83 F3
Chattahoochee →, *U.S.A.* 105 K3
Chattanooga, *U.S.A.* .. 105 H3
Chaturat, *Thailand* ... 58 E3
Chau Doc, *Vietnam* ... 59 G5
Chaudanne, Barr. de, *France* 27 E10
Chaudes-Aigues, *France* . 26 D7
Chauffailles, *France* ... 27 B8
Chauk, *Burma* 61 J19
Chaukan La, *Burma* ... 61 F20
Chaulnes, *France* 25 C9
Chaumont, *France* 25 D12
Chaumont, *U.S.A.* ... 107 B8
Chaumont-en-Vexin, *France* 25 C8
Chaumont-sur-Loire, *France* 24 E8
Chaunay, *France* 26 B4
Chauny, *France* 25 C10
Chausey, Is., *France* .. 24 D5
Chaussin, *France* 25 F12
Chautauqua L., *U.S.A.* . 106 D5
Chauvigny, *France* ... 24 F7
Chauvin, *Canada* 101 C6
Chavantina, *Brazil* 125 D7
Chaves, *Brazil* 122 B2
Chaves, *Portugal* 30 D3
Chavuma, *Zambia* 81 G4
Chawang, *Thailand* ... 59 H2
Chazelles-sur-Lyon, *France* 27 C8
Chazuta, *Peru* 124 B2
Chazy, *U.S.A.* 107 B11
Cheb, *Czech.* 20 E2
Cheboksarskoye Vdkhr., *Russia* 42 B8
Cheboksary, *Russia* ... 42 B8
Cheboygan, *U.S.A.* ... 104 C3
Chebsara, *Russia* 40 C10
Chech, Erg, *Africa* 74 D4
Chechaouen, *Morocco* . 74 A3
Chechen, Ostrov, *Russia* 43 H8
Chechenia □, *Russia* .. 43 J7
Checheno-Ingush Republic = Chechenia □, *Russia* . 43 J7

Chechnya = Chechenia □, Russia 43 J7
Chechon, S. Korea 51 F15
Chęciny, Poland 20 E10
Checleset B., Canada ... 100 C3
Checotah, U.S.A. 109 H7
Cheduba I., Burma 61 K18
Cheepie, Australia 91 D4
Chef-Boutonne, France .. 26 B3
Chegdomyn, Russia 45 D14
Chegga, Mauritania 74 C3
Chegutu, Zimbabwe 83 F3
Chehalis, U.S.A. 112 D4
Cheiron, Mt., France ... 27 E10
Cheju Do, S. Korea 51 H14
Chekalin, Russia 42 C3
Chekiang = Zhejiang □, China 53 C13
Chel = Kuru, Bahr el →, Sudan 77 F2
Chela, Sa. da, Angola ... 84 B1
Chelan, U.S.A. 110 C4
Chelan, L., U.S.A. 110 C3
Cheleken, Turkmenistan .. 44 F6
Chelforó, Argentina 128 A3
Chéliff, O. →, Algeria .. 75 A5
Chelkar = Shalqar, Kazakhstan 44 E6
Chelkar Tengiz, Solonchak, Kazakhstan 44 E7
Chellala Dahrania, Algeria 75 B5
Chelles, France 25 D9
Chełm, Poland 20 D13
Chełmek, Poland 20 E9
Chełmno, Poland 20 B8
Chelmsford, U.K. 13 F8
Chełmża, Poland 20 B8
Chelsea, Okla., U.S.A. .. 109 G7
Chelsea, Vt., U.S.A. ... 107 C12
Cheltenham, U.K. 13 F5
Chelva, Spain 28 F4
Chelyabinsk, Russia 44 D7
Chelyuskin, C., Russia .. 46 B14
Chemainus, Canada 100 D4
Chembar = Belinskiy, Russia 42 D6
Chemillé, France 24 E6
Chemnitz, Germany 18 E8
Chemult, U.S.A. 110 E3
Chen, Gora, Russia 45 C15
Chen Xian, China 53 E9
Chenab →, Pakistan ... 62 D4
Chenachane, O. →, Algeria 74 C4
Chenango Forks, U.S.A. . 107 D9
Chencha, Ethiopia 77 F4
Chenchiang = Zhenjiang, China 53 A12
Chênée, Belgium 17 G7
Cheney, U.S.A. 110 C5
Cheng Xian, China 50 H3
Chengbu, China 53 D8
Chengcheng, China 50 G5
Chengchou = Zhengzhou, China 50 G7
Chengde, China 51 D9
Chengdu, China 52 B5
Chenggong, China 52 E4
Chenggu, China 50 H4
Chengjiang, China 52 E4
Chengkou, China 52 B7
Ch'engtu = Chengdu, China 52 B5
Chengwu, China 50 G8
Chengxi Hu, China 53 A11
Chengyang, China 51 F11
Chenjiagang, China 51 G10
Chenkán, Mexico 115 D6
Chenxi, China 53 C8
Cheo Reo, Vietnam ... 58 F7
Cheom Ksan, Cambodia . 58 E5
Chepelare, Bulgaria ... 39 H7
Chepén, Peru 124 B2
Chepes, Argentina 126 C2
Chepo, Panama 116 E4
Cheptulil, Mt., Kenya .. 82 B4
Chequamegon B., U.S.A. 108 B9
Cher □, France 25 E9
Cher →, France 24 E7
Cherasco, Italy 32 D4
Cheratte, Belgium 17 G7
Cheraw, U.S.A. 105 H6
Cherbourg, France 24 C5
Cherchell, Algeria 75 A5
Cherdakly, Russia 42 C9
Cherdyn, Russia 44 C6
Cheremkhovo, Russia .. 45 D11
Cherepanovo, Russia .. 44 D9
Cherepovets, Russia ... 40 C9
Chergui, Chott ech, Algeria 75 B5
Cherikov = Cherykaw, Belarus 40 F6
Cherkasy, Ukraine 41 H7
Cherkessk, Russia 43 H6
Cherlak, Russia 44 D8
Chernaya, Russia 45 B9
Cherni, Bulgaria 38 G6
Chernigov = Chernihiv, Ukraine 41 G6
Chernihiv, Ukraine 41 G6
Chernivtsi, Ukraine ... 41 H3
Chernobyl = Chornobyl, Ukraine 41 G6
Chernogorsk, Russia ... 45 D10

Chernomorskoye = Chornomorske, Ukraine 41 K7
Chernovtsy = Chernivtsi, Ukraine 41 H3
Chernyakhovsk, Russia .. 9 J19
Chernyanka, Russia 42 E3
Chernyshovskiy, Russia .. 45 C12
Chernyye Zemli, Russia . 43 H8
Cherokee, Iowa, U.S.A. . 108 D7
Cherokee, Okla., U.S.A. . 109 G5
Cherokees, Lake O' The, U.S.A. 109 G7
Cherquenco, Chile 128 A2
Cherrapunji, India 61 G17
Cherry Creek, U.S.A. .. 110 G6
Cherry Valley, U.S.A. .. 113 M10
Cherskiy, Russia 45 C17
Cherskogo Khrebet, Russia 45 C15
Chertkovo, Russia 42 F5
Cherven, Belarus 40 F5
Cherven-Bryag, Bulgaria . 38 F7
Chervonohrad, Ukraine .. 41 G3
Cherykaw, Belarus 40 F6
Chesapeake, U.S.A. ... 104 G7
Chesapeake B., U.S.A. . 104 F7
Cheshire □, U.K. 12 D5
Cheshskaya Guba, Russia . 44 C5
Cheslatta L., Canada ... 100 C3
Chesley, Canada 106 B3
Cheste, Spain 29 F4
Chester, U.K. 12 D5
Chester, Calif., U.S.A. .. 110 F3
Chester, Ill., U.S.A. ... 109 G10
Chester, Mont., U.S.A. . 110 B8
Chester, Pa., U.S.A. ... 104 F8
Chester, S.C., U.S.A. .. 105 H5
Chesterfield, U.K. 12 D6
Chesterfield, Is., N. Cal. . 92 J7
Chesterfield Inlet, Canada 96 B10
Chesterton Ra., Australia 91 D4
Chesterville, Canada ... 107 A9
Chesuncook L., U.S.A. .. 99 C6
Chéticamp, Canada 99 C7
Chetumal, B. de, Mexico 115 D7
Chetwynd, Canada 100 B4
Chevanceaux, France .. 26 C3
Cheviot, The, U.K. 12 B5
Cheviot Hills, U.K. ... 12 B5
Cheviot Ra., Australia .. 90 D3
Chew Bahir, Ethiopia .. 77 G4
Chewelah, U.S.A. 110 B5
Cheyenne, Okla., U.S.A. . 109 H5
Cheyenne, Wyo., U.S.A. . 108 E2
Cheyenne →, U.S.A. .. 108 C4
Cheyenne Wells, U.S.A. . 108 F3
Cheyne B., Australia ... 89 F2
Chhabra, India 62 G7
Chhapra, India 63 G11
Chhata, India 62 F7
Chhatarpur, India 63 G8
Chhep, Cambodia 58 F5
Chhindwara, India 63 H8
Chhlong, Cambodia ... 59 F5
Chhuk, Cambodia 59 G5
Chi →, Thailand 58 E5
Chiamis, Indonesia ... 57 G13
Chiamussu = Jiamusi, China 54 B8
Chiang Dao, Thailand .. 58 C2
Chiang Kham, Thailand . 58 C3
Chiang Khan, Thailand . 58 D3
Chiang Khong, Thailand . 58 B3
Chiang Mai, Thailand .. 58 C2
Chiang Saen, Thailand .. 58 B3
Chiange, Angola 81 H2
Chiapa →, Mexico ... 115 D6
Chiapa de Corzo, Mexico 115 D6
Chiapas □, Mexico ... 115 D6
Chiaramonte Gulfi, Italy 35 E7
Chiaravalle, Italy 33 E10
Chiaravalle Centrale, Italy 35 D9
Chiari, Italy 32 C6
Chiasso, Switz. 23 E8
Chiatura, Georgia 43 J6
Chiautla, Mexico 115 D5
Chiávari, Italy 32 D6
Chiavenna, Italy 32 B6
Chiba, Japan 49 G10
Chibabava, Mozam. 85 C5
Chibatu, Indonesia ... 57 G12
Chibemba, Cunene, Angola 81 H2
Chibemba, Huila, Angola 84 B2
Chibia, Angola 81 H2
Chibougamau, Canada .. 98 C5
Chibougamau L., Canada 98 C5
Chibuk, Nigeria 79 C7
Chic-Chocs, Mts., Canada 99 C6
Chicacole = Srikakulam, India 61 K13
Chicago, U.S.A. 104 E2
Chicago Heights, U.S.A. 104 E2
Chichagof I., U.S.A. ... 100 B1
Chichaoua, Morocco ... 74 B3
Chicheng, China 50 D8
Chichester, U.K. 13 G7
Chichibu, Japan 49 F9
Ch'ich'ihaerh = Qiqihar, China 45 E13
Chickasha, U.S.A. 109 H5
Chiclana de la Frontera, Spain 31 J4
Chiclayo, Peru 124 B2
Chico, U.S.A. 112 F5
Chico →, Chubut, Argentina 128 B3

Chico →, Santa Cruz, Argentina 128 C3
Chicomo, Mozam. 85 C5
Chicontepec, Mexico .. 115 C5
Chicopee, U.S.A. 107 D12
Chicoutimi, Canada ... 99 C5
Chicualacuala, Mozam. . 85 C5
Chidambaram, India ... 60 P11
Chidenguele, Mozam. .. 85 C5
Chidley, C., Canada ... 97 B13
Chiede, Angola 84 B2
Chiefs Pt., Canada 106 B3
Chiem Hoa, Vietnam .. 58 A5
Chiemsee, Germany ... 19 H8
Chiengi, Zambia 83 D2
Chiengmai = Chiang Mai, Thailand 58 C2
Chienti →, Italy 33 E10
Chieri, Italy 32 D4
Chiers →, France 25 C11
Chiese →, Italy 32 C7
Chieti, Italy 33 F11
Chièvres, Belgium 17 G3
Chifeng, China 51 C10
Chigirin, Ukraine 41 H7
Chignecto B., Canada .. 99 C7
Chigorodó, Colombia .. 120 B2
Chiguana, Bolivia 126 A2
Chihli, G. of = Bo Hai, China 51 E10
Chihuahua, Mexico ... 114 B3
Chihuahua □, Mexico . 114 B3
Chiili, Kazakhstan 44 E7
Chik Bollapur, India .. 60 N10
Chikmagalur, India ... 60 N9
Chikwawa, Malawi 83 F3
Chilac, Mexico 115 D5
Chilako →, Canada .. 100 C4
Chilam Chavki, Pakistan 63 B6
Chilanga, Zambia 83 F2
Chilapa, Mexico 115 D5
Chilas, Pakistan 63 B6
Chilaw, Sri Lanka 60 R11
Chilcotin →, Canada .. 100 C4
Childers, Australia 91 D5
Childress, U.S.A. 109 H4
Chile ■, S. Amer. 128 B2
Chile Chico, Chile 128 C2
Chile Rise, Pac. Oc. ... 93 L18
Chilecito, Argentina ... 126 B2
Chilete, Peru 124 B2
Chilia, Brațul →, Romania 38 D12
Chililabombwe, Zambia . 83 E2
Chilin = Jilin, China .. 51 C14
Chilka L., India 61 K14
Chilko →, Canada ... 100 C4
Chilko, L., Canada 100 C4
Chillagoe, Australia ... 90 B3
Chillán, Chile 126 D1
Chillicothe, Ill., U.S.A. . 108 E10
Chillicothe, Mo., U.S.A. 108 F8
Chillicothe, Ohio, U.S.A. 104 F4
Chilliwack, Canada ... 100 D4
Chilo, India 62 E4
Chiloane, I., Mozam. .. 85 C5
Chiloé □, Chile 128 B2
Chiloé, I. de, Chile ... 128 B2
Chilpancingo, Mexico .. 115 D5
Chiltern Hills, U.K. ... 13 F7
Chilton, U.S.A. 104 C1
Chiluage, Angola 80 F4
Chilubi, Zambia 83 E2
Chilubula, Zambia 83 E3
Chilumba, Malawi 83 E3
Chilwa, L., Malawi ... 83 F4
Chimaltitán, Mexico .. 114 C4
Chimán, Panama 116 E4
Chimay, Belgium 17 H4
Chimbay, Uzbekistan .. 44 E6
Chimborazo, Ecuador .. 120 D2
Chimbote, Peru 124 B2
Chimkent = Shymkent, Kazakhstan 44 E7
Chimoio, Mozam. 83 F3
Chimpembe, Zambia .. 83 D2
Chin □, Burma 61 J18
Chin Ling Shan = Qinling Shandi, China 50 H5
China, Mexico 115 B5
China ■, Asia 50 E3
China Lake, U.S.A. ... 113 K9
Chinacota, Colombia .. 120 B3
Chinan = Jinan, China . 50 F9
Chinandega, Nic. 116 D2
Chinati Peak, U.S.A. .. 109 K2
Chincha Alta, Peru ... 124 C2
Chinchilla, Australia .. 91 D5
Chinchilla de Monte Aragón, Spain 29 G3
Chinchón, Spain 28 E1
Chinchorro, Banco, Mexico 115 D7
Chinchou = Jinzhou, China 51 D11
Chincoteague, U.S.A. .. 104 G8
Chinde, Mozam. 83 F4
Chindo, S. Korea 51 G14
Chindwin →, Burma .. 61 J19
Chineni, India 63 C6
Chinga, Mozam. 83 F4
Chingola, Zambia 83 E2
Chingole, Malawi 83 E3
Ch'ingtao = Qingdao, China 51 F11
Chinguar, Angola 81 G3
Chinguetti, Mauritania . 74 D2
Chingune, Mozam. 85 C5
Chinhae, S. Korea 51 G15

Chinhanguanine, Mozam. 85 D5
Chinhoyi, Zimbabwe .. 83 F3
Chiniot, Pakistan 62 D5
Chínipas, Mexico 114 B3
Chinju, S. Korea 51 G15
Chinle, U.S.A. 111 H9
Chinnampo, N. Korea . 51 E13
Chino, Japan 49 G9
Chino, U.S.A. 113 L9
Chino Valley, U.S.A. .. 111 J7
Chinon, France 24 E7
Chinook, Canada 101 C6
Chinook, U.S.A. 110 B9
Chinsali, Zambia 83 E3
Chióggia, Italy 33 C9
Chíos = Khíos, Greece . 39 L9
Chipata, Zambia 83 E3
Chipewyan L., Canada . 101 B9
Chipinge, Zimbabwe .. 83 G3
Chipiona, Spain 31 J4
Chipley, U.S.A. 105 K3
Chipman, Canada 99 C6
Chipoka, Malawi 83 E3
Chippenham, U.K. 13 F5
Chippewa →, U.S.A. . 108 C8
Chippewa Falls, U.S.A. . 108 C9
Chiquián, Peru 124 C2
Chiquimula, Guatemala 116 D2
Chiquinquira, Colombia 120 B3
Chiquitos, Llanos de, Bolivia 125 D5
Chir →, Russia 43 F6
Chirala, India 60 M12
Chiramba, Mozam. ... 83 F3
Chirawa, India 62 E6
Chirchiq, Uzbekistan .. 44 E7
Chirgua →, Venezuela 120 B4
Chiricahua Peak, U.S.A. 111 L9
Chiriquí, G. de, Panama 116 E3
Chiriquí, L. de, Panama 116 E3
Chirivira Falls, Zimbabwe 83 G3
Chirmiri, India 61 H13
Chiromo, Malawi 81 H7
Chirpan, Bulgaria 38 G8
Chirripó Grande, Cerro, Costa Rica 116 E3
Chisamba, Zambia 83 E2
Chisapani Garhi, Nepal . 61 F14
Chisasibi, Canada 98 B4
Chishtian Mandi, Pakistan 62 E5
Chishui, China 52 C5
Chishui He →, China . 52 C5
Chisimba Falls, Zambia . 83 E3
Chişinău, Moldova 41 J5
Chisone →, Italy 32 D4
Chisos Mts., U.S.A. ... 109 L3
Chistopol, Russia 42 C10
Chita, Colombia 120 B3
Chita, Russia 45 D12
Chitado, Angola 81 H2
Chitembo, Angola 81 G3
Chitipa, Malawi 83 D3
Chitose, Japan 48 C10
Chitral, Pakistan 60 B7
Chitré, Panama 116 E3
Chittagong, Bangla. ... 61 H17
Chittagong □, Bangla. . 61 G17
Chittaurgarh, India ... 62 G6
Chittoor, India 60 N11
Chitungwiza, Zimbabwe . 83 F3
Chiusa, Italy 33 B8
Chiusi, Italy 33 E8
Chiva, Spain 29 F4
Chivacoa, Venezuela .. 120 A4
Chivasso, Italy 32 C4
Chivay, Peru 124 D3
Chivhu, Zimbabwe 83 F3
Chivilcoy, Argentina .. 126 C4
Chiwanda, Tanzania .. 83 E3
Chixi, China 53 G9
Chizera, Zambia 83 E1
Chkalov = Orenburg, Russia 44 D6
Chkolovsk, Russia 42 B6
Chloride, U.S.A. 113 K12
Cho Bo, Vietnam 58 B5
Cho-do, N. Korea 51 E13
Cho Phuoc Hai, Vietnam 59 G6
Choba, Kenya 82 B4
Chobe National Park, Botswana 84 B3
Chochiwŏn, S. Korea .. 51 F14
Chociwel, Poland 20 B8
Chocó □, Colombia .. 120 B2
Chocontá, Colombia .. 120 B3
Choctawhatchee B., U.S.A. 103 D9
Chodecz, Poland 20 C9
Chodzież, Poland 20 C9
Choele Choel, Argentina 128 A3
Choisy-le-Roi, France .. 25 D9
Choix, Mexico 114 B3
Chojnice, Poland 20 B7
Chojnów, Poland 20 D5
Chōkai-San, Japan 48 E10
Choke, Ethiopia 77 E4
Chokurdakh, Russia ... 45 B15
Cholame, U.S.A. 112 K6
Cholet, France 24 E6
Choluteca, Honduras .. 116 D2
Choluteca □, Honduras 116 D2
Chom Bung, Thailand . 58 F2
Chom Thong, Thailand . 58 C2
Choma, Zambia 83 F2
Chomen Swamp, Ethiopia 77 F4
Chomun, India 62 F6
Chomutov, Czech. 20 E3

Chon Buri, Thailand ... 58 F3
Chon Thanh, Vietnam . 59 G6
Chonan, S. Korea 51 F14
Chone, Ecuador 120 D2
Chong Kai, Cambodia . 58 F4
Chong Mek, Thailand . 58 E5
Chong'an, China 53 D12
Chongde, China 53 B13
Chongdo, S. Korea ... 51 G15
Chŏngha, S. Korea ... 51 F15
Chŏngjin, N. Korea ... 51 D15
Chŏngju, N. Korea ... 51 E13
Chŏngju, S. Korea 51 F14
Chongli, China 50 D8
Chongming, China 53 B13
Chongming Dao, China 53 B13
Chongoyape, Peru 124 B2
Chongqing, Sichuan, China 52 C6
Chongqing, Sichuan, China 52 B4
Chongren, China 53 D11
Chŏngŭp, S. Korea ... 51 G14
Chongzuo, China 52 F6
Chŏnju, S. Korea 51 G14
Chonos, Arch. de los, Chile 128 C2
Chop, Ukraine 41 H2
Chopim →, Brazil ... 127 B5
Chorbat La, India 63 B7
Chorley, U.K. 12 D5
Chornobyl, Ukraine ... 41 G6
Chornomorske, Ukraine 41 K7
Choroque, Cerro, Bolivia 126 A2
Chorregon, Australia .. 90 C3
Chortkiv, Ukraine 41 H3
Chŏrwŏn, S. Korea ... 51 E14
Chorzów, Poland 20 E8
Chos-Malal, Argentina 126 D1
Chosan, N. Korea 51 D13
Choszczno, Poland ... 20 B5
Chota, Peru 124 B2
Choteau, U.S.A. 110 C7
Chotila, India 62 H4
Chowchilla, U.S.A. ... 111 H3
Choybalsan, Mongolia . 54 B6
Christchurch, N.Z. 87 K4
Christchurch, U.K. 13 G6
Christian I., Canada ... 106 B4
Christiana, S. Africa ... 84 D4
Christiansfeld, Denmark 11 J3
Christiansted, Virgin Is. . 117 C7
Christie B., Canada ... 101 A6
Christina →, Canada . 101 B6
Christmas Cr. →, Australia 88 C4
Christmas Creek, Australia 88 C4
Christmas I. = Kiritimati, Kiribati 93 G12
Christmas I., Ind. Oc. . 92 J2
Christopher L., Australia 89 D4
Chrudim, Czech. 20 F5
Chrzanów, Poland 20 E9
Chtimba, Malawi 83 E3
Chu = Shu, Kazakhstan 44 E8
Chu →, Vietnam 58 C5
Chu Chua, Canada ... 100 C4
Chu Lai, Vietnam 58 E7
Chu Xian, China 53 A12
Ch'uanchou = Quanzhou, China 53 E12
Chuankou, China 50 G6
Chūbu □, Japan 49 F8
Chubut □, Argentina . 128 B3
Chubut →, Argentina 128 B3
Chuchi L., Canada ... 100 B4
Chudovo, Russia 40 C6
Chudskoye, Oz., Russia . 9 G22
Chūgoku □, Japan ... 49 G6
Chūgoku-Sanchi, Japan 49 G6
Chuguyev = Chuhuyiv, Ukraine 41 H9
Chugwater, U.S.A. ... 108 E2
Chuhuyiv, Ukraine ... 41 H9
Chukchi Sea, Russia .. 45 C19
Chukotskoye Nagorye, Russia 45 C18
Chula Vista, U.S.A. ... 113 N9
Chulman, Russia 45 D13
Chulucanas, Peru 124 B1
Chulumani, Bolivia ... 124 D4
Chulym →, Russia ... 44 D9
Chum Phae, Thailand . 58 D4
Chum Saeng, Thailand . 58 E3
Chuma, Bolivia 124 D4
Chumar, India 63 C8
Chumbicha, Argentina . 126 B2
Chumerna, Bulgaria .. 38 G8
Chumikan, Russia 45 D14
Chumphon, Thailand . 59 G2
Chumpi, Peru 124 D3
Chumuare, Mozam. ... 83 E3
Chumunjin, S. Korea .. 51 F15
Chuna →, Russia 45 D10
Chun'an, China 53 C12
Chunchŏn, S. Korea .. 51 F14
Chunchura, India 63 H13
Chunga, Zambia 83 F2
Chunggang-ŭp, N. Korea 51 D14
Chunghwa, N. Korea .. 51 E13
Chungju, S. Korea 51 F14
Chungking = Chongqing, China 52 C6
Chunian, Pakistan 62 D6
Chunya, Tanzania 83 D3
Chunya □, Tanzania .. 82 D3
Chunyang, China 51 C15
Chuquibamba, Peru ... 124 D3

147

Chuquibambilla

Chuquibambilla, *Peru* 124 C3
Chuquicamata, *Chile* 126 A2
Chuquisaca □, *Bolivia* 125 E5
Chur, *Switz.* 23 C9
Churachandpur, *India* 61 G18
Churchill, *Canada* 101 B10
Churchill →, *Man., Canada* 101 B10
Churchill →, *Nfld., Canada* 99 B7
Churchill, C., *Canada* 101 B10
Churchill Falls, *Canada* 99 B7
Churchill L., *Canada* 101 B7
Churchill Pk., *Canada* 100 B3
Churfisten, *Switz.* 23 B8
Churu, *India* 62 E6
Churún Merú = Angel Falls, *Venezuela* 121 B5
Churwalden, *Switz.* 23 C9
Chushal, *India* 63 C8
Chusovoy, *Russia* 44 D6
Chuuronjang, *N. Korea* 51 D15
Chuvash Republic = Chuvashia □, *Russia* 42 C8
Chuvashia □, *Russia* 42 C8
Chuwārtah, *Iraq* 64 C5
Chuxiong, *China* 52 E3
Ci Xian, *China* 50 F8
Ciacova, *Romania* 38 D4
Cianjur, *Indonesia* 57 G12
Cibadok, *Indonesia* 57 G12
Cibatu, *Indonesia* 57 G12
Cibola, *U.S.A.* 113 M12
Cicero, *U.S.A.* 104 E2
Cícero Dantas, *Brazil* 122 D4
Cidacos →, *Spain* 28 C3
Cide, *Turkey* 66 B5
Ciechanów, *Poland* 20 C10
Ciego de Avila, *Cuba* 116 B4
Ciénaga, *Colombia* 120 A3
Ciénaga de Oro, *Colombia* 120 B2
Cienfuegos, *Cuba* 116 B3
Cieplice Śląskie Zdrój, *Poland* 20 E5
Cierp, *France* 26 F4
Cíes, Is., *Spain* 30 C2
Cieszyn, *Poland* 20 F8
Cieza, *Spain* 29 G3
Çifteler, *Turkey* 66 C4
Cifuentes, *Spain* 28 E2
Cihanbeyli, *Turkey* 66 C5
Cihuatlán, *Mexico* 114 D4
Cijara, Pantano de, *Spain* 31 F6
Cijulang, *Indonesia* 57 G13
Cikajang, *Indonesia* 57 G12
Cikampek, *Indonesia* 57 G12
Cilacap, *Indonesia* 57 G13
Çıldır, *Turkey* 67 B10
Çıldır Gölü, *Turkey* 67 B10
Cili, *China* 53 C8
Cilicia, *Turkey* 66 D5
Cill Chainnigh = Kilkenny, *Ireland* 15 D4
Cilo Dağı, *Turkey* 67 D10
Cima, *U.S.A.* 113 K11
Cimahi, *Indonesia* 57 G12
Cimarron, *Kans., U.S.A.* 109 G4
Cimarron, *N. Mex., U.S.A.* 109 G2
Cimarron →, *U.S.A.* 109 G6
Cimişlia, *Moldova* 41 J5
Cimone, Mte., *Italy* 32 D7
Cîmpina, *Romania* 38 D8
Cîmpulung, *Argeş, Romania* 38 D8
Cîmpulung, *Suceava, Romania* 38 B8
Çinar, *Turkey* 67 D9
Cinca →, *Spain* 28 D5
Cincinnati, *U.S.A.* 104 F3
Cîndeşti, *Romania* 38 D9
Çine, *Turkey* 66 D3
Ciney, *Belgium* 17 H6
Cíngoli, *Italy* 33 E10
Cinigiano, *Italy* 33 F8
Cinto, Mte., *France* 27 F12
Çiorani, *Romania* 38 E9
Čiovo, *Croatia* 33 E13
Cipó, *Brazil* 122 D4
Circeo, Mte., *Italy* 34 A6
Çirçir, *Turkey* 66 C7
Circle, *Alaska, U.S.A.* 96 B5
Circle, *Mont., U.S.A.* 108 B2
Circleville, *Ohio, U.S.A.* 104 F4
Circleville, *Utah, U.S.A.* 111 G7
Cirebon, *Indonesia* 57 G13
Cirencester, *U.K.* 13 F6
Cirey-sur-Vezouze, *France* 25 D13
Ciriè, *Italy* 32 C4
Cirium, *Cyprus* 37 E11
Cirò, *Italy* 35 C10
Ciron →, *France* 26 D3
Cisco, *U.S.A.* 109 J5
Cislău, *Romania* 38 D9
Cisneros, *Colombia* 120 B2
Cisterna di Latina, *Italy* 34 A5
Cisternino, *Italy* 35 B10
Citaré →, *Brazil* 121 C7
Citeli-Ckaro = Tsiteli-Tskaro, *Georgia* 43 K8
Citlaltépetl, *Mexico* 115 D5
Citrus Heights, *U.S.A.* 112 G5
Citrusdal, *S. Africa* 84 E2
Città della Pieve, *Italy* 33 F9
Città di Castello, *Italy* 33 E9
Città Sant' Angelo, *Italy* 33 F11
Cittadella, *Italy* 33 C8
Cittaducale, *Italy* 33 F9
Cittanova, *Italy* 35 D9
Ciucaş, *Romania* 38 D8
Ciudad Altamirano, *Mexico* 114 D4
Ciudad Bolívar, *Venezuela* 121 B5
Ciudad Camargo, *Mexico* 114 B3
Ciudad Chetumal, *Mexico* 115 D7
Ciudad de Valles, *Mexico* 115 C5
Ciudad del Carmen, *Mexico* 115 D6
Ciudad del Este, *Paraguay* 127 B5
Ciudad Delicias = Delicias, *Mexico* 114 B3
Ciudad Guayana, *Venezuela* 121 B5
Ciudad Guerrero, *Mexico* 114 B3
Ciudad Guzmán, *Mexico* 114 D4
Ciudad Juárez, *Mexico* 114 A3
Ciudad Madero, *Mexico* 115 C5
Ciudad Mante, *Mexico* 115 C5
Ciudad Obregón, *Mexico* 114 B3
Ciudad Ojeda, *Venezuela* 120 A3
Ciudad Real, *Spain* 31 G7
Ciudad Real □, *Spain* 31 G7
Ciudad Rodrigo, *Spain* 30 E4
Ciudad Trujillo = Santo Domingo, *Dom. Rep.* 117 C6
Ciudad Victoria, *Mexico* 115 C5
Ciudadela, *Spain* 36 B10
Ciulniţa, *Romania* 38 E10
Civa Burnu, *Turkey* 66 B7
Cividale del Friuli, *Italy* 33 B10
Cívita Castellana, *Italy* 33 F9
Civitanova Marche, *Italy* 33 E10
Civitavécchia, *Italy* 33 F8
Civitella del Tronto, *Italy* 33 F10
Civray, *France* 26 B4
Çivril, *Turkey* 66 C3
Cixerri →, *Italy* 34 C1
Cizre, *Turkey* 67 D10
Clacton-on-Sea, *U.K.* 13 F9
Clain →, *France* 24 F7
Claire, L., *Canada* 100 B6
Clairemont, *U.S.A.* 109 J4
Clairton, *U.S.A.* 106 F5
Clairvaux-les-Lacs, *France* 27 B9
Clallam Bay, *U.S.A.* 112 B2
Clamecy, *France* 25 E10
Clanton, *U.S.A.* 105 J2
Clanwilliam, *S. Africa* 84 E2
Clara, *Ireland* 15 C4
Clara →, *Australia* 90 B3
Claraville, *U.S.A.* 113 K8
Clare, *Australia* 91 E2
Clare, *U.S.A.* 104 D3
Clare □, *Ireland* 15 D3
Clare →, *Ireland* 15 C2
Clare I., *Ireland* 15 C2
Claremont, *Calif., U.S.A.* 113 L9
Claremont, *N.H., U.S.A.* 107 C12
Claremont Pt., *Australia* 90 A3
Claremore, *U.S.A.* 109 G7
Claremorris, *Ireland* 15 C3
Clarence →, *Australia* 91 D5
Clarence →, *N.Z.* 87 K4
Clarence, I., *Chile* 128 D2
Clarence I., *Antarctica* 5 C18
Clarence Str., *Australia* 88 B5
Clarence Str., *U.S.A.* 100 B2
Clarence Town, *Bahamas* 117 B5
Clarendon, *Ark., U.S.A.* 109 H9
Clarendon, *Tex., U.S.A.* 109 H4
Clarenville, *Canada* 99 C9
Claresholm, *Canada* 100 C6
Clarie Coast, *Antarctica* 5 C9
Clarinda, *U.S.A.* 108 E7
Clarion, *Iowa, U.S.A.* 108 D8
Clarion, *Pa., U.S.A.* 106 E5
Clarion →, *U.S.A.* 106 E5
Clark, *U.S.A.* 108 C6
Clark, Pt., *Canada* 106 B3
Clark Fork, *U.S.A.* 110 B5
Clark Fork →, *U.S.A.* 110 B5
Clark Hill Res., *U.S.A.* 105 J4
Clarkdale, *U.S.A.* 111 J7
Clarke City, *Canada* 99 B6
Clarke I., *Australia* 90 G4
Clarke L., *Canada* 101 C7
Clarke Ra., *Australia* 90 C4
Clark's Fork →, *U.S.A.* 110 D9
Clark's Harbour, *Canada* 99 D6
Clarks Summit, *U.S.A.* 107 E9
Clarksburg, *U.S.A.* 104 F5
Clarksdale, *U.S.A.* 109 H9
Clarkston, *U.S.A.* 110 C5
Clarksville, *Ark., U.S.A.* 109 H8
Clarksville, *Tenn., U.S.A.* 105 G2
Clarksville, *Tex., U.S.A.* 109 J7
Claro →, *Brazil* 123 E1
Clatskanie, *U.S.A.* 112 D3
Claude, *U.S.A.* 109 H4
Claveria, *Phil.* 55 B4
Clay, *U.S.A.* 112 G5
Clay Center, *U.S.A.* 108 F6
Claypool, *U.S.A.* 111 K8
Claysville, *U.S.A.* 106 F4
Clayton, *Idaho, U.S.A.* 110 D6
Clayton, *N. Mex., U.S.A.* 109 G3
Cle Elum, *U.S.A.* 110 C3
Clear, C., *Ireland* 15 E2
Clear I., *Ireland* 15 E2
Clear L., *U.S.A.* 112 F4
Clear Lake, *S. Dak., U.S.A.* 108 C6
Clear Lake, *Wash., U.S.A.* 110 B2
Clear Lake Reservoir, *U.S.A.* 110 F3
Clearfield, *Pa., U.S.A.* 104 E6
Clearfield, *Utah, U.S.A.* 110 F7
Clearlake Highlands, *U.S.A.* 112 G4
Clearmont, *U.S.A.* 110 D10
Clearwater, *Canada* 100 C4
Clearwater, *U.S.A.* 105 M4
Clearwater →, *Alta., Canada* 100 C6
Clearwater →, *Alta., Canada* 101 B6
Clearwater Cr. →, *Canada* 100 A3
Clearwater Mts., *U.S.A.* 110 C6
Clearwater Prov. Park, *Canada* 101 C8
Cleburne, *U.S.A.* 109 J6
Cleethorpes, *U.K.* 12 D7
Cleeve Hill, *U.K.* 13 F6
Clelles, *France* 27 D9
Clemency, *Lux.* 17 J7
Clerke Reef, *Australia* 88 C2
Clermont, *Australia* 90 C4
Clermont, *France* 25 C9
Clermont-en-Argonne, *France* 25 C12
Clermont-Ferrand, *France* 26 C7
Clermont-l'Hérault, *France* 26 E7
Clerval, *France* 25 E13
Clervaux, *Lux.* 17 H8
Cléry-St.-André, *France* 25 E8
Cles, *Italy* 32 B8
Cleveland, *Australia* 91 D5
Cleveland, *Miss., U.S.A.* 109 J9
Cleveland, *Ohio, U.S.A.* 106 E3
Cleveland, *Okla., U.S.A.* 109 G6
Cleveland, *Tenn., U.S.A.* 105 H3
Cleveland, *Tex., U.S.A.* 109 K7
Cleveland □, *U.K.* 12 C9
Cleveland, C., *Australia* 90 B4
Cleveland Heights, *U.S.A.* 106 E3
Clevelândia, *Brazil* 127 B5
Clevelândia do Norte, *Brazil* 121 C7
Clew B., *Ireland* 15 C2
Clewiston, *U.S.A.* 105 M5
Clifden, *Ireland* 15 C1
Clifden, *N.Z.* 87 M1
Cliffdell, *U.S.A.* 112 D5
Clifton, *Australia* 91 D5
Clifton, *Ariz., U.S.A.* 111 K9
Clifton, *Tex., U.S.A.* 109 K6
Clifton Beach, *Australia* 90 B4
Clifton Forge, *U.S.A.* 104 G6
Clifton Hills, *Australia* 91 D2
Climax, *Canada* 101 D7
Clinch →, *U.S.A.* 105 H3
Clingmans Dome, *U.S.A.* 105 H4
Clint, *U.S.A.* 111 L10
Clinton, *B.C., Canada* 100 C4
Clinton, *Ont., Canada* 98 D3
Clinton, *N.Z.* 87 M2
Clinton, *Ark., U.S.A.* 109 H8
Clinton, *Ill., U.S.A.* 108 E10
Clinton, *Ind., U.S.A.* 104 F2
Clinton, *Iowa, U.S.A.* 108 E9
Clinton, *Mass., U.S.A.* 107 D13
Clinton, *Mo., U.S.A.* 108 F8
Clinton, *N.C., U.S.A.* 105 H6
Clinton, *Okla., U.S.A.* 109 H5
Clinton, *S.C., U.S.A.* 105 H5
Clinton, *Tenn., U.S.A.* 105 G3
Clinton, *Wash., U.S.A.* 112 C4
Clinton C., *Australia* 90 C5
Clinton Colden L., *Canada* 96 B9
Clintonville, *U.S.A.* 108 C10
Clipperton, I., *Pac. Oc.* 93 F17
Clisson, *France* 24 E5
Clive L., *Canada* 100 A5
Cliza, *Bolivia* 125 D4
Cloates, Pt., *Australia* 88 D1
Clocolan, *S. Africa* 85 D4
Clodomira, *Argentina* 126 B3
Clonakilty, *Ireland* 15 E3
Clonakilty B., *Ireland* 15 E3
Cloncurry, *Australia* 90 C3
Cloncurry →, *Australia* 90 B3
Clones, *Ireland* 15 B4
Clonmel, *Ireland* 15 D4
Cloppenburg, *Germany* 18 C4
Cloquet, *U.S.A.* 108 B8
Clorinda, *Argentina* 126 B4
Cloud Peak, *U.S.A.* 110 D10
Cloudcroft, *U.S.A.* 111 K11
Cloverdale, *U.S.A.* 112 G4
Clovis, *Calif., U.S.A.* 111 H4
Clovis, *N. Mex., U.S.A.* 109 H3
Cloyes-sur-le-Loir, *France* 24 E8
Cluj-Napoca, *Romania* 38 C6
Clunes, *Australia* 91 F3
Cluny, *France* 27 B8
Cluses, *France* 27 B10
Clusone, *Italy* 32 C6
Clutha →, *N.Z.* 87 M2
Clwyd □, *U.K.* 12 D4
Clwyd →, *U.K.* 12 D4
Clyde, *N.Z.* 87 L2
Clyde, *U.S.A.* 106 C8
Clyde →, *U.K.* 14 F4
Clyde, Firth of, *U.K.* 14 F4
Clyde River, *Canada* 97 A13
Clydebank, *U.K.* 14 F4
Clymer, *U.S.A.* 106 D5
Côa →, *Portugal* 30 D3
Coachella, *U.S.A.* 113 M10
Coachella Canal, *U.S.A.* 113 N12
Coahoma, *U.S.A.* 109 J4
Coahuayana →, *Mexico* 114 D4
Coahuayutla, *Mexico* 114 D4
Coahuila □, *Mexico* 114 B4
Coal →, *Canada* 100 B3
Coalane, *Mozam.* 83 F4
Coalcomán, *Mexico* 114 D4
Coaldale, *Canada* 100 D6
Coalgate, *U.S.A.* 109 H6
Coalinga, *U.S.A.* 111 H3
Coalville, *U.K.* 12 E6
Coalville, *U.S.A.* 110 F8
Coaraci, *Brazil* 123 D4
Coari, *Brazil* 121 D5
Coari →, *Brazil* 121 D5
Coari, L. de, *Brazil* 121 D5
Coast □, *Kenya* 82 C4
Coast Mts., *Canada* 100 C3
Coast Ranges, *U.S.A.* 112 G4
Coatbridge, *U.K.* 14 F4
Coatepec, *Mexico* 115 D5
Coatepeque, *Guatemala* 116 D1
Coatesville, *U.S.A.* 104 F8
Coaticook, *Canada* 99 C5
Coats I., *Canada* 97 B11
Coats Land, *Antarctica* 5 D1
Coatzacoalcos, *Mexico* 115 D6
Cobalt, *Canada* 98 C4
Cobán, *Guatemala* 116 C1
Cobar, *Australia* 91 E4
Cóbh, *Ireland* 15 E3
Cobham, *Australia* 91 E3
Cobija, *Bolivia* 124 C4
Cobleskill, *U.S.A.* 107 D10
Coboconk, *Canada* 106 B6
Cobourg, *Canada* 98 D4
Cobourg Pen., *Australia* 88 B5
Cobram, *Australia* 91 F4
Cobre, *U.S.A.* 110 F6
Cóbué, *Mozam.* 83 E3
Coburg, *Germany* 19 E6
Coca, *Spain* 30 D6
Coca →, *Ecuador* 120 D2
Cocachacra, *Peru* 124 D3
Cocal, *Brazil* 122 B3
Cocanada = Kakinada, *India* 61 L13
Cocentaina, *Spain* 29 G4
Cochabamba, *Bolivia* 125 D4
Coche, I., *Venezuela* 121 A5
Cochem, *Germany* 19 E3
Cochemane, *Mozam.* 83 F3
Cochin, *India* 60 Q10
Cochin China = Nam-Phan, *Vietnam* 59 G6
Cochise, *U.S.A.* 111 K9
Cochran, *U.S.A.* 105 J4
Cochrane, *Alta., Canada* 100 C6
Cochrane, *Ont., Canada* 98 C3
Cochrane →, *Canada* 101 B8
Cochrane, L., *Chile* 128 C2
Cockburn, *Australia* 91 E3
Cockburn, Canal, *Chile* 128 D2
Cockburn I., *Canada* 98 C3
Cockburn Ra., *Australia* 88 C4
Cocklebiddy Motel, *Australia* 89 F4
Coco →, *Cent. Amer.* 116 D3
Coco, Pta., *Colombia* 120 C2
Cocoa, *U.S.A.* 105 L5
Cocobeach, *Gabon* 80 D1
Côcos, *Brazil* 123 D3
Côcos →, *Brazil* 123 D3
Cocos, I. del, *Pac. Oc.* 93 G19
Cocos Is., *Ind. Oc.* 92 J1
Cod, C., *U.S.A.* 103 B13
Codajás, *Brazil* 121 D5
Codera, C., *Venezuela* 120 A4
Coderre, *Canada* 101 C7
Codigoro, *Italy* 33 D9
Codó, *Brazil* 122 B3
Codogno, *Italy* 32 C6
Codpa, *Chile* 124 D4
Codroipo, *Italy* 33 C10
Cody, *U.S.A.* 110 D9
Coe Hill, *Canada* 98 D4
Coelemu, *Chile* 126 D1
Coelho Neto, *Brazil* 122 B3
Coen, *Australia* 90 A3
Coeroeni →, *Surinam* 121 C6
Coesfeld, *Germany* 18 D3
Cœur d'Alene, *U.S.A.* 110 C5
Cœur d'Alene L., *U.S.A.* 110 C5
Coevorden, *Neths.* 16 C9
Cofete, *Canary Is.* 36 F5
Coffeyville, *U.S.A.* 109 G7
Coffin B., *Australia* 91 E2
Coffin Bay Peninsula, *Australia* 91 E2
Coffs Harbour, *Australia* 91 E5
Cofrentes, *Spain* 29 F3
Cogealac, *Romania* 38 E11
Coghinas →, *Italy* 34 B1
Coghinas, L. di, *Italy* 34 B2
Cognac, *France* 26 C3
Cogne, *Italy* 32 C4
Cogolludo, *Spain* 28 E1
Cohagen, *U.S.A.* 110 C10
Cohoes, *U.S.A.* 107 D11
Cohuna, *Australia* 91 F3
Coiba, I., *Panama* 116 E3
Coig →, *Argentina* 128 D3
Coihaique, *Chile* 128 C2
Coimbatore, *India* 60 P10
Coimbra, *Brazil* 125 D6
Coimbra, *Portugal* 30 E2
Coimbra □, *Portugal* 30 E2
Coín, *Spain* 31 J6
Coipasa, L. de, *Bolivia* 124 D4
Coipasa, Salar de, *Bolivia* 124 D4
Cojata, *Peru* 124 D4
Cojedes □, *Venezuela* 120 B4
Cojedes →, *Venezuela* 120 B4
Cojimies, *Ecuador* 120 C1
Cojocna, *Romania* 38 C6
Cojutepequé, *El Salv.* 116 D2
Cokeville, *U.S.A.* 110 E8
Colac, *Australia* 91 F3
Colares, *Portugal* 31 G1
Colatina, *Brazil* 123 E3
Colbeck, C., *Antarctica* 5 D13
Colbinabbin, *Australia* 91 F3
Colborne, *Canada* 106 B7
Colby, *U.S.A.* 108 F4
Colchagua □, *Chile* 126 C1
Colchester, *U.K.* 13 F8
Coldstream, *U.K.* 14 F6
Coldwater, *Canada* 106 B5
Coldwater, *U.S.A.* 109 G5
Colebrook, *Australia* 90 G4
Colebrook, *U.S.A.* 107 B13
Coleman, *Canada* 100 D6
Coleman, *U.S.A.* 109 K5
Coleman →, *Australia* 90 B3
Colenso, *S. Africa* 85 D4
Coleraine, *Australia* 91 F3
Coleraine, *U.K.* 15 A5
Coleraine □, *U.K.* 15 A5
Coleridge, L., *N.Z.* 87 K3
Colesberg, *S. Africa* 84 E4
Coleville, *U.S.A.* 112 G7
Colfax, *Calif., U.S.A.* 112 F6
Colfax, *La., U.S.A.* 109 K8
Colfax, *Wash., U.S.A.* 110 C5
Colhué Huapi, L., *Argentina* 128 C3
Cólico, *Italy* 32 B6
Coligny, *France* 27 B9
Coligny, *S. Africa* 85 D4
Colima, *Mexico* 114 D4
Colima □, *Mexico* 114 D4
Colima, Nevado de, *Mexico* 114 D4
Colina, *Chile* 126 C1
Colina do Norte, *Guinea-Biss.* 78 C2
Colinas, *Goiás, Brazil* 123 D2
Colinas, *Maranhão, Brazil* 122 C3
Coll, *U.K.* 14 E2
Collaguasi, *Chile* 126 A2
Collarada, Peña, *Spain* 28 C4
Collarenebri, *Australia* 91 D4
Collbran, *U.S.A.* 111 G10
Colle di Val d'Elsa, *Italy* 33 E8
Colle Salvetti, *Italy* 32 E7
Colle Sannita, *Italy* 35 A7
Collécchio, *Italy* 32 D7
Colleen Bawn, *Zimbabwe* 83 G2
College Park, *U.S.A.* 105 J3
Collette, *Canada* 99 C6
Collie, *Australia* 89 F2
Collier B., *Australia* 88 C3
Collier Ra., *Australia* 88 D2
Colline Metallifere, *Italy* 32 E7
Collingwood, *Canada* 98 D3
Collingwood, *N.Z.* 87 J4
Collins, *Canada* 98 B2
Collinsville, *Australia* 90 C4
Collipulli, *Chile* 126 D1
Collo, *Algeria* 75 A6
Collonges, *France* 27 B9
Collooney, *Ireland* 15 B3
Colmar, *France* 25 D14
Colmars, *France* 27 D10
Colmenar, *Spain* 31 J6
Colmenar de Oreja, *Spain* 28 E1
Colmenar Viejo, *Spain* 30 E7
Colne, *U.K.* 12 D5
Colo →, *Australia* 91 E5
Cologna Véneta, *Italy* 33 C8
Cologne = Köln, *Germany* 18 E2
Colom, I., *Spain* 36 B11
Coloma, *U.S.A.* 112 G6
Colomb-Béchar = Béchar, *Algeria* 75 B4
Colombey-les-Belles, *France* 25 D12
Colombey-les-Deux-Églises, *France* 25 D11
Colômbia, *Brazil* 123 F2
Colombia ■, *S. Amer.* 120 C3
Colombier, *Switz.* 22 C3
Colombo, *Sri Lanka* 60 R11
Colome, *U.S.A.* 108 D5
Colón, *Argentina* 126 C4
Colón, *Cuba* 116 B3
Colón, *Panama* 116 E4
Colón, *Peru* 124 A1
Colona, *Australia* 89 F5
Colonella, *Italy* 33 F10
Colonia, *Uruguay* 126 C4
Colonia de Sant Jordi, *Spain* 36 B9
Colonia Dora, *Argentina* 126 B3
Colonial Heights, *U.S.A.* 104 G7
Colonne, C. delle, *Italy* 35 C10
Colonsay, *Canada* 101 C7
Colonsay, *U.K.* 14 E2
Colorado □, *U.S.A.* 111 G10
Colorado →, *Argentina* 128 A4
Colorado →, *N. Amer.* 111 L6
Colorado →, *U.S.A.* 109 L7
Colorado City, *U.S.A.* 109 J4
Colorado Desert, *U.S.A.* 102 D3
Colorado Plateau, *U.S.A.* 111 H8
Colorado River Aqueduct, *U.S.A.* 113 L12
Colorado Springs, *U.S.A.* 108 F2
Colorno, *Italy* 32 D7
Colotlán, *Mexico* 114 C4

Colquechaca, *Bolivia*	125	D4
Colton, *Calif., U.S.A.*	113	L9
Colton, *N.Y., U.S.A.*	107	B10
Colton, *Wash., U.S.A.*	110	C5
Columbia, *La., U.S.A.*	109	J8
Columbia, *Miss., U.S.A.*	109	K10
Columbia, *Mo., U.S.A.*	108	F8
Columbia, *Pa., U.S.A.*	107	F8
Columbia, *S.C., U.S.A.*	105	H5
Columbia, *Tenn., U.S.A.*	105	H2
Columbia →, *U.S.A.*	110	C1
Columbia, C., *Canada*	4	A4
Columbia, District of □, *U.S.A.*	104	F7
Columbia, Mt., *Canada*	100	C5
Columbia Basin, *U.S.A.*	110	C4
Columbia Falls, *U.S.A.*	110	B6
Columbia Heights, *U.S.A.*	108	C8
Columbiana, *U.S.A.*	106	F4
Columbretes, Is., *Spain*	28	F3
Columbus, *Ga., U.S.A.*	105	J3
Columbus, *Ind., U.S.A.*	104	F3
Columbus, *Kans., U.S.A.*	109	G7
Columbus, *Miss., U.S.A.*	105	J1
Columbus, *Mont., U.S.A.*	110	D9
Columbus, *N. Dak., U.S.A.*	108	A3
Columbus, *N. Mex., U.S.A.*	111	L10
Columbus, *Ohio, U.S.A.*	104	F4
Columbus, *Tex., U.S.A.*	109	L6
Columbus, *Wis., U.S.A.*	108	D10
Colunga, *Spain*	30	B5
Colusa, *U.S.A.*	112	F4
Colville, *U.S.A.*	110	B5
Colville →, *U.S.A.*	96	A4
Colville, C., *N.Z.*	87	G5
Colwyn Bay, *U.K.*	12	D4
Coma, *Ethiopia*	77	F4
Comácchio, *Italy*	33	D9
Comalcalco, *Mexico*	115	D6
Comallo, *Argentina*	128	B2
Comanche, *Okla., U.S.A.*	109	H6
Comanche, *Tex., U.S.A.*	109	K5
Comandante Luis Piedrabuena, *Argentina*	128	C3
Comănești, *Romania*	38	C9
Comarapa, *Bolivia*	125	D5
Comayagua, *Honduras*	116	D2
Combahee →, *U.S.A.*	105	J5
Combeaufontaine, *France*	25	E12
Comber, *Canada*	106	D2
Comblain-au-Pont, *Belgium*	17	H7
Combles, *France*	25	B9
Combourg, *France*	24	D5
Combronde, *France*	26	C7
Comeragh Mts., *Ireland*	15	D4
Comet, *Australia*	90	C4
Comilla, *Bangla.*	61	H17
Comines, *Belgium*	17	G1
Comino, *Malta*	37	C1
Comino, C., *Italy*	34	B2
Cómiso, *Italy*	35	F7
Comitán, *Mexico*	115	D6
Commentry, *France*	26	B6
Commerce, *Ga., U.S.A.*	105	H4
Commerce, *Tex., U.S.A.*	109	J7
Commercy, *France*	25	D12
Commewijne □, *Surinam*	121	B7
Committee B., *Canada*	97	B11
Commonwealth B., *Antarctica*	5	C10
Commoron Cr. →, *Australia*	91	D5
Communism Pk. = Kommunizma, Pik, *Tajikistan*	44	F8
Como, *Italy*	32	C6
Como, L. di, *Italy*	32	B6
Comodoro Rivadavia, *Argentina*	128	C3
Comorin, C., *India*	60	Q10
Comoro Is. = Comoros ■, *Ind. Oc.*	71	H8
Comoros ■, *Ind. Oc.*	71	H8
Comox, *Canada*	100	D4
Compiègne, *France*	25	C9
Comporta, *Portugal*	31	G2
Compostela, *Mexico*	114	C4
Comprida, I., *Brazil*	127	A6
Compton, *U.S.A.*	113	M8
Compton Downs, *Australia*	91	E4
Comrat, *Moldova*	41	J5
Con Cuong, *Vietnam*	58	C5
Con Son, *Vietnam*	59	H6
Cona Niyeu, *Argentina*	128	B3
Conakry, *Guinea*	78	D2
Conara Junction, *Australia*	90	G4
Concarneau, *France*	24	E3
Conceição, *Brazil*	122	C4
Conceição, *Mozam.*	83	F4
Conceição da Barra, *Brazil*	123	E4
Conceição do Araguaia, *Brazil*	122	C2
Conceição do Canindé, *Brazil*	122	C3
Concepción, *Argentina*	126	B2
Concepción, *Bolivia*	125	D5
Concepción, *Chile*	126	D1
Concepción, *Mexico*	115	D6
Concepción, *Paraguay*	126	A4
Concepción, *Peru*	124	C2
Concepción □, *Chile*	126	D1
Concepción →, *Mexico*	114	A2
Concepción, Est. de, *Chile*	128	D2
Concepción, L., *Bolivia*	125	D5
Concepción, Punta, *Mexico*	114	B2
Concepción del Oro, *Mexico*	114	C4
Concepción del Uruguay, *Argentina*	126	C4
Conception, Pt., *U.S.A.*	113	L6
Conception B., *Namibia*	84	C1
Conception I., *Bahamas*	117	B4
Concession, *Zimbabwe*	83	F3
Conchas Dam, *U.S.A.*	109	H2
Conche, *Canada*	99	B8
Conches-en-Ouche, *France*	24	D7
Concho, *U.S.A.*	111	J9
Concho →, *U.S.A.*	109	K5
Conchos →, *Chihuahua, Mexico*	114	B4
Conchos →, *Tamaulipas, Mexico*	115	B5
Concord, *Calif., U.S.A.*	112	H4
Concord, *N.C., U.S.A.*	105	H5
Concord, *N.H., U.S.A.*	107	C13
Concordia, *Argentina*	126	C4
Concórdia, *Brazil*	120	D4
Concordia, *Mexico*	114	C3
Concordia, *U.S.A.*	108	F6
Concots, *France*	26	D5
Concrete, *U.S.A.*	110	B3
Condamine, *Australia*	91	D5
Condat, *France*	26	C6
Conde, *Brazil*	123	D4
Condé, *U.S.A.*	108	C5
Condé-sur-l'Escaut, *France*	25	B10
Condé-sur-Noireau, *France*	24	D6
Condeúba, *Brazil*	123	D3
Condobolin, *Australia*	91	E4
Condom, *France*	26	E4
Condon, *U.S.A.*	110	D3
Condove, *Italy*	32	C4
Conegliano, *Italy*	33	C9
Conejera, I., *Spain*	36	B9
Conejos, *Mexico*	114	B4
Conflans-en-Jarnisy, *France*	25	C12
Confolens, *France*	26	B4
Confuso →, *Paraguay*	126	B4
Congjiang, *China*	52	E7
Congleton, *U.K.*	12	D5
Congo = Zaïre →, *Africa*	80	F2
Congo, *Brazil*	122	C4
Congo (Kinshasa) = Zaïre ■, *Africa*	80	E4
Congo ■, *Africa*	80	E3
Congo Basin, *Africa*	70	G6
Congonhas, *Brazil*	123	F3
Congress, *U.S.A.*	111	J7
Conil, *Spain*	31	J4
Coniston, *Canada*	98	C3
Conjeeveram = Kanchipuram, *India*	60	N11
Conjuboy, *Australia*	90	B3
Conklin, *Canada*	101	B6
Conlea, *Australia*	91	E3
Conn, L., *Ireland*	15	B2
Connacht □, *Ireland*	15	C3
Conneaut, *U.S.A.*	106	E4
Connecticut □, *U.S.A.*	107	E12
Connecticut →, *U.S.A.*	107	E12
Connell, *U.S.A.*	110	C4
Connellsville, *U.S.A.*	106	F5
Connemara, *Ireland*	15	C2
Connemaugh →, *U.S.A.*	106	F5
Connerré, *France*	24	D7
Connersville, *U.S.A.*	104	F3
Connors Ra., *Australia*	90	C4
Conoble, *Australia*	91	E3
Cononaco →, *Ecuador*	120	D2
Cononbridge, *U.K.*	14	D4
Conquest, *Canada*	101	C7
Conrad, *U.S.A.*	110	B8
Conran, C., *Australia*	91	F4
Conroe, *U.S.A.*	109	K7
Conselheiro Lafaiete, *Brazil*	123	F3
Conselheiro Pena, *Brazil*	123	E3
Consort, *Canada*	101	C6
Constance = Konstanz, *Germany*	19	H5
Constance, L. = Bodensee, *Europe*	23	A8
Constanța, *Romania*	38	E11
Constantina, *Spain*	31	H5
Constantine, *Algeria*	75	A6
Constitución, *Chile*	126	D1
Constitución, *Uruguay*	126	C4
Consuegra, *Spain*	31	F7
Consul, *Canada*	101	D7
Contact, *U.S.A.*	110	F6
Contai, *India*	63	J12
Contamana, *Peru*	124	B3
Contarina, *Italy*	33	C9
Contas →, *Brazil*	123	D4
Contes, *France*	27	E11
Conthey, *Switz.*	22	D4
Contoocook, *U.S.A.*	107	C13
Contra Costa, *Mozam.*	85	D5
Contres, *France*	24	E8
Contrexéville, *France*	25	D12
Contumazá, *Peru*	124	B2
Convención, *Colombia*	120	B3
Conversano, *Italy*	35	B10
Conway = Conwy, *U.K.*	12	D4
Conway = Conwy →, *U.K.*	12	D4
Conway, *Ark., U.S.A.*	109	H8
Conway, *N.H., U.S.A.*	107	C13
Conway, *S.C., U.S.A.*	105	J6
Conway, L., *Australia*	91	D2
Conwy, *U.K.*	12	D4
Conwy →, *U.K.*	12	D4
Coober Pedy, *Australia*	91	D1
Cooch Behar = Koch Bihar, *India*	61	F16
Coodardy, *Australia*	89	E2
Cook, *Australia*	89	F5
Cook, *U.S.A.*	108	B8
Cook, B., *Chile*	128	E2
Cook, Mt., *N.Z.*	87	K3
Cook Inlet, *U.S.A.*	96	C4
Cook Is., *Pac. Oc.*	93	J11
Cook Strait, *N.Z.*	87	J5
Cookeville, *U.S.A.*	105	G3
Cookhouse, *S. Africa*	84	E4
Cookshire, *Canada*	107	A13
Cookstown, *U.K.*	15	B5
Cookstown □, *U.K.*	15	B5
Cooksville, *Canada*	106	C5
Cooktown, *Australia*	90	B4
Coolabah, *Australia*	91	E4
Cooladdi, *Australia*	91	D4
Coolah, *Australia*	91	E4
Coolamon, *Australia*	91	E4
Coolangatta, *Australia*	91	D5
Coolgardie, *Australia*	89	F3
Coolibah, *Australia*	88	C5
Coolidge, *U.S.A.*	111	K8
Coolidge Dam, *U.S.A.*	111	K8
Cooma, *Australia*	91	F4
Coonabarabran, *Australia*	91	E4
Coonamble, *Australia*	91	E4
Coonana, *Australia*	89	F3
Coondapoor, *India*	60	N9
Coongie, *Australia*	91	D3
Coongoola, *Australia*	91	D4
Cooninie, L., *Australia*	91	D2
Cooper, *U.S.A.*	109	J7
Cooper →, *U.S.A.*	105	J6
Cooper Cr. →, *Australia*	91	D2
Cooperstown, *N. Dak., U.S.A.*	108	B5
Cooperstown, *N.Y., U.S.A.*	107	D10
Coorabie, *Australia*	89	F5
Coorabulka, *Australia*	90	C3
Coorow, *Australia*	89	E2
Cooroy, *Australia*	91	D5
Coos Bay, *U.S.A.*	110	E1
Cootamundra, *Australia*	91	E4
Cootehill, *Ireland*	15	B4
Cooyar, *Australia*	91	D5
Cooyeana, *Australia*	90	C2
Copahue Paso, *Argentina*	126	D1
Copainalá, *Mexico*	115	D6
Copán, *Honduras*	116	D2
Copatana, *Brazil*	120	D4
Cope, *U.S.A.*	108	F3
Cope, C., *Spain*	29	H3
Copenhagen = København, *Denmark*	11	J6
Copertino, *Italy*	35	B11
Copiapó, *Chile*	126	B1
Copiapó →, *Chile*	126	B1
Copley, *Australia*	91	E2
Copp L., *Canada*	100	A6
Copparo, *Italy*	33	D8
Copper Center, *U.S.A.*	96	B5
Copper Cliff, *Canada*	98	C3
Copper Harbor, *U.S.A.*	104	B2
Copper Queen, *Zimbabwe*	83	F2
Copperbelt □, *Zambia*	83	E2
Coppermine, *Canada*	96	B8
Coppermine →, *Canada*	96	B8
Copperopolis, *U.S.A.*	112	H6
Coquet →, *Surinam*	121	B6
Coquet →, *U.K.*	12	B6
Coquilhatville = Mbandaka, *Zaïre*	80	D3
Coquille, *U.S.A.*	110	E1
Coquimbo, *Chile*	126	B1
Coquimbo □, *Chile*	126	C1
Corabia, *Romania*	38	F7
Coração de Jesus, *Brazil*	123	E3
Coracora, *Peru*	124	D3
Coradi, Is., *Italy*	35	B10
Coral Gables, *U.S.A.*	105	N5
Coral Harbour, *Canada*	97	B11
Coral Sea, *Pac. Oc.*	92	J7
Corantijn →, *Surinam*	121	B6
Corato, *Italy*	35	A9
Corbeil-Essonnes, *France*	25	D9
Corbie, *France*	25	C9
Corbières, *France*	26	F6
Corbigny, *France*	25	E10
Corbin, *U.S.A.*	104	G3
Corbion, *Belgium*	17	J6
Corbones →, *Spain*	31	H5
Corby, *U.K.*	13	E7
Corby Glen, *U.K.*	13	E7
Corcaigh = Cork, *Ireland*	15	E3
Corcoles →, *Spain*	29	F1
Corcoran, *U.S.A.*	111	H4
Corcubión, *Spain*	30	C1
Cordele, *U.S.A.*	105	K4
Cordell, *U.S.A.*	109	H5
Cordenons, *Italy*	33	C9
Cordes, *France*	26	D5
Cordisburgo, *Brazil*	123	E3
Córdoba, *Argentina*	126	C3
Córdoba, *Mexico*	115	D5
Córdoba, *Spain*	31	H6
Córdoba □, *Argentina*	126	C3
Córdoba □, *Colombia*	120	B2
Córdoba □, *Spain*	31	G6
Córdoba, Sierra de, *Argentina*	126	C3
Cordon, *Phil.*	55	C4
Cordova, *Ala., U.S.A.*	105	J2
Cordova, *Alaska, U.S.A.*	96	B5
Corella, *Spain*	28	C3
Corella →, *Australia*	90	B3
Coremas, *Brazil*	122	C4
Corentyne →, *Guyana*	121	B6
Corfield, *Australia*	90	C3
Corfu = Kérkira, *Greece*	37	A3
Corfu, Str of, *Greece*	37	A4
Corgo, *Spain*	30	C3
Corguinho, *Brazil*	125	D7
Cori, *Italy*	34	A5
Coria, *Spain*	30	F4
Corigliano Cálabro, *Italy*	35	C9
Coringa Is., *Australia*	90	B4
Corinna, *Australia*	90	G4
Corinth = Kórinthos, *Greece*	39	M5
Corinth, *Miss., U.S.A.*	105	H1
Corinth, *N.Y., U.S.A.*	107	C11
Corinth, G. of = Korinthiakós Kólpos, *Greece*	39	L5
Corinth Canal, *Greece*	39	M6
Corinto, *Brazil*	123	E3
Corinto, *Nic.*	116	D2
Cork, *Ireland*	15	E3
Cork □, *Ireland*	15	E3
Cork Harbour, *Ireland*	15	E3
Corlay, *France*	24	D3
Corleone, *Italy*	34	E6
Corleto Perticara, *Italy*	35	B9
Çorlu, *Turkey*	66	B2
Cormack L., *Canada*	100	A4
Cormóns, *Italy*	33	C10
Cormorant, *Canada*	101	C8
Cormorant L., *Canada*	101	C8
Corn Is. = Maiz, Is. del, *Nic.*	116	D3
Cornélio Procópio, *Brazil*	127	A5
Cornell, *U.S.A.*	108	C9
Corner Brook, *Canada*	99	C8
Cornești, *Moldova*	41	J5
Corníglio, *Italy*	32	D7
Corning, *Ark., U.S.A.*	109	G9
Corning, *Calif., U.S.A.*	110	G2
Corning, *Iowa, U.S.A.*	108	E7
Corning, *N.Y., U.S.A.*	106	D7
Corno, Monte, *Italy*	33	F10
Cornwall, *Canada*	98	C5
Cornwall □, *U.K.*	13	G3
Corny Pt., *Australia*	91	E2
Coro, *Venezuela*	120	A4
Coroaci, *Brazil*	123	E3
Coroatá, *Brazil*	122	B3
Corocoro, *Bolivia*	124	D4
Corocoro, I., *Venezuela*	121	B5
Coroico, *Bolivia*	124	D4
Coromandel, *Brazil*	123	E2
Coromandel, *N.Z.*	87	G5
Coromandel Coast, *India*	60	N12
Corona, *Australia*	91	E3
Corona, *Calif., U.S.A.*	113	M9
Corona, *N. Mex., U.S.A.*	111	J11
Coronado, *U.S.A.*	113	N9
Coronado, B. de, *Costa Rica*	116	E3
Coronados, G. de los, *Chile*	128	B2
Coronados, Is. los, *U.S.A.*	113	N9
Coronation, *Canada*	100	C6
Coronation Gulf, *Canada*	96	B8
Coronation I., *Antarctica*	5	C18
Coronation I., *Australia*	88	B3
Coronation Is., *Australia*	88	B3
Coronda, *Argentina*	126	C3
Coronel, *Chile*	126	D1
Coronel Bogado, *Paraguay*	126	B4
Coronel Dorrego, *Argentina*	126	D3
Coronel Fabriciano, *Brazil*	123	E3
Coronel Murta, *Brazil*	123	E3
Coronel Oviedo, *Paraguay*	126	B4
Coronel Ponce, *Brazil*	125	D6
Coronel Pringles, *Argentina*	126	D3
Coronel Suárez, *Argentina*	126	D3
Coronel Vidal, *Argentina*	126	D4
Corongo, *Peru*	124	B2
Coronie □, *Surinam*	121	B6
Coropuna, Nevado, *Peru*	124	D3
Çorovoda, *Albania*	39	J3
Corowa, *Australia*	91	F4
Corozal, *Belize*	115	D7
Corozal, *Colombia*	120	B2
Corps, *France*	27	D9
Corpus, *Argentina*	127	B4
Corpus Christi, *U.S.A.*	109	M6
Corpus Christi, L., *U.S.A.*	109	L6
Corque, *Bolivia*	124	D4
Corral, *Chile*	128	A2
Corral de Almaguer, *Spain*	28	F1
Corralejo, *Canary Is.*	36	F6
Corréggio, *Italy*	32	D7
Corrente, *Brazil*	122	D2
Corrente →, *Brazil*	123	D3
Correntes →, *Brazil*	125	D6
Correntes, C. das, *Mozam.*	85	C6
Correntina, *Brazil*	123	D3
Corrèze □, *France*	26	C5
Corrèze →, *France*	26	C5
Corrib, L., *Ireland*	15	C2
Corrientes, *Argentina*	126	B4
Corrientes □, *Argentina*	126	B4
Corrientes →, *Peru*	120	D3
Corrientes, C., *Colombia*	120	B2
Corrientes, C., *Cuba*	116	B3
Corrientes, C., *Mexico*	114	C3
Corrigan, *U.S.A.*	109	K7
Corrigin, *Australia*	89	F2
Corry, *U.S.A.*	106	E5
Corse, *France*	27	F13
Corse, C., *France*	27	E13
Corse-du-Sud □, *France*	27	G13
Corsica = Corse, *France*	27	F13
Corsicana, *U.S.A.*	109	J6
Corte, *France*	27	F13
Corte do Pinto, *Portugal*	31	H3
Cortegana, *Spain*	31	H4
Cortez, *U.S.A.*	111	H9
Cortina d'Ampezzo, *Italy*	33	B9
Cortland, *U.S.A.*	107	D8
Cortona, *Italy*	33	E8
Coruche, *Portugal*	31	G2
Çoruh →, *Turkey*	43	K5
Çorum, *Turkey*	66	B6
Corumbá, *Brazil*	125	D6
Corumbá →, *Brazil*	123	E2
Corumbá de Goiás, *Brazil*	123	E2
Corumbaíba, *Brazil*	123	E2
Corunna = La Coruña, *Spain*	30	B2
Corvallis, *U.S.A.*	110	D2
Corvette, L. de la, *Canada*	98	B5
Corydon, *U.S.A.*	108	E8
Cosalá, *Mexico*	114	C3
Cosamaloapan, *Mexico*	115	D5
Cosenza, *Italy*	35	C9
Coshocton, *U.S.A.*	106	F3
Cosmo Newberry, *Australia*	89	E3
Cosne-sur-Loire, *France*	25	E9
Coso Junction, *U.S.A.*	113	J9
Coso Pk., *U.S.A.*	113	J9
Cospeito, *Spain*	30	B3
Cosquín, *Argentina*	126	C3
Cossato, *Italy*	32	C5
Cossé-le-Vivien, *France*	24	E6
Cosson →, *France*	24	E8
Costa Blanca, *Spain*	29	G4
Costa Brava, *Spain*	28	D8
Costa del Sol, *Spain*	31	J6
Costa Dorada, *Spain*	28	E6
Costa Mesa, *U.S.A.*	113	M9
Costa Rica ■, *Cent. Amer.*	116	D3
Costa Smeralda, *Italy*	34	A2
Costigliole d'Asti, *Italy*	32	D5
Costilla, *U.S.A.*	111	H11
Cosumnes →, *U.S.A.*	112	G5
Coswig, *Germany*	18	D8
Cotabato, *Phil.*	55	H6
Cotacajes →, *Bolivia*	124	D4
Cotagaita, *Bolivia*	126	A2
Cotahuasi, *Peru*	124	D3
Côte-d'Azur, *France*	27	E11
Côte-d'Ivoire = Ivory Coast ■, *Africa*	78	D3
Côte d'Or, *France*	25	E11
Côte-d'Or □, *France*	25	E11
Coteau des Prairies, *U.S.A.*	108	C6
Coteau du Missouri, *U.S.A.*	108	B4
Coteau Landing, *Canada*	107	A10
Cotegipe, *Brazil*	123	D3
Cotentin, *France*	24	C5
Côtes-d'Armor □, *France*	24	D4
Côtes de Meuse, *France*	25	C12
Côtes-du-Nord = Côtes-d'Armor □, *France*	24	D4
Cotiella, *Spain*	28	C5
Cotillo, *Canary Is.*	36	F5
Cotina →, *Bos.-H.*	21	M8
Cotoca, *Bolivia*	125	D5
Cotonou, *Benin*	79	D5
Cotopaxi, *Ecuador*	120	D2
Cotopaxi □, *Ecuador*	120	D2
Cotronei, *Italy*	35	C9
Cotswold Hills, *U.K.*	13	F5
Cottage Grove, *U.S.A.*	110	E2
Cottbus, *Germany*	18	D10
Cottingham, *U.K.*	12	D7
Cottonwood, *U.S.A.*	111	J7
Cotulla, *U.S.A.*	109	L5
Coubre, Pte. de la, *France*	26	C2
Couches, *France*	25	F11
Couço, *Portugal*	31	G2
Coudersport, *U.S.A.*	106	E6
Couedic, C. du, *Australia*	91	F2
Couëron, *France*	24	E5
Couesnon →, *France*	24	D5
Couhé, *France*	26	B4
Coulanges-sur-Yonne, *France*	25	E10
Coulee City, *U.S.A.*	110	C4
Coulman I., *Antarctica*	5	D11
Coulommiers, *France*	25	D10
Coulon →, *France*	27	E9
Coulonge →, *Canada*	98	C4
Coulonges-sur-l'Autize, *France*	26	B3
Coulterville, *U.S.A.*	112	H6
Council, *Alaska, U.S.A.*	96	B3
Council, *Idaho, U.S.A.*	110	D5
Council Bluffs, *U.S.A.*	108	E7
Council Grove, *U.S.A.*	108	F6
Coupeville, *U.S.A.*	112	B4
Courantyne →, *S. Amer.*	121	B6
Courcelles, *Belgium*	17	H4
Courçon, *France*	26	B3
Couronne, C., *France*	27	E9
Cours-la-Ville, *France*	27	B8
Coursan, *France*	26	E7
Courseulles-sur-Mer, *France*	24	C6
Court-St.-Etienne, *Belgium*	17	G5
Courtenay, *Canada*	100	D3
Courtland, *U.S.A.*	112	G5

Courtrai = Kortrijk, Belgium ... 17 G2
Courtright, Canada ... 106 D2
Courville-sur-Eure, France ... 24 D8
Coushatta, U.S.A. ... 109 J8
Coutances, France ... 24 C5
Couterne, France ... 24 D6
Coutras, France ... 26 C3
Coutts, Canada ... 100 D6
Couvet, Switz. ... 22 C3
Couvin, Belgium ... 17 H4
Covarrubias, Spain ... 28 C1
Coveñas, Colombia ... 120 B2
Coventry, U.K. ... 13 E6
Coventry L., Canada ... 101 A7
Covilhã, Portugal ... 30 E3
Covington, Ga., U.S.A. ... 105 J4
Covington, Ky., U.S.A. ... 104 F3
Covington, Okla., U.S.A. ... 109 G6
Covington, Tenn., U.S.A. ... 109 H10
Cowal, L., Australia ... 91 E4
Cowan, Canada ... 101 C8
Cowan, L., Australia ... 89 F3
Cowan L., Canada ... 101 C7
Cowangie, Australia ... 91 F3
Cowansville, Canada ... 107 A12
Cowarie, Australia ... 91 D2
Cowcowing Lakes, Australia ... 89 F2
Cowdenbeath, U.K. ... 14 E5
Cowell, Australia ... 91 E2
Cowes, U.K. ... 13 G6
Cowlitz →, U.S.A. ... 112 D4
Cowra, Australia ... 91 E4
Coxilha Grande, Brazil ... 127 B5
Coxim, Brazil ... 125 D7
Coxim →, Brazil ... 125 D7
Cox's Bazar, Bangla. ... 61 J17
Cox's Cove, Canada ... 99 C8
Coyame, Mexico ... 114 B3
Coyote Wells, U.S.A. ... 113 N11
Coyuca de Benítez, Mexico ... 115 D4
Coyuca de Catalan, Mexico ... 114 D4
Cozad, U.S.A. ... 108 E5
Cozumel, Mexico ... 115 C7
Cozumel, I. de, Mexico ... 115 C7
Craboon, Australia ... 91 E4
Cracow = Kraków, Poland ... 20 E9
Cracow, Australia ... 91 D5
Cradock, S. Africa ... 84 E4
Craig, Alaska, U.S.A. ... 100 B2
Craig, Colo., U.S.A. ... 110 F10
Craigavon, U.K. ... 15 B5
Craigmore, Zimbabwe ... 83 G3
Crailsheim, Germany ... 19 F6
Craiova, Romania ... 38 E6
Cramsie, Australia ... 90 C3
Cranberry Portage, Canada ... 101 C8
Cranbrook, Tas., Australia ... 90 G4
Cranbrook, W. Austral., Australia ... 89 F2
Cranbrook, Canada ... 100 D5
Crandon, U.S.A. ... 108 C10
Crane, Oreg., U.S.A. ... 110 E4
Crane, Tex., U.S.A. ... 109 K3
Cranston, U.S.A. ... 107 E13
Craon, France ... 24 E6
Craonne, France ... 25 C10
Craponne-sur-Arzon, France ... 26 C7
Crasna, Romania ... 38 C10
Crater L., U.S.A. ... 110 E2
Crateús, Brazil ... 122 C3
Crati →, Italy ... 35 C9
Crato, Brazil ... 122 C4
Crato, Portugal ... 31 F3
Cravo Norte, Colombia ... 120 B3
Cravo Norte →, Colombia ... 120 B3
Crawford, U.S.A. ... 108 D3
Crawfordsville, U.S.A. ... 104 E2
Crawley, U.K. ... 13 F7
Crazy Mts., U.S.A. ... 110 C8
Crean L., Canada ... 101 C7
Crécy-en-Brie, France ... 25 D9
Crécy-en-Ponthieu, France ... 25 B8
Crediton, Canada ... 106 C3
Credo, Australia ... 89 F3
Cree →, Canada ... 101 B7
Cree →, U.K. ... 14 G4
Cree L., Canada ... 101 B7
Creede, U.S.A. ... 111 H10
Creel, Mexico ... 114 B3
Creighton, U.S.A. ... 108 D6
Creil, France ... 25 C9
Crema, Italy ... 32 C6
Cremona, Italy ... 32 C7
Crepori →, Brazil ... 125 B6
Crépy, France ... 25 C10
Crépy-en-Valois, France ... 25 C9
Cres, Croatia ... 33 D11
Cresbard, U.S.A. ... 108 C5
Crescent, Okla., U.S.A. ... 109 H6
Crescent, Oreg., U.S.A. ... 110 E3
Crescent City, U.S.A. ... 110 F1
Crescentino, Italy ... 32 C5
Crespino, Italy ... 33 D8
Crespo, Argentina ... 126 C3
Cressy, Australia ... 91 F3
Crest, France ... 27 D9
Cresta, Mt., Phil. ... 55 C5
Crested Butte, U.S.A. ... 111 G10
Crestline, Calif., U.S.A. ... 113 L9
Crestline, Ohio, U.S.A. ... 106 F2
Creston, Canada ... 100 D5
Creston, Calif., U.S.A. ... 112 K6
Creston, Iowa, U.S.A. ... 108 E7
Creston, Wash., U.S.A. ... 110 C4

Crestview, Calif., U.S.A. ... 112 H8
Crestview, Fla., U.S.A. ... 105 K2
Crete = Kríti, Greece ... 37 D7
Crete, U.S.A. ... 108 E6
Crete, Sea of, Greece ... 39 N8
Creus, C. de, Spain ... 28 C8
Creuse □, France ... 26 B6
Creuse →, France ... 26 B4
Creuzburg, Germany ... 18 D6
Crevalcore, Italy ... 33 D8
Crèvecœur-le-Grand, France ... 25 C9
Crevillente, Spain ... 29 G4
Crewe, U.K. ... 12 D5
Criciúma, Brazil ... 127 B6
Crieff, U.K. ... 14 E5
Crikvenica, Croatia ... 33 C11
Crimea □, Ukraine ... 41 K8
Crimean Pen. = Krymskyy Pivostriv, Ukraine ... 41 K8
Crimmitschau, Germany ... 18 E8
Cristalândia, Brazil ... 122 D2
Cristino Castro, Brazil ... 122 C3
Crişul Alb →, Romania ... 38 C4
Crişul Negru →, Romania ... 38 C4
Crişul Repede →, Romania ... 38 C3
Crivitz, Germany ... 18 B7
Crixás, Brazil ... 123 D2
Crna Gora = Montenegro □, Yugoslavia ... 21 N9
Crni Drim →, Macedonia ... 39 H3
Črnomelj, Slovenia ... 33 C12
Croagh Patrick, Ireland ... 15 C2
Croatia ■, Europe ... 33 C13
Crocker, Banjaran, Malaysia ... 56 C5
Crockett, U.S.A. ... 109 K7
Crocodile = Krokodil →, Mozam. ... 85 D5
Crocodile Is., Australia ... 90 A1
Crocq, France ... 26 C6
Croisette, C., France ... 27 E9
Croisic, Pte. du, France ... 24 E4
Croix, L. La, Canada ... 98 C1
Croker, C., Australia ... 88 B5
Croker I., Australia ... 88 B5
Cromarty, Canada ... 101 B10
Cromarty, U.K. ... 14 D4
Cromer, U.K. ... 12 E9
Cromwell, N.Z. ... 87 L2
Cronat, France ... 25 F10
Cronulla, Australia ... 91 E5
Crooked →, Canada ... 100 C4
Crooked →, U.S.A. ... 110 D3
Crooked I., Bahamas ... 117 B5
Crooked Island Passage, Bahamas ... 117 B5
Crookston, Minn., U.S.A. ... 108 B6
Crookston, Nebr., U.S.A. ... 108 D4
Crooksville, U.S.A. ... 104 F4
Crookwell, Australia ... 91 E4
Crosby, Minn., U.S.A. ... 108 B8
Crosby, N. Dak., U.S.A. ... 101 D8
Crosby, Pa., U.S.A. ... 106 E6
Crosbyton, U.S.A. ... 109 J4
Cross →, Nigeria ... 79 E6
Cross City, U.S.A. ... 105 L4
Cross Fell, U.K. ... 12 C5
Cross L., Canada ... 101 C9
Cross Plains, U.S.A. ... 109 J5
Cross River □, Nigeria ... 79 D6
Cross Sound, U.S.A. ... 96 C6
Crossett, U.S.A. ... 109 J9
Crossfield, Canada ... 100 C6
Crosshaven, Ireland ... 15 E3
Croton-on-Hudson, U.S.A. ... 107 E11
Crotone, Italy ... 35 C10
Crow →, U.S.A. ... 100 B4
Crow Agency, U.S.A. ... 110 D10
Crow Hd., Ireland ... 15 E1
Crowell, U.S.A. ... 109 J5
Crowley, U.S.A. ... 109 K8
Crowley, L., U.S.A. ... 112 H8
Crown Point, U.S.A. ... 104 E2
Crows Landing, U.S.A. ... 112 H5
Crows Nest, Australia ... 91 D5
Crowsnest Pass, Canada ... 100 D6
Croydon, Australia ... 90 B3
Croydon, U.K. ... 13 F7
Crozet Is., Ind. Oc. ... 3 G12
Crozon, France ... 24 D2
Cruz, C., Cuba ... 116 C4
Cruz Alta, Brazil ... 127 B5
Cruz das Almas, Brazil ... 123 D4
Cruz de Malta, Brazil ... 122 C3
Cruz del Eje, Argentina ... 126 C3
Cruzeiro, Brazil ... 123 F2
Cruzeiro do Oeste, Brazil ... 127 A5
Cruzeiro do Sul, Brazil ... 124 B3
Cry L., Canada ... 100 B3
Crystal Bay, U.S.A. ... 112 F7
Crystal Brook, Australia ... 91 E2
Crystal City, Mo., U.S.A. ... 108 F9
Crystal City, Tex., U.S.A. ... 109 L5
Crystal Falls, U.S.A. ... 104 B1
Crystal River, U.S.A. ... 105 L4
Crystal Springs, U.S.A. ... 109 K9
Csongrád, Hungary ... 21 J10
Csorna, Hungary ... 21 H7
Csurgo, Hungary ... 21 J7
Cu Lao Hon, Vietnam ... 59 G7
Cua Rao, Vietnam ... 58 C5
Cuácua →, Mozam. ... 83 F4
Cuamato, Angola ... 84 B2
Cuamba, Mozam. ... 83 E4

Cuando →, Angola ... 81 H4
Cuando Cubango □, Angola ... 84 B3
Cuangar, Angola ... 84 B2
Cuanza →, Angola ... 70 G5
Cuarto →, Argentina ... 126 C3
Cuatrociénegas, Mexico ... 114 B4
Cuauhtémoc, Mexico ... 114 B3
Cuba, Portugal ... 31 G3
Cuba, N. Mex., U.S.A. ... 111 J10
Cuba, N.Y., U.S.A. ... 106 D6
Cuba ■, W. Indies ... 116 B4
Cuballing, Australia ... 89 F2
Cubango →, Africa ... 84 B3
Çubuk, Turkey ... 66 B5
Cucamonga, U.S.A. ... 113 L9
Cuchi, Angola ... 81 G3
Cuchillo-Có, Argentina ... 128 A4
Cuchivero →, Venezuela ... 120 B4
Cuchumatanes, Sierra de los, Guatemala ... 116 C1
Cucuí, Brazil ... 120 C4
Cucurpe, Mexico ... 114 A2
Cucurrupí, Colombia ... 120 C2
Cúcuta, Colombia ... 120 B3
Cudahy, U.S.A. ... 104 D2
Cudalbi, Romania ... 38 D10
Cuddalore, India ... 60 P11
Cuddapah, India ... 60 M11
Cuddapan, L., Australia ... 90 D3
Cudgewa, Australia ... 91 F4
Cue, Australia ... 89 E2
Cuéllar, Spain ... 30 D6
Cuenca, Ecuador ... 120 D2
Cuenca, Spain ... 28 E2
Cuenca □, Spain ... 28 F2
Cuenca, Serranía de, Spain ... 28 F3
Cuerdo del Pozo, Pantano de la, Spain ... 28 D2
Cuernavaca, Mexico ... 115 D5
Cuero, U.S.A. ... 109 L6
Cuers, France ... 27 E10
Cuervo, U.S.A. ... 109 H2
Cuesmes, Belgium ... 17 H3
Cuevas, Cerro, Bolivia ... 125 E4
Cuevas del Almanzora, Spain ... 29 H3
Cuevo, Bolivia ... 125 E5
Cuiabá, Brazil ... 125 D6
Cuiabá →, Brazil ... 125 D6
Cuilco, Guatemala ... 116 C1
Cuillin Hills, U.K. ... 14 D2
Cuillin Sd., U.K. ... 14 D2
Cuima, Angola ... 81 G3
Cuiseaux, France ... 27 B9
Cuité, Brazil ... 122 C4
Cuito →, Angola ... 84 B3
Cuitzeo, L. de, Mexico ... 114 D4
Cuiuni →, Brazil ... 121 D5
Çukai, Malaysia ... 59 K4
Culan, France ... 26 B6
Culasi, Phil. ... 55 F5
Culbertson, U.S.A. ... 108 A2
Culcairn, Australia ... 91 F4
Culebra, Sierra de la, Spain ... 30 D4
Culemborg, Neths. ... 16 E6
Culfa, Azerbaijan ... 67 C11
Culgoa →, Australia ... 91 D4
Culiacán, Mexico ... 114 C3
Culiacán →, Mexico ... 114 C3
Culion, Phil. ... 55 F4
Cullarin Ra., Australia ... 91 E4
Cúllar de Baza, Spain ... 29 H2
Cullen, U.K. ... 14 D6
Cullen Pt., Australia ... 90 A3
Cullera, Spain ... 29 F4
Cullman, U.S.A. ... 105 H2
Culloden, U.K. ... 14 D4
Culoz, France ... 27 C9
Culpeper, U.S.A. ... 104 F7
Culuene →, Brazil ... 125 C7
Culver, Pt., Australia ... 89 F3
Culverden, N.Z. ... 87 K4
Cumaná, Venezuela ... 121 A5
Cumare, Colombia ... 120 C3
Cumari, Brazil ... 123 E2
Cumberland, Canada ... 100 D3
Cumberland, Md., U.S.A. ... 104 F6
Cumberland, Wis., U.S.A. ... 108 C8
Cumberland →, U.S.A. ... 105 G2
Cumberland I., U.S.A. ... 105 K5
Cumberland Is., Australia ... 90 C4
Cumberland L., Canada ... 101 C8
Cumberland Pen., Canada ... 97 B13
Cumberland Plateau, U.S.A. ... 105 H3
Cumberland Sd., Canada ... 97 B13
Cumborah, Australia ... 91 D4
Cumbres Mayores, Spain ... 31 G4
Cumbria □, U.K. ... 12 C5
Cumbrian Mts., U.K. ... 12 C4
Cumbum, India ... 60 M11
Cuminá →, Brazil ... 121 D6
Cuminapanema →, Brazil ... 121 D7
Cummins, Australia ... 91 E2
Cummnock, Australia ... 91 E4
Cumnock, U.K. ... 14 F4
Cumpas, Mexico ... 114 A3
Cumplida, Pta., Canary Is. ... 36 F2
Çumra, Turkey ... 66 D5
Cundeelee, Australia ... 89 F3
Cunderdin, Australia ... 89 F2
Cundinamarca □, Colombia ... 120 C3
Cunene →, Angola ... 84 B1

Cúneo, Italy ... 32 D4
Cunillera, I., Spain ... 36 C7
Cunlhat, France ... 26 C7
Cunnamulla, Australia ... 91 D4
Cuorgnè, Italy ... 32 C4
Cupar, Canada ... 101 C8
Cupar, U.K. ... 14 E5
Cupica, G. de, Colombia ... 120 B2
Curaçá, Brazil ... 122 C4
Curaçao, Neth. Ant. ... 117 D6
Curacautín, Chile ... 128 A2
Curahuara de Carangas, Bolivia ... 124 D4
Curanilahue, Chile ... 126 D1
Curaray →, Peru ... 120 D3
Curatabaca, Venezuela ... 121 B5
Cure →, France ... 25 E10
Curepto, Chile ... 126 D1
Curiapo, Venezuela ... 121 B5
Curicó, Chile ... 126 C1
Curicó □, Chile ... 126 C1
Curicuriari →, Brazil ... 120 D4
Curimatá, Brazil ... 122 D3
Curiplaya, Colombia ... 120 C3
Curitiba, Brazil ... 127 B6
Currabubula, Australia ... 91 E5
Currais Novos, Brazil ... 122 C4
Curralinho, Brazil ... 122 B2
Currant, U.S.A. ... 110 G6
Curraweena, Australia ... 91 E4
Currawilla, Australia ... 90 D3
Current →, U.S.A. ... 109 G9
Currie, Australia ... 90 F3
Currie, U.S.A. ... 110 F6
Currituck Sd., U.S.A. ... 105 G8
Curtea de Argeş, Romania ... 38 D7
Curtis, Spain ... 30 B2
Curtis, U.S.A. ... 108 E4
Curtis Group, Australia ... 90 F4
Curtis I., Australia ... 90 C5
Curuá →, Pará, Brazil ... 121 D7
Curuá →, Pará, Brazil ... 125 B7
Curuá, I., Brazil ... 122 A1
Curuaés →, Brazil ... 125 B7
Curuápanema →, Brazil ... 121 D6
Curuçá, Brazil ... 122 B2
Curuguaty, Paraguay ... 127 A4
Curup, Indonesia ... 56 E2
Curupira, Serra, S. Amer. ... 121 C5
Cururu →, Brazil ... 125 B6
Cururupu, Brazil ... 122 B3
Curuzú Cuatiá, Argentina ... 126 B4
Curvelo, Brazil ... 123 E3
Cushing, U.S.A. ... 109 H6
Cushing, Mt., Canada ... 100 B3
Cusihuiriáchic, Mexico ... 114 B3
Cusna, Mte., Italy ... 32 D7
Cusset, France ... 26 B7
Custer, U.S.A. ... 108 D3
Cut Bank, U.S.A. ... 110 B7
Cutervo, Peru ... 124 B2
Cuthbert, U.S.A. ... 105 K3
Cutler, U.S.A. ... 112 J7
Cutral-Có, Argentina ... 128 A3
Cutro, Italy ... 35 C9
Cuttaburra →, Australia ... 91 D3
Cuttack, India ... 61 J14
Cuvier, C., Australia ... 89 D1
Cuvier I., N.Z. ... 87 G5
Cuxhaven, Germany ... 18 B4
Cuyabeno, Ecuador ... 120 D2
Cuyahoga Falls, U.S.A. ... 106 E3
Cuyapo, Phil. ... 55 D4
Cuyo, Phil. ... 55 F4
Cuyo East Pass, Phil. ... 55 F4
Cuyo West Pass, Phil. ... 55 F4
Cuyuni →, Guyana ... 121 B6
Cuzco, Bolivia ... 124 E4
Cuzco, Peru ... 124 C3
Cuzco □, Peru ... 124 C3
Cwmbran, U.K. ... 13 F4
Cyangugu, Rwanda ... 82 C2
Cyclades = Kikládhes, Greece ... 39 M7
Cygnet, Australia ... 90 G4
Cynthiana, U.S.A. ... 104 F3
Cypress Hills, Canada ... 101 D7
Cyprus ■, Asia ... 66 E5
Cyrenaica, Libya ... 73 C9
Cyrene = Shaḥḥāt, Libya ... 73 B9
Czar, Canada ... 101 C6
Czarne, Poland ... 20 B6
Czech Rep. ■, Europe ... 20 F4
Czersk, Poland ... 20 B7
Częstochowa, Poland ... 20 E9

D

Da →, Vietnam ... 58 B5
Da Hinggan Ling, China ... 54 B7
Da Lat, Vietnam ... 59 G7
Da Nang, Vietnam ... 58 D7
Da Qaidam, China ... 54 C4
Da Yunhe →, China ... 51 G11
Da'an, China ... 51 B13
Daarlerveen, Neths. ... 16 D9
Dab'a, Râs el, Egypt ... 76 H6
Daba Shan, China ... 52 B7
Dabajuro, Venezuela ... 120 A3
Dabakala, Ivory C. ... 78 D4
Dabeiba, Colombia ... 120 B2
Dabhoi, India ... 62 H5

Dąbie, Poland ... 20 B4
Dabie Shan, China ... 53 B10
Dabo, Indonesia ... 56 E2
Dabola, Guinea ... 78 C2
Dabou, Ivory C. ... 78 D4
Daboya, Ghana ... 79 D4
Dabrowa Tarnówska, Poland ... 20 E10
Dabu, China ... 53 E11
Dabung, Malaysia ... 59 K4
Dabus →, Ethiopia ... 77 E4
Dacato →, Ethiopia ... 77 F5
Dacca = Dhaka, Bangla. ... 63 H14
Dacca = Dhaka □, Bangla. ... 63 G14
Dachau, Germany ... 19 G7
Dadanawa, Guyana ... 121 C6
Daday, Turkey ... 66 B5
Dade City, U.S.A. ... 105 L4
Dades, Oued →, Morocco ... 74 B3
Dadiya, Nigeria ... 79 D7
Dadra and Nagar Haveli □, India ... 60 J8
Dadri = Charkhi Dadri, India ... 62 E7
Dadu, Pakistan ... 62 F2
Dadu He →, China ... 52 C4
Dăeni, Romania ... 38 E11
Daet, Phil. ... 55 D5
Dafang, China ... 52 D5
Dagana, Senegal ... 78 B1
Dagash, Sudan ... 76 D3
Dagestan □, Russia ... 43 J8
Dagestanskiye Ogni, Russia ... 43 J9
Daggett, U.S.A. ... 113 L10
Daghestan Republic = Dagestan □, Russia ... 43 J8
Daghfeli, Sudan ... 76 D3
Dağlıq Qarabağ = Nagorno-Karabakh, Azerbaijan ... 67 C12
Dagö = Hiiumaa, Estonia ... 9 G20
Dagu, China ... 51 E9
Daguan, China ... 52 D4
Dagupan, Phil. ... 55 C4
Dahab, Egypt ... 76 B3
Dahlak Kebir, Eritrea ... 68 D3
Dahlenburg, Germany ... 18 B6
Dahlonega, U.S.A. ... 105 H4
Dahme, Germany ... 18 D9
Dahod, India ... 62 H6
Dahomey = Benin ■, Africa ... 79 D5
Dahong Shan, China ... 53 B9
Dahra, Senegal ... 78 B1
Dahra, Massif de, Algeria ... 75 A5
Dai Hao, Vietnam ... 58 C6
Dai-Sen, Japan ... 49 G6
Dai Shan, China ... 53 B14
Dai Xian, China ... 50 E7
Daicheng, China ... 50 E9
Daimiel, Spain ... 29 F1
Daingean, Ireland ... 15 C4
Dainkog, China ... 52 A1
Daintree, Australia ... 90 B4
Daiō-Misaki, Japan ... 49 G8
Dairût, Egypt ... 76 B3
Daisetsu-Zan, Japan ... 48 C11
Dajarra, Australia ... 90 C2
Dajia, Taiwan ... 53 E13
Dajin Chuan →, China ... 52 B3
Dak Dam, Cambodia ... 58 F6
Dak Nhe, Vietnam ... 58 E6
Dak Pek, Vietnam ... 58 E6
Dak Song, Vietnam ... 59 F6
Dak Sui, Vietnam ... 58 E6
Dakar, Senegal ... 78 C1
Dakhla, W. Sahara ... 74 D1
Dakhla, El Wâhât el-, Egypt ... 76 B2
Dakingari, Nigeria ... 79 C5
Dakor, India ... 62 H5
Dakoro, Niger ... 79 C6
Dakota City, U.S.A. ... 108 D6
Đakovica, Serbia, Yug. ... 21 N10
Đakovo, Croatia ... 21 K8
Dalaba, Guinea ... 78 C2
Dalachi, China ... 50 F3
Dalai Nur, China ... 50 C9
Dālakī, Iran ... 65 D6
Dalälven, Sweden ... 9 F17
Dalaman, Turkey ... 66 D3
Dalaman →, Turkey ... 66 D3
Dalandzadgad, Mongolia ... 50 C3
Dalarna, Sweden ... 9 F16
Dālbandīn, Pakistan ... 60 E4
Dalbeattie, U.K. ... 14 G5
Dalbosjön, Sweden ... 11 F6
Dalby, Australia ... 91 D5
Dalby, Sweden ... 11 J7
Dalen, Neths. ... 16 C9
Dalen, Norway ... 10 E2
Dalfsen, Neths. ... 16 C8
Dalga, Egypt ... 76 B3
Dalgān, Iran ... 65 E9
Dalhart, U.S.A. ... 109 G3
Dalhousie, Canada ... 99 C6
Dalhousie, India ... 62 C6
Dali, Shaanxi, China ... 50 G5
Dali, Yunnan, China ... 52 E3
Dalian, China ... 51 E11
Daliang Shan, China ... 52 D4
Dalias, Spain ... 29 J2
Daling He →, China ... 51 D11
Dāliyat el Karmel, Israel ... 69 C4
Dalkeith, U.K. ... 14 F5
Dall I., U.S.A. ... 100 C2
Dallarnil, Australia ... 91 D5

Dergaon

Dallas, *Oreg., U.S.A.* 110 D2
Dallas, *Tex., U.S.A.* 109 J6
Dallol, *Ethiopia* 77 E5
Dalmacija, *Croatia* 21 M7
Dalmatia = Dalmacija, *Croatia* 21 M7
Dalmellington, *U.K.* 14 F4
Dalnegorsk, *Russia* 45 E14
Dalnerechensk, *Russia* 45 E14
Daloa, *Ivory C.* 78 D3
Dalou Shan, *China* 52 C6
Dalsjöfors, *Sweden* 11 G7
Dalskog, *Sweden* 11 F6
Dalsland, *Sweden* 9 G14
Daltenganj, *India* 63 G11
Dalton, *Canada* 98 C3
Dalton, *Ga., U.S.A.* 105 H3
Dalton, *Mass., U.S.A.* 107 D11
Dalton, *Nebr., U.S.A.* 108 E3
Dalton Iceberg Tongue, *Antarctica* 5 C9
Dalupiri I., *Phil.* 55 B4
Dalvík, *Iceland* 8 D4
Daly →, *Australia* 88 B5
Daly City, *U.S.A.* 112 H4
Daly L., *Canada* 101 B7
Daly Waters, *Australia* 90 B1
Dam Doi, *Vietnam* 59 H5
Dam Ha, *Vietnam* 58 B6
Daman, *India* 60 J8
Dāmaneh, *Iran* 65 C6
Damanhûr, *Egypt* 76 H7
Damanzhuang, *China* 50 E9
Damar, *Indonesia* 57 F7
Damaraland, *Namibia* 84 C2
Damascus = Dimashq, *Syria* 69 B5
Damaturu, *Nigeria* 79 C7
Damāvand, *Iran* 65 C7
Damāvand, Qolleh-ye, *Iran* 65 C7
Damba, *Angola* 80 F3
Dame Marie, *Haiti* 117 C5
Dāmghān, *Iran* 65 B7
Dămienesti, *Romania* 38 C10
Damietta = Dumyât, *Egypt* 76 H7
Daming, *China* 50 F8
Damīr Qābū, *Syria* 64 B4
Dammam = Ad Dammām, *Si. Arabia* 65 E6
Dammarie, *France* 24 D8
Dammartin-en-Goële, *France* 25 C9
Dammastock, *Switz.* 23 C6
Damme, *Germany* 18 C4
Damodar →, *India* 63 H12
Damoh, *India* 63 H8
Damous, *Algeria* 75 A5
Dampier, *Australia* 88 D2
Dampier, Selat, *Indonesia* 57 E8
Dampier Arch., *Australia* 88 D2
Damrei, Chuor Phnum, *Cambodia* 59 G4
Damville, *France* 24 D8
Damvillers, *France* 25 C12
Dan-Gulbi, *Nigeria* 79 C6
Dana, *Indonesia* 57 F6
Dana, L., *Canada* 98 B4
Dana, Mt., *U.S.A.* 112 H7
Danakil Depression, *Ethiopia* 77 E5
Danao, *Phil.* 55 F6
Danbury, *U.S.A.* 107 E11
Danby L., *U.S.A.* 111 J6
Dand, *Afghan.* 62 D1
Dandaragan, *Australia* 89 F2
Dandeldhura, *Nepal* 63 E9
Dandeli, *India* 60 M9
Dandenong, *Australia* 91 F4
Dandong, *China* 51 D13
Danfeng, *China* 50 H6
Danforth, *U.S.A.* 99 C6
Dangan Liedao, *China* 53 F10
Danger Is. = Pukapuka, *Cook Is.* 93 J11
Danger Pt., *S. Africa* 84 E2
Dangla, *Ethiopia* 77 E4
Dangora, *Nigeria* 79 C6
Dangrek, Phnom, *Thailand* 58 E5
Dangriga, *Belize* 115 D7
Dangshan, *China* 50 G9
Dangtu, *China* 53 B12
Dangyang, *China* 53 B8
Daniel, *U.S.A.* 110 E8
Daniel's Harbour, *Canada* 99 B8
Danielskuil, *S. Africa* 84 D3
Danielson, *U.S.A.* 107 E13
Danilov, *Russia* 42 A5
Danilovka, *Russia* 42 E7
Daning, *China* 50 F6
Danissa, *Kenya* 82 B5
Danja, *Nigeria* 79 C6
Dankalwa, *Nigeria* 79 C7
Dankama, *Nigeria* 79 C6
Dankhar Gompa, *India* 60 C11
Dankov, *Russia* 42 D4
Danleng, *China* 52 B4
Danlí, *Honduras* 116 D2
Dannemora, *U.S.A.* 107 B11
Dannenberg, *Germany* 18 B7
Dannevirke, *N.Z.* 87 J6
Dannhauser, *S. Africa* 85 D5
Danshui, *Taiwan* 53 E13
Dansville, *U.S.A.* 106 D7
Dantan, *India* 63 J12
Dante, *Somali Rep.* 68 E5
Danube = Dunărea →, *Europe* 41 K5
Danvers, *U.S.A.* 107 D14
Danville, *Ill., U.S.A.* 104 E2
Danville, *Ky., U.S.A.* 104 G3
Danville, *Va., U.S.A.* 105 G6
Danyang, *China* 53 B12
Danzhai, *China* 52 D6
Danzig = Gdańsk, *Poland* 20 A8
Dao, *Phil.* 57 B6
Dão →, *Portugal* 30 E2
Dao Xian, *China* 53 E8
Daocheng, *China* 52 C3
Daora, *W. Sahara* 74 C2
Daoud = Aïn Beïda, *Algeria* 75 A6
Daoulas, *France* 24 D2
Dapitan, *Phil.* 55 G5
Dapong, *Togo* 79 C5
Daqing Shan, *China* 50 D6
Daqu Shan, *China* 53 B14
Dar el Beida = Casablanca, *Morocco* 74 B3
Dar es Salaam, *Tanzania* 82 D4
Dar Mazār, *Iran* 65 D8
Dar'ā, *Syria* 69 C5
Dar'ā □, *Syria* 69 C5
Dārāb, *Iran* 65 D7
Daraj, *Libya* 75 B7
Dārān, *Iran* 65 C6
Daravica, *Serbia, Yug.* 21 N10
Daraw, *Egypt* 76 C3
Dārayyā, *Syria* 69 B5
Darazo, *Nigeria* 79 C7
Darband, *Pakistan* 62 B5
Darband, Kūh-e, *Iran* 65 D8
Darbhanga, *India* 63 F11
Darby, *U.S.A.* 110 C6
Dardanelle, *Ark., U.S.A.* 109 H8
Dardanelle, *Calif., U.S.A.* 112 G7
Dardanelles = Çanakkale Boğazı, *Turkey* 66 B2
Darende, *Turkey* 66 C7
Dārestān, *Iran* 65 D8
Darfo, *Italy* 32 C7
Dârfûr, *Sudan* 73 F9
Dargai, *Pakistan* 62 B4
Dargan Ata, *Uzbekistan* 44 E7
Dargaville, *N.Z.* 87 F4
Darhan Muminggan Lianheqi, *China* 50 D6
Dari, *Sudan* 77 F3
Darıca, *Turkey* 66 B3
Darién, G. del, *Colombia* 120 B2
Darién, Serranía del, *Colombia* 120 B2
Dariganga, *Mongolia* 50 B7
Darinskoye, *Kazakhstan* 42 E10
Darjeeling = Darjiling, *India* 63 F13
Darjiling, *India* 63 F13
Dark Cove, *Canada* 99 C9
Darkan, *Australia* 89 F2
Darkhazīneh, *Iran* 65 D6
Darkot Pass, *Pakistan* 63 A5
Darling →, *Australia* 91 E3
Darling Downs, *Australia* 91 D5
Darling Ra., *Australia* 89 F2
Darlington, *U.K.* 12 C6
Darlington, *S.C., U.S.A.* 105 H6
Darlington, *Wis., U.S.A.* 108 D9
Darlington, L., *S. Africa* 84 E4
Darlot, L., *Australia* 89 E3
Darłowo, *Poland* 20 A6
Darmstadt, *Germany* 19 F4
Darnah, *Libya* 73 B9
Darnall, *S. Africa* 85 D5
Darnétal, *France* 24 C8
Darney, *France* 25 D13
Darnley, C., *Antarctica* 5 C6
Darnley B., *Canada* 96 B7
Daroca, *Spain* 28 D3
Darr, *Australia* 90 C3
Darr →, *Australia* 90 C3
Darrington, *U.S.A.* 110 B3
Darsser Ort, *Germany* 18 A8
Dart →, *U.K.* 13 G4
Dart, C., *Antarctica* 5 D14
Dartmoor, *U.K.* 13 G4
Dartmouth, *Australia* 90 C3
Dartmouth, *Canada* 99 D7
Dartmouth, *U.K.* 13 G4
Dartmouth, L., *Australia* 91 D4
Dartuch, C., *Spain* 36 B10
Darvaza, *Turkmenistan* 44 E6
Darvel, Teluk, *Malaysia* 57 D5
Darwha, *India* 60 J10
Darwin, *Australia* 88 B5
Darwin, *U.S.A.* 113 J9
Darwin, Mt., *Chile* 128 D3
Darwin River, *Australia* 88 B5
Daryoi Amu = Amudarya →, *Uzbekistan* 44 E6
Dās, *U.A.E.* 65 E7
Dashetai, *China* 50 D5
Dashhowuz, *Turkmenistan* 44 E6
Dashkesan = Daşkäsän, *Azerbaijan* 43 K7
Dasht, *Iran* 65 B8
Dasht →, *Pakistan* 60 G2
Dasht-e Märgow, *Afghan.* 60 D3
Dasht-i-Nawar, *Afghan.* 62 C3
Daska, *Pakistan* 62 C6
Daşkäsän, *Azerbaijan* 43 K7
Dassa-Zoume, *Benin* 79 D5
Datça, *Turkey* 66 D2
Datia, *India* 63 G8
Datian, *China* 53 E11
Datong, *Anhui, China* 53 B11
Datong, *Shanxi, China* 50 D7
Datu, Tanjung, *Indonesia* 56 D3
Datu Piang, *Phil.* 55 H6
Daugava →, *Latvia* 9 H21
Daugavpils, *Latvia* 9 J22
Daule, *Ecuador* 120 D2
Daule →, *Ecuador* 120 D2
Daulpur, *India* 62 F7
Daun, *Germany* 19 E2
Dauphin, *Canada* 101 C8
Dauphin I., *U.S.A.* 105 K1
Dauphin L., *Canada* 101 C9
Dauphiné, *France* 27 C9
Daura, *Borno, Nigeria* 79 C7
Daura, *Kaduna, Nigeria* 79 C6
Dausa, *India* 62 F7
Däväçi, *Azerbaijan* 43 K9
Davangere, *India* 60 M9
Davao, *Phil.* 55 H6
Davao, G. of, *Phil.* 55 H6
Dāvar Panāh, *Iran* 65 E9
Davenport, *Calif., U.S.A.* 112 H4
Davenport, *Iowa, U.S.A.* 108 E9
Davenport, *Wash., U.S.A.* 110 C4
Davenport Downs, *Australia* 90 C3
Davenport Ra., *Australia* 90 C1
David, *Panama* 116 E3
David City, *U.S.A.* 108 E6
David Gorodok = Davyd Haradok, *Belarus* 41 F4
Davidson, *Canada* 101 C7
Davis, *U.S.A.* 112 G5
Davis Dam, *U.S.A.* 113 K12
Davis Inlet, *Canada* 99 A7
Davis Mts., *U.S.A.* 109 K2
Davis Sea, *Antarctica* 5 C7
Davis Str., *N. Amer.* 97 B14
Davos, *Switz.* 23 C9
Davy L., *Canada* 101 B7
Davyd Haradok, *Belarus* 41 F4
Dawa →, *Ethiopia* 77 G5
Dawaki, *Bauchi, Nigeria* 79 D6
Dawaki, *Kano, Nigeria* 79 C6
Dawes Ra., *Australia* 90 C5
Dawson, *Canada* 96 B6
Dawson, *Ga., U.S.A.* 105 K3
Dawson, *N. Dak., U.S.A.* 108 B5
Dawson, I., *Chile* 128 D2
Dawson Creek, *Canada* 100 B4
Dawson Inlet, *Canada* 101 A10
Dawson Ra., *Australia* 90 C4
Dawu, *China* 52 B3
Dax, *France* 26 E2
Daxi, *Taiwan* 53 E13
Daxian, *China* 52 B6
Daxin, *China* 52 F6
Daxindian, *China* 51 F11
Daxinggou, *China* 51 C15
Daxue Shan, *Sichuan, China* 52 B3
Daxue Shan, *Yunnan, China* 52 F2
Dayao, *China* 52 E3
Daye, *China* 53 B10
Dayi, *China* 52 B4
Daylesford, *Australia* 91 F3
Dayong, *China* 53 C8
Dayr az Zawr, *Syria* 67 E9
Daysland, *Canada* 100 C6
Dayton, *Nev., U.S.A.* 112 F7
Dayton, *Ohio, U.S.A.* 104 F3
Dayton, *Pa., U.S.A.* 106 F5
Dayton, *Tenn., U.S.A.* 105 H3
Dayton, *Wash., U.S.A.* 110 C4
Daytona Beach, *U.S.A.* 105 L5
Dayu, *China* 53 E10
Dayville, *U.S.A.* 110 D4
Dazhu, *China* 52 B6
Dazu, *China* 52 C5
De Aar, *S. Africa* 84 E3
De Bilt, *Neths.* 16 D6
De Funiak Springs, *U.S.A.* 105 K2
De Grey, *Australia* 88 D2
De Grey →, *Australia* 88 D2
De Kalb, *U.S.A.* 108 E10
De Koog, *Neths.* 16 B5
De Land, *U.S.A.* 105 L5
De Leon, *U.S.A.* 109 J5
De Panne, *Belgium* 17 F1
De Pere, *U.S.A.* 104 C1
De Queen, *U.S.A.* 109 H7
De Quincy, *U.S.A.* 109 K8
De Ridder, *U.S.A.* 109 K8
De Rijp, *Neths.* 16 C5
De Smet, *U.S.A.* 108 C6
De Soto, *U.S.A.* 108 F9
De Tour Village, *U.S.A.* 104 C4
De Witt, *U.S.A.* 109 H9
Dead Sea, *Asia* 69 D4
Deadwood, *U.S.A.* 108 C3
Deadwood L., *Canada* 100 B3
Deakin, *Australia* 89 F4
Deal, *U.K.* 13 F9
Deal I., *Australia* 90 F4
Dealesville, *S. Africa* 84 D4
De'an, *China* 53 C10
Dean, Forest of, *U.K.* 13 F5
Deán Funes, *Argentina* 126 C3
Dearborn, *U.S.A.* 98 D3
Dease →, *Canada* 100 B3
Dease L., *Canada* 100 B2
Dease Lake, *Canada* 100 B2
Death Valley, *U.S.A.* 113 J10
Death Valley Junction, *U.S.A.* 113 J10
Death Valley National Monument, *U.S.A.* 113 J10
Deauville, *France* 24 C7
Deba Habe, *Nigeria* 79 C7
Debaltsevo, *Ukraine* 41 H10
Debao, *China* 52 F6
Debar, *Macedonia* 39 H3
Debden, *Canada* 101 C7
Debdou, *Morocco* 75 B4
Dębica, *Poland* 20 E11
Dęblin, *Poland* 20 D11
Débo, L., *Mali* 78 B4
Debolt, *Canada* 100 B5
Deborah East, L., *Australia* 89 F2
Deborah West, L., *Australia* 89 F2
Debre Birhan, *Ethiopia* 77 F4
Debre Markos, *Ethiopia* 77 E4
Debre May, *Ethiopia* 77 E4
Debre Sina, *Ethiopia* 77 F4
Debre Tabor, *Ethiopia* 77 E4
Debre Zebit, *Ethiopia* 77 E4
Debrecen, *Hungary* 21 H11
Dečani, *Serbia, Yug.* 21 N10
Decatur, *Ala., U.S.A.* 105 H2
Decatur, *Ga., U.S.A.* 105 J3
Decatur, *Ill., U.S.A.* 108 F10
Decatur, *Ind., U.S.A.* 104 E3
Decatur, *Tex., U.S.A.* 109 J6
Decazeville, *France* 26 D6
Deccan, *India* 60 M10
Deception L., *Canada* 101 B8
Dechang, *China* 52 D4
Děčín, *Czech.* 20 E4
Decize, *France* 25 F10
Deckerville, *U.S.A.* 106 C2
Decollatura, *Italy* 35 C9
Decorah, *U.S.A.* 108 D9
Dedéagach = Alexandroúpolis, *Greece* 39 J8
Dedemsvaart, *Neths.* 16 C8
Dedham, *U.S.A.* 107 D13
Dédougou, *Burkina Faso* 78 C4
Dedovichi, *Russia* 40 D5
Dedza, *Malawi* 83 E3
Dee →, *Clwyd, U.K.* 12 D4
Dee →, *Gramp., U.K.* 14 D6
Deep B., *Canada* 100 A5
Deep Well, *Australia* 90 C1
Deepwater, *Australia* 91 D5
Deer →, *Canada* 101 B10
Deer Lake, *Nfld., Canada* 99 C8
Deer Lake, *Ont., Canada* 101 C10
Deer Lodge, *U.S.A.* 110 C7
Deer Park, *U.S.A.* 110 C5
Deer River, *U.S.A.* 108 B8
Deeral, *Australia* 90 B4
Deerdepoort, *S. Africa* 84 C4
Deerlijk, *Belgium* 17 G2
Deferiet, *U.S.A.* 107 B9
Defiance, *U.S.A.* 104 E3
Dêgê, *China* 52 B2
Degebe →, *Portugal* 31 G3
Degeh Bur, *Ethiopia* 68 F3
Degema, *Nigeria* 79 E6
Degersheim, *Switz.* 23 B8
Deggendorf, *Germany* 19 G8
Deh Bīd, *Iran* 65 D7
Deh-e Shīr, *Iran* 65 D7
Dehaj, *Iran* 65 D7
Dehdez, *Iran* 65 D6
Dehestān, *Iran* 65 D7
Dehgolān, *Iran* 67 E12
Dehi Titan, *Afghan.* 60 C3
Dehibat, *Tunisia* 75 B7
Dehlorān, *Iran* 67 F12
Dehnow-e Kūhestān, *Iran* 65 E8
Dehra Dun, *India* 62 D8
Dehri, *India* 63 G11
Dehua, *China* 53 E12
Dehui, *China* 51 B13
Deinze, *Belgium* 17 G3
Dej, *Romania* 38 B6
Dejiang, *China* 52 C7
Dekemhare, *Eritrea* 77 D4
Dekese, *Zaïre* 80 E4
Del Mar, *U.S.A.* 113 N9
Del Norte, *U.S.A.* 111 H10
Del Rio, *U.S.A.* 109 L4
Delai, *Sudan* 76 D4
Delano, *U.S.A.* 113 K7
Delareyville, *S. Africa* 84 D4
Delavan, *U.S.A.* 108 D10
Delaware, *U.S.A.* 104 E4
Delaware □, *U.S.A.* 104 F8
Delaware →, *U.S.A.* 104 F8
Delaware B., *U.S.A.* 103 C12
Delegate, *Australia* 91 F4
Delémont, *Switz.* 22 B4
Delft, *Neths.* 16 D4
Delfzijl, *Neths.* 16 B9
Delgado, C., *Mozam.* 83 E5
Delgerhet, *Mongolia* 50 B6
Delgo, *Sudan* 76 C3
Delhi, *Canada* 106 D4
Delhi, *India* 62 E7
Delhi, *U.S.A.* 107 D10
Delia, *Canada* 100 C6
Delice, *Turkey* 66 C6
Delicias, *Mexico* 114 B3
Delījān, *Iran* 65 C6
Delitzsch, *Germany* 18 D8
Dell City, *U.S.A.* 111 L11
Dell Rapids, *U.S.A.* 108 D6
Delle, *France* 25 E14
Dellys, *Algeria* 75 A5
Delmar, *U.S.A.* 107 D11
Delmenhorst, *Germany* 18 B4
Delmiro Gouveia, *Brazil* 122 C4
Delnice, *Croatia* 33 C11
Delong, Ostrova, *Russia* 45 B15
Deloraine, *Australia* 90 G4
Deloraine, *Canada* 101 D8
Delphi, *U.S.A.* 104 E2
Delphos, *U.S.A.* 104 E3
Delportshoop, *S. Africa* 84 D3
Delray Beach, *U.S.A.* 105 M5
Delsbo, *Sweden* 10 C10
Delta, *Colo., U.S.A.* 111 G9
Delta, *Utah, U.S.A.* 110 G7
Delta □, *Nigeria* 79 D6
Delta Amacuro □, *Venezuela* 121 B5
Delungra, *Australia* 91 D5
Delvinákion, *Greece* 39 K3
Delvinë, *Albania* 39 K3
Demanda, Sierra de la, *Spain* 28 C1
Demavand = Damāvand, *Iran* 65 C7
Demba, *Zaïre* 80 F4
Dembecha, *Ethiopia* 77 E4
Dembi, *Ethiopia* 77 F4
Dembia, *Zaïre* 82 B2
Dembidolo, *Ethiopia* 77 F3
Demer →, *Belgium* 17 G5
Demidov, *Russia* 40 E6
Deming, *N. Mex., U.S.A.* 111 K10
Deming, *Wash., U.S.A.* 112 B4
Demini →, *Brazil* 121 D5
Demirci, *Turkey* 66 C3
Demirköy, *Turkey* 66 B2
Demmin, *Germany* 18 B9
Demnate, *Morocco* 74 B3
Demonte, *Italy* 32 D4
Demopolis, *U.S.A.* 105 J2
Dempo, *Indonesia* 56 E2
Demyansk, *Russia* 40 D7
Den Burg, *Neths.* 16 B5
Den Chai, *Thailand* 58 D3
Den Dungen, *Neths.* 17 E6
Den Haag = 's-Gravenhage, *Neths.* 16 D4
Den Ham, *Neths.* 16 D8
Den Helder, *Neths.* 16 C5
Den Hulst, *Neths.* 16 C8
Den Oever, *Neths.* 16 C6
Denain, *France* 25 B10
Denair, *U.S.A.* 112 H6
Denau, *Uzbekistan* 44 F7
Denbigh, *U.K.* 12 D4
Dendang, *Indonesia* 56 E3
Dender →, *Belgium* 17 F4
Denderhoutem, *Belgium* 17 G4
Denderleeuw, *Belgium* 17 G4
Dendermonde, *Belgium* 17 F4
Deneba, *Ethiopia* 77 F4
Denekamp, *Neths.* 16 D10
Deng Xian, *China* 53 A9
Dengchuan, *China* 52 E3
Denge, *Nigeria* 79 C6
Dengfeng, *China* 50 G7
Dengi, *Nigeria* 79 D6
Dengkou, *China* 50 D4
Denham, *Australia* 89 E1
Denham Ra., *Australia* 90 C4
Denham Sd., *Australia* 89 E1
Denia, *Spain* 29 G5
Denial B., *Australia* 91 E1
Deniliquin, *Australia* 91 F3
Denison, *Iowa, U.S.A.* 108 D7
Denison, *Tex., U.S.A.* 109 J6
Denison Plains, *Australia* 88 C4
Denizli, *Turkey* 66 D3
Denman Glacier, *Antarctica* 5 C7
Denmark, *Australia* 89 F2
Denmark ■, *Europe* 11 J3
Denmark Str., *Atl. Oc.* 4 C6
Dennison, *U.S.A.* 106 F3
Denpasar, *Indonesia* 56 F5
Denton, *Mont., U.S.A.* 110 C9
Denton, *Tex., U.S.A.* 109 J6
D'Entrecasteaux, Pt., *Australia* 89 F2
Dents du Midi, *Switz.* 22 D3
Denu, *Ghana* 79 D5
Denver, *U.S.A.* 108 F2
Denver City, *U.S.A.* 109 J3
Deoband, *India* 62 E7
Deoghar, *India* 63 G12
Deolali, *India* 60 K8
Deoli = Devli, *India* 62 G6
Deoria, *India* 63 F10
Deosai Mts., *Pakistan* 63 B6
Deping, *China* 51 F9
Deposit, *U.S.A.* 107 D9
Depot Springs, *Australia* 89 E3
Deputatskiy, *Russia* 45 C14
Dêqên, *China* 52 C2
Deqing, *China* 53 F8
Dera Ghazi Khan, *Pakistan* 62 D4
Dera Ismail Khan, *Pakistan* 62 D4
Derbent, *Russia* 43 J9
Derby, *Australia* 88 C3
Derby, *U.K.* 12 E6
Derby, *Conn., U.S.A.* 107 E11
Derby, *N.Y., U.S.A.* 106 D6
Derbyshire □, *U.K.* 12 E6
Dereli, *Turkey* 67 B8
Derg →, *U.K.* 15 B4
Derg, L., *Ireland* 15 D3
Dergachi = Derhaci, *Ukraine* 41 G9
Dergaon, *India* 61 F19

Derhaci, *Ukraine* 41 G9
Derik, *Turkey* 67 D9
Derinkuyu, *Turkey* 66 C6
Dernieres, Isles, *U.S.A.* . 109 L9
Dêrong, *China* 52 C2
Derry = Londonderry,
  U.K. 15 B4
Derryveagh Mts., *Ireland* . 15 B3
Derudub, *Sudan* 76 D4
Derval, *France* 24 E5
Dervéni, *Greece* 39 L5
Derwent, *Canada* 101 C6
Derwent →, *Derby, U.K.* . 12 E6
Derwent →, *N. Yorks.,*
  U.K. 12 D7
Derwent Water, *U.K.* 12 C4
Des Moines, *Iowa, U.S.A.* 108 E8
Des Moines, *N. Mex.,*
  U.S.A. 109 G3
Des Moines →, *U.S.A.* .. 108 E9
Desaguadero →, *Argentina* 126 C2
Desaguadero →, *Bolivia* . 124 D4
Descanso, Pta., *Mexico* .. 113 N9
Descartes, *France* 26 B4
Deschaillons, *Canada* ... 99 C5
Descharme →, *Canada* .. 101 B7
Deschutes →, *U.S.A.* 110 D3
Dese, *Ethiopia* 68 E2
Deseado, C., *Chile* 128 D2
Desenzano del Garda, *Italy* 32 C7
Desert Center, *U.S.A.* ... 113 M11
Desert Hot Springs, *U.S.A.* 113 M10
Désirade, I., *Guadeloupe* . 117 C7
Deskenatlata L., *Canada* . 100 A6
Desna →, *Ukraine* 41 G6
Desnăţui →, *Romania* ... 38 E6
Desolación, I., *Chile* 128 D2
Despeñaperros, Paso, *Spain* 29 G1
Despotovac, *Serbia, Yug.* . 21 L11
Dessau, *Germany* 18 D8
Dessel, *Belgium* 17 F6
Dessye = Dese, *Ethiopia* . 68 E2
D'Estrees B., *Australia* .. 91 F2
Desuri, *India* 62 G5
Desvres, *France* 25 B8
Det Udom, *Thailand* 58 E5
Dete, *Zimbabwe* 83 F2
Detinja →, *Serbia, Yug.* . 21 M9
Detmold, *Germany* 18 D4
Detour, Pt., *U.S.A.* 104 C2
Detroit, *Mich., U.S.A.* ... 98 D4
Detroit, *Tex., U.S.A.* 109 J7
Detroit Lakes, *U.S.A.* 108 B7
Deurne, *Belgium* 17 F4
Deurne, *Neths.* 17 F7
Deutsche Bucht, *Germany* 18 A4
Deutschlandsberg, *Austria* 21 J5
Deux-Sèvres □, *France* ... 24 F6
Deva, *Romania* 38 D5
Devakottai, *India* 60 Q11
Devaprayag, *India* 63 D8
Dévaványa, *Hungary* 21 H10
Deveci Dağları, *Turkey* .. 66 B7
Develi, *Turkey* 66 C6
Deventer, *Neths.* 16 D8
Deveron →, *U.K.* 14 D6
Devgadh Bariya, *India* ... 62 H5
Devils Den, *U.S.A.* 112 K7
Devils Lake, *U.S.A.* 108 A5
Devils Paw, *Canada* 100 B2
Devizes, *U.K.* 13 F6
Devli, *India* 62 G6
Devnya, *Bulgaria* 38 F10
Devolii →, *Albania* 39 J3
Devon, *Canada* 100 C6
Devon □, *U.K.* 13 G4
Devon I., *Canada* 4 B3
Devonport, *Australia* 90 G4
Devonport, *N.Z.* 87 G5
Devonport, *U.K.* 13 G3
Devrek, *Turkey* 66 B4
Devrekâni, *Turkey* 66 B5
Devrez →, *Turkey* 66 B6
Dewas, *India* 62 H7
Dewetsdorp, *S. Africa* ... 84 D4
Dewsbury, *U.K.* 12 D6
Dexing, *China* 53 C11
Dexter, *Mo., U.S.A.* 109 G9
Dexter, *N. Mex., U.S.A.* . 109 J2
Dey-Dey, L., *Australia* ... 89 E5
Deyang, *China* 52 B5
Deyhūk, *Iran* 65 C8
Deyyer, *Iran* 65 E6
Dezadeash L., *Canada* ... 100 A1
Dezfūl, *Iran* 67 F13
Dezhneva, Mys, *Russia* .. 45 C19
Dezhou, *China* 50 F9
Dháfni, *Greece* 37 D7
Dhahaban, *Si. Arabia* ... 76 C4
Dhahiriya = Aẓ Ẓāhirīyah,
  West Bank 69 D3
Dhahran = Aẓ Ẓahrān,
  Si. Arabia 65 E6
Dhaka, *Bangla.* 63 H14
Dhaka □, *Bangla.* 63 G14
Dhali, *Cyprus* 37 D12
Dhamar, *Yemen* 68 E3
Dhamási, *Greece* 39 K5
Dhampur, *India* 63 E8
Dhamtari, *India* 61 J12
Dhanbad, *India* 63 H12
Dhangarhi, *Nepal* 61 E12
Dhankuta, *Nepal* 63 F12
Dhar, *India* 62 H6
Dharampur, *India* 62 H6
Dharamsala = Dharmsala,
  India 62 C7
Dharmapuri, *India* 60 N11
Dharmsala, *India* 62 C7
Dharwad, *India* 60 M9
Dhaulagiri, *Nepal* 63 E10
Dhebar, L., *India* 62 G6
Dheftera, *Cyprus* 37 D12
Dhenkanal, *India* 61 J14
Dhenoúsa, *Greece* 39 M8
Dherinia, *Cyprus* 37 D12
Dheskáti, *Greece* 39 K4
Dhespotikó, *Greece* 39 N7
Dhestina, *Greece* 39 L5
Dhiarrizos →, *Cyprus* .. 37 E11
Dhíbān, *Jordan* 69 D4
Dhíkti Óros, *Greece* 37 D7
Dhimitsána, *Greece* 39 M5
Dhodhekánisos, *Greece* . 39 N10
Dholiana, *Greece* 39 K3
Dholka, *India* 62 H5
Dhoraji, *India* 62 J4
Dhoxáton, *Greece* 39 H7
Dhráhstis, Ákra, *Greece* . 37 A3
Dhrápanon, Ákra, *Greece* 37 D6
Dhrol, *India* 62 H4
Dhuburi, *India* 61 F16
Dhule, *India* 60 J9
Dhut →, *Somali Rep.* ... 68 E5
Di Linh, *Vietnam* 59 G7
Di Linh, Cao Nguyen,
  Vietnam 59 G7
Día, *Greece* 37 D7
Diablo, Mt., *U.S.A.* 112 H5
Diablo Range, *U.S.A.* ... 112 J5
Diafarabé, *Mali* 78 C4
Diala, *Mali* 78 C3
Dialakoro, *Mali* 78 C3
Diallassagou, *Mali* 78 C4
Diamante, *Argentina* ... 126 C3
Diamante →, *Argentina* . 126 C2
Diamantina, *Brazil* 123 E3
Diamantina →, *Australia* . 91 D2
Diamantino, *Brazil* 125 C6
Diamond Harbour, *India* . 63 H13
Diamond Is., *Australia* ... 90 B5
Diamond Mts., *U.S.A.* ... 110 G6
Diamond Springs, *U.S.A.* 112 G6
Diamondville, *U.S.A.* 110 F8
Dianbai, *China* 53 G8
Diancheng, *China* 53 G8
Diano Marina, *Italy* 32 E5
Dianópolis, *Brazil* 123 D2
Dianra, *Ivory C.* 78 D3
Diapaga, *Burkina Faso* .. 79 C5
Diapangou, *Burkina Faso* . 79 C5
Diariguila, *Guinea* 78 C2
Dībā, *Oman* 65 E8
Dibaya, *Zaïre* 80 F4
Dibaya-Lubue, *Zaïre* 80 E3
Dibbi, *Ethiopia* 68 G3
Dibete, *Botswana* 84 C4
Dibrugarh, *India* 61 F19
Dickinson, *U.S.A.* 108 B3
Dickson, *Russia* 44 B9
Dickson, *U.S.A.* 105 G2
Dickson City, *U.S.A.* 107 E9
Dicle Nehri →, *Turkey* .. 67 D9
Dicomano, *Italy* 33 E8
Didam, *Neths.* 16 E8
Didesa, W. →, *Ethiopia* . 77 E4
Didiéni, *Mali* 78 C3
Didsbury, *Canada* 100 C6
Didwana, *India* 62 F6
Die, *France* 27 D9
Diébougou, *Burkina Faso* . 78 C4
Diefenbaker L., *Canada* . 101 C7
Diego Garcia, *Ind. Oc.* .. 3 E13
Diekirch, *Lux.* 17 J8
Diélette, *France* 24 C5
Diéma, *Mali* 78 C3
Diémbéring, *Senegal* 78 C1
Diemen, *Neths.* 16 D5
Dien Ban, *Vietnam* 58 E7
Dien Bien, *Vietnam* 58 B4
Dien Khanh, *Vietnam* ... 59 F7
Diepenbeek, *Belgium* 17 G6
Diepenheim, *Neths.* 16 D9
Diepenveen, *Neths.* 16 D8
Diepholz, *Germany* 18 C4
Dieppe, *France* 24 C8
Dieren, *Neths.* 16 D8
Dierks, *U.S.A.* 109 H7
Diessen, *Neths.* 17 F6
Diest, *Belgium* 17 G6
Dietikon, *Switz.* 23 B6
Dietto van, *Switz.* 23 A7
Dieulefit, *France* 27 D9
Dieuze, *France* 25 D13
Diever, *Neths.* 16 C8
Differdange, *Lux.* 17 J7
Dig, *India* 62 F7
Digba, *Zaïre* 82 B2
Digby, *Canada* 99 D6
Digges, *Canada* 101 B10
Digges Is., *Canada* 97 B12
Dighinala, *Bangla.* 61 H18
Dighton, *U.S.A.* 108 F4
Digne-les-Bains, *France* .. 27 D10
Digoin, *France* 26 B7
Digor, *Turkey* 67 B10
Digos, *Phil.* 55 H6
Digranes, *Iceland* 8 C6
Digul →, *Indonesia* 57 F9
Dihang →, *India* 61 F19
Dijlah, Nahr →, *Asia* 64 D5
Dijle →, *Belgium* 17 G5
Dijon, *France* 25 E12
Dikala, *Sudan* 77 G3
Dikimdya, *Russia* 45 D13
Dikkil, *Djibouti* 77 E5
Dikomu di Kai, *Botswana* 84 C3
Diksmuide, *Belgium* 17 F1
Dikson = Dickson, *Russia* 44 B9
Dikwa, *Nigeria* 79 C7
Dila, *Ethiopia* 77 F4
Dilbeek, *Belgium* 17 G4
Dili, *Indonesia* 57 F7
Dilijan, *Armenia* 43 K7
Dilizhan = Dilijan,
  Armenia 43 K7
Dillenburg, *Germany* 18 E4
Dilley, *U.S.A.* 109 L5
Dilling, *Sudan* 77 E2
Dillingen, *Germany* 19 G6
Dillingham, *U.S.A.* 96 C4
Dillon, *Canada* 101 B7
Dillon, *Mont., U.S.A.* ... 110 D7
Dillon, *S.C., U.S.A.* 105 H6
Dillon →, *Canada* 101 B7
Dilolo, *Zaïre* 80 G4
Dilsen, *Belgium* 17 F7
Dilston, *Australia* 90 G4
Dimas, *Mexico* 114 C3
Dimashq, *Syria* 69 B5
Dimashq □, *Syria* 69 B5
Dimbaza, *S. Africa* 85 E4
Dimbokro, *Ivory C.* 78 D4
Dimboola, *Australia* 91 F3
Dîmboviţa →, *Romania* .. 38 E9
Dîmbovnic →, *Romania* . 38 E8
Dimbulah, *Australia* 90 B4
Dimitrovgrad, *Bulgaria* .. 39 G8
Dimitrovgrad, *Russia* 42 C9
Dimitrovgrad, *Serbia, Yug.* 21 M12
Dimitrovo = Pernik,
  Bulgaria 38 G6
Dimmitt, *U.S.A.* 109 H3
Dimo, *Sudan* 77 F2
Dimona, *Israel* 69 D4
Dimovo, *Bulgaria* 38 F5
Dinagat, *Phil.* 55 F6
Dinajpur, *Bangla.* 61 G16
Dinan, *France* 24 D4
Dīnān Āb, *Iran* 65 C8
Dinant, *Belgium* 17 H5
Dinapur, *India* 63 G11
Dinar, *Turkey* 66 C4
Dīnār, Kūh-e, *Iran* 65 D6
Dinara Planina, *Croatia* . 33 E13
Dinard, *France* 24 D4
Dinaric Alps = Dinara
  Planina, *Croatia* 33 E13
Dinder, Nahr ed →, *Sudan* 77 E3
Dindigul, *India* 60 P11
Ding Xian, *China* 50 E8
Dingalan, *Phil.* 55 D4
Dingbian, *China* 50 F4
Dingelstädt, *Germany* ... 18 D6
Dinghai, *China* 53 B14
Dingle, *Ireland* 15 D1
Dingle B., *Ireland* 15 D1
Dingmans Ferry, *U.S.A.* . 107 E10
Dingnan, *China* 53 E10
Dingo, *Australia* 90 C4
Dingolfing, *Germany* 19 G8
Dingtao, *China* 50 G8
Dinguiraye, *Guinea* 78 C2
Dingwall, *U.K.* 14 D4
Dingxi, *China* 50 G3
Dingxiang, *China* 50 E7
Dingyuan, *China* 53 A11
Dinh, Mui, *Vietnam* 59 G7
Dinh Lap, *Vietnam* 58 B6
Dinokwe, *Botswana* 84 C4
Dinosaur National
  Monument, *U.S.A.* 110 F9
Dinslaken, *Germany* 17 E9
Dintel →, *Neths.* 17 E4
Dinteloord, *Neths.* 17 E4
Dinuba, *U.S.A.* 111 H4
Dinxperlo, *Neths.* 16 E9
Diósgyőr, *Hungary* 21 G10
Diourbel, *Senegal* 78 C1
Diplo, *Pakistan* 62 G3
Dipolog, *Phil.* 55 G5
Dipşa, *Romania* 38 C7
Dir, *Pakistan* 60 B7
Diré, *Mali* 78 B4
Dire Dawa, *Ethiopia* ... 68 F3
Diriamba, *Nic.* 116 D2
Dirico, *Angola* 81 H4
Dirk Hartog I., *Australia* . 89 E1
Dirranbandi, *Australia* ... 91 D4
Disa, *India* 62 G5
Disa, *Sudan* 77 E3
Disappointment, C.,
  U.S.A. 110 C1
Disappointment, L.,
  Australia 88 D3
Disaster B., *Australia* ... 91 F4
Discovery B., *Australia* ... 91 F3
Disentis, *Switz.* 23 C7
Dishna, *Egypt* 76 B3
Disina, *Nigeria* 79 C6
Disko, *Greenland* 4 C5
Disko Bugt, *Greenland* .. 4 C5
Disna = Dzisna →,
  Belarus 40 E5
Dison, *Belgium* 17 G7
Disteghil Sar, *Pakistan* .. 63 A6
Distrito Federal □, *Brazil* 123 E2
Distrito Federal □,
  Venezuela 120 A4
Disûq, *Egypt* 76 H7
Diu, *India* 62 J4
Dīvāndarreh, *Iran* 67 E12
Dives →, *France* 24 C6
Dives-sur-Mer, *France* .. 24 C6
Divichi = Dāvāçi,
  Azerbaijan 43 K9
Divide, *U.S.A.* 110 D7
Dividing Ra., *Australia* ... 89 E2
Divinópolis, *Brazil* 123 F3
Divisões, Serra dos, *Brazil* 123 E1
Divnoye, *Russia* 43 H6
Divo, *Ivory C.* 78 D3
Divriği, *Turkey* 67 C8
Dīwāl Kol, *Afghan.* 62 B2
Dixie Mt., *U.S.A.* 112 F6
Dixon, *Calif., U.S.A.* 112 G5
Dixon, *Ill., U.S.A.* 108 E10
Dixon, *Mont., U.S.A.* ... 110 C6
Dixon, *N. Mex., U.S.A.* . 111 H11
Dixon Entrance, *U.S.A.* . 100 C2
Dixonville, *Canada* 100 B5
Diyadin, *Turkey* 67 C10
Diyālā →, *Iraq* 67 F11
Diyarbakır, *Turkey* 67 D9
Djado, *Niger* 73 D7
Djakarta = Jakarta,
  Indonesia 57 G12
Djamâa, *Algeria* 75 B6
Djamba, *Angola* 84 B1
Djambala, *Congo* 80 E2
Djanet, *Algeria* 75 D6
Djawa = Jawa, *Indonesia* 57 G14
Djebiniana, *Tunisia* 75 A7
Djelfa, *Algeria* 75 B5
Djema, *C.A.R.* 82 A2
Djendel, *Algeria* 75 A5
Djeneïene, *Tunisia* 75 B7
Djenné, *Mali* 78 C4
Djenoun, Garet el, *Algeria* 75 D6
Djerba, *Tunisia* 75 B7
Djerba, I. de, *Tunisia* ... 73 B7
Djerid, Chott, *Tunisia* ... 75 B6
Djibo, *Burkina Faso* 79 C4
Djibouti, *Djibouti* 68 E3
Djibouti ■, *Africa* 68 E3
Djolu, *Zaïre* 80 D4
Djougou, *Benin* 79 D5
Djoum, *Cameroon* 80 D2
Djourab, *Chad* 73 E8
Djugu, *Zaïre* 82 B3
Djúpivogur, *Iceland* 8 D6
Djursholm, *Sweden* 10 E12
Djursland, *Denmark* 11 H4
Dmitriya Lapteva, Proliv,
  Russia 45 B15
Dmitriyev Lgovskiy, *Russia* 42 D2
Dmitrov, *Russia* 42 B3
Dmitrovsk-Orlovskiy,
  Russia 42 D2
Dnepr = Dnipro →,
  Ukraine 41 J7
Dneprodzerzhinsk =
  Dniprodzerzhynsk,
  Ukraine 41 H8
Dneprodzerzhinskoye
  Vdkhr. =
  Dniprodzerzhynske
  Vdskh., *Ukraine* 41 H8
Dnepropetrovsk =
  Dnipropetrovsk, *Ukraine* 41 H8
Dneprorudnoye =
  Dniprorudne, *Ukraine* . 41 J8
Dnestr = Dnister →,
  Europe 41 J6
Dnestrovski = Belgorod,
  Russia 42 E3
Dnieper = Dnipro →,
  Ukraine 41 J7
Dniester = Dnister →,
  Europe 41 J6
Dnipro →, *Ukraine* 41 J7
Dniprodzerzhynsk, *Ukraine* 41 H8
Dniprodzerzhynske Vdskh.,
  Ukraine 41 H8
Dnipropetrovsk, *Ukraine* . 41 H8
Dniprorudne, *Ukraine* ... 41 J8
Dnister →, *Europe* 41 J6
Dnistrovskyy Lyman,
  Ukraine 41 J6
Dno, *Russia* 40 D5
Dnyapro = Dnipro →,
  Ukraine 41 J7
Doan Hung, *Vietnam* ... 58 B5
Doba, *Chad* 73 G8
Dobbiaco, *Italy* 33 B9
Dobbyn, *Australia* 90 B3
Dobele, *Latvia* 9 H20
Döbeln, *Germany* 18 D9
Doberai, Jazirah, *Indonesia* 57 E8
Dobiegniew, *Poland* 20 C5
Doblas, *Argentina* 126 D3
Dobo, *Indonesia* 57 F8
Doboj, *Bos.-H.* 21 L8
Dobra, Dîmboviţa,
  Romania 38 E8
Dobra, Hunedoara,
  Romania 38 D5
Dobreta-Turnu-Severin,
  Romania 38 E5
Dobrich, *Bulgaria* 38 F10
Dobrinishta, *Bulgaria* ... 39 H6
Dobrodzień, *Poland* 20 E8
Dobropole, *Ukraine* 41 H9
Dobruja, *Romania* 38 E11
Dobrush, *Belarus* 41 F6
Dobtong, *Sudan* 77 F3
Doc, Mui, *Vietnam* 58 D6
Doce →, *Brazil* 123 E4
Doda, *India* 63 C6
Dodecanese =
  Dhodhekánisos, *Greece* . 39 N10
Dodewaard, *Neths.* 16 E7
Dodge Center, *U.S.A.* ... 108 C8
Dodge City, *U.S.A.* 109 G5
Dodge L., *Canada* 101 B7
Dodgeville, *U.S.A.* 108 D9
Dodo, *Sudan* 77 F2
Dodola, *Ethiopia* 77 F4
Dodoma, *Tanzania* 82 D4
Dodoma □, *Tanzania* ... 82 D4
Dodsland, *Canada* 101 C7
Dodson, *U.S.A.* 110 B9
Doesburg, *Neths.* 16 D8
Doetinchem, *Neths.* 16 E8
Dog Creek, *Canada* 100 C4
Dog L., *Man., Canada* ... 101 C9
Dog L., *Ont., Canada* ... 98 C2
Doğanşehir, *Turkey* 66 C7
Dogi, *Afghan.* 60 C3
Dogliani, *Italy* 32 D4
Dogondoutchi, *Niger* 79 C5
Doğubayazıt, *Turkey* 67 C11
Doguéraoua, *Niger* 79 C6
Doha = Ad Dawḩah, *Qatar* 65 E6
Dohazari, *Bangla.* 61 H18
Doi, *Indonesia* 57 D7
Doi Luang, *Thailand* 58 C3
Doi Saket, *Thailand* 58 C2
Doig →, *Canada* 100 B4
Dois Irmãos, Sa., *Brazil* . 122 C3
Dokka →, *Norway* 10 D4
Dokkum, *Neths.* 16 B7
Dokkumer Ee →, *Neths.* . 16 B7
Dokri, *Pakistan* 62 F3
Dokuchayevsk, *Ukraine* . 41 J9
Dol-de-Bretagne, *France* . 24 D5
Doland, *U.S.A.* 108 C5
Dolbeau, *Canada* 99 C5
Dole, *France* 25 E12
Doleib, Wadi →, *Sudan* . 77 E3
Dolgellau, *U.K.* 12 E4
Dolgelley = Dolgellau,
  U.K. 12 E4
Dolianova, *Italy* 34 C2
Dolinskaya = Dolynska,
  Ukraine 41 H7
Dollart, *Neths.* 16 B10
Dolna Banya, *Bulgaria* ... 38 G6
Dolni Dŭbnik, *Bulgaria* . 38 F7
Dolo, *Ethiopia* 77 G5
Dolo, *Italy* 33 C9
Dolomites = Dolomiti,
  Italy 33 B8
Dolomiti, *Italy* 33 B8
Dolores, *Argentina* 126 D4
Dolores, *Uruguay* 126 C4
Dolores, *U.S.A.* 111 H9
Dolores →, *U.S.A.* 111 G9
Dolphin, C., *Falk. Is.* ... 128 D5
Dolphin and Union Str.,
  Canada 96 B8
Dolynska, *Ukraine* 41 H7
Dolzhanskaya, *Russia* ... 43 J3
Dom, *Switz.* 22 D5
Dom Joaquim, *Brazil* ... 123 E3
Dom Pedrito, *Brazil* 127 C4
Dom Pedro, *Brazil* 122 B3
Doma, *Nigeria* 79 D6
Domaniç, *Turkey* 66 C3
Domasi, *Malawi* 83 F4
Domat Ems, *Switz.* 23 C8
Domažlice, *Czech.* 20 F2
Dombarovskiy, *Russia* ... 44 D6
Dombås, *Norway* 9 E13
Dombasle-sur-Meurthe,
  France 25 D13
Dombes, *France* 27 B8
Dombóvár, *Hungary* ... 21 J8
Domburg, *Neths.* 17 E3
Domérat, *France* 26 B6
Domeyko, *Chile* 126 B1
Domeyko, Cordillera, *Chile* 126 A2
Domfront, *France* 24 D6
Dominador, *Chile* 126 A2
Dominica ■, *W. Indies* .. 117 C7
Dominica Passage,
  W. Indies 117 C7
Dominican Rep. ■,
  W. Indies 117 C5
Dömitz, *Germany* 18 B7
Domme, *France* 26 D5
Dommel →, *Neths.* 17 E6
Domo, *Ethiopia* 68 F4
Domodóssola, *Italy* 32 B5
Dompaire, *France* 25 D13
Dompierre-sur-Besbre,
  France 26 B7
Dompim, *Ghana* 78 D4
Domrémy-la-Pucelle,
  France 25 D12
Domsjö, *Sweden* 10 A12
Domville, Mt., *Australia* . 91 D5
Domvraína, *Greece* 39 L5
Domžale, *Slovenia* 33 B11
Don →, *Russia* 43 G4
Don →, *Gramp., U.K.* ... 14 D6
Don →, *Humber., U.K.* .. 12 D7
Don, C., *Australia* 88 B5
Don Benito, *Spain* 31 G5

Dutton

Don Duong, *Vietnam* 59 G7
Don Martín, Presa de, *Mexico* 114 B4
Dona Ana = Nhamaabué, *Mozam.* 83 F4
Donaghadee, *U.K.* 15 B6
Donald, *Australia* 91 F3
Donalda, *Canada* 100 C6
Donaldsonville, *U.S.A.* 109 K9
Donalsonville, *U.S.A.* 105 K3
Donau = Dunărea →, *Europe* 41 K5
Donau →, *Austria* 21 G7
Donaueschingen, *Germany* 19 H4
Donauwörth, *Germany* 19 G6
Doncaster, *U.K.* 12 D6
Dondo, *Angola* 80 F2
Dondo, *Mozam.* 83 F3
Dondo, Teluk, *Indonesia* 57 D6
Dondra Head, *Sri Lanka* 60 S12
Donegal, *Ireland* 15 B3
Donegal □, *Ireland* 15 B4
Donegal B., *Ireland* 15 B3
Donets →, *Russia* 43 G5
Donetsk, *Ukraine* 41 J9
Dong Ba Thin, *Vietnam* 59 F7
Dong Dang, *Vietnam* 58 B6
Dong Giam, *Vietnam* 58 C5
Dong Ha, *Vietnam* 58 D6
Dong Hene, *Laos* 58 D5
Dong Hoi, *Vietnam* 58 D6
Dong Jiang →, *China* 53 F10
Dong Khe, *Vietnam* 58 A6
Dong Ujimqin Qi, *China* 50 B9
Dong Van, *Vietnam* 58 A5
Dong Xoai, *Vietnam* 59 G6
Donga, *Nigeria* 79 D7
Dong'an, *China* 53 D8
Dongara, *Australia* 89 E1
Dongbei, *China* 51 D13
Dongchuan, *China* 52 D4
Dongen, *Neths.* 17 E5
Donges, *France* 24 E4
Dongfang, *China* 58 C7
Dongfeng, *China* 51 C13
Donggala, *Indonesia* 57 E5
Donggan, *China* 52 F5
Donggou, *China* 51 E13
Dongguan, *China* 53 F9
Dongguang, *China* 50 F9
Donghai Dao, *China* 53 G8
Dongjingcheng, *China* 51 B15
Donglan, *China* 52 E6
Dongliu, *China* 53 B11
Dongmen, *China* 52 F6
Dongning, *China* 51 B16
Dongnyi, *China* 52 C3
Dongola, *Sudan* 76 D3
Dongou, *Congo* 80 D3
Dongping, *China* 50 G9
Dongshan, *China* 53 F11
Dongsheng, *China* 50 E6
Dongshi, *Taiwan* 53 E13
Dongtai, *China* 51 H11
Dongting Hu, *China* 53 C9
Dongxiang, *China* 53 C11
Dongxing, *China* 52 G7
Dongyang, *China* 53 C13
Dongzhi, *China* 53 B11
Donington, C., *Australia* 91 E2
Doniphan, *U.S.A.* 109 G9
Donja Stubica, *Croatia* 33 C13
Donji Dušnik, *Serbia, Yug.* 21 M12
Donji Miholjac, *Croatia* 21 K8
Donji Milanovac, *Serbia, Yug.* 21 L12
Donji Vakuf, *Bos.-H.* 21 L7
Dønna, *Norway* 8 C15
Donna, *U.S.A.* 109 M5
Donnaconna, *Canada* 99 C5
Donnelly's Crossing, *N.Z.* 87 F4
Donnybrook, *Australia* 89 F2
Donnybrook, *S. Africa* 85 D4
Donora, *U.S.A.* 106 F5
Donor's Hill, *Australia* 90 B3
Donostia = San Sebastián, *Spain* 28 B3
Donskoy, *Russia* 42 D4
Donsol, *Phil.* 55 E5
Donya Lendava, *Slovenia* 33 B13
Donzère, *France* 27 D8
Donzère-Mondragon, Barr. de, *France* 27 D8
Donzy, *France* 25 E10
Doon →, *U.K.* 14 F4
Doorn, *Neths.* 16 D6
Dora, L., *Australia* 88 D3
Dora Báltea →, *Italy* 32 C5
Dora Ripária →, *Italy* 32 C4
Doran L., *Canada* 101 A7
Dorchester, *U.K.* 13 G5
Dorchester, C., *Canada* 97 B12
Dordogne □, *France* 26 C4
Dordogne →, *France* 26 C3
Dordrecht, *Neths.* 16 E5
Dordrecht, *S. Africa* 84 E4
Dore →, *France* 26 C7
Dore, Mts., *France* 26 C6
Doré L., *Canada* 101 C7
Doré Lake, *Canada* 101 C7
Dores do Indaiá, *Brazil* 123 E2
Dorfen, *Germany* 19 G8
Dorgali, *Italy* 34 B2
Dori, *Burkina Faso* 79 C4
Doring →, *S. Africa* 84 E2
Doringbos, *S. Africa* 84 E2
Dorion, *Canada* 98 C5
Dormaa-Ahenkro, *Ghana* 78 D4
Dormo, Ras, *Eritrea* 77 E5
Dornach, *Switz.* 22 B5
Dornberg, *Slovenia* 33 C10
Dornbirn, *Austria* 19 H5
Dornes, *France* 25 F10
Dornoch, *U.K.* 14 D4
Dornoch Firth, *U.K.* 14 D4
Dornogovĭ □, *Mongolia* 50 B6
Doro, *Mali* 79 B4
Dorogobuzh, *Russia* 40 E7
Dorohoi, *Romania* 38 B9
Döröö Nuur, *Mongolia* 54 B4
Dorr, *Iran* 65 C6
Dorre I., *Australia* 89 E1
Dorrigo, *Australia* 91 E5
Dorris, *U.S.A.* 110 F3
Dorset, *Canada* 106 A6
Dorset, *U.S.A.* 106 E4
Dorset □, *U.K.* 13 G5
Dorsten, *Germany* 18 D2
Dortmund, *Germany* 18 D3
Dörtyol, *Turkey* 66 D7
Dorum, *Germany* 18 B4
Doruma, *Zaïre* 82 B2
Dorüneh, *Iran* 65 C8
Dos Bahías, C., *Argentina* 128 B3
Dos Hermanas, *Spain* 31 H5
Dos Palos, *U.S.A.* 112 J6
Dosso, *Niger* 79 C5
Dothan, *U.S.A.* 105 K3
Dottignies, *Belgium* 17 G2
Doty, *U.S.A.* 112 D3
Douai, *France* 25 B10
Douala, *Cameroon* 79 E6
Douarnenez, *France* 24 D2
Double Island Pt., *Australia* 91 D5
Doubrava →, *Czech.* 20 F5
Doubs □, *France* 25 E13
Doubs →, *France* 25 F12
Doubtful Sd., *N.Z.* 87 L1
Doubtless B., *N.Z.* 87 F4
Doudeville, *France* 24 C7
Doué-la-Fontaine, *France* 24 E6
Douentza, *Mali* 78 C4
Douglas, *S. Africa* 84 D3
Douglas, *U.K.* 12 C3
Douglas, *Alaska, U.S.A.* 100 B2
Douglas, *Ariz., U.S.A.* 111 L9
Douglas, *Ga., U.S.A.* 105 K4
Douglas, *Wyo., U.S.A.* 108 D2
Douglastown, *Canada* 99 C7
Douglasville, *U.S.A.* 105 J3
Douirat, *Morocco* 74 B4
Doukáton, Ákra, *Greece* 39 L3
Doulevant-le-Château, *France* 25 D11
Doullens, *France* 25 B9
Doumé, *Cameroon* 80 D2
Douna, *Mali* 78 C3
Dounan, *Taiwan* 53 F13
Dounreay, *U.K.* 14 C5
Dour, *Belgium* 17 H3
Dourada, Serra, *Brazil* 123 D2
Dourados, *Brazil* 127 A5
Dourados →, *Brazil* 127 A5
Dourdan, *France* 25 D9
Douro →, *Europe* 30 D2
Douvaine, *France* 27 B10
Douz, *Tunisia* 75 B6
Douze →, *France* 26 E3
Dove →, *U.K.* 12 E6
Dove Creek, *U.S.A.* 111 H9
Dover, *Australia* 90 G4
Dover, *U.K.* 13 F9
Dover, *Del., U.S.A.* 104 F8
Dover, *N.H., U.S.A.* 107 C14
Dover, *N.J., U.S.A.* 107 F10
Dover, *Ohio, U.S.A.* 106 F3
Dover, Pt., *Australia* 89 F4
Dover, Str. of, *Europe* 24 B8
Dover-Foxcroft, *U.S.A.* 99 C6
Dover Plains, *U.S.A.* 107 E11
Dovey = Dyfi →, *U.K.* 13 E4
Dovrefjell, *Norway* 10 B3
Dow Rūd, *Iran* 65 C6
Dowa, *Malawi* 83 E3
Dowagiac, *U.S.A.* 104 E2
Dowgha'i, *Iran* 65 B8
Dowlatābād, *Iran* 65 D8
Down □, *U.K.* 15 B6
Downey, *Calif., U.S.A.* 113 M8
Downey, *Idaho, U.S.A.* 110 E7
Downham Market, *U.K.* 13 E8
Downieville, *U.S.A.* 112 F6
Downpatrick, *U.K.* 15 B6
Downpatrick Hd., *Ireland* 15 B2
Dowsārī, *Iran* 65 D8
Doyle, *U.S.A.* 112 E6
Doylestown, *U.S.A.* 107 F9
Draa, C., *Morocco* 74 C2
Draa, Oued →, *Morocco* 74 C2
Drac →, *France* 27 C9
Drachten, *Neths.* 16 B8
Drăgănești, *Romania* 38 E7
Drăgănești-Viașca, *Romania* 38 E8
Dragaš, *Serbia, Yug.* 21 N10
Drăgășani, *Romania* 38 E7
Dragichyn, *Belarus* 41 F3
Dragonera, I., *Spain* 36 B9
Draguignan, *France* 27 E10
Drain, *U.S.A.* 110 E2
Drake, *Australia* 91 D5
Drake, *U.S.A.* 108 B4
Drake Passage, *S. Ocean* 5 B17
Drakensberg, *S. Africa* 85 E4
Dráma, *Greece* 39 H7
Drammen, *Norway* 10 E4
Drangajökull, *Iceland* 8 C2
Drangedal, *Norway* 10 E3
Dranov, Ostrov, *Romania* 38 E12
Dras, *India* 63 B6
Drau = Drava →, *Croatia* 21 K8
Drava →, *Croatia* 21 K8
Draveil, *France* 25 D9
Dravograd, *Slovenia* 33 B12
Drawa →, *Poland* 20 C5
Drawno, *Poland* 20 B5
Drayton Valley, *Canada* 100 C6
Dreibergen, *Neths.* 16 D6
Drenthe □, *Neths.* 16 C9
Drentsche Hoofdvaart, *Neths.* 16 C8
Drepanum, C., *Cyprus* 37 E11
Dresden, *Canada* 106 D2
Dresden, *Germany* 18 D9
Dreux, *France* 24 D8
Driel, *Neths.* 16 E7
Driffield, *U.K.* 12 C7
Driftwood, *U.S.A.* 106 E6
Driggs, *U.S.A.* 110 E8
Drin i zi →, *Albania* 39 H3
Drina →, *Bos.-H.* 21 L9
Drincea →, *Romania* 38 E5
Drini →, *Albania* 38 G3
Drinjača →, *Bos.-H.* 21 L9
Drissa = Vyerkhnyadzvinsk, *Belarus* 40 E4
Drivstua, *Norway* 10 B3
Drniš, *Croatia* 33 E13
Drøbak, *Norway* 10 E4
Drochia, *Moldova* 41 H4
Drogheda, *Ireland* 15 C5
Drogichin = Dragichyn, *Belarus* 41 F3
Drogobych = Drohobych, *Ukraine* 41 H2
Drohobych, *Ukraine* 41 H2
Droichead Atha = Drogheda, *Ireland* 15 C5
Droichead Nua, *Ireland* 15 C5
Droitwich, *U.K.* 13 E5
Drôme □, *France* 27 D9
Drôme →, *France* 27 D8
Dromedary, C., *Australia* 91 F5
Dronero, *Italy* 32 D4
Dronfield, *Australia* 90 C3
Dronne →, *France* 26 C3
Dronninglund, *Denmark* 11 G4
Dronrijp, *Neths.* 16 B7
Dropt →, *France* 26 D3
Drumbo, *Canada* 106 C4
Drumheller, *Canada* 100 C6
Drummond, *U.S.A.* 110 C7
Drummond I., *U.S.A.* 98 C3
Drummond Pt., *Australia* 91 E2
Drummond Ra., *Australia* 90 C4
Drummondville, *Canada* 98 C5
Drumright, *U.S.A.* 109 H6
Drunen, *Neths.* 17 E6
Druskininkai, *Lithuania* 9 J20
Drut →, *Belarus* 41 F6
Druten, *Neths.* 16 E7
Druya, *Belarus* 40 E4
Druzhina, *Russia* 45 C15
Drvar, *Bos.-H.* 33 D13
Drvenik, *Croatia* 33 E13
Dry Tortugas, *U.S.A.* 116 B3
Dryanovo, *Bulgaria* 38 G8
Dryden, *Canada* 101 D10
Dryden, *U.S.A.* 109 K3
Drygalski I., *Antarctica* 5 C7
Drysdale →, *Australia* 88 B4
Drysdale I., *Australia* 90 A2
Dschang, *Cameroon* 79 D7
Du Bois, *U.S.A.* 106 E6
Du Quoin, *U.S.A.* 108 G10
Duanesburg, *U.S.A.* 107 D10
Duaringa, *Australia* 90 C4
Ḍubā, *Si. Arabia* 64 E2
Dubai = Dubayy, *U.A.E.* 65 E7
Dubăsari, *Moldova* 41 J5
Dubăsari Vdkhr., *Moldova* 41 J5
Dubawnt →, *Canada* 101 A8
Dubawnt, L., *Canada* 101 A8
Dubayy, *U.A.E.* 65 E7
Dubbeldam, *Neths.* 16 E5
Dubbo, *Australia* 91 E4
Dubele, *Zaïre* 82 B2
Dübendorf, *Switz.* 23 B7
Dubica, *Croatia* 33 C13
Dublin, *Ireland* 15 C5
Dublin, *Ga., U.S.A.* 105 J4
Dublin, *Tex., U.S.A.* 109 J5
Dublin □, *Ireland* 15 C5
Dublin B., *Ireland* 15 C5
Dubna, *Russia* 42 B3
Dubno, *Ukraine* 41 G3
Dubois, *U.S.A.* 110 D7
Dubossary = Dubăsari, *Moldova* 41 J5
Dubossary Vdkhr. = Dubăsari Vdkhr., *Moldova* 41 J5
Dubovka, *Russia* 43 F7
Dubovskoye, *Russia* 43 G6
Dubrajpur, *India* 63 H12
Dubréka, *Guinea* 78 D2
Dubrovitsa = Dubrovytsya, *Ukraine* 41 G4
Dubrovnik, *Croatia* 21 N8
Dubrovskoye, *Russia* 45 D12
Dubrovytsya, *Ukraine* 41 G4
Dubuque, *U.S.A.* 108 D9
Duchang, *China* 53 C11
Duchesne, *U.S.A.* 110 F8
Duchess, *Australia* 90 C2
Ducie I., *Pac. Oc.* 93 K15
Duck Cr. →, *Australia* 88 D2
Duck Lake, *Canada* 101 C7
Duck Mountain Prov. Park, *Canada* 101 C8
Duckwall, Mt., *U.S.A.* 112 H6
Düdelange, *Lux.* 17 K8
Duderstadt, *Germany* 18 D6
Dudhi, *India* 61 G13
Düdingen, *Switz.* 22 C4
Dudinka, *Russia* 45 C9
Dudley, *U.K.* 13 E5
Dueñas, *Spain* 30 D6
Dueré, *Brazil* 123 D2
Duero = Douro →, *Europe* 30 D2
Duffel, *Belgium* 17 F5
Dufftown, *U.K.* 14 D5
Dufourspitz, *Switz.* 22 E5
Dugi Otok, *Croatia* 33 E12
Dugo Selo, *Croatia* 33 C13
Duifken Pt., *Australia* 90 A3
Duisburg, *Germany* 18 D2
Duitama, *Colombia* 120 B3
Duiveland, *Neths.* 17 E4
Duiwelskloof, *S. Africa* 85 C5
Dūkdamīn, *Iran* 65 C8
Duke I., *U.S.A.* 100 C2
Dukhān, *Qatar* 65 E6
Dukhovshchina, *Russia* 40 E7
Duki, *Pakistan* 60 D6
Duku, *Bauchi, Nigeria* 79 C7
Duku, *Sokoto, Nigeria* 79 C5
Dulag, *Phil.* 55 F6
Dulce →, *Argentina* 126 C3
Dulce, G., *Costa Rica* 116 E3
Dulf, *Iraq* 64 C5
Dŭlgopol, *Bulgaria* 38 F10
Dulit, Banjaran, *Malaysia* 56 D4
Duliu, *China* 50 E9
Dullewala, *Pakistan* 62 D4
Dülmen, *Germany* 18 D3
Dulovo, *Bulgaria* 38 F10
Dulq Maghār, *Syria* 67 D8
Dululu, *Australia* 90 C5
Duluth, *U.S.A.* 108 B8
Dum Dum, *India* 63 H13
Dum Duma, *India* 61 F19
Dum Hadjer, *Chad* 73 F8
Dūmā, *Lebanon* 69 A4
Dūmā, *Syria* 69 B5
Dumaguete, *Phil.* 55 G5
Dumai, *Indonesia* 56 D2
Dumaran, *Phil.* 55 F3
Dumas, *Ark., U.S.A.* 109 J9
Dumas, *Tex., U.S.A.* 109 H4
Dumbarton, *U.K.* 14 F4
Dumbleyung, *Australia* 89 F2
Dumfries, *U.K.* 14 F5
Dumfries & Galloway □, *U.K.* 14 F5
Dumka, *India* 63 G12
Dümmer See, *Germany* 18 C4
Dumoine →, *Canada* 98 C4
Dumoine L., *Canada* 98 C4
Dumraon, *India* 63 G11
Dumyât, *Egypt* 76 H7
Dumyât, Masabb, *Egypt* 76 H7
Dún Dealgan = Dundalk, *Ireland* 15 B5
Dun Laoghaire, *Ireland* 15 C5
Dun-le-Palestel, *France* 26 B5
Dun-sur-Auron, *France* 25 F9
Duna = Dunărea →, *Europe* 41 K5
Duna →, *Hungary* 21 K8
Dunaföldvár, *Hungary* 21 J8
Dunaj = Dunărea →, *Europe* 41 K5
Dunaj →, *Slovak Rep.* 21 H8
Dunajec →, *Poland* 20 E10
Dunajská Streda, *Slovak Rep.* 21 H7
Dunapatai, *Hungary* 21 J9
Dunărea →, *Europe* 41 K5
Dunaújváros, *Hungary* 21 J8
Dunav = Dunărea →, *Europe* 41 K5
Dunav →, *Serbia, Yug.* 21 L11
Dunay, *Russia* 48 C6
Dunback, *N.Z.* 87 L3
Dunbar, *Australia* 90 B3
Dunbar, *U.K.* 14 E6
Dunblane, *U.K.* 14 E5
Duncan, *Canada* 100 D4
Duncan, *Ariz., U.S.A.* 111 K9
Duncan, *Okla., U.S.A.* 109 H6
Duncan, L., *Canada* 98 B4
Duncan L., *Canada* 100 A6
Duncan Town, *Bahamas* 116 B4
Duncannon, *U.S.A.* 106 F7
Dundalk, *Canada* 106 B4
Dundalk, *Ireland* 15 B5
Dundalk Bay, *Ireland* 15 C5
Dundas, *Canada* 98 D4
Dundas, L., *Australia* 89 F3
Dundas I., *Canada* 100 C2
Dundas Str., *Australia* 88 B5
Dundee, *S. Africa* 85 D5
Dundee, *U.K.* 14 E6
Dundgovĭ □, *Mongolia* 50 B4
Dundoo, *Australia* 91 D3
Dundrum, *U.K.* 15 B6
Dundrum B., *U.K.* 15 B6
Dundwara, *India* 63 F8
Dunedin, *N.Z.* 87 L3
Dunedin, *U.S.A.* 105 L4
Dunedin →, *Canada* 100 B4
Dunfermline, *U.K.* 14 E5
Dungannon, *Canada* 106 C3
Dungannon, *U.K.* 15 B5
Dungannon □, *U.K.* 15 B5
Dungarpur, *India* 62 H5
Dungarvan, *Ireland* 15 D4
Dungarvan Harbour, *Ireland* 15 D4
Dungeness, *U.K.* 13 G8
Dungo, L. do, *Angola* 84 B2
Dungog, *Australia* 91 E5
Dungu, *Zaïre* 82 B2
Dungunâb, *Sudan* 76 C4
Dungunâb, Khalij, *Sudan* 76 C4
Dunhua, *China* 51 C15
Dunhuang, *China* 54 B4
Dunières, *France* 27 C8
Dunk I., *Australia* 90 B4
Dunkeld, *U.K.* 14 E5
Dunkerque, *France* 25 A9
Dunkery Beacon, *U.K.* 13 F4
Dunkirk = Dunkerque, *France* 25 A9
Dunkirk, *U.S.A.* 106 D5
Dunkuj, *Sudan* 77 E3
Dunkwa, *Central, Ghana* 78 D4
Dunkwa, *Central, Ghana* 79 D4
Dunlap, *U.S.A.* 108 E7
Dúnleary = Dun Laoghaire, *Ireland* 15 C5
Dunmanus B., *Ireland* 15 E2
Dunmara, *Australia* 90 B1
Dunmore, *U.S.A.* 107 E9
Dunmore Hd., *Ireland* 15 D1
Dunmore Town, *Bahamas* 116 A4
Dunn, *U.S.A.* 105 H6
Dunnellon, *U.S.A.* 105 L4
Dunnet Hd., *U.K.* 14 C5
Dunning, *U.S.A.* 108 E4
Dunnville, *Canada* 106 D5
Dunolly, *Australia* 91 F3
Dunoon, *U.K.* 14 F4
Dunqul, *Egypt* 76 C3
Duns, *U.K.* 14 F6
Dunseith, *U.S.A.* 108 A4
Dunsmuir, *U.S.A.* 110 F2
Dunstable, *U.K.* 13 F7
Dunstan Mts., *N.Z.* 87 L2
Dunster, *Canada* 100 C5
Dunvegan L., *Canada* 101 A7
Duolun, *China* 50 C9
Duong Dong, *Vietnam* 59 G4
Dupree, *U.S.A.* 108 C4
Dupuyer, *U.S.A.* 110 B7
Duque de Caxias, *Brazil* 123 F3
Duque de York, I., *Chile* 128 D1
Durack →, *Australia* 88 C4
Durack Ra., *Australia* 88 C4
Durağan, *Turkey* 66 B6
Durance →, *France* 27 E8
Durand, *U.S.A.* 104 D4
Durango = Victoria de Durango, *Mexico* 114 C4
Durango, *Spain* 28 B2
Durango, *U.S.A.* 111 H10
Durango □, *Mexico* 114 C4
Duranillin, *Australia* 89 F2
Durant, *U.S.A.* 109 J6
Duratón →, *Spain* 30 D6
Durazno, *Uruguay* 126 C4
Durazzo = Durrësi, *Albania* 39 H2
Durban, *France* 26 F6
Durban, *S. Africa* 85 D5
Dúrcal, *Spain* 31 J7
Düren, *Germany* 18 E2
Durg, *India* 61 J12
Durgapur, *India* 63 H12
Durham, *Canada* 98 D3
Durham, *U.K.* 12 C6
Durham, *Calif., U.S.A.* 112 F5
Durham, *N.C., U.S.A.* 105 G6
Durham □, *U.K.* 12 C6
Durham Downs, *Australia* 91 D4
Durmitor, *Montenegro, Yug.* 21 M9
Durness, *U.K.* 14 C4
Durrësi, *Albania* 39 H2
Durrie, *Australia* 90 D3
Dursunbey, *Turkey* 66 C3
Durtal, *France* 24 E6
Duru, *Zaïre* 82 B2
D'Urville, Tanjung, *Indonesia* 57 E9
D'Urville I., *N.Z.* 87 J4
Duryea, *U.S.A.* 107 E9
Dusa Mareb, *Somali Rep.* 68 F4
Dûsh, *Egypt* 76 C3
Dushak, *Turkmenistan* 44 F7
Dushan, *China* 52 E6
Dushanbe, *Tajikistan* 44 F7
Dusheti, *Georgia* 43 J7
Dusky Sd., *N.Z.* 87 L1
Dussejour, C., *Australia* 88 B4
Düsseldorf, *Germany* 18 D2
Dussen, *Neths.* 16 E5
Dutch Harbor, *U.S.A.* 96 C3
Dutlwe, *Botswana* 84 C3
Dutsan Wai, *Nigeria* 79 C6
Dutton, *Canada* 106 D3
Dutton →, *Australia* 90 C3

Duved

Duved, *Sweden* 10 A6
Duvno, *Bos.-H.* 21 M7
Duyun, *China* 52 D6
Düzce, *Turkey* 66 B4
Duzdab = Zāhedān, *Iran* 65 D9
Dvina, Severnaya →, *Russia* 44 C5
Dvinsk = Daugavpils, *Latvia* 9 J22
Dvor, *Croatia* 33 C13
Dwarka, *India* 62 H3
Dwellingup, *Australia* 89 F2
Dwight, *Canada* 106 A5
Dwight, *U.S.A.* 104 E1
Dyatkovo, *Russia* 42 D2
Dyatlovo = Dzyatlava, *Belarus* 40 F3
Dyer, C., *Canada* 97 B13
Dyer Plateau, *Antarctica* 5 D17
Dyersburg, *U.S.A.* 109 G10
Dyfed □, *U.K.* 13 E3
Dyfi →, *U.K.* 13 E4
Dyje →, *Czech.* 20 G6
Dyle →, *Belgium* 17 G5
Dymer, *Ukraine* 41 G6
Dynevor Downs, *Australia* 91 D3
Dynów, *Poland* 20 F12
Dysart, *Canada* 101 C8
Dzamin Üüd, *Mongolia* 50 C6
Dzerzhinsk, *Russia* 42 B6
Dzhalinda, *Russia* 45 D13
Dzhambul = Zhambyl, *Kazakhstan* 44 E8
Dzhankoy, *Ukraine* 41 K8
Dzhanybek, *Kazakhstan* 42 F8
Dzhardzhan, *Russia* 45 C13
Dzharylhach, Ostriv, *Ukraine* 41 J7
Dzhetygara = Zhetiqara, *Kazakhstan* 44 D7
Dzhezkazgan = Zhezqazghan, *Kazakhstan* 44 E7
Dzhizak = Jizzakh, *Uzbekistan* 44 E7
Dzhugdzur, Khrebet, *Russia* 45 D14
Dzhvari = Jvari, *Georgia* 43 J6
Działdowa, *Poland* 20 B10
Działoszyn, *Poland* 20 D8
Dzierzgoń, *Poland* 20 B9
Dzierzoniów, *Poland* 20 E6
Dzilam de Bravo, *Mexico* 115 C7
Dzioua, *Algeria* 75 B6
Dzisna, *Belarus* 40 E5
Dzisna →, *Belarus* 40 E5
Dzungaria = Junggar Pendi, *China* 54 B3
Dzungarian Gate = Alataw Shankou, *China* 54 B3
Dzuumod, *Mongolia* 54 B5
Dzyarzhynsk, *Belarus* 40 F4
Dzyatlava, *Belarus* 40 F3

E

Eabamet, L., *Canada* 98 B2
Eads, *U.S.A.* 108 F3
Eagle, *U.S.A.* 110 G10
Eagle →, *Canada* 99 B8
Eagle Butte, *U.S.A.* 108 C4
Eagle Grove, *U.S.A.* 108 D8
Eagle L., *Calif., U.S.A.* 110 F3
Eagle L., *Maine, U.S.A.* 99 C6
Eagle Lake, *U.S.A.* 109 L6
Eagle Mountain, *U.S.A.* 113 M11
Eagle Nest, *U.S.A.* 111 H11
Eagle Pass, *U.S.A.* 109 L4
Eagle Pk., *U.S.A.* 112 G7
Eagle Pt., *Australia* 88 C3
Eagle River, *U.S.A.* 108 C10
Ealing, *U.K.* 13 F7
Earaheedy, *Australia* 89 E3
Earl Grey, *Canada* 101 C8
Earle, *U.S.A.* 109 H9
Earlimart, *U.S.A.* 113 K7
Earn →, *U.K.* 14 E5
Earn, L., *U.K.* 14 E4
Earnslaw, Mt., *N.Z.* 87 L2
Earth, *U.S.A.* 109 H3
Easley, *U.S.A.* 105 H4
East Angus, *Canada* 99 C5
East Aurora, *U.S.A.* 106 D6
East B., *U.S.A.* 109 L10
East Bengal, *Bangla.* 61 G17
East Beskids = Vychodné Beskydy, *Europe* 41 H2
East Brady, *U.S.A.* 106 F5
East C., *N.Z.* 87 G7
East Chicago, *U.S.A.* 104 E2
East China Sea, *Asia* 54 C7
East Coulee, *Canada* 100 C6
East Falkland, *Falk. Is.* 128 D5
East Grand Forks, *U.S.A.* 108 B6
East Greenwich, *U.S.A.* 107 E13
East Hartford, *U.S.A.* 107 E12
East Helena, *U.S.A.* 110 C8
East Indies, *Asia* 57 E6
East Jordan, *U.S.A.* 104 C3
East Lansing, *U.S.A.* 104 D3
East Liverpool, *U.S.A.* 106 F4
East London, *S. Africa* 85 E4
East Main = Eastmain, *Canada* 98 B4
East Orange, *U.S.A.* 107 F10
East Pacific Ridge, *Pac. Oc.* 93 J17
East Pakistan = Bangladesh ■, *Asia* 61 H17
East Palestine, *U.S.A.* 106 F4
East Pine, *Canada* 100 B4
East Point, *U.S.A.* 105 J3
East Providence, *U.S.A.* 107 E13
East Pt., *Canada* 99 C7
East Retford = Retford, *U.K.* 12 D7
East St. Louis, *U.S.A.* 108 F9
East Schelde → = Oosterschelde, *Neths.* 17 E4
East Siberian Sea, *Russia* 45 B17
East Stroudsburg, *U.S.A.* 107 E9
East Sussex □, *U.K.* 13 G8
East Tawas, *U.S.A.* 104 C4
East Toorale, *Australia* 91 E4
East Walker →, *U.S.A.* 112 G7
Eastbourne, *N.Z.* 87 J5
Eastbourne, *U.K.* 13 G8
Eastend, *Canada* 101 D7
Easter Islands = Pascua, I. de, *Pac. Oc.* 93 K17
Eastern □, *Kenya* 82 B4
Eastern □, *Uganda* 82 B3
Eastern Cape, *S. Africa* 84 E4
Eastern Cr. →, *Australia* 90 C3
Eastern Ghats, *India* 60 N11
Eastern Group = Lau Group, *Fiji* 87 C9
Eastern Group, *Australia* 89 F3
Eastern Province □, *S. Leone* 78 D2
Eastern Transvaal □, *S. Africa* 85 B5
Easterville, *Canada* 101 C9
Easthampton, *U.S.A.* 107 D12
Eastland, *U.S.A.* 109 J5
Eastleigh, *U.K.* 13 G6
Eastmain, *Canada* 98 B4
Eastmain →, *Canada* 98 B4
Eastman, *Canada* 107 A12
Eastman, *U.S.A.* 105 J4
Easton, *Md., U.S.A.* 104 F7
Easton, *Pa., U.S.A.* 107 F9
Easton, *Wash., U.S.A.* 112 C5
Eastport, *U.S.A.* 99 D6
Eastsound, *U.S.A.* 112 B4
Eaton, *U.S.A.* 108 E2
Eatonia, *Canada* 101 C7
Eatonton, *U.S.A.* 105 J4
Eatontown, *U.S.A.* 107 F10
Eatonville, *U.S.A.* 112 D4
Eau Claire, *Fr. Guiana* 121 C7
Eau Claire, *U.S.A.* 108 C9
Eauze, *France* 26 E4
Ebagoola, *Australia* 90 A3
Eban, *Nigeria* 79 D5
Ebbw Vale, *U.K.* 13 F4
Ebeggui, *Algeria* 75 C6
Ebeltoft, *Denmark* 9 H14
Ebensburg, *U.S.A.* 106 F6
Ebensee, *Austria* 21 H3
Eber Gölü, *Turkey* 66 C4
Eberbach, *Germany* 19 F4
Eberswalde-Finow, *Germany* 18 C9
Ebetsu, *Japan* 48 C10
Ebian, *China* 52 C4
Ebikon, *Switz.* 23 B6
Ebingen, *Germany* 19 G5
Ebnat-Kappel, *Switz.* 23 B8
Eboli, *Italy* 35 B8
Ebolowa, *Cameroon* 79 E7
Ebrach, *Germany* 19 F6
Ébrié, Lagune, *Ivory C.* 78 D4
Ebro →, *Spain* 28 E5
Ebro, Pantano del, *Spain* 30 B7
Ebstorf, *Germany* 18 B6
Ecaussines-d' Enghien, *Belgium* 17 G4
Eceabat, *Turkey* 66 B2
Ech Cheliff, *Algeria* 75 A5
Echallens, *Switz.* 22 C3
Echeng, *China* 53 B10
Echigo-Sammyaku, *Japan* 49 F9
Echizen-Misaki, *Japan* 49 G7
Echmiadzin = Yejmiadzin, *Armenia* 43 K7
Echo Bay, *N.W.T., Canada* 96 B8
Echo Bay, *Ont., Canada* 98 C3
Echoing →, *Canada* 101 B10
Echt, *Neths.* 17 F7
Echternach, *Lux.* 17 J8
Echuca, *Australia* 91 F3
Ecija, *Spain* 31 H5
Eckernförde, *Germany* 18 A5
Eclipse Is., *Australia* 88 B4
Écommoy, *France* 24 E7
Ecoporanga, *Brazil* 123 E3
Écos, *France* 25 C8
Écouché, *France* 24 D6
Ecuador ■, *S. Amer.* 120 D2
Écueillé, *France* 24 E8
Ed, *Sweden* 11 F5
Ed Dabbura, *Sudan* 76 D3
Ed Dâmer, *Sudan* 76 D3
Ed Debba, *Sudan* 76 D3
Ed-Déffa, *Egypt* 76 A2
Ed Deim, *Sudan* 77 E2
Ed Dueim, *Sudan* 77 E3
Edah, *Australia* 89 E2
Edam, *Canada* 101 C7
Edam, *Neths.* 16 C6
Eday, *U.K.* 14 B6
Edd, *Eritrea* 68 E3
Eddrachillis B., *U.K.* 14 C3
Eddystone, *U.K.* 13 G3
Eddystone Pt., *Australia* 90 G4
Ede, *Neths.* 16 D7
Ede, *Nigeria* 79 D5
Édea, *Cameroon* 79 E7
Edegem, *Belgium* 17 F4
Edehon L., *Canada* 101 A9
Edekel, Adrar, *Algeria* 75 D6
Eden, *Australia* 91 F4
Eden, *N.C., U.S.A.* 105 G6
Eden, *N.Y., U.S.A.* 106 D6
Eden, *Tex., U.S.A.* 109 K5
Eden, *Wyo., U.S.A.* 110 E9
Eden →, *U.K.* 12 C4
Eden L., *Canada* 101 B8
Edenburg, *S. Africa* 84 D4
Edendale, *S. Africa* 85 D5
Edenderry, *Ireland* 15 C4
Edenton, *U.S.A.* 105 G7
Edenville, *S. Africa* 85 D4
Eder →, *Germany* 18 D5
Eder-Stausee, *Germany* 18 D4
Edgar, *U.S.A.* 108 E5
Edgartown, *U.S.A.* 107 E14
Edge Hill, *U.K.* 13 E6
Edgefield, *U.S.A.* 105 J5
Edgeley, *U.S.A.* 108 B5
Edgemont, *U.S.A.* 108 D3
Edgeøya, *Svalbard* 4 B9
Édhessa, *Greece* 39 J5
Edievale, *N.Z.* 87 L2
Edina, *Liberia* 78 D2
Edina, *U.S.A.* 108 E8
Edinburg, *U.S.A.* 109 M5
Edinburgh, *U.K.* 14 F5
Edinița, *Moldova* 41 H4
Edirne, *Turkey* 66 B2
Edison, *U.S.A.* 112 B4
Edithburgh, *Australia* 91 F2
Edjeleh, *Algeria* 75 C6
Edjudina, *Australia* 89 E3
Edmeston, *U.S.A.* 107 D9
Edmond, *U.S.A.* 109 H6
Edmonds, *U.S.A.* 112 C4
Edmonton, *Australia* 90 B4
Edmonton, *Canada* 100 C6
Edmund L., *Canada* 101 C10
Edmundston, *Canada* 99 C6
Edna, *U.S.A.* 109 L6
Edna Bay, *U.S.A.* 100 B2
Edo □, *Nigeria* 79 D6
Edolo, *Italy* 32 B7
Edremit, *Turkey* 66 C2
Edremit Körfezi, *Turkey* 66 C2
Edsbyn, *Sweden* 10 C9
Edsele, *Sweden* 10 A10
Edson, *Canada* 100 C5
Eduardo Castex, *Argentina* 126 D3
Edward →, *Australia* 91 F3
Edward, L., *Africa* 82 C2
Edward I., *Canada* 98 C2
Edward River, *Australia* 90 A3
Edward VII Land, *Antarctica* 5 E13
Edwards, *U.S.A.* 113 L9
Edwards Plateau, *U.S.A.* 109 K4
Edwardsville, *U.S.A.* 107 E9
Edzo, *Canada* 100 A5
Eefde, *Neths.* 16 D8
Eeklo, *Belgium* 17 F3
Eelde, *Neths.* 16 B9
Eem →, *Neths.* 16 D6
Eems →, *Neths.* 16 B9
Eems Kanaal, *Neths.* 16 B9
Eenrum, *Neths.* 16 B8
Eernegem, *Belgium* 17 F2
Eerste Valthermond, *Neths.* 16 C9
Eferi, *Algeria* 75 D6
Effingham, *U.S.A.* 104 F1
Effretikon, *Switz.* 23 B7
Eforie Sud, *Romania* 38 E11
Ega →, *Spain* 28 C3
Égadi, Isole, *Italy* 34 E5
Eganville, *Canada* 98 C4
Egeland, *U.S.A.* 108 A5
Egenolf L., *Canada* 101 B9
Eger = Cheb, *Czech.* 20 E2
Eger, *Hungary* 21 H10
Eger →, *Hungary* 21 H10
Egersund, *Norway* 9 G12
Egg L., *Canada* 101 B7
Eggenburg, *Austria* 20 G5
Eggenfelden, *Germany* 19 G8
Eggiwil, *Switz.* 22 C5
Éghezée, *Belgium* 17 G5
Eginbah, *Australia* 88 D2
Égletons, *France* 26 C6
Eglisau, *Switz.* 23 A7
Egmond-aan-Zee, *Neths.* 16 C5
Egmont, C., *N.Z.* 87 H4
Egmont, Mt., *N.Z.* 87 H5
Eğridir, *Turkey* 66 D4
Eğridir Gölü, *Turkey* 66 D4
Egtved, *Denmark* 11 J3
Éguas →, *Brazil* 123 D3
Egume, *Nigeria* 79 D6
Éguzon, *France* 26 B5
Egvekinot, *Russia* 45 C19
Egypt ■, *Africa* 76 J7
Eha Amufu, *Nigeria* 79 D6
Ehime □, *Japan* 49 H6
Ehingen, *Germany* 19 G5
Ehrenberg, *U.S.A.* 113 M12
Ehrwald, *Austria* 19 H6
Eibar, *Spain* 28 B2
Eibergen, *Neths.* 16 D9
Eichstätt, *Germany* 19 G7
Eider →, *Germany* 18 A4
Eidsvold, *Australia* 91 D5
Eidsvoll, *Norway* 9 F14
Eifel, *Germany* 19 E2
Eiffel Flats, *Zimbabwe* 83 F3
Eigg, *U.K.* 14 E2
Eighty Mile Beach, *Australia* 88 C3
Eil, *Somali Rep.* 68 F4
Eil, L., *U.K.* 14 E3
Eildon, L., *Australia* 91 F4
Eileen L., *Canada* 101 A7
Eilenburg, *Germany* 18 D8
Ein el Luweiqa, *Sudan* 77 E3
Einasleigh, *Australia* 90 B3
Einasleigh →, *Australia* 90 B3
Einbeck, *Germany* 18 D5
Eindhoven, *Neths.* 17 F6
Einsiedeln, *Switz.* 23 B7
Eire = Ireland ■, *Europe* 15 D4
Eiríksjökull, *Iceland* 8 D3
Eirlandsche Gat, *Neths.* 16 B5
Eirunepé, *Brazil* 124 B4
Eisden, *Belgium* 17 G7
Eisenach, *Germany* 18 E6
Eisenberg, *Germany* 18 E7
Eisenerz, *Austria* 21 H4
Eisenhüttenstadt, *Germany* 18 C10
Eisenstadt, *Austria* 21 H6
Eiserfeld, *Germany* 18 E3
Eisfeld, *Germany* 18 E6
Eisleben, *Germany* 18 D7
Eivissa = Ibiza, *Spain* 36 C7
Ejby, *Denmark* 11 J3
Eje, Sierra del, *Spain* 30 C4
Ejea de los Caballeros, *Spain* 28 C3
Ejutla, *Mexico* 115 D5
Ekalaka, *U.S.A.* 108 C2
Ekeren, *Belgium* 17 F4
Eket, *Nigeria* 79 E6
Eketahuna, *N.Z.* 87 J5
Ekhínos, *Greece* 39 H8
Ekibastuz, *Kazakhstan* 44 D8
Ekimchan, *Russia* 45 D14
Ekoli, *Zaïre* 82 C1
Eksel, *Belgium* 17 F6
Eksjö, *Sweden* 9 H16
Ekwan →, *Canada* 98 B3
Ekwan Pt., *Canada* 98 B3
El Aaiún, *W. Sahara* 74 C2
El Aargub, *Mauritania* 74 D1
El Abiodh-Sidi-Cheikh, *Algeria* 75 B5
El 'Agrûd, *Egypt* 69 E3
El Aïoun, *Morocco* 75 B4
El 'Aiyat, *Egypt* 76 J7
El Alamein, *Egypt* 76 H6
El Alto, *Peru* 124 A1
El 'Aqaba, W. →, *Egypt* 69 E2
El 'Arag, *Egypt* 76 B2
El Arahal, *Spain* 31 H5
El Arenal, *Spain* 36 B9
El Aricha, *Algeria* 75 B4
El Arīhā, *West Bank* 69 D4
El Arish, *Australia* 90 B4
El 'Arîsh, *Egypt* 69 D2
El 'Arîsh, W. →, *Egypt* 69 D2
El Arrouch, *Algeria* 75 A6
El Asnam = Ech Cheliff, *Algeria* 75 A5
El Astillero, *Spain* 30 B7
El Badâri, *Egypt* 76 B3
El Bahrein, *Egypt* 76 B2
El Ballâs, *Egypt* 76 B3
El Balyana, *Egypt* 76 B3
El Banco, *Colombia* 120 B3
El Baqeir, *Sudan* 76 D3
El Barco de Ávila, *Spain* 30 E5
El Barco de Valdeorras, *Spain* 30 C4
El Bauga, *Sudan* 76 D3
El Baúl, *Venezuela* 120 B4
El Bawiti, *Egypt* 76 J6
El Bayadh, *Algeria* 75 B5
El Bierzo, *Spain* 30 C4
El Bluff, *Nic.* 116 D3
El Bolsón, *Argentina* 128 B2
El Bonillo, *Spain* 29 G2
El Brûk, W. →, *Egypt* 69 E2
El Buheirat □, *Sudan* 77 F2
El Caín, *Argentina* 128 B3
El Cajon, *U.S.A.* 113 N10
El Callao, *Venezuela* 121 B5
El Camp, *Spain* 28 D6
El Campo, *U.S.A.* 109 L6
El Carmen, *Bolivia* 125 C5
El Carmen, *Venezuela* 120 C4
El Castillo, *Spain* 31 H4
El Centro, *U.S.A.* 113 N11
El Cerro, *Bolivia* 125 D5
El Cerro, *Spain* 31 H4
El Cocuy, *Colombia* 120 B3
El Compadre, *Mexico* 113 N10
El Corcovado, *Argentina* 128 B2
El Coronil, *Spain* 31 H5
El Cuy, *Argentina* 128 A3
El Cuyo, *Mexico* 115 C7
El Dab'a, *Egypt* 76 H6
El Daheir, *Egypt* 69 D3
El Deir, *Egypt* 76 B3
El Dere, *Somali Rep.* 68 G4
El Descanso, *Mexico* 113 N10
El Desemboque, *Mexico* 114 A2
El Dilingat, *Egypt* 76 H7
El Diviso, *Colombia* 120 C2
El Djem, *Tunisia* 75 A7
El Djouf, *Mauritania* 72 E3
El Dorado, *Ark., U.S.A.* 109 J8
El Dorado, *Kans., U.S.A.* 109 G6
El Dorado, *Venezuela* 121 B5
El Eglab, *Algeria* 74 C4
El Escorial, *Spain* 30 E6
El Eulma, *Algeria* 75 A6
El Faiyûm, *Egypt* 76 J7
El Fâsher, *Sudan* 77 E2
El Fashn, *Egypt* 76 J7
El Ferrol, *Spain* 30 B2
El Fifi, *Sudan* 77 E1
El Fuerte, *Mexico* 114 B3
El Gal, *Somali Rep.* 68 E5
El Gebir, *Sudan* 77 E2
El Gedida, *Egypt* 76 B2
El Geteina, *Sudan* 77 E3
El Gezira □, *Sudan* 77 E3
El Gîza, *Egypt* 76 H7
El Goléa, *Algeria* 75 B5
El Hadeb, *W. Sahara* 74 C2
El Hadjira, *Algeria* 75 B6
El Hagiz, *Sudan* 77 D4
El Hajeb, *Morocco* 74 B3
El Hammam, *Egypt* 76 H6
El Hammâmi, *Mauritania* 74 D2
El Hank, *Mauritania* 74 D3
El Hasian, *W. Sahara* 74 C2
El Hawata, *Sudan* 77 E3
El Heiz, *Egypt* 76 B2
El 'Idisât, *Egypt* 76 B3
El Iskandarîya, *Egypt* 76 H6
El Jadida, *Morocco* 74 B3
El Jebelein, *Sudan* 77 E3
El Kab, *Sudan* 76 D3
El Kabrît, G., *Egypt* 69 F2
El Kala, *Algeria* 75 A6
El Kalâa, *Morocco* 74 B3
El Kamlin, *Sudan* 77 D3
El Kantara, *Algeria* 75 A6
El Kantara, *Tunisia* 75 B7
El Karaba, *Sudan* 76 D3
El Kef, *Tunisia* 75 A6
El Khandaq, *Sudan* 76 D3
El Khârga, *Egypt* 76 B3
El Khartûm, *Sudan* 77 D3
El Khartûm □, *Sudan* 77 D3
El Khartûm Bahrî, *Sudan* 77 D3
El Khroub, *Algeria* 75 A6
El Kseur, *Algeria* 75 A5
El Ksiba, *Morocco* 74 B3
El Kuntilla, *Egypt* 69 E3
El Laqâwa, *Sudan* 77 E2
El Laqeita, *Egypt* 76 B3
El Leiya, *Sudan* 77 D4
El Mafâza, *Sudan* 77 E3
El Mahalla el Kubra, *Egypt* 76 H7
El Mahârîq, *Egypt* 76 B3
El Mahmûdîya, *Egypt* 76 H7
El Maitén, *Argentina* 128 B2
El Maiz, *Algeria* 75 C4
El-Maks el-Bahari, *Egypt* 76 C3
El Manshâh, *Egypt* 76 B3
El Mansour, *Algeria* 75 C4
El Mansûra, *Egypt* 76 H7
El Mantico, *Venezuela* 121 B5
El Manzala, *Egypt* 76 H7
El Marâgha, *Egypt* 76 B3
El Masid, *Sudan* 77 D3
El Matariya, *Egypt* 76 H8
El Medano, *Canary Is.* 36 F3
El Meghaier, *Algeria* 75 B6
El Meraguen, *Algeria* 75 C4
El Metemma, *Sudan* 77 D3
El Miamo, *Venezuela* 121 B5
El Milagro, *Argentina* 126 C2
El Milia, *Algeria* 75 A6
El Minyâ, *Egypt* 76 J7
El Molar, *Spain* 28 E1
El Mreyye, *Mauritania* 78 B3
El Obeid, *Sudan* 77 E3
El Odaiya, *Sudan* 77 E2
El Oro, *Mexico* 115 D4
El Oro □, *Ecuador* 120 D2
El Oued, *Algeria* 75 B6
El Palmar, *Bolivia* 125 D5
El Palmar, *Venezuela* 121 B5
El Palmito, Presa, *Mexico* 114 B3
El Panadés, *Spain* 28 D6
El Pardo, *Spain* 30 E7
El Paso, *U.S.A.* 111 L10
El Paso Robles, *U.S.A.* 112 K6
El Pedernoso, *Spain* 29 F2
El Pedroso, *Spain* 31 H5
El Pobo de Dueñas, *Spain* 28 E3
El Portal, *U.S.A.* 111 H4
El Porvenir, *Mexico* 114 A3
El Prat de Llobregat, *Spain* 28 D7
El Progreso, *Honduras* 116 C2
El Provencío, *Spain* 29 F2
El Pueblito, *Mexico* 114 B3
El Pueblo, *Canary Is.* 36 F2
El Puerto de Santa María, *Spain* 31 J4
El Qâhira, *Egypt* 76 H7
El Qantara, *Egypt* 69 E1
El Qasr, *Egypt* 76 B2
El Quseima, *Egypt* 69 E3
El Qusîya, *Egypt* 76 B3
El Râshda, *Egypt* 76 B2
El Reno, *U.S.A.* 109 H6
El Ribero, *Spain* 30 C2
El Rîdisiya, *Egypt* 76 C3
El Rio, *U.S.A.* 113 L7

Espéraza

El Ronquillo, *Spain* 31 H4
El Roque, Pta., *Canary Is.* 36 F4
El Rosarito, *Mexico* 114 B2
El Rubio, *Spain* 31 H5
El Saff, *Egypt* 76 J7
El Saheira, W. →, *Egypt* 69 E2
El Salto, *Mexico* 114 C3
El Salvador ■, *Cent. Amer.* 116 D2
El Sancejo, *Spain* 31 H5
El Sauce, *Nic.* 116 D2
El Shallal, *Egypt* 76 C3
El Simbillawein, *Egypt* 76 H7
El Sombrero, *Venezuela* 120 B4
El Suweis, *Egypt* 76 J8
El Tamarâni, W. →, *Egypt* 69 E3
El Thamad, *Egypt* 69 F3
El Tigre, *Venezuela* 121 B5
El Tîh, G., *Egypt* 69 F2
El Tîna, Khalîg, *Egypt* 69 D1
El Tocuyo, *Venezuela* 120 B4
El Tofo, *Chile* 126 B1
El Tránsito, *Chile* 126 B1
El Tûr, *Egypt* 76 J8
El Turbio, *Argentina* 128 D2
El Uqsur, *Egypt* 76 B3
El Vado, *Spain* 28 D1
El Vallés, *Spain* 28 D7
El Venado, *Mexico* 114 C4
El Vigía, *Venezuela* 120 B3
El Wabeira, *Egypt* 69 F2
El Wak, *Kenya* 82 B5
El Waqf, *Egypt* 76 B3
El Wâsta, *Egypt* 76 J7
El Weguet, *Ethiopia* 77 F5
El Wuz, *Sudan* 77 D3
Elafónisos, *Greece* 39 N5
Élassa, *Greece* 39 P9
Elassón, *Greece* 39 K5
Elat, *Israel* 69 F3
Elâzığ, *Turkey* 67 C8
Elba, *Italy* 32 F7
Elba, *U.S.A.* 105 K2
Elbasani, *Albania* 39 H3
Elbe, *U.S.A.* 112 D4
Elbe →, *Europe* 18 B4
Elbe-Seiten Kanal, *Germany* 18 C6
Elbert, Mt., *U.S.A.* 111 G10
Elberta, *U.S.A.* 104 C2
Elberton, *U.S.A.* 105 H4
Elbeuf, *France* 24 C8
Elbing = Elbląg, *Poland* 20 A9
Elbistan, *Turkey* 66 C7
Elbląg, *Poland* 20 A9
Elbow, *Canada* 101 C7
Elbrus, *Asia* 43 J6
Elburg, *Neths.* 16 D7
Elburz Mts. = Alborz, Reshteh-ye Kūhhā-ye, *Iran* 65 C7
Elche, *Spain* 29 G4
Elche de la Sierra, *Spain* 29 G2
Elcho I., *Australia* 90 A2
Elda, *Spain* 29 G4
Eldon, *Mo., U.S.A.* 108 F8
Eldon, *Wash., U.S.A.* 112 C3
Eldora, *U.S.A.* 108 D8
Eldorado, *Argentina* 127 B5
Eldorado, *Canada* 101 B7
Eldorado, *Mexico* 114 C3
Eldorado, *Ill., U.S.A.* 104 G1
Eldorado, *Tex., U.S.A.* 109 K4
Eldorado Springs, *U.S.A.* 109 G8
Eldoret, *Kenya* 82 B4
Eldred, *U.S.A.* 106 E6
Elea, C., *Cyprus* 37 D13
Electra, *U.S.A.* 109 H5
Elefantes →, *Mozam.* 85 C5
Elefantes, G., *Chile* 128 C2
Elektrogorsk, *Russia* 42 C4
Elektrostal, *Russia* 42 C4
Elele, *Nigeria* 79 D6
Elephant Butte Reservoir, *U.S.A.* 111 K10
Elephant I., *Antarctica* 5 C18
Elesbão Veloso, *Brazil* 122 C3
Eleşkirt, *Turkey* 67 C10
Eleuthera, *Bahamas* 116 A4
Elgepiggen, *Norway* 10 B5
Elgeyo-Marakwet □, *Kenya* 82 B4
Elgg, *Switz.* 23 B7
Elgin, *N.B., Canada* 99 C6
Elgin, *Ont., Canada* 107 B8
Elgin, *U.K.* 14 D5
Elgin, *Ill., U.S.A.* 104 D1
Elgin, *N. Dak., U.S.A.* 108 B4
Elgin, *Nebr., U.S.A.* 108 E5
Elgin, *Nev., U.S.A.* 111 H6
Elgin, *Oreg., U.S.A.* 110 D5
Elgin, *Tex., U.S.A.* 109 K6
Elgon, Mt., *Africa* 82 B3
Eliase, *Indonesia* 57 F8
Elida, *U.S.A.* 109 J3
Elikón, *Greece* 39 L5
Elim, *S. Africa* 84 E2
Elisabethville = Lubumbashi, *Zaïre* 83 E2
Eliseu Martins, *Brazil* 122 C3
Elista, *Russia* 43 G7
Elizabeth, *Australia* 91 E2
Elizabeth, *U.S.A.* 107 F10
Elizabeth City, *U.S.A.* 105 G7
Elizabethton, *U.S.A.* 105 G4
Elizabethtown, *Ky., U.S.A.* 104 G3
Elizabethtown, *N.Y., U.S.A.* 107 B11
Elizabethtown, *Pa., U.S.A.* 107 F8
Elizondo, *Spain* 28 B3
Ełk, *Poland* 20 B12
Elk City, *U.S.A.* 109 H5
Elk Creek, *U.S.A.* 112 F4
Elk Grove, *U.S.A.* 112 G5
Elk Island Nat. Park, *Canada* 100 C6
Elk Lake, *Canada* 98 C3
Elk Point, *Canada* 101 C6
Elk River, *Idaho, U.S.A.* 110 C5
Elk River, *Minn., U.S.A.* 108 C8
Elkedra, *Australia* 90 C2
Elkedra →, *Australia* 90 C2
Elkhart, *Ind., U.S.A.* 104 E3
Elkhart, *Kans., U.S.A.* 109 G4
Elkhorn, *Canada* 101 D8
Elkhorn →, *U.S.A.* 108 E6
Elkhovo, *Bulgaria* 38 G9
Elkin, *U.S.A.* 105 G5
Elkins, *U.S.A.* 104 F6
Elko, *Canada* 100 D5
Elko, *U.S.A.* 110 F6
Ell, L., *Australia* 89 E4
Ellecom, *Neths.* 16 D8
Ellef Ringnes I., *Canada* 4 B2
Ellendale, *Australia* 88 C3
Ellendale, *U.S.A.* 108 B5
Ellensburg, *U.S.A.* 110 C3
Ellenville, *U.S.A.* 107 E10
Ellery, Mt., *Australia* 91 F4
Ellesmere, L., *N.Z.* 87 M4
Ellesmere I., *Canada* 4 B4
Ellesmere Port, *U.K.* 12 D5
Ellezelles, *Belgium* 17 G3
Ellice Is. = Tuvalu ■, *Pac. Oc.* 92 H9
Ellinwood, *U.S.A.* 108 F5
Elliot, *Australia* 90 B1
Elliot, *S. Africa* 85 E4
Elliot Lake, *Canada* 98 C3
Elliotdale = Xhora, *S. Africa* 85 E4
Ellis, *U.S.A.* 108 F5
Elliston, *Australia* 91 E1
Ellisville, *U.S.A.* 109 K10
Ellon, *U.K.* 14 D6
Ellore = Eluru, *India* 61 L12
Ells →, *Canada* 100 B6
Ellsworth, *U.S.A.* 108 F5
Ellsworth Land, *Antarctica* 5 D16
Ellsworth Mts., *Antarctica* 5 D16
Ellwangen, *Germany* 19 G6
Ellwood City, *U.S.A.* 106 F4
Elm, *Switz.* 23 C8
Elma, *Canada* 101 D9
Elma, *U.S.A.* 112 D3
Elmadağ, *Turkey* 66 C5
Elmalı, *Turkey* 66 D3
Elmhurst, *U.S.A.* 104 E2
Elmina, *Ghana* 79 D4
Elmira, *Canada* 106 C4
Elmira, *U.S.A.* 106 D8
Elmore, *Australia* 91 F3
Elmore, *U.S.A.* 113 M11
Elmshorn, *Germany* 18 B5
Elmvale, *Canada* 106 B5
Elne, *France* 26 F6
Elora, *Canada* 106 C4
Elorza, *Venezuela* 120 B4
Eloúnda, *Greece* 37 D7
Eloy, *U.S.A.* 111 K8
Éloyes, *France* 25 D13
Elrose, *Canada* 101 C7
Elsas, *Canada* 98 C3
Elsie, *U.S.A.* 112 E3
Elsinore = Helsingør, *Denmark* 11 H6
Elsinore, *U.S.A.* 111 G7
Elspe, *Germany* 18 D4
Elspeet, *Neths.* 16 D7
Elst, *Neths.* 16 E7
Elster →, *Germany* 18 D7
Elsterwerda, *Germany* 18 D9
Elten, *Neths.* 16 E8
Eltham, *N.Z.* 87 H5
Elton, *Russia* 43 F8
Elton, Ozero, *Russia* 43 F8
Eluanbi, *Taiwan* 53 G13
Eluru, *India* 61 L12
Elvas, *Portugal* 31 G3
Elven, *France* 24 E4
Elverum, *Norway* 10 D5
Elvire →, *Australia* 88 C4
Elvo →, *Italy* 32 C5
Elvran, *Norway* 10 A5
Elwood, *Ind., U.S.A.* 104 E3
Elwood, *Nebr., U.S.A.* 108 E5
Elx = Elche, *Spain* 29 G4
Ely, *U.K.* 13 E8
Ely, *Minn., U.S.A.* 108 B9
Ely, *Nev., U.S.A.* 110 G6
Elyria, *U.S.A.* 106 E2
Elz →, *Germany* 19 G3
Emāmrūd, *Iran* 65 B7
Emba = Embi, *Kazakhstan* 44 E6
Emba = Embi →, *Kazakhstan* 44 E6
Embarcación, *Argentina* 126 A3
Embarras Portage, *Canada* 101 B6
Embetsu, *Japan* 48 B10
Embi, *Kazakhstan* 44 E6
Embi →, *Kazakhstan* 44 E6
Embira →, *Brazil* 124 B3
Embóna, *Greece* 37 C9
Embrach, *Switz.* 23 A7
Embrun, *France* 27 D10
Embu, *Kenya* 82 C4
Embu □, *Kenya* 82 C4
Emden, *Germany* 18 B3
Emerald, *Australia* 90 C4
Emerson, *Canada* 101 D9
Emery, *U.S.A.* 111 G8
Emet, *Turkey* 66 C3
Emi Koussi, *Chad* 73 E8
Emília-Romagna □, *Italy* 32 D7
Emílius, Mte., *Italy* 32 C4
Eminabad, *Pakistan* 62 C6
Emirdağ, *Turkey* 66 C4
Emlenton, *U.S.A.* 106 E5
Emlichheim, *Germany* 18 C2
Emme →, *Switz.* 22 B5
Emmeloord, *Neths.* 16 C7
Emmen, *Neths.* 16 C9
Emmendingen, *Germany* 19 G3
Emmental, *Switz.* 22 C4
Emmer-Compascuum, *Neths.* 16 C10
Emmerich, *Germany* 18 D2
Emmet, *Australia* 90 C3
Emmetsburg, *U.S.A.* 108 D7
Emmett, *U.S.A.* 110 E5
Empalme, *Mexico* 114 B2
Empangeni, *S. Africa* 85 D5
Empedrado, *Argentina* 126 B4
Emperor Seamount Chain, *Pac. Oc.* 92 D9
Empoli, *Italy* 32 E7
Emporia, *Kans., U.S.A.* 108 F6
Emporia, *Va., U.S.A.* 105 G7
Emporium, *U.S.A.* 106 E6
Empress, *Canada* 101 C6
Emptinne, *Belgium* 17 H6
Empty Quarter = Rub' al Khali, *Si. Arabia* 68 D4
Ems →, *Germany* 18 B3
Emsdale, *Canada* 106 A5
Emsdetten, *Germany* 18 C3
Emu, *China* 51 C15
Emu Park, *Australia* 90 C5
'En 'Avrona, *Israel* 69 F3
En Nahud, *Sudan* 77 E2
Ena, *Japan* 49 G8
Enafors, *Sweden* 10 A6
Enambú, *Colombia* 120 C3
Enana, *Namibia* 84 B2
Enånger, *Sweden* 10 C11
Enaratoli, *Indonesia* 57 E9
Enard B., *U.K.* 14 C3
Enare = Inarijärvi, *Finland* 8 B22
Encantadas, Serra, *Brazil* 127 C5
Encanto, C., *Phil.* 57 A6
Encarnación, *Paraguay* 127 B4
Encarnación de Diaz, *Mexico* 114 C4
Enchi, *Ghana* 78 D4
Encinal, *U.S.A.* 109 L5
Encinitas, *U.S.A.* 113 M9
Encino, *U.S.A.* 111 J11
Encontrados, *Venezuela* 120 B3
Encounter B., *Australia* 91 F2
Encruzilhada, *Brazil* 123 E3
Ende, *Indonesia* 57 F6
Endeavour, *Canada* 101 C8
Endeavour Str., *Australia* 90 A3
Endelave, *Denmark* 11 J4
Enderbury I., *Kiribati* 92 H10
Enderby, *Canada* 100 C5
Enderby I., *Australia* 88 D2
Enderby Land, *Antarctica* 5 C5
Enderlin, *U.S.A.* 108 B6
Endicott, *N.Y., U.S.A.* 107 D8
Endicott, *Wash., U.S.A.* 110 C5
Endimari →, *Brazil* 124 B4
Endyalgout I., *Australia* 88 B5
Ene →, *Peru* 124 C3
Enewetak Atoll, *Pac. Oc.* 92 F8
Enez, *Turkey* 66 B2
Enfield, *U.K.* 13 F7
Engadin, *Switz.* 19 J6
Engaño, C., *Dom. Rep.* 117 C6
Engaño, C., *Phil.* 57 A6
Engcobo, *S. Africa* 85 E4
Engelberg, *Switz.* 23 C6
Engels, *Russia* 42 E8
Engemann L., *Canada* 101 B7
Enger, *Norway* 10 D4
Enggano, *Indonesia* 56 F2
Enghien, *Belgium* 17 G4
Engil, *Morocco* 74 B4
Engkilili, *Malaysia* 56 D4
England, *U.S.A.* 109 H9
England □, *U.K.* 7 E5
Englee, *Canada* 99 B8
Englehart, *Canada* 98 C4
Engler L., *Canada* 101 B7
Englewood, *Colo., U.S.A.* 108 F2
Englewood, *Kans., U.S.A.* 109 G5
English →, *Canada* 101 C10
English Bazar = Ingraj Bazar, *India* 63 G13
English Channel, *Europe* 13 G6
English River, *Canada* 98 C1
Enguri →, *Georgia* 43 J5
Enid, *U.S.A.* 109 G6
Enipévs →, *Greece* 39 K5
Enkhuizen, *Neths.* 16 C6
Enköping, *Sweden* 10 E11
Enle, *China* 52 E3
Enna, *Italy* 35 E7
Ennadai, *Canada* 101 A8
Ennadai L., *Canada* 101 A8
Ennedi, *Chad* 73 E9
Enngonia, *Australia* 91 D4
Ennis, *Ireland* 15 D3
Ennis, *Mont., U.S.A.* 110 D8
Ennis, *Tex., U.S.A.* 109 J6
Enniscorthy, *Ireland* 15 D5
Enniskillen, *U.K.* 15 B4
Ennistimon, *Ireland* 15 D2
Enns →, *Austria* 21 G4
Enontekiö, *Finland* 8 B20
Enping, *China* 53 F9
Enriquillo, L., *Dom. Rep.* 117 C5
Ens, *Neths.* 16 C7
Enschede, *Neths.* 16 D9
Ensenada, *Argentina* 126 C4
Ensenada, *Mexico* 114 A1
Enshi, *China* 52 B7
Ensiola, Pta., *Spain* 36 B9
Ensisheim, *France* 25 E14
Entebbe, *Uganda* 82 B3
Enter, *Neths.* 16 D9
Enterprise, *Canada* 100 A5
Enterprise, *Oreg., U.S.A.* 110 D5
Enterprise, *Utah, U.S.A.* 111 H7
Entlebuch, *Switz.* 22 C6
Entre Ríos, *Bolivia* 126 A3
Entre Rios, *Bahia, Brazil* 123 D4
Entre Rios, *Pará, Brazil* 125 B7
Entre Ríos □, *Argentina* 126 C4
Entrepeñas, Pantano de, *Spain* 28 E2
Enugu, *Nigeria* 79 D6
Enugu □, *Nigeria* 79 D6
Enugu Ezike, *Nigeria* 79 D6
Enumclaw, *U.S.A.* 112 C5
Envermeu, *France* 24 C8
Envigado, *Colombia* 120 B2
Envira, *Brazil* 124 B3
Enz →, *Germany* 19 F5
Enza →, *Italy* 32 D7
Eólie, Ís., *Italy* 35 D7
Epanomí, *Greece* 39 J5
Epe, *Neths.* 16 D7
Epe, *Nigeria* 79 D5
Épernay, *France* 25 C10
Épernon, *France* 25 D8
Ephesus, *Turkey* 66 D2
Ephraim, *U.S.A.* 110 G8
Ephrata, *U.S.A.* 110 C4
Epila, *Spain* 28 D3
Épinac-les-Mines, *France* 25 F11
Épinal, *France* 25 D13
Epira, *Guyana* 121 B6
Episkopi, *Cyprus* 37 E11
Episkopí, *Greece* 37 D6
Episkopi Bay, *Cyprus* 37 E11
Eppan = Appiano, *Italy* 33 B8
Epping, *U.K.* 13 F8
Epukiro, *Namibia* 84 C2
Equatorial Guinea ■, *Africa* 80 D1
Equeipa, *Venezuela* 121 B5
Er Rahad, *Sudan* 77 E3
Er Rif, *Morocco* 75 A4
Er Roseires, *Sudan* 77 E3
Erāwadī Myit = Irrawaddy →, *Burma* 61 M19
Erba, *Italy* 32 C6
Erba, *Sudan* 76 D4
Erbaa, *Turkey* 66 B7
Erbil = Arbīl, *Iraq* 67 D11
Erçiş, *Turkey* 67 C10
Erdao Jiang →, *China* 51 C14
Erdek, *Turkey* 66 B2
Erdemli, *Turkey* 66 D6
Erdene, *Mongolia* 50 B6
Erding, *Germany* 19 G7
Erdre →, *France* 24 E5
Erebato →, *Venezuela* 121 B5
Erebus, Mt., *Antarctica* 5 D11
Erechim, *Brazil* 127 B5
Ereğli, *Konya, Turkey* 66 D6
Ereğli, *Zonguldak, Turkey* 66 B4
Erei, Monti, *Italy* 35 E7
Erembodegem, *Belgium* 17 G4
Erenhot, *China* 50 C7
Eresma →, *Spain* 30 D6
Erewadi Myitwanya, *Burma* 61 M19
Erfenisdam, *S. Africa* 84 D4
Erfoud, *Morocco* 74 B4
Erft →, *Germany* 18 D2
Erfurt, *Germany* 18 E7
Ergani, *Turkey* 67 C8
Ergeni Vozvyshennost, *Russia* 43 G7
Ērgli, *Latvia* 9 H21
Eria →, *Spain* 30 C5
Eriba, *Sudan* 77 D4
Eriboll, L., *U.K.* 14 C4
Erica, *Neths.* 16 C9
Érice, *Italy* 34 D5
Erie, *U.S.A.* 106 D4
Erie, L., *N. Amer.* 106 D3
Erie Canal, *U.S.A.* 106 C6
Erieau, *Canada* 106 D3
Erigavo, *Somali Rep.* 68 E4
Erikoúsa, *Greece* 37 A3
Eriksdale, *Canada* 101 C9
Eriksslund, *Sweden* 10 B9
Erímanthos, *Greece* 39 M4
Erimo-misaki, *Japan* 48 D11
Eriswil, *Switz.* 22 B5
Erithraí, *Greece* 39 L6
Eritrea ■, *Africa* 77 E4
Erjas →, *Portugal* 31 F3
Erlangen, *Germany* 19 F7
Erldunda, *Australia* 90 D1
Erlin, *Taiwan* 53 F13
Ermelo, *Neths.* 16 D7
Ermelo, *S. Africa* 85 D4
Ermenak, *Turkey* 66 D5
Ermióni, *Greece* 39 M6
Ermones, *Greece* 37 A3
Ermoúpolis = Síros, *Greece* 39 M7
Ernakulam = Cochin, *India* 60 Q10
Erne →, *Ireland* 15 B3
Erne, Lower L., *U.K.* 15 B4
Erne, Upper L., *U.K.* 15 B4
Ernée, *France* 24 D6
Ernest Giles Ra., *Australia* 89 E3
Ernstberg, *Germany* 19 E2
Erode, *India* 60 P10
Eromanga, *Australia* 91 D3
Erongo, *Namibia* 84 C2
Erp, *Neths.* 17 E7
Erquelinnes, *Belgium* 17 H4
Erquy, *France* 24 D4
Erquy, C. d', *France* 24 D4
Err, Piz d', *Switz.* 23 C9
Errabiddy, *Australia* 89 E2
Erramala Hills, *India* 60 M11
Errer →, *Ethiopia* 77 F5
Errigal, *Ireland* 15 A3
Erris Hd., *Ireland* 15 B1
Erseka, *Albania* 39 J3
Erskine, *U.S.A.* 108 B7
Erstein, *France* 25 D14
Erstfeld, *Switz.* 23 C7
Ertil, *Russia* 42 E5
Ertis = Irtysh →, *Russia* 44 C7
Ertvelde, *Belgium* 17 F3
Eruh, *Turkey* 67 D10
Eruwa, *Nigeria* 79 D5
Ervy-le-Châtel, *France* 25 D10
Erwin, *U.S.A.* 105 G4
Eryuan, *China* 52 D2
Erzgebirge, *Germany* 18 E9
Erzin, *Russia* 45 D10
Erzincan, *Turkey* 67 C8
Erzurum, *Turkey* 67 C9
Es Caló, *Spain* 36 C8
Es Caná, *Spain* 36 B8
Es Sahrâ' Esh Sharqîya, *Egypt* 76 B3
Es Sînâ', *Egypt* 76 J8
Es Sûkî, *Sudan* 77 E3
Esambo, *Zaïre* 82 C1
Esan-Misaki, *Japan* 48 D10
Esashi, *Hokkaidō, Japan* 48 B11
Esashi, *Hokkaidō, Japan* 48 D10
Esbjerg, *Denmark* 11 J2
Escada, *Brazil* 122 C4
Escalante, *U.S.A.* 111 H8
Escalante →, *U.S.A.* 111 H8
Escalón, *Mexico* 114 B4
Escalona, *Spain* 30 E6
Escambia →, *U.S.A.* 105 K2
Escanaba, *U.S.A.* 104 C2
Escaut →, *Belgium* 17 F3
Esch-sur-Alzette, *Lux.* 17 J7
Eschede, *Germany* 18 C6
Escholzmatt, *Switz.* 22 C5
Eschwege, *Germany* 18 D6
Eschweiler, *Germany* 18 E2
Escoma, *Bolivia* 124 D4
Escondido, *U.S.A.* 113 M9
Escuinapa, *Mexico* 114 C3
Escuintla, *Guatemala* 116 D1
Eséka, *Cameroon* 79 E7
Esens, *Germany* 18 B3
Esera →, *Spain* 28 C5
Eşfahān, *Iran* 65 C6
Esfīdeh, *Iran* 65 C8
Esgueva →, *Spain* 30 D6
Esh Sham = Dimashq, *Syria* 69 B5
Esh Shamâlîya □, *Sudan* 76 D2
Eshan, *China* 52 E4
Eshowe, *S. Africa* 85 D5
Esiama, *Ghana* 78 E4
Esil = Ishim →, *Russia* 44 D8
Esino →, *Italy* 33 E10
Esk →, *Cumb., U.K.* 14 G5
Esk →, *N. Yorks., U.K.* 12 C7
Eskifjörður, *Iceland* 8 D7
Eskilstuna, *Sweden* 10 E10
Eskimalatya, *Turkey* 67 C8
Eskimo Pt., *Canada* 101 A10
Eskişehir, *Turkey* 66 C4
Esla →, *Spain* 30 D4
Esla, Pantano del, *Spain* 30 D4
Eslāmābād-e Gharb, *Iran* 67 E12
Eslöv, *Sweden* 11 J7
Eşme, *Turkey* 66 C3
Esmeralda, I., *Chile* 128 C1
Esmeraldas, *Ecuador* 120 C2
Esmeraldas □, *Ecuador* 120 C2
Esmeraldas →, *Ecuador* 120 C2
Esneux, *Belgium* 17 G7
Espada, Pta., *Colombia* 120 A3
Espalion, *France* 26 D6
Espalmador, I., *Spain* 36 C7
Espanola, *Canada* 98 C3
Espardell, I. del, *Spain* 36 C7
Esparraguera, *Spain* 28 D6
Esparta, *Costa Rica* 116 E3
Espejo, *Spain* 31 H6
Esperança, *Brazil* 122 C4
Esperance, *Australia* 89 F3
Esperance B., *Australia* 89 F3
Esperantinópolis, *Brazil* 122 B3
Esperanza, *Santa Cruz, Argentina* 128 D2
Esperanza, *Santa Fe, Argentina* 126 C3
Esperanza, *Phil.* 55 G6
Espéraza, *France* 26 F6

Espichel, C., Portugal 31 G1
Espiel, Spain 31 G5
Espigão, Serra do, Brazil . 127 B5
Espinal, Colombia 120 C3
Espinar, Peru 124 C3
Espinazo, Sierra del = Espinhaço, Serra do, Brazil 123 E3
Espinhaço, Serra do, Brazil 123 E3
Espinho, Portugal 30 D2
Espinilho, Serra do, Brazil 127 B5
Espino, Venezuela 120 B4
Espinosa de los Monteros, Spain 30 B7
Espírito Santo □, Brazil . 123 F3
Espíritu Santo, B. del, Mexico 115 D7
Espíritu Santo, I., Mexico 114 C2
Espita, Mexico 115 C7
Espiye, Turkey 67 B8
Esplanada, Brazil 123 D4
Espluga de Francolí, Spain 28 D6
Espoo, Finland 9 F21
Espuña, Sierra, Spain ... 29 H3
Espungabera, Mozam. ... 85 C5
Esquel, Argentina 128 B2
Esquina, Argentina 126 B4
Essaouira, Morocco 74 B3
Essebie, Zaïre 82 B3
Essen, Belgium 17 F4
Essen, Germany 18 D2
Essendon, Mt., Australia . 89 E3
Essequibo →, Guyana ... 121 B6
Essex, Canada 106 D2
Essex, Calif., U.S.A. 113 L11
Essex, N.Y., U.S.A. 107 B11
Essex □, U.K. 13 F8
Esslingen, Germany 19 G5
Essonne □, France 25 D9
Essvik, Sweden 10 B11
Estaca, Pta. del, Spain .. 30 B3
Estadilla, Spain 28 C5
Estados, I. de Los, Argentina 128 D4
Estagel, France 26 F6
Eşfahbānāt, Iran 65 D7
Estallenchs, Spain 36 B9
Estância, Brazil 122 D4
Estancia, U.S.A. 111 J10
Estārm, Iran 65 D8
Estarreja, Portugal 30 E2
Estats, Pic d', Spain 28 C6
Estavayer-le-Lac, Switz. . 22 C3
Estcourt, S. Africa 85 D4
Este, Italy 33 C8
Esteban, Spain 30 B4
Estelí, Nic. 116 D2
Estella, Spain 28 C2
Estelline, S. Dak., U.S.A. 108 C6
Estelline, Tex., U.S.A. .. 109 H4
Estena →, Spain 31 F6
Estepa, Spain 31 H6
Estepona, Spain 31 J5
Esterhazy, Canada 101 C8
Esternay, France 25 D10
Esterri de Aneu, Spain .. 28 C6
Estevan, Canada 101 D8
Estevan Group, Canada . 100 C3
Estherville, U.S.A. 108 D7
Estissac, France 25 D10
Eston, Canada 101 C7
Estonia ■, Europe 9 G21
Estoril, Portugal 31 G1
Estouk, Mali 79 B5
Estrêla, Serra da, Portugal 30 E3
Estrella, Spain 29 G1
Estremoz, Portugal 31 G3
Estrondo, Serra do, Brazil 122 C2
Esztergom, Hungary ... 21 H8
Et Tîdra, Mauritania ... 78 B1
Étables-sur-Mer, France . 24 D4
Etadunna, Australia ... 91 D2
Etah, India 63 F8
Étain, France 25 C12
Etalle, Belgium 17 J6
Etamamu, Canada 99 B8
Étampes, France 25 D9
Étang-sur-Arroux, France 27 B8
Etanga, Namibia 84 B1
Étaples, France 25 B8
Etawah, India 63 F8
Etawah →, U.S.A. 105 H3
Etawney L., Canada ... 101 B9
Ete, Nigeria 79 D6
Éthe, Belgium 17 J7
Ethel, U.S.A. 112 D4
Ethel, Oued el =, Algeria 74 C4
Ethel Creek, Australia .. 88 D3
Ethelbert, Canada 101 C8
Ethiopia ■, Africa 68 F3
Ethiopian Highlands, Ethiopia 70 E7
Etive, L., U.K. 14 E3
Etna, Italy 35 E8
Etoile, Zaïre 83 E2
Etolin I., U.S.A. 100 B2
Etosha Pan, Namibia ... 84 B2
Etowah, U.S.A. 105 H3
Étrépagny, France 25 C8
Étretat, France 24 C7
Ettelbruck, Lux. 17 J8
Etten, Neths. 17 E5
Ettlingen, Germany ... 19 G4
Ettrick Water →, U.K. . 14 F6
Etuku, Zaïre 82 C2
Etzatlán, Mexico 114 C4
Eu, France 24 B8

Euboea = Évvoia, Greece . 39 L7
Eucla Motel, Australia .. 89 F4
Euclid, U.S.A. 106 E3
Euclides da Cunha, Brazil 122 D4
Eucumbene, L., Australia . 91 F4
Eudora, U.S.A. 109 J9
Eufaula, Ala., U.S.A. ... 105 K3
Eufaula, Okla., U.S.A. .. 109 H7
Eufaula L., U.S.A. 109 H7
Eugene, U.S.A. 110 E2
Eugowra, Australia 91 E4
Eulo, Australia 91 D4
Eunice, La., U.S.A. 109 K8
Eunice, N. Mex., U.S.A. . 109 J3
Eupen, Belgium 17 G8
Euphrates = Furāt, Nahr al →, Asia 64 D5
Eure □, France 24 C8
Eure →, France 24 C8
Eure-et-Loir □, France .. 24 D8
Eureka, Canada 4 B3
Eureka, Calif., U.S.A. .. 110 F1
Eureka, Kans., U.S.A. .. 109 G6
Eureka, Mont., U.S.A. .. 110 B6
Eureka, Nev., U.S.A. ... 110 G5
Eureka, S. Dak., U.S.A. . 108 C5
Eureka, Utah, U.S.A. ... 110 G7
Eureka, Mt., Australia .. 89 E3
Euroa, Australia 91 F4
Europa, I., Ind. Oc. 81 J8
Europa, Picos de, Spain . 30 B6
Europa, Pta. de, Gib. ... 31 J5
Europa Pt. = Europa, Pta. de, Gib. 31 J5
Europoort, Neths. 16 E4
Euskirchen, Germany ... 18 E2
Eustis, U.S.A. 105 L5
Eutin, Germany 18 A6
Eutsuk L., Canada 100 C3
Eva, Brazil 121 D6
Eva Downs, Australia ... 90 B1
Evale, Angola 84 B2
Evans, U.S.A. 108 E2
Evans Head, Australia .. 91 D5
Evans L., Canada 98 B4
Evans Mills, U.S.A. 107 B9
Evanston, Ill., U.S.A. ... 104 D2
Evanston, Wyo., U.S.A. . 110 F8
Evansville, Ind., U.S.A. . 104 F2
Evansville, Wis., U.S.A. . 108 D10
Évaux-les-Bains, France . 26 B6
Evaz, Iran 65 E7
Eveleth, U.S.A. 108 B8
Evensk, Russia 45 C16
Evenstad, Norway 10 C5
Everard, L., Australia .. 91 E1
Everard Park, Australia . 89 E5
Everard Ras., Australia . 89 E5
Evere, Belgium 17 G4
Everest, Mt., Nepal 63 E12
Everett, Pa., U.S.A. 106 F6
Everett, Wash., U.S.A. .. 112 C4
Evergem, Belgium 17 F3
Everglades, The, U.S.A. . 105 N5
Everglades City, U.S.A. . 105 N5
Everglades National Park, U.S.A. 105 N5
Evergreen, U.S.A. 105 K2
Everson, U.S.A. 110 B2
Evesham, U.K. 13 E6
Évian-les-Bains, France . 27 B10
Evinayong, Eq. Guin. .. 80 D2
Évinos →, Greece 39 L4
Évisa, France 27 F12
Evje, Norway 9 G12
Évora, Portugal 31 G3
Évora □, Portugal 31 G3
Evowghlī, Iran 67 C11
Évreux, France 24 C8
Évron, France 24 D6
Évros →, Bulgaria 39 N5
Evrótas →, Greece 39 N5
Évvoia, Greece 39 L7
Évvoia □, Greece 39 L6
Ewe, L., U.K. 14 D3
Ewing, U.S.A. 108 D5
Ewo, Congo 80 E2
Exaltación, Bolivia 125 C4
Excelsior Springs, U.S.A. 108 F7
Excideuil, France 26 C5
Exe →, U.K. 13 G4
Exeter, Canada 106 C3
Exeter, U.K. 13 G4
Exeter, Calif., U.S.A. ... 111 H4
Exeter, N.H., U.S.A. ... 107 D14
Exeter, Nebr., U.S.A. ... 108 E6
Exloo, Neths. 16 C9
Exmes, France 24 D7
Exmoor, U.K. 13 F4
Exmouth, Australia 88 D1
Exmouth, U.K. 13 G4
Exmouth G., Australia .. 88 D1
Expedition Ra., Australia 90 C4
Extremadura □, Spain .. 31 F4
Exuma Sound, Bahamas . 116 B4
Eyasi, L., Tanzania 82 E4
Eyeberry L., Canada ... 101 A8
Eyemouth, U.K. 14 F6
Eyre, Australia 89 F4
Eyre (North), L., Australia 91 D2
Eyre (South), L., Australia 91 D2
Eyre Cr. →, Australia .. 91 D2

Eyre Mts., N.Z. 87 L2
Eyre Pen., Australia ... 91 E2
Eysturoy, Færoe Is. 8 E9
Eyvānkī, Iran 65 C6
Ez Zeidab, Sudan 76 D3
Ezine, Turkey 66 C2
Ezmul, Mauritania 74 D1
Ezouza →, Cyprus 37 E11

F

F.Y.R.O.M. = Macedonia ■, Europe . 39 H4
Fabens, U.S.A. 111 L10
Fåborg, Denmark 11 J4
Fabriano, Italy 33 E9
Făcăeni, Romania 38 E10
Facatativá, Colombia ... 120 C3
Fachi, Niger 72 E7
Facture, France 26 D3
Fada, Chad 73 E9
Fada-n-Gourma, Burkina Faso 79 C5
Faddeyevskiy, Ostrov, Russia 45 B15
Fadghāmī, Syria 67 E9
Fadlab, Sudan 76 D3
Faenza, Italy 33 D8
Færoe Is. = Føroyar, Atl. Oc. 8 F9
Fafa, Mali 79 B5
Fafe, Portugal 30 D2
Fagam, Nigeria 79 C7
Făgăras, Romania 38 D7
Făgăras, Munţii, Romania 38 D7
Fågelsjö, Sweden 10 C8
Fagersta, Sweden 9 F16
Făget, Romania 38 D5
Fagnano, L., Argentina . 128 D3
Fagnano Castello, Italy . 35 C9
Fagnières, France 25 D11
Fahliān, Iran 65 D6
Fahraj, Kermān, Iran ... 65 D8
Fahraj, Yazd, Iran 65 D7
Faial, Madeira 36 D3
Faido, Switz. 23 D7
Fair Hd., U.K. 15 A5
Fair Oaks, U.S.A. 112 G5
Fairbank, U.S.A. 111 L8
Fairbanks, U.S.A. 96 B5
Fairbury, U.S.A. 108 E6
Fairfax, U.S.A. 109 G6
Fairfield, Ala., U.S.A. .. 105 J2
Fairfield, Calif., U.S.A. . 112 G4
Fairfield, Conn., U.S.A. . 107 E11
Fairfield, Idaho, U.S.A. . 110 E6
Fairfield, Ill., U.S.A. ... 104 F1
Fairfield, Iowa, U.S.A. .. 108 E9
Fairfield, Mont., U.S.A. . 110 C8
Fairfield, Tex., U.S.A. .. 109 K7
Fairford, Canada 101 C9
Fairhope, U.S.A. 105 K2
Fairlie, N.Z. 87 L3
Fairmead, U.S.A. 112 H6
Fairmont, Minn., U.S.A. 108 D7
Fairmont, W. Va., U.S.A. 104 F5
Fairmount, U.S.A. 113 L8
Fairplay, U.S.A. 111 G11
Fairport, U.S.A. 106 C7
Fairport Harbor, U.S.A. . 106 E3
Fairview, Australia 90 B3
Fairview, Canada 100 B5
Fairview, Mont., U.S.A. . 108 B2
Fairview, Okla., U.S.A. . 109 G5
Fairview, Utah, U.S.A. .. 110 G8
Fairweather, Mt., U.S.A. 96 C6
Faisalabad, Pakistan ... 62 D5
Faith, U.S.A. 108 C3
Faizabad, India 63 F10
Fajardo, Puerto Rico ... 117 C6
Fakfak, Indonesia 57 E8
Fakobli, Ivory C. 78 D3
Fakse, Denmark 11 J6
Fakse B., Denmark 11 J6
Fakse Ladeplads, Denmark 11 J6
Faku, China 51 C12
Falaise, France 24 D6
Falaise, Mui, Vietnam .. 58 B5
Falam, Burma 61 H18
Falces, Spain 28 C3
Fălciu, Romania 38 C11
Falcón □, Venezuela ... 120 A4
Falcon, C., Algeria 75 A4
Falcón, C., Spain 36 C7
Falcon Dam, U.S.A. ... 109 M5
Falconara Maríttima, Italy 33 E10
Falconer, U.S.A. 106 D5
Faléa, Mali 78 C2
Faleshty = Fălesti, Moldova 41 J4
Fălesti, Moldova 41 J4
Falfurrias, U.S.A. 109 M5
Falher, Canada 100 B5
Falirakí, Greece 37 C10
Falkenberg, Germany .. 18 D9
Falkenberg, Sweden ... 11 H6
Falkensee, Germany ... 18 C9
Falkenstein, Germany .. 18 E8
Falkirk, U.K. 14 F5
Falkland, East I., Falk. Is. 128 D5
Falkland, West, I., Falk. Is. 128 D4
Falkland Is. □, Atl. Oc. . 128 D5
Falkland Sd., Falk. Is. .. 128 D5

Falköping, Sweden 11 F7
Fall River, U.S.A. 107 E13
Fall River Mills, U.S.A. . 110 F3
Fallbrook, U.S.A. 111 K5
Fallbrook, Calif., U.S.A. . 113 M9
Fallon, Mont., U.S.A. .. 108 B2
Fallon, Nev., U.S.A. ... 110 G4
Falls City, Nebr., U.S.A. . 108 E7
Falls Creek, U.S.A. 106 E6
Falmouth, Jamaica 116 C4
Falmouth, U.K. 13 G2
Falmouth, U.S.A. 104 F3
False B., S. Africa 84 E2
Falso, C., Honduras ... 116 C3
Falset, Spain 28 D5
Falster, Denmark 11 K5
Falsterbo, Sweden 11 J6
Fălticeni, Romania 38 B9
Falun, Sweden 9 F16
Famagusta, Cyprus 66 E5
Famagusta Bay, Cyprus . 37 D13
Famatina, Sierra de, Argentina 126 B2
Family L., Canada 101 C9
Famoso, U.S.A. 113 K7
Fan Xian, China 50 G8
Fana, Mali 78 C3
Fandriana, Madag. ... 85 C8
Fang, Thailand 58 C2
Fang Xian, China 53 A8
Fangchang, China 53 B12
Fangcheng, Guangxi Zhuangzu, China 52 G7
Fangcheng, Henan, China 50 H7
Fangliao, Taiwan 53 F13
Fangshan, China 50 E6
Fangzi, China 51 F10
Fanjiatun, China 51 C13
Fani i Madh →, Albania 39 H3
Fannich, L., U.K. 14 D4
Fannūj, Iran 65 E8
Fano, Italy 33 E10
Fanø, Denmark 11 J2
Fanshaw, U.S.A. 100 B2
Fanshi, China 50 E7
Fao = Al Fāw, Iraq 65 D6
Faqirwala, Pakistan ... 62 E5
Fara in Sabina, Italy ... 33 F9
Faradje, Zaïre 82 B2
Farafangana, Madag. .. 85 C8
Farāfra, El Wâhât el-, Egypt 76 B2
Farah, Afghan. 60 C3
Farāh □, Afghan. 60 C3
Farahalana, Madag. ... 85 A9
Faraid, Gebel, Egypt ... 76 C4
Faramana, Burkina Faso 78 C4
Faranah, Guinea 78 C2
Farasān, Jazā'ir, Si. Arabia 68 D3
Farasan Is. = Farasān, Jazā'ir, Si. Arabia 68 D3
Faratsiho, Madag. 85 B8
Fardes →, Spain 29 H1
Fareham, U.K. 13 G6
Farewell, C., N.Z. 87 J4
Farewell C. = Farvel, Kap, Greenland 4 D5
Farghona, Uzbekistan . 44 E8
Fargo, U.S.A. 108 B6
Fār'iah, W. al →, West Bank 69 C4
Faribault, U.S.A. 108 C8
Faridkot, India 62 D6
Faridpur, Bangla. 63 H13
Fârila, Sweden 10 C9
Farim, Guinea-Biss. ... 78 C1
Farīmān, Iran 65 C8
Farina, Australia 91 E2
Farinha →, Brazil 122 C2
Fariones, Pta., Canary Is. 36 E6
Fâriskûr, Egypt 76 H7
Farmerville, U.S.A. ... 109 J8
Farmington, Calif., U.S.A. 112 H6
Farmington, N.H., U.S.A. 107 C13
Farmington, N. Mex., U.S.A. 111 H9
Farmington, Utah, U.S.A. 110 F8
Farmington →, U.S.A. . 107 E12
Farmville, U.S.A. 104 G6
Farnborough, U.K. 13 F7
Farne Is., U.K. 12 B6
Farnham, Canada 107 A12
Faro, Brazil 121 D6
Faro, Portugal 31 H3
Fårö, Sweden 9 H18
Faro □, Portugal 31 H2
Farquhar, C., Australia . 89 D1
Farrars Cr. →, Australia 90 D3
Farräshband, Iran 65 D7
Farrell, U.S.A. 106 E4
Farrell Flat, Australia .. 91 E2
Farrokhi, Iran 65 C8
Farruch, C., Spain 36 B10
Farrukhabad-cum-Fatehgarh, India 63 F8
Fārs □, Iran 65 D7
Fársala, Greece 39 K5
Farsø, Denmark 11 H3
Farsund, Norway 9 G12
Fartak, Râs, Si. Arabia . 64 D2
Fartura, Serra da, Brazil 127 B5
Faru, Nigeria 79 C6
Fārūj, Iran 65 B8
Farum, Denmark 11 J6

Farvel, Kap, Greenland . 4 D5
Farwell, U.S.A. 109 H3
Fasā, Iran 65 D7
Fasano, Italy 35 B10
Fashoda, Sudan 77 F3
Fastiv, Ukraine 41 G5
Fastnet Rock, Ireland .. 15 E2
Fastov = Fastiv, Ukraine . 41 G5
Fatagar, Tanjung, Indonesia 57 E8
Fatehgarh, India 63 F8
Fatehpur, Raj., India ... 62 F6
Fatehpur, Ut. P., India .. 63 G9
Fatesh, Russia 42 D2
Fatick, Senegal 78 C1
Fatima, Canada 99 C7
Fátima, Portugal 31 F2
Fatoya, Guinea 78 C3
Fatsa, Turkey 66 B7
Faucille, Col de la, France 27 B10
Faulkton, U.S.A. 108 C5
Faulquemont, France .. 25 C13
Fauquembergues, France 25 B9
Faure I., Australia 89 E1
Făurei, Romania 38 D10
Fauresmith, S. Africa .. 84 D4
Fauske, Norway 8 C16
Fauvillers, Belgium ... 17 J7
Favara, Italy 34 E6
Favaritx, C., Spain 36 A11
Favignana, Italy 34 E5
Favignana, I., Italy 34 E5
Favourable Lake, Canada 98 B1
Fawn →, Canada 98 A2
Fawnskin, U.S.A. 113 L10
Faxaflói, Iceland 8 D2
Faya-Largeau, Chad ... 73 E8
Fayd, Si. Arabia 64 E4
Fayence, France 27 E10
Fayette, Ala., U.S.A. ... 105 J2
Fayette, Mo., U.S.A. ... 108 F8
Fayetteville, Ark., U.S.A. 109 G7
Fayetteville, N.C., U.S.A. 105 H6
Fayetteville, Tenn., U.S.A. 105 H2
Fayón, Spain 28 D5
Fazenda Nova, Brazil .. 123 E1
Fazilka, India 62 D6
Fazilpur, Pakistan 62 E4
Fdérik, Mauritania 74 D2
Feale →, Ireland 15 D2
Fear, C., U.S.A. 105 J7
Feather →, U.S.A. ... 110 G3
Feather Falls, U.S.A. .. 112 F5
Featherston, N.Z. 87 J5
Featherstone, Zimbabwe 83 F3
Fécamp, France 24 C7
Fedala = Mohammedia, Morocco 74 B3
Federación, Argentina . 126 C4
Fedeshkūh, Iran 65 D7
Fedjadj, Chott el, Tunisia 75 B6
Fehmarn, Germany ... 18 A7
Fehmarn Bælt, Denmark 9 J14
Fei Xian, China 51 G9
Feijó, Brazil 124 B3
Feilding, N.Z. 87 J5
Feira de Santana, Brazil 123 D4
Feixiang, China 50 F8
Fejø, Denmark 11 K5
Feke, Turkey 66 D6
Felanitx, Spain 36 B10
Feldberg, Baden-W., Germany 19 H3
Feldberg, Mecklenburg-Vorpommern, Germany 18 B9
Feldkirch, Austria 19 H5
Felipe Carrillo Puerto, Mexico 115 D7
Felixlândia, Brazil 123 E3
Felixstowe, U.K. 13 F9
Felletin, France 26 C6
Felton, U.K. 12 B6
Felton, U.S.A. 112 H4
Feltre, Italy 33 B8
Femø, Denmark 11 K5
Femunden, Norway ... 10 B5
Fen He →, China 50 G6
Fenelon Falls, Canada . 106 B6
Feneroa, Ethiopia 77 E4
Feng Xian, Jiangsu, China 50 G9
Feng Xian, Shaanxi, China 50 H4
Fengári, Greece 39 J8
Fengcheng, Jiangxi, China 53 C10
Fengcheng, Liaoning, China 51 D13
Fengdu, China 52 C6
Fengfeng, China 50 F8
Fenggang, China 52 D6
Fenghua, China 53 C13
Fenghuang, China 52 D7
Fenghuangzui, China .. 52 A7
Fengjie, China 52 B7
Fengkai, China 53 F8
Fengle, China 53 B9
Fengning, China 50 D9
Fengqing, China 52 E2
Fengqiu, China 50 G8
Fengrun, China 51 E10
Fengshan, Guangxi Zhuangzu, China 52 E7
Fengshan, Guangxi Zhuangzu, China 52 E6
Fengtai, Anhui, China .. 53 A11
Fengtai, Beijing, China . 50 E9
Fengxian, China 53 B13

Foulpointe

Fengxiang, *China* **50 G4**
Fengxin, *China* **53 C10**
Fengyang, *China* **51 H9**
Fengyi, *China* **52 E3**
Fengzhen, *China* **50 D7**
Fenit, *Ireland* **15 D2**
Fennimore, *U.S.A.* **108 D9**
Feno, C. de, *France* **27 G12**
Fenoarivo Afovoany, *Madag.* **85 B8**
Fenoarivo Atsinanana, *Madag.* **85 B8**
Fens, The, *U.K.* **12 E8**
Fenton, *U.S.A.* **104 D4**
Fenxi, *China* **50 F6**
Fenyang, *China* **50 F6**
Fenyi, *China* **53 D10**
Feodosiya, *Ukraine* **41 K8**
Fer, C. de, *Algeria* **75 A6**
Ferdows, *Iran* **65 C8**
Fère-Champenoise, *France* **25 D10**
Fère-en-Tardenois, *France* **25 C10**
Ferentino, *Italy* **34 A6**
Ferfer, *Somali Rep.* **68 F4**
Fergana = Farghona, *Uzbekistan* **44 E8**
Fergus, *Canada* **98 D3**
Fergus Falls, *U.S.A.* **108 B6**
Fériana, *Tunisia* **75 B6**
Feričanci, *Croatia* **21 K8**
Ferkane, *Algeria* **75 B6**
Ferkéssédougou, *Ivory C.* **78 D3**
Ferlach, *Austria* **21 J4**
Ferland, *Canada* **98 B2**
Ferlo, Vallée du, *Senegal* **78 B2**
Fermanagh □, *U.K.* **15 B4**
Fermo, *Italy* **33 E10**
Fermoselle, *Spain* **30 D4**
Fermoy, *Ireland* **15 D3**
Fernán Nuñéz, *Spain* **31 H6**
Fernández, *Argentina* **126 B3**
Fernandina Beach, *U.S.A.* **105 K5**
Fernando de Noronha, *Brazil* **122 B5**
Fernando Póo = Bioko, *Eq. Guin.* **79 E6**
Fernandópolis, *Brazil* **123 F1**
Ferndale, *Calif., U.S.A.* **110 F1**
Ferndale, *Wash., U.S.A.* **112 B4**
Fernie, *Canada* **100 D5**
Fernlees, *Australia* **90 C4**
Fernley, *U.S.A.* **110 G4**
Ferozepore = Firozpur, *India* **62 D6**
Férrai, *Greece* **39 J9**
Ferrandina, *Italy* **35 B9**
Ferrara, *Italy* **33 D8**
Ferrato, C., *Italy* **34 C2**
Ferreira do Alentejo, *Portugal* **31 G2**
Ferreñafe, *Peru* **124 B2**
Ferrerías, *Spain* **36 B11**
Ferret, C., *France* **26 D2**
Ferrette, *France* **25 E14**
Ferriday, *U.S.A.* **109 K9**
Ferrières, *France* **25 D9**
Ferriete, *Italy* **32 D6**
Ferrol = El Ferrol, *Spain* **30 B2**
Ferrol, Pen. de, *Peru* **124 B2**
Ferron, *U.S.A.* **111 G8**
Ferros, *Brazil* **123 E3**
Ferryland, *Canada* **99 C9**
Fertile, *U.S.A.* **108 B6**
Fertília, *Italy* **34 B1**
Fès, *Morocco* **74 B4**
Feschaux, *Belgium* **17 H5**
Feshi, *Zaïre* **80 F3**
Fessenden, *U.S.A.* **108 B5**
Fetești, *Romania* **38 E10**
Fethiye, *Turkey* **66 D3**
Fetlar, *U.K.* **14 A8**
Feuerthalen, *Switz.* **23 A7**
Feuilles →, *Canada* **97 C12**
Feurs, *France* **27 C8**
Fezzan, *Libya* **73 C8**
Ffestiniog, *U.K.* **12 E4**
Fiambalá, *Argentina* **126 B2**
Fianarantsoa, *Madag.* **85 C8**
Fianarantsoa □, *Madag.* **85 B8**
Fianga, *Cameroon* **73 G8**
Fichtelgebirge, *Germany* **19 E7**
Ficksburg, *S. Africa* **85 D4**
Fidenza, *Italy* **32 D7**
Fiditi, *Nigeria* **79 D5**
Field, *Canada* **98 C3**
Field →, *Australia* **90 C2**
Field I., *Australia* **88 B5**
Fieri, *Albania* **39 J2**
Fiesch, *Switz.* **22 D6**
Fife □, *U.K.* **14 E5**
Fife Ness, *U.K.* **14 E6**
Fifth Cataract, *Sudan* **76 D3**
Figeac, *France* **26 D6**
Figline Valdarno, *Italy* **33 E8**
Figtree, *Zimbabwe* **83 G2**
Figueira Castelo Rodrigo, *Portugal* **30 E4**
Figueira da Foz, *Portugal* **30 E2**
Figueiró dos Vinhos, *Portugal* **30 F2**
Figueras, *Spain* **28 C7**
Figuig, *Morocco* **75 B4**
Fihaonana, *Madag.* **85 B8**
Fiherenana, *Madag.* **85 B8**
Fiherenana →, *Madag.* **85 C7**
Fiji ■, *Pac. Oc.* **87 C8**
Fika, *Nigeria* **79 C7**
Filabres, Sierra de los, *Spain* **29 H2**
Filadelfia, *Bolivia* **124 C4**
Filadélfia, *Brazil* **122 C2**
Filadélfia, *Italy* **35 D9**
Filer, *U.S.A.* **110 E6**
Filey, *U.K.* **12 C7**
Filfla, *Malta* **37 D1**
Filiași, *Romania* **38 E6**
Filiátes, *Greece* **39 K3**
Filiatrá, *Greece* **39 M4**
Filicudi, *Italy* **35 D7**
Filiourí →, *Greece* **39 H8**
Filipstad, *Sweden* **9 G16**
Filisur, *Switz.* **23 C9**
Fillmore, *Canada* **101 D8**
Fillmore, *Calif., U.S.A.* **113 L8**
Fillmore, *Utah, U.S.A.* **111 G7**
Filottrano, *Italy* **33 E10**
Finale Lígure, *Italy* **32 D5**
Finale nell' Emília, *Italy* **33 D8**
Fiñana, *Spain* **29 H2**
Finch, *Canada* **107 A9**
Findhorn →, *U.K.* **14 D5**
Findlay, *U.S.A.* **104 E4**
Finger L., *Canada* **101 C10**
Fíngõe, *Mozam.* **83 E3**
Finike, *Turkey* **66 D4**
Finistère □, *France* **24 D2**
Finisterre, *Spain* **30 C1**
Finisterre, C., *Spain* **30 C1**
Finke, *Australia* **90 D1**
Finke →, *Australia* **91 D2**
Finland ■, *Europe* **8 E22**
Finland, G. of, *Europe* **9 G21**
Finlay →, *Canada* **100 B3**
Finley, *Australia* **91 F4**
Finley, *U.S.A.* **108 B6**
Finn →, *Ireland* **15 B4**
Finnigan, Mt., *Australia* **90 B4**
Finniss, C., *Australia* **91 E1**
Finnmark, *Norway* **8 B20**
Finnsnes, *Norway* **8 B18**
Finspång, *Sweden* **9 G16**
Finsteraarhorn, *Switz.* **22 C6**
Finsterwalde, *Germany* **18 D9**
Finsterwolde, *Neths.* **16 B10**
Fiora →, *Italy* **33 F8**
Fiorenzuola d'Arda, *Italy* **32 D6**
Fīq, *Syria* **69 C4**
Firat = Furāt, Nahr al →, *Asia* **64 D5**
Fire River, *Canada* **98 C3**
Firebag →, *Canada* **101 B6**
Firebaugh, *U.S.A.* **112 J6**
Firedrake L., *Canada* **101 A8**
Firenze, *Italy* **33 E8**
Firk →, *Iraq* **64 D5**
Firmi, *France* **26 D6**
Firminy, *France* **27 C8**
Firozabad, *India* **63 F8**
Firozpur, *India* **62 D6**
Fīrūzābād, *Iran* **65 D7**
Fīrūzkūh, *Iran* **65 C7**
Firvale, *Canada* **100 C3**
Fish →, *Namibia* **84 D2**
Fish →, *S. Africa* **84 E3**
Fisher, *Australia* **89 F5**
Fisher B., *Canada* **101 C9**
Fishguard, *U.K.* **13 F3**
Fishing L., *Canada* **101 C9**
Fismes, *France* **25 C10**
Fitchburg, *U.S.A.* **107 D13**
Fitero, *Spain* **28 C3**
Fitri, L., *Chad* **73 F8**
Fitz Roy, *Argentina* **128 C3**
Fitzgerald, *Canada* **100 B6**
Fitzgerald, *U.S.A.* **105 K4**
Fitzmaurice →, *Australia* **88 B5**
Fitzroy →, *Queens., Australia* **90 C5**
Fitzroy →, *W. Austral., Australia* **88 C3**
Fitzroy Crossing, *Australia* **88 C4**
Fitzwilliam I., *Canada* **106 A3**
Fiume = Rijeka, *Croatia* **33 C11**
Fiumefreddo Brúzio, *Italy* **35 C9**
Five Points, *U.S.A.* **112 J6**
Fivizzano, *Italy* **32 D7**
Fizi, *Zaïre* **82 C2**
Fjellerup, *Denmark* **11 H4**
Fjerritslev, *Denmark* **11 G3**
Fkih ben Salah, *Morocco* **74 B3**
Flå, *Norway* **10 A4**
Flagler, *U.S.A.* **108 F3**
Flagstaff, *U.S.A.* **111 J8**
Flaherty I., *Canada* **98 A4**
Flåm, *Norway* **9 F12**
Flambeau →, *U.S.A.* **108 C9**
Flamborough Hd., *U.K.* **12 C7**
Flaming Gorge Dam, *U.S.A.* **110 F9**
Flaming Gorge Reservoir, *U.S.A.* **110 F9**
Flamingo, Teluk, *Indonesia* **57 F9**
Flanders = West-Vlaanderen □, *Belgium* **17 G2**
Flandre Occidentale = West-Vlaanderen □, *Belgium* **17 G2**
Flandre Orientale = Oost-Vlaanderen □, *Belgium* **17 F3**
Flandreau, *U.S.A.* **108 C6**
Flanigan, *U.S.A.* **112 E7**
Flannan Is., *U.K.* **14 C1**
Flåsjön, *Sweden* **8 D16**
Flat →, *Canada* **100 A3**
Flat River, *U.S.A.* **109 G9**
Flathead L., *U.S.A.* **110 C6**
Flattery, C., *Australia* **90 A4**
Flattery, C., *U.S.A.* **112 B2**
Flavy-le-Martel, *France* **25 C10**
Flawil, *Switz.* **23 B8**
Flaxton, *U.S.A.* **108 A3**
Fleetwood, *U.K.* **12 D4**
Flekkefjord, *Norway* **9 G12**
Flémalle, *Belgium* **17 G6**
Flemington, *U.S.A.* **106 E7**
Flensburg, *Germany* **18 A5**
Flensburger Förde, *Germany* **11 K3**
Flers, *France* **24 D6**
Flesherton, *Canada* **106 B4**
Flesko, Tanjung, *Indonesia* **57 D6**
Fleurance, *France* **26 E4**
Fleurier, *Switz.* **22 C3**
Fleurus, *Belgium* **17 H5**
Flevoland □, *Neths.* **16 C7**
Flims, *Switz.* **23 C8**
Flin Flon, *Canada* **101 C8**
Flinders →, *Australia* **90 B3**
Flinders B., *Australia* **89 F2**
Flinders Group, *Australia* **90 A3**
Flinders I., *Australia* **90 F4**
Flinders Ras., *Australia* **91 E2**
Flinders Reefs, *Australia* **90 B4**
Flint, *U.K.* **12 D4**
Flint, *U.S.A.* **104 D4**
Flint →, *U.S.A.* **105 K3**
Flint I., *Kiribati* **93 J12**
Flinton, *Australia* **91 D4**
Flix, *Spain* **28 D5**
Flixecourt, *France* **25 B9**
Flobecq, *Belgium* **17 G3**
Flodden, *U.K.* **12 B5**
Floodwood, *U.S.A.* **108 B8**
Flora, *Norway* **10 A5**
Flora, *U.S.A.* **104 F1**
Florac, *France* **26 D7**
Florala, *U.S.A.* **105 K2**
Florânia, *Brazil* **122 C4**
Floreffe, *Belgium* **17 H5**
Florence = Firenze, *Italy* **33 E8**
Florence, *Ala., U.S.A.* **105 H2**
Florence, *Ariz., U.S.A.* **111 K8**
Florence, *Colo., U.S.A.* **108 F2**
Florence, *Oreg., U.S.A.* **110 E1**
Florence, *S.C., U.S.A.* **105 H6**
Florence, L., *Australia* **91 D2**
Florennes, *Belgium* **17 H5**
Florensac, *France* **26 E7**
Florenville, *Belgium* **17 J6**
Flores, *Brazil* **122 C4**
Flores, *Guatemala* **116 C2**
Flores, *Indonesia* **57 F6**
Flores I., *Canada* **100 D3**
Flores Sea, *Indonesia* **57 F6**
Floresta, *Brazil* **122 C4**
Florești, *Moldova* **41 J5**
Floresville, *U.S.A.* **109 L5**
Floriano, *Brazil* **122 C3**
Florianópolis, *Brazil* **127 B6**
Florida, *Cuba* **116 B4**
Florida, *Uruguay* **127 C4**
Florida □, *U.S.A.* **105 L5**
Florida, Straits of, *U.S.A.* **116 B3**
Florida B., *U.S.A.* **116 A3**
Florida Keys, *U.S.A.* **103 F10**
Florídia, *Italy* **35 E8**
Floridsdorf, *Austria* **21 G6**
Flórina, *Greece* **39 J4**
Florø, *Norway* **9 F11**
Flower Station, *Canada* **107 A8**
Flower's Cove, *Canada* **99 B8**
Floydada, *U.S.A.* **109 J4**
Fluk, *Indonesia* **57 E7**
Flumen →, *Spain* **28 D4**
Flumendosa →, *Italy* **34 C2**
Fluminimaggiore, *Italy* **34 C1**
Flushing = Vlissingen, *Neths.* **17 F3**
Fluviá →, *Spain* **28 C8**
Flying Fish, C., *Antarctica* **5 D15**
Foam Lake, *Canada* **101 C8**
Foča, *Bos.-H.* **21 M8**
Foça, *Turkey* **66 C2**
Focșani, *Romania* **38 D10**
Fogang, *China* **53 F9**
Foggaret el Arab, *Algeria* **75 C5**
Foggaret ez Zoua, *Algeria* **75 C5**
Fóggia, *Italy* **35 A8**
Foggo, *Nigeria* **79 C6**
Foglia →, *Italy* **33 E9**
Fogo, *Canada* **99 C9**
Fogo I., *Canada* **99 C9**
Fohnsdorf, *Austria* **21 H4**
Föhr, *Germany* **18 A4**
Foia, *Portugal* **31 H2**
Foix, *France* **26 F5**
Fokino, *Russia* **42 D2**
Folda, *Nord-Trøndelag, Norway* **8 D14**
Folda, *Nordland, Norway* **8 C16**
Foleyet, *Canada* **98 C3**
Folgefonni, *Norway* **9 F12**
Foligno, *Italy* **33 F9**
Folkestone, *U.K.* **13 F9**
Folkston, *U.S.A.* **105 K5**
Follett, *U.S.A.* **109 G4**
Follónica, *Italy* **32 F7**
Follónica, G. di, *Italy* **32 F7**
Folsom Res., *U.S.A.* **112 G5**
Fond-du-Lac, *Canada* **101 B7**
Fond du Lac, *U.S.A.* **108 D10**
Fond-du-Lac →, *Canada* **101 B7**
Fonda, *U.S.A.* **107 D10**
Fondi, *Italy* **34 A6**
Fonfría, *Spain* **30 D4**
Fongen, *Norway* **10 A5**
Fonni, *Italy* **34 B2**
Fonsagrada, *Spain* **30 B3**
Fonseca, G. de, *Cent. Amer.* **116 D2**
Fontaine-Française, *France* **25 E12**
Fontainebleau, *France* **25 D9**
Fontana, L., *Argentina* **128 B2**
Fontas →, *Canada* **100 B4**
Fonte Boa, *Brazil* **120 D4**
Fontem, *Cameroon* **79 D6**
Fontenay-le-Comte, *France* **26 B3**
Fontur, *Iceland* **8 C6**
Fonyód, *Hungary* **21 J7**
Foochow = Fuzhou, *China* **53 D12**
Foping, *China* **50 H4**
Foppiano, *Italy* **32 B5**
Forbach, *France* **25 C13**
Forbes, *Australia* **91 E4**
Forbesganj, *India* **63 F12**
Forcados, *Nigeria* **79 D6**
Forcados →, *Nigeria* **79 D6**
Forcall →, *Spain* **28 E4**
Forcalquier, *France* **27 E9**
Forchheim, *Germany* **19 F7**
Forclaz, Col de la, *Switz.* **22 D4**
Ford City, *Calif., U.S.A.* **113 K7**
Ford City, *Pa., U.S.A.* **106 F5**
Førde, *Norway* **9 F11**
Ford's Bridge, *Australia* **91 D4**
Fordyce, *U.S.A.* **109 J8**
Forécariah, *Guinea* **78 D2**
Forel, Mt., *Greenland* **4 C6**
Foremost, *Canada* **100 D6**
Forenza, *Italy* **35 B8**
Forest, *Belgium* **17 G4**
Forest, *Canada* **106 C3**
Forest, *U.S.A.* **109 J10**
Forest City, *Iowa, U.S.A.* **108 D8**
Forest City, *N.C., U.S.A.* **105 H5**
Forest City, *Pa., U.S.A.* **107 E9**
Forest Grove, *U.S.A.* **112 E3**
Forestburg, *Canada* **100 C6**
Foresthill, *U.S.A.* **112 F6**
Forestier Pen., *Australia* **90 G4**
Forestville, *Canada* **99 C6**
Forestville, *Calif., U.S.A.* **112 G4**
Forestville, *Wis., U.S.A.* **104 C2**
Forez, Mts. du, *France* **26 C7**
Forfar, *U.K.* **14 E6**
Forges-les-Eaux, *France* **25 C8**
Forks, *U.S.A.* **112 C2**
Forlì, *Italy* **33 D9**
Forman, *U.S.A.* **108 B6**
Formazza, *Italy* **32 B5**
Formby Pt., *U.K.* **12 D4**
Formentera, *Spain* **36 C7**
Formentor, C. de, *Spain* **36 B10**
Former Yugoslav Republic of Macedonia = Macedonia ■, *Europe* **39 H4**
Fórmia, *Italy* **34 A6**
Formiga, *Brazil* **123 F2**
Formigine, *Italy* **32 D7**
Formiguères, *France* **26 F6**
Formosa = Taiwan ■, *Asia* **53 F13**
Formosa, *Argentina* **126 B4**
Formosa, *Brazil* **123 E2**
Formosa □, *Argentina* **126 B3**
Formosa, Serra, *Brazil* **125 C6**
Formosa Bay, *Kenya* **82 C5**
Formosa Strait, *Asia* **53 E12**
Formoso →, *Brazil* **123 D2**
Fornells, *Spain* **36 A11**
Fornos de Algodres, *Portugal* **30 E3**
Fornovo di Taro, *Italy* **32 D7**
Føroyar, *Atl. Oc.* **8 F9**
Forres, *U.K.* **14 D5**
Forrest, *Vic., Australia* **91 F3**
Forrest, *W. Austral., Australia* **89 F4**
Forrest, Mt., *Australia* **89 D4**
Forrest City, *U.S.A.* **109 H9**
Forrières, *Belgium* **17 H6**
Forsa, *Sweden* **10 C10**
Forsayth, *Australia* **90 B3**
Forsmo, *Sweden* **10 A11**
Forssa, *Finland* **9 F20**
Forst, *Germany* **18 D10**
Forster, *Australia* **91 E5**
Forsyth, *Ga., U.S.A.* **105 J4**
Forsyth, *Mont., U.S.A.* **110 C10**
Fort Albany, *Canada* **98 B3**
Fort Apache, *U.S.A.* **111 K9**
Fort Assiniboine, *Canada* **100 C6**
Fort Augustus, *U.K.* **14 D4**
Fort Beaufort, *S. Africa* **84 E4**
Fort Benton, *U.S.A.* **110 C8**
Fort Bragg, *U.S.A.* **110 G2**
Fort Bridger, *U.S.A.* **110 F8**
Fort Chipewyan, *Canada* **101 B6**
Fort Collins, *U.S.A.* **108 E2**
Fort-Coulonge, *Canada* **98 C4**
Fort Davis, *U.S.A.* **109 K3**
Fort-de-France, *Martinique* **117 D7**
Fort de Possel = Possel, *C.A.R.* **80 C3**
Fort Defiance, *U.S.A.* **111 J9**
Fort Dodge, *U.S.A.* **108 D7**
Fort Edward, *U.S.A.* **107 C11**
Fort Frances, *Canada* **101 D10**
Fort Franklin, *Canada* **96 B7**
Fort Garland, *U.S.A.* **111 H11**
Fort George = Chisasibi, *Canada* **98 B4**
Fort Good-Hope, *Canada* **96 B7**
Fort Hancock, *U.S.A.* **111 L11**
Fort Hertz = Putao, *Burma* **61 F20**
Fort Hope, *Canada* **98 B2**
Fort Irwin, *U.S.A.* **113 K10**
Fort Jameson = Chipata, *Zambia* **83 E3**
Fort Kent, *U.S.A.* **99 C6**
Fort Klamath, *U.S.A.* **110 E3**
Fort-Lamy = Ndjamena, *Chad* **73 F7**
Fort Laramie, *U.S.A.* **108 D2**
Fort Lauderdale, *U.S.A.* **105 M5**
Fort Liard, *Canada* **100 A4**
Fort Liberté, *Haiti* **117 C5**
Fort Lupton, *U.S.A.* **108 E2**
Fort Mackay, *Canada* **100 B6**
Fort McKenzie, *Canada* **99 A6**
Fort Macleod, *Canada* **100 D6**
Fort MacMahon, *Algeria* **75 C5**
Fort McMurray, *Canada* **100 B6**
Fort McPherson, *Canada* **96 B6**
Fort Madison, *U.S.A.* **108 E9**
Fort Meade, *U.S.A.* **105 M5**
Fort Miribel, *Algeria* **75 C5**
Fort Morgan, *U.S.A.* **108 E3**
Fort Myers, *U.S.A.* **105 M5**
Fort Nelson, *Canada* **100 B4**
Fort Nelson →, *Canada* **100 B4**
Fort Norman, *Canada* **96 B7**
Fort Payne, *U.S.A.* **105 H3**
Fort Peck, *U.S.A.* **110 B10**
Fort Peck Dam, *U.S.A.* **110 C10**
Fort Peck L., *U.S.A.* **110 C10**
Fort Pierce, *U.S.A.* **105 M5**
Fort Pierre, *U.S.A.* **108 C4**
Fort Pierre Bordes = Ti-n-Zaouaténe, *Algeria* **75 E5**
Fort Plain, *U.S.A.* **107 D10**
Fort Portal, *Uganda* **82 B3**
Fort Providence, *Canada* **100 A5**
Fort Qu'Appelle, *Canada* **101 C8**
Fort Resolution, *Canada* **100 A6**
Fort Rixon, *Zimbabwe* **83 G2**
Fort Rosebery = Mansa, *Zambia* **83 E2**
Fort Ross, *U.S.A.* **112 G3**
Fort Rupert = Waskaganish, *Canada* **98 B4**
Fort St. James, *Canada* **100 C4**
Fort St. John, *Canada* **100 B4**
Fort Sandeman, *Pakistan* **62 D3**
Fort Saskatchewan, *Canada* **100 C6**
Fort Scott, *U.S.A.* **109 G7**
Fort Severn, *Canada* **98 A2**
Fort Shevchenko, *Kazakhstan* **43 H10**
Fort Simpson, *Canada* **100 A4**
Fort Smith, *Canada* **100 B6**
Fort Smith, *U.S.A.* **109 H7**
Fort Stanton, *U.S.A.* **111 K11**
Fort Stockton, *U.S.A.* **109 K3**
Fort Sumner, *U.S.A.* **109 H2**
Fort Trinquet = Bir Mogrein, *Mauritania* **74 C2**
Fort Valley, *U.S.A.* **105 J4**
Fort Vermilion, *Canada* **100 B5**
Fort Walton Beach, *U.S.A.* **105 K2**
Fort Wayne, *U.S.A.* **104 E3**
Fort William, *U.K.* **14 E3**
Fort Worth, *U.S.A.* **109 J6**
Fort Yates, *U.S.A.* **108 B4**
Fort Yukon, *U.S.A.* **96 B5**
Fortaleza, *Bolivia* **124 C4**
Fortaleza, *Brazil* **122 B4**
Forteau, *Canada* **99 B8**
Forth →, *U.K.* **14 E5**
Forth, Firth of, *U.K.* **14 E6**
Forthassa Rharbia, *Algeria* **75 B4**
Fortín Coronel Eugenio Garay, *Paraguay* **125 E5**
Fortín Garrapatal, *Paraguay* **125 E5**
Fortín General Pando, *Paraguay* **125 D6**
Fortín Madrejón, *Paraguay* **125 E6**
Fortín Uno, *Argentina* **128 A3**
Fortore →, *Italy* **33 G12**
Fortrose, *U.K.* **14 D4**
Fortuna, *Spain* **29 G3**
Fortuna, *Calif., U.S.A.* **110 F1**
Fortuna, *N. Dak., U.S.A.* **108 A3**
Fortune B., *Canada* **99 C8**
Fos-sur-Mer, *France* **27 E8**
Foshan, *China* **53 F9**
Fosna, *Norway* **8 E14**
Fosnavåg, *Norway* **9 E11**
Fossacésia, *Italy* **33 F11**
Fossano, *Italy* **32 D4**
Fosses-la-Ville, *Belgium* **17 H5**
Fossil, *U.S.A.* **110 D3**
Fossilbrook, *Australia* **90 B3**
Fossombrone, *Italy* **33 E9**
Fosston, *U.S.A.* **108 B7**
Foster, *Canada* **107 A12**
Foster →, *Canada* **101 B7**
Fosters Ra., *Australia* **90 C1**
Fostoria, *U.S.A.* **104 E4**
Fougamou, *Gabon* **80 E2**
Fougères, *France* **24 D5**
Foul Pt., *Sri Lanka* **60 Q12**
Foula, *U.K.* **14 A6**
Foulness I., *U.K.* **13 F8**
Foulpointe, *Madag.* **85 B8**

Foum Assaka

Foum Assaka, *Morocco* .. 74 C2
Foum Zguid, *Morocco* ... 74 B3
Foumban, *Cameroon* 79 D7
Foundiougne, *Senegal* 78 C1
Fountain, *Colo., U.S.A.* .. 108 F2
Fountain, *Utah, U.S.A.* ... 110 G8
Fountain Springs, *U.S.A.* . 113 K8
Fourchambault, *France* ... 25 E10
Fourchu, *Canada* 99 C7
Fouriesburg, *S. Africa* 84 D4
Fourmies, *France* 25 B11
Foúrnoi, *Greece* 39 M9
Fours, *France* 25 F10
Fouta Djalon, *Guinea* 78 C2
Foux, Cap-à-, *Haiti* 117 C5
Foveaux Str., *N.Z.* 87 M2
Fowey, *U.K.* 13 G3
Fowler, *Calif., U.S.A.* 111 H4
Fowler, *Colo., U.S.A.* 108 F2
Fowler, *Kans., U.S.A.* ... 109 G4
Fowlers B., *Australia* 89 F5
Fowlerton, *U.S.A.* 109 L5
Fowman, *Iran* 67 D13
Fox →, *Canada* 101 B10
Fox Valley, *Canada* 101 C7
Foxe Basin, *Canada* 97 B12
Foxe Chan., *Canada* 97 B11
Foxe Pen., *Canada* 97 B12
Foxhol, *Neths.* 16 B9
Foxpark, *U.S.A.* 110 F10
Foxton, *N.Z.* 87 J5
Foyle, Lough, *U.K.* 15 A4
Foynes, *Ireland* 15 D2
Foz, *Spain* 30 B3
Fóz do Cunene, *Angola* .. 84 B1
Foz do Gregório, *Brazil* .. 124 B3
Foz do Iguaçu, *Brazil* 127 B5
Foz do Riosinho, *Brazil* .. 124 B3
Frackville, *U.S.A.* 107 F8
Fraga, *Spain* 28 D5
Fraire, *Belgium* 17 H5
Frameries, *Belgium* 17 H3
Framingham, *U.S.A.* 107 D13
Franca, *Brazil* 123 F2
Francavilla al Mare, *Italy* 33 F11
Francavilla Fontana, *Italy* . 35 B10
France ■, *Europe* 7 F6
Frances, *Australia* 91 F3
Frances →, *Canada* 100 A3
Frances L., *Canada* 100 A3
Francés Viejo, C., *Dom. Rep.* 117 C6
Franceville, *Gabon* 80 E2
Franche-Comté, *France* ... 25 F12
Franches Montagnes, *Switz.* 22 B4
Francisco de Orellana, *Ecuador* 120 D2
Francisco I. Madero, *Coahuila, Mexico* 114 B4
Francisco I. Madero, *Durango, Mexico* 114 C4
Francisco Sá, *Brazil* 123 E3
Francistown, *Botswana* ... 85 C4
Francofonte, *Italy* 35 E7
François, *Canada* 99 C8
François L., *Canada* 100 C3
Francorchamps, *Belgium* ... 17 H7
Franeker, *Neths.* 16 B7
Frankado, *Djibouti* 77 E5
Frankenberg, *Germany* ... 18 D4
Frankenthal, *Germany* ... 19 F4
Frankenwald, *Germany* ... 19 E7
Frankfort, *S. Africa* 85 D4
Frankfort, *Ind., U.S.A.* .. 104 E2
Frankfort, *Kans., U.S.A.* . 108 F6
Frankfort, *Ky., U.S.A.* ... 104 F3
Frankfort, *Mich., U.S.A.* . 104 C2
Frankfurt, *Brandenburg, Germany* 18 C10
Frankfurt, *Hessen, Germany* 19 E4
Fränkische Alb, *Germany* . 19 F7
Fränkische Rezal →, *Germany* 19 F7
Fränkische Saale →, *Germany* 19 E5
Fränkische Schweiz, *Germany* 19 F7
Frankland →, *Australia* .. 89 G2
Franklin, *Ky., U.S.A.* 105 G2
Franklin, *La., U.S.A.* 109 L9
Franklin, *Mass., U.S.A.* .. 107 D13
Franklin, *N.H., U.S.A.* ... 107 C13
Franklin, *Nebr., U.S.A.* .. 108 E5
Franklin, *Pa., U.S.A.* 106 E5
Franklin, *Tenn., U.S.A.* .. 105 H2
Franklin, *Va., U.S.A.* 105 G7
Franklin, *W. Va., U.S.A.* . 104 F6
Franklin B., *Canada* 96 B7
Franklin D. Roosevelt L., *U.S.A.* 110 B4
Franklin I., *Antarctica* 5 D11
Franklin L., *U.S.A.* 110 F6
Franklin Mts., *Canada* ... 96 B7
Franklin Str., *Canada* 96 A10
Franklinton, *U.S.A.* 109 K9
Franklinville, *U.S.A.* 106 D6
Franks Pk., *U.S.A.* 110 E9
Frankston, *Australia* 91 F4
Fränsta, *Sweden* 10 B10
Frantsa Iosifa, Zemlya, *Russia* 44 A6
Franz, *Canada* 98 C3
Franz Josef Land = Frantsa Iosifa, Zemlya, *Russia* .. 44 A6
Franzburg, *Germany* 18 A8
Frascati, *Italy* 34 A5
Fraser →, *B.C., Canada* . 100 D4
Fraser →, *Nfld., Canada* . 99 A7
Fraser, Mt., *Australia* 89 E2
Fraser I., *Australia* 91 D5
Fraser Lake, *Canada* 100 C4
Fraserburg, *S. Africa* 84 E3
Fraserburgh, *U.K.* 14 D6
Fraserdale, *Canada* 98 C3
Frasne, *France* 25 F13
Frauenfeld, *Switz.* 23 A7
Fray Bentos, *Uruguay* 126 C4
Frazier Downs, *Australia* . 88 C3
Frechilla, *Spain* 30 C6
Fredericia, *Denmark* 11 J3
Frederick, *Md., U.S.A.* ... 104 F7
Frederick, *Okla., U.S.A.* . 109 H5
Frederick, *S. Dak., U.S.A.* 108 C5
Frederick Sd., *U.S.A.* 100 B2
Fredericksburg, *Tex., U.S.A.* 109 K5
Fredericksburg, *Va., U.S.A.* 104 F7
Fredericktown, *U.S.A.* ... 109 G9
Frederico I. Madero, Presa, *Mexico* 114 B3
Fredericton, *Canada* 99 C6
Fredericton Junc., *Canada* 99 C6
Frederikshåb, *Greenland* .. 4 C5
Frederikshavn, *Denmark* .. 11 G4
Frederikssund, *Denmark* .. 11 J6
Frederiksted, *Virgin Is.* .. 117 C7
Fredonia, *Ariz., U.S.A.* .. 111 H7
Fredonia, *Kans., U.S.A.* .. 109 G7
Fredonia, *N.Y., U.S.A.* .. 106 D5
Fredrikstad, *Norway* 10 E4
Freehold, *U.S.A.* 107 F10
Freel Peak, *U.S.A.* 112 G7
Freeland, *U.S.A.* 107 E9
Freels, C., *Canada* 99 C9
Freeman, *Calif., U.S.A.* .. 113 K9
Freeman, *S. Dak., U.S.A.* 108 D6
Freeport, *Bahamas* 116 A4
Freeport, *Canada* 99 D6
Freeport, *Ill., U.S.A.* 108 D10
Freeport, *N.Y., U.S.A.* ... 107 F11
Freeport, *Tex., U.S.A.* ... 109 L7
Freetown, *S. Leone* 78 D2
Frégate, L., *Canada* 98 B5
Fregenal de la Sierra, *Spain* 31 G4
Fregene, *Italy* 34 A5
Fréhel, C., *France* 24 D4
Freiberg, *Germany* 18 E9
Freibourg = Fribourg, *Switz.* 22 C4
Freiburg, *Baden-W., Germany* 19 H3
Freiburg, *Niedersachsen, Germany* 18 B5
Freiburger Alpen, *Switz.* . 22 C4
Freire, *Chile* 128 A2
Freirina, *Chile* 126 B1
Freising, *Germany* 19 G7
Freistadt, *Austria* 20 G4
Freital, *Germany* 18 E9
Fréjus, *France* 27 E10
Fremantle, *Australia* 89 F2
Fremont, *Calif., U.S.A.* .. 111 H2
Fremont, *Mich., U.S.A.* .. 104 D3
Fremont, *Nebr., U.S.A.* .. 108 E6
Fremont, *Ohio, U.S.A.* ... 104 E4
Fremont →, *U.S.A.* 111 G8
Fremont L., *U.S.A.* 110 E9
French Camp, *U.S.A.* 112 H5
French Creek →, *U.S.A.* . 106 E5
French Guiana ■, *S. Amer.* 121 C7
French Pass, *N.Z.* 87 J4
French Polynesia ■, *Pac. Oc.* 93 J13
French Terr. of Afars & Issas = Djibouti ■, *Africa* 68 E3
Frenchglen, *U.S.A.* 110 E4
Frenchman Butte, *Canada* 101 C7
Frenchman Cr. →, *Mont., U.S.A.* 110 B10
Frenchman Cr. →, *Nebr., U.S.A.* 108 E4
Frenda, *Algeria* 75 A5
Fresco →, *Brazil* 125 B7
Freshfield, C., *Antarctica* . 5 C10
Fresnay-sur-Sarthe, *France* 24 D7
Fresnillo, *Mexico* 114 C4
Fresno, *U.S.A.* 111 H4
Fresno Alhandiga, *Spain* .. 30 E5
Fresno Reservoir, *U.S.A.* . 110 B9
Freudenstadt, *Germany* ... 19 G4
Freux, *Belgium* 17 J6
Frévent, *France* 25 B9
Frew →, *Australia* 90 C2
Frewena, *Australia* 90 B2
Freycinet Pen., *Australia* . 90 G4
Freyming-Merlebach, *France* 25 C13
Freyung, *Germany* 19 G9
Fria, *Guinea* 78 C2
Fria, C., *Namibia* 84 B1
Friant, *U.S.A.* 112 J7
Frías, *Argentina* 126 B2
Fribourg, *Switz.* 22 C4
Fribourg □, *Switz.* 22 C4
Frick, *Switz.* 22 A6
Friday Harbor, *U.S.A.* ... 112 B3
Friedberg, *Bayern, Germany* 19 G6
Friedberg, *Hessen, Germany* 19 E4
Friedland, *Germany* 18 B9
Friedrichshafen, *Germany* 19 H5
Friedrichskoog, *Germany* . 18 A4
Friedrichstadt, *Germany* .. 18 A5
Friendly Is. = Tonga ■, *Pac. Oc.* 87 D11
Friesack, *Germany* 18 C8
Friesche Wad, *Neths.* 16 B7
Friesland □, *Neths.* 16 B7
Friesoythe, *Germany* 18 B3
Frillesås, *Sweden* 11 G6
Frio →, *U.S.A.* 109 L5
Friona, *U.S.A.* 109 H3
Frisian Is., *Europe* 18 B2
Fristad, *Sweden* 11 G7
Fritch, *U.S.A.* 109 H4
Fritsla, *Sweden* 11 G6
Fritzlar, *Germany* 18 D5
Friuli-Venézia Giulia □, *Italy* 33 B10
Frobisher B., *Canada* 97 B13
Frobisher Bay = Iqaluit, *Canada* 97 B13
Frobisher L., *Canada* 101 B7
Frohavet, *Norway* 8 E13
Froid, *U.S.A.* 108 A2
Froid-Chapelle, *Belgium* .. 17 H4
Frolovo, *Russia* 42 F6
Fromberg, *U.S.A.* 110 D9
Frome, *U.K.* 13 F5
Frome, L., *Australia* 91 E2
Frome Downs, *Australia* .. 91 E2
Frómista, *Spain* 30 C6
Front Range, *U.S.A.* 110 G11
Front Royal, *U.S.A.* 104 F6
Fronteira, *Portugal* 31 F3
Fronteiras, *Brazil* 122 C3
Frontera, *Canary Is.* 36 G2
Frontera, *Mexico* 115 D6
Frontignan, *France* 26 E7
Frosinone, *Italy* 34 A6
Frosolone, *Italy* 35 A7
Frostburg, *U.S.A.* 104 F6
Frostisen, *Norway* 8 B17
Frouard, *France* 25 D13
Frøya, *Norway* 8 E13
Fruges, *France* 25 B9
Frumoasa, *Romania* 38 C8
Frunze = Bishkek, *Kyrgyzstan* 44 E8
Frutal, *Brazil* 123 F2
Frutigen, *Switz.* 22 C5
Frýdek-Místek, *Czech.* ... 20 F8
Frýdlant, *Czech.* 20 E5
Fu Jiang →, *China* 52 C6
Fu Xian, *Liaoning, China* . 51 E11
Fu Xian, *Shaanxi, China* .. 50 F5
Fu'an, *China* 53 D12
Fubian, *China* 52 B4
Fucécchio, *Italy* 32 E7
Fucheng, *China* 50 F9
Fuchou = Fuzhou, *China* . 53 D12
Fuchū, *Japan* 49 G6
Fuchuan, *China* 53 E8
Fuchun Jiang →, *China* .. 53 B13
Fúcino, Conca del, *Italy* .. 33 F10
Fuding, *China* 53 D13
Fuencaliente, *Canary Is.* .. 36 F2
Fuencaliente, *Spain* 31 G6
Fuencaliente, Pta., *Canary Is.* 36 F2
Fuengirola, *Spain* 31 J6
Fuente Alamo, *Albacete, Spain* 29 G3
Fuente Álamo, *Murcia, Spain* 29 H3
Fuente de Cantos, *Spain* .. 31 G4
Fuente del Maestre, *Spain* 31 G4
Fuente el Fresno, *Spain* .. 31 F7
Fuente Ovejuna, *Spain* ... 31 G5
Fuentes de Andalucía, *Spain* 31 H5
Fuentes de Ebro, *Spain* ... 28 D4
Fuentes de León, *Spain* ... 31 G4
Fuentes de Oñoro, *Spain* . 30 E4
Fuentesaúco, *Spain* 30 D5
Fuerte →, *Mexico* 114 B3
Fuerte Olimpo, *Paraguay* . 126 A4
Fuerteventura, *Canary Is.* . 36 F6
Fufeng, *China* 50 G4
Fuga I., *Phil.* 55 B4
Fugong, *China* 52 D2
Fugou, *China* 50 G8
Fugu, *China* 50 E6
Fuhai, *China* 54 B3
Fuḩaymī, *Iraq* 67 E10
Fuji, *Japan* 49 G9
Fuji-San, *Japan* 49 G9
Fuji-yoshida, *Japan* 49 G9
Fujian □, *China* 53 E12
Fujinomiya, *Japan* 49 G9
Fujisawa, *Japan* 49 G9
Fukien = Fujian □, *China* 53 E12
Fukuchiyama, *Japan* 49 G7
Fukue-Shima, *Japan* 49 H4
Fukui, *Japan* 49 F8
Fukui □, *Japan* 49 G8
Fukuoka, *Japan* 49 H5
Fukuoka □, *Japan* 49 H5
Fukushima, *Japan* 48 F10
Fukushima □, *Japan* 48 F10
Fukuyama, *Japan* 49 G6
Fulda, *Germany* 18 E5
Fulda →, *Germany* 18 D5
Fuling, *China* 52 C6
Fullerton, *Calif., U.S.A.* . 113 M9
Fullerton, *Nebr., U.S.A.* .. 108 E5
Fulongquan, *China* 51 B13
Fulton, *Mo., U.S.A.* 108 F9
Fulton, *N.Y., U.S.A.* 107 C8
Fulton, *Tenn., U.S.A.* 105 G1
Fuluälven →, *Sweden* 10 C7
Fulufjället, *Sweden* 10 C6
Fumay, *France* 25 C11
Fumel, *France* 26 D4
Fumin, *China* 52 E4
Funabashi, *Japan* 49 G10
Funchal, *Madeira* 36 D3
Fundación, *Colombia* 120 A3
Fundão, *Brazil* 123 E3
Fundão, *Portugal* 30 E3
Fundy, B. of, *Canada* 99 D6
Funing, *Hebei, China* 51 E10
Funing, *Jiangsu, China* ... 51 H10
Funing, *Yunnan, China* ... 52 F5
Funiu Shan, *China* 50 H7
Funsi, *Ghana* 78 C4
Funtua, *Nigeria* 79 C6
Fuping, *Hebei, China* 50 E8
Fuping, *Shaanxi, China* ... 50 G5
Fuqing, *China* 53 E12
Fuquan, *China* 52 D6
Fur, *Denmark* 11 H3
Furano, *Japan* 48 C11
Furāt, Nahr al →, *Asia* .. 64 D5
Fürg, *Iran* 65 D7
Furkapass, *Switz.* 23 C7
Furmanov, *Russia* 42 B5
Furmanovo, *Kazakhstan* .. 42 F9
Furnás, *Spain* 36 B8
Furnas, Represa de, *Brazil* 123 F2
Furneaux Group, *Australia* 90 G4
Furness, *U.K.* 12 C4
Furqlus, *Syria* 69 A6
Fürstenau, *Germany* 18 C3
Fürstenberg, *Germany* 18 B9
Fürstenfeld, *Austria* 21 H6
Fürstenfeldbruck, *Germany* 19 G7
Fürstenwalde, *Germany* .. 18 C10
Fürth, *Germany* 19 F6
Furth im Wald, *Germany* . 19 F8
Furtwangen, *Germany* 19 G4
Furukawa, *Japan* 48 E10
Furusund, *Sweden* 10 E12
Fury and Hecla Str., *Canada* 97 B11
Fusagasuga, *Colombia* 120 C3
Fuscaldo, *Italy* 35 C9
Fushan, *Shandong, China* . 51 F11
Fushan, *Shanxi, China* ... 50 G6
Fushun, *Liaoning, China* . 51 D12
Fushun, *Sichuan, China* .. 52 C5
Fusio, *Switz.* 23 D7
Fusong, *China* 51 C14
Füssen, *Germany* 19 H6
Fusui, *China* 52 F6
Futrono, *Chile* 128 B2
Futuna, *Wall. & F. Is.* ... 87 B8
Fuwa, *Egypt* 76 H7
Fuxin, *China* 51 C11
Fuyang, *Anhui, China* ... 50 H8
Fuyang, *Zhejiang, China* . 53 B12
Fuyang He →, *China* 50 E9
Fuying Dao, *China* 53 D13
Fuyu, *China* 51 B13
Fuyuan, *Heilongjiang, China* 54 B8
Fuyuan, *Yunnan, China* .. 52 E5
Fuzhou, *China* 53 D12
Fylde, *U.K.* 12 D5
Fyn, *Denmark* 11 J4
Fyne, L., *U.K.* 14 F3
Fyns Amtskommune □, *Denmark* 11 J4
Fyresvatn, *Norway* 10 E2

G

Gaanda, *Nigeria* 79 C7
Gabarin, *Nigeria* 79 C7
Gabas →, *France* 26 E3
Gabela, *Angola* 80 G2
Gabès, *Tunisia* 75 B7
Gabès, G. de, *Tunisia* 75 B7
Gabgaba, W. →, *Egypt* .. 76 C3
Gabon ■, *Africa* 80 E2
Gaborone, *Botswana* 84 C4
Gabriels, *U.S.A.* 107 B10
Gābrīk, *Iran* 65 E8
Gabrovo, *Bulgaria* 38 G8
Gacé, *France* 24 D7
Gāch Sār, *Iran* 65 B6
Gachsārān, *Iran* 65 D6
Gacko, *Bos.-H.* 21 M8
Gadag, *India* 60 M9
Gadamai, *Sudan* 77 D4
Gadap, *Pakistan* 62 G2
Gadarwara, *India* 63 H8
Gadebusch, *Germany* 18 B7
Gadein, *Sudan* 77 F2
Gadhada, *India* 62 J4
Gadmen, *Switz.* 23 C6
Gádor, Sierra de, *Spain* .. 29 J2
Gadsden, *Ala., U.S.A.* ... 105 H2
Gadsden, *Ariz., U.S.A.* .. 111 K6
Gadwal, *India* 60 L10
Gadyach = Hadyach, *Ukraine* 41 G8
Găeşti, *Romania* 38 E8
Gaeta, *Italy* 34 A6
Gaeta, G. di, *Italy* 34 A6
Gaffney, *U.S.A.* 105 H5
Gafsa, *Tunisia* 75 B6
Gagarin, *Russia* 42 C2
Gagetown, *Canada* 99 C6
Gagino, *Russia* 42 C7
Gagliano del Capo, *Italy* .. 35 C11
Gagnoa, *Ivory C.* 78 D3
Gagnon, *Canada* 99 B6
Gagnon, L., *Canada* 101 A6
Gagra, *Georgia* 43 J5
Gahini, *Rwanda* 82 C3
Gahmar, *India* 63 G10
Gai Xian, *China* 51 D12
Gaïdhouronísi, *Greece* 37 E7
Gail, *U.S.A.* 109 J4
Gail →, *Austria* 21 J3
Gaillac, *France* 26 E5
Gaillimh = Galway, *Ireland* 15 C2
Gaillon, *France* 24 C8
Gaimán, *Argentina* 128 B3
Gaines, *U.S.A.* 106 E7
Gainesville, *Fla., U.S.A.* . 105 L4
Gainesville, *Ga., U.S.A.* .. 105 H4
Gainesville, *Mo., U.S.A.* . 109 G8
Gainesville, *Tex., U.S.A.* . 109 J6
Gainsborough, *U.K.* 12 D7
Gairdner, L., *Australia* ... 91 E2
Gairloch, L., *U.K.* 14 D3
Gais, *Switz.* 23 B8
Gakuch, *Pakistan* 63 A5
Galán, Cerro, *Argentina* .. 126 B2
Galana →, *Kenya* 82 C5
Galangue, *Angola* 81 G3
Galápagos, *Pac. Oc.* 93 H18
Galashiels, *U.K.* 14 F6
Galaţi, *Romania* 38 D11
Galatia, *Turkey* 66 C5
Galatina, *Italy* 35 B11
Galátone, *Italy* 35 B11
Galax, *U.S.A.* 105 G5
Galaxídhion, *Greece* 39 L5
Galbraith, *Australia* 90 B3
Galcaio, *Somali Rep.* 68 F4
Galdhøpiggen, *Norway* ... 10 C2
Galeana, *Mexico* 114 C4
Galela, *Indonesia* 57 D7
Galera, *Spain* 29 H2
Galera, Pta., *Chile* 128 A2
Galera Point, *Trin. & Tob.* 117 D7
Galesburg, *U.S.A.* 108 E9
Galeton, *U.S.A.* 106 E7
Galheirão →, *Brazil* 123 D2
Galheiros, *Brazil* 123 D2
Gali, *Georgia* 43 J5
Galich, *Russia* 42 A6
Galiche, *Bulgaria* 38 F6
Galicia □, *Spain* 30 C3
Galilee = Hagalil, *Israel* .. 69 C4
Galilee, L., *Australia* 90 C4
Galilee, Sea of = Yam Kinneret, *Israel* 69 C4
Galinoporni, *Cyprus* 37 D13
Galion, *U.S.A.* 106 F2
Galite, Is. de la, *Tunisia* .. 75 A6
Galiuro Mts., *U.S.A.* 111 K8
Gallabat, *Sudan* 77 E4
Gallardon, *France* 25 D8
Gallarte, *Italy* 32 C5
Gallatin, *U.S.A.* 105 G2
Galle, *Sri Lanka* 60 R12
Gállego →, *Spain* 28 D4
Gallegos →, *Argentina* .. 128 D3
Galley Hd., *Ireland* 15 E3
Galliate, *Italy* 32 C5
Gallinas, Pta., *Colombia* . 120 A3
Gallipoli = Gelibolu, *Turkey* 66 B2
Gallípoli, *Italy* 35 B11
Gallipolis, *U.S.A.* 104 F4
Gällivare, *Sweden* 8 C19
Gallo, C., *Italy* 34 D6
Gallocanta, L. de, *Spain* .. 28 E3
Galloway, *U.K.* 14 G4
Galloway, Mull of, *U.K.* .. 14 G4
Gallup, *U.S.A.* 111 J9
Gallur, *Spain* 28 D3
Galong, *Australia* 91 E4
Galoya, *Sri Lanka* 60 Q12
Galt, *U.S.A.* 112 G5
Galtström, *Sweden* 10 B11
Galtür, *Austria* 19 J6
Galty Mts., *Ireland* 15 D3
Galtymore, *Ireland* 15 D3
Galva, *U.S.A.* 108 E9
Galvarino, *Chile* 128 A2
Galve de Sorbe, *Spain* ... 28 D1
Galveston, *U.S.A.* 109 L7
Galveston B., *U.S.A.* 109 L7
Gálvez, *Argentina* 126 C3
Gálvez, *Spain* 31 F6
Galway, *Ireland* 15 C2
Galway □, *Ireland* 15 C2
Galway B., *Ireland* 15 C2
Gam →, *Vietnam* 58 B5
Gamagori, *Japan* 49 G8
Gamari, L., *Ethiopia* 77 E5
Gamawa, *Nigeria* 79 C7
Gamay, *Phil.* 55 E6
Gambaga, *Ghana* 79 C4
Gambat, *Pakistan* 62 F3
Gambela, *Ethiopia* 77 F3
Gambia ■, *W. Afr.* 78 C1
Gambia →, *W. Afr.* 78 C1
Gambier, C., *Australia* ... 88 B5
Gambier Is., *Australia* ... 91 F2
Gamboli, *Pakistan* 62 E3
Gamboma, *Congo* 80 E3
Gamerco, *U.S.A.* 111 J9

Gamlakarleby = Kokkola, Finland 8 E20
Gammon →, Canada 101 C9
Gammouda, Tunisia 75 A6
Gamu-Gofa □, Ethiopia .. 77 F4
Gan, France 26 E3
Gan Gan, Argentina 128 B3
Gan Goriama, Mts., Cameroon 79 D7
Gan Jiang →, China 53 C10
Ganado, Ariz., U.S.A. 111 J9
Ganado, Tex., U.S.A. 109 L6
Gananoque, Canada 98 D4
Ganāveh, Iran 65 D6
Gäncä, Azerbaijan 43 K8
Gand = Gent, Belgium 17 F3
Ganda, Angola 81 G2
Gandak →, India 63 G11
Gandava, Pakistan 62 E2
Gander, Canada 99 C9
Gander L., Canada 99 C9
Ganderowe Falls, Zimbabwe 83 F2
Gandesa, Spain 28 D5
Gandhi Sagar, India 62 G6
Gandi, Nigeria 79 C6
Gandía, Spain 29 G4
Gandino, Italy 32 C6
Gando, Pta., Canary Is. .. 36 G4
Gandole, Nigeria 79 D7
Gandu, Brazil 123 D4
Ganedidalem = Gani, Indonesia 57 E7
Ganetti, Sudan 76 D3
Ganga →, India 63 H14
Ganga, Mouths of the, India 63 J13
Ganganagar, India 62 E5
Gangapur, India 62 F7
Gangara, Niger 79 C6
Gangaw, Burma 61 H19
Gangdisê Shan, China 61 D12
Ganges = Ganga →, India .. 63 H14
Ganges, France 26 E7
Gangoh, India 62 E7
Gangtok, India 61 F16
Gangu, China 50 G3
Gangyao, China 51 B14
Gani, Indonesia 57 E7
Ganj, India 63 F8
Gannat, France 26 B7
Gannett Peak, U.S.A. 110 E9
Gannvalley, U.S.A. 108 C5
Ganquan, China 50 F5
Gänserdorf, Austria 21 G6
Ganshui, China 52 C6
Gansu □, China 50 G3
Ganta, Liberia 78 D3
Gantheaume, C., Australia .. 91 F2
Gantheaume B., Australia .. 89 E1
Gantsevichi = Hantsavichy, Belarus 41 F4
Ganyem, Indonesia 57 E10
Ganyu, China 51 G10
Ganyushkino, Kazakhstan .. 43 G9
Ganzhou, China 53 E10
Gao, Mali 79 B5
Gao Xian, China 52 C5
Gao'an, China 53 C10
Gaohe, China 53 F9
Gaohebu, China 53 B11
Gaokeng, China 53 D9
Gaolan Dao, China 53 G9
Gaomi, China 51 F10
Gaoligong Shan, China .. 52 E2
Gaoping, China 50 G7
Gaotang, China 50 F9
Gaoua, Burkina Faso 78 C4
Gaoual, Guinea 78 C2
Gaoxiong, Taiwan 53 F13
Gaoyang, China 50 E8
Gaoyou, China 53 A12
Gaoyou Hu, China 51 H10
Gaoyuan, China 51 F9
Gaozhou, China 53 G8
Gap, France 27 D10
Gapan, Phil. 55 D4
Gar, China 54 C2
Garabogazköl Aylagy, Turkmenistan 44 E6
Garachico, Canary Is. 36 F3
Garachiné, Panama 116 E4
Garafia, Canary Is. 36 F2
Garajonay, Canary Is. 36 F2
Garanhuns, Brazil 122 C4
Garawe, Liberia 78 E3
Garba Tula, Kenya 82 B4
Garber, U.S.A. 109 G6
Garberville, U.S.A. 110 F2
Garça, Brazil 123 F2
Garças →, Mato Grosso, Brazil 125 D7
Garças →, Pernambuco, Brazil 122 C4
Garcias, Brazil 125 D7
Gard □, France 27 D8
Gard →, France 27 E8
Garda, L. di, Italy 32 C7
Gardanne, France 27 E9
Garde, L., Canada 101 A7
Gardelegen, Germany 18 C7
Garden City, Kans., U.S.A. .. 108 F4
Garden City, Tex., U.S.A. .. 109 K4
Garden Grove, U.S.A. 113 M9
Gardēz, Afghan. 62 C3
Gardiner, U.S.A. 110 D8

Gardiners I., U.S.A. 107 E12
Gardner, U.S.A. 107 D13
Gardner Canal, Canada 100 C3
Gardnerville, U.S.A. 112 G7
Gare Tigre, Fr. Guiana 121 C7
Garéssio, Italy 32 D5
Garey, U.S.A. 113 L6
Garfield, U.S.A. 110 C5
Gargan, Mt., France 26 C5
Gargano, Mte., Italy 35 A8
Gargouna, Mali 79 B5
Garhshankar, India 62 D7
Garibaldi Prov. Park, Canada 100 D4
Garies, S. Africa 84 E2
Garigliano →, Italy 34 A6
Garissa, Kenya 82 C4
Garissa □, Kenya 82 C5
Garkida, Nigeria 79 C7
Garko, Nigeria 79 C6
Garland, U.S.A. 110 F7
Garlasco, Italy 32 C5
Garm, Tajikistan 44 F8
Garmāb, Iran 65 C8
Garmisch-Partenkirchen, Germany 19 H7
Garmsār, Iran 65 C7
Garner, U.S.A. 108 D8
Garnett, U.S.A. 108 F7
Garo Hills, India 63 G14
Garoe, Somali Rep. 68 F4
Garonne →, France 26 C3
Garonne, Canal Latéral à la →, France 26 D4
Garoua, Cameroon 79 D7
Garrel, Germany 18 C3
Garrigue, France 26 E7
Garrison, Mont., U.S.A. .. 110 C7
Garrison, N. Dak., U.S.A. .. 108 B4
Garrison, Tex., U.S.A. 109 K7
Garrison Res. = Sakakawea, L., U.S.A. . 108 B3
Garrovillas, Spain 31 F4
Garrucha, Spain 29 H3
Garry →, U.K. 14 E5
Garry, L., Canada 96 B9
Garsen, Kenya 82 C5
Garson L., Canada 101 B6
Gartempe →, France 26 B4
Gartz, Germany 18 B10
Garu, Ghana 79 C4
Garub, Namibia 84 D2
Garut, Indonesia 57 G12
Garvão, Portugal 31 H2
Garvie Mts., N.Z. 87 L2
Garwa = Garoua, Cameroon 79 D7
Garwa, India 63 G10
Garwolin, Poland 20 D11
Gary, U.S.A. 104 E2
Garz, Germany 18 A9
Garzón, Colombia 120 C2
Garzê, China 52 B3
Gas-San, Japan 48 E10
Gasan Kuli = Hasan Kuli, Turkmenistan 44 F6
Gascogne, France 26 E4
Gascogne, G. de, Europe .. 28 B2
Gascony = Gascogne, France 26 E4
Gascoyne →, Australia .. 89 D1
Gascoyne Junc. T.O., Australia 89 E2
Gascueña, Spain 28 E2
Gash, Wadi →, Ethiopia .. 77 D4
Gashaka, Nigeria 79 D7
Gasherbrum, Pakistan 63 B7
Gashua, Nigeria 79 C7
Gaspé, Canada 99 C7
Gaspé, C. de, Canada 99 C7
Gaspé, Pén. de, Canada .. 99 C6
Gaspésie, Parc Prov. de la, Canada 99 C6
Gassaway, U.S.A. 104 F5
Gasselte, Neths. 16 C9
Gasselternijveen, Neths. .. 16 C9
Gássino Torinese, Italy .. 32 C4
Gassol, Nigeria 79 D7
Gasteiz = Vitoria, Spain .. 28 C2
Gastonia, U.S.A. 105 H5
Gastoúni, Greece 39 M4
Gastoúri, Greece 39 K2
Gastre, Argentina 128 B3
Gata, C., Cyprus 37 E12
Gata, C. de, Spain 29 J2
Gata, Sierra de, Spain 30 E4
Gataga →, Canada 100 B3
Gătaia, Romania 38 D4
Gatchina, Russia 40 C6
Gates, U.S.A. 106 C7
Gateshead, U.K. 12 C6
Gatesville, U.S.A. 109 K6
Gaths, Zimbabwe 83 G3
Gatico, Chile 126 A1
Gâtinais, France 25 D9
Gâtine, Hauteurs de, France 26 B3
Gatineau →, Canada 98 C4
Gatineau, Parc de la, Canada 98 C4
Gattaran, Phil. 55 B4
Gattinara, Italy 32 C5
Gatun, Panama 116 E4
Gatyana, S. Africa 85 E4
Gau, Fiji 87 D8
Gaucín, Spain 31 J5
Gauer L., Canada 101 B9

Gauhati, India 63 F14
Gauja →, Latvia 9 H21
Gaula →, Norway 8 E14
Gaurain-Ramecroix, Belgium 17 G3
Gausta, Norway 10 E2
Gauteng = P.W.V. □, S. Africa 85 D4
Gavá, Spain 28 D6
Gävakän, Iran 65 D7
Gavarnie, France 26 F3
Gaväter, Iran 65 E9
Gāvbandī, Iran 65 E7
Gavdhopoúla, Greece 37 E6
Gávdhos, Greece 37 E6
Gavere, Belgium 17 G3
Gavião, Portugal 31 F3
Gaviota, U.S.A. 113 L6
Gävle, Sweden 9 F17
Gävleborgs län □, Sweden . 10 C10
Gavorrano, Italy 32 F7
Gavray, France 24 D5
Gavrilov Yam, Russia 42 B4
Gawachab, Namibia 84 D2
Gawilgarh Hills, India 60 J10
Gawler, Australia 91 E2
Gaxun Nur, China 54 B5
Gaya, India 63 G11
Gaya, Niger 79 C5
Gaya, Nigeria 79 C6
Gaylord, U.S.A. 104 C3
Gayndah, Australia 91 D5
Gaysin = Haysyn, Ukraine .. 41 H5
Gayvoron = Hayvoron, Ukraine 41 H5
Gaza, Gaza Strip 69 D3
Gaza □, Mozam. 85 C5
Gaza Strip ■, Asia 69 D3
Gazaoua, Niger 79 C6
Gāzbor, Iran 65 D8
Gazi, Zaïre 82 B1
Gaziantep, Turkey 66 D7
Gazipaşa, Turkey 66 D5
Gazli, Uzbekistan 44 E7
Gbarnga, Liberia 78 D3
Gbekebo, Nigeria 79 D5
Gboko, Nigeria 79 D6
Gbongan, Nigeria 79 D5
Gcuwa, S. Africa 85 E4
Gdańsk, Poland 20 A8
Gdańska, Zatoka, Poland . 20 A9
Gdov, Russia 9 G22
Gdynia, Poland 20 A8
Gebe, Indonesia 57 D7
Gebeit Mine, Sudan 76 C4
Gebel Mûsa, Egypt 76 J8
Gebze, Turkey 66 B3
Gecha, Ethiopia 77 F4
Gedaref, Sudan 77 E4
Gede, Tanjung, Indonesia .. 56 F3
Gedinne, Belgium 17 J5
Gediz, Turkey 66 C3
Gediz →, Turkey 66 C2
Gedo, Ethiopia 77 F4
Gèdre, France 26 F4
Gedser, Denmark 11 K5
Gedser Odde, Denmark .. 11 K5
Geegully Cr. →, Australia .. 88 C3
Geel, Belgium 17 F5
Geelong, Australia 91 F3
Geelvink Chan., Australia .. 89 E1
Geer →, Belgium 17 G7
Geesthacht, Germany 18 B6
Geffen, Neths. 16 E6
Geidam, Nigeria 79 C7
Geikie →, Canada 101 B8
Geili, Sudan 77 D3
Geilo, Norway 10 D2
Geisingen, Germany 19 H4
Geislingen, Germany 19 G5
Geita, Tanzania 82 C3
Geita □, Tanzania 82 C3
Gejiu, China 52 F4
Gel →, Sudan 77 F2
Gel River, Sudan 77 F2
Gela, Italy 35 E7
Gela, G. di, Italy 35 F7
Geladi, Ethiopia 68 F4
Gelderland □, Neths. 16 D8
Geldermalsen, Neths. 16 E6
Geldern, Germany 18 D2
Geldrop, Neths. 17 F7
Geleen, Neths. 17 G7
Gelehun, S. Leone 78 D2
Gelendost, Turkey 66 C4
Gelendzhik, Russia 43 H4
Gelibolu, Turkey 66 B2
Gelnhausen, Germany 19 E5
Gelsenkirchen, Germany .. 18 D3
Gelting, Germany 18 A5
Gemas, Malaysia 59 L4
Gembloux, Belgium 17 G5
Gemena, Zaïre 80 D3
Gemerek, Turkey 66 C7
Gemert, Neths. 17 E7
Gemlik, Turkey 66 B3
Gemona del Friuli, Italy .. 33 B10
Gemsa, Egypt 76 B3
Gemünden, Germany 19 E5
Genale, Ethiopia 77 F5
Genappe, Belgium 17 G4
Genç, Turkey 67 C9
Gençay, France 26 B4
Gendringen, Neths. 16 E8
Gendt, Neths. 16 E7

Geneina, Gebel, Egypt ... 76 J8
General Acha, Argentina . 126 D3
General Alvear, Buenos Aires, Argentina 126 D3
General Alvear, Mendoza, Argentina 126 D2
General Artigas, Paraguay 126 B4
General Belgrano, Argentina 126 D4
General Cabrera, Argentina 126 C3
General Carrera, L., Chile 128 C2
General Cepeda, Mexico . 114 B4
General Conesa, Argentina 128 B4
General Guido, Argentina 126 D4
General Juan Madariaga, Argentina 126 D4
General La Madrid, Argentina 126 D3
General Lorenzo Vintter, Argentina 128 B4
General MacArthur, Phil. . 55 F6
General Martin Miguel de Güemes, Argentina 126 A3
General Paz, Argentina ... 126 B4
General Pico, Argentina ... 126 D3
General Pinedo, Argentina 126 B3
General Pinto, Argentina . 126 C3
General Sampaio, Brazil .. 122 B4
General Santos, Phil. 55 H6
General Toshevo, Bulgaria 38 F11
General Trevino, Mexico . 115 B5
General Trías, Mexico 114 B3
General Viamonte, Argentina 126 D3
General Villegas, Argentina 126 D3
General Vintter, L., Argentina 128 B2
Generoso, Mte., Switz. ... 23 E8
Genesee, Idaho, U.S.A. ... 110 C5
Genesee, Pa., U.S.A. 106 E7
Genesee →, U.S.A. 106 C7
Geneseo, Ill., U.S.A. 108 E9
Geneseo, Kans., U.S.A. .. 108 F5
Geneseo, N.Y., U.S.A. ... 106 D7
Geneva = Genève, Switz. . 22 D2
Geneva, Ala., U.S.A. 105 K3
Geneva, N.Y., U.S.A. 106 D7
Geneva, Nebr., U.S.A. ... 108 E6
Geneva, Ohio, U.S.A. 106 E4
Geneva, L. = Léman, L., Europe 22 D3
Geneva, L., U.S.A. 104 D1
Genève, Switz. 22 D2
Genève □, Switz. 22 D2
Genichesk = Henichesk, Ukraine 41 J8
Genil →, Spain 31 H5
Génissiat, Barr. de, France 27 B9
Genk, Belgium 17 G7
Genlis, France 25 E12
Gennargentu, Mti. del, Italy 34 C2
Gennep, Neths. 17 E7
Gennes, France 24 E6
Genoa = Génova, Italy .. 32 D5
Genoa, Australia 91 F4
Genoa, N.Y., U.S.A. 107 D8
Genoa, Nebr., U.S.A. 108 E6
Genoa, Nev., U.S.A. 112 F7
Genoa →, Argentina 128 B2
Génova, Italy 32 D5
Génova, G. di, Italy 32 E6
Gent, Belgium 17 F3
Gentbrugge, Belgium 17 F3
Genthin, Germany 18 C8
Gentio do Ouro, Brazil .. 122 D3
Geographe B., Australia .. 89 F2
Geographe Chan., Australia 89 D1
Geokchay = Göyçay, Azerbaijan 43 K8
Georga, Zemlya, Russia .. 44 A5
George, S. Africa 84 E3
George →, Canada 99 A6
George, L., N.S.W., Australia 91 F4
George, L., S. Austral., Australia 91 F3
George, L., W. Austral., Australia 88 D3
George, L., Uganda 82 B3
George, L., Fla., U.S.A. .. 105 L5
George, L., N.Y., U.S.A. . 107 C11
George Gill Ra., Australia 88 D5
George River = Kangiqsualujjuaq, Canada 97 C13
George Sound, N.Z. 87 L1
George Town, Bahamas .. 116 B4
George Town, Malaysia .. 59 K3
George V Land, Antarctica 5 C10
George VI Sound, Antarctica 5 D17
George West, U.S.A. 109 L5
Georgetown, Australia 90 B3
Georgetown, Ont., Canada 98 D4
Georgetown, P.E.I., Canada 99 C7
Georgetown, Cayman Is. . 116 C3
Georgetown, Gambia 78 C2
Georgetown, Guyana 121 B6
Georgetown, Calif., U.S.A. 112 G6
Georgetown, Colo., U.S.A. 110 G11
Georgetown, Ky., U.S.A. . 104 F3
Georgetown, S.C., U.S.A. 105 J6

Georgetown, Tex., U.S.A. 109 K6
Georgia □, U.S.A. 105 J4
Georgia ■, Asia 43 J6
Georgia, Str. of, Canada . 100 D4
Georgian B., Canada 98 C3
Georgina →, Australia 90 C2
Georgina Downs, Australia 90 C2
Georgiu-Dezh = Liski, Russia 42 E4
Georgiyevsk, Russia 43 H6
Gera, Germany 18 E8
Geraardsbergen, Belgium . 17 G3
Geral, Serra, Bahia, Brazil 123 D3
Geral, Serra, Goiás, Brazil 122 D2
Geral, Serra, Sta. Catarina, Brazil 127 B6
Geral de Goiás, Serra, Brazil 123 D2
Geral do Paraná, Serra, Brazil 123 E2
Geraldine, U.S.A. 110 C8
Geraldton, Australia 89 E1
Geraldton, Canada 98 C2
Gérardmer, France 25 D13
Gercüş, Turkey 67 D9
Gerede, Turkey 66 B5
Gereshk, Afghan. 60 D4
Gérgal, Spain 29 H2
Gerik, Malaysia 59 K3
Gering, U.S.A. 108 E3
Gerlach, U.S.A. 110 F4
Gerlachovka, Slovak Rep. . 20 F10
Gerlogubi, Ethiopia 68 F4
Germansen Landing, Canada 100 B4
Germany ■, Europe 18 E6
Germersheim, Germany .. 19 F4
Germī, Iran 67 C13
Germiston, S. Africa 85 D4
Gernsheim, Germany 19 F4
Gero, Japan 49 G8
Gerolstein, Germany 19 E2
Gerolzhofen, Germany 19 F6
Gerona, Spain 28 D7
Gerona □, Spain 28 C7
Gérouville, Belgium 17 J6
Gerrard, Canada 100 C5
Gers □, France 26 E4
Gers →, France 26 D4
Gersfeld, Germany 18 E5
Gerze, Turkey 66 B6
Geseke, Germany 18 D4
Geser, Indonesia 57 E8
Gesso →, Italy 32 D4
Gestro, Wabi →, Ethiopia 77 G5
Gesves, Belgium 17 H6
Getafe, Spain 30 E7
Gethsémani, Canada 99 B7
Gettysburg, Pa., U.S.A. .. 104 F7
Gettysburg, S. Dak., U.S.A. 108 C5
Getz Ice Shelf, Antarctica . 5 D14
Geul →, Neths. 17 G7
Gevaş, Turkey 67 C10
Gévaudan, France 26 D7
Gevgelija, Macedonia 39 H5
Gévora →, Spain 31 G4
Gex, France 27 B10
Geyser, U.S.A. 110 C8
Geyserville, U.S.A. 112 G4
Geyve, Turkey 66 B4
Ghâbat el Arab = Wang Kai, Sudan 77 F2
Ghaghara →, India 63 G11
Ghalla, Wadi el →, Sudan 77 E2
Ghallamane, Mauritania .. 74 D3
Ghana ■, W. Afr. 79 D4
Ghansor, India 63 H9
Ghanzi, Botswana 84 C3
Ghanzi □, Botswana 84 C3
Gharb el Istiwa'iya □, Sudan 77 F2
Gharbîya, Es Sahrâ el, Egypt 76 B2
Ghard Abû Muharik, Egypt 76 B2
Ghardaïa, Algeria 75 B5
Ghârib, G., Egypt 76 J8
Gharyān, Libya 75 B7
Gharyān □, Libya 75 B7
Ghat, Libya 75 D7
Ghatal, India 63 H12
Ghatampur, India 63 F9
Ghatti, Si. Arabia 64 D3
Ghawdex = Gozo, Malta . 37 C1
Ghazal, Bahr el →, Chad . 73 F8
Ghazâl, Bahr el →, Sudan 77 F3
Ghazaouet, Algeria 75 A4
Ghaziabad, India 62 E7
Ghazipur, India 63 G10
Ghaznî, Afghan. 62 C3
Ghaznî □, Afghan. 60 C6
Ghedi, Italy 32 C7
Ghèlinsor, Somali Rep. .. 68 F4
Ghent = Gent, Belgium .. 17 F3
Gheorghe Gheorghiu-Dej = Oneşti, Romania 38 C9
Gheorgheni, Romania 38 C8
Ghergani, Romania 38 E8
Gherla, Romania 38 B6
Ghilarza, Italy 34 B1
Ghisonaccia, France 27 F13
Ghisoni, France 27 F13
Ghizao, Afghan. 62 C1
Ghizar →, Pakistan 63 A5
Ghogha, India 62 J5
Ghot Ogrein, Egypt 76 A2
Ghotaru, India 62 F4

Ghotki, *Pakistan* 62 E3
Ghowr □, *Afghan.* 60 C4
Ghudaf, W. al →, *Iraq* . . 67 F10
Ghudāmis, *Libya* 75 B6
Ghughri, *India* 63 H9
Ghugus, *India* 60 K11
Ghulam Mohammad
  Barrage, *Pakistan* 62 G3
Ghūrīān, *Afghan.* 60 B2
Gia Dinh, *Vietnam* 59 G6
Gia Lai = Pleiku, *Vietnam* 58 F7
Gia Nghia, *Vietnam* 59 G6
Gia Ngoc, *Vietnam* 58 E7
Gia Vuc, *Vietnam* 58 E7
Gian, *Phil.* 57 C7
Giannutri, *Italy* 32 F8
Giant Forest, *U.S.A.* . . 112 J8
Giant Mts. = Krkonoše,
  Czech. 20 E5
Giants Causeway, *U.K.* . . 15 A5
Giarabub = Al Jaghbūb,
  Libya 73 C9
Giarre, *Italy* 35 E8
Giaveno, *Italy* 32 C4
Gibara, *Cuba* 116 B4
Gibb River, *Australia* . . . 88 C4
Gibbon, *U.S.A.* 108 E5
Gibe →, *Ethiopia* 77 F4
Gibellina, *Italy* 34 E6
Gibraléon, *Spain* 31 H4
Gibraltar ■, *Europe* 31 J5
Gibraltar, Str. of, *Medit. S.* 31 K5
Gibson Desert, *Australia* . 88 D4
Gibsons, *Canada* 100 D4
Gibsonville, *U.S.A.* 112 F6
Giddings, *U.S.A.* . . 109 K6
Gidole, *Ethiopia* 77 F4
Gien, *France* 25 E9
Giessen, *Germany* 18 E4
Gieten, *Neths.* 16 B9
Gīfān, *Iran* 65 B8
Gifatin, Geziret, *Egypt* . 76 B3
Gifford Creek, *Australia* . 88 D2
Gifhorn, *Germany* 18 C6
Gifu, *Japan* 49 G8
Gifu □, *Japan* 49 G8
Gigant, *Russia* 43 G5
Giganta, Sa. de la, *Mexico* 114 B2
Gigen, *Bulgaria* 38 F7
Gigha, *U.K.* 14 F3
Giglio, *Italy* 32 F7
Gignac, *France* 26 E7
Gigüela →, *Spain* 29 F1
Gijón, *Spain* 30 B5
Gil I., *Canada* 100 C3
Gila →, *U.S.A.* 111 K6
Gila Bend, *U.S.A.* 111 K7
Gila Bend Mts., *U.S.A.* . . 111 K7
Gīlān □, *Iran* 65 B6
Gilbert →, *Australia* 90 B3
Gilbert Is., *Kiribati* 92 G9
Gilbert Plains, *Canada* . . 101 C8
Gilbert River, *Australia* . 90 B3
Gilberton, *Australia* 90 B3
Gilbués, *Brazil* 122 C2
Gilf el Kebîr, Hadabat el,
  Egypt 76 C2
Gilford I., *Canada* 100 C3
Gilgandra, *Australia* 91 E4
Gilgil, *Kenya* 82 C4
Gilgit, *India* 63 B6
Gilgit →, *Pakistan* 63 B6
Giljeva Planina,
  Serbia, Yug. 21 M10
Gillam, *Canada* 101 B10
Gilleleje, *Denmark* 11 H6
Gillen, L., *Australia* 89 E3
Gilles, L., *Australia* 91 E2
Gillette, *U.S.A.* 108 C2
Gilliat, *Australia* 90 C3
Gillingham, *U.K.* 13 F8
Gilly, *Belgium* 17 H4
Gilmer, *U.S.A.* 109 J7
Gilmore, *Australia* 91 F4
Gilmore, L., *Australia* . . . 89 F3
Gilmour, *Canada* 98 D4
Gilo →, *Ethiopia* 77 F3
Gilort →, *Romania* 38 E6
Gilroy, *U.S.A.* 111 H3
Gilze, *Neths.* 17 E5
Gimbi, *Ethiopia* 77 F4
Gimigliano, *Italy* 35 D9
Gimli, *Canada* 101 C9
Gimone →, *France* 26 E5
Gimont, *France* 26 E4
Gin Gin, *Australia* 91 D5
Ginâh, *Egypt* 76 B3
Gindie, *Australia* 90 C4
Gingin, *Australia* 89 F2
Gîngiova, *Romania* 38 F6
Ginir, *Ethiopia* 68 F3
Ginosa, *Italy* 35 B9
Ginzo de Limia, *Spain* . . . 30 C3
Giohar, *Somali Rep.* 68 G4
Gióia, G. di, *Italy* 35 D8
Gióia del Colle, *Italy* 35 B9
Gióia Táuro, *Italy* 35 D8
Gioiosa Iónica, *Italy* 35 D9
Gióna, Óros, *Greece* 39 L5
Giovi, Passo dei, *Italy* . . . 32 D5
Giovinazzo, *Italy* 35 A9
Gir Hills, *India* 62 J4
Girab, *India* 62 F4
Girâfi, W. →, *Egypt* 69 F3
Giraltovce, *Slovak Rep.* . 20 F11
Girard, *Kans., U.S.A.* . . . 109 G7
Girard, *Ohio, U.S.A.* . . . 106 E4

Girard, *Pa., U.S.A.* 106 D4
Girardot, *Colombia* 120 C3
Girdle Ness, *U.K.* 14 D6
Giresun, *Turkey* 67 B8
Girga, *Egypt* 76 B3
Giridih, *India* 63 G12
Girifalco, *Italy* 35 D9
Girilambone, *Australia* . . 91 E4
Girne = Kyrenia, *Cyprus* . 66 E5
Giro, *Nigeria* 79 C5
Giromagny, *France* 25 E13
Girona = Gerona, *Spain* . 28 D7
Gironde □, *France* 26 D3
Gironde →, *France* 26 C2
Gironella, *Spain* 28 C6
Giru, *Australia* 90 B4
Girvan, *U.K.* 14 F4
Gisborne, *N.Z.* 87 H7
Gisenyi, *Rwanda* 82 C2
Gíslaved, *Sweden* 9 H15
Gisors, *France* 25 C8
Gistel, *Belgium* 17 F1
Giswil, *Switz.* 22 C6
Gitega, *Burundi* 82 C2
Gits, *Belgium* 17 F2
Giuba →, *Somali Rep.* . . . 68 G3
Giubiasco, *Switz.* 23 D8
Giugliano in Campania,
  Italy 35 B7
Giulianova, *Italy* 33 F10
Giurgeni, *Romania* 38 E10
Giurgiu, *Romania* 38 F8
Give, *Denmark* 11 J3
Givet, *France* 25 B11
Givors, *France* 27 C8
Givry, *Belgium* 17 H4
Givry, *France* 25 F11
Giyon, *Ethiopia* 77 F4
Giza = El Gîza, *Egypt* . . . 76 H7
Gizhiga, *Russia* 45 C17
Gizhiginskaya Guba, *Russia* 45 C16
Giżycko, *Poland* 20 A11
Gizzeria, *Italy* 35 D9
Gjegjan, *Albania* 39 H3
Gjerstad, *Norway* 10 F3
Gjirokastra, *Albania* 39 J3
Gjoa Haven, *Canada* 96 B10
Gjøl, *Denmark* 11 G3
Gjøvik, *Norway* 10 D4
Glace Bay, *Canada* 99 C8
Glacier Nat. Park, *Canada* 100 C5
Glacier Park, *U.S.A.* 110 B7
Glacier Peak, *U.S.A.* 110 B3
Gladewater, *U.S.A.* 109 J7
Gladstone, *Queens.,*
  Australia 90 C5
Gladstone, *S. Austral.,*
  Australia 91 E2
Gladstone, *W. Austral.,*
  Australia 89 E1
Gladstone, *Canada* 101 C9
Gladstone, *U.S.A.* 104 C2
Gladwin, *U.S.A.* 104 D3
Gladys L., *Canada* 100 B2
Glåma = Glomma →,
  Norway 10 E4
Gláma, *Iceland* 8 D2
Glamis, *U.S.A.* 113 N11
Glamoč, *Bos.-H.* 33 D13
Glan, *Sweden* 11 F10
Glanerbrug, *Neths.* 16 D9
Glarner Alpen, *Switz.* . . . 23 C8
Glärnisch, *Switz.* 23 C7
Glarus, *Switz.* 23 B8
Glarus □, *Switz.* 23 C8
Glasco, *Kans., U.S.A.* . . . 108 F6
Glasco, *N.Y., U.S.A.* . . . 107 D11
Glasgow, *U.K.* 14 F4
Glasgow, *Ky., U.S.A.* . . . 104 G3
Glasgow, *Mont., U.S.A.* . 110 B10
Glastonbury, *U.K.* 13 F5
Glastonbury, *U.S.A.* 107 E12
Glatt →, *Switz.* 23 B7
Glattfelden, *Switz.* 23 A7
Glauchau, *Germany* 18 E8
Glazov, *Russia* 42 A11
Gleiwitz = Gliwice, *Poland* 20 E8
Glen, *U.S.A.* 107 B13
Glen Affric, *U.K.* 14 D4
Glen Canyon Dam, *U.S.A.* 111 H8
Glen Canyon National
  Recreation Area, *U.S.A.* 111 H8
Glen Coe, *U.K.* 14 E3
Glen Cove, *U.S.A.* 107 F11
Glen Garry, *U.K.* 14 D3
Glen Innes, *Australia* . . . 91 D5
Glen Lyon, *U.S.A.* 107 E8
Glen Mor, *U.K.* 14 D4
Glen Moriston, *U.K.* 14 D4
Glen Orchy, *U.K.* 14 E4
Glen Spean, *U.K.* 14 E4
Glen Ullin, *U.S.A.* 108 B4
Glénan, Is. de, *France* . . . 24 E2
Glenburgh, *Australia* 89 E2
Glencoe, *Canada* 106 D3
Glencoe, *S. Africa* 85 D5
Glencoe, *U.S.A.* 108 C7
Glendale, *Ariz., U.S.A.* . . 111 K7
Glendale, *Calif., U.S.A.* . 113 L8
Glendale, *Oreg., U.S.A.* . 110 E2
Glendale, *Zimbabwe* 83 F3
Glendive, *U.S.A.* 108 B2
Glendo, *U.S.A.* 108 D2
Glenelg, *Australia* 91 E2
Glenelg →, *Australia* 91 F3
Glenflorrie, *Australia* 88 D2

Glengarriff, *Ireland* 15 E2
Glengyle, *Australia* 90 C2
Glenmora, *U.S.A.* 109 K8
Glenmorgan, *Australia* . . 91 D4
Glenn, *U.S.A.* 112 F4
Glenns Ferry, *U.S.A.* . . . 110 E6
Glenore, *Australia* 90 B3
Glenorchy, *Australia* 90 G4
Glenore, *Australia* 90 B3
Glenormiston, *Australia* . 90 C2
Glenreagh, *Australia* 91 E5
Glenrock, *U.S.A.* 110 E11
Glenrothes, *U.K.* 14 E5
Glens Falls, *U.S.A.* 107 C11
Glenties, *Ireland* 15 B3
Glenville, *U.S.A.* 104 F5
Glenwood, *Alta., Canada* 100 D6
Glenwood, *Nfld., Canada* . 99 C9
Glenwood, *Ark., U.S.A.* . 109 H8
Glenwood, *Hawaii, U.S.A.* 102 J17
Glenwood, *Iowa, U.S.A.* . 108 E7
Glenwood, *Minn., U.S.A.* 108 C7
Glenwood, *Wash., U.S.A.* 112 D5
Glenwood Springs, *U.S.A.* 110 G10
Gletsch, *Switz.* 23 C6
Glettinganes, *Iceland* 8 D7
Glina, *Croatia* 33 C13
Glittertind, *Norway* 10 C2
Gliwice, *Poland* 20 E8
Globe, *U.S.A.* 111 K8
Głodnitz, *Austria* 21 J4
Głogów, *Poland* 20 D6
Glomma →, *Norway* 10 E4
Glorieuses, Is., *Ind. Oc.* . 85 A8
Glossop, *U.K.* 12 D6
Gloucester, *Australia* . . . 91 E5
Gloucester, *U.K.* 13 F5
Gloucester I., *Australia* . . 90 B4
Gloucestershire □, *U.K.* . 13 F5
Gloversville, *U.S.A.* 107 C10
Glovertown, *Canada* 99 C9
Głowno, *Poland* 20 D9
Głubczyce, *Poland* 20 E7
Glubokiy, *Russia* 43 F5
Glubokoye = Hlybokaye,
  Belarus 40 E4
Głuchołazy, *Poland* 20 E7
Glücksburg, *Germany* . . . 18 A5
Glückstadt, *Germany* 18 B5
Glukhov = Hlukhiv,
  Ukraine 41 G7
Glusk, *Belarus* 41 F5
Glyngøre, *Denmark* 11 H2
Gmünd, *Kärnten, Austria* 21 J3
Gmünd, *Niederösterreich,*
  Austria 20 G5
Gnarp, *Sweden* 10 B11
Gnesta, *Sweden* 10 E11
Gniew, *Poland* 20 B8
Gniezno, *Poland* 20 C7
Gnoien, *Germany* 18 B8
Gnowangerup, *Australia* . 89 F2
Go Cong, *Vietnam* 59 G6
Go Quao, *Vietnam* 59 H5
Goa, *India* 60 M8
Goa □, *India* 60 M8
Goalen Hd., *Australia* . . . 91 F5
Goalpara, *India* 61 F17
Goalundo Ghat, *Bangla.* . 63 H13
Goaso, *Ghana* 78 D4
Goat Fell, *U.K.* 14 F3
Goba, *Ethiopia* 68 F2
Goba, *Mozam.* 85 D5
Gobabis, *Namibia* 84 C2
Gobernador Gregores,
  Argentina 128 C2
Gobi, *Asia* 50 C5
Gobō, *Japan* 49 H7
Gobo, *Sudan* 77 F3
Goch, *Germany* 18 D2
Gochas, *Namibia* 84 C2
Godavari →, *India* 61 L13
Godavari Point, *India* . . . 61 L13
Godbout, *Canada* 99 C6
Godda, *India* 63 G12
Godegård, *Sweden* 11 F9
Goderich, *Canada* 98 D3
Goderville, *France* 24 C7
Godhavn, *Greenland* 4 C5
Godhra, *India* 62 H5
Gödöllő, *Hungary* 21 H9
Godoy Cruz, *Argentina* . . 126 C2
Gods →, *Canada* 101 B10
Gods L., *Canada* 101 C10
Godthåb, *Greenland* 97 B14
Godwin Austen = K2, Mt.,
  Pakistan 63 B7
Goeie Hoop, Kaap die =
  Good Hope, C. of,
  S. Africa 84 E2
Goéland, L. au, *Canada* . . 98 C4
Goeree, *Neths.* 16 E4
Goes, *Neths.* 17 F3
Gogama, *Canada* 98 C3
Gogango, *Australia* 90 C5
Gogebic, L., *U.S.A.* 108 B10
Gogland, Ostrov, *Russia* . 9 F22
Gogra = Ghaghara →,
  India 63 G11
Gogrial, *Sudan* 77 F2
Goiana, *Brazil* 122 C5
Goianésia, *Brazil* 123 E2
Goiânia, *Brazil* 123 E2
Goiás, *Brazil* 123 E1
Goiás □, *Brazil* 122 D2
Goiatuba, *Brazil* 123 E2

Goio-Ere, *Brazil* 127 A5
Goirle, *Neths.* 17 E6
Góis, *Portugal* 30 E2
Gojam □, *Ethiopia* 77 E4
Gojeb, Wabi →, *Ethiopia* 77 F4
Gojō, *Japan* 49 G7
Gojra, *Pakistan* 62 D5
Gokarannath, *India* 63 F9
Gökçeada, *Turkey* 66 B1
Gökırmak →, *Turkey* . . . 66 B6
Göksu →, *Turkey* 66 D6
Göksun, *Turkey* 66 C7
Gokteik, *Burma* 61 H20
Gokurt, *Pakistan* 62 E2
Gola, *India* 63 E9
Golakganj, *India* 63 F13
Golan Heights = Hagolan,
  Syria 69 B4
Golāshkerd, *Iran* 65 E8
Golaya Pristen = Hola
  Pristan, *Ukraine* 41 J7
Gölbaşı, *Adıyaman, Turkey* 66 D7
Gölbaşı, *Ankara, Turkey* . 66 C5
Golchikha, *Russia* 4 B12
Golconda, *U.S.A.* 110 F5
Gölcük, *Kocaeli, Turkey* . 66 B3
Gölcük, *Niğde, Turkey* . . 66 C6
Gold Beach, *U.S.A.* 110 E1
Gold Coast, *Australia* . . . 91 D5
Gold Coast, *W. Afr.* 79 E4
Gold Hill, *U.S.A.* 110 E2
Goldach, *Switz.* 23 B8
Goldau, *Switz.* 23 B7
Goldberg, *Germany* 18 B8
Golden, *Canada* 100 C5
Golden, *U.S.A.* 108 F2
Golden B., *N.Z.* 87 J4
Golden Gate, *U.S.A.* 110 H2
Golden Hinde, *Canada* . . 100 D3
Golden Lake, *Canada* . . . 106 A7
Golden Prairie, *Canada* . . 101 C7
Golden Vale, *Ireland* 15 D3
Goldendale, *U.S.A.* 110 D3
Goldfield, *U.S.A.* 111 H5
Goldfields, *Canada* 101 B7
Goldsand L., *Canada* 101 B8
Goldsboro, *U.S.A.* 105 H7
Goldsmith, *U.S.A.* 109 K3
Goldsworthy, *Australia* . . 88 D2
Goldthwaite, *U.S.A.* 109 K5
Goleǧā, *Portugal* 31 F2
Goleniów, *Poland* 20 B4
Golestānak, *Iran* 65 D7
Goleta, *U.S.A.* 113 L7
Golfito, *Costa Rica* 116 E3
Golfo Aranci, *Italy* 34 B2
Gölgeli Dağları, *Turkey* . 66 D3
Goliad, *U.S.A.* 109 L6
Golija, *Serbia, Yug.* 21 M10
Gölköy, *Turkey* 66 B7
Golo →, *France* 27 F13
Golpāyegān, *Iran* 65 C6
Gölpazarı, *Turkey* 66 B4
Golra, *Pakistan* 62 C5
Golspie, *U.K.* 14 D5
Golyama Kamchiya →,
  Bulgaria 38 F10
Goma, *Rwanda* 82 C2
Goma, *Zaïre* 82 C2
Gomati →, *India* 63 G10
Gombari, *Zaïre* 82 B2
Gombe, *Nigeria* 79 C7
Gombe →, *Tanzania* 82 C3
Gombi, *Nigeria* 79 C7
Gomel = Homyel, *Belarus* 41 F6
Gomera, *Canary Is.* 36 F2
Gómez Palacio, *Mexico* . . 114 B4
Gomīshān, *Iran* 65 B7
Gommern, *Germany* 18 C7
Gomogomo, *Indonesia* . . 57 F8
Gomoh, *India* 61 H15
Gompa = Ganta, *Liberia* . 78 D3
Goms, *Switz.* 22 D6
Gonābād, *Iran* 65 C8
Gonaïves, *Haiti* 117 C5
Gonâve, G. de la, *Haiti* . . 117 C5
Gonâve, I. de la, *Haiti* . . . 117 C5
Gonbad-e Kāvūs, *Iran* . . . 65 B7
Gonda, *India* 63 F9
Gondal, *India* 62 J4
Gonder, *Ethiopia* 77 E4
Gonder □, *Ethiopia* 77 E4
Gondia, *India* 60 J12
Gondola, *Mozam.* 83 F3
Gondomar, *Portugal* 30 D2
Gondomar, *Spain* 30 C2
Gondrecourt-le-Château,
  France 25 D12
Gönen, *Turkey* 66 B2
Gong Xian, *China* 52 C5
Gong'an, *China* 53 B9
Gongcheng, *China* 53 E8
Gongga Shan, *China* 52 C3
Gongguan, *China* 52 G7
Gonghe, *China* 54 C5
Gongola →, *Nigeria* 79 D7
Gongolgon, *Australia* . . . 91 E4
Gongshan, *China* 52 D2
Gongtan, *China* 52 C7
Goniadz, *Poland* 20 B12
Goniri, *Nigeria* 79 C7
Gonjo, *China* 52 B2
Gonnesa, *Italy* 34 C1
Gónnos, *Greece* 39 K5
Gonnosfanádiga, *Italy* . . . 34 C1
Gonzaga, *Phil.* 55 B5
Gonzales, *Calif., U.S.A.* . 111 H3

Gonzales, *Tex., U.S.A.* . . . 109 L6
González Chaves,
  Argentina 126 D3
Good Hope, C. of,
  S. Africa 84 E2
Gooderham, *Canada* 98 D4
Goodeve, *Canada* 101 C8
Gooding, *U.S.A.* 110 E6
Goodland, *U.S.A.* 108 F4
Goodnight, *U.S.A.* 109 H4
Goodooga, *Australia* 91 D4
Goodsoil, *Canada* 101 C7
Goodsprings, *U.S.A.* 111 J6
Goole, *U.K.* 12 D7
Goolgowi, *Australia* 91 E4
Goomalling, *Australia* . . . 89 F2
Goombalie, *Australia* 91 D4
Goonda, *Mozam.* 83 F3
Goondiwindi, *Australia* . . 91 D5
Goongarrie, L., *Australia* . 89 F3
Goonyella, *Australia* 90 C4
Goor, *Neths.* 16 D9
Gooray, *Australia* 91 D5
Goose →, *Canada* 99 B7
Goose L., *U.S.A.* 110 F3
Gop, *India* 60 H6
Gopalganj, *India* 63 F11
Goppenstein, *Switz.* 22 D5
Göppingen, *Germany* 19 G5
Gor, *Spain* 29 H2
Góra, *Poland* 20 D6
Gorakhpur, *India* 63 F10
Gorbatov, *Russia* 42 B6
Gorbea, Peña, *Spain* 28 B2
Gorda, *U.S.A.* 112 K5
Gorda, Pta., *Canary Is.* . . 36 F2
Gorda, Pta., *Nic.* 116 D3
Gordan B., *Australia* 88 B5
Gordon, *U.S.A.* 108 D3
Gordon →, *Australia* 90 G4
Gordon, I., *Chile* 128 D3
Gordon Downs, *Australia* 88 C4
Gordon L., *Alta., Canada* 101 B6
Gordon L., *N.W.T.,*
  Canada 100 A6
Gordonvale, *Australia* . . . 90 B4
Gore, *Australia* 91 D5
Goré, *Chad* 73 G8
Gore, *Ethiopia* 77 F4
Gore, *N.Z.* 87 M2
Gore Bay, *Canada* 98 C3
Görele, *Turkey* 67 B8
Goreme, *Turkey* 66 C6
Gorey, *Ireland* 15 D5
Gorg, *Iran* 65 D8
Gorgān, *Iran* 65 B7
Gorgona, isola, *Italy* 32 E6
Gorgora, *Ethiopia* 77 E4
Gorham, *U.S.A.* 107 B13
Gori, *Georgia* 43 J7
Gorinchem, *Neths.* 16 E5
Gorinhatã, *Brazil* 123 E2
Goris, *Armenia* 67 C12
Goritsy, *Russia* 42 B3
Gorízia, *Italy* 33 C10
Gorki = Horki, *Belarus* . . 40 E6
Gorki = Nizhniy
  Novgorod, *Russia* 42 B7
Gorkiy = Nizhniy
  Novgorod, *Russia* 42 B7
Gorkovskoye Vdkhr.,
  Russia 42 B6
Gørlev, *Denmark* 11 J5
Gorlice, *Poland* 20 F11
Görlitz, *Germany* 18 D10
Gorlovka = Horlivka,
  Ukraine 41 H10
Gorman, *Calif., U.S.A.* . . 113 L8
Gorman, *Tex., U.S.A.* . . . 109 J5
Gorna Dzhumayo =
  Blagoevgrad, *Bulgaria* . 39 G6
Gorna Oryakhovitsa,
  Bulgaria 38 F8
Gorna Radgona, *Slovenia* 33 B13
Gornja Tuzla, *Bos.-H.* . . . 21 L8
Gornji Grad, *Slovenia* . . . 33 B11
Gornji Milanovac,
  Serbia, Yug. 21 M10
Gornji Vakuf, *Bos.-H.* . . . 21 M7
Gorno-Altay □, *Russia* . . 44 D9
Gorno-Altaysk, *Russia* . . 44 D9
Gorno Slinkino =
  Gornopravdinsk, *Russia* 44 C8
Gornopravdinsk, *Russia* . 44 C8
Gornyatskiy, *Russia* 43 F5
Gornyi, *Russia* 48 B6
Gornyy, *Russia* 42 E9
Gorodenka = Horodenka,
  Ukraine 41 H3
Gorodets, *Russia* 42 B6
Gorodishche =
  Horodyshche, *Ukraine* . 41 H6
Gorodishche, *Russia* 42 D7
Gorodnya = Horodnya,
  Ukraine 41 G6
Gorodok = Haradok,
  Belarus 40 E6
Gorodok = Horodok,
  Ukraine 41 H2
Gorodovikovsk, *Russia* . . 43 G5
Gorokhov = Horokhiv,
  Ukraine 41 G3
Gorokhovets, *Russia* 42 B6
Gorom Gorom,
  Burkina Faso 79 C4
Goromonzi, *Zimbabwe* . . 83 F3
Gorongose →, *Mozam.* . . 85 C5

Gorongoza, Mozam. 83 F3
Gorongoza, Sa. da, Mozam. 83 F3
Gorontalo, Indonesia .. 57 D6
Goronyo, Nigeria 79 C6
Gorredijk, Neths. 16 C8
Gorron, France 24 D6
Gorshechnoye, Russia .. 42 E4
Gorssel, Neths. 16 D8
Gort, Ireland 15 C3
Gortis, Greece 37 D6
Goryachiy Klyuch, Russia . 43 H4
Gorzkowice, Poland 20 D9
Gorzów Śląski, Poland .. 20 D8
Gorzów Wielkopolski, Poland 20 C5
Göschenen, Switz. 23 C7
Gosford, Australia 91 E5
Goshen, Calif., U.S.A. .. 112 J7
Goshen, Ind., U.S.A. ... 104 E3
Goshen, N.Y., U.S.A. .. 107 E10
Goshogawara, Japan ... 48 D10
Goslar, Germany 18 D6
Gospič, Croatia 33 D12
Gosport, U.K. 13 G6
Gossau, Switz. 23 B8
Gosse →, Australia 90 B1
Gostivar, Macedonia ... 39 H3
Gostyń, Poland 20 D7
Gostynin, Poland 20 C9
Göta älv →, Sweden 11 G5
Göta kanal, Sweden 9 G16
Götaland, Sweden 9 G15
Göteborg, Sweden 11 G5
Götene, Sweden 11 F7
Gotha, Germany 18 E6
Gothenburg = Göteborg, Sweden 11 G5
Gothenburg, U.S.A. ... 108 E4
Gotland, Sweden 9 H18
Gotse Delchev, Bulgaria . 39 H6
Gotska Sandön, Sweden . 9 G18
Gōtsu, Japan 49 G6
Göttingen, Germany ... 18 D5
Gottwald = Zmiyev, Ukraine 41 H9
Gottwaldov = Zlín, Czech. 20 F7
Goubangzi, China 51 D11
Gouda, Neths. 16 D5
Goúdhoura, Ákra, Greece 37 E8
Goudiry, Senegal 78 C2
Gough I., Atl. Oc. 2 G9
Gouin, Rés., Canada ... 98 C5
Gouitafla, Ivory C. 78 D3
Goulburn, Australia ... 91 E4
Goulburn Is., Australia . 90 A1
Goulia, Ivory C. 78 C3
Goulimine, Morocco ... 74 C3
Goulmina, Morocco ... 74 B4
Gounou-Gaya, Chad ... 73 G9
Goúra, Greece 39 M5
Gouraya, Algeria 75 A5
Gourdon, France 26 D5
Gouré, Niger 79 C7
Gouri, Chad 73 E8
Gourits →, S. Africa ... 84 E3
Gourma Rharous, Mali . 79 B4
Goúrnais, Greece 37 D7
Goursi, Burkina Faso .. 78 C4
Gournay-en-Bray, France . 25 C8
Gourock Ra., Australia . 91 F4
Gouverneur, U.S.A. ... 107 B9
Gouviá, Greece 37 A3
Gouzon, France 26 B6
Govan, Canada 101 C8
Governador Valadares, Brazil 123 E3
Governor's Harbour, Bahamas 116 A4
Gowan Ra., Australia .. 90 C4
Gowanda, U.S.A. 106 D6
Gowd-e Zirreh, Afghan. . 60 E3
Gower, U.K. 13 F3
Gowna, L., Ireland 15 C4
Goya, Argentina 126 B4
Göyçay, Azerbaijan 43 K8
Goyder Lagoon, Australia 91 D2
Goyllarisquisga, Peru .. 124 C2
Göynük, Turkey 66 B4
Goz Beïda, Chad 73 F9
Goz Regeb, Sudan 77 D4
Gozo, Malta 37 C1
Graaff-Reinet, S. Africa . 84 E3
Grabow, Germany 18 B7
Grabs, Switz. 23 B8
Gračac, Croatia 33 D12
Gračanica, Bos.-H. 21 L8
Graçay, France 25 E8
Grace, U.S.A. 110 E8
Graceville, U.S.A. 108 C6
Gracias a Dios, C., Honduras 116 C3
Graciosa, I., Canary Is. . 36 E6
Gradaús, Brazil 122 C1
Gradaús, Serra dos, Brazil 122 C1
Gradets, Bulgaria 38 G9
Grado, Italy 33 C10
Grado, Spain 30 B4
Gradule, Australia 91 D4
Grady, U.S.A. 109 H3
Graeca, Lacul, Romania . 38 E9
Grafenau, Germany ... 19 G9
Gräfenberg, Germany .. 19 F7
Grafton, Australia 91 D5
Grafton, U.S.A. 108 A6
Gragnano, Italy 35 B7

Graham, Canada 98 C1
Graham, N.C., U.S.A. .. 105 G6
Graham, Tex., U.S.A. .. 109 J5
Graham →, Canada ... 100 B4
Graham, Mt., U.S.A. .. 111 K9
Graham Bell, Os., Russia . 44 A7
Graham I., Canada 100 C2
Graham Land, Antarctica . 5 C17
Grahamdale, Canada .. 101 C9
Grahamstown, S. Africa . 84 E4
Graïba, Tunisia 75 B7
Graide, Belgium 17 J6
Graie, Alpi, Europe ... 32 C4
Grain Coast, W. Afr. .. 78 E3
Grajaú, Brazil 122 C2
Grajaú →, Brazil 122 B3
Grajewo, Poland 20 B12
Gramada, Bulgaria 38 F5
Gramat, France 26 D5
Grammichele, Italy 35 E7
Grampian □, U.K. 14 D6
Grampian Highlands = Grampian Mts., U.K. . 14 E5
Grampian Mts., U.K. .. 14 E5
Gran →, Surinam 121 C6
Gran Altiplanicie Central, Argentina 128 C3
Gran Canaria, Canary Is. . 36 F4
Gran Chaco, S. Amer. . 126 B3
Gran Paradiso, Italy ... 32 C4
Gran Sasso d'Italia, Italy . 33 F10
Granada, Nic. 116 D2
Granada, Spain 29 H1
Granada, U.S.A. 109 F3
Granada □, Spain 31 H7
Granadilla de Abona, Canary Is. 36 F3
Granard, Ireland 15 C4
Granbury, U.S.A. 109 J6
Granby, Canada 98 C5
Grand →, Mo., U.S.A. . 108 F8
Grand →, S. Dak., U.S.A. . 108 C4
Grand Bahama, Bahamas 116 A4
Grand Bank, Canada .. 99 C8
Grand Bassam, Ivory C. . 78 D4
Grand Béréby, Ivory C. .. 78 E3
Grand-Bourg, Guadeloupe 117 C7
Grand Canal = Yun Ho →, China 51 E9
Grand Canyon, U.S.A. .. 111 H7
Grand Canyon National Park, U.S.A. 111 H7
Grand Cayman, Cayman Is. 116 C3
Grand Cess, Liberia ... 78 E3
Grand Coulee, U.S.A. .. 110 C4
Grand Coulee Dam, U.S.A. 110 C4
Grand Erg Occidental, Algeria 75 B5
Grand Erg Oriental, Algeria 75 C6
Grand Falls, Canada ... 99 C8
Grand Forks, Canada .. 100 D5
Grand Forks, U.S.A. ... 108 B6
Grand-Fougeray, France . 24 E5
Grand Haven, U.S.A. .. 104 D2
Grand I., U.S.A. 104 B2
Grand Island, U.S.A. .. 108 E5
Grand Isle, U.S.A. 109 L10
Grand Junction, U.S.A. . 111 G9
Grand L., N.B., Canada . 99 C6
Grand L., Nfld., Canada . 99 C8
Grand L., Nfld., Canada . 99 B7
Grand L., U.S.A. 109 L8
Grand Lac Victoria, Canada 98 C4
Grand Lahou, Ivory C. . 78 D3
Grand Lake, U.S.A. ... 110 F11
Grand-Leez, Belgium .. 17 G5
Grand-Lieu, L. de, France 24 E5
Grand Manan I., Canada . 99 D6
Grand Marais, Canada . 108 B9
Grand Marais, U.S.A. .. 104 B3
Grand-Mère, Canada .. 98 C5
Grand Popo, Benin ... 79 D5
Grand Portage, U.S.A. . 98 C2
Grand Rapids, Canada . 101 C9
Grand Rapids, Mich., U.S.A. 104 D2
Grand Rapids, Minn., U.S.A. 108 B8
Grand St.-Bernard, Col du, Europe 22 E4
Grand Santi, Fr. Guiana . 121 C7
Grand Teton, U.S.A. .. 110 E8
Grand Valley, U.S.A. .. 110 G9
Grand View, Canada .. 101 C8
Grandas de Salime, Spain . 30 B4
Grande →, Jujuy, Argentina 126 A2
Grande →, Mendoza, Argentina 126 D2
Grande →, Bolivia 125 D5
Grande →, Bahia, Brazil 122 D3
Grande →, Minas Gerais, Brazil 123 F1
Grande →, Spain 29 F4
Grande →, Venezuela . 121 B5
Grande, B., Argentina . 128 D3
Grande, I., Brazil 123 F3
Grande, Rio →, U.S.A. . 109 N6
Grande, Serra, Piauí, Brazil 122 C2
Grande, Serra, Tocantins, Brazil 122 D2
Grande Baie, Canada ... 99 C5

Grande Baleine, R. de la →, Canada 98 A4
Grande Cache, Canada . 100 C5
Grande de Santiago →, Mexico 114 C3
Grande Dixence, Barr. de la, Switz. 22 D4
Grande-Entrée, Canada . 99 C7
Grande Prairie, Canada . 100 B5
Grande-Rivière, Canada . 99 C7
Grande Sauldre →, France 25 E9
Grande-Vallée, Canada .. 99 C6
Grandes-Bergeronnes, Canada 99 C6
Grandfalls, U.S.A. 109 K3
Grandoe Mines, Canada . 100 B3
Grândola, Portugal ... 31 G2
Grandpré, France 25 C11
Grandson, Switz. 22 C3
Grandview, U.S.A. 110 C4
Grandvilliers, France .. 25 C8
Graneros, Chile 126 C1
Grangemouth, U.K. ... 14 E5
Granger, Wash., U.S.A. . 110 C3
Granger, Wyo., U.S.A. . 110 F9
Grangeville, U.S.A. ... 110 D5
Granite City, U.S.A. .. 108 F9
Granite Falls, U.S.A. .. 108 C7
Granite Mt., U.S.A. ... 113 M10
Granite Peak, Australia . 89 E3
Granite Peak, U.S.A. .. 110 D9
Granity, N.Z. 87 J3
Granja, Brazil 122 B3
Granja de Moreruela, Spain 30 D5
Granja de Torrehermosa, Spain 31 G5
Granollers, Spain 28 D7
Gransee, Germany 18 B9
Grant, U.S.A. 108 E4
Grant, Mt., U.S.A. 110 G4
Grant City, U.S.A. 108 E7
Grant I., Australia 88 B5
Grant Range, U.S.A. .. 111 G6
Grantham, U.K. 12 E7
Grantown-on-Spey, U.K. . 14 D5
Grants, U.S.A. 111 J10
Grants Pass, U.S.A. ... 110 E2
Grantsburg, U.S.A. ... 108 C8
Grantsville, U.S.A. ... 110 F7
Granville, France 24 D5
Granville, N. Dak., U.S.A. . 108 A4
Granville, N.Y., U.S.A. . 104 D9
Granville L., Canada .. 101 B8
Grao de Gandía, Spain . 29 F4
Grapeland, U.S.A. 109 K7
Gras, L. de, Canada ... 96 B8
Graskop, S. Africa 85 C5
Grass →, Canada 101 B9
Grass Range, U.S.A. .. 110 C9
Grass River Prov. Park, Canada 101 C8
Grass Valley, Calif., U.S.A. 112 F6
Grass Valley, Oreg., U.S.A. 110 D3
Grassano, Italy 35 B9
Grasse, France 27 E10
Grassmere, Australia .. 91 E3
Graubünden □, Switz. . 23 C9
Graulhet, France 26 E5
Graus, Spain 28 C5
Gravatá, Brazil 122 C4
Grave, Neths. 16 E7
Grave, Pte. de, France . 26 C2
's-Graveland, Neths. ... 16 D6
Gravelbourg, Canada .. 101 D7
Gravelines, France 25 B9
's-Gravendeel, Neths. .. 16 E5
's-Gravenhage, Neths. .. 16 D4
Gravenhurst, Canada .. 106 B5
's-Gravenpolder, Neths. . 17 F3
's-Gravensande, Neths. . 16 D4
Gravesend, Australia .. 91 D5
Gravesend, U.K. 13 F8
Gravina di Púglia, Italy . 35 B9
Gravois, Pointe-à-, Haiti . 117 C5
Gravone →, France ... 27 G12
Gray, France 25 E12
Grayling, U.S.A. 104 C3
Grayling →, Canada .. 100 B3
Grays Harbor, U.S.A. .. 110 C1
Grays L., U.S.A. 110 E8
Grays River, U.S.A. ... 112 D3
Grayson, Canada 101 C8
Grayvoron, Russia 42 E2
Graz, Austria 21 H5
Grazalema, Spain 31 J5
Greasy L., Canada 100 A4
Great Abaco I., Bahamas 116 A4
Great Artesian Basin, Australia 90 C3
Great Australian Bight, Australia 89 F5
Great Bahama Bank, Bahamas 116 B4
Great Barrier I., N.Z. .. 87 G5
Great Barrier Reef, Australia 90 B4
Great Barrington, U.S.A. . 107 D11
Great Basin, U.S.A. ... 110 G5
Great Bear →, Canada . 96 B7
Great Bear L., Canada . 96 B7
Great Belt = Store Bælt, Denmark 11 J5
Great Bend, Kans., U.S.A. 108 F5
Great Bend, Pa., U.S.A. . 107 E9
Great Blasket I., Ireland .. 15 D1

Great Britain, Europe 6 E5
Great Central, Canada ... 100 D3
Great Dividing Ra., Australia 90 C4
Great Driffield = Driffield, U.K. 12 C7
Great Exuma I., Bahamas 116 B4
Great Falls, Canada ... 101 C9
Great Falls, U.S.A. ... 110 C8
Great Fish = Groot Vis →, S. Africa ... 84 E4
Great Guana Cay, Bahamas 116 B4
Great Harbour Deep, Canada 99 B8
Great I., Canada 101 B9
Great Inagua I., Bahamas 117 B5
Great Indian Desert = Thar Desert, India ... 62 F4
Great Karoo, S. Africa .. 84 E3
Great Lake, Australia .. 90 G4
Great Malvern, U.K. .. 13 E5
Great Ormes Head, U.K. . 12 D4
Great Ouse →, U.K. .. 12 E8
Great Palm I., Australia . 90 B4
Great Plains, N. Amer. . 102 A6
Great Ruaha →, Tanzania 82 D4
Great Saint Bernard P. = Grand St.-Bernard, Col du, Europe 22 E4
Great Salt L., U.S.A. .. 110 F7
Great Salt Lake Desert, U.S.A. 110 F7
Great Salt Plains L., U.S.A. 109 G5
Great Sandy Desert, Australia 88 D3
Great Sangi = Sangihe, P., Indonesia 57 D7
Great Scarcies →, S. Leone 78 D2
Great Slave L., Canada .. 100 A5
Great Smoky Mts. Nat. Pk., U.S.A. 105 H4
Great Stour = Stour →, U.K. 13 F9
Great Victoria Desert, Australia 89 E4
Great Wall, China 50 E5
Great Whernside, U.K. . 12 C6
Great Yarmouth, U.K. . 12 E9
Greater Antilles, W. Indies 117 C5
Greater London □, U.K. . 13 F7
Greater Manchester □, U.K. 12 D5
Greater Sunda Is., Indonesia 56 F4
Grebbestad, Sweden .. 11 F5
Grebenka = Hrebenka, Ukraine 41 G7
Greco, C., Cyprus 37 E13
Greco, Mte., Italy 34 A6
Gredos, Sierra de, Spain . 30 E5
Greece, U.S.A. 106 C7
Greece ■, Europe 39 K6
Greeley, Colo., U.S.A. . 108 E2
Greeley, Nebr., U.S.A. . 108 E5
Green →, Ky., U.S.A. . 104 G2
Green →, Utah, U.S.A. . 111 G9
Green B., U.S.A. 104 C2
Green Bay, U.S.A. 104 C2
Green C., Australia ... 91 F5
Green Cove Springs, U.S.A. 105 L5
Green River, U.S.A. ... 111 G8
Greenbank, U.S.A. ... 112 B4
Greenbush, Mich., U.S.A. 106 B1
Greenbush, Minn., U.S.A. 108 A6
Greencastle, U.S.A. ... 104 F2
Greene, U.S.A. 107 D9
Greenfield, Calif., U.S.A. . 112 J5
Greenfield, Calif., U.S.A. . 113 K8
Greenfield, Ind., U.S.A. . 104 F3
Greenfield, Iowa, U.S.A. . 108 E7
Greenfield, Mass., U.S.A. 107 D12
Greenfield, Mo., U.S.A. . 109 G8
Greenfield Park, Canada . 107 A11
Greenland ■, N. Amer. . 4 C5
Greenland Sea, Arctic ... 4 B7
Greenock, U.K. 14 F4
Greenore, Ireland 15 B5
Greenore Pt., Ireland .. 15 D5
Greenough →, Australia . 89 E1
Greenport, U.S.A. 107 E12
Greensboro, Ga., U.S.A. . 105 J4
Greensboro, N.C., U.S.A. . 105 G6
Greensburg, Ind., U.S.A. . 104 F3
Greensburg, Kans., U.S.A. 109 G5
Greensburg, Pa., U.S.A. . 106 F5
Greenville, Liberia ... 78 D3
Greenville, Ala., U.S.A. . 105 K2
Greenville, Calif., U.S.A. . 112 E6
Greenville, Ill., U.S.A. . 108 F10
Greenville, Maine, U.S.A. 99 C6
Greenville, Mich., U.S.A. 104 D3
Greenville, Miss., U.S.A. 109 J9
Greenville, N.C., U.S.A. . 105 H7
Greenville, Ohio, U.S.A. . 104 E3
Greenville, Pa., U.S.A. .. 106 E4
Greenville, S.C., U.S.A. . 105 H4
Greenville, Tenn., U.S.A. 105 G4
Greenville, Tex., U.S.A. . 109 J6
Greenwater Lake Prov. Park, Canada 101 C8
Greenwich, U.K. 13 F8
Greenwich, Conn., U.S.A. 107 E11
Greenwich, N.Y., U.S.A. . 107 C11

Greenwich, Ohio, U.S.A. 106 E2
Greenwood, Canada ... 100 D5
Greenwood, Miss., U.S.A. 109 J9
Greenwood, S.C., U.S.A. 105 H4
Greenwood, Mt., Australia 88 B5
Gregório →, Brazil ... 124 B3
Gregory, U.S.A. 108 D5
Gregory →, Australia . 90 B2
Gregory, L., S. Austral., Australia 91 D2
Gregory, L., W. Austral., Australia 89 D3
Gregory Downs, Australia 90 B2
Gregory L., Australia .. 88 D4
Gregory Ra., Queens., Australia 90 B3
Gregory Ra., W. Austral., Australia 88 D3
Greiffenberg, Germany .. 18 B9
Greifswald, Germany .. 18 A9
Greifswalder Bodden, Germany 18 A9
Grein, Austria 21 G4
Greiz, Germany 18 E8
Gremikha, Russia 44 C4
Grenå, Denmark 11 H4
Grenada, U.S.A. 109 J10
Grenada ■, W. Indies . 117 D7
Grenade, France 26 E5
Grenadines, W. Indies . 117 D7
Grenchen, Switz. 22 B4
Grenen, Denmark 11 G4
Grenfell, Australia ... 91 E4
Grenfell, Canada 101 C8
Grenoble, France 27 C9
Grenora, U.S.A. 108 A3
Grenville, C., Australia . 90 A3
Grenville Chan., Canada . 100 C3
Gréoux-les-Bains, France . 27 E9
Gresham, U.S.A. 112 E4
Gresik, Indonesia 57 G15
Gréssoney St. Jean, Italy . 32 C4
Gretna Green, U.K. ... 14 F5
Grevelingen Krammer, Neths. 16 E4
Greven, Germany 18 C3
Grevená, Greece 39 J4
Grevenbroich, Germany . 18 D2
Grevenmacher, Lux. ... 17 J8
Grevesmühlen, Germany . 18 B7
Grevie, Sweden 11 H6
Grey →, N.Z. 87 K3
Grey, C., Australia ... 90 A2
Grey Ra., Australia ... 91 D3
Grey Res., Canada ... 99 C8
Greybull, U.S.A. 110 D9
Greymouth, N.Z. 87 K3
Greytown, N.Z. 87 J5
Greytown, S. Africa .. 85 D5
Gribanovskiy, Russia .. 42 E5
Gribbell I., Canada ... 100 C3
Gridley, U.S.A. 112 F5
Griekwastad, S. Africa . 84 D3
Griffin, U.S.A. 105 J3
Griffith, Australia 91 E4
Grijpskerk, Neths. 16 B8
Grillby, Sweden 10 E11
Grimari, C.A.R. 73 G9
Grimaylov = Hrymayliv, Ukraine 41 H4
Grimbergen, Belgium . 17 G4
Grimes, U.S.A. 112 F5
Grimma, Germany 18 D8
Grimmen, Germany .. 18 A9
Grimsby, Canada 106 C5
Grimsby, U.K. 12 D7
Grimselpass, Switz. ... 23 C6
Grímsey, Iceland 8 C5
Grimshaw, Canada ... 100 B5
Grimstad, Norway 11 F2
Grindelwald, Switz. ... 22 C6
Grindsted, Denmark .. 11 J2
Grindu, Romania 38 E9
Grinnell, U.S.A. 108 E8
Griñón, Spain 30 E7
Grintavec, Slovenia ... 33 B11
Grip, Norway 10 A1
Gris-Nez, C., France .. 25 B8
Grisolles, France 26 E5
Grisons = Graubünden □, Switz. 23 C9
Grivegnée, Belgium ... 17 G7
Grmeč Planina, Bos.-H. . 33 D13
Groais I., Canada 99 B8
Groblersdal, S. Africa . 85 D4
Grobming, Austria ... 21 H3
Grodno = Hrodna, Belarus 40 F2
Grodzisk Mazowiecki, Poland 20 C10
Grodzisk Wielkopolski, Poland 20 C6
Grodzyanka = Hrodzyanka, Belarus 40 F5
Groenlo, Neths. 16 D9
Groesbeck, U.S.A. 109 K6
Groesbeek, Neths. 16 E7
Groix, France 24 E3
Groix, Î. de, France ... 24 E3
Grójec, Poland 20 D10
Grolloo, Neths. 16 C9
Gronau, Niedersachsen, Germany 18 C5
Gronau, Nordrhein-Westfalen, Germany 18 C3
Grong, Norway 8 D15
Groningen, Neths. 16 B9

Groningen

Groningen, Surinam 121 B6
Groningen □, Neths. 16 B9
Groninger Wad, Neths. 16 B9
Gronsveld, Neths. 17 G7
Groom, U.S.A. 109 H4
Groot →, S. Africa 84 E3
Groot Berg →, S. Africa 84 E2
Groot-Brakrivier, S. Africa 84 E3
Groot-Kei →, S. Africa 85 E4
Groot Vis →, S. Africa 84 E4
Groote Eylandt, Australia 90 A2
Grootebroek, Neths. 16 C6
Grootfontein, Namibia 84 B2
Grootlaagte →, Africa 84 C3
Grootvloer →, S. Africa 84 E3
Gros C., Canada 100 A6
Grosa, Pta., Spain 36 B8
Grósio, Italy 32 B7
Grosne →, France 27 B8
Gross Glockner, Austria 21 H2
Grossenbrode, Germany 18 A7
Grossenhain, Germany 18 D9
Grosseto, Italy 32 F8
Groswater B., Canada 99 B8
Grote Gette →, Neths. 17 G6
Grote Nete →, Belgium 17 F5
Groton, Conn., U.S.A. 107 E12
Groton, S. Dak., U.S.A. 108 C5
Grottáglie, Italy 35 B10
Grottaminarda, Italy 35 A8
Grottammare, Italy 33 F10
Grouard Mission, Canada 100 B5
Grouin, Pte. du, France 24 D5
Groundhog →, Canada 98 C3
Grouse Creek, U.S.A. 110 F7
Grouw, Neths. 16 B7
Grove City, U.S.A. 106 E4
Groveland, U.S.A. 112 H6
Grover City, U.S.A. 113 K6
Groveton, N.H., U.S.A. 107 B13
Groveton, Tex., U.S.A. 109 K7
Grožnjan, Croatia 33 C10
Groznyy, Russia 43 J7
Grubbenvorst, Neths. 17 F8
Grudziądz, Poland 20 B8
Gruissan, France 26 E7
Grumo Áppula, Italy 35 A9
Grünberg, Germany 18 E4
Grundy Center, U.S.A. 108 D8
Gruver, U.S.A. 109 G4
Gruyères, Switz. 22 C4
Gryazi, Russia 42 D4
Gryazovets, Russia 40 C11
Gstaad, Switz. 22 C4
Gua, India 61 H14
Gua Musang, Malaysia 59 K3
Guacanayabo, G. de, Cuba 116 B4
Guacara, Venezuela 120 A4
Guachípas →, Argentina 126 B2
Guachiría →, Colombia 120 B3
Guadajoz →, Spain 31 H6
Guadalajara, Mexico 114 C4
Guadalajara, Spain 28 E1
Guadalajara □, Spain 28 E2
Guadalcanal, Solomon Is. 92 H8
Guadalcanal, Spain 31 G5
Guadalén →, Spain 31 G2
Guadales, Argentina 126 C2
Guadalete →, Spain 31 J4
Guadalhorce →, Spain 31 J6
Guadalimar →, Spain 29 G1
Guadalmena →, Spain 29 G2
Guadalmez →, Spain 31 G5
Guadalope →, Spain 28 D4
Guadalquivir →, Spain 31 J4
Guadalupe = Guadeloupe ■, W. Indies 117 C7
Guadalupe, Brazil 122 C3
Guadalupe, Mexico 113 N10
Guadalupe, Spain 31 F5
Guadalupe, U.S.A. 113 L6
Guadalupe →, Mexico 113 N10
Guadalupe →, U.S.A. 109 L6
Guadalupe, Sierra de, Spain 31 F5
Guadalupe Bravos, Mexico 114 A3
Guadalupe Peak, U.S.A. 111 L11
Guadalupe y Calvo, Mexico 114 B3
Guadarrama, Sierra de, Spain 30 E6
Guadauta, Georgia 43 J5
Guadeloupe ■, W. Indies 117 C7
Guadeloupe Passage, W. Indies 117 C7
Guadiamar →, Spain 31 J4
Guadiana →, Portugal 31 H3
Guadiana Menor →, Spain 29 H1
Guadiaro →, Spain 31 J5
Guadiato →, Spain 31 H5
Guadiela →, Spain 28 E2
Guadix, Spain 29 H1
Guafo, Boca del, Chile 128 B2
Guafo, I., Chile 128 B2
Guaíba, Brazil 127 C5
Guainía □, Colombia 120 C4
Guainía →, Colombia 120 C4
Guaíra, Brazil 127 A5
Guaitecas, Is., Chile 128 B2
Guajará-Mirim, Brazil 125 C4
Guajira □, Colombia 120 A3
Guajira, Pen. de la, Colombia 120 A3
Gualaceo, Ecuador 120 D2
Gualán, Guatemala 116 C2
Gualdo Tadino, Italy 33 E9
Gualeguay, Argentina 126 C4
Gualeguaychú, Argentina 126 C4
Gualicho, Salina, Argentina 128 B3

Gualjaina, Argentina 128 B2
Guam ■, Pac. Oc. 92 F6
Guamá, Brazil 122 B2
Guamá →, Brazil 122 B2
Guamblin, I., Chile 128 B1
Guaminí, Argentina 126 D3
Guamote, Ecuador 120 D2
Guampí, Sierra de, Venezuela 121 B4
Guamúchil, Mexico 114 B3
Guan Xian, China 52 B4
Guanabacoa, Cuba 116 B3
Guanacaste, Cordillera del, Costa Rica 116 D2
Guanaceví, Mexico 114 B3
Guanahani = San Salvador, Bahamas 117 B5
Guanajay, Cuba 116 B3
Guanajuato, Mexico 114 C4
Guanajuato □, Mexico 114 C4
Guanambi, Brazil 123 D3
Guanare, Venezuela 120 B4
Guanare →, Venezuela 120 B4
Guandacol, Argentina 126 B2
Guane, Cuba 116 B3
Guang'an, China 52 B6
Guangchang, China 53 D11
Guangde, China 53 B12
Guangdong □, China 53 F9
Guangfeng, China 53 C12
Guanghan, China 52 B5
Guanghua, China 53 A8
Guangji, China 53 C10
Guangling, China 50 E8
Guangning, China 53 F9
Guangrao, China 51 F10
Guangshun, China 52 D6
Guangwu, China 50 F3
Guangxi Zhuangzu Zizhiqu □, China 52 E7
Guangyuan, China 52 A5
Guangze, China 53 D11
Guangzhou, China 53 F9
Guanhães, Brazil 123 E3
Guanipa →, Venezuela 121 B5
Guanling, China 52 E5
Guannan, China 51 G10
Guanta, Venezuela 121 A5
Guantánamo, Cuba 117 B4
Guantao, China 50 F8
Guanyang, China 53 E8
Guanyun, China 51 G10
Guapí, Colombia 120 C2
Guápiles, Costa Rica 116 D3
Guaporé →, Brazil 125 C4
Guaqui, Bolivia 124 D4
Guara, Sierra de, Spain 28 C4
Guarabira, Brazil 122 C4
Guaranda, Ecuador 120 D2
Guarapari, Brazil 123 F3
Guarapuava, Brazil 123 G1
Guaratinguetá, Brazil 127 A6
Guaratuba, Brazil 127 B6
Guarda, Portugal 30 E3
Guarda □, Portugal 30 E3
Guardafui, C. = Asir, Ras, Somali Rep. 68 E5
Guardamar del Segura, Spain 29 G4
Guardavalle, Italy 35 D9
Guardiagrele, Italy 33 F11
Guardo, Spain 30 C6
Guareña, Spain 31 G4
Guareña →, Spain 30 D5
Guaria □, Paraguay 126 B4
Guárico □, Venezuela 120 B4
Guarujá, Brazil 127 A6
Guarus, Brazil 123 F3
Guasave, Mexico 114 B3
Guascama, Pta., Colombia 120 C2
Guasdualito, Venezuela 120 B3
Guasipati, Venezuela 121 B5
Guastalla, Italy 32 D7
Guatemala, Guatemala 116 D1
Guatemala ■, Cent. Amer. 116 C1
Guatire, Venezuela 120 A4
Guaviare □, Colombia 120 C3
Guaviare →, Colombia 120 C4
Guaxupé, Brazil 127 A6
Guayabero →, Colombia 120 C3
Guayama, Puerto Rico 117 C6
Guayaneco, Arch., Chile 128 C1
Guayaquil, Ecuador 120 D2
Guayaquil, G. de, Ecuador 120 D1
Guayaramerín, Bolivia 125 C4
Guayas →, Ecuador 120 D2
Guaymas, Mexico 114 B2
Guazhou, China 53 A12
Guba, Zaïre 83 E2
Gûbâl, Madîq, Egypt 76 B3
Gubat, Phil. 55 E6
Gúbbio, Italy 33 E9
Gubio, Nigeria 79 C7
Gubkin, Russia 42 E3
Gudata = Guadauta, Georgia 43 J5
Gudbrandsdalen, Norway 9 F14
Guddu Barrage, Pakistan 60 E6
Gudenå, Denmark 11 H3
Gudermes, Russia 43 J8
Gudivada, India 61 L12
Gudur, India 60 M11
Guebwiller, France 25 E14
Guecho, Spain 28 B2
Guékédou, Guinea 78 D2
Guelma, Algeria 75 A6

Guelph, Canada 98 D3
Guemar, Algeria 75 B6
Guémené-Penfao, France 24 E5
Guémené-sur-Scorff, France 24 D3
Guéné, Benin 79 C5
Guépi, Peru 120 D2
Guer, France 24 E4
Güer Aike, Argentina 128 D3
Guérande, France 24 E4
Guercif, Morocco 75 B4
Guéréda, Chad 73 F9
Guéret, France 26 B5
Guérigny, France 25 E10
Guerneville, U.S.A. 112 G4
Guernica, Spain 28 B2
Guernsey, U.K. 13 H5
Guernsey, U.S.A. 108 D2
Guerrara, Oasis, Algeria 75 B5
Guerrara, Saoura, Algeria 75 B5
Guerrero □, Mexico 115 D5
Guerzim, Algeria 75 C4
Gueugnon, France 27 B8
Gueydan, U.S.A. 109 K8
Güğher, Iran 65 D8
Guglionesi, Italy 35 A7
Gui Jiang →, China 53 F8
Gui Xian, China 52 F7
Guia, Canary Is. 36 F4
Guia de Isora, Canary Is. 36 F3
Guia Lopes da Laguna, Brazil 127 A4
Guichi, China 53 B11
Guider, Cameroon 79 D7
Guidimouni, Niger 79 C6
Guiding, China 52 D6
Guidong, China 53 D9
Guiglo, Ivory C. 78 D3
Guijá, Mozam. 85 C5
Guijo de Coria, Spain 30 E4
Guildford, U.K. 13 F7
Guilford, U.S.A. 99 C6
Guilin, China 53 E8
Guillaumes, France 27 D10
Guillestre, France 27 D10
Guilvinec, France 24 E2
Güimar, Canary Is. 36 F3
Guimarães, Brazil 122 B3
Guimarães, Portugal 30 D2
Guimaras, Phil. 55 F5
Guinda, U.S.A. 112 G4
Guinea ■, W. Afr. 78 C2
Guinea, Gulf of, Atl. Oc. 79 E5
Guinea-Bissau ■, Africa 78 C2
Güines, Cuba 116 B3
Guingamp, France 24 D3
Guipavas, France 24 D2
Guiping, China 53 F8
Guipúzcoa □, Spain 28 B2
Guir, O. →, Algeria 75 B4
Guiratinga, Brazil 125 D7
Güiria, Venezuela 121 A5
Guiscard, France 25 C10
Guise, France 25 C10
Guitiriz, Spain 30 B3
Guiuan, Phil. 55 F6
Guixi, China 53 C11
Guiyang, Guizhou, China 52 D6
Guiyang, Hunan, China 53 E9
Guizhou □, China 52 D6
Gujan-Mestras, France 26 D2
Gujarat □, India 62 H4
Gujiang, China 53 D10
Gujranwala, Pakistan 62 C6
Gujrat, Pakistan 62 C6
Gukovo, Russia 43 F5
Gulbarga, India 60 L10
Gulbene, Latvia 9 H22
Gulf, The, Asia 65 E6
Gulfport, U.S.A. 109 K10
Gulgong, Australia 91 E4
Gulin, China 52 C5
Gulistan, Pakistan 62 D2
Gull Lake, Canada 101 C7
Gullegem, Belgium 17 G2
Güllük, Turkey 66 D2
Gulma, Nigeria 79 C5
Gulmarg, India 63 B6
Gülnar, Turkey 66 D5
Gulpen, Neths. 17 G7
Gülşehir, Turkey 66 C6
Gulshad, Kazakhstan 44 E8
Gulsvik, Norway 10 D3
Gulu, Uganda 82 B3
Gulwe, Tanzania 82 D4
Gulyaypole = Hulyaypole, Ukraine 41 J9
Gum Lake, Australia 91 E3
Gumal →, Pakistan 62 D4
Gumbaz, Pakistan 62 D3
Gumel, Nigeria 79 C6
Gumiel de Hizán, Spain 28 D1
Gumlu, Australia 90 B4
Gumma □, Japan 49 F9
Gummersbach, Germany 18 D3
Gummi, Nigeria 79 C6
Gumzai, Indonesia 57 F8
Guna, India 62 G7
Guna, Ethiopia 77 E4
Gundagai, Australia 91 F4
Gundelfingen, Germany 19 G6
Gundih, Indonesia 57 G14
Güneydoğu Toroslar, Turkey 67 C9
Gungu, Zaïre 80 F3
Gunisao →, Canada 101 C9

Gunisao L., Canada 101 C9
Gunnbjørn Fjeld, Greenland 4 C6
Gunnedah, Australia 91 E5
Gunningbar Cr. →, Australia 91 E4
Gunnison, Colo., U.S.A. 111 G10
Gunnison, Utah, U.S.A. 110 G8
Gunnison →, U.S.A. 111 G9
Gunpowder, Australia 90 B2
Guntakal, India 60 M10
Guntersville, U.S.A. 105 H2
Guntong, Malaysia 59 K3
Guntur, India 61 L12
Gunungapi, Indonesia 57 F7
Gunungsitoli, Indonesia 56 D1
Günz →, Germany 19 G6
Günzburg, Germany 19 G6
Gunzenhausen, Germany 19 F6
Guo He →, China 51 H9
Guoyang, China 50 H9
Gupis, Pakistan 63 A5
Gura Humorului, Romania 38 B8
Gurag, Ethiopia 77 F4
Gurdaspur, India 62 C6
Gurdon, U.S.A. 109 J8
Gurdzhaani, Georgia 43 K7
Gürgentepe, Turkey 66 B7
Gurgueia →, Brazil 122 C3
Gurha, India 62 G4
Guri, Embalse de, Venezuela 121 B5
Gurk →, Austria 21 J4
Gurkha, Nepal 63 E11
Gurley, Australia 91 D4
Gürpınar, Turkey 67 C10
Gurué, Mozam. 83 F4
Gurun, Malaysia 59 K3
Gürün, Turkey 66 C7
Gurupá, Brazil 121 D7
Gurupá, I. Grande de, Brazil 121 D7
Gurupi, Brazil 123 D2
Gurupi →, Brazil 122 B2
Gurupi, Serra do, Brazil 122 C2
Guryev = Atyraū, Kazakhstan 44 E6
Gus-Khrustalnyy, Russia 42 C5
Gusau, Nigeria 79 C6
Gusev, Russia 9 J20
Gushan, China 51 E12
Gushgy, Turkmenistan 44 F7
Gushi, China 53 A10
Gushiago, Ghana 79 D4
Gusinje, Montenegro, Yug. 21 N9
Gusinoozersk, Russia 45 D11
Gúspini, Italy 34 C1
Gustanj, Slovenia 33 B11
Gustine, U.S.A. 111 H3
Güstrow, Germany 18 B8
Gusum, Sweden 11 F10
Guta = Kalárovo, Slovak Rep. 21 H7
Gütersloh, Germany 18 D4
Gutha, Australia 89 E2
Guthalongra, Australia 90 B4
Guthrie, U.S.A. 109 H6
Gutian, China 53 D12
Gutiérrez, Bolivia 125 D5
Guttannen, Switz. 23 C6
Guttenberg, U.S.A. 108 D9
Guyana ■, S. Amer. 121 B6
Guyane française = French Guiana ■, S. Amer. 121 C7
Guyang, China 50 D6
Guyenne, France 26 D4
Guymon, U.S.A. 109 G4
Guyra, Australia 91 E5
Guyuan, Hebei, China 50 D8
Guyuan, Ningxia Huizu, China 50 F4
Guzhang, China 52 C7
Guzhen, China 51 H9
Guzmán, L. de, Mexico 114 A3
Gvardeysk, Russia 9 J19
Gvardeyskoye, Ukraine 41 K8
Gwa, Burma 61 L19
Gwaai, Zimbabwe 83 F2
Gwabegar, Australia 91 E4
Gwadabawa, Nigeria 79 C6
Gwädar, Pakistan 60 G3
Gwagwada, Nigeria 79 C6
Gwalia, Australia 89 E3
Gwalior, India 62 F8
Gwanda, Zimbabwe 83 G2
Gwandu, Nigeria 79 C5
Gwane, Zaïre 82 B2
Gwaram, Nigeria 79 C7
Gwarzo, Nigeria 79 C6
Gweebarra B., Ireland 15 B3
Gweedore, Ireland 15 A3
Gwent □, U.K. 13 F5
Gweru, Zimbabwe 83 F2
Gwi, Nigeria 79 D6
Gwinn, U.S.A. 104 B2
Gwio Kura, Nigeria 79 C7
Gwol, Ghana 78 C4
Gwoza, Nigeria 79 C7
Gwydir →, Australia 91 D4
Gwynedd □, U.K. 12 E4
Gyandzha = Gäncä, Azerbaijan 43 K8
Gyaring Hu, China 54 C4
Gydanskiy P-ov., Russia 44 C8
Gympie, Australia 91 D5

Gyoma, Hungary 21 J10
Gyöngyös, Hungary 21 H9
Györ, Hungary 21 H7
Gypsum Pt., Canada 100 A6
Gypsumville, Canada 101 C9
Gyula, Hungary 21 J11
Gyumri, Armenia 43 K6
Gyzylarbat, Turkmenistan 44 F7
Gzhatsk = Gagarin, Russia 42 C2

H

Ha 'Arava →, Israel 69 E4
Ha Coi, Vietnam 58 B6
Ha Dong, Vietnam 58 B5
Ha Giang, Vietnam 58 A5
Ha Tien, Vietnam 59 G5
Ha Tinh, Vietnam 58 C5
Ha Trung, Vietnam 58 C5
Haacht, Belgium 17 G5
Haag, Germany 19 G8
Haaksbergen, Neths. 16 D9
Haaltert, Belgium 17 G4
Haamstede, Neths. 17 E3
Haapsalu, Estonia 9 G20
Haarlem, Neths. 16 D5
Haast →, N.Z. 87 K2
Haast Bluff, Australia 88 D5
Haastrecht, Neths. 16 E5
Hab Nadi Chauki, Pakistan 62 G2
Habaswein, Kenya 82 B4
Habay, Canada 100 B5
Habay-la-Neuve, Belgium 17 J7
Ḥabbānīyah, Iraq 67 F10
Ḥabbānīyah, Hawr al, Iraq 67 F10
Haboro, Japan 48 B10
Haccourt, Belgium 17 G7
Hachenburg, Germany 18 E3
Hachijō-Jima, Japan 49 H9
Hachinohe, Japan 48 D10
Hachiōji, Japan 49 G9
Hachŏn, N. Korea 51 D15
Hachy, Belgium 17 J7
Hacıbektaş, Turkey 66 C6
Hacılar, Turkey 66 C6
Hackensack, U.S.A. 107 F10
Hadali, Pakistan 62 C5
Hadarba, Ras, Sudan 76 C4
Hadarom □, Israel 69 E3
Haddington, U.K. 14 F6
Hadejia, Nigeria 79 C7
Hadejia →, Nigeria 79 C7
Haden, Australia 91 D5
Ḥadera, Israel 69 C3
Ḥadera, N. →, Israel 69 C3
Haderslev, Denmark 11 J3
Hadhramaut = Ḥadramawt, Yemen 68 D4
Hadim, Turkey 66 D5
Hadjeb El Aïoun, Tunisia 75 A6
Hadong, S. Korea 51 G14
Ḥadramawt, Yemen 68 D4
Ḥadrānīyah, Iraq 64 C4
Hadrian's Wall, U.K. 12 C5
Hadsten, Denmark 11 H4
Hadsund, Denmark 11 H4
Hadyach, Ukraine 41 G8
Haeju, N. Korea 51 E13
Haenam, S. Korea 51 G14
Haerhpin = Harbin, China 51 B14
Hafar al Bāṭin, Si. Arabia 64 D5
Hafik, Turkey 66 C7
Ḥafīrat al 'Aydā, Si. Arabia 64 E3
Hafizabad, Pakistan 62 C5
Haflong, India 61 G18
Hafnarfjörður, Iceland 8 D3
Hafun, Ras, Somali Rep. 68 E5
Hagalil, Israel 69 C4
Hagen, Germany 18 D3
Hagenow, Germany 18 B7
Hagerman, U.S.A. 109 J2
Hagerstown, U.S.A. 104 F7
Hagetmau, France 26 E3
Hagfors, Sweden 9 F15
Häggenås, Sweden 10 A8
Hagi, Japan 49 G5
Hagolan, Syria 69 B4
Hagondange-Briey, France 25 C13
Hags Hd., Ireland 15 D2
Hague, C. de la, France 24 C5
Hague, The = 's-Gravenhage, Neths. 16 D4
Haguenau, France 25 D14
Hai □, Tanzania 82 C4
Hai Duong, Vietnam 58 B6
Hai'an, Guangdong, China 53 G8
Hai'an, Jiangsu, China 53 A13
Haicheng, Fujian, China 53 E11
Haicheng, Liaoning, China 51 D12
Haifa = Ḥefa, Israel 69 C3
Haifeng, China 53 F10
Haig, Australia 89 F4
Haiger, Germany 18 E4
Haikang, China 53 G8
Haikou, China 54 D6
Hāʾil, Si. Arabia 64 E4
Hailar, China 54 B6
Hailey, U.S.A. 110 E6
Haileybury, Canada 98 C4
Hailin, China 51 B15
Hailing Dao, China 53 G8
Hailong, China 51 C13
Hailun, China 54 B7

Hazebrouck

Hailuoto, *Finland* 8 D21
Haimen, *Guangdong, China* 53 F11
Haimen, *Jiangsu, China* 53 B13
Haimen, *Zhejiang, China* 53 C13
Hainan □, *China* 54 E5
Hainaut □, *Belgium* 17 H4
Haines, *U.S.A.* 110 D5
Haines City, *U.S.A.* 105 L5
Haines Junction, *Canada* 100 A1
Haining, *China* 53 B13
Haiphong, *Vietnam* 54 D5
Haiti ■, *W. Indies* 117 C5
Haiya Junction, *Sudan* 76 D4
Haiyan, *China* 53 B13
Haiyang, *China* 51 F11
Haiyuan, *Guangxi Zhuangzu, China* 52 F6
Haiyuan, *Ningxia Huizu, China* 50 F3
Haizhou, *China* 51 G10
Haizhou Wan, *China* 51 G10
Hajar Bangar, *Sudan* 73 F9
Hajdúböszörmény, *Hungary* 21 H11
Hajdúszobaszló, *Hungary* 21 H11
Hajipur, *India* 63 G11
Ḥājjī Muḥsin, *Iraq* 64 C5
Ḥājjīābād, *Eṣfahan, Iran* 65 C7
Ḥājjīābād, *Hormozgān, Iran* 65 D7
Hakansson, Mts., *Zaïre* 83 D2
Håkantorp, *Sweden* 11 F6
Hakkâri, *Turkey* 67 D10
Hakkâri Dağları, *Turkey* 67 C10
Hakken-Zan, *Japan* 49 G7
Hakodate, *Japan* 48 D10
Haku-San, *Japan* 49 F8
Hakui, *Japan* 49 F8
Hala, *Pakistan* 60 G6
Ḥalab, *Syria* 66 D7
Ḥalabjah, *Iraq* 67 E11
Halaib, *Sudan* 76 C4
Halanzy, *Belgium* 17 J7
Ḥālat 'Ammār, *Si. Arabia* 64 D3
Halbā, *Lebanon* 69 A5
Halberstadt, *Germany* 18 D7
Halcombe, *N.Z.* 87 J5
Halcon, Mt., *Phil.* 57 B6
Halden, *Norway* 10 E5
Haldensleben, *Germany* 18 C7
Haldia, *India* 61 H16
Haldwani, *India* 63 E8
Hale →, *Australia* 90 C2
Haleakala Crater, *U.S.A.* 102 H16
Halen, *Belgium* 17 G6
Haleyville, *U.S.A.* 105 H2
Half Assini, *Ghana* 78 D4
Halfway →, *Canada* 100 B4
Haliburton, *Canada* 98 C4
Halifax, *Australia* 90 B4
Halifax, *Canada* 99 D7
Halifax, *U.K.* 12 D6
Halifax B., *Australia* 90 B4
Halifax I., *Namibia* 84 D2
Halīl →, *Iran* 65 E8
Hall, *Austria* 19 H7
Hall Beach, *Canada* 97 B11
Hall Pt., *Australia* 88 C3
Halland, *Sweden* 9 H15
Hallands län □, *Sweden* 11 H6
Hallands Väderö, *Sweden* 11 H6
Hallandsås, *Sweden* 11 H7
Halle, *Belgium* 17 G4
Halle, *Nordrhein-Westfalen, Germany* 18 C4
Halle, *Sachsen-Anhalt, Germany* 18 D7
Hällefors, *Sweden* 9 G16
Hallein, *Austria* 21 H3
Hällekis, *Sweden* 11 F7
Hallett, *Australia* 91 E2
Hallettsville, *U.S.A.* 109 L6
Hällevadsholm, *Sweden* 11 F5
Halliday, *U.S.A.* 108 B3
Halliday L., *Canada* 101 A7
Hallim, *S. Korea* 51 H14
Hallingdalselva →, *Norway* 9 F13
Hallock, *U.S.A.* 101 D9
Halls Creek, *Australia* 88 C4
Hallsberg, *Sweden* 9 G16
Hallstahammar, *Sweden* 10 E10
Hallstead, *U.S.A.* 107 E9
Halmahera, *Indonesia* 57 D7
Halmeu, *Romania* 38 B6
Halmstad, *Sweden* 11 H6
Halq el Oued, *Tunisia* 75 A7
Hals, *Denmark* 11 H4
Halsafjorden, *Norway* 10 A2
Hälsingborg = Helsingborg, *Sweden* 11 H6
Hälsingland, *Sweden* 9 F16
Halstad, *U.S.A.* 108 B6
Haltdalen, *Norway* 10 B5
Haltern, *Germany* 18 D3
Halti, *Finland* 8 B19
Halul, *Qatar* 65 E7
Ḥalvān, *Iran* 65 C8
Ham, *France* 25 C10
Ham Tan, *Vietnam* 59 G6
Ham Yen, *Vietnam* 58 A5
Hamab, *Namibia* 84 D2
Hamad, *Sudan* 77 D3
Hamada, *Japan* 49 G6
Hamadān, *Iran* 67 E13
Hamadān □, *Iran* 65 C6
Hamadia, *Algeria* 75 A5
Hamāh, *Syria* 66 E7
Hamamatsu, *Japan* 49 G8
Hamar, *Norway* 10 D5
Hamâta, Gebel, *Egypt* 76 C3
Hambantota, *Sri Lanka* 60 R12
Hamber Prov. Park, *Canada* 100 C5
Hamburg, *Germany* 18 B5
Hamburg, *Ark., U.S.A.* 109 J9
Hamburg, *Iowa, U.S.A.* 108 E7
Hamburg, *N.Y., U.S.A.* 106 D6
Hamburg, *Pa., U.S.A.* 107 F9
Hamburg □, *Germany* 18 B6
Ḥamḍ, W. al →, *Si. Arabia* 64 E3
Hamden, *U.S.A.* 107 E12
Häme, *Finland* 9 F20
Hämeenlinna, *Finland* 9 F21
Hamélé, *Ghana* 78 C4
Hamelin Pool, *Australia* 89 E1
Hameln, *Germany* 18 C5
Hamer Koke, *Ethiopia* 77 F4
Hamerkaz □, *Israel* 69 C3
Hamersley Ra., *Australia* 88 D2
Hamhung, *N. Korea* 51 E14
Hami, *China* 54 B4
Hamilton, *Australia* 91 F3
Hamilton, *Canada* 98 D4
Hamilton, *N.Z.* 87 G5
Hamilton, *U.K.* 14 F4
Hamilton, *Mo., U.S.A.* 108 F8
Hamilton, *Mont., U.S.A.* 110 C6
Hamilton, *N.Y., U.S.A.* 107 D9
Hamilton, *Ohio, U.S.A.* 104 F3
Hamilton, *Tex., U.S.A.* 109 K5
Hamilton →, *Australia* 90 C2
Hamilton City, *U.S.A.* 112 F4
Hamilton Hotel, *Australia* 90 C3
Hamilton Inlet, *Canada* 99 B8
Hamina, *Finland* 9 F22
Hamiota, *Canada* 101 C8
Hamlet, *U.S.A.* 105 H6
Hamley Bridge, *Australia* 91 E2
Hamlin = Hameln, *Germany* 18 C5
Hamlin, *N.Y., U.S.A.* 106 C7
Hamlin, *Tex., U.S.A.* 109 J4
Hamm, *Germany* 18 D3
Hammam Bouhadjar, *Algeria* 75 A4
Hammamet, *Tunisia* 75 A7
Hammamet, G. de, *Tunisia* 75 A7
Hammarstrand, *Sweden* 10 A10
Hamme, *Belgium* 17 F4
Hamme-Mille, *Belgium* 17 G5
Hammel, *Denmark* 11 H3
Hammelburg, *Germany* 19 E5
Hammerfest, *Norway* 8 A20
Hammond, *Ind., U.S.A.* 104 E2
Hammond, *La., U.S.A.* 109 K9
Hammonton, *U.S.A.* 104 F8
Hamoir, *Belgium* 17 H7
Hamont, *Belgium* 17 F7
Hamoyet, Jebel, *Sudan* 76 D4
Hampden, *N.Z.* 87 L3
Hampshire □, *U.K.* 13 F6
Hampshire Downs, *U.K.* 13 F6
Hampton, *Ark., U.S.A.* 109 J8
Hampton, *Iowa, U.S.A.* 108 D8
Hampton, *N.H., U.S.A.* 107 D14
Hampton, *S.C., U.S.A.* 105 J5
Hampton, *Va., U.S.A.* 104 G7
Hampton Tableland, *Australia* 89 F4
Hamrat esh Sheykh, *Sudan* 77 E2
Hamur, *Turkey* 67 C10
Hamyang, *S. Korea* 51 G14
Han Jiang →, *China* 53 F11
Han Shui →, *China* 53 B10
Hana, *U.S.A.* 102 H17
Hanak, *Si. Arabia* 64 E3
Hanamaki, *Japan* 48 E10
Hanang, *Tanzania* 82 C4
Hanau, *Germany* 19 E4
Hanbogd, *Mongolia* 50 C4
Hancheng, *China* 50 G6
Hanchuan, *China* 53 B9
Hancock, *Mich., U.S.A.* 108 B10
Hancock, *Minn., U.S.A.* 108 C7
Hancock, *N.Y., U.S.A.* 107 E9
Handa, *Japan* 49 G8
Handa, *Somali Rep.* 68 E5
Handan, *China* 50 F8
Handen, *Sweden* 10 E12
Handeni, *Tanzania* 82 D4
Handeni □, *Tanzania* 82 D4
Handub, *Sudan* 76 D4
Handwara, *India* 63 B6
Handzame, *Belgium* 17 F2
Hanegev, *Israel* 69 E3
Haney, *Canada* 100 D4
Hanford, *U.S.A.* 111 H4
Hang Chat, *Thailand* 58 C2
Hang Dong, *Thailand* 58 C2
Hangang →, *S. Korea* 51 F14
Hangayn Nuruu, *Mongolia* 54 B4
Hangchou = Hangzhou, *China* 53 B13
Hanggin Houqi, *China* 50 D4
Hanggin Qi, *China* 50 E5
Hangu, *China* 51 E9
Hangzhou, *China* 53 B13
Hangzhou Wan, *China* 53 B13
Hanhongor, *Mongolia* 50 C3
Ḥanīdh, *Si. Arabia* 65 E6
Ḥanīsh, *Yemen* 68 E3
Hanjiang, *China* 53 E12
Hankinson, *U.S.A.* 108 B6
Hanko, *Finland* 9 G20
Hankou, *China* 53 B10
Hanksville, *U.S.A.* 111 G8
Hanle, *India* 63 C8
Hanmer Springs, *N.Z.* 87 K4
Hann →, *Australia* 88 C4
Hann, Mt., *Australia* 88 C4
Hanna, *Canada* 100 C6
Hannaford, *U.S.A.* 108 B5
Hannah, *U.S.A.* 108 A5
Hannah B., *Canada* 98 B4
Hannibal, *U.S.A.* 108 F9
Hannik, *Sudan* 76 D3
Hannover, *Germany* 18 C5
Hannut, *Belgium* 17 G6
Hanoi, *Vietnam* 54 D5
Hanover = Hannover, *Germany* 18 C5
Hanover, *Canada* 106 B3
Hanover, *S. Africa* 84 E3
Hanover, *N.H., U.S.A.* 107 C12
Hanover, *Ohio, U.S.A.* 106 F2
Hanover, *Pa., U.S.A.* 104 F7
Hanover, I., *Chile* 128 D2
Hanshou, *China* 53 C8
Hansi, *India* 62 E6
Hanson, L., *Australia* 91 E2
Hantsavichy, *Belarus* 41 F4
Hanyang, *China* 53 B10
Hanyin, *China* 52 A7
Hanyuan, *China* 52 C4
Hanzhong, *China* 50 H4
Hanzhuang, *China* 51 G9
Haora, *India* 63 H13
Haoxue, *China* 53 B9
Haparanda, *Sweden* 8 D21
Hapert, *Neths.* 17 F6
Happy, *U.S.A.* 109 H4
Happy Camp, *U.S.A.* 110 F2
Happy Valley-Goose Bay, *Canada* 99 B7
Hapsu, *N. Korea* 51 D15
Hapur, *India* 62 E7
Ḥaql, *Si. Arabia* 69 F3
Haquira, *Peru* 124 C3
Har, *Indonesia* 57 F8
Har-Ayrag, *Mongolia* 50 B5
Har Hu, *China* 54 C4
Har Us Nuur, *Mongolia* 54 B4
Har Yehuda, *Israel* 69 D3
Ḥaraḍ, *Si. Arabia* 68 C4
Haradok, *Belarus* 40 E6
Haranomachi, *Japan* 48 F10
Harardera, *Somali Rep.* 68 G4
Harare, *Zimbabwe* 83 F3
Harat, *Eritrea* 77 D4
Harazé, *Chad* 73 F8
Harbin, *China* 51 B14
Harbiye, *Turkey* 66 D7
Harboør, *Denmark* 11 H2
Harbor Beach, *U.S.A.* 104 D4
Harbor Springs, *U.S.A.* 104 C3
Harbour Breton, *Canada* 99 C8
Harbour Grace, *Canada* 99 C9
Harburg, *Germany* 18 B5
Hårby, *Denmark* 11 J4
Harda, *India* 62 H7
Hardangerfjorden, *Norway* 9 F12
Hardangervidda, *Norway* 9 F12
Hardap Dam, *Namibia* 84 C2
Hardegarijp, *Neths.* 16 B7
Hardenberg, *Neths.* 16 C9
Harderwijk, *Neths.* 16 D7
Hardey →, *Australia* 88 D2
Hardin, *U.S.A.* 110 D10
Harding, *S. Africa* 85 E4
Harding Ra., *Australia* 88 C3
Hardisty, *Canada* 100 C6
Hardman, *U.S.A.* 110 D4
Hardoi, *India* 63 F9
Hardwar = Haridwar, *India* 62 E8
Hardwick, *U.S.A.* 107 B12
Hardy, *U.S.A.* 109 G9
Hardy, Pen., *Chile* 128 E3
Hare B., *Canada* 99 B8
Hareid, *Norway* 9 E12
Harelbeke, *Belgium* 17 G2
Haren, *Germany* 18 C3
Haren, *Neths.* 16 B9
Harer, *Ethiopia* 68 F3
Harerge □, *Ethiopia* 77 F5
Hareto, *Ethiopia* 77 F4
Harfleur, *France* 24 C7
Hargeisa, *Somali Rep.* 68 F3
Hari →, *Indonesia* 56 E2
Haria, *Canary Is.* 36 E6
Haricha, Hamada el, *Mali* 74 D4
Haridwar, *India* 62 E8
Haringhata →, *Bangla.* 61 J16
Haringvliet, *Neths.* 16 E4
Harīrūd →, *Asia* 60 A2
Härjedalen, *Sweden* 9 E15
Harlan, *Iowa, U.S.A.* 108 E7
Harlan, *Ky., U.S.A.* 105 G4
Harlech, *U.K.* 12 E3
Harlem, *U.S.A.* 110 B9
Harlingen, *Neths.* 16 B6
Harlingen, *U.S.A.* 109 M6
Harlowton, *U.S.A.* 110 C9
Harmånger, *Sweden* 10 C11
Harmil, *Eritrea* 77 D5
Harney Basin, *U.S.A.* 110 E4
Harney L., *U.S.A.* 110 E4
Harney Peak, *U.S.A.* 108 D3
Härnön, *Sweden* 10 B12
Härnösand, *Sweden* 10 B11
Haro, *Spain* 28 C2
Harp L., *Canada* 99 A7
Harper, *Liberia* 78 E3
Harplinge, *Sweden* 11 H6
Harrand, *Pakistan* 62 E4
Harriman, *U.S.A.* 105 H3
Harrington Harbour, *Canada* 99 B8
Harris, *U.K.* 14 D2
Harris, Sd. of, *U.K.* 14 D1
Harris L., *Australia* 91 E2
Harrisburg, *Ill., U.S.A.* 109 G10
Harrisburg, *Nebr., U.S.A.* 108 E3
Harrisburg, *Oreg., U.S.A.* 110 D2
Harrisburg, *Pa., U.S.A.* 106 F8
Harrismith, *S. Africa* 85 D4
Harrison, *Ark., U.S.A.* 109 G8
Harrison, *Idaho, U.S.A.* 110 C5
Harrison, *Nebr., U.S.A.* 108 D3
Harrison, C., *Canada* 99 B8
Harrison Bay, *U.S.A.* 96 A4
Harrison L., *Canada* 100 D4
Harrisonburg, *U.S.A.* 104 F6
Harrisonville, *U.S.A.* 108 F7
Harriston, *Canada* 98 D3
Harrisville, *U.S.A.* 106 B1
Harrogate, *U.K.* 12 D6
Harrow, *U.K.* 13 F7
Harsefeld, *Germany* 18 B5
Harsīn, *Iran* 67 E12
Harskamp, *Neths.* 16 D7
Harstad, *Norway* 8 B17
Hart, *U.S.A.* 104 D2
Hart, L., *Australia* 91 E2
Hartbees →, *S. Africa* 84 D3
Hartberg, *Austria* 21 H5
Hartford, *Conn., U.S.A.* 107 E12
Hartford, *Ky., U.S.A.* 104 G2
Hartford, *S. Dak., U.S.A.* 108 D6
Hartford, *Wis., U.S.A.* 108 D10
Hartford City, *U.S.A.* 104 E3
Hartland, *Canada* 99 C6
Hartland Pt., *U.K.* 13 F3
Hartlepool, *U.K.* 12 C6
Hartley Bay, *Canada* 100 C3
Hartmannberge, *Namibia* 84 B1
Hartney, *Canada* 101 D8
Harts →, *S. Africa* 84 D3
Hartselle, *U.S.A.* 105 H2
Hartshorne, *U.S.A.* 109 H7
Hartsville, *U.S.A.* 105 H5
Hartwell, *U.S.A.* 105 H4
Harunabad, *Pakistan* 62 E5
Harvand, *Iran* 65 D7
Harvey, *Australia* 89 F2
Harvey, *Ill., U.S.A.* 104 E2
Harvey, *N. Dak., U.S.A.* 108 B5
Harwich, *U.K.* 13 F9
Haryana □, *India* 62 E7
Haryn →, *Belarus* 41 F4
Harz, *Germany* 18 D6
Harzé, *Belgium* 17 H7
Harzgerode, *Germany* 18 D7
Hasaheisa, *Sudan* 77 E3
Hasan Kīādeh, *Iran* 65 B6
Hasan Kuli, *Turkmenistan* 44 F6
Ḥasanābād, *Iran* 65 C7
Hasanpur, *India* 62 E8
Haselünne, *Germany* 18 C3
Hashimoto, *Japan* 49 G7
Hashtjerd, *Iran* 65 C6
Håsjö, *Sweden* 10 A10
Haskell, *Okla., U.S.A.* 109 H7
Haskell, *Tex., U.S.A.* 109 J5
Haslach, *Germany* 19 G4
Haslev, *Denmark* 11 J5
Hasparren, *France* 26 E2
Hassa, *Turkey* 66 D7
Hasselt, *Belgium* 17 G6
Hasselt, *Neths.* 16 C8
Hassene, Adrar, *Algeria* 75 D5
Hassfurt, *Germany* 19 E6
Hassi bou Khelala, *Algeria* 75 B4
Hassi Djafou, *Algeria* 75 B5
Hassi el Abiod, *Algeria* 75 B5
Hassi el Biod, *Algeria* 75 C6
Hassi el Hadjar, *Algeria* 75 B5
Hassi Imoulaye, *Algeria* 75 C6
Hassi Inifel, *Algeria* 75 C5
Hassi Messaoud, *Algeria* 75 B6
Hassi Tartrat, *Algeria* 75 B6
Hassi Zerzour, *Morocco* 74 B4
Hässleholm, *Sweden* 9 H15
Hastière-Lavaux, *Belgium* 17 H5
Hastings, *N.Z.* 87 H6
Hastings, *U.K.* 13 G8
Hastings, *Mich., U.S.A.* 104 D3
Hastings, *Minn., U.S.A.* 108 C8
Hastings, *Nebr., U.S.A.* 108 E5
Hastings Ra., *Australia* 91 E5
Hat Yai, *Thailand* 59 J3
Hatanbulag, *Mongolia* 50 C5
Hatay = Antalya, *Turkey* 66 D4
Hatch, *U.S.A.* 111 K10
Hatches Creek, *Australia* 90 C2
Hatchet L., *Canada* 101 B8
Haţeg, *Romania* 38 D5
Haţeg, Mţii., *Romania* 38 D6
Hatert, *Neths.* 16 E7
Hateruma-Shima, *Japan* 49 M1
Hatfield P.O., *Australia* 91 E3
Hatgal, *Mongolia* 54 A5
Hathras, *India* 62 F8
Hatia, *Bangla.* 61 H17
Hato de Corozal, *Colombia* 120 B3
Hato Mayor, *Dom. Rep.* 117 C6
Hattah, *Australia* 91 E3
Hattem, *Neths.* 16 D8
Hatteras, C., *U.S.A.* 105 H8
Hattiesburg, *U.S.A.* 109 K10
Hatvan, *Hungary* 21 H9
Hau Bon = Cheo Reo, *Vietnam* 58 F7
Hau Duc, *Vietnam* 58 E7
Haug, *Norway* 10 D4
Haugastøl, *Norway* 10 D1
Haugesund, *Norway* 9 G11
Haukipudas, *Finland* 8 D21
Haulerwijk, *Neths.* 16 B8
Haultain →, *Canada* 101 B7
Hauraki G., *N.Z.* 87 G5
Haut Atlas, *Morocco* 74 B3
Haut-Rhin □, *France* 25 E14
Haut Zaïre □, *Zaïre* 82 B2
Haute-Corse □, *France* 27 F13
Haute-Garonne □, *France* 26 E5
Haute-Loire □, *France* 26 C7
Haute-Marne □, *France* 25 D12
Haute-Saône □, *France* 25 E13
Haute-Savoie □, *France* 27 C10
Haute-Vienne □, *France* 26 C5
Hauterive, *Canada* 99 C6
Hautes-Alpes □, *France* 27 D10
Hautes Fagnes = Hohe Venn, *Belgium* 17 H8
Hautes-Pyrénées □, *France* 26 F4
Hauteville-Lompnès, *France* 27 C9
Hautmont, *France* 25 B10
Hautrage, *Belgium* 17 H3
Hauts-de-Seine □, *France* 25 D9
Hauts Plateaux, *Algeria* 75 B4
Hauzenberg, *Germany* 19 G9
Havana = La Habana, *Cuba* 116 B3
Havana, *U.S.A.* 108 E9
Havant, *U.K.* 13 G7
Havasu, L., *U.S.A.* 113 L12
Havel →, *Germany* 18 C8
Havelange, *Belgium* 17 H6
Havelian, *Pakistan* 62 B5
Havelock, *N.B., Canada* 99 C6
Havelock, *Ont., Canada* 98 D4
Havelock, *N.Z.* 87 J4
Havelte, *Neths.* 16 C8
Haverfordwest, *U.K.* 13 F3
Haverhill, *U.S.A.* 107 D13
Havering, *U.K.* 13 F8
Haverstraw, *U.S.A.* 107 E11
Håverud, *Sweden* 11 F6
Havlíčkův Brod, *Czech.* 20 F5
Havneby, *Denmark* 11 J2
Havre, *U.S.A.* 110 B9
Havre-Aubert, *Canada* 99 C7
Havre-St.-Pierre, *Canada* 99 B7
Havza, *Turkey* 66 B6
Haw →, *U.S.A.* 105 H6
Hawaii □, *U.S.A.* 102 H16
Hawaii I., *Pac. Oc.* 102 J17
Hawaiian Is., *Pac. Oc.* 102 H17
Hawaiian Ridge, *Pac. Oc.* 93 E11
Hawarden, *Canada* 101 C7
Hawarden, *U.S.A.* 108 D6
Hawea, L., *N.Z.* 87 L2
Hawera, *N.Z.* 87 H5
Hawick, *U.K.* 14 F6
Hawk Junction, *Canada* 98 C3
Hawke B., *N.Z.* 87 H6
Hawker, *Australia* 91 E2
Hawkesbury, *Canada* 98 C5
Hawkesbury I., *Canada* 100 C3
Hawkesbury Pt., *Australia* 90 A1
Hawkinsville, *U.S.A.* 105 J4
Hawkwood, *Australia* 91 D5
Hawley, *U.S.A.* 108 B6
Hawrān, *Syria* 69 C5
Ḥawrān, W. →, *Iraq* 67 F10
Hawsh Mūssá, *Lebanon* 69 B4
Hawthorne, *U.S.A.* 110 G4
Hawzen, *Ethiopia* 77 E4
Haxtun, *U.S.A.* 108 E3
Hay, *Australia* 91 E3
Hay →, *Australia* 90 C2
Hay →, *Canada* 100 A5
Hay, C., *Australia* 88 B4
Hay L., *Canada* 100 B5
Hay Lakes, *Canada* 100 C6
Hay-on-Wye, *U.K.* 13 E4
Hay River, *Canada* 100 A5
Hay Springs, *U.S.A.* 108 D3
Haya, *Indonesia* 57 E7
Hayachine-San, *Japan* 48 E10
Hayange, *France* 25 C13
Hayden, *Ariz., U.S.A.* 111 K8
Hayden, *Colo., U.S.A.* 110 F10
Haydon, *Australia* 90 B3
Hayes, *U.S.A.* 108 C4
Hayes →, *Canada* 101 B10
Haymana, *Turkey* 66 C5
Haynesville, *U.S.A.* 109 J8
Hayrabolu, *Turkey* 66 B2
Hays, *Canada* 100 C6
Hays, *U.S.A.* 108 F5
Haysyn, *Ukraine* 41 H5
Hayvoron, *Ukraine* 41 H5
Hayward, *Calif., U.S.A.* 112 H4
Hayward, *Wis., U.S.A.* 108 B9
Haywards Heath, *U.K.* 13 F7
Hazafon □, *Israel* 69 C4
Hazarām, Kūh-e, *Iran* 65 D8
Hazard, *U.S.A.* 104 G4
Hazaribag, *India* 63 H11
Hazaribag Road, *India* 63 G11
Hazebrouck, *France* 25 B9

Hazelton, *Canada*	100	B3
Hazelton, *U.S.A.*	108	B4
Hazen, *N. Dak., U.S.A.*	108	B4
Hazen, *Nev., U.S.A.*	110	G4
Hazerswoude, *Neths.*	16	D5
Hazlehurst, *Ga., U.S.A.*	105	K4
Hazlehurst, *Miss., U.S.A.*	109	K9
Hazleton, *U.S.A.*	107	F9
Hazlett, L., *Australia*	88	D4
Hazor, *Israel*	69	B4
He Xian, *Anhui, China*	53	B12
He Xian, *Guangxi Zhuangzu, China*	53	E8
Head of Bight, *Australia*	89	F5
Headlands, *Zimbabwe*	83	F3
Healdsburg, *U.S.A.*	112	G4
Healdton, *U.S.A.*	109	H6
Healesville, *Australia*	91	F4
Heanor, *U.K.*	12	D6
Heard I., *Ind. Oc.*	3	G13
Hearne, *U.S.A.*	109	K6
Hearne B., *Canada*	101	A9
Hearne L., *Canada*	100	A6
Hearst, *Canada*	98	C3
Heart →, *U.S.A.*	108	B4
Heart's Content, *Canada*	99	C9
Heath →, *Bolivia*	124	C4
Heath Pt., *Canada*	99	C7
Heath Steele, *Canada*	99	C6
Heavener, *U.S.A.*	109	H7
Hebbronville, *U.S.A.*	109	M5
Hebei □, *China*	50	E9
Hebel, *Australia*	91	D4
Heber, *U.S.A.*	113	N11
Heber Springs, *U.S.A.*	109	H9
Hebert, *Canada*	101	C7
Hebgen L., *U.S.A.*	110	D8
Hebi, *China*	50	G8
Hebrides, *U.K.*	14	D1
Hebron = Al Khalīl, *West Bank*	69	D4
Hebron, *Canada*	97	C13
Hebron, *N. Dak., U.S.A.*	108	B3
Hebron, *Nebr., U.S.A.*	108	E6
Hecate Str., *Canada*	100	C2
Hechi, *China*	52	E7
Hechingen, *Germany*	19	G4
Hechtel, *Belgium*	17	F6
Hechuan, *China*	52	B6
Hecla, *U.S.A.*	108	C5
Hecla I., *Canada*	101	C9
Heddal, *Norway*	10	E3
Hédé, *France*	24	D5
Hede, *Sweden*	10	B7
Hedemora, *Sweden*	9	F16
Hedley, *U.S.A.*	109	H4
Hedmark fylke □, *Norway*	10	C5
Hedrum, *Norway*	10	E4
Heeg, *Neths.*	16	C7
Heegermeer, *Neths.*	16	C7
Heemskerk, *Neths.*	16	C5
Heemstede, *Neths.*	16	D5
Heer, *Neths.*	17	G7
Heerde, *Neths.*	16	D8
's Heerenburg, *Neths.*	16	E8
Heerenveen, *Neths.*	16	C7
Heerhugowaard, *Neths.*	16	C5
Heerlen, *Neths.*	17	G7
Heers, *Belgium*	17	G6
Heesch, *Neths.*	16	E7
Heestert, *Belgium*	17	G2
Heeze, *Neths.*	17	F7
Hefa, *Israel*	69	C4
Hefa □, *Israel*	69	C4
Hefei, *China*	53	B11
Hegang, *China*	54	B8
Hegyalja, *Hungary*	21	G11
Heichengzhen, *China*	50	F4
Heide, *Germany*	18	A5
Heidelberg, *Germany*	19	F4
Heidelberg, *S. Africa*	84	E3
Heidenheim, *Germany*	19	G6
Heijing, *China*	52	E3
Heilbron, *S. Africa*	85	D4
Heilbronn, *Germany*	19	F5
Heiligenblut, *Austria*	21	H2
Heiligenhafen, *Germany*	18	A6
Heiligenstadt, *Germany*	18	D6
Heilongjiang □, *China*	51	B14
Heilunkiang = Heilongjiang □, *China*	51	B14
Heimaey, *Iceland*	8	E3
Heino, *Neths.*	16	D8
Heinola, *Finland*	9	F22
Heinsch, *Belgium*	17	J7
Heinze Is., *Burma*	61	M20
Heishan, *China*	51	D12
Heishui, *Liaoning, China*	51	C10
Heishui, *Sichuan, China*	52	A4
Heist, *Belgium*	17	F2
Heist-op-den-Berg, *Belgium*	17	F5
Hejaz = Al Hijāz, *Si. Arabia*	68	B2
Hejian, *China*	50	E9
Hejiang, *China*	52	C5
Hejin, *China*	50	G6
Hekelgem, *Belgium*	17	G4
Hekimhan, *Turkey*	66	C7
Hekla, *Iceland*	8	E4
Hekou, *Gansu, China*	50	F2
Hekou, *Guangdong, China*	53	F9
Hekou, *Yunnan, China*	54	D5
Helagsfjället, *Sweden*	10	B6
Helan Shan, *China*	50	E3
Helchteren, *Belgium*	17	F6
Helden, *Neths.*	17	F7
Helechosa, *Spain*	31	F6
Helena, *Ark., U.S.A.*	109	H9
Helena, *Mont., U.S.A.*	110	C7
Helendale, *U.S.A.*	113	L9
Helensburgh, *U.K.*	14	E4
Helensville, *N.Z.*	87	G5
Helgeland, *Norway*	8	C15
Helgeroa, *Norway*	10	F3
Helgoland, *Germany*	18	A3
Heligoland = Helgoland, *Germany*	18	A3
Heligoland B. = Deutsche Bucht, *Germany*	18	A4
Heliopolis, *Egypt*	76	H7
Hella, *Iceland*	8	E3
Hellebæk, *Denmark*	11	H6
Hellendoorn, *Neths.*	16	D8
Hellevoetsluis, *Neths.*	16	E4
Hellín, *Spain*	29	G3
Helmand □, *Afghan.*	60	D4
Helmand →, *Afghan.*	60	D2
Helme →, *Germany*	18	D7
Helmond, *Neths.*	17	F7
Helmsdale, *U.K.*	14	C5
Helmstedt, *Germany*	18	C7
Helnæs, *Denmark*	11	J4
Helong, *China*	51	C15
Helper, *U.S.A.*	110	G8
Helsingborg, *Sweden*	11	H6
Helsinge, *Denmark*	11	H6
Helsingfors = Helsinki, *Finland*	9	F21
Helsingør, *Denmark*	11	H6
Helsinki, *Finland*	9	F21
Helston, *U.K.*	13	G2
Helvellyn, *U.K.*	12	C4
Helvoirt, *Neths.*	17	E6
Helwân, *Egypt*	76	J7
Hemet, *U.S.A.*	113	M10
Hemingford, *U.S.A.*	108	D3
Hemphill, *U.S.A.*	109	K8
Hempstead, *U.S.A.*	109	K6
Hemse, *Sweden*	9	H18
Hemsö, *Sweden*	10	B12
Henan □, *China*	50	G8
Henares →, *Spain*	28	E1
Henashi-Misaki, *Japan*	48	D9
Hendaye, *France*	26	E2
Hendek, *Turkey*	66	B4
Henderson, *Argentina*	126	D3
Henderson, *Ky., U.S.A.*	104	G2
Henderson, *N.C., U.S.A.*	105	G6
Henderson, *Nev., U.S.A.*	113	J12
Henderson, *Tenn., U.S.A.*	105	H1
Henderson, *Tex., U.S.A.*	109	J7
Hendersonville, *U.S.A.*	105	H4
Hendījān, *Iran*	65	D6
Hendon, *Australia*	91	D5
Heng Xian, *China*	52	F7
Hengcheng, *China*	50	E4
Hengdaohezi, *China*	51	B15
Hengelo, *Gelderland, Neths.*	16	D8
Hengelo, *Overijssel, Neths.*	16	D9
Hengfeng, *China*	53	C10
Hengshan, *Hunan, China*	53	D9
Hengshan, *Shaanxi, China*	50	F5
Hengshui, *China*	50	F8
Hengyang, *Hunan, China*	53	D9
Hengyang, *Hunan, China*	53	D9
Henichesk, *Ukraine*	41	J8
Hénin-Beaumont, *France*	25	B9
Henlopen, C., *U.S.A.*	104	F8
Hennan, *Sweden*	10	B9
Hennebont, *France*	24	E3
Hennenman, *S. Africa*	84	D4
Hennessey, *U.S.A.*	109	G6
Hennigsdorf, *Germany*	18	C9
Henrichemont, *France*	25	E9
Henrietta, *U.S.A.*	109	J5
Henrietta, Ostrov, *Russia*	45	B16
Henrietta Maria, C., *Canada*	98	A3
Henry, *U.S.A.*	108	E10
Henryetta, *U.S.A.*	109	H6
Hensall, *Canada*	106	C3
Hentiyn Nuruu, *Mongolia*	54	B5
Henty, *Australia*	91	F4
Henzada, *Burma*	61	L19
Heping, *China*	53	E10
Heppner, *U.S.A.*	110	D4
Hepu, *China*	52	G7
Hepworth, *Canada*	106	B3
Heqing, *China*	52	D3
Hequ, *China*	50	E6
Héradsflói, *Iceland*	8	D6
Héradsvötn →, *Iceland*	8	D4
Herald Cays, *Australia*	90	B4
Herāt, *Afghan.*	60	B3
Herāt □, *Afghan.*	60	B3
Hérault □, *France*	26	E7
Hérault →, *France*	26	E7
Herbault, *France*	24	E8
Herbert →, *Australia*	90	B4
Herbert Downs, *Australia*	90	C2
Herberton, *Australia*	90	B4
Herbignac, *France*	24	E4
Herborn, *Germany*	18	E4
Herby, *Poland*	20	E8
Hercegnovi, *Montenegro, Yug.*	21	N8
Herðubreið, *Iceland*	8	D5
Hereford, *U.K.*	13	E5
Hereford, *U.S.A.*	109	H3
Hereford and Worcester □, *U.K.*	13	E5
Herefoss, *Norway*	11	F2
Herent, *Belgium*	17	G5
Herentals, *Belgium*	17	F5
Herenthout, *Belgium*	17	F5
Herfølge, *Denmark*	11	J6
Herford, *Germany*	18	C4
Héricourt, *France*	25	E13
Herington, *U.S.A.*	108	F6
Herisau, *Switz.*	23	B8
Hérisson, *France*	26	B6
Herk →, *Belgium*	17	G6
Herkenbosch, *Neths.*	17	F8
Herkimer, *U.S.A.*	107	D10
Herlong, *U.S.A.*	112	E6
Herm, *U.K.*	24	C4
Hermagor-Pressegger See, *Austria*	21	J3
Herman, *U.S.A.*	108	C6
Hermann, *U.S.A.*	108	F9
Hermannsburg, *Germany*	18	C6
Hermannsburg Mission, *Australia*	88	D5
Hermanus, *S. Africa*	84	E2
Herment, *France*	26	C6
Hermidale, *Australia*	91	E4
Hermiston, *U.S.A.*	110	D4
Hermitage, *N.Z.*	87	K3
Hermite, I., *Chile*	128	E3
Hermon, Mt. = Ash Shaykh, J., *Lebanon*	69	B4
Hermosillo, *Mexico*	114	B2
Hernád →, *Hungary*	21	H11
Hernandarias, *Paraguay*	127	B5
Hernandez, *U.S.A.*	112	J6
Hernando, *Argentina*	126	C3
Hernando, *U.S.A.*	109	H10
Herne, *Belgium*	17	G4
Herne, *Germany*	17	E10
Herne Bay, *U.K.*	13	F9
Herning, *Denmark*	11	H2
Heroica = Caborca, *Mexico*	114	A2
Heroica Nogales = Nogales, *Mexico*	114	A2
Heron Bay, *Canada*	98	C2
Herradura, Pta. de la, *Canary Is.*	36	F5
Herreid, *U.S.A.*	108	C4
Herrera, *Spain*	31	H6
Herrera de Alcántar, *Spain*	31	F3
Herrera de Pisuerga, *Spain*	30	C6
Herrera del Duque, *Spain*	31	F5
Herrick, *Australia*	90	G4
Herrin, *U.S.A.*	109	G10
Herrljunga, *Sweden*	11	F7
Hersbruck, *Germany*	19	F7
Herseaux, *Belgium*	17	G2
Herselt, *Belgium*	17	F5
Hersonissos, *Greece*	37	D7
Herstal, *Belgium*	17	G7
Hertford, *U.K.*	13	F7
Hertfordshire □, *U.K.*	13	F7
's-Hertogenbosch, *Neths.*	17	E6
Hertzogville, *S. Africa*	84	D4
Hervás, *Spain*	30	E5
Herve, *Belgium*	17	G7
Herwijnen, *Neths.*	16	E6
Herzberg, *Brandenburg, Germany*	18	D9
Herzberg, *Niedersachsen, Germany*	18	D6
Herzele, *Belgium*	17	G3
Herzliyya, *Israel*	69	C3
Herzogenbuchsee, *Switz.*	22	B5
Heşār, *Fārs, Iran*	65	D6
Heşār, *Markazī, Iran*	65	C6
Hesdin, *France*	25	B9
Hesel, *Germany*	18	B3
Heshui, *China*	50	G5
Heshun, *China*	50	F7
Hesperange, *Lux.*	17	J8
Hesperia, *U.S.A.*	113	L9
Hesse = Hessen □, *Germany*	18	E5
Hessen □, *Germany*	18	E5
Hetch Hetchy Aqueduct, *U.S.A.*	112	H5
Hettinger, *U.S.A.*	108	C3
Hettstedt, *Germany*	18	D7
Heugem, *Neths.*	17	G7
Heule, *Belgium*	17	G2
Heusden, *Belgium*	17	F6
Heusden, *Neths.*	16	E6
Hève, C. de la, *France*	24	C7
Heverlee, *Belgium*	17	G5
Hewett, C., *Canada*	97	A13
Hexham, *U.K.*	12	C5
Hexi, *Yunnan, China*	52	E4
Hexi, *Zhejiang, China*	53	D12
Hexigten Qi, *China*	51	C9
Heyderābād, *Iran*	65	D7
Heyfield, *Australia*	91	F4
Heysham, *U.K.*	12	C5
Heythuysen, *Neths.*	17	F7
Heyuan, *China*	53	F10
Heywood, *Australia*	91	F3
Heze, *China*	50	G8
Hezhang, *China*	52	D5
Hi Vista, *U.S.A.*	113	L9
Hialeah, *U.S.A.*	105	N5
Hiawatha, *Kans., U.S.A.*	108	F7
Hiawatha, *Utah, U.S.A.*	110	G8
Hibbing, *U.S.A.*	108	B8
Hibbs B., *Australia*	90	G4
Hibernia Reef, *Australia*	88	B3
Hickory, *U.S.A.*	105	H5
Hicks, Pt., *Australia*	91	F4
Hicksville, *U.S.A.*	107	F11
Hida, *Romania*	38	B6
Hida-Gawa →, *Japan*	49	G8
Hida-Sammyaku, *Japan*	49	F8
Hidaka-Sammyaku, *Japan*	48	C11
Hidalgo, *Mexico*	115	C5
Hidalgo □, *Mexico*	115	C5
Hidalgo, Presa M., *Mexico*	114	B3
Hidalgo, Pta. del, *Canary Is.*	36	F3
Hidalgo del Parral, *Mexico*	114	B3
Hidrolândia, *Brazil*	123	E2
Hieflau, *Austria*	21	H4
Hiendelaencina, *Spain*	28	D1
Hierro, *Canary Is.*	36	G1
Higashiajima-San, *Japan*	48	F10
Higashiōsaka, *Japan*	49	G7
Higgins, *U.S.A.*	109	G4
Higgins Corner, *U.S.A.*	112	F5
Higginsville, *Australia*	89	F3
High Atlas = Haut Atlas, *Morocco*	74	B3
High I., *Canada*	99	A7
High Island, *U.S.A.*	109	L7
High Level, *Canada*	100	B5
High Point, *U.S.A.*	105	H6
High Prairie, *Canada*	100	B5
High River, *Canada*	100	C6
High Springs, *U.S.A.*	105	L4
High Tatra = Tatry, *Slovak Rep.*	20	F9
High Wycombe, *U.K.*	13	F7
Highbury, *Australia*	90	B3
Highland □, *U.K.*	14	D4
Highland Park, *U.S.A.*	104	D2
Highmore, *U.S.A.*	108	C5
Highrock L., *Canada*	101	B7
Higüay, *Dom. Rep.*	117	C6
Hihya, *Egypt*	76	H7
Hiiumaa, *Estonia*	9	G20
Híjar, *Spain*	28	D4
Hijāz □, *Si. Arabia*	68	C2
Hijken, *Neths.*	16	C8
Hijo = Tagum, *Phil.*	55	H6
Hikari, *Japan*	49	H5
Hiko, *U.S.A.*	111	H6
Hikone, *Japan*	49	G8
Hikurangi, *N.Z.*	87	F5
Hikurangi, Mt., *N.Z.*	87	H6
Hildburghausen, *Germany*	19	E6
Hildesheim, *Germany*	18	C5
Hill →, *Australia*	89	F2
Hill City, *Idaho, U.S.A.*	110	E6
Hill City, *Kans., U.S.A.*	108	F5
Hill City, *Minn., U.S.A.*	108	B8
Hill City, *S. Dak., U.S.A.*	108	D3
Hill Island L., *Canada*	101	A7
Hillared, *Sweden*	11	G7
Hillcrest Center, *U.S.A.*	113	K8
Hillegom, *Neths.*	16	D5
Hillerød, *Denmark*	11	J6
Hillingdon, *U.K.*	13	F7
Hillman, *U.S.A.*	104	C4
Hillmond, *Canada*	101	C7
Hillsboro, *Kans., U.S.A.*	108	F6
Hillsboro, *N. Dak., U.S.A.*	108	B6
Hillsboro, *N.H., U.S.A.*	107	C13
Hillsboro, *N. Mex., U.S.A.*	111	K10
Hillsboro, *Oreg., U.S.A.*	112	E4
Hillsboro, *Tex., U.S.A.*	109	J6
Hillsborough, *Grenada*	117	D7
Hillsdale, *Mich., U.S.A.*	104	E3
Hillsdale, *N.Y., U.S.A.*	107	D11
Hillside, *Australia*	88	D2
Hillsport, *Canada*	98	C2
Hillston, *Australia*	91	E4
Hilo, *U.S.A.*	102	J17
Hilton, *U.S.A.*	106	C7
Hilvan, *Turkey*	67	D8
Hilvarenbeek, *Neths.*	17	F6
Hilversum, *Neths.*	16	D6
Himachal Pradesh □, *India*	62	D7
Himalaya, *Asia*	63	E11
Himamaylan, *Phil.*	55	F5
Himara, *Albania*	39	J2
Himatnagar, *India*	60	H8
Himeji, *Japan*	49	G7
Himi, *Japan*	49	F8
Himmerland, *Denmark*	11	H3
Ḥimṣ, *Syria*	69	A5
Ḥimṣ □, *Syria*	69	A5
Hinche, *Haiti*	117	C5
Hinchinbrook I., *Australia*	90	B4
Hinckley, *U.K.*	13	E6
Hinckley, *U.S.A.*	110	G7
Hindås, *Sweden*	11	G6
Hindaun, *India*	62	F7
Hindmarsh, L., *Australia*	91	F3
Hindsholm, *Denmark*	11	J4
Hindu Bagh, *Pakistan*	62	D2
Hindu Kush, *Asia*	60	B7
Hindubagh, *Pakistan*	60	D5
Hindupur, *India*	60	N10
Hines Creek, *Canada*	100	B5
Hinganghat, *India*	60	J11
Hingeon, *Belgium*	17	G5
Hingham, *U.S.A.*	110	B8
Hingoli, *India*	60	K10
Hinigaran, *Phil.*	55	F5
Hinis, *Turkey*	67	C9
Hinna = Imi, *Ethiopia*	68	F3
Hinna, *Nigeria*	79	C7
Hinnøya, *Norway*	8	B16
Hinojosa del Duque, *Spain*	31	G5
Hinsdale, *U.S.A.*	110	B10
Hinterrhein →, *Switz.*	23	C8
Hinton, *Canada*	100	C5
Hinton, *U.S.A.*	104	G5
Hinwil, *Switz.*	23	B7
Hınzır Burnu, *Turkey*	66	D6
Hippolytushoef, *Neths.*	16	C5
Hirado, *Japan*	49	H4
Hirakud Dam, *India*	61	J13
Hiratsuka, *Japan*	49	G9
Hirfanlı Baraji, *Turkey*	66	C5
Hirhafok, *Algeria*	75	D6
Hîrlău, *Romania*	38	B9
Hiroo, *Japan*	48	C11
Hirosaki, *Japan*	48	D10
Hiroshima, *Japan*	49	G6
Hiroshima □, *Japan*	49	G6
Hirsholmene, *Denmark*	11	G4
Hirson, *France*	25	C11
Hirtshals, *Denmark*	11	G3
Hisar, *India*	62	E6
Hisb →, *Iraq*	64	D5
Ḥismá, *Si. Arabia*	64	D3
Hispaniola, *W. Indies*	117	C5
Ḥīt, *Iraq*	67	F10
Hita, *Japan*	49	H5
Hitachi, *Japan*	49	F10
Hitchin, *U.K.*	13	F7
Hitoyoshi, *Japan*	49	H5
Hitra, *Norway*	8	E13
Hitzacker, *Germany*	18	B7
Ḥiyyon, N. →, *Israel*	69	E4
Hjalmar L., *Canada*	101	A7
Hjälmare kanal, *Sweden*	10	E9
Hjälmaren, *Sweden*	10	E9
Hjartdal, *Norway*	10	E2
Hjerkinn, *Norway*	10	B3
Hjørring, *Denmark*	11	G3
Hjortkvarn, *Sweden*	11	F9
Hlinsko, *Czech.*	20	F5
Hluhluwe, *S. Africa*	85	D5
Hlukhiv, *Ukraine*	41	G7
Hlyboka, *Ukraine*	41	H3
Hlybokaye, *Belarus*	40	E4
Ho, *Ghana*	79	D5
Ho Chi Minh City = Phanh Bho Ho Chi Minh, *Vietnam*	59	G6
Ho Thuong, *Vietnam*	58	C5
Hoa Binh, *Vietnam*	58	B5
Hoa Da, *Vietnam*	59	G7
Hoa Hiep, *Vietnam*	59	G5
Hoai Nhon, *Vietnam*	58	E7
Hoang Lien Son, *Vietnam*	58	A4
Hoare B., *Canada*	97	B13
Hobart, *Australia*	90	G4
Hobart, *U.S.A.*	109	H5
Hobbs, *U.S.A.*	109	J3
Hobbs Coast, *Antarctica*	5	D14
Hobo, *Colombia*	120	C2
Hoboken, *Belgium*	17	F4
Hoboken, *U.S.A.*	107	F10
Hobro, *Denmark*	11	H3
Hobscheid, *Lux.*	17	J7
Hoburgen, *Sweden*	9	H18
Hochdorf, *Switz.*	23	B6
Hochschwab, *Austria*	21	H5
Höchstadt, *Germany*	19	F6
Hockenheim, *Germany*	19	F4
Hodaka-Dake, *Japan*	49	F8
Hodgson, *Canada*	101	C9
Hódmezővásárhely, *Hungary*	21	J10
Hodna, Chott el, *Algeria*	75	A5
Hodna, Monts du, *Algeria*	75	A5
Hodonín, *Czech.*	20	G7
Hoeamdong, *N. Korea*	51	C16
Hœdic, I. de, *France*	24	E4
Hoek van Holland, *Neths.*	16	E4
Hoeksche Waard, *Neths.*	16	E4
Hoenderloo, *Neths.*	16	D7
Hoengsŏng, *S. Korea*	51	F14
Hoensbroek, *Neths.*	17	G7
Hoeryong, *N. Korea*	51	C15
Hoeselt, *Belgium*	17	G6
Hoeven, *Neths.*	17	E5
Hoeyang, *N. Korea*	51	E14
Hof, *Germany*	19	E7
Höfðakaupstaður, *Iceland*	8	D3
Hofgeismar, *Germany*	18	D5
Hofmeyr, *S. Africa*	84	E4
Höfn, *Iceland*	8	D6
Hofors, *Sweden*	9	F17
Hofsjökull, *Iceland*	8	D4
Hōfu, *Japan*	49	G5
Hogan Group, *Australia*	90	F4
Hogansville, *U.S.A.*	105	J3
Hogeland, *U.S.A.*	110	B9
Hoggar = Ahaggar, *Algeria*	75	D6
Högsäter, *Sweden*	11	F6
Hogsty Reef, *Bahamas*	117	B5
Hoh →, *U.S.A.*	112	C2
Hoh Xil Shan, *China*	54	C3
Hohe Rhön, *Germany*	19	E5
Hohe Tauern, *Austria*	21	H2
Hohe Venn, *Belgium*	17	H8
Hohenau, *Austria*	20	G6
Hohenems, *Austria*	19	H5
Hohenstein-Ernstthal, *Germany*	18	E8
Hohenwald, *U.S.A.*	105	H2
Hohenwestedt, *Germany*	18	A5
Hohhot, *China*	50	D6
Hóhlakas, *Greece*	37	D9
Hohoe, *Ghana*	79	D5
Hoi An, *Vietnam*	58	E7
Hoi Xuan, *Vietnam*	58	B5

Hoisington, U.S.A. 108 F5
Højer, Denmark 11 K2
Hōjō, Japan 49 H6
Hökerum, Sweden 11 G7
Hokianga Harbour, N.Z. 87 F4
Hokitika, N.Z. 87 K3
Hokkaidō □, Japan 48 C11
Hokksund, Norway 10 E3
Hol-Hol, Djibouti 77 E5
Hola Pristan, Ukraine 41 J7
Holbæk, Denmark 11 J5
Holbrook, Australia 91 F4
Holbrook, U.S.A. 111 J8
Holden, Canada 100 C6
Holden, U.S.A. 110 G7
Holdenville, U.S.A. 109 H6
Holderness, U.K. 12 D7
Holdfast, Canada 101 C7
Holdrege, U.S.A. 108 E5
Holguín, Cuba 116 B4
Hollabrunn, Austria 20 G6
Hollams Bird I., Namibia 84 C1
Holland = Jayapura, Indonesia 57 E10
Hollandsch Diep, Neths. 17 E5
Hollandsch IJssel →, Neths. 16 E5
Hollfeld, Germany 19 F7
Hollidaysburg, U.S.A. 106 F6
Hollis, U.S.A. 109 H5
Hollister, Calif., U.S.A. 111 H3
Hollister, Idaho, U.S.A. 110 E6
Hollum, Neths. 16 B7
Holly, U.S.A. 108 F3
Holly Hill, U.S.A. 105 L5
Holly Springs, U.S.A. 109 H10
Hollywood, Calif., U.S.A. 111 J4
Hollywood, Fla., U.S.A. 105 N5
Holm, Sweden 10 B10
Holman Island, Canada 96 A8
Hólmavík, Iceland 8 D3
Holmes Reefs, Australia 90 B4
Holmestrand, Norway 10 E4
Holmsbu, Norway 10 E4
Holmsjön, Sweden 10 B9
Holmsland Klit, Denmark 11 J2
Holmsund, Sweden 8 E19
Holroyd →, Australia 90 A3
Holstebro, Denmark 11 H2
Holsworthy, U.K. 13 G3
Holte, Denmark 11 J6
Holten, Neths. 16 D8
Holton, Canada 99 B8
Holton, U.S.A. 108 F7
Holtville, U.S.A. 113 N11
Holwerd, Neths. 16 B7
Holy Cross, U.S.A. 96 B4
Holy I., Gwynedd, U.K. 12 D3
Holy I., Northumb., U.K. 12 B6
Holyhead, U.K. 12 D3
Holyoke, Colo., U.S.A. 108 E3
Holyoke, Mass., U.S.A. 107 D12
Holyrood, Canada 99 C9
Holzkirchen, Germany 19 H7
Holzminden, Germany 18 D5
Homa Bay, Kenya 82 C3
Homa Bay □, Kenya 82 C3
Homalin, Burma 61 G19
Homand, Iran 65 C8
Homberg, Germany 18 D5
Hombori, Mali 79 B4
Homburg, Germany 19 F3
Home B., Canada 97 B13
Home Hill, Australia 90 B4
Homedale, U.S.A. 110 E5
Homer, Alaska, U.S.A. 96 C4
Homer, La., U.S.A. 109 J8
Homestead, Australia 90 C4
Homestead, Fla., U.S.A. 105 N5
Homestead, Oreg., U.S.A. 110 D5
Homewood, U.S.A. 112 F6
Hominy, U.S.A. 109 G6
Homoine, Mozam. 85 C6
Homoljske Planina, Serbia, Yug. 21 L11
Homorod, Romania 38 C8
Homs = Ḥimṣ, Syria 69 A5
Homyel, Belarus 41 F6
Hon Chong, Vietnam 59 G5
Hon Me, Vietnam 58 C5
Hon Quan, Vietnam 59 G6
Honan = Henan □, China 50 G8
Honbetsu, Japan 48 C11
Honcut, U.S.A. 112 F5
Honda, Colombia 120 B3
Honda Bay, Phil. 55 G3
Hondeklipbaai, S. Africa 84 E2
Hondo, Japan 49 H5
Hondo, U.S.A. 109 L5
Hondo →, Belize 115 D7
Honduras ■, Cent. Amer. 116 D2
Honduras, G. de, Caribbean 116 C2
Hønefoss, Norway 9 F14
Honesdale, U.S.A. 107 E9
Honey L., U.S.A. 112 F6
Honfleur, France 24 C7
Hong Gai, Vietnam 58 B6
Hong He →, China 50 H8
Hong Kong ■, Asia 53 F10
Hong'an, China 53 B10
Hongch'ŏn, S. Korea 51 F14
Honghai Wan, China 53 F10
Honghu, China 53 C9

Hongjiang, China 52 D7
Hongliu He →, China 50 F5
Hongor, Mongolia 50 B7
Hongsa, Laos 58 C3
Hongshui He →, China 52 F7
Hongsŏng, S. Korea 51 F14
Hongtong, China 50 F6
Honguedo, Détroit d', Canada 99 C7
Hongwon, N. Korea 51 E14
Hongya, China 52 C4
Hongyuan, China 52 A4
Hongze Hu, China 51 H10
Honiara, Solomon Is. 92 H7
Honiton, U.K. 13 G4
Honjō, Japan 48 E10
Honkorâb, Ras, Egypt 76 C4
Honningsvåg, Norway 8 A21
Honolulu, U.S.A. 102 H16
Honshū, Japan 49 G9
Hontoria del Pinar, Spain 28 D1
Hood, Mt., U.S.A. 110 D3
Hood, Pt., Australia 89 F2
Hood River, U.S.A. 110 D3
Hoodsport, U.S.A. 112 C3
Hooge, Germany 18 A4
Hoogerheide, Neths. 17 F4
Hoogeveen, Neths. 16 C8
Hoogeveensche Vaart, Neths. 16 C8
Hoogezand, Neths. 16 B9
Hooghly = Hughli →, India 63 J13
Hooghly-Chinsura = Chunchura, India 63 H13
Hoogkerk, Neths. 16 B9
Hooglede, Belgium 17 G2
Hoogstraten, Belgium 17 F5
Hoogvliet, Neths. 16 E4
Hook Hd., Ireland 15 D5
Hook I., Australia 90 C4
Hook of Holland = Hoek van Holland, Neths. 16 E4
Hooker, U.S.A. 109 G4
Hooker Creek, Australia 88 C5
Hoopeston, U.S.A. 104 E2
Hoopstad, S. Africa 84 D4
Hoorn, Neths. 16 C6
Hoover Dam, U.S.A. 113 K12
Hooversville, U.S.A. 106 F6
Hop Bottom, U.S.A. 107 E9
Hopa, Turkey 67 B9
Hope, Canada 100 D4
Hope, Ariz., U.S.A. 113 M13
Hope, Ark., U.S.A. 109 J8
Hope, N. Dak., U.S.A. 108 B6
Hope, L., Australia 91 D2
Hope, Pt., U.S.A. 96 B3
Hope Town, Bahamas 116 A4
Hopedale, Canada 99 A7
Hopefield, S. Africa 84 E2
Hopei = Hebei □, China 50 E9
Hopelchén, Mexico 115 D7
Hopetoun, Vic., Australia 91 F3
Hopetoun, W. Austral., Australia 89 F3
Hopetown, S. Africa 84 D3
Hopkins, U.S.A. 108 E7
Hopkins, L., Australia 88 D4
Hopkinsville, U.S.A. 105 G2
Hopland, U.S.A. 112 G3
Hoptrup, Denmark 11 J3
Hoquiam, U.S.A. 112 D3
Horasan, Turkey 67 B10
Horcajo de Santiago, Spain 28 F1
Horden Hills, Australia 88 D5
Horezu, Romania 38 D6
Horgen, Switz. 23 B7
Horinger, China 50 D6
Horki, Belarus 40 E6
Horlick Mts., Antarctica 5 E15
Horlivka, Ukraine 41 H10
Hormoz, Iran 65 E7
Hormoz, Jaz. ye, Iran 65 E8
Hormuz, Str. of, The Gulf 65 E8
Horn, Iceland 8 C2
Horn, Neths. 17 F7
Horn →, Canada 100 A5
Horn, Cape = Hornos, C. de, Chile 128 E3
Horn Head, Ireland 15 A3
Horn I., Australia 90 A3
Horn I., U.S.A. 105 K1
Horn Mts., Canada 100 A5
Hornachuelos, Spain 31 H5
Hornavan, Sweden 8 C17
Hornbæk, Denmark 11 H6
Hornbeck, U.S.A. 109 K8
Hornbrook, U.S.A. 110 F2
Hornburg, Germany 18 C6
Horncastle, U.K. 12 D7
Hornell, U.S.A. 106 D7
Hornell L., Canada 100 A5
Hornepayne, Canada 98 C3
Hornitos, U.S.A. 112 H6
Hornos, C. de, Chile 128 E3
Hornoy, France 25 C8
Hornsby, Australia 91 E5
Hornsea, U.K. 12 D7
Hornslandet, Sweden 10 C11
Hornslet, Denmark 11 H4
Hornu, Belgium 17 H3
Hörnum, Germany 18 A4
Horobetsu, Japan 48 C10
Horodenka, Ukraine 41 H3
Horodnya, Ukraine 41 G6

Horodok, Khmelnytskyy, Ukraine 41 H4
Horodok, Lviv, Ukraine 41 H2
Horodyshche, Ukraine 41 H6
Horokhiv, Ukraine 41 G3
Horqin Youyi Qianqi, China 51 A12
Horqueta, Paraguay 126 A4
Horred, Sweden 11 G6
Horse Creek, U.S.A. 108 E3
Horse Is., Canada 99 B8
Horsefly L., Canada 100 C4
Horsens, Denmark 11 J3
Horsens Fjord, Denmark 11 J4
Horsham, Australia 91 F3
Horsham, U.K. 13 F7
Horst, Neths. 17 F8
Horten, Norway 10 E4
Hortobágy →, Hungary 21 H11
Horton, U.S.A. 108 F7
Horton →, Canada 96 B7
Horw, Switz. 23 B6
Horwood, L., Canada 98 C3
Hosaina, Ethiopia 77 F4
Hose, Gunung-Gunung, Malaysia 56 D4
Ḥoseynābād, Khuzestān, Iran 65 C6
Ḥoseynābād, Kordestān, Iran 67 E12
Hoshangabad, India 62 H7
Hoshiarpur, India 62 D6
Hosingen, Lux. 17 H8
Hosmer, U.S.A. 108 C5
Hospental, Switz. 23 C7
Hospet, India 60 M10
Hospitalet de Llobregat, Spain 28 D7
Hoste, I., Chile 128 E3
Hostens, France 26 D3
Hot, Thailand 58 C2
Hot Creek Range, U.S.A. 110 G5
Hot Springs, Ark., U.S.A. 109 H8
Hot Springs, S. Dak., U.S.A. 108 D3
Hotagen, Sweden 8 E16
Hotan, China 54 C2
Hotazel, S. Africa 84 D3
Hotchkiss, U.S.A. 111 G10
Hotham, C., Australia 88 B5
Hoting, Sweden 8 D17
Hotte, Massif de la, Haiti 117 C5
Hottentotsbaai, Namibia 84 D1
Hotton, Belgium 17 H6
Houat, I. de, France 24 E4
Houck, U.S.A. 111 J9
Houdan, France 25 D8
Houdeng-Goegnies, Belgium 17 H4
Houei Sai, Laos 58 B3
Houffalize, Belgium 17 H7
Houghton, U.S.A. 104 B10
Houghton L., U.S.A. 104 C3
Houghton-le-Spring, U.K. 12 C6
Houhora Heads, N.Z. 87 F4
Houille →, Belgium 17 H5
Houlton, U.S.A. 99 C6
Houma, China 50 G6
Houma, U.S.A. 109 L9
Houndé, Burkina Faso 78 C4
Hourtin, France 26 C2
Hourtin-Carcans, Étang d', France 26 C2
Houston, Canada 100 C3
Houston, Mo., U.S.A. 109 G9
Houston, Tex., U.S.A. 109 L7
Houten, Neths. 16 D6
Houthalen, Belgium 17 F6
Houthem, Belgium 17 G1
Houthulst, Belgium 17 G2
Houtman Abrolhos, Australia 89 E1
Houyet, Belgium 17 H6
Hov, Denmark 11 J4
Hova, Sweden 11 F8
Høvåg, Norway 11 F2
Hovd, Mongolia 54 B4
Hove, U.K. 13 G7
Hoveyzeh, Iran 65 D6
Hövsgöl, Mongolia 50 C5
Hövsgöl Nuur, Mongolia 50 A5
Howakil, Eritrea 77 D5
Howar, Wadi →, Sudan 77 D2
Howard, Australia 91 D5
Howard, Kans., U.S.A. 109 G6
Howard, Pa., U.S.A. 106 E7
Howard, S. Dak., U.S.A. 108 C6
Howard I., Australia 90 A2
Howard L., Canada 101 A7
Howe, U.S.A. 110 E7
Howe, C., Australia 91 F5
Howell, U.S.A. 104 D4
Howick, Canada 107 A11
Howick, S. Africa 85 D5
Howick Group, Australia 90 A4
Howitt, L., Australia 91 D2
Howland I., Pac. Oc. 92 G10
Howley, Canada 99 C8
Howrah = Haora, India 63 H13
Howth Hd., Ireland 15 C5
Höxter, Germany 18 D5
Hoy, U.K. 14 C5
Hoya, Germany 18 B5
Høyanger, Norway 9 F12
Hoyerswerda, Germany 18 D10
Hoyos, Spain 30 E4
Hpungan Pass, Burma 61 F20

Hradec Králové, Czech. 20 E5
Hranice, Czech. 20 F7
Hrazdan, Armenia 43 K7
Hrebenka, Ukraine 41 G7
Hrodna, Belarus 40 F2
Hrodzyanka, Belarus 40 F5
Hron →, Slovak Rep. 21 H8
Hrubieszów, Poland 20 E13
Hrvatska = Croatia ■, Europe 33 C13
Hrymayliv, Ukraine 41 H4
Hsenwi, Burma 61 H20
Hsiamen = Xiamen, China 53 E12
Hsian = Xi'an, China 50 G5
Hsinhailien = Lianyungang, China 51 G10
Hsisha Chuntao, Pac. Oc. 56 A4
Hsüchou = Xuzhou, China 51 G9
Hu Xian, China 50 G5
Hua Hin, Thailand 58 F2
Hua Xian, Henan, China 50 G8
Hua Xian, Shaanxi, China 50 G5
Hua'an, China 53 E11
Huacaya, Bolivia 125 E5
Huacheng, China 53 E10
Huachinera, Mexico 114 A3
Huacho, Peru 124 C2
Huachón, Peru 124 C2
Huade, China 50 D7
Huadian, China 51 C14
Huai He →, China 53 A12
Huai Yot, Thailand 59 J2
Huai'an, Hebei, China 50 D8
Huai'an, Jiangsu, China 51 H10
Huaibei, China 50 G9
Huaide, China 51 C13
Huaidezhen, China 51 C13
Huaihua, China 52 D7
Huaiji, China 53 F9
Huainan, China 53 A11
Huaining, China 53 B11
Huairen, China 50 E7
Huairou, China 50 D9
Huaiyang, China 50 H8
Huaiyuan, Anhui, China 51 H9
Huaiyuan, Guangxi Zhuangzu, China 52 E7
Huajianzi, China 51 D13
Huajuapan de Leon, Mexico 115 D5
Hualapai Peak, U.S.A. 111 J7
Hualian, Taiwan 53 F13
Huallaga →, Peru 124 B2
Huallanca, Peru 124 B2
Huamachuco, Peru 124 B2
Huambo, Angola 81 G3
Huan Jiang →, China 50 G5
Huan Xian, China 50 F4
Huancabamba, Peru 124 B2
Huancane, Peru 124 D4
Huancapi, Peru 124 C3
Huancavelica, Peru 124 C2
Huancavelica □, Peru 124 C3
Huancayo, Peru 124 C2
Huanchaca, Bolivia 124 E4
Huanchaca, Serranía de, Bolivia 125 C5
Huang Hai = Yellow Sea, China 51 G12
Huang He →, China 51 F10
Huang Xian, China 51 F11
Huangchuan, China 53 A10
Huanggang, China 53 B10
Huangling, China 50 G5
Huangliu, China 54 F5
Huanglong, China 50 G5
Huanglongtan, China 53 A8
Huangmei, China 53 B10
Huangpi, China 53 B10
Huangping, China 52 D6
Huangshi, China 53 B10
Huangsongdian, China 51 C14
Huangyan, China 53 C13
Huangyangsi, China 53 D8
Huaning, China 52 E4
Huanjiang, China 52 E7
Huanta, Peru 124 C3
Huantai, China 51 F9
Huánuco, Peru 124 B2
Huánuco □, Peru 124 B2
Huanuni, Bolivia 124 D4
Huanzo, Cordillera de, Peru 124 C3
Huaping, China 52 D3
Huaral, Peru 124 C2
Huaraz, Peru 124 B2
Huari, Peru 124 B2
Huarmey, Peru 124 C2
Huarochiri, Peru 124 C2
Huarong, China 53 C9
Huascarán, Nevado, Peru 124 B2
Huasco, Chile 126 B1
Huasco →, Chile 126 B1
Huasna, U.S.A. 113 K6
Huatabampo, Mexico 114 B3
Huauchinango, Mexico 115 C5
Huautla de Jiménez, Mexico 115 D5
Huaxi, China 52 D6
Huay Namota, Mexico 114 C4
Huayin, China 50 G6
Huaylas, Peru 124 B2
Huayuan, China 52 C7
Huazhou, China 53 G8

Hubbard, U.S.A. 109 K6
Hubbart Pt., Canada 101 B10
Hubei □, China 53 B9
Hubli-Dharwad = Dharwad, India 60 M9
Huchang, N. Korea 51 D14
Hückelhoven, Germany 18 D2
Huddersfield, U.K. 12 D6
Hudi, Sudan 76 D3
Hudiksvall, Sweden 10 C11
Hudson, Canada 101 C10
Hudson, Mass., U.S.A. 107 D13
Hudson, Mich., U.S.A. 104 E3
Hudson, N.Y., U.S.A. 107 D11
Hudson, Wis., U.S.A. 108 C8
Hudson, Wyo., U.S.A. 110 E9
Hudson →, U.S.A. 107 F10
Hudson Bay, N.W.T., Canada 97 C11
Hudson Bay, Sask., Canada 101 C8
Hudson Falls, U.S.A. 107 C11
Hudson Mts., Antarctica 5 D16
Hudson Str., Canada 97 B13
Hudson's Hope, Canada 100 B4
Hue, Vietnam 58 D6
Huebra →, Spain 30 D4
Huechucuicui, Pta., Chile 128 B2
Huedin, Romania 38 C6
Huehuetenango, Guatemala 116 C1
Huejúcar, Mexico 114 C4
Huelgoat, France 24 D3
Huelma, Spain 29 H1
Huelva, Spain 31 H4
Huelva □, Spain 31 H4
Huelva →, Spain 31 H5
Huentelauquén, Chile 126 C1
Huércal Overa, Spain 29 H3
Huerta, Sa. de la, Argentina 126 C2
Huertas, C. de las, Spain 29 G4
Huerva →, Spain 28 D4
Huesca, Spain 28 C5
Huesca □, Spain 28 C5
Huéscar, Spain 29 H2
Huetamo, Mexico 114 D4
Huete, Spain 28 E2
Hugh →, Australia 90 D1
Hughenden, Australia 90 C3
Hughes, Australia 89 F4
Hughli →, India 63 J13
Hugo, U.S.A. 108 F3
Hugoton, U.S.A. 109 G4
Hui Xian, Gansu, China 50 H4
Hui Xian, Henan, China 50 G7
Hui'an, China 53 E12
Hui'anbu, China 50 F4
Huichang, China 53 E10
Huichapán, Mexico 115 C5
Huidong, China 52 D4
Huifa He →, China 51 C14
Huila □, Colombia 120 C2
Huila, Nevado del, Colombia 120 C2
Huilai, China 53 F11
Huili, China 52 D4
Huimin, China 51 F9
Huinan, China 51 C14
Huinca Renancó, Argentina 126 C3
Huining, China 50 G3
Huinong, China 50 E4
Huise, Belgium 17 G3
Huishui, China 52 D6
Huisne →, France 24 E7
Huissen, Neths. 16 E7
Huiting, China 50 G9
Huitong, China 52 D7
Huixtla, Mexico 115 D6
Huize, China 52 D4
Huizen, Neths. 16 D6
Huizhou, China 53 F10
Hukawng Valley, Burma 61 F20
Hukou, China 53 C11
Hukuntsi, Botswana 84 C3
Hula, Ethiopia 77 F4
Hulan, China 54 B7
Ḥulayfā', Si. Arabia 64 E4
Huld, Mongolia 50 B3
Hulin He →, China 51 B12
Hull = Kingston upon Hull, U.K. 12 D7
Hull, Canada 98 C4
Hull →, U.K. 12 D7
Hulst, Neths. 17 F4
Hulun Nur, China 54 B6
Hulyaypole, Ukraine 41 J9
Humahuaca, Argentina 126 A2
Humaitá, Brazil 125 B5
Humaitá, Paraguay 126 B4
Humansdorp, S. Africa 84 E3
Humbe, Angola 84 B1
Humber →, U.K. 12 D7
Humberside □, U.K. 12 D7
Humbert River, Australia 88 C5
Humble, U.S.A. 109 L8
Humboldt, Canada 101 C7
Humboldt, Iowa, U.S.A. 108 D7
Humboldt, Tenn., U.S.A. 109 H10
Humboldt →, U.S.A. 110 F4
Humboldt Gletscher, Greenland 4 B4
Hume, U.S.A. 112 J8
Hume, L., Australia 91 F4
Humenné, Slovak Rep. 20 G11
Humphreys, Mt., U.S.A. 112 H8
Humphreys Peak, U.S.A. 111 J8
Humpolec, Czech. 20 F5
Humptulips, U.S.A. 112 C3

Hūn, *Libya* 73 C8
Hun Jiang →, *China* 51 D13
Húnaflói, *Iceland* 8 D3
Hunan □, *China* 53 D9
Hunchun, *China* 51 C16
Hundested, *Denmark* 11 J5
Hundred Mile House, *Canada* 100 C4
Hunedoara, *Romania* 38 D5
Hünfeld, *Germany* 18 E5
Hung Yen, *Vietnam* 58 B6
Hungary ■, *Europe* 21 H9
Hungary, Plain of, *Europe* 6 F9
Hungerford, *Australia* 91 D3
Hŭngnam, *N. Korea* 51 E14
Huni Valley, *Ghana* 78 D4
Hunsberge, *Namibia* 84 D2
Hunsrück, *Germany* 19 F3
Hunstanton, *U.K.* 12 E8
Hunte →, *Germany* 18 C4
Hunter, *N. Dak., U.S.A.* 108 B6
Hunter, *N.Y., U.S.A.* 107 D10
Hunter I., *Australia* 90 G4
Hunter I., *Canada* 100 C3
Hunter Ra., *Australia* 91 E5
Hunters Road, *Zimbabwe* 83 F2
Hunterville, *N.Z.* 87 H5
Huntingburg, *U.S.A.* 104 F2
Huntingdon, *Canada* 98 C5
Huntingdon, *U.K.* 13 E7
Huntingdon, *U.S.A.* 106 F6
Huntington, *Ind., U.S.A.* 104 E3
Huntington, *N.Y., U.S.A.* 107 F11
Huntington, *Oreg., U.S.A.* 110 D5
Huntington, *Utah, U.S.A.* 110 G8
Huntington, *W. Va., U.S.A.* 104 F4
Huntington Beach, *U.S.A.* 113 M8
Huntington Park, *U.S.A.* 111 K4
Huntly, *N.Z.* 87 G5
Huntly, *U.K.* 14 D6
Huntsville, *Canada* 98 C4
Huntsville, *Ala., U.S.A.* 105 H2
Huntsville, *Tex., U.S.A.* 109 K7
Hunyani →, *Zimbabwe* 83 F3
Hunyuan, *China* 50 E7
Hunza →, *India* 63 B6
Huo Xian, *China* 50 F6
Huong Hoa, *Vietnam* 58 D6
Huong Khe, *Vietnam* 58 C5
Huonville, *Australia* 90 G4
Huoqiu, *China* 53 A11
Huoshan, *Anhui, China* 53 A12
Huoshan, *Anhui, China* 53 B11
Huoshan Dao, *Taiwan* 53 F13
Hupeh = Hubei □, *China* 53 B9
Ḩūr, *Iran* 65 D8
Hure Qi, *China* 51 C11
Hurezani, *Romania* 38 E6
Hurghada, *Egypt* 76 B3
Hurley, *N. Mex., U.S.A.* 111 K9
Hurley, *Wis., U.S.A.* 108 B9
Huron, *Calif., U.S.A.* 112 J6
Huron, *Ohio, U.S.A.* 106 E2
Huron, *S. Dak., U.S.A.* 108 C5
Huron, L., *U.S.A.* 106 C2
Hurricane, *U.S.A.* 111 H7
Hurso, *Ethiopia* 77 F5
Hurum, *Norway* 10 C2
Hurunui →, *N.Z.* 87 K4
Hurup, *Denmark* 11 H2
Húsavík, *Iceland* 8 C5
Huşi, *Romania* 38 C11
Huskvarna, *Sweden* 9 H16
Hussar, *Canada* 100 C6
Hustadvika, *Norway* 8 E12
Husum, *Germany* 18 A5
Husum, *Sweden* 10 A13
Hutchinson, *Kans., U.S.A.* 109 F6
Hutchinson, *Minn., U.S.A.* 108 C7
Huttig, *U.S.A.* 109 J8
Hutton, Mt., *Australia* 91 D4
Huttwil, *Switz.* 22 B5
Huwun, *Ethiopia* 77 G5
Huy, *Belgium* 17 G6
Hvammstangi, *Iceland* 8 D3
Hvar, *Croatia* 33 E13
Hvarski Kanal, *Croatia* 33 E13
Hvítá →, *Iceland* 8 D3
Hwachon-chosuji, *S. Korea* 51 E14
Hwang Ho = Huang He →, *China* 51 F10
Hwange, *Zimbabwe* 83 F2
Hwange Nat. Park, *Zimbabwe* 84 B4
Hyannis, *U.S.A.* 108 E4
Hyargas Nuur, *Mongolia* 54 B4
Hybo, *Sweden* 10 C10
Hyde Park, *Guyana* 121 B6
Hyden, *Australia* 89 F2
Hyderabad, *India* 60 L11
Hyderabad, *Pakistan* 62 G3
Hyères, *France* 27 E10
Hyères, Is. d', *France* 27 E10
Hyesan, *N. Korea* 51 D15
Hyland →, *Canada* 100 B3
Hyltebruk, *Sweden* 11 H7
Hymia, *India* 63 C8
Hyndman Peak, *U.S.A.* 110 E6
Hyōgo □, *Japan* 49 G7
Hyrum, *U.S.A.* 110 F8
Hysham, *U.S.A.* 110 C10
Hythe, *U.K.* 13 F9
Hyūga, *Japan* 49 H5
Hyvinge = Hyvinkää, *Finland* 9 F21
Hyvinkää, *Finland* 9 F21

I

I-n-Échaï, *Mali* 74 D4
I-n-Gall, *Niger* 79 B6
Iabès, Erg, *Algeria* 75 C4
Iaco →, *Brazil* 124 B4
Iaçu, *Brazil* 123 D3
Iakora, *Madag.* 85 C8
Iaşi, *Romania* 38 B10
Iauaretê, *Colombia* 120 C4
Iba, *Phil.* 55 D3
Ibadan, *Nigeria* 79 D5
Ibagué, *Colombia* 120 C2
Ibaiti, *Brazil* 123 F1
Iballja, *Albania* 38 G3
Ibănești, *Romania* 38 C7
Ibar →, *Serbia, Yug.* 21 M10
Ibaraki □, *Japan* 49 F10
Ibarra, *Ecuador* 120 C2
Ibba, *Sudan* 77 G2
Ibba, Bahr el →, *Sudan* 77 F2
Ibbenbüren, *Germany* 18 C3
Ibembo, *Zaïre* 82 B1
Ibera, L., *Argentina* 126 B4
Iberian Peninsula, *Europe* 6 G5
Iberico, Sistema, *Spain* 28 E2
Iberville, *Canada* 98 C5
Iberville, Lac d', *Canada* 98 A5
Ibi, *Nigeria* 79 D6
Ibiá, *Brazil* 123 E2
Ibicaraí, *Brazil* 123 D4
Ibicuí, *Brazil* 123 D4
Ibicuy, *Argentina* 126 C4
Ibioapaba, Sa. da, *Brazil* 122 B3
Ibipetuba, *Brazil* 122 D3
Ibitiara, *Brazil* 123 D3
Ibiza, *Spain* 36 C7
Íblei, Monti, *Italy* 35 E7
Ibo, *Mozam.* 83 E5
Ibonma, *Indonesia* 57 E8
Ibotirama, *Brazil* 123 D3
Ibrāhīm →, *Lebanon* 69 A4
Ibshawâi, *Egypt* 76 J7
Ibu, *Indonesia* 57 D7
Iburg, *Germany* 18 C4
Ibusuki, *Japan* 49 J5
Icá, *Peru* 124 C2
Ica →, *Peru* 124 C2
Içá →, *Brazil* 124 A4
Icabarú, *Venezuela* 121 C5
Icabarú →, *Venezuela* 121 C5
Içana, *Brazil* 120 C4
Içana →, *Brazil* 120 C4
Icatu, *Brazil* 122 B3
İçel = Mersin, *Turkey* 66 D6
Iceland ■, *Europe* 8 D4
Icha, *Russia* 45 D16
Ich'ang = Yichang, *China* 53 B8
Ichchapuram, *India* 61 K14
Ichihara, *Japan* 49 G10
Ichikawa, *Japan* 49 G9
Ichilo →, *Bolivia* 125 D5
Ichinohe, *Japan* 48 D10
Ichinomiya, *Japan* 49 G8
Ichinoseki, *Japan* 48 E10
Ichnya, *Ukraine* 41 G7
Ichŏn, *S. Korea* 51 F14
Icht, *Morocco* 74 C3
Ichtegem, *Belgium* 17 F2
Icó, *Brazil* 122 C4
Icod, *Canary Is.* 36 F3
Icoraci, *Brazil* 122 B2
Icy Str., *U.S.A.* 100 B1
Ida Grove, *U.S.A.* 108 D7
Ida Valley, *Australia* 89 E3
Idabel, *U.S.A.* 109 J7
Idaga Hamus, *Ethiopia* 77 E4
Idah, *Nigeria* 79 D6
Idaho □, *U.S.A.* 110 D6
Idaho City, *U.S.A.* 110 E6
Idaho Falls, *U.S.A.* 110 E7
Idaho Springs, *U.S.A.* 110 G11
Idanha-a-Nova, *Portugal* 30 F3
Idar-Oberstein, *Germany* 19 F3
Idd el Ghanam, *Sudan* 73 F9
Iddan, *Somali Rep.* 68 F4
Idehan, *Libya* 75 C7
Idehan Marzūq, *Libya* 73 D7
Idelès, *Algeria* 75 D6
Idfû, *Egypt* 76 C3
Ídhi Óros, *Greece* 37 D6
Ídhra, *Greece* 39 M6
Idi, *Indonesia* 56 C1
Idiofa, *Zaïre* 80 E3
Idku, Bahra el, *Egypt* 76 H7
Idlib, *Syria* 66 E7
Idria, *U.S.A.* 112 J6
Idrija, *Slovenia* 33 B11
Idritsa, *Russia* 40 D5
Idstein, *Germany* 19 E4
Idutywa, *S. Africa* 85 E4
Ieper, *Belgium* 17 G1
Ierápetra, *Greece* 37 E7
Ierissós, *Greece* 39 J6
Ierzu, *Italy* 34 C2
Iesi, *Italy* 33 E10
Ifach, Punta, *Spain* 29 G5
'Ifāl, W. al →, *Si. Arabia* 64 D2
Ifanadiana, *Madag.* 85 C8
Ife, *Nigeria* 79 D5
Iférouâne, *Niger* 79 B6
Iffley, *Australia* 90 B3
Ifni, *Morocco* 74 C2
Ifon, *Nigeria* 79 D6
Iforas, Adrar des, *Mali* 79 B5
Ifould, L., *Australia* 89 F5

Ifrane, *Morocco* 74 B3
Iganga, *Uganda* 82 B3
Igara Paraná →, *Colombia* 120 D3
Igarapava, *Brazil* 123 F2
Igarapé Açu, *Brazil* 122 B2
Igarapé-Mirim, *Brazil* 122 B2
Igarka, *Russia* 44 C9
Igatimi, *Paraguay* 127 A4
Igbetti, *Nigeria* 79 D5
Igbo-Ora, *Nigeria* 79 D5
Igboho, *Nigeria* 79 D5
Iğdır, *Turkey* 67 C11
Iggesund, *Sweden* 10 C11
Ighil Izane, *Algeria* 75 A5
Iglésias, *Italy* 34 C1
Igli, *Algeria* 75 C6
Igloolik, *Canada* 97 B11
Igma, Gebel el, *Egypt* 76 J8
Ignace, *Canada* 98 C1
İğneada Burnu, *Turkey* 66 B3
Igra, *Russia* 42 B11
Iguaçu →, *Brazil* 127 B5
Iguaçu, Cat. del, *Brazil* 127 B5
Iguaçu Falls = Iguaçu, Cat. del, *Brazil* 127 B5
Iguala, *Mexico* 115 D5
Igualada, *Spain* 28 D6
Iguape, *Brazil* 123 F2
Iguassu = Iguaçu →, *Brazil* 127 B5
Iguatu, *Brazil* 122 C4
Iguéla, *Gabon* 80 E1
Igunga □, *Tanzania* 82 C3
Iheya-Shima, *Japan* 49 L3
Ihiala, *Nigeria* 79 D6
Ihosy, *Madag.* 85 C8
Ihotry, L., *Madag.* 85 C7
Ii, *Finland* 8 D21
Ii-Shima, *Japan* 49 L3
Iida, *Japan* 49 G8
Iijoki →, *Finland* 8 D21
Iisalmi, *Finland* 8 E22
Iiyama, *Japan* 49 F9
Iizuka, *Japan* 49 H5
Ijâfene, *Mauritania* 74 D3
Ijebu-Igbo, *Nigeria* 79 D5
Ijebu-Ode, *Nigeria* 79 D5
IJmuiden, *Neths.* 16 D5
IJssel →, *Neths.* 16 C7
IJsselmeer, *Neths.* 16 C6
IJsselmuiden, *Neths.* 16 C7
IJsselstein, *Neths.* 16 D6
Ijuí, *Brazil* 127 B4
IJzendijke, *Neths.* 17 F3
IJzer →, *Belgium* 17 F1
Ikale, *Nigeria* 79 D6
Ikare, *Nigeria* 79 D6
Ikaría, *Greece* 39 M9
Ikast, *Denmark* 11 H3
Ikeda, *Japan* 49 G6
Ikeja, *Nigeria* 79 D5
Ikela, *Zaïre* 80 E4
Ikerre-Ekiti, *Nigeria* 79 D6
Ikhtiman, *Bulgaria* 38 G6
Iki, *Japan* 49 H4
Ikimba L., *Tanzania* 82 C3
Ikire, *Nigeria* 79 D5
Ikizdere, *Turkey* 67 B9
Ikom, *Nigeria* 79 D6
Ikopa →, *Madag.* 85 B8
Ikot Ekpene, *Nigeria* 79 D6
Ikungu, *Tanzania* 82 C3
Ikurun, *Nigeria* 79 D5
Ila, *Nigeria* 79 D5
Ilagan, *Phil.* 55 C4
Ïlām, *Iran* 67 F12
Ilam, *Nepal* 63 F12
Ilanskiy, *Russia* 45 D10
Ilanz, *Switz.* 23 C8
Ilaro, *Nigeria* 79 D5
Iława, *Poland* 20 B9
Ilbilbie, *Australia* 90 C4
Ile-à-la-Crosse, *Canada* 101 B7
Ile-à-la-Crosse, Lac, *Canada* 101 B7
Île-de-France, *France* 25 D9
Ilebo, *Zaïre* 80 E4
Ileje □, *Tanzania* 83 D3
Ilek, *Russia* 44 D6
Ilek →, *Russia* 44 D6
Ilero, *Nigeria* 79 D5
Ilesha, *Kwara, Nigeria* 79 D5
Ilesha, *Oyo, Nigeria* 79 D5
Ilford, *Canada* 101 B9
Ilfracombe, *Australia* 90 C3
Ilfracombe, *U.K.* 13 F3
Ilgaz, *Turkey* 66 B5
Ilgaz Dağları, *Turkey* 66 B5
Ilgın, *Turkey* 66 C4
Ilha Grande, *Brazil* 121 D4
Ilha Grande, B. da, *Brazil* 123 F3
Ílhavo, *Portugal* 30 E2
Ilhéus, *Brazil* 123 D4
Ili →, *Kazakhstan* 44 E8
Iliç, *Turkey* 67 C8
Ilich, *Kazakhstan* 44 E7
Ilichevsk, *Azerbaijan* 67 C11
Iliff, *U.S.A.* 108 E3
Iligan, *Phil.* 55 G6
Iliodhrómia, *Greece* 39 L6
Ilion, *U.S.A.* 107 D9
Ilirska-Bistrica, *Slovenia* 33 C11
Ilkeston, *U.K.* 12 E6

Illampu = Ancohuma, Nevada, *Bolivia* 124 D4
Illana B., *Phil.* 55 H5
Illapel, *Chile* 126 C1
Ille-et-Vilaine □, *France* 24 D5
Ille-sur-Têt, *France* 26 F6
Iller →, *Germany* 19 G5
Illescas, *Spain* 30 E7
Illetas, *Spain* 36 B9
Illichivsk, *Ukraine* 41 J6
Illiers-Combray, *France* 24 D8
Illimani, *Bolivia* 124 D4
Illinois □, *U.S.A.* 103 C9
Illinois →, *U.S.A.* 103 C8
Illium = Troy, *Turkey* 66 C2
Illizi, *Algeria* 75 C6
Illora, *Spain* 31 H7
Ilm →, *Germany* 18 D7
Ilmajoki, *Finland* 9 E20
Ilmen, Ozero, *Russia* 40 C6
Ilmenau, *Germany* 18 E6
Ilo, *Peru* 124 D3
Ilobu, *Nigeria* 79 D5
Iloilo, *Phil.* 55 F5
Ilora, *Nigeria* 79 D5
Ilorin, *Nigeria* 79 D5
Ilovatka, *Russia* 42 E7
Ilovlya, *Russia* 43 F7
Ilovlya →, *Russia* 43 F7
Ilubabor □, *Ethiopia* 77 F3
Ilva Mică, *Romania* 38 B7
Ilwaco, *U.S.A.* 112 D2
Ilwaki, *Indonesia* 57 F7
Ilyichevsk = Illichivsk, *Ukraine* 41 J6
Imabari, *Japan* 49 G6
Imaloto →, *Madag.* 85 C8
Imamoğlu, *Turkey* 66 D6
Imandra, Ozero, *Russia* 44 C4
Imari, *Japan* 49 H4
Imasa, *Sudan* 76 D4
Imatra, *Finland* 40 B5
Imbâbah, *Egypt* 76 H7
Imbabura □, *Ecuador* 120 C2
Imbaimadai, *Guyana* 121 B5
Imbler, *U.S.A.* 110 D5
Imdahane, *Morocco* 74 B3
imeni 26 Bakinskikh Komissarov = Neftçala, *Azerbaijan* 67 C13
Imeni Poliny Osipenko, *Russia* 45 D14
Imeri, Serra, *Brazil* 120 C4
Imerimandroso, *Madag.* 85 B8
Imesan, *Mauritania* 74 D1
Imi, *Ethiopia* 68 F3
Imishly = Imişli, *Azerbaijan* 43 L9
Imişli, *Azerbaijan* 43 L9
Imitek, *Morocco* 74 C3
Imlay, *U.S.A.* 110 F4
Imlay City, *U.S.A.* 106 C1
Immenstadt, *Germany* 19 H6
Immingham, *U.K.* 12 D7
Immokalee, *U.S.A.* 105 M5
Imo □, *Nigeria* 79 D6
Imola, *Italy* 33 D8
Imotski, *Croatia* 21 M7
Imperatriz, *Amazonas, Brazil* 124 B4
Imperatriz, *Maranhão, Brazil* 122 C2
Impéria, *Italy* 32 E5
Imperial, *Canada* 101 C7
Imperial, *Peru* 124 C2
Imperial, *Calif., U.S.A.* 113 N11
Imperial, *Nebr., U.S.A.* 108 E4
Imperial Beach, *U.S.A.* 113 N9
Imperial Dam, *U.S.A.* 113 N12
Imperial Reservoir, *U.S.A.* 113 N12
Imperial Valley, *U.S.A.* 113 N11
Imperieuse Reef, *Australia* 88 C2
Impfondo, *Congo* 80 D3
Imphal, *India* 61 G18
Imphy, *France* 26 B7
Imroz = Gökçeada, *Turkey* 66 B1
Imst, *Austria* 19 H6
Imuruan B., *Phil.* 57 B5
In Belbel, *Algeria* 75 C5
In Delimane, *Mali* 79 B5
In Rhar, *Algeria* 75 C5
In Salah, *Algeria* 75 C5
In Tallak, *Mali* 79 B5
Ina, *Japan* 49 G8
Inajá, *Brazil* 122 C4
Inangahua Junction, *N.Z.* 87 J3
Inanwatan, *Indonesia* 57 E8
Iñapari, *Peru* 124 C4
Inari, *Finland* 8 B22
Inarijärvi, *Finland* 8 B22
Inawashiro-Ko, *Japan* 48 F10
Inca, *Spain* 36 B9
Incaguasi, *Chile* 126 B1
Ince-Burnu, *Turkey* 66 A6
Incekum Burnu, *Turkey* 66 D5
Inchon, *S. Korea* 51 F14
Incio, *Spain* 30 C3
Incirliova, *Turkey* 66 D2
Incomáti →, *Mozam.* 85 D5
Inda Silase, *Ethiopia* 77 E4
Indalsälven →, *Sweden* 10 B11
Indaw, *Burma* 61 G20
Independence, *Calif., U.S.A.* 111 H4

Independence, *Iowa, U.S.A.* 108 D9
Independence, *Kans., U.S.A.* 109 G7
Independence, *Mo., U.S.A.* 108 F7
Independence, *Oreg., U.S.A.* 110 D2
Independence Fjord, *Greenland* 4 A6
Independence Mts., *U.S.A.* 110 F5
Independência, *Brazil* 122 C3
Independenţa, *Romania* 38 D10
Index, *U.S.A.* 112 C5
India ■, *Asia* 60 K11
Indian →, *U.S.A.* 105 M5
Indian Cabins, *Canada* 100 B5
Indian Harbour, *Canada* 99 B8
Indian Head, *Canada* 101 C8
Indian Ocean 46 J10
Indian Springs, *U.S.A.* 113 J11
Indiana, *U.S.A.* 106 F5
Indiana □, *U.S.A.* 104 E3
Indianapolis, *U.S.A.* 104 F2
Indianola, *Iowa, U.S.A.* 108 E8
Indianola, *Miss., U.S.A.* 109 J9
Indiapora, *Brazil* 123 E1
Indiga, *Russia* 44 C5
Indigirka →, *Russia* 45 B15
Indija, *Serbia, Yug.* 21 K10
Indio, *U.S.A.* 113 M10
Indonesia ■, *Asia* 56 F5
Indore, *India* 62 H6
Indramayu, *Indonesia* 57 G13
Indravati →, *India* 61 K12
Indre □, *France* 25 F8
Indre →, *France* 24 E7
Indre-et-Loire □, *France* 24 E7
Indus →, *Pakistan* 62 G2
Indus, Mouth of the, *Pakistan* 62 H2
İnebolu, *Turkey* 66 B5
İnegöl, *Turkey* 66 B3
Inés, Mt., *Argentina* 128 C3
Ineu, *Romania* 38 C4
Inezgane, *Morocco* 74 B3
Infantes, *Spain* 29 G1
Infiernillo, Presa del, *Mexico* 114 D4
Infiesto, *Spain* 30 B5
Ingapirca, *Ecuador* 120 D2
Ingelmunster, *Belgium* 17 G2
Ingende, *Zaïre* 80 E3
Ingeniero Jacobacci, *Argentina* 128 B3
Ingenio, *Canary Is.* 36 G4
Ingenio Santa Ana, *Argentina* 126 B2
Ingersoll, *Canada* 106 C4
Ingham, *Australia* 90 B4
Ingleborough, *U.K.* 12 C5
Inglewood, *Queens., Australia* 91 D5
Inglewood, *Vic., Australia* 91 F3
Inglewood, *N.Z.* 87 H5
Inglewood, *U.S.A.* 113 M8
Ingólfshöfði, *Iceland* 8 E5
Ingolstadt, *Germany* 19 G7
Ingomar, *U.S.A.* 110 C10
Ingonish, *Canada* 99 C7
Ingore, *Guinea-Biss.* 78 C1
Ingraj Bazar, *India* 63 G13
Ingrid Christensen Coast, *Antarctica* 5 C6
Ingul = Inhul →, *Ukraine* 41 J6
Ingulec = Inhulec, *Ukraine* 41 J7
Ingulets = Inhulets →, *Ukraine* 41 J7
Inguri = Enguri →, *Georgia* 43 J5
Ingushetia □, *Russia* 43 J7
Ingwavuma, *S. Africa* 85 D5
Inhaca, I., *Mozam.* 85 D5
Inhafenga, *Mozam.* 85 C5
Inhambane, *Mozam.* 85 C6
Inhambane □, *Mozam.* 85 C5
Inhambupe, *Brazil* 123 D4
Inhaminga, *Mozam.* 83 F3
Inharrime, *Mozam.* 85 C6
Inharrime →, *Mozam.* 85 C6
Inhul →, *Ukraine* 41 J7
Inhulec, *Ukraine* 41 J7
Inhulets →, *Ukraine* 41 J7
Inhuma, *Brazil* 122 C3
Inhumas, *Brazil* 123 E2
Iniesta, *Spain* 29 F3
Ining = Yining, *China* 44 E9
Inini □, *Fr. Guiana* 121 C7
Inírida →, *Colombia* 120 C4
Inishbofin, *Ireland* 15 C1
Inishmore, *Ireland* 15 C2
Inishowen Pen., *Ireland* 15 A4
Injune, *Australia* 91 D4
Inklin, *Canada* 100 B2
Inklin →, *Canada* 100 B2
Inkom, *U.S.A.* 110 E7
Inle L., *Burma* 61 J20
Inn →, *Austria* 19 G9
Innamincka, *Australia* 91 D3
Inner Hebrides, *U.K.* 14 D2
Inner Mongolia = Nei Monggol Zizhiqu □, *China* 50 C6
Inner Sound, *U.K.* 14 D3
Innerkip, *Canada* 106 C4
Innerkirchen, *Switz.* 22 C6
Innerste →, *Germany* 18 C5
Innetalling I., *Canada* 98 A4

Innisfail, *Australia* 90 B4
Innisfail, *Canada* 100 C6
In'no-shima, *Japan* 49 G6
Innsbruck, *Austria* 19 H7
Inny →, *Ireland* 15 C4
Inocência, *Brazil* 123 E1
Inongo, *Zaïre* 80 E3
Inoucdjouac = Inukjuak,
  Canada 97 C12
Inowrocław, *Poland* 20 C8
Inpundong, *N. Korea* 51 D14
Inquisivi, *Bolivia* 124 D4
Ins, *Switz.* 22 B4
Inscription, C., *Australia* . 89 E1
Insein, *Burma* 61 L20
Însurăţei, *Romania* 38 E10
Intendente Alvear,
  Argentina 126 D3
Interior, *U.S.A.* 108 D4
Interlaken, *Switz.* 22 F14
International Falls, *U.S.A.* 108 A8
Intiyaco, *Argentina* 126 B3
Intragna, *Switz.* 23 D7
Intutu, *Peru* 120 D3
Inukjuak, *Canada* 97 C12
Inútil, B., *Chile* 128 D2
Inuvik, *Canada* 96 B6
Inveraray, *U.K.* 14 E3
Inverbervie, *U.K.* 14 E6
Invercargill, *N.Z.* 87 M2
Inverell, *Australia* 91 D5
Invergordon, *U.K.* 14 D4
Invermere, *Canada* 100 C5
Inverness, *Canada* 99 C7
Inverness, *U.K.* 14 D4
Inverness, *U.S.A.* 105 L4
Inverurie, *U.K.* 14 D6
Inverway, *Australia* 88 C4
Investigator Group,
  Australia 91 E1
Investigator Str., *Australia* 91 F2
Inya, *Russia* 44 D9
Inyanga, *Zimbabwe* 83 F3
Inyangani, *Zimbabwe* 83 F3
Inyantue, *Zimbabwe* 83 F2
Inyo Mts., *U.S.A.* 111 H5
Inyokern, *U.S.A.* 113 K9
Inza, *Russia* 42 D8
Inzhavino, *Russia* 42 D5
Iō-Jima, *Japan* 49 J5
Ioánnina, *Greece* 39 K3
Iola, *U.S.A.* 109 G7
Ion Corvin, *Romania* 38 E10
Iona, *U.K.* 14 E2
Ione, *Calif., U.S.A.* 112 G6
Ione, *Wash., U.S.A.* 110 B5
Ionia, *U.S.A.* 104 D3
Ionian Is. = Iónioi Nísoi,
  Greece 39 L3
Ionian Sea, *Medit. S.* ... 6 H9
Iónioi Nísoi, *Greece* 39 L3
Íos, *Greece* 39 N8
Iowa □, *U.S.A.* 108 D8
Iowa City, *U.S.A.* 108 E9
Iowa Falls, *U.S.A.* 108 D8
Ipala, *Tanzania* 82 C3
Ipameri, *Brazil* 123 E2
Iparía, *Peru* 124 B3
Ipáti, *Greece* 39 L5
Ipatinga, *Brazil* 123 E3
Ipatovo, *Russia* 43 H6
Ipel →, *Europe* 21 G9
Ipiales, *Colombia* 120 C2
Ipiaú, *Brazil* 123 D4
Ipin = Yibin, *China* 52 C5
Ipirá, *Brazil* 123 D4
Ipiranga, *Brazil* 120 D4
Ipixuna, *Brazil* 124 B3
Ipixuna →, *Amazonas,*
  Brazil 124 B3
Ipixuna →, *Amazonas,*
  Brazil 125 B5
Ipoh, *Malaysia* 59 K3
Iporá, *Brazil* 123 D1
Ippy, *C.A.R.* 73 G9
Ipsala, *Turkey* 66 B2
Ipsárion Óros, *Greece* ... 39 J7
Ipswich, *Australia* 91 D5
Ipswich, *U.K.* 13 E9
Ipswich, *Mass., U.S.A.* .. 107 D14
Ipswich, *S. Dak., U.S.A.* . 108 C5
Ipu, *Brazil* 122 B3
Ipueiras, *Brazil* 122 B3
Ipupiara, *Brazil* 123 D3
Iqaluit, *Canada* 97 B13
Iquique, *Chile* 124 E3
Iquitos, *Peru* 120 D3
Irabu-Jima, *Japan* 49 M2
Iracoubo, *Fr. Guiana* 121 B7
Irafshān, *Iran* 65 E9
Irahuan, *Phil.* 55 G3
Iráklia, *Greece* 39 N8
Iráklion, *Greece* 37 D7
Iráklion □, *Greece* 37 D7
Irala, *Paraguay* 127 B5
Iramba □, *Tanzania* 82 C3
Iran ■, *Asia* 65 C7
Iran, Gunung-Gunung,
  Malaysia 56 D4
Iran Ra. = Iran, Gunung-
  Gunung, *Malaysia* 56 D4
Īrānshahr, *Iran* 65 E9
Irapa, *Venezuela* 121 A5
Irapuato, *Mexico* 114 C4
Iraq ■, *Asia* 67 F10
Irarrar, O. →, *Mali* 75 D5
Irati, *Brazil* 127 B5

Irbid, *Jordan* 69 C4
Irbid □, *Jordan* 69 C5
Irebu, *Zaïre* 80 E3
Irecê, *Brazil* 122 D3
Iregua →, *Spain* 28 C7
Ireland ■, *Europe* 15 D4
Ireland's Eye, *Ireland* ... 15 C5
Irele, *Nigeria* 79 D6
Ireng →, *Brazil* 121 C6
Iret, *Russia* 45 C16
Irgiz, Bolshaya →, *Russia* 42 D9
Irhârharene, *Algeria* 75 C6
Irharrar, O. →, *Algeria* . 75 C6
Irherm, *Morocco* 74 B3
Irhil Mgoun, *Morocco* ... 74 B3
Irhyangdong, *N. Korea* .. 51 D15
Iri, *S. Korea* 51 G14
Irian Jaya □, *Indonesia* .. 57 E9
Irié, *Guinea* 78 D3
Iriga, *Phil.* 55 E5
Iringa, *Tanzania* 82 D4
Iringa □, *Tanzania* 82 D4
Iriomote-Jima, *Japan* ... 49 M1
Iriona, *Honduras* 116 C2
Iriri →, *Brazil* 121 D7
Iriri Novo →, *Brazil* 125 B7
Irish Republic ■, *Europe* . 15 D4
Irish Sea, *U.K.* 12 D3
Irkineyeva, *Russia* 45 D10
Irkutsk, *Russia* 45 D11
Irma, *Canada* 101 C6
Irō-Zaki, *Japan* 49 G9
Iroise, Mer d', *France* ... 24 D2
Iron Baron, *Australia* 91 E2
Iron Gate = Portile de
  Fier, *Europe* 38 E5
Iron Knob, *Australia* 91 E2
Iron Mountain, *U.S.A.* .. 104 C1
Iron Ra., *Australia* 90 A3
Iron River, *U.S.A.* 108 B10
Ironbridge, *U.K.* 13 E5
Irondequoit, *U.S.A.* 106 C7
Ironstone Kopje, *Botswana* 84 D3
Ironton, *Mo., U.S.A.* 109 G9
Ironton, *Ohio, U.S.A.* ... 104 F4
Ironwood, *U.S.A.* 108 B9
Iroquois Falls, *Canada* .. 98 C3
Irosin, *Phil.* 55 E6
Irpin, *Ukraine* 41 G6
Irrara Cr. →, *Australia* .. 91 D4
Irrawaddy □, *Burma* 61 L19
Irrawaddy →, *Burma* ... 61 M19
Irsina, *Italy* 35 B9
Irtysh →, *Russia* 44 C7
Irumu, *Zaïre* 82 B2
Irún, *Spain* 28 B3
Irunea = Pamplona, *Spain* 28 C3
Irurzun, *Spain* 28 C3
Irvine, *Canada* 101 D6
Irvine, *U.K.* 14 F4
Irvine, *Calif., U.S.A.* 113 M9
Irvine, *Ky., U.S.A.* 104 G4
Irvinestown, *U.K.* 15 B4
Irving, *U.S.A.* 109 J6
Irvona, *U.S.A.* 106 F6
Irwin →, *Australia* 89 E1
Irymple, *Australia* 91 E3
Is-sur-Tille, *France* 25 E12
Isa, *Nigeria* 79 C6
Isaac →, *Australia* 90 C4
Isabel, *U.S.A.* 108 C4
Isabela, I., *Mexico* 114 C3
Isabela, *Phil.* 55 H5
Isabella, Cord., *Nic.* 116 D2
Isabella Ra., *Australia* ... 88 D3
Ísafjarðardjúp, *Iceland* .. 8 C2
Ísafjörður, *Iceland* 8 C2
Isagarh, *India* 62 G7
Isahaya, *Japan* 49 H5
Isaka, *Tanzania* 82 C3
Isakly, *Russia* 42 C10
Isana = Içana →, *Brazil* . 120 C4
Isangi, *Zaïre* 80 D4
Isar →, *Germany* 19 G8
Ísarco →, *Italy* 33 B8
Ísari, *Greece* 39 M5
Isbergues, *France* 25 B9
Iscayachi, *Bolivia* 125 E4
Iscuandé, *Colombia* 120 C2
Isdell →, *Australia* 88 C3
Ise, *Japan* 49 G8
Ise-Wan, *Japan* 49 G8
Isefjord, *Denmark* 11 J5
Iseltwald, *Switz.* 22 C5
Isenthal, *Switz.* 23 C7
Iseo, *Italy* 32 C7
Iseo, L. d', *Italy* 32 C7
Iseramagazi, *Tanzania* .. 82 C3
Isère □, *France* 27 C9
Isère →, *France* 27 D8
Iserlohn, *Germany* 18 D3
Isérnia, *Italy* 35 A7
Iseyin, *Nigeria* 79 D5
Isherton, *Guyana* 121 C6
Ishigaki-Shima, *Japan* .. 49 M2
Ishikari-Gawa →, *Japan* . 48 C10
Ishikari-Sammyaku, *Japan* 48 C11
Ishikari-Wan, *Japan* 48 C10
Ishikawa □, *Japan* 49 F8
Ishim, *Russia* 44 D7
Ishim →, *Russia* 44 D8
Ishinomaki, *Japan* 48 E10
Ishioka, *Japan* 49 F10
Ishkuman, *Pakistan* 63 A5
Ishpeming, *U.S.A.* 104 B2

Isigny-sur-Mer, *France* .. 24 C5
Isil Kul, *Russia* 44 D8
Isiolo, *Kenya* 82 B4
Isiolo □, *Kenya* 82 B4
Isiro, *Zaïre* 82 B2
Isisford, *Australia* 90 C3
Iskenderun, *Turkey* 66 D7
Iskenderun Körfezi, *Turkey* 66 D6
Iskilip, *Turkey* 66 B6
Iskŭr →, *Bulgaria* 38 F7
Iskut →, *Canada* 100 B2
Isla →, *U.K.* 14 E5
Isla Cristina, *Spain* 31 H3
Isla Vista, *U.S.A.* 113 L7
Islâhiye, *Turkey* 66 D7
Islamabad, *Pakistan* 62 C5
Islamkot, *Pakistan* 62 G4
Island →, *Canada* 100 A4
Island Falls, *Canada* 98 C3
Island Falls, *U.S.A.* 99 C6
Island L., *Canada* 101 C10
Island Lagoon, *Australia* . 91 E2
Island Pond, *U.S.A.* 107 B13
Islands, B. of, *Canada* ... 99 C8
Islay, *U.K.* 14 F2
Isle →, *France* 26 D3
Isle aux Morts, *Canada* .. 99 C8
Isle of Wight □, *U.K.* ... 13 G6
Isle Royale, *U.S.A.* 108 A10
Isleta, *U.S.A.* 111 J10
Isleton, *U.S.A.* 112 G5
Ismail = Izmayil, *Ukraine* 41 K5
Ismâ'ilîya, *Egypt* 76 H8
Ismaning, *Germany* 19 G7
Ismay, *U.S.A.* 108 B2
Isna, *Egypt* 76 B3
Isogstalo, *India* 63 B8
Isola del Gran Sasso
  d'Italia, *Italy* 33 F10
Ísola del Liri, *Italy* 34 A6
Ísola della Scala, *Italy* ... 32 C8
Ísola di Capo Rizzuto, *Italy* 35 D10
Isparta, *Turkey* 66 D4
Isperikh, *Bulgaria* 38 F9
Íspica, *Italy* 35 F7
Israel ■, *Asia* 69 D3
Issano, *Guyana* 121 B6
Issia, *Ivory C.* 78 D3
Issoire, *France* 26 C7
Issoudun, *France* 25 F8
Issyk-Kul, Ozero = Ysyk-
  Köl, *Kyrgyzstan* 44 E8
Ist, *Croatia* 33 D11
Istaihah, *U.A.E.* 65 F7
Istanbul, *Turkey* 66 B3
Istmina, *Colombia* 120 B2
Istok, *Serbia, Yug.* 21 N10
Istokpoga, L., *U.S.A.* 105 M5
Istra, *Croatia* 33 C11
Istranca Dağları, *Turkey* . 66 B2
Istres, *France* 27 E8
Istria = Istra, *Croatia* ... 33 C11
Itá, *Paraguay* 126 B4
Itabaiana, *Paraíba, Brazil* . 122 C4
Itabaiana, *Sergipe, Brazil* . 122 D4
Itabaianinha, *Brazil* 122 D4
Itaberaba, *Brazil* 123 D3
Itaberaí, *Brazil* 123 E2
Itabira, *Brazil* 123 E3
Itabirito, *Brazil* 123 F3
Itaboca, *Brazil* 121 D6
Itabuna, *Brazil* 123 D4
Itacajá, *Brazil* 122 C2
Itacaunas →, *Brazil* 122 C2
Itacoatiara, *Brazil* 121 D6
Itacuaí →, *Brazil* 124 A3
Itaguaçu, *Brazil* 123 E3
Itaguari →, *Brazil* 123 D3
Itaguatins, *Brazil* 122 C2
Itaim →, *Brazil* 122 C3
Itaínópolis, *Brazil* 122 C3
Itaipú, Reprêsa de, *Brazil* 127 B5
Itaituba, *Brazil* 121 D6
Itajaí, *Brazil* 127 B6
Itajubá, *Brazil* 123 F2
Itajuípe, *Brazil* 123 D4
Itaka, *Tanzania* 83 D3
Italy ■, *Europe* 7 G8
Itamataré, *Brazil* 122 B2
Itambacuri, *Brazil* 123 E3
Itambé, *Brazil* 123 E3
Itampolo, *Madag.* 85 C7
Itanhauã →, *Brazil* 121 D5
Itanhém, *Brazil* 123 E3
Itapaci, *Brazil* 123 D2
Itapagé, *Brazil* 122 B4
Itaparica, I. de, *Brazil* ... 123 D4
Itapebi, *Brazil* 123 E4
Itapecuru-Mirim, *Brazil* . 122 B3
Itaperuna, *Brazil* 123 F3
Itapetinga, *Brazil* 123 E3
Itapetininga, *Brazil* 127 A6
Itapeva, *Brazil* 127 A6
Itapicuru →, *Bahia, Brazil* 122 D4
Itapicuru →, *Maranhão,*
  Brazil 122 B3
Itapinima, *Brazil* 125 B5
Itapipoca, *Brazil* 122 B4
Itapiranga, *Brazil* 121 D6
Itápolis, *Brazil* 123 F2
Itaporanga, *Brazil* 122 C4
Itapuá □, *Paraguay* 127 B4
Itapuranga, *Brazil* 123 E2
Itaquari, *Brazil* 123 F3
Itaquatiara, *Brazil* 121 D6
Itaquí, *Brazil* 126 B4

Itararé, *Brazil* 127 A6
Itarsi, *India* 62 H7
Itarumã, *Brazil* 123 E1
Itatí, *Argentina* 126 B4
Itatira, *Brazil* 122 B4
Itatuba, *Brazil* 125 B5
Itatupa, *Brazil* 121 D7
Itaueira, *Brazil* 122 C3
Itaueira →, *Brazil* 122 C3
Itaúna, *Brazil* 123 F3
Itbayat, *Phil.* 55 A4
Ite, *Peru* 124 D3
Itezhi Tezhi, L., *Zambia* . 83 F2
Ithaca = Itháki, *Greece* .. 39 L3
Ithaca, *U.S.A.* 107 D8
Itháki, *Greece* 39 L3
Itinga, *Brazil* 123 E3
Itiquira, *Brazil* 125 D7
Itiquira →, *Brazil* 125 D6
Itiruçu, *Brazil* 123 D3
Itiúba, *Brazil* 122 D4
Ito, *Japan* 49 G9
Itoigawa, *Japan* 49 F8
Iton →, *France* 24 C8
Itonamas →, *Bolivia* ... 125 C5
Itsa, *Egypt* 76 J7
Ittoqqortoormiit =
  Scoresbysund, *Greenland* 4 B6
Itu, *Brazil* 127 A6
Itu, *Nigeria* 79 D6
Ituaçu, *Brazil* 123 D3
Ituango, *Colombia* 120 B2
Ituiutaba, *Brazil* 123 E2
Itumbiara, *Brazil* 123 E2
Ituna, *Canada* 101 C8
Itunge Port, *Tanzania* ... 83 D3
Ituni, *Guyana* 121 B6
Itupiranga, *Brazil* 122 C2
Iturama, *Brazil* 123 E1
Iturbe, *Argentina* 126 A2
Ituri →, *Zaïre* 82 B2
Iturup, Ostrov, *Russia* ... 45 E15
Ituverava, *Brazil* 123 F2
Ituxi →, *Brazil* 125 B5
Ituyuro →, *Argentina* ... 126 A3
Itzehoe, *Germany* 18 B5
Ivaí →, *Brazil* 127 A5
Ivalo, *Finland* 8 B22
Ivalojoki →, *Finland* 8 B22
Ivanava, *Belarus* 41 F3
Ivangorod, *Russia* 40 C5
Ivanhoe, *N.S.W., Australia* 91 E3
Ivanhoe, W. Austral.,
  Australia 88 C4
Ivanhoe, *U.S.A.* 112 J7
Ivanhoe L., *Canada* 101 A7
Ivanić Grad, *Croatia* 33 C13
Ivanjica, *Serbia, Yug.* ... 21 M10
Ivanjščice, *Croatia* 33 B13
Ivankoyskoye Vdkhr.,
  Russia 42 B3
Ivano-Frankivsk, *Ukraine* . 41 H3
Ivano-Frankovsk = Ivano-
  Frankivsk, *Ukraine* ... 41 H3
Ivanovo = Ivanava, *Belarus* 41 F3
Ivanovo, *Russia* 42 B5
Ivato, *Madag.* 85 C8
Ivatsevichy, *Belarus* 41 F3
Ivaylovgrad, *Bulgaria* ... 39 H9
Ivinheima →, *Brazil* 127 A5
Iviza = Ibiza, *Spain* 36 C7
Ivohibe, *Madag.* 85 C8
Ivolândia, *Brazil* 123 E1
Ivory Coast ■, *Africa* ... 78 D3
Ivrea, *Italy* 32 C4
Ivujivik, *Canada* 97 B12
Ivvavik National Park,
  Canada 96 B6
Ivyanets, *Belarus* 40 F4
Iwahig, *Phil.* 56 C5
Iwaizumi, *Japan* 48 E10
Iwaki, *Japan* 49 F10
Iwakuni, *Japan* 49 G6
Iwamizawa, *Japan* 48 C10
Iwanai, *Japan* 48 C10
Iwata, *Japan* 49 G8
Iwate □, *Japan* 48 E10
Iwate-San, *Japan* 48 E10
Iwo, *Nigeria* 79 D5
Ixiamas, *Bolivia* 124 C4
Ixopo, S. *Africa* 85 E5
Ixtepec, *Mexico* 115 D5
Ixtlán del Río, *Mexico* ... 114 C4
Iyo, *Japan* 49 H6
Izabal, L. de, *Guatemala* . 116 C2
Izamal, *Mexico* 115 C7
Izberbash, *Russia* 43 J8
Izegem, *Belgium* 17 G2
Izena-Shima, *Japan* 49 L3
Izhevsk, *Russia* 44 D6
Izmayil, *Ukraine* 41 K5
Izmir, *Turkey* 66 C2
Izmit, *Turkey* 66 B3
Iznajar, *Spain* 31 H6
Iznalloz, *Spain* 29 H1
Iznik, *Turkey* 66 B3
Iznik Gölü, *Turkey* 66 B3
Izobil'nyy, *Russia* 43 H5
Izola, *Slovenia* 33 C10
Izozog, Bañados de, *Bolivia* 125 D5
Izra, *Syria* 69 C5
Iztochni Rodopi, *Bulgaria* . 39 H8
Izu-Shotō, *Japan* 49 G10
Izumi-sano, *Japan* 49 G7
Izumo, *Japan* 49 G6
Izyaslav, *Ukraine* 41 G4
Izyum, *Ukraine* 41 H9

J

J.F. Rodrigues, *Brazil* 122 B1
Jaba, *Ethiopia* 77 F4
Jabal el Awlîya, *Sudan* ... 77 D3
Jabal Lubnān, *Lebanon* .. 69 B4
Jabalón →, *Spain* 31 G6
Jabalpur, *India* 63 H8
Jabbūl, *Syria* 64 B3
Jablah, *Syria* 66 E6
Jablanac, *Croatia* 33 D11
Jablonec, *Czech.* 20 E5
Jabłonowo, *Poland* 20 B9
Jaboatão, *Brazil* 122 C4
Jaboticabal, *Brazil* 127 A6
Jaburu, *Brazil* 125 B5
Jaca, *Spain* 28 C4
Jacaré →, *Brazil* 122 D3
Jacareí, *Brazil* 127 A6
Jacarèzinho, *Brazil* 127 A6
Jaciara, *Brazil* 125 D7
Jacinto, *Brazil* 123 E3
Jaciparaná, *Brazil* 125 B5
Jackman, *U.S.A.* 99 C5
Jacksboro, *U.S.A.* 109 J5
Jackson, *Australia* 91 D4
Jackson, *Ala., U.S.A.* 105 K2
Jackson, *Calif., U.S.A.* ... 112 G6
Jackson, *Ky., U.S.A.* 104 G4
Jackson, *Mich., U.S.A.* .. 104 D3
Jackson, *Minn., U.S.A.* .. 108 D7
Jackson, *Miss., U.S.A.* ... 109 J9
Jackson, *Mo., U.S.A.* 109 G10
Jackson, *Ohio, U.S.A.* ... 104 F4
Jackson, *Tenn., U.S.A.* .. 105 H1
Jackson, *Wyo., U.S.A.* ... 110 E8
Jackson B., *N.Z.* 87 K2
Jackson L., *U.S.A.* 110 E8
Jacksons, *N.Z.* 87 K3
Jacksonville, *Ala., U.S.A.* . 105 J3
Jacksonville, *Calif., U.S.A.* 112 H6
Jacksonville, *Fla., U.S.A.* . 105 K5
Jacksonville, *Ill., U.S.A.* .. 108 F9
Jacksonville, *N.C., U.S.A.* . 105 H7
Jacksonville, *Oreg., U.S.A.* 110 E2
Jacksonville, *Tex., U.S.A.* . 109 K7
Jacksonville Beach, *U.S.A.* 105 K5
Jacmel, *Haiti* 117 C5
Jacob Lake, *U.S.A.* 111 H7
Jacobabad, *Pakistan* 62 E3
Jacobina, *Brazil* 122 D3
Jacques-Cartier, Mt.,
  Canada 99 C6
Jacqueville, *Ivory C.* 78 D4
Jacuí →, *Brazil* 127 C5
Jacumba, *U.S.A.* 113 N10
Jacundá, →, *Brazil* 122 B1
Jade, *Germany* 18 B4
Jadebusen, *Germany* ... 18 B4
Jadoigne, *Belgium* 17 G5
Jadotville = Likasi, *Zaïre* . 83 E2
Jadraque, *Spain* 28 E2
Jādū, *Libya* 75 B7
Jaén, *Peru* 124 B2
Jaén, *Spain* 31 H7
Jaén □, *Spain* 31 H7
Jafène, *Africa* 74 D3
Jaffa = Tel Aviv-Yafo,
  Israel 69 C3
Jaffa, C., *Australia* 91 F2
Jaffna, *Sri Lanka* 60 Q12
Jagadhri, *India* 62 D7
Jagadishpur, *India* 63 G11
Jagdalpur, *India* 61 K12
Jagersfontein, S. *Africa* .. 84 D4
Jagraon, *India* 60 D9
Jagst →, *Germany* 19 F5
Jagtial, *India* 60 K11
Jaguaquara, *Brazil* 123 D4
Jaguariaíva, *Brazil* 127 A6
Jaguaribe, *Brazil* 122 C4
Jaguaribe →, *Brazil* 122 B4
Jaguaruana, *Brazil* 122 B4
Jagüey Grande, *Cuba* ... 116 B3
Jahangirabad, *India* 62 E8
Jahrom, *Iran* 65 D7
Jaicós, *Brazil* 122 C3
Jailolo, *Indonesia* 57 D7
Jailolo, Selat, *Indonesia* . 57 D7
Jaipur, *India* 62 F6
Jājarm, *Iran* 65 B8
Jajce, *Bos.-H.* 21 L7
Jakarta, *Indonesia* 57 G12
Jakobstad = Pietarsaari,
  Finland 8 E20
Jakupica, *Macedonia* ... 39 H4
Jal, *U.S.A.* 109 J3
Jalalabad, *Afghan.* 62 B4
Jalalabad, *India* 63 F8
Jalalpur Jattan, *Pakistan* . 62 C6
Jalama, *U.S.A.* 113 L6
Jalapa, *Guatemala* 116 D2
Jalapa Enríquez, *Mexico* . 115 D5
Jalasjärvi, *Finland* 9 E20
Jalaun, *India* 63 F8
Jales, *Brazil* 123 F1
Jaleswar, *Nepal* 63 F11
Jalgaon, *Maharashtra, India* 60 J10
Jalgaon, *Maharashtra, India* 60 J9
Jalhay, *Belgium* 17 G7
Jalībah, *Iraq* 64 D5
Jalingo, *Nigeria* 79 D7
Jalisco □, *Mexico* 114 C4
Jalkot, *Pakistan* 63 B5
Jallas →, *Spain* 30 C1
Jalna, *India* 60 K9

Jalón →, *Spain* 28 D3
Jalpa, *Mexico* 114 C4
Jalpaiguri, *India* 61 F16
Jaluit I., *Pac. Oc.* 92 G8
Jalūlā, *Iraq* 67 E11
Jamaari, *Nigeria* 79 C6
Jamaica ■, *W. Indies* 116 C4
Jamalpur, *Bangla.* 61 G16
Jamalpur, *India* 63 G12
Jamalpurganj, *India* 63 H13
Jamanxim →, *Brazil* 125 A6
Jamari, *Brazil* 125 B5
Jamari →, *Brazil* 125 B5
Jambe, *Indonesia* 57 E8
Jambes, *Belgium* 17 H5
Jambi, *Indonesia* 56 E2
Jambi □, *Indonesia* 56 E2
Jambusar, *India* 62 H5
James →, *U.S.A.* 108 D6
James B., *Canada* 97 C11
James Ras., *Australia* ... 88 D5
James Ross I., *Antarctica* . 5 C18
Jamestown, *Australia* 91 E2
Jamestown, *S. Africa* 84 E4
Jamestown, *Ky., U.S.A.* .. 104 G3
Jamestown, *N. Dak.,*
  U.S.A. 108 B5
Jamestown, *N.Y., U.S.A.* . 106 D5
Jamestown, *Pa., U.S.A.* .. 106 E4
Jamestown, *Tenn., U.S.A.* 105 G3
Jamīlābād, *Iran* 65 C6
Jamiltepec, *Mexico* 115 D5
Jamkhandi, *India* 60 L9
Jammerbugt, *Denmark* ... 11 G3
Jammu, *India* 62 C6
Jammu & Kashmir □, *India* 63 B7
Jamnagar, *India* 62 H4
Jamoigne, *Belgium* 17 J6
Jampur, *Pakistan* 62 E4
Jamrud, *Pakistan* 62 C4
Jämsä, *Finland* 9 F21
Jamshedpur, *India* 63 H12
Jamtara, *India* 63 H12
Jämtland, *Sweden* 8 E15
Jämtlands län □, *Sweden* . 10 B7
Jan L., *Canada* 101 C8
Jan Mayen, *Arctic* 4 B7
Janakkala, *Finland* 9 F21
Janaúba, *Brazil* 123 E3
Janaucu, I., *Brazil* 122 A1
Jand, *Pakistan* 62 C5
Janda, L. de la, *Spain* ... 31 J5
Jandaia, *Brazil* 123 E1
Jandaq, *Iran* 65 C7
Jandia, *Canary Is.* 36 F5
Jandia, Pta. de, *Canary Is.* 36 F5
Jandiatuba →, *Brazil* 120 D4
Jandola, *Pakistan* 62 C4
Jandowae, *Australia* 91 D5
Jandrain-Jandrenouilles,
  Belgium 17 G5
Jándula →, *Spain* 31 G6
Janesville, *U.S.A.* 108 D10
Janga, *Ghana* 79 C4
Jango, *Brazil* 125 E6
Janin, *West Bank* 69 C4
Janjina, *Croatia* 21 N7
Janos, *Mexico* 114 A3
Jánoshálza, *Hungary* 21 H7
Janów Podlaski, *Poland* .. 20 C13
Januária, *Brazil* 123 E3
Janub Dârfûr □, *Sudan* .. 77 E2
Janub Kordofân □, *Sudan* 77 E3
Janubio, *Canary Is.* 36 F6
Janville, *France* 25 D8
Janzé, *France* 24 E5
Jaora, *India* 62 H6
Japan ■, *Asia* 49 G8
Japan, Sea of, *Asia* 48 E7
Japan Trench, *Pac. Oc.* ... 92 G4
Japen = Yapen, *Indonesia* 57 E9
Japurá →, *Brazil* 120 D4
Jaque, *Panama* 120 B2
Jarābulus, *Syria* 67 D8
Jaraguá, *Brazil* 123 E2
Jaraguari, *Brazil* 125 E7
Jaraicejo, *Spain* 31 F5
Jaraiz, *Spain* 30 E5
Jarama →, *Spain* 28 E1
Jaramānah, *Syria* 66 F7
Jaramillo, *Argentina* 128 C3
Jarandilla, *Spain* 30 E5
Jaranwala, *Pakistan* 62 D5
Jarash, *Jordan* 69 C4
Jarauçu →, *Brazil* 121 D7
Jardim, *Brazil* 126 A4
Jardín →, *Spain* 29 G2
Jardines de la Reina, Is.,
  Cuba 116 B4
Jargalang, *China* 51 C12
Jargalant = Hovd,
  Mongolia 54 B4
Jargeau, *France* 25 E9
Jari →, *Brazil* 121 D7
Jarīr, W. al →, *Si. Arabia* 64 E4
Jarmen, *Germany* 18 B9
Jarnac, *France* 26 C3
Jarny, *France* 25 C12
Jarocin, *Poland* 20 D7
Jarosław, *Poland* 20 E12
Järpås, *Sweden* 11 F6
Järpen, *Sweden* 10 A7
Jarrahdale, *Australia* ... 89 F2
Jarres, Plaine des, *Laos* .. 58 C4
Jarso, *Ethiopia* 77 F4
Jartai, *China* 50 E3
Jaru, *Brazil* 125 C5

Jaru →, *Brazil* 125 C5
Jarud Qi, *China* 51 B11
Järvenpää, *Finland* 9 F21
Jarvis, *Canada* 106 D4
Jarvis I., *Pac. Oc.* 93 H12
Jarwa, *India* 63 F10
Jaša Tomić, *Serbia, Yug.* . 21 K10
Jāsimīyah, *Iraq* 67 F11
Jasin, *Malaysia* 59 L4
Jāsk, *Iran* 65 E8
Jasło, *Poland* 20 F11
Jason, Is., *Falk. Is.* 128 D4
Jasper, *Alta., Canada* 100 C5
Jasper, *Ont., Canada* 107 B9
Jasper, *Ala., U.S.A.* 105 J2
Jasper, *Fla., U.S.A.* 105 K4
Jasper, *Minn., U.S.A.* ... 108 D6
Jasper, *Tex., U.S.A.* 109 K8
Jasper Nat. Park, *Canada* . 100 C5
Jassy = Iaşi, *Romania* ... 38 B10
Jastrebarsko, *Croatia* 33 C12
Jastrzębie Zdrój, *Poland* . 20 F8
Jászárokszállás, *Hungary* . 21 H10
Jászberény, *Hungary* 21 H9
Jászladány, *Hungary* 21 H10
Jataí, *Brazil* 123 E1
Jatapu →, *Brazil* 121 D6
Jati, *Pakistan* 62 G3
Jatibarang, *Indonesia* ... 57 G13
Jatinegara, *Indonesia* ... 57 G12
Játiva, *Spain* 29 G4
Jatobal, *Brazil* 122 B2
Jaú, *Brazil* 127 A6
Jaú →, *Brazil* 121 D5
Jauaperí →, *Brazil* 121 D5
Jauche, *Belgium* 17 G5
Jauja, *Peru* 124 C2
Jaunpur, *India* 63 G10
Jauru →, *Brazil* 125 D6
Java = Jawa, *Indonesia* .. 57 G14
Java Sea, *Indonesia* 56 E3
Java Trench, *Ind. Oc.* 92 H2
Jávea, *Spain* 29 G5
Javhlant = Ulyasutay,
  Mongolia 54 B4
Javier, I., *Chile* 128 C2
Javron, *France* 24 D6
Jawa, *Indonesia* 57 G14
Jawor, *Poland* 20 D6
Jaworzno, *Poland* 20 E9
Jay, *U.S.A.* 109 G7
Jaya, Puncak, *Indonesia* . 57 E9
Jayanca, *Peru* 124 B2
Jayanti, *India* 61 F16
Jayapura, *Indonesia* 57 E10
Jayawijaya, Pegunungan,
  Indonesia 57 E9
Jaynagar, *India* 61 F15
Jayrūd, *Syria* 66 F7
Jayton, *U.S.A.* 109 J4
Jāzīreh-ye Shīf, *Iran* 65 D6
Jazminal, *Mexico* 114 C4
Jazzīn, *Lebanon* 69 B4
Jean, *U.S.A.* 113 K11
Jean Marie River, *Canada* 100 A4
Jean Rabel, *Haiti* 117 C5
Jeanerette, *U.S.A.* 109 L9
Jeanette, Ostrov, *Russia* .. 45 B16
Jeannette, *U.S.A.* 106 F5
Jebba, *Morocco* 74 A4
Jebba, *Nigeria* 79 D5
Jebel, Bahr el →, *Sudan* . 77 F3
Jebel Qerri, *Sudan* 77 D3
Jeberos, *Peru* 124 B2
Jedburgh, *U.K.* 14 F6
Jedda = Jiddah, *Si. Arabia* 68 C2
Jędrzejów, *Poland* 20 E10
Jedway, *Canada* 100 C2
Jeetzel →, *Germany* 18 B7
Jefferson, *Iowa, U.S.A.* .. 108 D7
Jefferson, *Ohio, U.S.A.* .. 106 E4
Jefferson, *Tex., U.S.A.* ... 109 J7
Jefferson, *Wis., U.S.A.* .. 108 D10
Jefferson, Mt., *Nev.,*
  U.S.A. 110 G5
Jefferson, Mt., *Oreg.,*
  U.S.A. 110 D3
Jefferson City, *Mo., U.S.A.* 108 F8
Jefferson City, *Tenn.,*
  U.S.A. 105 G4
Jeffersonville, *U.S.A.* 104 F3
Jega, *Nigeria* 79 C5
Jēkabpils, *Latvia* 9 H21
Jelenia Góra, *Poland* 20 E5
Jelgava, *Latvia* 9 H20
Jelli, *Sudan* 77 F3
Jellicoe, *Canada* 98 C2
Jemaja, *Indonesia* 56 D3
Jemaluang, *Malaysia* 59 L4
Jemappes, *Belgium* 17 H3
Jember, *Indonesia* 57 H15
Jembongan, *Malaysia* ... 56 C5
Jemeppe, *Belgium* 17 G7
Jemnice, *Czech.* 20 F5
Jena, *Germany* 18 E7
Jena, *U.S.A.* 109 K8
Jendouba, *Tunisia* 75 A6
Jenkins, *U.S.A.* 104 G4
Jenner, *U.S.A.* 112 G3
Jennings, *U.S.A.* 109 K8
Jennings →, *Canada* 100 B2
Jeparit, *Australia* 91 F3
Jequié, *Brazil* 123 D3
Jequitaí →, *Brazil* 123 E3
Jequitinhonha, *Brazil* ... 123 E3
Jequitinhonha →, *Brazil* . 123 E4
Jerada, *Morocco* 75 B4

Jerantut, *Malaysia* 59 L4
Jérémie, *Haiti* 117 C5
Jeremoabo, *Brazil* 122 D4
Jerez, Punta, *Mexico* 115 C5
Jerez de García Salinas,
  Mexico 114 C4
Jerez de la Frontera, *Spain* 31 J4
Jerez de los Caballeros,
  Spain 31 G4
Jericho = Arīḥā, *Syria* ... 64 C3
Jericho = El Arīḥā,
  West Bank 69 D4
Jericho, *Australia* 90 C4
Jerichow, *Germany* 18 C8
Jerilderie, *Australia* 91 F4
Jermyn, *U.S.A.* 107 E9
Jerome, *U.S.A.* 111 J8
Jersey, *U.K.* 13 H5
Jersey City, *U.S.A.* 107 F10
Jersey Shore, *U.S.A.* 106 E7
Jerseyville, *U.S.A.* 108 F9
Jerusalem, *Israel* 69 D4
Jervis B., *Australia* 91 F5
Jesenice, *Slovenia* 33 B11
Jesenké, *Slovak Rep.* 21 G10
Jesselton = Kota Kinabalu,
  Malaysia 56 C5
Jessnitz, *Germany* 18 D8
Jessore, *Bangla.* 61 H16
Jesup, *U.S.A.* 105 K5
Jesús, *Peru* 124 B2
Jesús Carranza, *Mexico* .. 115 D5
Jesús María, *Argentina* .. 126 C3
Jetmore, *U.S.A.* 109 F5
Jetpur, *India* 62 J4
Jette, *Belgium* 17 G4
Jevnaker, *Norway* 10 D4
Jewett, *Ohio, U.S.A.* 106 F3
Jewett, *Tex., U.S.A.* 109 K6
Jewett City, *U.S.A.* 107 E13
Jeyḥūnābād, *Iran* 65 C6
Jeypore, *India* 61 K13
Jeziorany, *Poland* 20 B10
Jhajjar, *India* 62 E7
Jhal Jhao, *Pakistan* 60 F4
Jhalawar, *India* 62 G7
Jhang Maghiana, *Pakistan* 62 D5
Jhansi, *India* 63 G8
Jharia, *India* 63 H12
Jharsaguda, *India* 61 J14
Jhelum, *Pakistan* 62 C5
Jhelum →, *Pakistan* 62 D5
Jhunjhunu, *India* 62 E6
Ji Xian, *Hebei, China* ... 50 F8
Ji Xian, *Henan, China* ... 50 G8
Ji Xian, *Shanxi, China* ... 50 F6
Jia Xian, *Henan, China* .. 50 H7
Jia Xian, *Shaanxi, China* . 50 E6
Jiading, *China* 53 B13
Jiahe, *China* 53 E9
Jiali, *Taiwan* 53 F13
Jialing Jiang →, *China* ... 52 C6
Jiamusi, *China* 54 B8
Ji'an, *Jiangxi, China* 53 D10
Ji'an, *Jilin, China* 51 D14
Jianchang, *China* 51 D11
Jianchangying, *China* ... 51 D10
Jianchuan, *China* 52 D2
Jiande, *China* 53 C12
Jiangbei, *China* 52 C6
Jiangcheng, *China* 52 F3
Jiangdi, *China* 52 D4
Jiange, *China* 52 A5
Jiangjin, *China* 52 C6
Jiangkou, *China* 52 D7
Jiangle, *China* 53 D11
Jiangling, *China* 53 B9
Jiangmen, *China* 53 F9
Jiangshan, *China* 53 C12
Jiangsu □, *China* 51 H10
Jiangxi □, *China* 53 D10
Jiangyin, *China* 53 B13
Jiangyong, *China* 53 E8
Jiangyou, *China* 52 B5
Jianhe, *China* 52 D7
Jianli, *China* 53 C9
Jianning, *China* 53 D11
Jian'ou, *China* 53 D12
Jianshi, *China* 52 B7
Jianshui, *China* 52 F4
Jianyang, *Fujian, China* . 53 D12
Jianyang, *Sichuan, China* 52 B5
Jiao Xian, *China* 51 F11
Jiaohe, *Hebei, China* 50 E9
Jiaohe, *Jilin, China* 51 C14
Jiaoling, *China* 53 E11
Jiaozhou Wan, *China* ... 51 F11
Jiaozuo, *China* 50 G7
Jiashan, *China* 53 A11
Jiawang, *China* 51 G9
Jiaxiang, *China* 50 G9
Jiaxing, *China* 53 B13
Jiayi, *Taiwan* 53 F13
Jiayu, *China* 53 C9
Jibão, Serra do, *Brazil* ... 123 D3
Jibiya, *Nigeria* 79 C6
Jibou, *Romania* 38 B6
Jibuti = Djibouti ■, *Africa* 68 E3
Jicarón, I., *Panama* 116 E3
Jičín, *Czech.* 20 E5
Jiddah, *Si. Arabia* 68 C2
Jido, *India* 61 E19
Jieshou, *China* 50 H8
Jiexiu, *China* 50 F6
Jieyang, *China* 53 F11
Jigawa □, *Nigeria* 79 C6
Jiggalong, *Australia* 88 D3

Jihlava, *Czech.* 20 F5
Jijel, *Algeria* 75 A6
Jijiga, *Ethiopia* 68 F3
Jijona, *Spain* 29 G4
Jikamshi, *Nigeria* 79 C6
Jilin, *China* 51 C14
Jilin □, *China* 51 C13
Jiloca →, *Spain* 28 D3
Jilong, *Taiwan* 53 E13
Jima, *Ethiopia* 77 F4
Jimbolia, *Romania* 38 D3
Jimena de la Frontera,
  Spain 31 J5
Jiménez, *Mexico* 114 B4
Jimo, *China* 51 F11
Jin Jiang →, *China* 53 C10
Jin Xian, *Hebei, China* .. 50 E8
Jin Xian, *Liaoning, China* 51 E11
Jinan, *China* 50 F9
Jincheng, *China* 50 G7
Jinchuan, *China* 52 B4
Jind, *India* 62 E7
Jindabyne, *Australia* 91 F4
Jindrichuv Hradec, *Czech.* 20 F5
Jing He →, *China* 50 G5
Jing Shan, *China* 53 B8
Jing Xian, *Anhui, China* . 53 B12
Jing Xian, *Hunan, China* . 52 D7
Jing'an, *China* 53 C10
Jingbian, *China* 50 F5
Jingchuan, *China* 50 G4
Jingde, *China* 53 B12
Jingdezhen, *China* 53 C11
Jingdong, *China* 52 E3
Jinggu, *China* 52 F3
Jinghai, *China* 50 E9
Jinghong, *China* 52 F3
Jingjiang, *China* 53 A13
Jingle, *China* 50 E6
Jingmen, *China* 53 B9
Jingning, *China* 50 G3
Jingpo Hu, *China* 51 C15
Jingshan, *China* 53 B9
Jingtai, *China* 50 F3
Jingxi, *China* 52 F6
Jingxing, *China* 50 E8
Jingyang, *China* 50 G5
Jingyu, *China* 51 C14
Jingyuan, *China* 50 F3
Jingziguan, *China* 50 H6
Jinhua, *China* 53 C12
Jining,
  Nei Mongol Zizhiqu,
  China 50 D7
Jining, *Shandong, China* . 50 G9
Jinja, *Uganda* 82 B3
Jinjang, *Malaysia* 59 L3
Jinji, *China* 50 F4
Jinjiang, *Fujian, China* .. 53 E12
Jinjiang, *Yunnan, China* . 52 D3
Jinjie, *China* 50 E6
Jinjini, *Ghana* 78 D4
Jinkou, *China* 53 B10
Jinmen Dao, *China* 53 E12
Jinnah Barrage, *Pakistan* 60 C7
Jinning, *China* 52 E4
Jinotega, *Nic.* 116 D2
Jinotepe, *Nic.* 116 D2
Jinping, *Guizhou, China* . 52 D7
Jinping, *Yunnan, China* .. 52 F4
Jinsha, *China* 52 D6
Jinsha Jiang →, *China* ... 52 C5
Jinshan, *China* 53 B13
Jinshi, *China* 53 C8
Jintan, *China* 53 B12
Jinxi, *Jiangxi, China* 53 D11
Jinxi, *Liaoning, China* ... 51 D11
Jinxian, *China* 53 C11
Jinxiang, *China* 50 G9
Jinyun, *China* 53 C13
Jinzhai, *China* 53 B10
Jinzhou, *China* 51 D11
Jiparaná →, *Brazil* 125 B5
Jipijapa, *Ecuador* 120 D1
Jiquilpan, *Mexico* 114 D4
Jishan, *China* 50 G6
Jishou, *China* 52 C7
Jishui, *China* 53 D10
Jisr ash Shughūr, *Syria* .. 66 E7
Jitarning, *Australia* 89 F2
Jitra, *Malaysia* 59 J3
Jiu →, *Romania* 38 F6
Jiudengkou, *China* 50 E4
Jiujiang, *Guangdong, China* 53 F9
Jiujiang, *Jiangxi, China* .. 53 C10
Jiuling Shan, *China* 53 C10
Jiulong, *China* 52 C3
Jiuquan, *China* 54 C4
Jiutai, *China* 51 B13
Jiuxiangcheng, *China* ... 50 H8
Jiuxincheng, *China* 50 E8
Jiuyuhang, *China* 53 B12
Jixi, *Anhui, China* 53 B12
Jixi, *Heilongjiang, China* . 51 B16
Jiyang, *China* 51 F9
Jīzān, *Si. Arabia* 68 D3
Jize, *China* 50 F8
Jizera →, *Czech.* 20 E4
Jizō-Zaki, *Japan* 49 G6
Jizzakh, *Uzbekistan* 44 E7
Joaçaba, *Brazil* 127 B5
Joaíma, *Brazil* 123 E3
João, *Brazil* 122 B1
João Amaro, *Brazil* 123 D3
João Câmara, *Brazil* 122 C4
João Pessoa, *Brazil* 122 C5
João Pinheiro, *Brazil* 123 E2

Joaquim Távora, *Brazil* ... 123 F2
Joaquín V. González,
  Argentina 126 B3
Jobourg, Nez de, *France* .. 24 C5
Jódar, *Spain* 29 H1
Jodhpur, *India* 62 F5
Jœuf, *France* 25 C13
Jofane, *Mozam.* 85 C5
Jõgeva, *Estonia* 9 G22
Joggins, *Canada* 99 C7
Jogjakarta = Yogyakarta,
  Indonesia 57 G14
Johannesburg, *S. Africa* .. 85 D4
Johannesburg, *U.S.A.* ... 113 K9
John Day, *U.S.A.* 110 D4
John Day →, *U.S.A.* 110 D3
John H. Kerr Reservoir,
  U.S.A. 105 G6
John o' Groats, *U.K.* 14 C5
Johnnie, *U.S.A.* 113 J10
John's Ra., *Australia* 90 C1
Johnson, *U.S.A.* 109 G4
Johnson City, *N.Y., U.S.A.* 107 D9
Johnson City, *Tenn.,*
  U.S.A. 105 G4
Johnson City, *Tex., U.S.A.* 109 K5
Johnsonburg, *U.S.A.* 106 E6
Johnsondale, *U.S.A.* 113 K8
Johnson's Crossing, *Canada* 100 A2
Johnston, L., *Australia* ... 89 F3
Johnston Falls =
  Mambilima Falls, *Zambia* 83 E2
Johnston I., *Pac. Oc.* 93 F11
Johnstone Str., *Canada* .. 100 C3
Johnstown, *N.Y., U.S.A.* . 107 C10
Johnstown, *Pa., U.S.A.* .. 106 F6
Johor Baharu, *Malaysia* . 59 M4
Jõhvi, *Estonia* 9 G22
Joigny, *France* 25 E10
Joinvile, *Brazil* 127 B6
Joinville, *France* 25 D12
Joinville I., *Antarctica* ... 5 C18
Jojutla, *Mexico* 115 D5
Jokkmokk, *Sweden* 8 C18
Jökulsá á Bru →, *Iceland* 8 D6
Jökulsá á Fjöllum →,
  Iceland 8 C5
Jolfā, *Āzarbājān-e Sharqī,*
  Iran 67 C11
Jolfā, *Eşfahan, Iran* 65 C6
Joliet, *U.S.A.* 104 E1
Joliette, *Canada* 98 C5
Jolo, *Phil.* 55 J4
Jolon, *U.S.A.* 112 K5
Jomalig, *Phil.* 55 D5
Jombang, *Indonesia* 57 G15
Jomda, *China* 52 B2
Jome, *Indonesia* 57 E7
Jomfruland, *Norway* 11 F3
Jönåker, *Sweden* 11 F10
Jonava, *Lithuania* 9 J21
Jones Sound, *Canada* ... 4 B3
Jonesboro, *Ark., U.S.A.* .. 109 H9
Jonesboro, *Ill., U.S.A.* ... 109 G10
Jonesboro, *La., U.S.A.* ... 109 J8
Jonesport, *U.S.A.* 99 D6
Jonglei, *Sudan* 77 F3
Jonglei □, *Sudan* 77 F3
Joniškis, *Lithuania* 9 H20
Jönköping, *Sweden* 9 H16
Jonquière, *Canada* 99 C5
Jonsberg, *Sweden* 11 F10
Jonsered, *Sweden* 11 G6
Jonzac, *France* 26 C3
Joplin, *U.S.A.* 109 G7
Jordan, *U.S.A.* 110 C10
Jordan ■, *Asia* 69 E5
Jordan →, *Asia* 69 D4
Jordan Valley, *U.S.A.* ... 110 E5
Jordânia, *Brazil* 123 E3
Jorge, C., *Chile* 128 D1
Jorhat, *India* 61 F19
Jörn, *Sweden* 8 D19
Jorong, *Indonesia* 56 E4
Jørpeland, *Norway* 9 G11
Jorquera →, *Chile* 126 B2
Jos, *Nigeria* 79 D6
José Batlle y Ordóñez,
  Uruguay 127 C4
José de San Martín,
  Argentina 128 B2
Joseph, *U.S.A.* 110 D5
Joseph, L., *Nfld., Canada* . 99 B6
Joseph, L., *Ont., Canada* . 106 A5
Joseph Bonaparte G.,
  Australia 88 B4
Joseph City, *U.S.A.* 111 J8
Joshua Tree, *U.S.A.* 113 L10
Joshua Tree National
  Monument, *U.S.A.* .. 113 M10
Josselin, *France* 24 E4
Jostedalsbreen, *Norway* . 9 F12
Jotunheimen, *Norway* ... 10 C2
Jourdanton, *U.S.A.* 109 L5
Joure, *Neths.* 16 C7
Joussard, *Canada* 100 B5
Joutseno, *Finland* 40 B5
Jovellanos, *Cuba* 116 B3
Joyeuse, *France* 27 D8
Józefów, *Poland* 20 C11
Ju Xian, *China* 51 F10
Juan Aldama, *Mexico* ... 114 C4
Juan Bautista Alberdi,
  Argentina 126 C3
Juan de Fuca Str., *Canada* 112 B2
Juan de Nova, *Ind. Oc.* .. 85 B7

Juan Fernández, Arch. de, Pac. Oc. ... 93 L20
Juan José Castelli, Argentina ... 126 B3
Juan L. Lacaze, Uruguay ... 126 C4
Juanjuí, Peru ... 124 B2
Juankoski, Finland ... 8 E23
Juárez, Argentina ... 126 D4
Juárez, Mexico ... 113 N11
Juárez, Sierra de, Mexico ... 114 A1
Juatinga, Ponta de, Brazil ... 123 F3
Jùazeiro, Brazil ... 122 C3
Juàzeiro do Norte, Brazil ... 122 C4
Jubayl, Lebanon ... 69 A4
Jubbah, Si. Arabia ... 64 D4
Jubbulpore = Jabalpur, India ... 63 H8
Jübek, Germany ... 18 A5
Jubga, Russia ... 43 H4
Jubilee L., Australia ... 89 E4
Juby, C., Morocco ... 74 C2
Júcar →, Spain ... 29 F4
Júcaro, Cuba ... 116 B4
Juchitán, Mexico ... 115 D5
Judaea = Har Yehuda, Israel ... 69 D3
Judenburg, Austria ... 21 H4
Judith →, U.S.A. ... 110 C9
Judith, Pt., U.S.A. ... 107 E13
Judith Gap, U.S.A. ... 110 C9
Jufari →, Brazil ... 121 D5
Jugoslavia = Yugoslavia ■, Europe ... 21 M10
Juigalpa, Nic. ... 116 D2
Juillac, France ... 26 C5
Juist, Germany ... 18 B2
Juiz de Fora, Brazil ... 123 F3
Jujuy □, Argentina ... 126 A2
Julesburg, U.S.A. ... 108 E3
Juli, Peru ... 124 D4
Julia Cr. →, Australia ... 90 C3
Julia Creek, Australia ... 90 C3
Juliaca, Peru ... 124 D3
Julian, U.S.A. ... 113 M10
Julian Alps = Julijske Alpe, Slovenia ... 33 B11
Julianakanaal, Neths. ... 17 F7
Julianatop, Surinam ... 121 C6
Julianehåb, Greenland ... 4 C5
Jülich, Germany ... 18 E2
Julierpass, Switz. ... 23 D9
Julijske Alpe, Slovenia ... 33 B11
Julimes, Mexico ... 114 B3
Jullundur, India ... 62 D6
Julu, China ... 50 F8
Jumbo, Zimbabwe ... 83 F3
Jumbo Pk., U.S.A. ... 113 J12
Jumentos Cays, Bahamas ... 117 B4
Jumet, Belgium ... 17 H4
Jumilla, Spain ... 29 G3
Jumla, Nepal ... 63 E10
Jumna = Yamuna →, India ... 63 G9
Junagadh, India ... 62 J4
Junction, Tex., U.S.A. ... 109 K5
Junction, Utah, U.S.A. ... 111 G7
Junction B., Australia ... 90 A1
Junction City, Kans., U.S.A. ... 108 F6
Junction City, Oreg., U.S.A. ... 110 D2
Junction Pt., Australia ... 90 A1
Jundah, Australia ... 90 C3
Jundiaí, Brazil ... 127 A6
Juneau, U.S.A. ... 96 C6
Junee, Australia ... 91 E4
Jungfrau, Switz. ... 22 C5
Junggar Pendi, China ... 54 B3
Junglinster, Lux. ... 17 J8
Jungshahi, Pakistan ... 62 G2
Juniata →, U.S.A. ... 106 F7
Junín, Argentina ... 126 C3
Junín, Peru ... 124 C2
Junín □, Peru ... 124 C3
Junín de los Andes, Argentina ... 128 A2
Jūniyah, Lebanon ... 69 B4
Juntura, U.S.A. ... 110 E4
Juparanã, L., Brazil ... 123 E3
Jupiter →, Canada ... 99 C7
Juquiá, Brazil ... 123 F2
Jur, Nahr el →, Sudan ... 77 F2
Jura = Jura, Mts. du, Europe ... 27 B10
Jura = Schwäbische Alb, Germany ... 19 G5
Jura, Europe ... 25 F13
Jura, U.K. ... 14 F3
Jura, France ... 25 F12
Jura, Mts. du, Europe ... 27 B10
Jura, Sd. of, U.K. ... 14 F3
Jura Suisse, Switz. ... 22 B3
Jurado, Colombia ... 120 B2
Jurbarkas, Lithuania ... 9 J20
Jurilovca, Romania ... 38 E11
Jūrmala, Latvia ... 9 H20
Jurong, China ... 53 B12
Juruá →, Brazil ... 120 D4
Juruena, Brazil ... 125 C6
Juruena →, Brazil ... 125 B6
Juruti, Brazil ... 121 D6
Jussey, France ... 25 E12
Justo Daract, Argentina ... 126 C2
Jutaí, Brazil ... 124 B4
Jutaí →, Brazil ... 120 D4
Jüterbog, Germany ... 18 D9
Juticalpa, Honduras ... 116 D2

Jutland = Jylland, Denmark ... 11 H3
Jutphaas, Neths. ... 16 D6
Juventud, I. de la, Cuba ... 116 B3
Juvigny-sous-Andaine, France ... 24 D6
Juvisy-sur-Orge, France ... 25 D9
Juwain, Afghan. ... 60 D2
Jüy Zar, Iran ... 67 F12
Juye, China ... 50 G9
Juzennecourt, France ... 25 D11
Jvari, Georgia ... 43 J6
Jylland, Denmark ... 11 H3
Jyväskylä, Finland ... 9 E21

K

K2, Mt., Pakistan ... 63 B7
Kaap Plateau, S. Africa ... 84 D3
Kaapkruis, Namibia ... 84 C1
Kaapstad = Cape Town, S. Africa ... 84 E2
Kaatsheuvel, Neths. ... 17 E6
Kabaena, Indonesia ... 57 F6
Kabala, S. Leone ... 78 D2
Kabale, Uganda ... 82 C3
Kabalo, Zaïre ... 82 D2
Kabambare, Zaïre ... 82 C2
Kabango, Zaïre ... 83 D2
Kabanjahe, Indonesia ... 56 D1
Kabankalan, Phil. ... 55 G5
Kabara, Mali ... 78 B4
Kabardinka, Russia ... 43 H4
Kabardino-Balkar Republic = Kabardino Balkaria □, Russia ... 43 J6
Kabardino Balkaria □, Russia ... 43 J6
Kabare, Indonesia ... 57 E8
Kabarega Falls, Uganda ... 82 B3
Kabasalan, Phil. ... 55 H5
Kabba, Nigeria ... 79 D6
Kabin Buri, Thailand ... 58 F3
Kabinakagami L., Canada ... 98 C3
Kabīr, Zab al →, Iraq ... 67 D10
Kabna, Sudan ... 76 D3
Kabompo, Zambia ... 83 E1
Kabompo →, Zambia ... 81 G4
Kabondo, Zaïre ... 83 D2
Kabongo, Zaïre ... 82 D2
Kabou, Togo ... 79 D5
Kaboudia, Rass, Tunisia ... 75 A7
Kabra, Australia ... 90 C5
Kabūd Gonbad, Iran ... 65 B8
Kabugao, Phil. ... 55 B4
Kābul, Afghan. ... 62 B3
Kābul □, Afghan. ... 60 B6
Kabul →, Pakistan ... 62 C5
Kabunga, Zaïre ... 82 C2
Kaburuang, Indonesia ... 57 D7
Kabushiya, Sudan ... 77 D3
Kabwe, Zambia ... 83 E2
Kačanik, Serbia, Yug. ... 21 N11
Kachchh, Gulf of, India ... 62 H3
Kachchh, Rann of, India ... 62 G4
Kachebera, Zambia ... 83 E3
Kachin □, Burma ... 61 F20
Kachira, L., Uganda ... 82 C3
Kachiry, Kazakhstan ... 44 D8
Kachisi, Ethiopia ... 77 F4
Kachot, Cambodia ... 59 G4
Kaçkar, Turkey ... 67 B9
Kadan Kyun, Burma ... 56 B1
Kadanai →, Afghan. ... 62 D1
Kadarkút, Hungary ... 21 J7
Kade, Ghana ... 79 D4
Kadi, India ... 62 H5
Kadina, Australia ... 91 E2
Kadınhanı, Turkey ... 66 C5
Kadirli, Turkey ... 66 D7
Kadiyevka = Stakhanov, Ukraine ... 41 H10
Kadoka, U.S.A. ... 108 D4
Kadom, Russia ... 42 C6
Kadoma, Zimbabwe ... 83 F2
Kâdugli, Sudan ... 77 E2
Kaduna, Nigeria ... 79 C6
Kaduna □, Nigeria ... 79 C6
Kaduy, Russia ... 40 C9
Kaédi, Mauritania ... 78 B2
Kaélé, Cameroon ... 79 C7
Kaeng Khoï, Thailand ... 58 E3
Kaesŏng, N. Korea ... 51 F14
Kāf, Si. Arabia ... 64 D3
Kafakumba, Zaïre ... 80 F4
Kafan = Kapan, Armenia ... 67 C12
Kafanchan, Nigeria ... 79 D6
Kafareti, Nigeria ... 79 C7
Kaffrine, Senegal ... 78 C1
Kafia Kingi, Sudan ... 73 G9
Kafinda, Zambia ... 83 E3
Kafirévs, Ákra, Greece ... 39 L7
Kafr el Dawâr, Egypt ... 76 H7
Kafr el Sheikh, Egypt ... 76 H7
Kafue, Zambia ... 83 F2
Kafue →, Zambia ... 81 H5
Kafue Flats, Zambia ... 83 F2
Kafue Nat. Park, Zambia ... 83 F2
Kafulwe, Zambia ... 83 D2
Kaga, Afghan. ... 62 B4
Kaga Bandoro, C.A.R. ... 73 G8
Kagan, Uzbekistan ... 44 F7
Kagawa □, Japan ... 49 G6

Kagera □, Tanzania ... 82 C3
Kagera →, Uganda ... 82 C3
Kağizman, Turkey ... 67 B10
Kagoshima, Japan ... 49 J5
Kagoshima □, Japan ... 49 J5
Kagul = Cahul, Moldova ... 41 K5
Kahak, Iran ... 65 B6
Kahama, Tanzania ... 82 C3
Kahama □, Tanzania ... 82 C3
Kahang, Malaysia ... 59 L4
Kahayan →, Indonesia ... 56 E4
Kahe, Tanzania ... 82 C4
Kahemba, Zaïre ... 80 F3
Kahil, Djebel bou, Algeria ... 75 B5
Kahniah →, Canada ... 100 B4
Kahnūj, Iran ... 65 E8
Kahoka, U.S.A. ... 108 E9
Kahoolawe, U.S.A. ... 102 H16
Kahramanmaraş, Turkey ... 66 D7
Kâhta, Turkey ... 67 D8
Kahuta, Pakistan ... 62 C5
Kai, Kepulauan, Indonesia ... 57 F8
Kai Besar, Indonesia ... 57 F8
Kai Is. = Kai, Kepulauan, Indonesia ... 57 F8
Kai Kecil, Indonesia ... 57 F8
Kai Xian, China ... 52 B7
Kaiama, Nigeria ... 79 D5
Kaiapoi, N.Z. ... 87 K4
Kaieteur Falls, Guyana ... 121 B6
Kaifeng, China ... 50 G8
Kaihua, China ... 53 C12
Kaikohe, N.Z. ... 87 F4
Kaikoura, N.Z. ... 87 K4
Kaikoura Ra., N.Z. ... 87 J4
Kailahun, S. Leone ... 78 D2
Kaili, China ... 52 D6
Kailu, China ... 51 C11
Kailua Kona, U.S.A. ... 102 J17
Kaimana, Indonesia ... 57 E8
Kaimanawa Mts., N.Z. ... 87 H5
Kaimganj, India ... 63 F8
Kaimur Hills, India ... 63 G9
Kaingaroa Forest, N.Z. ... 87 H6
Kainji Res., Nigeria ... 79 C5
Kainuu, Finland ... 8 D23
Kaipara Harbour, N.Z. ... 87 G5
Kaiping, China ... 53 F9
Kaipokok B., Canada ... 99 B8
Kairana, India ... 62 E7
Kaironi, Indonesia ... 57 E8
Kairouan, Tunisia ... 75 A7
Kaiserslautern, Germany ... 19 F3
Kaitaia, N.Z. ... 87 F4
Kaitangata, N.Z. ... 87 M2
Kaithal, India ... 62 E7
Kaitu →, Pakistan ... 62 C4
Kaiwi Channel, U.S.A. ... 102 H16
Kaiyang, China ... 52 D6
Kaiyuan, Liaoning, China ... 51 C13
Kaiyuan, Yunnan, China ... 52 F4
Kajaani, Finland ... 8 D22
Kajabbi, Australia ... 90 B3
Kajana = Kajaani, Finland ... 8 D22
Kajang, Malaysia ... 59 L3
Kajaran, Armenia ... 67 C12
Kajiado, Kenya ... 82 C4
Kajiado □, Kenya ... 82 C4
Kajo Kaji, Sudan ... 77 G3
Kaka, Sudan ... 77 E3
Kakabeka Falls, Canada ... 98 C2
Kakamas, S. Africa ... 84 D3
Kakamega, Kenya ... 82 B3
Kakamega □, Kenya ... 82 B3
Kakanj, Bos.-H. ... 21 L8
Kakanui Mts., N.Z. ... 87 L3
Kake, Japan ... 49 G6
Kakegawa, Japan ... 49 G9
Kakeroma-Jima, Japan ... 49 K4
Kakhib, Russia ... 43 J8
Kakhovka, Ukraine ... 41 J7
Kakhovske Vdskh., Ukraine ... 41 J7
Kakinada, India ... 61 L13
Kakisa →, Canada ... 100 A5
Kakisa L., Canada ... 100 A5
Kakogawa, Japan ... 49 G7
Kakwa →, Canada ... 100 C5
Kāl Gūsheh, Iran ... 65 D8
Kal Safīd, Iran ... 67 E12
Kala, Pakistan ... 62 C7
Kalaa-Kebira, Tunisia ... 75 A7
Kalabagh, Pakistan ... 62 C4
Kalabahi, Indonesia ... 57 F6
Kalabáka, Greece ... 39 K4
Kalabo, Zambia ... 81 G4
Kalach, Russia ... 42 E5
Kalach na Donu, Russia ... 43 F6
Kaladan →, Burma ... 61 J18
Kaladar, Canada ... 106 B7
Kalahari, Africa ... 84 C3
Kalahari Gemsbok Nat. Park, S. Africa ... 84 D3
Kalajoki, Finland ... 8 D20
Kalak, Iran ... 65 E8
Kalakamati, Botswana ... 85 C4
Kalakan, Russia ... 45 D12
Kalakh, Syria ... 64 C3
K'alak'unlun Shank'ou, Pakistan ... 63 B8
Kalam, Pakistan ... 63 B5
Kalama, U.S.A. ... 112 C4
Kalama, Zaïre ... 82 C2
Kalámai, Greece ... 39 M5
Kalamariá, Greece ... 39 J5
Kalamata = Kalámai, Greece ... 39 M5

Kalamazoo, U.S.A. ... 104 D3
Kalamazoo →, U.S.A. ... 104 D2
Kalambo Falls, Tanzania ... 83 D3
Kálamos, Greece ... 39 L3
Kalannie, Australia ... 89 F2
Kalāntarī, Iran ... 65 C7
Kalao, Indonesia ... 57 F6
Kalaotoa, Indonesia ... 57 F6
Kälarne, Sweden ... 10 B10
Kalárovo, Slovak Rep. ... 21 H7
Kalasin, Thailand ... 58 D4
Kalat, Pakistan ... 60 E5
Kalāteh, Iran ... 65 B7
Kalāteh-ye-Ganj, Iran ... 65 E8
Kálathos, Greece ... 39 N11
Kalaus →, Russia ... 43 H7
Kalávrita, Greece ... 39 L5
Kalbarri, Australia ... 89 E1
Kale, Turkey ... 66 D3
Kalecik, Turkey ... 66 B5
Kalegauk Kyun, Burma ... 61 M20
Kalehe, Zaïre ... 82 C2
Kalema, Tanzania ... 82 C3
Kalemie, Zaïre ... 82 D2
Kalety, Poland ... 20 E8
Kalewa, Burma ... 61 H19
Kalgan = Zhangjiakou, China ... 50 D8
Kalgoorlie-Boulder, Australia ... 89 F3
Kaliakra, Nos, Bulgaria ... 38 F11
Kalianda, Indonesia ... 56 F3
Kalibo, Phil. ... 55 F5
Kaliganj, Bangla. ... 63 H13
Kalima, Zaïre ... 82 C2
Kalimantan, Indonesia ... 56 E4
Kalimantan Barat □, Indonesia ... 56 E4
Kalimantan Selatan □, Indonesia ... 56 E5
Kalimantan Tengah □, Indonesia ... 56 E4
Kalimantan Timur □, Indonesia ... 56 D5
Kálimnos, Greece ... 39 N10
Kalimpong, India ... 63 F13
Kalinin = Tver, Russia ... 42 B2
Kaliningrad, Russia ... 9 J19
Kalininsk, Russia ... 42 E7
Kalinkavichy, Belarus ... 41 F5
Kalinkovichi = Kalinkavichy, Belarus ... 41 F5
Kalinovik, Bos.-H. ... 21 M8
Kalipetrovo, Bulgaria ... 38 E10
Kaliro, Uganda ... 82 B3
Kalispell, U.S.A. ... 110 B6
Kalisz, Poland ... 20 D8
Kaliua, Tanzania ... 82 D3
Kalix, Sweden ... 8 D20
Kalix →, Sweden ... 8 D20
Kalka, India ... 62 D7
Kalkan, Turkey ... 66 D3
Kalkaska, U.S.A. ... 104 C3
Kalkfeld, Namibia ... 84 C2
Kalkfontein, Botswana ... 84 C3
Kalkrand, Namibia ... 84 C2
Kållandsö, Sweden ... 11 F7
Kallavesi, Finland ... 8 E22
Kallithéa, Greece ... 39 M6
Kallonís, Kólpos, Greece ... 39 K9
Kallsjön, Sweden ... 8 E15
Kalmalo, Nigeria ... 79 C6
Kalmar, Sweden ... 9 H17
Kalmthout, Belgium ... 17 F4
Kalmyk Republic = Kalmykia □, Russia ... 43 G8
Kalmykia □, Russia ... 43 G8
Kalmykovo, Kazakhstan ... 44 E6
Kalna, India ... 63 H13
Kalocsa, Hungary ... 21 J9
Kalokhorio, Cyprus ... 37 E12
Kaloko, Zaïre ... 82 D2
Kalol, Gujarat, India ... 62 H5
Kalol, Gujarat, India ... 62 H5
Kalolímnos, Greece ... 39 M10
Kalomo, Zambia ... 83 F2
Kalpi, India ... 63 F8
Kaltbrunn, Switz. ... 23 B8
Kaltern = Caldaro, Italy ... 33 B8
Kaltungo, Nigeria ... 79 D7
Kalu, Pakistan ... 62 G2
Kalulushi, Zambia ... 83 E2
Kalundborg, Denmark ... 11 J5
Kalush, Ukraine ... 41 H3
Kalutara, Sri Lanka ... 60 R11
Kalyazin, Russia ... 42 B3
Kama, Zaïre ... 82 C2
Kama →, Russia ... 44 D6
Kamachumu, Tanzania ... 82 C3
Kamaishi, Japan ... 48 E10
Kamalia, Pakistan ... 62 D5
Kaman, Turkey ... 66 C5
Kamapanda, Zambia ... 83 E1
Kamaran, Yemen ... 68 D3
Kamativi, Zimbabwe ... 83 F2
Kamba, Nigeria ... 79 C5
Kambalda, Australia ... 89 F3
Kambar, Pakistan ... 62 F3
Kambia, S. Leone ... 78 D2
Kambolé, Zambia ... 83 D3
Kambos, Cyprus ... 37 D11
Kamchatka, P-ov., Russia ... 45 D16
Kamchatka Pen. = Kamchatka, P-ov., Russia ... 45 D16

Kamen, Russia ... 44 D9
Kamen-Rybolov, Russia ... 48 B6
Kamenjak, Rt., Croatia ... 33 D10
Kamenka = Kaminka, Ukraine ... 41 H7
Kamenka, Kazakhstan ... 42 E10
Kamenka, Russia ... 42 D6
Kamenka, Russia ... 42 E4
Kamenka Bugskaya = Kamyanka-Buzka, Ukraine ... 41 G3
Kamenka Dneprovskaya = Kamyanka-Dniprovska, Ukraine ... 41 J8
Kamennomostskiy, Russia ... 43 H5
Kamenolomni, Russia ... 43 G5
Kamensk-Shakhtinskiy, Russia ... 43 F5
Kamensk Uralskiy, Russia ... 44 D7
Kamenskiy, Russia ... 42 E7
Kamenskoye, Russia ... 45 C17
Kamenyak, Bulgaria ... 38 F9
Kamenz, Germany ... 18 D10
Kameoka, Japan ... 49 G7
Kamiah, U.S.A. ... 110 C5
Kamień Pomorski, Poland ... 20 B4
Kamieskroon, S. Africa ... 84 E2
Kamilukuak, L., Canada ... 101 A8
Kamin-Kashyrskyy, Ukraine ... 41 G3
Kamina, Zaïre ... 83 D1
Kaminak L., Canada ... 101 A9
Kaminka, Ukraine ... 41 H7
Kaminoyama, Japan ... 48 E10
Kamiros, Greece ... 37 C9
Kamituga, Zaïre ... 82 C2
Kamloops, Canada ... 100 C4
Kamnik, Slovenia ... 33 B11
Kamo, Armenia ... 43 K7
Kamo, Japan ... 48 F9
Kamoa Mts., Guyana ... 121 C6
Kamoke, Pakistan ... 62 C6
Kamp →, Austria ... 21 G5
Kampala, Uganda ... 82 B3
Kampar, Malaysia ... 59 K3
Kampar →, Indonesia ... 56 D2
Kampen, Neths. ... 16 C7
Kamperland, Neths. ... 17 E3
Kamphaeng Phet, Thailand ... 58 D2
Kampolombo, L., Zambia ... 83 E2
Kampong To, Thailand ... 59 J3
Kampot, Cambodia ... 59 G5
Kampuchea = Cambodia ■, Asia ... 58 F5
Kampung →, Indonesia ... 57 F9
Kampung Air Putih, Malaysia ... 59 K4
Kampung Jerangau, Malaysia ... 59 K4
Kampung Raja, Malaysia ... 59 K4
Kampungbaru = Tolitoli, Indonesia ... 57 D6
Kamrau, Teluk, Indonesia ... 57 E8
Kamsack, Canada ... 101 C8
Kamskoye Ustye, Russia ... 42 C9
Kamuchawie L., Canada ... 101 B8
Kamui-Misaki, Japan ... 48 C10
Kamyanets-Podilskyy, Ukraine ... 41 H4
Kamyanka-Buzka, Ukraine ... 41 G3
Kamyanka-Dniprovska, Ukraine ... 41 J8
Kāmyārān, Iran ... 67 E12
Kamyshin, Russia ... 42 E7
Kamyzyak, Russia ... 43 G9
Kanaaupscow, Canada ... 98 B4
Kanab, U.S.A. ... 111 H7
Kanab →, U.S.A. ... 111 H7
Kanagi, Japan ... 48 D10
Kanairiktok →, Canada ... 99 A7
Kanália, Greece ... 39 K5
Kananga, Zaïre ... 80 F4
Kanarraville, U.S.A. ... 111 H7
Kanash, Russia ... 42 C8
Kanaskat, U.S.A. ... 112 C5
Kanawha →, U.S.A. ... 104 F4
Kanazawa, Japan ... 49 F8
Kanchanaburi, Thailand ... 58 E2
Kanchenjunga, Nepal ... 63 F13
Kanchipuram, India ... 60 N11
Kanda Kanda, Zaïre ... 80 F4
Kandahar = Qandahār, Afghan. ... 60 D4
Kandalaksha, Russia ... 44 C4
Kandalu, Afghan. ... 60 E3
Kandangan, Indonesia ... 56 E5
Kandanos, Greece ... 37 D5
Kander →, Switz. ... 22 C5
Kandersteg, Switz. ... 22 D5
Kandhila, India ... 62 E7
Kandhkot, Pakistan ... 62 E3
Kandhla, India ... 62 E7
Kandi, Benin ... 79 C5
Kandi, India ... 63 H13
Kandira, Turkey ... 66 B4
Kandla, India ... 62 H4
Kandos, Australia ... 91 E4
Kandy, Sri Lanka ... 60 R12
Kane, U.S.A. ... 106 E6
Kane Basin, Greenland ... 4 B4
Kanevskaya, Russia ... 43 G4
Kanfanar, Croatia ... 33 C10
Kangaba, Mali ... 78 C3
Kangal, Turkey ... 66 C7
Kangān, Fārs, Iran ... 65 E7
Kangān, Hormozgān, Iran ... 65 E8
Kangar, Malaysia ... 59 J3

Kangaroo I.

Kangaroo I., *Australia* 91 F2
Kangasala, *Finland* 9 F21
Kangāvar, *Iran* 67 E12
Kangding, *China* 52 B3
Kăngdong, *N. Korea* 51 E14
Kangean, Kepulauan, *Indonesia* 56 F5
Kangean Is. = Kangean, Kepulauan, *Indonesia* .. 56 F5
Kanggye, *N. Korea* 51 D14
Kanggyŏng, *S. Korea* 51 F14
Kanghwa, *S. Korea* 51 F14
Kangiqsualujjuaq, *Canada* 97 C13
Kangiqsujuaq, *Canada* ... 97 B12
Kangirsuk, *Canada* 97 B13
Kangnŭng, *S. Korea* 51 F15
Kango, *Gabon* 80 D2
Kangping, *China* 51 C12
Kangto, *India* 61 F18
Kani, *Ivory C.* 78 D3
Kaniama, *Zaïre* 82 D1
Kaniapiskau →, *Canada* .. 99 A6
Kaniapiskau L., *Canada* .. 99 B6
Kanin, Poluostrov, *Russia* 44 C5
Kanin Nos, Mys, *Russia* .. 44 C5
Kanin Pen. = Kanin, Poluostrov, *Russia* 44 C5
Kaniva, *Australia* 91 F3
Kanjiža, *Serbia, Yug.* 21 J10
Kanjut Sar, *Pakistan* 63 A6
Kankaanpää, *Finland* 9 F20
Kankakee, *U.S.A.* 104 E2
Kankakee →, *U.S.A.* 104 E1
Kankan, *Guinea* 78 C3
Kankendy = Xankändi, *Azerbaijan* 67 C12
Kanker, *India* 61 J12
Kankunskiy, *Russia* 45 D13
Kannapolis, *U.S.A.* 105 H5
Kannauj, *India* 63 F8
Kannod, *India* 60 H10
Kano, *Nigeria* 79 C6
Kano □, *Nigeria* 79 C6
Kan'onji, *Japan* 49 G6
Kanoroba, *Ivory C.* 78 D3
Kanowit, *Malaysia* 56 D4
Kanowna, *Australia* 89 F3
Kanoya, *Japan* 49 J5
Kanpetlet, *Burma* 61 J18
Kanpur, *India* 63 F9
Kansas □, *U.S.A.* 108 F6
Kansas →, *U.S.A.* 108 F7
Kansas City, *Kans., U.S.A.* 108 F7
Kansas City, *Mo., U.S.A.* 108 F7
Kansenia, *Zaïre* 83 E2
Kansk, *Russia* 45 D10
Kansŏng, *S. Korea* 51 E15
Kansu = Gansu □, *China* 50 G3
Kantang, *Thailand* 59 J2
Kantché, *Niger* 79 C6
Kanté, *Togo* 79 D5
Kantemirovka, *Russia* 42 F4
Kantharalak, *Thailand* .. 58 E5
Kantō □, *Japan* 49 F9
Kantō-Sanchi, *Japan* 49 G9
Kanturk, *Ireland* 15 D3
Kanuma, *Japan* 49 F9
Kanus, *Namibia* 84 D2
Kanye, *Botswana* 84 C4
Kanzenze, *Zaïre* 83 E2
Kanzi, Ras, *Tanzania* 82 D4
Kaohsiung = Gaoxiong, *Taiwan* 53 F13
Kaokoveld, *Namibia* 84 B1
Kaolack, *Senegal* 78 C1
Kaoshan, *China* 51 B13
Kapadvanj, *India* 62 H5
Kapan, *Armenia* 67 C12
Kapanga, *Zaïre* 80 F4
Kapchagai = Qapshaghay, *Kazakhstan* 44 E8
Kapellen, *Belgium* 17 F4
Kapéllo, Ákra, *Greece* ... 39 N6
Kapema, *Zaïre* 83 E2
Kapfenberg, *Austria* 21 H5
Kapiri Mposhi, *Zambia* .. 83 E2
Kapiskau →, *Canada* .. 98 B3
Kapit, *Malaysia* 56 D4
Kapiti I., *N.Z.* 87 J5
Kaplice, *Czech.* 20 G4
Kapoe, *Thailand* 59 H2
Kapoeta, *Sudan* 77 G3
Kapos →, *Hungary* 21 J8
Kaposvár, *Hungary* 21 J7
Kapowsin, *U.S.A.* 112 D4
Kappeln, *Germany* 18 A5
Kapps, *Namibia* 84 C2
Kaprije, *Croatia* 33 E12
Kaprijke, *Belgium* 17 F3
Kapsan, *N. Korea* 51 D15
Kapsukas = Marijampolė, *Lithuania* 9 J20
Kapuas →, *Indonesia* .. 56 E3
Kapuas Hulu, Pegunungan, *Malaysia* 56 D4
Kapuas Hulu Ra. = Kapuas Hulu, Pegunungan, *Malaysia* .. 56 D4
Kapulo, *Zaïre* 83 D2
Kapunda, *Australia* 91 E2
Kapuni, *N.Z.* 87 H5
Kapurthala, *India* 62 D6
Kapuskasing, *Canada* ... 98 C3
Kapuskasing →, *Canada* 98 C3
Kapustin Yar, *Russia* 43 F7
Kaputar, *Australia* 91 E5
Kaputir, *Kenya* 82 B4

Kapuvár, *Hungary* 21 H7
Kara, *Russia* 44 C7
Kara Bogaz Gol, Zaliv = Garabogazköl Aylagy, *Turkmenistan* 44 E6
Kara Kalpak Republic = Karakalpakstan □, *Uzbekistan* 44 E6
Kara Kum, *Turkmenistan* . 44 F6
Kara Sea, *Russia* 44 B7
Karabiğa, *Turkey* 66 B2
Karabük, *Turkey* 66 B5
Karaburun, *Turkey* 66 C2
Karaburuni, *Albania* 39 J2
Karabutak = Qarabutaq, *Kazakhstan* 44 E7
Karacabey, *Turkey* 66 B3
Karacasu, *Turkey* 66 D3
Karachala = Qaraçala, *Azerbaijan* 43 L9
Karachayevsk, *Russia* 43 J5
Karachev, *Russia* 42 D2
Karachey-Cherkessia □, *Russia* 43 J5
Karachi, *Pakistan* 62 G2
Karad, *India* 60 L9
Karadeniz Boğazı, *Turkey* 66 B3
Karaga, *Ghana* 79 D4
Karaganda = Qaraghandy, *Kazakhstan* 44 E8
Karagayly, *Kazakhstan* .. 44 E8
Karaginskiy, Ostrov, *Russia* 45 D17
Karagüney Dağları, *Turkey* 66 B6
Karagwe □, *Tanzania* 82 C3
Karaikal, *India* 60 P11
Karaikkudi, *India* 60 P11
Karaisali, *Turkey* 66 D6
Karaj, *Iran* 65 C6
Karak, *Malaysia* 59 L4
Karakalpakstan □, *Uzbekistan* 44 E6
Karakas, *Kazakhstan* 44 E9
Karakitang, *Indonesia* ... 57 D7
Karaklis = Vanadzor, *Armenia* 43 K7
Karakoçan, *Turkey* 67 C9
Karakoram Pass, *Pakistan* 63 B7
Karakoram Ra., *Pakistan* . 63 B7
Karakurt, *Turkey* 67 B10
Karalon, *Russia* 45 D12
Karaman, *Turkey* 66 D5
Karamay, *China* 54 B3
Karambu, *Indonesia* 56 E5
Karamea Bight, *N.Z.* 87 J3
Karamsad, *India* 62 H5
Karand, *Iran* 67 E12
Karanganyar, *Indonesia* .. 57 G13
Karapinar, *Turkey* 66 D5
Karasburg, *Namibia* 84 D2
Karasino, *Russia* 44 C9
Karasjok, *Norway* 8 B21
Karasu, *Turkey* 66 B4
Karasuk, *Russia* 44 D8
Karasuyama, *Japan* 49 F10
Karataş, *Turkey* 66 D6
Karataş Burnu, *Turkey* .. 66 D6
Karatau = Qarataū, *Kazakhstan* 44 E8
Karatau, Khrebet, *Kazakhstan* 44 E7
Karauli, *India* 62 F7
Karavostasi, *Cyprus* 37 D11
Karawang, *Indonesia* 57 G12
Karawanken, *Europe* 21 J4
Karayazı, *Turkey* 67 C10
Karazhal, *Kazakhstan* 44 E8
Karbalā, *Iraq* 67 F11
Kårböle, *Sweden* 10 C9
Karcag, *Hungary* 21 H10
Karcha →, *Pakistan* 63 B7
Karda, *Russia* 45 D11
Kardhámila, *Greece* 39 L9
Kardhítsa, *Greece* 39 K4
Kärdla, *Estonia* 9 G20
Kareeberge, *S. Africa* .. 84 E3
Kareima, *Sudan* 76 D3
Karelia □, *Russia* 44 C4
Karelian Republic = Karelia □, *Russia* 44 C4
Kārevāndar, *Iran* 65 E9
Kargasok, *Russia* 44 D9
Kargat, *Russia* 44 D9
Kargı, *Turkey* 66 B6
Kargil, *India* 63 B7
Kargopol, *Russia* 40 B10
Karguéri, *Niger* 79 C7
Karia ba Mohammed, *Morocco* 74 B3
Kariān, *Iran* 65 E8
Kariba, *Zimbabwe* 83 F2
Kariba, L., *Zimbabwe* ... 83 F2
Kariba Dam, *Zimbabwe* . 83 F2
Kariba Gorge, *Zambia* .. 83 F2
Karibib, *Namibia* 84 C2
Karimata, Kepulauan, *Indonesia* 56 E3
Karimata, Selat, *Indonesia* 56 E3
Karimata Is. = Karimata, Kepulauan, *Indonesia* .. 56 E3
Karimnagar, *India* 60 K11
Karimunjawa, Kepulauan, *Indonesia* 56 F4
Karin, *Somali Rep.* 68 E4
Karīt, *Iran* 65 C8
Kariya, *Japan* 49 G8
Karjala, *Finland* 40 A5

Karkaralinsk = Qarqaraly, *Kazakhstan* 44 E8
Karkinitska Zatoka, *Ukraine* 41 K7
Karkinitskiy Zaliv = Karkinitska Zatoka, *Ukraine* 41 K7
Karkur Tohl, *Egypt* 76 C2
Karl Liebknecht, *Russia* .. 42 E2
Karl-Marx-Stadt = Chemnitz, *Germany* ... 18 E8
Karla, L. = Voiviïs Límni, *Greece* 39 K5
Karlivka, *Ukraine* 41 H8
Karlobag, *Croatia* 33 D12
Karlovac, *Croatia* 33 C12
Karlovka = Karlivka, *Ukraine* 41 H8
Karlovo, *Bulgaria* 38 G7
Karlovy Vary, *Czech.* 20 E2
Karlsbad = Karlovy Vary, *Czech.* 20 E2
Karlsborg, *Sweden* 11 F8
Karlshamn, *Sweden* 9 H16
Karlskoga, *Sweden* 9 G16
Karlskrona, *Sweden* 9 H16
Karlsruhe, *Germany* 19 F4
Karlstad, *Sweden* 9 G15
Karlstad, *U.S.A.* 108 A6
Karlstadt, *Germany* 19 F5
Karnal, *India* 62 E7
Karnali →, *Nepal* 63 E9
Karnaphuli Res., *Bangla.* . 61 H18
Karnataka □, *India* 60 N10
Karnes City, *U.S.A.* 109 L6
Karnische Alpen, *Europe* . 21 J3
Karo, *Mali* 78 C4
Karoi, *Zimbabwe* 83 F2
Karonga, *Malawi* 83 D3
Karoonda, *Australia* 91 F2
Karora, *Sudan* 76 D4
Káros, *Greece* 39 N8
Karousádhes, *Greece* 39 K2
Karpasia □, *Cyprus* 37 D13
Kárpathos, *Greece* 39 P10
Kárpathos, Stenón, *Greece* 39 P10
Karpuz Burnu = Apostolos Andreas, C., *Cyprus* .. 66 E6
Karrebæk, *Denmark* 11 J5
Kars, *Turkey* 67 B10
Karsakpay, *Kazakhstan* .. 44 E7
Karsha, *Kazakhstan* 42 F10
Karshi = Qarshi, *Uzbekistan* 44 F7
Karsiyang, *India* 63 F13
Karst, *Croatia* 33 C11
Kartaly, *Russia* 44 D7
Kartapur, *India* 62 D6
Karthaus, *U.S.A.* 106 E6
Kartuzy, *Poland* 20 A8
Karufa, *Indonesia* 57 E8
Karumba, *Australia* 90 B3
Karumo, *Tanzania* 82 C3
Karumwa, *Tanzania* 82 C3
Karungu, *Kenya* 82 C3
Karup, *Denmark* 11 H3
Karviná, *Czech.* 20 F8
Karwar, *India* 60 M9
Karwi, *India* 63 G9
Kasache, *Malawi* 83 E3
Kasai →, *Zaïre* 80 E3
Kasai Oriental □, *Zaïre* .. 82 C1
Kasaji, *Zaïre* 83 E1
Kasama, *Zambia* 83 E3
Kasan-dong, *N. Korea* .. 51 D14
Kasane, *Namibia* 84 B3
Kasanga, *Tanzania* 83 D3
Kasangulu, *Zaïre* 80 E3
Kasaragod, *India* 60 N9
Kasba L., *Canada* 101 A8
Kasba Tadla, *Morocco* .. 74 B3
Käseh Garān, *Iran* 64 C5
Kasempa, *Zambia* 83 E2
Kasenga, *Zaïre* 83 E2
Kasese, *Uganda* 82 B3
Kasewa, *Zambia* 83 E2
Kasganj, *India* 63 F8
Kashabowie, *Canada* ... 98 C1
Kāshān, *Iran* 65 C6
Kashi, *China* 54 C2
Kashimbo, *Zaïre* 83 E2
Kashin, *Russia* 42 B3
Kashipur, *India* 63 E8
Kashira, *Russia* 42 C4
Kashiwazaki, *Japan* 49 F9
Kashk-e Kohneh, *Afghan.* 60 B3
Kashmar, *Iran* 65 C8
Kashmir, *Asia* 63 C7
Kashmor, *Pakistan* 62 E3
Kashpirovka, *Russia* 42 D9
Kashun Noerh = Gaxun Nur, *China* 54 B9
Kasimov, *Russia* 42 C5
Kasinge, *Zaïre* 82 D2
Kasiruta, *Indonesia* 57 E7
Kaskaskia →, *U.S.A.* .. 108 G10
Kaskattama →, *Canada* 101 B10
Kaskinen, *Finland* 9 E19
Kaslo, *Canada* 100 D5
Kasmere L., *Canada* 101 B8
Kasongo, *Zaïre* 82 C2
Kasongo Lunda, *Zaïre* .. 80 F3
Kásos, *Greece* 39 P9
Kásos, Stenón, *Greece* ... 39 P9
Kaspi, *Georgia* 43 K7
Kaspiysk, *Russia* 43 J8

Kaspiyskiy, *Russia* 43 H8
Kassab ed Doleib, *Sudan* . 77 E3
Kassaba, *Egypt* 76 C2
Kassalâ, *Sudan* 77 D4
Kassalâ □, *Sudan* 77 D4
Kassel, *Germany* 18 D5
Kassinger, *Sudan* 76 D3
Kassiópi, *Greece* 37 A3
Kassue, *Indonesia* 57 F9
Kastamonu, *Turkey* 66 B5
Kastav, *Croatia* 33 C11
Kastéllion, *Greece* 37 D7
Kastélli, *Greece* 37 D5
Kastellou, Ákra, *Greece* .. 39 P10
Kasterlee, *Belgium* 17 F5
Kastóri, *Greece* 39 M5
Kastoría, *Greece* 39 J4
Kastornoye, *Russia* 42 F4
Kástron, *Greece* 39 K8
Kastsyukovichy, *Belarus* . 40 F7
Kasulu, *Tanzania* 82 C3
Kasulu □, *Tanzania* 82 C3
Kasumi, *Japan* 49 G7
Kasungu, *Malawi* 83 E3
Kasur, *Pakistan* 62 D6
Kata, *Russia* 45 D11
Kataba, *Zambia* 83 F2
Katako Kombe, *Zaïre* 82 C1
Katákolon, *Greece* 39 M4
Katale, *Tanzania* 82 C3
Katamatite, *Australia* 91 F4
Katanda, *Kivu, Zaïre* 82 C2
Katanda, *Shaba, Zaïre* .. 82 D1
Katanga = Shaba □, *Zaïre* 82 D2
Katangi, *India* 60 J11
Katangli, *Russia* 45 D15
Katavi Swamp, *Tanzania* . 82 D3
Katerini, *Greece* 39 J5
Katha, *Burma* 61 G20
Katherîna, Gebel, *Egypt* . 76 J8
Katherine, *Australia* 88 B5
Kathiawar, *India* 62 H4
Kathikas, *Cyprus* 37 E11
Kati, *Mali* 78 C3
Katihar, *India* 63 G12
Katima Mulilo, *Zambia* .. 84 B3
Katimbira, *Malawi* 83 E3
Katingan = Mendawai →, *Indonesia* 56 E4
Katiola, *Ivory C.* 78 D3
Katmandu, *Nepal* 63 F11
Kato Akhaïa, *Greece* 39 L4
Káto Arkhánai, *Greece* ... 37 D7
Káto Khorió, *Greece* 37 D7
Kato Pyrgos, *Cyprus* 37 D11
Káto Stavros, *Greece* 39 J6
Katompe, *Zaïre* 82 D2
Katonga →, *Uganda* 82 B3
Katoomba, *Australia* 91 E5
Katowice, *Poland* 20 E9
Katrine, L., *U.K.* 14 E4
Katrineholm, *Sweden* ... 10 E10
Katsepe, *Madag.* 85 B8
Katsina, *Nigeria* 79 C6
Katsina □, *Nigeria* 79 C6
Katsina Ala →, *Nigeria* . 79 D6
Katsumoto, *Japan* 49 H4
Katsuura, *Japan* 49 G10
Katsuyama, *Japan* 49 F8
Kattaviá, *Greece* 37 D9
Kattegat, *Denmark* 11 H5
Katumba, *Zaïre* 82 D2
Katungu, *Kenya* 82 C5
Katwa, *India* 63 H13
Katwijk-aan-Zee, *Neths.* . 16 D4
Kaub, *Germany* 19 E3
Kaufbeuren, *Germany* ... 19 H6
Kaufman, *U.S.A.* 109 J6
Kauhajoki, *Finland* 9 E20
Kauhava, *Finland* 9 E20
Kaukauna, *U.S.A.* 104 C1
Kaukauveld, *Namibia* .. 84 C3
Kaunas, *Lithuania* 9 J20
Kaura Namoda, *Nigeria* . 79 C6
Kautokeino, *Norway* 8 B20
Kavacha, *Russia* 45 C17
Kavadarci, *Macedonia* ... 39 H5
Kavaja, *Albania* 39 H2
Kavak, *Turkey* 66 B7
Kavalerovo, *Russia* 48 B7
Kavali, *India* 60 M12
Kavála, *Greece* 39 J7
Kavār, *Iran* 65 D7
Kavarna, *Bulgaria* 38 F11
Kavkaz, *Russia* 43 H3
Kavos, *Greece* 37 B4
Kaw, *Fr. Guiana* 121 C7
Kawa, *Sudan* 77 E3
Kawagama L., *Canada* .. 106 A6
Kawagoe, *Japan* 49 G9
Kawaguchi, *Japan* 49 G9
Kawaihae, *U.S.A.* 102 H17
Kawambwa, *Zambia* 83 D2
Kawanoe, *Japan* 49 G6
Kawardha, *India* 63 J9
Kawasaki, *Japan* 49 G9
Kawene, *Canada* 98 C1
Kawerau, *N.Z.* 87 H6
Kawhia Harbour, *N.Z.* .. 87 H5
Kawio, Kepulauan, *Indonesia* 57 D7
Kawnro, *Burma* 61 H21
Kawthoolei = Kawthule □, *Burma* 61 L20
Kawthule □, *Burma* 61 L20

Kaya, *Burkina Faso* 79 C4
Kayah □, *Burma* 61 K20
Kayan →, *Indonesia* 56 D5
Kaycee, *U.S.A.* 110 E10
Kayeli, *Indonesia* 57 E7
Kayenta, *U.S.A.* 111 H8
Kayes, *Mali* 78 C2
Kayima, *S. Leone* 78 D2
Kayl, *Lux.* 17 K8
Kayoa, *Indonesia* 57 D7
Kayomba, *Zambia* 83 E1
Kayoro, *Ghana* 79 C4
Kayrunnera, *Australia* .. 91 E3
Kaysatskoye, *Russia* 42 F8
Kayseri, *Turkey* 66 C6
Kaysville, *U.S.A.* 110 F8
Kayuagung, *Indonesia* .. 56 E2
Kazachye, *Russia* 45 B14
Kazakhstan ■, *Asia* 44 E7
Kazan, *Russia* 42 C9
Kazan-Rettō, *Pac. Oc.* .. 92 E6
Kazanlŭk, *Bulgaria* 38 G8
Kazanskaya, *Russia* 42 F5
Kazatin = Kozyatyn, *Ukraine* 41 H5
Kazbek, *Russia* 43 J7
Kāzerūn, *Iran* 65 D6
Kazi Magomed = Qazimämmäd, *Azerbaijan* 43 K9
Kazincbarcika, *Hungary* .. 21 G10
Kaztalovka, *Kazakhstan* . 42 F9
Kazumba, *Zaïre* 80 F4
Kazuno, *Japan* 48 D10
Kazym →, *Russia* 44 C7
Kcynia, *Poland* 20 C7
Ké-Macina, *Mali* 78 C3
Kéa, *Greece* 39 M7
Keams Canyon, *U.S.A.* .. 111 J8
Kearney, *U.S.A.* 108 E5
Keban, *Turkey* 67 C8
Keban Baraji, *Turkey* ... 67 C8
Kebbi □, *Nigeria* 79 C6
Kébi, *Ivory C.* 78 D3
Kebili, *Tunisia* 75 B6
Kebnekaise, *Sweden* 8 C18
Kebri Dehar, *Ethiopia* .. 68 F3
Kebumen, *Indonesia* 57 G13
Kecel, *Hungary* 21 J9
Kechika →, *Canada* 100 B3
Kecskemét, *Hungary* 21 J9
Kedada, *Ethiopia* 77 F4
Kedgwick, *Canada* 99 C6
Kedia Hill, *Botswana* .. 84 C3
Kedainiai, *Lithuania* 9 J21
Kediri, *Indonesia* 57 G15
Kédougou, *Senegal* 78 C2
Kedzierzyn, *Poland* 20 E8
Keeler, *U.S.A.* 112 J9
Keeley L., *Canada* 101 C7
Keeling Is. = Cocos Is., *Ind. Oc.* 92 J1
Keene, *Calif., U.S.A.* 113 K8
Keene, *N.H., U.S.A.* 107 D12
Keeper Hill, *Ireland* 15 D3
Keerbergen, *Belgium* 17 F5
Keeseville, *U.S.A.* 107 B11
Keeten Mastgat, *Neths.* .. 17 E4
Keetmanshoop, *Namibia* . 84 D2
Keewatin, *U.S.A.* 108 B8
Keewatin □, *Canada* 101 A9
Keewatin □, *Canada* 101 B8
Kefa □, *Ethiopia* 77 F4
Kefallinía, *Greece* 39 L3
Kefamenanu, *Indonesia* . 57 F6
Keffi, *Nigeria* 79 D6
Keflavík, *Iceland* 8 D2
Keg River, *Canada* 100 B5
Kegaska, *Canada* 99 B7
Kehl, *Germany* 19 G3
Keighley, *U.K.* 12 D6
Keila, *Estonia* 9 G21
Keimoes, *S. Africa* 84 D3
Keita, *Niger* 79 C6
Keitele, *Finland* 8 E22
Keith, *Australia* 91 F3
Keith, *U.K.* 14 D6
Keith Arm, *Canada* 96 B7
Kejser Franz Joseph Fjord = Kong Franz Joseph Fd., *Greenland* . 4 B6
Kekri, *India* 62 G6
Kël, *Russia* 45 C13
Kelamet, *Eritrea* 77 D4
Kelan, *China* 50 E6
Kelang, *Malaysia* 59 L3
Kelantan →, *Malaysia* .. 59 J4
Kelheim, *Germany* 19 G7
Kelibia, *Tunisia* 75 A7
Kellé, *Congo* 80 E2
Keller, *U.S.A.* 110 B4
Kellerberrin, *Australia* .. 89 F2
Kellett, C., *Canada* 4 B1
Kelleys I., *U.S.A.* 106 E2
Kellogg, *U.S.A.* 110 C5
Kells = Ceanannus Mor, *Ireland* 15 C5
Kélo, *Chad* 73 G8
Kelokedhara, *Cyprus* ... 37 E11
Kelowna, *Canada* 100 D5
Kelsey Bay, *Canada* 100 C3
Kelseyville, *U.S.A.* 112 G4
Kelso, *N.Z.* 87 L2

Kelso, *U.K.* 14 F6
Kelso, *U.S.A.* 112 D4
Keluang, *Malaysia* 59 L4
Kelvington, *Canada* 101 C8
Kem, *Russia* 44 C4
Kem-Kem, *Morocco* 74 B4
Kema, *Indonesia* 57 D7
Kemah, *U.S.A.* 112 D4
Kemaliye, *Turkey* 67 C8
Kemano, *Canada* 100 C3
Kemasik, *Malaysia* 59 K4
Kembolcha, *Ethiopia* 77 E4
Kemer, *Turkey* 66 D4
Kemerovo, *Russia* 44 D9
Kemi, *Finland* 8 D21
Kemi älv = Kemijoki →,
   Finland 8 D21
Kemijärvi, *Finland* 8 C22
Kemijoki →, *Finland* 8 D21
Kemmel, *Belgium* 17 G1
Kemmerer, *U.S.A.* 110 F8
Kemmuna = Comino,
   Malta 37 C1
Kemp, L., *U.S.A.* 109 J5
Kemp Land, *Antarctica* .. 5 C5
Kempsey, *Australia* 91 E5
Kempt, L., *Canada* 98 C5
Kempten, *Germany* 19 H6
Kemptville, *Canada* 98 C4
Kenadsa, *Algeria* 75 B4
Kendal, *Indonesia* 56 F4
Kendal, *U.K.* 12 C5
Kendall, *Australia* 91 E5
Kendall →, *Australia* ... 90 A3
Kendallville, *U.S.A.* ... 104 E3
Kendari, *Indonesia* 57 E6
Kendawangan, *Indonesia* . 56 E4
Kende, *Nigeria* 79 C5
Kendenup, *Australia* 89 F2
Kendrapara, *India* 61 J15
Kendrew, *S. Africa* 84 E3
Kendrick, *U.S.A.* 110 C5
Kene Thao, *Laos* 58 D3
Kenedy, *U.S.A.* 109 L6
Kenema, *S. Leone* 78 D2
Keng Kok, *Laos* 58 D5
Keng Tawng, *Burma* 61 J21
Keng Tung, *Burma* 61 J21
Kenge, *Zaïre* 80 E3
Kengeja, *Tanzania* 82 D4
Kenhardt, *S. Africa* 84 D3
Kenitra, *Morocco* 74 B3
Kenli, *China* 51 F10
Kenmare, *Ireland* 15 E2
Kenmare, *U.S.A.* 108 A3
Kenmare →, *Ireland* 15 E2
Kennebec, *U.S.A.* 108 D5
Kennedy, *Zimbabwe* 83 F2
Kennedy Ra., *Australia* . 89 D2
Kennedy Taungdeik,
   Burma 61 H18
Kennet →, *U.K.* 13 F7
Kenneth Ra., *Australia* . 88 D2
Kennett, *U.S.A.* 109 G9
Kennewick, *U.S.A.* 110 C4
Kénogami, *Canada* 99 C5
Kenogami →, *Canada* 98 B3
Kenora, *Canada* 101 D10
Kenosha, *U.S.A.* 104 D2
Kensington, *Canada* 99 C7
Kensington, *U.S.A.* 108 F5
Kensington Downs,
   Australia 90 C3
Kent, *Ohio, U.S.A.* 106 E3
Kent, *Oreg., U.S.A.* 110 D3
Kent, *Tex., U.S.A.* 109 K2
Kent, *Wash., U.S.A.* 112 C4
Kent □, *U.K.* 13 F8
Kent Group, *Australia* .. 90 F4
Kent Pen., *Canada* 96 B9
Kentau, *Kazakhstan* 44 E7
Kentland, *U.S.A.* 104 E2
Kenton, *U.S.A.* 104 E4
Kentucky □, *U.S.A.* 104 G3
Kentucky →, *U.S.A.* 104 F3
Kentucky L., *U.S.A.* 105 G2
Kentville, *Canada* 99 C7
Kentwood, *U.S.A.* 109 K9
Kenya ■, *Africa* 82 B4
Kenya, Mt., *Kenya* 82 C4
Keo Neua, Deo, *Vietnam* . 58 C5
Keokuk, *U.S.A.* 108 E9
Kep, *Cambodia* 59 G5
Kep, *Vietnam* 58 B6
Kepi, *Indonesia* 57 F9
Kępno, *Poland* 20 D7
Kerala □, *India* 60 P10
Kerama-Rettō, *Japan* 49 L3
Keran, *Pakistan* 63 B5
Kerang, *Australia* 91 F3
Keraudren, C., *Australia* 88 C2
Kerava, *Finland* 9 F21
Kerch, *Ukraine* 41 K9
Kerchenskiy Proliv,
   Black Sea 41 K9
Kerchoual, *Mali* 79 B5
Kerempe Burnu, *Turkey* .. 66 A5
Keren, *Eritrea* 77 D4
Kerewan, *Gambia* 78 C1
Kerguelen, *Ind. Oc.* 3 G13
Keri Kera, *Sudan* 77 E3
Kericho, *Kenya* 82 C4
Kericho □, *Kenya* 82 C4
Kerinci, *Indonesia* 56 E2
Kerkdriel, *Neths.* 16 E6
Kerkenna, Is., *Tunisia* . 75 B7
Kerki, *Turkmenistan* 44 F7

Kérkira, *Greece* 37 A3
Kerkrade, *Neths.* 17 G8
Kerma, *Sudan* 76 D3
Kermadec Is., *Pac. Oc.* . 92 K10
Kermadec Trench, *Pac. Oc.* 92 L10
Kermān, *Iran* 65 D8
Kerman, *U.S.A.* 112 J6
Kermān □, *Iran* 65 D8
Kermānshāh = Bākhtarān,
   Iran 67 E12
Kerme Körfezi, *Turkey* .. 66 D2
Kermit, *U.S.A.* 109 K3
Kern →, *U.S.A.* 113 K7
Kerns, *Switz.* 23 C6
Kernville, *U.S.A.* 113 K8
Keroh, *Malaysia* 59 K3
Kerrobert, *Canada* 101 C7
Kerrville, *U.S.A.* 109 K5
Kerry □, *Ireland* 15 D2
Kerry Hd., *Ireland* 15 D2
Kersa, *Ethiopia* 77 F5
Kerteminde, *Denmark* 11 J4
Kertosono, *Indonesia* ... 57 G15
Kerulen →, *Asia* 54 B6
Kerzaz, *Algeria* 75 C4
Kerzers, *Switz.* 22 C4
Kesagami →, *Canada* 98 B4
Kesagami L., *Canada* 98 B3
Keşan, *Turkey* 66 B2
Kesch, Piz, *Switz.* 23 C9
Kesennuma, *Japan* 48 E10
Keshit, *Iran* 65 D8
Keşiş Dağ, *Turkey* 67 C8
Keskin, *Turkey* 66 C5
Kessel, *Belgium* 17 F5
Kessel, *Neths.* 17 F8
Kessel-Lo, *Belgium* 17 G5
Kestell, *S. Africa* 85 D4
Kestenga, *Russia* 44 C4
Kesteren, *Neths.* 16 E7
Keswick, *U.K.* 12 C4
Keszthely, *Hungary* 21 J7
Ket →, *Russia* 44 D9
Keta, *Ghana* 79 D5
Ketapang, *Indonesia* 56 E4
Ketchikan, *U.S.A.* 96 C6
Ketchum, *U.S.A.* 110 E6
Kete Krachi, *Ghana* 79 D4
Ketef, Khalîg Umm el,
   Egypt 76 C4
Ketelmeer, *Neths.* 16 C7
Keti Bandar, *Pakistan* .. 62 G2
Ketri, *India* 62 E6
Kętrzyn, *Poland* 20 A11
Kettering, *U.K.* 13 E7
Kettle →, *Canada* 101 B11
Kettle Falls, *U.S.A.* ... 110 B4
Kettleman City, *U.S.A.* . 112 J7
Keurusselkä, *Finland* ... 9 E21
Keuruu, *Finland* 9 E21
Kevin, *U.S.A.* 110 B8
Kewanee, *U.S.A.* 108 E10
Kewaunee, *U.S.A.* 104 C2
Keweenaw B., *U.S.A.* 104 B1
Keweenaw Pen., *U.S.A.* .. 104 B2
Keweenaw Pt., *U.S.A.* ... 104 B2
Key Harbour, *Canada* 98 C3
Key West, *U.S.A.* 103 F10
Keyser, *U.S.A.* 104 F6
Keystone, *U.S.A.* 108 D3
Kezhma, *Russia* 45 D11
Kežmarok, *Slovak Rep.* .. 20 F10
Khabarovo, *Russia* 44 C7
Khabarovsk, *Russia* 45 E14
Khabr, *Iran* 65 D8
Khābūr →, *Syria* 67 E9
Khachmas = Xaçmaz,
   Azerbaijan 43 K9
Khachrod, *India* 62 H6
Khadari, W. el →, *Sudan* 77 E2
Khadro, *Pakistan* 62 F3
Khadyzhensk, *Russia* 43 H4
Khadzhilyangar, *India* .. 63 B8
Khagaria, *India* 63 G12
Khaipur, *Bahawalpur,
   Pakistan* 62 E5
Khaipur, *Hyderabad,
   Pakistan* 62 F3
Khair, *India* 62 F7
Khairabad, *India* 63 F9
Khairagarh, *India* 63 J9
Khairpur, *Pakistan* 60 F6
Khakassia □, *Russia* 44 D9
Khakhea, *Botswana* 84 C3
Khalafābād, *Iran* 65 D6
Khalafallah, *Algeria* ... 75 B5
Khalilabad, *India* 63 F10
Khalīlī, *Iran* 65 E7
Khalkhāl, *Iran* 67 D13
Khálki, *Greece* 39 K5
Khalkís, *Greece* 39 L6
Khalmer-Sede = Tazovskiy,
   Russia 44 C8
Khalmer Yu, *Russia* 44 C7
Khalturin, *Russia* 44 D5
Khalūf, *Oman* 68 C6
Kham Keut, *Laos* 58 C5
Khamas Country, *Botswana* 84 C4
Khambat, G. of, *India* .. 62 J5
Khambhaliya, *India* 62 H3
Khambhat, *India* 62 H5
Khamilonísion, *Greece* .. 39 P9
Khamîr, *Iran* 65 E7
Khamir, *Yemen* 68 D3
Khamsa, *Egypt* 69 E1
Khān Abū Shāmat, *Syria* . 69 B5
Khān Āzād, *Iraq* 64 C5
Khān Mujiddah, *Iraq* 64 C4

Khān Shaykhūn, *Syria* ... 66 E7
Khān Yūnis, *Gaza Strip* . 69 D3
Khānaqīn, *Iraq* 67 E11
Khānbāghī, *Iran* 65 B7
Khandrá, *Greece* 39 P9
Khandwa, *India* 60 J10
Khandyga, *Russia* 45 C14
Khāneh, *Iran* 64 B5
Khanewal, *Pakistan* 62 D4
Khanh Duong, *Vietnam* ... 58 F7
Khaniá, *Greece* 37 D6
Khaniá □, *Greece* 37 D6
Khaníon, Kólpos, *Greece* 37 D5
Khanka, Ozero, *Asia* 45 E14
Khankendy = Xankändi,
   Azerbaijan 67 C12
Khanna, *India* 62 D7
Khanpur, *Pakistan* 62 E4
Khanty-Mansiysk, *Russia* 44 C7
Khapalu, *Pakistan* 63 B7
Khapcheranga, *Russia* ... 45 E12
Kharabali, *Russia* 43 G8
Kharagpur, *India* 63 H12
Kharan Kalat, *Pakistan* . 60 E4
Kharānaq, *Iran* 65 C7
Kharda, *India* 60 K9
Khardung La, *India* 63 B7
Khârga, El Wâhât el, *Egypt* 76 B3
Khargon, *India* 60 J9
Kharit, Wadi el →, *Egypt* 76 C3
Khārk, Jazireh, *Iran* ... 65 D6
Kharkiv, *Ukraine* 41 H9
Kharkov = Kharkiv,
   Ukraine 41 H9
Kharmanli, *Bulgaria* 39 H8
Kharovsk, *Russia* 40 C11
Kharta, *Turkey* 66 B3
Khartoum = El Khartûm,
   Sudan 77 D3
Khasan, *Russia* 48 C5
Khasavyurt, *Russia* 43 J8
Khāsh, *Iran* 60 E2
Khashm el Girba, *Sudan* . 77 E4
Khashuri, *Georgia* 43 J6
Khaskovo, *Bulgaria* 39 H8
Khatanga, *Russia* 45 B11
Khatanga →, *Russia* 45 B11
Khatauli, *India* 62 E7
Khātūnābād, *Iran* 65 C6
Khatyrka, *Russia* 45 C18
Khaybar, Harrat,
   Si. Arabia 64 E4
Khāzimiyah, *Iraq* 64 C4
Khazzân Jabal el Awliyâ,
   Sudan 77 D3
Khe Bo, *Vietnam* 58 C5
Khe Long, *Vietnam* 58 B5
Khed Brahma, *India* 60 G8
Khekra, *India* 62 E7
Khemarak Phouminville,
   Cambodia 59 G4
Khemelnik, *Ukraine* 41 H4
Khemis Miliana, *Algeria* 75 A5
Khemissèt, *Morocco* 74 B3
Khemmarat, *Thailand* 58 D5
Khenāmān, *Iran* 65 D8
Khenchela, *Algeria* 75 A6
Khenifra, *Morocco* 74 B3
Kherrata, *Algeria* 75 A6
Kherson, *Ukraine* 41 J7
Khersónisos Akrotíri,
   Greece 37 D6
Kheta →, *Russia* 45 B11
Khilok, *Russia* 45 D12
Khimki, *Russia* 42 C3
Khíos, *Greece* 39 L9
Khirbat Qanāfār, *Lebanon* 69 B4
Khiuma = Hiiumaa,
   Estonia 9 G20
Khiva, *Uzbekistan* 44 E7
Khīyāv, *Iran* 64 B5
Khlong Khlung, *Thailand* 58 D2
Khmelnitskiy =
   Khmelnytskyy, *Ukraine* 41 H4
Khmelnytskyy, *Ukraine* .. 41 H4
Khmer Rep. =
   Cambodia ■, *Asia* 58 F5
Khoai, Hon, *Vietnam* 59 H5
Khodoriv, *Ukraine* 41 H3
Khodzent = Khudzhand,
   Tajikistan 44 E7
Khojak P., *Afghan.* 60 D5
Khok Kloi, *Thailand* 59 H2
Khok Pho, *Thailand* 59 J3
Kholm, *Russia* 40 D6
Kholmsk, *Russia* 45 E15
Khomas Hochland,
   Namibia 84 C2
Khomeyn, *Iran* 65 C6
Khon Kaen, *Thailand* 58 D4
Khong, *Laos* 58 E5
Khong Sedone, *Laos* 58 E5
Khonuu, *Russia* 45 C15
Khoper →, *Russia* 42 F6
Khor el 'Atash, *Sudan* .. 77 E3
Khóra, *Greece* 39 M4
Khóra Sfakíon, *Greece* .. 37 D6
Khorāsān □, *Iran* 65 C8
Khorat = Nakhon
   Ratchasima, *Thailand* . 58 E4
Khorat, Cao Nguyen,
   Thailand 58 E4
Khorb el Ethel, *Algeria* 74 C3
Khorixas, *Namibia* 84 C1
Khorol, *Ukraine* 41 H7

Khorramābād, *Khorāsān,
   Iran* 65 C8
Khorramābād, *Lorestān,
   Iran* 67 F13
Khorrāmshahr, *Iran* 65 D6
Khorugh, *Tajikistan* 44 F8
Khosravī, *Iran* 65 D6
Khosrowābād, *Khuzestān,
   Iran* 65 D6
Khosrowābād, *Kordestān,
   Iran* 67 E12
Khosūyeh, *Iran* 65 D7
Khotyn, *Ukraine* 41 H4
Khouribga, *Morocco* 74 B3
Khowai, *Bangla.* 61 G17
Khoyniki, *Belarus* 41 G5
Khrami →, *Georgia* 43 K7
Khrenovoye, *Russia* 42 E5
Khristianá, *Greece* 39 N8
Khrysokhou B., *Cyprus* .. 37 D11
Khu Khan, *Thailand* 58 E5
Khudzhand, *Tajikistan* .. 44 E7
Khuff, *Si. Arabia* 64 E5
Khūgīānī, *Afghan.* 62 D1
Khulna, *Bangla.* 61 H16
Khulna □, *Bangla.* 61 H16
Khulo, *Georgia* 43 K6
Khumago, *Botswana* 84 C3
Khūnsorkh, *Iran* 65 E8
Khūr, *Iran* 65 C8
Khurai, *India* 62 G8
Khurayş, *Si. Arabia* 65 E6
Khūrīyā Mūrīyā, Jazā 'ir,
   Oman 68 D6
Khurja, *India* 62 E7
Khūsf, *Iran* 65 C8
Khush, *Afghan.* 60 C3
Khushab, *Pakistan* 62 C5
Khust, *Ukraine* 41 H2
Khuzdar, *Pakistan* 62 F2
Khūzestān □, *Iran* 65 D6
Khvājeh, *Iran* 64 B5
Khvalynsk, *Russia* 42 D9
Khvānsār, *Iran* 65 D7
Khvatovka, *Russia* 42 D8
Khvor, *Iran* 65 C7
Khvorgū, *Iran* 65 E8
Khvormūj, *Iran* 65 D6
Khvoy, *Iran* 67 C11
Khvoynaya, *Russia* 40 C8
Khyber Pass, *Afghan.* ... 62 B4
Kiabukwa, *Zaïre* 83 D1
Kiama, *Australia* 91 E5
Kiamba, *Phil.* 55 H6
Kiambi, *Zaïre* 82 D2
Kiambu, *Kenya* 82 C4
Kiangsi = Jiangxi □, *China* 53 D10
Kiangsu = Jiangsu □,
   China 51 H10
Kibæk, *Denmark* 11 J2
Kibanga Port, *Uganda* ... 82 B3
Kibangou, *Congo* 80 E2
Kibara, *Tanzania* 82 C3
Kibare, Mts., *Zaïre* 82 D2
Kibombo, *Zaïre* 82 C2
Kibondo, *Tanzania* 82 C3
Kibondo □, *Tanzania* 82 C3
Kibumbu, *Burundi* 82 C2
Kibungu, *Rwanda* 82 C3
Kibuye, *Burundi* 82 C2
Kibuye, *Rwanda* 82 C2
Kibwesa, *Tanzania* 82 D2
Kibwezi, *Kenya* 82 C4
Kichiga, *Russia* 45 D17
Kicking Horse Pass,
   Canada 100 C5
Kidal, *Mali* 79 B5
Kidderminster, *U.K.* 13 E5
Kidete, *Tanzania* 82 D4
Kidira, *Senegal* 78 C2
Kidnappers, C., *N.Z.* ... 87 H6
Kidston, *Australia* 90 B3
Kidugallo, *Tanzania* 82 D4
Kiel, *Germany* 18 A6
Kiel Kanal = Nord-Ostsee-
   Kanal →, *Germany* 18 A5
Kielce, *Poland* 20 E10
Kieldrecht, *Belgium* 17 F4
Kieler Bucht, *Germany* .. 18 A6
Kien Binh, *Vietnam* 59 H5
Kien Tan, *Vietnam* 59 G5
Kienge, *Zaïre* 83 E2
Kiessé, *Niger* 79 C5
Kiev = Kyyiv, *Ukraine* .. 41 G6
Kiffa, *Mauritania* 78 B2
Kifisós →, *Greece* 39 L6
Kifrī, *Iraq* 67 E11
Kigali, *Rwanda* 82 C3
Kigarama, *Tanzania* 82 C3
Kigoma □, *Tanzania* 82 D2
Kigoma-Ujiji, *Tanzania* . 82 C2
Kigomasha, Ras, *Tanzania* 82 C4
Kihee, *Australia* 91 D3
Kihnu, *Estonia* 9 G21
Kii-Sanchi, *Japan* 49 G8
Kii-Suidō, *Japan* 49 H7
Kikaiga-Shima, *Japan* ... 49 K4
Kikinda, *Serbia, Yug.* .. 21 K10
Kikládhes, *Greece* 39 M7
Kikwit, *Zaïre* 80 E3
Kílalki, *Greece* 39 N10
Kilauea Crater, *U.S.A.* . 102 J17
Kilchberg, *Switz.* 23 B7
Kilcoy, *Australia* 91 D5
Kildare, *Ireland* 15 C5
Kildare □, *Ireland* 15 C5

Kilgore, *U.S.A.* 109 J7
Kilifi, *Kenya* 82 C4
Kilifi □, *Kenya* 82 C4
Kilimanjaro, *Tanzania* .. 82 C4
Kilimanjaro □, *Tanzania* . 82 C4
Kilimli, *Turkey* 66 B4
Kilindini, *Kenya* 82 C4
Kilis, *Turkey* 66 D7
Kiliya, *Ukraine* 41 K5
Kilju, *N. Korea* 51 D15
Kilkee, *Ireland* 15 D2
Kilkenny, *Ireland* 15 D4
Kilkenny □, *Ireland* 15 D4
Kilkieran B., *Ireland* .. 15 C2
Kilkís, *Greece* 39 J5
Killala, *Ireland* 15 B2
Killala B., *Ireland* 15 B2
Killaloe, *Ireland* 15 D3
Killaloe Sta., *Canada* .. 106 A7
Killam, *Canada* 100 C6
Killarney, *Australia* ... 91 D5
Killarney, *Canada* 98 C3
Killarney, *Ireland* 15 D2
Killarney, Lakes of, *Ireland* 15 E2
Killary Harbour, *Ireland* 15 C2
Killdeer, *Canada* 101 D7
Killdeer, *U.S.A.* 108 B3
Killeen, *U.S.A.* 109 K6
Killiecrankie, Pass of, *U.K.* 14 E5
Killin, *U.K.* 14 E4
Killíni, Ilía, *Greece* .. 39 M4
Killíni, Korinthía, *Greece* 39 M5
Killybegs, *Ireland* 15 B3
Kilmarnock, *U.K.* 14 F4
Kilmez, *Russia* 42 B10
Kilmez →, *Russia* 42 B10
Kilmore, *Australia* 91 F3
Kilondo, *Tanzania* 83 D3
Kilosa, *Tanzania* 82 D4
Kilosa □, *Tanzania* 82 D4
Kilrush, *Ireland* 15 D2
Kilwa □, *Tanzania* 83 D4
Kilwa Kisiwani, *Tanzania* 83 D4
Kilwa Kivinje, *Tanzania* 83 D4
Kilwa Masoko, *Tanzania* . 83 D4
Kim, *U.S.A.* 109 G3
Kimaam, *Indonesia* 57 F9
Kimamba, *Tanzania* 82 D4
Kimba, *Australia* 91 E2
Kimball, *Nebr., U.S.A.* . 108 E3
Kimball, *S. Dak., U.S.A.* 108 D5
Kimberley, *Canada* 100 D5
Kimberley, *S. Africa* ... 84 D3
Kimberley Downs,
   Australia 88 C3
Kimberly, *U.S.A.* 110 E6
Kimchaek, *N. Korea* 51 D15
Kimchŏn, *S. Korea* 51 F15
Kími, *Greece* 39 L7
Kimje, *S. Korea* 51 G14
Kímolos, *Greece* 39 N7
Kimovsk, *Russia* 42 C3
Kimparana, *Mali* 78 C4
Kimry, *Russia* 42 B3
Kimsquit, *Canada* 100 C3
Kimstad, *Sweden* 11 F9
Kinabalu, Gunong,
   Malaysia 56 C5
Kínaros, *Greece* 39 N9
Kinaskan L., *Canada* 100 B2
Kinbasket L., *Canada* ... 100 C5
Kincaid, *Canada* 101 D7
Kincardine, *Canada* 98 D3
Kinda, *Zaïre* 83 D2
Kinder Scout, *U.K.* 12 D6
Kindersley, *Canada* 101 C7
Kindia, *Guinea* 78 C2
Kindu, *Zaïre* 82 C2
Kinel, *Russia* 42 D10
Kineshma, *Russia* 42 B6
Kinesi, *Tanzania* 82 C3
King, L., *Australia* 89 F2
King, Mt., *Australia* ... 90 D4
King City, *U.S.A.* 111 H3
King Cr. →, *Australia* .. 90 C2
King Edward →, *Australia* 88 B4
King Frederick VI Land =
   Kong Frederik VI.s Kyst,
   Greenland* 4 C5
King George B., *Falk. Is.* 128 D4
King George I., *Antarctica* 5 C18
King George Is., *Canada* 97 C11
King I. = Kadan Kyun,
   Burma 56 B1
King I., *Australia* 90 F3
King I., *Canada* 100 C3
King Leopold Ras.,
   Australia 88 C4
King Sd., *Australia* 88 C3
King William I., *Canada* 96 B10
King William's Town,
   S. Africa 84 E4
Kingaroy, *Australia* 91 D5
Kingfisher, *U.S.A.* 109 H6
Kingirbān, *Iraq* 64 C5
Kingisepp = Kuressaare,
   Estonia 9 G20
Kingisepp = Kuressaare,
   Russia 40 C5
Kingman, *Ariz., U.S.A.* . 113 K12
Kingman, *Kans., U.S.A.* . 109 G5
Kingoonya, *Australia* ... 91 E2
Kings →, *U.S.A.* 111 H4
Kings Canyon National
   Park, *U.S.A.* 111 H4
King's Lynn, *U.K.* 12 E8
Kings Mountain, *U.S.A.* . 105 H5

King's Peak, *U.S.A.* 110 F8
Kingsbridge, *U.K.* 13 G4
Kingsburg, *U.S.A.* 111 H4
Kingscote, *Australia* 91 F2
Kingscourt, *Ireland* 15 C5
Kingsley, *U.S.A.* 108 D7
Kingsport, *U.S.A.* 105 G4
Kingston, *Canada* 98 D4
Kingston, *Jamaica* 116 C4
Kingston, *N.Z.* 87 L2
Kingston, *N.Y., U.S.A.* 107 E10
Kingston, *Pa., U.S.A.* 107 E9
Kingston, *R.I., U.S.A.* 107 E13
Kingston Pk., *U.S.A.* 113 K11
Kingston South East,
  Australia 91 F2
Kingston upon Hull, *U.K.* 12 D7
Kingston-upon-Thames,
  U.K. 13 F7
Kingstown, *St. Vincent* 117 D7
Kingstree, *U.S.A.* 105 J6
Kingsville, *Canada* 98 D3
Kingsville, *U.S.A.* 109 M6
Kingussie, *U.K.* 14 D4
Kınık, *Turkey* 66 C2
Kinistino, *Canada* 101 C7
Kinkala, *Congo* 80 E2
Kinki □, *Japan* 49 H8
Kinleith, *N.Z.* 87 H5
Kinmount, *Canada* 106 B6
Kinna, *Sweden* 11 G6
Kinnaird, *Canada* 100 D5
Kinnairds Hd., *U.K.* 14 D7
Kinnared, *Sweden* 11 G7
Kinnarodden, *Norway* 6 A11
Kino, *Mexico* 114 B2
Kinoje →, *Canada* 98 B3
Kinomoto, *Japan* 49 G8
Kinoni, *Uganda* 82 C3
Kinrooi, *Belgium* 17 F7
Kinross, *U.K.* 14 E5
Kinsale, *Ireland* 15 E3
Kinsale, Old Hd. of,
  Ireland 15 E3
Kinsha = Chang Jiang →,
  China 53 B13
Kinshasa, *Zaïre* 80 E3
Kinsley, *U.S.A.* 109 G5
Kinston, *U.S.A.* 105 H7
Kintampo, *Ghana* 79 D4
Kintap, *Indonesia* 56 E5
Kintore Ra., *Australia* 88 D4
Kintyre, *U.K.* 14 F3
Kintyre, Mull of, *U.K.* 14 F3
Kinushseo →, *Canada* 98 A3
Kinuso, *Canada* 100 B5
Kinyangiri, *Tanzania* 82 C3
Kiparissía, *Greece* 39 M4
Kiparissiakós Kólpos,
  Greece 39 M4
Kipembawe, *Tanzania* 82 D3
Kipengere Ra., *Tanzania* 83 D3
Kipili, *Tanzania* 82 D3
Kipini, *Kenya* 82 C5
Kipling, *Canada* 101 C8
Kippure, *Ireland* 15 C5
Kipushi, *Zaïre* 83 E2
Kiratpur, *India* 62 E8
Kirchberg, *Switz.* 22 B5
Kirchhain, *Germany* 18 E4
Kirchheim, *Germany* 19 G5
Kirchheim-Bolanden,
  Germany 19 F4
Kirensk, *Russia* 45 D11
Kirgella Rocks, *Australia* 89 F3
Kirghizia = Kyrgyzstan ■,
  Asia 44 E8
Kirghizstan =
  Kyrgyzstan ■, *Asia* 44 E8
Kiri, *Zaïre* 80 E3
Kiribati ■, *Pac. Oc.* 92 H10
Kırıkhan, *Turkey* 66 D7
Kırıkkale, *Turkey* 66 C5
Kirillov, *Russia* 40 C10
Kirin = Jilin, *China* 51 C14
Kirin = Jilin □, *China* 51 C13
Kirishi, *Russia* 40 C7
Kiritimati, *Kiribati* 93 G12
Kirka, *Turkey* 66 C4
Kirkcaldy, *U.K.* 14 E5
Kirkcudbright, *U.K.* 14 G4
Kirkee, *India* 60 K8
Kirkenær, *Norway* 10 D6
Kirkenes, *Norway* 8 B23
Kirkintilloch, *U.K.* 14 F4
Kirkjubæjarklaustur,
  Iceland 8 E4
Kirkkonummi, *Finland* 9 F21
Kirkland, *U.S.A.* 111 J7
Kirkland Lake, *Canada* 98 C3
Kırklareli, *Turkey* 66 B2
Kirksville, *U.S.A.* 108 E8
Kirkūk, *Iraq* 67 E11
Kirkwall, *U.K.* 14 C6
Kirkwood, *S. Africa* 84 E4
Kirn, *Germany* 19 F3
Kirov, *Russia* 42 C2
Kirov, *Russia* 44 D5

Kirovabad = Gäncä,
  Azerbaijan 43 K8
Kirovakan = Vanadzor,
  Armenia 43 K7
Kirovograd = Kirovohrad,
  Ukraine 41 H7
Kirovohrad, *Ukraine* 41 H7
Kirovsk = Babadayhan,
  Turkmenistan 44 F7
Kirovsk, *Russia* 44 C4
Kirovskiy, *Russia* 43 H9
Kirovskiy, *Kamchatka,
  Russia* 45 D16
Kirovskiy, *Primorsk, Russia* 48 B6
Kirriemuir, *U.K.* 14 E6
Kirsanov, *Russia* 42 D6
Kırşehir, *Turkey* 66 C6
Kirtachi, *Niger* 79 C5
Kirthar Range, *Pakistan* 62 F2
Kiruna, *Sweden* 8 C19
Kirundu, *Zaïre* 82 C2
Kirup, *Australia* 89 F2
Kirya, *Russia* 42 C8
Kiryū, *Japan* 49 F9
Kisaga, *Tanzania* 82 C3
Kisalaya, *Nic.* 116 D3
Kisámou, Kólpos, *Greece* 37 D5
Kisanga, *Zaïre* 82 B2
Kisangani, *Zaïre* 82 B2
Kisar, *Indonesia* 57 F7
Kisaran, *Indonesia* 56 D1
Kisarawe, *Tanzania* 82 D4
Kisarawe □, *Tanzania* 82 D4
Kisarazu, *Japan* 49 G9
Kisbér, *Hungary* 21 H8
Kiselevsk, *Russia* 44 D9
Kishanganga →, *Pakistan* 63 B5
Kishanganj, *India* 63 F13
Kishangarh, *India* 62 F4
Kishi, *Nigeria* 79 D5
Kishinev = Chişinău,
  Moldova 41 J5
Kishiwada, *Japan* 49 G7
Kishtwar, *India* 63 C6
Kisii, *Kenya* 82 C3
Kisii □, *Kenya* 82 C3
Kisiju, *Tanzania* 82 D4
Kisir, *Turkey* 67 B10
Kisizi, *Uganda* 82 C2
Kiska I., *U.S.A.* 96 C1
Kiskatinaw →, *Canada* 100 B4
Kiskittogisu L., *Canada* 101 C9
Kiskörös, *Hungary* 21 J9
Kiskundorozsma, *Hungary* 21 J10
Kiskunfélegyháza, *Hungary* 21 J9
Kiskunhalas, *Hungary* 21 J9
Kiskunmajsa, *Hungary* 21 J9
Kislovodsk, *Russia* 43 J6
Kiso-Gawa →, *Japan* 49 G8
Kiso-Sammyaku, *Japan* 49 G8
Kisofukushima, *Japan* 49 G8
Kisoro, *Uganda* 82 C2
Kispest, *Hungary* 21 H9
Kissidougou, *Guinea* 78 D2
Kissimmee, *U.S.A.* 105 L5
Kissimmee →, *U.S.A.* 105 M5
Kississing L., *Canada* 101 B8
Kissónerga, *Cyprus* 37 E11
Kistanje, *Croatia* 33 E12
Kisújszállás, *Hungary* 21 H10
Kisumu, *Kenya* 82 C3
Kisvárda, *Hungary* 21 G12
Kiswani, *Tanzania* 82 C4
Kiswere, *Tanzania* 83 D4
Kit Carson, *U.S.A.* 108 F3
Kita, *Mali* 78 C3
Kitab, *Uzbekistan* 44 F7
Kitaibaraki, *Japan* 49 F10
Kitakami, *Japan* 48 E10
Kitakami-Gawa →, *Japan* 48 E10
Kitakami-Sammyaku, *Japan* 48 E10
Kitakata, *Japan* 48 F9
Kitakyūshū, *Japan* 49 H5
Kitale, *Kenya* 82 B4
Kitami, *Japan* 48 C11
Kitami-Sammyaku, *Japan* 48 B11
Kitangiri, L., *Tanzania* 82 C3
Kitaya, *Tanzania* 83 E5
Kitchener, *Australia* 89 F3
Kitchener, *Canada* 98 D3
Kitee, *Finland* 40 E4
Kitega = Gitega, *Burundi* 82 C2
Kitengo, *Zaïre* 82 D1
Kiteto □, *Tanzania* 82 C4
Kitgum, *Uganda* 82 B3
Kíthira, *Greece* 39 N7
Kíthnos, *Greece* 39 M7
Kiti, *Cyprus* 37 E12
Kiti, C., *Cyprus* 37 E12
Kitikmeot □, *Canada* 96 A9
Kitimat, *Canada* 100 C3
Kitinen →, *Finland* 8 C22
Kitiyab, *Sudan* 77 D3
Kítros, *Greece* 39 J5
Kitsuki, *Japan* 49 H5
Kittakittaooloo, L.,
  Australia 91 D2
Kittanning, *U.S.A.* 106 F5
Kittatinny Mts., *U.S.A.* 107 E10
Kittery, *U.S.A.* 105 D10
Kittilä, *Finland* 8 C21
Kitui, *Kenya* 82 C4
Kitui □, *Kenya* 82 C4
Kitwe, *Zambia* 83 E2
Kitzbühel, *Austria* 19 H8
Kitzingen, *Germany* 19 F6
Kivarli, *India* 62 G5

Kivertsi, *Ukraine* 41 G3
Kividhes, *Cyprus* 37 E11
Kivu □, *Zaïre* 82 C2
Kivu, L., *Zaïre* 82 C2
Kiyev = Kyyiv, *Ukraine* 41 G6
Kiyevskoye Vdkhr. =
  Kyyivske Vdskh.,
  Ukraine 41 G6
Kiziguru, *Rwanda* 82 C3
Kizil Irmak →, *Turkey* 66 B6
Kizil Jilga, *India* 63 B8
Kizil Yurt, *Russia* 43 J8
Kızılcahamam, *Turkey* 66 B5
Kızılhisar, *Turkey* 66 D3
Kızılırmak, *Turkey* 66 B5
Kızıltepe, *Turkey* 67 D9
Kizimkazi, *Tanzania* 82 D4
Kizlyar, *Russia* 43 J8
Kizyl-Arvat = Gyzylarbat,
  Turkmenistan 44 F6
Kjellerup, *Denmark* 11 H3
Kjölur, *Iceland* 8 D4
Klaeng, *Thailand* 58 F3
Klagenfurt, *Austria* 21 J4
Klagshamn, *Sweden* 11 J6
Klagstorp, *Sweden* 11 J7
Klaipėda, *Lithuania* 9 J19
Klaksvík, *Færoe Is.* 8 E9
Klamath →, *U.S.A.* 110 F1
Klamath Falls, *U.S.A.* 110 E3
Klamath Mts., *U.S.A.* 110 F2
Klanjec, *Croatia* 33 B12
Klappan →, *Canada* 100 B3
Klarälven →, *Sweden* 9 G15
Klaten, *Indonesia* 57 G14
Klatovy, *Czech.* 20 F3
Klausen = Chiusa, *Italy* 33 B8
Klawer, *S. Africa* 84 E2
Klawock, *U.S.A.* 100 B2
Klazienaveen, *Neths.* 16 C10
Kleczew, *Poland* 20 C8
Kleena Kleene, *Canada* 100 C4
Klein, *U.S.A.* 110 C9
Klein-Karas, *Namibia* 84 D2
Kleine Gette →, *Belgium* 17 G6
Kleine Nete →, *Belgium* 17 F5
Klekovača, *Bos.-H.* 33 D13
Klenovec, *Macedonia* 39 H3
Klenovec, *Slovak Rep.* 20 G9
Klerksdorp, *S. Africa* 84 D4
Kletnya, *Russia* 40 F7
Kletsk = Klyetsk, *Belarus* 41 F4
Kletskiy, *Russia* 43 F6
Kleve, *Germany* 18 D2
Klickitat, *U.S.A.* 110 D3
Klickitat →, *U.S.A.* 112 E5
Klidhes, *Cyprus* 37 D13
Klimovichi, *Belarus* 40 F6
Klin, *Russia* 42 B3
Klinaklini →, *Canada* 100 C3
Klintsy, *Russia* 41 F7
Klipdale, *S. Africa* 84 E2
Klipplaat, *S. Africa* 84 E3
Klitmøller, *Denmark* 11 G2
Kljajićevo, *Serbia, Yug.* 21 K9
Ključ, *Bos.-H.* 33 D13
Kłobuck, *Poland* 20 E8
Kłodzko, *Poland* 20 E6
Kloetinge, *Neths.* 17 F3
Klondike, *Canada* 96 B6
Kloosterzande, *Neths.* 17 F4
Klosterneuburg, *Austria* 21 G6
Klosters, *Switz.* 23 C9
Kloten, *Switz.* 23 B7
Klötze, *Germany* 18 C7
Klouto, *Togo* 79 D5
Kluane L., *Canada* 96 B6
Kluczbork, *Poland* 20 E8
Klundert, *Neths.* 17 E5
Klyetsk, *Belarus* 41 F4
Klyuchevskaya, Gora,
  Russia 45 D17
Knaresborough, *U.K.* 12 C6
Knee L., *Man., Canada* 101 B10
Knee L., *Sask., Canada* 101 B7
Kneïss, Is., *Tunisia* 75 B7
Knesselare, *Belgium* 17 F2
Knezha, *Bulgaria* 38 F7
Knić, *Serbia, Yug.* 21 M10
Knight Inlet, *Canada* 100 C3
Knighton, *U.K.* 13 E4
Knights Ferry, *U.S.A.* 112 H6
Knights Landing, *U.S.A.* 112 G5
Knin, *Croatia* 33 D13
Knittelfeld, *Austria* 21 H4
Knjaževac, *Serbia, Yug.* 21 M12
Knob, C., *Australia* 89 F2
Knockmealdown Mts.,
  Ireland 15 D4
Knokke, *Belgium* 17 F2
Knossós, *Greece* 37 D7
Knox, *U.S.A.* 104 E2
Knox, C., *Canada* 100 C2
Knox Coast, *Antarctica* 5 C8
Knoxville, *Iowa, U.S.A.* 108 E8
Knoxville, *Tenn., U.S.A.* 105 H4
Knutshø, *Norway* 10 B3
Knysna, *S. Africa* 84 E3
Knyszyn, *Poland* 20 B12
Ko Kha, *Thailand* 58 C2
Ko Tao, *Thailand* 59 G2

Koba, *Aru, Indonesia* 57 F8
Koba, *Bangka, Indonesia* 56 E3
Kobarid, *Slovenia* 33 B10
Kobayashi, *Japan* 49 J5
Kōbe, *Japan* 49 G7
Kobelyaky, *Ukraine* 41 H8
København, *Denmark* 11 J6
Kōbi-Sho, *Japan* 49 M1
Koblenz, *Germany* 19 E3
Koblenz, *Switz.* 22 A6
Kobo, *Ethiopia* 77 E4
Kobroor, Kepulauan,
  Indonesia 57 F8
Kobryn, *Belarus* 41 F3
Kobuleti, *Georgia* 43 K5
Kobyłka, *Poland* 20 C11
Kobylkino, *Russia* 42 C6
Kocaeli = İzmit, *Turkey* 66 B3
Kočani, *Macedonia* 39 H5
Koçarlı, *Turkey* 66 D2
Koceljevo, *Serbia, Yug.* 21 L9
Kočevje, *Slovenia* 33 C11
Koch Bihar, *India* 61 F16
Kochang, *S. Korea* 51 G14
Kochas, *India* 63 G10
Kocher →, *Germany* 19 F5
Kocheva, *Russia* 45 D13
Kōchi, *Japan* 49 H6
Kōchi □, *Japan* 49 H6
Kochiu = Gejiu, *China* 52 F4
Kodiak, *U.S.A.* 96 C4
Kodiak I., *U.S.A.* 96 C4
Kodinar, *India* 62 J4
Kodori →, *Georgia* 43 J5
Koekelare, *Belgium* 17 F1
Koersel, *Belgium* 17 F6
Koes, *Namibia* 84 D2
Koffiefontein, *S. Africa* 84 D4
Kofiau, *Indonesia* 57 E7
Koforidua, *Ghana* 79 D4
Kōfu, *Japan* 49 G9
Koga, *Japan* 49 F9
Kogaluk →, *Canada* 99 A7
Kogan, *Australia* 91 D5
Køge, *Denmark* 9 J15
Kogi □, *Nigeria* 79 D6
Kogin Baba, *Nigeria* 79 D7
Koh-i-Bābā, *Afghan.* 60 B5
Koh-i-Khurd, *Afghan.* 62 C1
Kohat, *Pakistan* 62 C4
Kohima, *India* 61 G19
Kohkīlūyeh va Būyer
  Aḥmadi □, *Iran* 65 D6
Kohler Ra., *Antarctica* 5 D15
Kohtla-Järve, *Estonia* 9 G22
Koillismaa, *Finland* 8 D23
Koin-dong, *N. Korea* 51 D14
Kojŏ, *N. Korea* 51 E14
Kojonup, *Australia* 89 F2
Kojūr, *Iran* 65 B6
Koka, *Sudan* 76 C3
Kokand = Qŭqon,
  Uzbekistan 44 E8
Kokanee Glacier Prov.
  Park, *Canada* 100 D5
Kokas, *Indonesia* 57 E8
Kokchetav = Kökshetaū,
  Kazakhstan 44 D7
Kokemäenjoki →, *Finland* 9 F19
Kokerite, *Guyana* 121 B6
Kokhma, *Russia* 42 B5
Kokkola, *Finland* 8 E20
Koko, *Nigeria* 79 C5
Koko Kyunzu, *Burma* 61 M18
Kokolopozo, *Ivory C.* 78 D3
Kokomo, *U.S.A.* 104 E2
Kokonau, *Indonesia* 57 E9
Kokoro, *Niger* 79 C5
Koksan, *N. Korea* 51 E14
Kökshetaū, *Kazakhstan* 44 D7
Koksoak →, *Canada* 97 C13
Kokstad, *S. Africa* 85 E4
Kokubu, *Japan* 49 J5
Kokuora, *Russia* 45 B15
Kola, *Indonesia* 57 F8
Kola, *Russia* 44 C4
Kola Pen. = Kolskiy
  Poluostrov, *Russia* 44 C4
Kolahoi, *India* 63 B6
Kolahun, *Liberia* 78 D2
Kolaka, *Indonesia* 57 E6
Kolar, *India* 60 N11
Kolar Gold Fields, *India* 60 N11
Kolari, *Finland* 8 C20
Kolayat, *India* 60 F8
Kolby Kås, *Denmark* 11 J4
Kolchugino = Leninsk-
  Kuznetskiy, *Russia* 44 D9
Kolchugino, *Russia* 42 B4
Kolda, *Senegal* 78 C2
Kolding, *Denmark* 11 J3
Kole, *Zaïre* 80 E4
Koléa, *Algeria* 75 A5
Kolepom = Yos Sudarso,
  Pulau, *Indonesia* 57 F9
Kolguyev, Ostrov, *Russia* 44 C5
Kolham, *Neths.* 16 B9
Kolhapur, *India* 60 L9
Kolia, *Ivory C.* 78 D3
Kolín, *Czech.* 20 E5
Kolind, *Denmark* 11 H4
Kolkas Rags, *Latvia* 9 H20
Kolleda, *Germany* 18 D7
Kollum, *Neths.* 16 B8
Kolmanskop, *Namibia* 84 D2
Köln, *Germany* 18 E2
Koło, *Poland* 20 C8

Kołobrzeg, *Poland* 20 A5
Kolokani, *Mali* 78 C3
Kolomna, *Russia* 42 C4
Kolomyya, *Ukraine* 41 H3
Kolondiéba, *Mali* 78 C3
Kolonodale, *Indonesia* 57 E6
Kolosib, *India* 61 G18
Kolpashevo, *Russia* 44 D9
Kolpino, *Russia* 40 C6
Kolpny, *Russia* 42 D3
Kolskiy Poluostrov, *Russia* 44 C4
Kolubara →, *Serbia, Yug.* 21 L10
Koluszki, *Poland* 20 D9
Kolwezi, *Zaïre* 83 E2
Kolyma →, *Russia* 45 C17
Kolymskoye Nagorye,
  Russia 45 C16
Kôm Ombo, *Egypt* 76 C3
Komandorskie Is. =
  Komandorskiye Ostrova,
  Russia 45 D17
Komandorskiye Ostrova,
  Russia 45 D17
Komárno, *Slovak Rep.* 21 H8
Komárom, *Hungary* 21 H8
Komatipoort, *S. Africa* 85 D5
Komatou Yialou, *Cyprus* 37 D13
Komatsu, *Japan* 49 F8
Komatsujima, *Japan* 49 H7
Kombissiri, *Burkina Faso* 79 C4
Kombori, *Burkina Faso* 78 C4
Komen, *Slovenia* 33 C10
Komenda, *Ghana* 79 D4
Komi □, *Russia* 44 C6
Komiža, *Croatia* 33 E13
Komló, *Hungary* 21 J8
Kommunarsk = Alchevsk,
  Ukraine 41 H10
Kommunizma, Pik,
  Tajikistan 44 F8
Komodo, *Indonesia* 57 F5
Komoé, *Ivory C.* 78 D4
Komono, *Congo* 80 E2
Komoran, Pulau, *Indonesia* 57 F9
Komoro, *Japan* 49 F9
Komotini, *Greece* 39 H8
Kompasberg, *S. Africa* 84 E3
Kompong Bang, *Cambodia* 59 F5
Kompong Cham, *Cambodia* 59 F5
Kompong Chhnang,
  Cambodia 59 F5
Kompong Chikreng,
  Cambodia 58 F5
Kompong Kleang,
  Cambodia 58 F5
Kompong Luong,
  Cambodia 59 G5
Kompong Pranak,
  Cambodia 58 F5
Kompong Som, *Cambodia* 59 G4
Kompong Som, Chhung,
  Cambodia 59 G4
Kompong Speu, *Cambodia* 59 G5
Kompong Sralao,
  Cambodia 58 E5
Kompong Thom, *Cambodia* 58 F5
Kompong Trabeck,
  Cambodia 58 F5
Kompong Trabeck,
  Cambodia 59 G5
Kompong Trach, *Cambodia* 59 G5
Kompong Tralach,
  Cambodia 59 G5
Komrat = Comrat,
  Moldova 41 J5
Komsberg, *S. Africa* 84 E3
Komsomolets, Ostrov,
  Russia 45 A10
Komsomolsk, *Russia* 42 B5
Komsomolsk, *Russia* 45 D14
Komsomolskiy, *Russia* 42 C7
Konakovo, *Russia* 42 B3
Konarhá □, *Afghan.* 60 B7
Konārī, *Iran* 65 D6
Konawa, *U.S.A.* 109 H6
Konch, *India* 63 G8
Kondakovo, *Russia* 45 C16
Konde, *Tanzania* 82 C4
Kondinin, *Australia* 89 F2
Kondoa, *Tanzania* 82 C4
Kondoa □, *Tanzania* 82 D4
Kondókali, *Greece* 37 A3
Kondopaga, *Russia* 40 A8
Kondratyevo, *Russia* 45 D10
Kondrovo, *Russia* 42 C2
Konduga, *Nigeria* 79 C7
Köneürgench,
  Turkmenistan 44 E6
Konevo, *Russia* 40 A8
Kong, *Ivory C.* 78 D4
Kong →, *Cambodia* 58 F5
Kong, Koh, *Cambodia* 59 G4
Kong Christian IX.s Land,
  Greenland 4 C6
Kong Christian X.s Land,
  Greenland 4 B6
Kong Franz Joseph Fd.,
  Greenland 4 B6
Kong Frederik IX.s Land,
  Greenland 4 C5
Kong Frederik VI.s Kyst,
  Greenland 4 C5
Kong Frederik VIII.s Land,
  Greenland 4 B6
Kong Oscar Fjord,
  Greenland 4 B6
Kongeå →, *Denmark* 11 J3

Kongju, S. Korea 51 F14
Konglu, Burma 61 F20
Kongolo, Kasai Or., Zaïre 82 D1
Kongolo, Shaba, Zaïre .. 82 D2
Kongor, Sudan 77 F3
Kongoussi, Burkina Faso . 79 C4
Kongsberg, Norway 10 E3
Kongsvinger, Norway ... 10 D6
Kongwa, Tanzania 82 D4
Koni, Zaïre 83 E2
Koni, Mts., Zaïre 83 E2
Königsberg = Kaliningrad, Russia 9 J19
Königslutter, Germany .. 18 C6
Königswusterhausen, Germany 18 C9
Konin, Poland 20 C8
Kónitsa, Greece 39 J3
Köniz, Switz. 22 C4
Konjice, Slovenia 33 B12
Konkiep, Namibia 84 D2
Konkouré →, Guinea ... 78 D2
Konnern, Germany 18 D7
Kono, S. Leone 78 D2
Konolfingen, Switz. 22 C5
Konongo, Ghana 79 D4
Konosha, Russia 40 B11
Kōnosu, Japan 49 F9
Konotop, Ukraine 41 G7
Konqi He →, China 54 B4
Końskie, Poland 20 D10
Konstantinovka = Kostyantynivka, Ukraine 41 H9
Konstantinovsk, Russia . 43 G5
Konstanz, Germany 19 H5
Kont, Iran 65 E9
Kontagora, Nigeria 79 C6
Kontich, Belgium 17 F4
Kontum, Vietnam 58 E7
Kontum, Plateau du, Vietnam 58 E7
Konya, Turkey 66 D5
Konya Ovası, Turkey .. 66 C5
Konz, Germany 19 F2
Konza, Kenya 82 C4
Kookynie, Australia 89 E3
Kooline, Australia 88 D2
Kooloonong, Australia .. 91 E3
Koolyanobbing, Australia 89 F2
Koondrook, Australia ... 91 F3
Koonibba, Australia 91 E1
Koorawatha, Australia .. 91 E4
Koorda, Australia 89 F2
Kooskia, U.S.A. 110 C6
Kootenai →, Canada ... 110 B5
Kootenay L., Canada ... 100 D5
Kootenay Nat. Park, Canada 100 C5
Kootjieskolk, S. Africa .. 84 E3
Kopanovka, Russia 43 G8
Kopaonik, Serbia, Yug. . 21 M11
Kópavogur, Iceland 8 D3
Koper, Slovenia 33 C10
Kopervik, Norway 9 G11
Kopeysk, Russia 44 D7
Kopi, Australia 91 E2
Köping, Sweden 10 E10
Kopiste, Croatia 33 F13
Köpmanholmen, Sweden . 10 A12
Koppang, Norway 10 C5
Kopperå, Norway 10 A5
Koppies, S. Africa 85 D4
Koprivnica, Croatia 33 B13
Kopychyntsi, Ukraine .. 41 H3
Korab, Macedonia 39 H3
Korakiána, Greece 37 A3
Korba, India 63 H10
Korbach, Germany 18 D4
Korbu, G., Malaysia ... 59 K3
Korça, Albania 39 J3
Korce = Korça, Albania . 39 J3
Korčula, Croatia 33 F14
Korčulanski Kanal, Croatia 33 E13
Kord Küy, Iran 65 B7
Kord Sheykh, Iran 65 D7
Kordestān □, Iran 64 C5
Kordofân □, Sudan 73 F10
Korea, North ■, Asia ... 51 E14
Korea, South ■, Asia ... 51 F15
Korea Bay, Korea 51 E13
Korea Strait, Asia 51 G15
Korenevo, Russia 42 E2
Korenovsk, Russia 43 H4
Korets, Ukraine 41 G4
Korgan, Turkey 66 B7
Korgus, Sudan 76 D3
Korhogo, Ivory C. 78 D3
Koribundu, S. Leone ... 78 D2
Korim, Indonesia 57 E9
Korinthiakós Kólpos, Greece 39 L5
Kórinthos, Greece 39 M5
Korioumé, Mali 78 B4
Koríssa, Límni, Greece . 37 B3
Kōriyama, Japan 48 F10
Korkuteli, Turkey 66 D4
Kormakiti, C., Cyprus .. 37 D11
Körmend, Hungary 21 H6
Kornat, Croatia 33 E12
Korneshty = Corneşti, Moldova 41 J5
Kornsjø, Norway 10 F5
Kornstad, Norway 10 A1
Koro, Fiji 87 C8
Koro, Ivory C. 78 D3
Koro, Mali 78 C4
Koro Sea, Fiji 87 C9

Korocha, Russia 42 E3
Köroğlu Dağları, Turkey .. 66 B5
Korogwe, Tanzania 82 D4
Korogwe □, Tanzania ... 82 D4
Koroit, Australia 91 F3
Koronadal, Phil. 55 H6
Koronowo, Poland 20 B7
Koror, Pac. Oc. 57 C8
Körös →, Hungary 21 J10
Korosten, Ukraine 41 G5
Korostyshev, Ukraine ... 41 G5
Korotoyak, Russia 42 E4
Korraraika, Helodranon' i, Madag. 85 B7
Korsakov, Russia 45 E15
Korshunovo, Russia 45 D12
Korsør, Denmark 9 J14
Korsun Shevchenkovskiy, Ukraine 41 H6
Korsze, Poland 20 A11
Kortemark, Belgium 17 F2
Kortessem, Belgium 17 G6
Korti, Sudan 76 D3
Kortrijk, Belgium 17 G2
Korwai, India 62 G8
Koryakskoye Nagorye, Russia 45 C18
Koryŏng, S. Korea 51 G15
Koryukovka, Ukraine ... 41 G7
Kos, Greece 39 N10
Kosa, Ethiopia 77 F4
Kosaya Gora, Russia ... 42 C3
Kościan, Poland 20 C6
Kościerzyna, Poland ... 20 A7
Kosciusko, U.S.A. 109 J10
Kosciusko, Mt., Australia . 91 F4
Kosciusko I., U.S.A. ... 100 B2
Kösély →, Hungary 21 H11
Kosha, Sudan 76 C3
K'oshih = Kashi, China .. 54 C2
Koshiki-Rettō, Japan ... 49 J4
Kosi, India 62 F7
Košice, Slovak Rep. 20 G11
Kosjerić, Serbia, Yug. .. 21 M9
Koskhinoú, Greece 37 C10
Kosŏng, N. Korea 51 E15
Kosovska-Mitrovica = Titova-Mitrovica, Serbia, Yug. 21 N10
Kostajnica, Croatia 33 C13
Kostanjevica, Slovenia .. 33 C12
Kostelec, Czech. 20 E6
Koster, S. Africa 84 D4
Kôstî, Sudan 77 E3
Kostopil, Ukraine 41 G4
Kostroma, Russia 42 B5
Kostromskoye Vdkhr., Russia 42 B5
Kostyantynivka, Ukraine .. 41 H9
Kostyukovichi = Kastsyukovichy, Belarus 40 F7
Koszalin, Poland 20 A6
Kőszeg, Hungary 21 H6
Kot Addu, Pakistan 62 D4
Kot Moman, Pakistan .. 62 C5
Kota, India 62 G6
Kota Baharu, Malaysia .. 59 J4
Kota Belud, Malaysia ... 56 C5
Kota Kinabalu, Malaysia . 56 C5
Kota Tinggi, Malaysia .. 59 M4
Kotaagung, Indonesia .. 56 F2
Kotabaru, Indonesia ... 56 E5
Kotabumi, Indonesia ... 56 E2
Kotagede, Indonesia ... 57 G14
Kotamobagu, Indonesia . 57 D6
Kotaneelee →, Canada . 100 A4
Kotawaringin, Indonesia . 56 E4
Kotcho L., Canada 100 B4
Kotelnich, Russia 42 A9
Kotelnikovo, Russia 43 G6
Kotelnyy, Ostrov, Russia 45 B14
Köthen, Germany 18 D7
Kothi, India 63 G9
Kotiro, Pakistan 62 F2
Kotka, Finland 9 F22
Kotlas, Russia 44 C5
Kotli, Pakistan 62 C5
Kotmul, Pakistan 63 B6
Kotonkoro, Nigeria 79 C6
Kotor, Montenegro, Yug. . 21 N8
Kotoriba, Croatia 33 B13
Kotovo, Russia 42 E7
Kotovsk, Russia 42 D5
Kotovsk, Ukraine 41 J5
Kotputli, India 62 F7
Kotri, Pakistan 62 G3
Kótronas, Greece 39 N5
Kottayam, India 60 Q10
Kotturu, India 60 M10
Kotuy →, Russia 45 B11
Kotzebue, U.S.A. 96 B3
Kouango, C.A.R. 80 C4
Koudekerke, Neths. 17 F3
Koudougou, Burkina Faso 78 C4
Koufonísi, Greece 37 E8
Kougaberg, S. Africa ... 84 E3
Kouibli, Ivory C. 78 D3
Kouilou →, Congo 80 E2
Kouki, C.A.R. 80 C3
Koula Moutou, Gabon .. 80 E2
Koulen, Cambodia 58 F5
Koulikoro, Mali 78 C3
Koúm-bournoú, Ákra, Greece 37 C10
Koumala, Australia 90 C4
Koumankou, Mali 78 C3

Koumbia, Burkina Faso .. 78 C4
Koumbia, Guinea 78 C2
Koumboum, Guinea 78 C2
Koumpenntoum, Senegal . 78 C2
Koumra, Chad 73 G8
Koundara, Guinea 78 C2
Kounradskiy, Kazakhstan . 44 E8
Kountze, U.S.A. 109 K7
Koupéla, Burkina Faso .. 79 C4
Kouris →, Cyprus 37 E11
Kourou, Fr. Guiana 121 B7
Kouroussa, Guinea 78 C3
Koussané, Mali 78 C2
Kousséri, Cameroon 73 F7
Koutiala, Mali 78 C3
Kouto, Ivory C. 78 D3
Kouvé, Togo 79 D5
Kouvola, Finland 9 F22
Kovačica, Serbia, Yug. .. 21 K10
Kovel, Ukraine 41 G3
Kovin, Serbia, Yug. 21 L10
Kovrov, Russia 42 B5
Kowanyama, Australia .. 90 B3
Kowkash, Canada 98 B2
Kowloon, H.K. 53 F10
Kowŏn, N. Korea 51 E14
Kowuk →, U.S.A. 96 B4
Koyulhisar, Turkey 66 B7
Koza, Japan 49 L3
Kozan, Turkey 66 D6
Kozáni, Greece 39 J4
Kozara, Bos.-H. 33 D14
Kozarac, Bos.-H. 33 D13
Kozelets, Ukraine 41 G6
Kozelsk, Russia 42 C3
Kozhikode = Calicut, India 60 P9
Kozje, Slovenia 33 B12
Kozlovka, Russia 42 C9
Kozlu, Turkey 66 B4
Kozluk, Turkey 67 C9
Koźmin, Poland 20 D7
Kozmodemyansk, Russia . 42 B8
Kozyatyn, Ukraine 41 H5
Kpabia, Ghana 79 D4
Kpalimé, Togo 79 D5
Kpandae, Ghana 79 D4
Kpessi, Togo 79 D5
Kra, Isthmus of = Kra, Kho Khot, Thailand .. 59 G2
Kra, Kho Khot, Thailand . 59 G2
Kra Buri, Thailand 59 G2
Krabbendijke, Neths. ... 17 F4
Krabi, Thailand 59 H2
Kragan, Indonesia 57 G14
Kragerø, Norway 10 F3
Kragujevac, Serbia, Yug. . 21 L10
Krajina, Bos.-H. 33 D13
Krakatau = Rakata, Pulau, Indonesia 56 F3
Krakor, Cambodia 58 F5
Kraków, Poland 20 E9
Kraksaan, Indonesia ... 57 G15
Kråkstad, Norway 10 E4
Kralanh, Cambodia 58 F4
Králíky, Czech. 20 E6
Kraljevo, Serbia, Yug. .. 21 M10
Kralovice, Czech. 20 F3
Kralupy, Czech. 20 E4
Kramatorsk, Ukraine ... 41 H9
Kramfors, Sweden 10 B11
Kramis, C., Algeria 75 A5
Krångede, Sweden 10 A10
Kranj, Slovenia 33 B11
Kranjska Gora, Slovenia . 33 B10
Krankskop, S. Africa ... 85 D5
Krapina, Croatia 33 B12
Krapina →, Croatia 33 C12
Krapkowice, Poland ... 20 E7
Kraskino, Russia 45 E14
Krāslava, Latvia 40 E4
Kraslice, Czech. 20 E2
Krasnaya Gorbatka, Russia 42 C5
Krasnaya Polyana, Russia . 43 J5
Kraśnik, Poland 20 E12
Kraśnik Fabryczny, Poland 20 E12
Krasnoarmeisk, Ukraine . 41 H9
Krasnoarmeysk, Russia .. 42 E7
Krasnoarmeyskiy, Russia . 43 G6
Krasnodar, Russia 43 H4
Krasnodon, Ukraine ... 41 H10
Krasnogorskiy, Russia .. 42 B9
Krasnograd = Krasnohrad, Ukraine 41 H8
Krasnogvardeyskoye, Russia 43 H5
Krasnogvardeysk, Ukraine 41 K8
Krasnohrad, Ukraine ... 41 H8
Krasnokutsk, Ukraine .. 41 G8
Krasnolesnyy, Russia ... 42 E4
Krasnoperekopsk, Ukraine 41 J7
Krasnorechenskiy, Russia 48 B7
Krasnoselkupsk, Russia . 44 C9
Krasnoslobodsk, Russia . 42 C6
Krasnoslobodsk, Russia . 43 F7
Krasnoturinsk, Russia .. 44 D7
Krasnoufimsk, Russia .. 44 D6
Krasnouralsk, Russia .. 44 D7
Krasnovodsk = Krasnowodsk, Turkmenistan 44 E6
Krasnowodsk, Turkmenistan 44 E6
Krasnoyarsk, Russia ... 45 D10

Krasnoye = Krasnyy, Russia 40 E6
Krasnozavodsk, Russia .. 42 B4
Krasny Sulin, Russia ... 43 G5
Krasnystaw, Poland 20 E13
Krasnyy, Russia 40 E6
Krasnyy Kholm, Russia . 42 A3
Krasnyy Kut, Russia ... 42 E8
Krasnyy Liman, Ukraine . 41 H9
Krasnyy Luch, Ukraine .. 41 H10
Krasnyy Profintern, Russia 42 B5
Krasnyy Yar, Russia ... 42 D10
Krasnyy Yar, Russia ... 42 E7
Krasnyy Yar, Russia ... 43 G9
Krasnyye Baki, Russia .. 42 B7
Krasnyyoskolske Vdskh., Ukraine 41 H9
Kraszna →, Hungary ... 21 G12
Kratie, Cambodia 58 F6
Krau, Indonesia 57 E10
Kravanh, Chuor Phnum, Cambodia 59 G4
Krefeld, Germany 18 D2
Krémaston, Límni, Greece 39 L4
Kremenchug = Kremenchuk, Ukraine .. 41 H7
Kremenchuk, Ukraine ... 41 H7
Kremenchuksk Vdskh., Ukraine 41 H7
Kremenets, Ukraine ... 41 G3
Kremennaya, Ukraine .. 41 H10
Kremges = Svitlovodsk, Ukraine 41 H7
Kremikovtsi, Bulgaria .. 38 G6
Kremmen, Germany 18 C9
Krems, Austria 21 G5
Kremsmünster, Austria . 21 G4
Kretinga, Lithuania 9 J19
Krettamia, Algeria 74 C4
Krettsy, Russia 40 C7
Kreuzberg, Germany ... 19 E5
Kreuzlingen, Switz. 23 A8
Kribi, Cameroon 79 E6
Krichem, Bulgaria 38 G7
Krichev = Krychaw, Belarus 40 F6
Krim, Slovenia 33 C11
Krimpen, Neths. 16 E5
Kriós, Ákra, Greece 37 D5
Krishna →, India 61 M12
Krishnanagar, India 63 H13
Kristiansand, Norway .. 9 G13
Kristianstad, Sweden .. 9 H16
Kristiansund, Norway .. 10 A1
Kristiinankaupunki, Finland 9 E19
Kristinehamn, Sweden . 9 G16
Kristinestad = Kristiinankaupunki, Finland 9 E19
Kríti, Greece 37 D7
Kritsá, Greece 37 D7
Kriva →, Macedonia ... 38 G4
Kriva Palanka, Macedonia 38 G5
Krivaja →, Bos.-H. 21 L8
Krivoy Rog = Kryvyy Rih, Ukraine 41 J7
Križevci, Croatia 33 B13
Krk, Croatia 33 C11
Krka →, Slovenia 33 C12
Krkonoše, Czech. 20 E5
Krnov, Czech. 20 E7
Krobia, Poland 20 D6
Krokeaí, Greece 39 N5
Krokodil →, Mozam. .. 85 D5
Krokom, Sweden 10 A8
Krolevets, Ukraine 41 G7
Kroměříž, Czech. 20 F7
Krommenie, Neths. ... 16 D5
Kromy, Russia 42 D2
Kronach, Germany 19 E7
Kronprins Olav Kyst, Antarctica 5 C5
Kronshtadt, Russia ... 40 C5
Kroonstad, S. Africa .. 84 D4
Kröpelin, Germany ... 18 A7
Kropotkin, Irkutsk, Russia 45 D12
Kropotkin, Krasnodar, Russia 43 H5
Kropp, Germany 18 A5
Krościenko, Poland ... 20 F10
Krosno, Poland 20 F11
Krosno Odrzańskie, Poland 20 C5
Krotoszyn, Poland 20 D7
Krotovka, Russia 42 D10
Kroussón, Greece 37 D6
Krško, Slovenia 33 C12
Kruger Nat. Park, S. Africa 85 C5
Krugersdorp, S. Africa . 85 D4
Kruiningen, Neths. 17 F4
Kruisfontein, S. Africa . 84 E3
Kruishoutem, Belgium . 17 G3
Kruisland, Neths. 17 F4
Kruja, Albania 39 H2
Krulevshchina = Krulyewshchyna, Belarus 40 E4
Krulyewshchyna, Belarus . 40 E4
Kruma, Albania 38 G3
Krumbach, Germany .. 19 G6
Krung Thep = Bangkok, Thailand 58 F3
Krupanj, Serbia, Yug. ... 21 L9
Krupinia, Slovak Rep. .. 21 G8
Krupki, Belarus 40 E5
Kruševac, Serbia, Yug. .. 21 M11
Kruzof I., U.S.A. 100 B1
Krychaw, Belarus 40 F6

Krymsk, Russia 43 H4
Krymskiy Poluostrov = Krymskyy Pivostriv, Ukraine 41 K8
Krymskyy Pivostriv, Ukraine 41 K8
Krynica Morska, Poland .. 20 A9
Krynki, Poland 20 B13
Kryvyy Rih, Ukraine ... 41 J7
Krzywiń, Poland 20 D6
Krzyz, Poland 20 C6
Ksabi, Morocco 74 B4
Ksar Chellala, Algeria .. 75 A5
Ksar el Boukhari, Algeria 75 A5
Ksar el Kebir, Morocco .. 74 B3
Ksar es Souk = Ar Rachidiya, Morocco 74 B4
Ksar Rhilane, Tunisia ... 75 B6
Ksour, Mts. des, Algeria . 75 B4
Kstovo, Russia 42 B7
Kuala, Indonesia 56 D3
Kuala Berang, Malaysia .. 59 K4
Kuala Dungun, Malaysia . 59 K4
Kuala Kangsar, Malaysia . 59 K3
Kuala Kelawang, Malaysia 59 L4
Kuala Kerai, Malaysia .. 59 K4
Kuala Kubu Baharu, Malaysia 59 L3
Kuala Lipis, Malaysia .. 59 K4
Kuala Lumpur, Malaysia . 59 L3
Kuala Nerang, Malaysia . 59 J3
Kuala Pilah, Malaysia .. 59 L4
Kuala Rompin, Malaysia . 59 L4
Kuala Selangor, Malaysia 59 L3
Kuala Terengganu, Malaysia 59 K4
Kualajelai, Indonesia ... 56 E4
Kualakapuas, Indonesia . 56 E4
Kualakurun, Indonesia .. 56 E4
Kualapembuang, Indonesia 56 E4
Kualasimpang, Indonesia . 56 D1
Kuancheng, China 51 D10
Kuandang, Indonesia ... 57 D6
Kuandian, China 51 D13
Kuangchou = Guangzhou, China 53 F9
Kuantan, Malaysia 59 L4
Kuba = Quba, Azerbaijan 43 K9
Kuban →, Russia 43 H3
Kubenskoye, Ozero, Russia 40 C10
Kubokawa, Japan 49 H6
Kubrat, Bulgaria 38 F9
Kučevo, Serbia, Yug. ... 21 L11
Kucha Gompa, India ... 63 B7
Kuchaman, India 62 F6
Kuchino-eruba-Jima, Japan 49 J5
Kuchino-Shima, Japan .. 49 K4
Kuchinotsu, Japan 49 H5
Kucing, Malaysia 56 D4
Kuçova, Albania 39 J2
Kud →, Pakistan 62 F2
Kuda, India 60 H7
Kudat, Malaysia 56 C5
Kudus, Indonesia 57 G14
Kudymkar, Russia 44 D6
Kueiyang = Guiyang, China 52 D6
Kufstein, Austria 19 H8
Kugong I., Canada 98 A4
Kūh-e-Hazārām, Iran .. 65 D8
Kūhak, Iran 60 F4
Kūhbonān, Iran 65 D8
Kūhestak, Iran 65 E8
Kūhīn, Iran 65 C6
Kūhīrī, Iran 65 E9
Kuhnsdorf, Austria 21 J4
Kūhpāyeh, Eşfahan, Iran . 65 C7
Kūhpāyeh, Kermān, Iran . 65 D8
Kui Buri, Thailand 59 F2
Kuinre, Neths. 16 C7
Kuito, Angola 81 G3
Kujang, N. Korea 51 E14
Kuji, Japan 48 D10
Kujū-San, Japan 49 H5
Kukawa, Nigeria 79 C7
Kukerin, Australia 89 F2
Kukmor, Russia 42 B10
Kukup, Malaysia 59 M4
Kukvidze, Russia 42 E6
Kula, Serbia, Yug. 21 K9
Kula, Turkey 66 C3
Kulai, Malaysia 59 M4
Kulal, Mt., Kenya 82 B4
Kulaly, Ostrov, Kazakhstan 43 H10
Kulasekarappattinam, India 60 Q11
Kuldiga, Latvia 9 H19
Kuldja = Yining, China .. 44 E9
Kuldu, Sudan 77 E2
Kulebaki, Russia 42 C6
Kulen Vakuf, Bos.-H. ... 33 D13
Kulgam, India 63 C6
Kulim, Malaysia 59 K3
Kulin, Australia 89 F2
Kulja, Australia 89 F2
Kulm, U.S.A. 108 B5
Kulmbach, Germany .. 19 E7
Kŭlob, Tajikistan 44 F7
Kulp, Turkey 67 C9
Kulsary, Kazakhstan .. 44 E6
Kulti, India 63 H12
Kulu, Turkey 66 C5
Kulu, India 62 C7
Kulumbura, Australia .. 88 B4
Kulunda, Russia 44 D8
Kulungar, Afghan. 62 C3
Kŭlvand, Iran 65 D7
Kulwin, Australia 91 F3
Kulyab = Kŭlob, Tajikistan 44 F7

Kum Tekei

Kum Tekei, *Kazakhstan* 44 E8
Kuma →, *Russia* 43 H8
Kumaganum, *Nigeria* 79 C7
Kumagaya, *Japan* 49 F9
Kumai, *Indonesia* 56 E4
Kumamba, Kepulauan, *Indonesia* 57 E9
Kumamoto, *Japan* 49 H5
Kumamoto □, *Japan* 49 H5
Kumanovo, *Macedonia* 38 G4
Kumara, *N.Z.* 87 K3
Kumarl, *Australia* 89 F3
Kumasi, *Ghana* 78 D4
Kumayri = Gyumri, *Armenia* 43 K6
Kumba, *Cameroon* 79 E6
Kumbakonam, *India* 60 P11
Kumbarilla, *Australia* 91 D5
Kumbo, *Cameroon* 79 D7
Kŭmchŏn, *N. Korea* 51 E14
Kumdok, *India* 63 C8
Kume-Shima, *Japan* 49 L3
Kumeny, *Russia* 42 A9
Kŭmhwa, *S. Korea* 51 E14
Kumi, *Uganda* 82 B3
Kumla, *Sweden* 9 G16
Kumluca, *Turkey* 66 D4
Kummerower See, *Germany* 18 B8
Kumo, *Nigeria* 79 C7
Kumon Bum, *Burma* 61 F20
Kumylzhenskaya, *Russia* 42 F6
Kunama, *Australia* 91 F4
Kunashir, Ostrov, *Russia* 45 E15
Kunda, *Estonia* 9 G22
Kundla, *India* 62 J4
Kungala, *Australia* 91 D5
Kungälv, *Sweden* 11 G5
Kunghit I., *Canada* 100 C2
Kungrad = Qŭnghirot, *Uzbekistan* 44 E6
Kungsbacka, *Sweden* 11 G6
Kungur, *Russia* 44 D6
Kungurri, *Australia* 90 C4
Kunhar →, *Pakistan* 63 B5
Kunhegyes, *Hungary* 21 H10
Kuningan, *Indonesia* 57 G13
Kunlong, *Burma* 61 H21
Kunlun Shan, *Asia* 54 C3
Kunming, *China* 52 E4
Kunrade, *Neths.* 17 G7
Kunsan, *S. Korea* 51 G14
Kunshan, *China* 53 B13
Kununurra, *Australia* 88 C4
Kunwarara, *Australia* 90 C5
Kunya-Urgench = Köneürgench, *Turkmenistan* 44 E6
Künzelsau, *Germany* 19 F5
Kuopio, *Finland* 8 E22
Kupa →, *Croatia* 33 C13
Kupang, *Indonesia* 57 F6
Kupres, *Bos.-H.* 21 L7
Kupyansk, *Ukraine* 41 H9
Kupyansk-Uzlovoi, *Ukraine* 41 H9
Kuqa, *China* 54 B3
Kür →, *Azerbaijan* 67 C13
Kura = Kür →, *Azerbaijan* 67 C13
Kuranda, *Australia* 90 B4
Kurashiki, *Japan* 49 G6
Kurayoshi, *Japan* 49 G6
Kürdämir, *Azerbaijan* 43 K9
Kurdistan, *Asia* 67 D10
Kŭrdzhali, *Bulgaria* 39 H8
Kure, *Japan* 49 G6
Küre, *Turkey* 66 B5
Küre Dağları, *Turkey* 66 B6
Kuressaare, *Estonia* 9 G20
Kuressaare, *Russia* 40 C5
Kurgaldzhinskiy, *Kazakhstan* 44 D8
Kurgan, *Russia* 44 D7
Kurganinsk, *Russia* 43 H5
Kurgannaya = Kurganinsk, *Russia* 43 H5
Kuria Maria Is. = Khūrīyā Mūrīyā, Jazā 'ir, *Oman* 68 D6
Kuridala, *Australia* 90 C3
Kurigram, *Bangla.* 61 G16
Kurikka, *Finland* 9 E20
Kuril Is. = Kurilskiye Ostrova, *Russia* 45 E15
Kuril Trench, *Pac. Oc.* 92 C7
Kurilsk, *Russia* 45 E15
Kurilskiye Ostrova, *Russia* 45 E15
Kuringen, *Belgium* 17 G6
Kurino, *Japan* 49 J5
Kurinskaya Kosa, *Azerbaijan* 67 C13
Kurkur, *Egypt* 76 C3
Kurlovskiy, *Russia* 42 C5
Kurmuk, *Sudan* 77 E3
Kurnool, *India* 60 M10
Kuro-Shima, *Kagoshima, Japan* 49 J4
Kuro-Shima, *Okinawa, Japan* 49 M2
Kurow, *N.Z.* 87 L3
Kurrajong, *Australia* 91 E5
Kurram →, *Pakistan* 62 C4
Kurri Kurri, *Australia* 91 E5
Kursavka, *Russia* 43 H6
Kurshskiy Zaliv, *Russia* 9 J19
Kursk, *Russia* 42 E3
Kuršumlija, *Serbia, Yug.* 21 M11
Kurşunlu, *Turkey* 66 B5
Kurtalan, *Turkey* 67 D9
Kuru, Bahr el →, *Sudan* 77 F2
Kurucaşile, *Turkey* 66 B5
Kuruktag, *China* 54 B3
Kuruman, *S. Africa* 84 D3
Kuruman →, *S. Africa* 84 D3
Kurume, *Japan* 49 H5
Kurunegala, *Sri Lanka* 60 R12
Kurupukari, *Guyana* 121 C6
Kurya, *Russia* 45 C11
Kus Gölü, *Turkey* 66 B2
Kuşadası, *Turkey* 66 D2
Kusatsu, *Japan* 49 F9
Kusawa L., *Canada* 100 A1
Kusel, *Germany* 19 F3
Kushchevskaya, *Russia* 43 G4
Kushikino, *Japan* 49 J5
Kushima, *Japan* 49 J5
Kushimoto, *Japan* 49 H7
Kushiro, *Japan* 48 C12
Kushiro →, *Japan* 48 C12
Kūshk, *Iran* 65 D8
Kushka = Gushgy, *Turkmenistan* 44 F7
Kūshkī, *Īlām, Iran* 64 C5
Kūshkī, *Khorāsān, Iran* 65 B8
Kūshkū, *Iran* 65 E7
Kushol, *India* 63 C7
Kushtia, *Bangla.* 61 H16
Kushum →, *Kazakhstan* 42 F10
Kuskokwim →, *U.S.A.* 96 B3
Kuskokwim B., *U.S.A.* 96 C3
Küsnacht, *Switz.* 23 B7
Kussharo-Ko, *Japan* 48 C12
Küssnacht, *Switz.* 23 B6
Kustanay = Qostanay, *Kazakhstan* 44 D7
Kut, Ko, *Thailand* 59 G4
Kütahya, *Turkey* 66 C4
Kutaisi, *Georgia* 43 J6
Kutaraja = Banda Aceh, *Indonesia* 56 C1
Kutch, Gulf of = Kachchh, Gulf of, *India* 62 H3
Kutch, Rann of = Kachchh, Rann of, *India* 62 G4
Kutina, *Croatia* 33 C13
Kutiyana, *India* 62 J4
Kutkashen, *Azerbaijan* 43 K8
Kutná Hora, *Czech.* 20 F5
Kutno, *Poland* 20 C9
Kuttabul, *Australia* 90 C4
Kutu, *Zaïre* 80 E3
Kutum, *Sudan* 77 E1
Kuujjuaq, *Canada* 97 C13
Kuŭp-tong, *N. Korea* 51 D14
Kuurne, *Belgium* 17 G2
Kuusamo, *Finland* 8 D23
Kuusankoski, *Finland* 9 F22
Kuvshinovo, *Russia* 42 B2
Kuwait = Al Kuwayt, *Kuwait* 64 D5
Kuwait ■, *Asia* 64 D5
Kuwana, *Japan* 49 G8
Kuybyshev = Samara, *Russia* 42 D10
Kuybyshev, *Russia* 44 D8
Kuybyshevo, *Ukraine* 41 J9
Kuybyshevskoye Vdkhr., *Russia* 42 C9
Kuye He →, *China* 50 E6
Kūyeh, *Iran* 64 B5
Kūysanjaq, *Iraq* 67 D11
Kuyumba, *Russia* 45 C10
Kuzey Anadolu Dağları, *Turkey* 66 B7
Kuznetsk, *Russia* 42 D8
Kvænangen, *Norway* 8 A19
Kvaløy, *Norway* 8 B18
Kvam, *Norway* 10 C3
Kvareli = Qvareli, *Georgia* 43 K7
Kvarner, *Croatia* 33 D11
Kvarnerič, *Croatia* 33 D11
Kviteseid, *Norway* 10 E2
Kwabhaca, *S. Africa* 85 E4
Kwadacha →, *Canada* 100 B3
Kwakhanai, *Botswana* 84 C3
Kwakoegron, *Surinam* 121 B6
Kwale, *Kenya* 82 C4
Kwale, *Nigeria* 79 D6
Kwale □, *Kenya* 82 C4
KwaMashu, *S. Africa* 85 D5
Kwamouth, *Zaïre* 80 E3
Kwando →, *Africa* 84 B3
Kwangdaeri, *N. Korea* 51 D14
Kwangju, *S. Korea* 51 G14
Kwangsi-Chuang = Guangxi Zhuangzu Zizhiqu □, *China* 52 E7
Kwangtung = Guangdong □, *China* 53 F9
Kwara □, *Nigeria* 79 D5
Kwataboahegan →, *Canada* 98 B3
Kwatisore, *Indonesia* 57 E8
KwaZulu Natal □, *S. Africa* 85 D5
Kweichow = Guizhou □, *China* 52 D6
Kwekwe, *Zimbabwe* 83 F2
Kwimba □, *Tanzania* 82 C3
Kwinana New Town, *Australia* 89 F2
Kwoka, *Indonesia* 57 E8
Kyabé, *Chad* 73 G8
Kyabra Cr. →, *Australia* 91 D3
Kyabram, *Australia* 91 F4
Kyaikto, *Burma* 58 D1
Kyakhta, *Russia* 45 D11
Kyancutta, *Australia* 91 E2
Kyangin, *Burma* 61 K19
Kyaukpadaung, *Burma* 61 J19
Kyaukpyu, *Burma* 61 K18
Kyaukse, *Burma* 61 J20
Kyburz, *U.S.A.* 112 G6
Kyenjojo, *Uganda* 82 B3
Kyle Dam, *Zimbabwe* 83 G3
Kyle of Lochalsh, *U.K.* 14 D3
Kyll →, *Germany* 19 F2
Kyllburg, *Germany* 19 E2
Kymijoki →, *Finland* 9 F22
Kyneton, *Australia* 91 F3
Kynuna, *Australia* 90 C3
Kyō-ga-Saki, *Japan* 49 G7
Kyoga, L., *Uganda* 82 B3
Kyogle, *Australia* 91 D5
Kyongju, *S. Korea* 51 G15
Kyongpyaw, *Burma* 61 L19
Kyŏngsŏng, *N. Korea* 51 D15
Kyōto, *Japan* 49 G7
Kyōto □, *Japan* 49 G7
Kyparissovouno, *Cyprus* 37 D12
Kyperounda, *Cyprus* 37 E11
Kyren, *Russia* 45 D11
Kyrenia, *Cyprus* 66 E5
Kyrgyzstan ■, *Asia* 44 E8
Kyritz, *Germany* 18 C8
Kyrönjoki →, *Finland* 8 E19
Kystatyam, *Russia* 45 C13
Kytal Ktakh, *Russia* 45 C13
Kythréa, *Cyprus* 37 D12
Kyulyunken, *Russia* 45 C14
Kyunhla, *Burma* 61 H19
Kyuquot, *Canada* 100 C3
Kyurdamir = Kürdämir, *Azerbaijan* 43 K9
Kyūshū, *Japan* 49 H5
Kyūshū □, *Japan* 49 H5
Kyūshū-Sanchi, *Japan* 49 H5
Kyustendil, *Bulgaria* 38 G5
Kyusyur, *Russia* 45 B13
Kywong, *Australia* 91 E4
Kyyiv, *Ukraine* 41 G6
Kyyivske Vdskh., *Ukraine* 41 G6
Kyzyl, *Russia* 45 D10
Kyzyl Kum, *Uzbekistan* 44 E7
Kyzyl-Kyya, *Kyrgyzstan* 44 E8
Kzyl-Orda = Qyzylorda, *Kazakhstan* 44 E7

L

La Albuera, *Spain* 31 G4
La Albufera, *Spain* 29 F4
La Alcarria, *Spain* 28 E2
La Algaba, *Spain* 31 H4
La Almarcha, *Spain* 28 F2
La Almunia de Doña Godina, *Spain* 28 D3
La Asunción, *Venezuela* 121 A5
La Banda, *Argentina* 126 B3
La Bañeza, *Spain* 30 C5
La Barca, *Mexico* 114 C4
La Barge, *U.S.A.* 110 E8
La Bassée, *France* 25 B9
La Bastide-Puylaurent, *France* 26 D7
La Baule, *France* 24 E4
La Belle, *U.S.A.* 105 M5
La Biche →, *Canada* 100 B4
La Bisbal, *Spain* 28 D8
La Blanquilla, *Venezuela* 121 A5
La Bomba, *Mexico* 114 A1
La Bresse, *France* 25 D13
La Bureba, *Spain* 28 C1
La Cal →, *Bolivia* 125 D6
La Calera, *Chile* 126 C1
La Campiña, *Spain* 31 H6
La Canal, *Spain* 36 C7
La Cañiza, *Spain* 30 C2
La Capelle, *France* 25 C10
La Carlota, *Argentina* 126 C3
La Carlota, *Phil.* 55 F5
La Carolina, *Spain* 31 G7
La Cavalerie, *France* 26 D7
La Ceiba, *Honduras* 116 C2
La Chaise-Dieu, *France* 26 C7
La Chaize-le-Vicomte, *France* 24 F5
La Chapelle d'Angillon, *France* 25 E9
La Chapelle-Glain, *France* 24 E5
La Charité-sur-Loire, *France* 25 E10
La Chartre-sur-le-Loir, *France* 24 E7
La Châtaigneraie, *France* 26 B3
La Châtre, *France* 26 B5
La Chaux de Fonds, *Switz.* 22 B3
La Chorrera, *Colombia* 120 D3
La Ciotat, *France* 27 E9
La Clayette, *France* 27 B8
La Cocha, *Argentina* 126 B2
La Concepción = Ri-Aba, *Eq. Guin.* 79 E6
La Concepción, *Venezuela* 120 A3
La Concordia, *Mexico* 115 D6
La Conner, *U.S.A.* 110 B2
La Coruña, *Spain* 30 B2
La Coruña □, *Spain* 30 B2
La Côte, *Switz.* 22 D2
La Côte-St.-André, *France* 27 C9
La Courtine-le-Trucq, *France* 26 C6
La Crau, *France* 27 E8
La Crete, *Canada* 100 B5
La Crosse, *Kans., U.S.A.* 108 F5
La Crosse, *Wis., U.S.A.* 108 D9
La Cruz, *Costa Rica* 116 D2
La Cruz, *Mexico* 114 C3
La Dorada, *Colombia* 120 B3
La Ensenada, *Chile* 128 B2
La Escondida, *Mexico* 114 C5
La Esmeralda, *Paraguay* 126 A3
La Esperanza, *Argentina* 128 B3
La Esperanza, *Cuba* 116 B3
La Esperanza, *Honduras* 116 D2
La Estrada, *Spain* 30 C2
La Fayette, *U.S.A.* 105 H3
La Fé, *Cuba* 116 B3
La Fère, *France* 25 C10
La Ferté-Bernard, *France* 24 D7
La Ferté-Macé, *France* 24 D6
La Ferté-St.-Aubin, *France* 25 E8
La Ferté-sous-Jouarre, *France* 25 D10
La Ferté-Vidame, *France* 24 D7
La Flèche, *France* 24 E6
La Follette, *U.S.A.* 105 G3
La Fregeneda, *Spain* 30 E4
La Fría, *Venezuela* 120 B3
La Fuente de San Esteban, *Spain* 30 E4
La Gineta, *Spain* 29 F2
La Gloria, *Colombia* 120 B3
La Gran Sabana, *Venezuela* 121 B5
La Grand-Combe, *France* 27 D8
La Grande, *U.S.A.* 110 D4
La Grande-Motte, *France* 27 E8
La Grange, *Calif., U.S.A.* 112 H6
La Grange, *Ga., U.S.A.* 105 J3
La Grange, *Ky., U.S.A.* 104 F3
La Grange, *Tex., U.S.A.* 109 L6
La Grita, *Venezuela* 120 B3
La Guaira, *Venezuela* 120 A4
La Guardia, *Spain* 30 D2
La Gudiña, *Spain* 30 C3
La Güera, *Mauritania* 74 D1
La Guerche-de-Bretagne, *France* 24 E5
La Guerche-sur-l'Aubois, *France* 25 F9
La Habana, *Cuba* 116 B3
La Harpe, *U.S.A.* 108 E9
La Haye-du-Puits, *France* 24 C5
La Horqueta, *Venezuela* 121 B5
La Horra, *Spain* 30 D7
La Independencia, *Mexico* 115 D6
La Isabela, *Dom. Rep.* 117 C5
La Jara, *U.S.A.* 111 H11
La Joya, *Peru* 124 D3
La Junquera, *Spain* 28 C7
La Junta, *U.S.A.* 109 F3
La Laguna, *Canary Is.* 36 F3
La Libertad, *Guatemala* 116 C1
La Libertad, *Mexico* 114 B2
La Libertad □, *Peru* 124 B2
La Ligua, *Chile* 126 C1
La Línea de la Concepción, *Spain* 31 J5
La Loche, *Canada* 101 B7
La Londe-les-Maures, *France* 27 E10
La Lora, *Spain* 30 C7
La Loupe, *France* 24 D8
La Louvière, *Belgium* 17 H4
La Machine, *France* 25 F10
La Maddalena, *Italy* 34 A2
La Malbaie, *Canada* 99 C5
La Mancha, *Spain* 29 F2
La Mariña, *Spain* 30 B3
La Mesa, *Calif., U.S.A.* 113 N9
La Mesa, *N. Mex., U.S.A.* 111 K10
La Misión, *Mexico* 114 A1
La Mothe-Achard, *France* 24 F5
La Motte, *France* 27 D10
La Motte-Chalançon, *France* 27 D9
La Moure, *U.S.A.* 108 B5
La Muela, *Spain* 28 D3
La Mure, *France* 27 D9
La Negra, *Chile* 126 A1
La Neuveville, *Switz.* 22 B4
La Oliva, *Canary Is.* 36 F6
La Oraya, *Peru* 124 C2
La Orotava, *Canary Is.* 36 F3
La Pacaudière, *France* 26 B7
La Palma, *Canary Is.* 36 F2
La Palma, *Panama* 116 E4
La Palma del Condado, *Spain* 31 H4
La Paloma, *Chile* 126 C1
La Pampa □, *Argentina* 126 D2
La Paragua, *Venezuela* 121 B5
La Paz, *Entre Ríos, Argentina* 126 C4
La Paz, *San Luis, Argentina* 126 C2
La Paz, *Bolivia* 124 D4
La Paz, *Honduras* 116 D2
La Paz, *Mexico* 114 C2
La Paz, *Phil.* 55 D4
La Paz □, *Bolivia* 124 D4
La Paz Centro, *Nic.* 116 D2
La Pedrera, *Colombia* 120 D4
La Perouse Str., *Asia* 48 B11
La Pesca, *Mexico* 115 C5
La Piedad, *Mexico* 114 C4
La Pine, *U.S.A.* 110 E3
La Plant, *U.S.A.* 108 C4
La Plata, *Argentina* 126 D4
La Plata, *Colombia* 120 C2
La Plata, L., *Argentina* 128 B2
La Pobla de Lillet, *Spain* 28 C6
La Pola de Gordón, *Spain* 30 C5
La Porte, *U.S.A.* 104 E2
La Puebla, *Spain* 28 F8
La Puebla de Cazalla, *Spain* 31 H5
La Puebla de los Infantes, *Spain* 31 H5
La Puebla de Montalbán, *Spain* 30 F6
La Puerta, *Spain* 29 G2
La Punt, *Switz.* 23 C9
La Purísima, *Mexico* 114 B2
La Push, *U.S.A.* 112 C2
La Quiaca, *Argentina* 126 A2
La Rambla, *Spain* 31 H6
La Reine, *Canada* 98 C4
La Réole, *France* 26 D3
La Restinga, *Canary Is.* 36 G2
La Rioja, *Argentina* 126 B2
La Rioja □, *Argentina* 126 B2
La Rioja □, *Spain* 28 C2
La Robla, *Spain* 30 C5
La Roche, *Switz.* 22 C4
La Roche-Bernard, *France* 24 E4
La Roche-Canillac, *France* 26 C5
La Roche-en-Ardenne, *Belgium* 17 H7
La Roche-sur-Yon, *France* 24 F5
La Rochefoucauld, *France* 26 C4
La Rochelle, *France* 26 B2
La Roda, *Albacete, Spain* 29 F2
La Roda, *Sevilla, Spain* 31 H6
La Romana, *Dom. Rep.* 117 C6
La Ronge, *Canada* 101 B7
La Rumorosa, *Mexico* 113 N10
La Sabina, *Spain* 36 C7
La Sagra, *Spain* 29 H2
La Salle, *U.S.A.* 108 E10
La Sanabria, *Spain* 30 C4
La Santa, *Canary Is.* 36 E6
La Sarraz, *Switz.* 22 C3
La Sarre, *Canada* 98 C4
La Scie, *Canada* 99 C8
La Selva, *Spain* 28 D7
La Selva Beach, *U.S.A.* 112 J5
La Serena, *Chile* 126 B1
La Serena, *Spain* 31 G5
La Seyne-sur-Mer, *France* 27 E9
La Sila, *Italy* 35 C9
La Solana, *Spain* 29 G1
La Souterraine, *France* 26 B5
La Spézia, *Italy* 32 D6
La Suze-sur-Sarthe, *France* 24 E7
La Tagua, *Colombia* 120 C3
La Teste, *France* 26 D2
La Tortuga, *Venezuela* 117 D6
La Tour-du-Pin, *France* 27 C9
La Tranche-sur-Mer, *France* 24 F5
La Tremblade, *France* 26 C2
La Tuque, *Canada* 98 C5
La Unión, *Chile* 128 B2
La Unión, *Colombia* 120 C2
La Unión, *El Salv.* 116 D2
La Unión, *Mexico* 114 D4
La Unión, *Peru* 124 B2
La Unión, *Spain* 29 H4
La Urbana, *Venezuela* 120 B4
La Vecilla, *Spain* 30 C5
La Vega, *Dom. Rep.* 117 C5
La Vega, *Peru* 124 C2
La Vela, *Venezuela* 120 A4
La Veleta, *Spain* 31 H7
La Venta, *Mexico* 115 D6
La Ventura, *Mexico* 114 C4
La Venturosa, *Colombia* 120 B4
La Victoria, *Venezuela* 120 A4
La Voulte-sur-Rhône, *France* 27 D8
La Zarza, *Spain* 31 H4
Laaber →, *Germany* 19 G8
Laage, *Germany* 18 B8
Laba →, *Russia* 43 H4
Labason, *Phil.* 55 G5
Labastide-Murat, *France* 26 D5
Labastide-Rouairoux, *France* 26 E6
Labbézenga, *Mali* 79 B5
Labe = Elbe →, *Europe* 18 B4
Labé, *Guinea* 78 C2
Laberec →, *Slovak Rep.* 20 G11
Laberge, L., *Canada* 100 A1
Labin, *Croatia* 33 C11
Labinsk, *Russia* 43 H5
Labis, *Malaysia* 59 L4
Labo, *Phil.* 55 D5
Laboe, *Germany* 18 A6
Labouheyre, *France* 26 D3
Laboulaye, *Argentina* 126 C3
Labra, Peña, *Spain* 30 B6
Labrador, Coast of □, *Canada* 99 B7
Labrador City, *Canada* 99 B6
Lábrea, *Brazil* 125 B5
Labrède, *France* 26 D3
Labuan, Pulau, *Malaysia* 56 C5
Labuha, *Indonesia* 57 E7
Labuhan, *Indonesia* 57 G11
Labuhanbajo, *Indonesia* 57 F6
Labuissière, *Belgium* 17 H4
Labuk, Telok, *Malaysia* 56 C5

Labyrinth, L., *Australia* . . 91 E2
Labytnangi, *Russia* 44 C7
Lac Allard, *Canada* 99 B7
Lac Bouchette, *Canada* . . . 99 C5
Lac du Flambeau, *U.S.A.* . . 108 B10
Lac Édouard, *Canada* 98 C5
Lac La Biche, *Canada* 100 C6
Lac la Martre, *Canada* 96 B8
Lac-Mégantic, *Canada* 99 C5
Lac Seul, Res., *Canada* . . . 98 B1
Lac Thien, *Vietnam* 58 F7
Lacanau, *France* 26 D2
Lacanau, Étang de, *France* . 26 D2
Lacantúm →, *Mexico* . . . 115 D6
Lacara →, *Spain* 31 G4
Lacaune, *France* 26 E6
Lacaune, Mts. de, *France* . 26 E6
Laccadive Is. =
   Lakshadweep Is.,
   Ind. Oc. 46 H11
Lacepede B., *Australia* . . . 91 F2
Lacepede Is., *Australia* . . . 88 C3
Lacerdónia, *Mozam.* 83 F4
Lacey, *U.S.A.* 112 C4
Lachay, Pta., *Peru* 124 C2
Lachen, *Switz.* 23 B7
Lachhmangarh, *India* 62 F6
Lachi, *Pakistan* 62 C4
Lachine, *Canada* 98 C5
Lachlan →, *Australia* 91 E3
Lachute, *Canada* 98 C5
Lackawanna, *U.S.A.* 106 D6
Lacolle, *Canada* 107 A11
Lacombe, *Canada* 100 C6
Lacona, *U.S.A.* 107 C8
Láconi, *Italy* 34 C2
Laconia, *U.S.A.* 107 C13
Lacq, *France* 26 E3
Lacrosse, *U.S.A.* 110 C5
Ladakh Ra., *India* 63 B8
Ladário, *Brazil* 125 D6
Ládhon →, *Greece* 39 M4
Ladik, *Turkey* 66 B6
Ladismith, *S. Africa* 84 E3
Lādīz, *Iran* 65 D9
Ladnun, *India* 62 F6
Ladoga, L. = Ladozhskoye
   Ozero, *Russia* 40 B6
Ladon, *France* 25 D9
Ladozhskoye Ozero, *Russia* 40 B6
Ladrillero, G., *Chile* 128 C1
Lady Grey, *S. Africa* 84 E4
Ladybrand, *S. Africa* 84 D4
Ladysmith, *Canada* 100 D4
Ladysmith, *S. Africa* 85 D4
Ladysmith, *U.S.A.* 108 C9
Lae, *Papua N. G.* 92 H6
Laem Ngop, *Thailand* 59 F4
Laem Pho, *Thailand* 59 J3
Læsø, *Denmark* 11 G4
Læsø Rende, *Denmark* . . . 11 G4
Lafayette, Colo., *U.S.A.* . . 108 F2
Lafayette, Ind., *U.S.A.* . . 104 E2
Lafayette, La., *U.S.A.* . . . 109 K9
Lafayette, Tenn., *U.S.A.* . 105 G3
Laferte →, *Canada* 100 A5
Lafia, *Nigeria* 79 D6
Lafiagi, *Nigeria* 79 D6
Lafleche, *Canada* 101 D7
Lafon, *Sudan* 77 F3
Laforsen, *Sweden* 10 C9
Lagan →, *Sweden* 11 H4
Lagan →, *U.K.* 15 B6
Lagarfljót →, *Iceland* 8 D6
Lagarto, *Brazil* 122 D4
Lage, *Germany* 18 D4
Lage, *Spain* 30 B2
Lage-Mierde, *Neths.* 17 F6
Lågen →, *Oppland,
   Norway* 9 F14
Lågen →, *Vestfold,
   Norway* 9 G14
Lägerdorf, *Germany* 18 B5
Laghouat, *Algeria* 75 B5
Lagnieu, *France* 27 C9
Lagny, *France* 25 D9
Lago, *Italy* 35 C9
Lago Posadas, *Argentina* . 128 C2
Lago Ranco, *Chile* 128 B2
Lagôa, *Portugal* 31 H2
Lagoaça, *Portugal* 30 D4
Lagodekhi, *Georgia* 43 K8
Lagonegro, *Italy* 35 B8
Lagonoy Gulf, *Phil.* 55 E5
Lagos, *Nigeria* 79 D5
Lagos, *Portugal* 31 H2
Lagos de Moreno, *Mexico* 114 C4
Lagrange, *U.S.A.* 88 C3
Lagrange B., *Australia* . . . 88 C3
Laguardia, *Spain* 28 C2
Laguépie, *France* 26 D5
Laguna, *Brazil* 127 B6
Laguna, *U.S.A.* 111 J10
Laguna Beach, *U.S.A.* . . . 113 M9
Laguna de la Janda, *Spain* 31 J5
Laguna Limpia, *Argentina* 126 B4
Laguna Madre, *U.S.A.* . . . 115 B5
Lagunas, *Chile* 126 A2
Lagunas, *Peru* 124 B2
Lagunillas, *Bolivia* 125 D5
Lahad Datu, *Malaysia* 57 C5
Lahan Sai, *Thailand* 58 E4
Lahanam, *Laos* 58 D5
Laharpur, *India* 63 F9
Lahat, *Indonesia* 56 E2
Lahewa, *Indonesia* 56 D1
Lahiang Lahiang, *Phil.* . . . 55 H4

Lāhījān, *Iran* 65 B6
Lahn →, *Germany* 19 E3
Laholm, *Sweden* 11 H7
Laholmsbukten, *Sweden* . . 11 H6
Lahontan Reservoir,
   U.S.A. 110 G4
Lahore, *Pakistan* 62 D6
Lahr, *Germany* 19 G3
Lahti, *Finland* 9 F21
Lahtis = Lahti, *Finland* . . 9 F21
Laï, *Chad* 73 G8
Lai Chau, *Vietnam* 58 A4
Lai'an, *China* 53 A12
Laibin, *China* 52 F7
Laidley, *Australia* 91 D5
Laifeng, *China* 52 C7
L'Aigle, *France* 24 D7
Laignes, *France* 25 E11
L'Aiguillon-sur-Mer, *France* 26 B2
Laikipia □, *Kenya* 82 B4
Laingsburg, *S. Africa* 84 E3
Lainio älv →, *Sweden* 8 C20
Lairg, *U.K.* 14 C4
Laishui, *China* 50 E8
Laiwu, *China* 51 F9
Laixi, *China* 51 F11
Laiyang, *China* 51 F11
Laiyuan, *China* 50 E8
Laizhou Wan, *China* 51 F10
Laja →, *Mexico* 114 C4
Lajere, *Nigeria* 79 C7
Lajes, *Rio Grande do N.,
   Brazil* 122 C4
Lajes, *Sta. Catarina, Brazil* 127 B5
Lajinha, *Brazil* 123 F3
Lajkovac, *Serbia, Yug.* . . . 21 L10
Lajosmizse, *Hungary* 21 H9
Lak Sao, *Laos* 58 C5
Lakaband, *Pakistan* 62 D3
Lake Alpine, *U.S.A.* 112 G7
Lake Andes, *U.S.A.* 108 D5
Lake Anse, *U.S.A.* 104 B1
Lake Arthur, *U.S.A.* 109 K8
Lake Cargelligo, *Australia* . 91 E4
Lake Charles, *U.S.A.* 109 K8
Lake City, Colo., *U.S.A.* . . 111 G10
Lake City, Fla., *U.S.A.* . . . 105 K4
Lake City, Iowa, *U.S.A.* . . 108 D7
Lake City, Mich., *U.S.A.* . 104 C3
Lake City, Minn., *U.S.A.* . 108 C8
Lake City, Pa., *U.S.A.* . . . 106 D4
Lake City, S.C., *U.S.A.* . . 105 J6
Lake George, *U.S.A.* . . . 107 C11
Lake Grace, *Australia* 89 F2
Lake Harbour, *Canada* . . . 97 B13
Lake Havasu City, *U.S.A.* 113 L12
Lake Hughes, *U.S.A.* . . . 113 L8
Lake Isabella, *U.S.A.* . . . 113 K8
Lake King, *Australia* 89 F2
Lake Lenore, *Canada* . . . 101 C8
Lake Louise, *Canada* 100 C5
Lake Mead National
   Recreation Area, *U.S.A.* 113 K12
Lake Mills, *U.S.A.* 108 D8
Lake Nash, *Australia* 90 C2
Lake Providence, *U.S.A.* . 109 J9
Lake River, *Canada* 98 B3
Lake Superior Prov. Park,
   Canada 98 C3
Lake Village, *U.S.A.* 109 J9
Lake Wales, *U.S.A.* 105 M5
Lake Worth, *U.S.A.* 105 M5
Lakefield, *Canada* 98 D4
Lakeland, *Australia* 90 B3
Lakeland, *U.S.A.* 105 L5
Lakemba, *Fiji* 87 D9
Lakeport, *U.S.A.* 112 F4
Lakes Entrance, *Australia* . 91 F4
Lakeside, Ariz., *U.S.A.* . . 111 J9
Lakeside, Calif., *U.S.A.* . . 113 N10
Lakeside, Nebr., *U.S.A.* . . 108 D3
Lakeview, *U.S.A.* 110 E3
Lakewood, Colo., *U.S.A.* . 108 F2
Lakewood, N.J., *U.S.A.* . . 107 F10
Lakewood, Ohio, *U.S.A.* . 106 E3
Lakewood Center, *U.S.A.* 112 C4
Lakhaniá, *Greece* 37 D9
Lakhonpheng, *Laos* 58 E5
Lakhpat, *India* 62 H3
Läki, *Azerbaijan* 43 K8
Lakin, *U.S.A.* 109 G4
Lakitusaki →, *Canada* . . . 98 B3
Lákkoi, *Greece* 37 D5
Lakonikós Kólpos, *Greece* . 39 N5
Lakor, *Indonesia* 57 F7
Lakota, *Ivory C.* 78 D3
Lakota, *U.S.A.* 108 A5
Laksefjorden, *Norway* . . . 8 A22
Lakselv, *Norway* 8 A21
Lakshadweep Is., *Ind. Oc.* 46 H11
Lakshmikantapur, *India* . . 63 H13
Lala Ghat, *India* 61 G18
Lala Musa, *Pakistan* 62 C5
Lalago, *Tanzania* 82 C3
Lalapanzi, *Zimbabwe* 83 F3
Lalganj, *India* 63 G11
Lalibela, *Ethiopia* 77 E4
Lalin, *China* 51 B14
Lalín, *Spain* 30 C2
Lalin He →, *China* 51 B13
Lalinde, *France* 26 D4
Lalitapur = Patan, *Nepal* . 61 F14
Lalitpur, *India* 63 G8
Lam, *Vietnam* 58 B6
Lam Pao Res., *Thailand* . . 58 D4
Lama Kara, *Togo* 79 D5
Lamaing, *Burma* 61 M20

Lamar, *Colo., U.S.A.* . . . 108 F3
Lamar, *Mo., U.S.A.* 109 G7
Lamarque, *Argentina* . . . 128 A3
Lamas, *Peru* 124 B2
Lamastre, *France* 27 D8
Lamballe, *France* 24 D4
Lambaréné, *Gabon* 80 E2
Lambasa, *Fiji* 87 C8
Lambay I., *Ireland* 15 C5
Lambayeque □, *Peru* . . . 124 B2
Lambert, *U.S.A.* 108 B2
Lambert Glacier, *Antarctica* 5 D6
Lamberts Bay, *S. Africa* . . 84 E2
Lambesc, *France* 27 E9
Lámbia, *Greece* 39 M4
Lambro →, *Italy* 32 C6
Lame, *Nigeria* 79 C6
Lame Deer, *U.S.A.* 110 D10
Lamego, *Portugal* 30 D3
Lamèque, *Canada* 99 C7
Lameroo, *Australia* 91 F3
Lamesa, *U.S.A.* 109 J4
Lamía, *Greece* 39 L5
Lamitan, *Phil.* 55 H5
Lammermuir Hills, *U.K.* . . 14 F6
Lamon Bay, *Phil.* 55 D5
Lamont, *Canada* 100 C6
Lamont, *U.S.A.* 113 K8
Lampa, *Peru* 124 D3
Lampang, *Thailand* 58 C2
Lampasas, *U.S.A.* 109 K5
Lampaul, *France* 24 D1
Lampazos de Naranjo,
   Mexico 114 B4
Lampeter, *U.K.* 13 E3
Lampione, *Medit. S.* 75 A7
Lampman, *Canada* 101 D8
Lamprey, *Canada* 101 B10
Lampung □, *Indonesia* . . . 56 F2
Lamu, *Kenya* 82 C5
Lamu □, *Kenya* 82 C5
Lamud, *Peru* 124 B2
Lamy, *U.S.A.* 111 J11
Lan Xian, *China* 50 E6
Lan Yu, *Taiwan* 53 F13
Lanai I., *U.S.A.* 102 H16
Lanak La, *India* 63 B8
Lanak'o Shank'ou = Lanak
   La, *India* 63 B8
Lanao, L., *Phil.* 55 H6
Lanark, *Canada* 107 A8
Lanark, *U.K.* 14 F5
Lancang, *China* 52 F2
Lancang Jiang →, *China* . . 52 G3
Lancashire □, *U.K.* 12 D5
Lancaster, *Canada* 107 A10
Lancaster, *U.K.* 12 C5
Lancaster, Calif., *U.S.A.* . 113 L8
Lancaster, Ky., *U.S.A.* . . 104 G3
Lancaster, N.H., *U.S.A.* . . 107 B13
Lancaster, N.Y., *U.S.A.* . . 106 D6
Lancaster, Pa., *U.S.A.* . . . 107 F8
Lancaster, S.C., *U.S.A.* . . 105 H5
Lancaster, Wis., *U.S.A.* . . 108 D9
Lancaster Sd., *Canada* . . . 97 A11
Lancer, *Canada* 101 C7
Lanchow = Lanzhou,
   China 50 F2
Lanciano, *Italy* 33 F11
Lanco, *Chile* 128 A2
Lancones, *Peru* 124 A1
Lancun, *China* 51 F11
Łancut, *Poland* 20 E12
Lancy, *Switz.* 22 D2
Landau, *Bayern, Germany* 19 G8
Landau, *Rhld-Pfz.,
   Germany* 19 F4
Landeck, *Austria* 19 H6
Landen, *Belgium* 17 G6
Lander, *U.S.A.* 110 E9
Lander →, *Australia* 88 D5
Landerneau, *France* 24 D2
Landeryd, *Sweden* 11 G7
Landes, *France* 26 D3
Landes □, *France* 26 E3
Landete, *Spain* 28 F3
Landi Kotal, *Pakistan* 62 B4
Landivisiau, *France* 24 D2
Landor, *Australia* 89 E2
Landquart, *Switz.* 23 C9
Landquart →, *Switz.* 23 C9
Landrecies, *France* 25 B10
Land's End, *U.K.* 13 G2
Landsberg, *Germany* 19 G6
Landsborough Cr. →,
   Australia 90 C3
Landshut, *Germany* 19 G8
Landskrona, *Sweden* 11 J6
Landstuhl, *Germany* 19 F3
Landvetter, *Sweden* 11 G6
Laneffe, *Belgium* 17 H5
Lanesboro, *U.S.A.* 107 E9
Lanett, *U.S.A.* 105 J3
Lang Bay, *Canada* 100 D4
Lang Qua, *Vietnam* 58 A5
Lang Shan, *China* 50 D4
Lang Son, *Vietnam* 58 B6
Lang Suan, *Thailand* 59 H2
La'nga Co, *China* 61 D12
Langádhás, *Greece* 39 J6
Langádhia, *Greece* 39 M5
Långan →, *Sweden* 10 A8
Langar, *Iran* 65 C9
Langara I., *Canada* 100 C2
Langarabbetje, *Surinam* . . 121 C7
Langdai, *China* 52 D5

Langdon, *U.S.A.* 108 A5
Langdorp, *Belgium* 17 G5
Langeac, *France* 26 C7
Langeais, *France* 24 E7
Langeb Baraka →, *Sudan* . 76 D4
Langeberg, *S. Africa* 84 E3
Langeberge, *S. Africa* 84 D3
Langeland, *Denmark* 11 K4
Langemark, *Belgium* 17 G1
Langen, *Germany* 19 F4
Langenburg, *Canada* . . . 101 C8
Langeneß, *Germany* 18 A4
Langenthal, *Switz.* 22 B5
Langeoog, *Germany* 18 B3
Langeskov, *Denmark* 11 J4
Langesund, *Norway* 10 F3
Länghem, *Sweden* 11 G7
Langhirano, *Italy* 32 D7
Langholm, *U.K.* 14 F6
Langhus, *Norway* 10 E4
Langjökull, *Iceland* 8 D3
Langkawi, P., *Malaysia* . . . 59 J2
Langklip, *S. Africa* 84 D3
Langkon, *Malaysia* 56 C5
Langlade, St- P. & M. 99 C8
Langlois, *U.S.A.* 110 E1
Langnau, *Switz.* 22 C5
Langogne, *France* 26 D7
Langon, *France* 26 D3
Langøya, *Norway* 8 B16
Langres, *France* 25 E12
Langres, Plateau de, *France* 25 E12
Langsa, *Indonesia* 56 D1
Långsele, *Sweden* 10 A11
Langtry, *U.S.A.* 109 L4
Langu, *Thailand* 59 J2
Languedoc, *France* 26 E7
Langxi, *China* 53 B12
Langzhong, *China* 52 B5
Lanigan, *Canada* 101 C7
Lankao, *China* 50 G8
Länkäran, *Azerbaijan* 67 C13
Lannemezan, *France* 26 E4
Lannilis, *France* 24 D2
Lannion, *France* 24 D3
L'Annonciation, *Canada* . . 98 C5
Lanouaille, *France* 26 C5
Lanping, *China* 52 D2
Lansdale, *U.S.A.* 107 F9
Lansdowne, *Australia* 91 E5
Lansdowne, *Canada* 107 B8
Lansdowne House, *Canada* 98 B2
L'Anse, *U.S.A.* 98 C2
L'Anse au Loup, *Canada* . 99 B8
Lansford, *U.S.A.* 107 F9
Lanshan, *China* 53 E9
Lansing, *U.S.A.* 104 D3
Lanslebourg-Mont-Cenis,
   France 27 C10
Lanta Yai, Ko, *Thailand* . . 59 J2
Lanus, *Argentina* 126 C4
Lanusei, *Italy* 34 C2
Lanuza, *Phil.* 55 G7
Lanxi, *China* 53 C12
Lanzarote, *Canary Is.* 36 E6
Lanzhou, *China* 50 F2
Lanzo Torinese, *Italy* 32 C4
Lao →, *Italy* 35 C8
Lao Bao, *Laos* 58 D6
Lao Cai, *Vietnam* 58 A4
Laoag, *Phil.* 55 B4
Laoang, *Phil.* 55 E6
Laoha He →, *China* 51 C11
Laois □, *Ireland* 15 D4
Laon, *France* 25 C10
Laona, *U.S.A.* 104 C1
Laos ■, *Asia* 58 D5
Lapa, *Brazil* 127 B6
Lapalisse, *France* 26 B7
Laparan, *Phil.* 57 C6
Laporte, *U.S.A.* 107 E8
Lapovo, *Serbia, Yug.* 21 L11
Lappeenranta, *Finland* . . . 9 F23
Lappland, *Europe* 8 B21
Laprida, *Argentina* 126 D3
Lapseki, *Turkey* 66 B2
Laptev Sea, *Russia* 45 B13
Lapua, *Finland* 8 E20
Lāpusul →, *Romania* 38 B6
L'Aquila, *Italy* 33 F10
Lār, *Āzarbājān-e Sharqī,
   Iran* 64 B5
Lār, *Fārs, Iran* 65 E7
Lara □, *Venezuela* 120 A4
Larabanga, *Ghana* 78 D4
Laracha, *Spain* 30 B2
Larache, *Morocco* 74 A3
Laragne-Montéglin, *France* 27 D9
Laramie, *U.S.A.* 108 E2
Laramie Mts., *U.S.A.* 108 E2
Laranjeiras, *Brazil* 122 D4
Laranjeiras do Sul, *Brazil* . 127 B5
Larantuka, *Indonesia* 57 F6
Larap, *Phil.* 55 D5
Larat, *Indonesia* 57 F8
L'Arbresle, *France* 27 C8
Larde, *Mozam.* 83 F4
Larder Lake, *Canada* 98 C4
Lardhos, Ákra, *Greece* . . . 37 C10
Lardhos, Órmos, *Greece* . 37 C10

Laredo, *Spain* 28 B1
Laredo, *U.S.A.* 109 M5
Laredo Sd., *Canada* 100 C3
Laren, *Neths.* 16 D6
Largentière, *France* 27 D8
L'Argentière-la-Bessée,
   France 27 D10
Largs, *U.K.* 14 F4
Lari, *Italy* 32 E7
Lariang, *Indonesia* 57 E5
Larimore, *U.S.A.* 108 B6
Lārīn, *Iran* 65 C7
Larino, *Italy* 35 A7
Lárisa, *Greece* 39 K5
Larkana, *Pakistan* 62 F3
Larnaca, *Cyprus* 66 E5
Larnaca Bay, *Cyprus* 37 E12
Larne, *U.K.* 15 B6
Larned, *U.S.A.* 108 F5
Larochette, *Belgium* 17 J8
Laroquebrou, *France* 26 D6
Larrimah, *Australia* 88 C5
Larsen Ice Shelf, *Antarctica* 5 C17
Larvik, *Norway* 10 E4
Laryak, *Russia* 44 C8
Larzac, Causse du, *France* 26 E7
Las Alpujarras, *Spain* . . . 29 J1
Las Animas, *U.S.A.* 108 F3
Las Anod, *Somali Rep.* . . . 68 F4
Las Blancos, *Spain* 29 H4
Las Brenãs, *Argentina* . . . 126 B3
Las Cabezas de San Juan,
   Spain 31 J5
Las Chimeneas, *Mexico* . . 113 N10
Las Coloradas, *Argentina* . 128 A2
Las Cruces, *U.S.A.* 111 K10
Las Flores, *Argentina* . . . 126 D4
Las Heras, *Argentina* . . . 126 C2
Las Horquetas, *Argentina* . 128 C2
Las Khoreh, *Somali Rep.* . 68 E4
Las Lajas, *Argentina* 128 A2
Las Lomas, *Peru* 124 A1
Las Lomitas, *Argentina* . . 126 A3
Las Marismas, *Spain* 31 H4
Las Mercedes, *Venezuela* . 120 B4
Las Navas de la
   Concepción, *Spain* 31 H5
Las Navas de Tolosa, *Spain* 31 G7
Las Navas del Marqués,
   Spain 30 E6
Las Palmas, *Argentina* . . . 126 B4
Las Palmas, *Canary Is.* . . . 36 F4
Las Palmas →, *Mexico* . . . 113 N10
Las Piedras, *Uruguay* . . . 127 C4
Las Pipinas, *Argentina* . . . 126 D4
Las Plumas, *Argentina* . . . 128 B3
Las Rosas, *Argentina* . . . 126 C3
Las Tablas, *Panama* 116 E3
Las Termas, *Argentina* . . . 126 B3
Las Truchas, *Mexico* 114 D4
Las Varillas, *Argentina* . . 126 C3
Las Vegas, N. Mex.,
   U.S.A. 111 J11
Las Vegas, Nev., *U.S.A.* . 113 J11
Lascano, *Uruguay* 127 C5
Lashburn, *Canada* 101 C7
Lashio, *Burma* 61 H20
Lashkar, *India* 62 F8
Łasin, *Poland* 20 B9
Lasíthi □, *Greece* 37 D7
Lasíthi □, *Greece* 37 D7
Laško, *Slovenia* 33 B12
Lassance, *Brazil* 123 E3
Lassay, *France* 24 D6
Lassen Pk., *U.S.A.* 110 F3
Last Mountain L., *Canada* 101 C7
Lastchance Cr. →, *U.S.A.* 112 E5
Lastoursville, *Gabon* 80 E2
Lastovo, *Croatia* 33 F13
Lastovski Kanal, *Croatia* . 33 F13
Lat Yao, *Thailand* 58 E2
Latacunga, *Ecuador* 120 D2
Latakia = Al Lādhiqīyah,
   Syria 66 E6
Latchford, *Canada* 98 C4
Laterza, *Italy* 35 B9
Latham, *Australia* 89 E2
Lathen, *Germany* 18 C3
Lathrop Wells, *U.S.A.* . . . 113 J10
Latiano, *Italy* 35 B10
Latina, *Italy* 34 A5
Latisana, *Italy* 33 C10
Latium = Lazio □, *Italy* . . 33 F9
Laton, *U.S.A.* 112 J7
Latorica →, *Slovak Rep.* . 21 G11
Latouche Treville, C.,
   Australia 88 C3
Latrobe, *Australia* 90 G4
Latrobe, *U.S.A.* 106 F5
Latrónico, *Italy* 35 B9
Latvia ■, *Europe* 9 H20
Lau Group, *Fiji* 87 C9
Lauca →, *Bolivia* 124 D4
Lauchhammer, *Germany* . 18 D9
Lauenburg, *Germany* 18 B6
Läufelfingen, *Switz.* 22 B5
Laufen, *Switz.* 22 B5
Lauffen, *Germany* 19 F5
Laujar, *Spain* 29 J2
Laukaa, *Finland* 9 E21
Launceston, *Australia* . . . 90 G4
Launceston, *U.K.* 13 G3
Laune →, *Ireland* 15 D2
Laupheim, *Germany* 19 G5
Laura, *Australia* 90 B3
Laura, *Australia* 90 B3
Laureana di Borrello, *Italy* 35 D9
Laurel, *Miss., U.S.A.* . . . 109 K10

Laurel, *Mont., U.S.A.* 110 D9
Laurencekirk, *U.K.* 14 E6
Laurens, *U.S.A.* 105 H4
Laurentian Plateau, *Canada* 99 B6
Laurentides, Parc Prov.
des, *Canada* 99 C5
Lauria, *Italy* 35 B8
Laurie L., *Canada* 101 B8
Laurinburg, *U.S.A.* 105 H6
Laurium, *U.S.A.* 104 B1
Lausanne, *Switz.* 22 C3
Laut, *Indonesia* 56 D3
Laut Kecil, Kepulauan,
Indonesia 56 E5
Lautaro, *Chile* 128 A2
Lauterbach, *Germany* ... 18 E5
Lauterbrunnen, *Switz.* 22 C5
Lauterecken, *Germany* 19 F3
Lautoka, *Fiji* 87 C7
Lauwe, *Belgium* 17 G2
Lauwers, *Neths.* 16 A8
Lauwers Zee, *Neths.* 16 B8
Lauzon, *Canada* 99 C5
Lava Hot Springs, *U.S.A.* 110 E7
Lavadores, *Spain* 30 C2
Lavagna, *Italy* 32 D6
Laval, *France* 24 D6
Lavalle, *Argentina* 126 B2
Lávara, *Greece* 39 H9
Lavardac, *France* 26 D4
Lavaur, *France* 26 E5
Lavaux, *Switz.* 22 D3
Lavelanet, *France* 26 F5
Lavello, *Italy* 35 A8
Laverne, *U.S.A.* 109 G5
Laverton, *Australia* 89 E3
Lavos, *Portugal* 30 E2
Lavras, *Brazil* 123 F3
Lavre, *Portugal* 31 G2
Lavrentiya, *Russia* 45 C19
Lávrion, *Greece* 39 M7
Lávris, *Greece* 37 D6
Lavumisa, *Swaziland* 85 D5
Lawas, *Malaysia* 56 D5
Lawele, *Indonesia* 57 F6
Lawn Hill, *Australia* 90 B2
Lawng Pit, *Burma* 61 G20
Lawqah, *Si. Arabia* 64 D4
Lawra, *Ghana* 78 C4
Lawrence, *N.Z.* 87 L2
Lawrence, *Kans., U.S.A.* .. 108 F7
Lawrence, *Mass., U.S.A.* . 107 D13
Lawrenceburg, *Ind.,*
U.S.A. 104 F3
Lawrenceburg, *Tenn.,*
U.S.A. 105 H2
Lawrenceville, *U.S.A.* ... 105 J4
Laws, *U.S.A.* 112 H8
Lawton, *U.S.A.* 109 H5
Lawu, *Indonesia* 57 G14
Laxford, L., *U.K.* 14 C3
Lay →, *France* 26 B2
Laylān, *Iraq* 64 C5
Layon →, *France* 24 E6
Laysan I., *Pac. Oc.* 93 E11
Laytonville, *U.S.A.* 110 G2
Lazarevskoye, *Russia* 43 J4
Lazio □, *Italy* 33 F9
Lazo, *Russia* 48 C6
Le Barcarès, *France* 26 F7
Le Beausset, *France* 27 E9
Le Blanc, *France* 26 B5
Le Bleymard, *France* 26 D7
Le Bourgneuf-la-Fôret,
France 24 D6
Le Bouscat, *France* 26 D3
Le Brassus, *Switz.* 22 C2
Le Bugue, *France* 26 D4
Le Canourgue, *France* 26 D7
Le Cateau, *France* 25 B10
Le Chambon-Feugerolles,
France 27 C8
Le Château-d'Oléron,
France 26 C2
Le Châtelard, *Switz.* 22 D3
Le Châtelet, *France* 26 B6
Le Châtelet-en-Brie, *France* 25 D9
Le Chesne, *France* 25 C11
Le Cheylard, *France* 27 D8
Le Conquet, *France* 24 D2
Le Creusot, *France* 25 F11
Le Croisic, *France* 24 E4
Le Donjon, *France* 26 B7
Le Dorat, *France* 26 B5
Le François, *Martinique* .. 117 D7
Le Grand-Lucé, *France* ... 24 E7
Le Grand-Pressigny, *France* 24 F7
Le Havre, *France* 24 C7
Le Lavandou, *France* 27 E10
Le Lion-d'Angers, *France* . 24 E6
Le Locle, *Switz.* 22 B3
Le Louroux-Béconnais,
France 24 E6
Le Luc, *France* 27 E10
Le Madonie, *Italy* 34 E6
Le Maire, Estr. de,
Argentina 128 D4
Le Mans, *France* 24 D7
Le Mars, *U.S.A.* 108 D6
Le Mêle-sur-Sarthe, *France* 24 D7
Le Merlerault, *France* 24 D7
Le Monastier-sur-Gazeille,
France 26 D7
Le Monêtier-les-Bains,
France 27 D10
Le Mont d'Or, *France* 25 F13
Le Mont-Dore, *France* 26 C6

Le Mont-St.-Michel, *France* 24 D5
Le Moule, *Guadeloupe* ... 117 C7
Le Muy, *France* 27 E10
Le Palais, *France* 24 E3
Le Perthus, *France* 26 F6
Le Pont, *Switz.* 22 C2
Le Pouldu, *France* 24 E3
Le Puy-en-Velay, *France* . 26 C7
Le Quesnoy, *France* 25 B10
Le Roy, *U.S.A.* 109 F7
Le Sentier, *Switz.* 22 C2
Le Sueur, *U.S.A.* 108 C8
Le Teil, *France* 27 D8
Le Teilleul, *France* 24 D6
Le Theil, *France* 24 D7
Le Thillot, *France* 25 E13
Le Thuy, *Vietnam* 58 D6
Le Touquet-Paris-Plage,
France 25 B8
Le Tréport, *France* 24 B8
Le Val-d'Ajol, *France* ... 25 E13
Le Verdon-sur-Mer, *France* 26 C2
Le Vigan, *France* 26 E7
Lea →, *U.K.* 13 F7
Leach, *Cambodia* 59 F4
Lead, *U.S.A.* 108 C3
Leader, *Canada* 101 C7
Leadhills, *U.K.* 14 F5
Leadville, *U.S.A.* 111 G10
Leaf →, *U.S.A.* 109 K10
Leakey, *U.S.A.* 109 L5
Leamington, *Canada* 98 D3
Leamington, *U.S.A.* 110 G7
Leamington Spa = Royal
Leamington Spa, *U.K.* . 13 E6
Le'an, *China* 53 D10
Leandro Norte Alem,
Argentina 127 B4
Learmonth, *Australia* 88 D1
Leask, *Canada* 101 C7
Leavenworth, *Kans.,*
U.S.A. 108 F7
Leavenworth, *Wash.,*
U.S.A. 110 C3
Łeba, *Poland* 20 A7
Lebak, *Phil.* 55 H6
Lebam, *U.S.A.* 112 D3
Lebanon, *Ind., U.S.A.* ... 104 E2
Lebanon, *Kans., U.S.A.* .. 108 F5
Lebanon, *Ky., U.S.A.* 104 G3
Lebanon, *Mo., U.S.A.* ... 109 G8
Lebanon, *Oreg., U.S.A.* .. 110 D2
Lebanon, *Pa., U.S.A.* 107 F8
Lebanon, *Tenn., U.S.A.* .. 105 G2
Lebanon ■, *Asia* 69 B4
Lebbeke, *Belgium* 17 G4
Lebec, *U.S.A.* 113 L8
Lebedyan, *Russia* 42 D4
Lebedyn, *Ukraine* 41 G8
Lebomboberge, *S. Africa* . 85 C5
Lębork, *Poland* 20 A7
Lebrija, *Spain* 31 J4
Lebu, *Chile* 126 D1
Lecce, *Italy* 35 B11
Lecco, *Italy* 32 C6
Lecco, L. di, *Italy* 32 C6
Lécera, *Spain* 28 D4
Lech, *Austria* 19 H6
Lech →, *Germany* 19 G6
Lechang, *China* 53 E9
Lechtaler Alpen, *Austria* . 19 H6
Lectoure, *France* 26 E4
Łęczyca, *Poland* 20 C9
Ledbury, *U.K.* 13 E5
Lede, *Belgium* 17 G3
Ledeberg, *Belgium* 17 F3
Ledesma, *Spain* 30 D5
Ledong, *China* 58 C7
Leduc, *Canada* 100 C6
Ledyczek, *Poland* 20 B6
Lee, *U.S.A.* 107 D11
Lee →, *Ireland* 15 E3
Lee Vining, *U.S.A.* 112 H7
Leech L., *U.S.A.* 108 B7
Leedey, *U.S.A.* 109 H5
Leeds, *U.K.* 12 D6
Leek, *Neths.* 16 B8
Leek, *U.K.* 12 D5
Leende, *Neths.* 17 F7
Leer, *Germany* 18 B3
Leerdam, *Neths.* 16 E6
Leersum, *Neths.* 16 E6
Leesburg, *U.S.A.* 105 L5
Leeton, *Australia* 91 E4
Leetonia, *U.S.A.* 106 F4
Leeu Gamka, *S. Africa* ... 84 E3
Leeuwarden, *Neths.* 16 B7
Leeuwin, C., *Australia* ... 89 F2
Leeward Is., *Atl. Oc.* 117 C7
Lefka, *Cyprus* 37 D11
Lefkoniko, *Cyprus* 37 D12
Lefors, *U.S.A.* 109 H4
Lefroy, L., *Australia* 89 F3
Legal, *Canada* 100 C6
Leganés, *Spain* 30 E7
Legazpi, *Phil.* 55 E5
Legendre I., *Australia* ... 88 D2
Leghorn = Livorno, *Italy* . 32 E7
Legionowo, *Poland* 20 C10
Léglise, *Belgium* 17 J7
Legnago, *Italy* 33 C8
Legnano, *Italy* 32 C5
Legnica, *Poland* 20 D6
Legrad, *Croatia* 33 B13
Legume, *Australia* 91 D5

Leh, *India* 63 B7
Lehi, *U.S.A.* 110 F8
Lehighton, *U.S.A.* 107 F9
Lehrte, *Germany* 18 C5
Lei Shui →, *China* 53 D9
Leiah, *Pakistan* 62 D4
Leibnitz, *Austria* 21 J5
Leibo, *China* 52 C4
Leicester, *U.K.* 13 E6
Leicestershire □, *U.K.* ... 13 E6
Leichhardt →, *Australia* . 90 B2
Leichhardt Ra., *Australia* . 90 C4
Leiden, *Neths.* 16 D5
Leiderdorp, *Neths.* 16 D5
Leidschendam, *Neths.* 16 D4
Leie →, *Belgium* 25 A10
Leignon, *Belgium* 17 H6
Leinster, *Australia* 89 E3
Leinster □, *Ireland* 15 C4
Leinster, Mt., *Ireland* ... 15 D5
Leipzig, *Germany* 18 D8
Leiria, *Portugal* 31 F2
Leiria □, *Portugal* 31 F2
Leirvik, *Norway* 9 G11
Leisler, Mt., *Australia* ... 88 D4
Leith, *U.K.* 14 F5
Leith Hill, *U.K.* 13 F7
Leitha →, *Europe* 21 H7
Leitrim, *Ireland* 15 B3
Leitrim □, *Ireland* 15 B3
Leiyang, *China* 53 D9
Leiza, *Spain* 28 B3
Leizhou Bandao, *China* ... 54 D6
Leizhou Wan, *China* 53 G8
Lek →, *Neths.* 16 E5
Leka, *Norway* 8 D14
Leke, *Belgium* 17 F1
Lekkerkerk, *Neths.* 16 E5
Leksula, *Indonesia* 57 E7
Lékva Ori, *Greece* 37 D6
Leland, *U.S.A.* 109 J9
Leland Lakes, *Canada* ... 101 A6
Leleque, *Argentina* 128 E2
Lelystad, *Neths.* 16 D6
Lema, *Nigeria* 79 C5
Léman, L., *Europe* 22 D3
Lemelerveld, *Neths.* 16 D8
Lemera, *Zaïre* 82 C2
Lemery, *Phil.* 55 E4
Lemgo, *Germany* 18 C4
Lemhi Ra., *U.S.A.* 110 D7
Lemmer, *Neths.* 16 C7
Lemmon, *U.S.A.* 108 C3
Lemon Grove, *U.S.A.* 113 N9
Lemoore, *U.S.A.* 111 H4
Lempdes, *France* 26 C7
Lemsid, *W. Sahara* 74 C2
Lemvig, *Denmark* 11 H2
Lena →, *Russia* 45 B13
Lencloître, *France* 24 B7
Lençóis, *Brazil* 123 D3
Léndas, *Greece* 37 E6
Lendeh, *Iran* 65 D6
Lendelede, *Belgium* 17 G2
Lendinara, *Italy* 33 C8
Lengerich, *Germany* 18 C3
Lenggong, *Malaysia* 59 K3
Lenggries, *Germany* 19 H7
Lengua de Vaca, Pta.,
Chile 126 C1
Lenina, Kanal →, *Russia* . 43 J7
Leninabad = Khudzhand,
Tajikistan 44 E7
Leninakan = Gyumri,
Armenia 43 K6
Leningrad = Sankt-
Peterburg, *Russia* 40 C6
Leninogorsk = Ridder,
Kazakhstan 44 D9
Leninsk, *Russia* 43 F7
Leninsk-Kuznetskiy, *Russia* 44 D9
Leninskoye, *Russia* 42 A8
Leninskoye, *Russia* 45 E14
Lenk, *Switz.* 22 D4
Lenmalu, *Indonesia* 57 E8
Lenne →, *Germany* 18 D3
Lennox, I., *Chile* 128 E3
Lennoxville, *Canada* 107 A13
Leno, *Italy* 32 C7
Lenoir, *U.S.A.* 105 H5
Lenoir City, *U.S.A.* 105 H3
Lenora, *U.S.A.* 108 F4
Lenore L., *Canada* 101 C8
Lenox, *U.S.A.* 107 D11
Lens, *Belgium* 17 G3
Lens, *France* 25 B9
Lens St. Remy, *Belgium* .. 17 G6
Lensk, *Russia* 45 C12
Lent, *Neths.* 16 E7
Lentekhi, *Georgia* 43 J6
Lentini, *Italy* 35 E8
Lenwood, *U.S.A.* 113 L9
Lenzburg, *Switz.* 22 B6
Lenzen, *Germany* 18 B7
Lenzerheide, *Switz.* 23 C9
Leoben, *Austria* 21 H5
Leodhas = Lewis, *U.K.* ... 14 C2
Leola, *U.S.A.* 108 C5
Leominster, *U.K.* 13 E5
Leominster, *U.S.A.* 107 D13
León, *France* 26 E2

León, *Mexico* 114 C4
León, *Nic.* 116 D2
León, *Spain* 30 C5
Leon, *U.S.A.* 108 E8
León □, *Spain* 30 C5
León, Montañas de, *Spain* 30 C4
Leonardtown, *U.S.A.* 104 F7
Leone, Mte., *Switz.* 22 D6
Leonforte, *Italy* 35 E7
Leongatha, *Australia* 91 F4
Leonídhion, *Greece* 39 M5
Leonora, *Australia* 89 E3
Léopold II, Lac = Mai-
Ndombe, L., *Zaïre* 80 E3
Leopoldina, *Brazil* 123 F3
Leopoldo Bulhões, *Brazil* . 123 E2
Leopoldsburg, *Belgium* ... 17 F6
Léopoldville = Kinshasa,
Zaïre 80 E3
Leoti, *U.S.A.* 108 F4
Leova, *Moldova* 41 J5
Leoville, *Canada* 101 C7
Lépa, L. do, *Angola* 84 B2
Lepe, *Spain* 31 H3
Lepel = Lyepyel, *Belarus* . 40 E5
Lepikha, *Russia* 45 C13
Leping, *China* 53 C11
Lepontine, Alpi, *Italy* ... 23 D6
Leppävirta, *Finland* 9 E22
Lequeitio, *Spain* 28 B2
Lercara Friddi, *Italy* 34 E6
Lerdo, *Mexico* 114 B4
Léré, *Chad* 73 G7
Lere, *Nigeria* 79 D6
Leribe, *Lesotho* 85 D4
Lérici, *Italy* 32 D6
Lérida, *Spain* 28 D5
Lérida □, *Spain* 28 C6
Lérins, Is. de, *France* ... 27 E11
Lerma, *Spain* 30 C7
Léros, *Greece* 39 M9
Lérouville, *France* 25 D12
Lerwick, *U.K.* 14 A7
Les Abrets, *France* 27 C9
Les Andelys, *France* 24 C8
Les Arcs, *France* 27 E10
Les Baux-de-Provence,
France 27 E8
Les Bois, *Switz.* 22 B3
Les Cayes, *Haiti* 117 C5
Les Diablerets, *Switz.* ... 22 D4
Les Échelles, *France* 27 C9
Les Essarts, *France* 24 F5
Les Étroits, *Canada* 99 C6
Les Eyzies-de-Tayac-
Sireuil, *France* 26 D5
Les Herbiers, *France* 24 F5
Les Minquiers, Chan. Is. .. 24 D4
Les Ponts-de-Cé, *France* . 24 E6
Les Riceys, *France* 25 E11
Les Sables-d'Olonne,
France 26 B2
Les Vans, *France* 27 D8
Les Verrières, *Switz.* 22 C2
Lesbos = Lésvos, *Greece* . 39 K9
Leshan, *China* 52 C4
Lésina, L. di, *Italy* 33 G12
Lesja, *Norway* 10 B2
Lesjaverk, *Norway* 10 B2
Leskov I., *Antarctica* 5 B1
Leskovac, *Serbia, Yug.* ... 21 M11
Leslie, *U.S.A.* 109 H8
Lesneven, *France* 24 D2
Lešnica, *Serbia, Yug.* 21 L9
Lesopilnoye, *Russia* 48 A7
Lesotho ■, *Africa* 85 D4
Lesozavodsk, *Russia* 45 E14
Lesparre-Médoc, *France* .. 26 C3
Lessay, *France* 24 C5
Lesse →, *Belgium* 17 H5
Lesser Antilles, *W. Indies* . 117 C7
Lesser Slave L., *Canada* .. 100 B5
Lesser Sunda Is., *Indonesia* 57 F6
Lessines, *Belgium* 17 G3
Lester, *U.S.A.* 112 C5
Lestock, *Canada* 101 C8
Lesuer I., *Australia* 88 B4
Lésvos, *Greece* 39 K9
Leszno, *Poland* 20 D6
Letchworth, *U.K.* 13 F7
Letea, Ostrov, *Romania* .. 38 D12
Lethbridge, *Canada* 100 D6
Lethem, *Guyana* 121 C6
Leti, Kepulauan, *Indonesia* 57 F7
Leti Is. = Leti, Kepulauan,
Indonesia 57 F7
Letiahau →, *Botswana* ... 84 C3
Leticia, *Colombia* 120 D4
Leting, *China* 51 E10
Letjiesbos, *S. Africa* 84 E3
Letlhakane, *Botswana* 84 C4
Letlhakeng, *Botswana* 84 C3
Letpadan, *Burma* 61 L19
Letpan, *Burma* 61 K19
Letterkenny, *Ireland* 15 B4
Leu, *Romania* 38 E7
Leucadia, *U.S.A.* 113 M9
Leucate, *France* 26 F7
Leucate, Étang de, *France* 26 F7
Leuk, *Switz.* 22 D5
Leukerbad, *Switz.* 22 D5
Leupegem, *Belgium* 17 G3
Leuser, G., *Indonesia* 56 D1
Leutkirch, *Germany* 19 H6
Leuven, *Belgium* 17 G5
Leuze, *Hainaut, Belgium* . 17 G3
Leuze, *Namur, Belgium* .. 17 G5

Lev Tolstoy, *Russia* 42 D4
Leváдhia, *Greece* 39 L5
Levan, *U.S.A.* 110 G8
Levanger, *Norway* 8 E14
Levant, I. du, *France* 27 E10
Lévanto, *Italy* 32 D6
Levanzo, *Italy* 34 E5
Levelland, *U.S.A.* 109 J3
Leven, *U.K.* 14 E6
Leven, L., *U.K.* 14 E5
Leven, Toraka, *Madag.* ... 85 A8
Levens, *France* 27 E11
Leveque C., *Australia* 88 C3
Leverano, *Italy* 35 B10
Leverkusen, *Germany* 18 D2
Levet, *France* 25 F9
Levice, *Slovak Rep.* 21 G8
Levico, *Italy* 33 C8
Levie, *France* 27 G13
Levier, *France* 25 F13
Levin, *N.Z.* 87 J5
Lévis, *Canada* 99 C5
Levis, L., *Canada* 100 A5
Levítha, *Greece* 39 M9
Levittown, *N.Y., U.S.A.* . 107 F11
Levittown, *Pa., U.S.A.* .. 107 F10
Levkás, *Greece* 39 L3
Levkímmi, *Greece* 37 B4
Levkímmi, Ákra, *Greece* . 37 B4
Levkôsia = Nicosia, *Cyprus* 37 D12
Levoča, *Slovak Rep.* 20 F10
Levroux, *France* 25 F8
Levski, *Bulgaria* 38 F8
Levskigrad = Karlovo,
Bulgaria 38 G7
Lewellen, *U.S.A.* 108 E3
Lewes, *U.K.* 13 G8
Lewes, *U.S.A.* 104 F8
Lewis, *U.K.* 14 C2
Lewis →, *U.S.A.* 112 C4
Lewis, Butt of, *U.K.* 14 C2
Lewis Ra., *Australia* 88 D4
Lewis Range, *U.S.A.* 110 C7
Lewisburg, *Pa., U.S.A.* .. 106 F8
Lewisburg, *Tenn., U.S.A.* 105 H2
Lewisporte, *Canada* 99 C8
Lewiston, *Idaho, U.S.A.* . 110 C5
Lewiston, *Maine, U.S.A.* . 105 C11
Lewistown, *Mont., U.S.A.* 110 C9
Lewistown, *Pa., U.S.A.* .. 106 F7
Lexington, *Ill., U.S.A.* .. 108 E10
Lexington, *Ky., U.S.A.* .. 104 F3
Lexington, *Miss., U.S.A.* . 109 J9
Lexington, *Mo., U.S.A.* .. 108 F8
Lexington, *N.C., U.S.A.* . 105 H5
Lexington, *Nebr., U.S.A.* . 108 E5
Lexington, *Ohio, U.S.A.* . 106 F2
Lexington, *Oreg., U.S.A.* . 110 D4
Lexington, *Tenn., U.S.A.* 105 H1
Lexington Park, *U.S.A.* .. 104 F7
Leye, *China* 52 E6
Leyre →, *France* 26 D2
Leysin, *Switz.* 22 D4
Leyte, *Phil.* 55 F6
Leyte Gulf, *Phil.* 55 F6
Lezay, *France* 26 B4
Lezha, *Albania* 39 H2
Lezhi, *China* 52 B5
Lézignan-Corbières, *France* 26 E6
Lezoux, *France* 26 C7
Lgov, *Russia* 42 F3
Lhasa, *China* 54 D4
Lhazê, *China* 54 D3
Lhokkruet, *Indonesia* 56 D1
Lhokseumawe, *Indonesia* . 56 C1
Lhuntsi Dzong, *India* 61 F17
Li, *Thailand* 58 D2
Li Shui →, *China* 53 C8
Li Xian, *Gansu, China* ... 50 G3
Li Xian, *Hebei, China* ... 50 E8
Li Xian, *Hunan, China* .. 53 C8
Li Xian, *Sichuan, China* . 52 B4
Lian Xian, *China* 53 E9
Liancheng, *China* 53 E11
Lianga, *Phil.* 55 G7
Liangcheng,
Nei Mongol Zizhiqu,
China 50 D7
Liangcheng, *Shandong,*
China 51 G10
Liangdang, *China* 50 H4
Lianghekou, *China* 52 C7
Liangping, *China* 52 B6
Lianhua, *China* 53 D9
Lianjiang, *Fujian, China* . 53 D12
Lianjiang, *Guangdong,*
China 53 G8
Lianping, *China* 53 E10
Lianshan, *China* 53 E9
Lianshanguan, *China* 51 D12
Lianshui, *China* 51 H10
Lianyuan, *China* 53 D8
Lianyungang, *China* 51 G10
Liao He →, *China* 51 D11
Liaocheng, *China* 50 F8
Liaodong Bandao, *China* . 51 E12
Liaodong Wan, *China* 51 D11
Liaoning □, *China* 51 D12
Liaoyang, *China* 51 D12
Liaoyuan, *China* 51 C13
Liaozhong, *China* 51 D12
Liari, *Pakistan* 62 G2
Liard →, *Canada* 100 A4
Liari, *Pakistan* 62 G2
Líbano, *Colombia* 120 C2
Libau = Liepāja, *Latvia* .. 9 H19

Libby, *U.S.A.* 110 B6
Libenge, *Zaïre* 80 D3
Liberal, *Kans., U.S.A.* . . . 109 G4
Liberal, *Mo., U.S.A.* 109 G7
Liberdade, *Brazil* 124 C3
Liberdade →, *Brazil* 125 B7
Liberec, *Czech.* 20 E5
Liberia, *Costa Rica* 116 D2
Liberia ■, *W. Afr.* 78 D3
Libertad, *Venezuela* 120 B4
Liberty, *Mo., U.S.A.* 108 F7
Liberty, *Tex., U.S.A.* 109 K7
Libin, *Belgium* 17 J6
Lîbîya, Sahrâ', *Africa* 73 C9
Libo, *China* 52 E6
Libobo, Tanjung, *Indonesia* 57 E7
Libode, *S. Africa* 85 E4
Libonda, *Zambia* 81 G4
Libourne, *France* 26 D3
Libramont, *Belgium* 17 J6
Libreville, *Gabon* 80 D1
Libya ■, *N. Afr.* 73 C8
Libyan Desert = Lîbîya,
　Sahrâ', *Africa* 73 C9
Libyan Plateau = Ed-
　Déffa, *Egypt* 76 A2
Licantén, *Chile* 126 D1
Licata, *Italy* 34 E6
Lice, *Turkey* 67 C9
Licheng, *China* 50 F7
Lichfield, *U.K.* 12 E6
Lichinga, *Mozam.* 83 E4
Lichtaart, *Belgium* 17 F5
Lichtenburg, *S. Africa* . . . 84 D4
Lichtenfels, *Germany* 19 E7
Lichtenvoorde, *Neths.* 16 E9
Lichtervelde, *Belgium* 17 F2
Lichuan, *Hubei, China* . . . 52 B7
Lichuan, *Jiangxi, China* . . 53 D11
Licosa, Punta, *Italy* 35 B7
Lida, *Belarus* 9 K21
Lida, *U.S.A.* 111 H5
Lidingö, *Sweden* 10 E12
Lidköping, *Sweden* 11 F7
Lido, *Italy* 33 C9
Lido, *Niger* 79 C5
Lido di Roma = Óstia,
　Lido di, *Italy* 34 A5
Lidzbark Warminski,
　Poland 20 A10
Liebenwalde, *Germany* . . . 18 C9
Lieberose, *Germany* 18 D10
Liebig, Mt., *Australia* 88 D5
Liechtenstein ■, *Europe* . . 23 B9
Liederkerke, *Belgium* 17 G4
Liège, *Belgium* 17 G7
Liège □, *Belgium* 17 G7
Liegnitz = Legnica, *Poland* 20 D6
Liempde, *Neths.* 17 E6
Lienart, *Zaïre* 82 B2
Lienyünchiangshih =
　Lianyungang, *China* 51 G10
Lienz, *Austria* 21 J2
Liepāja, *Latvia* 9 H19
Lier, *Belgium* 17 F5
Lierneux, *Belgium* 17 H7
Lieshout, *Neths.* 17 E7
Liestal, *Switz.* 22 B5
Liévin, *France* 25 B9
Lièvre →, *Canada* 98 C4
Liezen, *Austria* 21 H4
Liffey →, *Ireland* 15 C5
Lifford, *Ireland* 15 B4
Liffré, *France* 24 D5
Lifjell, *Norway* 10 E2
Lifudzin, *Russia* 48 B7
Ligao, *Phil.* 55 E5
Lightning Ridge, *Australia* 91 D4
Lignano Sabbiadoro, *Italy* 33 C10
Ligny-en-Barrois, *France* . . 25 D12
Ligny-le-Châtel, *France* . . . 25 E10
Ligoúrion, *Greece* 39 M6
Ligueil, *France* 24 E7
Liguria □, *Italy* 32 D6
Ligurian Sea, *Medit. S.* . . . 32 E5
Lihou Reefs and Cays,
　Australia 90 B5
Lihue, *U.S.A.* 102 H15
Lijiang, *China* 52 D3
Likasi, *Zaïre* 83 E2
Likati, *Zaïre* 80 D4
Likhoslavl, *Russia* 42 B2
Likhovskoy, *Russia* 43 F5
Likoma I., *Malawi* 83 E3
Likumburu, *Tanzania* 83 D4
L'Ile-Bouchard, *France* . . . 24 E7
L'Ile-Rousse, *France* 27 F12
Liling, *China* 53 D9
Lille, *Belgium* 17 F5
Lille, *France* 25 B10
Lille Bælt, *Denmark* 11 J3
Lillebonne, *France* 24 C7
Lillehammer, *Norway* 10 C4
Lillers, *France* 25 B9
Lillesand, *Norway* 11 F2
Lilleshall, *U.K.* 13 E5
Lillestrøm, *Norway* 10 E5
Lillian Point, Mt., *Australia* 89 E4
Lillo, *Spain* 28 F1
Lillooet →, *Canada* 100 D4
Lilongwe, *Malawi* 83 E3
Liloy, *Phil.* 57 C6
Lim →, *Bos.-H.* 21 M9
Lima, *Indonesia* 57 E7
Lima, *Peru* 124 C2
Lima, *Mont., U.S.A.* 110 D7
Lima, *Ohio, U.S.A.* 104 E3

Lima □, *Peru* 124 C2
Lima →, *Portugal* 30 D2
Limages, *Canada* 107 A9
Liman, *Russia* 43 H8
Limassol, *Cyprus* 66 E5
Limavady, *U.K.* 15 A5
Limavady □, *U.K.* 15 B5
Limay →, *Argentina* 128 A3
Limay Mahuida, *Argentina* 126 D2
Limbang, *Brunei* 56 D5
Limbara, Mte., *Italy* 34 B2
Limbaži, *Latvia* 9 H21
Limbdi, *India* 62 H4
Limbe, *Cameroon* 79 E6
Limbourg, *Belgium* 17 G7
Limbri, *Australia* 91 E5
Limburg, *Germany* 19 E4
Limburg □, *Belgium* 17 F6
Limburg □, *Neths.* 17 F7
Limeira, *Brazil* 127 A6
Limerick, *Ireland* 15 D3
Limerick □, *Ireland* 15 D3
Limestone, *U.S.A.* 106 D6
Limestone →, *Canada* 101 B10
Limfjorden, *Denmark* 11 H3
Limia = Lima →, *Portugal* . 30 D2
Limingen, *Norway* 8 D15
Limmared, *Sweden* 11 G7
Limmat →, *Switz.* 23 B6
Limmen, *Neths.* 16 C5
Limmen Bight, *Australia* . . 90 A2
Limmen Bight →,
　Australia 90 B2
Límni, *Greece* 39 L6
Límnos, *Greece* 39 K8
Limoeiro, *Brazil* 122 C4
Limoeiro do Norte, *Brazil* . 122 C4
Limoges, *France* 26 C5
Limón, *Costa Rica* 116 D3
Limon, *U.S.A.* 108 F3
Limone Piemonte, *Italy* . . . 32 D4
Limousin, *France* 26 C5
Limousin, Plateaux du,
　France 26 C5
Limoux, *France* 26 E6
Limpopo →, *Africa* 85 D5
Limuru, *Kenya* 82 C4
Lin Xian, *China* 50 F6
Lin'an, *China* 53 B12
Linapacan I., *Phil.* 55 F3
Linapacan Str., *Phil.* 55 F3
Linares, *Chile* 126 D1
Linares, *Colombia* 120 C2
Linares, *Mexico* 115 C5
Linares, *Spain* 29 G1
Linares □, *Chile* 126 D1
Línas Mte., *Italy* 34 C1
Lincang, *China* 52 F3
Lincheng, *China* 50 F8
Linchuan, *China* 53 D11
Lincoln, *Argentina* 126 C3
Lincoln, *N.Z.* 87 K4
Lincoln, *U.K.* 12 D7
Lincoln, *Calif., U.S.A.* . . . 112 G5
Lincoln, *Ill., U.S.A.* 108 E10
Lincoln, *Kans., U.S.A.* . . . 108 F5
Lincoln, *Maine, U.S.A.* . . . 99 C6
Lincoln, *N.H., U.S.A.* 107 B13
Lincoln, *N. Mex., U.S.A.* . 111 K11
Lincoln, *Nebr., U.S.A.* . . . 108 E6
Lincoln Hav = Lincoln
　Sea, *Arctic* 4 A5
Lincoln Sea, *Arctic* 4 A5
Lincolnshire □, *U.K.* 12 D7
Lincolnshire Wolds, *U.K.* . . 12 D7
Lincolnton, *U.S.A.* 105 H5
L'Incudine, *France* 27 G13
Lind, *U.S.A.* 110 C4
Linda, *U.S.A.* 112 F5
Lindau, *Germany* 19 H5
Linde →, *Neths.* 16 C7
Linden, *Guyana* 121 B6
Linden, *Calif., U.S.A.* 112 G5
Linden, *Tex., U.S.A.* 109 J7
Lindenheuvel, *Neths.* 17 G7
Lindenhurst, *U.S.A.* 107 F11
Linderöd, *Sweden* 11 J7
Linderödsåsen, *Sweden* . . . 11 J7
Lindesnes, *Norway* 9 H12
Líndhos, *Greece* 66 D3
Lindi, *Tanzania* 83 D4
Lindi □, *Tanzania* 83 D4
Lindi →, *Zaïre* 82 B2
Lindoso, *Portugal* 30 D2
Lindow, *Germany* 18 C8
Lindsay, *Canada* 98 D4
Lindsay, *Calif., U.S.A.* . . . 111 H4
Lindsay, *Okla., U.S.A.* . . . 109 H6
Lindsborg, *U.S.A.* 108 F6
Linfen, *China* 50 F6
Ling Xian, *Hunan, China* . 53 D9
Ling Xian, *Shandong,
　China* 50 F9
Lingao, *China* 58 C7
Lingayen, *Phil.* 57 A6
Lingayen G., *Phil.* 55 C4
Lingbi, *China* 51 H9
Lingchuan,
　*Guangxi Zhuangzu,
　China* 53 E8
Lingchuan, *Shanxi, China* . 50 G7
Lingen, *Germany* 18 C3
Lingga, *Indonesia* 56 E2
Lingga, Kepulauan,
　Indonesia 56 E2

Lingga Arch. = Lingga,
　Kepulauan, *Indonesia* . . 56 E2
Lingle, *U.S.A.* 108 D2
Lingling, *China* 53 D8
Lingqiu, *China* 50 E8
Lingshan, *China* 52 F7
Lingshi, *China* 50 F6
Lingshou, *China* 50 E8
Lingshui, *China* 58 C8
Lingtai, *China* 50 G4
Linguéré, *Senegal* 78 B1
Lingwu, *China* 50 E4
Lingyuan, *China* 51 D10
Lingyun, *China* 52 E6
Linh Cam, *Vietnam* 58 C5
Linh, *China* 50 D4
Linhai, *China* 53 C13
Linhares, *Brazil* 123 E3
Linhe, *China* 50 D4
Linjiang, *China* 51 D14
Linköping, *Sweden* 11 F9
Linkou, *China* 51 B16
Linli, *China* 53 C8
Linlithgow, *U.K.* 14 F5
Linnhe, L., *U.K.* 14 E3
Linosa, I., *Medit. S.* 75 A7
Linqi, *China* 50 G7
Linqing, *China* 50 F8
Linqu, *China* 51 F10
Linru, *China* 50 G7
Lins, *Brazil* 127 A6
Linshui, *China* 52 B6
Lintao, *China* 50 G2
Linth →, *Switz.* 19 H5
Linthal, *Switz.* 23 C8
Linton, *Canada* 99 C5
Linton, *Ind., U.S.A.* 104 F2
Linton, *N. Dak., U.S.A.* . . 108 B4
Lintong, *China* 50 G5
Linville, *Australia* 91 D5
Linwood, *Canada* 106 C4
Linwu, *China* 53 E9
Linxi, *China* 51 C10
Linxia, *China* 54 C5
Linxiang, *China* 53 C9
Linyanti →, *Africa* 84 B4
Linyi, *China* 51 G10
Linz, *Austria* 21 G4
Linz, *Germany* 18 E3
Linzhenzhen, *China* 50 F5
Linzi, *China* 51 F10
Lion, G. du, *France* 27 E8
Lionárisso, *Cyprus* 37 D13
Lioni, *Italy* 35 B8
Lions, G. of = Lion, G.
　du, *France* 27 E8
Lion's Den, *Zimbabwe* . . . 83 F3
Lion's Head, *Canada* 98 D3
Liozno = Lyozna, *Belarus* . 40 E6
Lipa, *Phil.* 55 E4
Lipali, *Mozam.* 83 F4
Lípari, *Italy* 35 D7
Lípari, Is. = Eólie, Ís.,
　Italy 35 D7
Lipcani, *Moldova* 41 H4
Lipetsk, *Russia* 42 D4
Liping, *China* 52 D7
Lipkany = Lipcani,
　Moldova 41 H4
Lipljan, *Serbia, Yug.* 21 N11
Lipno, *Poland* 20 C9
Lipova, *Romania* 38 C4
Lipovcy Manzovka, *Russia* 48 B6
Lipovets, *Ukraine* 41 H5
Lippe →, *Germany* 18 D2
Lippstadt, *Germany* 18 D4
Lipscomb, *U.S.A.* 109 G4
Lipsko, *Poland* 20 D11
Lipsói, *Greece* 39 M9
Liptovsky Svaty Mikuláš,
　Slovak Rep. 20 F9
Liptrap C., *Australia* 91 F4
Lipu, *China* 53 E8
Lira, *Uganda* 82 B3
Liri →, *Italy* 34 A6
Liria, *Spain* 28 F4
Lisala, *Zaïre* 80 D4
Lisboa, *Portugal* 31 G1
Lisboa □, *Portugal* 31 G1
Lisbon = Lisboa, *Portugal* . 31 G1
Lisbon, *N. Dak., U.S.A.* . . 108 B6
Lisbon, *N.H., U.S.A.* 107 B13
Lisbon, *Ohio, U.S.A.* 106 F4
Lisburn, *U.K.* 15 B5
Lisburne, C., *U.S.A.* 96 B3
Liscannor, B., *Ireland* 15 D2
Liscia →, *Italy* 34 A2
Lishe Jiang →, *China* 52 E3
Lishi, *China* 50 F6
Lishu, *China* 51 C13
Lishui, *Jiangsu, China* . . . 53 B12
Lishui, *Zhejiang, China* . . 53 C12
Lisianski I., *Pac. Oc.* 92 E10
Lisichansk = Lysychansk,
　Ukraine 41 H10
Lisieux, *France* 24 C7
Liski, *Russia* 42 E4
L'Isle-Adam, *France* 25 C9
L'Isle-Jourdain, *Gers,
　France* 26 E5
L'Isle-Jourdain, *Vienne,
　France* 26 B4
L'Isle-sur-le-Doubs, *France* 25 E13
Lisle-sur-Tarn, *France* . . . 26 E5
Lismore, *Australia* 91 D5
Lismore, *Ireland* 15 D4
Lisse, *Neths.* 16 D5

List, *Germany* 18 A4
Lista, *Norway* 9 G12
Lister, Mt., *Antarctica* 5 D11
Liston, *Australia* 91 D5
Listowel, *Canada* 98 D3
Listowel, *Ireland* 15 D2
Lit-et-Mixe, *France* 26 D2
Litang, *Guangxi Zhuangzu,
　China* 52 F7
Litang, *Sichuan, China* . . . 52 B3
Litang, *Malaysia* 57 C5
Litang Qu →, *China* 52 C3
Litani →, *Lebanon* 69 B4
Litchfield, *Calif., U.S.A.* . . 112 E6
Litchfield, *Conn., U.S.A.* . 107 E11
Litchfield, *Ill., U.S.A.* 108 F10
Litchfield, *Minn., U.S.A.* . 108 C7
Lithgow, *Australia* 91 E5
Líthinon, Ákra, *Greece* . . . 37 E6
Lithuania ■, *Europe* 9 J20
Litija, *Slovenia* 33 B11
Litókhoron, *Greece* 39 J5
Litoměřice, *Czech.* 20 E4
Little Abaco I., *Bahamas* . . 116 A4'
Little Barrier I., *N.Z.* 87 G5
Little Belt Mts., *U.S.A.* . . . 110 C8
Little Blue →, *U.S.A.* 108 F6
Little Cadotte →, *Canada* . 100 B5
Little Cayman, I.,
　Cayman Is. 116 C3
Little Churchill →, *Canada* 101 B9
Little Colorado →, *U.S.A.* . 111 H8
Little Current, *Canada* 98 C3
Little Current →, *Canada* . 98 B3
Little Falls, *Minn., U.S.A.* . 108 C7
Little Falls, *N.Y., U.S.A.* . 107 C10
Little Fork →, *U.S.A.* 108 A8
Little Grand Rapids,
　Canada 101 C9
Little Humboldt →,
　U.S.A. 110 F5
Little Inagua I., *Bahamas* . 117 B5
Little Karoo, *S. Africa* . . . 84 E3
Little Lake, *U.S.A.* 113 K9
Little Laut Is. = Laut
　Kecil, Kepulauan,
　Indonesia 56 E5
Little Minch, *U.K.* 14 D2
Little Missouri →, *U.S.A.* . 108 B3
Little Ouse →, *U.K.* 13 E8
Little Rann, *India* 62 H4
Little Red →, *U.S.A.* 109 H9
Little River, *N.Z.* 87 K4
Little Rock, *U.S.A.* 109 H8
Little Ruaha →, *Tanzania* . 82 D4
Little Sable Pt., *U.S.A.* . . . 104 D2
Little Sioux →, *U.S.A.* . . . 108 E6
Little Smoky →, *Canada* . . 100 C5
Little Snake →, *U.S.A.* . . . 110 F9
Little Valley, *U.S.A.* 106 D6
Little Wabash →, *U.S.A.* . . 104 G1
Littlefield, *U.S.A.* 109 J3
Littlefork, *U.S.A.* 108 A8
Littlehampton, *U.K.* 13 G7
Littleton, *U.S.A.* 107 B13
Liu He →, *China* 51 D11
Liu Jiang →, *China* 52 F7
Liuba, *China* 50 H4
Liucheng, *China* 52 E7
Liugou, *China* 51 D10
Liuhe, *China* 51 C13
Liuheng Dao, *China* 53 C14
Liukang Tenggaja,
　Indonesia 57 F5
Liuli, *Tanzania* 83 E3
Liuwa Plain, *Zambia* 81 G4
Liuyang, *China* 53 C9
Liuzhou, *China* 52 E7
Liuzhuang, *China* 51 H11
Livadherón, *Greece* 39 J4
Livadhia, *Cyprus* 37 E12
Livarot, *France* 24 D7
Live Oak, *Calif., U.S.A.* . . 112 F5
Live Oak, *Fla., U.S.A.* . . . 105 K4
Liveras, *Cyprus* 37 D11
Liveringa, *Australia* 88 C3
Livermore, *U.S.A.* 112 H5
Livermore, Mt., *U.S.A.* . . . 109 K2
Liverpool, *Canada* 99 D7
Liverpool, *U.K.* 12 D5
Liverpool Plains, *Australia* 91 E5
Liverpool Ra., *Australia* . . 91 E5
Livingston, *Guatemala* . . . 116 C2
Livingston, *Calif., U.S.A.* . 112 H6
Livingston, *Mont., U.S.A.* . 110 D8
Livingston, *Tex., U.S.A.* . . 109 K7
Livingstone, *Zambia* 83 F2
Livingstone Mts., *Tanzania* 83 D3
Livingstonia, *Malawi* 83 E3
Livny, *Russia* 42 D3
Livonia, *U.S.A.* 104 D4
Livorno, *Italy* 32 C4
Livramento, *Brazil* 127 C4
Livramento do Brumado,
　Brazil 123 D3
Livron-sur-Drôme, *France* . 27 D8
Liwale, *Tanzania* 83 D4
Liwale □, *Tanzania* 83 D4
Lixi, *China* 52 D3
Liyang, *China* 53 B12
Lizard I., *Australia* 90 A4
Lizard Pt., *U.K.* 13 H2
Lizarda, *Brazil* 122 C2
Lizzano, *Italy* 35 B10
Ljubija, *Bos.-H.* 33 D13
Ljubljana, *Slovenia* 33 B11

Ljubno, *Slovenia* 33 B11
Ljubuški, *Bos.-H.* 21 M7
Ljung, *Sweden* 11 F7
Ljungan →, *Sweden* 10 B11
Ljungaverk, *Sweden* 10 B10
Ljungby, *Sweden* 9 H15
Ljusdal, *Sweden* 10 C10
Ljusnan →, *Sweden* 9 F17
Ljusne, *Sweden* 9 F17
Ljutomer, *Slovenia* 33 B13
Llagostera, *Spain* 28 D7
Llamellín, *Peru* 124 B2
Llancanelo, Salina,
　Argentina 126 D2
Llandeilo, *U.K.* 13 F3
Llandovery, *U.K.* 13 F4
Llandrindod Wells, *U.K.* . . 13 E4
Llandudno, *U.K.* 12 D4
Llanelli, *U.K.* 13 F3
Llanes, *Spain* 30 B6
Llangollen, *U.K.* 12 E4
Llanidloes, *U.K.* 13 E4
Llano, *U.S.A.* 109 K5
Llano →, *U.S.A.* 109 K5
Llano Estacado, *U.S.A.* . . . 109 J3
Llanos, *S. Amer.* 118 C3
Llanquihue, *Chile* 128 B2
Llanquihue, L., *Chile* 128 B1
Llebetx, C., *Spain* 36 B9
Lleida = Lérida, *Spain* . . . 28 D5
Llentrisca, C., *Spain* 36 C7
Llera, *Mexico* 115 C5
Llerena, *Spain* 31 G4
Llica, *Bolivia* 124 D4
Llico, *Chile* 126 C1
Llobregat →, *Spain* 28 D7
Lloret de Mar, *Spain* 28 D7
Lloyd B., *Australia* 90 A3
Lloyd L., *Canada* 101 B7
Lloydminster, *Canada* 101 C6
Lluchmayor, *Spain* 36 B9
Llullaillaco, Volcán,
　S. Amer. 126 A2
Lo, *Belgium* 17 G1
Lo →, *Vietnam* 58 B5
Loa, *U.S.A.* 111 G8
Loa →, *Chile* 126 A1
Loano, *Italy* 32 D5
Lobatse, *Botswana* 84 D4
Löbau, *Germany* 18 D10
Lobbes, *Belgium* 17 H4
Lobenstein, *Germany* 18 E7
Lobería, *Argentina* 126 D4
Lobito, *Angola* 81 G2
Lobón, Canal de, *Spain* . . 31 G4
Lobos, *Argentina* 126 D4
Lobos, I., *Mexico* 114 B2
Lobos, I. de, *Canary Is.* . . 36 F6
Lobos de Tierra, I., *Peru* . . 124 B1
Loc Binh, *Vietnam* 58 B6
Loc Ninh, *Vietnam* 59 G6
Locarno, *Switz.* 23 D7
Loch Garman = Wexford,
　Ireland 15 D5
Lochaber, *U.K.* 14 E4
Lochcarron, *U.K.* 14 D3
Lochem, *Neths.* 16 D8
Loches, *France* 24 E7
Lochgelly, *U.K.* 14 E5
Lochgilphead, *U.K.* 14 E3
Lochinver, *U.K.* 14 C3
Lochnagar, *Australia* 90 C4
Lochnagar, *U.K.* 14 E5
Łochów, *Poland* 20 C11
Lochy →, *U.K.* 14 E3
Lock, *Australia* 91 E2
Lock Haven, *U.S.A.* 106 E7
Lockeford, *U.S.A.* 112 G5
Lockeport, *Canada* 99 D6
Lockerbie, *U.K.* 14 F5
Lockhart, *U.S.A.* 109 L6
Lockhart, L., *Australia* 89 F2
Lockney, *U.S.A.* 109 H4
Lockport, *U.S.A.* 106 C6
Locminé, *France* 24 E4
Locri, *Italy* 35 D9
Locronan, *France* 24 D2
Loctudy, *France* 24 E2
Lod, *Israel* 69 D3
Lodeinoye Pole, *Russia* . . . 40 B7
Lodève, *France* 26 E7
Lodge Grass, *U.S.A.* 110 D10
Lodgepole, *U.S.A.* 108 E3
Lodgepole Cr. →, *U.S.A.* . 108 E2
Lodhran, *Pakistan* 62 E4
Lodi, *Italy* 32 C6
Lodi, *U.S.A.* 112 G5
Lodja, *Zaïre* 82 C1
Lodosa, *Spain* 28 C2
Lödöse, *Sweden* 11 F6
Lodwar, *Kenya* 82 B4
Łódź, *Poland* 20 D9
Loei, *Thailand* 58 D3
Loenen, *Neths.* 16 D8
Loengo, *Zaïre* 82 C2
Loeriesfontein, *S. Africa* . . 84 E2
Lofoten, *Norway* 8 B15
Lofsdalen, *Sweden* 10 B7
Lofsen →, *Sweden* 10 B7
Logan, *Kans., U.S.A.* 108 F5
Logan, *Ohio, U.S.A.* 104 F4
Logan, *Utah, U.S.A.* 110 F8
Logan, *W. Va., U.S.A.* . . . 104 G5
Logan, Mt., *Canada* 96 B5
Logan Pass, *U.S.A.* 100 D6
Logandale, *U.S.A.* 113 J12
Logansport, *Ind., U.S.A.* . 104 E2

Logansport, La., U.S.A.	109	K8
Logo, Sudan	77	F3
Logone →, Chad	73	F8
Logroño, Spain	28	C2
Logrosán, Spain	31	F5
Løgstør, Denmark	11	H3
Lohardaga, India	63	H11
Lohja, Finland	9	F21
Lohr, Germany	19	F5
Loi-kaw, Burma	61	K20
Loimaa, Finland	9	F20
Loir →, France	24	E6
Loir-et-Cher □, France	24	E8
Loire □, France	27	C8
Loire →, France	24	E4
Loire-Atlantique □, France	24	E5
Loiret □, France	25	E9
Loitz, Germany	18	B9
Loja, Ecuador	124	A2
Loja, Spain	31	H6
Loja □, Ecuador	120	D2
Loji, Indonesia	57	E7
Loka, Sudan	77	G3
Lokandu, Zaïre	82	C2
Løken, Norway	10	E5
Lokeren, Belgium	17	F3
Lokhvitsa, Ukraine	41	G7
Lokichokio, Kenya	82	B3
Lokitaung, Kenya	82	B4
Lokkan tekojärvi, Finland	8	C22
Løkken, Denmark	11	G3
Løkken, Norway	10	A3
Loknya, Russia	40	D6
Lokoja, Nigeria	79	D6
Lokolama, Zaïre	80	E3
Lokot, Russia	42	D2
Lol →, Sudan	77	F2
Lola, Guinea	78	D3
Lola, Mt., U.S.A.	112	F6
Lolibai, Gebel, Sudan	77	G3
Lolimi, Sudan	77	G3
Loliondo, Tanzania	82	C4
Lolland, Denmark	11	K5
Lollar, Germany	18	E4
Lolo, U.S.A.	110	C6
Lolodorf, Cameroon	79	E7
Lom, Bulgaria	38	F6
Lom →, Bulgaria	38	F6
Lom Kao, Thailand	58	D3
Lom Sak, Thailand	58	D3
Loma, U.S.A.	110	C8
Loma Linda, U.S.A.	113	L9
Lomami →, Zaïre	82	B1
Lomas de Zamora, Argentina	126	C4
Lombadina, Australia	88	C3
Lombárdia □, Italy	32	C6
Lombardy = Lombárdia □, Italy	32	C6
Lombez, France	26	E4
Lomblen, Indonesia	57	F6
Lombok, Indonesia	56	F5
Lomé, Togo	79	D5
Lomela, Zaïre	80	E4
Lomela →, Zaïre	80	E4
Lomello, Italy	32	C5
Lomié, Cameroon	80	D2
Lomma, Sweden	11	J7
Lomme →, Belgium	17	H6
Lommel, Belgium	17	F6
Lomond, Canada	100	C6
Lomond, L., U.K.	14	E4
Lomphat, Cambodia	58	F6
Lompobatang, Indonesia	57	F5
Lompoc, U.S.A.	113	L6
Lomsegga, Norway	10	C2
Łomza, Poland	20	B12
Loncoche, Chile	128	A2
Loncopuè, Argentina	128	A2
Londa, India	60	M9
Londerzeel, Belgium	17	G4
Londiani, Kenya	82	C4
Londinières, France	24	C8
London, Canada	98	D3
London, U.K.	13	F7
London, Ky., U.S.A.	104	G3
London, Ohio, U.S.A.	104	F4
London, Greater □, U.K.	13	F7
Londonderry, U.K.	15	B4
Londonderry □, U.K.	15	B4
Londonderry, C., Australia	88	B4
Londonderry, I., Chile	128	E2
Londrina, Brazil	127	A5
Lone Pine, U.S.A.	111	H4
Long Beach, Calif., U.S.A.	113	M8
Long Beach, N.Y., U.S.A.	107	F11
Long Beach, Wash., U.S.A.	112	D2
Long Branch, U.S.A.	107	F11
Long Creek, U.S.A.	110	D4
Long Eaton, U.K.	12	E6
Long I., Australia	90	C4
Long I., Bahamas	117	B4
Long I., U.S.A.	107	F11
Long Island Sd., U.S.A.	107	E12
Long L., Canada	98	C2
Long Lake, U.S.A.	107	C10
Long Pine, U.S.A.	108	D5
Long Point B., Canada	106	D4
Long Pt., Nfld., Canada	99	C8
Long Pt., Ont., Canada	106	D4
Long Range Mts., Canada	99	C8
Long Reef, Australia	88	B4
Long Str. = Longa, Proliv, Russia	4	C16
Long Thanh, Vietnam	59	G6
Long Xian, China	50	G4
Long Xuyen, Vietnam	59	G5
Longá, Greece	39	N4
Longa, Proliv, Russia	4	C16
Long'an, China	52	F6
Longarone, Italy	33	B9
Longchang, China	52	C5
Longchi, China	52	C4
Longchuan, Guangdong, China	53	E10
Longchuan, Yunnan, China	52	E1
Longde, China	50	G4
Longeau, France	25	E12
Longford, Australia	90	G4
Longford, Ireland	15	C4
Longford □, Ireland	15	C4
Longguan, China	50	D8
Longhua, China	51	D9
Longhui, China	53	D8
Longido, Tanzania	82	C4
Longiram, Indonesia	56	E5
Longkou, Jiangxi, China	53	D10
Longkou, Shandong, China	51	F11
Longlac, Canada	98	C2
Longli, China	52	D6
Longlier, Belgium	17	J6
Longlin, China	52	E5
Longling, China	52	E2
Longmen, China	53	F10
Longming, China	52	F6
Longmont, U.S.A.	108	E2
Longnan, China	53	E10
Longnawan, Indonesia	56	D4
Longobucco, Italy	35	C9
Longquan, China	53	C12
Longreach, Australia	90	C3
Longshan, China	52	C7
Longsheng, China	53	E8
Longton, Australia	90	C4
Longtown, U.K.	13	F5
Longué-Jumelles, France	24	E6
Longueau, France	25	C9
Longueuil, Canada	107	A11
Longuyon, France	25	C12
Longview, Canada	100	C6
Longview, Tex., U.S.A.	109	J7
Longview, Wash., U.S.A.	112	D4
Longvilly, Belgium	17	H7
Longwy, France	25	C12
Longxi, China	50	G3
Longyou, China	53	C12
Longzhou, China	52	F6
Lonigo, Italy	33	C8
Löningen, Germany	18	C3
Lonja →, Croatia	33	C13
Lonoke, U.S.A.	109	H9
Lonquimay, Chile	128	A2
Lons-le-Saunier, France	25	F12
Lønstrup, Denmark	11	G3
Lookout, C., Canada	98	A3
Lookout, C., U.S.A.	105	H7
Loolmalasin, Tanzania	82	C4
Loon →, Alta., Canada	100	B5
Loon →, Man., Canada	101	B8
Loon Lake, Canada	101	C7
Loon-op-Zand, Neths.	17	E6
Loongana, Australia	89	F4
Loop Hd., Ireland	15	D2
Loosduinen, Neths.	16	D4
Lop Buri, Thailand	58	E3
Lop Nor = Lop Nur, China	54	B4
Lop Nur, China	54	B4
Lopare, Bos.-H.	21	L8
Lopatin, Russia	43	J8
Lopatina, G., Russia	45	D15
Lopaye, Sudan	77	F3
Lopera, Spain	31	H6
Lopez, Phil.	55	E5
Lopez, C., Gabon	80	E1
Loppersum, Neths.	16	B9
Lopphavet, Norway	8	A19
Lora →, Afghan.	60	D4
Lora, Hamun-i-, Pakistan	60	E4
Lora Cr. →, Australia	91	D2
Lora del Río, Spain	31	H5
Lorain, U.S.A.	106	E2
Loralai, Pakistan	62	D3
Lorca, Spain	29	H3
Lord Howe I., Pac. Oc.	92	L7
Lord Howe Ridge, Pac. Oc.	92	L8
Lordsburg, U.S.A.	111	K9
Loreto, Bolivia	125	D5
Loreto, Brazil	122	C2
Loreto, Italy	33	E10
Loreto, Mexico	114	B2
Loreto →, Peru	120	D3
Loreto Aprutino, Italy	33	F10
Lorgues, France	27	E10
Lorica, Colombia	120	B2
Lorient, France	24	E3
Lorn, U.K.	14	E3
Lorn, Firth of, U.K.	14	E3
Lorne, Australia	91	F3
Lorovouno, Cyprus	37	D11
Lörrach, Germany	19	H3
Lorraine, France	25	D12
Lorrainville, Canada	98	C4
Los, Îles de, Guinea	78	D2
Los Alamos, Calif., U.S.A.	113	L6
Los Alamos, N. Mex., U.S.A.	111	J10
Los Altos, U.S.A.	112	H4
Los Andes, Chile	126	C1
Los Angeles, Chile	126	D1
Los Angeles, U.S.A.	113	L8
Los Angeles Aqueduct, U.S.A.	113	K9
Los Antiguos, Argentina	128	C2
Los Banos, U.S.A.	111	H3
Los Barrios, Spain	31	J5
Los Blancos, Argentina	126	A3
Los Cristianos, Canary Is.	36	F3
Los Gatos, U.S.A.	112	H5
Los Hermanos, Venezuela	117	D7
Los Islotes, Canary Is.	36	E6
Los Lagos, Chile	128	A2
Los Llanos de Aridane, Canary Is.	36	F2
Los Lomas, Peru	124	A1
Los Lunas, U.S.A.	111	J10
Los Menucos, Argentina	128	B3
Los Mochis, Mexico	114	B3
Los Monegros, Spain	28	D4
Los Monos, Argentina	128	C3
Los Olivos, U.S.A.	113	L6
Los Palacios, Cuba	116	B3
Los Palacios y Villafranca, Spain	31	H5
Los Reyes, Mexico	114	D4
Los Ríos □, Ecuador	120	D2
Los Roques, Venezuela	120	A4
Los Santos de Maimona, Spain	31	G4
Los Teques, Venezuela	120	A4
Los Testigos, Venezuela	121	A5
Los Vilos, Chile	126	C1
Los Yébenes, Spain	31	F7
Losada →, Colombia	120	C3
Loshkalakh, Russia	45	C15
Lošinj, Croatia	33	D11
Losser, Neths.	16	D10
Lossiemouth, U.K.	14	D5
Lot □, France	26	D5
Lot →, France	26	D4
Lot-et-Garonne □, France	26	D4
Lota, Chile	126	D1
Løten, Norway	10	D5
Lotfābād, Iran	65	B8
Lothair, S. Africa	85	D5
Lothian □, U.K.	14	F5
Lothiers, France	25	F8
Lötschbergtunnel, Switz.	22	D5
Lottefors, Sweden	10	C10
Lotzwil, Switz.	22	B5
Loubomo, Congo	80	E2
Loudéac, France	24	D4
Loudi, China	53	D8
Loudon, U.S.A.	105	H3
Loudonville, U.S.A.	106	F2
Loudun, France	24	E7
Loué, France	24	E6
Loue →, France	25	E12
Louga, Senegal	78	B1
Loughborough, U.K.	12	E6
Loughrea, Ireland	15	C3
Loughros More B., Ireland	15	B3
Louhans, France	27	B9
Louis Trichardt, S. Africa	85	C4
Louis XIV, Pte., Canada	98	B4
Louisa, U.S.A.	104	F4
Louisbourg, Canada	99	C8
Louise I., Canada	100	C2
Louiseville, Canada	98	C5
Louisiade Arch., Papua N. G.	92	J7
Louisiana, U.S.A.	108	F9
Louisiana □, U.S.A.	109	K9
Louisville, Ky., U.S.A.	104	F3
Louisville, Miss., U.S.A.	109	J10
Loulay, France	26	B3
Loulé, Portugal	31	H2
Louny, Czech.	20	E3
Loup City, U.S.A.	108	E5
Lourdes, France	26	E3
Lourdes-du-Blanc-Sablon, Canada	99	B8
Lourenço, Brazil	121	C7
Lourenço-Marques = Maputo, Mozam.	85	D5
Loures, Portugal	31	G1
Lourinhã, Portugal	31	F1
Lousã, Portugal	30	E2
Louth, Australia	91	E4
Louth, Ireland	15	C5
Louth, U.K.	12	D7
Louth □, Ireland	15	C5
Louvain = Leuven, Belgium	17	G5
Louveigné, Belgium	17	G7
Louviers, France	24	C8
Louwsburg, S. Africa	85	D5
Lovat →, Russia	40	C6
Love, Canada	101	C8
Lovech, Bulgaria	38	F7
Loveland, U.S.A.	108	E2
Lovell, U.S.A.	110	D9
Lovelock, U.S.A.	110	F4
Lóvere, Italy	32	C7
Loviisa, Finland	9	F22
Loving, U.S.A.	109	J2
Lovington, U.S.A.	109	J3
Lovios, Spain	30	D2
Lovisa = Loviisa, Finland	9	F22
Lovran, Croatia	33	C11
Low Pt., Australia	89	F4
Low Tatra = Nízké Tatry, Slovak Rep.	20	G9
Lowa, Zaïre	82	C2
Lowa →, Zaïre	82	C2
Lowell, U.S.A.	107	D13
Lower Arrow L., Canada	100	D5
Lower California = Baja California, Mexico	114	A1
Lower Hutt, N.Z.	87	J5
Lower L., U.S.A.	110	F3
Lower Lake, U.S.A.	112	G4
Lower Post, Canada	100	B3
Lower Red L., U.S.A.	108	B7
Lower Saxony = Niedersachsen □, Germany	18	C5
Lower Tunguska = Tunguska, Nizhnyaya →, Russia	45	C9
Lowestoft, U.K.	13	E9
Łowicz, Poland	20	C9
Lowville, U.S.A.	107	C9
Loxton, Australia	91	E3
Loxton, S. Africa	84	E3
Loyalton, U.S.A.	112	F6
Loyalty Is. = Loyauté, Is., N. Cal.	92	K8
Loyang = Luoyang, China	50	G7
Loyauté, Is., N. Cal.	92	K8
Loyev = Loyew, Belarus	41	G6
Loyew, Belarus	41	G6
Lož, Slovenia	33	C11
Lozère □, France	26	D7
Loznica, Serbia, Yug.	21	L9
Lozova, Ukraine	41	H9
Luachimo, Angola	80	F4
Luacono, Angola	80	G4
Lualaba →, Zaïre	82	B5
Luampa, Zambia	83	F1
Lu'an, China	53	B11
Luan Chau, Vietnam	58	B4
Luan He →, China	51	E10
Luan Xian, China	51	E10
Luancheng, Guangxi Zhuangzu, China	52	F7
Luancheng, Hebei, China	50	F8
Luanda, Angola	80	F2
Luang Prabang, Laos	58	C4
Luang Thale, Thailand	59	J3
Luangwa, Zambia	83	F3
Luangwa →, Zambia	83	E3
Luangwa Valley, Zambia	83	E3
Luanne, China	51	D9
Luanping, China	51	D9
Luanshya, Zambia	83	E2
Luapula □, Zambia	83	E2
Luapula →, Africa	83	D2
Luarca, Spain	30	B4
Luashi, Zaïre	83	E1
Luau, Angola	80	G4
Lubalo, Angola	80	F3
Lubań, Poland	20	D5
Lubana, Ozero = Lubānas Ezers, Latvia	9	H22
Lubānas Ezers, Latvia	9	H22
Lubang, Phil.	55	E4
Lubang Is., Phil.	57	B6
Lubartów, Poland	20	D12
Lubawa, Poland	20	B9
Lubbeek, Belgium	17	G5
Lübben, Germany	18	D9
Lübbenau, Germany	18	D9
Lubbock, U.S.A.	109	J4
Lübeck, Germany	18	B6
Lübecker Bucht, Germany	18	A7
Lubefu, Zaïre	82	C1
Lubefu →, Zaïre	82	C1
Lubero = Luofu, Zaïre	82	C2
Lubicon L., Canada	100	B5
Lublin, Poland	20	D12
Lubliniec, Poland	20	E8
Lubnān □, Lebanon	69	B4
Lubny, Ukraine	41	G7
Lubon, Poland	20	C6
Lubongola, Zaïre	82	C2
Lubsko, Poland	20	D4
Lübtheen, Germany	18	B7
Lubuagan, Phil.	55	C4
Lubudi, Zaïre	83	D2
Lubudi →, Zaïre	83	D2
Lubuk Antu, Malaysia	56	D4
Lubukklinggau, Indonesia	56	E2
Lubuksikaping, Indonesia	56	D2
Lubumbashi, Zaïre	83	E2
Lubunda, Zaïre	82	D2
Lubungu, Zambia	83	E2
Lubutu, Zaïre	82	C2
Luc An Chau, Vietnam	58	A5
Luc-en-Diois, France	27	D9
Lucan, Canada	106	C3
Lucban, Phil.	55	D4
Lucca, Italy	32	E7
Luce Bay, U.K.	14	G4
Lucea, Jamaica	116	C4
Lucedale, U.S.A.	105	K1
Lucena, Phil.	55	E4
Lucena, Spain	31	H6
Lucena del Cid, Spain	28	E4
Lučenec, Slovak Rep.	21	G9
Lucera, Italy	35	A8
Lucerne = Luzern, Switz.	23	B6
Lucerne, U.S.A.	112	F4
Lucerne Valley, U.S.A.	113	L10
Lucero, Mexico	114	A3
Luchena →, Spain	29	H3
Lucheng, China	50	F7
Lucheringo →, Mozam.	83	E4
Lüchow, Germany	18	C7
Luchuan, China	53	F8
Lucie →, Surinam	121	C6
Lucira, Angola	81	G2
Luckau, Germany	18	D9
Luckenwalde, Germany	18	C9
Lucknow, India	63	F9
Luçon, France	26	B2
Lüda = Dalian, China	51	E11
Luda Kamchiya →, Bulgaria	38	F10
Ludbreg, Croatia	33	B13
Lüdenscheid, Germany	18	D3
Lüderitz, Namibia	84	D2
Ludewe □, Tanzania	83	D3
Ludhiana, India	62	D6
Ludian, China	52	D4
Luding Qiao, China	52	C4
Lüdinghausen, Germany	18	D3
Ludington, U.S.A.	104	D2
Ludlow, U.K.	13	E5
Ludlow, Calif., U.S.A.	113	L10
Ludlow, Vt., U.S.A.	107	C12
Ludus, Romania	38	C7
Ludvika, Sweden	9	F16
Ludwigsburg, Germany	19	G5
Ludwigshafen, Germany	19	F4
Ludwigslust, Germany	18	B7
Ludza, Latvia	40	D4
Luebo, Zaïre	80	F4
Lueki, Zaïre	82	C2
Luena, Zaïre	83	D2
Luena, Zambia	83	E3
Luepa, Venezuela	121	B5
Lüeyang, China	50	H4
Lufeng, Guangdong, China	53	F10
Lufeng, Yunnan, China	52	E4
Lufira →, Zaïre	83	D2
Lufkin, U.S.A.	109	K7
Lufupa, Zaïre	83	E1
Luga, Russia	40	C5
Luga →, Russia	40	C5
Lugang, Taiwan	53	E13
Lugano, Switz.	23	D7
Lugano, L. di, Switz.	23	E8
Lugansk = Luhansk, Ukraine	41	H10
Lugard's Falls, Kenya	82	C4
Lugela, Mozam.	83	F4
Lugenda →, Mozam.	83	E4
Lugh Ganana, Somali Rep.	68	G3
Lugnaquilla, Ireland	15	D5
Lugnvik, Sweden	10	B11
Lugo, Italy	33	D8
Lugo, Spain	30	B3
Lugo □, Spain	30	C3
Lugoj, Romania	38	D4
Lugones, Spain	30	B5
Lugovoy, Kazakhstan	44	E8
Luhansk, Ukraine	41	H10
Luhe →, Germany	18	B6
Luhuo, China	52	B3
Luiana, Angola	84	B3
Luimneach = Limerick, Ireland	15	D3
Luino, Italy	32	C5
Luís Correia, Brazil	122	B3
Luís Gonçalves, Brazil	122	C1
Luitpold Coast, Antarctica	5	D1
Luiza, Zaïre	80	F4
Luizi, Zaïre	82	D2
Luján, Argentina	126	C4
Lujiang, China	53	B11
Lukanga Swamp, Zambia	83	E2
Lukenie →, Zaïre	80	E3
Lukhisaral, India	63	G12
Lüki, Bulgaria	39	H7
Lukolela, Equateur, Zaïre	80	E3
Lukolela, Kasai Or., Zaïre	82	D1
Lukosi, Zimbabwe	83	F2
Lukovit, Bulgaria	38	F7
Łuków, Poland	20	D12
Lukoyanov, Russia	42	C7
Lule älv →, Sweden	8	D19
Luleå, Sweden	8	D20
Lüleburgaz, Turkey	66	B2
Luliang, China	52	E4
Luling, U.S.A.	109	L6
Lulong, China	51	E10
Lulonga →, Zaïre	80	D3
Lulua →, Zaïre	80	E4
Luluabourg = Kananga, Zaïre	80	F4
Lumai, Angola	81	G4
Lumajang, Indonesia	57	H15
Lumbala N'guimbo, Angola	81	G4
Lumberton, Miss., U.S.A.	109	K10
Lumberton, N.C., U.S.A.	105	H6
Lumberton, N. Mex., U.S.A.	111	H10
Lumbres, France	25	B9
Lumbwa, Kenya	82	C4
Lummen, Belgium	17	G6
Lumsden, N.Z.	87	L2
Lumut, Malaysia	59	K3
Lumut, Tg., Indonesia	56	E3
Luna, Phil.	55	C4
Lunan, China	52	E4
Lunavada, India	62	H5
Lunca, Romania	38	B8
Lund, Sweden	11	J7
Lund, U.S.A.	110	G6
Lundazi, Zambia	83	E3
Lunderskov, Denmark	11	J3
Lundi →, Zimbabwe	83	G3
Lundu, Malaysia	56	D3
Lundy, U.K.	13	F3
Lune →, U.K.	12	C5
Lüneburg, Germany	18	B6
Lüneburg Heath = Lüneburger Heide, Germany	18	C6

Lüneburger Heide,
  Germany 18 C6
Lunel, France 27 E8
Lünen, Germany 18 D3
Lunenburg, Canada 99 D7
Lunéville, France 25 D13
Lunga →, Zambia 83 E2
Lungern, Switz. 22 C6
Lungi Airport, S. Leone . 78 D2
Lunglei, India 61 H18
Luni, India 62 F5
Luni →, India 62 G4
Luninets = Luninyets,
  Belarus 41 F4
Luning, U.S.A. 110 G4
Lunino, Russia 42 D7
Luninyets, Belarus 41 F4
Lunner, Norway 10 D4
Lunsemfwa →, Zambia . 83 E3
Lunsemfwa Falls, Zambia . 83 E2
Lunteren, Neths. 16 D7
Luo He →, China 50 G6
Luocheng, China 52 E7
Luochuan, China 50 G5
Luoci, China 52 E4
Luodian, China 52 E6
Luoding, China 53 F8
Luodong, Taiwan 53 E13
Luofu, Zaïre 82 C2
Luohe, China 50 H8
Luojiang, China 52 B5
Luonan, China 50 G6
Luoning, China 50 G6
Luoyang, China 50 G7
Luoyuan, China 53 D12
Luozi, Zaïre 80 E2
Luozigou, China 51 C16
Lupanshui, China 52 D5
Lupeni, Romania 38 D6
Lupilichi, Mozam. 83 E4
Lupoing, China 52 E5
Luquan, China 52 E4
Luque, Paraguay 126 B4
Luque, Spain 31 H6
Luray, U.S.A. 104 F6
Lure, France 25 E13
Luremo, Angola 80 F3
Lurgan, U.K. 15 B5
Luri, France 27 F13
Luribay, Bolivia 124 D4
Lurin, Peru 124 C2
Lusaka, Zambia 83 F2
Lusambo, Zaïre 82 C1
Lusangaye, Zaïre 82 C2
Luseland, Canada 101 C7
Lushan, Henan, China . 50 H7
Lushan, Sichuan, China . 52 B4
Lushi, China 50 G6
Lushnja, Albania 39 J2
Lushoto, Tanzania 82 C4
Lushoto □, Tanzania ... 82 C4
Lushui, China 52 E2
Lüshun, China 51 E11
Lusignan, France 26 B4
Lusigny-sur-Barse, France 25 D11
Lusk, U.S.A. 108 D2
Lussac-les-Châteaux,
  France 26 B4
Lussanvira, Brazil 123 F1
Luta = Dalian, China .. 51 E11
Luton, U.K. 13 F7
Lutong, Malaysia 56 D4
Lutry, Switz. 22 C3
Lutsk, Ukraine 41 G3
Lützow Holmbukta,
  Antarctica 5 C4
Lutzputs, S. Africa ... 84 D3
Luverne, U.S.A. 108 D6
Luvua, Zaïre 83 D2
Luvua →, Zaïre 82 D2
Luwegu →, Tanzania .. 83 D4
Luwuk, Indonesia 57 E6
Luxembourg, Lux. 17 J8
Luxembourg □, Belgium . 17 J7
Luxembourg ■, Europe . 17 J8
Luxeuil-les-Bains, France . 25 E13
Luxi, Hunan, China ... 53 C8
Luxi, Yunnan, China .. 52 E4
Luxi, Yunnan, China .. 52 E2
Luxor = El Uqsur, Egypt . 76 B3
Luy →, France 26 E2
Luy-de-Béarn →, France 26 E3
Luy-de-France →, France 26 E3
Luyi, China 50 H8
Luyksgestel, Neths. ... 17 F6
Luz-St.-Sauveur, France . 26 F4
Luzern, Switz. 23 B6
Luzern □, Switz. 22 B5
Luzhai, China 52 E7
Luzhou, China 52 C5
Luziânia, Brazil 123 E2
Luzilândia, Brazil ... 122 B3
Luzon, Phil. 55 D4
Luzy, France 25 F10
Luzzi, Italy 35 C9
Lviv, Ukraine 41 H3
Lvov = Lviv, Ukraine .. 41 H3
Lyakhavichy, Belarus .. 41 F4
Lyakhovskiye, Ostrova,
  Russia 45 B15
Lyaki = Läki, Azerbaijan 43 K8
Lyallpur = Faisalabad,
  Pakistan 62 D5
Lycaonia, Turkey 66 D5
Lychen, Germany 18 B9

Lychkova, Russia 40 D7
Lycia, Turkey 66 D3
Lycksele, Sweden 8 D18
Lydda = Lod, Israel ... 69 D3
Lydenburg, S. Africa .. 85 D5
Lydia, Turkey 66 C3
Lyell, N.Z. 87 J4
Lyell I., Canada 100 C2
Lyepyel, Belarus 40 E5
Lygnern, Sweden 11 G6
Lyman, U.S.A. 110 F8
Lyme Regis, U.K. 13 G5
Lymington, U.K. 13 G6
Łyna →, Poland 9 J19
Lynchburg, U.S.A. 104 G6
Lynd →, Australia 90 B3
Lynd Ra., Australia ... 91 D4
Lynden, Canada 106 C4
Lynden, U.S.A. 112 B4
Lyndhurst, Queens.,
  Australia 90 B3
Lyndhurst, S. Austral.,
  Australia 91 E2
Lyndon →, Australia .. 89 D1
Lyndonville, N.Y., U.S.A. 106 C6
Lyndonville, Vt., U.S.A. 107 B12
Lyngdal, Norway 10 F9
Lyngen, Norway 8 B19
Lynher Reef, Australia . 88 C3
Lynn, U.S.A. 107 D14
Lynn Canal, U.S.A. ... 100 B1
Lynn Lake, Canada 101 B8
Lynnwood, U.S.A. 112 C4
Lynton, U.K. 13 F4
Lyntupy, Belarus 9 J22
Lynx L., Canada 101 A7
Lyø, Denmark 11 J4
Lyon, France 27 C8
Lyonnais, France 27 C8
Lyons = Lyon, France .. 27 C8
Lyons, Colo., U.S.A. .. 108 E2
Lyons, Ga., U.S.A. ... 105 J4
Lyons, Kans., U.S.A. .. 108 F5
Lyons, N.Y., U.S.A. .. 106 C4
Lyozna, Belarus 40 E6
Lyrestad, Sweden 11 F8
Lys = Leie →, Belgium . 25 A10
Lysekil, Sweden 11 F5
Lyskovo, Russia 42 B7
Lyss, Switz. 22 B4
Lysychansk, Ukraine .. 41 H10
Lytle, U.S.A. 109 L5
Lyttelton, N.Z. 87 K4
Lytton, Canada 100 C4
Lyuban, Russia 40 C6
Lyubertsy, Russia 42 C4
Lyubim, Russia 42 A5
Lyuboml, Ukraine 41 G3
Lyubotyn, Ukraine 41 H8
Lyubytino, Russia 40 C7
Lyudinovo, Russia 42 D2

M

Ma →, Vietnam 58 C5
Ma'adaba, Jordan 69 E4
Maamba, Zambia 84 B4
Ma'ān, Jordan 69 E4
Ma'ān □, Jordan 69 F5
Maanselkä, Finland ... 8 C23
Ma'anshan, China 53 B12
Maarheeze, Neths. 17 F7
Maarianhamina, Finland . 9 F18
Maarn, Neths. 16 D6
Maarssen, Neths. 16 D6
Maartensdijk, Neths. .. 16 D6
Maas →, Neths. 16 E5
Maasbracht, Belgium .. 17 F7
Maasbree, Neths. 17 F8
Maasdam, Neths. 16 E5
Maasdijk, Neths. 16 E4
Maaseik, Belgium 17 F7
Maasland, Neths. 16 E4
Maasniel, Neths. 17 F8
Maassluis, Neths. 16 E4
Maastricht, Neths. ... 17 G7
Maave, Mozam. 85 C5
Mabaruma, Guyana 121 B6
Mabel L., Canada 100 C5
Mabenge, Zaïre 82 B1
Mabian, China 52 C4
Mablethorpe, U.K. 12 D8
Maboma, Zaïre 82 B2
Mabrouk, Mali 79 B4
Mabton, U.S.A. 110 C3
Mac Bac, Vietnam 59 H6
Macachín, Argentina .. 126 D3
Macaé, Brazil 123 F3
Macaíba, Brazil 122 C4
Macajuba, Brazil 123 D3
McAlester, U.S.A. 109 H7
McAllen, U.S.A. 109 M5
Macamic, Canada 98 C4
Macao = Macau ■, China 53 F9
Macão, Portugal 31 F3
Macapá, Brazil 121 C7
Macará, Ecuador 120 D2
Macarani, Brazil 123 E3
Macarena, Serranía de la,
  Colombia 120 C3
McArthur →, Australia . 90 B2
McArthur, Port, Australia 90 B2
McArthur River, Australia 90 B2

Macas, Ecuador 120 D2
Macate, Peru 124 B2
Macau, Brazil 122 C4
Macau ■, China 53 F9
Macaúbas, Brazil 123 D3
Macaya →, Colombia .. 120 C3
McBride, Canada 100 C4
McCall, U.S.A. 110 D5
McCamey, U.S.A. 109 K3
McCammon, U.S.A. 110 E7
McCauley I., Canada .. 100 C2
McCleary, U.S.A. 112 C3
Macclesfield, U.K. ... 12 D5
McClintock, Canada ... 101 B10
M'Clintock Chan., Canada 96 A9
McClintock Ra., Australia 88 C4
McCloud, U.S.A. 110 F2
McCluer I., Australia . 88 B5
McClure, U.S.A. 106 F7
McClure, L., U.S.A. .. 112 H6
M'Clure Str., Canada . 4 B2
McClusky, U.S.A. 108 B4
McComb, U.S.A. 109 K9
McConaughy, L., U.S.A. 108 E4
McCook, U.S.A. 108 E4
McCullough Mt., U.S.A. 113 K11
McCusker →, Canada .. 101 B7
McDame, Canada 100 B3
McDermitt, U.S.A. 110 F5
Macdonald, L., Australia 88 D4
McDonald Is., Ind. Oc. 3 G13
Macdonnell Ras., Australia 88 D5
McDouall Peak, Australia 91 D1
Macdougall L., Canada . 96 B10
MacDowell L., Canada . 98 B1
Maceda, Spain 30 C3
Macedonia ■, Europe .. 39 H4
Maceió, Brazil 122 C4
Maceira, Portugal 31 F2
Macenta, Guinea 78 D3
Macerata, Italy 33 E10
McFarland, U.S.A. 113 K7
McFarlane →, Canada . 101 B7
Macfarlane, L., Australia 91 E2
McGehee, U.S.A. 109 J9
McGill, U.S.A. 110 G6
Macgillycuddy's Reeks,
  Ireland 15 D2
MacGregor, Canada 101 D9
McGregor, U.S.A. 108 D9
McGregor →, Canada .. 100 B4
McGregor Ra., Australia 91 D3
Mach, Pakistan 60 E5
Māch Kowr, Iran 65 E9
Machacalis, Brazil ... 123 E3
Machado = Jiparaná →,
  Brazil 125 B5
Machagai, Argentina .. 126 B3
Machakos, Kenya 82 C4
Machakos □, Kenya 82 C4
Machala, Ecuador 120 D2
Machanga, Mozam. 85 C6
Machattie, L., Australia 90 C2
Machava, Mozam. 85 D5
Machece, Mozam. 83 F4
Machecoul, France 24 F5
Machelen, Belgium 17 G4
Macheng, China 53 B10
Machevna, Russia 45 C18
Machezo, Spain 31 F6
Machias, U.S.A. 99 D6
Machichaco, C., Spain . 28 B2
Machichi →, Canada .. 101 B10
Machico, Madeira 36 D3
Machilipatnam, India . 61 L12
Machiques, Venezuela . 120 A3
Machupicchu, Peru 124 C3
Machynlleth, U.K. 13 E4
McIlwraith Ra., Australia 90 A3
Macina, Mali 78 C4
McIntosh, U.S.A. 108 C4
McIntosh L., Canada .. 101 B8
Macintosh Ra., Australia 89 E4
Macintyre →, Australia 91 D5
Macizo Galaico, Spain . 30 C3
Mackay, Australia 90 C4
Mackay, U.S.A. 110 E7
MacKay →, Canada ... 100 B6
Mackay, L., Australia . 88 D4
McKay Ra., Australia . 88 D3
McKeesport, U.S.A. ... 106 F5
McKenna, U.S.A. 112 C4
Mackenzie, Canada 100 B4
Mackenzie, Guyana 121 B6
McKenzie, U.S.A. 105 G1
Mackenzie →, Australia 90 C4
Mackenzie →, Canada . 96 B6
McKenzie →, U.S.A. .. 110 D2
Mackenzie Bay, Canada . 4 B1
Mackenzie City = Linden,
  Guyana 121 B6
Mackenzie Highway,
  Canada 100 B5
Mackenzie Mts., Canada 96 B6
Mackinaw City, U.S.A. . 104 C3
McKinlay, Australia .. 90 C3
McKinlay →, Australia 90 C3
McKinley, Mt., U.S.A. . 96 B4
McKinley Sea, Arctic .. 4 A7
McKinney, U.S.A. 109 J6
Mackinnon Road, Kenya . 82 C4
Macksville, Australia . 91 E5
McLaughlin, U.S.A. ... 108 C4
Maclean, Australia ... 91 D5
McLean, U.S.A. 109 H4

McLeansboro, U.S.A. .. 108 F10
Maclear, S. Africa ... 85 E4
Macleay →, Australia . 91 E5
McLennan, Canada 100 B5
MacLeod, B., Canada .. 101 A7
McLeod, L., Australia . 89 D1
MacLeod Lake, Canada . 100 C4
McLoughlin, Mt., U.S.A. 110 E2
McLure, Canada 100 C4
McMechen, U.S.A. 106 G4
McMillan, L., U.S.A. . 109 J2
McMinnville, Oreg., U.S.A. 110 D2
McMinnville, Tenn.,
  U.S.A. 105 H3
McMorran, Canada 101 C7
McMurdo Sd., Antarctica 5 D11
McMurray = Fort
  McMurray, Canada ... 100 B6
McMurray, U.S.A. 112 B4
McNary, U.S.A. 111 J9
MacNutt, Canada 101 C8
Macodoene, Mozam. 85 C6
Macomb, U.S.A. 108 E9
Macomer, Italy 34 B1
Mâcon, France 27 B8
Macon, Ga., U.S.A. ... 105 J4
Macon, Miss., U.S.A. . 105 J1
Macon, Mo., U.S.A. ... 108 F8
Macondo, Angola 81 G4
Macossa, Mozam. 83 F3
Macoun L., Canada 101 B8
Macovane, Mozam. 85 C6
McPherson, U.S.A. 108 F6
McPherson Pk., U.S.A. . 113 L7
McPherson Ra., Australia 91 D5
Macquarie Harbour,
  Australia 90 G4
Macquarie Is., Pac. Oc. 92 N7
MacRobertson Land,
  Antarctica 5 D6
Macroom, Ireland 15 E3
Macroy, Australia 88 D2
MacTier, Canada 106 A5
Macubela, Mozam. 83 F4
Macugnaga, Italy 32 C4
Macuiza, Mozam. 83 F3
Macujer, Colombia 120 C3
Macusani, Peru 124 C3
Macuse, Mozam. 83 F4
Macuspana, Mexico 115 D6
Macusse, Angola 84 B3
McVille, U.S.A. 108 B5
Madadeni, S. Africa .. 85 D5
Madagali, Nigeria 79 C7
Madagascar ■, Africa . 85 C8
Madā'in Sālih, Si. Arabia 64 E3
Madama, Niger 73 D7
Madame I., Canada 99 C7
Madaoua, Niger 79 C6
Madara, Nigeria 79 C7
Madaripur, Bangla. ... 61 H17
Madauk, Burma 61 L20
Madawaska, Canada 106 A7
Madawaska →, Canada . 98 C4
Madaya, Burma 61 H20
Madbar, Sudan 77 F3
Maddaloni, Italy 35 A7
Made, Neths. 17 E5
Madeira, Atl. Oc. 36 D3
Madeira →, Brazil 121 D6
Madeleine, Is. de la,
  Canada 99 C7
Maden, Turkey 67 C8
Madera, U.S.A. 111 H3
Madha, India 60 L9
Madhubani, India 63 F12
Madhya Pradesh □, India 62 J7
Madian, China 53 A11
Madidi →, Bolivia 124 C4
Madikeri, India 60 N9
Madill, U.S.A. 109 H6
Madimba, Zaïre 80 E3
Ma'din, Syria 67 E8
Madīnat ash Sha'b, Yemen 68 E3
Madingou, Congo 80 E2
Madirovalo, Madag. ... 85 B8
Madison, Calif., U.S.A. 112 G5
Madison, Fla., U.S.A. . 105 K4
Madison, Ind., U.S.A. . 104 F3
Madison, Nebr., U.S.A. 108 E6
Madison, Ohio, U.S.A. . 106 E3
Madison, S. Dak., U.S.A. 108 D6
Madison, Wis., U.S.A. . 108 D10
Madison →, U.S.A. ... 110 D8
Madisonville, Ky., U.S.A. 104 G2
Madisonville, Tex., U.S.A. 109 K7
Madista, Botswana 84 C4
Madiun, Indonesia 57 G14
Madley, U.K. 13 E5
Madol, Sudan 77 F2
Madon →, France 25 D13
Madona, Latvia 9 H22
Madras = Tamil Nadu □,
  India 60 P10
Madras, India 60 N12
Madras, U.S.A. 110 D3
Madre, L., Mexico 115 B5
Madre, Sierra, Phil. . 55 C5
Madre de Dios □, Peru . 124 C3
Madre de Dios →, Bolivia 124 C4
Madre de Dios, I., Chile 128 D1
Madre del Sur, Sierra,
  Mexico 115 D5
Madre Occidental, Sierra,
  Mexico 114 B3

Madre Oriental, Sierra,
  Mexico 114 C4
Madri, India 62 G5
Madrid, Spain 30 E7
Madrid □, Spain 30 E7
Madridejos, Spain 31 F7
Madrigal de las Altas
  Torres, Spain 30 D6
Madrona, Sierra, Spain 31 G6
Madroñera, Spain 31 F5
Madu, Sudan 77 E2
Madura, Selat, Indonesia 57 G15
Madura Motel, Australia 89 F4
Madurai, India 60 Q11
Madurantakam, India .. 60 N11
Madzhalis, Russia 43 J8
Mae Chan, Thailand ... 58 B2
Mae Hong Son, Thailand 58 C2
Mae Khlong →, Thailand 58 F3
Mae Phrik, Thailand .. 58 D2
Mae Ramat, Thailand .. 58 D2
Mae Rim, Thailand 58 C2
Mae Sot, Thailand 58 D2
Mae Suai, Thailand ... 58 C2
Mae Tha, Thailand 58 C2
Maebashi, Japan 49 F9
Maella, Spain 28 D5
Măeruş, Romania 38 D8
Maesteg, U.K. 13 F4
Maestra, Sierra, Cuba . 116 B4
Maestrazgo, Mts. del, Spain 28 E4
Maevatanana, Madag. .. 85 B8
Mafeking = Mafikeng,
  S. Africa 84 D4
Mafeking, Canada 101 C8
Maféré, Ivory C. 78 D4
Mafeteng, Lesotho 84 D4
Maffe, Belgium 17 H6
Maffra, Australia 91 F4
Mafia I., Tanzania ... 82 D4
Mafikeng, S. Africa .. 84 D4
Mafra, Brazil 127 B6
Mafra, Portugal 31 G1
Mafungabusi Plateau,
  Zimbabwe 83 F2
Magadan, Russia 45 D16
Magadi, Kenya 82 C4
Magadi, L., Kenya 82 C4
Magaliesburg, S. Africa 85 D4
Magallanes □, Chile .. 128 D2
Magallanes, Estrecho de,
  Chile 128 D2
Magangué, Colombia ... 120 B3
Magaria, Niger 79 C6
Magburaka, S. Leone .. 78 D2
Magdalen Is. = Madeleine,
  Is. de la, Canada .. 99 C7
Magdalena, Argentina . 126 D4
Magdalena, Bolivia ... 125 C5
Magdalena, Malaysia .. 56 D5
Magdalena, Mexico 114 A2
Magdalena, U.S.A. 111 J10
Magdalena □, Colombia 120 A3
Magdalena →, Colombia 120 A3
Magdalena →, Mexico . 114 A2
Magdalena, B., Mexico . 114 C2
Magdalena, I., Chile .. 128 B2
Magdalena, Llano de la,
  Mexico 114 C2
Magdeburg, Germany ... 18 C7
Magdelaine Cays, Australia 90 B5
Magdub, Sudan 77 E2
Magee, U.S.A. 109 K10
Magee, I., U.K. 15 B6
Magelang, Indonesia .. 57 G14
Magellan's Str. =
  Magallanes, Estrecho de,
  Chile 128 D2
Magenta, Italy 32 C5
Magenta, L., Australia 89 F2
Magerøya, Norway 8 A21
Maggia, Switz. 23 D7
Maggia →, Switz. 23 D7
Maggiorasca, Mte., Italy 32 D6
Maggiore, L., Italy .. 32 C5
Maghama, Mauritania .. 78 B2
Magherafelt, U.K. 15 B5
Maghnia, Algeria 75 B4
Magione, Italy 33 E9
Magistralnyy, Russia . 45 D11
Magliano in Toscana, Italy 33 F8
Máglie, Italy 35 B11
Magnac-Laval, France . 26 B5
Magnetic Pole (North) =
  North Magnetic Pole,
  Canada 4 B2
Magnetic Pole (South) =
  South Magnetic Pole,
  Antarctica 5 C9
Magnitogorsk, Russia . 44 D6
Magnolia, Ark., U.S.A. 109 J8
Magnolia, Miss., U.S.A. 109 K9
Magnor, Norway 10 E6
Magny-en-Vexin, France 25 C8
Magog, Canada 99 C5
Magoro, Uganda 82 B3
Magosa = Famagusta,
  Cyprus 66 E5
Magouládhes, Greece .. 37 A3
Magoye, Zambia 83 F2
Magpie L., Canada 99 B7
Magrath, Canada 100 D6
Magro →, Spain 29 F4
Magrur, Wadi →, Sudan 77 D2
Magu □, Tanzania 82 C3
Maguan, China 52 F5
Maguarinho, C., Brazil 122 B2

Mağusa

Mağusa = Famagusta, Cyprus ... 66 E5
Maguse L., Canada ... 101 A9
Maguse Pt., Canada ... 101 A10
Magwe, Burma ... 61 J19
Maha Sarakham, Thailand ... 58 D4
Mahābād, Iran ... 67 D11
Mahabharat Lekh, Nepal ... 63 E9
Mahabo, Madag. ... 85 C7
Mahadeo Hills, India ... 62 H8
Mahagi, Zaïre ... 82 B3
Mahaicony, Guyana ... 121 B6
Mahajamba →, Madag. ... 85 B8
Mahajamba, Helodranon' i, Madag. ... 85 B8
Mahajan, India ... 62 E5
Mahajanga, Madag. ... 85 B8
Mahajanga □, Madag. ... 85 B8
Mahajilo →, Madag. ... 85 B8
Mahakam →, Indonesia ... 56 E5
Mahalapye, Botswana ... 84 C4
Maḥallāt, Iran ... 65 C6
Māhān, Iran ... 65 D8
Mahanadi →, India ... 61 J15
Mahanoro, Madag. ... 85 B8
Mahanoy City, U.S.A. ... 107 F8
Maharashtra □, India ... 60 J9
Maharès, Tunisia ... 75 B7
Mahari Mts., Tanzania ... 82 D2
Mahasham, W. →, Egypt ... 69 E3
Mahasolo, Madag. ... 85 B8
Mahattat ash Shīdīyah, Jordan ... 69 F4
Mahattat 'Unayzah, Jordan ... 69 E4
Mahaxay, Laos ... 58 D5
Mahbes, W. Sahara ... 74 C3
Mahbubnagar, India ... 60 L10
Maḥḍah, Oman ... 65 E7
Mahdia, Guyana ... 121 B6
Mahdia, Tunisia ... 75 A7
Mahe, India ... 63 C8
Mahenge, Tanzania ... 83 D4
Maheno, N.Z. ... 87 L3
Mahesana, India ... 62 H5
Mahia Pen., N.Z. ... 87 H6
Mahilyow, Belarus ... 40 F6
Mahirija, Morocco ... 75 B4
Mahmiya, Sudan ... 77 D3
Mahmud Kot, Pakistan ... 62 D4
Mahmudia, Romania ... 38 D12
Mahnomen, U.S.A. ... 108 B7
Mahoba, India ... 63 G8
Mahón, Spain ... 36 B11
Mahone Bay, Canada ... 99 D7
Mahuta, Nigeria ... 79 C5
Mai-Ndombe, L., Zaïre ... 80 E3
Mai-Sai, Thailand ... 58 B2
Maicao, Colombia ... 120 A3
Maîche, France ... 25 E13
Maici →, Brazil ... 125 B5
Maicurú →, Brazil ... 121 D7
Máida, Italy ... 35 D9
Maidan Khula, Afghan. ... 62 C3
Maidenhead, U.K. ... 13 F7
Maidi, Yemen ... 77 D5
Maidstone, Canada ... 101 C7
Maidstone, U.K. ... 13 F8
Maiduguri, Nigeria ... 79 C7
Maigo, Phil. ... 55 G5
Maigualida, Sierra, Venezuela ... 121 B4
Maigudo, Ethiopia ... 77 F4
Maijdi, Bangla. ... 61 H17
Maikala Ra., India ... 61 J12
Mailly-le-Camp, France ... 25 D11
Mailsi, Pakistan ... 62 E5
Main →, Germany ... 19 F4
Main →, U.K. ... 15 B5
Main Centre, Canada ... 101 C7
Mainburg, Germany ... 19 G7
Maine, France ... 24 E6
Maine □, U.S.A. ... 99 C6
Maine →, Ireland ... 15 D2
Maine-et-Loire □, France ... 24 E6
Maïne-Soroa, Niger ... 79 C7
Maingkwan, Burma ... 61 F20
Mainit, L., Phil. ... 55 G6
Mainland, Orkney, U.K. ... 14 C5
Mainland, Shet., U.K. ... 14 A7
Mainpuri, India ... 63 F8
Maintenon, France ... 25 D8
Maintirano, Madag. ... 85 B7
Mainvault, Belgium ... 17 G3
Mainz, Germany ... 19 F4
Maipú, Argentina ... 126 D4
Maiquetía, Venezuela ... 120 A4
Maira →, Italy ... 32 D4
Mairabari, India ... 61 F18
Mairipotaba, Brazil ... 123 E2
Maisí, Cuba ... 117 B5
Maisi, Pta. de, Cuba ... 117 B5
Maisse, France ... 25 D9
Maissin, Belgium ... 17 J6
Maitland, N.S.W., Australia ... 91 E5
Maitland, S. Austral., Australia ... 91 E2
Maitland →, Canada ... 106 C3
Maiyema, Nigeria ... 79 C5
Maiyuan, China ... 53 E11
Maíz, Is. del, Nic. ... 116 D3
Maizuru, Japan ... 49 G7
Majagual, Colombia ... 120 B3
Majalengka, Indonesia ... 57 G13
Majari →, Brazil ... 121 C5
Majene, Indonesia ... 57 E5
Majes →, Peru ... 124 D3

Maji, Ethiopia ... 77 F4
Majiang, China ... 52 D6
Major, Canada ... 101 C7
Majorca = Mallorca, Spain ... 36 B10
Majuriã, Brazil ... 125 B5
Maka, Senegal ... 78 C2
Makak, Cameroon ... 79 E7
Makale, Indonesia ... 57 E5
Makamba, Burundi ... 82 C2
Makari, Cameroon ... 80 B2
Makarikari = Makgadikgadi Salt Pans, Botswana ... 84 C4
Makarovo, Russia ... 45 D11
Makarska, Croatia ... 21 M7
Makaryev, Russia ... 42 B6
Makasar = Ujung Pandang, Indonesia ... 57 F5
Makasar, Selat, Indonesia ... 57 E5
Makasar, Str. of = Makasar, Selat, Indonesia ... 57 E5
Makat, Kazakhstan ... 44 E6
Makedonija = Macedonia ■, Europe ... 39 H4
Makena, U.S.A. ... 102 H16
Makeni, S. Leone ... 78 D2
Makeyevka = Makiyivka, Ukraine ... 41 H9
Makgadikgadi Salt Pans, Botswana ... 84 C4
Makhachkala, Russia ... 43 J8
Makharadze = Ozurgeti, Georgia ... 43 K5
Makhmūr, Iraq ... 67 E10
Makian, Indonesia ... 57 D7
Makindu, Kenya ... 82 C4
Makinsk, Kazakhstan ... 44 D8
Makiyivka, Ukraine ... 41 H9
Makkah, Si. Arabia ... 68 C2
Makkovik, Canada ... 99 A8
Makkum, Neths. ... 16 B6
Makó, Hungary ... 21 J10
Makokou, Gabon ... 80 D2
Makongo, Zaïre ... 82 B2
Makoro, Zaïre ... 82 B2
Makoua, Congo ... 80 E3
Makrá, Greece ... 39 N8
Makrai, India ... 60 H10
Makran Coast Range, Pakistan ... 60 G4
Makrana, India ... 62 F6
Makriyialos, Greece ... 37 D7
Maksimkin Yar, Russia ... 44 D9
Maktar, Tunisia ... 75 A6
Mākū, Iran ... 67 C11
Makumbi, Zaïre ... 80 F4
Makunda, Botswana ... 84 C3
Makurazaki, Japan ... 49 J5
Makurdi, Nigeria ... 79 D6
Makūyeh, Iran ... 65 D7
Makwassie, S. Africa ... 84 D4
Mal B., Ireland ... 15 D2
Mal i Nemërçkës, Albania ... 39 J3
Mala, Peru ... 124 C2
Mala, Pta., Panama ... 116 E3
Mala Belozërka, Ukraine ... 41 J8
Mala Kapela, Croatia ... 33 D12
Mala Vyska, Ukraine ... 41 H6
Malabang, Phil. ... 55 H6
Malabar Coast, India ... 60 P9
Malabo = Rey Malabo, Eq. Guin. ... 79 E6
Malacca, Str. of, Indonesia ... 59 L3
Malacky, Slovak Rep. ... 21 G7
Malad City, U.S.A. ... 110 E7
Maladzyechna, Belarus ... 40 E4
Málaga, Colombia ... 120 B3
Málaga, Spain ... 31 J6
Málaga, U.S.A. ... 109 J2
Málaga □, Spain ... 31 J6
Malagarasi, Tanzania ... 82 D3
Malagarasi →, Tanzania ... 82 D2
Malagón, Spain ... 31 F7
Malagón →, Spain ... 31 H3
Malaimbandy, Madag. ... 85 C8
Malakâl, Sudan ... 77 F3
Malakand, Pakistan ... 62 B4
Malakoff, U.S.A. ... 109 J7
Malamyzh, Russia ... 45 E14
Malang, Indonesia ... 57 G15
Malangen, Norway ... 8 B18
Malanje, Angola ... 80 F3
Mälaren, Sweden ... 10 E11
Malargüe, Argentina ... 126 D2
Malartic, Canada ... 98 C4
Malaryta, Belarus ... 41 G3
Malatya, Turkey ... 67 C8
Malawi ■, Africa ... 83 E3
Malawi, L., Africa ... 83 E3
Malay Pen., Asia ... 59 J3
Malaya Belozërka = Mala Belozërka, Ukraine ... 41 J8
Malaya Vishera, Russia ... 40 C7
Malaya Viska = Mala Vyska, Ukraine ... 41 H6
Malaybalay, Phil. ... 55 G6
Malāyer, Iran ... 67 E13
Malaysia ■, Asia ... 56 D4
Malbon, Australia ... 90 C3
Malbooma, Australia ... 91 E1
Malbork, Poland ... 20 A9
Malcésine, Italy ... 32 C7
Malchin, Germany ... 18 B8
Malchow, Germany ... 18 B8
Malcolm, Australia ... 89 E3

Malcolm, Pt., Australia ... 89 F3
Maldegem, Belgium ... 17 F2
Malden, Mass., U.S.A. ... 107 D13
Malden, Mo., U.S.A. ... 109 G10
Malden I., Kiribati ... 93 H12
Maldives ■, Ind. Oc. ... 47 J11
Maldonado, Uruguay ... 127 C5
Maldonado, Punta, Mexico ... 115 D5
Malè, Italy ... 32 B7
Maléa, Ákra, Greece ... 39 N6
Malegaon, India ... 60 J9
Malei, Mozam. ... 83 F4
Malek Kandī, Iran ... 67 D12
Malela, Zaïre ... 82 C2
Malema, Mozam. ... 83 E4
Máleme, Greece ... 37 D5
Malerkotla, India ... 62 D6
Máles, Greece ... 37 D7
Malesherbes, France ... 25 D9
Malestroit, France ... 24 E4
Malfa, Italy ... 35 D7
Malgobek, Russia ... 43 J7
Malgomaj, Sweden ... 8 D17
Malgrat, Spain ... 28 D7
Malha, Sudan ... 77 D2
Malheur →, U.S.A. ... 110 D5
Malheur L., U.S.A. ... 110 E4
Mali, Guinea ... 78 C2
Mali ■, Africa ... 78 B4
Mali →, Burma ... 61 G20
Mali Kanal, Serbia, Yug. ... 21 K9
Malibu, U.S.A. ... 113 L8
Malik, Indonesia ... 57 E6
Malili, Indonesia ... 57 E6
Malimba, Mts., Zaïre ... 82 D2
Malin Hd., Ireland ... 15 A4
Malindi, Kenya ... 82 C5
Malines = Mechelen, Belgium ... 17 F4
Malino, Indonesia ... 57 D6
Malinyi, Tanzania ... 83 D4
Malipo, China ... 52 F5
Maliqi, Albania ... 39 J3
Malita, Phil. ... 57 C7
Malkara, Turkey ... 66 B2
Malkinia Górna, Poland ... 20 C12
Malko Tŭrnovo, Bulgaria ... 39 H10
Mallacoota, Australia ... 91 F4
Mallacoota Inlet, Australia ... 91 F4
Mallaig, U.K. ... 14 E3
Mallawan, India ... 63 F9
Mallawi, Egypt ... 76 B3
Malleco □, Chile ... 128 A2
Mallemort, France ... 27 E9
Málles Venosta, Italy ... 32 B7
Mállia, Greece ... 37 D7
Mallión, Kólpos, Greece ... 37 D7
Mallorca, Spain ... 36 B10
Mallorytown, Canada ... 107 B9
Mallow, Ireland ... 15 D3
Malmberget, Sweden ... 8 C19
Malmédy, Belgium ... 17 H8
Malmesbury, S. Africa ... 84 E2
Malmö, Sweden ... 11 J6
Malmöhus län □, Sweden ... 11 J7
Malmslätt, Sweden ... 11 F9
Malmyzh, Russia ... 42 B10
Maloarkhangelsk, Russia ... 42 D3
Maloca, Brazil ... 121 C6
Maloja, Switz. ... 23 D9
Maloja, P., Switz. ... 23 D9
Malolos, Phil. ... 57 B6
Malombe L., Malawi ... 83 E4
Malone, U.S.A. ... 107 B10
Malong, China ... 52 E4
Mâløy, Norway ... 9 F11
Maloyaroslavets, Russia ... 42 C3
Malpartida, Spain ... 31 F4
Malpaso, Canary Is. ... 36 G1
Malpica, Spain ... 30 B2
Mals = Málles Venosta, Italy ... 32 B7
Malta, Brazil ... 122 C4
Malta, Idaho, U.S.A. ... 110 E7
Malta, Mont., U.S.A. ... 110 B10
Malta ■, Europe ... 37 D1
Malta Channel, Medit. S. ... 34 F6
Maltahöhe, Namibia ... 84 C2
Malters, Switz. ... 22 B6
Malton, Canada ... 106 C5
Malton, U.K. ... 12 C7
Maluku, Indonesia ... 57 E7
Maluku □, Indonesia ... 57 E7
Maluku Sea = Molucca Sea, Indonesia ... 57 E6
Malumfashi, Nigeria ... 79 C6
Malvan, India ... 60 L8
Malvern, U.S.A. ... 109 H8
Malvern Hills, U.K. ... 13 E5
Malvik, Norway ... 10 A4
Malvinas, Is. = Falkland Is. □, Atl. Oc. ... 128 D5
Malya, Tanzania ... 82 C3
Malyn, Ukraine ... 41 G5
Malyy Lyakhovskiy, Ostrov, Russia ... 45 B15
Malyy Nimnyr, Russia ... 45 D13
Mama, Russia ... 45 D12
Mamadysh, Russia ... 42 C10
Mamanguape, Brazil ... 122 C4
Mambasa, Zaïre ... 82 B2
Mambilima Falls, Zambia ... 83 E2
Mambirima, Zaïre ... 83 E2
Mambo, Tanzania ... 82 C4
Mambrui, Kenya ... 82 C5

Mamburao, Phil. ... 55 E4
Mameigwess L., Canada ... 98 B2
Mamer, Lux. ... 17 J8
Mamers, France ... 24 D7
Mamfe, Cameroon ... 79 D6
Mamiña, Chile ... 124 E4
Mámmola, Italy ... 35 D9
Mammoth, U.S.A. ... 111 K8
Mamoré →, Bolivia ... 125 C4
Mamou, Guinea ... 78 C2
Mampatá, Guinea-Biss. ... 78 C2
Mampong, Ghana ... 79 D4
Mamuil Malal, Paso, S. Amer. ... 128 A2
Mamuju, Indonesia ... 57 E5
Man, Ivory C. ... 78 D3
Man, I. of, U.K. ... 12 C3
Man Na, Burma ... 61 H20
Mana, Fr. Guiana ... 121 B7
Mana →, Fr. Guiana ... 121 B7
Måna →, Norway ... 10 E2
Manaar, G. of = Mannar, G. of, Asia ... 60 Q11
Manabí □, Ecuador ... 120 D1
Manacacías →, Colombia ... 120 C3
Manacapuru, Brazil ... 121 D5
Manacapuru →, Brazil ... 121 D5
Manacor, Spain ... 36 B10
Manado, Indonesia ... 57 D6
Manage, Belgium ... 17 G4
Managua, Nic. ... 116 D2
Managua, L., Nic. ... 116 D2
Manakara, Madag. ... 85 C8
Manama = Al Manāmah, Bahrain ... 65 E6
Manambao →, Madag. ... 85 B7
Manambato, Madag. ... 85 A8
Manambolo →, Madag. ... 85 B7
Manambolosy, Madag. ... 85 B8
Manamara, Madag. ... 85 B8
Mananara →, Madag. ... 85 C8
Mananjary, Madag. ... 85 C8
Manantenina, Madag. ... 85 C8
Manaos = Manaus, Brazil ... 121 D6
Manapire →, Venezuela ... 120 B4
Manapouri, N.Z. ... 87 L1
Manapouri, L., N.Z. ... 87 L1
Manas, China ... 54 B3
Manas →, India ... 61 F17
Manaslu, Nepal ... 63 E11
Manasquan, U.S.A. ... 107 F10
Manassa, U.S.A. ... 111 H11
Manaung, Burma ... 61 K18
Manaus, Brazil ... 121 D6
Manavgat, Turkey ... 66 D4
Manawan L., Canada ... 101 B8
Manay, Phil. ... 55 H7
Manbij, Syria ... 66 D7
Mancelona, U.S.A. ... 104 C3
Mancha Real, Spain ... 31 H7
Manche □, France ... 24 C5
Manchester, U.K. ... 12 D5
Manchester, Calif., U.S.A. ... 112 G3
Manchester, Conn., U.S.A. ... 107 E12
Manchester, Ga., U.S.A. ... 105 J3
Manchester, Iowa, U.S.A. ... 108 D9
Manchester, Ky., U.S.A. ... 104 G4
Manchester, N.H., U.S.A. ... 107 D13
Manchester, N.Y., U.S.A. ... 106 D7
Manchester, Vt., U.S.A. ... 107 C11
Manchester L., Canada ... 101 A7
Manchuria = Dongbei, China ... 51 D13
Manciano, Italy ... 33 F8
Mancifa, Ethiopia ... 77 F5
Mancora, Pta., Peru ... 124 A1
Mand →, Iran ... 65 D7
Manda, Chunya, Tanzania ... 82 D3
Manda, Ludewe, Tanzania ... 83 E3
Mandabé, Madag. ... 85 C7
Mandaguari, Brazil ... 127 A5
Mandah, Mongolia ... 50 B5
Mandal, Norway ... 9 G12
Mandalay, Burma ... 61 J20
Mandale = Mandalay, Burma ... 61 J20
Mandalgovi, Mongolia ... 50 B4
Mandalī, Iraq ... 67 F11
Mandan, U.S.A. ... 108 B4
Mandaon, Phil. ... 55 E5
Mandar, Teluk, Indonesia ... 57 E5
Mandas, Italy ... 34 C2
Mandasor = Mandsaur, India ... 62 G6
Mandaue, Phil. ... 55 F5
Mandelieu-la-Napoule, France ... 27 E10
Mandera, Kenya ... 82 B5
Mandera □, Kenya ... 82 B5
Manderfeld, Belgium ... 17 H8
Mandi, India ... 62 D7
Mandimba, Mozam. ... 83 E4
Mandioli, Indonesia ... 57 E7
Mandioré, L., S. Amer. ... 125 D6
Mandla, India ... 63 H9
Mandø, Denmark ... 11 J2
Mandoto, Madag. ... 85 B8
Mandoúdhion, Greece ... 39 L6
Mandra, Pakistan ... 62 C5
Mandrare →, Madag. ... 85 D8
Mandritsara, Madag. ... 85 B8
Mandsaur, India ... 62 G6
Mandurah, Australia ... 89 F2
Mandúria, Italy ... 35 B10
Mandvi, India ... 62 H3
Mandya, India ... 60 N10
Mandzai, Pakistan ... 62 D2

Mané, Burkina Faso ... 79 C4
Maneh, Iran ... 65 B8
Manengouba, Mts., Cameroon ... 79 D6
Maneroo, Australia ... 90 C3
Maneroo Cr. →, Australia ... 90 C3
Manfalût, Egypt ... 76 B3
Manfred, Australia ... 91 E3
Manfredónia, Italy ... 35 A8
Manfredónia, G. di, Italy ... 35 A9
Manga, Brazil ... 123 D3
Manga, Burkina Faso ... 79 C4
Manga, Niger ... 79 C7
Mangabeiras, Chapada das, Brazil ... 122 D2
Mangalia, Romania ... 38 F11
Mangalore, India ... 60 N9
Manganeses, Spain ... 30 D5
Mangaweka, N.Z. ... 87 H5
Manggar, Indonesia ... 56 E3
Manggawitu, Indonesia ... 57 E8
Mangkalihat, Tanjung, Indonesia ... 57 D5
Mangla Dam, Pakistan ... 63 C5
Manglares, C., Colombia ... 120 C2
Manglaur, India ... 62 E7
Mangnai, China ... 54 C4
Mango, Togo ... 79 C5
Mangoche, Malawi ... 83 E4
Mangoky →, Madag. ... 85 C7
Mangole, Indonesia ... 57 E7
Mangombe, Zaïre ... 82 C2
Mangonui, N.Z. ... 87 F4
Mangualde, Portugal ... 30 E3
Mangueigne, Chad ... 73 F9
Mangueira, L. da, Brazil ... 127 C5
Manguéni, Hamada, Niger ... 75 D7
Mangum, U.S.A. ... 109 H5
Mangyshlak Poluostrov, Kazakhstan ... 44 E6
Manhattan, U.S.A. ... 108 F6
Manhiça, Mozam. ... 85 D5
Manhuaçu, Brazil ... 123 F3
Manhumirim, Brazil ... 123 F3
Maní, Colombia ... 120 C3
Mania →, Madag. ... 85 B8
Maniago, Italy ... 33 B9
Manica, Mozam. ... 85 B5
Manica e Sofala □, Mozam. ... 85 B5
Manicaland □, Zimbabwe ... 83 F3
Manicoré, Brazil ... 125 B5
Manicoré →, Brazil ... 125 B5
Manicouagan →, Canada ... 99 C6
Manīfah, Si. Arabia ... 65 E6
Manifold, Australia ... 90 C5
Manifold, C., Australia ... 90 C5
Maniganggo, China ... 52 B2
Manigotagan, Canada ... 101 C9
Manihiki, Cook Is. ... 93 J11
Manika, Plateau de la, Zaïre ... 83 E2
Manila, Phil. ... 55 D4
Manila, U.S.A. ... 110 F9
Manila B., Phil. ... 55 D4
Manilla, Australia ... 91 E5
Manimpé, Mali ... 78 C3
Maningrida, Australia ... 90 A1
Manipur □, India ... 61 G18
Manipur →, Burma ... 61 H19
Manisa, Turkey ... 66 C2
Manistee, U.S.A. ... 104 C2
Manistee →, U.S.A. ... 104 C2
Manistique, U.S.A. ... 104 C2
Manito L., Canada ... 101 C7
Manitoba □, Canada ... 101 B9
Manitoba, L., Canada ... 101 C9
Manitou, Canada ... 101 D9
Manitou I., U.S.A. ... 98 C2
Manitou Is., U.S.A. ... 104 C2
Manitou L., Canada ... 99 B6
Manitou Springs, U.S.A. ... 108 F2
Manitoulin I., Canada ... 98 C3
Manitowaning, Canada ... 98 C3
Manitowoc, U.S.A. ... 104 C2
Manitsauá-Missu →, Brazil ... 125 C7
Manizales, Colombia ... 120 B2
Manja, Madag. ... 85 C7
Manjacaze, Mozam. ... 85 C5
Manjakandriana, Madag. ... 85 B8
Manjhand, Pakistan ... 62 G3
Manjil, Iran ... 65 B6
Manjimup, Australia ... 89 F2
Manjra →, India ... 60 K10
Mankato, Kans., U.S.A. ... 108 F5
Mankato, Minn., U.S.A. ... 108 C8
Mankayane, Swaziland ... 85 D5
Mankono, Ivory C. ... 78 D3
Mankota, Canada ... 101 D7
Manlay, Mongolia ... 50 B4
Manlleu, Spain ... 28 C7
Manly, Australia ... 91 E5
Manmad, India ... 60 J9
Mann Ras., Australia ... 89 E5
Manna, Indonesia ... 56 E2
Mannahill, Australia ... 91 E3
Mannar, Sri Lanka ... 60 Q11
Mannar, G. of, Asia ... 60 Q11
Mannar I., Sri Lanka ... 60 Q11
Männedorf, Switz. ... 23 B7
Mannheim, Germany ... 19 F4
Manning, Canada ... 100 B5
Manning, Oreg., U.S.A. ... 112 E3
Manning, S.C., U.S.A. ... 105 J5
Manning Prov. Park, Canada ... 100 D4
Mannington, U.S.A. ... 104 F5

Mannu →, Italy ... 34 C2
Mannu, C., Italy ... 34 B1
Mannum, Australia ... 91 E2
Mano, S. Leone ... 78 D2
Manoa, Bolivia ... 125 B4
Manokwari, Indonesia ... 57 E8
Manombo, Madag. ... 85 C7
Manono, Zaïre ... 82 D2
Manosque, France ... 27 E9
Manouane, L., Canada ... 99 B5
Manpojin, N. Korea ... 51 D14
Manresa, Spain ... 28 D6
Mansa, Gujarat, India ... 62 H5
Mansa, Punjab, India ... 62 E6
Mansa, Zambia ... 83 E2
Mansehra, Pakistan ... 62 B5
Mansel I., Canada ... 97 B11
Mansfield, Australia ... 91 F4
Mansfield, U.K. ... 12 D6
Mansfield, La., U.S.A. ... 109 J8
Mansfield, Mass., U.S.A. ... 107 D13
Mansfield, Ohio, U.S.A. ... 106 F2
Mansfield, Pa., U.S.A. ... 106 E7
Mansfield, Wash., U.S.A. ... 110 C4
Mansidão, Brazil ... 122 D3
Mansilla de las Mulas, Spain ... 30 C5
Mansle, France ... 26 C4
Manso →, Brazil ... 123 D2
Mansoa, Guinea-Biss. ... 78 C1
Manson Creek, Canada ... 100 B4
Mansoura, Algeria ... 75 A5
Manta, Ecuador ... 120 D1
Manta, B. de, Ecuador ... 120 D1
Mantalingajan, Mt., Phil. ... 55 G2
Mantare, Tanzania ... 82 C3
Manteca, U.S.A. ... 111 H3
Mantecal, Venezuela ... 120 B4
Mantena, Brazil ... 123 E3
Manteo, U.S.A. ... 105 H8
Mantes-la-Jolie, France ... 25 D8
Manthani, India ... 60 K11
Manthelan, France ... 24 E7
Manti, U.S.A. ... 110 G8
Mantiqueira, Serra da, Brazil ... 123 F3
Manton, U.S.A. ... 104 C3
Mantorp, Sweden ... 11 F9
Mántova, Italy ... 32 C7
Mänttä, Finland ... 9 E21
Mantua = Mántova, Italy ... 32 C7
Manturovo, Russia ... 42 A7
Manu, Peru ... 124 C3
Manu →, Peru ... 124 C3
Manua Is., Amer. Samoa ... 87 B14
Manuae, Cook Is. ... 93 J12
Manuel Alves →, Brazil ... 123 D2
Manuel Alves Grande →, Brazil ... 122 C2
Manuel Urbano, Brazil ... 124 B4
Manui, Indonesia ... 57 E6
Manuripi →, Bolivia ... 124 C4
Manville, U.S.A. ... 108 D2
Many, U.S.A. ... 109 K8
Manyara, L., Tanzania ... 82 C4
Manych →, Russia ... 43 G5
Manych-Gudilo, Ozero, Russia ... 43 G6
Manyonga →, Tanzania ... 82 C3
Manyoni, Tanzania ... 82 D3
Manyoni □, Tanzania ... 82 D3
Manzai, Pakistan ... 62 C4
Manzala, Bahra el, Egypt ... 76 H7
Manzanares, Spain ... 29 F1
Manzaneda, Cabeza de, Spain ... 30 C3
Manzanillo, Cuba ... 116 B4
Manzanillo, Mexico ... 114 D4
Manzanillo, Pta., Panama ... 116 E4
Manzano Mts., U.S.A. ... 111 J10
Manzariyeh, Iran ... 65 C6
Manzhouli, China ... 54 B6
Manzini, Swaziland ... 85 D5
Mao, Chad ... 73 F8
Maoke, Pegunungan, Indonesia ... 57 E9
Maolin, China ... 51 C12
Maoming, China ... 53 G8
Maowen, China ... 52 B4
Maoxing, China ... 51 B13
Mapam Yumco, China ... 54 C3
Mapastepec, Mexico ... 115 D6
Mapia, Kepulauan, Indonesia ... 57 D8
Mapimí, Mexico ... 114 B4
Mapimí, Bolsón de, Mexico ... 114 B4
Maping, China ... 53 B9
Mapinga, Tanzania ... 82 D4
Mapinhane, Mozam. ... 85 C6
Mapire, Venezuela ... 121 B5
Maple Creek, Canada ... 101 D7
Maple Valley, U.S.A. ... 112 C4
Mapleton, U.S.A. ... 110 D2
Mapuera →, Brazil ... 121 D6
Maputo, Mozam. ... 85 D5
Maputo, B. de, Mozam. ... 85 D5
Maqiaohe, China ... 51 B16
Maqnā, Si. Arabia ... 64 D2
Maqteïr, Mauritania ... 74 D2
Maquela do Zombo, Angola ... 80 F3
Maquinchao, Argentina ... 128 B3
Maquoketa, U.S.A. ... 108 D9
Mar, Serra do, Brazil ... 127 B6
Mar Chiquita, L., Argentina ... 126 C3
Mar del Plata, Argentina ... 126 D4

Mar Menor, Spain ... 29 H4
Mara, Guyana ... 121 B6
Mara, Tanzania ... 82 C3
Mara □, Tanzania ... 82 C3
Maraã, Brazil ... 120 D4
Marabá, Brazil ... 122 C2
Maracá, I. de, Brazil ... 121 C7
Maracaibo, Venezuela ... 120 A3
Maracaibo, L. de, Venezuela ... 120 B3
Maracaju, Brazil ... 127 A4
Maracajú, Serra de, Brazil ... 125 E6
Maracanã, Brazil ... 122 B2
Maracás, Brazil ... 123 D3
Maracay, Venezuela ... 120 A4
Marādah, Libya ... 73 C8
Maradi, Niger ... 79 C6
Maradun, Nigeria ... 79 C6
Marāgheh, Iran ... 67 D12
Maragogipe, Brazil ... 123 D4
Marāh, Si. Arabia ... 64 E5
Marajó, B. de, Brazil ... 122 B2
Marajó, I. de, Brazil ... 122 B2
Marākand, Iran ... 64 B5
Maralal, Kenya ... 82 B4
Maralinga, Australia ... 89 F5
Marama, Australia ... 91 F3
Marampa, S. Leone ... 78 D2
Maran, Malaysia ... 59 L4
Marana, U.S.A. ... 111 K8
Maranboy, Australia ... 88 B5
Maranchón, Spain ... 28 D2
Marand, Iran ... 67 C11
Marang, Malaysia ... 59 K4
Maranguape, Brazil ... 122 B4
Maranhão = São Luís, Brazil ... 122 B3
Maranhão □, Brazil ... 122 B2
Marano, L. di, Italy ... 33 C10
Maranoa →, Australia ... 91 D4
Marañón →, Peru ... 124 A3
Marão, Mozam. ... 85 C5
Marapi →, Brazil ... 121 C6
Marari, Brazil ... 124 B4
Maraş = Kahramanmaraş, Turkey ... 66 D7
Mărăşeşti, Romania ... 38 D10
Maratea, Italy ... 35 C8
Marateca, Portugal ... 31 G2
Marathasa □, Cyprus ... 37 E11
Marathókambos, Greece ... 39 M9
Marathon, Australia ... 90 C3
Marathon, Canada ... 98 C2
Marathon, Greece ... 39 L6
Marathon, N.Y., U.S.A. ... 107 D8
Marathon, Tex., U.S.A. ... 109 K3
Marathóvouno, Cyprus ... 37 D12
Maratua, Indonesia ... 57 D5
Maraú, Brazil ... 123 D4
Maravatío, Mexico ... 114 D4
Marawi City, Phil. ... 55 G6
Marāwih, U.A.E. ... 65 E7
Marbella, Spain ... 31 J6
Marble Bar, Australia ... 88 D2
Marble Falls, U.S.A. ... 109 K5
Marblehead, U.S.A. ... 107 D14
Marburg, Germany ... 18 E4
Marby, Sweden ... 10 A8
Marcal →, Hungary ... 21 H7
Marcapata, Peru ... 124 C3
Marcaria, Italy ... 32 C7
March, U.K. ... 13 E8
Marchand = Rommani, Morocco ... 74 B3
Marche, France ... 26 B5
Marche □, Italy ... 33 E10
Marche-en-Famenne, Belgium ... 17 H6
Marchena, Spain ... 31 H5
Marches = Marche □, Italy ... 33 E10
Marciana Marina, Italy ... 32 F7
Marcianise, Italy ... 35 A7
Marcigny, France ... 27 B8
Marcillat-en-Combraille, France ... 26 B6
Marcinelle, Belgium ... 17 H4
Marck, France ... 25 B8
Marckolsheim, France ... 25 D14
Marcona, Peru ... 124 D2
Marcos Juárez, Argentina ... 126 C3
Marcus I. = Minami-Tori-Shima, Pac. Oc. ... 92 E7
Marcus Necker Ridge, Pac. Oc. ... 92 F9
Marcy, Mt., U.S.A. ... 107 B11
Mardan, Pakistan ... 62 B5
Mardie, Australia ... 88 D2
Mardin, Turkey ... 67 D9
Marechal Deodoro, Brazil ... 122 C4
Maree, L., U.K. ... 14 D3
Mareeba, Australia ... 90 B4
Marek = Stanke Dimitrov, Bulgaria ... 38 G6
Marek, Indonesia ... 57 E6
Maremma, Italy ... 32 F8
Maréna, Mali ... 78 C3
Marenberg, Slovenia ... 33 B12
Marengo, U.S.A. ... 108 E8
Marennes, France ... 26 C2
Marenyi, Kenya ... 82 C4
Marerano, Madag. ... 85 C7
Maréttimo, Italy ... 34 E5
Mareuil-sur-Lay, France ... 24 B2
Marfa, U.S.A. ... 109 K2
Marfa Pt., Malta ... 37 D1
Marganets = Marhanets, Ukraine ... 41 J8

Margaret →, Australia ... 88 C4
Margaret Bay, Canada ... 100 C3
Margaret L., Canada ... 100 B5
Margaret River, Australia ... 88 C4
Margarita, I. de, Venezuela ... 121 A5
Margarítion, Greece ... 39 K3
Margaritovo, Russia ... 48 C7
Margate, S. Africa ... 85 E5
Margate, U.K. ... 13 F9
Margelan = Marghilon, Uzbekistan ... 44 E8
Margeride, Mts. de la, France ... 26 D7
Margherita di Savola, Italy ... 35 A9
Marghilon, Uzbekistan ... 44 E8
Margosatubig, Phil. ... 55 H5
Marguerite, Canada ... 100 C4
Marhanets, Ukraine ... 41 J8
Marhoum, Algeria ... 75 B4
Mari El □, Russia ... 42 B8
Mari Republic = Mari El □, Russia ... 42 B8
María Elena, Chile ... 126 A2
María Grande, Argentina ... 126 C4
Maria I., N. Terr., Australia ... 90 A2
Maria I., Tas., Australia ... 90 G4
Maria van Diemen, C., N.Z. ... 87 F4
Mariager, Denmark ... 11 H4
Mariager Fjord, Denmark ... 11 H4
Mariakani, Kenya ... 82 C4
Marian L., Canada ... 100 A5
Mariana Trench, Pac. Oc. ... 92 F6
Marianao, Cuba ... 116 B3
Marianna, Ark., U.S.A. ... 109 H9
Marianna, Fla., U.S.A. ... 105 K3
Mariánské Lázně, Czech. ... 20 F2
Marias →, U.S.A. ... 110 C8
Mariato, Punta, Panama ... 116 E3
Mariazell, Austria ... 21 H5
Ma'rib, Yemen ... 68 D4
Maribo, Denmark ... 11 K5
Maribor, Slovenia ... 33 B12
Marico →, Africa ... 84 C4
Maricopa, Ariz., U.S.A. ... 111 K7
Maricopa, Calif., U.S.A. ... 113 K7
Maricourt, Canada ... 97 C12
Marīdī, Sudan ... 77 G2
Maridi, Wadi →, Sudan ... 77 F2
Marié →, Brazil ... 120 D4
Marie Byrd Land, Antarctica ... 5 D14
Marie-Galante, Guadeloupe ... 117 C7
Mariecourt = Kangiqsujuaq, Canada ... 97 B12
Mariefred, Sweden ... 10 E11
Marienbad = Mariánské Lázně, Czech. ... 20 F2
Marienberg, Germany ... 18 E9
Marienberg, Neths. ... 16 D9
Marienbourg, Belgium ... 17 H5
Mariental, Namibia ... 84 C2
Marienville, U.S.A. ... 106 E5
Mariestad, Sweden ... 11 F7
Marietta, Ga., U.S.A. ... 105 J3
Marietta, Ohio, U.S.A. ... 104 F5
Marieville, Canada ... 107 A11
Marignane, France ... 27 E9
Marihatag, Phil. ... 55 G7
Mariinsk, Russia ... 44 D9
Mariinskiy Posad, Russia ... 42 B8
Marijampolė, Lithuania ... 9 J20
Marília, Brazil ... 127 A5
Marillana, Australia ... 88 D2
Marín, Spain ... 30 C2
Marina, U.S.A. ... 112 J5
Marina di Cirò, Italy ... 35 C10
Marina Plains, Australia ... 90 A3
Marinduque, Phil. ... 55 E5
Marine City, U.S.A. ... 104 D4
Marineo, Italy ... 34 E6
Marinette, U.S.A. ... 104 C2
Maringá, Brazil ... 127 A5
Marinha Grande, Portugal ... 31 F2
Marion, Ala., U.S.A. ... 105 J2
Marion, Ill., U.S.A. ... 109 G10
Marion, Ind., U.S.A. ... 104 E3
Marion, Iowa, U.S.A. ... 108 D9
Marion, Kans., U.S.A. ... 108 F6
Marion, Mich., U.S.A. ... 104 C3
Marion, N.C., U.S.A. ... 105 H4
Marion, Ohio, U.S.A. ... 104 E4
Marion, S.C., U.S.A. ... 105 H6
Marion, Va., U.S.A. ... 105 G5
Marion, L., U.S.A. ... 105 J5
Maripa, Venezuela ... 121 B4
Maripasoula, Fr. Guiana ... 121 C7
Mariposa, U.S.A. ... 111 H4
Mariscal Estigarribia, Paraguay ... 126 A3
Maritime Alps = Maritimes, Alpes, Europe ... 27 D11
Maritimes, Alpes, Europe ... 27 D11
Maritsa = Évros →, Bulgaria ... 66 B2
Maritsa, Greece ... 37 C10
Mariupol, Ukraine ... 41 J9
Marīvān, Iran ... 67 E12
Markam, China ... 52 C2
Markazī □, Iran ... 65 C6
Markdale, Canada ... 106 B4
Marke, Belgium ... 17 G2
Marked Tree, U.S.A. ... 109 H9
Markelsdorfer Huk, Germany ... 18 A6

Marken, Neths. ... 16 D6
Markermeer, Neths. ... 16 C6
Market Drayton, U.K. ... 12 E5
Market Harborough, U.K. ... 13 E7
Markham, Canada ... 106 C5
Markham, Mt., Antarctica ... 5 E11
Markham L., Canada ... 101 A8
Marki, Poland ... 20 C11
Markleeville, U.S.A. ... 112 G7
Markovo, Russia ... 45 C17
Markoye, Burkina Faso ... 79 C5
Marks, Russia ... 42 E8
Marksville, U.S.A. ... 109 K8
Markt Schwaben, Germany ... 19 G7
Marktredwitz, Germany ... 19 E8
Marla, Australia ... 91 D1
Marlboro, U.S.A. ... 107 D13
Marlborough, Australia ... 90 C4
Marlborough Downs, U.K. ... 13 F6
Marle, France ... 25 C10
Marlin, U.S.A. ... 109 K6
Marlow, Germany ... 18 A8
Marlow, U.S.A. ... 109 H6
Marly-le-Grand, Switz. ... 22 C4
Marmagao, India ... 60 M8
Marmande, France ... 26 D4
Marmara, Turkey ... 66 B2
Marmara, Sea of = Marmara Denizi, Turkey ... 66 B3
Marmara Denizi, Turkey ... 66 B3
Marmaris, Turkey ... 66 D3
Marmarth, U.S.A. ... 108 B3
Marmelos →, Brazil ... 125 B5
Marmion, Mt., Australia ... 89 E2
Marmion L., Canada ... 98 C1
Marmolada, Mte., Italy ... 33 B8
Marmolejo, Spain ... 31 G6
Marmora, Canada ... 98 D4
Marnay, France ... 25 E12
Marne □, Germany ... 18 B5
Marne □, France ... 25 D11
Marne →, France ... 25 D9
Marneuli, Georgia ... 43 K7
Maroa, Venezuela ... 120 C4
Maroala, Madag. ... 85 B8
Maroantsetra, Madag. ... 85 B8
Maromandia, Madag. ... 85 A8
Marondera, Zimbabwe ... 83 F3
Maroni →, Fr. Guiana ... 121 B7
Maronne →, France ... 26 C5
Maroochydore, Australia ... 91 D5
Maroona, Australia ... 91 F3
Maros →, Hungary ... 21 J10
Marosakoa, Madag. ... 85 B8
Marostica, Italy ... 33 C8
Maroua, Cameroon ... 79 C7
Marovoay, Madag. ... 85 B8
Marowijne □, Surinam ... 121 C7
Marowijne →, Surinam ... 121 B7
Marquard, S. Africa ... 84 D4
Marqueira, Portugal ... 31 G1
Marquesas Is. = Marquises, Is., Pac. Oc. ... 93 H14
Marquette, U.S.A. ... 104 B2
Marquise, France ... 25 B8
Marquises, Is., Pac. Oc. ... 93 H14
Marra, Gebel, Sudan ... 77 F2
Marracuene, Mozam. ... 85 D5
Marradi, Italy ... 33 D8
Marrakech, Morocco ... 74 B3
Marrawah, Australia ... 90 G3
Marrecas, Serra das, Brazil ... 122 C3
Marree, Australia ... 91 D2
Marrilla, Australia ... 88 D1
Marrimane, Mozam. ... 85 C5
Marromeu, Mozam. ... 85 B6
Marroquí, Punta, Spain ... 31 K5
Marrowie Cr. →, Australia ... 91 E4
Marrubane, Mozam. ... 83 F4
Marrum, Neths. ... 16 B7
Marrupa, Mozam. ... 83 E4
Marsá Matrûh, Egypt ... 76 A2
Marsá Susah, Libya ... 73 B9
Marsabit, Kenya ... 82 B4
Marsabit □, Kenya ... 82 B4
Marsala, Italy ... 34 E5
Marsalforn, Malta ... 37 C1
Marsberg, Germany ... 18 D4
Marsciano, Italy ... 33 F9
Marsden, Australia ... 91 E4
Marsdiep, Neths. ... 16 C5
Marseillan, France ... 26 E7
Marseille, France ... 27 E9
Marseilles = Marseille, France ... 27 E9
Marsh I., U.S.A. ... 109 L9
Marsh L., U.S.A. ... 108 C6
Marshall, Liberia ... 78 D2
Marshall, Ark., U.S.A. ... 109 H8
Marshall, Mich., U.S.A. ... 104 D3
Marshall, Minn., U.S.A. ... 108 C7
Marshall, Mo., U.S.A. ... 108 F8
Marshall, Tex., U.S.A. ... 109 J7
Marshall →, Australia ... 90 C2
Marshall Is. ■, Pac. Oc. ... 92 G9
Marshalltown, U.S.A. ... 108 D8
Marshfield, Mo., U.S.A. ... 109 G8
Marshfield, Wis., U.S.A. ... 108 C9
Marshün, Iran ... 65 B6
Mársico Nuovo, Italy ... 35 B8
Märsta, Sweden ... 10 E11
Marstal, Denmark ... 11 K4
Marstrand, Sweden ... 11 G5
Mart, U.S.A. ... 109 K6
Marta →, Italy ... 33 F8
Martaban, Burma ... 61 L20

Martaban, G. of, Burma ... 61 L20
Martano, Italy ... 35 B11
Martapura, Kalimantan, Indonesia ... 56 E4
Martapura, Sumatera, Indonesia ... 56 E2
Marte, Nigeria ... 79 C7
Martel, France ... 26 D5
Martelange, Belgium ... 17 J7
Martés, Sierra, Spain ... 29 F4
Martha's Vineyard, U.S.A. ... 107 E14
Martigné-Ferchaud, France ... 24 E5
Martigny, Switz. ... 22 D4
Martigues, France ... 27 E9
Martil, Morocco ... 74 A3
Martin, Slovak Rep. ... 20 F8
Martin, S. Dak., U.S.A. ... 108 D4
Martin, Tenn., U.S.A. ... 109 G10
Martín →, Spain ... 28 D4
Martin L., U.S.A. ... 105 J3
Martina, Switz. ... 23 C10
Martina Franca, Italy ... 35 B10
Martinborough, N.Z. ... 87 J5
Martinez, U.S.A. ... 112 G4
Martinho Campos, Brazil ... 123 E2
Martinique ■, W. Indies ... 117 D7
Martinique Passage, W. Indies ... 117 C7
Martínon, Greece ... 39 L6
Martinópolis, Brazil ... 127 A5
Martins Ferry, U.S.A. ... 106 F4
Martinsburg, Pa., U.S.A. ... 106 F6
Martinsburg, W. Va., U.S.A. ... 104 F7
Martinsville, Ind., U.S.A. ... 104 F2
Martinsville, Va., U.S.A. ... 105 G6
Marton, N.Z. ... 87 J5
Martorell, Spain ... 28 D6
Martos, Spain ... 31 H7
Martuni, Armenia ... 43 K7
Maru, Nigeria ... 79 C6
Marudi, Malaysia ... 56 D4
Ma'ruf, Afghan. ... 60 D5
Marugame, Japan ... 49 G6
Maruim, Brazil ... 122 D4
Marulan, Australia ... 91 E5
Marum, Neths. ... 16 B8
Marunga, Angola ... 84 B3
Marungu, Mts., Zaïre ... 82 D2
Marvast, Iran ... 65 D7
Marvejols, France ... 26 D7
Marwar, India ... 62 G5
Mary, Turkmenistan ... 44 F7
Mary Frances L., Canada ... 101 A7
Mary Kathleen, Australia ... 90 C2
Maryborough = Port Laoise, Ireland ... 15 C4
Maryborough, Queens., Australia ... 91 D5
Maryborough, Vic., Australia ... 91 F3
Maryfield, Canada ... 101 D8
Maryland □, U.S.A. ... 104 F7
Maryland Junction, Zimbabwe ... 83 F3
Maryport, U.K. ... 12 C4
Mary's Harbour, Canada ... 99 B8
Marystown, Canada ... 99 C8
Marysvale, U.S.A. ... 111 G7
Marysville, Canada ... 100 D5
Marysville, Calif., U.S.A. ... 112 F5
Marysville, Kans., U.S.A. ... 108 F6
Marysville, Mich., U.S.A. ... 106 D2
Marysville, Ohio, U.S.A. ... 104 E4
Marysville, Wash., U.S.A. ... 112 B4
Maryvale, Australia ... 91 D5
Maryville, U.S.A. ... 105 H4
Marzo, Punta, Colombia ... 120 B2
Marzûq, Libya ... 73 C7
Masahunga, Tanzania ... 82 C3
Masai, Malaysia ... 59 M4
Masai Steppe, Tanzania ... 82 C4
Masaka, Uganda ... 82 C3
Masalembo, Kepulauan, Indonesia ... 56 F4
Masalima, Kepulauan, Indonesia ... 56 F5
Masallı, Azerbaijan ... 67 C13
Masamba, Indonesia ... 57 E6
Masan, S. Korea ... 51 G15
Masanasa, Spain ... 29 F4
Masasi, Tanzania ... 83 E4
Masasi □, Tanzania ... 83 E4
Masaya, Nic. ... 116 D2
Masba, Nigeria ... 79 C7
Masbate, Phil. ... 55 E5
Mascara, Algeria ... 75 A5
Mascota, Mexico ... 114 C4
Masela, Indonesia ... 57 F7
Maseru, Lesotho ... 84 D4
Mashaba, Zimbabwe ... 83 G3
Mashābih, Si. Arabia ... 64 E3
Mashan, China ... 52 F7
Mashhad, Iran ... 65 B8
Mashi, Nigeria ... 79 C6
Mashī, Nigeria ... 65 D8
Mashkel, Hamun-i-, Pakistan ... 60 E3
Mashki Chāh, Pakistan ... 60 E3
Mashonaland Central □, Zimbabwe ... 85 B5
Mashonaland East □, Zimbabwe ... 85 B5
Mashonaland West □, Zimbabwe ... 85 B4

Mashtaga

Mashtaga = Maştağa,
  Azerbaijan 43 K10
Masi Manimba, *Zaïre* .. 80 E3
Masindi, *Uganda* 82 B3
Masindi Port, *Uganda* 82 B3
Masisea, *Peru* 124 B3
Masisi, *Zaïre* 82 C2
Masjed Soleyman, *Iran* .. 65 D6
Mask, L., *Ireland* 15 C2
Maslinica, *Croatia* 33 E13
Masnou, *Spain* 28 D7
Masoala, Tanjon' i, *Madag.* 85 B9
Masoarivo, *Madag.* 85 B7
Masohi, *Indonesia* 57 E7
Masomeloka, *Madag.* 85 C8
Mason, *Nev., U.S.A.* 112 G4
Mason, *Tex., U.S.A.* 109 K5
Mason City, *U.S.A.* 108 D8
Maspalomas, *Canary Is.* .. 36 G4
Maspalomas, Pta.,
  Canary Is. 36 G4
Masqat, *Oman* 68 C6
Massa, *Italy* 32 D7
Massa, O. →, *Morocco* .. 74 B3
Massa Maríttima, *Italy* .. 32 E7
Massachusetts □, *U.S.A.* . 107 D12
Massachusetts B., *U.S.A.* . 107 D14
Massafra, *Italy* 35 B10
Massaguet, *Chad* 73 F8
Massakory, *Chad* 73 F8
Massanella, *Spain* 36 B9
Massangena, *Mozam.* 85 C5
Massapê, *Brazil* 122 B3
Massarosa, *Italy* 32 E7
Massat, *France* 26 F5
Massawa = Mitsiwa,
  Eritrea 77 D4
Massena, *U.S.A.* 107 B10
Massénya, *Chad* 73 F8
Masset, *Canada* 100 C2
Massiac, *France* 26 C7
Massif Central, *France* .. 26 D7
Massillon, *U.S.A.* 106 F3
Massinga, *Mozam.* 85 C6
Masson, *Canada* 107 A9
Masson I., *Antarctica* .. 5 C7
Maştağa, *Azerbaijan* .. 43 K10
Mastanli = Momchilgrad,
  Bulgaria 39 H8
Masterton, *N.Z.* 87 J5
Mástikho, Ákra, *Greece* . 39 L9
Mastuj, *Pakistan* 63 A5
Mastung, *Pakistan* 60 E5
Mastūrah, *Si. Arabia* .. 76 C4
Masty, *Belarus* 40 F3
Masuda, *Japan* 49 G5
Masvingo, *Zimbabwe* 83 G3
Masvingo □, *Zimbabwe* . 83 G3
Maswa □, *Tanzania* 82 C3
Maşyāf, *Syria* 66 E7
Mata de São João, *Brazil* . 123 D4
Matabeleland North □,
  Zimbabwe 83 F2
Matabeleland South □,
  Zimbabwe 83 G2
Mataboor, *Indonesia* 57 E9
Matachel →, *Spain* 31 G4
Matachewan, *Canada* 98 C3
Matacuni →, *Venezuela* . 121 C4
Matad, *Mongolia* 54 B6
Matadi, *Zaïre* 80 F2
Matagalpa, *Nic.* 116 D2
Matagami, *Canada* 98 C4
Matagami, L., *Canada* .. 98 C4
Matagorda, *U.S.A.* 109 L7
Matagorda B., *U.S.A.* .. 109 L6
Matagorda I., *U.S.A.* .. 109 L6
Matak, P., *Indonesia* .. 59 L6
Matakana, *Australia* .. 91 E4
Mátala, *Greece* 37 E6
Matalaque, *Peru* 124 D3
Matam, *Senegal* 78 B2
Matameye, *Niger* 79 C6
Matamoros, *Campeche,*
  Mexico 115 D6
Matamoros, *Coahuila,*
  Mexico 114 B4
Matamoros, *Puebla, Mexico* 115 D5
Matamoros, *Tamaulipas,*
  Mexico 115 B5
Ma'ţan as Sarra, *Libya* .. 73 D9
Matandu →, *Tanzania* .. 83 D3
Matane, *Canada* 99 C6
Matang, *China* 52 F5
Matankari, *Niger* 79 C5
Matanzas, *Cuba* 116 B3
Matapan, C. = Taínaron,
  Ákra, *Greece* 39 N5
Matapédia, *Canada* 99 C6
Matara, *Sri Lanka* 60 S12
Mataram, *Indonesia* .. 56 F5
Matarani, *Peru* 124 D3
Mataranka, *Australia* .. 88 B5
Matarma, Râs, *Egypt* .. 69 E1
Mataró, *Spain* 28 D7
Matarraña →, *Spain* .. 28 D5
Matatiele, *S. Africa* .. 85 E4
Mataura, *N.Z.* 87 M2
Matehuala, *Mexico* 114 C4
Mateira, *Brazil* 123 E1
Matélica, *Italy* 33 E10
Matera, *Italy* 35 B9
Mátészalka, *Hungary* .. 21 H12
Matetsi, *Zimbabwe* 83 F2
Mateur, *Tunisia* 75 A6

Matfors, *Sweden* 10 B11
Matha, *France* 26 C3
Matheson Island, *Canada* . 101 C9
Mathis, *U.S.A.* 109 L6
Mathura, *India* 62 F7
Mati, *Phil.* 55 H7
Mati →, *Albania* 39 H2
Matías Romero, *Mexico* . 115 D5
Matibane, *Mozam.* 83 E5
Matima, *Botswana* 84 C3
Matiri Ra., *N.Z.* 87 J4
Matlock, *U.K.* 12 D6
Matmata, *Tunisia* 75 B6
Matna, *Sudan* 77 E4
Mato →, *Venezuela* 121 B4
Mato, Serrania de,
  Venezuela 120 B4
Mato Grosso □, *Brazil* . 125 C6
Mato Grosso, Planalto do,
  Brazil 125 C7
Mato Grosso do Sul □,
  Brazil 125 D7
Matochkin Shar, *Russia* .. 44 B6
Matopo Hills, *Zimbabwe* . 83 G2
Matopos, *Zimbabwe* 83 G2
Matosinhos, *Portugal* .. 30 D2
Matour, *France* 27 B8
Matsena, *Nigeria* 79 C7
Matsesta, *Russia* 43 J4
Matsue, *Japan* 49 G6
Matsumae, *Japan* 48 D10
Matsumoto, *Japan* 49 F9
Matsusaka, *Japan* 49 G8
Matsuura, *Japan* 49 H4
Matsuyama, *Japan* 49 H6
Mattagami →, *Canada* .. 98 B3
Mattancheri, *India* 60 Q10
Mattawa, *Canada* 98 C4
Mattawamkeag, *U.S.A.* .. 99 C6
Matterhorn, *Switz.* 22 E5
Matthew Town, *Bahamas* . 117 B5
Matthew's Ridge, *Guyana* 121 B5
Mattice, *Canada* 98 C3
Mattituck, *U.S.A.* 107 F12
Mattmar, *Sweden* 10 A7
Matuba, *Mozam.* 85 C5
Matucana, *Peru* 124 C2
Matun, *Afghan.* 62 C3
Maturín, *Venezuela* 121 B5
Mau, *India* 63 G10
Mau Escarpment, *Kenya* . 82 C4
Mau Ranipur, *India* .. 63 G8
Maubeuge, *France* 25 B10
Maubourguet, *France* .. 26 E4
Maud, Pt., *Australia* .. 88 D1
Maude, *Australia* 91 E3
Maudin Sun, *Burma* .. 61 M19
Maués, *Brazil* 121 D6
Maui, *U.S.A.* 102 H16
Maulamyaing = Moulmein,
  Burma 61 L20
Maule □, *Chile* 126 D1
Mauléon-Licharre, *France* 26 E3
Maullín, *Chile* 128 B2
Maumee, *U.S.A.* 104 E4
Maumee →, *U.S.A.* 104 E4
Maumere, *Indonesia* .. 57 F6
Maun, *Botswana* 84 B3
Mauna Kea, *U.S.A.* 102 J17
Mauna Loa, *U.S.A.* 102 J17
Maungmagan Kyunzu,
  Burma 61 M20
Maupin, *U.S.A.* 110 D3
Maure-de-Bretagne, *France* 24 E5
Maurepas, L., *U.S.A.* .. 109 K9
Maures, *France* 27 E10
Mauriac, *France* 26 C6
Maurice, L., *Australia* .. 89 E5
Maurienne, *France* 27 C10
Mauritania ■, *Africa* .. 74 D3
Mauritius ■, *Ind. Oc.* .. 71 J9
Mauron, *France* 24 D4
Maurs, *France* 26 D6
Mauston, *U.S.A.* 108 D9
Mauterndorf, *Austria* .. 21 H3
Mauvezin, *France* 26 E4
Mauzé-sur-le-Mignon,
  France 26 B3
Mavaca →, *Venezuela* .. 121 C4
Mavinga, *Angola* 81 H4
Mavli, *India* 62 G5
Mavrova, *Albania* 39 J2
Mavuradonha Mts.,
  Zimbabwe 83 F3
Mawa, *Zaïre* 82 B2
Mawana, *India* 62 E7
Mawand, *Pakistan* 62 E3
Mawk Mai, *Burma* 61 J20
Mawlaik, *Burma* 61 H19
Mawquq, *Si. Arabia* .. 64 E4
Mawson Coast, *Antarctica* 5 C6
Max, *U.S.A.* 108 B4
Maxcanú, *Mexico* 115 C6
Maxesibeni, *S. Africa* .. 85 E4
Maxhamish L., *Canada* . 100 B4
Maxixe, *Mozam.* 85 C6
Maxville, *Canada* 107 A10
Maxwell, *U.S.A.* 112 F4
Maxwelton, *Australia* .. 90 C3
May Downs, *Australia* .. 90 C4
May Pen, *Jamaica* 116 C4
Maya, *Spain* 28 B3
Maya →, *Russia* 45 D14
Maya Mts., *Belize* 115 D7
Mayaguana, *Bahamas* . 117 B5

Mayagüez, *Puerto Rico* ... 117 C6
Mayahi, *Niger* 79 C6
Mayals, *Spain* 28 D5
Mayâmey, *Iran* 65 B7
Mayang, *China* 52 D7
Mayarí, *Cuba* 117 B4
Maybell, *U.S.A.* 110 F9
Maychew, *Ethiopia* 77 E4
Maydān, *Iraq* 67 E11
Maydena, *Australia* .. 90 G4
Mayen, *Germany* 19 E3
Mayenne, *France* 24 D6
Mayenne □, *France* 24 D6
Mayenne →, *France* .. 24 E6
Mayer, *U.S.A.* 111 J7
Mayerthorpe, *Canada* .. 100 C5
Mayfield, *U.S.A.* 105 G1
Mayhill, *U.S.A.* 111 K11
Maykop, *Russia* 43 H5
Maymyo, *Burma* 58 A1
Maynard, *U.S.A.* 112 C4
Maynard Hills, *Australia* . 89 E2
Mayne →, *Australia* .. 90 C3
Maynooth, *Ireland* 15 C5
Mayo, *Canada* 96 B6
Mayo □, *Ireland* 15 C2
Mayo →, *Argentina* .. 128 C3
Mayo →, *Peru* 124 B2
Mayo L., *Canada* 96 B6
Mayon Volcano, *Phil.* .. 55 E5
Mayor I., *N.Z.* 87 G6
Mayorga, *Spain* 30 C5
Mayraira Pt., *Phil.* 55 B4
Mayskiy, *Russia* 43 J7
Mayson L., *Canada* 101 B7
Maysville, *U.S.A.* 104 F4
Mayu, *Indonesia* 57 D7
Mayville, *N. Dak., U.S.A.* 108 B6
Mayville, *N.Y., U.S.A.* .. 106 D5
Mayya, *Russia* 45 C14
Mazabuka, *Zambia* 83 F2
Mazagán = El Jadida,
  Morocco 74 B3
Mazagão, *Brazil* 121 D7
Mazamet, *France* 26 E6
Mazán, *Peru* 120 D3
Māzandarān □, *Iran* .. 65 B7
Mazapil, *Mexico* 114 C4
Mazar, O. →, *Algeria* .. 75 B5
Mazara del Vallo, *Italy* .. 34 E5
Mazarredo, *Argentina* .. 128 C3
Mazarrón, *Spain* 29 H3
Mazarrón, G. de, *Spain* . 29 H3
Mazaruni →, *Guyana* .. 121 B6
Mazatán, *Mexico* 114 B2
Mazatenango, *Guatemala* 116 D1
Mazatlán, *Mexico* 114 C3
Mažeikiai, *Lithuania* .. 9 H20
Māzhān, *Iran* 65 C8
Mazīnān, *Iran* 65 B8
Mazoe, *Mozam.* 83 F3
Mazoe →, *Mozam.* 83 F3
Mazoe Dam, *Zimbabwe* . 83 F3
Mazrûb, *Sudan* 77 E2
Mazu Dao, *China* 53 D12
Mazurian Lakes =
  Mazurski, Pojezierze,
  Poland 20 B10
Mazurski, Pojezierze,
  Poland 20 B10
Mazyr, *Belarus* 41 F5
Mazzarino, *Italy* 35 E7
Mbaba, *Senegal* 78 C1
Mbabane, *Swaziland* .. 85 D5
Mbagne, *Mauritania* .. 78 B2
M'bahiakro, *Ivory C.* .. 78 D4
Mbaïki, *C.A.R.* 80 D3
Mbala, *Zambia* 83 D3
Mbale, *Uganda* 82 B3
Mbalmayo, *Cameroon* .. 79 E7
Mbamba Bay, *Tanzania* . 83 E3
Mbandaka, *Zaïre* 80 D3
Mbanga, *Cameroon* .. 79 E6
Mbanza Congo, *Angola* . 80 F2
Mbanza Ngungu, *Zaïre* . 80 F2
Mbarara, *Uganda* 82 C3
Mbashe →, *S. Africa* .. 85 E4
Mbatto, *Ivory C.* 78 D4
Mbenkuru →, *Tanzania* . 83 D4
Mberengwa, *Zimbabwe* . 83 G2
Mberengwa, Mt.,
  Zimbabwe 83 G2
Mberubu, *Nigeria* 79 D6
Mbesuma, *Zambia* 83 D3
Mbeya, *Tanzania* 83 D3
Mbeya □, *Tanzania* 82 D3
Mbinga, *Tanzania* 83 E4
Mbinga □, *Tanzania* 83 E3
Mbini □, *Eq. Guin.* 80 D2
Mboki, *C.A.R.* 77 F2
Mboro, *Senegal* 78 B1
Mboune, *Senegal* 78 C2
Mbour, *Senegal* 78 C1
Mbout, *Mauritania* 78 B2
Mbozi □, *Tanzania* 83 D3
Mbuji-Mayi, *Zaïre* 80 D1
Mbulu, *Tanzania* 82 C4
Mbulu □, *Tanzania* 82 C4
Mburucuyá, *Argentina* . 126 B4
Mcherrah, *Algeria* 74 C4
Mchinja, *Tanzania* 83 D4
Mchinji, *Malawi* 83 E3
Mdennah, *Mauritania* .. 74 D3
Mead, L., *U.S.A.* 113 J12
Meade, *U.S.A.* 109 G4
Meadow, *Australia* 89 E1
Meadow Lake, *Canada* . 101 C7

Meadow Lake Prov. Park,
  Canada 101 C7
Meadow Valley Wash →,
  U.S.A. 113 J12
Meadville, *U.S.A.* 106 E4
Meaford, *Canada* 98 D3
Mealhada, *Portugal* .. 30 E2
Mealy Mts., *Canada* .. 99 B8
Meander River, *Canada* . 100 B5
Meares, C., *U.S.A.* 110 D2
Mearim →, *Brazil* 122 B3
Meath □, *Ireland* 15 C5
Meath Park, *Canada* .. 101 C7
Meaulne, *France* 26 B6
Meaux, *France* 25 D9
Mebechi-Gawa →, *Japan* 48 D10
Mecanhelas, *Mozam.* .. 83 F4
Mecaya →, *Colombia* .. 120 C2
Mecca = Makkah,
  Si. Arabia 68 C2
Mecca, *U.S.A.* 113 M10
Mechanicsburg, *U.S.A.* . 106 F8
Mechanicville, *U.S.A.* . 107 D11
Mechara, *Ethiopia* 77 F5
Mechelen, *Antwerpen,*
  Belgium 17 F4
Mechelen, *Limburg,*
  Belgium 17 G7
Mecheria, *Algeria* 75 B4
Mechernich, *Germany* .. 18 E2
Mechetinskaya, *Russia* . 43 G5
Mechra Benâbbou,
  Morocco 74 B3
Mecitözü, *Turkey* 66 B6
Mecklenburg-
  Vorpommern □,
  Germany 18 B8
Mecklenburger Bucht,
  Germany 18 A7
Meconta, *Mozam.* 83 E4
Meda, *Australia* 88 C3
Meda, *Portugal* 30 E3
Medan, *Indonesia* 56 D1
Médanos, *Argentina* .. 128 A4
Medanosa, Pta., *Argentina* 128 C3
Médéa, *Algeria* 75 A5
Medeiros Neto, *Brazil* .. 123 E3
Medel, Pic, *Switz.* 23 C7
Medellín, *Colombia* 120 B2
Medelpad, *Sweden* 9 E17
Medemblik, *Neths.* 16 C6
Médenine, *Tunisia* 75 B7
Mederdra, *Mauritania* .. 78 B1
Medford, *Mass., U.S.A.* . 107 D13
Medford, *Oreg., U.S.A.* . 110 E2
Medford, *Wis., U.S.A.* .. 108 C9
Medgidia, *Romania* 38 E11
Medi, *Sudan* 77 F3
Media Agua, *Argentina* . 126 C2
Media Luna, *Argentina* . 126 C2
Mediaş, *Romania* 38 C7
Medical Lake, *U.S.A.* .. 110 C5
Medicina, *Italy* 33 D8
Medicine Bow, *U.S.A.* .. 110 F10
Medicine Bow Pk., *U.S.A.* 110 F10
Medicine Bow Ra., *U.S.A.* 110 F10
Medicine Hat, *Canada* .. 101 D6
Medicine Lake, *U.S.A.* .. 108 A2
Medicine Lodge, *U.S.A.* . 109 G5
Medina = Al Madīnah,
  Si. Arabia 64 E3
Medina, *Brazil* 123 E3
Medina, *Colombia* 120 C3
Medina, *N. Dak., U.S.A.* 108 B5
Medina, *N.Y., U.S.A.* .. 106 C6
Medina, *Ohio, U.S.A.* .. 106 E3
Medina →, *U.S.A.* 109 L5
Medina de Ríoseco, *Spain* 30 D5
Medina del Campo, *Spain* 30 D6
Medina L., *U.S.A.* 109 L5
Medina-Sidonia, *Spain* . 31 J5
Medinaceli, *Spain* 28 D2
Medinipur, *India* 63 H12
Mediterranean Sea, *Europe* 70 C5
Medjerda, O. →, *Tunisia* . 75 A7
Medley, *Canada* 101 C6
Médoc, *France* 26 C3
Medstead, *Canada* 101 C7
Medulin, *Croatia* 33 D10
Medveda, *Serbia, Yug.* . 21 N11
Medvedevo, *Russia* 42 B8
Medveditsa →, *Russia* .. 42 F6
Medveditsa →, *Russia* .. 42 B3
Medvedok, *Russia* 42 B10
Medvezhi, Ostrava, *Russia* 45 B17
Medvezhyegorsk, *Russia* . 44 C4
Medway →, *U.K.* 13 F8
Medzilaborce, *Slovak Rep.* 20 F11
Meeberrie, *Australia* .. 89 E2
Meekatharra, *Australia* . 89 E2
Meeker, *U.S.A.* 110 F10
Meer, *Belgium* 17 F5
Meerane, *Germany* 18 E8
Meerhout, *Belgium* 17 F6
Meerle, *Belgium* 17 F5
Meersburg, *Germany* .. 19 H5
Meerssen, *Neths.* 17 G7
Meerut, *India* 62 E7
Meeteetse, *U.S.A.* 110 D9
Meeuwen, *Belgium* 17 F6
Mega, *Ethiopia* 77 G4
Megálo Petalí, *Greece* .. 39 M7
Megalópolis, *Greece* 39 M5
Meganísi, *Greece* 39 L3
Mégara, *Greece* 39 M6
Mègève, *France* 27 C10

Meghalaya □, *India* 61 G17
Meghezez, *Ethiopia* 77 F4
Mégiscane, L., *Canada* .. 98 C4
Megra, *Russia* 40 B9
Mehadia, *Romania* 38 E5
Mehaigne →, *Belgium* .. 17 G6
Mehaïguene, O. →,
  Algeria 75 B5
Meheisa, *Sudan* 76 D3
Mehndawal, *India* 63 F10
Mehr Jān, *Iran* 65 C7
Mehrābād, *Iran* 67 D12
Mehrān, *Iran* 67 F12
Mehrīz, *Iran* 65 D7
Mehun-sur-Yèvre, *France* . 25 E9
Mei Jiang →, *China* .. 53 E11
Mei Xian, *Guangdong,*
  China 53 E11
Mei Xian, *Shaanxi, China* . 50 G4
Meia Ponte →, *Brazil* .. 123 E2
Meichang, *China* 53 C8
Meichengzhen, *China* .. 53 C8
Meichuan, *China* 53 B10
Meiganga, *Cameroon* .. 80 C2
Meijel, *Neths.* 17 F7
Meiktila, *Burma* 61 J19
Meilen, *Switz.* 23 B7
Meiningen, *Germany* .. 18 E6
Meio →, *Brazil* 123 D3
Meira, Sierra de, *Spain* . 30 B3
Meiringen, *Switz.* 22 C6
Meishan, *China* 52 B4
Meissen, *Germany* 18 D9
Meissner, *Germany* 18 D5
Meitan, *China* 52 D6
Mejillones, *Chile* 126 A1
Meka, *Australia* 89 E2
Mékambo, *Gabon* 80 D2
Mekdela, *Ethiopia* 77 E4
Mekele, *Ethiopia* 77 E4
Mekhtar, *Pakistan* 60 D6
Meknès, *Morocco* 74 B3
Meko, *Nigeria* 79 D5
Mekong →, *Asia* 59 H6
Mekongga, *Indonesia* .. 57 E6
Mekvari = Kür →,
  Azerbaijan 67 C13
Melagiri Hills, *India* .. 60 N10
Melah, Sebkhet el, *Algeria* 75 C4
Melaka, *Malaysia* 59 L4
Melalap, *Malaysia* 56 C5
Mélambes, *Greece* 37 D6
Melanesia, *Pac. Oc.* .. 92 H7
Melbourne, *Australia* .. 91 F3
Melbourne, *U.S.A.* 105 L5
Melchor Múzquiz, *Mexico* 114 B4
Melchor Ocampo, *Mexico* 114 C4
Méldola, *Italy* 33 D9
Meldorf, *Germany* 18 A5
Melegnano, *Italy* 32 C6
Melenci, *Serbia, Yug.* .. 21 K10
Melenki, *Russia* 42 C5
Mélèzes →, *Canada* 97 C12
Melfi, *Chad* 73 F8
Melfi, *Italy* 35 B8
Melfort, *Canada* 101 C8
Melfort, *Zimbabwe* 83 F3
Melgaço, *Madeira* 30 C2
Melgar de Fernamental,
  Spain 30 C6
Melhus, *Norway* 10 A4
Melick, *Neths.* 17 F8
Melide, *Switz.* 23 E7
Meligalá, *Greece* 39 M4
Melilla, *N. Afr.* 75 A4
Melipilla, *Chile* 126 C1
Mélissa, Ákra, *Greece* .. 37 D6
Melita, *Canada* 101 D8
Mélito di Porto Salvo, *Italy* 35 E8
Melitopol, *Ukraine* 41 J8
Melk, *Austria* 21 G5
Mellansel, *Sweden* 8 E18
Melle, *Belgium* 17 G3
Melle, *France* 26 B3
Melle, *Germany* 18 C4
Mellégue, O. →, *Tunisia* . 75 A6
Mellen, *U.S.A.* 108 B9
Mellerud, *Sweden* 11 F6
Mellette, *U.S.A.* 108 C5
Mellid, *Spain* 30 C2
Mellieha, *Malta* 37 D1
Mellit, *Sudan* 77 E2
Mellizo Sur, Cerro, *Chile* . 128 C2
Mellrichstadt, *Germany* . 19 E6
Melnik, *Bulgaria* 39 H6
Mělník, *Czech.* 20 E4
Melo, *Uruguay* 127 C5
Melolo, *Indonesia* 57 F6
Melouprey, *Cambodia* .. 58 F5
Melrhir, Chott, *Algeria* . 75 B6
Melrose, *N.S.W., Australia* 91 E4
Melrose, *W. Austral.,*
  Australia 89 E3
Melrose, *U.K.* 14 F6
Melrose, *U.S.A.* 109 H3
Mels, *Switz.* 23 B8
Melsele, *Belgium* 17 F4
Melstone, *U.S.A.* 110 C10
Melsungen, *Germany* .. 18 D5
Melton Mowbray, *U.K.* . 12 E7
Melun, *France* 25 D9
Melut, *Sudan* 77 E3
Melville, *Canada* 101 C8
Melville, C., *Australia* .. 90 A3
Melville, L., *Canada* .. 99 B8
Melville B., *Australia* .. 90 A2
Melville I., *Australia* .. 88 B5

Melville I., *Canada* 4 B2
Melville Pen., *Canada* .. 97 B11
Melvin →, *Canada* 100 B5
Memaliaj, *Albania* 39 J2
Memba, *Mozam.* 83 E5
Memboro, *Indonesia* 57 F5
Membrilla, *Spain* 29 G1
Memel = Klaipėda,
  Lithuania 9 J19
Memel, *S. Africa* 85 D4
Memmingen, *Germany* .. 19 H6
Mempawah, *Indonesia* .. 56 D3
Memphis, *Tenn., U.S.A.* 109 H10
Memphis, *Tex., U.S.A.* . 109 H4
Mena, *Ukraine* 41 G7
Mena, *U.S.A.* 109 H7
Mena →, *Ethiopia* 77 F5
Menai Strait, *U.K.* 12 D3
Ménaka, *Mali* 79 B5
Menaldum, *Neths.* 16 B7
Menan = Chao Phraya →,
  Thailand 58 F3
Menarandra →, *Madag.* . 85 D7
Menard, *U.S.A.* 109 K5
Menasha, *U.S.A.* 104 C1
Menate, *Indonesia* 56 E4
Mendawai →, *Indonesia* . 56 E4
Mende, *France* 26 D7
Mendebo, *Ethiopia* 77 F4
Mendez, *Mexico* 115 B5
Mendhar, *India* 63 C6
Mendi, *Ethiopia* 77 F4
Mendip Hills, *U.K.* 13 F5
Mendocino, *U.S.A.* 110 G2
Mendocino, C., *U.S.A.* . 110 F1
Mendota, *Calif., U.S.A.* 111 H3
Mendota, *Ill., U.S.A.* . 108 E10
Mendoza, *Argentina* .. 126 C2
Mendoza □, *Argentina* . 126 C2
Mendrisio, *Switz.* 23 E7
Mene Grande, *Venezuela* 120 B3
Menemen, *Turkey* 66 C2
Menen, *Belgium* 17 G2
Menéndez, L., *Argentina* 128 B2
Menfi, *Italy* 34 E5
Mengcheng, *China* 53 A11
Mengdingjie, *China* 52 F2
Mengeš, *Slovenia* 33 B11
Menggala, *Indonesia* .. 56 E3
Menghai, *China* 52 G3
Mengíbar, *Spain* 31 H7
Mengjin, *China* 50 G7
Mengla, *China* 52 G3
Menglian, *China* 52 F2
Mengoub, *Algeria* 74 C3
Mengshan, *China* 53 E8
Mengyin, *China* 51 G9
Mengzhe, *China* 52 F3
Mengzi, *China* 52 F4
Menihek L., *Canada* 99 B6
Menin = Menen, *Belgium* 17 G2
Menindee, *Australia* .. 91 E3
Menindee L., *Australia* . 91 E3
Meningie, *Australia* 91 F2
Menlo Park, *U.S.A.* 112 H4
Menominee, *U.S.A.* 104 C2
Menominee →, *U.S.A.* . 104 C2
Menomonie, *U.S.A.* 108 C9
Menongue, *Angola* 81 G3
Menorca, *Spain* 36 B11
Mentakab, *Malaysia* 59 L4
Mentawai, Kepulauan,
  Indonesia 56 E1
Menton, *France* 27 E11
Mentor, *U.S.A.* 106 E3
Menzel-Bourguiba, *Tunisia* 75 A6
Menzel Chaker, *Tunisia* . 75 B7
Menzel-Temime, *Tunisia* . 75 A7
Menzies, *Australia* 89 E3
Me'ona, *Israel* 69 B4
Meoqui, *Mexico* 114 B3
Mepaco, *Mozam.* 83 F3
Meppel, *Neths.* 16 C8
Meppen, *Germany* 18 C3
Mequinenza, *Spain* 28 D5
Mer, *France* 24 E8
Mer Rouge, *U.S.A.* 109 J9
Merabéllou, Kólpos, *Greece* 37 D7
Meramangye, L., *Australia* 89 E5
Meran = Merano, *Italy* . 33 B8
Merano, *Italy* 33 B8
Merate, *Italy* 32 C6
Merauke, *Indonesia* 57 F10
Merbabu, *Indonesia* 57 G14
Merbein, *Australia* 91 E3
Merca, *Somali Rep.* 68 G3
Mercadal, *Spain* 36 B11
Mercato Saraceno, *Italy* . 33 E9
Merced, *U.S.A.* 111 H3
Merced Pk., *U.S.A.* 112 H7
Mercedes, *Buenos Aires,
  Argentina* 126 C4
Mercedes, *Corrientes,
  Argentina* 126 B4
Mercedes, *San Luis,
  Argentina* 126 C2
Mercedes, *Uruguay* 126 C4
Merceditas, *Chile* 126 B1
Mercer, *N.Z.* 87 G5
Mercer, *U.S.A.* 106 E4
Merchtem, *Belgium* 17 G4
Mercier, *Bolivia* 124 C4
Mercury, *U.S.A.* 113 J11
Mercy C., *Canada* 97 B13
Merdrignac, *France* 24 D4
Mere, *Belgium* 17 G3
Meredith, C., *Falk. Is.* . 128 D4

Meredith, L., *U.S.A.* 109 H4
Merefa, *Ukraine* 41 H9
Merelbeke, *Belgium* 17 G3
Méréville, *France* 25 D9
Merga = Nukheila, *Sudan* 76 D2
Mergui Arch. = Myeik
  Kyunzu, *Burma* 59 G1
Mérida, *Mexico* 115 C7
Mérida, *Spain* 31 G4
Mérida, *Venezuela* 120 B3
Mérida □, *Venezuela* .. 120 B3
Mérida, Cord. de,
  Venezuela 120 B3
Meriden, *U.S.A.* 107 E12
Meridian, *Calif., U.S.A.* 112 F5
Meridian, *Idaho, U.S.A.* 110 E5
Meridian, *Miss., U.S.A.* 105 J1
Meridian, *Tex., U.S.A.* . 109 K6
Mering, *Germany* 19 G7
Meriruma, *Brazil* 121 C7
Merkel, *U.S.A.* 109 J4
Merksem, *Belgium* 17 F4
Merksplas, *Belgium* 17 F5
Mermaid Reef, *Australia* . 88 C2
Mern, *Denmark* 11 J6
Merowe, *Sudan* 76 D3
Merredin, *Australia* 89 F2
Merrick, *U.K.* 14 F4
Merrickville, *Canada* .. 107 B9
Merrill, *Oreg., U.S.A.* . 110 E3
Merrill, *Wis., U.S.A.* . 108 C10
Merriman, *U.S.A.* 108 D4
Merritt, *Canada* 100 C4
Merriwa, *Australia* 91 E5
Merriwagga, *Australia* . 91 E4
Merrygoen, *Australia* .. 91 E4
Merryville, *U.S.A.* 109 K8
Merry I., *Canada* 98 A4
Mersa Fatma, *Eritrea* .. 68 E3
Mersch, *Lux.* 17 J8
Merseburg, *Germany* .. 18 D7
Mersey →, *U.K.* 12 D5
Merseyside □, *U.K.* 12 D5
Mersin, *Turkey* 66 D6
Mersing, *Malaysia* 59 L4
Merta, *India* 62 F6
Mertert, *Lux.* 17 J8
Merthyr Tydfil, *U.K.* . 13 F4
Mértola, *Portugal* 31 H3
Mertzig, *Lux.* 17 J8
Mertzon, *U.S.A.* 109 K4
Méru, *France* 25 C9
Meru, *Kenya* 82 B4
Meru, *Tanzania* 82 C4
Meru □, *Kenya* 82 B4
Merville, *France* 25 B9
Méry-sur-Seine, *France* . 25 D10
Merzifon, *Turkey* 66 B6
Merzig, *Germany* 19 F2
Merzouga, Erg Tin, *Algeria* 75 D7
Mesa, *U.S.A.* 111 K8
Mesach Mellet, *Libya* . 75 D7
Mesagne, *Italy* 35 B10
Mesanagrós, *Greece* 37 C9
Mesaoría □, *Cyprus* 37 D12
Mesarás, Kólpos, *Greece* . 37 D6
Meschede, *Germany* 18 D4
Mescit, *Turkey* 67 B9
Mesfinto, *Ethiopia* 77 E4
Mesgouez, L., *Canada* . 98 B4
Meshchovsk, *Russia* 42 C2
Meshed = Mashhad, *Iran* 65 B8
Meshoppen, *U.S.A.* 107 E8
Meshra er Req, *Sudan* . 77 F2
Mesick, *U.S.A.* 104 C3
Mesilinka →, *Canada* .. 100 B4
Mesilla, *U.S.A.* 111 K10
Meslay-du-Maine, *France* 24 E6
Mesocco, *Switz.* 23 D8
Mesolóngion, *Greece* .. 39 L4
Mesopotamia = Al Jazirah,
  Iraq 67 E10
Mesoraca, *Italy* 35 C9
Mesquite, *U.S.A.* 111 H6
Mess Cr. →, *Canada* .. 100 B2
Messac, *France* 24 E5
Messad, *Algeria* 75 B5
Messalo →, *Mozam.* 83 E4
Méssaména, *Cameroon* . 79 E7
Messancy, *Belgium* 17 J7
Messier, Canal, *Chile* . 128 C2
Messina, *Italy* 35 D8
Messina, *S. Africa* 85 C5
Messina, Str. di, *Italy* . 35 D8
Messíni, *Greece* 39 M5
Messiniakós Kólpos, *Greece* 39 N5
Messkirch, *Germany* 19 H5
Messonghi, *Greece* 37 B3
Mesta →, *Bulgaria* 39 H7
Mestanza, *Spain* 31 G6
Mestre, *Italy* 33 C9
Mestre, Espigão, *Brazil* . 123 D2
Městys Zelezná Ruda,
  Czech. 20 F3
Mesudiye, *Turkey* 66 B7
Meta □, *Colombia* 120 C3
Meta →, *S. Amer.* 120 B4
Metairie, *U.S.A.* 109 L9
Metaline Falls, *U.S.A.* . 110 B5
Metán, *Argentina* 126 B2
Metangula, *Mozam.* 83 E3
Metáuro →, *Italy* 33 E10
Metema, *Ethiopia* 77 E4
Metengobalame, *Mozam.* . 83 E3
Méthana, *Greece* 39 M6
Methven, *N.Z.* 87 K3
Methy L., *Canada* 101 B7

Metil, *Mozam.* 83 F4
Metlakatla, *U.S.A.* 100 B2
Metlaoui, *Tunisia* 75 B6
Metlika, *Slovenia* 33 C12
Metropolis, *U.S.A.* 109 G10
Mettet, *Belgium* 17 H5
Mettur Dam, *India* 60 P10
Metz, *France* 25 C13
Meulaboh, *Indonesia* .. 56 D1
Meulan, *France* 25 C8
Meung-sur-Loire, *France* . 25 E8
Meureudu, *Indonesia* .. 56 C1
Meurthe →, *France* 25 D13
Meurthe-et-Moselle □,
  France 25 D13
Meuse □, *France* 25 C12
Meuse →, *Europe* 17 G7
Meuselwitz, *Germany* .. 18 D8
Mexborough, *U.K.* 12 D6
Mexia, *U.S.A.* 109 K6
Mexiana, I., *Brazil* 122 A2
Mexicali, *Mexico* 114 A1
México, *Mexico* 115 D5
Mexico, *Maine, U.S.A.* . 107 B14
Mexico, *Mo., U.S.A.* .. 108 F9
México □, *Mexico* 114 D5
Mexico ■, *Cent. Amer.* . 114 C4
Mexico, G. of, *Cent. Amer.* 115 C7
Meyenburg, *Germany* .. 18 B8
Meymac, *France* 26 C6
Meymaneh, *Afghan.* 60 B4
Meyrargues, *France* 27 E9
Meyrueis, *France* 26 D7
Meyssac, *France* 26 C5
Mezdra, *Bulgaria* 38 F6
Mèze, *France* 26 E7
Mezen, *Russia* 44 C5
Mezen →, *Russia* 44 C5
Mézène, *France* 27 D8
Mézidon, *France* 24 C6
Mézilhac, *France* 27 D8
Mézin, *France* 26 D4
Mezöberény, *Hungary* . 21 J11
Mezökövácsháza, *Hungary* 21 J10
Mezökövesd, *Hungary* . 21 H10
Mézos, *France* 26 D2
Mezötúr, *Hungary* 21 J10
Mezquital, *Mexico* 114 C4
Mezzolombardo, *Italy* . 32 B8
Mgeta, *Tanzania* 83 D4
Mglin, *Russia* 41 F7
Mhlaba Hills, *Zimbabwe* . 83 F3
Mhow, *India* 62 H6
Miahuatlán, *Mexico* 115 D5
Miajadas, *Spain* 31 F5
Miallo, *Australia* 90 B4
Miami, *Ariz., U.S.A.* .. 111 K8
Miami, *Fla., U.S.A.* 105 N5
Miami, *Tex., U.S.A.* .. 109 H4
Miami →, *U.S.A.* 104 F3
Miami Beach, *U.S.A.* .. 105 N5
Miamisburg, *U.S.A.* .. 104 F3
Mian Xian, *China* 50 H4
Mianchi, *China* 50 G6
Mīāndowāb, *Iran* 67 D12
Miandrivazo, *Madag.* .. 85 B8
Mīāneh, *Iran* 67 D12
Mianning, *China* 52 C4
Mianwali, *Pakistan* 62 C4
Mianyang, *Hubei, China* 53 B9
Mianyang, *Sichuan, China* 52 B5
Mianzhu, *China* 52 B5
Miaoli, *Taiwan* 53 E13
Miarinarivo, *Madag.* .. 85 B8
Miass, *Russia* 44 D7
Miastko, *Poland* 20 A6
Michalovce, *Slovak Rep.* 20 G11
Michelstadt, *Germany* . 19 F5
Michigan □, *U.S.A.* 104 C3
Michigan, L., *U.S.A.* .. 104 C2
Michigan City, *U.S.A.* . 104 E2
Michikamau L., *Canada* . 99 B7
Michipicoten, *Canada* .. 98 C3
Michipicoten I., *Canada* . 98 C2
Michoacan □, *Mexico* .. 114 D4
Michurin, *Bulgaria* 38 G10
Michurinsk, *Russia* 42 D5
Miclere, *Australia* 90 C4
Mico, Pta., *Nic.* 116 D3
Micronesia, Federated
  States of ■, *Pac. Oc.* . 92 G7
Mid Glamorgan □, *U.K.* . 13 F4
Midai, P., *Indonesia* .. 59 L6
Midale, *Canada* 101 D8
Middagsfjället, *Sweden* . 10 A6
Middelbeers, *Neths.* 17 F6
Middelburg, *Neths.* 17 F3
Middelburg, *Eastern Cape,
  S. Africa* 84 E3
Middelburg,
  Eastern Trans., S. Africa 85 D4
Middelfart, *Denmark* .. 11 J3
Middelharnis, *Neths.* .. 16 E4
Middelkerke, *Belgium* . 17 F1
Middelrode, *Neths.* 17 E6
Middelwit, *S. Africa* .. 84 C4
Middle Alkali L., *U.S.A.* 110 F3
Middle Fork Feather →,
  U.S.A. 112 F5
Middle I., *Australia* 89 F3
Middle Loup →, *U.S.A.* 108 E5
Middleboro, *U.S.A.* .. 107 E14
Middleburg, *N.Y., U.S.A.* 107 D10
Middleburg, *Pa., U.S.A.* 106 F7
Middleburg, *U.S.A.* 107 B11
Middleport, *U.S.A.* 104 F4
Middlesboro, *Ky., U.S.A.* 103 C10

Middlesboro, *Ky., U.S.A.* 105 G4
Middlesbrough, *U.K.* .. 12 C6
Middlesex, *Belize* 116 C2
Middlesex, *U.S.A.* 107 F10
Middleton, *Australia* .. 90 C3
Middleton, *Canada* 99 D6
Middletown, *Calif., U.S.A.* 112 G4
Middletown, *Conn., U.S.A.* 107 E12
Middletown, *N.Y., U.S.A.* 107 E10
Middletown, *Ohio, U.S.A.* 104 F3
Middletown, *Pa., U.S.A.* 107 F8
Midelt, *Morocco* 74 B4
Midi, Canal du →, *France* 26 E5
Midi d'Ossau, Pic du,
  France 26 F3
Midland, *Canada* 98 D4
Midland, *Calif., U.S.A.* 113 M12
Midland, *Mich., U.S.A.* . 104 D3
Midland, *Pa., U.S.A.* .. 106 F4
Midland, *Tex., U.S.A.* . 109 K3
Midlands □, *Zimbabwe* . 83 F2
Midleton, *Ireland* 15 E3
Midlothian, *U.S.A.* 109 J6
Midongy, Tangorombohitr'
  i, *Madag.* 85 C8
Midongy Atsimo, *Madag.* 85 C8
Midou →, *France* 26 E3
Midouze →, *France* 26 E3
Midsayap, *Phil.* 55 H6
Midu, *China* 52 E3
Midway Is., *Pac. Oc.* .. 92 E10
Midway Wells, *U.S.A.* 113 N11
Midwest, *U.S.A.* 103 B9
Midwest, *Wyo., U.S.A.* . 110 E10
Midwolda, *Neths.* 16 B9
Midyat, *Turkey* 67 D9
Midzör, *Bulgaria* 38 G10
Mie □, *Japan* 49 G8
Miechów, *Poland* 20 E10
Międzychód, *Poland* 20 C5
Międzyrzec Podlaski,
  Poland 20 D12
Międzyrzecz, *Poland* .. 20 C5
Miélan, *France* 26 E4
Mielec, *Poland* 20 E11
Mienga, *Angola* 84 B2
Miercurea Ciuc, *Romania* 38 C8
Mieres, *Spain* 30 B5
Mierlo, *Neths.* 17 F7
Mieso, *Ethiopia* 77 F5
Mifflintown, *U.S.A.* 106 F7
Mifraz Hefa, *Israel* 69 C4
Migdâl, *Israel* 69 C4
Migennes, *France* 25 E10
Migliarino, *Italy* 33 D8
Miguel Alemán, Presa,
  Mexico 115 D5
Miguel Alves, *Brazil* .. 122 B3
Miguel Calmon, *Brazil* . 122 D3
Mihaliçcik, *Turkey* 66 C4
Mihara, *Japan* 49 G6
Mijares →, *Spain* 28 F4
Mijas, *Spain* 31 J6
Mikese, *Tanzania* 82 D4
Mikha-Tskhakaya =
  Senaki, *Georgia* 43 J6
Mikhailovka =
  Mykhaylivka, *Ukraine* . 41 J8
Mikhaylov, *Russia* 42 C4
Mikhaylovgrad, *Bulgaria* 38 F6
Mikhaylovska, *Russia* .. 42 E6
Mikhnevo, *Russia* 42 C3
Mikínai, *Greece* 39 M5
Mikkeli, *Finland* 9 F22
Mikkwa →, *Canada* 100 B6
Mikniya, *Sudan* 77 D3
Mikołajki, *Poland* 20 B11
Míkonos, *Greece* 39 M8
Mikrón Dhérion, *Greece* . 39 H9
Mikulov, *Czech.* 20 G6
Mikumi, *Tanzania* 82 D4
Milaca, *U.S.A.* 108 C8
Milagro, *Ecuador* 120 D2
Milagros, *Phil.* 55 E5
Milan = Milano, *Italy* . 32 C6
Milan, *Mo., U.S.A.* 108 E8
Milan, *Tenn., U.S.A.* .. 105 H1
Milang, *Australia* 91 E2
Milange, *Mozam.* 83 F4
Milano, *Italy* 32 C6
Milås, *Turkey* 66 D2
Milazzo, *Italy* 35 D8
Milbank, *U.S.A.* 108 C6
Milden, *Canada* 101 C7
Mildmay, *Canada* 106 B3
Mildura, *Australia* 91 E3
Mile, *China* 52 E4
Miléai, *Greece* 39 K6
Miles, *Australia* 91 D5
Miles, *U.S.A.* 109 K4
Miles City, *U.S.A.* 108 B2
Milestone, *Canada* 101 D8
Mileto, *Italy* 35 D9
Miletto, Mte., *Italy* 35 A7
Miletus, *Turkey* 66 D2
Mileura, *Australia* 89 E2
Milford, *Calif., U.S.A.* 112 E6
Milford, *Conn., U.S.A.* 107 E11
Milford, *Del., U.S.A.* . 104 F8
Milford, *Mass., U.S.A.* 107 D13
Milford, *N.Y., U.S.A.* . 107 D10
Milford, *Utah, U.S.A.* 111 G7
Milford Haven, *U.K.* .. 13 F2
Milford Sd., *N.Z.* 87 L1
Milgun, *Australia* 89 D2
Milh, Bahr al, *Iraq* 67 F10
Miliana, Aïn Salah, *Algeria* 75 C5

Miliana, *Médéa, Algeria* . 75 A5
Miling, *Australia* 89 F2
Militello in Val di Catánia,
  Italy 35 E7
Milk →, *U.S.A.* 110 B10
Milk, Wadi el →, *Sudan* . 76 D3
Milk River, *Canada* 100 D6
Mill, *Neths.* 17 E7
Mill City, *U.S.A.* 110 D2
Mill I., *Antarctica* 5 C8
Mill Valley, *U.S.A.* 112 H4
Millau, *France* 26 D7
Millbridge, *Canada* 106 B7
Millbrook, *Canada* 106 B6
Mille Lacs, L. des, *Canada* 98 C1
Mille Lacs L., *U.S.A.* .. 108 B8
Milledgeville, *U.S.A.* .. 105 J4
Millen, *U.S.A.* 105 J5
Miller, *U.S.A.* 108 C5
Millerovo, *Russia* 43 F5
Millersburg, *Ohio, U.S.A.* 106 F3
Millersburg, *Pa., U.S.A.* 106 F8
Millerton, *U.S.A.* 107 E11
Millerton L., *U.S.A.* .. 112 J7
Millevaches, Plateau de,
  France 26 C6
Millicent, *Australia* 91 F3
Millingen, *Neths.* 16 E8
Millinocket, *U.S.A.* 99 C6
Millmerran, *Australia* . 91 D5
Mills L., *Canada* 100 A5
Millsboro, *U.S.A.* 106 G4
Milltown Malbay, *Ireland* . 15 D2
Millville, *U.S.A.* 104 F8
Millwood L., *U.S.A.* .. 109 J8
Milly-la-Forêt, *France* . 25 D9
Milna, *Croatia* 33 E13
Milne →, *Australia* 90 C2
Milne Inlet, *Canada* 97 A11
Milnor, *U.S.A.* 108 B6
Milo, *Canada* 100 C6
Mílos, *Greece* 39 N7
Miloševo, *Serbia, Yug.* . 21 K10
Milparinka P.O., *Australia* 91 D3
Miltenberg, *Germany* .. 19 F5
Milton, *Canada* 106 C5
Milton, *N.Z.* 87 M2
Milton, *U.K.* 14 D4
Milton, *Calif., U.S.A.* . 112 G6
Milton, *Fla., U.S.A.* .. 105 K2
Milton, *Pa., U.S.A.* .. 106 F8
Milton-Freewater, *U.S.A.* 110 D4
Milton Keynes, *U.K.* .. 13 E7
Miltou, *Chad* 73 F8
Milverton, *Canada* 106 C4
Milwaukee, *U.S.A.* 104 D2
Milwaukee Deep, *Atl. Oc.* 117 C6
Milwaukie, *U.S.A.* 112 E4
Mim, *Ghana* 78 D4
Mimizan, *France* 26 D2
Mimoso, *Brazil* 123 E2
Min →, *Fujian, China* .. 53 E12
Min Jiang →, *China* 52 C5
Min Xian, *China* 50 G3
Mina, *U.S.A.* 111 G4
Mina Pirquitas, *Argentina* 126 A2
Mīnā Su'ud, *Si. Arabia* . 65 D6
Mīnā'al Ahmadī, *Kuwait* . 65 D6
Mīnāb, *Iran* 65 E8
Minago →, *Canada* 101 C9
Minaki, *Canada* 101 D10
Minamata, *Japan* 49 H5
Minami-Tori-Shima,
  Pac. Oc. 92 E7
Minas, *Uruguay* 127 C4
Minas, Sierra de las,
  Guatemala 116 C2
Minas Basin, *Canada* .. 99 C7
Minas de Rio Tinto, *Spain* 31 H4
Minas de San Quintín,
  Spain 31 G6
Minas Gerais □, *Brazil* . 123 E2
Minas Novas, *Brazil* .. 123 E3
Minatitlán, *Mexico* 115 D6
Minbu, *Burma* 61 J19
Mincio →, *Italy* 32 C7
Mindanao, *Phil.* 55 H6
Mindanao Sea = Bohol
  Sea, *Phil.* 57 C6
Mindanao Trench, *Pac. Oc.* 55 F7
Mindel →, *Germany* 19 G6
Mindelheim, *Germany* . 19 G6
Minden, *Canada* 106 B6
Minden, *Germany* 18 C4
Minden, *La., U.S.A.* .. 109 J8
Minden, *Nev., U.S.A.* . 112 G7
Mindiptana, *Indonesia* . 57 F10
Mindoro, *Phil.* 55 E4
Mindoro Str., *Phil.* 55 E4
Mindouli, *Congo* 80 E2
Mine, *Japan* 49 G5
Minehead, *U.K.* 13 F4
Mineiros, *Brazil* 125 D7
Mineola, *U.S.A.* 109 J7
Mineral King, *U.S.A.* . 112 J8
Mineral Wells, *U.S.A.* . 109 J5
Mineralnyye Vody, *Russia* 43 H6
Minersville, *Pa., U.S.A.* 107 F8
Minersville, *Utah, U.S.A.* 111 G7
Minerva, *U.S.A.* 106 F3
Minervino Murge, *Italy* . 35 A9
Minetto, *U.S.A.* 107 C8
Mingäçevir, *Azerbaijan* . 43 K8
Mingäçevir Su Anbarı,
  Azerbaijan 43 K8
Mingan, *Canada* 99 B7

Mingechaur = Mingäçevir, Azerbaijan 43 K8
Mingechaurskoye Vdkhr. = Mingäçevir Su Anbarı, Azerbaijan 43 K8
Mingela, Australia 90 B4
Mingenew, Australia 89 E2
Mingera Cr. →, Australia 90 C2
Minggang, China 53 A10
Mingin, Burma 61 H19
Minglanilla, Spain 28 F3
Minglun, China 52 E7
Mingorria, Spain 30 E6
Mingt'iehkaitafan = Mintaka Pass, Pakistan 63 A6
Mingxi, China 53 D11
Mingyuegue, China 51 C15
Minho = Miño →, Spain . 30 D2
Minhou, China 53 E12
Miniĉevo, Serbia, Yug. . 21 M12
Minidoka, U.S.A. 110 E7
Minigwal, L., Australia .. 89 E3
Minilya, Australia 89 D1
Minilya →, Australia ... 89 D1
Minipi, L., Canada 99 B7
Mink L., Canada 100 A5
Minna, Nigeria 79 D6
Minneapolis, Kans., U.S.A. 108 F6
Minneapolis, Minn., U.S.A. 108 C8
Minnedosa, Canada 101 C9
Minnesota □, U.S.A. 108 B7
Minnesund, Norway 10 D5
Minnie Creek, Australia . 89 D2
Minnipa, Australia 91 E2
Minnitaki L., Canada ... 98 C1
Mino, Japan 49 G8
Miño →, Spain 30 D2
Minorca = Menorca, Spain 36 B11
Minore, Australia 91 E4
Minot, U.S.A. 108 A4
Minqin, China 50 E2
Minqing, China 53 D12
Minsen, Germany 18 B3
Minsk, Belarus 40 F4
Mińsk Mazowiecki, Poland 20 C11
Mintaka Pass, Pakistan . 63 A6
Minto, Canada 96 B5
Minton, Canada 101 D8
Minturn, U.S.A. 110 G10
Minturno, Italy 34 A6
Minûf, Egypt 76 H7
Minusinsk, Russia 45 D10
Minutang, India 61 E20
Minvoul, Gabon 80 D2
Minya el Qamh, Egypt .. 76 H7
Mionica, Serbia, Yug. .. 21 L10
Mir, Niger 79 C7
Mīr Kūh, Iran 65 E8
Mīr Shahdād, Iran 65 E8
Mira, Italy 33 C9
Mira, Portugal 30 E2
Mira →, Colombia 120 C2
Mira →, Portugal 31 H2
Mira por vos Cay, Bahamas 117 B5
Mirabella Eclano, Italy . 35 A7
Miracema do Norte, Brazil 122 C2
Mirador, Brazil 122 C3
Miraflores, Colombia .. 120 C3
Miraj, India 60 L9
Miram Shah, Pakistan .. 62 C4
Miramar, Argentina 126 D4
Miramar, Mozam. 85 C6
Miramas, France 27 E8
Mirambeau, France 26 C3
Miramichi B., Canada .. 99 C7
Miramont-de-Guyenne, France 26 D4
Miranda, Brazil 125 E6
Miranda □, Venezuela .. 120 A4
Miranda →, Brazil 125 D6
Miranda de Ebro, Spain . 28 C2
Miranda do Corvo, Spain 30 E2
Miranda do Douro, Portugal 30 D4
Mirande, France 26 E4
Mirandela, Portugal ... 30 D3
Mirando City, U.S.A. .. 109 M5
Mirándola, Italy 32 D8
Mirandópolis, Brazil .. 127 A5
Mirango, Malawi 83 E3
Mirani, Australia 90 C4
Mirano, Italy 33 C9
Mirassol, Brazil 127 A6
Mirbāţ, Oman 68 D5
Mirear, Egypt 76 C4
Mirebeau, Côte-d'Or, France 25 E12
Mirebeau, Vienne, France . 24 F7
Mirecourt, France 25 D13
Mirgorod = Myrhorod, Ukraine 41 H7
Miri, Malaysia 56 D4
Miriam Vale, Australia . 90 C5
Mirim, L., S. Amer. ... 127 C5
Mirimire, Venezuela ... 120 A4
Miriti, Brazil 125 B6
Mirnyy, Russia 45 C12
Mirond L., Canada 101 B8
Mirpur, Pakistan 63 C5
Mirpur Bibiwari, Pakistan 62 E2
Mirpur Khas, Pakistan . 62 G3
Mirpur Sakro, Pakistan 62 G2
Mirria, Niger 79 C6
Mirror, Canada 100 C6
Mîrşani, Romania 38 E6
Miryang, S. Korea 51 G15
Mirzaani, Georgia 43 K8

Mirzapur, India 63 G10
Mirzapur-cum-Vindhyachal = Mirzapur, India 63 G10
Misantla, Mexico 115 D5
Misawa, Japan 48 D10
Miscou I., Canada 99 C7
Mish'āb, Ra's al, Si. Arabia 65 D6
Mishagua →, Peru 124 C3
Mishan, China 54 B8
Mishawaka, U.S.A. 104 E2
Mishbih, Gebel, Egypt . 76 C3
Mishima, Japan 49 G9
Misilmeri, Italy 34 D6
Misión, Mexico 113 N10
Misión Fagnano, Argentina 128 D3
Misiones □, Argentina . 127 B5
Misiones □, Paraguay .. 126 B4
Miskah, Si. Arabia 64 E4
Miskitos, Cayos, Nic. . 116 D3
Miskolc, Hungary 21 G10
Misoke, Zaïre 82 C2
Misool, Indonesia 57 E8
Misrātah, Libya 73 B8
Missanabie, Canada ... 98 C3
Missão Velha, Brazil .. 122 C4
Missinaibi →, Canada .. 98 B3
Missinaibi L., Canada . 98 C3
Mission, S. Dak., U.S.A. 108 D4
Mission, Tex., U.S.A. . 109 M5
Mission City, Canada .. 100 D4
Mission Viejo, U.S.A. . 113 M9
Missisa L., Canada ... 98 B2
Mississagi →, Canada .. 98 C3
Mississippi □, U.S.A. . 109 J10
Mississippi →, U.S.A. . 109 L10
Mississippi L., Canada 107 A8
Mississippi River Delta, U.S.A. 109 L9
Mississippi Sd., U.S.A. 109 K10
Missoula, U.S.A. 110 C6
Missour, Morocco 74 B4
Missouri □, U.S.A. 108 F8
Missouri →, U.S.A. 108 F9
Missouri Valley, U.S.A. 108 E7
Mist, U.S.A. 112 E3
Mistake B., Canada ... 101 A10
Mistassini →, Canada .. 99 C5
Mistassini L., Canada . 98 B5
Mistastin L., Canada .. 99 A7
Mistatim, Canada 101 C8
Mistelbach, Austria ... 20 G6
Misterbianco, Italy ... 35 E7
Mistretta, Italy 35 E7
Misty L., Canada 101 B8
Misurata = Misrātah, Libya 73 B8
Mît Ghamr, Egypt 76 H7
Mitatib, Sudan 77 D4
Mitchell, Australia ... 91 D4
Mitchell, Canada 106 C3
Mitchell, Ind., U.S.A. 104 F2
Mitchell, Nebr., U.S.A. 108 E3
Mitchell, Oreg., U.S.A. 110 D3
Mitchell, S. Dak., U.S.A. 108 D5
Mitchell →, Australia . 90 B3
Mitchell, Mt., U.S.A. . 105 H4
Mitchell Ras., Australia 90 A2
Mitchelstown, Ireland . 15 D3
Mitha Tiwana, Pakistan 62 C5
Mitilíni, Greece 39 K9
Mito, Japan 49 F10
Mitrofanovka, Russia .. 42 F4
Mitrovica = Titova-Mitrovica, Serbia, Yug. 21 N10
Mitsinjo, Madag. 85 B8
Mitsiwa, Eritrea 77 D4
Mitsiwa Channel, Eritrea 77 D5
Mitsukaidō, Japan 49 F9
Mittagong, Australia .. 91 E5
Mittelland, Switz. ... 22 C4
Mittellandkanal →, Germany 18 C3
Mittenwalde, Germany .. 18 C9
Mitterteich, Germany .. 19 F8
Mittweida, Germany ... 18 E8
Mitú, Colombia 120 C3
Mituas, Colombia 120 C4
Mitumba, Tanzania 82 D3
Mitumba, Chaîne des, Zaïre 82 D2
Mitumba Mts. = Mitumba, Chaîne des, Zaïre .. 82 D2
Mitwaba, Zaïre 83 D2
Mityana, Uganda 82 B3
Mitzic, Gabon 80 D2
Mixteco →, Mexico 115 D5
Miyagi □, Japan 48 E10
Miyāh, W. el →, Egypt . 76 B3
Miyāh, W. el →, Syria . 64 C3
Miyake-Jima, Japan ... 49 G9
Miyako, Japan 48 E10
Miyako-Jima, Japan ... 49 M2
Miyako-Rettō, Japan .. 49 M2
Miyakonojō, Japan 49 J5
Miyanoura-Dake, Japan 49 J5
Miyazaki, Japan 49 J5
Miyazaki □, Japan 49 H5
Miyazu, Japan 49 G7
Miyet, Bahr el = Dead Sea, Asia 69 D4
Miyi, China 52 D4
Miyoshi, Japan 49 G6
Miyun, China 50 D9
Miyun Shuiku, China .. 51 D9
Mizamis = Ozamiz, Phil. 55 G5
Mizdah, Libya 75 B7

Mizen Hd., Cork, Ireland . 15 E2
Mizen Hd., Wick., Ireland 15 D5
Mizhi, China 50 F6
Mizil, Romania 38 E9
Mizoram □, India 61 H18
Mizpe Ramon, Israel .. 69 E3
Mizusawa, Japan 48 E10
Mjöbäck, Sweden 11 G6
Mjölby, Sweden 11 F9
Mjörn, Sweden 11 G6
Mjøsa, Norway 10 D5
Mkata, Tanzania 82 D4
Mkokotoni, Tanzania .. 82 D4
Mkomazi, Tanzania 82 C4
Mkomazi →, S. Africa .. 85 E5
Mkulwe, Tanzania 83 D3
Mkumbi, Ras, Tanzania 82 D4
Mkushi, Zambia 83 E2
Mkushi River, Zambia . 83 E2
Mkuze, S. Africa 85 D5
Mladá Boleslav, Czech. 20 E4
Mladenovac, Serbia, Yug. 21 L10
Mlala Hills, Tanzania . 82 D3
Mlange, Malawi 83 F4
Mlava →, Serbia, Yug. . 21 L11
Mława, Poland 20 B10
Mlinište, Bos.-H. 33 D13
Mljet, Croatia 21 N7
Młynary, Poland 20 A9
Mmabatho, S. Africa .. 84 D4
Mme, Cameroon 79 D7
Mo i Rana, Norway 8 C16
Moa, Indonesia 57 F7
Moa →, S. Leone 78 D2
Moab, U.S.A. 111 G9
Moabi, Gabon 80 E2
Moaco →, Brazil 124 B4
Moala, Fiji 87 D8
Moalie Park, Australia 91 D3
Moaña, Spain 30 C2
Moba, Zaïre 82 D2
Mobārakābād, Iran 65 D7
Mobārakīyeh, Iran 65 C6
Mobaye, C.A.R. 80 D4
Mobayi, Zaïre 80 D4
Moberly, U.S.A. 108 F8
Moberly →, Canada 100 B4
Mobile, U.S.A. 105 K1
Mobile B., U.S.A. 105 K2
Mobridge, U.S.A. 108 C4
Mobutu Sese Seko, L. = Albert L., Africa ... 82 B3
Moc Chau, Vietnam 58 B5
Moc Hoa, Vietnam 59 G5
Mocabe Kasari, Zaïre . 83 D2
Mocajuba, Brazil 122 B2
Moçambique, Mozam. ... 83 F5
Moçâmedes = Namibe, Angola 81 H2
Mocapra →, Venezuela . 120 B4
Mocha, I., Chile 128 A2
Mochudi, Botswana 84 C4
Mocimboa da Praia, Mozam. 83 E5
Moclips, U.S.A. 112 C2
Mocoa, Colombia 120 C2
Mococa, Brazil 127 A6
Mocorito, Mexico 114 B3
Moctezuma, Mexico 114 B3
Moctezuma →, Mexico .. 115 C5
Mocuba, Mozam. 83 F4
Mocúzari, Presa, Mexico 114 B3
Modane, France 27 C10
Modasa, India 62 H5
Modave, Belgium 17 H6
Modder →, S. Africa .. 84 D3
Modderrivier, S. Africa 84 D3
Módena, Italy 32 D7
Modena, U.S.A. 111 H7
Modesto, U.S.A. 111 H3
Módica, Italy 35 F7
Modigliana, Italy 33 D8
Modo, Sudan 77 F3
Modra, Slovak Rep. ... 21 G7
Moe, Australia 91 F4
Moebase, Mozam. 83 F4
Moëlan-sur-Mer, France 24 E3
Moengo, Surinam 121 B7
Moerbeke, Neths. 17 E6
Moergestel, Neths. ... 17 E6
Moers, Germany 17 F9
Moësa →, Switz. 23 D8
Moffat, U.K. 14 F5
Moga, India 62 D6
Mogadishu = Muqdisho, Somali Rep. 68 G4
Mogador = Essaouira, Morocco 74 B3
Mogadouro, Portugal .. 30 D4
Mogalakwena →, S. Africa 85 C4
Mogami →, Japan 48 E10
Mogán, Canary Is. 36 G4
Mogaung, Burma 61 G20
Møgeltønder, Denmark . 11 K2
Mogente, Spain 29 G4
Mogho, Ethiopia 77 G5
Mogi das Cruzes, Brazil 127 A6
Mogi-Guaçu →, Brazil . 127 A6
Mogi-Mirim, Brazil ... 127 A6
Mogielnica, Poland ... 20 D10
Mogilev = Mahilyow, Belarus 40 F6
Mogilev-Podolskiy = Mohyliv-Podilskyy, Ukraine 41 H4
Mogilno, Poland 20 C7
Mogincual, Mozam. 83 F5
Mogliano Véneto, Italy 33 C9

Mogocha, Russia 45 D12
Mogoi, Indonesia 57 E8
Mogok, Burma 61 H20
Moguer, Spain 31 H4
Mogumber, Australia .. 89 F2
Mohács, Hungary 21 K8
Mohales Hoek, Lesotho 84 E4
Mohall, U.S.A. 108 A4
Mohammadābād, Iran ... 65 B8
Mohammadia, Algeria .. 75 A5
Mohammedia, Morocco .. 74 B3
Mohave, L., U.S.A. ... 113 K12
Mohawk →, U.S.A. 107 D11
Möhne →, Germany 18 D3
Moholm, Sweden 11 F8
Mohoro, Tanzania 82 D4
Mohyliv-Podilskyy, Ukraine 41 H4
Moia, Sudan 77 F2
Moidart, L., U.K. 14 E3
Moinești, Romania 38 C9
Mointy, Kazakhstan ... 44 E8
Moirans, France 27 C9
Moirans-en-Montagne, France 27 B9
Moíres, Greece 37 D6
Moisaküla, Estonia ... 9 G21
Moisie, Canada 99 B6
Moisie →, Canada 99 B6
Moissac, France 26 D5
Moïssala, Chad 73 G8
Moita, Portugal 31 G2
Mojácar, Spain 29 H3
Mojados, Spain 30 D6
Mojave, U.S.A. 113 K8
Mojave Desert, U.S.A. 113 L10
Mojiang, China 52 F3
Mojo, Bolivia 126 A2
Mojo, Ethiopia 77 F4
Mojokerto, Indonesia . 57 G15
Moju →, Brazil 122 B2
Mokai, N.Z. 87 H5
Mokambo, Zaïre 83 E2
Mokameh, India 63 G11
Mokelumne →, U.S.A. .. 112 G5
Mokelumne Hill, U.S.A. 112 G6
Mokhós, Greece 37 D7
Mokhotlong, Lesotho .. 85 D4
Moknine, Tunisia 75 A7
Mokokchung, India 61 F19
Mokra Gora, Serbia, Yug. 21 N10
Mokronog, Slovenia ... 33 C12
Moksha →, Russia 42 C6
Mokshan, Russia 42 D7
Mol, Belgium 17 F6
Mola, C. de la, Spain . 28 F9
Mola di Bari, Italy .. 35 A10
Moláoi, Greece 39 N5
Molat, Croatia 33 D11
Molchanovo, Russia ... 44 D9
Mold, U.K. 12 D4
Moldavia = Moldova ■, Europe 41 J5
Molde, Norway 8 E12
Moldova ■, Europe 41 J5
Moldova Nouă, Romania 38 E4
Moldoveanu, Romania .. 38 D7
Molepolole, Botswana . 84 C4
Moléson, Switz. 22 C4
Molfetta, Italy 35 A9
Molina de Aragón, Spain 28 E3
Moline, U.S.A. 108 E9
Molinella, Italy 33 D8
Molinos, Argentina ... 126 B2
Moliro, Zaïre 82 D3
Molise □, Italy 33 G11
Moliterno, Italy 35 B8
Mollahat, Bangla. 63 H13
Mölle, Sweden 11 H6
Molledo, Spain 30 B6
Mollendo, Peru 124 D3
Mollerin, L., Australia 89 F2
Mollerusa, Spain 28 D5
Mollina, Spain 31 H6
Mölln, Germany 18 B6
Mölltorp, Sweden 11 F8
Mölndal, Sweden 11 G6
Molochansk, Ukraine .. 41 J8
Molochnoye, Ozero, Ukraine 41 J8
Molodechno = Maladzyechna, Belarus 40 E4
Molokai, U.S.A. 102 H16
Molong, Australia 91 E4
Molopo →, Africa 84 D3
Mólos, Greece 39 L5
Molotov = Perm, Russia 44 D6
Moloundou, Cameroon .. 80 D3
Molsheim, France 25 D14
Molson L., Canada 101 C9
Molteno, S. Africa ... 84 E4
Molu, Indonesia 57 F8
Molucca Sea, Indonesia 57 E6
Moluccas = Maluku, Indonesia 57 E7
Moma, Mozam. 83 F4
Moma, Zaïre 82 C1
Mombaça, Brazil 122 C4
Mombasa, Kenya 82 C4
Mombetsu, Japan 48 B11
Mombuey, Spain 30 C4
Momchilgrad, Bulgaria 39 H8
Momi, Zaïre 82 C2
Momignies, Belgium ... 17 H4
Mompós, Colombia 120 B3
Møn, Denmark 11 K6

Mon →, Burma 61 J19
Mona, Canal de la, W. Indies 117 C6
Mona, Isla, Puerto Rico 117 C6
Mona, Pta., Costa Rica 116 E3
Mona, Pta., Spain 31 J7
Monach Is., U.K. 14 D1
Monaco ■, Europe 27 E11
Monadhliath Mts., U.K. 14 D4
Monagas □, Venezuela . 121 B5
Monaghan, Ireland 15 B5
Monaghan □, Ireland .. 15 B5
Monahans, U.S.A. 109 K3
Monapo, Mozam. 83 E5
Monarch Mt., Canada .. 100 C3
Monastir = Bitola, Macedonia 39 H4
Monastir, Tunisia 75 A7
Moncada, Phil. 55 D4
Moncada, Spain 28 F4
Moncalieri, Italy 32 C4
Moncalvo, Italy 32 C5
Monção, Portugal 30 C2
Moncarapacho, Portugal 31 H3
Moncayo, Sierra del, Spain 28 D3
Mönchengladbach, Germany 18 D2
Monchique, Portugal .. 31 H2
Monclova, Mexico 114 B4
Moncontour, France ... 24 D4
Moncoutant, France ... 26 B3
Moncton, Canada 99 C7
Mondego →, Portugal .. 30 E2
Mondego, C., Portugal 30 E2
Mondeodo, Indonesia .. 57 E6
Mondolfo, Italy 33 E10
Mondoñedo, Spain 30 B3
Mondovì, Italy 32 D4
Mondovi, U.S.A. 108 C9
Mondragon, France 27 D8
Mondragón, Phil. 55 E6
Mondragone, Italy 34 A6
Mondrain I., Australia 89 F3
Monduli □, Tanzania .. 82 C4
Monemvasía, Greece ... 39 N6
Monessen, U.S.A. 106 F5
Monesterio, Spain 31 G4
Monestier-de-Clermont, France 27 D9
Monett, U.S.A. 109 G8
Monfalcone, Italy 33 C10
Monflanquin, France .. 26 D4
Monforte, Portugal ... 31 F3
Monforte de Lemos, Spain 30 C3
Mong Hsu, Burma 61 J21
Mong Kung, Burma 61 J20
Mong Nai, Burma 61 J20
Mong Pawk, Burma 61 H21
Mong Ton, Burma 61 J21
Mong Wa, Burma 61 J22
Mong Yai, Burma 61 H21
Mongalla, Sudan 77 F3
Mongers, L., Australia 89 E2
Monghyr = Munger, India 63 G12
Mongibello = Etna, Italy 35 E8
Mongo, Chad 73 F8
Mongolia ■, Asia 45 B10
Mongonu, Nigeria 79 C7
Mongororo, Chad 73 F9
Mongu, Zambia 81 H4
Môngua, Angola 84 B2
Monistrol-d'Allier, France 26 D7
Monistrol-sur-Loire, France 27 C8
Monkey Bay, Malawi ... 83 E4
Monkey River, Belize . 115 D7
Monkira, Australia ... 90 C3
Monkoto, Zaïre 80 E4
Monmouth, U.K. 13 F5
Monmouth, U.S.A. 108 E9
Mono L., U.S.A. 111 H4
Monolith, U.S.A. 113 K8
Monólithos, Greece ... 37 C9
Monongahela, U.S.A. .. 106 F5
Monópoli, Italy 35 B10
Monor, Hungary 21 H9
Monóvar, Spain 29 G4
Monqoumba, C.A.R. 80 D3
Monreal del Campo, Spain 28 E3
Monreale, Italy 34 D6
Monroe, Ga., U.S.A. .. 105 J4
Monroe, La., U.S.A. .. 109 J8
Monroe, Mich., U.S.A. 104 E4
Monroe, N.C., U.S.A. . 105 H5
Monroe, N.Y., U.S.A. . 107 E10
Monroe, Utah, U.S.A. . 111 G7
Monroe, Wash., U.S.A. 112 C5
Monroe, Wis., U.S.A. . 108 D10
Monroe City, U.S.A. .. 108 F9
Monroeville, Ala., U.S.A. 105 K2
Monroeville, Pa., U.S.A. 106 F5
Monrovia, Liberia 78 D2
Monrovia, U.S.A. 111 J4
Mons, Belgium 17 H3
Monsaraz, Portugal ... 31 G3
Monse, Indonesia 57 E6
Monsefú, Peru 124 B2
Monségur, France 26 D4
Monsélice, Italy 33 C8
Monster, Neths. 16 D4
Mont Cenis, Col du, France 27 C10
Mont-de-Marsan, France 26 E3
Mont-Joli, Canada 99 C6
Mont-Laurier, Canada . 98 C4
Mont-St.-Michel, Le = Le Mont-St.-Michel, France 24 D5
Mont-sous-Vaudrey, France 25 F12

Mont-sur-Marchienne, Belgium ... 17 H4
Mont Tremblant Prov. Park, Canada ... 98 C5
Montabaur, Germany ... 18 E3
Montagnac, France ... 26 E7
Montagnana, Italy ... 33 C8
Montagu, S. Africa ... 84 E3
Montagu I., Antarctica ... 5 B1
Montague, Canada ... 99 C7
Montague, U.S.A. ... 110 F2
Montague, I., Mexico ... 114 A2
Montague Ra., Australia ... 89 E2
Montague Sd., Australia ... 88 B4
Montaigu, France ... 24 F5
Montalbán, Spain ... 28 E3
Montalbano di Elicona, Italy ... 35 D8
Montalbano Iónico, Italy ... 35 B9
Montalbo, Spain ... 28 F2
Montalcino, Italy ... 33 E8
Montalegre, Portugal ... 30 D3
Montalto di Castro, Italy ... 33 F8
Montalto Uffugo, Italy ... 35 C9
Montalvo, U.S.A. ... 113 L7
Montamarta, Spain ... 30 D5
Montaña, Peru ... 124 B3
Montana, Switz. ... 22 D4
Montana □, U.S.A. ... 110 C9
Montaña Clara, I., Canary Is. ... 36 E6
Montánchez, Spain ... 31 F4
Montañita, Colombia ... 120 C2
Montargis, France ... 25 E9
Montauban, France ... 26 D5
Montauk, U.S.A. ... 107 E13
Montauk Pt., U.S.A. ... 107 E13
Montbard, France ... 25 E11
Montbéliard, France ... 25 E13
Montblanch, Spain ... 28 D6
Montbrison, France ... 27 C8
Montcalm, Pic de, France ... 26 F5
Montceau-les-Mines, France ... 25 F11
Montchanin, France ... 27 D8
Montclair, U.S.A. ... 107 F10
Montcornet, France ... 25 C11
Montcuq, France ... 26 D5
Montdidier, France ... 25 C9
Monte Albán, Mexico ... 115 D5
Monte Alegre, Brazil ... 121 D7
Monte Alegre de Goiás, Brazil ... 123 D2
Monte Alegre de Minas, Brazil ... 123 E2
Monte Azul, Brazil ... 123 E3
Monte Bello Is., Australia ... 88 D2
Monte Carmelo, Brazil ... 123 E2
Monte Caseros, Argentina ... 126 C4
Monte Comán, Argentina ... 126 C2
Monte Cristi, Dom. Rep. ... 117 C5
Monte Dinero, Argentina ... 128 D3
Monte Lindo →, Paraguay ... 126 A4
Monte Quemado, Argentina ... 126 B3
Monte Redondo, Portugal ... 30 F2
Monte Rio, U.S.A. ... 112 G4
Monte San Giovanni Campano, Italy ... 34 A6
Monte San Savino, Italy ... 33 E8
Monte Sant' Ángelo, Italy ... 35 A8
Monte Santu, C. di, Italy ... 34 B2
Monte Vista, U.S.A. ... 111 H10
Monteagudo, Argentina ... 127 B5
Monteagudo, Bolivia ... 125 D5
Montealegre, Spain ... 29 G3
Montebello, Canada ... 98 C5
Montebelluna, Italy ... 33 C9
Montebourg, France ... 24 C5
Montecastrilli, Italy ... 33 F9
Montecatini Terme, Italy ... 32 E7
Montecito, U.S.A. ... 113 L7
Montecristi, Ecuador ... 120 D1
Montecristo, Italy ... 32 F7
Montefalco, Italy ... 33 F9
Montefiascone, Italy ... 33 F9
Montefrío, Spain ... 31 H6
Montegnée, Belgium ... 17 G7
Montego Bay, Jamaica ... 116 C4
Montegranaro, Italy ... 33 E10
Monteiro, Brazil ... 122 C4
Montejicar, Spain ... 29 H1
Montejinnie, Australia ... 88 C5
Montelíbano, Colombia ... 120 B2
Montélimar, France ... 27 D8
Montella, Italy ... 35 B8
Montello, U.S.A. ... 110 F6
Montellano, Spain ... 31 J5
Montello, U.S.A. ... 110 D10
Montelupo Fiorentino, Italy ... 32 E8
Montemor-o-Novo, Portugal ... 31 G2
Montemor-o-Velho, Portugal ... 30 E2
Montemorelos, Mexico ... 115 B5
Montendre, France ... 26 C3
Montenegro, Brazil ... 127 B5
Montenegro □, Yugoslavia ... 21 N9
Montenero di Bisáccia, Italy ... 33 G11
Montepuez, Mozam. ... 83 E4
Montepuez →, Mozam. ... 83 E5
Montepulciano, Italy ... 33 E8
Montereale, Italy ... 33 F10
Montereau-Fault-Yonne, France ... 25 D9
Monterey, U.S.A. ... 111 H3
Monterey B., U.S.A. ... 112 J5
Montería, Colombia ... 120 B2

Montero, Bolivia ... 125 D5
Monteros, Argentina ... 126 B2
Monterotondo, Italy ... 33 F9
Monterrey, Mexico ... 114 B4
Montes Altos, Brazil ... 122 C2
Montes Claros, Brazil ... 123 E3
Montesano, U.S.A. ... 112 D3
Montesárchio, Italy ... 35 A7
Montescaglioso, Italy ... 35 B9
Montesilvano Marina, Italy ... 33 F11
Montevarchi, Italy ... 33 E8
Montevideo, Uruguay ... 127 C4
Montevideo, U.S.A. ... 108 C7
Montezuma, U.S.A. ... 108 E8
Montfaucon, France ... 25 C12
Montfaucon-en-Velay, France ... 27 C8
Montfort, France ... 24 D5
Montfort, Neths. ... 17 F7
Montfort-l'Amaury, France ... 25 D8
Montgenèvre, France ... 27 D10
Montgomery = Sahiwal, Pakistan ... 62 D5
Montgomery, U.K. ... 13 E4
Montgomery, Ala., U.S.A. ... 105 J2
Montgomery, W. Va., U.S.A. ... 104 F5
Montguyon, France ... 26 C3
Monthey, Switz. ... 22 D3
Monticelli d'Ongina, Italy ... 32 C6
Monticello, Ark., U.S.A. ... 109 J9
Monticello, Fla., U.S.A. ... 105 K4
Monticello, Ind., U.S.A. ... 104 E2
Monticello, Iowa, U.S.A. ... 108 D9
Monticello, Ky., U.S.A. ... 105 G3
Monticello, Minn., U.S.A. ... 108 C8
Monticello, Miss., U.S.A. ... 109 K9
Monticello, N.Y., U.S.A. ... 107 E10
Monticello, Utah, U.S.A. ... 111 H9
Montichiari, Italy ... 32 C7
Montier-en-Der, France ... 25 D11
Montignac, France ... 26 C5
Montignies-sur-Sambre, Belgium ... 17 H4
Montigny, France ... 25 C13
Montigny-sur-Aube, France ... 25 E11
Montijo, Spain ... 31 G4
Montijo, Presa de, Spain ... 31 G4
Montilla, Spain ... 31 H6
Montlhéry, France ... 25 D9
Montluçon, France ... 26 B6
Montmagny, Canada ... 99 C5
Montmarault, France ... 26 B6
Montmartre, Canada ... 101 C8
Montmédy, France ... 25 C12
Montmélian, France ... 27 C10
Montmirail, France ... 25 D10
Montmoreau-St.-Cybard, France ... 26 C4
Montmorency, Canada ... 99 C5
Montmorillon, France ... 26 B4
Montmort, France ... 25 D10
Monto, Australia ... 90 C5
Montoir-sur-le-Loir, France ... 24 E7
Montório al Vomano, Italy ... 33 F10
Montoro, Spain ... 31 G6
Montour Falls, U.S.A. ... 106 D8
Montpelier, Idaho, U.S.A. ... 110 E8
Montpelier, Ohio, U.S.A. ... 104 E3
Montpelier, Vt., U.S.A. ... 107 B12
Montpellier, France ... 26 E7
Montpezat-de-Quercy, France ... 26 D5
Montpon-Ménestérol, France ... 26 D4
Montréal, Canada ... 98 C5
Montréal, France ... 26 E6
Montreal L., Canada ... 101 C7
Montreal Lake, Canada ... 101 C7
Montredon-Labessonnié, France ... 26 E6
Montréjeau, France ... 26 E4
Montrésor, France ... 24 E8
Montreuil, France ... 25 B8
Montreuil-Bellay, France ... 24 E6
Montreux, Switz. ... 22 D3
Montrevault, France ... 24 E5
Montrevel-en-Bresse, France ... 27 B9
Montrichard, France ... 24 E8
Montrose, U.K. ... 14 E6
Montrose, Colo., U.S.A. ... 111 G10
Montrose, Pa., U.S.A. ... 107 E9
Monts, Pte. des, Canada ... 99 C6
Monts-sur-Guesnes, France ... 24 F7
Montsalvy, France ... 26 D6
Montsant, Sierra de, Spain ... 28 D5
Montsauche, France ... 25 E11
Montsech, Sierra del, Spain ... 28 C5
Montseny, Spain ... 28 D7
Montserrat, Spain ... 28 D6
Montserrat ■, W. Indies ... 117 C7
Montuenga, Spain ... 30 D6
Montuiri, Spain ... 36 B9
Monveda, Zaïre ... 80 D4
Monywa, Burma ... 61 H19
Monza, Italy ... 32 C6
Monze, Zambia ... 83 F2
Monze, C., Pakistan ... 62 G2
Monzón, Spain ... 28 D5
Mooi River, S. Africa ... 85 D4
Mook, Neths. ... 16 E7
Moolawatana, Australia ... 91 D2
Mooliabeenee, Australia ... 89 F2
Mooloogool, Australia ... 89 E3
Moomin Cr. →, Australia ... 91 D4
Moonah →, Australia ... 90 C2

Moonbeam, Canada ... 98 C3
Moonda, L., Australia ... 90 D3
Moonie, Australia ... 91 D5
Moonie →, Australia ... 91 D4
Moonta, Australia ... 91 E2
Moora, Australia ... 89 F2
Mooraberree, Australia ... 90 D3
Moorarie, Australia ... 89 E2
Moorcroft, U.S.A. ... 108 C2
Moore →, Australia ... 89 F2
Moore, L., Australia ... 89 E2
Moore Reefs, Australia ... 90 B4
Moorefield, U.S.A. ... 104 F6
Moores Res., U.S.A. ... 107 B13
Mooresville, U.S.A. ... 105 H5
Moorfoot Hills, U.K. ... 14 F5
Moorhead, U.S.A. ... 108 B6
Mooroopna, Australia ... 91 F4
Moorpark, U.S.A. ... 113 L8
Moorreesburg, S. Africa ... 84 E2
Moorslede, Belgium ... 17 G2
Moosburg, Germany ... 19 G7
Moose →, Canada ... 98 B3
Moose Factory, Canada ... 98 B3
Moose I., Canada ... 101 C9
Moose Jaw, Canada ... 101 C7
Moose Jaw →, Canada ... 101 C7
Moose Lake, Canada ... 101 C8
Moose Lake, U.S.A. ... 108 B8
Moose Mountain Cr. →, Canada ... 101 D8
Moose Mountain Prov. Park, Canada ... 101 D8
Moose River, Canada ... 98 B3
Moosehead L., U.S.A. ... 99 C6
Moosomin, Canada ... 101 C8
Moosonee, Canada ... 98 B3
Moosup, U.S.A. ... 107 E13
Mopeia Velha, Mozam. ... 83 F4
Mopipi, Botswana ... 84 C3
Mopoi, C.A.R. ... 82 A2
Mopti, Mali ... 78 C4
Moqatta, Sudan ... 77 E4
Moquegua, Peru ... 124 D3
Moquegua □, Peru ... 124 D3
Mór, Hungary ... 21 H8
Móra, Portugal ... 31 G2
Mora, Sweden ... 9 F16
Mora, Minn., U.S.A. ... 108 C8
Mora, N. Mex., U.S.A. ... 111 J11
Mora de Ebro, Spain ... 28 D5
Mora de Rubielos, Spain ... 28 E4
Mora la Nueva, Spain ... 28 D5
Moraca →, Montenegro, Yug. ... 21 N9
Morada Nova, Brazil ... 122 C4
Morada Nova de Minas, Brazil ... 123 E2
Moradabad, India ... 63 E8
Morafenobe, Madag. ... 85 B7
Morag, Poland ... 20 B9
Moral de Calatrava, Spain ... 29 G1
Moraleja, Spain ... 30 E4
Morales, Colombia ... 120 C2
Moramanga, Madag. ... 85 B8
Moran, Kans., U.S.A. ... 109 G7
Moran, Wyo., U.S.A. ... 110 E8
Moranbah, Australia ... 90 C4
Morano Cálabro, Italy ... 35 C9
Morant Cays, Jamaica ... 116 C4
Morant Pt., Jamaica ... 116 C4
Morar, L., U.K. ... 14 E3
Moratalla, Spain ... 29 G3
Moratuwa, Sri Lanka ... 60 R11
Morava →, Slovak Rep. ... 20 G6
Morava →, Serbia, Yug. ... 21 M10
Moravia, Czech. ... 20 F7
Moravia, Romania ... 21 K11
Moravita, Romania ... 21 K11
Moravská Třebová, Czech. ... 20 F6
Morawa, Australia ... 89 E2
Morawhanna, Guyana ... 121 B6
Moray Firth, U.K. ... 14 D5
Morbach, Germany ... 19 F3
Morbegno, Italy ... 32 B6
Morbi, India ... 62 H4
Morbihan □, France ... 24 E4
Morcenx, France ... 26 D3
Mordelles, France ... 24 D5
Morden, Canada ... 101 D9
Mordovian Republic = Mordvinia □, Russia ... 42 C7
Mordovo, Russia ... 42 D5
Mordvinia □, Russia ... 42 C7
Møre og Romsdal fylke □, Norway ... 9 B2
Morea, Australia ... 91 F3
Morea, Greece ... 6 H10
Moreau →, U.S.A. ... 108 C4
Morecambe, U.K. ... 12 C5
Morecambe B., U.K. ... 12 C5
Moree, Australia ... 91 D4
Morehead, U.S.A. ... 104 F4
Morehead City, U.S.A. ... 105 H7
Morelia, Mexico ... 114 D4
Morella, Australia ... 90 C3
Morella, Spain ... 28 E4
Morelos, Mexico ... 114 B3
Morelos □, Mexico ... 115 D5
Morena, Sierra, Spain ... 31 G6
Morenci, U.S.A. ... 111 K9
Moreni, Romania ... 38 E8
Morero, Bolivia ... 125 C5
Moreru →, Brazil ... 125 C6

Moresby I., Canada ... 100 C2
Morestel, France ... 27 C9
Moret-sur-Loing, France ... 25 D9
Moreton, Australia ... 90 A3
Moreton I., Australia ... 91 D5
Moreuil, France ... 25 C9
Morey, Spain ... 36 B10
Morez, France ... 27 B10
Morgan, Australia ... 91 E2
Morgan, U.S.A. ... 110 F8
Morgan City, U.S.A. ... 109 L9
Morgan Hill, U.S.A. ... 112 H5
Morganfield, U.S.A. ... 104 G2
Morganton, U.S.A. ... 105 H5
Morgantown, U.S.A. ... 104 F6
Morgat, France ... 24 D2
Morgenzon, S. Africa ... 85 D4
Morges, Switz. ... 22 C2
Morghak, Iran ... 65 D8
Morhange, France ... 25 D13
Mori, Italy ... 32 C7
Morialmée, Belgium ... 17 H5
Morice L., Canada ... 100 C3
Morichal, Colombia ... 120 C3
Morichal Largo →, Venezuela ... 121 B5
Moriki, Nigeria ... 79 C6
Morinville, Canada ... 100 C6
Morioka, Japan ... 48 E10
Moris, Mexico ... 114 B3
Morlaàs, France ... 26 E3
Morlaix, France ... 24 D3
Morlanwelz, Belgium ... 17 H4
Mormanno, Italy ... 35 C8
Mormant, France ... 25 D9
Mornington, Vic., Australia ... 91 F4
Mornington, W. Austral., Australia ... 88 C4
Mornington, I., Chile ... 128 C1
Mornington I., Australia ... 90 B2
Mórnos →, Greece ... 39 L4
Moro, Sudan ... 77 E3
Moro G., Phil. ... 55 H5
Morocco ■, N. Afr. ... 74 B3
Morococha, Peru ... 124 C2
Morogoro, Tanzania ... 82 D4
Morogoro □, Tanzania ... 82 D4
Moroleón, Mexico ... 114 C4
Morombe, Madag. ... 85 C7
Moron, Argentina ... 126 C4
Morón, Cuba ... 116 B4
Mörön, Mongolia ... 54 B6
Morón de Almazán, Spain ... 28 D2
Morón de la Frontera, Spain ... 31 H5
Morona →, Peru ... 120 D2
Morona-Santiago □, Ecuador ... 120 D2
Morondava, Madag. ... 85 C7
Morondo, Ivory C. ... 78 D3
Morongo Valley, U.S.A. ... 113 L10
Moronou, Ivory C. ... 78 D4
Morotai, Indonesia ... 57 D7
Moroto, Uganda ... 82 B3
Moroto Summit, Kenya ... 82 B3
Morozovsk, Russia ... 43 F5
Morpeth, U.K. ... 12 B6
Morphou, Cyprus ... 66 E5
Morphou Bay, Cyprus ... 37 D11
Morrilton, U.S.A. ... 109 H8
Morrinhos, Ceara, Brazil ... 122 B3
Morrinhos, Minas Gerais, Brazil ... 123 E2
Morrinsville, N.Z. ... 87 G5
Morris, Canada ... 101 D9
Morris, Ill., U.S.A. ... 104 E1
Morris, Minn., U.S.A. ... 108 C7
Morris, Mt., Australia ... 89 E5
Morrisburg, Canada ... 98 D4
Morrison, U.S.A. ... 108 E10
Morristown, Ariz., U.S.A. ... 111 K7
Morristown, N.J., U.S.A. ... 107 F10
Morristown, S. Dak., U.S.A. ... 108 C4
Morristown, Tenn., U.S.A. ... 105 G4
Morro, Pta., Chile ... 126 B1
Morro Bay, U.S.A. ... 111 J3
Morro del Jable, Canary Is. ... 36 F5
Morro do Chapéu, Brazil ... 123 D3
Morro Jable, Pta. de, Canary Is. ... 36 F5
Morros, Brazil ... 122 B3
Morrosquillo, G. de, Colombia ... 116 E4
Morrumbene, Mozam. ... 85 C6
Mors, Nykøbing, Denmark ... 11 H2
Morshansk, Russia ... 42 D5
Mörsil, Sweden ... 10 A7
Mortagne →, France ... 25 D13
Mortagne-au-Perche, France ... 24 D7
Mortagne-sur-Gironde, France ... 26 C3
Mortagne-sur-Sèvre, France ... 24 F6
Mortain, France ... 24 D6
Mortara, Italy ... 32 C5
Morteau, France ... 25 E13
Morteros, Argentina ... 126 C3
Mortes, R. das →, Brazil ... 123 D1
Mortlake, Australia ... 91 F3
Morton, Tex., U.S.A. ... 109 J3
Morton, Wash., U.S.A. ... 112 D4
Mortsel, Belgium ... 17 F4
Morundah, Australia ... 91 E4
Moruya, Australia ... 91 F5
Morvan, France ... 25 E11
Morven, Australia ... 91 D4

Morvern, U.K. ... 14 E3
Morwell, Australia ... 91 F4
Mosalsk, Russia ... 42 C2
Mosbach, Germany ... 19 F5
Mošćenice, Croatia ... 33 C11
Mosciano Sant' Ángelo, Italy ... 33 F10
Moscos Is., Burma ... 58 E1
Moscow = Moskva, Russia ... 42 C3
Moscow, U.S.A. ... 110 C5
Mosel →, Europe ... 19 E3
Moselle = Mosel →, Europe ... 19 E3
Moselle □, France ... 25 D13
Moses Lake, U.S.A. ... 110 C4
Mosgiel, N.Z. ... 87 L3
Moshi, Tanzania ... 82 C4
Moshi □, Tanzania ... 82 C4
Moshupa, Botswana ... 84 C4
Mosjøen, Norway ... 8 D15
Moskenesøya, Norway ... 8 C15
Moskenstraumen, Norway ... 8 C15
Moskva, Russia ... 42 C3
Moskva →, Russia ... 42 C4
Moslavačka Gora, Croatia ... 33 C13
Mosomane, Botswana ... 84 C4
Moson-magyaróvár, Hungary ... 21 H7
Mospino, Ukraine ... 41 J9
Mosquera, Colombia ... 120 C2
Mosquero, U.S.A. ... 109 H3
Mosqueruela, Spain ... 28 E4
Mosquitia, Honduras ... 116 C3
Mosquitos, G. de los, Panama ... 116 E3
Moss, Norway ... 10 E4
Moss Vale, Australia ... 91 E5
Mossaka, Congo ... 80 E3
Mossâmedes, Brazil ... 123 E1
Mossbank, Canada ... 101 D7
Mossburn, N.Z. ... 87 L2
Mosselbaai, S. Africa ... 84 E3
Mossendjo, Congo ... 80 E2
Mosses, Col des, Switz. ... 22 D4
Mossgiel, Australia ... 91 E3
Mossman, Australia ... 90 B4
Mossoró, Brazil ... 122 C4
Mossuril, Mozam. ... 83 E5
Mossy →, Canada ... 101 C8
Most, Czech. ... 20 E3
Mosta, Malta ... 37 D1
Mostaganem, Algeria ... 75 A5
Mostar, Bos.-H. ... 21 M7
Mostardas, Brazil ... 127 C5
Mostefa, Rass, Tunisia ... 75 A7
Mostiska = Mostyska, Ukraine ... 41 H2
Móstoles, Spain ... 30 E7
Mosty = Masty, Belarus ... 40 F3
Mostyska, Ukraine ... 41 H2
Mosul = Al Mawşil, Iraq ... 67 D10
Mosulpo, S. Korea ... 51 H14
Mota del Cuervo, Spain ... 28 F2
Mota del Marqués, Spain ... 30 D5
Motagua →, Guatemala ... 116 C2
Motala, Sweden ... 11 F9
Motherwell, U.K. ... 14 F5
Motihari, India ... 63 F11
Motilla del Palancar, Spain ... 29 F3
Motnik, Slovenia ... 33 B11
Motocurunya, Venezuela ... 121 C5
Motovun, Croatia ... 33 C10
Motozintla de Mendoza, Mexico ... 115 D6
Motril, Spain ... 29 J1
Motru, Romania ... 38 E6
Mott, U.S.A. ... 108 B3
Móttola, Italy ... 35 B10
Motueka, N.Z. ... 87 J4
Motueka →, N.Z. ... 87 J4
Motul, Mexico ... 115 C7
Mouanda, Gabon ... 80 E2
Mouchalagane →, Canada ... 99 B6
Mouding, China ... 52 E3
Moudjeria, Mauritania ... 78 B2
Moudon, Switz. ... 22 C3
Mouila, Gabon ... 80 E2
Moulamein, Australia ... 91 F3
Mouliana, Greece ... 37 D7
Moulins, France ... 26 B7
Moulmein, Burma ... 61 L20
Moulouya, O. →, Morocco ... 75 A4
Moulton, U.S.A. ... 109 L6
Moultrie, U.S.A. ... 105 K4
Moultrie, L., U.S.A. ... 105 J5
Mound City, Mo., U.S.A. ... 108 E7
Mound City, S. Dak., U.S.A. ... 108 C4
Moúnda, Ákra, Greece ... 39 L3
Moundou, Chad ... 73 G8
Moundsville, U.S.A. ... 106 G4
Moung, Cambodia ... 58 F4
Mount Airy, U.S.A. ... 105 G5
Mount Albert, Canada ... 106 B5
Mount Amherst, Australia ... 88 C4
Mount Augustus, Australia ... 88 D2
Mount Angel, U.S.A. ... 110 D2
Mount Barker, S. Austral., Australia ... 91 F2
Mount Barker, W. Austral., Australia ... 89 F2
Mount Carmel, U.S.A. ... 104 F2
Mount Clemens, U.S.A. ... 98 D3
Mount Coolon, Australia ... 90 C4
Mount Darwin, Zimbabwe ... 83 F3
Mount Desert I., U.S.A. ... 99 D6

Mount Dora, *U.S.A.* 105 L5
Mount Douglas, *Australia* . 90 C4
Mount Eba, *Australia* 91 E2
Mount Edgecumbe, *U.S.A.* 100 B1
Mount Elizabeth, *Australia* 88 C4
Mount Fletcher, *S. Africa* . 85 E4
Mount Forest, *Canada* 98 D3
Mount Gambier, *Australia* . 91 F3
Mount Garnet, *Australia* .. 90 B4
Mount Hope, *N.S.W.,*
  Australia 91 E4
Mount Hope, *S. Austral.,*
  Australia 91 E2
Mount Hope, *U.S.A.* 104 G5
Mount Horeb, *U.S.A.* 108 D10
Mount Howitt, *Australia* .. 91 D3
Mount Isa, *Australia* 90 C2
Mount Keith, *Australia* ... 89 E3
Mount Laguna, *U.S.A.* ... 113 N10
Mount Larcom, *Australia* . 90 C5
Mount Lofty Ra., *Australia* 91 E2
Mount McKinley National
  Park, *U.S.A.* 96 B5
Mount Magnet, *Australia* . 89 E2
Mount Maunganui, *N.Z.* .. 87 G6
Mount Molloy, *Australia* .. 90 B4
Mount Monger, *Australia* . 89 F3
Mount Morgan, *Australia* . 90 C5
Mount Morris, *U.S.A.* 106 D7
Mount Mulligan, *Australia* 90 B3
Mount Narryer, *Australia* . 89 E2
Mount Olympus = Uludağ,
  Turkey 66 B3
Mount Oxide Mine,
  Australia 90 B2
Mount Pearl, *Canada* 99 C9
Mount Perry, *Australia* ... 91 D5
Mount Phillips, *Australia* . 88 D2
Mount Pleasant, *Iowa,*
  U.S.A. 108 E9
Mount Pleasant, *Mich.,*
  U.S.A. 104 D3
Mount Pleasant, *Pa.,*
  U.S.A. 106 F5
Mount Pleasant, *S.C.,*
  U.S.A. 105 J6
Mount Pleasant, *Tenn.,*
  U.S.A. 105 H2
Mount Pleasant, *Tex.,*
  U.S.A. 109 J7
Mount Pleasant, *Utah,*
  U.S.A. 110 G8
Mount Pocono, *U.S.A.* ... 107 E9
Mount Rainier National
  Park, *U.S.A.* 112 D5
Mount Revelstoke Nat.
  Park, *Canada* 100 C5
Mount Robson Prov. Park,
  Canada 100 C5
Mount Sandiman, *Australia* 89 D2
Mount Shasta, *U.S.A.* 110 F2
Mount Signal, *U.S.A.* 113 N11
Mount Sterling, *Ill., U.S.A.* 108 F9
Mount Sterling, *Ky.,*
  U.S.A. 104 F4
Mount Surprise, *Australia* . 90 B3
Mount Union, *U.S.A.* 106 F7
Mount Vernon, *Australia* . 88 D2
Mount Vernon, *Ind.,*
  U.S.A. 108 F10
Mount Vernon, *N.Y.,*
  U.S.A. 107 F11
Mount Vernon, *Ohio,*
  U.S.A. 106 F2
Mount Vernon, *Wash.,*
  U.S.A. 112 B4
Mountain Center, *U.S.A.* . 113 M10
Mountain City, *Nev.,*
  U.S.A. 110 F6
Mountain City, *Tenn.,*
  U.S.A. 105 G5
Mountain Grove, *U.S.A.* . 109 G8
Mountain Home, *Ark.,*
  U.S.A. 109 G8
Mountain Home, *Idaho,*
  U.S.A. 110 E6
Mountain Iron, *U.S.A.* ... 108 B8
Mountain Park, *Canada* .. 100 C5
Mountain Pass, *U.S.A.* ... 113 K11
Mountain View, *Ark.,*
  U.S.A. 109 H8
Mountain View, *Calif.,*
  U.S.A. 111 H2
Mountainair, *U.S.A.* 111 J10
Mountmellick, *Ireland* ... 15 C4
Moura, *Australia* 90 C4
Moura, *Brazil* 121 D5
Moura, *Portugal* 31 G3
Mourão, *Portugal* 31 G3
Mourdi, Dépression du,
  Chad 73 E9
Mourdiah, *Mali* 78 C3
Mourenx-Ville-Nouvelle,
  France 26 E3
Mouri, *Ghana* 79 D4
Mourilyan, *Australia* 90 B4
Mourmelon-le-Grand,
  France 25 C11
Mourne →, *U.K.* 15 B4
Mourne Mts., *U.K.* 15 B5
Mournies, *Greece* 37 D6
Mouscron, *Belgium* 17 G2
Moussoro, *Chad* 73 F8
Mouthe, *France* 25 F13
Moutier, *Switz.* 22 B4
Moûtiers, *France* 27 C10

Moutohara, *N.Z.* 87 H6
Moutong, *Indonesia* 57 D6
Mouy, *France* 25 C9
Mouzáki, *Greece* 39 K4
Movas, *Mexico* 114 B3
Moville, *Ireland* 15 A4
Moxhe, *Belgium* 17 G6
Moxotó →, *Brazil* 122 C4
Moy →, *Ireland* 15 B3
Moyale, *Kenya* 68 G2
Moyamba, *S. Leone* 78 D2
Moyen Atlas, *Morocco* . 74 B3
Moyle □, *U.K.* 15 A5
Moyo, *Indonesia* 56 F5
Moyobamba, *Peru* 124 B2
Moyyero →, *Russia* ... 45 C11
Mozambique =
  Moçambique, *Mozam.* 83 F5
Mozambique ■, *Africa* . 83 F4
Mozambique Chan., *Africa* 85 B7
Mozdok, *Russia* 43 J7
Mozdūrān, *Iran* 65 B9
Mozhaysk, *Russia* 42 C3
Mozhga, *Russia* 42 B11
Mozhnābād, *Iran* 65 C9
Mozirje, *Slovenia* 33 B11
Mozyr = Mazyr, *Belarus* 41 F5
Mpanda, *Tanzania* 82 D3
Mpanda □, *Tanzania* ... 82 D3
Mpésoba, *Mali* 78 C3
Mpika, *Zambia* 83 E3
Mpulungu, *Zambia* 83 D3
Mpumalanga, *S. Africa* . 85 D5
Mpwapwa, *Tanzania* ... 82 D4
Mpwapwa □, *Tanzania* . 82 D4
Mqinvartsveri = Kazbek,
  Russia 43 J7
Mrągowo, *Poland* 20 B11
Mramor, *Serbia, Yug.* . 21 M11
Mrimina, *Morocco* 74 C3
Mrkonjić Grad, *Bos.-H.* . 21 L7
Mrkopalj, *Croatia* 33 C11
Msab, Oued en →, *Algeria* 75 B6
Msaken, *Tunisia* 75 A7
Msambansovu, *Zimbabwe* 83 F3
M'sila, *Algeria* 75 A5
Msoro, *Zambia* 83 E3
Msta →, *Russia* 40 C6
Mstislavl = Mstsislaw,
  Belarus 40 E6
Mstsislaw, *Belarus* 40 E6
Mtama, *Tanzania* 83 E4
Mtilikwe →, *Zimbabwe* . 83 G3
Mtsensk, *Russia* 42 D3
Mtskheta, *Georgia* 43 K7
Mtubatuba, *S. Africa* ... 85 D5
Mtwara-Mikindani,
  Tanzania 83 E5
Mu Gia, Deo, *Vietnam* . 58 D5
Mu Us Shamo, *China* .. 50 E5
Muaná, *Brazil* 122 B2
Muang Chiang Rai,
  Thailand 58 C2
Muang Lamphun, *Thailand* 58 C2
Muang Pak Beng, *Laos* . 58 C3
Muar, *Malaysia* 59 L4
Muarabungo, *Indonesia* . 56 E2
Muaraenim, *Indonesia* .. 56 E2
Muarajuloi, *Indonesia* .. 56 E4
Muarakaman, *Indonesia* . 56 E5
Muaratebo, *Indonesia* .. 56 E2
Muaratembesi, *Indonesia* 56 E2
Muaratewe, *Indonesia* .. 56 E4
Mubarakpur, *India* 63 F10
Mubarraz = Al Mubarraz,
  Si. Arabia 65 E6
Mubende, *Uganda* 82 B3
Mubi, *Nigeria* 79 C7
Mubur, P., *Indonesia* ... 59 L6
Mucajaí, *Brazil* 121 C5
Mucajaí, Serra do, *Brazil* 121 C5
Muchachos, Roque de los,
  Canary Is. 36 F2
Mücheln, *Germany* 18 D7
Muchinga Mts., *Zambia* 83 E3
Muchkapskiy, *Russia* ... 42 E6
Muck, *U.K.* 14 E2
Muckadilla, *Australia* ... 91 D4
Muco →, *Colombia* 120 C3
Mucuim →, *Brazil* 125 B5
Mucur, *Turkey* 66 C6
Mucuri, *Brazil* 123 E4
Mucurici, *Brazil* 123 E3
Mucusso, *Angola* 84 B3
Muda, *Canary Is.* 36 F6
Mudanjiang →, *China* .. 51 A15
Mudanjiang, *China* 51 B15
Mudanya, *Turkey* 66 B3
Muddy Cr. →, *U.S.A.* . 111 H8
Mudgee, *Australia* 91 E4
Mudjatik →, *Canada* .. 101 B7
Mudurnu, *Turkey* 66 B4
Muecate, *Mozam.* 83 E4
Mueda, *Mozam.* 83 E4
Mueller Ra., *Australia* .. 88 C4
Muende, *Mozam.* 83 E3
Muerto, Mar, *Mexico* .. 115 D6
Muertos, Punta de los,
  Spain 29 J3
Mufindi □, *Tanzania* ... 83 D4
Mufu Shan, *China* 53 C10
Mufulira, *Zambia* 83 E2
Mufumbiro Range, *Africa* 82 C2
Mugardos, *Spain* 30 B2
Muge, *Portugal* 31 F2

Muge →, *Portugal* 31 F2
Múggia, *Italy* 33 C10
Mughayrā', *Si. Arabia* .. 64 D3
Mugi, *Japan* 49 H7
Mugia, *Spain* 30 B1
Mugila, Mts., *Zaïre* 82 D2
Muğla, *Turkey* 66 D3
Müglizh, *Bulgaria* 38 G8
Mugu, *Nepal* 63 E10
Muhammad, Râs, *Egypt* . 76 B3
Muhammad Qol, *Sudan* . 76 C4
Muhammadabad, *India* . 63 F10
Muhesi →, *Tanzania* ... 82 D4
Muheza □, *Tanzania* ... 82 C4
Mühldorf, *Germany* 19 G8
Mühlhausen, *Germany* . 18 D6
Mühlig Hofmann fjella,
  Antarctica 5 D3
Muhos, *Finland* 8 D22
Muhu, *Estonia* 9 G20
Muhutwe, *Tanzania* 82 C3
Muiden, *Neths.* 16 D6
Muikamachi, *Japan* 49 F9
Muine Bheag, *Ireland* .. 15 D5
Muiños, *Spain* 30 D3
Muir, L., *Australia* 89 F2
Mukachevo, *Ukraine* ... 41 H2
Mukacheve = Mukacheve,
  Ukraine 41 H2
Mukah, *Malaysia* 56 D4
Mukawwa, Geziret, *Egypt* 76 C4
Mukdahan, *Thailand* ... 58 D5
Mukden = Shenyang,
  China 51 D12
Mukhtolovo, *Russia* 42 C6
Mukhtuya = Lensk, *Russia* 45 C12
Mukinbudin, *Australia* .. 89 F2
Mukishi, *Zaïre* 83 D1
Mukomuko, *Indonesia* .. 56 E2
Mukomwenze, *Zaïre* ... 82 D2
Muktsar, *India* 62 D6
Mukur, *Afghan.* 62 C2
Mukutawa →, *Canada* . 101 C9
Mukwela, *Zambia* 83 F2
Mula, *Spain* 29 G3
Mulange, *Zaïre* 82 C2
Mulchén, *Chile* 126 D1
Mulde →, *Germany* 18 D8
Mule Creek, *U.S.A.* 108 D2
Muleba, *Tanzania* 82 C3
Muleba □, *Tanzania* 82 C3
Mulegns, *Switz.* 23 C9
Muleshoe, *U.S.A.* 109 H3
Mulgathing, *Australia* .. 91 E1
Mulgrave, *Canada* 99 C7
Mulhacén, *Spain* 29 H1
Mülheim, *Germany* 18 D2
Mulhouse, *France* 25 E14
Muli, *China* 52 D3
Muling, *China* 51 B16
Mull, *U.K.* 14 E3
Mullaittivu, *Sri Lanka* .. 60 Q12
Mullen, *U.S.A.* 108 D4
Mullengudgery, *Australia* 91 E4
Mullens, *U.S.A.* 104 G5
Muller, Pegunungan,
  Indonesia 56 D4
Mullet Pen., *Ireland* 15 B1
Mullewa, *Australia* 89 E2
Müllheim, *Germany* 19 H3
Mulligan →, *Australia* .. 90 C2
Mullin, *U.S.A.* 109 K5
Mullingar, *Ireland* 15 C4
Mullins, *U.S.A.* 105 H6
Mullumbimby, *Australia* 91 D5
Mulobezi, *Zambia* 83 F2
Multan, *Pakistan* 62 D4
Multrå, *Sweden* 10 A11
Mulumbe, Mts., *Zaïre* .. 83 D2
Mulungushi Dam, *Zambia* 83 E2
Mulvane, *U.S.A.* 109 G6
Mulwad, *Sudan* 76 D3
Mulwala, *Australia* 91 F4
Mumbaï = Bombay, *India* 60 K8
Mumbwa, *Zambia* 83 E2
Mumra, *Russia* 43 H8
Mun →, *Thailand* 58 E5
Muna, *Indonesia* 57 F6
Munamagi, *Estonia* 9 H22
Münchberg, *Germany* .. 19 E7
Müncheberg, *Germany* . 18 C10
München, *Germany* 19 G7
Munchen-Gladbach =
  Mönchengladbach,
  Germany 18 D2
Muncho Lake, *Canada* . 100 B3
Munchŏn, *N. Korea* 51 E14
Münchwilen, *Switz.* 23 B7
Muncie, *U.S.A.* 104 E3
Muncoonie, L., *Australia* 90 D2
Mundala, *Indonesia* 57 E10
Mundare, *Canada* 100 C6
Munday, *U.S.A.* 109 J5
Münden, *Germany* 18 D5
Mundindi, *Australia* 88 D3
Mundo →, *Spain* 29 G2
Mundo Novo, *Brazil* ... 123 D3
Mundra, *India* 62 H3
Mundrabilla, *Australia* .. 89 F4
Munducurus, *Brazil* 121 D6
Munera, *Spain* 29 F2
Mungallala, *Australia* ... 91 D4
Mungallala Cr. →,
  Australia 91 D4
Mungana, *Australia* 90 B3
Mungaoli, *India* 62 G8
Mungari, *Mozam.* 83 F3

Mungbere, *Zaïre* 82 B2
Munger, *India* 63 G12
Mungindi, *Australia* 91 D4
Mungo, *Australia* 81 G3
Munhango, *Angola* 81 G3
Munich = München,
  Germany 19 G7
Munising, *U.S.A.* 104 B2
Munka-Ljungby, *Sweden* 11 H6
Munkedal, *Sweden* 11 F5
Munku-Sardyk, *Russia* . 45 D11
Münnerstadt, *Germany* . 19 E6
Muñoz Gamero, Pen.,
  Chile 128 D2
Munroe L., *Canada* 101 B9
Munsan, *S. Korea* 51 F14
Münsingen, *Switz.* 22 C5
Munster, *France* 25 D14
Munster, *Niedersachsen,*
  Germany 18 C6
Münster,
  Nordrhein-Westfalen,
  Germany 18 D3
Münster, *Switz.* 23 D6
Munster □, *Ireland* 15 D3
Muntadgin, *Australia* ... 89 F2
Muntele Mare, *Romania* 38 C6
Muntok, *Indonesia* 56 E3
Munyama, *Zambia* 83 F2
Munzur Dağları, *Turkey* 67 C8
Muong Beng, *Laos* 58 B3
Muong Et, *Laos* 58 B5
Muong Hai, *Laos* 58 B3
Muong Hiem, *Laos* 58 B4
Muong Houn, *Laos* 58 B3
Muong Hung, *Vietnam* . 58 B4
Muong Kau, *Laos* 58 E5
Muong Khao, *Laos* 58 C4
Muong Khoua, *Laos* ... 58 B4
Muong Liep, *Laos* 58 C3
Muong May, *Laos* 58 E6
Muong Ngeun, *Laos* ... 58 B3
Muong Ngoi, *Laos* 58 B4
Muong Nhie, *Vietnam* .. 58 A4
Muong Nong, *Laos* 58 D6
Muong Ou Tay, *Laos* .. 58 A3
Muong Oua, *Laos* 58 C3
Muong Peun, *Laos* 58 B4
Muong Phalane, *Laos* .. 58 D5
Muong Phieng, *Laos* ... 58 C3
Muong Phine, *Laos* 58 D6
Muong Sai, *Laos* 58 B3
Muong Saiapoun, *Laos* . 58 C3
Muong Sen, *Vietnam* ... 58 C5
Muong Sing, *Laos* 58 B3
Muong Son, *Laos* 58 B4
Muong Soui, *Laos* 58 C4
Muong Va, *Laos* 58 B4
Muong Xia, *Vietnam* ... 58 B5
Muonio, *Finland* 8 C20
Muonionjoki →, *Finland* . 8 C20
Muotathal, *Switz.* 23 C7
Mupa, *Angola* 81 H3
Muping, *China* 51 F11
Muqaddam, Wadi →,
  Sudan 76 D3
Muqdisho, *Somali Rep.* . 68 G4
Mur-de-Bretagne, *France* 24 D4
Mura →, *Slovenia* 33 B13
Muradiye, *Turkey* 67 C10
Murakami, *Japan* 48 E9
Murallón, Cuerro, *Chile* . 128 C2
Muralto, *Switz.* 23 D7
Muranda, *Rwanda* 82 C2
Murang'a, *Kenya* 82 C4
Murashi, *Russia* 44 D5
Murat, *France* 26 C6
Murat →, *Turkey* 67 C9
Muratlı, *Turkey* 66 B2
Muravera, *Italy* 34 C2
Murayama, *Japan* 48 E10
Murban, *U.A.E.* 65 F7
Murça, *Portugal* 30 D3
Murchison →, *Australia* 89 E1
Murchison, Mt., *Antarctica* 5 D11
Murchison Falls =
  Kabarega Falls, *Uganda* 82 B3
Murchison House, *Australia* 89 E1
Murchison Ra., *Australia* . 90 C1
Murchison Rapids, *Malawi* 83 F3
Murcia, *Spain* 29 G3
Murcia □, *Spain* 29 H3
Murdo, *U.S.A.* 108 D4
Murdoch Pt., *Australia* .. 90 A3
Mureş →, *Romania* 38 C3
Mureşul = Mureş →,
  Romania 38 C3
Muret, *France* 26 E5
Murfatlar, *Romania* 38 E11
Murfreesboro, *U.S.A.* ... 105 H2
Murg, *Switz.* 23 B8
Murg →, *Germany* 19 G4
Murgab = Murghob,
  Tajikistan 44 F8
Murgenthal, *Switz.* 22 B5
Murghob, *Tajikistan* 44 F8
Murgon, *Australia* 91 D5
Murgoo, *Australia* 89 E2
Muri, *Switz.* 23 B6
Muria, *Indonesia* 57 G14
Muriaé, *Brazil* 123 F3
Murias de Paredes, *Spain* 30 C4
Murici, *Brazil* 122 C4
Muriel Mine, *Zimbabwe* . 83 F3
Müritz-see, *Germany* ... 18 B8
Murka, *Kenya* 82 C4
Murmansk, *Russia* 44 C4

Murmerwoude, *Neths.* .. 16 B8
Murnau, *Germany* 19 H7
Muro, *France* 27 F12
Muro, *Spain* 36 B10
Muro, C. de, *France* 27 G12
Muro Lucano, *Italy* 35 B8
Murom, *Russia* 42 C6
Muroran, *Japan* 48 C10
Muros, *Spain* 30 C1
Muros y de Noya, Ría de,
  Spain 30 C2
Muroto, *Japan* 49 H7
Muroto-Misaki, *Japan* .. 49 H7
Murphy, *U.S.A.* 110 E5
Murphys, *U.S.A.* 112 G6
Murphysboro, *U.S.A.* .. 109 G10
Murrat, *Sudan* 76 D2
Murray, *Ky., U.S.A.* ... 105 G1
Murray, *Utah, U.S.A.* .. 110 F8
Murray →, *Australia* ... 91 F2
Murray →, *Canada* 100 B4
Murray, L., *U.S.A.* 105 H5
Murray Bridge, *Australia* . 91 F2
Murray Downs, *Australia* 90 C1
Murray Harbour, *Canada* . 99 C7
Murraysburg, *S. Africa* .. 84 E3
Murree, *Pakistan* 62 C5
Murrieta, *U.S.A.* 113 M9
Murrin Murrin, *Australia* . 89 E3
Murrumbidgee →,
  Australia 91 E3
Murrumburrah, *Australia* 91 E4
Murrurundi, *Australia* ... 91 E5
Murshid, *Sudan* 76 C3
Murshidabad, *India* 63 G13
Murska Sobota, *Slovenia* 33 B13
Murten, *Switz.* 22 C4
Murtensee, *Switz.* 22 C4
Murtle L., *Canada* 100 C5
Murtoa, *Australia* 91 F3
Murtosa, *Portugal* 30 E2
Muru →, *Brazil* 124 B3
Murungu, *Tanzania* 82 C3
Murwara, *India* 63 H9
Murwillumbah, *Australia* 91 D5
Mürz →, *Austria* 21 H5
Mürzzuschlag, *Austria* .. 21 H5
Muş, *Turkey* 67 C9
Mûsa, G., *Egypt* 76 J8
Musa Khel, *Pakistan* 62 D3
Mūsá Qal'eh, *Afghan.* .. 60 C4
Musaffargarh, *Pakistan* . 60 D7
Musala, *Bulgaria* 38 G6
Musala, *Indonesia* 56 D1
Musan, *N. Korea* 51 C15
Musangu, *Zaïre* 83 E1
Musasa, *Tanzania* 82 C3
Musay'īd, *Qatar* 65 E6
Muscat = Masqat, *Oman* . 68 C6
Muscat & Oman =
  Oman ■, *Asia* 68 C6
Muscatine, *U.S.A.* 108 E9
Musel, *Spain* 30 B5
Musgrave, *Australia* 90 A3
Musgrave Ras., *Australia* 89 E5
Mushie, *Zaïre* 80 E3
Mushin, *Nigeria* 79 D5
Musi →, *Indonesia* 56 E2
Muskeg →, *Canada* ... 100 A4
Muskegon, *U.S.A.* 104 D2
Muskegon →, *U.S.A.* .. 104 D2
Muskegon Heights, *U.S.A.* 104 D2
Muskogee, *U.S.A.* 109 H7
Muskwa →, *Canada* ... 100 B4
Muslimiyah, *Syria* 64 B3
Musmar, *Sudan* 76 D4
Musoma, *Tanzania* 82 C3
Musoma □, *Tanzania* ... 82 C3
Musquaro, L., *Canada* .. 99 B7
Musquodoboit Harbour,
  Canada 99 D7
Musselburgh, *U.K.* 14 F5
Musselkanaal, *Neths.* ... 16 C10
Musselshell →, *U.S.A.* . 110 C10
Mussidan, *France* 26 C4
Mussomeli, *Italy* 34 E6
Musson, *Belgium* 17 J7
Mussoorie, *India* 62 D8
Mussuco, *Angola* 84 B2
Mustafakemalpaşa, *Turkey* 66 B3
Mustang, *Nepal* 63 E10
Musters, L., *Argentina* .. 128 C3
Musudan, *N. Korea* 51 D15
Muswellbrook, *Australia* . 91 E5
Mût, *Egypt* 76 B2
Mut, *Turkey* 66 D5
Mutanda, *Mozam.* 85 C5
Mutanda, *Zambia* 83 E2
Mutare, *Zimbabwe* 83 F3
Muting, *Indonesia* 57 F10
Mutoray, *Russia* 45 C11
Mutshatsha, *Zaïre* 83 E1
Mutsu, *Japan* 48 D10
Mutsu-Wan, *Japan* 48 D10
Muttaburra, *Australia* ... 90 C3
Mutuáli, *Mozam.* 83 E4
Mutunópolis, *Brazil* 123 D2
Muweilih, *Egypt* 69 E3
Muxima, *Angola* 80 F2
Muy Muy, *Nic.* 116 D2
Muyinga, *Burundi* 82 C3
Muynak, *Uzbekistan* 44 E6
Muzaffarabad, *Pakistan* . 63 B5
Muzaffargarh, *Pakistan* . 62 D4
Muzaffarnagar, *India* ... 62 E7
Muzaffarpur, *India* 63 F11

Navarra

Muzhi, *Russia* 44 C7
Muzillac, *France* 24 E4
Muzon, C., *U.S.A.* 100 C2
Muztag, *China* 54 C3
Mvôlô, *Sudan* 77 F2
Mvuma, *Zimbabwe* 83 F3
Mvurwi, *Zimbabwe* 83 F3
Mwadui, *Tanzania* 82 C3
Mwambo, *Tanzania* 83 E5
Mwandi, *Zambia* 83 F1
Mwanza, *Tanzania* 82 C3
Mwanza, *Zaïre* 82 D2
Mwanza, *Zambia* 83 F1
Mwanza □, *Tanzania* 82 C3
Mwaya, *Tanzania* 83 D3
Mweelrea, *Ireland* 15 C2
Mweka, *Zaïre* 80 E4
Mwenezi, *Zimbabwe* 83 G3
Mwenezi →, *Mozam.* 83 G3
Mwenga, *Zaïre* 82 C2
Mweru, L., *Zambia* 83 D2
Mweza Range, *Zimbabwe* 83 G3
Mwilambwe, *Zaïre* 82 D5
Mwimbi, *Tanzania* 83 D3
Mwinilunga, *Zambia* 83 E1
My Tho, *Vietnam* 59 G6
Mya, O. →, *Algeria* 75 B5
Myajlar, *India* 62 F4
Myanaung, *Burma* 61 K19
Myanmar = Burma ■, *Asia* 61 J20
Myaungmya, *Burma* 61 L19
Myeik Kyunzu, *Burma* 59 G1
Myerstown, *U.S.A.* 107 F8
Myingyan, *Burma* 61 J19
Myitkyina, *Burma* 61 G20
Myjava, *Slovak Rep.* 20 G7
Mykhaylivka, *Ukraine* 41 J8
Mykines, *Færoe Is.* 8 E9
Mykolayiv, *Ukraine* 41 J7
Mymensingh, *Bangla.* 61 G17
Mynydd Du, *U.K.* 13 F4
Mýrdalsjökull, *Iceland* 8 E4
Myrhorod, *Ukraine* 41 H7
Myroodah, *Australia* 88 C3
Myrtle Beach, *U.S.A.* 105 J6
Myrtle Creek, *U.S.A.* 110 E2
Myrtle Point, *U.S.A.* 110 E1
Myrtou, *Cyprus* 37 D12
Mysen, *Norway* 10 E5
Mysia, *Turkey* 66 C2
Myslenice, *Poland* 20 F9
Myślibórz, *Poland* 20 C4
Mysłowice, *Poland* 20 E9
Mysore = Karnataka □, *India* 60 N10
Mysore, *India* 60 N10
Mystic, *U.S.A.* 107 E13
Myszków, *Poland* 20 E9
Mythen, *Switz.* 23 B7
Mytishchi, *Russia* 42 C3
Myton, *U.S.A.* 110 F8
Mývatn, *Iceland* 8 D5
Mzimba, *Malawi* 83 E3
Mzimkulu →, *S. Africa* 85 E5
Mzimvubu →, *S. Africa* 85 E4
Mzuzu, *Malawi* 83 E3

N

N' Dioum, *Senegal* 78 B2
Na Hearadh = Harris, *U.K.* 14 D2
Na Noi, *Thailand* 58 C3
Na Phao, *Laos* 58 D5
Na Sam, *Vietnam* 58 A6
Na San, *Vietnam* 58 B5
Naab →, *Germany* 19 F8
Naaldwijk, *Neths.* 16 E4
Na'am, *Sudan* 77 F2
Naantali, *Finland* 9 F19
Naarden, *Neths.* 16 D6
Naas, *Ireland* 15 C5
Nababiep, *S. Africa* 84 D2
Nabadwip = Navadwip, *India* 63 H13
Nabari, *Japan* 49 G8
Nabawa, *Australia* 89 E1
Nabberu, L., *Australia* 89 E3
Nabburg, *Germany* 19 F8
Naberezhnyye Chelny, *Russia* 42 C11
Nabeul, *Tunisia* 75 A7
Nabha, *India* 62 D7
Nabīd, *Iran* 65 D8
Nabire, *Indonesia* 57 E9
Nabisar, *Pakistan* 62 G3
Nabisipi →, *Canada* 99 B7
Nabiswera, *Uganda* 82 B3
Nablus = Nābulus, *West Bank* 69 C4
Naboomspruit, *S. Africa* 85 C4
Nabua, *Phil.* 55 E5
Nābulus, *West Bank* 69 C4
Nacala, *Mozam.* 83 E5
Nacala-Velha, *Mozam.* 83 E5
Nacaome, *Honduras* 116 D2
Nacaroa, *Mozam.* 83 E4
Naches, *U.S.A.* 110 C3
Naches →, *U.S.A.* 112 D6
Nachingwea, *Tanzania* 83 E4
Nachingwea □, *Tanzania* 83 E4
Nachna, *India* 62 F4
Náchod, *Czech.* 20 E6
Nacimiento Reservoir, *U.S.A.* 112 K6
Nacka, *Sweden* 10 E12
Nackara, *Australia* 91 E2
Naco, *Mexico* 114 A3
Naco, *U.S.A.* 111 L9
Nacogdoches, *U.S.A.* 109 K7
Nácori Chico, *Mexico* 114 B3
Nacozari, *Mexico* 114 A3
Nadi, *Sudan* 76 D3
Nadiad, *India* 62 H5
Nădlac, *Romania* 38 C3
Nador, *Morocco* 75 A4
Nadur, *Malta* 37 C1
Nadūshan, *Iran* 65 C7
Nadvirna, *Ukraine* 41 H3
Nadvornaya = Nadvirna, *Ukraine* 41 H3
Nadym, *Russia* 44 C8
Nadym →, *Russia* 44 C8
Nærbø, *Norway* 9 G11
Næstved, *Denmark* 11 J5
Nafada, *Nigeria* 79 C7
Näfels, *Switz.* 23 B8
Naftshahr, *Iran* 67 E11
Nafud Desert = An Nafūd, *Si. Arabia* 64 D4
Nafūsah, Jabal, *Libya* 75 B7
Nag Hammâdi, *Egypt* 76 B3
Naga, *Phil.* 55 E5
Naga, Kreb en, *Africa* 74 D3
Nagagami →, *Canada* 98 C3
Nagahama, *Japan* 49 G8
Nagai, *Japan* 48 E10
Nagaland □, *India* 61 F19
Nagano, *Japan* 49 F9
Nagano □, *Japan* 49 F9
Nagaoka, *Japan* 49 F9
Nagappattinam, *India* 60 P11
Nagar Parkar, *Pakistan* 62 G4
Nagasaki, *Japan* 49 H4
Nagasaki □, *Japan* 49 H4
Nagato, *Japan* 49 G5
Nagaur, *India* 62 F5
Nagercoil, *India* 60 Q10
Nagina, *India* 63 E8
Nagīneh, *Iran* 65 C8
Nagir, *Pakistan* 63 A6
Nagold, *Germany* 19 G4
Nagold →, *Germany* 19 G4
Nagoorin, *Australia* 90 C5
Nagorno-Karabakh, *Azerbaijan* 67 C12
Nagornyy, *Russia* 45 D13
Nagoya, *Japan* 49 G8
Nagpur, *India* 60 J11
Nagua, *Dom. Rep.* 117 C6
Nagykanizsa, *Hungary* 21 J7
Nagykörös, *Hungary* 21 H9
Nagyléta, *Hungary* 21 H11
Naha, *Japan* 49 L3
Nahanni Butte, *Canada* 100 A4
Nahanni Nat. Park, *Canada* 100 A3
Nahariyya, *Israel* 66 F6
Nahāvand, *Iran* 67 E13
Nahe →, *Germany* 19 F3
Nahîya, W. →, *Egypt* 76 J7
Nahlin, *Canada* 100 B2
Nahuel Huapi, L., *Argentina* 128 B2
Naicá, *Mexico* 114 B3
Naicam, *Canada* 101 C8
Nā'ifah, *Si. Arabia* 68 D5
Naila, *Germany* 19 E7
Nain, *Canada* 99 A7
Nā'īn, *Iran* 65 C7
Naini Tal, *India* 63 E8
Nainpur, *India* 60 H12
Naintré, *France* 24 F7
Naipu, *Romania* 38 E8
Naira, *Indonesia* 57 E7
Nairn, *U.K.* 14 D5
Nairobi, *Kenya* 82 C4
Naissaar, *Estonia* 9 G21
Naivasha, *Kenya* 82 C4
Naivasha, L., *Kenya* 82 C4
Najac, *France* 26 D5
Najafābād, *Iran* 65 C6
Nájera, *Spain* 28 C2
Najerilla →, *Spain* 28 C2
Najibabad, *India* 62 E8
Najin, *N. Korea* 51 C16
Najmah, *Si. Arabia* 65 E6
Naju, *S. Korea* 51 G14
Nakadōri-Shima, *Japan* 49 H4
Nakalagba, *Zaïre* 82 B2
Nakaminato, *Japan* 49 F10
Nakamura, *Japan* 49 H6
Nakano, *Japan* 49 F9
Nakano-Shima, *Japan* 49 K4
Nakashibetsu, *Japan* 48 C12
Nakfa, *Eritrea* 77 D4
Nakhichevan = Naxçıvan, *Azerbaijan* 67 C11
Nakhichevan Republic = Naxçıvan □, *Azerbaijan* 67 C11
Nakhl, *Egypt* 69 F2
Nakhl-e Taqī, *Iran* 65 E7
Nakhodka, *Russia* 45 E14
Nakhon Nayok, *Thailand* 58 E3
Nakhon Pathom, *Thailand* 58 F3
Nakhon Phanom, *Thailand* 58 D5
Nakhon Ratchasima, *Thailand* 58 E4
Nakhon Sawan, *Thailand* 58 E3
Nakhon Si Thammarat, *Thailand* 59 H3
Nakhon Thai, *Thailand* 58 D3
Nakina, *B.C., Canada* 100 B2
Nakina, *Ont., Canada* 98 B2
Nakło nad Noteią, *Poland* 20 B7
Nakodar, *India* 62 D6
Nakskov, *Denmark* 11 K5
Näkten, *Sweden* 10 B8
Naktong →, *S. Korea* 51 G15
Nakuru, *Kenya* 82 C4
Nakuru □, *Kenya* 82 C4
Nakuru, L., *Kenya* 82 C4
Nakusp, *Canada* 100 C5
Nal →, *Pakistan* 62 G1
Nalchik, *Russia* 43 J6
Nälden, *Sweden* 10 A8
Näldsjön, *Sweden* 10 A8
Nalerigu, *Ghana* 79 C4
Nalgonda, *India* 60 L11
Nalhati, *India* 63 G12
Nalinnes, *Belgium* 17 H4
Nallamalai Hills, *India* 60 M11
Nallıhan, *Turkey* 66 B4
Nalón →, *Spain* 30 B4
Nālūt, *Libya* 75 B7
Nam Can, *Vietnam* 59 H5
Nam Co, *China* 54 C4
Nam Dinh, *Vietnam* 58 B6
Nam Du, Hon, *Vietnam* 59 H5
Nam Ngum Dam, *Laos* 58 C4
Nam-Phan, *Vietnam* 59 G6
Nam Phong, *Thailand* 58 D4
Nam Tha, *Laos* 58 B3
Nam Tok, *Thailand* 58 E2
Namacunde, *Angola* 84 B2
Namacurra, *Mozam.* 85 B6
Namak, Daryācheh-ye, *Iran* 65 C7
Namak, Kavir-e, *Iran* 65 C8
Namaland, *Namibia* 84 C2
Namangan, *Uzbekistan* 44 E8
Namapa, *Mozam.* 83 E4
Namaqualand, *S. Africa* 84 D2
Namasagali, *Uganda* 82 B3
Namber, *Indonesia* 57 E8
Nambour, *Australia* 91 D5
Nambucca Heads, *Australia* 91 E5
Namche Bazar, *Nepal* 63 F12
Namchonjŏm, *N. Korea* 51 E14
Namêche, *Belgium* 17 H6
Namecunda, *Mozam.* 83 E4
Nameh, *Indonesia* 56 D5
Nameponda, *Mozam.* 83 F4
Nametil, *Mozam.* 83 F4
Namew L., *Canada* 101 C8
Namib Desert = Namibwoestyn, *Namibia* 84 C2
Namibe, *Angola* 81 H2
Namibe □, *Angola* 84 B1
Namibia ■, *Africa* 84 C2
Namibwoestyn, *Namibia* 84 C2
Namīn, *Iran* 67 C13
Namlea, *Indonesia* 57 E7
Namoi →, *Australia* 91 E4
Namous, O. en →, *Algeria* 75 B4
Nampa, *U.S.A.* 110 E5
Nampō-Shotō, *Japan* 49 J10
Nampula, *Mozam.* 83 F4
Namrole, *Indonesia* 57 E7
Namse Shankou, *China* 61 E13
Namsen →, *Norway* 8 D14
Namsos, *Norway* 8 D14
Namtsy, *Russia* 45 C13
Namtu, *Burma* 61 H20
Namtumbo, *Tanzania* 83 E4
Namu, *Canada* 100 C3
Namur, *Belgium* 17 H5
Namur □, *Belgium* 17 H6
Namutoni, *Namibia* 84 B2
Namwala, *Zambia* 83 F2
Namwŏn, *S. Korea* 51 G14
Namysłów, *Poland* 20 D7
Nan, *Thailand* 58 C3
Nan →, *Thailand* 58 E3
Nan Xian, *China* 53 C9
Nanaimo, *Canada* 100 D4
Nanam, *N. Korea* 51 D15
Nanan, *China* 53 E12
Nanango, *Australia* 91 D5
Nan'ao, *China* 53 F11
Nanao, *Japan* 49 F8
Nanbu, *China* 52 B6
Nanchang, *China* 53 C10
Nancheng, *China* 53 D11
Nanching = Nanjing, *China* 53 A12
Nanchong, *China* 52 B6
Nanchuan, *China* 52 C6
Nancy, *France* 25 D13
Nanda Devi, *India* 63 D8
Nandan, *China* 52 E6
Nandan, *Japan* 49 G7
Nanded, *India* 60 K10
Nandewar Ra., *Australia* 91 E5
Nandi, *Fiji* 87 C7
Nandi □, *Kenya* 82 B4
Nandurbar, *India* 60 J9
Nandyal, *India* 60 M11
Nanfeng, *Guangdong, China* 53 F8
Nanfeng, *Jiangxi, China* 53 D11
Nanga, *Australia* 89 E1
Nanga-Eboko, *Cameroon* 79 E7
Nanga Parbat, *Pakistan* 63 B6
Nangade, *Mozam.* 83 E4
Nangapinoh, *Indonesia* 56 E4
Nangarhár □, *Afghan.* 60 B7
Nangatayap, *Indonesia* 56 E4
Nangeya Mts., *Uganda* 82 B3
Nangis, *France* 25 D10
Nangong, *China* 50 F8
Nanhua, *China* 52 E3
Nanhuang, *China* 51 F11
Nanhui, *China* 53 B13
Nanjeko, *Zambia* 83 F1
Nanji Shan, *China* 53 D13
Nanjian, *China* 52 E3
Nanjiang, *China* 52 A6
Nanjing, *Fujian, China* 53 E11
Nanjing, *Jiangsu, China* 53 A12
Nanjirinji, *Tanzania* 83 D4
Nankana Sahib, *Pakistan* 62 D5
Nankang, *China* 53 E10
Nanking = Nanjing, *China* 53 A12
Nankoku, *Japan* 49 H6
Nanling, *China* 53 B12
Nanning, *China* 52 F7
Nannup, *Australia* 89 F2
Nanpan Jiang →, *China* 52 E6
Nanpara, *India* 63 F9
Nanpi, *China* 50 E9
Nanping, *Fujian, China* 53 D12
Nanping, *Henan, China* 53 C9
Nanri Dao, *China* 53 E12
Nanripe, *Mozam.* 83 E4
Nansei-Shotō = Ryūkyū-rettō, *Japan* 49 M2
Nansen Sd., *Canada* 4 A3
Nansio, *Tanzania* 82 C3
Nant, *France* 26 D7
Nantes, *France* 24 E5
Nanteuil-le-Haudouin, *France* 25 C9
Nantiat, *France* 26 B5
Nanticoke, *U.S.A.* 107 E8
Nanton, *Canada* 100 C6
Nantong, *China* 53 A13
Nantua, *France* 27 B9
Nantucket I., *U.S.A.* 94 E12
Nanuque, *Brazil* 123 E3
Nanutarra, *Australia* 88 D2
Nanxiong, *China* 53 E10
Nanyang, *China* 50 H7
Nanyi Hu, *China* 53 B12
Nanyuan, *China* 50 E9
Nanyuki, *Kenya* 82 B4
Nanzhang, *China* 53 B8
Nao, C. de la, *Spain* 29 G5
Naococane L., *Canada* 99 B5
Naoetsu, *Japan* 49 F9
Náousa, *Greece* 39 J5
Naozhou Dao, *China* 53 G8
Napa, *U.S.A.* 112 G4
Napa →, *U.S.A.* 112 G4
Napanee, *Canada* 98 D4
Napanoch, *U.S.A.* 107 E10
Nape, *Laos* 58 C5
Nape Pass = Keo Neua, Deo, *Vietnam* 58 C5
Napf, *Switz.* 22 B5
Napier, *N.Z.* 87 H6
Napier Broome B., *Australia* 88 B4
Napier Downs, *Australia* 88 C3
Napier Pen., *Australia* 90 A2
Naples = Nápoli, *Italy* 35 B7
Naples, *U.S.A.* 105 M5
Napo, *China* 52 F5
Napo □, *Ecuador* 120 D2
Napo →, *Peru* 120 D3
Napoleon, *N. Dak., U.S.A.* 108 B5
Napoleon, *Ohio, U.S.A.* 104 E3
Nápoli, *Italy* 35 B7
Nápoli, G. di, *Italy* 35 B7
Napopo, *Zaïre* 82 B2
Nappa Merrie, *Australia* 91 D3
Naqâda, *Egypt* 76 B3
Naqadeh, *Iran* 67 D11
Naqqāsh, *Iran* 65 C6
Nara, *Japan* 49 G7
Nara, *Mali* 78 B3
Nara □, *Japan* 49 G8
Nara Canal, *Pakistan* 62 G3
Nara Visa, *U.S.A.* 109 H3
Naracoorte, *Australia* 91 F3
Naradhan, *Australia* 91 E4
Narasapur, *India* 61 L12
Narathiwat, *Thailand* 59 J3
Narayanganj, *Bangla.* 61 H17
Narayanpet, *India* 60 L10
Narbonne, *France* 26 E7
Narcea →, *Spain* 30 B4
Nardīn, *Iran* 65 B7
Nardò, *Italy* 35 B11
Narembeen, *Australia* 89 F2
Nares Str., *Arctic* 94 B13
Naretha, *Australia* 89 F3
Narew →, *Poland* 20 C10
Nari →, *Pakistan* 62 E2
Narin, *Afghan.* 60 A6
Narindra, Helodranon' i, *Madag.* 85 A8
Narino □, *Colombia* 120 C2
Narita, *Japan* 49 G10
Narmada →, *India* 62 J5
Narman, *Turkey* 67 B9
Narmland, *Sweden* 9 F15
Narnaul, *India* 62 E7
Narni, *Italy* 33 F9
Naro, *Ghana* 78 C4
Naro, *Italy* 34 E6
Naro Fominsk, *Russia* 42 C3
Narodnaya, *Russia* 6 B17
Narok, *Kenya* 82 C4
Narok □, *Kenya* 82 C4
Narón, *Spain* 30 B2
Narooma, *Australia* 91 F5
Narowal, *Pakistan* 62 C6
Narrabri, *Australia* 91 E4
Narran →, *Australia* 91 D4
Narrandera, *Australia* 91 E4
Narraway →, *Canada* 100 B5
Narrogin, *Australia* 89 F2
Narromine, *Australia* 91 E4
Narsimhapur, *India* 63 H8
Nartkala, *Russia* 43 J6
Naruto, *Japan* 49 G7
Narva, *Estonia* 40 C5
Narva →, *Russia* 9 G22
Narvik, *Norway* 8 B17
Narvskoye Vdkhr., *Russia* 40 C5
Narwana, *India* 62 E7
Naryan-Mar, *Russia* 44 C6
Naryilco, *Australia* 91 D3
Narym, *Russia* 44 D9
Narymskoye, *Kazakhstan* 44 E9
Naryn, *Kyrgyzstan* 44 E8
Nasa, *Norway* 8 C16
Nasarawa, *Nigeria* 79 D6
Năsăud, *Romania* 38 B7
Naseby, *N.Z.* 87 L3
Naselle, *U.S.A.* 112 D3
Naser, Buheirat en, *Egypt* 76 C3
Nashua, *Iowa, U.S.A.* 108 D8
Nashua, *Mont., U.S.A.* 110 B10
Nashua, *N.H., U.S.A.* 107 D13
Nashville, *Ark., U.S.A.* 109 J8
Nashville, *Ga., U.S.A.* 105 K4
Nashville, *Tenn., U.S.A.* 105 G2
Našice, *Croatia* 21 K8
Nasielsk, *Poland* 20 C10
Nasik, *India* 60 K8
Nasipit, *Phil.* 55 G6
Nasirabad, *India* 62 F6
Naskaupi →, *Canada* 99 B7
Naso, *Italy* 35 D7
Naşriān-e Pā'īn, *Iran* 64 C5
Nass →, *Canada* 100 B3
Nassau, *Bahamas* 116 A4
Nassau, *U.S.A.* 107 D11
Nassau, B., *Chile* 128 E3
Nasser, L. = Naser, Buheirat en, *Egypt* 76 C3
Nasser City = Kôm Ombo, *Egypt* 76 C3
Nassian, *Ivory C.* 78 D4
Nässjö, *Sweden* 9 H16
Nasugbu, *Phil.* 55 D4
Näsviken, *Sweden* 10 C10
Nat Kyizin, *Burma* 61 M20
Nata, *Botswana* 84 C4
Natagaima, *Colombia* 120 C2
Natal, *Brazil* 122 C4
Natal, *Canada* 100 D6
Natal, *Indonesia* 56 D1
Natalinci, *Serbia, Yug.* 21 L10
Naţanz, *Iran* 65 C6
Natashquan, *Canada* 99 B7
Natashquan →, *Canada* 99 B7
Natchez, *U.S.A.* 109 K9
Natchitoches, *U.S.A.* 109 K8
Naters, *Switz.* 22 D5
Nathalia, *Australia* 91 F4
Nathdwara, *India* 62 G5
Nati, Pta., *Spain* 36 A10
Natimuk, *Australia* 91 F3
Nation →, *Canada* 100 B4
National City, *U.S.A.* 113 N9
Natitingou, *Benin* 79 C5
Natividad, I., *Mexico* 114 B1
Natoma, *U.S.A.* 108 F5
Natron, L., *Tanzania* 82 C4
Natrona Heights, *U.S.A.* 106 F5
Natrûn, W. el →, *Egypt* 76 H7
Natuna Besar, Kepulauan, *Indonesia* 59 L7
Natuna Is. = Natuna Besar, Kepulauan, *Indonesia* 59 L7
Natuna Selatan, Kepulauan, *Indonesia* 59 L7
Natural Bridge, *U.S.A.* 107 B9
Naturaliste, C., *Australia* 90 G4
Nau Qala, *Afghan.* 62 B3
Naubinway, *U.S.A.* 98 C2
Naucelle, *France* 26 D6
Nauders, *Austria* 19 J6
Nauen, *Germany* 18 C8
Naugatuck, *U.S.A.* 107 E11
Naumburg, *Germany* 18 D7
Nā'ūr at Tunayb, *Jordan* 69 D4
Nauru ■, *Pac. Oc.* 92 H8
Naushahra = Nowshera, *Pakistan* 60 B8
Nauta, *Peru* 120 D3
Nautanwa, *India* 61 F13
Nautla, *Mexico* 115 C5
Nava, *Mexico* 114 B4
Nava del Rey, *Spain* 30 D5
Navacerrada, Puerto de, *Spain* 30 E7
Navadwip, *India* 63 H13
Navahermosa, *Spain* 31 F6
Navahrudak, *Belarus* 40 F3
Navajo Reservoir, *U.S.A.* 111 H10
Navalcarnero, *Spain* 30 E6
Navalmoral de la Mata, *Spain* 30 F5
Navalvillar de Pela, *Spain* 31 F5
Navan = An Uaimh, *Ireland* 15 C5
Navapolatsk, *Belarus* 40 E5
Navarino, I., *Chile* 128 E3
Navarra □, *Spain* 28 C3

Navarre, *U.S.A.* 106 F3
Navarrenx, *France* 26 E3
Navarro →, *U.S.A.* 112 F3
Navasota, *U.S.A.* 109 K6
Navassa, *W. Indies* 117 C4
Nave, *Italy* 32 C7
Naver →, *U.K.* 14 C4
Navia, *Spain* 30 B4
Navia →, *Spain* 30 B4
Navia de Suarna, *Spain* 30 C4
Navidad, *Chile* 126 C1
Navlya, *Russia* 42 D2
Navoi = Nawoiy, *Uzbekistan* 44 E7
Navojoa, *Mexico* 114 B3
Navolato, *Mexico* 114 C4
Návpaktos, *Greece* 39 L4
Návplion, *Greece* 39 M5
Navrongo, *Ghana* 79 C4
Navsari, *India* 60 J8
Nawa Kot, *Pakistan* 62 E4
Nawabganj, *Ut. P., India* 63 F9
Nawabganj, *Ut. P., India* 63 E8
Nawabshah, *Pakistan* 62 F3
Nawada, *India* 63 G11
Nawakot, *Nepal* 63 F11
Nawalgarh, *India* 62 F6
Nawanshahr, *India* 63 C6
Nawi, *Sudan* 76 D3
Nawoiy, *Uzbekistan* 44 E7
Naxçivan, *Azerbaijan* 67 C11
Naxçivan □, *Azerbaijan* 67 C11
Náxos, *Greece* 39 M8
Nay, *France* 26 E3
Nāy Band, *Iran* 65 E7
Naya →, *Colombia* 120 C2
Nayakhan, *Russia* 45 C16
Nayarit □, *Mexico* 114 C4
Nayong, *China* 52 D5
Nayoro, *Japan* 48 B11
Nayyāl, W. →, *Si. Arabia* 64 D3
Nazaré, *Bahia, Brazil* 123 D4
Nazaré, *Pará, Brazil* 125 B7
Nazaré, *Tocantins, Brazil* 122 C2
Nazaré, *Portugal* 31 F1
Nazareth = Nazerat, *Israel* 69 C4
Nazas, *Mexico* 114 B4
Nazas →, *Mexico* 114 B4
Naze, The, *U.K.* 13 F9
Nazerat, *Israel* 69 C4
Nāzik, *Iran* 67 C11
Nazilli, *Turkey* 66 D3
Nazir Hat, *Bangla.* 61 H17
Nazko, *Canada* 100 C4
Nazko →, *Canada* 100 C4
Nazret, *Ethiopia* 77 F4
Nchanga, *Zambia* 83 E2
Ncheu, *Malawi* 83 E3
Ndala, *Tanzania* 82 C3
Ndalatando, *Angola* 80 F2
Ndali, *Benin* 79 D5
Ndareda, *Tanzania* 82 C4
Ndélé, *C.A.R.* 73 G9
Ndendé, *Gabon* 80 E2
Ndjamena, *Chad* 73 F7
Ndjolé, *Gabon* 80 E2
Ndola, *Zambia* 83 E2
Ndoto Mts., *Kenya* 82 B4
Nduguti, *Tanzania* 82 C3
Nea →, *Norway* 10 A5
Néa Flippiás, *Greece* 39 K3
Neagh, Lough, *U.K.* 15 B5
Neah Bay, *U.S.A.* 112 B2
Neale, L., *Australia* 88 D5
Neápolis, *Kozan, Greece* 39 J4
Neápolis, *Kríti, Greece* 37 D7
Neápolis, *Lakonia, Greece* 39 N6
Near Is., *U.S.A.* 96 C1
Neath, *U.K.* 13 F4
Nebbou, *Burkina Faso* 79 C4
Nebine Cr. →, *Australia* 91 D4
Nebitdag, *Turkmenistan* 44 F6
Nebolchy, *Russia* 40 C7
Nebraska □, *U.S.A.* 108 E5
Nebraska City, *U.S.A.* 108 E7
Nébrodi, Monti, *Italy* 35 E7
Necedah, *U.S.A.* 108 C9
Nechako →, *Canada* 100 C4
Neches →, *U.S.A.* 109 L8
Neckar →, *Germany* 19 F4
Necochea, *Argentina* 126 D4
Nedelišće, *Croatia* 33 B13
Neder Rijn →, *Neths.* 16 E8
Nederbrakel, *Belgium* 17 G3
Nederweert, *Neths.* 17 F7
Nédha →, *Greece* 39 M4
Nedroma, *Algeria* 75 A4
Neede, *Neths.* 16 D9
Needles, *U.S.A.* 113 L12
Needles, The, *U.K.* 13 G6
Neembucú □, *Paraguay* 126 B4
Neemuch = Nimach, *India* 62 G6
Neenah, *U.S.A.* 104 C1
Neepawa, *Canada* 101 C9
Neer, *Neths.* 17 F7
Neerpelt, *Belgium* 17 F6
Nefta, *Tunisia* 75 B6
Neftah Sidi Boubekeur, *Algeria* 75 A5
Neftçala, *Azerbaijan* 67 C13
Neftegorsk, *Russia* 43 H4
Neftekumsk, *Russia* 43 H7
Neftenbach, *Switz.* 23 A7
Negapatam = Nagappattinam, *India* 60 P11
Negaunee, *U.S.A.* 104 B2

Negele, *Ethiopia* 68 F2
Negev Desert = Hanegev, *Israel* 69 E3
Negombo, *Sri Lanka* 60 R11
Negotin, *Serbia, Yug.* 21 L12
Negra, Peña, *Spain* 30 C4
Negra, Pta., *Mauritania* 74 D1
Negra, Pta., *Peru* 124 B1
Negra Pt., *Phil.* 57 A6
Negrais, C. = Maudin Sun, *Burma* 61 M19
Negreira, *Spain* 30 C2
Négrine, *Algeria* 75 B6
Negro →, *Argentina* 128 B4
Negro →, *Bolivia* 125 C5
Negro →, *Brazil* 121 D6
Negro →, *Uruguay* 127 C4
Negros, *Phil.* 55 G5
Nehalem →, *U.S.A.* 112 E3
Nehāvand, *Iran* 65 C6
Nehbandān, *Iran* 65 D9
Neheim, *Germany* 18 D3
Nehoiaşu, *Romania* 38 D9
Nei Monggol Zizhiqu □, *China* 50 C6
Neidpath, *Canada* 101 C7
Neihart, *U.S.A.* 110 C8
Neijiang, *China* 52 C5
Neilton, *U.S.A.* 110 C2
Neiqiu, *China* 50 F8
Neira de Jusá, *Spain* 30 C3
Neiva, *Colombia* 120 C2
Neixiang, *China* 50 H6
Nejanilini L., *Canada* 101 B9
Nejo, *Ethiopia* 77 F4
Nekā, *Iran* 65 B7
Nekemte, *Ethiopia* 77 F4
Nekheb, *Egypt* 76 B3
Neksø, *Denmark* 9 J16
Nelas, *Portugal* 30 E3
Nelia, *Australia* 90 C3
Nelidovo, *Russia* 40 D7
Neligh, *U.S.A.* 108 D5
Nelkan, *Russia* 45 D14
Nellore, *India* 60 M11
Nelma, *Russia* 45 E14
Nelson, *Canada* 100 D5
Nelson, *N.Z.* 87 J4
Nelson, *U.K.* 12 D5
Nelson, *U.S.A.* 111 J7
Nelson →, *Canada* 101 C9
Nelson, C., *Australia* 91 F3
Nelson, Estrecho, *Chile* 128 D2
Nelson Forks, *Canada* 100 B4
Nelson House, *Canada* 101 B9
Nelson L., *Canada* 101 B8
Nelspoort, *S. Africa* 84 E3
Nelspruit, *S. Africa* 85 D5
Néma, *Mauritania* 78 B3
Neman →, *Lithuania* 9 J19
Nemeiben L., *Canada* 101 B7
Nemira, *Romania* 38 C9
Nemours, *France* 25 D9
Nemunas = Neman →, *Lithuania* 9 J19
Nemuro, *Japan* 48 C12
Nemuro-Kaikyō, *Japan* 48 C12
Nemuy, *Russia* 45 D14
Nen Jiang →, *China* 51 B13
Nenagh, *Ireland* 15 D3
Nenana, *U.S.A.* 96 B5
Nenasi, *Malaysia* 59 L4
Nene →, *U.K.* 12 E8
Nenjiang, *China* 54 B7
Neno, *Malawi* 83 F3
Nenusa, Kepulauan, *Indonesia* 57 D7
Neodesha, *U.S.A.* 109 G7
Neópolis, *Brazil* 122 D4
Neosho, *U.S.A.* 109 G7
Neosho →, *U.S.A.* 109 H7
Nepal ■, *Asia* 63 F11
Nepalganj, *Nepal* 63 E9
Nephi, *U.S.A.* 110 G8
Nephin, *Ireland* 15 B2
Neptune, *U.S.A.* 107 F10
Néra →, *Romania* 38 E4
Nérac, *France* 26 D4
Nerchinsk, *Russia* 45 D12
Nerchinskiy Zavod, *Russia* 45 D12
Nereju, *Romania* 38 D9
Nerekhta, *Russia* 42 B5
Néret L., *Canada* 99 B5
Neringa, *Lithuania* 9 J19
Nerja, *Spain* 31 J7
Nerl →, *Russia* 42 B5
Nerpio, *Spain* 29 G2
Nerva, *Spain* 31 H4
Nes, *Neths.* 16 B7
Nesbyen, *Norway* 10 D3
Nesebǔr, *Bulgaria* 38 G10
Nesland, *Norway* 10 E1
Neslandsvatn, *Norway* 10 F3
Nesle, *France* 25 C9
Nesodden, *Norway* 10 E4
Nesque →, *France* 27 E8
Ness, L., *U.K.* 14 D4
Nesslau, *Switz.* 23 B8
Nesterov, *Ukraine* 41 G2
Néstos →, *Greece* 39 H7
Nesvizh = Nyasvizh, *Belarus* 41 F4
Netanya, *Israel* 69 C3
Nète →, *Belgium* 17 F4
Netherdale, *Australia* 90 C4
Netherlands ■, *Europe* 16 E6

Netherlands Antilles ■, *W. Indies* 120 A4
Neto →, *Italy* 35 C10
Nettancourt, *France* 25 D11
Nettilling L., *Canada* 97 B12
Nettuno, *Italy* 34 A5
Netzahualcoyotl, Presa, *Mexico* 115 D6
Neu-Isenburg, *Germany* 19 E4
Neu-Ulm, *Germany* 19 G6
Neubrandenburg, *Germany* 18 B9
Neubukow, *Germany* 18 A7
Neuburg, *Germany* 19 G7
Neuchâtel, *Switz.* 22 C3
Neuchâtel □, *Switz.* 22 C3
Neuchâtel, Lac de, *Switz.* 22 C3
Neudau, *Austria* 21 H6
Neuenegg, *Switz.* 22 C4
Neuenhaus, *Germany* 18 C2
Neuf-Brisach, *France* 25 D14
Neufahrn, *Germany* 19 G8
Neufchâteau, *Belgium* 17 J6
Neufchâteau, *France* 25 D12
Neufchâtel-en-Bray, *France* 24 C8
Neufchâtel-sur-Aisne, *France* 25 C11
Neuhaus, *Germany* 18 B6
Neuhausen, *Switz.* 23 A7
Neuillé-Pont-Pierre, *France* 24 E7
Neuilly-St.-Front, *France* 25 C10
Neukalen, *Germany* 18 B8
Neumarkt, *Germany* 19 F7
Neumarkt-Sankt Veit, *Germany* 19 G8
Neumünster, *Germany* 18 A5
Neung-sur-Beuvron, *France* 25 E8
Neunkirchen, *Austria* 21 H6
Neunkirchen, *Germany* 19 F3
Neuquén, *Argentina* 128 A3
Neuquén □, *Argentina* 126 D2
Neuquén →, *Argentina* 128 A3
Neuruppin, *Germany* 18 C8
Neuse →, *U.S.A.* 105 H7
Neusiedler See, *Austria* 21 H6
Neuss, *Germany* 17 F9
Neussargues-Moissac, *France* 26 C7
Neustadt, *Baden-W., Germany* 19 H4
Neustadt, *Bayern, Germany* 19 F8
Neustadt, *Bayern, Germany* 19 G7
Neustadt, *Bayern, Germany* 19 F6
Neustadt, *Bayern, Germany* 19 E7
Neustadt, *Brandenburg, Germany* 18 C8
Neustadt, *Hessen, Germany* 18 E5
Neustadt, *Niedersachsen, Germany* 18 C5
Neustadt, *Rhld.-Pfz., Germany* 19 F4
Neustadt, *Schleswig-Holstein, Germany* 18 A6
Neustadt, *Thüringen, Germany* 18 E7
Neustrelitz, *Germany* 18 B9
Neuvic, *France* 26 C6
Neuville, *Belgium* 17 H5
Neuville-aux-Bois, *France* 25 D9
Neuville-de-Poitou, *France* 26 B4
Neuville-sur-Saône, *France* 27 C8
Neuvy-le-Roi, *France* 24 E7
Neuvy-St.-Sépulchre, *France* 26 B5
Neuvy-sur-Barangeon, *France* 25 E9
Neuwerk, *Germany* 18 B4
Neuwied, *Germany* 18 E3
Neva →, *Russia* 40 C6
Nevada, *U.S.A.* 109 G7
Nevada □, *U.S.A.* 110 G5
Nevada, Sierra, *Spain* 29 H1
Nevada, Sierra, *U.S.A.* 110 G3
Nevada City, *U.S.A.* 112 F6
Nevado, Cerro, *Argentina* 126 D2
Nevanka, *Russia* 45 D10
Nevel, *Russia* 40 D5
Nevele, *Belgium* 17 F3
Nevers, *France* 25 F10
Nevertire, *Australia* 91 E4
Neville, *Canada* 101 D7
Nevinnomyssk, *Russia* 43 H6
Nevis, *W. Indies* 117 C7
Nevrokop = Gotse Delchev, *Bulgaria* 39 H6
Nevşehir, *Turkey* 66 C6
New →, *Guyana* 121 C6
New →, *U.S.A.* 104 G5
New Albany, *Ind., U.S.A.* 104 F3
New Albany, *Miss., U.S.A.* 109 H10
New Albany, *Pa., U.S.A.* 107 E8
New Amsterdam, *Guyana* 121 B6
New Angledool, *Australia* 91 D4
New Bedford, *U.S.A.* 107 E14
New Bern, *U.S.A.* 105 H7
New Bethlehem, *U.S.A.* 106 E5
New Bloomfield, *U.S.A.* 106 F7
New Boston, *U.S.A.* 109 J7
New Braunfels, *U.S.A.* 109 L5
New Brighton, *N.Z.* 87 K4
New Brighton, *U.S.A.* 106 F4
New Britain, *Papua N. G.* 92 H7
New Britain, *U.S.A.* 107 E12
New Brunswick, *U.S.A.* 107 F10
New Brunswick □, *Canada* 99 C6
New Bussa, *Nigeria* 79 D5
New Caledonia ■, *Pac. Oc.* 92 K8
New Castle, *Ind., U.S.A.* 104 F3

New Castle, *Pa., U.S.A.* 106 E4
New City, *U.S.A.* 107 E11
New Cumberland, *U.S.A.* 106 F4
New Cuyama, *U.S.A.* 113 L7
New Delhi, *India* 62 E7
New Denver, *Canada* 100 D5
New Don Pedro Reservoir, *U.S.A.* 112 H6
New England, *U.S.A.* 108 B3
New England Ra., *Australia* 91 E5
New Forest, *U.K.* 13 G6
New Glasgow, *Canada* 99 C7
New Guinea, *Oceania* 92 H5
New Hamburg, *Canada* 106 C4
New Hampshire □, *U.S.A.* 107 C13
New Hampton, *U.S.A.* 108 D8
New Hanover, *S. Africa* 85 D5
New Haven, *Conn., U.S.A.* 107 E12
New Haven, *Mich., U.S.A.* 106 D2
New Hazelton, *Canada* 100 B3
New Hebrides = Vanuatu ■, *Pac. Oc.* 92 J8
New Iberia, *U.S.A.* 109 K9
New Ireland, *Papua N. G.* 92 H7
New Jersey □, *U.S.A.* 107 F10
New Kensington, *U.S.A.* 106 F5
New Lexington, *U.S.A.* 104 F4
New Liskeard, *Canada* 98 C4
New London, *Conn., U.S.A.* 107 E12
New London, *Minn., U.S.A.* 108 C7
New London, *Ohio, U.S.A.* 106 E2
New London, *Wis., U.S.A.* 108 C10
New Madrid, *U.S.A.* 109 G10
New Meadows, *U.S.A.* 110 D5
New Melones L., *U.S.A.* 112 H6
New Mexico □, *U.S.A.* 111 J10
New Milford, *Conn., U.S.A.* 107 E11
New Milford, *Pa., U.S.A.* 107 E9
New Norcia, *Australia* 89 F2
New Norfolk, *Australia* 90 G4
New Orleans, *U.S.A.* 109 K9
New Philadelphia, *U.S.A.* 106 F3
New Plymouth, *N.Z.* 87 H5
New Plymouth, *U.S.A.* 110 E5
New Providence, *Bahamas* 116 A4
New Radnor, *U.K.* 13 E4
New Richmond, *U.S.A.* 108 C8
New Roads, *U.S.A.* 109 K9
New Rochelle, *U.S.A.* 107 F11
New Rockford, *U.S.A.* 108 B5
New Ross, *Ireland* 15 D5
New Salem, *U.S.A.* 108 B4
New Scone, *U.K.* 14 E5
New Siberian Is. = Novosibirskiye Ostrova, *Russia* 45 B15
New Smyrna Beach, *U.S.A.* 105 L5
New South Wales □, *Australia* 91 E4
New Springs, *Australia* 89 E3
New Town, *U.S.A.* 108 A3
New Ulm, *U.S.A.* 108 C7
New Waterford, *Canada* 99 C7
New Westminster, *Canada* 100 D4
New York □, *U.S.A.* 107 D9
New York City, *U.S.A.* 107 F11
New Zealand ■, *Oceania* 87 J5
Newala, *Tanzania* 83 E4
Newala □, *Tanzania* 83 E4
Newark, *Del., U.S.A.* 104 F8
Newark, *N.J., U.S.A.* 107 F10
Newark, *N.Y., U.S.A.* 106 C7
Newark, *Ohio, U.S.A.* 106 F2
Newark-on-Trent, *U.K.* 12 D7
Newaygo, *U.S.A.* 104 D3
Newberg, *U.S.A.* 110 D2
Newberry, *Mich., U.S.A.* 104 B3
Newberry, *S.C., U.S.A.* 105 H5
Newberry Springs, *U.S.A.* 113 L10
Newbridge = Droichead Nua, *Ireland* 15 C5
Newbrook, *Canada* 100 C6
Newburgh, *U.S.A.* 107 E10
Newbury, *U.K.* 13 F6
Newbury, *U.S.A.* 107 B12
Newburyport, *U.S.A.* 107 D14
Newcastle, *Australia* 91 E5
Newcastle, *Canada* 99 C6
Newcastle, *S. Africa* 85 D4
Newcastle, *U.K.* 15 B6
Newcastle, *Calif., U.S.A.* 112 G5
Newcastle, *Wyo., U.S.A.* 108 D2
Newcastle Emlyn, *U.K.* 13 E3
Newcastle Ra., *Australia* 88 C5
Newcastle-under-Lyme, *U.K.* 12 D5
Newcastle-upon-Tyne, *U.K.* 12 C6
Newcastle Waters, *Australia* 90 B1
Newdegate, *Australia* 89 F2
Newell, *U.S.A.* 108 C3
Newfoundland □, *Canada* 99 B8
Newhalem, *U.S.A.* 100 B4
Newhall, *U.S.A.* 113 L8
Newham, *U.K.* 13 F8
Newhaven, *U.K.* 13 G8
Newkirk, *U.S.A.* 109 G6
Newman, *Australia* 88 D2
Newman, *U.S.A.* 112 H5
Newmarket, *Canada* 106 B5
Newmarket, *Ireland* 15 D3
Newmarket, *U.K.* 13 E8
Newmarket, *U.S.A.* 107 C14
Newnan, *U.S.A.* 105 J3

Newport, *Gwent, U.K.* 13 F5
Newport, *I. of W., U.K.* 13 G6
Newport, *Ark., U.S.A.* 109 H9
Newport, *Ky., U.S.A.* 104 F3
Newport, *N.H., U.S.A.* 107 C12
Newport, *Oreg., U.S.A.* 110 D1
Newport, *Pa., U.S.A.* 106 F7
Newport, *R.I., U.S.A.* 107 E13
Newport, *Tenn., U.S.A.* 105 H4
Newport, *Vt., U.S.A.* 107 B12
Newport, *Wash., U.S.A.* 110 B5
Newport Beach, *U.S.A.* 113 M9
Newport News, *U.S.A.* 104 G7
Newquay, *U.K.* 13 G2
Newry, *U.K.* 15 B5
Newry & Mourne □, *U.K.* 15 B5
Newton, *Iowa, U.S.A.* 108 E8
Newton, *Mass., U.S.A.* 107 D13
Newton, *Miss., U.S.A.* 109 J10
Newton, *N.C., U.S.A.* 105 H5
Newton, *N.J., U.S.A.* 107 E10
Newton, *Tex., U.S.A.* 109 K8
Newton Abbot, *U.K.* 13 G4
Newton Boyd, *Australia* 91 D5
Newton Stewart, *U.K.* 14 G4
Newtonmore, *U.K.* 14 D4
Newtown, *U.K.* 13 E4
Newtownabbey □, *U.K.* 15 B6
Newtownards, *U.K.* 15 B6
Newville, *U.S.A.* 106 F7
Nexon, *France* 26 C5
Neya, *Russia* 42 A6
Neyrīz, *Iran* 65 D7
Neyshābūr, *Iran* 65 B8
Nezhin = Nizhyn, *Ukraine* 41 G6
Nezperce, *U.S.A.* 110 C5
Ngabang, *Indonesia* 56 D3
Ngabordamlu, Tanjung, *Indonesia* 57 F8
Ngambé, *Cameroon* 79 D7
Ngami Depression, *Botswana* 84 C3
Ngamo, *Zimbabwe* 83 F2
Nganglong Kangri, *China* 61 C12
Nganjuk, *Indonesia* 57 G14
Ngao, *Thailand* 58 C2
Ngaoundéré, *Cameroon* 80 C2
Ngapara, *N.Z.* 87 L3
Ngara, *Tanzania* 82 C3
Ngara □, *Tanzania* 82 C3
Ngawi, *Indonesia* 57 G14
Ngoma, *Malawi* 83 E3
Ngomahura, *Zimbabwe* 83 G3
Ngomba, *Tanzania* 83 D3
Ngop, *Sudan* 77 F3
Ngoring Hu, *China* 54 C4
Ngorkou, *Mali* 78 B4
Ngorongoro, *Tanzania* 82 C4
Ngozi, *Burundi* 82 C2
Ngudu, *Tanzania* 82 C3
Nguigmi, *Niger* 73 F7
Ngukurr, *Australia* 90 A1
Ngunga, *Tanzania* 82 D3
Nguru, *Nigeria* 79 C7
Nguru Mts., *Tanzania* 82 D4
Nguyen Binh, *Vietnam* 58 A5
Nha Trang, *Vietnam* 59 F7
Nhacoongo, *Mozam.* 85 C6
Nhamaabué, *Mozam.* 83 F4
Nhambiquara, *Brazil* 125 C6
Nhamundá, *Brazil* 121 D6
Nhamundá →, *Brazil* 121 D6
Nhangutazi, L., *Mozam.* 85 C5
Nhecolândia, *Brazil* 125 D6
Nhill, *Australia* 91 F3
Nho Quan, *Vietnam* 58 B5
Nhulunbuy, *Australia* 90 A2
Nia-nia, *Zaïre* 82 B2
Niafounké, *Mali* 78 B4
Niagara, *U.S.A.* 104 C1
Niagara Falls, *Canada* 98 D4
Niagara Falls, *U.S.A.* 106 C5
Niagara-on-the-Lake, *Canada* 106 C5
Niah, *Malaysia* 56 D4
Niamey, *Niger* 79 C5
Nianforando, *Guinea* 78 D2
Nianfors, *Sweden* 10 C10
Niangara, *Zaïre* 82 B2
Nias, *Indonesia* 56 D1
Niassa □, *Mozam.* 83 E4
Nibbiano, *Italy* 32 D6
Nibe, *Denmark* 11 H3
Nicaragua ■, *Cent. Amer.* 116 D2
Nicaragua, L. de, *Nic.* 116 D2
Nicastro, *Italy* 35 D9
Nice, *France* 27 E11
Niceville, *U.S.A.* 105 K2
Nichinan, *Japan* 49 J5
Nicholás, Canal, *W. Indies* 116 B3
Nicholasville, *U.S.A.* 104 G3
Nichols, *U.S.A.* 107 D8
Nicholson, *Australia* 88 C4
Nicholson, *U.S.A.* 107 E9
Nicholson →, *Australia* 90 B2
Nicholson Ra., *Australia* 89 E2
Nickerie □, *Surinam* 121 C6
Nickerie →, *Surinam* 121 B6
Nicobar Is., *Ind. Oc.* 46 J13
Nicoclí, *Colombia* 120 B2
Nicola, *Canada* 100 C4
Nicolet, *Canada* 98 C5
Nicolls Town, *Bahamas* 116 A4
Nicosia, *Cyprus* 66 E5
Nicosia, *Italy* 35 E7
Nicótera, *Italy* 35 D8

Norway

Nicoya, *Costa Rica* 116 D2
Nicoya, G. de, *Costa Rica* 116 E3
Nicoya, Pen. de, *Costa Rica* 116 E2
Nidau, *Switz.* 22 B4
Nidd →, *U.K.* 12 C6
Nidda, *Germany* 18 E5
Nidda →, *Germany* 19 E4
Nidwalden □, *Switz.* 23 C6
Nidzica, *Poland* 20 B10
Niebüll, *Germany* 18 A4
Nied →, *Germany* 25 C13
Niederaula, *Germany* 18 E5
Niederbipp, *Switz.* 22 B5
Niederbronn-les-Bains, *France* 25 D14
Niedere Tauern, *Austria* 21 H4
Niedersachsen □, *Germany* 18 C5
Niekerkshoop, *S. Africa* 84 D3
Niel, *Belgium* 17 F4
Niellé, *Ivory C.* 78 C3
Niemba, *Zaïre* 82 D2
Niemen = Neman →, *Lithuania* 9 J19
Nienburg, *Germany* 18 C5
Niers →, *Germany* 18 D2
Niesen, *Switz.* 22 C5
Niesky, *Germany* 18 D10
Nieu Bethesda, *S. Africa* 84 E3
Nieuw-Amsterdam, *Neths.* 16 C9
Nieuw Amsterdam, *Surinam* 121 B6
Nieuw Beijerland, *Neths.* 16 E4
Nieuw-Dordrecht, *Neths.* 16 C9
Nieuw Loosdrecht, *Neths.* 16 D6
Nieuw Nickerie, *Surinam* 121 B6
Nieuw-Schoonebeek, *Neths.* 16 C10
Nieuw-Vennep, *Neths.* 16 D5
Nieuw-Vossemeer, *Neths.* 17 E4
Nieuwe-Niedorp, *Neths.* 16 C5
Nieuwe-Pekela, *Neths.* 16 B9
Nieuwe-Schans, *Neths.* 16 B10
Nieuwendijk, *Neths.* 16 E5
Nieuwerkerken, *Belgium* 17 G6
Nieuwkoop, *Neths.* 16 D5
Nieuwleusen, *Neths.* 16 C8
Nieuwnamen, *Neths.* 17 F4
Nieuwolda, *Neths.* 16 B9
Nieuwoudtville, *S. Africa* 84 E2
Nieuwpoort, *Belgium* 17 F1
Nieuwveen, *Neths.* 16 D5
Nieves, *Spain* 30 C2
Nieves, Pico de las, *Canary Is.* 36 G4
Nièvre □, *France* 25 E10
Niğde, *Turkey* 66 D6
Nigel, *S. Africa* 85 D4
Niger □, *Nigeria* 79 C6
Niger ■, *W. Afr.* 79 B6
Niger →, *W. Afr.* 79 D6
Nigeria ■, *W. Afr.* 79 D6
Nightcaps, *N.Z.* 87 L2
Nigríta, *Greece* 39 J6
Nihtaur, *India* 63 E8
Nii-Jima, *Japan* 49 G9
Niigata, *Japan* 48 F9
Niigata □, *Japan* 49 F9
Niihama, *Japan* 49 H6
Niihau, *U.S.A.* 102 H14
Niimi, *Japan* 49 G6
Niitsu, *Japan* 48 F9
Níjar, *Spain* 29 J2
Nijil, *Jordan* 69 E4
Nijkerk, *Neths.* 16 D7
Nijlen, *Belgium* 17 F5
Nijmegen, *Neths.* 16 E7
Nijverdal, *Neths.* 16 D8
Nīk Pey, *Iran* 67 D13
Nike, *Nigeria* 79 D6
Nikiniki, *Indonesia* 57 F6
Nikki, *Benin* 79 D5
Nikkō, *Japan* 49 F9
Nikolayev = Mykolayiv, *Ukraine* 41 J7
Nikolayevsk, *Russia* 42 E7
Nikolayevsk-na-Amur, *Russia* 45 D15
Nikolsk, *Russia* 42 D8
Nikolskoye, *Russia* 45 D17
Nikopol, *Bulgaria* 38 F7
Nikopol, *Ukraine* 41 J8
Niksar, *Turkey* 66 B7
Nīkshahr, *Iran* 65 E9
Nikšić, *Montenegro, Yug.* 21 N8
Nîl, Nahr en →, *Africa* 76 H7
Nîl el Abyad →, *Sudan* 77 D3
Nîl el Azraq →, *Sudan* 77 D3
Niland, *U.S.A.* 113 M11
Nile = Nîl, Nahr en →, *Africa* 76 H7
Nile Delta, *Egypt* 76 H7
Niles, *U.S.A.* 106 E4
Nilo Peçanha, *Brazil* 123 D4
Nimach, *India* 62 G6
Nimbahera, *India* 62 G6
Nîmes, *France* 27 E8
Nimfaíon, Ákra = Pínnes, Ákra, *Greece* 39 J7
Nimmitabel, *Australia* 91 F4
Nimule, *Sudan* 77 G3
Nin, *Croatia* 33 D12
Nīnawá, *Iraq* 67 D10
Nindigully, *Australia* 91 D4
Ninemile, *U.S.A.* 100 B2
Nineveh = Nīnawá, *Iraq* 67 D10
Ning Xian, *China* 50 G4
Ningaloo, *Australia* 88 D1
Ning'an, *China* 51 B15
Ningbo, *China* 53 C13
Ningcheng, *China* 51 D10
Ningde, *China* 53 D12
Ningdu, *China* 53 D10
Ninggang, *China* 53 D9
Ningguo, *China* 53 B12
Ninghai, *China* 53 C13
Ninghua, *China* 53 D11
Ningjin, *China* 50 F8
Ningjing Shan, *China* 52 B2
Ninglang, *China* 52 D3
Ningling, *China* 50 G8
Ningming, *China* 52 F6
Ningnan, *China* 52 D4
Ningpo = Ningbo, *China* 53 C13
Ningqiang, *China* 50 H4
Ningshan, *China* 50 H5
Ningsia Hui A.R. = Ningxia Huizu Zizhiqu □, *China* 50 E3
Ningwu, *China* 50 E7
Ningxia Huizu Zizhiqu □, *China* 50 E3
Ningxiang, *China* 53 C9
Ningyang, *China* 50 G9
Ningyuan, *China* 53 E8
Ninh Binh, *Vietnam* 58 B5
Ninh Giang, *Vietnam* 58 B6
Ninh Hoa, *Vietnam* 58 F7
Ninh Ma, *Vietnam* 58 F7
Ninove, *Belgium* 17 G4
Nioaque, *Brazil* 127 A4
Niobrara, *U.S.A.* 108 D6
Niobrara →, *U.S.A.* 108 D6
Niono, *Mali* 78 C3
Nioro du Rip, *Senegal* 78 C1
Nioro du Sahel, *Mali* 78 B3
Niort, *France* 26 B3
Nipawin, *Canada* 101 C8
Nipawin Prov. Park, *Canada* 101 C8
Nipigon, *Canada* 98 C2
Nipigon, L., *Canada* 98 C2
Nipin →, *Canada* 101 B7
Nipishish L., *Canada* 99 B7
Nipissing L., *Canada* 98 C4
Nipomo, *U.S.A.* 113 K6
Nipton, *U.S.A.* 113 K11
Niquelândia, *Brazil* 123 D2
Nīr, *Iran* 67 C12
Nirasaki, *Japan* 49 G9
Nirmal, *India* 60 K11
Nirmali, *India* 63 F12
Niš, *Serbia, Yug.* 21 M11
Nisa, *Portugal* 31 F3
Nişāb, *Si. Arabia* 64 D5
Nişāb, *Yemen* 68 E4
Nišava →, *Serbia, Yug.* 21 M11
Niscemi, *Italy* 35 E7
Nishinomiya, *Japan* 49 G7
Nishin'omote, *Japan* 49 J5
Nishiwaki, *Japan* 49 G7
Nísíros, *Greece* 39 N10
Niskibi →, *Canada* 98 A2
Nispen, *Neths.* 17 F4
Nisqually →, *U.S.A.* 112 C4
Nissáki, *Greece* 37 A3
Nissan →, *Sweden* 11 H6
Nissedal, *Norway* 10 E2
Nisser, *Norway* 10 E2
Nissum Bredning, *Denmark* 9 H13
Nissum Fjord, *Denmark* 11 H2
Nistelrode, *Neths.* 17 E7
Nistru = Dnister →, *Europe* 41 J6
Nisutlin →, *Canada* 100 A2
Nitchequon, *Canada* 99 B5
Niterói, *Brazil* 123 F3
Nith →, *U.K.* 14 F5
Nitra, *Slovak Rep.* 21 G8
Nittedal, *Norway* 10 D4
Nittenau, *Germany* 19 F8
Niuafo'ou, *Tonga* 87 B11
Niue, *Cook Is.* 93 J11
Niulan Jiang →, *China* 52 D4
Niut, *Indonesia* 56 D4
Niutou Shan, *China* 53 C13
Niuzhuang, *China* 51 D12
Nivala, *Finland* 8 E21
Nivelles, *Belgium* 17 G4
Nivernais, *France* 25 E10
Nixon, *U.S.A.* 109 L6
Nizamabad, *India* 60 K11
Nizamghat, *India* 61 E19
Nizhne Kolymsk, *Russia* 45 C17
Nizhne-Vartovsk, *Russia* 44 C8
Nizhneangarsk, *Russia* 45 D11
Nizhnegorskiy = Nyzhnohirskyy, *Ukraine* 41 K8
Nizhnekamsk, *Russia* 42 C10
Nizhneudinsk, *Russia* 45 D10
Nizhneyansk, *Russia* 45 B14
Nizhniy Chir, *Russia* 43 F6
Nizhniy Lomov, *Russia* 42 D6
Nizhniy Novgorod, *Russia* 42 B7
Nizhniy Tagil, *Russia* 44 D6
Nizhyn, *Ukraine* 41 G6
Nizip, *Turkey* 66 D7
Nízké Tatry, *Slovak Rep.* 20 G9
Nizza Monferrato, *Italy* 32 D5
Njakwa, *Malawi* 83 E3
Njanji, *Zambia* 83 E3
Njinjo, *Tanzania* 83 D4
Njombe, *Tanzania* 83 D3
Njombe □, *Tanzania* 83 D3
Njombe →, *Tanzania* 82 D4
Nkambe, *Cameroon* 79 D7
Nkana, *Zambia* 83 E2
Nkawkaw, *Ghana* 79 D4
Nkayi, *Zimbabwe* 83 F2
Nkhata Bay, *Malawi* 80 G6
Nkhota Kota, *Malawi* 83 E3
Nkongsamba, *Cameroon* 79 E6
Nkurenkuru, *Namibia* 84 B2
Nkwanta, *Ghana* 78 D4
Nmai →, *Burma* 61 G20
Noakhali = Maijdi, *Bangla.* 61 H17
Noatak, *U.S.A.* 96 B3
Nobel, *Canada* 106 A4
Nobeoka, *Japan* 49 H5
Noblejas, *Spain* 28 F1
Noblesville, *U.S.A.* 104 E3
Noce →, *Italy* 32 B8
Nocera Inferiore, *Italy* 35 B7
Nocera Terinese, *Italy* 35 C9
Nocera Umbra, *Italy* 33 E9
Noci, *Italy* 35 B10
Nockatunga, *Australia* 91 D3
Nocona, *U.S.A.* 109 J6
Noda, *Japan* 49 G9
Noel, *U.S.A.* 109 G7
Nogales, *Mexico* 114 A2
Nogales, *U.S.A.* 111 L8
Nōgata, *Japan* 49 H5
Nogent-en-Bassigny, *France* 25 D12
Nogent-le-Rotrou, *France* 24 D7
Nogent-sur-Seine, *France* 25 D10
Noggerup, *Australia* 89 F2
Noginsk, *Moskva, Russia* 42 C4
Noginsk, *Sib., Russia* 45 C10
Nogoa →, *Australia* 90 C4
Nogoyá, *Argentina* 126 C4
Nogueira de Ramuin, *Spain* 30 C3
Noguera Pallaresa →, *Spain* 28 D5
Noguera Ribagorzana →, *Spain* 28 D5
Nohar, *India* 62 E6
Noire, Montagne, *France* 26 E6
Noire, Mt., *France* 24 D3
Noirétable, *France* 26 C7
Noirmoutier, I. de, *France* 24 F4
Noirmoutier-en-l'Ile, *France* 24 F4
Nojane, *Botswana* 84 C3
Nojima-Zaki, *Japan* 49 G9
Nok Kundi, *Pakistan* 60 E3
Nokaneng, *Botswana* 84 B3
Nokhtuysk, *Russia* 45 C12
Nokia, *Finland* 9 F20
Nokomis, *Canada* 101 C8
Nokomis L., *Canada* 101 B8
Nol, *Sweden* 11 G6
Nola, *C.A.R.* 80 D3
Nola, *Italy* 35 B7
Nolay, *France* 25 F11
Noli, C. di, *Italy* 32 D5
Nolinsk, *Russia* 42 B9
Noma Omuramba →, *Namibia* 84 B3
Noman L., *Canada* 101 A7
Nombre de Dios, *Panama* 116 E4
Nome, *U.S.A.* 96 B3
Nomo-Zaki, *Japan* 49 H4
Nonacho L., *Canada* 101 A7
Nonancourt, *France* 24 D8
Nonant-le-Pin, *France* 24 D7
Nonda, *Australia* 90 C3
Nong Chang, *Thailand* 58 E2
Nong Het, *Laos* 58 C4
Nong Khai, *Thailand* 58 D4
Nong'an, *China* 51 B13
Nongoma, *S. Africa* 85 D5
Nonoava, *Mexico* 114 B3
Nonthaburi, *Thailand* 58 F3
Nontron, *France* 26 C4
Nonza, *France* 27 F13
Noonamah, *Australia* 88 B5
Noonan, *U.S.A.* 108 A3
Noondoo, *Australia* 91 D4
Noonkanbah, *Australia* 88 C3
Noord-Bergum, *Neths.* 16 B8
Noord Brabant □, *Neths.* 17 E6
Noord Holland □, *Neths.* 16 D5
Noordbeveland, *Neths.* 17 E3
Noordeloos, *Neths.* 16 E5
Noordhollandsch Kanaal, *Neths.* 16 C5
Noordhorn, *Neths.* 16 B8
Noordoostpolder, *Neths.* 16 C7
Noordwijk aan Zee, *Neths.* 16 D4
Noordwijk-Binnen, *Neths.* 16 D4
Noordwijkerhout, *Neths.* 16 D5
Noordzee Kanaal, *Neths.* 16 D5
Noorwolde, *Neths.* 16 C8
Nootka, *Canada* 100 D3
Nootka I., *Canada* 100 D3
Nóqui, *Angola* 80 F2
Nora, *Eritrea* 77 D5
Noranda, *Canada* 98 C4
Nórcia, *Italy* 33 F10
Norco, *U.S.A.* 113 M9
Nord □, *France* 25 B10
Nord-Ostsee-Kanal →, *Germany* 18 A5
Nordagutu, *Norway* 10 E3
Nordaustlandet, *Svalbard* 4 B9
Nordborg, *Denmark* 11 J3
Nordby, *Århus, Denmark* 11 J4
Nordby, *Ribe, Denmark* 11 J2
Norddeich, *Germany* 18 B3
Nordegg, *Canada* 100 C5
Norden, *Germany* 18 B3
Nordenham, *Germany* 18 B4
Norderhov, *Norway* 10 D4
Norderney, *Germany* 18 B3
Nordfjord, *Norway* 9 F11
Nordfriesische Inseln, *Germany* 18 A4
Nordhausen, *Germany* 18 D6
Nordhorn, *Germany* 18 C3
Norðoyar, *Færoe Is.* 8 E9
Nordjyllands Amtskommune □, *Denmark* 11 H4
Nordkapp, *Norway* 8 A21
Nordkapp, *Svalbard* 4 A9
Nordkinn = Kinnarodden, *Norway* 6 A11
Nordkinn-halvøya, *Norway* 8 A22
Nördlingen, *Germany* 19 G6
Nordrhein-Westfalen □, *Germany* 18 D3
Nordstrand, *Germany* 18 A4
Nordvik, *Russia* 45 B12
Nore, *Norway* 10 D3
Norefjell, *Norway* 10 D3
Norembega, *Canada* 98 C3
Noresund, *Norway* 10 D3
Norfolk, *Nebr., U.S.A.* 108 D6
Norfolk, *Va., U.S.A.* 104 G7
Norfolk □, *U.K.* 12 E9
Norfolk Broads, *U.K.* 12 E9
Norfolk I., *Pac. Oc.* 92 K8
Norfork Res., *U.S.A.* 109 G8
Norg, *Neths.* 16 B8
Norilsk, *Russia* 45 C9
Norley, *Australia* 91 D3
Norma, Mt., *Australia* 90 C3
Normal, *U.S.A.* 108 E10
Norman, *U.S.A.* 109 H6
Norman →, *Australia* 90 B3
Norman Wells, *Canada* 96 B7
Normanby →, *Australia* 90 A3
Normandie, *France* 24 D7
Normandie, Collines de, *France* 24 D6
Normandin, *Canada* 98 C5
Normandy = Normandie, *France* 24 D7
Normanhurst, Mt., *Australia* 89 E3
Normanton, *Australia* 90 B3
Norquay, *Canada* 101 C8
Norquinco, *Argentina* 128 B2
Norrbotten □, *Sweden* 8 C19
Nørre Åby, *Denmark* 11 J3
Nørre Nebel, *Denmark* 11 J2
Nørresundby, *Denmark* 11 G3
Norris, *U.S.A.* 110 D8
Norristown, *U.S.A.* 107 F9
Norrköping, *Sweden* 11 F10
Norrland, *Sweden* 9 E16
Norrtälje, *Sweden* 10 E12
Norseman, *Australia* 89 F3
Norsholm, *Sweden* 11 F9
Norsk, *Russia* 45 D14
Norte, Pta., *Argentina* 128 B4
Norte, Pta. del, *Canary Is.* 36 G2
Norte de Santander □, *Colombia* 120 B3
Nortelândia, *Brazil* 125 C6
North Adams, *U.S.A.* 107 D11
North Battleford, *Canada* 101 C7
North Bay, *Canada* 98 C4
North Belcher Is., *Canada* 98 A4
North Bend, *Canada* 100 D4
North Bend, *Oreg., U.S.A.* 110 E1
North Bend, *Pa., U.S.A.* 106 E7
North Bend, *Wash., U.S.A.* 112 C5
North Berwick, *U.K.* 14 E6
North Berwick, *U.S.A.* 107 C14
North C., *Canada* 99 C7
North C., *N.Z.* 87 F4
North Canadian →, *U.S.A.* 109 H7
North Cape = Nordkapp, *Norway* 8 A21
North Cape = Nordkapp, *Svalbard* 4 A9
North Caribou L., *Canada* 98 B1
North Carolina □, *U.S.A.* 105 H5
North Channel, *Canada* 98 C3
North Channel, *U.K.* 14 G3
North Chicago, *U.S.A.* 104 D2
North Dakota □, *U.S.A.* 108 B5
North Dandalup, *Australia* 89 F2
North Down □, *U.K.* 15 B6
North Downs, *U.K.* 13 F8
North East, *U.S.A.* 106 D5
North East Frontier Agency = Arunachal Pradesh □, *India* 61 E19
North East Providence Chan., *W. Indies* 116 A4
North Eastern □, *Kenya* 82 B5
North Esk →, *U.K.* 14 E6
North European Plain, *Europe* 6 D11
North Foreland, *U.K.* 13 F9
North Fork, *U.S.A.* 112 H7
North Fork American →, *U.S.A.* 112 G5
North Fork Feather →, *U.S.A.* 112 F5
North Frisian Is. = Nordfriesische Inseln, *Germany* 18 A4
North Henik L., *Canada* 101 A9
North Highlands, *U.S.A.* 112 G5
North Horr, *Kenya* 82 B4
North I., *Kenya* 82 B4
North I., *N.Z.* 87 H5
North Kingsville, *U.S.A.* 106 E4
North Knife →, *Canada* 101 B10
North Koel →, *India* 63 G10
North Korea ■, *Asia* 51 E14
North Lakhimpur, *India* 61 F19
North Las Vegas, *U.S.A.* 113 J11
North Loup →, *U.S.A.* 108 E5
North Magnetic Pole, *Canada* 4 B2
North Minch, *U.K.* 14 C3
North Nahanni →, *Canada* 100 A4
North Olmsted, *U.S.A.* 106 E3
North Ossetia □, *Russia* 43 J7
North Pagai, I. = Pagai Utara, *Indonesia* 56 E2
North Palisade, *U.S.A.* 111 H4
North Platte, *U.S.A.* 108 E4
North Platte →, *U.S.A.* 108 E4
North Pole, *Arctic* 4 A
North Portal, *Canada* 101 D8
North Powder, *U.S.A.* 110 D5
North Pt., *Canada* 99 C7
North Rhine Westphalia = Nordrhein-Westfalen □, *Germany* 18 D3
North Ronaldsay, *U.K.* 14 B6
North Saskatchewan →, *Canada* 101 C7
North Sea, *Europe* 6 D6
North Sporades = Voríai Sporádhes, *Greece* 39 K6
North Sydney, *Canada* 99 C7
North Taranaki Bight, *N.Z.* 87 H5
North Thompson →, *Canada* 100 C4
North Tonawanda, *U.S.A.* 106 C6
North Troy, *U.S.A.* 107 B12
North Truchas Pk., *U.S.A.* 111 J11
North Twin I., *Canada* 98 B3
North Tyne →, *U.K.* 12 C5
North Uist, *U.K.* 14 D1
North Vancouver, *Canada* 100 D4
North Vernon, *U.S.A.* 104 F3
North Wabasca L., *Canada* 100 B6
North Walsham, *U.K.* 12 E9
North-West □, *S. Africa* 84 D4
North West C., *Australia* 88 D1
North West Christmas I. Ridge, *Pac. Oc.* 93 G11
North West Frontier □, *Pakistan* 62 C4
North West Highlands, *U.K.* 14 D3
North West Providence Channel, *W. Indies* 116 A4
North West River, *Canada* 99 B7
North West Territories □, *Canada* 96 B9
North Western □, *Zambia* 83 E2
North York Moors, *U.K.* 12 C7
North Yorkshire □, *U.K.* 12 C6
Northallerton, *U.K.* 12 C6
Northam, *S. Africa* 84 C4
Northampton, *Australia* 89 E1
Northampton, *U.K.* 13 E7
Northampton, *Mass., U.S.A.* 107 D12
Northampton, *Pa., U.S.A.* 107 F9
Northampton Downs, *Australia* 90 C4
Northamptonshire □, *U.K.* 13 E7
Northbridge, *U.S.A.* 107 D13
Northcliffe, *Australia* 89 F2
Northeim, *Germany* 18 D6
Northern □, *Malawi* 83 E3
Northern □, *Uganda* 82 B3
Northern □, *Zambia* 83 E3
Northern Cape □, *S. Africa* 84 D3
Northern Circars, *India* 61 L13
Northern Indian L., *Canada* 101 B9
Northern Ireland □, *U.K.* 15 B5
Northern Light, L., *Canada* 98 C1
Northern Marianas ■, *Pac. Oc.* 92 F6
Northern Province □, *S. Leone* 78 D2
Northern Territory □, *Australia* 88 D5
Northern Transvaal □, *S. Africa* 85 C4
Northfield, *U.S.A.* 108 C8
Northland □, *N.Z.* 87 F4
Northome, *U.S.A.* 108 B7
Northport, *Ala., U.S.A.* 105 J2
Northport, *Mich., U.S.A.* 104 C3
Northport, *Wash., U.S.A.* 110 B5
Northumberland □, *U.K.* 12 B5
Northumberland, C., *Australia* 91 F3
Northumberland Is., *Australia* 90 C4
Northumberland Str., *Canada* 99 C7
Northwich, *U.K.* 12 D5
Northwood, *Iowa, U.S.A.* 108 D8
Northwood, *N. Dak., U.S.A.* 108 B6
Norton, *U.S.A.* 108 F5
Norton, *Zimbabwe* 83 F3
Norton Sd., *U.S.A.* 96 B3
Nortorf, *Germany* 18 A5
Norwalk, *Calif., U.S.A.* 113 M8
Norwalk, *Conn., U.S.A.* 107 E11
Norwalk, *Ohio, U.S.A.* 106 E2
Norway, *U.S.A.* 104 C2

Norway ■, *Europe* 8 E14
Norway House, *Canada* . . 101 C9
Norwegian Sea, *Atl. Oc.* . . 4 C8
Norwich, *Canada* 106 D4
Norwich, *U.K.* 12 E9
Norwich, *Conn., U.S.A.* . . 107 E12
Norwich, *N.Y., U.S.A.* . . 107 D9
Norwood, *Canada* 106 B7
Noshiro, *Japan* 48 D10
Nosivka, *Ukraine* 41 G6
Nosok, *Russia* 44 B9
Nosovka = Nosivka,
 Ukraine 41 G6
Noss Hd., *U.K.* 14 C5
Nossa Senhora da Glória,
 Brazil 122 D4
Nossa Senhora das Dores,
 Brazil 122 D4
Nossa Senhora do
 Livramento, *Brazil* . . 125 D6
Nossebro, *Sweden* 11 F6
Nossob →, *S. Africa* 84 D3
Nosy Bé, *Madag.* 81 G9
Nosy Boraha, *Madag.* . . . 85 B8
Nosy Mitsio, *Madag.* . . . 81 G9
Nosy Varika, *Madag.* . . . 85 C8
Noteć →, *Poland* 20 C5
Notigi Dam, *Canada* . . . 101 B9
Notikewin →, *Canada* . . 100 B5
Notios Evvoïkos Kólpos,
 Greece 39 L7
Noto, *Italy* 35 F8
Noto, G. di, *Italy* 35 F8
Notodden, *Norway* 10 E3
Notre-Dame, *Canada* . . . 99 C7
Notre Dame B., *Canada* . . 99 C8
Notre Dame de Koartac =
 Quaqtaq, *Canada* 97 B13
Notre Dame d'Ivugivic =
 Ivujivik, *Canada* 97 B12
Notsé, *Togo* 79 D5
Nottaway →, *Canada* 98 B4
Nøtterøy, *Norway* 10 E4
Nottingham, *U.K.* 12 E6
Nottinghamshire □, *U.K.* . 12 D7
Nottoway →, *U.S.A.* . . . 104 G7
Notwane →, *Botswana* . . 84 C4
Nouâdhibou, *Mauritania* . . 74 D1
Nouâdhibou, Ras,
 Mauritania 74 D1
Nouakchott, *Mauritania* . . 78 B1
Nouméa, *N. Cal.* 92 K8
Noupoort, *S. Africa* 84 E3
Nouveau Comptoir =
 Wemindji, *Canada* 98 B4
Nouvelle-Calédonie = New
 Caledonia ■, *Pac. Oc.* . 92 K8
Nouzonville, *France* 25 C11
Nová Baňa, *Slovak Rep.* . 21 G8
Nová Bystřice, *Czech.* . . 20 F5
Nova Casa Nova, *Brazil* . 122 C3
Nova Cruz, *Brazil* 122 C4
Nova Era, *Brazil* 123 E3
Nova Esperança, *Brazil* . 127 A5
Nova Friburgo, *Brazil* . . 123 F3
Nova Gaia = Cambundi-
 Catembo, *Angola* 80 G3
Nova Gradiška, *Croatia* . . 21 K7
Nova Granada, *Brazil* . . 123 F2
Nova Iguaçu, *Brazil* . . . 123 F3
Nova Iorque, *Brazil* . . . 122 C3
Nova Kakhovka, *Ukraine* . 41 J7
Nova Lamego, *Guinea-Biss.* 78 C2
Nova Lima, *Brazil* 127 A7
Nova Lisboa = Huambo,
 Angola 81 G3
Nova Lusitânia, *Mozam.* . 83 F3
Nova Mambone, *Mozam.* . 85 C6
Nova Odesa, *Ukraine* . . . 41 J6
Nova Ponte, *Brazil* 123 E2
Nova Scotia □, *Canada* . . 99 C7
Nova Sofala, *Mozam.* . . . 85 C5
Nova Venécia, *Brazil* . . . 123 E3
Nova Vida, *Brazil* 125 C5
Nova Zagora, *Bulgaria* . . 38 G8
Novaleksandrovskaya =
 Novoaleksandrovsk,
 Russia 43 H5
Novannenskiy =
 Novoannenskiy, *Russia* . 42 E6
Novara, *Italy* 32 C5
Novato, *U.S.A.* 112 G4
Novaya Kakhovka = Nova
 Kakhovka, *Ukraine* . . . 41 J7
Novaya Kazanka,
 Kazakhstan 43 F9
Novaya Ladoga, *Russia* . . 40 B7
Novaya Lyalya, *Russia* . . 44 D7
Novaya Zemlya, *Russia* . . 44 B6
Novelda, *Spain* 29 G4
Novellara, *Italy* 32 D7
Noventa Vicentina, *Italy* . 33 C8
Novgorod, *Russia* 40 C6
Novgorod-Severskiy =
 Novhorod-Siverskyy,
 Ukraine 41 G7
Novhorod-Siverskyy,
 Ukraine 41 G7
Novi Bečej, *Serbia, Yug.* . 21 K10
Novi Grad, *Croatia* 33 C10
Novi Krichim, *Bulgaria* . . 38 G7
Novi Lígure, *Italy* 32 D5
Novi Pazar, *Bulgaria* . . . 38 F10
Novi Pazar, *Serbia, Yug.* . 21 M10
Novi Sad, *Serbia, Yug.* . . 21 K9
Novi Vinodolski, *Croatia* . 33 C11
Novigrad, *Croatia* 33 D12

Noville, *Belgium* 17 H7
Novo Acôrdo, *Brazil* . . . 122 D2
Novo Aripuanã, *Brazil* . . 121 E5
Nôvo Cruzeiro, *Brazil* . . 123 E3
Nôvo Hamburgo, *Brazil* . 127 B5
Novo Horizonte, *Brazil* . 123 F2
Novo Mesto, *Slovenia* . . . 33 C12
Novo Remanso, *Brazil* . . 122 C3
Novoaleksandrovsk, *Russia* 43 H5
Novoannenskiy, *Russia* . . 42 E6
Novoataysk, *Russia* 44 D9
Novoazovsk, *Ukraine* . . . 41 J10
Novocheboksarsk, *Russia* . 42 B8
Novocherkassk, *Russia* . . 43 G5
Novodevichye, *Russia* . . . 42 D9
Novogrudok =
 Navahrudak, *Belarus* . . 40 F3
Novohrad-Volynskyy,
 Ukraine 41 G4
Novokachalinsk, *Russia* . . 48 B6
Novokazalinsk =
 Zhangaqazaly,
 Kazakhstan 44 E7
Novokhopersk, *Russia* . . . 42 E5
Novokuybyshevsk, *Russia* . 42 D9
Novokuznetsk, *Russia* . . . 44 D9
Novomirgorod, *Ukraine* . . 41 H6
Novomoskovsk, *Russia* . . 42 C4
Novomoskovsk, *Ukraine* . . 41 H8
Novopolotsk =
 Navapolatsk, *Belarus* . . 40 E5
Novorossiysk, *Russia* . . . 43 H3
Novorybnoye, *Russia* . . . 45 B11
Novorzhev, *Russia* 40 D5
Novoselytsya, *Ukraine* . . 41 H4
Novoshakhtinsk, *Russia* . . 43 G4
Novosibirsk, *Russia* 44 D9
Novosibirskiye Ostrova,
 Russia 45 B15
Novosil, *Russia* 42 D3
Novosokolniki, *Russia* . . . 40 D6
Novotitarovskaya, *Russia* . 43 H4
Novotroitsk, *Russia* 44 D6
Novoukrayinka, *Ukraine* . 41 H6
Novouljanovsk, *Russia* . . 42 C9
Novouzensk, *Russia* 42 E9
Novovolynsk, *Ukraine* . . . 41 G3
Novovoronezhskiy, *Russia* . 42 E4
Novozybkov, *Russia* 41 F6
Novska, *Croatia* 21 K6
Novy Bug = Novyy Buh,
 Ukraine 41 J7
Nový Bydzov, *Czech.* . . . 20 E5
Novy Dwór Mazowiecki,
 Poland 20 C10
Novyy Afon, *Georgia* . . . 43 J5
Novyy Buh, *Ukraine* 41 J7
Novyy Oskol, *Russia* 42 E3
Novyy Port, *Russia* 44 C8
Now Shahr, *Iran* 65 B6
Nowa Deba, *Poland* 20 E11
Nowa Ruda, *Poland* 20 E6
Nowa Sól, *Poland* 20 D5
Nowbarān, *Iran* 65 C6
Nowe, *Poland* 20 B8
Nowghāb, *Iran* 65 C8
Nowgong, *India* 61 F18
Nowogard, *Poland* 20 B5
Nowogród, *Poland* 20 B11
Nowra, *Australia* 91 E5
Nowshera, *Pakistan* 60 B8
Nowy Korczyn, *Poland* . . 20 E10
Nowy Sącz, *Poland* 20 F10
Noxen, *U.S.A.* 107 E8
Noxon, *U.S.A.* 110 C6
Noya, *Spain* 30 C2
Noyant, *France* 24 E7
Noyers, *France* 25 E10
Noyes I., *U.S.A.* 100 B2
Noyon, *France* 25 C9
Noyon, *Mongolia* 50 C2
Nozay, *France* 24 E5
Nsa, O. en →, *Algeria* . . . 75 B6
Nsanje, *Malawi* 83 F4
Nsawam, *Ghana* 79 D4
Nsomba, *Zambia* 83 E2
Nsukka, *Nigeria* 79 D6
Nu Jiang →, *China* 52 C1
Nu Shan, *China* 52 D2
Nuba Mts. = Nubah,
 Jibalan, *Sudan* 77 E3
Nubah, Jibalan, *Sudan* . . 77 E3
Nubian Desert = Nûbîya,
 Es Sahrâ En, *Sudan* . . . 76 C3
Nûbîya, Es Sahrâ En,
 Sudan 76 C3
Ñuble □, *Chile* 126 D1
Nuboai, *Indonesia* 57 E9
Nubra →, *India* 63 B7
Nueces →, *U.S.A.* 109 M6
Nueltin L., *Canada* 101 A9
Nueva, *I., Chile* 128 E3
Nueva Antioquia,
 Colombia 120 B4
Nueva Asunción □,
 Paraguay 126 A3
Nueva Esparta □,
 Venezuela 121 A5
Nueva Gerona, *Cuba* . . . 116 B3
Nueva Imperial, *Chile* . . 128 A2
Nueva Palmira, *Uruguay* . 126 C4
Nueva Rosita, *Mexico* . . 114 B4
Nueva San Salvador,
 El Salv. 116 D2
Nuéve de Julio, *Argentina* 126 D3
Nuevitas, *Cuba* 116 B4

Nuevo, G., *Argentina* . . . 128 B4
Nuevo Guerrero, *Mexico* . 115 B5
Nuevo Laredo, *Mexico* . . 115 B5
Nuevo León □, *Mexico* . . 114 C4
Nuevo Mundo, Cerro,
 Bolivia 124 E4
Nuevo Rocafuerte, *Ecuador* 120 D2
Nugget Pt., *N.Z.* 87 M2
Nugrus, Gebel, *Egypt* . . . 76 C3
Nuhaka, *N.Z.* 87 H6
Nuits-St.-Georges, *France* . 25 E11
Nukey Bluff, *Australia* . . 91 E2
Nukheila, *Sudan* 76 D2
Nukhuyb, *Iraq* 67 F10
Nuku'alofa, *Tonga* 87 E11
Nukus, *Uzbekistan* 44 E6
Nuland, *Neths.* 16 E6
Nulato, *U.S.A.* 96 B4
Nules, *Spain* 28 F4
Nullagine →, *Australia* . . 88 D3
Nullarbor, *Australia* 89 F5
Nullarbor Plain, *Australia* . 89 F4
Numalla, L., *Australia* . . . 91 D3
Numan, *Nigeria* 79 D7
Numansdorp, *Neths.* 16 E4
Numata, *Japan* 49 F9
Numatinna →, *Sudan* . . . 77 F2
Numazu, *Japan* 49 G9
Numbulwar, *Australia* . . . 90 A2
Numfoor, *Indonesia* 57 E8
Numurkah, *Australia* . . . 91 F4
Nunaksaluk I., *Canada* . . 99 A7
Nuneaton, *U.K.* 13 E6
Nungo, *Mozam.* 83 E4
Nungwe, *Tanzania* 82 C3
Nunivak I., *U.S.A.* 96 B3
Nunkun, *India* 63 C7
Nunspeet, *Neths.* 16 D7
Núoro, *Italy* 34 B2
Nuquí, *Colombia* 120 B2
Nūrābād, *Iran* 65 E8
Nure →, *Italy* 32 C6
Nuremburg = Nürnberg,
 Germany 19 F7
Nuri, *Mexico* 114 B3
Nurina, *Australia* 89 F4
Nuriootpa, *Australia* 91 E2
Nurlat, *Russia* 42 C10
Nurmes, *Finland* 8 E23
Nürnberg, *Germany* 19 F7
Nurran, L. = Terewah, L.,
 Australia 91 D4
Nurrari Lakes, *Australia* . 89 E5
Nurri, *Italy* 34 C2
Nusa Barung, *Indonesia* . 57 H15
Nusa Kambangan,
 Indonesia 57 G13
Nusa Tenggara Barat □,
 Indonesia 56 F5
Nusa Tenggara Timur □,
 Indonesia 57 F6
Nusaybin, *Turkey* 67 D9
Nushki, *Pakistan* 62 E2
Nutak, *Canada* 97 C13
Nuth, *Neths.* 17 G7
Nutwood Downs, *Australia* 90 B1
Nuuk = Godthåb,
 Greenland 97 B14
Nuwakot, *Nepal* 63 E10
Nuweiba', *Egypt* 76 B3
Nuweveldberge, *S. Africa* . 84 E3
Nuyts, C., *Australia* 89 F5
Nuyts Arch., *Australia* . . 91 E1
Nxau-Nxau, *Botswana* . . 84 B3
Nyaake, *Liberia* 78 E3
Nyack, *U.S.A.* 107 E11
Nyadal, *Sweden* 10 B11
Nyah West, *Australia* . . . 91 F3
Nyahanga, *Tanzania* 82 C3
Nyahua, *Tanzania* 82 D3
Nyahururu, *Kenya* 82 B4
Nyainqentanglha Shan,
 China 54 C4
Nyakanazi, *Tanzania* . . . 82 C3
Nyakrom, *Ghana* 79 D4
Nyâlâ, *Sudan* 77 E1
Nyamandhlovu, *Zimbabwe* 83 F2
Nyambiti, *Tanzania* 82 C3
Nyamwaga, *Tanzania* . . . 82 C3
Nyandekwa, *Tanzania* . . 82 C3
Nyanding →, *Sudan* 77 F3
Nyandoma, *Russia* 40 B11
Nyangana, *Namibia* 84 B3
Nyanguge, *Tanzania* 82 C3
Nyankpala, *Ghana* 79 D4
Nyanza, *Burundi* 82 C2
Nyanza, *Rwanda* 82 C2
Nyanza □, *Kenya* 82 C3
Nyarling →, *Canada* . . . 100 A6
Nyasa, L. = Malawi, L.,
 Africa 83 E3
Nyasvizh, *Belarus* 41 F4
Nyazura, *Zimbabwe* 83 F3
Nyazwidzi →, *Zimbabwe* . 83 F3
Nybro, *Sweden* 9 H16
Nyda, *Russia* 44 C8
Nyeri, *Kenya* 82 C4
Nyerol, *Sudan* 77 F3
Nyhem, *Sweden* 10 B9
Nyiel, *Sudan* 77 F3
Nyinahin, *Ghana* 78 D4
Nyírbátor, *Hungary* 21 H12
Nyíregyháza, *Hungary* . . 21 H11
Nykøbing, Sjælland,
 Denmark 11 J5

Nykøbing, Storstrøm,
 Denmark 11 K5
Nykøbing, Viborg,
 Denmark 11 H2
Nyköping, *Sweden* 11 F11
Nykvarn, *Sweden* 10 E11
Nyland, *Sweden* 10 A11
Nylstroom, *S. Africa* 85 C4
Nymagee, *Australia* 91 E4
Nymburk, *Czech.* 20 E5
Nynäshamn, *Sweden* . . . 10 F11
Nyngan, *Australia* 91 E4
Nyoman = Neman →,
 Lithuania 9 J19
Nyon, *Switz.* 22 D2
Nyong →, *Cameroon* 79 E6
Nyons, *France* 27 D9
Nyord, *Denmark* 11 J6
Nyou, *Burkina Faso* 79 C4
Nysa, *Poland* 20 E7
Nysa →, *Europe* 18 C10
Nyssa, *U.S.A.* 110 E5
Nysted, *Denmark* 11 K5
Nyunzu, *Zaïre* 82 D2
Nyurba, *Russia* 45 C12
Nyzhnohirskyy, *Ukraine* . 41 K8
Nzega, *Tanzania* 82 C3
Nzega □, *Tanzania* 82 C3
N'Zérékoré, *Guinea* 78 D3
Nzeto, *Angola* 80 F2
Nzilo, Chutes de, *Zaïre* . . 83 E2
Nzubuka, *Tanzania* 82 C3

O

Ō-Shima, *Nagasaki, Japan* . 49 G4
Ō-Shima, *Shizuoka, Japan* . 49 G9
Oacoma, *U.S.A.* 108 D5
Oahe, L., *U.S.A.* 108 C4
Oahe Dam, *U.S.A.* 108 C4
Oahu, *U.S.A.* 102 H16
Oak Creek, *U.S.A.* 110 F10
Oak Harbor, *U.S.A.* 112 B4
Oak Hill, *U.S.A.* 104 G5
Oak Park, *U.S.A.* 104 E2
Oak Ridge, *U.S.A.* 105 G3
Oak View, *U.S.A.* 113 L7
Oakan-Dake, *Japan* 48 C12
Oakbank, *Australia* 91 E3
Oakdale, *Calif., U.S.A.* . . 111 H3
Oakdale, *La., U.S.A.* . . . 109 K8
Oakengates, *U.K.* 12 E5
Oakes, *U.S.A.* 108 B5
Oakesdale, *U.S.A.* 110 C5
Oakey, *Australia* 91 D5
Oakham, *U.K.* 12 E7
Oakhurst, *U.S.A.* 112 H7
Oakland, *Calif., U.S.A.* . . 111 H2
Oakland, *Oreg., U.S.A.* . . 110 E2
Oakland City, *U.S.A.* . . . 104 F2
Oakley, *Idaho, U.S.A.* . . . 110 E7
Oakley, *Kans., U.S.A.* . . . 108 F4
Oakover →, *Australia* . . . 88 D3
Oakridge, *U.S.A.* 110 E2
Oakville, *U.S.A.* 112 D3
Oamaru, *N.Z.* 87 L3
Oasis, *Calif., U.S.A.* . . . 113 M10
Oasis, *Nev., U.S.A.* 112 H9
Oates Land, *Antarctica* . . 5 C11
Oatman, *U.S.A.* 113 K12
Oaxaca, *Mexico* 115 D5
Oaxaca □, *Mexico* 115 D5
Ob →, *Russia* 44 C7
Oba, *Canada* 98 C3
Obala, *Cameroon* 79 E7
Obama, *Japan* 49 G7
Oban, *U.K.* 14 E3
Obbia, *Somali Rep.* 68 F4
Obdam, *Neths.* 16 C5
Obed, *Canada* 100 C5
Ober-Aagau, *Switz.* 22 B5
Obera, *Argentina* 127 B4
Oberalppass, *Switz.* 23 C7
Oberalpstock, *Switz.* . . . 23 C7
Oberammergau, *Germany* . 19 H7
Oberdrauburg, *Austria* . . 21 J2
Oberengadin, *Switz.* 23 C9
Oberentfelden, *Switz.* . . . 22 B6
Oberhausen, *Germany* . . 18 D2
Oberkirch, *Germany* 19 G4
Oberland, *Switz.* 22 C5
Oberlin, *Kans., U.S.A.* . . 108 F4
Oberlin, *La., U.S.A.* 109 K8
Oberlin, *Ohio, U.S.A.* . . 106 E2
Obernai, *France* 25 D14
Oberndorf, *Germany* 19 G4
Oberon, *Australia* 91 E4
Oberpfälzer Wald,
 Germany 19 F8
Obersiggenthal, *Switz.* . . 23 B6
Oberstdorf, *Germany* . . . 19 H6
Oberwil, *Switz.* 22 A5
Obi, Kepulauan, *Indonesia* 57 E7
Obi Is. = Obi, Kepulauan,
 Indonesia 57 E7
Obiaruku, *Nigeria* 79 D6
Óbidos, *Brazil* 121 D6
Óbidos, *Portugal* 31 F1
Obihiro, *Japan* 48 C11
Obilatu, *Indonesia* 57 E7
Obilnoye, *Russia* 43 G7
Obing, *Germany* 19 H8
Obisfelde, *Germany* 18 C6
Objat, *France* 26 C5

Obluchye, *Russia* 45 E14
Obninsk, *Russia* 42 C3
Obo, *C.A.R.* 82 A2
Obo, *Ethiopia* 77 G4
Obock, *Djibouti* 77 E5
Oborniki, *Poland* 20 C6
Oboyan, *Russia* 42 E3
Obozerskaya =
 Obozerskiy, *Russia* . . . 44 C5
Obozerskiy, *Russia* 44 C5
Obrovac, *Croatia* 33 D12
Obruk, *Turkey* 66 C5
Observatory Inlet, *Canada* 100 B3
Obshchi Syrt, *Russia* 6 D16
Obskaya Guba, *Russia* . . 44 C8
Obuasi, *Ghana* 79 D4
Obubra, *Nigeria* 79 D6
Obwalden □, *Switz.* 22 C6
Obzor, *Bulgaria* 38 G10
Ocala, *U.S.A.* 105 L4
Ocamo →, *Venezuela* . . . 121 C4
Ocampo, *Mexico* 114 B3
Ocaña, *Colombia* 120 B3
Ocaña, *Spain* 28 F1
Ocanomowoc, *U.S.A.* . . . 108 D10
Ocate, *U.S.A.* 109 G2
Occidental, Cordillera,
 Colombia 120 C3
Occidental, Cordillera,
 Peru 124 C3
Ocean City, *N.J., U.S.A.* . 104 F8
Ocean City, *Wash., U.S.A.* 112 C2
Ocean I. = Banaba,
 Kiribati 92 H8
Ocean Park, *U.S.A.* 112 D2
Oceano, *U.S.A.* 113 K6
Oceanport, *U.S.A.* 107 F10
Oceanside, *U.S.A.* 113 M9
Ochagavia, *Spain* 28 C3
Ochamchira, *Georgia* . . . 43 J5
Ochamps, *Belgium* 17 J6
Ochil Hills, *U.K.* 14 E5
Ochre River, *Canada* . . . 101 C9
Ochsenfurt, *Germany* . . . 19 F6
Ochsenhausen, *Germany* . 19 G5
Ocilla, *U.S.A.* 105 K4
Ocmulgee →, *U.S.A.* . . . 105 K4
Ocna Sibiului, *Romania* . 38 D7
Ocnița, *Moldova* 41 H4
Ocoña, *Peru* 124 D3
Ocoña →, *Peru* 124 D3
Oconee →, *U.S.A.* 105 K4
Oconto, *U.S.A.* 104 C2
Oconto Falls, *U.S.A.* . . . 104 C1
Ocosingo, *Mexico* 115 D6
Ocotal, *Nic.* 116 D2
Ocotlán, *Mexico* 114 C4
Ocquier, *Belgium* 17 H6
Ocreza →, *Portugal* 31 F3
Octave, *U.S.A.* 111 J7
Octeville, *France* 24 C5
Ocumare del Tuy,
 Venezuela 120 A4
Ocuri, *Bolivia* 125 D4
Oda, *Ghana* 79 D4
Ōda, *Japan* 49 G6
Oda, J., *Sudan* 76 C4
Ódáðahraun, *Iceland* . . . 8 D5
Ödåkra, *Sweden* 11 H6
Odate, *Japan* 48 D10
Odawara, *Japan* 49 G9
Odda, *Norway* 9 F12
Odder, *Denmark* 11 J4
Oddur, *Somali Rep.* 68 G3
Ödeborg, *Sweden* 11 F5
Odei →, *Canada* 101 B9
Odemira, *Portugal* 31 H2
Ödemiş, *Turkey* 66 C3
Odendaalsrus, *S. Africa* . 84 D4
Odense, *Denmark* 11 J4
Odenwald, *Germany* 19 F5
Oder →, *Germany* 18 B10
Oderzo, *Italy* 33 C9
Odesa, *Ukraine* 41 J6
Odessa = Odesa, *Ukraine* . 41 J6
Odessa, *Canada* 107 B8
Odessa, *Tex., U.S.A.* . . . 109 K3
Odessa, *Wash., U.S.A.* . . 110 C4
Odiakwe, *Botswana* 84 C4
Odiel →, *Spain* 31 H4
Odienné, *Ivory C.* 78 D3
Odintsovo, *Russia* 42 C3
Odiongan, *Phil.* 55 E4
Odobești, *Romania* 38 D10
O'Donnell, *U.S.A.* 109 J4
Odoorn, *Neths.* 16 C9
Odorheiu Secuiesc,
 Romania 38 C8
Odoyevo, *Russia* 42 D3
Odra = Oder →, *Germany* . 18 B10
Odra →, *Poland* 20 B4
Odra →, *Spain* 30 C6
Odžaci, *Serbia, Yug.* . . . 21 K9
Odzi, *Zimbabwe* 85 B5
Oedelem, *Belgium* 17 F2
Oegstgeest, *Neths.* 16 D4
Oeiras, *Brazil* 122 C3
Oeiras, *Portugal* 31 G1
Oelrichs, *U.S.A.* 108 D3
Oelsnitz, *Germany* 18 E8
Oelwein, *U.S.A.* 108 D9
Oenpelli, *Australia* 88 B5
Of, *Turkey* 67 B9
Ofanto →, *Italy* 35 A9
Offa, *Nigeria* 79 D5

Offaly □, *Ireland* 15 C4
Offenbach, *Germany* 19 E4
Offenburg, *Germany* 19 G3
Offerdal, *Sweden* 10 A8
Offida, *Italy* 33 F10
Offranville, *France* 24 C8
Ofidhousa, *Greece* 39 N9
Ofotfjorden, *Norway* 8 B17
Ōfunato, *Japan* 48 E10
Oga, *Japan* 48 E9
Oga-Hantō, *Japan* 48 E9
Ogahalla, *Canada* 98 B2
Ōgaki, *Japan* 49 G8
Ogallala, *U.S.A.* 108 E4
Ogasawara Gunto,
  Pac. Oc. 92 E6
Ogbomosho, *Nigeria* 79 D5
Ogden, *Iowa, U.S.A.* 108 D8
Ogden, *Utah, U.S.A.* 110 F7
Ogdensburg, *U.S.A.* 107 B9
Ogeechee →, *U.S.A.* 105 K5
Ogilby, *U.S.A.* 113 N12
Oglio →, *Italy* 32 C7
Ogmore, *Australia* 90 C4
Ognon →, *France* 25 E12
Ogoja, *Nigeria* 79 D6
Ogoki →, *Canada* 98 B2
Ogoki L., *Canada* 98 B2
Ogoki Res., *Canada* 98 B2
Ogooué →, *Gabon* 80 E1
Ogosta →, *Bulgaria* 38 F6
Ogowe = Ogooué →,
  Gabon 80 E1
Ogr = Sharafa, *Sudan* ... 77 E2
Ogre, *Latvia* 9 H21
Ogrein, *Sudan* 76 D3
Ogulin, *Croatia* 33 C12
Ogun □, *Nigeria* 79 D5
Oguta, *Nigeria* 79 D6
Ogwashi-Uku, *Nigeria* .. 79 D6
Ogwe, *Nigeria* 79 E6
Ohai, *N.Z.* 87 L2
Ohakune, *N.Z.* 87 H5
Ohanet, *Algeria* 75 C6
Ohata, *Japan* 48 D10
Ohau, L., *N.Z.* 87 L2
Ohey, *Belgium* 17 H6
Ohio □, *U.S.A.* 104 E3
Ohio →, *U.S.A.* 104 G1
Ohře →, *Czech.* 20 E4
Ohre →, *Germany* 18 C7
Ohrid, *Macedonia* 39 H3
Ohridsko Jezero,
  Macedonia 39 H3
Ohrigstad, *S. Africa* 85 C5
Öhringen, *Germany* 19 F5
Oiapoque →, *Brazil* 121 C7
Oikou, *China* 51 E9
Oil City, *U.S.A.* 106 E5
Oildale, *U.S.A.* 113 K7
Oirschot, *Neths.* 17 E6
Oise □, *France* 25 C9
Oise →, *France* 25 D9
Oisterwijk, *Neths.* 17 E6
Ōita, *Japan* 49 H5
Ōita □, *Japan* 49 H5
Oiticica, *Brazil* 122 C3
Ojai, *U.S.A.* 113 L7
Ojinaga, *Mexico* 114 B4
Ojiya, *Japan* 49 F9
Ojos del Salado, Cerro,
  Argentina 126 B2
Oka →, *Russia* 42 B7
Okaba, *Indonesia* 57 F9
Okahandja, *Namibia* ... 84 C2
Okahukura, *N.Z.* 87 H5
Okanagan L., *Canada* .. 100 C5
Okandja, *Gabon* 80 E2
Okanogan, *U.S.A.* 110 B4
Okanogan →, *U.S.A.* .. 110 B4
Okaputa, *Namibia* 84 C2
Okara, *Pakistan* 62 D5
Okarito, *N.Z.* 87 K3
Okaukuejo, *Namibia* ... 84 B2
Okavango Swamps,
  Botswana 84 B3
Okaya, *Japan* 49 F9
Okayama, *Japan* 49 G6
Okayama □, *Japan* 49 G6
Okazaki, *Japan* 49 G8
Oke-Iho, *Nigeria* 79 D5
Okeechobee, *U.S.A.* ... 105 M5
Okeechobee, L., *U.S.A.* . 105 M5
Okefenokee Swamp,
  U.S.A. 105 K4
Okehampton, *U.K.* 13 G3
Okene, *Nigeria* 79 D6
Oker →, *Germany* 18 C6
Okha, *Russia* 45 D15
Ókhi Óros, *Greece* 39 L7
Okhotsk, *Russia* 45 D15
Okhotsk, Sea of, *Asia* .. 45 D15
Okhotskiy Perevoz, *Russia* 45 C14
Okhtyrka, *Ukraine* 41 G8
Oki-Shotō, *Japan* 49 F6
Okiep, *S. Africa* 84 D2
Okigwi, *Nigeria* 79 D6
Okija, *Nigeria* 79 D6
Okinawa □, *Japan* 49 L3
Okinawa-Guntō, *Japan* . 49 L3
Okinawa-Jima, *Japan* .. 49 L4
Okino-erabu-Shima, *Japan* 49 L4
Okitipupa, *Nigeria* 79 D5
Oklahoma □, *U.S.A.* ... 109 H6
Oklahoma City, *U.S.A.* . 109 H6
Okmulgee, *U.S.A.* 109 H7
Oknitsa = Ocniţa, *Moldova* 41 H4

Okolo, *Uganda* 82 B3
Okolona, *U.S.A.* 109 H10
Okrika, *Nigeria* 79 E6
Oktabrsk = Oktyabrsk,
  Kazakhstan 44 E6
Oktyabrsk, *Kazakhstan* .. 44 E6
Oktyabrsk, *Russia* 42 D9
Oktyabrskiy = Aktsyabrski,
  Belarus 41 F5
Oktyabrskiy, *Russia* 43 G5
Oktyabrskoy Revolyutsii,
  Os., *Russia* 45 B10
Oktyabrskoye =
  Zhovtneve, *Ukraine* ... 41 J7
Oktyabrskoye, *Russia* ... 44 C7
Okulovka, *Russia* 40 C7
Okuru, *N.Z.* 87 K2
Okushiri-Tō, *Japan* 48 C9
Okuta, *Nigeria* 79 D5
Okwa →, *Botswana* ... 84 C3
Ola, *U.S.A.* 109 H8
Ólafsfjörður, *Iceland* ... 8 C4
Ólafsvík, *Iceland* 8 D2
Olancha, *U.S.A.* 113 J8
Olancha Pk., *U.S.A.* 113 J8
Olanchito, *Honduras* ... 116 C2
Öland, *Sweden* 9 H17
Olargues, *France* 26 E6
Olary, *Australia* 91 E3
Olascoaga, *Argentina* .. 126 D3
Olathe, *U.S.A.* 108 F7
Olavarría, *Argentina* ... 126 D3
Oława, *Poland* 20 E7
Ólbia, *Italy* 34 B2
Ólbia, G. di, *Italy* 34 B2
Old Bahama Chan. =
  Bahama, Canal Viejo de,
  W. Indies 116 B4
Old Baldy Pk. = San
  Antonio, Mt., *U.S.A.* .. 113 L9
Old Cork, *Australia* 90 C3
Old Crow, *Canada* 96 B6
Old Dale, *U.S.A.* 113 L11
Old Dongola, *Sudan* ... 76 D3
Old Fletton, *U.K.* 13 E7
Old Forge, *N.Y., U.S.A.* . 107 C10
Old Forge, *Pa., U.S.A.* .. 107 E9
Old Fort →, *Canada* ... 101 B6
Old Shinyanga, *Tanzania* 82 C3
Old Speck Mt., *U.S.A.* .. 107 B14
Old Town, *U.S.A.* 99 D6
Old Wives L., *Canada* .. 101 C7
Oldbury, *U.K.* 13 F5
Oldcastle, *Ireland* 15 C4
Oldeani, *Tanzania* 82 C4
Oldenburg, *Niedersachsen,
  Germany* 18 B4
Oldenburg,
  *Schleswig-Holstein,
  Germany* 18 A6
Oldenzaal, *Neths.* 16 D9
Oldham, *U.K.* 12 D5
Oldman →, *Canada* ... 100 D6
Olds, *Canada* 100 C6
Olean, *U.S.A.* 106 D6
Oléggio, *Italy* 32 C5
Oleiros, *Portugal* 30 F3
Olekma →, *Russia* 45 C13
Olekminsk, *Russia* 45 C13
Oleksandriya, *Ukraine* .. 41 H7
Oleksandriya, *Ukraine* .. 41 G4
Oleksandrovka, *Ukraine* . 41 H7
Olema, *U.S.A.* 112 G4
Olen, *Belgium* 17 F5
Olenek, *Russia* 45 C12
Olenek →, *Russia* 45 B13
Olenino, *Russia* 42 B1
Oléron, I. d', *France* ... 26 C2
Oleśnica, *Poland* 20 D7
Olesno, *Poland* 20 E8
Olevsk, *Ukraine* 41 G4
Olga, *Russia* 45 E14
Olga, L., *Canada* 98 C4
Olga, Mt., *Australia* 89 E5
Ølgod, *Denmark* 11 J2
Olhão, *Portugal* 31 H3
Olib, *Croatia* 33 D11
Oliena, *Italy* 34 B2
Oliete, *Spain* 28 D4
Olifants →, *Africa* 85 C5
Olifantshoek, *S. Africa* .. 84 D3
Ólimbos, *Greece* 39 P10
Ólimbos, Óros, *Greece* . 39 J5
Olímpia, *Brazil* 127 A6
Olinda, *Brazil* 122 C5
Olindiná, *Brazil* 122 D4
Olite, *Spain* 28 C3
Oliva, *Argentina* 126 C3
Oliva, *Spain* 29 G4
Oliva, Punta del, *Spain* . 30 B5
Oliva de la Frontera, *Spain* 31 G4
Olivares, *Spain* 28 F2
Olivehurst, *U.S.A.* 112 F5
Oliveira, *Brazil* 123 F3
Oliveira de Azemeis,
  Portugal 30 E2
Oliveira dos Brejinhos,
  Brazil 123 D3
Olivenza, *Spain* 31 G3
Oliver, *Canada* 100 D5
Oliver L., *Canada* 101 B8
Olivone, *Switz.* 23 C7
Olkhovka, *Russia* 42 F7
Olkusz, *Poland* 20 E9
Ollagüe, *Chile* 126 A2
Olloy, *Belgium* 17 H5
Olmedo, *Spain* 30 D6

Olmos, *Peru* 124 B2
Olney, *Ill., U.S.A.* 104 F1
Olney, *Tex., U.S.A.* 109 J5
Oloma, *Cameroon* 79 E7
Olomane →, *Canada* .. 99 B7
Olomouc, *Czech.* 20 F7
Olonets, *Russia* 40 B7
Olongapo, *Phil.* 55 D4
Olot, *Spain* 28 C7
Olovo, *Bos.-H.* 21 L8
Olovyannaya, *Russia* ... 45 D12
Oloy →, *Russia* 45 C16
Olpe, *Germany* 18 D3
Olshanka, *Ukraine* 41 H6
Olshany, *Ukraine* 41 G8
Olst, *Neths.* 16 D8
Olsztyn, *Poland* 20 B10
Olt →, *Romania* 38 F7
Olten, *Switz.* 22 B5
Olteniţa, *Romania* 38 E9
Olton, *U.S.A.* 109 H3
Oltu, *Turkey* 67 B9
Olur, *Turkey* 67 B10
Olutanga, *Phil.* 55 H5
Olvega, *Spain* 28 D3
Olvera, *Spain* 31 J5
Olymbos, *Cyprus* 37 D12
Olympia, *Greece* 39 M4
Olympia, *U.S.A.* 112 D4
Olympic Mts., *U.S.A.* ... 112 C3
Olympic Nat. Park, *U.S.A.* 112 C3
Olympus, *Cyprus* 66 E5
Olympus, Mt. = Ólimbos,
  Óros, *Greece* 39 J5
Olympus, Mt., *U.S.A.* ... 112 C3
Olyphant, *U.S.A.* 107 E9
Om →, *Russia* 44 D8
Om Hajer, *Eritrea* 77 E4
Om Koi, *Thailand* 58 D2
Ōma, *Japan* 48 D10
Ōmachi, *Japan* 49 F8
Omae-Zaki, *Japan* 49 G9
Ōmagari, *Japan* 48 E10
Omagh, *U.K.* 15 B4
Omagh □, *U.K.* 15 B4
Omaha, *U.S.A.* 108 E7
Omak, *U.S.A.* 110 B4
Omalos, *Greece* 37 D5
Oman ■, *Asia* 68 C6
Oman, G. of, *Asia* 65 E8
Omaruru, *Namibia* 84 C2
Omaruru →, *Namibia* .. 84 C1
Omate, *Peru* 124 D3
Ombai, Selat, *Indonesia* . 57 F6
Ombooué, *Gabon* 80 E1
Ombrone →, *Italy* 32 F8
Omdurmân, *Sudan* 77 D3
Omegna, *Italy* 32 C5
Omeonga, *Zaïre* 82 C1
Ometepe, I. de, *Nic.* ... 116 D2
Ometepec, *Mexico* 115 D5
Ominato, *Japan* 48 D10
Omineca →, *Canada* .. 100 B4
Omiš, *Croatia* 33 E13
Omišalj, *Croatia* 33 C11
Omitara, *Namibia* 84 C2
Ōmiya, *Japan* 49 G9
Omme →, *Denmark* ... 11 J2
Ommen, *Neths.* 16 C8
Ömnögovī □, *Mongolia* . 50 C3
Omo →, *Ethiopia* 77 F4
Omodhos, *Cyprus* 37 E11
Omolon →, *Russia* 45 C16
Omono-Gawa →, *Japan* 48 E10
Omsk, *Russia* 44 D8
Omsukchan, *Russia* 45 C16
Ōmu, *Japan* 48 B11
Omul, Vf., *Romania* 38 D8
Ōmura, *Japan* 49 H4
Omuramba Omatako →,
  Namibia 81 H4
Omurtag, *Bulgaria* 38 F9
Ōmuta, *Japan* 49 H5
On, *Belgium* 17 H6
Onaga, *U.S.A.* 108 F6
Onalaska, *U.S.A.* 108 D9
Onamia, *U.S.A.* 108 B8
Onancock, *U.S.A.* 104 G8
Onang, *Indonesia* 57 E5
Onaping L., *Canada* 98 C3
Oñate, *Spain* 28 B2
Onavas, *Mexico* 114 B3
Onawa, *U.S.A.* 108 D6
Oncócua, *Angola* 84 B1
Onda, *Spain* 28 F4
Ondaejin, *N. Korea* 51 D15
Ondangua, *Namibia* ... 84 B2
Ondárroa, *Spain* 28 B2
Ondas →, *Brazil* 123 D3
Ondava →, *Slovak Rep.* . 20 G11
Onderdijk, *Neths.* 16 C6
Ondjiva, *Angola* 84 B2
Ondo, *Nigeria* 79 D5
Ondo □, *Nigeria* 79 D5
Öndörhaan, *Mongolia* .. 54 B6
Öndörshil, *Mongolia* ... 50 B5
Öndverðarnes, *Iceland* . 8 D1
Onega, *Russia* 6 C13
Onega →, *Russia* 6 C13
Onega, G. of =
  Onezhskaya Guba,
  Russia 44 C4

Onega, L. = Onezhskoye
  Ozero, *Russia* 40 B8
Onehunga, *N.Z.* 87 G5
Oneida, *U.S.A.* 107 C9
Oneida L., *U.S.A.* 107 C9
O'Neill, *U.S.A.* 108 D5
Onema, *Zaïre* 82 C1
Oneonta, *Ala., U.S.A.* .. 105 J2
Oneonta, *N.Y., U.S.A.* .. 107 D9
Oneşti, *Romania* 38 C9
Onezhskaya Guba, *Russia* 44 C4
Onezhskoye Ozero, *Russia* 40 B8
Ongarue, *N.Z.* 87 H5
Ongerup, *Australia* 89 F2
Ongjin, *N. Korea* 51 F13
Ongkharak, *Thailand* ... 58 E3
Ongniud Qi, *China* 51 C10
Ongoka, *Zaïre* 82 C2
Ongole, *India* 60 M12
Ongon, *Mongolia* 50 B7
Onguren, *Russia* 45 D11
Onhaye, *Belgium* 17 H5
Oni, *Georgia* 43 J6
Onida, *U.S.A.* 108 C4
Onilahy →, *Madag.* ... 85 C7
Onitsha, *Nigeria* 79 D6
Onoda, *Japan* 49 G5
Onpyŏng-ni, *S. Korea* .. 51 H14
Ons, Is. d', *Spain* 30 C2
Onsala, *Sweden* 11 G6
Onslow, *Australia* 88 D2
Onslow B., *U.S.A.* 105 H7
Onstwedde, *Neths.* 16 B10
Ontake-San, *Japan* 49 G8
Ontaneda, *Spain* 30 B7
Ontario, *Calif., U.S.A.* .. 113 L9
Ontario, *Oreg., U.S.A.* .. 110 D5
Ontario □, *Canada* 98 B2
Ontario, L., *U.S.A.* 98 D4
Onteniente, *Spain* 29 G4
Ontonagon, *U.S.A.* 108 B10
Ontur, *Spain* 29 G3
Onyx, *U.S.A.* 113 K8
Oodnadatta, *Australia* .. 91 D2
Ooldea, *Australia* 89 F5
Ooltgensplaat, *Neths.* .. 17 E4
Oombulgurri, *Australia* .. 88 C4
Oona River, *Canada* ... 100 C2
Oordegem, *Belgium* ... 17 G3
Oorindi, *Australia* 90 C3
Oost-Vlaanderen □,
  Belgium 17 F3
Oost-Vlieland, *Neths.* .. 16 B6
Oostakker, *Belgium* 17 F3
Oostburg, *Neths.* 17 F3
Oostduinkerke, *Belgium* . 17 F1
Oostelijk-Flevoland, *Neths.* 16 C7
Oostende, *Belgium* 17 F1
Oosterbeek, *Neths.* 16 C6
Oosterdijk, *Neths.* 16 C6
Oosterend, *Friesland,
  Neths.* 16 B6
Oosterend, *Noord-Holland,
  Neths.* 16 B5
Oosterhout, *Neths.* 17 E5
Oosterschelde, *Neths.* .. 17 E4
Oosterwolde, *Neths.* ... 16 B8
Oosterzele, *Belgium* ... 17 G3
Oostkamp, *Belgium* ... 17 F2
Oostmalle, *Belgium* ... 17 F5
Oostrozebekke, *Belgium* 17 G2
Oostvleteren, *Belgium* .. 17 G1
Oostvoorne, *Neths.* 16 E4
Oostzaan, *Neths.* 16 D5
Ootacamund, *India* 60 P10
Ootmarsum, *Neths.* ... 16 D9
Ootsa L., *Canada* 100 C3
Opala, *Russia* 45 D16
Opala, *Zaïre* 82 C1
Opanake, *Sri Lanka* ... 60 R12
Opasatika, *Canada* 98 C3
Opasquia, *Canada* 101 C10
Opémisca, L., *Canada* .. 98 C5
Opheim, *U.S.A.* 110 B10
Ophthalmia Ra., *Australia* 88 D2
Opi, *Nigeria* 79 D6
Opinaca →, *Canada* ... 98 B4
Opinaca L., *Canada* 98 B4
Opiskotish, L., *Canada* . 99 B6
Ploo, *Neths.* 16 E7
Opmeer, *Neths.* 16 C6
Opobo, *Nigeria* 79 E6
Opochka, *Russia* 40 D5
Opoczno, *Poland* 20 D10
Opol, *Phil.* 55 G6
Opole, *Poland* 20 E7
Oporto = Porto, *Portugal* 30 D2
Opotiki, *N.Z.* 87 H6
Opp, *U.S.A.* 105 K2
Oppdal, *Norway* 9 E13
Oppenheim, *Germany* .. 19 F4
Opperdoes, *Neths.* 16 C6
Óppido Mamertina, *Italy* 35 D8
Oppland fylke □, *Norway* 10 C3
Oppstad, *Norway* 10 D5
Oprtalj, *Croatia* 33 C10
Opua, *N.Z.* 87 F5
Opunake, *N.Z.* 87 H4
Opuzen, *Croatia* 21 M7
Ora, *Cyprus* 37 E12
Ora, *Italy* 33 B8

Ora Banda, *Australia* ... 89 F3
Oracle, *U.S.A.* 111 K8
Oradea, *Romania* 38 B4
Öræfajökull, *Iceland* 8 D5
Orahovac, *Serbia, Yug.* .. 21 N10
Orai, *India* 63 G8
Oraison, *France* 27 E9
Oral = Zhayyq →,
  Kazakhstan 44 E6
Oral, *Kazakhstan* 42 E10
Oran, *Algeria* 75 A4
Oran, *Argentina* 126 A3
Orange = Oranje →,
  S. Africa 84 D2
Orange, *Australia* 91 E4
Orange, *France* 27 D8
Orange, *Calif., U.S.A.* .. 113 M9
Orange, *Mass., U.S.A.* .. 107 D12
Orange, *Tex., U.S.A.* ... 109 K8
Orange, *Va., U.S.A.* 104 F6
Orange, C., *Brazil* 121 C7
Orange Cove, *U.S.A.* ... 112 J7
Orange Free State □,
  S. Africa 84 D4
Orange Grove, *U.S.A.* .. 109 M6
Orange Walk, *Belize* ... 115 D7
Orangeburg, *U.S.A.* 105 J5
Orangeville, *Canada* ... 98 D3
Orani, *Phil.* 55 D4
Oranienburg, *Germany* . 18 C9
Oranje →, *S. Africa* 84 D2
Oranje Vrystaat = Orange
  Free State □, *S. Africa* . 84 D4
Oranjemund, *Namibia* .. 84 D2
Oranjerivier, *S. Africa* ... 84 D3
Oras, *Phil.* 55 E6
Orăştie, *Romania* 38 D6
Oraşul Stalin = Braşov,
  Romania 38 D8
Orava →, *Slovak Rep.* .. 20 F9
Oravita, *Romania* 38 D4
Orb →, *France* 26 E7
Orba →, *Italy* 32 D5
Ørbæk, *Denmark* 11 J4
Orbe, *Switz.* 22 C3
Orbec, *France* 24 C7
Orbetello, *Italy* 33 F8
Órbigo →, *Spain* 30 C5
Orbost, *Australia* 91 F4
Orce, *Spain* 29 H2
Orce →, *Spain* 29 H2
Orchies, *France* 25 B10
Orchila, I., *Venezuela* ... 120 A4
Orco →, *Italy* 32 C4
Orcopampa, *Peru* 124 D3
Orcutt, *U.S.A.* 113 L6
Ord →, *Australia* 88 C4
Ord, Mt., *Australia* 88 C4
Ordenes, *Spain* 30 B2
Orderville, *U.S.A.* 111 H7
Ording = St-Peter-Ording,
  Germany 18 A4
Ordos = Mu Us Shamo,
  China 50 E5
Ordu, *Turkey* 66 B7
Ordubad, *Azerbaijan* ... 67 C12
Orduña, *Álava, Spain* ... 28 C7
Orduña, *Granada, Spain* . 29 H1
Ordway, *U.S.A.* 108 F3
Ordzhonikidze =
  Vladikavkaz, *Russia* ... 43 J7
Ordzhonikidze, *Ukraine* . 41 J8
Ore, *Zaïre* 82 B2
Ore Mts. = Erzgebirge,
  Germany 18 E9
Orealla, *Guyana* 121 B6
Orebić, *Croatia* 21 M7
Örebro, *Sweden* 9 G16
Oregon, *U.S.A.* 108 D10
Oregon □, *U.S.A.* 110 E3
Oregon City, *U.S.A.* ... 112 E4
Orekhov = Orikhiv,
  Ukraine 41 J8
Orekhovo-Zuyevo, *Russia* 42 C4
Orel, *Russia* 42 D3
Orel →, *Ukraine* 41 H8
Orellana, Canal de, *Spain* 31 F5
Orellana, Pantano de,
  Spain 31 F5
Orellana la Vieja, *Spain* . 31 F5
Orem, *U.S.A.* 110 F8
Ören, *Turkey* 66 D2
Orenburg, *Russia* 44 D6
Orense, *Spain* 30 C3
Orense □, *Spain* 30 C3
Orepuki, *N.Z.* 87 M1
Orestiás, *Greece* 39 H9
Øresund, *Europe* 11 J6
Orford Ness, *U.K.* 13 E9
Organ̄á, *Spain* 28 C6
Organos, Pta. de los,
  Canary Is. 36 F2
Orgaz, *Spain* 31 F7
Orgeyev = Orhei, *Moldova* 41 J5
Orhaneli, *Turkey* 66 C3
Orhangazi, *Turkey* 66 B3
Orhei, *Moldova* 41 J5
Orhon Gol →, *Mongolia* . 54 A5
Ória, *Italy* 35 B10
Orient, *Australia* 91 D3
Oriental, Cordillera,
  Bolivia 125 D4
Oriental, Cordillera,
  Colombia 120 B3
Oriente, *Argentina* 126 D3
Origny-Ste.-Benoîte, *France* 25 C10

Orihuela, *Spain* 29 G4
Orihuela del Tremedal, *Spain* 28 E3
Orikhiv, *Ukraine* 41 J8
Oriku, *Albania* 39 J2
Orinduik, *Guyana* 121 C5
Orinoco →, *Venezuela* ... 121 B5
Orissa □, *India* 61 K14
Orissaare, *Estonia* 9 G20
Oristano, *Italy* 34 C1
Oristano, G. di, *Italy* 34 C1
Orituco →, *Venezuela* 120 B4
Orizaba, *Mexico* 115 D5
Orizona, *Brazil* 123 E2
Orjen, *Bos.-H.* 21 N8
Orjiva, *Spain* 29 J1
Orkanger, *Norway* 10 A3
Örkelljunga, *Sweden* 11 H7
Örkény, *Hungary* 21 H9
Orkla →, *Norway* 10 A3
Orkney, *S. Africa* 84 D4
Orkney □, *U.K.* 14 C6
Orkney Is., *U.K.* 14 C6
Orland, *U.S.A.* 112 F4
Orlando, *U.S.A.* 105 L5
Orlando, C. d', *Italy* 35 D7
Orléanais, *France* 25 E8
Orléans, *France* 25 E8
Orleans, *U.S.A.* 107 B12
Orléans, I. d', *Canada* ... 99 C5
Orlice →, *Czech.* 20 E6
Orlov, *Slovak Rep.* 20 F10
Orlov Gay, *Russia* 42 E9
Ormara, *Pakistan* 60 G4
Ormea, *Italy* 32 D4
Ormília, *Greece* 39 J6
Ormoc, *Phil.* 55 F6
Ormond, *N.Z.* 87 H6
Ormond Beach, *U.S.A.* ... 105 L5
Ormož, *Slovenia* 33 B13
Ormstown, *Canada* 107 A11
Ormans, *France* 25 E13
Orne □, *France* 24 D7
Orne →, *France* 24 C6
Ørnhøj, *Denmark* 11 H2
Ornö, *Sweden* 10 E12
Örnsköldsvik, *Sweden* 10 A12
Oro, *N. Korea* 51 D14
Oro →, *Mexico* 114 B3
Oro Grande, *U.S.A.* 113 L9
Orobie, Alpi, *Italy* 32 B6
Orocué, *Colombia* 120 C3
Orodo, *Nigeria* 79 D6
Orogrande, *U.S.A.* 111 K10
Orol, *Spain* 30 B3
Orol Dengizi = Aral Sea, *Asia* 44 E7
Oromocto, *Canada* 99 C6
Oron, *Nigeria* 79 E6
Oron, *Switz.* 22 C3
Orono, *Canada* 106 C6
Oropesa, *Spain* 30 F5
Oroquieta, *Phil.* 55 G5
Orós, *Brazil* 122 C4
Orosei, *Italy* 34 B2
Orosei, G. di, *Italy* 34 B2
Orosháza, *Hungary* 21 J10
Orotukan, *Russia* 45 C16
Oroville, Calif., *U.S.A.* .. 112 F5
Oroville, Wash., *U.S.A.* .. 110 B4
Oroville, L., *U.S.A.* 112 F5
Orroroo, *Australia* 91 E2
Orrville, *U.S.A.* 106 F3
Orsara di Púglia, *Italy* ... 35 A8
Orsha, *Belarus* 40 E6
Orsières, *Switz.* 22 D4
Orsk, *Russia* 44 D6
Ørslev, *Denmark* 11 J5
Orsogna, *Italy* 33 F11
Orşova, *Romania* 38 E6
Ørsted, *Denmark* 11 H4
Orta, L. d', *Italy* 32 C5
Orta Nova, *Italy* 35 A8
Ortaca, *Turkey* 66 D3
Ortaköy, Çorum, *Turkey* . 66 B6
Ortaköy, Niğde, *Turkey* .. 66 C6
Orte, *Italy* 33 F9
Ortegal, C., *Spain* 30 B3
Orteguaza →, *Colombia* . 120 C2
Orthez, *France* 26 E3
Ortho, *Belgium* 17 H7
Ortigueira, *Spain* 30 B3
Orting, *U.S.A.* 112 C4
Ortles, *Italy* 32 B7
Ortón →, *Bolivia* 124 C4
Ortona, *Italy* 33 F11
Orūmīyeh, *Iran* 67 D11
Orūmīyeh, Daryācheh-ye, *Iran* 67 D11
Orune, *Italy* 34 B2
Oruro, *Bolivia* 124 D4
Oruro □, *Bolivia* 124 D4
Orust, *Sweden* 11 F5
Oruzgān □, *Afghan.* 60 C5
Orvault, *France* 24 E5
Orvieto, *Italy* 33 F9
Orwell, *U.S.A.* 106 E4
Orwell →, *U.K.* 13 E9
Oryakhovo, *Bulgaria* 38 F6
Orzinuovi, *Italy* 32 C6
Orzysz, *Poland* 20 B11
Osa, Pen. de, *Costa Rica* . 116 E3
Osage, Iowa, *U.S.A.* 108 D8
Osage, Wyo., *U.S.A.* 108 D2
Osage →, *U.S.A.* 108 F9
Osage City, *U.S.A.* 108 F7
Ōsaka, *Japan* 49 G7

Osawatomie, *U.S.A.* 108 F7
Osborne, *U.S.A.* 108 F5
Osceola, Ark., *U.S.A.* ... 109 H10
Osceola, Iowa, *U.S.A.* .. 108 E8
Oschatz, *Germany* 18 D9
Oschersleben, *Germany* . 18 C7
Óschiri, *Italy* 34 B2
Oscoda, *U.S.A.* 106 B1
Ösel = Saaremaa, *Estonia* 9 G20
Osery, *Russia* 42 C4
Osh, *Kyrgyzstan* 44 E8
Oshawa, *Canada* 98 D4
Oshkosh, Nebr., *U.S.A.* . 108 E3
Oshkosh, Wis., *U.S.A.* .. 108 C10
Oshmyany = Ashmyany, *Belarus* 9 J21
Oshnovīyeh, *Iran* 64 B5
Oshogbo, *Nigeria* 79 D5
Oshtorīnān, *Iran* 67 E13
Oshwe, *Zaïre* 80 E3
Osijek, *Croatia* 21 K8
Ósilo, *Italy* 34 B1
Ósimo, *Italy* 33 E10
Osintorf, *Belarus* 40 E6
Osipenko = Berdyansk, *Ukraine* 41 J9
Osipovichi = Asipovichy, *Belarus* 40 F5
Osizweni, *S. Africa* 85 D5
Oskaloosa, *U.S.A.* 108 E8
Oskarshamn, *Sweden* ... 9 H17
Oskélanéo, *Canada* 98 C4
Öskemen, *Kazakhstan* .. 44 E9
Oskol →, *Ukraine* 41 H9
Oslo, *Norway* 10 E4
Oslob, *Phil.* 55 G5
Oslofjorden, *Norway* 10 E4
Osmanabad, *India* 60 K10
Osmancık, *Turkey* 66 B6
Osmaniye, *Turkey* 66 D7
Ösmo, *Sweden* 10 F11
Osnabrück, *Germany* ... 18 C4
Osor, *Italy* 33 D11
Osorio, *Brazil* 127 B5
Osorno, *Chile* 128 B2
Osorno, *Spain* 30 C6
Osorno □, *Chile* 128 B2
Osorno, Vol., *Chile* 128 B2
Osøyri, *Norway* 9 F11
Ospika →, *Canada* 100 B4
Osprey Reef, *Australia* .. 90 A4
Oss, *Neths.* 16 E7
Ossa, Mt., *Australia* 90 G4
Óssa, Oros, *Greece* 39 K5
Ossa de Montiel, *Spain* . 29 G2
Osse →, *France* 26 D4
Ossabaw I., *U.S.A.* 105 K5
Ossendrecht, *Neths.* 17 F4
Ossining, *U.S.A.* 107 E11
Ossipee, *U.S.A.* 107 C13
Ossokmanuan L., *Canada* 99 B7
Ossora, *Russia* 45 D17
Ostashkov, *Russia* 42 B1
Oste →, *Germany* 18 B5
Ostend = Oostende, *Belgium* 17 F1
Oster, *Ukraine* 41 G6
Osterburg, *Germany* 18 C7
Osterburken, *Germany* .. 19 F5
Österdalälven, *Sweden* .. 9 F16
Österdalen, *Norway* 9 F14
Östergötlands län □, *Sweden* 11 F9
Osterholz-Scharmbeck, *Germany* 18 B4
Østerild, *Denmark* 11 G2
Ostermundigen, *Switz.* .. 22 C4
Östersund, *Sweden* 10 A8
Østfold fylke □, *Norway* . 10 E5
Ostfriesische Inseln, *Germany* 18 B3
Ostfriesland, *Germany* .. 18 B3
Óstia, Lido di, *Italy* 34 A5
Ostíglia, *Italy* 33 C8
Ostra, *Italy* 33 E10
Ostrava, *Czech.* 20 F8
Ostróda, *Poland* 20 B9
Ostrogozhsk, *Russia* 42 E4
Ostrogróg Szamotuły, *Poland* 20 C5
Ostroh, *Ukraine* 41 G4
Ostrołęka, *Poland* 20 B11
Ostrov, *Bulgaria* 38 F7
Ostrov, *Romania* 38 E10
Ostrov, *Russia* 40 D5
Ostrów Mazowiecka, *Poland* 20 C11
Ostrów Wielkopolski, *Poland* 20 D7
Ostrowiec-Świętokrzyski, *Poland* 20 E11
Ostrzeszów, *Poland* 20 D7
Ostseebad Kühlungsborn, *Germany* 18 A7
Osttirol □, *Austria* 19 J8
Ostuni, *Italy* 35 B10
Osum →, *Bulgaria* 38 F7
Osumi →, *Albania* 39 J3
Ōsumi-Kaikyō, *Japan* ... 49 J5
Ōsumi-Shotō, *Japan* 49 J5
Osun □, *Nigeria* 79 D5
Osuna, *Spain* 31 H5
Oswego, *U.S.A.* 107 C8
Oswestry, *U.K.* 12 E4
Oświęcim, *Poland* 20 E9
Otago □, *N.Z.* 87 L2

Otago Harbour, *N.Z.* 87 L3
Ōtake, *Japan* 49 G6
Otaki, *N.Z.* 87 J5
Otaru, *Japan* 48 C10
Otaru-Wan = Ishikari-Wan, *Japan* 48 C10
Otava →, *Czech.* 20 F4
Otavalo, *Ecuador* 120 C2
Otavi, *Namibia* 84 B2
Otchinjau, *Angola* 84 B1
Otelec, *Romania* 38 D3
Otero de Rey, *Spain* 30 B3
Othello, *U.S.A.* 110 C4
Othonoí, *Greece* 39 K1
Óthris, Óros, *Greece* 39 K5
Otira Gorge, *N.Z.* 87 K3
Otis, *U.S.A.* 108 E3
Otjiwarongo, *Namibia* .. 84 C2
Otočac, *Croatia* 33 D12
Otoineppu, *Japan* 48 B11
Otorohanga, *N.Z.* 87 H5
Otoskwin →, *Canada* ... 98 B2
Otosquen, *Canada* 101 C8
Otra →, *Norway* 9 G13
Otradnyy, *Russia* 42 D10
Otranto, *Italy* 35 B11
Otranto, C. d', *Italy* 35 B11
Otranto, Str. of, *Italy* ... 35 B11
Otse, *S. Africa* 84 D4
Ōtsu, *Japan* 49 G7
Ōtsuki, *Japan* 49 G9
Otta, *Norway* 10 C3
Ottawa = Outaouais →, *Canada* 98 C5
Ottawa, *Canada* 98 C4
Ottawa, Ill., *U.S.A.* 108 E10
Ottawa, Kans., *U.S.A.* .. 108 F7
Ottawa Is., *Canada* 97 C11
Ottélé, *Cameroon* 79 E7
Otter L., *Canada* 101 B8
Otter Rapids, Ont., *Canada* 98 B3
Otter Rapids, Sask., *Canada* 101 B8
Otterndorf, *Germany* ... 18 B4
Otterup, *Denmark* 11 J4
Otterville, *Canada* 106 D4
Ottignies, *Belgium* 17 G5
Otto Beit Bridge, *Zimbabwe* 83 F2
Ottosdal, *S. Africa* 84 D4
Ottsjön, *Sweden* 10 A7
Ottumwa, *U.S.A.* 108 E8
Otu, *Nigeria* 79 D5
Otukpa, *Nigeria* 79 D6
Oturkpo, *Nigeria* 79 D6
Otway, B., *Chile* 128 D2
Otway, C., *Australia* 91 F3
Otwock, *Poland* 20 C11
Ötz, *Austria* 19 H6
Ötz →, *Austria* 19 H6
Ötztaler Alpen, *Austria* . 19 J7
Ou →, *Laos* 58 B4
Ou Neua, *Laos* 58 A3
Ou-Sammyaku, *Japan* .. 48 E10
Ouachita →, *U.S.A.* 109 K9
Ouachita, L., *U.S.A.* 109 H8
Ouachita Mts., *U.S.A.* .. 109 H7
Ouâdane, *Mauritania* ... 74 D2
Ouadda, *C.A.R.* 73 G9
Ouagadougou, *Burkina Faso* 79 C4
Ouahigouya, *Burkina Faso* 78 C4
Ouahila, *Algeria* 74 C3
Ouahran = Oran, *Algeria* 75 A4
Ouaïnâta, *Mauritania* .. 78 B3
Ouallene, *Algeria* 75 D5
Ouanda Djallé, *C.A.R.* .. 73 G9
Ouango, *C.A.R.* 80 D4
Ouarâne, *Mauritania* ... 74 D2
Ouargla, *Algeria* 75 B6
Ouarkziz, Djebel, *Algeria* 74 C3
Ouarzazate, *Morocco* ... 74 B3
Ouatagouna, *Mali* 79 B5
Oubangi →, *Zaïre* 80 E3
Oubarakai, O. →, *Algeria* 75 C6
Ouche →, *France* 25 E12
Oud-Beijerland, *Neths.* . 16 E4
Oud-Gastel, *Neths.* 17 E4
Oud Turnhout, *Belgium* . 17 F6
Ouddorp, *Neths.* 16 E3
Oude-Pekela, *Neths.* 16 B10
Oude Rijn →, *Neths.* ... 16 D4
Oudega, *Neths.* 16 B8
Oudenaarde, *Belgium* ... 17 G3
Oudenbosch, *Neths.* 17 E5
Oudenburg, *Belgium* 17 F2
Ouderkerk, Utrecht, *Neths.* 16 D5
Ouderkerk, Zuid-Holland, *Neths.* 16 E5
Oudeschild, *Neths.* 16 B5
Oudewater, *Neths.* 16 D5
Oudkarspel, *Neths.* 16 C5
Oudon, *France* 24 E5
Oudon →, *France* 24 E6
Oudtshoorn, *S. Africa* ... 84 E3
Oued Zem, *Morocco* 74 B3
Ouellé, *Ivory C.* 78 D4
Ouenza, *Algeria* 75 A6
Ouessa, *Burkina Faso* ... 78 C4
Ouessant, I. d', *France* .. 24 D1
Ouesso, *Congo* 80 D3
Ouest, Pte., *Canada* 99 C7
Ouezzane, *Morocco* 74 B3
Ouffet, *Belgium* 17 H6
Ouidah, *Benin* 79 D5
Ouistreham, *France* 24 C6
Oujda, *Morocco* 75 B4

Oujeft, *Mauritania* 74 D2
Oulainen, *Finland* 8 D21
Ould Yenjé, *Mauritania* . 78 B2
Ouled Djellal, *Algeria* ... 75 B6
Ouled Naïl, Mts. des, *Algeria* 75 B5
Oulmès, *Morocco* 74 B3
Oulu, *Finland* 8 D21
Oulujärvi, *Finland* 8 D22
Oulujoki →, *Finland* 8 D21
Oulx, *Italy* 32 C5
Oum Chalouba, *Chad* ... 73 E9
Oum-el-Bouaghi, *Algeria* 75 A6
Oum el Ksi, *Algeria* 74 C3
Oum-er-Rbia, O. →, *Morocco* 74 B3
Oumè, *Ivory C.* 78 D3
Ounane, Dj., *Algeria* 75 C6
Ounasjoki →, *Finland* ... 8 C21
Ounguati, *Namibia* 84 C2
Ounianga-Kébir, *Chad* .. 73 E9
Ounianga Sérir, *Chad* ... 73 E9
Our →, *Lux.* 17 J8
Ouray, *U.S.A.* 111 G10
Ourcq →, *France* 25 C10
Ourém, *Brazil* 122 B2
Ourense = Orense, *Spain* 30 C3
Ouricuri, *Brazil* 122 C3
Ourinhos, *Brazil* 127 A6
Ourique, *Portugal* 31 H2
Ouro Fino, *Brazil* 127 A6
Ouro Prêto, *Brazil* 123 F3
Ouro Sogui, *Senegal* 78 B2
Oursi, *Burkina Faso* 79 C4
Ourthe →, *Belgium* 17 H7
Ouse, *Australia* 90 G4
Ouse →, E. Susx., *U.K.* . 13 G8
Ouse →, N. Yorks., *U.K.* . 12 C8
Oust, *France* 26 F5
Oust →, *France* 24 E4
Outaouais →, *Canada* .. 98 C5
Outardes →, *Canada* ... 99 C6
Outat Oulad el Haj, *Morocco* 75 B4
Outer Hebrides, *U.K.* ... 14 D1
Outer I., *Canada* 99 B8
Outes, *Spain* 30 C2
Outjo, *Namibia* 84 C2
Outlook, *Canada* 101 C7
Outlook, *U.S.A.* 108 A2
Outokumpu, *Finland* ... 8 E23
Outreau, *France* 25 B8
Outremont →, *France* ... 25 E8
Ouvèze →, *France* 27 E8
Ouyen, *Australia* 91 F3
Ouzouer-le-Marché, *France* 25 E8
Ovada, *Italy* 32 D5
Ovalau, *Fiji* 87 C8
Ovalle, *Chile* 126 C1
Ovamboland, *Namibia* .. 84 B2
Ovar, *Portugal* 30 E2
Ovejas, *Colombia* 120 B2
Overdinkel, *Neths.* 16 D10
Overflakkee, *Neths.* 16 E4
Overijse, *Belgium* 17 G5
Overijssel □, *Neths.* 16 D9
Overijsselsch Kanaal →, *Neths.* 16 C8
Overpelt, *Belgium* 17 F6
Overton, *U.S.A.* 113 J12
Övertorneå, *Sweden* 8 C20
Ovid, *U.S.A.* 108 E3
Ovidiopol, *Ukraine* 41 J6
Oviedo, *Spain* 30 B5
Oviedo □, *Spain* 30 B5
Oviken, *Sweden* 10 A8
Oviksfjällen, *Sweden* ... 10 B7
Oviši, *Latvia* 9 H19
Övör Hangay □, *Mongolia* 50 B5
Øvre Årdal, *Norway* 9 F12
Ovruch, *Ukraine* 41 G5
Owaka, *N.Z.* 87 M2
Owambo = Ovamboland, *Namibia* 84 B2
Owase, *Japan* 49 G8
Owatonna, *U.S.A.* 108 C8
Owbeh, *Afghan.* 60 B3
Owego, *U.S.A.* 107 D8
Owen Falls Dam, *Uganda* 82 B3
Owen Sound, *Canada* ... 98 D3
Owendo, *Gabon* 80 D1
Owens →, *U.S.A.* 112 J9
Owens L., *U.S.A.* 113 J9
Owensboro, *U.S.A.* 104 G2
Owensville, *U.S.A.* 108 F9
Owerri, *Nigeria* 79 D6
Owl →, *Canada* 101 B10
Owo, *Nigeria* 79 D6
Owosso, *U.S.A.* 104 D3
Owyhee, *U.S.A.* 110 F5
Owyhee →, *U.S.A.* 110 E5
Owyhee, L., *U.S.A.* 110 E5
Oxapampa, *Peru* 124 C2
Oxelösund, *Sweden* 11 F11
Oxford, *N.Z.* 87 K4
Oxford, *U.K.* 13 F6
Oxford, Miss., *U.S.A.* .. 109 H10
Oxford, N.C., *U.S.A.* ... 105 G6
Oxford, Ohio, *U.S.A.* ... 104 F3
Oxford L., *Canada* 101 C9
Oxfordshire □, *U.K.* 13 F6
Oxley, *Australia* 91 E3
Oxnard, *U.S.A.* 113 L7
Oxus = Amudarya →, *Uzbekistan* 44 E6
Oya, *Malaysia* 56 D4
Oyama, *Japan* 49 F9

Oyapock →, *Fr. Guiana* . 121 C7
Oyem, *Gabon* 80 D2
Oyen, *Canada* 101 C6
Øyeren, *Norway* 10 E5
Oykel →, *U.K.* 14 D4
Oymyakon, *Russia* 45 C15
Oyo, *Nigeria* 79 D5
Oyo □, *Nigeria* 79 D5
Oyón, *Peru* 124 C2
Oyonnax, *France* 27 B9
Oyster Bay, *U.S.A.* 107 F11
Ōyūbari, *Japan* 48 C11
Özalp, *Turkey* 67 C10
Ozamiz, *Phil.* 55 G5
Ozark, Ala., *U.S.A.* 105 K3
Ozark, Ark., *U.S.A.* 109 H8
Ozark, Mo., *U.S.A.* 109 G8
Ozark Plateau, *U.S.A.* .. 109 G9
Ozarks, L. of the, *U.S.A.* 108 G10
Ózd, *Hungary* 21 G10
Ozernoye, *Russia* 42 E10
Ozery, *Russia* 42 E9
Ozette L., *U.S.A.* 112 B2
Ozieri, *Italy* 34 B2
Ozinki, *Russia* 42 E9
Ozona, *U.S.A.* 109 K4
Ozorków, *Poland* 20 D9
Ozuluama, *Mexico* 115 C5
Ozurgeti, *Georgia* 43 K5

P

P.W.V. □, *S. Africa* 85 D4
Pa, *Burkina Faso* 78 C4
Pa-an, *Burma* 61 L20
Pa Mong Dam, *Thailand* . 58 D4
Paal, *Belgium* 17 F6
Paamiut = Frederikshåb, *Greenland* 4 C5
Paar →, *Germany* 19 G6
Paarl, *S. Africa* 84 E2
Paauilo, *U.S.A.* 102 H17
Pab Hills, *Pakistan* 62 F2
Pabianice, *Poland* 20 D9
Pabna, *Bangla.* 61 G16
Pabo, *Uganda* 82 B3
Pacaás Novos, Serra dos, *Brazil* 125 C5
Pacaipampa, *Peru* 124 B2
Pacaja →, *Brazil* 122 B1
Pacajus, *Brazil* 122 B4
Pacaraima, Sierra, *Venezuela* 121 C5
Pacarán, *Peru* 124 C2
Pacaraos, *Peru* 124 C2
Pacasmayo, *Peru* 124 B2
Paceco, *Italy* 34 E5
Pachacamac, *Peru* 124 C2
Pachhar, *India* 62 G7
Pachino, *Italy* 35 F8
Pachitea →, *Peru* 124 B3
Pachiza, *Peru* 124 B2
Pacho, *Colombia* 120 B3
Pachpadra, *India* 60 G8
Pachuca, *Mexico* 115 C5
Pacific, *Canada* 100 C3
Pacific-Antarctic Ridge, *Pac. Oc.* 93 M16
Pacific Grove, *U.S.A.* ... 111 H3
Pacific Ocean, *Pac. Oc.* . 93 G14
Pacifica, *U.S.A.* 112 H4
Pacitan, *Indonesia* 57 H14
Packwood, *U.S.A.* 112 D5
Pacuí →, *Brazil* 123 E2
Pacy-sur-Eure, *France* .. 24 C8
Padaido, Kepulauan, *Indonesia* 57 E9
Padang, *Indonesia* 56 E2
Padangpanjang, *Indonesia* 56 E2
Padangsidempuan, *Indonesia* 56 D1
Padauari →, *Brazil* 121 D5
Padborg, *Denmark* 11 K3
Padcaya, *Bolivia* 125 E5
Paddockwood, *Canada* . 101 C7
Paderborn, *Germany* ... 18 D4
Padilla, *Bolivia* 125 D5
Padloping Island, *Canada* 97 B13
Pádova, *Italy* 33 C8
Padra, *India* 62 H5
Padrauna, *India* 63 F10
Padre I., *U.S.A.* 109 M6
Padro, Mte., *France* 27 F12
Padrón, *Spain* 30 C2
Padstow, *U.K.* 13 G3
Padua = Pádova, *Italy* .. 33 C8
Paducah, Ky., *U.S.A.* ... 104 G1
Paducah, Tex., *U.S.A.* .. 109 H4
Padul, *Spain* 31 H7
Padula, *Italy* 35 B8
Paengnyong-do, *S. Korea* 51 F13
Paeroa, *N.Z.* 87 G5
Paesana, *Italy* 32 D4
Pafúri, *Mozam.* 85 C5
Pag, *Croatia* 33 D11
Pagadian, *Phil.* 55 H5
Pagai Selatan, P., *Indonesia* 56 E2
Pagai Utara, *Indonesia* .. 56 E2
Pagalu = Annobón, *Atl. Oc.* 71 G4
Pagastikós Kólpos, *Greece* 39 K6
Pagatan, *Indonesia* 56 E5
Page, Ariz., *U.S.A.* 111 H8
Page, N. Dak., *U.S.A.* .. 108 B6

Paglieta, *Italy* 33 F11
Pagny-sur-Moselle, *France* . . 25 D13
Pago Pago, *Amer. Samoa* . . 87 B13
Pagosa Springs, *U.S.A.* . . 111 H10
Pagwa River, *Canada* 98 B2
Pahala, *U.S.A.* 102 J17
Pahang →, *Malaysia* 59 L4
Pahiatua, *N.Z.* 87 J5
Pahokee, *U.S.A.* 105 M5
Pahrump, *U.S.A.* 113 J11
Pahute Mesa, *U.S.A.* . . . 112 H10
Pai, *Thailand* 58 C2
Paia, *U.S.A.* 102 H16
Paicines, *U.S.A.* 112 J5
Paide, *Estonia* 9 G21
Paignton, *U.K.* 13 G4
Paiján, *Peru* 124 B2
Päijänne, *Finland* 9 F21
Paimbœuf, *France* 24 E4
Paimpol, *France* 24 D3
Painan, *Indonesia* 56 E2
Painesville, *U.S.A.* 106 E3
Paint Hills = Wemindji,
  Canada 98 B4
Paint L., *Canada* 101 B9
Paint Rock, *U.S.A.* 109 K5
Painted Desert, *U.S.A.* . . 111 J8
Paintsville, *U.S.A.* 104 G4
País Vasco □, *Spain* 28 C2
Paisley, *Canada* 106 B3
Paisley, *U.K.* 14 F4
Paisley, *U.S.A.* 110 E3
Paita, *Peru* 124 B1
Paiva →, *Portugal* 30 D2
Paizhou, *China* 53 B9
Pajares, *Spain* 30 B5
Pajares, Puerto de, *Spain* . 30 C5
Pak Lay, *Laos* 58 C3
Pak Phanang, *Thailand* . . 59 H3
Pak Sane, *Laos* 58 C4
Pak Song, *Laos* 58 E6
Pak Suong, *Laos* 58 C4
Pakaraima Mts., *Guyana* . 121 B5
Pákhnes, *Greece* 37 D6
Pakistan ■, *Asia* 62 E3
Pakistan, East =
  Bangladesh ■, *Asia* . . . 61 H17
Pakkading, *Laos* 58 C4
Pakokku, *Burma* 61 J19
Pakpattan, *Pakistan* 62 D5
Pakrac, *Croatia* 21 K7
Paks, *Hungary* 21 J8
Pakse, *Laos* 58 E5
Paktiā □, *Afghan.* 60 C6
Pakwach, *Uganda* 82 B3
Pala, *Chad* 73 G8
Pala, *U.S.A.* 113 M9
Pala, *Zaïre* 82 D2
Palabek, *Uganda* 82 B3
Palacios, *U.S.A.* 109 L6
Palafrugell, *Spain* 28 D8
Palagiano, *Italy* 35 B10
Palagonía, *Italy* 35 E7
Palagruža, *Croatia* 33 F13
Palaiokastron, *Greece* . . . 37 D8
Palaiokhóra, *Greece* 37 D5
Palam, *India* 60 K10
Palamás, *Greece* 39 K5
Palamós, *Spain* 28 D8
Palampur, *India* 62 C7
Palana, *Australia* 90 F4
Palana, *Russia* 45 D16
Palanan, *Phil.* 55 C5
Palanan Pt., *Phil.* 55 C5
Palandri, *Pakistan* 63 C5
Palanga, *Lithuania* 9 J19
Palangkaraya, *Indonesia* . 56 E4
Palani Hills, *India* 60 P10
Palanpur, *India* 62 G5
Palanro, *Indonesia* 57 E5
Palapye, *Botswana* 84 C4
Palas, *Pakistan* 63 B5
Palatka, *Russia* 45 C16
Palatka, *U.S.A.* 105 L5
Palau = Belau ■, *Pac. Oc.* 92 G5
Palawan, *Phil.* 55 G3
Palayankottai, *India* 60 Q10
Palazzo San Gervásio, *Italy* 35 B8
Palazzolo Acréide, *Italy* . . 35 E7
Palca, *Chile* 124 D4
Paldiski, *Estonia* 9 G21
Paleleh, *Indonesia* 57 D6
Palembang, *Indonesia* . . . 56 E2
Palena →, *Chile* 128 B2
Palena, L., *Chile* 128 B2
Palencia, *Spain* 30 C6
Palencia □, *Spain* 30 C6
Paleokastrítsa, *Greece* . . . 37 A3
Paleometokho, *Cyprus* . . . 37 D12
Palermo, *Colombia* 120 C2
Palermo, *Italy* 34 D6
Palermo, *U.S.A.* 110 G3
Palestine, *Asia* 69 D4
Palestine, *U.S.A.* 109 K7
Palestrina, *Italy* 34 A5
Paletwa, *Burma* 61 J18
Palghat, *India* 60 P10
Palgrave, Mt., *Australia* . . 88 D2
Pali, *India* 62 G5
Palinuro, C., *Italy* 35 B8
Palisade, *U.S.A.* 108 E4
Paliseul, *Belgium* 17 J6
Palitana, *India* 62 J4
Palizada, *Mexico* 115 D6
Palizzi Marina, *Italy* 35 E8
Palk Bay, *Asia* 60 Q11

Palk Strait, *Asia* 60 Q11
Palkānah, *Iraq* 64 C5
Palla Road = Dinokwe,
  Botswana 84 C4
Pallanza = Verbánia, *Italy* . 32 C5
Pallasovka, *Russia* 42 E8
Pallisa, *Uganda* 82 B3
Pallu, *India* 62 E6
Palm Beach, *U.S.A.* 105 M6
Palm Desert, *U.S.A.* . . . 113 M10
Palm Is., *Australia* 90 B4
Palm Springs, *U.S.A.* . . . 113 M10
Palma, *Mozam.* 83 E5
Palma →, *Brazil* 123 D2
Palma, B. de, *Spain* 36 B9
Palma de Mallorca, *Spain* . 36 B9
Palma del Río, *Spain* 31 H5
Palma di Montechiaro, *Italy* 34 E6
Palma Soriano, *Cuba* . . . 116 B4
Palmanova, *Italy* 33 C10
Palmares, *Brazil* 122 C4
Palmarito, *Venezuela* . . . 120 B3
Palmarola, *Italy* 34 B5
Palmas, *Brazil* 127 B5
Palmas, C., *Liberia* 78 E3
Pálmas, G. di, *Italy* 34 C1
Palmas de Monte Alto,
  Brazil 123 D3
Palmdale, *U.S.A.* 113 L8
Palmeira, *Brazil* 123 G2
Palmeira dos Índios, *Brazil* 122 C4
Palmeirais, *Brazil* 122 C3
Palmeiras →, *Brazil* 123 D2
Palmeirinhas, Pta. das,
  Angola 80 F2
Palmela, *Portugal* 31 G2
Palmelo, *Brazil* 123 E2
Palmer, *U.S.A.* 96 B5
Palmer →, *Australia* 90 B3
Palmer Arch., *Antarctica* . 5 C17
Palmer Lake, *U.S.A.* 108 F2
Palmer Land, *Antarctica* . . 5 D18
Palmerston, *Canada* 106 C4
Palmerston, *N.Z.* 87 L3
Palmerston North, *N.Z.* . . 87 J5
Palmerton, *U.S.A.* 107 F9
Palmetto, *U.S.A.* 105 M4
Palmi, *Italy* 35 D8
Palmira, *Argentina* 126 C2
Palmira, *Colombia* 120 C2
Palmyra = Tudmur, *Syria* . 67 E8
Palmyra, *Mo., U.S.A.* . . . 108 F9
Palmyra, *N.Y., U.S.A.* . . . 106 C7
Palmyra Is., *Pac. Oc.* . . . 93 G11
Palo Alto, *U.S.A.* 111 H2
Palo del Colle, *Italy* 35 A9
Palo Verde, *U.S.A.* 113 M12
Palombara Sabina, *Italy* . . 33 F9
Palompon, *Phil.* 55 F6
Palopo, *Indonesia* 57 E6
Palos, C. de, *Spain* 29 H4
Palos Verdes, *U.S.A.* . . . 113 M8
Palos Verdes, Pt., *U.S.A.* . 113 M8
Palouse, *U.S.A.* 110 C5
Palpa, *Peru* 124 C2
Palparara, *Australia* 90 C3
Pålsboda, *Sweden* 10 E9
Palu, *Indonesia* 57 E5
Palu, *Turkey* 67 C9
Paluan, *Phil.* 57 B6
Palwal, *India* 62 E7
Pama, *Burkina Faso* 79 C5
Pamanukan, *Indonesia* . . 57 G12
Pamekasan, *Indonesia* . . 57 G15
Pamiers, *France* 26 E5
Pamirs, *Tajikistan* 44 F8
Pamlico →, *U.S.A.* 105 H7
Pamlico Sd., *U.S.A.* 105 H8
Pampa, *U.S.A.* 109 H4
Pampa de Agma, *Argentina* 128 B3
Pampa de las Salinas,
  Argentina 126 C2
Pampa Grande, *Bolivia* . . 125 D5
Pampa Hermosa, *Peru* . . 124 B2
Pampanua, *Indonesia* . . . 57 E6
Pamparato, *Italy* 32 D4
Pampas, *Argentina* 126 D3
Pampas, *Peru* 124 C3
Pampas →, *Peru* 124 C3
Pamphylia, *Turkey* 66 D4
Pamplona, *Colombia* 120 B3
Pamplona, *Spain* 28 C3
Pampoenpoort, *S. Africa* . 84 E3
Pan Xian, *China* 52 E5
Pana, *U.S.A.* 108 F10
Panabo, *Phil.* 55 H6
Panaca, *U.S.A.* 111 H6
Panagyurishte, *Bulgaria* . . 38 G7
Panaitan, *Indonesia* 57 G11
Panaji, *India* 60 M8
Panamá, *Panama* 116 E4
Panama ■, *Cent. Amer.* . . 116 E4
Panamá, G. de, *Panama* . 116 E4
Panama Canal, *Panama* . . 116 E4
Panama City, *U.S.A.* 105 K3
Panamint Range, *U.S.A.* . 113 J9
Panamint Springs, *U.S.A.* . 113 J9
Panão, *Peru* 124 B2
Panaon I., *Phil.* 55 F6
Panare, *Thailand* 59 J3
Panarea, *Italy* 35 D8
Panaro →, *Italy* 32 D8
Panay, *Phil.* 55 F5
Panay, G., *Phil.* 57 B6
Pancake Range, *U.S.A.* . . 111 G6
Pančevo, *Serbia, Yug.* . . . 21 L10

Pancorbo, Paso, *Spain* . . . 28 C1
Pandan, *Antique, Phil.* . . . 55 F5
Pandan, *Catanduanes, Phil.* 55 D6
Pandegelang, *Indonesia* . . 57 G12
Pandharpur, *India* 60 L9
Pandilla, *Spain* 28 D1
Pando, *Uruguay* 127 C4
Pando □, *Bolivia* 124 C4
Pando, L. = Hope, L.,
  Australia 91 D2
Pandokrátor, *Greece* 37 A3
Pandora, *Costa Rica* 116 E3
Panevėžys, *Lithuania* . . . 9 J21
Panfilov, *Kazakhstan* 44 E8
Panfilovo, *Russia* 42 E6
Pang-Long, *Burma* 61 H21
Pang-Yang, *Burma* 61 H21
Panga, *Zaïre* 82 B2
Pangalanes, Canal des,
  Madag. 85 C8
Pangani, *Tanzania* 82 D4
Pangani □, *Tanzania* 82 D4
Pangani →, *Tanzania* . . . 82 D4
Pangfou = Bengbu, *China* . 51 H9
Pangil, *Zaïre* 82 C2
Pangkah, Tanjung,
  Indonesia 57 G15
Pangkajene, *Indonesia* . . 57 E5
Pangkalanbrandan,
  Indonesia 56 D1
Pangkalanbuun, *Indonesia* 56 E4
Pangkalansusu, *Indonesia* 56 D1
Pangkalpinang, *Indonesia* . 56 E3
Pangkoh, *Indonesia* 56 E4
Pangnirtung, *Canada* . . . 97 B13
Pangrango, *Indonesia* . . . 57 G12
Panguipulli, *Chile* 128 A2
Panguitch, *U.S.A.* 111 H7
Pangutaran Group, *Phil.* . . 55 H4
Panhandle, *U.S.A.* 109 H4
Pani Mines, *India* 62 H5
Pania-Mutombo, *Zaïre* . . . 82 D1
Panipat, *India* 62 E7
Panjal Range, *India* 62 C7
Panjgur, *Pakistan* 60 F4
Panjim = Panaji, *India* . . . 60 M8
Panjinad Barrage, *Pakistan* 60 E7
Panjwai, *Afghan.* 62 D1
Pankshin, *Nigeria* 79 D6
Panmunjŏm, *N. Korea* . . . 51 F14
Panna, *India* 63 G9
Panna Hills, *India* 63 G9
Pano Lefkara, *Cyprus* . . . 37 E12
Pano Panayia, *Cyprus* . . . 37 E11
Panorama, *Brazil* 127 A5
Pánormon, *Greece* 37 D6
Panshan, *China* 51 D12
Panshi, *China* 51 C14
Pantar, *Indonesia* 57 F6
Pante Macassar, *Indonesia* 57 F6
Pantelleria, *Italy* 34 F5
Pantón, *Spain* 30 C3
Pánuco, *Mexico* 115 C5
Panyam, *Nigeria* 79 D6
Panyu, *China* 53 F9
Pao →, *Anzoátegui,*
  Venezuela 121 B5
Pao →, *Apure, Venezuela* 120 B4
Páola, *Italy* 35 C9
Paola, *Malta* 37 D2
Paola, *U.S.A.* 108 F7
Paonia, *U.S.A.* 111 G10
Paoting = Baoding, *China* . 50 E8
Paot'ou = Baotou, *China* . 50 D6
Paoua, *C.A.R.* 73 G8
Pápa, *Hungary* 21 H7
Papagayo →, *Mexico* . . . 115 D5
Papagayo, G. de,
  Costa Rica 116 D2
Papakura, *N.Z.* 87 G5
Papantla, *Mexico* 115 C5
Papar, *Malaysia* 56 C5
Pápas, Ákra, *Greece* 39 L4
Papenburg, *Germany* 18 B3
Paphlagonia, *Turkey* 66 B5
Paphos, *Cyprus* 66 E5
Papien Chiang = Da →,
  Vietnam 58 B5
Papigochic →, *Mexico* . . . 114 B3
Paposo, *Chile* 126 B1
Papoutsa, *Cyprus* 37 E12
Papua New Guinea ■,
  Oceania 92 H6
Papuča, *Croatia* 33 D12
Papudo, *Chile* 126 C1
Papuk, *Croatia* 21 K7
Papun, *Burma* 61 K20
Papunya, *Australia* 88 D5
Pará = Belém, *Brazil* 122 B2
Pará □, *Brazil* 125 A7
Pará □, *Surinam* 121 B6
Parábita, *Italy* 35 B11
Paraburdoo, *Australia* . . . 88 D2
Paracale, *Phil.* 55 D5
Paracas, Pen. de, *Peru* . . 124 C2
Paracatu, *Brazil* 123 E2
Paracatu →, *Brazil* 123 E2
Paracel Is. = Hsisha
  Chuntao, *Pac. Oc.* . . . 56 A4
Parachilna, *Australia* 91 E2
Parachinar, *Pakistan* 62 C4
Paraćin, *Serbia, Yug.* . . . 21 M11
Paracuru, *Brazil* 122 B4
Parada, Punta, *Peru* 124 D2
Paradas, *Spain* 31 H5
Paradela, *Spain* 30 C3
Paradhísi, *Greece* 37 C10

Paradip, *India* 61 J15
Paradise, *Calif., U.S.A.* . . 112 F5
Paradise, *Mont., U.S.A.* . . 110 C6
Paradise, *Nev., U.S.A.* . . 113 J11
Paradise →, *Canada* 99 B8
Paradise Valley, *U.S.A.* . . 110 F5
Parado, *Indonesia* 57 F5
Paragould, *U.S.A.* 109 G9
Paraguá →, *Bolivia* 125 C5
Paragua →, *Venezuela* . . 121 B5
Paraguaçu →, *Brazil* 123 D4
Paraguaçu Paulista, *Brazil* 127 A5
Paraguaipoa, *Venezuela* . 120 A3
Paraguaná, Pen. de,
  Venezuela 120 A3
Paraguarí, *Paraguay* 126 B4
Paraguarí □, *Paraguay* . . 126 B4
Paraguay ■, *S. Amer.* . . . 126 A4
Paraguay →, *Paraguay* . . 126 B4
Paraíba = João Pessoa,
  Brazil 122 C5
Paraíba □, *Brazil* 122 C4
Paraíba do Sul →, *Brazil* . 123 F3
Parainen, *Finland* 9 F20
Paraiso, *Mexico* 115 D6
Parak, *Iran* 65 E7
Parakhino Paddubye,
  Russia 40 C7
Parakou, *Benin* 79 D5
Paralimni, *Cyprus* 37 D12
Paramaribo, *Surinam* 121 B6
Parambu, *Brazil* 122 C3
Paramillo, Nudo del,
  Colombia 120 B2
Paramirim, *Brazil* 123 D3
Paramirim →, *Brazil* 123 D3
Paramithiá, *Greece* 39 K3
Paramushir, Ostrov, *Russia* 45 D16
Paran →, *Israel* 69 E4
Paraná, *Argentina* 126 C3
Paraná, *Brazil* 123 D2
Paraná □, *Brazil* 127 A5
Paraná →, *Argentina* 126 C4
Paranaguá, *Brazil* 127 B6
Paranaíba →, *Brazil* 123 F1
Paranapanema →, *Brazil* . 127 A5
Paranapiacaba, Serra do,
  Brazil 127 A6
Paranavaí, *Brazil* 127 A5
Parang, Jolo, *Phil.* 55 J4
Parang, Mindanao, *Phil.* . . 55 C6
Parangaba, *Brazil* 122 B4
Parápola, *Greece* 39 N6
Parapóri, Ákra, *Greece* . . 39 P10
Paratinga, *Brazil* 123 D3
Paratoo, *Australia* 91 E2
Parattah, *Australia* 90 G4
Paraúna, *Brazil* 123 E1
Paray-le-Monial, *France* . . 27 B8
Parbati →, *India* 62 G7
Parbhani, *India* 60 K10
Parchim, *Germany* 18 B7
Parczew, *Poland* 20 D12
Pardes Hanna, *Israel* 69 C3
Pardilla, *Spain* 30 D7
Pardo →, *Bahia, Brazil* . . 123 E4
Pardo →, *Mato Grosso,*
  Brazil 127 A5
Pardo →, *Minas Gerais,*
  Brazil 123 E3
Pardo →, *São Paulo,*
  Brazil 123 F2
Pardubice, *Czech.* 20 E5
Pare, *Indonesia* 57 G15
Pare □, *Tanzania* 82 C4
Pare Mts., *Tanzania* 82 C4
Parecis, Serra dos, *Brazil* . 125 C6
Paredes de Nava, *Spain* . 30 C6
Pareh, *Iran* 64 B5
Parelhas, *Brazil* 122 C4
Paren, *Russia* 45 C17
Parent, *Canada* 98 C5
Parent, L., *Canada* 98 C4
Parentis-en-Born, *France* . 26 D2
Parepare, *Indonesia* 57 E5
Parfino, *Russia* 40 D6
Pargo, Pta. do, *Madeira* . . 36 D2
Paria, G. de, *Venezuela* . . 121 A5
Paria, Pen. de, *Venezuela* . 121 A5
Pariaguán, *Venezuela* . . . 121 B5
Pariaman, *Indonesia* 56 E2
Paricatuba, *Brazil* 121 D5
Paricutín, Cerro, *Mexico* . 114 D4
Parigi, *Java, Indonesia* . . 57 G13
Parigi, *Sulawesi, Indonesia* 57 E6
Parika, *Guyana* 121 B6
Parikkala, *Finland* 40 B5
Parima, Serra, *Brazil* . . . 121 C5
Parinari, *Peru* 124 A3
Paríngul Mare, *Romania* . . 38 D6
Parintins, *Brazil* 121 D6
Pariparit Kyun, *Burma* . . . 61 M18
Paris, *Canada* 98 D3
Paris, *France* 25 D9
Paris, *Idaho, U.S.A.* 110 E8
Paris, *Ky., U.S.A.* 104 F3
Paris, *Tenn., U.S.A.* 105 G1
Paris, *Tex., U.S.A.* 109 J7
Paris, Ville de □, *France* . 25 D9
Parish, *U.S.A.* 107 C8
Park, *U.S.A.* 112 B4
Park City, *U.S.A.* 109 G6
Park Falls, *U.S.A.* 108 C9
Park Range, *U.S.A.* 110 G10
Park Rapids, *U.S.A.* 108 B7
Park River, *U.S.A.* 108 A6

Park Rynie, *S. Africa* 85 E5
Parkā Bandar, *Iran* 65 E8
Parkano, *Finland* 9 E20
Parker, *Ariz., U.S.A.* 113 L12
Parker, *S. Dak., U.S.A.* . . 108 D6
Parker Dam, *U.S.A.* 113 L12
Parkersburg, *U.S.A.* 104 F5
Parkerview, *Canada* 101 C8
Parkes, *Australia* 91 E4
Parkfield, *U.S.A.* 112 K6
Parkland, *U.S.A.* 112 C4
Parkside, *Canada* 101 C7
Parkston, *U.S.A.* 108 D5
Parksville, *Canada* 100 D4
Parma, *Italy* 32 D7
Parma, *Idaho, U.S.A.* . . . 110 E5
Parma, *Ohio, U.S.A.* 106 E3
Parma →, *Italy* 32 D7
Parnaguá, *Brazil* 122 D3
Parnaíba, *Piauí, Brazil* . . 122 B3
Parnaíba, *São Paulo, Brazil* 125 D7
Parnaíba →, *Brazil* 122 B3
Parnamirim, *Brazil* 122 C4
Parnarama, *Brazil* 122 C3
Parnassós, *Greece* 39 L5
Párnis, *Greece* 39 L6
Párnon Óros, *Greece* . . . 39 M5
Pärnu, *Estonia* 9 G21
Paroo →, *Australia* 91 E3
Páros, *Greece* 39 M8
Parowan, *U.S.A.* 111 H7
Parpaillon, *France* 27 D10
Parral, *Chile* 126 D1
Parramatta, *Australia* . . . 91 E5
Parras, *Mexico* 114 B4
Parrett →, *U.K.* 13 F5
Parris I., *U.S.A.* 105 J5
Parrsboro, *Canada* 99 C7
Parry Is., *Canada* 4 B2
Parry Sound, *Canada* . . . 98 C3
Parsberg, *Germany* 19 F7
Parshall, *U.S.A.* 108 B3
Parsnip →, *Canada* 100 B4
Parsons, *U.S.A.* 109 G7
Parsons Ra., *Australia* . . . 90 A2
Partanna, *Italy* 34 E5
Parthenay, *France* 24 F6
Partinico, *Italy* 34 D6
Paru →, *Brazil* 121 D7
Parú →, *Venezuela* 120 C4
Paru de Oeste →, *Brazil* . 121 C6
Parucito →, *Venezuela* . . 120 B4
Paruro, *Peru* 124 C3
Parván □, *Afghan.* 60 B6
Parvatipuram, *India* 61 K13
Parys, *S. Africa* 84 D4
Pas-de-Calais □, *France* . 25 B9
Pasadena, *Calif., U.S.A.* . 113 L8
Pasadena, *Tex., U.S.A.* . . 109 L7
Pasaje, *Ecuador* 120 D2
Pasaje →, *Argentina* 126 B3
Pasay, *Phil.* 55 D4
Pascagoula, *U.S.A.* 109 K10
Pascagoula →, *U.S.A.* . . 109 K10
Paşcani, *Romania* 38 B9
Pasco, *U.S.A.* 110 C4
Pasco □, *Peru* 124 C2
Pasco, Cerro de, *Peru* . . . 124 C2
Pascua, I. de, *Pac. Oc.* . . 93 K17
Pasewalk, *Germany* 18 B10
Pasfield L., *Canada* 101 B7
Pasha →, *Russia* 40 B7
Pashiwari, *Pakistan* 63 B6
Pashmakli = Smolyan,
  Bulgaria 39 H7
Pasinler, *Turkey* 67 C9
Pasirian, *Indonesia* 57 H15
Pasley, C., *Australia* 89 F3
Pašman, *Croatia* 33 E12
Pasni, *Pakistan* 60 G3
Paso Cantinela, *Mexico* . . 113 N11
Paso de Indios, *Argentina* . 128 B3
Paso de los Libres,
  Argentina 126 B4
Paso de los Toros, *Uruguay* 126 C4
Paso Flores, *Argentina* . . 128 B2
Paso Robles, *U.S.A.* 111 J3
Pasorapa, *Bolivia* 125 D5
Paspébiac, *Canada* 99 C6
Pasrur, *Pakistan* 62 C6
Passage West, *Ireland* . . . 15 E3
Passaic, *U.S.A.* 107 F10
Passau, *Germany* 19 G9
Passendale, *Belgium* 17 G2
Passero, C., *Italy* 35 F8
Passo Fundo, *Brazil* 127 B5
Passos, *Brazil* 123 F2
Passow, *Germany* 18 B10
Passwang, *Switz.* 22 B5
Passy, *France* 27 C10
Pastavy, *Belarus* 9 J22
Pastaza □, *Ecuador* 120 D2
Pastaza →, *Peru* 120 D2
Pastęk, *Poland* 20 A9
Pasto, *Colombia* 120 C2
Pastos Bons, *Brazil* 122 C3
Pastrana, *Spain* 28 E2
Pasuruan, *Indonesia* 57 G15
Patagones, *Argentina* . . . 128 B4
Patagonia, *U.S.A.* 111 L8
Patambar, *Iran* 65 D9
Patan, *India* 60 H8
Patan, *Maharashtra, India* . 62 H5
Patan, *Nepal* 61 F14
Patani, *Indonesia* 57 D7
Pataudi, *India* 62 E7

Patay

Patay, *France* 25 D8
Patchewollock, *Australia* 91 F3
Patchogue, *U.S.A.* 107 F11
Patea, *N.Z.* 87 H5
Pategi, *Nigeria* 79 D6
Patensie, *S. Africa* 84 E3
Paternò, *Italy* 35 E7
Pateros, *U.S.A.* 110 B4
Paterson, *U.S.A.* 107 F10
Paterson Ra., *Australia* 88 D3
Paterswolde, *Neths.* 16 B9
Pathankot, *India* 62 C6
Pathfinder Reservoir, *U.S.A.* 110 E10
Pathiu, *Thailand* 59 G2
Pathum Thani, *Thailand* 58 E3
Pati, *Indonesia* 57 G14
Patía, *Colombia* 120 C2
Patía →, *Colombia* 120 C2
Patiala, *India* 62 D7
Patine Kouka, *Senegal* 78 C2
Pativilca, *Peru* 124 C2
Patkai Bum, *India* 61 F19
Pátmos, *Greece* 39 M9
Patna, *India* 63 G11
Patnos, *Turkey* 67 C10
Patonga, *Uganda* 82 B3
Patos, *Brazil* 122 C4
Patos, L. dos, *Brazil* 127 C5
Patos de Minas, *Brazil* 123 E2
Patquía, *Argentina* 126 C2
Pátrai, *Greece* 39 L4
Pátraikós Kólpos, *Greece* 39 L4
Patras = Pátrai, *Greece* 39 L4
Patricio Lynch, I., *Chile* 128 C1
Patrocínio, *Brazil* 123 E2
Patta, *Kenya* 82 C5
Pattada, *Italy* 34 B2
Pattani, *Thailand* 59 J3
Patten, *U.S.A.* 99 C6
Patterson, *Calif., U.S.A.* 111 H3
Patterson, *La., U.S.A.* 109 L9
Patterson, Mt., *U.S.A.* 112 G7
Patti, *India* 62 D6
Patti, *Italy* 35 D7
Pattoki, *Pakistan* 62 D5
Patton, *U.S.A.* 106 F6
Patu, *Brazil* 122 C4
Patuakhali, *Bangla.* 61 H17
Patuca →, *Honduras* 116 C3
Patuca, Punta, *Honduras* 116 C3
Pâturages, *Belgium* 17 H3
Pátzcuaro, *Mexico* 114 D4
Pau, *France* 26 E3
Pau, Gave de →, *France* 26 E2
Pau d' Arco, *Brazil* 122 C2
Pau dos Ferros, *Brazil* 122 C4
Paucartambo, *Peru* 124 C3
Pauillac, *France* 26 C3
Pauini, *Brazil* 124 B4
Pauini →, *Brazil* 121 D5
Pauk, *Burma* 61 J19
Paul I., *Canada* 99 A7
Paul Isnard, *Fr. Guiana* 121 C7
Paulhan, *France* 26 E7
Paulis = Isiro, *Zaïre* 82 B2
Paulista, *Brazil* 122 C5
Paulistana, *Brazil* 122 C3
Paullina, *U.S.A.* 108 D7
Paulo Afonso, *Brazil* 122 C4
Paulo de Faria, *Brazil* 123 F2
Paulpietersburg, *S. Africa* 85 D5
Pauls Valley, *U.S.A.* 109 H6
Pauma Valley, *U.S.A.* 113 M10
Pausa, *Peru* 124 D3
Pauto →, *Colombia* 120 B3
Pāveh, *Iran* 67 E12
Pavelets, *Russia* 42 D4
Pavia, *Italy* 32 C6
Pāvilosta, *Latvia* 9 H19
Pavlikeni, *Bulgaria* 38 F8
Pavlodar, *Kazakhstan* 44 D8
Pavlograd = Pavlohrad, *Ukraine* 41 H8
Pavlohrad, *Ukraine* 41 H8
Pavlovo, *Russia* 42 C6
Pavlovo, *Russia* 45 C12
Pavlovsk, *Russia* 42 E5
Pavlovskaya, *Russia* 43 G4
Pavlovskiy-Posad, *Russia* 42 C4
Pavullo nel Frignano, *Italy* 32 D7
Pawhuska, *U.S.A.* 109 G6
Pawling, *U.S.A.* 107 E11
Pawnee, *U.S.A.* 109 G6
Pawnee City, *U.S.A.* 108 E6
Pawtucket, *U.S.A.* 107 E13
Paximádhia, *Greece* 37 D6
Paxoí, *Greece* 39 K3
Paxton, *Ill., U.S.A.* 104 E1
Paxton, *Nebr., U.S.A.* 108 E4
Payakumbuh, *Indonesia* 56 E2
Payerne, *Switz.* 22 C3
Payette, *U.S.A.* 110 D5
Paymogo, *Spain* 31 H3
Payne Bay = Kangirsuk, *Canada* 97 B13
Paynes Find, *Australia* 89 E2
Paynesville, *Liberia* 78 D2
Paynesville, *U.S.A.* 108 C7
Paysandú, *Uruguay* 126 C4
Payson, *Ariz., U.S.A.* 111 J8
Payson, *Utah, U.S.A.* 110 F8
Paz →, *Guatemala* 116 D1
Paz, B. la, *Mexico* 114 C2
Pāzanān, *Iran* 65 D6
Pazar, *Turkey* 67 B9
Pazarcık, *Turkey* 66 D7
Pazardzhik, *Bulgaria* 38 G7
Pazaryolu, *Turkey* 67 B9
Pazin, *Croatia* 33 C10
Pazña, *Bolivia* 124 D4
Pčinja →, *Macedonia* 39 H4
Pe Ell, *U.S.A.* 112 D3
Peabody, *U.S.A.* 107 D14
Peace →, *Canada* 100 B6
Peace Point, *Canada* 100 B6
Peace River, *Canada* 100 B5
Peach Springs, *U.S.A.* 111 J7
Peak, The = Kinder Scout, *U.K.* 12 D6
Peak Downs, *Australia* 90 C4
Peak Downs Mine, *Australia* 90 C4
Peak Hill, *N.S.W., Australia* 91 E4
Peak Hill, *W. Austral., Australia* 89 E2
Peak Ra., *Australia* 90 C4
Peake, *Australia* 91 F2
Peake Cr. →, *Australia* 91 D2
Peale, Mt., *U.S.A.* 111 G9
Pearblossom, *U.S.A.* 113 L9
Pearl →, *U.S.A.* 109 K10
Pearl City, *U.S.A.* 102 H16
Pearsall, *U.S.A.* 109 L5
Pearse I., *Canada* 100 C2
Peary Land, *Greenland* 4 A6
Pease →, *U.S.A.* 109 H5
Pebane, *Mozam.* 83 F4
Pebas, *Peru* 120 D3
Pebble, I., *Falk. Is.* 128 D5
Pebble Beach, *U.S.A.* 112 J5
Peć, *Serbia, Yug.* 21 N10
Peçanha, *Brazil* 123 E3
Péccioli, *Italy* 32 E7
Pechea, *Romania* 38 D10
Pechenga, *Russia* 44 C4
Pechenizhyn, *Ukraine* 41 H3
Pechiguera, Pta., *Canary Is.* 36 F6
Pechnezhskoye Vdkhr., *Ukraine* 41 G9
Pechora →, *Russia* 44 C6
Pechorskaya Guba, *Russia* 44 C6
Pecica, *Romania* 38 C4
Pečka, *Serbia, Yug.* 21 L9
Pécora, C., *Italy* 34 C1
Pečory, *Russia* 9 H22
Pecos, *U.S.A.* 109 K3
Pecos →, *U.S.A.* 109 L3
Pécs, *Hungary* 21 J8
Pedder, L., *Australia* 90 G4
Peddie, *S. Africa* 85 E4
Pédernales, *Dom. Rep.* 117 C5
Pedieos →, *Cyprus* 37 D12
Pedirka, *Australia* 91 D2
Pedra Azul, *Brazil* 123 E3
Pedra Grande, Recifes de, *Brazil* 123 E4
Pedras Negras, *Brazil* 125 C5
Pedreiras, *Brazil* 122 B3
Pedro Afonso, *Brazil* 122 C2
Pedro Cays, *Jamaica* 116 C4
Pedro Chico, *Colombia* 120 C3
Pedro de Valdivia, *Chile* 126 A2
Pedro Juan Caballero, *Paraguay* 127 A4
Pedro Muñoz, *Spain* 29 F2
Pedrógão Grande, *Portugal* 30 F2
Peebinga, *Australia* 91 E3
Peebles, *U.K.* 14 F5
Peekskill, *U.S.A.* 107 E11
Peel, *U.K.* 12 C3
Peel →, *Australia* 91 E5
Peel →, *Canada* 96 B6
Peene →, *Germany* 18 A9
Peera Peera Poolanna L., *Australia* 91 D2
Peers, *Canada* 100 C5
Pegasus Bay, *N.Z.* 87 K4
Pegnitz, *Germany* 19 F7
Pegnitz →, *Germany* 19 F6
Pego, *Spain* 29 G4
Pegu, *Burma* 61 L20
Pegu Yoma, *Burma* 61 K19
Pehuajó, *Argentina* 126 D3
Pei Xian, *China* 50 G9
Peine, *Chile* 126 A2
Peine, *Germany* 18 C6
Peip'ing = Beijing, *China* 50 E9
Peipus, L. = Chudskoye, Oz., *Russia* 9 G22
Peissenberg, *Germany* 19 H7
Peitz, *Germany* 18 D10
Peixe, *Brazil* 123 D2
Peixe →, *Brazil* 123 F1
Peixoto de Azeredo →, *Brazil* 125 C6
Peize, *Neths.* 16 B8
Pek →, *Serbia, Yug.* 21 L11
Pekalongan, *Indonesia* 57 G13
Pekan, *Malaysia* 59 L4
Pekanbaru, *Indonesia* 56 D2
Pekin, *U.S.A.* 108 E10
Peking = Beijing, *China* 50 E9
Pelabuhan Kelang, *Malaysia* 59 L3
Pelabuhan Ratu, Teluk, *Indonesia* 57 G12
Pelabuhanratu, *Indonesia* 57 G12
Pélagos, *Greece* 39 K7
Pelaihari, *Indonesia* 56 E4
Pelat, Mt., *France* 27 D10
Peleaga, Vf., *Romania* 38 D5
Pelechuco, *Bolivia* 124 C4
Pelée, Mt., *Martinique* 117 D7
Pelee, Pt., *Canada* 98 D3
Pelee I., *Canada* 98 D3
Pelejo, *Peru* 124 B2
Pelekech, *Kenya* 82 B4
Peleng, *Indonesia* 57 E6
Pelham, *U.S.A.* 105 K3
Pelhřimov, *Czech.* 20 F5
Pelican L., *Canada* 101 C8
Pelican Narrows, *Canada* 101 B8
Pelican Rapids, *Canada* 101 C8
Pelkosenniemi, *Finland* 8 C22
Pella, *S. Africa* 84 D2
Pella, *U.S.A.* 108 E8
Pellaro, *Italy* 35 D8
Pello, *Finland* 8 C21
Pellworm, *Germany* 18 A4
Pelly →, *Canada* 96 B6
Pelly Bay, *Canada* 97 B11
Pelly L., *Canada* 96 B9
Peloponnese = Pelopónnisos □, *Greece* 39 M5
Pelopónnisos □, *Greece* 39 M5
Peloritani, Monti, *Italy* 35 D8
Peloro, C., *Italy* 35 D8
Pelorus Sd., *N.Z.* 87 J4
Pelotas, *Brazil* 127 C5
Pelvoux, Massif du, *France* 27 D10
Pemalang, *Indonesia* 57 G13
Pematangsiantar, *Indonesia* 56 D1
Pemba, *Mozam.* 83 E5
Pemba, *Zambia* 83 F2
Pemba Channel, *Tanzania* 82 D4
Pemba I., *Tanzania* 82 D4
Pemberton, *Australia* 89 F2
Pemberton, *Canada* 100 C4
Pembina, *U.S.A.* 108 A6
Pembina →, *U.S.A.* 101 D9
Pembine, *U.S.A.* 104 C2
Pembroke, *Canada* 98 C4
Pembroke, *U.K.* 13 F3
Pembroke, *U.S.A.* 105 J5
Pen-y-Ghent, *U.K.* 12 C5
Peña, Sierra de la, *Spain* 28 C4
Peña de Francia, Sierra de, *Spain* 30 E4
Penafiel, *Portugal* 30 D2
Peñafiel, *Spain* 30 D6
Peñaflor, *Spain* 31 H5
Peñalara, Pico, *Spain* 30 E7
Penalva, *Brazil* 122 B2
Penamacôr, *Portugal* 30 E3
Penang = Pinang, *Malaysia* 59 K3
Penápolis, *Brazil* 127 A6
Peñaranda de Bracamonte, *Spain* 30 E5
Peñarroya-Pueblonuevo, *Spain* 31 G5
Peñas, C. de, *Spain* 30 B5
Penas, G. de, *Chile* 128 C2
Peñas, Pta., *Venezuela* 121 A5
Peñas de San Pedro, *Spain* 29 G2
Peñas del Chache, *Canary Is.* 36 E6
Peñausende, *Spain* 30 D5
Pench'i = Benxi, *China* 51 D12
Pend Oreille →, *U.S.A.* 110 B5
Pend Oreille L., *U.S.A.* 110 C5
Pendembu, *S. Leone* 78 D2
Pendências, *Brazil* 122 C4
Pender B., *Australia* 88 C3
Pendleton, *Calif., U.S.A.* 113 M9
Pendleton, *Oreg., U.S.A.* 110 D4
Penedo, *Brazil* 122 D4
Penetanguishene, *Canada* 98 D4
Peng Xian, *China* 52 B4
Pengalengan, *Indonesia* 57 G12
Penge, *Kasai Or., Zaïre* 82 D1
Penge, *Kivu, Zaïre* 82 C2
Penglai, *China* 51 F11
Pengshui, *China* 52 C7
Penguin, *Australia* 90 G4
Pengxi, *China* 52 B5
Pengze, *China* 53 C11
Penhalonga, *Zimbabwe* 83 F3
Peniche, *Portugal* 31 F1
Penicuik, *U.K.* 14 F5
Penida, *Indonesia* 56 F5
Peninsular Malaysia □, *Malaysia* 59 L4
Peñíscola, *Spain* 28 E5
Penitente, Serra dos, *Brazil* 122 C2
Penmarch, *France* 24 E2
Penmarch, Pte. de, *France* 24 E2
Penn Hills, *U.S.A.* 106 F5
Penn Yan, *U.S.A.* 106 D7
Pennabilli, *Italy* 33 E9
Pennant, *Canada* 101 C7
Penne, *Italy* 33 F10
Penner →, *India* 60 M12
Pennine, Alpi, *Alps* 32 B4
Pennines, *U.K.* 12 C5
Pennington, *U.S.A.* 112 F5
Pennino, Mte., *Italy* 33 E9
Pennsylvania □, *U.S.A.* 104 E6
Penny, *Canada* 100 C4
Peno, *Russia* 42 B1
Penola, *Australia* 91 F3
Penong, *Australia* 89 F5
Penonomé, *Panama* 116 E3
Penrith, *Australia* 91 E5
Penrith, *U.K.* 12 C5
Pensacola, *U.S.A.* 105 K2
Pensacola Mts., *Antarctica* 5 E1
Pense, *Canada* 101 C8
Penshurst, *Australia* 91 F3
Pentecoste, *Brazil* 122 B4
Penticton, *Canada* 100 D5
Pentland, *Australia* 90 C4
Pentland Firth, *U.K.* 14 C5
Pentland Hills, *U.K.* 14 F5
Penylan L., *Canada* 101 A7
Penza, *Russia* 42 D7
Penzance, *U.K.* 13 G2
Penzberg, *Germany* 19 H7
Penzhino, *Russia* 45 C17
Penzhinskaya Guba, *Russia* 45 C17
Penzlin, *Germany* 18 B9
Peoria, *Ariz., U.S.A.* 111 K7
Peoria, *Ill., U.S.A.* 108 E10
Pepingen, *Belgium* 17 G4
Pepinster, *Belgium* 17 G7
Pera Hd., *Australia* 90 A3
Perabumulih, *Indonesia* 56 E2
Perakhóra, *Greece* 39 L5
Perales de Alfambra, *Spain* 28 E3
Perales del Puerto, *Spain* 30 E4
Peralta, *Spain* 28 C3
Pérama, *Kérkira, Greece* 37 A3
Pérama, *Kríti, Greece* 37 D6
Peräpohjola, *Finland* 8 C22
Percé, *Canada* 99 C7
Perche, *France* 24 D8
Perche, Collines du, *France* 24 D7
Percival Lakes, *Australia* 88 D4
Percy, *France* 24 D5
Percy Is., *Australia* 90 C5
Perdido →, *Argentina* 128 B3
Perdido, Mte., *Spain* 26 F4
Perdu, Mt. = Perdido, Mte., *Spain* 26 F4
Pereira, *Colombia* 120 C2
Pereira Barreto, *Brazil* 123 F1
Perekerten, *Australia* 91 E3
Perelazovskiy, *Russia* 43 F6
Perené →, *Peru* 124 C3
Perenjori, *Australia* 89 E2
Pereslavl-Zalesskiy, *Russia* 42 B4
Pereyaslav-Khmelnytskyy, *Ukraine* 41 G6
Pérez, I., *Mexico* 115 C7
Pergamino, *Argentina* 126 C3
Pergau →, *Malaysia* 59 K3
Pérgine Valsugana, *Italy* 33 B8
Pérgola, *Italy* 33 E9
Perham, *U.S.A.* 108 B7
Perhentian, Kepulauan, *Malaysia* 59 K4
Periam, *Romania* 38 C3
Péribonca →, *Canada* 99 C5
Péribonca, L., *Canada* 99 B5
Perico, *Argentina* 126 A2
Pericos, *Mexico* 114 B3
Périers, *France* 24 C5
Périgord, *France* 26 D4
Périgueux, *France* 26 C4
Perijá, Sierra de, *Colombia* 120 B3
Peristéra, *Greece* 39 K6
Peristerona →, *Cyprus* 37 D12
Perito Moreno, *Argentina* 128 C2
Peritoró, *Brazil* 122 B3
Perković, *Croatia* 33 E13
Perlas, Arch. de las, *Panama* 116 E4
Perlas, Punta de, *Nic.* 116 D3
Perleberg, *Germany* 18 B7
Perm, *Russia* 44 D6
Pernambuco = Recife, *Brazil* 122 C5
Pernambuco □, *Brazil* 122 C4
Pernatty Lagoon, *Australia* 91 E2
Pernik, *Bulgaria* 38 G6
Peron, C., *Australia* 89 E1
Peron Is., *Australia* 88 B5
Peron Pen., *Australia* 89 E1
Péronne, *France* 25 C9
Péronnes, *Belgium* 17 H4
Perosa Argentina, *Italy* 32 D4
Perow, *Canada* 100 C3
Perpendicular Pt., *Australia* 91 E5
Perpignan, *France* 26 F6
Perris, *U.S.A.* 113 M9
Perros-Guirec, *France* 24 D3
Perry, *Fla., U.S.A.* 105 K4
Perry, *Ga., U.S.A.* 105 J4
Perry, *Iowa, U.S.A.* 108 E7
Perry, *Maine, U.S.A.* 105 C12
Perry, *Okla., U.S.A.* 109 G6
Perryton, *U.S.A.* 109 G4
Perryville, *U.S.A.* 109 G10
Perşembe, *Turkey* 66 B7
Perseverancia, *Bolivia* 125 C5
Pershotravensk, *Ukraine* 41 G4
Persia = Iran ■, *Asia* 65 C7
Persian Gulf = Gulf, The, *Asia* 65 E6
Perstorp, *Sweden* 11 H7
Pertek, *Turkey* 67 C8
Perth, *Australia* 89 F2
Perth, *Canada* 98 D4
Perth, *U.K.* 14 E5
Perth Amboy, *U.S.A.* 107 F10
Pertuis, *France* 27 E9
Peru, *Ill., U.S.A.* 108 E10
Peru, *Ind., U.S.A.* 104 E2
Peru ■, *S. Amer.* 120 D2
Peru-Chile Trench, *Pac. Oc.* 93 K20
Perúgia, *Italy* 33 E9
Perušić, *Croatia* 33 D12
Péruwelz, *Belgium* 17 G3
Pervomaysk, *Russia* 42 C6
Pervomaysk, *Ukraine* 41 H6
Pervouralsk, *Russia* 44 D6
Perwez, *Belgium* 17 G5
Pes, Pta. del, *Spain* 36 C7
Pésaro, *Italy* 33 E9
Pescara, *Italy* 33 F11
Pescara →, *Italy* 33 F11
Peschanokopskoye, *Russia* 43 G5
Péscia, *Italy* 32 E7
Pescina, *Italy* 33 G10
Peseux, *Switz.* 22 C3
Peshawar, *Pakistan* 62 B4
Peshtigo, *U.S.A.* 104 C2
Peski, *Russia* 42 E6
Pêso da Régua, *Portugal* 30 D3
Pesqueira, *Brazil* 122 C4
Pessac, *France* 26 D3
Pessoux, *Belgium* 17 H6
Pestovo, *Russia* 40 C8
Pestravka, *Russia* 42 D9
Petah Tiqwa, *Israel* 69 C3
Petaling Jaya, *Malaysia* 59 L3
Petaloudhes, *Greece* 37 C10
Petaluma, *U.S.A.* 112 G4
Petange, *Lux.* 17 J7
Petatlán, *Mexico* 114 D4
Petauke, *Zambia* 83 E3
Petawawa, *Canada* 98 C4
Petegem, *Belgium* 17 G3
Petén Itzá, L., *Guatemala* 116 C2
Peter I.s Øy, *Antarctica* 5 C16
Peter Pond L., *Canada* 101 B7
Peterbell, *Canada* 98 C3
Peterborough, *Australia* 91 E2
Peterborough, *Canada* 97 D12
Peterborough, *U.K.* 13 E7
Peterborough, *U.S.A.* 107 D13
Peterhead, *U.K.* 14 D7
Petermann Bjerg, *Greenland* 94 B17
Peter's Mine, *Guyana* 121 B6
Petersburg, *Alaska, U.S.A.* 100 B2
Petersburg, *Ind., U.S.A.* 104 F2
Petersburg, *Va., U.S.A.* 104 G7
Petersburg, *W. Va., U.S.A.* 104 F6
Petford, *Australia* 90 B3
Petília Policastro, *Italy* 35 C9
Petit Bois I., *U.S.A.* 105 K1
Petit-Cap, *Canada* 99 C7
Petit Goâve, *Haiti* 117 C5
Petit Lac Manicouagan, *Canada* 99 B6
Petit Saint Bernard, Col du, *Italy* 32 C3
Petitcodiac, *Canada* 99 C6
Petite Baleine →, *Canada* 98 A4
Petite Saguenay, *Canada* 99 C5
Petitsikapau, L., *Canada* 99 B6
Petlad, *India* 62 H5
Peto, *Mexico* 115 C7
Petone, *N.Z.* 87 J5
Petoskey, *U.S.A.* 104 C3
Petra, *Jordan* 69 E4
Petra, *Spain* 36 B10
Petra, Ostrova, *Russia* 4 B13
Petra Velikogo, Zaliv, *Russia* 48 C5
Petralia Sottana, *Italy* 35 E7
Petrel, *Spain* 29 G4
Petreto-Bicchisano, *France* 27 G12
Petrich, *Bulgaria* 39 H6
Petrijanec, *Croatia* 33 B13
Petrikov = Pyetrikaw, *Belarus* 41 F5
Petrinja, *Croatia* 33 C13
Petrodvorets, *Russia* 40 C5
Petrograd = Sankt-Peterburg, *Russia* 40 C6
Petrolândia, *Brazil* 122 C4
Petrolia, *Canada* 98 D3
Petrolina, *Brazil* 122 C3
Petropavl, *Kazakhstan* 44 D7
Petropavlovsk = Petropavl, *Kazakhstan* 44 D7
Petropavlovsk-Kamchatskiy, *Russia* 45 D16
Petropavlovskiy = Akhtubinsk, *Russia* 43 F8
Petrópolis, *Brazil* 123 F3
Petroşani, *Romania* 38 D6
Petrova Gora, *Croatia* 33 C12
Petrovac, *Montenegro, Yug.* 21 N8
Petrovsk, *Russia* 42 D7
Petrovsk-Zabaykalskiy, *Russia* 45 D11
Petrovskaya, *Russia* 43 H3
Petrovskoye = Svetlograd, *Russia* 43 H6
Petrozavodsk, *Russia* 40 B8
Petrus Steyn, *S. Africa* 85 D4
Petrusburg, *S. Africa* 84 D4
Peumo, *Chile* 126 C1
Peureulak, *Indonesia* 56 D1
Pevek, *Russia* 45 C18
Peveragno, *Italy* 32 D4
Peyrehorade, *France* 26 E2
Peyruis, *France* 27 D9
Pézenas, *France* 26 E7
Pfaffenhofen, *Germany* 19 G7
Pfäffikon, *Switz.* 23 B7
Pfarrkirchen, *Germany* 19 G8
Pfeffenhausen, *Germany* 19 G7
Pforzheim, *Germany* 19 G4
Pfullendorf, *Germany* 19 H5
Pfungstadt, *Germany* 19 F4
Phagwara, *India* 60 D9
Phaistós, *Greece* 37 D6
Phala, *Botswana* 84 C4

Phalera = Phulera, India . 62 F6
Phalodi, India 62 F5
Phalsbourg, France . . . 25 D14
Phan, Thailand 58 C2
Phan Rang, Vietnam . . . 59 G7
Phan Ri = Hoa Da,
Vietnam 59 G7
Phan Thiet, Vietnam . . . 59 G7
Phanat Nikhom, Thailand . 58 F3
Phangan, Ko, Thailand . . 59 H3
Phangnga, Thailand . . . 59 H2
Phanh Bho Ho Chi Minh,
Vietnam 59 G6
Phanom Sarakham,
Thailand 58 F3
Pharenda, India 63 F10
Phatthalung, Thailand . 59 J3
Phayao, Thailand 58 C2
Phelps, N.Y., U.S.A. . . . 106 D7
Phelps, Wis., U.S.A. . . . 108 B10
Phelps L., Canada 101 B8
Phenix City, U.S.A. 105 J3
Phet Buri, Thailand 58 F2
Phetchabun, Thailand . . 58 D3
Phetchabun, Thiu Khao,
Thailand 58 E3
Phetchaburi = Phet Buri,
Thailand 58 F2
Phi Phi, Ko, Thailand . . . 59 J2
Phiafay, Laos 58 E6
Phibun Mangsahan,
Thailand 58 E5
Phichai, Thailand 58 D3
Phichit, Thailand 58 D3
Philadelphia, Miss., U.S.A. 109 J10
Philadelphia, N.Y., U.S.A. 107 B9
Philadelphia, Pa., U.S.A. 107 F9
Philip, U.S.A. 108 C4
Philippeville, Belgium . . 17 H5
Philippi L., Australia . . . 90 C2
Philippines ■, Asia 55 F5
Philippolis, S. Africa . . . 84 E4
Philippopolis = Plovdiv,
Bulgaria 38 G7
Philipsburg, Mont., U.S.A. 110 C7
Philipsburg, Pa., U.S.A. . 106 F6
Philipstown = Daingean,
Ireland 15 C4
Philipstown, S. Africa . . 84 E3
Phillip I., Australia 91 F4
Phillips, Tex., U.S.A. . . . 109 H4
Phillips, Wis., U.S.A. . . . 108 C9
Phillipsburg, Kans., U.S.A. 108 F5
Phillipsburg, N.J., U.S.A. 107 F9
Phillott, Australia 91 D4
Philmont, U.S.A. 107 D11
Philomath, U.S.A. 110 D2
Phimai, Thailand 58 E4
Phitsanulok, Thailand . . 58 D3
Phnom Dangrek, Thailand 58 E5
Phnom Penh, Cambodia . 59 G5
Phoenix, Ariz., U.S.A. . . 111 K7
Phoenix, N.Y., U.S.A. . . 107 C8
Phoenix Is., Kiribati . . . 92 H10
Phoenixville, U.S.A. . . . 107 F9
Phon, Thailand 58 E4
Phon Tiou, Laos 58 D5
Phong →, Thailand 58 D4
Phong Saly, Laos 58 B4
Phong Tho, Vietnam . . . 58 A4
Phonhong, Laos 58 C4
Phonum, Thailand 59 H2
Phosphate Hill, Australia . 90 C2
Photharam, Thailand . . . 58 F2
Phra Chedi Sam Ong,
Thailand 58 E2
Phra Nakhon Si Ayutthaya,
Thailand 58 E3
Phra Thong, Ko, Thailand 59 H2
Phrae, Thailand 58 C3
Phrom Phiram, Thailand . 58 D3
Phrygia, Turkey 66 C4
Phu Dien, Vietnam 58 C5
Phu Loi, Laos 58 B4
Phu Ly, Vietnam 58 B5
Phu Tho, Vietnam 58 B5
Phuc Yen, Vietnam 58 B5
Phuket, Thailand 59 J2
Phuket, Ko, Thailand . . . 59 J2
Phulera, India 62 F6
Phumiphon, Khuan,
Thailand 58 D2
Phun Phin, Thailand . . . 59 H2
Piacá, Brazil 122 C2
Piacenza, Italy 32 C6
Piaçabuçu, Brazil 122 C4
Piádena, Italy 32 C7
Pialba, Australia 91 D5
Pian Cr. →, Australia . . 91 E4
Piana, France 27 F12
Pianella, Italy 33 F11
Pianoro, Italy 33 D8
Pianosa, Puglia, Italy . . 33 F12
Pianosa, Toscana, Italy . 32 F7
Piapot, Canada 101 D7
Piare →, Italy 33 C9
Pias, Portugal 31 G3
Piaseczno, Poland 20 C11
Piatã, Brazil 123 D3
Piatra, Romania 38 F8
Piatra Neamţ, Romania . 38 C8
Piauí □, Brazil 122 C3
Piauí →, Brazil 122 C3
Piave →, Italy 33 C9
Piazza Ármerina, Italy . . 35 E7
Pibor →, Sudan 77 F3
Pibor Post, Sudan 77 F3

Pica, Chile 124 E4
Picardie, France 25 C9
Picardie, Plaine de, France 25 C9
Picardy = Picardie, France 25 C9
Picayune, U.S.A. 109 K10
Picerno, Italy 35 B8
Pichilemu, Chile 126 C1
Pichincha, □, Ecuador . . 120 D2
Pickerel L., Canada . . . 98 C1
Pickle Lake, Canada . . . 98 B1
Pico Truncado, Argentina 128 C3
Picos, Brazil 122 C3
Picos Ancares, Sierra de,
Spain 30 C4
Picota, Peru 124 B2
Picquigny, France 25 C9
Picton, Australia 91 E5
Picton, Canada 98 D4
Picton, N.Z. 87 J5
Picton, I., Chile 128 E3
Pictou, Canada 99 C7
Picture Butte, Canada . . 100 D6
Picuí, Brazil 122 C4
Picún Leufú, Argentina . 128 A3
Pidurutalagala, Sri Lanka . 60 R12
Piedecuesta, Colombia . 120 B3
Piedicavallo, Italy 32 C4
Piedmont = Piemonte □,
Italy 32 D4
Piedmont, U.S.A. 105 J3
Piedmont Plateau, U.S.A. 105 J5
Piedmonte d'Alife, Italy . 35 A7
Piedra →, Spain 28 D3
Piedra del Anguila,
Argentina 128 B2
Piedra Lais, Venezuela . 120 C4
Piedrabuena, Spain . . . 31 F6
Piedrahita, Spain 30 E5
Piedras, R. de las →, Peru 124 C4
Piedras Negras, Mexico . 114 B4
Pieksämäki, Finland . . . 9 E22
Piemonte □, Italy 32 D4
Pierce, U.S.A. 110 C6
Piercefield, U.S.A. 107 B10
Pierre, U.S.A. 108 C4
Pierre Bénite, Barrage de
la, France 27 C8
Pierre-de-Bresse, France . 27 B9
Pierrefeu-du-Var, France . 27 E10
Pierrefonds, France . . . 25 C9
Pierrefontaine-les-Varans,
France 25 E13
Pierrefort, France 26 D6
Pierrelatte, France 27 D8
Piešťany, Slovak Rep. . . 20 G7
Piesting →, Austria . . . 21 G6
Piet Retief, S. Africa . . . 85 D5
Pietarsaari, Finland . . . 8 E20
Pietermaritzburg, S. Africa 85 D5
Pietersburg, S. Africa . . 85 C4
Pietraperzía, Italy 35 E7
Pietrasanta, Italy 32 E7
Pietrosul, Romania 38 B8
Pietrosul, Romania 38 B7
Pieve di Cadore, Italy . . 33 B9
Pieve di Teco, Italy . . . 32 D4
Pievepélago, Italy 32 D7
Pigádhia, Greece 39 P10
Pigeon, U.S.A. 104 D4
Piggott, U.S.A. 109 G9
Pigna, Italy 32 E4
Pigüe, Argentina 126 D3
Pihani, India 63 F9
Pihlajavesi, Finland . . . 9 F23
Pijnacker, Neths. 16 D4
Pikalevo, Russia 40 C8
Pikes Peak, U.S.A. 108 F2
Piketberg, S. Africa . . . 84 E2
Pikeville, U.S.A. 104 G4
Pikou, China 51 E12
Pikwitonei, Canada . . . 101 B9
Piła, Poland 20 B6
Pila, Spain 29 G3
Pilani, India 62 E6
Pilar, Brazil 122 C4
Pilar, Paraguay 126 B4
Pilas Group, Phil. 57 C6
Pilaya →, Bolivia 125 E5
Pilcomayo →, Paraguay . 126 B4
Pilibhit, India 63 E8
Pilica →, Poland 20 D11
Pilkhawa, India 62 E7
Pillaro, Ecuador 120 D2
Pílos, Greece 39 N4
Pilot Mound, Canada . . 101 D9
Pilot Point, U.S.A. 109 J6
Pilot Rock, U.S.A. 110 D4
Pilsen = Plzeň, Czech. . 20 F3
Pilštanj, Slovenia 33 B12
Pima, U.S.A. 111 K9
Pimba, Australia 91 E2
Pimenta Bueno, Brazil . 125 C5
Pimentel, Peru 124 B2
Pina, Spain 28 D4
Pinamalayan, Phil. 55 E4
Pinang, Malaysia 59 K3
Pinar, C. del, Spain . . . 36 B10
Pinar del Río, Cuba . . . 116 B3
Pinarbaşı, Turkey 66 C7
Pınarhisar, Turkey 66 B2
Pinchang, China 52 B6
Pincher Creek, Canada . 100 D6
Pinchi L., Canada 100 C4
Pinckneyville, U.S.A. . . 108 F10
Pîncota, Romania 38 C4
Pind Dadan Khan, Pakistan 62 C5
Pindar, Australia 89 E2

Pindaré →, Brazil 122 B3
Pindaré Mirim, Brazil . . 122 B2
Pindi Gheb, Pakistan . . 62 C5
Pindiga, Nigeria 79 D7
Pindobal, Brazil 122 B2
Pindos Óros, Greece . . . 39 K4
Pindus Mts. = Pindos
Óros, Greece 39 K4
Pine, U.S.A. 111 J8
Pine →, Canada 101 B7
Pine, C., Canada 99 C9
Pine Bluff, U.S.A. 109 H8
Pine City, U.S.A. 108 C8
Pine Falls, Canada 101 C9
Pine Flat L., U.S.A. 112 J7
Pine Pass, Canada 100 B4
Pine Point, Canada . . . 100 A6
Pine Ridge, U.S.A. 108 D3
Pine River, Canada . . . 101 C8
Pine River, U.S.A. 108 B7
Pine Valley, U.S.A. 113 N10
Pinecrest, U.S.A. 112 G6
Pinedale, U.S.A. 112 J7
Pinehill, Australia 90 C4
Pinerolo, Italy 32 D4
Pineto, Italy 33 F11
Pinetop, U.S.A. 111 J9
Pinetown, S. Africa 85 D5
Pinetree, U.S.A. 110 E11
Pineville, Ky., U.S.A. . . . 105 G4
Pineville, La., U.S.A. . . . 109 K8
Piney, France 25 D11
Ping →, Thailand 58 E3
Pingaring, Australia . . . 89 F2
Pingba, China 52 D6
Pingchuan, China 52 D3
Pingding, China 50 F7
Pingdingshan, China . . 50 H7
Pingdong, Taiwan 53 F13
Pingdu, China 51 F10
Pingelly, Australia 89 F2
Pingguo, China 52 F6
Pinghe, China 53 E11
Pingjiang, China 53 C9
Pingle, China 53 E8
Pingli, China 52 A7
Pingliang, China 50 G4
Pinglu, China 50 E7
Pingluo, China 50 E4
Pingnan, Fujian, China . . 53 D12
Pingnan,
Guangxi Zhuangzu,
China 53 F8
Pingquan, China 51 D10
Pingrup, Australia 89 F2
Pingtan, China 53 E12
Pingtang, China 52 E6
Pingwu, China 50 H3
Pingxiang,
Guangxi Zhuangzu,
China 52 F6
Pingxiang, Jiangxi, China . 53 D9
Pingyao, China 50 F7
Pingyi, China 51 G9
Pingyin, China 50 F9
Pingyuan, Guangdong,
China 53 E10
Pingyuan, Shandong, China 50 F9
Pingyuanjie, China 52 F4
Pinhal, Brazil 127 A6
Pinheiro, Brazil 122 B2
Pinheiro Machado, Brazil 127 C5
Pinhel, Portugal 30 E3
Pinhuá →, Brazil 125 B4
Pini, Indonesia 56 D1
Piniós →, Ilía, Greece . . 39 M4
Piniós →, Trikkala, Greece 39 K5
Pinjarra, Australia 89 F2
Pink →, Canada 101 B8
Pinnacles, Australia . . . 89 E3
Pinnacles, U.S.A. 112 J5
Pinnaroo, Australia . . . 91 F3
Pinneberg, Germany . . . 18 B5
Pínnes, Ákra, Greece . . 39 J7
Pino Hachado, Paso,
S. Amer. 128 A2
Pinon Hills, U.S.A. 113 L9
Pinos, Mexico 114 C4
Pinos, Mt., U.S.A. 113 L7
Pinos Pt., U.S.A. 111 H3
Pinos Puente, Spain . . . 31 H7
Pinotepa Nacional, Mexico 115 D5
Pinrang, Indonesia 57 E5
Pins, Pte. aux, Canada . 98 D3
Pinsk, Belarus 41 F4
Pintados, Chile 124 E4
Pintumba, Australia . . . 89 F5
Pinyang, China 53 D13
Pinyug, Russia 44 C5
Pio XII, Brazil 122 B2
Pioche, U.S.A. 111 H6
Piombino, Italy 32 F7
Piombino, Canale di, Italy 32 F7
Pioner, Os., Russia 45 B10
Pionki, Poland 20 D11
Piorini →, Brazil 121 D5
Piorini, L., Brazil 121 D5
Piotrków Trybunalski,
Poland 20 D9
Piove di Sacco, Italy . . . 33 C9
Pip, Iran 65 E9
Pipar, India 62 F5
Piparia, India 62 H8
Pipestone, U.S.A. 108 D6
Pipestone →, Canada . . 98 B2
Pipestone Cr. →, Canada 101 D8

Pipmuacan, Rés., Canada . 99 C5
Pippingarra, Australia . . 88 D2
Pipriac, France 24 E5
Piqua, U.S.A. 104 E3
Piquet Carneiro, Brazil . 122 C4
Piquiri →, Brazil 127 A5
Pīr Sohrāb, Iran 65 E9
Piracanjuba, Brazil 123 E2
Piracicaba, Brazil 127 A6
Piracuruca, Brazil 122 B3
Piræus = Piraiévs, Greece 39 M6
Piraiévs, Greece 39 M6
Piráino, Italy 35 D7
Pirajuí, Brazil 127 A6
Pirané, Argentina 126 B4
Piranhas, Brazil 122 C4
Pirapemas, Brazil 122 B3
Pirapora, Brazil 123 E3
Piray →, Bolivia 125 D5
Pires do Rio, Brazil . . . 123 E2
Pírgos, Ilía, Greece . . . 39 M4
Pírgos, Messinia, Greece 39 N5
Pirgovo, Bulgaria 38 F8
Piriac-sur-Mer, France . . 24 E4
Piribebuy, Paraguay . . . 126 B4
Pirin Planina, Bulgaria . 39 H6
Pirineos, Spain 28 C6
Piripiri, Brazil 122 B3
Piritu, Venezuela 120 B4
Pirmasens, Germany . . 19 F3
Pirna, Germany 18 E9
Pirot, Serbia, Yug. 21 M12
Piru, Indonesia 57 E7
Piru, U.S.A. 113 L8
Piryatin = Pyryatyn,
Ukraine 41 G7
Pisa, Italy 32 E7
Pisac, Peru 124 C3
Pisagua, Chile 124 D3
Pisarovina, Croatia 33 C12
Pisciotta, Italy 35 B8
Pisco, Peru 124 C2
Písek, Czech. 20 F4
Pishan, China 54 C2
Pishin Lora →, Pakistan . 62 E1
Pisidia, Turkey 66 D4
Pising, Indonesia 57 F6
Pismo Beach, U.S.A. . . . 113 K6
Pissis, Cerro, Argentina . 126 B2
Pissos, France 26 D3
Pissouri, Cyprus 37 E11
Pisticci, Italy 35 B9
Pistóia, Italy 32 E7
Pistol B., Canada 101 A10
Pisuerga →, Spain 30 D6
Pisz, Poland 20 B11
Pitalito, Colombia 120 C2
Pitanga, Brazil 123 F1
Pitangui, Brazil 123 E3
Pitarpunga, L., Australia . 91 E3
Pitcairn I., Pac. Oc. . . . 93 K14
Pite älv →, Sweden . . . 8 D19
Piteå, Sweden 8 D19
Piterka, Russia 42 E8
Piteşti, Romania 38 E7
Pithapuram, India 61 L13
Pithara, Australia 89 F2
Píthion, Greece 39 H9
Pithiviers, France 25 D9
Pitigliano, Italy 33 F8
Pitkyaranta, Russia . . . 40 B6
Pitlochry, U.K. 14 E5
Pitrufquén, Chile 128 A2
Pitt I., Canada 100 C3
Pittem, Belgium 17 F2
Pittsburg, Kans., U.S.A. . 109 G7
Pittsburg, Tex., U.S.A. . . 109 J7
Pittsburgh, U.S.A. 106 F5
Pittsfield, Ill., U.S.A. . . . 108 F9
Pittsfield, Mass., U.S.A. . 107 D11
Pittsfield, N.H., U.S.A. . . 107 C13
Pittston, U.S.A. 107 E9
Pittsworth, Australia . . . 91 D5
Pituri →, Australia 90 C2
Piuí, Brazil 123 F2
Pium, Brazil 122 D2
Piura, Peru 124 B1
Piura □, Peru 124 A2
Pivijay, Colombia 120 A3
Pizarro, Colombia 120 C2
Pizol, Switz. 23 C8
Pizzo, Italy 35 D9
Placentia, Canada 99 C9
Placentia B., Canada . . 99 C9
Placer, Phil. 55 F5
Placerville, U.S.A. 112 G6
Placetas, Cuba 116 B4
Plaffeien, Switz. 22 C4
Plain Dealing, U.S.A. . . 109 J8
Plainfield, U.S.A. 107 F10
Plains, Kans., U.S.A. . . . 109 G4
Plains, Mont., U.S.A. . . . 110 C6
Plains, Tex., U.S.A. 109 J3
Plainview, Nebr., U.S.A. . 108 D6
Plainview, Tex., U.S.A. . . 109 H4
Plainville, U.S.A. 108 F5
Plainwell, U.S.A. 104 D3
Plaisance, France 26 E4
Pláka, Greece 39 J8
Pláka, Ákra, Greece . . . 37 D8
Plakhino, Russia 44 C9
Plana Cays, Bahamas . . 117 B5

Planada, U.S.A. 112 H6
Plancoët, France 24 D4
Plandište, Serbia, Yug. . 21 K11
Planeta Rica, Colombia . 120 B2
Planina, Slovenia 33 B12
Planina, Slovenia 33 C11
Plankinton, U.S.A. 108 D5
Plano, U.S.A. 109 J6
Plant City, U.S.A. 105 L4
Plaquemine, U.S.A. . . . 109 K9
Plasencia, Spain 30 E4
Plaški, Croatia 33 C12
Plaster City, U.S.A. 113 N11
Plaster Rock, Canada . . 99 C6
Plastun, Russia 48 B8
Plata, Río de la, S. Amer. 126 C4
Platani →, Italy 34 E6
Plátanos, Greece 37 D5
Plateau □, Nigeria 79 D6
Plateau du Coteau du
Missouri, U.S.A. 108 B4
Plato, Colombia 120 B3
Platta, Piz, Switz. 23 D9
Platte, U.S.A. 108 D5
Platte →, U.S.A. 108 F7
Platteville, U.S.A. 108 E2
Plattling, Germany 19 G8
Plattsburgh, U.S.A. 107 B11
Plattsmouth, U.S.A. . . . 108 E7
Plau, Germany 18 B8
Plauen, Germany 18 E8
Plavinas, Latvia 9 H21
Plavnica, Montenegro, Yug. 21 N9
Plavsk, Russia 42 D3
Playa Blanca, Canary Is. . 36 F6
Playa Blanca Sur,
Canary Is. 36 F6
Playa de las Americas,
Canary Is. 36 F3
Playa de Mogán, Canary Is. 36 G4
Playa del Inglés, Canary Is. 36 G4
Playa Esmerelda,
Canary Is. 36 F5
Playgreen L., Canada . . 101 C9
Pleasant Bay, Canada . . 99 C7
Pleasant Hill, Calif.,
U.S.A. 112 H4
Pleasant Hill, Mo., U.S.A. 108 F7
Pleasanton, U.S.A. 109 L5
Pleasantville, U.S.A. . . . 104 F8
Pléaux, France 26 C6
Pleiku, Vietnam 58 F7
Plélan-le-Grand, France . 24 D4
Plémet-la-Pierre, France . 24 D4
Pléneuf-Val-André, France 24 D4
Plenița, Romania 38 E6
Plenty →, Australia . . . 90 C2
Plenty, B. of, N.Z. 87 G6
Plentywood, U.S.A. . . . 108 A2
Plessisville, Canada . . . 99 C5
Plestin-les-Grèves, France 24 D3
Pleszew, Poland 20 D7
Pleternica, Croatia 21 K7
Pletipi L., Canada 99 B5
Pleven, Bulgaria 38 F8
Plevlja, Montenegro, Yug. 21 M9
Płock, Poland 20 C9
Plöcken Passo, Italy . . . 33 B9
Ploegsteert, Belgium . . 17 G1
Ploemeur, France 24 E3
Ploërmel, France 24 E4
Ploiești, Romania 38 E9
Plombières-les-Bains,
France 25 E13
Plomin, Croatia 33 C11
Plön, Germany 18 A6
Plöner See, Germany . . 18 A6
Plonge, Lac la, Canada . 101 B7
Płońsk, Poland 20 C10
Ploty, Poland 20 B5
Plouaret, France 24 D3
Plouay, France 24 E3
Ploudalmézeau, France . 24 D2
Plougasnou, France . . . 24 D3
Plouha, France 24 D4
Plouhinec, France 24 E2
Plovdiv, Bulgaria 38 G7
Plum, U.S.A. 106 F5
Plum I., U.S.A. 107 E12
Plumas, U.S.A. 112 F7
Plummer, U.S.A. 110 C5
Plumtree, Zimbabwe . . 83 G2
Plunge, Lithuania 9 J19
Pluvigner, France 24 E3
Plymouth, U.K. 13 G3
Plymouth, Calif., U.S.A. . 112 G6
Plymouth, Ind., U.S.A. . 104 E2
Plymouth, Mass., U.S.A. 107 E14
Plymouth, N.C., U.S.A. . 105 H7
Plymouth, N.H., U.S.A. . 107 C13
Plymouth, Pa., U.S.A. . . 107 E9
Plymouth, Wis., U.S.A. . 104 D2
Plynlimon = Pumlumon
Fawr, U.K. 13 E4
Plyusa, Russia 40 C5
Plyusa →, Russia 40 C5
Plyussa = Plyusa, Russia . 40 C5
Plyussa = Plyusa →,
Russia 40 C5
Plzeň, Czech. 20 F3
Pniewy, Poland 20 C6
Pô, Burkina Faso 79 C4
Po →, Italy 33 D9
Po, Foci del, Italy 33 D9
Po Hai = Bo Hai, China . 51 E10
Pobé, Benin 79 D5
Pobeda, Russia 45 C15

Pobedino, *Russia*	45	E15
Pobedy Pik, *Kyrgyzstan*	44	E8
Pobiedziska, *Poland*	20	C7
Pobla de Segur, *Spain*	28	C5
Pobladura de Valle, *Spain*	30	C5
Pocahontas, *Ark., U.S.A.*	109	G9
Pocahontas, *Iowa, U.S.A.*	108	D7
Pocatello, *U.S.A.*	110	E7
Pochep, *Russia*	41	F7
Pochinki, *Russia*	42	C7
Pochinok, *Russia*	40	E7
Pochutla, *Mexico*	115	D5
Poci, *Venezuela*	121	B5
Pocinhos, *Brazil*	122	C4
Pocito Casas, *Mexico*	114	B2
Poções, *Brazil*	123	D3
Pocomoke City, *U.S.A.*	104	F8
Poconé, *Brazil*	125	D6
Poços de Caldas, *Brazil*	127	A6
Poddębice, *Poland*	20	D8
Poděbrady, *Czech.*	20	E5
Podensac, *France*	26	D3
Podgorica, *Montenegro, Yug.*	21	N9
Podilska Vysochyna, *Ukraine*	41	H4
Podkamennaya Tunguska →, *Russia*	45	C10
Podlapac, *Croatia*	33	D12
Podolsk, *Russia*	42	C3
Podor, *Senegal*	78	B1
Podporozhy, *Russia*	40	B8
Podravska Slatina, *Croatia*	21	K7
Podujevo, *Serbia, Yug.*	21	N11
Poel, *Germany*	18	B7
Pofadder, *S. Africa*	84	D2
Pogamasing, *Canada*	98	C3
Poggiardo, *Italy*	35	B11
Poggibonsi, *Italy*	33	E8
Pogoanele, *Romania*	38	E9
Pogradeci, *Albania*	39	J3
Pogranitšnyi, *Russia*	48	B5
Poh, *Indonesia*	57	E6
Pohang, *S. Korea*	51	F15
Pohjanmaa, *Finland*	8	E20
Pohnpei, *Pac. Oc.*	92	G7
Pohorelá, *Slovak Rep.*	20	G10
Pohorje, *Slovenia*	33	B12
Poiana Mare, *Romania*	38	F6
Poinsett, C., *Antarctica*	5	C8
Point Edward, *Canada*	98	D3
Point Pedro, *Sri Lanka*	60	Q12
Point Pleasant, *N.J., U.S.A.*	107	F10
Point Pleasant, *W. Va., U.S.A.*	104	F4
Pointe-à-la-Hache, *U.S.A.*	109	L10
Pointe-à-Pitre, *Guadeloupe*	117	C7
Pointe Noire, *Congo*	80	E2
Poirino, *Italy*	32	D4
Poisonbush Ra., *Australia*	88	D3
Poissy, *France*	25	D9
Poitiers, *France*	24	F7
Poitou, *France*	26	B3
Poitou, Seuil du, *France*	26	B4
Poix de Picardie, *France*	25	C8
Poix-Terron, *France*	25	C11
Pojoaque Valley, *U.S.A.*	111	J11
Pokaran, *India*	60	F7
Pokataroo, *Australia*	91	D4
Pokhvistnevo, *Russia*	42	D11
Poko, *Sudan*	77	F3
Poko, *Zaïre*	82	B2
Pokrov, *Russia*	42	C4
Pokrovsk = Engels, *Russia*	42	E8
Pokrovsk, *Russia*	45	C13
Pokrovskoye, *Russia*	43	G4
Pol, *Spain*	30	B3
Pola = Pula, *Croatia*	33	D10
Pola, *Russia*	40	D7
Pola de Allande, *Spain*	30	B4
Pola de Lena, *Spain*	30	B5
Pola de Siero, *Spain*	30	B5
Pola de Somiedo, *Spain*	30	B4
Polacca, *U.S.A.*	111	J8
Polan, *Iran*	65	E9
Poland ■, *Europe*	20	C9
Polanów, *Poland*	20	A6
Polatlı, *Turkey*	66	C5
Polatsk, *Belarus*	40	E5
Polcura, *Chile*	126	D1
Polden Hills, *U.K.*	13	F5
Polessk, *Russia*	9	J19
Polesye = Pripet Marshes, *Europe*	41	F5
Polgar, *Hungary*	21	H11
Pŏlgyo-ri, *S. Korea*	51	G14
Poli, *Cameroon*	80	C2
Políaigos, *Greece*	39	N7
Policastro, G. di, *Italy*	35	C8
Police, *Poland*	20	B4
Polignano a Mare, *Italy*	35	B10
Poligny, *France*	25	F12
Políkhnitas, *Greece*	39	K9
Polillo Is., *Phil.*	55	D4
Polillo Strait, *Phil.*	55	D4
Polis, *Cyprus*	37	D11
Polístena, *Italy*	35	D9
Políyiros, *Greece*	39	J6
Polk, *U.S.A.*	106	E5
Polla, *Italy*	35	B8
Pollachi, *India*	60	P10
Pollensa, *Spain*	36	B10
Pollensa, B. de, *Spain*	36	B10
Póllica, *Italy*	35	B8
Pollino, Mte., *Italy*	35	C9
Pollock, *U.S.A.*	108	C4
Polna, *Russia*	40	C5
Polnovat, *Russia*	44	C7
Polo, *U.S.A.*	108	E10
Pology, *Ukraine*	41	J9
Polonne, *Ukraine*	41	G4
Polonnoye = Polonne, *Ukraine*	41	G4
Polson, *U.S.A.*	110	C6
Poltava, *Ukraine*	41	H8
Põltsamaa, *Estonia*	9	G21
Polunochnoye, *Russia*	44	C7
Põlva, *Estonia*	9	G22
Polynesia, *Pac. Oc.*	93	H11
Polynésie française = French Polynesia ■, *Pac. Oc.*	93	J13
Pomarance, *Italy*	32	E7
Pomárico, *Italy*	35	B9
Pomaro, *Mexico*	114	D4
Pombal, *Brazil*	122	C4
Pombal, *Portugal*	30	F2
Pómbia, *Greece*	37	D6
Pomeroy, *Ohio, U.S.A.*	104	F4
Pomeroy, *Wash., U.S.A.*	110	C5
Pomichna, *Ukraine*	41	H6
Pomona, *U.S.A.*	113	L9
Pomorie, *Bulgaria*	38	G10
Pomos, *Cyprus*	37	D11
Pomos, C., *Cyprus*	37	D11
Pompano Beach, *U.S.A.*	105	M5
Pompei, *Italy*	35	B7
Pompey, *France*	25	D13
Pompeys Pillar, *U.S.A.*	110	D10
Ponape = Pohnpei, *Pac. Oc.*	92	G7
Ponask, L., *Canada*	98	B1
Ponass L., *Canada*	101	C8
Ponca, *U.S.A.*	108	D6
Ponca City, *U.S.A.*	109	G6
Ponce, *Puerto Rico*	117	C6
Ponchatoula, *U.S.A.*	109	K9
Poncheville, L., *Canada*	98	B4
Poncin, *France*	27	B9
Pond, *U.S.A.*	113	K7
Pond Inlet, *Canada*	97	A12
Pondicherry, *India*	60	P11
Pondrôme, *Belgium*	17	H6
Ponds, I. of, *Canada*	99	B8
Ponferrada, *Spain*	30	C4
Pongo, Wadi →, *Sudan*	77	F2
Pongo, Wadi →, *Sudan*	77	F2
Ponnyadaung, *Burma*	61	J19
Ponoka, *Canada*	100	C6
Ponorogo, *Indonesia*	57	G14
Ponoy, →, *Russia*	44	C5
Pons, *France*	26	C3
Pons, *Spain*	28	D6
Ponsul →, *Portugal*	31	F3
Pont-à-Celles, *Belgium*	17	G4
Pont-à-Mousson, *France*	25	D13
Pont-Audemer, *France*	24	C7
Pont-Aven, *France*	24	E3
Pont Canavese, *Italy*	32	C4
Pont-de-Roide, *France*	25	E13
Pont-de-Salars, *France*	26	D6
Pont-de-Vaux, *France*	25	F11
Pont-de-Veyle, *France*	27	B8
Pont-l'Abbé, *France*	24	E2
Pont-l'Évêque, *France*	24	C7
Pont-St.-Esprit, *France*	27	D8
Pont-Saint-Martin, *Italy*	32	C4
Pont-sur-Yonne, *France*	25	D10
Ponta de Pedras, *Brazil*	122	B2
Ponta do Sol, *Madeira*	36	D2
Ponta Grossa, *Brazil*	127	B5
Ponta Pora, *Brazil*	127	A4
Pontacq, *France*	26	E3
Pontailler-sur-Saône, *France*	25	E12
Pontal →, *Brazil*	122	C3
Pontalina, *Brazil*	123	E2
Pontarlier, *France*	25	F13
Pontassieve, *Italy*	33	E8
Pontaubault, *France*	24	D5
Pontaumur, *France*	26	C6
Pontcharra, *France*	27	C10
Pontchartrain L., *U.S.A.*	109	K9
Pontchâteau, *France*	24	E4
Ponte Alta, Serra do, *Brazil*	123	E2
Ponte Alta do Norte, *Brazil*	122	D2
Ponte Branca, *Brazil*	125	D7
Ponte da Barca, *Portugal*	30	D2
Ponte de Sor, *Portugal*	31	F3
Ponte dell'Ólio, *Italy*	32	D6
Ponte di Legno, *Italy*	32	B7
Ponte do Lima, *Portugal*	30	D2
Ponte do Pungué, *Mozam.*	83	F3
Ponte-Leccia, *France*	27	F13
Ponte nelle Alpi, *Italy*	33	B9
Ponte Nova, *Brazil*	123	F3
Ponte San Pietro, *Italy*	32	C6
Pontebba, *Italy*	33	B10
Pontecorvo, *Italy*	34	A6
Pontedera, *Italy*	32	E7
Pontefract, *U.K.*	12	D6
Ponteix, *Canada*	101	D7
Pontelandolfo, *Italy*	35	A7
Pontevedra, *Spain*	30	C2
Pontevedra □, *Spain*	30	C2
Pontevedra, R. de →, *Spain*	30	C2
Pontévico, *Italy*	32	C7
Ponthierville = Ubundu, *Zaïre*		
Pontiac, *Ill., U.S.A.*	108	E10
Pontiac, *Mich., U.S.A.*	104	D4
Pontian Kecil, *Malaysia*	59	M4
Pontianak, *Indonesia*	56	E3
Pontic Mts. = Kuzey Anadolu Dağları, *Turkey*	66	B7
Pontine Is. = Ponziane, Ísole, *Italy*	34	B5
Pontine Mts. = Kuzey Anadolu Dağları, *Turkey*	66	B7
Pontínia, *Italy*	34	A6
Pontivy, *France*	24	D4
Pontoise, *France*	25	C9
Ponton →, *Canada*	100	B5
Pontorson, *France*	24	D5
Pontrémoli, *Italy*	32	D6
Pontresina, *Switz.*	23	D9
Pontrieux, *France*	24	D3
Pontypool, *Canada*	106	B6
Pontypool, *U.K.*	13	F4
Pontypridd, *U.K.*	13	F4
Ponza, *Italy*	34	B5
Ponziane, Ísole, *Italy*	34	B5
Poochera, *Australia*	91	E1
Poole, *U.K.*	13	G6
Pooley I., *Canada*	100	C3
Poona = Pune, *India*	60	K8
Pooncarie, *Australia*	91	E3
Poopelloe L., *Australia*	91	E3
Poopó, *Bolivia*	124	D4
Poopó, L. de, *Bolivia*	124	D4
Popanyinning, *Australia*	89	F2
Popayán, *Colombia*	120	C2
Poperinge, *Belgium*	17	G1
Popilta, L., *Australia*	91	E3
Popio L., *Australia*	91	E3
Poplar, *U.S.A.*	108	A2
Poplar →, *Man., Canada*	101	C9
Poplar →, *N.W.T., Canada*	100	A4
Poplar Bluff, *U.S.A.*	109	G9
Poplarville, *U.S.A.*	109	K10
Popocatépetl, Volcán, *Mexico*	115	D5
Popokabaka, *Zaïre*	80	F3
Pópoli, *Italy*	33	F10
Popovača, *Croatia*	33	C13
Popovo, *Bulgaria*	38	F9
Poppel, *Belgium*	17	F6
Poprád, *Slovak Rep.*	20	F10
Poprád →, *Slovak Rep.*	20	F10
Porali →, *Pakistan*	62	G2
Porangaba, *Brazil*	124	B3
Porangatu, *Brazil*	123	D2
Porbandar, *India*	62	J3
Porce →, *Colombia*	120	B3
Porcher I., *Canada*	100	C2
Porco, *Bolivia*	125	D4
Porcos →, *Brazil*	123	D2
Porcuna, *Spain*	31	H6
Porcupine →, *Canada*	101	B8
Porcupine →, *U.S.A.*	96	B5
Pordenone, *Italy*	33	C9
Poreč, *Croatia*	33	C10
Porecatu, *Brazil*	123	F1
Poretskoye, *Russia*	42	C8
Pori, *Finland*	9	F19
Porkhov, *Russia*	40	D5
Porlamar, *Venezuela*	121	A5
Porlezza, *Italy*	32	B6
Porma →, *Spain*	30	C5
Pornic, *France*	24	E4
Poronaysk, *Russia*	45	E15
Póros, *Greece*	39	M6
Poroshiri-Dake, *Japan*	48	C11
Poroto Mts., *Tanzania*	83	D3
Porpoise B., *Antarctica*	5	C9
Porquerolles, I. de, *France*	27	F10
Porrentruy, *Switz.*	22	B4
Porreras, *Spain*	36	B10
Porretta, Passo di, *Italy*	32	D7
Porsangen, *Norway*	8	A21
Porsgrunn, *Norway*	10	E3
Port Adelaide, *Australia*	91	E2
Port Alberni, *Canada*	100	D4
Port Alfred, *Canada*	99	C5
Port Alfred, *S. Africa*	84	E4
Port Alice, *Canada*	100	C3
Port Allegany, *U.S.A.*	106	E6
Port Allen, *U.S.A.*	109	K9
Port Alma, *Australia*	90	C5
Port Angeles, *U.S.A.*	112	B3
Port Antonio, *Jamaica*	116	C4
Port Aransas, *U.S.A.*	109	M6
Port Arthur = Lüshun, *China*	51	E11
Port Arthur, *Australia*	90	G4
Port Arthur, *U.S.A.*	109	L8
Port au Port B., *Canada*	99	C8
Port-au-Prince, *Haiti*	117	C5
Port Augusta, *Australia*	91	E2
Port Augusta West, *Australia*	91	E2
Port Austin, *U.S.A.*	98	D3
Port Bell, *Uganda*	82	B3
Port Bergé Vaovao, *Madag.*	85	B8
Port Blandford, *Canada*	99	C9
Port Bou, *Spain*	28	C8
Port Bouët, *Ivory C.*	78	D4
Port Bradshaw, *Australia*	90	A2
Port Broughton, *Australia*	91	E2
Port Burwell, *Canada*	98	D3
Port Canning, *India*	63	H13
Port-Cartier, *Canada*	99	B6
Port Chalmers, *N.Z.*	87	L3
Port Chester, *U.S.A.*	107	F11
Port Clements, *Canada*	100	C2
Port Clinton, *U.S.A.*	104	E4
Port Colborne, *Canada*	98	D4
Port Coquitlam, *Canada*	100	D4
Port Credit, *Canada*	106	C5
Port Curtis, *Australia*	90	C5
Port Dalhousie, *Canada*	106	C5
Port Darwin, *Australia*	88	B5
Port Darwin, *Falk. Is.*	128	D5
Port Davey, *Australia*	90	G4
Port-de-Bouc, *France*	27	E8
Port-de-Paix, *Haiti*	117	C5
Port Dickson, *Malaysia*	59	L3
Port Douglas, *Australia*	90	B4
Port Dover, *Canada*	106	D4
Port Edward, *Canada*	100	C2
Port Elgin, *Canada*	98	D3
Port Elizabeth, *S. Africa*	84	E4
Port Ellen, *U.K.*	14	F2
Port-en-Bessin, *France*	24	C6
Port Erin, *U.K.*	12	C3
Port Essington, *Australia*	88	B5
Port Etienne = Nouâdhibou, *Mauritania*	74	D1
Port Fairy, *Australia*	91	F3
Port Fouâd = Bûr Fuad, *Egypt*	76	H8
Port Gamble, *U.S.A.*	112	C4
Port-Gentil, *Gabon*	80	E1
Port Gibson, *U.S.A.*	109	K9
Port Glasgow, *U.K.*	14	F4
Port Harcourt, *Nigeria*	79	E6
Port Hardy, *Canada*	100	C3
Port Harrison = Inukjuak, *Canada*	97	C12
Port Hawkesbury, *Canada*	99	C7
Port Hedland, *Australia*	88	D2
Port Henry, *U.S.A.*	107	B11
Port Hood, *Canada*	99	C7
Port Hope, *Canada*	98	D4
Port Hueneme, *U.S.A.*	113	L7
Port Huron, *U.S.A.*	104	D4
Port Iliç, *Azerbaijan*	67	C13
Port Isabel, *U.S.A.*	109	M6
Port Jefferson, *U.S.A.*	107	F11
Port Jervis, *U.S.A.*	107	E10
Port-Joinville, *France*	24	F4
Port Katon, *Russia*	43	G4
Port Kelang = Pelabuhan Kelang, *Malaysia*	59	L3
Port Kembla, *Australia*	91	E5
Port Kenny, *Australia*	91	E1
Port-la-Nouvelle, *France*	26	E7
Port Laoise, *Ireland*	15	C4
Port Lavaca, *U.S.A.*	109	L6
Port-Leucate, *France*	26	F7
Port Lincoln, *Australia*	91	E2
Port Loko, *S. Leone*	78	D2
Port Louis, *France*	24	E3
Port Lyautey = Kenitra, *Morocco*	74	B3
Port MacDonnell, *Australia*	91	F3
Port Macquarie, *Australia*	91	E5
Port Maria, *Jamaica*	116	C4
Port Mellon, *Canada*	100	D4
Port-Menier, *Canada*	99	C7
Port Morant, *Jamaica*	116	C4
Port Moresby, *Papua N. G.*	92	H6
Port Mourant, *Guyana*	121	B6
Port Mouton, *Canada*	99	D7
Port Musgrave, *Australia*	90	A3
Port-Navalo, *France*	24	E4
Port Nelson, *Canada*	101	B10
Port Nolloth, *S. Africa*	84	D2
Port Nouveau-Québec = Kangiqsualujjuaq, *Canada*	97	C13
Port O'Connor, *U.S.A.*	109	L6
Port of Spain, *Trin. & Tob.*	117	D7
Port Orchard, *U.S.A.*	112	C4
Port Orford, *U.S.A.*	110	E1
Port Pegasus, *N.Z.*	87	M1
Port Perry, *Canada*	98	D4
Port Phillip B., *Australia*	91	F3
Port Pirie, *Australia*	91	E2
Port Radium = Echo Bay, *Canada*	96	B8
Port Renfrew, *Canada*	100	D4
Port Roper, *Australia*	90	A2
Port Rowan, *Canada*	98	D3
Port Safaga = Bûr Safâga, *Egypt*	76	B3
Port Said = Bûr Sa'îd, *Egypt*	76	H8
Port St. Joe, *U.S.A.*	105	L3
Port St. Johns, *S. Africa*	85	E4
Port-St.-Louis-du-Rhône, *France*	27	E8
Port San Vicente, *Phil.*	55	B5
Port Sanilac, *U.S.A.*	98	D3
Port Saunders, *Canada*	99	B8
Port Severn, *Canada*	106	B5
Port Shepstone, *S. Africa*	85	E5
Port Simpson, *Canada*	100	C2
Port Stanley = Stanley, *Falk. Is.*	128	D5
Port Stanley, *Canada*	98	D3
Port Sudan = Bûr Sûdân, *Sudan*	76	D4
Port-sur-Saône, *France*	25	E13
Port Talbot, *U.K.*	13	F4
Port Taufiq = Bûr Taufiq, *Egypt*	76	J8
Port Townsend, *U.S.A.*	112	B4
Port-Vendres, *France*	26	F7
Port Wakefield, *Australia*	91	E2
Port Washington, *U.S.A.*	104	D2
Port Weld, *Malaysia*	59	K3
Portachuelo, *Bolivia*	125	D5
Portadown, *U.K.*	15	B5
Portage, *U.S.A.*	108	D10
Portage La Prairie, *Canada*	101	D9
Portageville, *U.S.A.*	109	G10
Portalegre, *Portugal*	31	F3
Portalegre □, *Portugal*	31	F3
Portales, *U.S.A.*	109	H3
Portarlington, *Ireland*	15	C4
Porteirinha, *Brazil*	123	E3
Portel, *Brazil*	122	B1
Portel, *Portugal*	31	G3
Porter L., *N.W.T., Canada*	101	A7
Porter L., *Sask., Canada*	101	B7
Porterville, *S. Africa*	84	E2
Porterville, *U.S.A.*	111	H4
Porthcawl, *U.K.*	13	F4
Porthill, *U.S.A.*	110	B5
Portile de Fier, *Europe*	38	E5
Portimão, *Portugal*	31	H2
Portland, *N.S.W., Australia*	91	E4
Portland, *Vic., Australia*	91	F3
Portland, *Canada*	107	B8
Portland, *Conn., U.S.A.*	107	E12
Portland, *Maine, U.S.A.*	99	D5
Portland, *Mich., U.S.A.*	104	D3
Portland, *Oreg., U.S.A.*	112	E4
Portland, I. of, *U.K.*	13	G5
Portland B., *Australia*	91	F3
Portland Bill, *U.K.*	13	G5
Portland Prom., *Canada*	97	C12
Portlands Roads, *Australia*	90	A3
Portneuf, *Canada*	99	C5
Pôrto, *Brazil*	122	B2
Porto, *France*	27	F12
Porto, *Portugal*	30	D2
Porto □, *Portugal*	30	D2
Porto, G. de, *France*	27	F12
Pôrto Acre, *Brazil*	124	B4
Pôrto Alegre, *Pará, Brazil*	121	D7
Pôrto Alegre, *Rio Grande do S., Brazil*	127	C5
Porto Amboim = Gunza, *Angola*	80	G2
Porto Argentera, *Italy*	32	D4
Porto Azzurro, *Italy*	32	F7
Porto Botte, *Italy*	34	C1
Pôrto Cajueiro, *Brazil*	125	C6
Porto Civitanova, *Italy*	33	E10
Porto Cristo, *Spain*	36	B10
Pôrto da Fôlha, *Brazil*	122	C4
Pôrto de Móz, *Brazil*	121	D7
Pôrto de Pedras, *Brazil*	122	C4
Pôrto des Meinacos, *Brazil*	125	C7
Pôrto Empédocle, *Italy*	34	E6
Pôrto Esperança, *Brazil*	125	D6
Pôrto Esperidão, *Brazil*	125	D6
Pôrto Franco, *Brazil*	122	C2
Porto Garibaldi, *Italy*	33	D9
Pôrto Grande, *Brazil*	121	C7
Pôrto Jofre, *Brazil*	125	D6
Pórto Lágo, *Greece*	39	J8
Porto Mendes, *Brazil*	127	A5
Porto Moniz, *Madeira*	36	D2
Pôrto Murtinho, *Brazil*	125	E6
Pôrto Nacional, *Brazil*	122	D2
Porto Novo, *Benin*	79	D5
Porto Petro, *Spain*	36	B10
Porto Recanati, *Italy*	33	E10
Pôrto San Giórgio, *Italy*	33	E10
Pôrto Santana, *Brazil*	121	D7
Porto Santo, *Madeira*	72	B1
Porto Santo Stéfano, *Italy*	32	F8
Pôrto São José, *Brazil*	127	A5
Pôrto Seguro, *Brazil*	123	E4
Porto Tolle, *Italy*	33	D9
Pôrto Tórres, *Italy*	34	B1
Pôrto União, *Brazil*	127	B5
Pôrto Válter, *Brazil*	124	B3
Porto-Vecchio, *France*	27	G13
Pôrto Velho, *Brazil*	125	B5
Portobelo, *Panama*	116	E4
Portoferráio, *Italy*	32	F7
Portogruaro, *Italy*	33	C9
Portola, *U.S.A.*	112	F6
Portomaggiore, *Italy*	33	D8
Portoscuso, *Italy*	34	C1
Portovénere, *Italy*	32	D6
Portoviejo, *Ecuador*	120	D1
Portpatrick, *U.K.*	14	G3
Portree, *U.K.*	14	D2
Portrush, *U.K.*	15	A5
Portsall, *France*	24	D2
Portsmouth, *Domin.*	117	C7
Portsmouth, *U.K.*	13	G6
Portsmouth, *N.H., U.S.A.*	107	C14
Portsmouth, *Ohio, U.S.A.*	104	F4
Portsmouth, *R.I., U.S.A.*	107	E13
Portsmouth, *Va., U.S.A.*	104	G7
Portsoy, *U.K.*	14	D6
Porttipahtan tekojärvi, *Finland*	8	B22
Portugal ■, *Europe*	30	F3
Portugalete, *Spain*	28	B1
Portuguesa □, *Venezuela*	120	B4
Portumna, *Ireland*	15	C3
Portville, *U.S.A.*	106	D6
Porvenir, *Bolivia*	124	C4
Porvenir, *Chile*	128	D2
Porvoo, *Finland*	9	F21
Porzuna, *Spain*	31	F6
Posada →, *Italy*	34	B2
Posadas, *Argentina*	127	B4
Posadas, *Spain*	31	H5
Poschiavo, *Switz.*	23	D10

Place	Region	Page	Grid
Posets,	*Spain*	28	C5
Poshan = Boshan,	*China*	51	F9
Posht-e-Badam,	*Iran*	65	C7
Posídhion, Ákra,	*Greece*	39	K6
Poso,	*Indonesia*	57	E6
Posoegroenoe,	*Surinam*	121	C6
Posong,	*S. Korea*	51	G14
Posse,	*Brazil*	123	D2
Possel,	*C.A.R.*	80	C3
Possession I.,	*Antarctica*	5	D11
Pössneck,	*Germany*	18	E7
Post,	*U.S.A.*	109	J4
Post Falls,	*U.S.A.*	110	C5
Postavy = Pastavy,	*Belarus*	9	J22
Poste Maurice Cortier,	*Algeria*	75	D5
Postmasburg,	*S. Africa*	84	D3
Postojna,	*Slovenia*	33	C11
Poston,	*U.S.A.*	113	M12
Potchefstroom,	*S. Africa*	84	D4
Poté,	*Brazil*	123	E3
Poteau,	*U.S.A.*	109	H7
Poteet,	*U.S.A.*	109	L5
Potelu, Lacul,	*Romania*	38	F7
Potenza,	*Italy*	35	B8
Potenza →,	*Italy*	33	E10
Potenza Picena,	*Italy*	33	E10
Poteriteri, L.,	*N.Z.*	87	M1
Potes,	*Spain*	30	B6
Potgietersrus,	*S. Africa*	85	C4
Poti,	*Georgia*	43	J5
Potiraguá,	*Brazil*	123	E4
Potiskum,	*Nigeria*	79	C7
Potomac →,	*U.S.A.*	104	F7
Potosí,	*Bolivia*	125	D4
Potosí □,	*Bolivia*	124	E4
Potosi Mt.,	*U.S.A.*	113	K11
Pototan,	*Phil.*	55	F5
Potrerillos,	*Chile*	126	B2
Potsdam,	*Germany*	18	C9
Potsdam,	*U.S.A.*	107	B10
Pottenstein,	*Germany*	19	F7
Potter,	*U.S.A.*	108	E3
Pottery Hill = Abû Ballas,	*Egypt*	76	C2
Pottstown,	*U.S.A.*	107	F9
Pottsville,	*U.S.A.*	107	F8
Pottuvil,	*Sri Lanka*	60	R12
Pouancé,	*France*	24	E5
Pouce Coupé,	*Canada*	100	B4
Poughkeepsie,	*U.S.A.*	107	E11
Pouilly-sur-Loire,	*France*	25	E9
Poulaphouca Res.,	*Ireland*	15	C5
Poulsbo,	*U.S.A.*	112	C4
Pourri, Mt.,	*France*	27	C10
Pouso Alegre, *Mato Grosso,*	*Brazil*	125	C6
Pouso Alegre, *Minas Gerais,*	*Brazil*	127	A6
Pouzauges,	*France*	24	F6
Povenets,	*Russia*	44	C4
Poverty B.,	*N.Z.*	87	H7
Póvoa de Lanhosa,	*Portugal*	30	D2
Póvoa de Varzim,	*Portugal*	30	D2
Povorino,	*Russia*	42	E6
Powassan,	*Canada*	98	C4
Poway,	*U.S.A.*	113	N9
Powder →,	*U.S.A.*	108	B2
Powder River,	*U.S.A.*	110	E10
Powell,	*U.S.A.*	110	D9
Powell L.,	*U.S.A.*	111	H8
Powell River,	*Canada*	100	D4
Powers, *Mich.,*	*U.S.A.*	104	C2
Powers, *Oreg.,*	*U.S.A.*	110	E1
Powers Lake,	*U.S.A.*	108	A3
Powys □,	*U.K.*	13	E4
Poxoreu,	*Brazil*	125	D7
Poyang Hu,	*China*	53	C11
Poyarkovo,	*Russia*	45	E13
Poza de la Sal,	*Spain*	28	C1
Poza Rica,	*Mexico*	115	C5
Pozanti,	*Turkey*	66	D6
Požarevac, *Serbia,*	*Yug.*	21	L11
Pozi,	*Taiwan*	53	F13
Poznań,	*Poland*	20	C6
Pozo,	*U.S.A.*	113	K6
Pozo Alcón,	*Spain*	29	H2
Pozo Almonte,	*Chile*	124	E4
Pozo Colorado,	*Paraguay*	126	A4
Pozo del Dátil,	*Mexico*	114	B2
Pozoblanco,	*Spain*	31	G5
Pozuzo,	*Peru*	124	C2
Pozzallo,	*Italy*	35	F7
Pozzuoli,	*Italy*	35	B7
Pra →,	*Ghana*	79	D4
Prachin Buri,	*Thailand*	58	E3
Prachuap Khiri Khan,	*Thailand*	59	G2
Pradelles,	*France*	26	D7
Pradera,	*Colombia*	120	C2
Prades,	*France*	26	F6
Prado,	*Brazil*	123	E4
Prado del Rey,	*Spain*	31	J5
Præstø,	*Denmark*	11	J6
Pragersko,	*Slovenia*	33	B12
Prague = Praha,	*Czech.*	20	E4
Praha,	*Czech.*	20	E4
Prahecq,	*France*	26	B3
Prahova □,	*Romania*	38	E8
Prahovo, *Serbia,*	*Yug.*	21	L12
Praid,	*Romania*	38	C8
Prainha, *Amazonas,*	*Brazil*	125	B6
Prainha, *Pará,*	*Brazil*	121	D7
Prairie,	*Australia*	90	C3
Prairie →,	*U.S.A.*	109	H5
Prairie City,	*U.S.A.*	110	D4
Prairie du Chien,	*U.S.A.*	108	D9
Prairies,	*Canada*	96	C9
Pramánda,	*Greece*	39	K4
Pran Buri,	*Thailand*	58	F2
Prang,	*Ghana*	79	D4
Prapat,	*Indonesia*	56	D1
Prasonísi, Ákra,	*Greece*	37	D9
Prata,	*Brazil*	123	E2
Pratapgarh,	*India*	62	G6
Prática di Mare,	*Italy*	34	A5
Prätigau,	*Switz.*	23	C9
Prato,	*Italy*	32	E8
Prátola Peligna,	*Italy*	33	F10
Pratovécchio,	*Italy*	33	E8
Prats-de-Mollo-la-Preste,	*France*	26	F6
Pratt,	*U.S.A.*	109	G5
Pratteln,	*Switz.*	22	A5
Prattville,	*U.S.A.*	105	J2
Pravdinsk,	*Russia*	42	B6
Pravia,	*Spain*	30	B4
Praya,	*Indonesia*	56	F5
Pré-en-Pail,	*France*	24	D6
Pré-Saint-Didier,	*Italy*	32	C4
Precordillera,	*Argentina*	126	C2
Predáppio,	*Italy*	33	D8
Predazzo,	*Italy*	33	B8
Predejane, *Serbia,*	*Yug.*	21	N12
Preeceville,	*Canada*	101	C8
Préfailles,	*France*	24	E4
Pregonero,	*Venezuela*	120	B3
Pregrada,	*Croatia*	33	B12
Preiļi,	*Latvia*	9	H22
Preko,	*Croatia*	33	D12
Prelate,	*Canada*	101	C7
Prelog,	*Croatia*	33	B13
Premer,	*Canada*	100	B3
Premont,	*U.S.A.*	109	M5
Premuda,	*Croatia*	33	D11
Prenjasi,	*Albania*	39	H3
Prentice,	*U.S.A.*	108	C9
Prenzlau,	*Germany*	18	B9
Preobrazheniye,	*Russia*	48	C6
Preparis North Channel,	*Ind. Oc.*	61	M18
Preparis South Channel,	*Ind. Oc.*	61	M18
Přerov,	*Czech.*	20	F7
Presanella,	*Italy*	32	B7
Prescott,	*Canada*	98	D4
Prescott, *Ariz.,*	*U.S.A.*	111	J7
Prescott, *Ark.,*	*U.S.A.*	109	J8
Preservation Inlet,	*N.Z.*	87	M1
Preševo, *Serbia,*	*Yug.*	21	N11
Presho,	*U.S.A.*	108	D4
Presicce,	*Italy*	35	C11
Presidencia de la Plaza,	*Argentina*	126	B4
Presidencia Roque Saenz Peña,	*Argentina*	126	B3
Presidente Epitácio,	*Brazil*	123	F1
Presidente Hayes □,	*Paraguay*	126	A4
Presidente Hermes,	*Brazil*	125	C5
Presidente Prudente,	*Brazil*	127	A5
Presidio,	*Mexico*	114	B4
Presidio,	*U.S.A.*	109	L2
Preslav,	*Bulgaria*	38	F9
Prešov,	*Slovak Rep.*	20	F11
Prespa, L. = Prespansko Jezero,	*Macedonia*	39	J4
Prespansko Jezero,	*Macedonia*	39	J4
Presque Isle,	*U.S.A.*	99	C6
Prestbury,	*U.K.*	13	F5
Prestea,	*Ghana*	78	D4
Presteigne,	*U.K.*	13	E5
Presto,	*Bolivia*	125	D5
Preston,	*Canada*	106	C4
Preston,	*U.K.*	12	D5
Preston, *Idaho,*	*U.S.A.*	110	E8
Preston, *Minn.,*	*U.S.A.*	108	D8
Preston, *Nev.,*	*U.S.A.*	110	G6
Preston, C.,	*Australia*	88	D2
Prestonpans,	*U.K.*	14	F6
Prestwick,	*U.K.*	14	F4
Prêto →, *Amazonas,*	*Brazil*	121	D5
Prêto →, *Bahia,*	*Brazil*	122	D3
Prêto do Igapó-Açu →,	*Brazil*	121	D6
Pretoria,	*S. Africa*	85	D4
Preuilly-sur-Claise,	*France*	24	F7
Préveza,	*Greece*	39	L3
Priazovskoye,	*Ukraine*	41	J8
Pribilof Is.,	*Bering S.*	4	D17
Priboj, *Serbia,*	*Yug.*	21	M9
Příbram,	*Czech.*	20	F4
Price,	*U.S.A.*	110	G8
Price I.,	*Canada*	100	C3
Prichard,	*U.S.A.*	105	K1
Priego,	*Spain*	28	E2
Priego de Córdoba,	*Spain*	31	H6
Priekule,	*Latvia*	9	H19
Prien,	*Germany*	19	H8
Prienai,	*Lithuania*	9	J20
Prieska,	*S. Africa*	84	D3
Priest →,	*U.S.A.*	110	B5
Priest L.,	*U.S.A.*	110	B5
Priest Valley,	*U.S.A.*	111	J6
Priestly,	*Canada*	100	C3
Prievidza,	*Slovak Rep.*	20	G8
Prijedor,	*Bos.-H.*	33	D13
Prikaspiyskaya Nizmennost = Caspian Depression,	*Eurasia*	43	G9
Prikubanskaya Nizmennost,	*Russia*	43	H4
Prilep,	*Macedonia*	39	H4
Priluki = Pryluky,	*Ukraine*	41	G7
Prime Seal I.,	*Australia*	90	G4
Primeira Cruz,	*Brazil*	122	B3
Primorsk,	*Russia*	40	B5
Primorsko-Akhtarsk,	*Russia*	43	G4
Primorskoye,	*Ukraine*	41	J9
Primrose L.,	*Canada*	101	C7
Prince Albert,	*Canada*	101	C7
Prince Albert,	*S. Africa*	84	E3
Prince Albert Mts.,	*Antarctica*	5	D11
Prince Albert Nat. Park,	*Canada*	101	C7
Prince Albert Pen.,	*Canada*	96	A8
Prince Albert Sd.,	*Canada*	96	A8
Prince Alfred, C.,	*Canada*	4	B1
Prince Charles I.,	*Canada*	97	B12
Prince Charles Mts.,	*Antarctica*	5	D6
Prince Edward I. □,	*Canada*	99	C7
Prince Edward Is.,	*Ind. Oc.*	3	G11
Prince George,	*Canada*	100	C4
Prince of Wales, C.,	*U.S.A.*	94	C3
Prince of Wales I.,	*Australia*	90	A3
Prince of Wales I.,	*Canada*	96	A10
Prince of Wales I.,	*U.S.A.*	100	B2
Prince Patrick I.,	*Canada*	4	B2
Prince Regent Inlet,	*Canada*	4	B3
Prince Rupert,	*Canada*	100	C2
Princenhage,	*Neths.*	17	F5
Princesa Isabel,	*Brazil*	122	C4
Princess Charlotte B.,	*Australia*	90	A3
Princess May Ras.,	*Australia*	88	C4
Princess Royal I.,	*Canada*	100	C3
Princeton,	*Canada*	100	D4
Princeton, *Calif.,*	*U.S.A.*	112	F4
Princeton, *Ill.,*	*U.S.A.*	108	E10
Princeton, *Ind.,*	*U.S.A.*	104	F2
Princeton, *Ky.,*	*U.S.A.*	104	G2
Princeton, *Mo.,*	*U.S.A.*	108	E8
Princeton, *N.J.,*	*U.S.A.*	107	F10
Princeton, *W. Va.,*	*U.S.A.*	104	G5
Principe, I. de,	*Atl. Oc.*	70	F4
Principe Chan.,	*Canada*	100	C2
Principe da Beira,	*Brazil*	125	C5
Prineville,	*U.S.A.*	110	D3
Prins Harald Kyst,	*Antarctica*	5	D4
Prinsesse Astrid Kyst,	*Antarctica*	5	D3
Prinsesse Ragnhild Kyst,	*Antarctica*	5	D4
Prinzapolca,	*Nic.*	116	D3
Prior, C.,	*Spain*	30	B2
Priozersk,	*Russia*	40	B6
Pripet = Prypyat →,	*Europe*	41	G6
Pripet Marshes,	*Europe*	41	F5
Pripyat Marshes = Pripet Marshes,	*Europe*	41	F5
Pripyats = Prypyat →,	*Europe*	41	G6
Prislop, Pasul,	*Romania*	38	B8
Pristen,	*Russia*	42	E3
Priština, *Serbia,*	*Yug.*	21	N11
Pritzwalk,	*Germany*	18	B8
Privas,	*France*	27	D8
Priverno,	*Italy*	34	A6
Privolzhsk,	*Russia*	42	B5
Privolzhskaya Vozvyshennost,	*Russia*	42	E7
Privolzhskiy,	*Russia*	42	E8
Privolzhye,	*Russia*	42	D9
Priyutnoye,	*Russia*	43	G6
Prizren, *Serbia,*	*Yug.*	21	N10
Prizzi,	*Italy*	34	E6
Prnjavor,	*Bos.-H.*	21	L7
Probolinggo,	*Indonesia*	57	G15
Próchromos,	*Cyprus*	37	E11
Proddatur,	*India*	60	M11
Prodhromos,	*Cyprus*	37	E11
Proença-a-Nova,	*Portugal*	31	F3
Prof. Van Blommestein Meer,	*Surinam*	121	C6
Profítis Ilías,	*Greece*	37	C9
Profondeville,	*Belgium*	17	H5
Progreso,	*Mexico*	115	C7
Prohladnyy,	*Russia*	43	J7
Prokletije,	*Albania*	38	G2
Prokopyevsk,	*Russia*	44	D9
Prokuplje, *Serbia,*	*Yug.*	21	M11
Proletarsk,	*Russia*	43	G5
Proletarskaya = Proletarsk,	*Russia*	43	G5
Prome = Pyè,	*Burma*	61	K19
Prophet →,	*Canada*	100	B4
Propriá,	*Brazil*	122	D4
Propriano,	*France*	27	G12
Proserpine,	*Australia*	90	C4
Proston,	*Australia*	91	D5
Prosser,	*U.S.A.*	110	C4
Prostějov,	*Czech.*	20	F7
Protection,	*U.S.A.*	109	G5
Próti,	*Greece*	39	M4
Provadiya,	*Bulgaria*	38	F10
Proven,	*Belgium*	17	G1
Provence,	*France*	27	E9
Providence, *Ky.,*	*U.S.A.*	104	G2
Providence, *R.I.,*	*U.S.A.*	107	E13
Providence Bay,	*Canada*	98	C3
Providence Mts.,	*U.S.A.*	111	J6
Providencia,	*Ecuador*	120	D2
Providencia, I. de,	*Colombia*	116	D3
Provideniya,	*Russia*	45	C19
Provins,	*France*	25	D10
Provo,	*U.S.A.*	110	F8
Provost,	*Canada*	101	C6
Prozor,	*Bos.-H.*	21	M7
Prudentópolis,	*Brazil*	123	G1
Prud'homme,	*Canada*	101	C7
Prudnik,	*Poland*	20	E7
Prüm,	*Germany*	19	E2
Pruszcz Gdański,	*Poland*	20	A8
Pruszków,	*Poland*	20	C10
Prut →,	*Romania*	38	D11
Pruzhany,	*Belarus*	41	F3
Prvić,	*Croatia*	33	D11
Prydz B.,	*Antarctica*	5	C6
Pryluky,	*Ukraine*	41	G7
Pryor,	*U.S.A.*	109	G7
Prypyat →,	*Europe*	41	G6
Przasnysz,	*Poland*	20	B10
Przedbórz,	*Poland*	20	D9
Przemyśl,	*Poland*	20	F12
Przeworsk,	*Poland*	20	E12
Przewóz,	*Poland*	20	D4
Przhevalsk,	*Kyrgyzstan*	44	E8
Przysuchla,	*Poland*	20	D10
Psakhná,	*Greece*	39	L6
Psará,	*Greece*	39	L8
Psel →,	*Ukraine*	41	H7
Pserimos,	*Greece*	39	N10
Psíra,	*Greece*	37	D7
Pskov,	*Russia*	40	D5
Pskovskoye, Ozero,	*Russia*	9	H22
Psunj,	*Croatia*	21	K7
Pszczyna,	*Poland*	20	F8
Pteleón,	*Greece*	39	K5
Ptich = Ptsich →,	*Belarus*	41	F5
Ptolemaís,	*Greece*	39	J4
Ptsich →,	*Belarus*	41	F5
Ptuj,	*Slovenia*	33	B12
Ptujska Gora,	*Slovenia*	33	B12
Pu Xian,	*China*	50	F6
Pua,	*Thailand*	58	C3
Puán,	*Argentina*	126	D3
Pu'an,	*China*	52	E5
Pubei,	*China*	52	F7
Pucacuro →,	*Peru*	120	D3
Pucallpa,	*Peru*	124	B3
Pucará,	*Bolivia*	125	D5
Pucará,	*Peru*	124	C3
Pucarani,	*Bolivia*	124	D4
Pucheng,	*China*	53	D12
Pučišće,	*Croatia*	33	E13
Pucka, Zatoka,	*Poland*	20	A8
Puding,	*China*	52	D5
Pudozh,	*Russia*	40	B9
Pudukkottai,	*India*	60	P11
Puebla,	*Mexico*	115	D5
Puebla □,	*Mexico*	115	D5
Puebla de Alcocer,	*Spain*	31	G5
Puebla de Don Fadrique,	*Spain*	29	H2
Puebla de Don Rodrigo,	*Spain*	31	F6
Puebla de Guzmán,	*Spain*	31	H3
Puebla de Sanabria,	*Spain*	30	C4
Puebla de Trives,	*Spain*	30	C3
Puebla del Caramiñal,	*Spain*	30	C2
Pueblo,	*U.S.A.*	108	F2
Pueblo Hundido,	*Chile*	126	B1
Pueblo Nuevo,	*Venezuela*	120	B3
Puelches,	*Argentina*	126	D2
Puelén,	*Argentina*	126	D2
Puente Alto,	*Chile*	126	C1
Puente del Arzobispo,	*Spain*	30	F5
Puente-Genil,	*Spain*	31	H6
Puente la Reina,	*Spain*	28	C3
Puenteareas,	*Spain*	30	C2
Puentedeume,	*Spain*	30	B2
Puentes de Garcia Rodriguez,	*Spain*	30	B3
Pu'er,	*China*	52	F3
Puerco →,	*U.S.A.*	111	J10
Puerto,	*Canary Is.*	36	F2
Puerto Acosta,	*Bolivia*	124	D4
Puerto Aisén,	*Chile*	128	C2
Puerto Ángel,	*Mexico*	115	D5
Puerto Arista,	*Mexico*	115	D6
Puerto Armuelles,	*Panama*	116	E3
Puerto Ayacucho,	*Venezuela*	120	B4
Puerto Barrios,	*Guatemala*	116	C2
Puerto Bermejo,	*Argentina*	126	B4
Puerto Bermúdez,	*Peru*	124	C3
Puerto Bolívar,	*Ecuador*	120	D2
Puerto Cabello,	*Venezuela*	120	A4
Puerto Cabezas,	*Nic.*	116	D3
Puerto Cabo Gracias á Dios,	*Nic.*	116	D3
Puerto Capaz = Jebba,	*Morocco*	74	A4
Puerto Carreño,	*Colombia*	120	B4
Puerto Castilla,	*Honduras*	116	C2
Puerto Chicama,	*Peru*	124	B2
Puerto Coig,	*Argentina*	128	D3
Puerto Cortés,	*Costa Rica*	116	E3
Puerto Cortés,	*Honduras*	116	C2
Puerto Cumarebo,	*Venezuela*	120	A4
Puerto de Alcudia,	*Spain*	36	B10
Puerto de Andraitx,	*Spain*	36	B9
Puerto de Cabrera,	*Spain*	36	B9
Puerto de Gran Tarajal,	*Canary Is.*	36	F5
Puerto de la Cruz,	*Canary Is.*	36	F3
Puerto de Pozo Negro,	*Canary Is.*	36	F6
Puerto de Sóller,	*Spain*	36	B9
Puerto del Carmen,	*Canary Is.*	36	F6
Puerto del Rosario,	*Canary Is.*	36	F6
Puerto Deseado,	*Argentina*	128	C3
Puerto Guaraní,	*Paraguay*	125	E6
Puerto Heath,	*Bolivia*	124	C4
Puerto Huitoto,	*Colombia*	120	C3
Puerto Inca,	*Peru*	124	B3
Puerto Juárez,	*Mexico*	115	C7
Puerto La Cruz,	*Venezuela*	121	A5
Puerto Leguízamo,	*Colombia*	120	D3
Puerto Límon,	*Colombia*	120	C3
Puerto Lobos,	*Argentina*	128	B3
Puerto López,	*Colombia*	120	C3
Puerto Lumbreras,	*Spain*	29	H3
Puerto Madryn,	*Argentina*	128	B3
Puerto Maldonado,	*Peru*	124	C4
Puerto Manotí,	*Cuba*	116	B4
Puerto Mazarrón,	*Spain*	29	H3
Puerto Mercedes,	*Colombia*	120	C3
Puerto Miraña,	*Colombia*	120	D3
Puerto Montt,	*Chile*	128	B2
Puerto Morelos,	*Mexico*	115	C7
Puerto Nariño,	*Colombia*	120	C4
Puerto Natales,	*Chile*	128	D2
Puerto Nuevo,	*Colombia*	120	B4
Puerto Nutrias,	*Venezuela*	120	B4
Puerto Ordaz,	*Venezuela*	121	B5
Puerto Padre,	*Cuba*	116	B4
Puerto Páez,	*Venezuela*	120	B4
Puerto Peñasco,	*Mexico*	114	A2
Puerto Pinasco,	*Paraguay*	126	A4
Puerto Pirámides,	*Argentina*	128	B4
Puerto Plata,	*Dom. Rep.*	117	C5
Puerto Pollensa,	*Spain*	36	B10
Puerto Portillo,	*Peru*	124	B3
Puerto Princesa,	*Phil.*	55	G3
Puerto Quellón,	*Chile*	128	B2
Puerto Quepos,	*Costa Rica*	116	E3
Puerto Real,	*Spain*	31	J4
Puerto Rico,	*Bolivia*	124	C4
Puerto Rico,	*Canary Is.*	36	G4
Puerto Rico ■,	*W. Indies*	117	C6
Puerto Rico Trench,	*Atl. Oc.*	117	C6
Puerto Saavedra,	*Chile*	128	A2
Puerto Sastre,	*Paraguay*	126	A4
Puerto Siles,	*Bolivia*	125	C4
Puerto Suárez,	*Bolivia*	125	D6
Puerto Tejada,	*Colombia*	120	C2
Puerto Umbría,	*Colombia*	120	C2
Puerto Vallarta,	*Mexico*	114	C3
Puerto Varas,	*Chile*	128	B2
Puerto Villazón,	*Bolivia*	125	C5
Puerto Wilches,	*Colombia*	120	B3
Puertollano,	*Spain*	31	G6
Puertomarín,	*Spain*	30	C3
Puesto Cunambo,	*Peru*	120	D2
Pueyrredón, L.,	*Argentina*	128	C2
Pugachev,	*Russia*	42	D9
Puge,	*China*	52	D4
Puge,	*Tanzania*	82	C3
Puget Sound,	*U.S.A.*	110	C2
Puget-Théniers,	*France*	27	E10
Púglia □,	*Italy*	35	B9
Pugödong,	*N. Korea*	51	C16
Pugu,	*Tanzania*	82	D4
Pügünzï,	*Iran*	65	E8
Pui,	*Romania*	38	D6
Puica,	*Peru*	124	C3
Puig Mayor,	*Spain*	36	B9
Puigcerdá,	*Spain*	28	C6
Puigmal,	*Spain*	28	C7
Puigpuñent,	*Spain*	36	B9
Puisaye, Collines de la,	*France*	25	E10
Puiseaux,	*France*	25	D9
Pujilí,	*Ecuador*	120	D2
Pujon-chosuji,	*N. Korea*	51	D14
Puka,	*Albania*	38	G2
Pukaki L.,	*N.Z.*	87	L3
Pukapuka,	*Cook Is.*	93	J11
Pukatawagan,	*Canada*	101	B8
Pukchin,	*N. Korea*	51	D13
Pukchŏng,	*N. Korea*	51	D15
Pukekohe,	*N.Z.*	87	G5
Pukou,	*China*	53	A12
Pula,	*Croatia*	33	D10
Pula,	*Italy*	34	D2
Pulacayo,	*Bolivia*	124	E4
Pulaski, *N.Y.,*	*U.S.A.*	107	C8
Pulaski, *Tenn.,*	*U.S.A.*	105	H2
Pulaski, *Va.,*	*U.S.A.*	104	G5
Puławy,	*Poland*	20	D11
Pulga,	*U.S.A.*	112	F5
Pulicat, L.,	*India*	60	N12
Pullman,	*U.S.A.*	110	C5
Pulog,	*Phil.*	55	C4
Pułtusk,	*Poland*	20	C11
Pülümür,	*Turkey*	67	C8
Pumlumon Fawr,	*U.K.*	13	E4
Puna,	*Bolivia*	125	D4
Puná, I.,	*Ecuador*	120	D1
Punakha,	*Bhutan*	61	F16
Punasar,	*India*	62	F5

Punata, *Bolivia* 125 D4
Punch, *India* 63 C6
Pune, *India* 60 K8
Pungsan, *N. Korea* 51 D15
Pungue, Ponte de, *Mozam.* 83 F3
Puning, *China* 53 F11
Punjab □, *India* 62 D6
Punjab □, *Pakistan* 62 E6
Puno, *Peru* 124 D3
Punta Alta, *Argentina* 128 A4
Punta Arenas, *Chile* 128 D2
Punta Cardón, *Venezuela* . 120 A3
Punta Coles, *Peru* 124 D3
Punta de Bombón, *Peru* .. 124 D3
Punta de Díaz, *Chile* 126 B1
Punta Delgado, *Argentina* 128 B4
Punta Gorda, *Belize* 115 D7
Punta Gorda, *U.S.A.* 105 M5
Punta Prieta, *Mexico* 114 B2
Punta Prima, *Spain* 36 B11
Puntabie, *Australia* 91 E1
Puntarenas, *Costa Rica* .. 116 E3
Punto Fijo, *Venezuela* ... 120 A3
Punxsatawney, *U.S.A.* ... 106 F5
Puqi, *China* 53 C9
Puquio, *Peru* 124 C3
Pur →, *Russia* 44 C8
Purace, Vol., *Colombia* .. 120 C2
Puralia = Puruliya, *India* . 63 H12
Purbeck, Isle of, *U.K.* ... 13 G5
Purcell, *U.S.A.* 109 H6
Purchena Tetica, *Spain* .. 29 H2
Puri, *India* 61 K14
Purificación, *Colombia* ... 120 C3
Purmerend, *Neths.* 16 C5
Purnia, *India* 63 G12
Purukcahu, *Indonesia* 56 E4
Puruliya, *India* 63 H12
Purus →, *Brazil* 121 D5
Puruvesi, *Finland* 40 B5
Pūrvomay, *Bulgaria* 38 G8
Purwakarta, *Indonesia* ... 57 G12
Purwodadi, *Jawa, Indonesia* 57 G13
Purwodadi, *Jawa, Indonesia* 57 G14
Purwokerto, *Indonesia* ... 57 G13
Purworejo, *Indonesia* 57 G14
Puryŏng, *N. Korea* 51 C15
Pusan, *S. Korea* 51 G15
Pushchino, *Russia* 45 D16
Pushkin, *Russia* 40 C6
Pushkino, *Russia* 42 E8
Pushkino, *Russia* 42 B3
Püspökladány, *Hungary* . 21 H11
Pustoshka, *Russia* 40 D5
Putahow L., *Canada* 101 B8
Putao, *Burma* 61 F20
Putaruru, *N.Z.* 87 H5
Putbus, *Germany* 18 A9
Puthein Myit →, *Burma* .. 61 M19
Putian, *China* 53 E12
Putignano, *Italy* 35 B10
Putina, *Peru* 124 C4
Puting, Tanjung, *Indonesia* 56 E4
Putlitz, *Germany* 18 B8
Putna →, *Romania* 38 D10
Putnam, *U.S.A.* 107 E13
Putorana, Gory, *Russia* .. 45 C10
Putre, *Chile* 124 D4
Puttalam, *Sri Lanka* 60 Q11
Putte, *Neths.* 17 F4
Putten, *Neths.* 16 D7
Puttgarden, *Germany* 18 A7
Putumayo →, *S. Amer.* .. 120 D4
Putuo, *China* 53 C14
Putussibau, *Indonesia* ... 56 D4
Puurs, *Belgium* 17 F4
Puy-de-Dôme, *France* 26 C6
Puy-de-Dôme □, *France* .. 26 C7
Puy-Guillaume, *France* ... 26 C7
Puy-l'Évêque, *France* 26 D5
Puyallup, *U.S.A.* 112 C4
Puyang, *China* 50 G8
Puyehue, *Chile* 128 B2
Puylaurens, *France* 26 E6
Puyo, *Ecuador* 120 D2
Pūzeh Rīg, *Iran* 65 E8
Pwani □, *Tanzania* 82 D4
Pweto, *Zaïre* 83 D2
Pwllheli, *U.K.* 12 E3
Pyana →, *Russia* 42 C8
Pyapon, *Burma* 61 L19
Pyasina →, *Russia* 45 B9
Pyatigorsk, *Russia* 43 H6
Pyatykhatky, *Ukraine* 41 H7
Pyè, *Burma* 61 K19
Pyetrikaw, *Belarus* 41 F5
Pyhäjoki, *Finland* 8 D21
Pyinmana, *Burma* 61 K20
Pyla, *Cyprus* 37 E12
Pyŏktong, *N. Korea* 51 D13
Pyŏnggang, *N. Korea* 51 E14
Pyŏngtaek, *S. Korea* 51 F14
P'yŏngyang, *N. Korea* 51 E13
Pyote, *U.S.A.* 109 K3
Pyramid L., *U.S.A.* 110 G4
Pyramid Pk., *U.S.A.* 113 J10
Pyramids, *Egypt* 76 J7
Pyrénées, *Europe* 26 F4
Pyrénées-Atlantiques □,
  France 26 E3
Pyrénées-Orientales □,
  France 26 F6
Pyryatyn, *Ukraine* 41 G7
Pyrzyce, *Poland* 20 B4
Pytalovo, *Russia* 40 D4
Pyttegga, *Norway* 10 B1
Pyu, *Burma* 61 K20

Q

Qaanaaq = Thule,
  Greenland 4 B4
Qabirri →, *Azerbaijan* 43 K8
Qachasnek, *S. Africa* 85 E4
Qādib, *Yemen* 68 E5
Qa'el Jafr, *Jordan* 69 E5
Qa'emābād, *Iran* 65 D9
Qā'emshahr, *Iran* 65 B7
Qagan Nur, *China* 50 C8
Qahar Youyi Zhongqi,
  China 50 D7
Qahremānshahr =
  Bākhtarān, *Iran* 67 E12
Qaidam Pendi, *China* 54 C4
Qajarīyeh, *Iran* 65 D6
Qala, Ras il, *Malta* 37 C1
Qala-i-Jadid, *Afghan.* 62 D2
Qala Yangi, *Afghan.* 62 B2
Qal'at al Akhḍar,
  Si. Arabia 64 E3
Qal'at Dīzah, *Iraq* 67 D11
Qal'at Sukkar, *Iraq* 67 G12
Qal'eh Darreh, *Iran* 64 B5
Qal'eh Shaharak, *Afghan.* 60 B4
Qalyûb, *Egypt* 76 H7
Qamar, Ghubbat al, *Yemen* 68 D5
Qamdo, *China* 52 B1
Qamruddin Karez, *Pakistan* 62 D3
Qandahār, *Afghan.* 60 D4
Qandahār □, *Afghan.* 60 D4
Qapān, *Iran* 65 B7
Qapshaghay, *Kazakhstan* . 44 E8
Qâra, *Egypt* 76 B2
Qara Qash →, *India* 63 B8
Qarabutaq, *Kazakhstan* .. 44 E7
Qaraçala, *Azerbaijan* 43 L9
Qaraghandy, *Kazakhstan* . 44 E8
Qārah, *Si. Arabia* 64 D4
Qaratau̇, *Kazakhstan* 44 E8
Qardud, *Sudan* 77 E2
Qareh →, *Iran* 67 C12
Qareh Tekān, *Iran* 65 B6
Qarqan, *China* 54 C3
Qarqan He →, *China* 54 C3
Qarqaraly, *Kazakhstan* ... 44 E8
Qarrasa, *Sudan* 77 E3
Qarshi, *Uzbekistan* 44 F7
Qartabā, *Lebanon* 69 A4
Qaryat al Gharab, *Iraq* .. 64 D5
Qaryat al 'Ulyā, *Si. Arabia* 64 E5
Qasr 'Amra, *Jordan* 64 D3
Qasr-e Qand, *Iran* 65 E9
Qasr Farâfra, *Egypt* 76 B2
Qatanā, *Syria* 69 B5
Qatar ■, *Asia* 65 E6
Qatlīsh, *Iran* 65 B8
Qattâra, *Egypt* 76 A2
Qattâra, Munkhafed el,
  Egypt 76 B2
Qattâra Depression =
  Qattâra, Munkhafed el,
  Egypt 76 B2
Qawām al Ḥamzah, *Iraq* . 64 D5
Qāyen, *Iran* 65 C8
Qazaqstan =
  Kazakhstan ■, *Asia* ... 44 E7
Qazimämmäd, *Azerbaijan* 43 K9
Qazvin, *Iran* 65 B6
Qena, *Egypt* 76 B3
Qena, W. →, *Egypt* 76 B3
Qeqertarsuaq = Disko,
  Greenland 4 C5
Qeqertarsuaq = Godhavn,
  Greenland 4 C5
Qeshlāq, *Iran* 67 E12
Qeshm, *Iran* 65 E8
Qezi'ot, *Israel* 69 E3
Qi Xian, *China* 50 G8
Qian Gorlos, *China* 51 B13
Qian Xian, *China* 50 G5
Qiancheng, *China* 52 D7
Qianjiang,
  *Guangxi Zhuangzu,
  China* 52 F7
Qianjiang, *Hubei, China* . 53 B9
Qianjiang, *Sichuan, China* 52 C7
Qianshan, *China* 53 B11
Qianwei, *China* 52 C4
Qianxi, *China* 52 D6
Qianyang, *Hunan, China* . 53 D8
Qianyang, *Shaanxi, China* 50 G4
Qianyang, *Zhejiang, China* 53 B12
Qiaojia, *China* 52 D4
Qībā', *Si. Arabia* 64 E5
Qichun, *China* 53 B10
Qidong, *Hunan, China* ... 53 D9
Qidong, *Jiangsu, China* .. 53 B13
Qijiang, *China* 52 C6
Qila Safed, *Pakistan* 60 E2
Qila Saifullāh, *Pakistan* .. 62 D3
Qilian Shan, *China* 54 C4
Qimen, *China* 53 C11
Qin He →, *China* 50 G7
Qin Jiang →, *China* 53 D10
Qin Ling = Qinling Shandi,
  China 50 H5
Qin'an, *China* 50 G3
Qing Xian, *China* 50 E9
Qingcheng, *China* 51 F9
Qingdao, *China* 51 F11
Qingfeng, *China* 50 G8
Qinghai □, *China* 54 C4

Qinghai Hu, *China* 54 C5
Qinghecheng, *China* 51 D13
Qinghemen, *China* 51 D11
Qingjian, *China* 50 F6
Qingjiang, *Jiangsu, China* 51 H10
Qingjiang, *Jiangxi, China* 53 C10
Qingliu, *China* 53 D11
Qinglong, *China* 52 E5
Qingping, *China* 52 D6
Qingpu, *China* 53 B13
Qingshui, *China* 50 G4
Qingshuihe, *China* 50 E6
Qingtian, *China* 53 C13
Qingtongxia Shuiku, *China* 50 F3
Qingxi, *China* 52 D7
Qingxu, *China* 50 F7
Qingyang, *Anhui, China* . 53 B11
Qingyang, *Gansu, China* . 50 F4
Qingyi Jiang →, *China* ... 52 C4
Qingyuan, *Guangdong,
  China* 53 F9
Qingyuan, *Liaoning, China* 51 C13
Qingyuan, *Zhejiang, China* 53 D12
Qingyun, *China* 51 F9
Qinhuangdao, *China* 51 E10
Qinling Shandi, *China* ... 50 H5
Qinshui, *China* 50 G7
Qinyang, *China* 50 G7
Qinyuan, *China* 50 F7
Qinzhou, *China* 52 G7
Qionghai, *China* 58 C8
Qionglai, *China* 52 B4
Qiongshan, *China* 58 C8
Qiongzhou Haixia, *China* . 58 B8
Qiqihar, *China* 45 E13
Qiraïya, W. →, *Egypt* 69 E3
Qiryat Ata, *Israel* 69 C4
Qiryat Gat, *Israel* 69 D3
Qiryat Mal'akhi, *Israel* ... 69 D3
Qiryat Shemona, *Israel* .. 69 B4
Qiryat Yam, *Israel* 69 C4
Qishan, *China* 50 G4
Qishan, *Taiwan* 53 F13
Qitai, *China* 54 B3
Qiubei, *China* 52 E5
Qixia, *China* 51 F11
Qiyang, *China* 53 D8
Qızlağac Körfäzi,
  Azerbaijan 67 C13
Qojūr, *Iran* 64 B5
Qom, *Iran* 65 C6
Qomsheh, *Iran* 65 D6
Qorveh, *Iran* 67 E12
Qostanay, *Kazakhstan* ... 44 D7
Qoṭūr, *Iran* 67 C11
Qu Jiang →, *China* 52 B6
Qu Xian, *Sichuan, China* . 52 B6
Qu Xian, *Zhejiang, China* 53 C12
Quairading, *Australia* 89 F2
Quakenbrück, *Germany* .. 18 C3
Quakertown, *U.S.A.* 107 F9
Qualeup, *Australia* 89 F2
Quambatook, *Australia* .. 91 F3
Quambone, *Australia* 91 E4
Quamby, *Australia* 90 C3
Quan Long, *Vietnam* 59 H5
Quanah, *U.S.A.* 109 H5
Quandialla, *Australia* 91 E4
Quang Ngai, *Vietnam* 58 E7
Quang Yen, *Vietnam* 58 B6
Quannan, *China* 53 E10
Quantock Hills, *U.K.* 13 F4
Quanzhou,
  Fujian, China 53 E12
Quanzhou,
  *Guangxi Zhuangzu,
  China* 53 E8
Quaqtaq, *Canada* 97 B13
Quaraí, *Brazil* 126 C4
Quarré-les-Tombes, *France* 25 E10
Quartu Sant'Elena, *Italy* . 34 C1
Quartzsite, *U.S.A.* 113 M12
Quatsino, *Canada* 100 C3
Quatsino Sd., *Canada* ... 100 C3
Quba, *Azerbaijan* 43 K9
Qūchān, *Iran* 65 B8
Queanbeyan, *Australia* .. 91 F4
Québec, *Canada* 99 C5
Québec □, *Canada* 99 B6
Quedlinburg, *Germany* ... 18 D7
Queen Alexandra Ra.,
  Antarctica 5 E11
Queen Charlotte, *Canada* . 100 C2
Queen Charlotte Bay,
  Falk. Is. 128 D4
Queen Charlotte Is.,
  Canada 100 C2
Queen Charlotte Str.,
  Canada 100 C3
Queen Elizabeth Is.,
  Canada 94 B10
Queen Elizabeth Nat. Park,
  Uganda 82 C3
Queen Mary Land,
  Antarctica 5 D7
Queen Maud G., *Canada* . 96 B9
Queen Maud Land,
  Antarctica 5 D3
Queen Maud Mts.,
  Antarctica 5 E13
Queens Chan., *Australia* . 88 C4
Queenscliff, *Australia* ... 91 F3
Queensland □, *Australia* . 90 C3
Queenstown, *Australia* ... 90 G4
Queenstown, *N.Z.* 87 L2
Queenstown, *S. Africa* ... 84 E4

Queets, *U.S.A.* 112 C2
Queguay Grande →,
  Uruguay 126 C4
Queimadas, *Brazil* 122 D4
Quela, *Angola* 80 F3
Quelimane, *Mozam.* 83 F4
Quelpart = Cheju Do,
  S. Korea 51 H14
Quemado, *N. Mex., U.S.A.* 111 J9
Quemado, *Tex., U.S.A.* .. 109 L4
Quemú-Quemú, *Argentina* 126 D3
Quequén, *Argentina* 126 D4
Querco, *Peru* 124 C3
Querétaro, *Mexico* 114 C4
Querétaro □, *Mexico* 114 C5
Querfurt, *Germany* 18 D7
Quesada, *Spain* 29 H1
Questembert, *France* 24 E4
Quetena, *Bolivia* 124 E4
Quetico Prov. Park,
  Canada 98 C1
Quetrequile, *Argentina* .. 128 B3
Quetta, *Pakistan* 62 D2
Quevedo, *Ecuador* 120 D2
Quezaltenango, *Guatemala* 116 D1
Quezon City, *Phil.* 55 D4
Qufār, *Si. Arabia* 64 E4
Qui Nhon, *Vietnam* 58 F7
Quibaxe, *Angola* 80 F2
Quibdo, *Colombia* 120 B2
Quiberon, *France* 24 E3
Quibor, *Venezuela* 120 B4
Quick, *Canada* 100 C3
Quickborn, *Germany* 18 B5
Quiet L., *Canada* 100 A2
Quiévrain, *Belgium* 17 H3
Quiindy, *Paraguay* 126 B4
Quila, *Mexico* 114 C3
Quilán, C., *Chile* 128 B2
Quilcene, *U.S.A.* 112 C4
Quilengues, *Angola* 81 G2
Quilimarí, *Chile* 126 C1
Quilino, *Argentina* 126 C3
Quillabamba, *Peru* 124 C3
Quillacollo, *Bolivia* 124 D4
Quillagua, *Chile* 126 A2
Quillaicillo, *Chile* 126 C1
Quillan, *France* 26 F6
Quillebeuf-sur-Seine,
  France 24 C7
Quillota, *Chile* 126 C1
Quilmes, *Argentina* 126 C4
Quilon, *India* 60 Q10
Quilpie, *Australia* 91 D3
Quilpué, *Chile* 126 C1
Quilua, *Mozam.* 83 F4
Quime, *Bolivia* 124 D4
Quimilí, *Argentina* 126 B3
Quimper, *France* 24 D2
Quimperlé, *France* 24 E3
Quinault →, *U.S.A.* 112 C2
Quincemil, *Peru* 124 C3
Quincy, *Calif., U.S.A.* ... 112 F6
Quincy, *Fla., U.S.A.* 105 K3
Quincy, *Ill., U.S.A.* 108 F9
Quincy, *Mass., U.S.A.* .. 107 D14
Quincy, *Wash., U.S.A.* .. 110 C4
Quines, *Argentina* 126 C2
Quinga, *Mozam.* 83 F5
Quingey, *France* 25 E12
Quintana de la Serena,
  Spain 31 G5
Quintana Roo □, *Mexico* . 115 D7
Quintanar de la Orden,
  Spain 28 F1
Quintanar de la Sierra,
  Spain 28 D2
Quintanar del Rey, *Spain* . 29 F3
Quintero, *Chile* 126 C1
Quintin, *France* 24 D4
Quinto, *Spain* 28 D4
Quinyambie, *Australia* ... 91 E3
Quípar →, *Spain* 29 G3
Quipungo, *Angola* 81 G2
Quirihue, *Chile* 126 D1
Quirindi, *Australia* 91 E5
Quiroga, *Spain* 30 C3
Quiruvilca, *Peru* 124 B2
Quissac, *France* 27 E8
Quissanga, *Mozam.* 83 E5
Quitilipi, *Argentina* 126 B3
Quitman, *Ga., U.S.A.* ... 105 K4
Quitman, *Miss., U.S.A.* .. 105 J1
Quitman, *Tex., U.S.A.* .. 109 J7
Quito, *Ecuador* 120 D2
Quixadá, *Brazil* 122 C4
Quixaxe, *Mozam.* 83 F5
Quixeramobim, *Brazil* ... 122 C4
Qujing, *China* 52 E4
Qul'ân, Jazā'ir, *Egypt* 76 C4
Qumbu, *S. Africa* 85 E4
Quneitra, *Syria* 69 B4
Qûngirot, *Uzbekistan* 44 E6
Quoin I., *Australia* 88 B4
Quoin Pt., *S. Africa* 84 E2
Quondong, *Australia* 91 E2
Quorn, *Australia* 91 E2
Qŭqon, *Uzbekistan* 44 E8
Qurein, *Sudan* 77 E3
Qurnat as Sawdā', *Lebanon* 69 A5
Qûs, *Egypt* 76 B3
Qusar, *Azerbaijan* 43 K9

Qusaybah, *Iraq* 67 E9
Quseir, *Egypt* 76 B3
Qūshchī, *Iran* 67 D11
Quthing, *Lesotho* 85 E4
Qūṭīābād, *Iran* 67 E13
Quwo, *China* 50 G6
Quyang, *China* 50 E8
Quynh Nhai, *Vietnam* 58 B4
Quzi, *China* 50 F4
Qvareli, *Georgia* 43 K7
Qytet Stalin = Kuçova,
  Albania 39 J2
Qyzylorda, *Kazakhstan* .. 44 E7

R

Ra, Ko, *Thailand* 59 H2
Råå, *Sweden* 11 J6
Raahe, *Finland* 8 D21
Raalte, *Neths.* 16 D8
Raamsdonksveer, *Neths.* . 17 E5
Raasay, *U.K.* 14 D2
Raasay, Sd. of, *U.K.* 14 D2
Rab, *Croatia* 33 D11
Raba, *Indonesia* 57 F5
Rába →, *Hungary* 21 H7
Rabaçal →, *Portugal* 30 D3
Rabah, *Nigeria* 79 C6
Rabai, *Kenya* 82 C4
Rabastens, *France* 26 E5
Rabastens-de-Bigorre,
  France 26 E4
Rabat, *Malta* 37 D1
Rabat, *Morocco* 74 B3
Rabaul, *Papua N. G.* 92 H7
Rabbit →, *Canada* 100 B3
Rabbit Lake, *Canada* 101 C7
Rabbitskin →, *Canada* ... 100 A4
Rabka, *Poland* 20 F9
Rābor, *Iran* 65 D8
Rácale, *Italy* 35 C11
Racalmuto, *Italy* 34 E6
Racconigi, *Italy* 32 D4
Race, C., *Canada* 99 C9
Rach Gia, *Vietnam* 59 G5
Raciąż, *Poland* 20 C10
Racibórz, *Poland* 20 E8
Racine, *U.S.A.* 104 D2
Rackerby, *U.S.A.* 112 F5
Radama, Nosy, *Madag.* .. 85 A8
Radama, Saikanosy,
  Madag. 85 A8
Rădăuți, *Romania* 38 B8
Radbuza →, *Czech.* 20 F3
Radeburg, *Germany* 18 D9
Radeče, *Slovenia* 33 B12
Radekhiv, *Ukraine* 41 G3
Radekhov = Radekhiv,
  Ukraine 41 G3
Radford, *U.S.A.* 104 G5
Radhanpur, *India* 62 H4
Radiska →, *Macedonia* ... 39 H3
Radisson, *Canada* 101 C7
Radium Hot Springs,
  Canada 100 C5
Radna, *Romania* 38 C4
Radnor Forest, *U.K.* 13 E4
Radolfzell, *Germany* 19 H4
Radom, *Poland* 20 D11
Radomir, *Bulgaria* 38 G6
Radomsko, *Poland* 20 D9
Radomyshl, *Ukraine* 41 G5
Radoviš, *Macedonia* 39 H5
Radovljica, *Slovenia* 33 B11
Radstock, *U.K.* 13 F5
Radstock, C., *Australia* .. 91 E1
Răducăneni, *Romania* ... 38 C10
Radviliškis, *Lithuania* 9 J20
Radville, *Canada* 101 D8
Rae, *Canada* 100 A5
Rae Bareli, *India* 63 F9
Rae Isthmus, *Canada* ... 97 B11
Raeren, *Belgium* 17 G8
Raeside, L., *Australia* ... 89 E3
Raetihi, *N.Z.* 87 H5
Rafaela, *Argentina* 126 C3
Rafah, *Gaza Strip* 69 D3
Rafai, *C.A.R.* 82 B1
Raffadali, *Italy* 34 E6
Rafḥā, *Si. Arabia* 64 D4
Rafsanjān, *Iran* 65 D8
Raft Pt., *Australia* 88 C3
Ragachow, *Belarus* 41 F6
Ragag, *Sudan* 77 E1
Ragama, *Sri Lanka* 60 R11
Ragged, Mt., *Australia* ... 89 F3
Raglan, *Australia* 90 C5
Raglan, *N.Z.* 87 G5
Ragunda, *Sweden* 8 A10
Ragusa, *Italy* 35 F7
Raha, *Indonesia* 57 E6
Rahad, Nahr ed →, *Sudan* 77 E3
Rahad al Bardī, *Sudan* ... 73 F9
Rahaeng = Tak, *Thailand* . 58 D2
Rahden, *Germany* 18 C4
Raheita, *Eritrea* 77 E5
Raḥīmah, *Si. Arabia* 65 E6
Rahimyar Khan, *Pakistan* . 62 E4
Rāhjerd, *Iran* 65 C6
Raichur, *India* 60 L10
Raiganj, *India* 63 G13
Raigarh, *India* 61 J13
Raijua, *Indonesia* 57 F6
Railton, *Australia* 90 G4

Rainbow Lake, Canada	100	B5	
Rainier, U.S.A.	112	D4	
Rainier, Mt., U.S.A.	112	D5	
Rainy L., Canada	101	D10	
Rainy River, Canada	101	D10	
Raippaluoto, Finland	8	E19	
Raipur, India	61	J12	
Raisio, Finland	9	F20	
Raj Nandgaon, India	61	J12	
Raja, Ujung, Indonesia	56	D1	
Raja Ampat, Kepulauan, Indonesia	57	E7	
Rajahmundry, India	61	L12	
Rajapalaiyam, India	60	Q10	
Rajasthan □, India	62	F5	
Rajasthan Canal, India	62	E5	
Rajauri, India	63	C6	
Rajgarh, Mad. P., India	62	G7	
Rajgarh, Raj., India	62	E6	
Rajhenburg, Slovenia	33	B12	
Rajkot, India	62	H4	
Rajmahal Hills, India	63	G12	
Rajpipla, India	60	J8	
Rajpura, India	62	D7	
Rajshahi, Bangla.	61	G16	
Rajshahi □, Bangla.	63	G13	
Rakaia, N.Z.	87	K4	
Rakaia →, N.Z.	87	K4	
Rakan, Ra's, Qatar	65	E6	
Rakaposhi, Pakistan	63	A6	
Rakata, Pulau, Indonesia	56	F3	
Rakhiv, Ukraine	41	H3	
Rakhni, Pakistan	62	D3	
Rakitnoye, Russia	48	B7	
Rakkestad, Norway	10	E5	
Rakops, Botswana	84	C3	
Rákospalota, Hungary	21	H9	
Rakovica, Croatia	33	D12	
Rakovník, Czech.	20	E3	
Rakovski, Bulgaria	38	G7	
Rakvere, Estonia	9	G22	
Raleigh, U.S.A.	105	H6	
Raleigh B., U.S.A.	105	H7	
Ralja, Serbia, Yug.	21	L10	
Ralls, U.S.A.	109	J4	
Ram →, Canada	100	A4	
Rām Allāh, West Bank	69	D4	
Ram Hd., Australia	91	F4	
Rama, Nic.	116	D3	
Ramacca, Italy	35	E7	
Ramales de la Victoria, Spain	28	B1	
Ramalho, Serra do, Brazil	123	D3	
Raman, Thailand	59	J3	
Ramanathapuram, India	60	Q11	
Ramanetaka, B. de, Madag.	85	A8	
Ramat Gan, Israel	69	C3	
Ramatlhabama, S. Africa	84	D4	
Ramban, India	63	C6	
Rambervillers, France	25	D13	
Rambipuji, Indonesia	57	H15	
Rambouillet, France	25	D8	
Ramea, Canada	99	C8	
Ramechhap, Nepal	63	F12	
Ramelau, Indonesia	57	F7	
Ramenskoye, Russia	42	C4	
Ramgarh, Bihar, India	63	H11	
Ramgarh, Raj., India	62	F6	
Ramgarh, Raj., India	62	F4	
Rāmhormoz, Iran	65	D6	
Ramiān, Iran	65	B7	
Ramingining, Australia	90	A2	
Ramla, Israel	69	D3	
Ramlu, Eritrea	77	E5	
Ramme, Denmark	11	H2	
Ramnad = Ramanathapuram, India	60	Q11	
Ramnagar, India	63	C6	
Ramnäs, Sweden	10	E10	
Ramon, Russia	42	E4	
Ramona, U.S.A.	113	M10	
Ramore, Canada	98	C3	
Ramotswa, Botswana	84	C4	
Rampur, H.P., India	62	D7	
Rampur, Mad. P., India	62	H5	
Rampur, Ut. P., India	63	E8	
Rampur Hat, India	63	G12	
Rampura, India	62	G6	
Ramree I. = Ramree Kyun, Burma	61	K18	
Ramree Kyun, Burma	61	K18	
Rāmsar, Iran	65	B6	
Ramsel, Belgium	17	F5	
Ramsey, Canada	98	C3	
Ramsey, U.K.	12	C3	
Ramsgate, U.K.	13	F9	
Ramsjö, Sweden	10	B9	
Ramtek, India	60	J11	
Ramvik, Sweden	10	B11	
Ranaghat, India	63	H13	
Ranahu, Pakistan	62	G3	
Ranau, Malaysia	56	C5	
Rancagua, Chile	126	C1	
Rance, Belgium	17	H4	
Rance →, France	24	D5	
Rance, Barrage de la, France	24	D4	
Rancharia, Brazil	123	F1	
Rancheria →, Canada	100	A3	
Ranchester, U.S.A.	110	D10	
Ranchi, India	63	H11	
Ranco, L., Chile	128	B2	
Randan, France	26	B7	
Randazzo, Italy	35	E7	
Randers, Denmark	11	H4	
Randers Fjord, Denmark	11	H4	
Randfontein, S. Africa	85	D4	
Randle, U.S.A.	112	D5	
Randolph, Mass., U.S.A.	107	D13	
Randolph, N.Y., U.S.A.	106	D6	
Randolph, Utah, U.S.A.	110	F8	
Randolph, Vt., U.S.A.	107	C12	
Randsfjorden, Norway	10	D4	
Råne älv →, Sweden	8	D20	
Rangae, Thailand	59	J3	
Rangaunu B., N.Z.	87	F4	
Rångedala, Sweden	11	G7	
Rangeley, U.S.A.	107	B14	
Rangely, U.S.A.	110	F9	
Ranger, U.S.A.	109	J5	
Rangia, India	61	F17	
Rangiora, N.Z.	87	K4	
Rangitaiki →, N.Z.	87	G6	
Rangitata →, N.Z.	87	K3	
Rangkasbitung, Indonesia	57	G12	
Rangon →, Burma	61	L20	
Rangoon, Burma	61	L20	
Rangpur, Bangla.	61	G16	
Rangsit, Thailand	58	F3	
Ranibennur, India	60	M9	
Raniganj, India	63	H12	
Raniwara, India	60	G8	
Rānīyah, Iraq	64	B5	
Ranken →, Australia	90	C2	
Rankin, U.S.A.	109	K4	
Rankin Inlet, Canada	96	B10	
Rankins Springs, Australia	91	E4	
Rannoch, L., U.K.	14	E4	
Rannoch Moor, U.K.	14	E4	
Ranobe, Helodranon' i, Madag.	85	C7	
Ranohira, Madag.	85	C8	
Ranomafana, Toamasina, Madag.	85	B8	
Ranomafana, Toliara, Madag.	85	C8	
Ranong, Thailand	59	H2	
Rānsa, Iran	65	C6	
Ransiki, Indonesia	57	E8	
Rantau, Indonesia	56	E5	
Rantauprapat, Indonesia	56	D1	
Rantemario, Indonesia	57	E5	
Rantoul, U.S.A.	104	E1	
Ranum, Denmark	11	H3	
Raon l'Étape, France	25	D13	
Raoui, Erg er, Algeria	75	C4	
Raoyang, China	50	E8	
Rapa, Pac. Oc.	93	K13	
Rapallo, Italy	32	D6	
Rāpch, Iran	65	E8	
Rapid →, Canada	100	B3	
Rapid City, U.S.A.	108	D3	
Rapid River, U.S.A.	104	C2	
Rapides des Joachims, Canada	98	C4	
Rapla, Estonia	9	G21	
Rapperswil, Switz.	23	B7	
Rapu Rapu I., Phil.	55	E6	
Ra's al 'Ayn, Syria	67	D9	
Ra's al Khaymah, U.A.E.	65	E8	
Ra's al-Unuf, Libya	73	B8	
Ra's an Naqb, Jordan	69	F4	
Rasa, Punta, Argentina	128	B4	
Rasca, Pta. de la, Canary Is.	36	G3	
Raseiniai, Lithuania	9	J20	
Rashad, Sudan	77	E3	
Rashīd, Egypt	76	H7	
Rashīd, Masabb, Egypt	76	H7	
Rasht, Iran	67	D13	
Rasi Salai, Thailand	58	E5	
Raška, Serbia, Yug.	21	M10	
Rason L., Australia	89	E3	
Rașova, Romania	38	E10	
Rasra, India	63	G10	
Rass el Oued, Algeria	75	A6	
Rasskazovo, Russia	42	D5	
Rastatt, Germany	19	G4	
Rat →, Canada	100	B4	
Rat Buri, Thailand	58	F2	
Rat Islands, U.S.A.	96	C1	
Rat River, Canada	100	A6	
Ratangarh, India	62	E6	
Rath, India	63	G8	
Rath Luirc, Ireland	15	D3	
Rathdrum, Ireland	15	D5	
Rathenow, Germany	18	C8	
Rathkeale, Ireland	15	D3	
Rathlin, U.K.	15	A5	
Rathlin O'Birne I., Ireland	15	B3	
Ratibor = Racibórz, Poland	20	E8	
Ratlam, India	62	H6	
Ratnagiri, India	60	L8	
Raton, U.S.A.	109	G2	
Rattaphum, Thailand	59	J3	
Rattray Hd., U.K.	14	D7	
Ratz, Mt., Canada	100	B2	
Ratzeburg, Germany	18	B6	
Raub, Malaysia	59	L3	
Rauch, Argentina	126	D4	
Raufarhöfn, Iceland	8	C6	
Raufoss, Norway	10	D4	
Raukumara Ra., N.Z.	87	H6	
Raul Soares, Brazil	123	F3	
Rauland, Norway	10	E2	
Rauma, Finland	9	F19	
Rauma →, Norway	10	B1	
Raurkela, India	63	H11	
Rausu-Dake, Japan	48	B12	
Rava-Ruska, Ukraine	41	G2	
Rava Russkaya = Rava-Ruska, Ukraine	41	G2	
Ravānsar, Iran	67	E12	
Ravanusa, Italy	34	E6	
Rāvar, Iran	65	D8	
Ravels, Belgium	17	F6	
Ravena, U.S.A.	107	D11	
Ravenna, Italy	33	D9	
Ravenna, Nebr., U.S.A.	108	E5	
Ravenna, Ohio, U.S.A.	106	E3	
Ravensburg, Germany	19	H5	
Ravenshoe, Australia	90	B4	
Ravensthorpe, Australia	89	F3	
Ravenswood, Australia	90	C4	
Ravenswood, U.S.A.	104	F5	
Ravi →, Pakistan	62	D4	
Ravna Gora, Croatia	33	C11	
Rawa Mazowiecka, Poland	20	D10	
Rawalpindi, Pakistan	62	C5	
Rawāndūz, Iraq	67	D11	
Rawang, Malaysia	59	L3	
Rawdon, Canada	98	C5	
Rawene, N.Z.	87	F4	
Rawicz, Poland	20	D6	
Rawlinna, Australia	89	F4	
Rawlins, U.S.A.	110	F10	
Rawlinson Ra., Australia	89	D4	
Rawson, Argentina	128	B3	
Ray, U.S.A.	108	A3	
Ray, C., Canada	99	C8	
Rayadurg, India	60	M10	
Rayagada, India	61	K13	
Raychikhinsk, Russia	45	E13	
Rāyen, Iran	65	D8	
Raymond, Canada	100	D6	
Raymond, Calif., U.S.A.	112	H7	
Raymond, Wash., U.S.A.	112	D3	
Raymondville, U.S.A.	109	M6	
Raymore, Canada	101	C8	
Rayne, U.S.A.	109	K8	
Rayón, Mexico	114	B2	
Rayong, Thailand	58	F3	
Rayville, U.S.A.	109	J9	
Raz, Pte. du, France	24	D2	
Razan, Iran	67	E13	
Ražana, Serbia, Yug.	21	L9	
Ražanj, Serbia, Yug.	21	M11	
Razdel'naya = Rozdilna, Ukraine	41	J6	
Razdolnoye, Russia	48	C5	
Razdolnoye, Ukraine	41	K7	
Razeh, Iran	65	C6	
Razelm, Lacul, Romania	38	E12	
Razgrad, Bulgaria	38	F9	
Razmak, Pakistan	62	C3	
Ré, I. de, France	26	B2	
Reading, U.K.	13	F7	
Reading, U.S.A.	107	F9	
Real, Cordillera, Bolivia	124	D4	
Realicó, Argentina	126	D3	
Réalmont, France	26	E6	
Reata, Mexico	114	B4	
Rebais, France	25	D10	
Rebecca, L., Australia	89	F3	
Rebi, Indonesia	57	F8	
Rebiana, Libya	73	D9	
Rebun-Tō, Japan	48	B10	
Recanati, Italy	33	E10	
Recaș, Romania	38	D4	
Recherche, Arch. of the, Australia	89	F3	
Recht, Belgium	17	H8	
Rechytsa, Belarus	41	F6	
Recife, Brazil	122	C5	
Recklinghausen, Germany	17	E10	
Reconquista, Argentina	126	B4	
Recreio, Brazil	125	B6	
Recreo, Argentina	126	B2	
Recuay, Peru	124	B2	
Red →, La., U.S.A.	109	K9	
Red →, N. Dak., U.S.A.	108	A6	
Red Bank, U.S.A.	107	F10	
Red Bay, Canada	99	B8	
Red Bluff, U.S.A.	110	F2	
Red Bluff L., U.S.A.	109	K3	
Red Cliffs, Australia	91	E3	
Red Cloud, U.S.A.	108	E5	
Red Deer, Canada	100	C6	
Red Deer →, Alta., Canada	101	C6	
Red Deer →, Man., Canada	101	C8	
Red Deer L., Canada	101	C8	
Red Indian L., Canada	99	C8	
Red Lake, Canada	101	C10	
Red Lake Falls, U.S.A.	108	B6	
Red Lodge, U.S.A.	110	D9	
Red Mountain, U.S.A.	113	K9	
Red Oak, U.S.A.	108	E7	
Red Rock, Canada	98	C2	
Red Rock, L., U.S.A.	108	E8	
Red Rocks Pt., Australia	89	F4	
Red Sea, Asia	68	C2	
Red Slate Mt., U.S.A.	112	H8	
Red Sucker L., Canada	101	C10	
Red Tower Pass = Turnu Roșu, Romania	38	D7	
Red Wing, U.S.A.	108	C8	
Rédange, Lux.	17	J7	
Redbridge, U.K.	13	F8	
Redcar, U.K.	12	C6	
Redcliff, Canada	101	C6	
Redcliffe, Australia	91	D5	
Redcliffe, Mt., Australia	89	E3	
Reddersburg, S. Africa	84	D4	
Redding, U.S.A.	110	F2	
Redditch, U.K.	13	E6	
Redenção, Brazil	122	B4	
Redfield, U.S.A.	108	C5	
Redkino, Russia	42	B3	
Redknife →, Canada	100	A5	
Redlands, U.S.A.	113	M9	
Redmond, Australia	89	F2	
Redmond, Oreg., U.S.A.	110	D3	
Redmond, Wash., U.S.A.	112	C4	
Redon, France	24	E4	
Redonda, Antigua	117	C7	
Redondela, Spain	30	C2	
Redondo, Portugal	31	G3	
Redondo Beach, U.S.A.	113	M8	
Redrock Pt., Canada	100	A5	
Redruth, U.K.	13	G2	
Redvers, Canada	101	D8	
Redwater, Canada	100	C6	
Redwood, U.S.A.	107	B9	
Redwood City, U.S.A.	111	H2	
Redwood Falls, U.S.A.	108	C7	
Ree, L., Ireland	15	C4	
Reed, L., Canada	101	C8	
Reed City, U.S.A.	104	D3	
Reeder, U.S.A.	108	B3	
Reedley, U.S.A.	111	H4	
Reedsburg, U.S.A.	108	D9	
Reedsport, U.S.A.	110	E1	
Reefton, N.Z.	87	K3	
Refahiye, Turkey	67	C8	
Refugio, U.S.A.	109	L6	
Rega →, Poland	20	A5	
Regalbuto, Italy	35	E7	
Regen, Germany	19	G9	
Regen →, Germany	19	F8	
Regensburg, Germany	19	F8	
Regensdorf, Switz.	23	B6	
Réggio di Calábria, Italy	35	D8	
Réggio nell'Emília, Italy	32	D7	
Regina, Canada	101	C8	
Régina, Fr. Guiana	121	C7	
Registro, Brazil	127	A6	
Reguengos de Monsaraz, Portugal	31	G3	
Rehar →, India	63	H10	
Rehoboth, Namibia	84	C2	
Rehovot, Israel	69	D3	
Rei-Bouba, Cameroon	73	G7	
Reichenbach, Germany	18	E8	
Reichenbach, Switz.	22	C5	
Reid, Australia	89	F4	
Reid River, Australia	90	B4	
Reiden, Switz.	22	B5	
Reidsville, U.S.A.	105	G6	
Reigate, U.K.	13	F7	
Reillo, Spain	28	F3	
Reims, France	25	C11	
Reina Adelaida, Arch., Chile	128	D2	
Reinach, Aargau, Switz.	22	B5	
Reinach, Basel, Switz.	22	B5	
Reinbeck, U.S.A.	108	D8	
Reindeer →, Canada	101	B8	
Reindeer I., Canada	101	C9	
Reindeer L., Canada	101	B8	
Reinga, C., N.Z.	87	F4	
Reinosa, Spain	30	B6	
Reinosa, Paso, Spain	30	C6	
Reitdiep, Neths.	16	B8	
Reitz, S. Africa	85	D4	
Reivilo, S. Africa	84	D3	
Rejmyre, Sweden	11	F9	
Reka →, Slovenia	33	C11	
Rekinniki, Russia	45	C17	
Reliance, Canada	101	A7	
Remad, Oued →, Algeria	75	B4	
Rémalard, France	24	D7	
Remarkable, Mt., Australia	91	E2	
Rembang, Indonesia	57	G14	
Remchi, Algeria	75	A4	
Remedios, Colombia	120	B3	
Remedios, Panama	116	E3	
Remeshk, Iran	65	E8	
Remich, Lux.	17	J8	
Rémire, Fr. Guiana	121	C7	
Remiremont, France	25	D13	
Remo, Ethiopia	77	F5	
Remontnoye, Russia	43	G6	
Remoulins, France	27	E8	
Remscheid, Germany	18	D3	
Ren Xian, China	50	F8	
Renascença, Brazil	120	D4	
Rende, Italy	35	C9	
Rendeux, Belgium	17	H7	
Rendína, Greece	39	K4	
Rendsburg, Germany	18	A5	
Rene, Russia	45	C19	
Renfrew, Canada	98	C4	
Renfrew, U.K.	14	F4	
Rengat, Indonesia	56	E2	
Rengo, Chile	126	C1	
Renhua, China	53	E9	
Renhuai, China	52	D6	
Reni, Ukraine	41	K5	
Renk, Sudan	77	E3	
Renkum, Neths.	16	E7	
Renmark, Australia	91	E3	
Rennell Sd., Canada	100	C2	
Renner Springs T.O., Australia	90	B1	
Rennes, France	24	D5	
Rennes, Bassin de, France	24	E5	
Reno, U.S.A.	112	F7	
Reno →, Italy	33	D9	
Renovo, U.S.A.	106	E7	
Renqiu, China	50	E9	
Rensselaer, Ind., U.S.A.	104	E2	
Rensselaer, N.Y., U.S.A.	107	D11	
Rentería, Spain	28	B3	
Renton, U.S.A.	112	C4	
Réo, Burkina Faso	78	C4	
Reotipur, India	63	G10	
Republic, Mich., U.S.A.	104	B2	
Republic, Wash., U.S.A.	110	B4	
Republican →, U.S.A.	108	F6	
Republican City, U.S.A.	108	E5	
Repulse Bay, Canada	97	B11	
Requena, Peru	124	B3	
Requena, Spain	29	F3	
Reşadiye = Datça, Turkey	66	D2	
Reşadiye, Turkey	66	B7	
Resele, Sweden	10	A11	
Reserve, Canada	101	C8	
Reserve, U.S.A.	111	K9	
Resht = Rasht, Iran	67	D13	
Resistencia, Argentina	126	B4	
Reşiţa, Romania	38	D4	
Resolution I., Canada	97	B13	
Resolution I., N.Z.	87	L1	
Resplandes, Brazil	122	C2	
Resplendor, Brazil	123	E3	
Ressano Garcia, Mozam.	85	D5	
Reston, Canada	101	D8	
Retalhuleu, Guatemala	116	D1	
Reteag, Romania	38	B7	
Retenue, L. de, Zaïre	83	E2	
Retford, U.K.	12	D7	
Rethel, France	25	C11	
Rethem, Germany	18	C5	
Réthímnon, Greece	37	D6	
Réthímnon □, Greece	37	D6	
Retiche, Alpi, Switz.	23	D10	
Retie, Belgium	17	F6	
Retiers, France	24	E5	
Retortillo, Spain	30	E4	
Reuland, Belgium	17	H8	
Réunion ■, Ind. Oc.	71	J9	
Reus, Spain	28	D6	
Reusel, Neths.	17	F6	
Reuss →, Switz.	23	B6	
Reutlingen, Germany	19	G5	
Reutte, Austria	19	H6	
Reuver, Neths.	17	F8	
Reval = Tallinn, Estonia	9	G21	
Revel, France	26	E6	
Revelganj, India	63	G11	
Revelstoke, Canada	100	C5	
Reventazón, Peru	124	B1	
Revigny-sur-Ornain, France	25	D11	
Revilla Gigedo, Is., Pac. Oc.	93	F16	
Revillagigedo I., U.S.A.	100	B2	
Revin, France	25	C11	
Revúè →, Mozam.	83	F3	
Rewa, India	63	G9	
Rewa →, Guyana	121	C6	
Rewari, India	62	E7	
Rexburg, U.S.A.	110	E8	
Rey, Iran	65	C6	
Rey, Rio del →, Nigeria	79	E6	
Rey Malabo, Eq. Guin.	79	E6	
Reyes, Bolivia	124	C4	
Reyes, Pt., U.S.A.	112	H3	
Reyhanlı, Turkey	66	D7	
Reykjahlið, Iceland	8	D5	
Reykjanes, Iceland	8	E2	
Reykjavík, Iceland	8	D3	
Reynolds, Canada	101	D9	
Reynolds Ra., Australia	88	D5	
Reynoldsville, U.S.A.	106	E6	
Reynosa, Mexico	115	B5	
Rēzekne, Latvia	9	H22	
Rezvān, Iran	65	E8	
Rharis, O. →, Algeria	75	C6	
Rhayader, U.K.	13	E4	
Rheden, Neths.	16	D8	
Rhein, Canada	101	C8	
Rhein →, Europe	16	E8	
Rhein-Main-Donau-Kanal, Germany	19	F7	
Rheinbach, Germany	18	E2	
Rheine, Germany	18	C3	
Rheineck, Switz.	23	B9	
Rheinfelden, Switz.	22	A5	
Rheinland-Pfalz □, Germany	19	E2	
Rheinsberg, Germany	18	B8	
Rheinwaldhorn, Switz.	23	D8	
Rhenen, Neths.	16	E7	
Rheriss, Oued →, Morocco	74	B4	
Rheydt, Germany	18	D2	
Rhin = Rhein →, Europe	16	E8	
Rhinau, France	25	D14	
Rhine = Rhein →, Europe	16	E8	
Rhineland-Palatinate = Rheinland-Pfalz □, Germany	19	E2	
Rhinelander, U.S.A.	108	C10	
Rhino Camp, Uganda	82	B3	
Rhir, Cap, Morocco	74	B3	
Rhisnes, Belgium	17	G5	
Rho, Italy	32	C6	
Rhode Island □, U.S.A.	107	E13	
Rhodes = Ródhos, Greece	37	C10	

Place	Pg	Ref
Rhodesia = Zimbabwe ■, *Africa*	83	F2
Rhodope Mts. = Rhodopi Planina, *Bulgaria*	39	H7
Rhodopi Planina, *Bulgaria*	39	H7
Rhön = Hohe Rhön, *Germany*	19	E5
Rhondda, *U.K.*	13	F4
Rhône □, *France*	27	C8
Rhône →, *France*	27	E8
Rhum, *U.K.*	14	E2
Rhyl, *U.K.*	12	D4
Rhymney, *U.K.*	13	F4
Ri-Aba, *Eq. Guin.*	79	E6
Riachão, *Brazil*	122	C2
Riacho de Santana, *Brazil*	123	D3
Rialma, *Brazil*	123	E2
Riaño, *Spain*	30	C5
Rians, *France*	27	E9
Riansares →, *Spain*	28	F1
Riasi, *India*	63	C6
Riau □, *Indonesia*	56	D2
Riau, Kepulauan, *Indonesia*	56	D2
Riau Arch. = Riau, Kepulauan, *Indonesia*	56	D2
Riaza, *Spain*	28	D1
Riaza →, *Spain*	28	D1
Riba de Saelices, *Spain*	28	E2
Ribadavia, *Spain*	30	C2
Ribadeo, *Spain*	30	B3
Ribadesella, *Spain*	30	B5
Ribamar, *Brazil*	122	B3
Ribas, *Spain*	28	C7
Ribas do Rio Pardo, *Brazil*	125	E7
Ribble →, *U.K.*	12	C5
Ribe, *Denmark*	11	J2
Ribeauvillé, *France*	25	D14
Ribécourt, *France*	25	C9
Ribeira, *Spain*	30	C2
Ribeira Brava, *Madeira*	36	D2
Ribeira do Pombal, *Brazil*	122	D4
Ribeirão Prêto, *Brazil*	127	A6
Ribeiro Gonçalves, *Brazil*	122	C2
Ribemont, *France*	25	C10
Ribera, *Italy*	34	E6
Ribérac, *France*	26	C4
Riberalta, *Bolivia*	125	C4
Ribnica, *Slovenia*	33	C11
Rîbniţa, *Moldova*	41	J5
Ribnitz-Damgarten, *Germany*	18	A8
Riccarton, *N.Z.*	87	K4
Riccia, *Italy*	35	A7
Riccione, *Italy*	33	D9
Rice, *U.S.A.*	113	L12
Rice L., *Canada*	106	B6
Rice Lake, *U.S.A.*	108	C9
Rich, *Morocco*	74	B4
Rich Hill, *U.S.A.*	109	F7
Richards Bay, *S. Africa*	85	D5
Richards L., *Canada*	101	B7
Richardson →, *Canada*	101	B6
Richardson Springs, *U.S.A.*	112	F5
Richardton, *U.S.A.*	108	B3
Riche, C., *Australia*	89	F2
Richelieu, *France*	24	E7
Richey, *U.S.A.*	108	B2
Richfield, *U.S.A.*	110	E6
Richfield, Utah, *U.S.A.*	111	G8
Richford, *U.S.A.*	107	B12
Richibucto, *Canada*	99	C7
Richland, Ga., *U.S.A.*	105	J3
Richland, Oreg., *U.S.A.*	110	D5
Richland, Wash., *U.S.A.*	110	C4
Richland Center, *U.S.A.*	108	D9
Richlands, *U.S.A.*	104	G5
Richmond, N.S.W., *Australia*	91	E5
Richmond, Queens., *Australia*	90	C3
Richmond, *N.Z.*	87	J4
Richmond, *U.K.*	12	C6
Richmond, Calif., *U.S.A.*	112	H4
Richmond, Ind., *U.S.A.*	104	F3
Richmond, Ky., *U.S.A.*	104	G3
Richmond, Mich., *U.S.A.*	106	D2
Richmond, Mo., *U.S.A.*	108	F8
Richmond, Tex., *U.S.A.*	109	L7
Richmond, Utah, *U.S.A.*	110	F8
Richmond, Va., *U.S.A.*	104	G7
Richmond Ra., *Australia*	91	D5
Richmond-upon-Thames, *U.K.*	13	F7
Richterswil, *Switz.*	23	B7
Richton, *U.S.A.*	105	K1
Richwood, *U.S.A.*	104	F5
Ricla, *Spain*	28	D3
Ridder, *Kazakhstan*	44	D9
Ridderkerk, *Neths.*	16	E5
Riddes, *Switz.*	22	D4
Ridgecrest, *U.S.A.*	113	K9
Ridgedale, *Canada*	101	C8
Ridgefield, *U.S.A.*	112	E4
Ridgeland, *U.S.A.*	105	J5
Ridgelands, *Australia*	90	C5
Ridgetown, *Canada*	98	D3
Ridgewood, *U.S.A.*	107	F10
Ridgway, *U.S.A.*	106	E6
Riding Mountain Nat. Park, *Canada*	101	C8
Ridley, Mt., *Australia*	89	F3
Ried, *Austria*	21	G3
Riedlingen, *Germany*	19	G5
Riel, *Neths.*	17	E6
Rienza →, *Italy*	32	B4
Riesa, *Germany*	18	D9
Riesco, I., *Chile*	128	D2
Riesi, *Italy*	35	E7
Riet →, *S. Africa*	84	D3
Rieti, *Italy*	33	F9
Rieupeyroux, *France*	26	D6
Riez, *France*	27	E10
Riffe L., *U.S.A.*	112	D4
Rifle, *U.S.A.*	110	G10
Rift Valley □, *Kenya*	82	B4
Rig Rig, *Chad*	73	F7
Rīga, *Latvia*	9	H21
Riga, G. of, *Latvia*	9	H20
Rīgān, *Iran*	65	D8
Rīgas Jūras Līcis = Riga, G. of, *Latvia*	9	H20
Rigaud, *Canada*	107	A10
Rigby, *U.S.A.*	110	E8
Rīgestān □, *Afghan.*	60	D4
Riggins, *U.S.A.*	110	D5
Rignac, *France*	26	D6
Rigolet, *Canada*	99	B8
Riihimäki, *Finland*	9	F21
Riiser-Larsen-halvøya, *Antarctica*	5	C4
Rijau, *Nigeria*	79	C6
Rijeka, *Croatia*	33	C11
Rijen, *Neths.*	17	E5
Rijkevorsel, *Belgium*	17	F5
Rijn →, *Neths.*	16	D4
Rijnsberg, *Neths.*	16	D4
Rijsbergen, *Neths.*	17	E5
Rijssen, *Neths.*	16	D9
Rijswijk, *Neths.*	16	D4
Rike, *Ethiopia*	77	E4
Rikuzentakada, *Japan*	48	E10
Rila Planina, *Bulgaria*	38	G6
Riley, *U.S.A.*	110	E4
Rima →, *Nigeria*	79	C6
Rimah, Wadi ar →, *Si. Arabia*	64	E4
Rimavská Sobota, *Slovak Rep.*	21	G10
Rimbey, *Canada*	100	C6
Rimbo, *Sweden*	10	E12
Rimi, *Nigeria*	79	C6
Rímini, *Italy*	33	D9
Rîmnicu Sărat, *Romania*	38	D10
Rîmnicu Vîlcea, *Romania*	38	D7
Rimouski, *Canada*	99	C6
Rimrock, *U.S.A.*	112	D5
Rinca, *Indonesia*	57	F5
Rincón de Romos, *Mexico*	114	C4
Rinconada, *Argentina*	126	A2
Ringarum, *Sweden*	11	F10
Ringe, *Denmark*	11	J4
Ringim, *Nigeria*	79	C6
Ringkøbing, *Denmark*	11	H2
Ringling, *U.S.A.*	110	C8
Ringsaker, *Norway*	10	D4
Ringsted, *Denmark*	11	J5
Ringvassøy, *Norway*	8	B18
Rinjani, *Indonesia*	56	F5
Rinteln, *Germany*	18	C5
Río, Punta del, *Spain*	29	J2
Rio Branco, *Brazil*	124	B4
Río Branco, *Uruguay*	127	C5
Rio Brilhante, *Brazil*	127	A5
Rio Bueno, *Chile*	128	B2
Río Chico, *Venezuela*	120	A4
Rio Claro, *Brazil*	127	A6
Rio Claro, *Trin. & Tob.*	117	D7
Río Colorado, *Argentina*	128	A4
Río Cuarto, *Argentina*	126	C3
Rio das Pedras, *Mozam.*	85	C6
Rio de Contas, *Brazil*	123	D3
Rio de Janeiro, *Brazil*	123	F3
Rio de Janeiro □, *Brazil*	123	F3
Rio do Prado, *Brazil*	123	E3
Rio do Sul, *Brazil*	127	B6
Río Gallegos, *Argentina*	128	D3
Río Grande, *Argentina*	128	D3
Río Grande, *Bolivia*	124	E4
Río Grande, *Brazil*	127	C5
Río Grande, *Mexico*	114	C4
Río Grande, *Nic.*	116	D3
Rio Grande →, *U.S.A.*	109	N6
Rio Grande City, *U.S.A.*	109	M5
Río Grande del Norte →, *N. Amer.*	103	E7
Rio Grande do Norte □, *Brazil*	122	C4
Rio Grande do Sul □, *Brazil*	127	C5
Río Hato, *Panama*	116	E3
Rio Lagartos, *Mexico*	115	C7
Rio Largo, *Brazil*	122	C4
Rio Maior, *Portugal*	31	F2
Rio Marina, *Italy*	32	F7
Río Mayo, *Argentina*	128	C2
Río Mulatos, *Bolivia*	124	D4
Río Muni = Mbini □, *Eq. Guin.*	80	D2
Rio Negro, *Brazil*	127	B6
Rio Negro, *Chile*	128	B3
Rio Negro, Pantanal do, *Brazil*	125	D6
Río Pardo, *Brazil*	127	C5
Río Pico, *Argentina*	128	B2
Río Real, *Brazil*	123	D4
Río Segundo, *Argentina*	126	C3
Río Tercero, *Argentina*	126	C3
Rio Tinto, *Brazil*	122	C4
Rio Tinto, *Portugal*	30	D2
Rio Verde, *Brazil*	123	E1
Río Verde, *Mexico*	115	C5
Rio Verde de Mato Grosso, *Brazil*	125	D7
Rio Vista, *U.S.A.*	112	G5
Ríobamba, *Ecuador*	120	D2
Ríohacha, *Colombia*	120	A3
Rioja, *Peru*	124	B2
Riom, *France*	26	C7
Riom-ès-Montagnes, *France*	26	C6
Rion-des-Landes, *France*	26	E3
Rionegro, *Colombia*	120	B2
Rionero in Vúlture, *Italy*	35	B8
Rioni →, *Georgia*	43	J5
Rios, *Spain*	30	D3
Ríosucio, Caldas, *Colombia*	120	B2
Ríosucio, Choco, *Colombia*	120	B2
Riou L., *Canada*	101	B7
Rioz, *France*	25	E13
Riozinho →, *Brazil*	120	D4
Riparia, Dora →, *Italy*	32	C4
Ripatransone, *Italy*	33	F10
Ripley, *Canada*	106	B3
Ripley, Calif., *U.S.A.*	113	M12
Ripley, N.Y., *U.S.A.*	106	D5
Ripley, Tenn., *U.S.A.*	109	H10
Ripoll, *Spain*	28	C7
Ripon, *U.K.*	12	C6
Ripon, Calif., *U.S.A.*	112	H5
Ripon, Wis., *U.S.A.*	104	D1
Riposto, *Italy*	35	E8
Risalpur, *Pakistan*	62	B4
Risan, Montenegro, *Yug.*	21	N8
Risaralda □, *Colombia*	120	B2
Riscle, *France*	26	E3
Rishã', W. ar →, *Si. Arabia*	64	E5
Rishiri-Tō, *Japan*	48	B10
Rishon le Ziyyon, *Israel*	69	D3
Risle →, *France*	24	C7
Rison, *U.S.A.*	109	J8
Risør, *Norway*	11	F3
Rissani, *Morocco*	74	B4
Riti, *Nigeria*	79	D6
Rittman, *U.S.A.*	106	F3
Ritzville, *U.S.A.*	110	C4
Riva Bella, *France*	24	C6
Riva del Garda, *Italy*	32	C7
Rivadavia, Buenos Aires, *Argentina*	126	D3
Rivadavia, Mendoza, *Argentina*	126	C2
Rivadavia, Salta, *Argentina*	126	A3
Rivadavia, *Chile*	126	B1
Rivarolo Canavese, *Italy*	32	C4
Rivas, *Nic.*	116	D2
Rive-de-Gier, *France*	27	C8
River Cess, *Liberia*	78	D3
Rivera, *Uruguay*	127	C4
Riverdale, *U.S.A.*	112	J7
Riverhead, *U.S.A.*	107	F12
Riverhurst, *Canada*	101	C7
Riverina, *Australia*	89	E3
Rivers, *Canada*	101	C8
Rivers □, *Nigeria*	79	E6
Rivers, L. of the, *Canada*	101	D7
Rivers Inlet, *Canada*	100	C3
Riversdale, *S. Africa*	84	E3
Riverside, Calif., *U.S.A.*	113	M9
Riverside, Wyo., *U.S.A.*	110	F10
Riversleigh, *Australia*	90	B2
Riverton, *Australia*	91	E2
Riverton, *Canada*	101	C9
Riverton, *N.Z.*	87	M1
Riverton, *U.S.A.*	110	E9
Riverton Heights, *U.S.A.*	112	C4
Rives, *France*	27	C9
Rivesaltes, *France*	26	F6
Riviera, *Europe*	32	E5
Riviera di Levante, *Italy*	32	D6
Riviera di Ponente, *Italy*	32	D5
Rivière-à-Pierre, *Canada*	99	C5
Rivière-au-Renard, *Canada*	99	C7
Rivière-du-Loup, *Canada*	99	C6
Rivière-Pentecôte, *Canada*	99	C6
Rivière-Pilote, *Martinique*	117	D7
Rivne, *Ukraine*	41	G4
Rívoli, *Italy*	32	C4
Rivoli B., *Australia*	91	F3
Rixensart, *Belgium*	17	G5
Riyadh = Ar Riyāḍ, *Si. Arabia*	64	E5
Rize, *Turkey*	67	B9
Rizhao, *China*	51	G10
Rizokarpaso, *Cyprus*	66	E6
Rizzuto, C., *Italy*	35	D10
Rjukan, *Norway*	10	E2
Roa, *Norway*	10	D4
Roa, *Spain*	30	D7
Road Town, *Virgin Is.*	117	C7
Roag, L., *U.K.*	14	C2
Roanne, *France*	27	B8
Roanoke, Ala., *U.S.A.*	105	J3
Roanoke, Va., *U.S.A.*	104	G6
Roanoke →, *U.S.A.*	105	H7
Roanoke I., *U.S.A.*	105	H8
Roanoke Rapids, *U.S.A.*	105	G7
Roatán, *Honduras*	116	C2
Robbins I., *Australia*	90	G4
Robe →, *Australia*	88	D2
Robe →, *Ireland*	15	C2
Röbel, *Germany*	18	B8
Robert Lee, *U.S.A.*	109	K4
Roberts, *U.S.A.*	110	E7
Robertsganj, *India*	63	G10
Robertson, *S. Africa*	84	E2
Robertson I., *Antarctica*	5	C18
Robertson Ra., *Australia*	88	D3
Robertstown, *Australia*	91	E2
Roberval, *Canada*	99	C5
Robeson Chan., *Greenland*	4	A4
Robinson →, *Australia*	90	B2
Robinson Ra., *Australia*	89	E2
Robinson River, *Australia*	90	B2
Robinvale, *Australia*	91	E3
Roblin, *Canada*	101	C8
Roboré, *Bolivia*	125	D6
Robson, Mt., *Canada*	100	C5
Robstown, *U.S.A.*	109	M6
Roca, C. da, *Portugal*	6	H4
Roca Partida, I., *Mexico*	114	D2
Rocas, I., *Brazil*	122	B5
Rocca d'Aspidé, *Italy*	35	B8
Rocca San Casciano, *Italy*	33	D8
Roccalbegna, *Italy*	33	F8
Roccastrada, *Italy*	33	F8
Roccella Iónica, *Italy*	35	D9
Rocha, *Uruguay*	127	C5
Rochdale, *U.K.*	12	D5
Rochechouart, *France*	26	C4
Rochedo, *Brazil*	125	D7
Rochefort, *Belgium*	17	H6
Rochefort, *France*	26	C3
Rochefort-en-Terre, *France*	24	E4
Rochelle, *U.S.A.*	108	E10
Rocher River, *Canada*	100	A6
Rocherath, *Belgium*	17	H8
Rocheservière, *France*	24	F5
Rochester, *Canada*	100	C6
Rochester, *U.K.*	13	F8
Rochester, Ind., *U.S.A.*	104	E2
Rochester, Minn., *U.S.A.*	108	C8
Rochester, N.H., *U.S.A.*	107	C14
Rochester, N.Y., *U.S.A.*	106	C7
Rociana, *Spain*	31	H4
Rociu, *Romania*	38	E8
Rock →, *Canada*	100	A3
Rock Hill, *U.S.A.*	105	H5
Rock Island, *U.S.A.*	108	E9
Rock Rapids, *U.S.A.*	108	D6
Rock River, *U.S.A.*	110	F11
Rock Sound, *Bahamas*	116	B4
Rock Springs, Mont., *U.S.A.*	110	C10
Rock Springs, Wyo., *U.S.A.*	110	F9
Rock Valley, *U.S.A.*	108	D6
Rockall, *Atl. Oc.*	6	D3
Rockanje, *Neths.*	16	E4
Rockdale, Tex., *U.S.A.*	109	K6
Rockdale, Wash., *U.S.A.*	112	C5
Rockefeller Plateau, *Antarctica*	5	E14
Rockford, *U.S.A.*	108	D10
Rockglen, *Canada*	101	D7
Rockhampton, *Australia*	90	C5
Rockhampton Downs, *Australia*	90	B2
Rockingham, *Australia*	89	F2
Rockingham B., *Australia*	90	B4
Rockingham Forest, *U.K.*	13	E7
Rocklake, *U.S.A.*	108	A5
Rockland, *Canada*	107	A9
Rockland, Idaho, *U.S.A.*	110	E7
Rockland, Maine, *U.S.A.*	99	D6
Rockland, Mich., *U.S.A.*	108	B10
Rocklin, *U.S.A.*	112	G5
Rockmart, *U.S.A.*	105	H3
Rockport, Mo., *U.S.A.*	108	E7
Rockport, Tex., *U.S.A.*	109	L6
Rocksprings, *U.S.A.*	109	K4
Rockville, Conn., *U.S.A.*	107	E12
Rockville, Md., *U.S.A.*	104	F7
Rockwall, *U.S.A.*	109	J6
Rockwell City, *U.S.A.*	108	D7
Rockwood, *U.S.A.*	105	H3
Rocky Ford, *U.S.A.*	108	F3
Rocky Gully, *Australia*	89	F2
Rocky Lane, *Canada*	100	B5
Rocky Mount, *U.S.A.*	105	H7
Rocky Mountain House, *Canada*	100	C6
Rocky Mts., *N. Amer.*	100	C4
Rockyford, *Canada*	100	C6
Rocroi, *France*	25	C11
Rod, *Pakistan*	60	E3
Rødberg, *Norway*	10	D2
Rødby, *Denmark*	11	K5
Rødbyhavn, *Denmark*	11	K5
Roddickton, *Canada*	99	B8
Rødding, *Denmark*	11	J3
Rødekro, *Denmark*	11	J3
Roden, *Neths.*	16	B8
Rodenkirchen, *Germany*	18	B4
Roderick I., *Canada*	100	C3
Rodez, *France*	26	D6
Rodholívos, *Greece*	39	J6
Rodhopoú, *Greece*	37	D5
Ródhos, *Greece*	37	C10
Rodi Gargánico, *Italy*	35	A8
Rodna, *Romania*	38	B7
Rodney, *Canada*	106	D3
Rodney, C., *N.Z.*	87	G5
Rodniki, *Russia*	42	B5
Rodriguez, *Ind. Oc.*	3	E13
Roe →, *U.K.*	15	A5
Roebling, *U.S.A.*	107	F10
Roebourne, *Australia*	88	D2
Roebuck B., *Australia*	88	C3
Roebuck Plains, *Australia*	88	C3
Roer →, *Neths.*	17	F7
Roermond, *Neths.*	17	F7
Roes Welcome Sd., *Canada*	97	B11
Roeselare, *Belgium*	17	G2
Rœulx, *Belgium*	17	G4
Rogachev = Ragachow, *Belarus*	41	F6
Rogagua, L., *Bolivia*	124	C4
Rogaška Slatina, *Slovenia*	33	B12
Rogatec, *Slovenia*	33	B12
Rogatyn, *Ukraine*	41	H3
Rogdhia, *Greece*	37	D7
Rogers, *U.S.A.*	109	G7
Rogers City, *U.S.A.*	104	C4
Rogerson, *U.S.A.*	110	E6
Rogersville, *U.S.A.*	105	G4
Roggan River, *Canada*	98	B4
Roggel, *Neths.*	17	F7
Roggeveldberge, *S. Africa*	84	E3
Roggiano Gravina, *Italy*	35	C9
Rogliano, *France*	27	F13
Rogliano, *Italy*	35	C9
Rogoaguado, L., *Bolivia*	125	C4
Rogue →, *U.S.A.*	110	E1
Rohan, *France*	24	D4
Róhda, *Greece*	37	A3
Rohnert Park, *U.S.A.*	112	G4
Rohrbach-lès-Bitche, *France*	25	C14
Rohri, *Pakistan*	62	F3
Rohri Canal, *Pakistan*	62	F3
Rohtak, *India*	62	E7
Roi Et, *Thailand*	58	D4
Roisel, *France*	25	C10
Roja, *Latvia*	9	H20
Rojas, *Argentina*	126	C3
Rojo, C., *Mexico*	115	C5
Rokan →, *Indonesia*	56	D2
Rokeby, *Australia*	90	A3
Rokiškis, *Lithuania*	9	J21
Rokitno, *Russia*	42	E2
Rolândia, *Brazil*	127	A5
Rolde, *Neths.*	16	C9
Rolla, Kans., *U.S.A.*	109	G4
Rolla, Mo., *U.S.A.*	108	G9
Rolla, N. Dak., *U.S.A.*	108	A5
Rollag, *Norway*	10	D3
Rolle, *Switz.*	22	D2
Rolleston, *Australia*	90	C4
Rollingstone, *Australia*	90	B4
Rom, *Sudan*	77	F3
Roma, *Australia*	91	D4
Roma, *Italy*	34	A5
Roma, *Sweden*	9	H18
Roman, *Romania*	38	C9
Roman, *Russia*	45	C12
Roman-Kosh, Gora, *Ukraine*	41	K8
Romanche →, *France*	27	C9
Romang, *Indonesia*	57	F7
Români, *Egypt*	69	E1
Romania ■, *Europe*	38	D8
Romano, Cayo, *Cuba*	116	B4
Romano di Lombárdia, *Italy*	32	C6
Romanovka = Basarabeasca, *Moldova*	41	J5
Romans-sur-Isère, *France*	27	C9
Romanshorn, *Switz.*	23	A8
Romblon, *Phil.*	55	E5
Rombo □, *Tanzania*	82	C4
Rome = Roma, *Italy*	34	A5
Rome, Ga., *U.S.A.*	105	H3
Rome, N.Y., *U.S.A.*	107	C9
Romeleåsen, *Sweden*	11	J7
Romenay, *France*	27	B9
Romerike, *Norway*	10	D5
Romilly-sur-Seine, *France*	25	D10
Romîni, *Romania*	38	E7
Rommani, *Morocco*	74	B3
Romney, *U.S.A.*	104	F6
Romney Marsh, *U.K.*	13	F8
Romny, *Ukraine*	41	G7
Rømø, *Denmark*	11	J2
Romodan, *Ukraine*	41	G7
Romodanovo, *Russia*	42	C7
Romont, *Switz.*	22	C3
Romorantin-Lanthenay, *France*	25	E8
Romsdalen, *Norway*	10	B2
Ron, *Vietnam*	58	D6
Rona, *U.K.*	14	D3
Ronan, *U.S.A.*	110	C6
Roncador, Cayos, *Caribbean*	116	D3
Roncador, Serra do, *Brazil*	123	D1
Roncesvalles, Paso, *Spain*	28	B3
Ronceverte, *U.S.A.*	104	G5
Ronciglione, *Italy*	33	F9
Ronco →, *Italy*	33	D9
Ronda, *Spain*	31	J5
Ronda, Serranía de, *Spain*	31	J5
Rondane, *Norway*	10	C3
Rondón, *Colombia*	120	B3
Rondônia, *Brazil*	125	C5
Rondônia □, *Brazil*	125	C5
Rondonópolis, *Brazil*	125	D7
Rong Jiang →, *China*	52	E7
Rong Xian, Guangxi Zhuangzu, *China*	53	F8
Rong'an, *China*	52	E7
Rongjiang, *China*	52	E7
Rongshui, *China*	52	E7
Rønne, *Denmark*	9	J16
Ronne Ice Shelf, *Antarctica*	5	D18
Ronsard, C., *Australia*	89	D1
Ronse, *Belgium*	17	G3
Ronuro →, *Brazil*	125	C7
Roodepoort, *S. Africa*	85	D4

Sahara

Roodeschool, *Neths.* 16 B9
Roof Butte, *U.S.A.* 111 H9
Roompot, *Neths.* 17 E3
Roorkee, *India* 62 E7
Roosendaal, *Neths.* 17 E4
Roosevelt, *Minn., U.S.A.* 108 A7
Roosevelt, *Utah, U.S.A.* 110 F8
Roosevelt →, *Brazil* 125 B5
Roosevelt, Mt., *Canada* 100 B3
Roosevelt I., *Antarctica* 5 D12
Roosevelt Res., *U.S.A.* 111 K8
Roper →, *Australia* 90 A2
Ropesville, *U.S.A.* 109 J3
Roque Pérez, *Argentina* 126 D4
Roquefort, *France* 26 D3
Roquemaure, *France* 27 D8
Roquetas, *Spain* 28 E5
Roquevaire, *France* 27 E9
Roraima □, *Brazil* 121 C5
Roraima, Mt., *Venezuela* 121 B5
Rorketon, *Canada* 101 C9
Røros, *Norway* 10 B5
Rorschach, *Switz.* 23 B8
Rosa, *Zambia* 83 D3
Rosa, C., *Algeria* 75 A6
Rosa, Monte, *Europe* 22 E5
Rosal, *Spain* 30 D2
Rosal de la Frontera, *Spain* 31 H3
Rosalia, *U.S.A.* 110 C5
Rosamond, *U.S.A.* 113 L8
Rosans, *France* 27 D9
Rosario, *Argentina* 126 C3
Rosário, *Brazil* 122 B3
Rosario, *Baja Calif. Mexico* 114 A1
Rosario, *Sinaloa, Mexico* 114 C3
Rosario, *Paraguay* 126 A4
Rosario, Villa del, *Venezuela* 120 A3
Rosario de la Frontera, *Argentina* 126 B3
Rosario de Lerma, *Argentina* 126 A2
Rosario del Tala, *Argentina* 126 C4
Rosário do Sul, *Brazil* 127 C5
Rosário Oeste, *Brazil* 125 C6
Rosarito, *Mexico* 113 N9
Rosarno, *Italy* 35 D8
Rosas, *Spain* 28 C8
Rosas, G. de, *Spain* 28 C8
Roscoe, *U.S.A.* 108 C5
Roscoff, *France* 24 D3
Roscommon, *Ireland* 15 C3
Roscommon, *U.S.A.* 104 C3
Roscommon □, *Ireland* 15 C3
Roscrea, *Ireland* 15 D4
Rose →, *Australia* 90 A2
Rose Blanche, *Canada* 99 C8
Rose Harbour, *Canada* 100 C2
Rose Pt., *Canada* 100 C2
Rose Valley, *Canada* 101 C8
Roseau, *Domin.* 117 C7
Roseau, *U.S.A.* 108 A7
Rosebery, *Australia* 90 G4
Rosebud, *U.S.A.* 109 K6
Roseburg, *U.S.A.* 110 E2
Rosedale, *Australia* 90 C5
Rosedale, *U.S.A.* 109 J9
Rosée, *Belgium* 17 H5
Roseland, *U.S.A.* 112 G4
Rosemary, *Canada* 100 C6
Rosenberg, *U.S.A.* 109 L7
Rosendaël, *France* 25 A9
Rosenheim, *Germany* 19 H8
Roseto degli Abruzzi, *Italy* 33 F11
Rosetown, *Canada* 101 C7
Rosetta = Rashîd, *Egypt* 76 H7
Roseville, *U.S.A.* 112 G5
Rosewood, *N. Terr., Australia* 88 C4
Rosewood, *Queens., Australia* 91 D5
Roshkhvār, *Iran* 65 C8
Rosières-en-Santerre, *France* 25 C9
Rosignano Marittimo, *Italy* 32 E7
Rosignol, *Guyana* 121 B6
Roşiori de Vede, *Romania* 38 E8
Rositsa, *Bulgaria* 38 F10
Rositsa →, *Bulgaria* 38 F8
Roskilde, *Denmark* 11 J6
Roskilde Amtskommune □, *Denmark* 11 J6
Roskilde Fjord, *Denmark* 11 J6
Roslavl, *Russia* 40 F7
Roslyn, *Australia* 91 E4
Rosmaninhal, *Portugal* 31 F3
Rosmead, *S. Africa* 84 E4
Røsnæs, *Denmark* 11 J4
Rosolini, *Italy* 35 F7
Rosporden, *France* 24 E3
Ross, *Australia* 90 G4
Ross, *N.Z.* 87 K3
Ross I., *Antarctica* 5 D11
Ross Ice Shelf, *Antarctica* 5 E12
Ross L., *U.S.A.* 110 B3
Ross-on-Wye, *U.K.* 13 F5
Ross Sea, *Antarctica* 5 D11
Rossa, *Switz.* 23 D8
Rossan Pt., *Ireland* 15 B3
Rossano Cálabro, *Italy* 35 C9
Rossburn, *Canada* 101 C8
Rosseau, *Canada* 106 A5
Rossignol, L., *Canada* 98 B5
Rossignol Res., *Canada* 99 D6
Rossland, *Canada* 100 D5
Rosslare, *Ireland* 15 D5
Rosslau, *Germany* 18 D8
Rosso, *Mauritania* 78 B1
Rosso, C., *France* 27 F12
Rossosh, *Russia* 42 E4
Rossport, *Canada* 98 C2
Rossum, *Neths.* 16 E6
Røssvatnet, *Norway* 8 D16
Rossville, *Australia* 90 B4
Røst, *Norway* 8 C15
Rosthern, *Canada* 101 C7
Rostock, *Germany* 18 A8
Rostov, *Don, Russia* 43 G4
Rostov, *Yarosl., Russia* 42 B4
Rostrenen, *France* 24 D3
Roswell, *U.S.A.* 109 J2
Rosyth, *U.K.* 14 E5
Rota, *Spain* 31 J4
Rotälven →, *Sweden* 10 C8
Rotan, *U.S.A.* 109 J4
Rotem, *Belgium* 17 F7
Rotenburg, *Germany* 18 B5
Roth, *Germany* 19 F7
Rothaargebirge, *Germany* 18 E4
Rothenburg, *Switz.* 23 B6
Rothenburg ob der Tauber, *Germany* 19 F6
Rother →, *U.K.* 13 G8
Rotherham, *U.K.* 12 D6
Rothes, *U.K.* 14 D5
Rothesay, *Canada* 99 C6
Rothesay, *U.K.* 14 F3
Rothrist, *Switz.* 22 B5
Roti, *Indonesia* 57 F6
Roto, *Australia* 91 E4
Rotondella, *Italy* 35 B9
Rotoroa, L., *N.Z.* 87 J4
Rotorua, *N.Z.* 87 H6
Rotorua, L., *N.Z.* 87 H6
Rotselaar, *Belgium* 17 G5
Rott →, *Germany* 19 G9
Rotten →, *Switz.* 22 D5
Rottenburg, *Germany* 19 G4
Rotterdam, *Neths.* 16 E5
Rottnest I., *Australia* 89 F2
Rottumeroog, *Neths.* 16 A9
Rottweil, *Germany* 19 G4
Rotuma, *Fiji* 92 J9
Roubaix, *France* 25 B10
Rouen, *France* 24 C8
Rouergue, *France* 26 D5
Rouillac, *France* 26 C3
Rouleau, *Canada* 101 C8
Round Mountain, *U.S.A.* 110 G5
Round Mt., *Australia* 91 E5
Roundup, *U.S.A.* 110 C9
Roura, *Fr. Guiana* 121 C7
Rousay, *U.K.* 14 B5
Rouses Point, *U.S.A.* 107 B11
Roussillon, *Isère, France* 27 C8
Roussillon, *Pyrénées-Or., France* 26 F6
Rouveen, *Neths.* 16 C8
Rouxville, *S. Africa* 84 E4
Rouyn, *Canada* 98 C4
Rovaniemi, *Finland* 8 C21
Rovato, *Italy* 32 C7
Rovenki, *Ukraine* 41 H10
Rovereto, *Italy* 32 C8
Rovigo, *Italy* 33 C8
Rovinari, *Romania* 38 E6
Rovinj, *Croatia* 33 C10
Rovira, *Colombia* 120 C2
Rovno = Rivne, *Ukraine* 41 G4
Rovnoye, *Russia* 42 E8
Rovuma →, *Tanzania* 83 E5
Row'ān, *Iran* 65 C6
Rowena, *Australia* 91 D4
Rowley Shoals, *Australia* 88 C2
Roxa, *Guinea-Biss.* 78 C1
Roxas, *Capiz, Phil.* 55 F5
Roxas, *Isabela, Phil.* 55 C4
Roxas, *Mindoro, Phil.* 55 E4
Roxboro, *U.S.A.* 105 G6
Roxborough Downs, *Australia* 90 C2
Roxburgh, *N.Z.* 87 L2
Roxen, *Sweden* 11 F9
Roy, *Mont., U.S.A.* 110 C9
Roy, *N. Mex., U.S.A.* 109 H2
Roy Hill, *Australia* 88 D2
Roya, Peña, *Spain* 28 E4
Royal Leamington Spa, *U.K.* 13 E6
Royal Tunbridge Wells, *U.K.* 13 F8
Royan, *France* 26 C2
Roye, *France* 25 C9
Røyken, *Norway* 10 E4
Rožaj, *Montenegro, Yug.* 21 N10
Rozay-en-Brie, *France* 25 D9
Rozdilna, *Ukraine* 41 J6
Rozhyshche, *Ukraine* 41 G3
Rožňava, *Slovak Rep.* 20 G10
Rozoy-sur-Serre, *France* 25 C11
Rtishchevo, *Russia* 42 D6
Rúa, *Spain* 30 C3
Ruacaná, *Angola* 84 B1
Ruahine Ra., *N.Z.* 87 H6
Ruapehu, *N.Z.* 87 H5
Ruapuke I., *N.Z.* 87 M2
Ruâq, W. →, *Egypt* 69 F2
Rub' al Khali, *Si. Arabia* 68 D4
Rubeho Mts., *Tanzania* 82 D4
Rubezhnoye = Rubizhne, *Ukraine* 41 H10
Rubh a' Mhail, *U.K.* 14 F2
Rubha Hunish, *U.K.* 14 D2
Rubha Robhanais = Lewis, Butt of, *U.K.* 14 C2
Rubiataba, *Brazil* 123 E2
Rubicon →, *U.S.A.* 112 G5
Rubicone →, *Italy* 33 D9
Rubinéia, *Brazil* 123 F1
Rubino, *Ivory C.* 78 D4
Rubio, *Venezuela* 120 B3
Rubizhne, *Ukraine* 41 H10
Rubtsovsk, *Russia* 44 D9
Ruby L., *U.S.A.* 110 F6
Ruby Mts., *U.S.A.* 110 F6
Rucheng, *China* 53 E9
Rud, *Norway* 10 D4
Rūd Sar, *Iran* 65 B6
Ruda Śląska, *Poland* 20 E8
Rudall, *Australia* 91 E2
Rudall →, *Australia* 88 D3
Ruden, *Germany* 18 A9
Rüdersdorf, *Germany* 18 C9
Rudewa, *Tanzania* 83 E3
Rudkøbing, *Denmark* 11 K4
Rudnik, *Serbia, Yug.* 21 L10
Rudnogorsk, *Russia* 45 D11
Rudnya, *Russia* 40 E6
Rudnyy, *Kazakhstan* 44 D7
Rudolf, Ostrov, *Russia* 44 A6
Rudolstadt, *Germany* 18 E7
Rudong, *China* 53 A13
Rudozem, *Bulgaria* 39 H7
Rudyard, *U.S.A.* 104 B3
Rue, *France* 25 B8
Ruelle, *France* 26 C4
Rufa'a, *Sudan* 77 E3
Ruffec, *France* 26 B4
Rufiji □, *Tanzania* 82 D4
Rufiji →, *Tanzania* 82 D4
Rufino, *Argentina* 126 C3
Rufisque, *Senegal* 78 C1
Rufunsa, *Zambia* 83 F2
Rugao, *China* 53 A13
Rugby, *U.K.* 13 E6
Rugby, *U.S.A.* 108 A5
Rügen, *Germany* 18 A9
Rugles, *France* 24 D7
Ruhengeri, *Rwanda* 82 C2
Ruhla, *Germany* 18 E6
Ruhland, *Germany* 18 D9
Ruhnu saar, *Estonia* 9 H20
Ruhr →, *Germany* 18 D2
Ruhuhu →, *Tanzania* 83 E3
Rui Barbosa, *Brazil* 123 D3
Rui'an, *China* 53 D13
Ruichang, *China* 53 C10
Ruidosa, *U.S.A.* 109 L2
Ruidoso, *U.S.A.* 111 K11
Ruili, *China* 52 E1
Ruinen, *Neths.* 16 C8
Ruinerwold, *Neths.* 16 C8
Ruiten A Kanaal →, *Neths.* 16 C10
Ruivo, Pico, *Madeira* 36 D3
Rujm Tal'at al Jamā'ah, *Jordan* 69 E4
Ruk, *Pakistan* 62 F3
Rukwa □, *Tanzania* 82 D3
Rukwa L., *Tanzania* 82 D3
Rulhieres, C., *Australia* 88 B4
Rulles, *Belgium* 17 J7
Rum Cay, *Bahamas* 117 B5
Rum Jungle, *Australia* 88 B5
Ruma, *Serbia, Yug.* 21 K9
Rumāḩ, *Si. Arabia* 64 E5
Rumania = Romania ■, *Europe* 38 D8
Rumaylah, *Iraq* 64 D5
Rumbalara, *Australia* 90 D1
Rumbêk, *Sudan* 77 F2
Rumbeke, *Belgium* 17 G2
Rumelange, *Lux.* 17 K8
Rumford, *U.S.A.* 107 B14
Rumilly, *France* 27 C9
Rumoi, *Japan* 48 C10
Rumonge, *Burundi* 82 C2
Rumsey, *Canada* 100 C6
Rumula, *Australia* 90 B4
Rumuruti, *Kenya* 82 B4
Runan, *China* 50 H8
Runanga, *N.Z.* 87 K3
Runaway, C., *N.Z.* 87 G6
Runcorn, *U.K.* 12 D5
Rungwa, *Tanzania* 82 D3
Rungwa →, *Tanzania* 82 D3
Rungwe, *Tanzania* 83 D3
Rungwe □, *Tanzania* 83 D3
Runka, *Nigeria* 79 C6
Runton Ra., *Australia* 88 D3
Ruokolahti, *Finland* 40 B5
Ruoqiang, *China* 54 C3
Rupa, *India* 61 F18
Rupar, *India* 62 D7
Rupat, *Indonesia* 56 D2
Rupert →, *Canada* 98 B4
Rupert House = Waskaganish, *Canada* 98 B4
Rupununi →, *Guyana* 121 C6
Rur →, *Germany* 18 E2
Rurrenabaque, *Bolivia* 124 C4
Rus →, *Spain* 29 F2
Rusambo, *Zimbabwe* 83 F3
Rusape, *Zimbabwe* 83 F3
Ruschuk = Ruse, *Bulgaria* 38 F8
Ruse, *Bulgaria* 38 F8
Ruşeţu, *Romania* 38 E10
Rushan, *China* 51 F11
Rushden, *U.K.* 13 E7
Rushford, *U.S.A.* 108 D9
Rushville, *Ill., U.S.A.* 108 E9
Rushville, *Ind., U.S.A.* 104 F3
Rushville, *Nebr., U.S.A.* 108 D3
Rushworth, *Australia* 91 F4
Russas, *Brazil* 122 B4
Russell, *Canada* 101 C8
Russell, *U.S.A.* 108 F5
Russell L., *Man., Canada* 101 B8
Russell L., *N.W.T., Canada* 100 A5
Russellkonda, *India* 61 K14
Russellville, *Ala., U.S.A.* 105 H2
Russellville, *Ark., U.S.A.* 109 H8
Russellville, *Ky., U.S.A.* 105 G2
Russi, *Italy* 33 D9
Russia ■, *Eurasia* 45 C11
Russian →, *U.S.A.* 112 G3
Russkaya Polyana, *Kazakhstan* 44 D8
Russkoye Ustie, *Russia* 4 B15
Rustam, *Pakistan* 62 B5
Rustam Shahr, *Pakistan* 62 F2
Rustavi, *Georgia* 43 K7
Rustenburg, *S. Africa* 84 D4
Ruston, *U.S.A.* 109 J8
Ruswil, *Switz.* 22 B6
Rutana, *Burundi* 82 C2
Rute, *Spain* 31 H6
Ruteng, *Indonesia* 57 F6
Ruth, *Mich., U.S.A.* 106 C2
Ruth, *Nev., U.S.A.* 110 G6
Rutherford, *U.S.A.* 112 G4
Rutherglen, *U.K.* 14 F4
Rüti, *Switz.* 23 B7
Rutigliano, *Italy* 35 A10
Rutland Plains, *Australia* 90 B3
Rutledge →, *Canada* 101 A6
Rutledge L., *Canada* 101 A6
Rutqa, W. →, *Syria* 67 E9
Rutshuru, *Zaïre* 82 C2
Ruurlo, *Neths.* 16 D8
Ruvo di Púglia, *Italy* 35 A9
Ruvu, *Tanzania* 82 D4
Ruvu →, *Tanzania* 82 D4
Ruvuma □, *Tanzania* 83 E4
Ruwais, *U.A.E.* 65 E7
Ruwenzori, *Africa* 82 B2
Ruyigi, *Burundi* 82 C3
Ruyuan, *China* 53 E9
Ruzayevka, *Russia* 42 C7
Ružomberok, *Slovak Rep.* 20 F9
Rwanda ■, *Africa* 82 C3
Ry, *Denmark* 11 H3
Ryakhovo, *Bulgaria* 38 F9
Ryan, L., *U.K.* 14 G3
Ryazan, *Russia* 42 C4
Ryazhsk, *Russia* 42 D5
Rybache = Rybachye, *Kazakhstan* 44 E9
Rybachye, *Kazakhstan* 44 E9
Rybinsk, *Russia* 42 A4
Rybinskoye Vdkhr., *Russia* 40 C10
Rybnik, *Poland* 20 E8
Rybnitsa = Rîbniţa, *Moldova* 41 J5
Rybnoye, *Russia* 42 C4
Rychwał, *Poland* 20 C8
Ryde, *U.K.* 13 G6
Ryderwood, *U.S.A.* 112 D3
Rydöbruk, *Sweden* 11 H7
Rydułtowy, *Poland* 20 E8
Rye, *U.K.* 13 G8
Rye →, *U.K.* 12 C7
Rye Patch Reservoir, *U.S.A.* 110 F4
Ryegate, *U.S.A.* 110 C9
Rylsk, *Russia* 42 E2
Rylstone, *Australia* 91 E4
Ryn Peski, *Kazakhstan* 43 G9
Ryōthu, *Japan* 48 E9
Rypin, *Poland* 20 B9
Ryūgasaki, *Japan* 49 G10
Ryūkyū Is. = Ryūkyū-rettō, *Japan* 49 M2
Ryūkyū-rettō, *Japan* 49 M2
Rzeszów, *Poland* 20 E11
Rzhev, *Russia* 42 B2

S

Sa, *Thailand* 58 C3
Sa Dec, *Vietnam* 59 G5
Sa'ādatābād, *Fārs, Iran* 65 D7
Sa'ādatābād, *Kermān, Iran* 65 D7
Saale →, *Germany* 18 D7
Saaler Bodden, *Germany* 18 A8
Saalfeld, *Germany* 18 E7
Saane →, *Switz.* 22 B4
Saar →, *Europe* 25 C13
Saarbrücken, *Germany* 19 F2
Saarburg, *Germany* 19 F2
Saaremaa, *Estonia* 9 G20
Saarijärvi, *Finland* 9 E21
Saariselkä, *Finland* 8 B23
Saarland □, *Germany* 25 C13
Saarlouis, *Germany* 19 F2
Saas Fee, *Switz.* 22 D5
Sab 'Ābar, *Syria* 66 F7
Saba, *W. Indies* 117 C7
Šabac, *Serbia, Yug.* 21 L9
Sabadell, *Spain* 28 D7
Sabah □, *Malaysia* 56 C5
Sabak Bernam, *Malaysia* 59 L3
Sabalān, Kūhhā-ye, *Iran* 67 C12
Sábana de la Mar, *Dom. Rep.* 117 C6
Sábanalarga, *Colombia* 120 A3
Sabang, *Indonesia* 56 C1
Sabará, *Brazil* 123 E3
Sabattis, *U.S.A.* 107 B10
Sabáudia, *Italy* 34 A6
Sabaya, *Bolivia* 124 D4
Saberania, *Indonesia* 57 E9
Sabhah, *Libya* 73 C7
Sabie, *S. Africa* 85 D5
Sabinal, *Mexico* 114 A3
Sabinal, *U.S.A.* 109 L5
Sabinal, Punta del, *Spain* 29 J2
Sabinas, *Mexico* 114 B4
Sabinas →, *Mexico* 114 B4
Sabinas Hidalgo, *Mexico* 114 B4
Sabine →, *U.S.A.* 109 L8
Sabine L., *U.S.A.* 109 L8
Sabine Pass, *U.S.A.* 109 L8
Sabinópolis, *Brazil* 123 E3
Sabinov, *Slovak Rep.* 20 F11
Sabirabad, *Azerbaijan* 43 K9
Sabkhet el Bardawîl, *Egypt* 69 D2
Sablayan, *Phil.* 55 E4
Sable, C., *Canada* 99 D6
Sable, C., *U.S.A.* 103 E10
Sable I., *Canada* 99 D8
Sablé-sur-Sarthe, *France* 24 E6
Saboeiro, *Brazil* 122 C4
Sabor →, *Portugal* 30 D3
Sabou, *Burkina Faso* 78 C4
Sabrātah, *Libya* 75 B7
Sabria, *Tunisia* 75 B6
Sabrina Coast, *Antarctica* 5 C9
Sabugal, *Portugal* 30 E3
Sabulubek, *Indonesia* 56 E1
Sabzevār, *Iran* 65 B8
Sabzvārān, *Iran* 65 D8
Sac City, *U.S.A.* 108 D7
Sacedón, *Spain* 28 E2
Sachigo →, *Canada* 98 A2
Sachigo, L., *Canada* 98 B1
Sachkhere, *Georgia* 43 J6
Sachseln, *Switz.* 23 C6
Sachsen □, *Germany* 18 E9
Sachsen-Anhalt □, *Germany* 18 D8
Sacile, *Italy* 33 C9
Sackets Harbor, *U.S.A.* 107 C8
Saco, *Maine, U.S.A.* 105 D10
Saco, *Mont., U.S.A.* 110 B10
Sacramento, *Brazil* 123 E2
Sacramento, *U.S.A.* 112 G5
Sacramento →, *U.S.A.* 112 G5
Sacramento Mts., *U.S.A.* 111 K11
Sacramento Valley, *U.S.A.* 112 G5
Sacratif, C., *Spain* 29 J1
Săcueni, *Romania* 38 B5
Sada, *Spain* 30 B2
Sádaba, *Spain* 28 C3
Sadani, *Tanzania* 82 D4
Sadao, *Thailand* 59 J3
Sadd el Aali, *Egypt* 76 C3
Saddle Mt., *U.S.A.* 112 E3
Sade, *Nigeria* 79 C7
Sadimi, *Zaïre* 83 D1
Sa'dīyah, Hawr as, *Iraq* 67 F12
Sado, *Japan* 48 E9
Sado →, *Portugal* 31 G2
Sadon, *Burma* 61 G20
Sadon, *Russia* 43 J6
Sæby, *Denmark* 11 G4
Saegerstown, *U.S.A.* 106 E4
Saelices, *Spain* 28 F2
Safaga, *Egypt* 76 B3
Şafājah, *Si. Arabia* 64 E3
Säffle, *Sweden* 9 G15
Safford, *U.S.A.* 111 K9
Saffron Walden, *U.K.* 13 E8
Safi, *Morocco* 74 B3
Şafīābād, *Iran* 65 B8
Safīd Dasht, *Iran* 65 C6
Safīd Kūh, *Afghan.* 60 B3
Safonovo, *Russia* 40 E7
Safranbolu, *Turkey* 66 B5
Safwān, *Iraq* 64 D5
Sag Harbor, *U.S.A.* 107 F12
Saga, *Indonesia* 57 E8
Saga, *Japan* 49 H5
Saga □, *Japan* 49 H5
Sagae, *Japan* 48 E10
Sagala, *Mali* 78 C3
Sagar, *India* 60 M9
Sagara, L., *Tanzania* 82 D3
Sagay, *Phil.* 55 F5
Sagil, *Mongolia* 54 A4
Saginaw, *U.S.A.* 104 D4
Saginaw B., *U.S.A.* 104 D4
Şagīr, Zāb aş →, *Iraq* 67 E10
Sagleipie, *Liberia* 78 D3
Saglouc = Salluit, *Canada* 97 B12
Sagŏ-ri, *S. Korea* 51 G14
Sagone, *France* 27 F12
Sagone, G. de, *France* 27 F12
Sagres, *Portugal* 31 J2
Sagua la Grande, *Cuba* 116 B3
Saguache, *U.S.A.* 111 G10
Saguenay →, *Canada* 99 C5
Sagunto, *Spain* 28 F4
Sahaba, *Sudan* 76 D3
Sahagún, *Colombia* 120 B2
Sahagún, *Spain* 30 C5
Saḩam al Jawlān, *Syria* 69 C4
Sahand, Kūh-e, *Iran* 67 D12
Sahara, *Africa* 72 D5

Saharan Atlas = Saharien, Atlas, *Algeria* ... 75 B5
Saharanpur, *India* ... 62 E7
Saharien, Atlas, *Algeria* ... 75 B5
Sahasinaka, *Madag.* ... 85 C8
Sahaswan, *India* ... 63 E8
Sahel, Canal du, *Mali* ... 78 C3
Sahibganj, *India* ... 63 G12
Sāḩilīyah, *Iraq* ... 67 F10
Sahiwal, *Pakistan* ... 62 D5
Şahneh, *Iran* ... 67 E12
Sahtaneh →, *Canada* ... 100 B4
Sahuaripa, *Mexico* ... 114 B3
Sahuarita, *U.S.A.* ... 111 L8
Sahuayo, *Mexico* ... 114 C4
Sahy, *Slovak Rep.* ... 21 G8
Sai Buri, *Thailand* ... 59 J3
Sai-Cinza, *Brazil* ... 125 B6
Sa'id Bundas, *Sudan* ... 73 G9
Saïda, *Algeria* ... 75 B5
Sa'īdābād, *Kermān, Iran* ... 65 D7
Sa'īdābād, *Semnān, Iran* ... 65 B7
Saïdia, *Morocco* ... 75 A4
Sa'īdīyeh, *Iran* ... 65 B6
Saidpur, *Bangla.* ... 61 G16
Saidu, *Pakistan* ... 63 B5
Saignelégier, *Switz.* ... 22 B3
Saignes, *France* ... 26 C6
Saigon = Phanh Bho Ho Chi Minh, *Vietnam* ... 59 G6
Saijō, *Japan* ... 49 H6
Saikhoa Ghat, *India* ... 61 F19
Saiki, *Japan* ... 49 H5
Saillans, *France* ... 27 D9
Sailolof, *Indonesia* ... 57 E8
Saimaa, *Finland* ... 9 F23
Saimbeyli, *Turkey* ... 66 D7
Şa'in Dezh, *Iran* ... 67 D12
St. Abb's Head, *U.K.* ... 14 F6
St. Aegyd, *Austria* ... 21 H5
St.-Affrique, *France* ... 26 E6
St.-Agrève, *France* ... 27 C8
St.-Aignan, *France* ... 24 E8
St. Alban's, *Canada* ... 99 C8
St. Albans, *U.K.* ... 13 F7
St. Albans, *Vt., U.S.A.* ... 107 B11
St. Albans, *W. Va., U.S.A.* ... 104 F5
St. Alban's Head, *U.K.* ... 13 G5
St. Albert, *Canada* ... 100 C6
St.-Amand-en-Puisaye, *France* ... 25 E10
St.-Amand-les-Eaux, *France* ... 25 B10
St.-Amand-Mont-Rond, *France* ... 26 B6
St.-Amarin, *France* ... 25 E14
St.-Amour, *France* ... 27 B9
St.-André-de-Cubzac, *France* ... 26 D3
St.-André-de-l'Eure, *France* ... 24 D8
St.-André-les-Alpes, *France* ... 27 E10
St. Andrew's, *Canada* ... 99 C8
St. Andrews, *U.K.* ... 14 E6
St.-Anicet, *Canada* ... 107 A10
St. Ann B., *Canada* ... 99 C7
St. Anne, *U.K.* ... 24 C4
St. Ann's Bay, *Jamaica* ... 116 C4
St. Anthony, *Canada* ... 99 B8
St. Anthony, *U.S.A.* ... 110 E8
St.-Antonin-Noble-Val, *France* ... 26 D5
St. Arnaud, *Australia* ... 91 F3
St. Arthur, *Canada* ... 99 C6
St. Asaph, *U.K.* ... 12 D4
St.-Astier, *France* ... 26 C4
St. Aubin, *Switz.* ... 22 C3
St.-Aubin-du-Cormier, *France* ... 24 D5
St-Augustin-Saguenay, *Canada* ... 99 B8
St. Augustine, *U.S.A.* ... 105 L5
St. Austell, *U.K.* ... 13 G3
St.-Avold, *France* ... 25 C13
St.-Barthélemy, I., *W. Indies* ... 117 C7
St. Bee's Hd., *U.K.* ... 12 C4
St.-Benoît-du-Sault, *France* ... 26 B5
St.-Bernard, Col du Grand, *Europe* ... 22 E4
St.-Bernard, Col du Petit, *France* ... 27 C10
St.-Blaise, *Switz.* ... 22 B3
St. Boniface, *Canada* ... 101 D9
St.-Bonnet, *France* ... 27 D10
St.-Brévin-les-Pins, *France* ... 24 E4
St.-Brice-en-Coglès, *France* ... 24 D5
St. Bride's, *Canada* ... 99 C9
St. Brides B., *U.K.* ... 13 F2
St.-Brieuc, *France* ... 24 D4
St.-Calais, *France* ... 24 E7
St-Cast-le-Guildo, *France* ... 24 D4
St. Catharines, *Canada* ... 98 D4
St. Catherines I., *U.S.A.* ... 105 K5
St. Catherine's Pt., *U.K.* ... 13 G6
St.-Céré, *France* ... 26 D5
St.-Cergue, *Switz.* ... 22 D2
St.-Cernin, *France* ... 26 C6
St.-Chamond, *France* ... 27 C8
St. Charles, *Ill., U.S.A.* ... 104 E1
St. Charles, *Mo., U.S.A.* ... 108 F9
St.-Chély-d'Apcher, *France* ... 26 D7
St.-Chinian, *France* ... 26 E6
St. Christopher = St. Kitts, *W. Indies* ... 117 C7
St. Christopher-Nevis ■, *W. Indies* ... 117 C7

St.-Ciers-sur-Gironde, *France* ... 26 C3
St. Clair, *Mich., U.S.A.* ... 106 D2
St. Clair, *Pa., U.S.A.* ... 107 F8
St. Clair, L., *Canada* ... 98 D3
St. Clairsville, *U.S.A.* ... 106 F4
St.-Claud, *France* ... 26 C4
St.-Claude, *Canada* ... 101 D9
St.-Claude, *France* ... 27 B9
St. Cloud, *Fla., U.S.A.* ... 105 L5
St. Cloud, *Minn., U.S.A.* ... 108 C7
St-Coeur de Marie, *Canada* ... 99 C5
St. Cricq, C., *Australia* ... 89 E1
St. Croix, *Virgin Is.* ... 117 C7
St. Croix →, *U.S.A.* ... 108 C8
St. Croix Falls, *U.S.A.* ... 108 C8
St.-Cyr-sur-Mer, *France* ... 27 E9
St. David's, *Canada* ... 99 C8
St. David's, *U.K.* ... 13 F2
St. David's Head, *U.K.* ... 13 F2
St.-Denis, *France* ... 25 D9
St.-Denis-d'Orques, *France* ... 24 D6
St.-Dié, *France* ... 25 D13
St.-Dizier, *France* ... 25 D11
St.-Égrève, *France* ... 27 C9
St. Elias, Mt., *U.S.A.* ... 96 B5
St. Elias Mts., *Canada* ... 100 A1
St.-Élie, *Fr. Guiana* ... 121 C7
St.-Eloy-les-Mines, *France* ... 26 B6
St.-Émilion, *France* ... 26 D3
St.-Étienne, *France* ... 27 C8
St.-Étienne-de-Tinée, *France* ... 27 D10
St. Eugène, *Canada* ... 107 A10
St. Eustatius, *W. Indies* ... 117 C7
St-Félicien, *Canada* ... 98 C5
St.-Florent, *France* ... 27 F13
St.-Florent, G. de, *France* ... 27 F13
St.-Florent-sur-Cher, *France* ... 25 F9
St.-Florentin, *France* ... 25 D10
St.-Flour, *France* ... 26 C7
St.-Fons, *France* ... 27 C8
St. Francis, *U.S.A.* ... 108 F4
St. Francis →, *U.S.A.* ... 109 H9
St. Francis, C., *S. Africa* ... 84 E3
St. Francisville, *U.S.A.* ... 109 K9
St-François, L., *Canada* ... 107 A10
St.-Fulgent, *France* ... 24 F5
St-Gabriel-de-Brandon, *Canada* ... 98 C5
St. Gallen = Sankt Gallen, *Switz.* ... 23 B8
St.-Gaudens, *France* ... 26 E4
St.-Gengoux-le-National, *France* ... 27 B8
St.-Geniez-d'Olt, *France* ... 26 D6
St. George, *Australia* ... 91 D4
St. George, *Canada* ... 99 C6
St. George, *S.C., U.S.A.* ... 105 J5
St. George, *Utah, U.S.A.* ... 111 H7
St. George, C., *Canada* ... 99 C8
St. George, C., *U.S.A.* ... 105 L3
St. George Ra., *Australia* ... 88 C4
St.-Georges, *Belgium* ... 17 G6
St-Georges, *Canada* ... 99 C5
St.-Georges, *Fr. Guiana* ... 121 C7
St. George's, *Grenada* ... 117 D7
St. George's B., *Canada* ... 99 C8
St. Georges Basin, *Australia* ... 88 C4
St. George's Channel, *Europe* ... 15 E6
St.-Georges-de-Didonne, *France* ... 26 C3
St. Georges Hd., *Australia* ... 91 F5
St.-Gérard, *Belgium* ... 17 H5
St.-Germain-de-Calberte, *France* ... 26 D7
St.-Germain-des-Fossés, *France* ... 26 B7
St.-Germain-du-Plain, *France* ... 25 F11
St.-Germain-en-Laye, *France* ... 25 D9
St.-Germain-Laval, *France* ... 27 C8
St.-Germain-Lembron, *France* ... 26 C7
St.-Gervais-d'Auvergne, *France* ... 26 B6
St.-Gervais-les-Bains, *France* ... 27 C10
St.-Gildas, Pte. de, *France* ... 24 E4
St.-Gilles, *France* ... 27 E8
St.-Gilles-Croix-de-Vie, *France* ... 26 B2
St.-Gingolph, *Switz.* ... 22 D3
St.-Girons, *France* ... 26 F5
St. Gotthard P. = San Gottardo, P. del, *Switz.* ... 23 C7
St.-Gualtier, *France* ... 24 F8
St.-Guénolé, *France* ... 24 E2
St. Helena, *U.S.A.* ... 110 G2
St. Helena ■, *Atl. Oc.* ... 2 E9
St. Helena, Mt., *U.S.A.* ... 112 G4
St. Helena B., *S. Africa* ... 84 E2
St. Helens, *Australia* ... 90 G4
St. Helens, *U.K.* ... 12 D5
St. Helens, *U.S.A.* ... 112 E4
St. Helens, Mt., *U.S.A.* ... 112 D4
St. Helier, *U.K.* ... 13 H5
St.-Hilaire-du-Harcouët, *France* ... 24 D5
St.-Hippolyte, *France* ... 25 E13
St.-Hippolyte-du-Fort, *France* ... 26 E7

St.-Honoré-les-Bains, *France* ... 25 F10
St-Hubert, *Belgium* ... 17 H6
St.-Hyacinthe, *Canada* ... 98 C5
St. Ignace, *U.S.A.* ... 104 C3
St. Ignace I., *Canada* ... 98 C2
St. Ignatius, *U.S.A.* ... 110 C6
St.-Imier, *Switz.* ... 22 B3
St. Ives, *Cambs., U.K.* ... 13 E7
St. Ives, *Corn., U.K.* ... 13 G2
St. James, *France* ... 24 D5
St. James, *U.S.A.* ... 108 D7
St-Jean, *Canada* ... 98 C5
St-Jean →, *Canada* ... 99 B7
St-Jean, L., *Canada* ... 99 C5
St. Jean Baptiste, *Canada* ... 101 D9
St.-Jean-d'Angély, *France* ... 26 C3
St-Jean-de-Bournay, *France* ... 27 C9
St.-Jean-de-Luz, *France* ... 26 E2
St.-Jean-de-Maurienne, *France* ... 27 C10
St.-Jean-de-Monts, *France* ... 24 F4
St.-Jean-du-Gard, *France* ... 26 D7
St.-Jean-en-Royans, *France* ... 27 C9
St.-Jean-Port-Joli, *Canada* ... 99 C5
St-Jérôme, *Qué., Canada* ... 98 C5
St-Jérôme, *Qué., Canada* ... 99 C5
St. John, *Canada* ... 99 C6
St. John, *Kans., U.S.A.* ... 109 G5
St. John →, *U.S.A.* ... 99 C6
St. John, C., *Canada* ... 99 B8
St. John's, *Antigua* ... 117 C7
St. John's, *Canada* ... 99 C9
St. Johns, *Ariz., U.S.A.* ... 111 J9
St. Johns, *Mich., U.S.A.* ... 104 D3
St. Johns →, *U.S.A.* ... 105 K5
St. Johnsbury, *U.S.A.* ... 107 B12
St. Johnsville, *U.S.A.* ... 107 C10
St. Joseph, *La., U.S.A.* ... 109 K9
St. Joseph, *Mich., U.S.A.* ... 104 D2
St. Joseph, *Mo., U.S.A.* ... 108 F7
St. Joseph →, *U.S.A.* ... 104 D2
St. Joseph, I., *Canada* ... 98 C3
St. Joseph, L., *Canada* ... 98 B1
St-Jovite, *Canada* ... 98 C5
St.-Juéry, *France* ... 26 E6
St.-Julien-Chapteuil, *France* ... 27 C8
St.-Julien-du-Sault, *France* ... 25 D10
St.-Julien-en-Genevois, *France* ... 27 B10
St.-Junien, *France* ... 26 C4
St.-Just-en-Chaussée, *France* ... 25 C9
St.-Just-en-Chevalet, *France* ... 26 C7
St.-Justin, *France* ... 26 E3
St. Kilda, *N.Z.* ... 87 L3
St. Kitts, *W. Indies* ... 117 C7
St. Kitts-Nevis = St. Christopher-Nevis ■, *W. Indies* ... 117 C7
St. Laurent, *Canada* ... 101 C9
St. Laurent, *Fr. Guiana* ... 121 B7
St.-Laurent-du-Pont, *France* ... 27 C9
St.-Laurent-en-Grandvaux, *France* ... 27 B9
St. Lawrence, *Australia* ... 90 C4
St. Lawrence, *Canada* ... 99 C8
St. Lawrence →, *Canada* ... 99 C6
St. Lawrence, Gulf of, *Canada* ... 99 C7
St. Lawrence I., *U.S.A.* ... 96 B3
St.-Léger, *Belgium* ... 17 J7
St. Leonard, *Canada* ... 99 C6
St.-Léonard-de-Noblat, *France* ... 26 C5
St. Lewis →, *Canada* ... 99 B8
St.-Lô, *France* ... 24 C5
St. Louis, *Senegal* ... 78 B1
St. Louis, *Mich., U.S.A.* ... 104 D3
St. Louis, *Mo., U.S.A.* ... 108 F9
St. Louis →, *U.S.A.* ... 108 B8
St.-Loup-sur-Semouse, *France* ... 25 E13
St. Lucia ■, *W. Indies* ... 117 D7
St. Lucia, L., *S. Africa* ... 85 D5
St. Lucia Channel, *W. Indies* ... 117 D7
St. Lunaire-Griquet, *Canada* ... 99 B8
St. Maarten, *W. Indies* ... 117 C7
St.-Maixent-l'École, *France* ... 26 B3
St.-Malo, *France* ... 24 D4
St.-Malo, G. de, *France* ... 24 D4
St.-Mandrier-sur-Mer, *France* ... 27 E9
St-Marc, *Haiti* ... 117 C5
St.-Marcellin, *France* ... 27 C9
St.-Marcouf, Is., *France* ... 24 C5
St. Maries, *U.S.A.* ... 110 C5
St-Martin, *W. Indies* ... 117 C7
St. Martin, L., *Canada* ... 101 C9
St.-Martin-de-Ré, *France* ... 26 B2
St.-Martin-Vésubie, *France* ... 27 D11
St. Martins, *Canada* ... 99 C6
St. Martinville, *U.S.A.* ... 109 K9
St. Mary Pk., *Australia* ... 91 E2
St. Marys, *Australia* ... 90 G4
St. Marys, *Canada* ... 106 C3
St. Mary's, *U.K.* ... 13 H1
St. Marys, *U.S.A.* ... 106 M6
St. Mary's, C., *Canada* ... 99 C9
St. Mary's B., *Canada* ... 99 C9
St. Marys Bay, *Canada* ... 99 D6
St-Mathieu, Pte., *France* ... 24 D2

St. Matthews, I. = Zadetkyi Kyun, *Burma* ... 59 H2
St.-Maur-des-Fossés, *France* ... 25 D9
St.-Maurice, *Switz.* ... 22 D4
St-Maurice →, *Canada* ... 98 C5
St.-Médard-de-Guizières, *France* ... 26 C3
St.-Méen-le-Grand, *France* ... 24 D4
St. Michael's Mount, *U.K.* ... 13 G2
St.-Michel-de-Maurienne, *France* ... 27 C10
St.-Mihiel, *France* ... 25 D12
St.-Nazaire, *France* ... 24 E4
St. Neots, *U.K.* ... 13 E7
St.-Nicolas-de-Port, *France* ... 25 D13
St. Niklass = Sint Niklaas, *Belgium* ... 17 F4
St. Niklaus, *Switz.* ... 22 D5
St.-Omer, *France* ... 25 B9
St-Pacome, *Canada* ... 99 C6
St.-Palais-sur-Mer, *France* ... 26 C2
St.-Pamphile, *Canada* ... 99 C6
St.-Pardoux-la-Rivière, *France* ... 26 C4
St. Pascal, *Canada* ... 99 C6
St. Paul, *Canada* ... 100 C6
St. Paul, *Minn., U.S.A.* ... 108 C8
St. Paul, *Nebr., U.S.A.* ... 108 E5
St. Paul, I., *Ind. Oc.* ... 3 F13
St. Paul →, *Canada* ... 99 C7
St.-Paul-de-Fenouillet, *France* ... 26 F6
St. Paul I., *Canada* ... 99 C7
St.-Paul-lès-Dax, *France* ... 26 E2
St.-Péray, *France* ... 27 D8
St.-Père-en-Retz, *France* ... 24 E4
St. Peter, *U.S.A.* ... 108 C8
St-Peter-Ording, *Germany* ... 18 A4
St. Peter Port, *U.K.* ... 13 H5
St. Peters, *N.S., Canada* ... 99 C7
St. Peters, *P.E.I., Canada* ... 99 C7
St. Petersburg = Sankt-Peterburg, *Russia* ... 40 C6
St. Petersburg, *U.S.A.* ... 105 M4
St.-Philbert-de-Grand-Lieu, *France* ... 24 E5
St.-Pierre, *St-P. & M.* ... 99 C8
St-Pierre, L., *Canada* ... 98 C5
St.-Pierre-d'Oléron, *France* ... 26 C2
St.-Pierre-Église, *France* ... 24 C5
St.-Pierre-en-Port, *France* ... 24 C7
St.-Pierre et Miquelon □, *St-P. & M.* ... 99 C8
St.-Pierre-le-Moûtier, *France* ... 25 F10
St.-Pieters Leew, *Belgium* ... 17 G4
St.-Pol-de-Léon, *France* ... 24 D2
St.-Pol-sur-Mer, *France* ... 25 A9
St.-Pol-sur-Ternoise, *France* ... 25 B9
St.-Pons, *France* ... 26 E6
St.-Pourçain-sur-Sioule, *France* ... 26 B7
St.-Quay-Portrieux, *France* ... 24 D4
St.-Quentin, *France* ... 25 C10
St.-Rambert-d'Albon, *France* ... 27 C8
St.-Raphaël, *France* ... 27 E10
St. Regis, *U.S.A.* ... 110 C6
St.-Rémy-de-Provence, *France* ... 27 E8
St.-Renan, *France* ... 24 D2
St.-Saëns, *France* ... 24 C8
St.-Sauveur-en-Puisaye, *France* ... 25 E10
St.-Sauveur-le-Vicomte, *France* ... 24 C5
St.-Savin, *France* ... 26 B4
St.-Savinien, *France* ... 26 C3
St. Sebastien, Tanjon' i, *Madag.* ... 85 A8
St.-Seine-l'Abbaye, *France* ... 25 E11
St.-Sernin-sur-Rance, *France* ... 26 E6
St.-Servan-sur-Mer, *France* ... 24 D4
St.-Sever, *France* ... 26 E3
St.-Sever-Calvados, *France* ... 24 D5
St.-Siméon, *Canada* ... 99 C6
St. Stephen, *Canada* ... 99 C6
St.-Sulpice, *France* ... 26 E5
St.-Sulpice-Laurière, *France* ... 26 B5
St.-Syprien, *France* ... 26 F7
St.-Thégonnec, *France* ... 24 D3
St. Thomas, *Canada* ... 98 D3
St. Thomas I., *Virgin Is.* ... 117 C7
St-Tite, *Canada* ... 98 C5
St-Tropez, *France* ... 27 E10
St. Troud = Sint Truiden, *Belgium* ... 17 G6
St.-Vaast-la-Hougue, *France* ... 24 C5
St.-Valéry-en-Caux, *France* ... 24 C7
St.-Valéry-sur-Somme, *France* ... 25 B8
St.-Vallier, *France* ... 27 C8
St.-Vallier-de-Thiey, *France* ... 27 E10
St.-Varent, *France* ... 24 F6
St. Vincent, *W. Indies* ... 117 D7
St. Vincent, G., *Australia* ... 91 F2
St. Vincent & the Grenadines ■, *W. Indies* ... 117 D7
St.-Vincent-de-Tyrosse, *France* ... 26 E2
St. Vincent Passage, *W. Indies* ... 117 D7
St.-Vith, *Belgium* ... 17 H8
St.-Yrieix-la-Perche, *France* ... 26 C5
Ste.-Adresse, *France* ... 24 C7

Ste-Agathe-des-Monts, *Canada* ... 98 C5
Ste-Anne de Beaupré, *Canada* ... 99 C5
Ste-Anne-des-Monts, *Canada* ... 99 C6
Ste-Croix, *Switz.* ... 22 C3
Ste.-Enimie, *France* ... 26 D7
Ste.-Foy-la-Grande, *France* ... 26 D4
Ste. Genevieve, *U.S.A.* ... 108 G9
Ste.-Hermine, *France* ... 26 B3
Ste.-Livrade-sur-Lot, *France* ... 26 D4
Ste-Marguerite →, *Canada* ... 99 B6
Ste.-Marie, *Martinique* ... 117 D7
Ste.-Marie-aux-Mines, *France* ... 25 D14
Ste-Marie de la Madeleine, *Canada* ... 99 C5
Ste.-Maure-de-Touraine, *France* ... 24 E7
Ste.-Maxime, *France* ... 27 E10
Ste.-Menehould, *France* ... 25 C11
Ste.-Mère-Église, *France* ... 24 C5
Ste.-Rose, *Guadeloupe* ... 117 C7
Ste. Rose du Lac, *Canada* ... 101 C9
Saintes, *France* ... 26 C3
Saintes, I. des, *Guadeloupe* ... 117 C7
Stes.-Maries-de-la-Mer, *France* ... 27 E8
Saintonge, *France* ... 26 C3
Saipan, *Pac. Oc.* ... 92 F6
Sairang, *India* ... 61 H18
Sairecábur, Cerro, *Bolivia* ... 126 A2
Saitama □, *Japan* ... 49 F9
Sajama, *Bolivia* ... 124 D4
Sajum, *India* ... 63 C8
Sak →, *S. Africa* ... 84 E3
Sakai, *Japan* ... 49 G7
Sakaide, *Japan* ... 49 G6
Sakaiminato, *Japan* ... 49 G6
Sakākah, *Si. Arabia* ... 64 D4
Sakakawea, L., *U.S.A.* ... 108 B3
Sakami, L., *Canada* ... 98 B4
Sākāne, 'Erg i-n, *Mali* ... 74 D4
Sakania, *Zaïre* ... 83 E2
Sakarya = Adapazarı, *Turkey* ... 66 B4
Sakarya →, *Turkey* ... 66 B4
Sakashima-Guntō, *Japan* ... 49 M2
Sakata, *Japan* ... 48 E9
Sakchu, *N. Korea* ... 51 D13
Sakeny →, *Madag.* ... 85 C8
Sakété, *Benin* ... 79 D5
Sakha □, *Russia* ... 45 C13
Sakhalin, *Russia* ... 45 D15
Sakhalinskiy Zaliv, *Russia* ... 45 D15
Şaki, *Azerbaijan* ... 43 K8
Šakiai, *Lithuania* ... 9 J20
Sakon Nakhon, *Thailand* ... 58 D5
Sakrand, *Pakistan* ... 62 F3
Sakrivier, *S. Africa* ... 84 E3
Sakskøbing, *Denmark* ... 11 K5
Sakuma, *Japan* ... 49 G8
Sakurai, *Japan* ... 49 G7
Saky, *Ukraine* ... 41 K7
Sal →, *Russia* ... 43 G5
Sal, *Sweden* ... 9 G17
Sala Consilina, *Italy* ... 35 B7
Sala-y-Gómez, *Pac. Oc.* ... 93 K17
Salaberry-de-Valleyfield, *Canada* ... 98 C5
Saladas, *Argentina* ... 126 B4
Saladillo, *Argentina* ... 126 D4
Salado →, *Buenos Aires, Argentina* ... 126 D4
Salado →, *La Pampa, Argentina* ... 128 A3
Salado →, *Río Negro, Argentina* ... 128 B3
Salado →, *Santa Fe, Argentina* ... 126 C3
Salado →, *Mexico* ... 114 B5
Salaga, *Ghana* ... 79 D4
Şalāh, *Syria* ... 69 C5
Sálakhos, *Greece* ... 37 C9
Salala, *Liberia* ... 78 D2
Salala, *Sudan* ... 76 C4
Salālah, *Oman* ... 68 D5
Salamanca, *Chile* ... 126 C1
Salamanca, *Spain* ... 30 E5
Salamanca, *U.S.A.* ... 106 D6
Salamanca □, *Spain* ... 30 E5
Salāmatābād, *Iran* ... 64 C5
Salamina, *Colombia* ... 120 B2
Salamis, *Cyprus* ... 37 D12
Salamís, *Greece* ... 39 M6
Salar de Atacama, *Chile* ... 126 A2
Salar de Uyuni, *Bolivia* ... 124 E4
Sălard, *Romania* ... 38 B5
Salas, *Spain* ... 30 B4
Salas de los Infantes, *Spain* ... 28 C1
Salatiga, *Indonesia* ... 57 G14
Salaverry, *Peru* ... 124 B2
Salawati, *Indonesia* ... 57 E8
Salayar, *Indonesia* ... 57 F6
Salazar →, *Spain* ... 28 C3
Salbris, *France* ... 25 E9
Salcombe, *U.K.* ... 13 G4
Saldaña, *Spain* ... 30 C6
Saldanha, *S. Africa* ... 84 E2
Saldanha B., *S. Africa* ... 84 E2
Saldus, *Latvia* ... 9 H20
Sale, *Australia* ... 91 F4
Salé, *Morocco* ... 74 B3
Sale, *U.K.* ... 12 D5
Salekhard, *Russia* ... 44 C7

Salem, India 60 P11
Salem, Ind., U.S.A. 104 F2
Salem, Mass., U.S.A. .. 107 D14
Salem, Mo., U.S.A. 109 G9
Salem, N.J., U.S.A. 104 F8
Salem, Ohio, U.S.A. ... 106 F4
Salem, Oreg., U.S.A. .. 110 D2
Salem, S. Dak., U.S.A. . 108 D6
Salem, Va., U.S.A. 104 G5
Salemi, Italy 34 E5
Salernes, France 27 E10
Salerno, Italy 35 B7
Salerno, G. di, Italy ... 35 B7
Salford, U.K. 12 D5
Salgir →, Ukraine 41 K8
Salgótarján, Hungary ... 21 G9
Salgueiro, Brazil 122 C4
Salida, U.S.A. 102 C5
Salies-de-Béarn, France . 26 E3
Salihli, Turkey 66 C3
Salihorsk, Belarus 41 F4
Salima, Malawi 81 G6
Salina, Italy 35 D7
Salina, U.S.A. 108 F6
Salina Cruz, Mexico 115 D5
Salinas, Brazil 123 E3
Salinas, Chile 126 A2
Salinas, Ecuador 120 D1
Salinas, U.S.A. 111 H3
Salinas →, Guatemala ... 115 D6
Salinas →, U.S.A. 111 H3
Salinas, B. de, Nic. ... 116 D2
Salinas, C. de, Spain ... 36 B10
Salinas, Pampa de las, Argentina 126 C2
Salinas Ambargasta, Argentina 126 B3
Salinas de Hidalgo, Mexico 114 C4
Salinas Grandes, Argentina 126 B3
Saline →, Ark., U.S.A. . 109 J8
Saline →, Kans., U.S.A. . 108 F6
Salines, Spain 36 B10
Salinópolis, Brazil 122 B2
Salins-les-Bains, France . 25 F12
Salir, Portugal 31 H2
Salisbury = Harare, Zimbabwe 83 F3
Salisbury, Australia ... 91 E2
Salisbury, U.K. 13 F6
Salisbury, Md., U.S.A. . 104 F8
Salisbury, N.C., U.S.A. 105 H5
Salisbury Plain, U.K. .. 13 F6
Săliște, Romania 38 D6
Salitre →, Brazil 122 C3
Salka, Nigeria 79 C5
Şalkhad, Syria 69 C5
Salla, Finland 8 C23
Sallent, Spain 28 D6
Salles-Curan, France ... 26 D6
Salling, Denmark 11 H2
Sallisaw, U.S.A. 109 H7
Sallom Junction, Sudan . 76 D4
Salluit, Canada 97 B12
Salmās, Iran 67 C11
Salmerón, Spain 28 E2
Salmo, Canada 100 D5
Salmon, U.S.A. 110 D7
Salmon →, Canada 100 C4
Salmon →, U.S.A. 110 D5
Salmon Arm, Canada 100 C5
Salmon Falls, U.S.A. ... 110 E6
Salmon Gums, Australia . 89 F3
Salmon Res., Canada 99 C8
Salmon River Mts., U.S.A. 110 D6
Salo, Finland 9 F20
Salò, Italy 32 C7
Salobreña, Spain 31 J7
Salome, U.S.A. 113 M13
Salon-de-Provence, France 27 E9
Salonica = Thessaloníki, Greece 39 J5
Salonta, Romania 38 C4
Salor →, Spain 31 F3
Salou, C., Spain 28 D6
Salpausselkä, Finland .. 9 F22
Salsacate, Argentina ... 126 C2
Salses, France 26 F6
Salsk, Russia 43 G5
Salso →, Italy 34 E6
Salsomaggiore Terme, Italy 32 D6
Salt →, Canada 100 B6
Salt →, U.S.A. 111 K7
Salt Creek, Australia .. 91 F2
Salt Fork Arkansas →, U.S.A. 109 G6
Salt Lake City, U.S.A. . 110 F8
Salt Range, Pakistan ... 62 C5
Salta, Argentina 126 A2
Salta □, Argentina 126 A2
Saltcoats, U.K. 14 F4
Saltee Is., Ireland 15 D5
Saltfjellet, Norway 8 C16
Saltfjorden, Norway 8 C16
Saltholm, Denmark 11 J6
Saltillo, Mexico 114 B4
Salto, Argentina 126 C3
Salto, Uruguay 126 C4
Salto da Divisa, Brazil 123 E4
Salton City, U.S.A. 113 M11
Salton Sea, U.S.A. 113 M11
Saltpond, Ghana 79 D4
Saltsjöbaden, Sweden ... 10 E12
Saltville, U.S.A. 104 G5
Saluda →, U.S.A. 105 H5
Salûm, Egypt 76 A2
Salûm, Khâlig el, Egypt . 76 A2
Salur, India 61 K13

Salut, Is. du, Fr. Guiana .. 121 B7
Saluzzo, Italy 32 D4
Salvación, B., Chile ... 128 D1
Salvador, Brazil 123 D4
Salvador, Canada 101 C7
Salvador, L., U.S.A. ... 109 L9
Salvaterra, Brazil 122 B2
Salvaterra de Magos, Portugal 31 F2
Sálvora, I., Spain 30 C2
Salween →, Burma 61 L20
Salyan, Azerbaijan 67 C13
Salyersville, U.S.A. ... 104 G4
Salza →, Austria 21 H4
Salzach →, Austria 21 G2
Salzburg, Austria 21 H3
Salzgitter, Germany 18 C6
Salzwedel, Germany 18 C7
Sam Neua, Laos 58 B5
Sam Ngao, Thailand 58 D2
Sam Rayburn Reservoir, U.S.A. 109 K7
Sam Son, Vietnam 58 C5
Sam Teu, Laos 58 C5
Sama, Russia 44 C7
Sama de Langreo, Spain . 30 B5
Samagaltay, Russia 45 D10
Samaipata, Bolivia 125 D5
Samales Group, Phil. ... 55 J4
Samâlût, Egypt 76 J7
Samana, India 62 D7
Samana Cay, Bahamas 117 B5
Samanâ, Turkey 66 D6
Samanga, Tanzania 83 D4
Samangwa, Zaïre 82 C1
Samani, Japan 48 C11
Samar, Phil. 55 F6
Samara, Russia 42 D10
Samara →, Russia 42 D10
Samara →, Ukraine 41 H8
Samaria = Shōmrōn, West Bank 69 C4
Samariá, Greece 37 D5
Samarinda, Indonesia ... 56 E5
Samarkand = Samarqand, Uzbekistan 44 F7
Samarqand, Uzbekistan .. 44 F7
Sāmarrā, Iraq 67 E10
Samastipur, India 63 G11
Samatan, France 26 E4
Samaúma, Brazil 125 B5
Şamaxi, Azerbaijan 43 K9
Samba, India 63 C6
Samba, Zaïre 82 C2
Sambaíba, Brazil 122 C2
Sambalpur, India 61 J14
Sambar, Tanjung, Indonesia .. 56 E4
Sambas, Indonesia 56 D3
Sambava, Madag. 85 A9
Sambawizi, Zimbabwe 83 F2
Sambhal, India 63 E8
Sambhar, India 62 F6
Sambiase, Italy 35 D9
Sambir, Ukraine 41 H2
Sambonifacio, Italy 32 C8
Sambor, Cambodia 58 F6
Sambre →, Europe 17 H5
Sambuca di Sicília, Italy .. 34 E6
Samburu □, Kenya 82 B4
Samchŏk, S. Korea 51 F15
Samchonpo, S. Korea 51 G15
Same, Tanzania 82 C4
Samedan, Switz. 23 C9
Samer, France 25 B8
Samfya, Zambia 83 E2
Sámi, Greece 39 L3
Şämkir, Azerbaijan 43 K8
Samnah, Si. Arabia 64 E3
Samnaun, Switz. 23 C10
Samo Alto, Chile 126 C1
Samobor, Croatia 33 C12
Samoëns, France 27 B10
Samokov, Bulgaria 38 G6
Samoorombón, B., Argentina 126 D4
Samorogouan, Burkina Faso 78 C4
Sámos, Greece 39 M9
Samoš, Serbia, Yug. 21 K10
Samos, Spain 30 C3
Samothráki, Évros, Greece .. 39 J8
Samothráki, Kérkira, Greece 37 A3
Samoylovka, Russia 42 E6
Sampa, Ghana 78 D4
Sampacho, Argentina 126 C3
Sampang, Indonesia 57 G15
Samper de Calanda, Spain .. 28 D4
Sampit, Indonesia 56 E4
Sampit, Teluk, Indonesia . 56 E4
Samrée, Belgium 17 H7
Samrong, Cambodia 58 E4
Samrong, Thailand 58 E3
Samsø, Denmark 11 J4
Samsø Bælt, Denmark 11 J4
Samsun, Turkey 66 B7
Samtredia, Georgia 43 J6
Samui, Ko, Thailand 59 H3
Samur →, Russia 43 K9
Samurskiy Khrebet, Russia .. 43 K8
Samusole, Zaïre 83 E1
Samut Prakan, Thailand . 58 F3
Samut Sakhon, Thailand . 58 F3
Samut Songkhram →, Thailand 58 F3
Samwari, Pakistan 62 E2
San, Mali 78 C4

San →, Cambodia 58 F5
San →, Poland 20 E11
San Adrián, C. de, Spain . 30 B2
San Agustín, Colombia .. 120 C2
San Agustin, C., Phil. . 55 H7
San Agustín de Valle Fértil, Argentina 126 C2
San Ambrosio, Pac. Oc. . 93 K20
San Andreas, U.S.A. 112 G6
San Andrés, I. de, Caribbean 116 D3
San Andres Mts., U.S.A. 111 K10
San Andrés Tuxtla, Mexico 115 D5
San Angelo, U.S.A. 109 K4
San Anselmo, U.S.A. 112 H4
San Antonio, Belize 115 D7
San Antonio, Chile 126 C1
San Antonio, Phil. 55 D4
San Antonio, Spain 36 C7
San Antonio, N. Mex., U.S.A. 111 K10
San Antonio, Tex., U.S.A. 109 L5
San Antonio, Venezuela . 120 C4
San Antonio →, U.S.A. .. 109 L6
San Antonio, C., Argentina .. 126 D4
San Antonio, C., Cuba .. 116 B3
San Antonio, C. de, Spain 29 G5
San Antonio de los Baños, Cuba 116 B3
San Antonio de los Cobres, Argentina 126 A2
San Antonio Oeste, Argentina 128 B4
San Arcángelo, Italy ... 35 B9
San Ardo, U.S.A. 112 J6
San Augustín, Canary Is. .. 36 G4
San Augustine, U.S.A. .. 109 K7
San Bartolomé, Canary Is. .. 36 F6
San Bartolomé de Tirajana, Canary Is. 36 G4
San Bartolomeo in Galdo, Italy 35 A8
San Benedetto del Tronto, Italy 33 F10
San Benedetto Po, Italy . 32 C7
San Benedicto, I., Mexico 114 D2
San Benito, U.S.A. 109 M6
San Benito →, U.S.A. ... 112 J5
San Benito Mt., U.S.A. . 112 J6
San Bernardino, U.S.A. . 113 L9
San Bernardino, Paso del, Switz. 23 D8
San Bernardino Mts., U.S.A. 113 L10
San Bernardino Str., Phil. .. 55 E6
San Bernardo, Chile 126 C1
San Bernardo, I. de, Colombia 120 B2
San Blas, Mexico 114 B3
San Blas, Arch. de, Panama 116 E4
San Blas, C., U.S.A. ... 105 L3
San Borja, Bolivia 124 C4
San Buenaventura, Bolivia 124 C4
San Buenaventura, Mexico 114 B4
San Carlos = Butuku-Luba, Eq. Guin. 79 E6
San Carlos, Argentina .. 126 C2
San Carlos, Bolivia 125 D5
San Carlos, Chile 126 D1
San Carlos, Mexico 114 B4
San Carlos, Nic. 116 D3
San Carlos, Negros, Phil. .. 55 F5
San Carlos, Pangasinan, Phil. 55 D4
San Carlos, Spain 36 B8
San Carlos, Uruguay 127 C5
San Carlos, U.S.A. 111 K8
San Carlos, Amazonas, Venezuela 120 C4
San Carlos, Cojedes, Venezuela 120 B4
San Carlos de Bariloche, Argentina 128 B2
San Carlos de la Rápita, Spain 28 E5
San Carlos del Zulia, Venezuela 120 B3
San Carlos L., U.S.A. .. 111 K8
San Cataldo, Italy 34 E6
San Celoni, Spain 28 D7
San Clemente, Chile 126 D1
San Clemente, Spain 29 F2
San Clemente, U.S.A. ... 113 M9
San Clemente I., U.S.A. 113 N8
San Costanzo, Italy 33 E10
San Cristóbal, Argentina .. 126 C3
San Cristóbal, Colombia . 120 D3
San Cristóbal, Dom. Rep. .. 117 C5
San Cristóbal, Mexico .. 115 D6
San Cristóbal, Spain ... 36 B11
San Cristóbal, Venezuela .. 120 B3
San Damiano d'Asti, Italy .. 32 D5
San Daniele del Friuli, Italy .. 33 B10
San Demétrio Corone, Italy .. 35 C9
San Diego, Calif., U.S.A. .. 113 N9
San Diego, Tex., U.S.A. . 109 M5
San Diego, C., Argentina .. 128 D3
San Diego de la Unión, Mexico 114 C4
San Dimitri, Ras, Malta . 37 C1
San Donà di Piave, Italy .. 33 C9
San Elpídio a Mare, Italy .. 33 E10
San Esteban de Gormaz, Spain 28 D1

San Felice sul Panaro, Italy .. 32 D8
San Felipe, Chile 126 C1
San Felipe, Colombia ... 120 C4
San Felipe, Mexico 114 A2
San Felipe, Venezuela .. 120 A4
San Felipe →, U.S.A. ... 113 M11
San Felíu de Guíxols, Spain .. 28 D8
San Felíu de Llobregat, Spain 28 D7
San Félix, Pac. Oc. 93 K20
San Fernando, Chile 126 C1
San Fernando, Mexico ... 114 B1
San Fernando, La Union, Phil. 55 C4
San Fernando, Pampanga, Phil. 55 D4
San Fernando, Baleares, Spain 36 C7
San Fernando, Cádiz, Spain .. 31 J4
San Fernando, Trin. & Tob. 117 D7
San Fernando, U.S.A. ... 113 L8
San Fernando →, Mexico . 114 C5
San Fernando de Apure, Venezuela 120 B4
San Fernando de Atabapo, Venezuela 120 C4
San Fernando di Púglia, Italy 35 A9
San Francisco, Argentina . 126 C3
San Francisco, Bolivia . 125 D4
San Francisco, U.S.A. .. 111 H2
San Francisco →, U.S.A. . 111 K9
San Francisco, Paso de, S. Amer. 126 B2
San Francisco de Macorís, Dom. Rep. 117 C5
San Francisco del Monte de Oro, Argentina 126 C2
San Francisco del Oro, Mexico 114 B3
San Francisco Javier, Spain .. 36 C7
San Francisco Solano, Pta., Colombia 120 B2
San Fratello, Italy 35 D7
San Gabriel, Ecuador ... 120 C2
San Gavino Monreale, Italy .. 34 C1
San Gil, Colombia 120 B3
San Gimignano, Italy ... 32 E8
San Giórgio di Nogaro, Italy 33 C10
San Giórgio Iónico, Italy .. 35 B10
San Giovanni Bianco, Italy .. 32 C6
San Giovanni in Fiore, Italy .. 35 C9
San Giovanni in Persiceto, Italy 33 D8
San Giovanni Rotondo, Italy 35 A8
San Giovanni Valdarno, Italy 33 E8
San Giuliano Terme, Italy .. 32 E7
San Gorgonio Mt., U.S.A. .. 113 L10
San Gottardo, P. del, Switz. 23 C7
San Gregorio, Uruguay .. 127 C4
San Gregorio, U.S.A. ... 112 H4
San Guiseppe Iato, Italy .. 34 E6
San Ignacio, Belize 115 D7
San Ignacio, Bolivia ... 125 D5
San Ignacio, Mexico 114 B2
San Ignacio, Paraguay .. 126 B4
San Ignacio, L., Mexico . 114 B2
San Ildefonso, C., Phil. . 55 C5
San Isidro, Argentina .. 126 C4
San Jacinto, Colombia .. 120 B2
San Jacinto, U.S.A. 113 M10
San Jaime, Spain 36 B11
San Javier, Misiones, Argentina 127 B4
San Javier, Santa Fe, Argentina 126 C4
San Javier, Beni, Bolivia .. 125 C5
San Javier, Santa Cruz, Bolivia 125 D5
San Javier, Chile 126 D1
San Javier, Spain 29 H4
San Jerónimo, Sa. de, Colombia 120 B2
San Jeronimo Taviche, Mexico 115 D5
San Joaquín, Bolivia ... 125 C5
San Joaquín, U.S.A. 112 J6
San Joaquín, Venezuela . 120 A4
San Joaquín →, Bolivia . 125 C5
San Joaquin →, U.S.A. .. 111 G3
San Joaquin Valley, U.S.A. .. 112 J6
San Jordi, Spain 36 B9
San Jorge, Argentina ... 126 C3
San Jorge, Spain 36 C7
San Jorge, B. de, Mexico .. 114 A2
San Jorge, G., Argentina .. 128 C3
San Jorge, G. de, Spain . 28 E4
San José, Bolivia 125 D5
San José, Costa Rica ... 116 E3
San José, Guatemala 116 D1
San José, Mexico 114 C2
San Jose, Phil. 55 D4
San José, Spain 36 C7
San Jose, U.S.A. 111 H3
San Jose →, U.S.A. 111 J10
San Jose de Buenovista, Phil. 55 E4
San José de Feliciano, Argentina 126 C4
San José de Jáchal, Argentina 126 C2
San José de Mayo, Uruguay 126 C4

San José de Ocune, Colombia 120 C3
San José de Uchapiamonas, Bolivia 124 C4
San José del Cabo, Mexico 114 C3
San José del Guaviare, Colombia 120 C3
San José do Anauá, Brazil 121 C5
San Juan, Argentina 126 C2
San Juan, Colombia 120 B2
San Juan, Ica, Peru 124 D2
San Juan, Puno, Peru ... 124 C4
San Juan, Phil. 55 G7
San Juan, Puerto Rico .. 117 C6
San Juan □, Argentina .. 126 C2
San Juan →, Argentina .. 126 C2
San Juan →, Bolivia 125 E4
San Juan →, Colombia ... 120 C2
San Juan →, Nic. 116 D3
San Juan →, U.S.A. 111 H8
San Juan →, Venezuela .. 121 A5
San Juan, C., Eq. Guin. .. 80 D1
San Juan Bautista, Paraguay 126 B4
San Juan Bautista, Spain . 36 B8
San Juan Bautista, U.S.A. 111 H3
San Juan Bautista Valle Nacional, Mexico 115 D5
San Juan Capistrano, U.S.A. 113 M9
San Juan Cr. →, U.S.A. . 112 J5
San Juan de Guadalupe, Mexico 114 C4
San Juan de los Morros, Venezuela 120 B4
San Juan del César, Colombia 120 A3
San Juan del Norte, Nic. .. 116 D3
San Juan del Norte, B. de, Nic. 116 D3
San Juan del Puerto, Spain .. 31 H4
San Juan del Río, Mexico .. 115 C5
San Juan del Sur, Nic. . 116 D2
San Juan I., U.S.A. 112 B3
San Juan Mts., U.S.A. .. 111 H10
San Julián, Argentina .. 128 C3
San Just, Sierra de, Spain .. 28 E4
San Justo, Argentina ... 126 C3
San Kamphaeng, Thailand . 58 C2
San Lázaro, C., Mexico . 114 C2
San Lázaro, Sa., Mexico . 114 C3
San Leandro, U.S.A. 111 H2
San Leonardo, Spain 28 D1
San Lorenzo, Argentina . 126 C3
San Lorenzo, Beni, Bolivia 125 D4
San Lorenzo, Tarija, Bolivia 125 E5
San Lorenzo, Ecuador ... 120 C2
San Lorenzo, Paraguay .. 126 B4
San Lorenzo, Spain 36 B10
San Lorenzo, Venezuela . 120 B3
San Lorenzo →, Mexico .. 114 C3
San Lorenzo, I., Mexico . 114 B2
San Lorenzo, I., Peru .. 124 C2
San Lorenzo, Mt., Argentina 128 C2
San Lorenzo de la Parrilla, Spain 28 F2
San Lorenzo de Morunys, Spain 28 C6
San Lucas, Bolivia 125 E4
San Lucas, Baja Calif. S., Mexico 114 C3
San Lucas, Baja Calif. S., Mexico 114 B2
San Lucas, U.S.A. 112 J5
San Lucas, C., Mexico .. 114 C3
San Lúcido, Italy 35 C9
San Luis, Argentina 126 C2
San Luis, Cuba 116 B3
San Luis, Guatemala 116 C2
San Luis, U.S.A. 111 H11
San Luis □, Argentina .. 126 C2
San Luis, I., Mexico ... 114 B2
San Luis, L. de, Bolivia .. 125 C5
San Luis, Sierra de, Argentina 126 C2
San Luis de la Paz, Mexico 114 C4
San Luis Obispo, U.S.A. .. 113 K6
San Luis Potosí, Mexico . 114 C4
San Luis Potosí □, Mexico 114 C4
San Luis Reservoir, U.S.A. 112 H5
San Luis Río Colorado, Mexico 114 A2
San Marco dei Cavoti, Italy 35 C9
San Marco in Lámis, Italy . 35 A8
San Marcos, Colombia ... 120 B2
San Marcos, Guatemala .. 116 D1
San Marcos, Mexico 114 B2
San Marcos, U.S.A. 109 L6
San Marino ■, Europe ... 33 E9
San Martín, Argentina .. 126 C2
San Martín, Colombia ... 120 C3
San Martin →, Bolivia .. 125 C5
San Martín, L., Argentina 128 C2
San Martín de los Andes, Argentina 128 B2
San Martín de Valdeiglesias, Spain 30 E6
San Martino de Calvi, Italy 32 C6
San Mateo, Phil. 55 C4
San Mateo, Baleares, Spain 36 B7
San Mateo, Valencia, Spain 28 E5
San Mateo, U.S.A. 111 H2
San Matías, Bolivia 125 D6

San Matías, G.

San Matías, G., *Argentina* 128 B4
San Miguel, *El Salv.* 116 D2
San Miguel, *Panama* 116 E4
San Miguel, *Spain* 36 B7
San Miguel, *U.S.A.* 111 J3
San Miguel, *Venezuela* 120 B4
San Miguel →, *Bolivia* 125 C5
San Miguel →, *S. Amer.* 120 C2
San Miguel de Huachi, *Bolivia* 124 D4
San Miguel de Salinas, *Spain* 29 H4
San Miguel de Tucumán, *Argentina* 126 B2
San Miguel del Monte, *Argentina* 126 D4
San Miguel I., *U.S.A.* 113 L6
San Miniato, *Italy* 32 E7
San Narciso, *Phil.* 55 D4
San Nicolás, *Canary Is.* 36 G4
San Nicolas, *Phil.* 55 B4
San Nicolás de los Arroyas, *Argentina* 126 C3
San Nicolas I., *U.S.A.* 113 M7
San Onofre, *Colombia* 120 B2
San Onofre, *U.S.A.* 113 M9
San Pablo, *Bolivia* 126 A2
San Pablo, *Phil.* 55 D4
San Páolo di Civitate, *Italy* 35 A8
San Pedro, *Buenos Aires, Argentina* 127 B5
San Pedro, *Jujuy, Argentina* 126 A3
San Pedro, *Colombia* 120 C3
San-Pédro, *Ivory C.* 78 E3
San Pedro, *Mexico* 114 C2
San Pedro, *Peru* 124 C3
San Pedro □, *Paraguay* 126 A4
San Pedro →, *Chihuahua, Mexico* 114 B3
San Pedro →, *Michoacan, Mexico* 114 D4
San Pedro →, *Nayarit, Mexico* 114 C3
San Pedro →, *U.S.A.* 111 K8
San Pedro, Pta., *Chile* 126 B1
San Pedro, Sierra de, *Spain* 31 F4
San Pedro Channel, *U.S.A.* 113 M8
San Pedro de Arimena, *Colombia* 120 C3
San Pedro de Atacama, *Chile* 126 A2
San Pedro de Jujuy, *Argentina* 126 A3
San Pedro de las Colonias, *Mexico* 114 B4
San Pedro de Lloc, *Peru* 124 B2
San Pedro de Macorís, *Dom. Rep.* 117 C6
San Pedro del Norte, *Nic.* 116 D3
San Pedro del Paraná, *Paraguay* 126 B4
San Pedro del Pinatar, *Spain* 29 H4
San Pedro Mártir, Sierra, *Mexico* 114 A1
San Pedro Mixtepec, *Mexico* 115 D5
San Pedro Ocampo = Melchor Ocampo, *Mexico* 114 C4
San Pedro Sula, *Honduras* 116 C2
San Pieto, *Italy* 34 C1
San Pietro Vernótico, *Italy* 35 B11
San Quintín, *Mexico* 114 A1
San Rafael, *Argentina* 126 C2
San Rafael, *Calif., U.S.A.* 112 H4
San Rafael, *N. Mex., U.S.A.* 111 J10
San Rafael, *Venezuela* 120 A3
San Rafael Mt., *U.S.A.* 113 L7
San Rafael Mts., *U.S.A.* 113 L7
San Ramón, *Bolivia* 125 C5
San Ramón, *Peru* 124 C2
San Ramón de la Nueva Orán, *Argentina* 126 A3
San Remo, *Italy* 32 E4
San Román, C., *Venezuela* 120 A3
San Roque, *Argentina* 126 B4
San Roque, *Spain* 31 J5
San Rosendo, *Chile* 126 D1
San Saba, *U.S.A.* 109 K5
San Salvador, *Bahamas* 117 B5
San Salvador, *El Salv.* 116 D2
San Salvador, *Spain* 36 B10
San Salvador de Jujuy, *Argentina* 126 A3
San Salvador I., *Bahamas* 117 B5
San Sebastián, *Argentina* 128 D3
San Sebastián, *Spain* 28 B3
San Sebastián, *Venezuela* 120 B4
San Sebastian de la Gomera, *Canary Is.* 36 F2
San Serra, *Spain* 36 B10
San Serverino Marche, *Italy* 33 E10
San Simeon, *U.S.A.* 112 K5
San Simon, *U.S.A.* 111 K9
San Stéfano di Cadore, *Italy* 33 B9
San Telmo, *Mexico* 114 A1
San Telmo, *Spain* 36 B9
San Tiburcio, *Mexico* 114 C4
San Valentin, Mte., *Chile* 128 C2
San Vicente de Alcántara, *Spain* 31 F3
San Vicente de la Barquera, *Spain* 30 B6
San Vicente del Caguán, *Colombia* 120 C3
San Vincenzo, *Italy* 32 E7
San Vito, *Italy* 34 C2
San Vito, C., *Italy* 34 D5
San Vito al Tagliamento, *Italy* 33 C9
San Vito Chietino, *Italy* 33 F11
San Vito dei Normanni, *Italy* 35 B10
San Yanaro, *Colombia* 120 C4
San Ygnacio, *U.S.A.* 109 M5
Saña, *Peru* 124 B2
Sana', *Yemen* 68 D3
Sana →, *Bos.-H.* 33 C13
Sanaba, *Burkina Faso* 78 C4
Şanāfīr, *Si. Arabia* 76 B3
Sanaga →, *Cameroon* 79 E6
Sanaloa, Presa, *Mexico* 114 C3
Sanana, *Indonesia* 57 E7
Sanand, *India* 62 H5
Sanandaj, *Iran* 67 E12
Sanandita, *Bolivia* 126 A3
Sanary-sur-Mer, *France* 27 E9
Sanawad, *India* 62 H7
Sancellas, *Spain* 36 B9
Sancergues, *France* 25 E9
Sancerre, *France* 25 E9
Sancerrois, Collines du, *France* 25 E9
Sancha He →, *China* 52 D6
Sanchahe, *China* 51 B14
Sánchez, *Dom. Rep.* 117 C6
Sanchor, *India* 62 G4
Sanco Pt., *Phil.* 57 C7
Sancoins, *France* 25 F9
Sancti-Spíritus, *Cuba* 116 B4
Sancy, Puy de, *France* 26 C6
Sand →, *S. Africa* 85 C5
Sand Springs, *U.S.A.* 109 G6
Sanda, *Japan* 49 G7
Sandakan, *Malaysia* 56 C5
Sandan = Sambor, *Cambodia* 58 F6
Sandanski, *Bulgaria* 39 H6
Sandaré, *Mali* 78 C2
Sanday, *U.K.* 14 B6
Sandefjord, *Norway* 10 E4
Sanders, *U.S.A.* 111 J9
Sanderson, *U.S.A.* 109 K3
Sandfly L., *Canada* 101 B7
Sandgate, *Australia* 91 D5
Sandía, *Peru* 124 C4
Sandıklı, *Turkey* 66 C4
Sandnes, *Norway* 9 G11
Sandness, *U.K.* 14 A7
Sandnessjøen, *Norway* 8 C15
Sandoa, *Zaïre* 80 F4
Sandona, *Colombia* 120 C2
Sandover →, *Australia* 90 C2
Sandoway, *Burma* 61 K19
Sandoy, *Færoe Is.* 8 F9
Sandpoint, *U.S.A.* 110 B5
Sandringham, *U.K.* 12 E8
Sandslån, *Sweden* 10 A11
Sandspit, *Canada* 100 C2
Sandstone, *Australia* 89 E2
Sandu, *China* 52 E6
Sandusky, *Mich., U.S.A.* 98 D3
Sandusky, *Ohio, U.S.A.* 106 E2
Sandvig, *Sweden* 11 J8
Sandviken, *Sweden* 9 F17
Sandwich, C., *Australia* 90 B4
Sandwich B., *Canada* 99 B8
Sandwich B., *Namibia* 84 C1
Sandwip Chan., *Bangla.* 61 H17
Sandy, *Nev., U.S.A.* 113 K11
Sandy, *Oreg., U.S.A.* 112 E4
Sandy Bight, *Australia* 89 F3
Sandy C., *Queens., Australia* 90 C5
Sandy C., *Tas., Australia* 90 G3
Sandy Cay, *Bahamas* 117 B4
Sandy Cr. →, *U.S.A.* 110 F9
Sandy L., *Canada* 98 B1
Sandy Lake, *Canada* 98 B1
Sandy Narrows, *Canada* 101 B8
Sanford, *Fla., U.S.A.* 105 L5
Sanford, *Maine, U.S.A.* 107 C14
Sanford, *N.C., U.S.A.* 105 H6
Sanford →, *Australia* 89 E2
Sanford, Mt., *U.S.A.* 96 B5
Sang-i-Masha, *Afghan.* 62 C2
Sanga, *Mozam.* 83 E4
Sanga →, *Congo* 80 E3
Sanga-Tolon, *Russia* 45 C15
Sangamner, *India* 60 K9
Sangar, *Afghan.* 62 C1
Sangar, *Russia* 45 C13
Sangar Sarai, *Afghan.* 62 B4
Sangasangadalam, *Indonesia* 56 E5
Sangatte, *France* 25 B8
Sangay, *Ecuador* 120 D2
Sange, *Zaïre* 82 D2
Sangeang, *Indonesia* 57 F5
Sanger, *U.S.A.* 111 H4
Sangerhausen, *Germany* 18 D7
Sanggan He →, *China* 50 E9
Sanggau, *Indonesia* 56 D4
Sangihe, Kepulauan, *Indonesia* 57 D7
Sangihe, P., *Indonesia* 57 D7
Sangju, *S. Korea* 51 F15
Sangkapura, *Indonesia* 56 F4
Sangkhla, *Thailand* 58 E2
Sangli, *India* 60 L9
Sangmélina, *Cameroon* 79 E7
Sangonera →, *Spain* 29 H3
Sangre de Cristo Mts., *U.S.A.* 109 G2
Sangro →, *Italy* 33 F11
Sangudo, *Canada* 100 C6
Sangue →, *Brazil* 125 C6
Sangüesa, *Spain* 28 C3
Sanguinaires, Is., *France* 27 G12
Sangzhi, *China* 53 C8
Sanhala, *Ivory C.* 78 C3
Sanje, *Uganda* 82 C3
Sanjiang, *China* 52 E7
Sanjo, *Japan* 48 F9
Sankt Antönien, *Switz.* 23 C9
Sankt Blasien, *Germany* 19 H4
Sankt Gallen, *Switz.* 23 B8
Sankt Gallen □, *Switz.* 23 B8
Sankt Goar, *Germany* 19 E3
Sankt Ingbert, *Germany* 19 F3
Sankt Margrethen, *Switz.* 23 B9
Sankt Moritz, *Switz.* 23 D9
Sankt-Peterburg, *Russia* 40 C6
Sankt Pölten, *Austria* 21 G5
Sankt Valentin, *Austria* 21 G4
Sankt Veit, *Austria* 21 J4
Sankt Wendel, *Germany* 19 F3
Sankuru →, *Zaïre* 80 E4
Sanliurfa, *Turkey* 67 D8
Sanlúcar de Barrameda, *Spain* 31 J4
Sanlúcar la Mayor, *Spain* 31 H4
Sanluri, *Italy* 34 C1
Sanmenxia, *China* 50 G6
Sanming, *China* 53 D11
Sannaspos, *S. Africa* 84 D4
Sannicandro Gargánico, *Italy* 35 A8
Sannidal, *Norway* 10 F3
Sannieshof, *S. Africa* 84 D4
Sannīn, J., *Lebanon* 69 B4
Sanok, *Poland* 20 F12
Sanquhar, *U.K.* 14 F5
Sansanding Dam, *Mali* 78 C3
Sansepolcro, *Italy* 33 E9
Sansha, *China* 53 D13
Sanshui, *China* 53 F9
Sanski Most, *Bos.-H.* 33 D13
Sansui, *China* 52 D7
Santa, *Peru* 124 B2
Sant' Ágata de Goti, *Italy* 35 A7
Sant' Ágata di Militello, *Italy* 35 D7
Santa Ana, *Beni, Bolivia* 125 C4
Santa Ana, *Santa Cruz, Bolivia* 125 D6
Santa Ana, *Santa Cruz, Bolivia* 125 D5
Santa Ana, *Ecuador* 120 D1
Santa Ana, *El Salv.* 116 D2
Santa Ana, *Mexico* 114 A2
Santa Ana, *U.S.A.* 113 M9
Santa Ana →, *Venezuela* 120 B3
Sant' Ángelo Lodigiano, *Italy* 32 C6
Sant' Antíoco, *Italy* 34 C1
Sant' Arcángelo di Romagna, *Italy* 33 D9
Santa Bárbara, *Colombia* 120 B2
Santa Bárbara, *Honduras* 116 D2
Santa Bárbara, *Mexico* 114 B3
Santa Bárbara, *Spain* 28 E5
Santa Barbara, *U.S.A.* 113 L7
Santa Bárbara, *Venezuela* 120 B3
Santa Bárbara, Mt., *Spain* 29 H2
Santa Barbara Channel, *U.S.A.* 113 L7
Santa Barbara I., *U.S.A.* 113 M7
Santa Catalina, *Colombia* 120 A2
Santa Catalina, *Mexico* 114 B2
Santa Catalina, Gulf of, *U.S.A.* 113 N9
Santa Catalina I., *U.S.A.* 113 M8
Santa Catarina □, *Brazil* 127 B6
Santa Catarina, I. de, *Brazil* 127 B6
Santa Caterina Villarmosa, *Italy* 35 E7
Santa Cecília, *Brazil* 127 B5
Santa Clara, *Cuba* 116 B4
Santa Clara, *Calif., U.S.A.* 111 H3
Santa Clara, *Utah, U.S.A.* 111 H7
Santa Clara de Olimar, *Uruguay* 127 C5
Santa Clotilde, *Peru* 120 D3
Santa Coloma de Farners, *Spain* 28 D7
Santa Coloma de Gramanet, *Spain* 28 D7
Santa Comba, *Spain* 30 B2
Santa Croce Camerina, *Italy* 35 F7
Santa Croce di Magliano, *Italy* 35 A7
Santa Cruz, *Argentina* 128 D3
Santa Cruz, *Bolivia* 125 D5
Santa Cruz, *Brazil* 122 C4
Santa Cruz, *Chile* 126 C1
Santa Cruz, *Costa Rica* 116 D2
Santa Cruz, *Madeira* 36 D3
Santa Cruz, *Peru* 124 B2
Santa Cruz, *Phil.* 55 D4
Santa Cruz, *U.S.A.* 111 H2
Santa Cruz, *Venezuela* 121 B5
Santa Cruz □, *Argentina* 128 C3
Santa Cruz □, *Bolivia* 125 D5
Santa Cruz →, *Argentina* 128 D3
Santa Cruz Cabrália, *Brazil* 123 E4
Santa Cruz de la Palma, *Canary Is.* 36 F2
Santa Cruz de Mudela, *Spain* 29 G1
Santa Cruz de Tenerife, *Canary Is.* 36 F3
Santa Cruz del Norte, *Cuba* 116 B3
Santa Cruz del Retamar, *Spain* 30 E6
Santa Cruz del Sur, *Cuba* 116 B4
Santa Cruz do Rio Pardo, *Brazil* 127 A6
Santa Cruz do Sul, *Brazil* 127 B5
Santa Cruz I., *Solomon Is.* 92 J8
Santa Cruz I., *U.S.A.* 113 M7
Santa Domingo, Cay, *Bahamas* 116 B4
Santa Elena, *Argentina* 126 C4
Santa Elena, *Ecuador* 120 D1
Santa Elena, C., *Costa Rica* 116 D2
Sant' Eufémia, G. di, *Italy* 35 D9
Santa Eugenia, Pta., *Mexico* 114 B1
Santa Eulalia, *Spain* 36 C8
Santa Fe, *Argentina* 126 C3
Santa Fe, *Spain* 31 H7
Santa Fe, *U.S.A.* 111 J11
Santa Fé □, *Argentina* 126 C3
Santa Filomena, *Brazil* 122 C2
Santa Galdana, *Spain* 36 B10
Santa Gertrudis, *Spain* 36 B7
Santa Helena, *Brazil* 122 B2
Santa Helena de Goiás, *Brazil* 123 E1
Santa Inês, *Brazil* 123 D4
Santa Inés, *Baleares, Spain* 36 B7
Santa Inés, *Extremadura, Spain* 31 G5
Santa Inés, I., *Chile* 128 D2
Santa Isabel = Rey Malabo, *Eq. Guin.* 79 E6
Santa Isabel, *Argentina* 126 D2
Santa Isabel, *Brazil* 123 D1
Santa Isabel, Pico, *Eq. Guin.* 79 E6
Santa Isabel do Araguaia, *Brazil* 122 C2
Santa Isabel do Morro, *Brazil* 123 D1
Santa Lucía, *Corrientes, Argentina* 126 B4
Santa Lucía, *San Juan, Argentina* 126 C2
Santa Lucía, *Spain* 29 H4
Santa Lucía, *Uruguay* 126 C4
Santa Lucia Range, *U.S.A.* 111 J3
Santa Magdalena, I., *Mexico* 114 C2
Santa Margarita, *Argentina* 126 D3
Santa Margarita, *Mexico* 114 C2
Santa Margarita, *Spain* 36 B10
Santa Margarita, *U.S.A.* 112 K6
Santa Margarita →, *U.S.A.* 113 M9
Santa Margherita, *Italy* 32 D6
Santa María, *Argentina* 126 B2
Santa Maria, *Brazil* 127 B5
Santa Maria, *Phil.* 55 C4
Santa Maria, *Spain* 36 B9
Santa Maria, *Switz.* 23 C10
Santa Maria, *U.S.A.* 113 L6
Santa María →, *Mexico* 114 A3
Santa María, B. de, *Mexico* 114 B3
Santa Maria, C. de, *Portugal* 31 J3
Santa Maria Cápua Vétere, *Italy* 35 A7
Santa Maria da Vitória, *Brazil* 123 D3
Santa María de Ipire, *Venezuela* 121 B4
Santa Maria di Leuca, C., *Italy* 35 C11
Santa Maria do Suaçuí, *Brazil* 123 E3
Santa Maria dos Marmelos, *Brazil* 125 B5
Santa María la Real de Nieva, *Spain* 30 D6
Santa Marta, *Colombia* 120 A3
Santa Marta, *Spain* 31 G4
Santa Marta, Ría de, *Spain* 30 B3
Santa Marta, Sierra Nevada de, *Colombia* 120 A3
Santa Marta Grande, C., *Brazil* 127 B6
Santa Maura = Levkás, *Greece* 39 L3
Santa Monica, *U.S.A.* 113 M8
Santa Olalla, *Huelva, Spain* 31 H4
Santa Olalla, *Toledo, Spain* 30 E6
Sant' Onofrio, *Italy* 35 D9
Santa Pola, *Spain* 29 G4
Santa Ponsa, *Spain* 36 B9
Santa Quitéria, *Brazil* 122 B3
Santa Rita, *U.S.A.* 111 K10
Santa Rita, *Guarico, Venezuela* 120 B4
Santa Rita, *Zulia, Venezuela* 120 A3
Santa Rita do Araquaia, *Brazil* 125 D7
Santa Rosa, *La Pampa, Argentina* 126 D3
Santa Rosa, *San Luis, Argentina* 126 C2
Santa Rosa, *Bolivia* 124 C4
Santa Rosa, *Brazil* 127 B5
Santa Rosa, *Colombia* 120 C4
Santa Rosa, *Ecuador* 120 D2
Santa Rosa, *Peru* 124 C3
Santa Rosa, *Calif., U.S.A.* 112 G4
Santa Rosa, *N. Mex., U.S.A.* 109 H2
Santa Rosa, *Venezuela* 120 C4
Santa Rosa de Cabal, *Colombia* 120 C2
Santa Rosa de Copán, *Honduras* 116 D2
Santa Rosa de Osos, *Colombia* 120 B2
Santa Rosa de Río Primero, *Argentina* 126 C3
Santa Rosa de Viterbo, *Colombia* 120 B3
Santa Rosa del Palmar, *Bolivia* 125 D5
Santa Rosa I., *Calif., U.S.A.* 113 M6
Santa Rosa I., *Fla., U.S.A.* 105 K2
Santa Rosa Range, *U.S.A.* 110 F5
Santa Rosalía, *Mexico* 114 B2
Santa Sofia, *Italy* 33 E8
Santa Sylvina, *Argentina* 126 B3
Santa Tecla = Nueva San Salvador, *El Salv.* 116 D2
Santa Teresa, *Argentina* 126 C3
Santa Teresa, *Brazil* 123 E3
Santa Teresa, *Mexico* 115 B5
Santa Teresa, *Venezuela* 121 C5
Santa Teresa di Riva, *Italy* 35 E8
Santa Teresa Gallura, *Italy* 34 A2
Santa Vitória, *Brazil* 123 E1
Santa Vitória do Palmar, *Brazil* 127 C5
Santa Ynez →, *U.S.A.* 113 L6
Santa Ynez Mts., *U.S.A.* 113 L6
Santa Ysabel, *U.S.A.* 113 M10
Santadi, *Italy* 34 C1
Santai, *China* 52 B5
Santaluz, *Brazil* 122 D4
Santana, *Brazil* 123 D3
Santana, *Madeira* 36 D3
Santana, Coxilha de, *Brazil* 127 C4
Santana do Ipanema, *Brazil* 122 C4
Santana do Livramento, *Brazil* 127 C4
Santanayi, *Spain* 36 B10
Santander, *Colombia* 120 C2
Santander, *Spain* 30 B7
Santander Jiménez, *Mexico* 115 C5
Santaquin, *U.S.A.* 110 G8
Santarém, *Brazil* 121 D7
Santarém, *Portugal* 31 F2
Santarém □, *Portugal* 31 F2
Santaren Channel, *W. Indies* 116 B4
Santee, *U.S.A.* 113 N10
Santéramo in Colle, *Italy* 35 B9
Santerno →, *Italy* 33 D8
Santhià, *Italy* 32 C5
Santiago, *Bolivia* 125 D6
Santiago, *Brazil* 127 B5
Santiago, *Chile* 126 C1
Santiago, *Panama* 116 E3
Santiago, *Peru* 124 C2
Santiago, *Phil.* 55 C4
Santiago □, *Chile* 126 C1
Santiago →, *Peru* 120 D2
Santiago, C., *Chile* 128 D1
Santiago, Punta de, *Eq. Guin.* 79 E6
Santiago, Serranía de, *Bolivia* 125 D6
Santiago de Chuco, *Peru* 124 B2
Santiago de Compostela, *Spain* 30 C2
Santiago de Cuba, *Cuba* 116 C4
Santiago de los Cabelleros, *Dom. Rep.* 117 C5
Santiago del Estero, *Argentina* 126 B3
Santiago del Estero □, *Argentina* 126 B3
Santiago del Teide, *Canary Is.* 36 F3
Santiago do Cacém, *Portugal* 31 G2
Santiago Ixcuintla, *Mexico* 114 C3
Santiago Papasquiaro, *Mexico* 114 B3
Santiaguillo, L. de, *Mexico* 114 C4
Santillana del Mar, *Spain* 30 B6
Säntis, *Switz.* 23 B8
Santisteban del Puerto, *Spain* 29 G1
Santo →, *Peru* 124 B2
Santo Amaro, *Brazil* 123 D4
Santo Anastácio, *Brazil* 127 A5
Santo André, *Brazil* 127 A6
Santo Ângelo, *Brazil* 127 B5
Santo Antonio, *Brazil* 125 D6
Santo Antônio de Jesus, *Brazil* 123 D4
Santo Antônio do Içá, *Brazil* 120 D4
Santo Antônio do Leverger, *Brazil* 125 D6
Santo Corazón, *Bolivia* 125 D6
Santo Domingo, *Dom. Rep.* 117 C6
Santo Domingo, *Baja Calif. Mexico* 114 A1

Santo Domingo, Baja Calif. S., Mexico .. 114 B2
Santo Domingo, Nic. 116 D3
Santo Domingo de la Calzada, Spain 28 C2
Santo Domingo de los Colorados, Ecuador 120 D2
Santo Stéfano di Camastro, Italy 35 D7
Santo Stino di Livenza, Italy 33 C9
Santo Tirso, Portugal 30 D2
Santo Tomás, Mexico 114 A1
Santo Tomás, Peru 124 C3
Santo Tomé, Argentina ... 127 B4
Santo Tomé de Guayana = Ciudad Guayana, Venezuela 121 B5
Santoña, Spain 30 B7
Santoríni = Thíra, Greece . 39 N8
Santos, Brazil 127 A6
Santos, Sierra de los, Spain 31 G5
Santos Dumont, Brazil .. 123 F3
Santpoort, Neths. 16 D5
Sanvignes-les-Mines, France 25 F11
Sanyuan, China 50 G5
Sanza Pombo, Angola 80 F3
São Anastácio, Brazil 127 A5
São Bartolomeu de Messines, Portugal ... 31 H2
São Benedito, Brazil 122 B3
São Bento, Brazil 123 E3
São Bento do Norte, Brazil 122 C4
São Bernado de Campo, Brazil 123 F2
São Borja, Brazil 127 B4
São Bras d'Alportel, Portugal 31 H3
São Caitano, Brazil 122 C4
São Carlos, Brazil 127 A6
São Cristóvão, Brazil 122 D4
São Domingos, Brazil 123 D2
São Domingos do Maranhão, Brazil 123 D1
São Félix, Brazil 123 D1
São Francisco, Brazil 123 E3
São Francisco →, Brazil . 122 D4
São Francisco do Maranhão, Brazil 122 C3
São Francisco do Sul, Brazil 127 B6
São Gabriel, Brazil 127 C5
São Gabriel da Palha, Brazil 123 E3
São Gonçalo, Brazil 123 F3
São Gotardo, Brazil 123 E2
Sao Hill, Tanzania 83 D4
São João da Boa Vista, Brazil 127 A6
São João da Pesqueira, Portugal 30 D3
São João da Ponte, Brazil 123 E3
São João del Rei, Brazil . 123 F3
São João do Araguaia, Brazil 122 C2
São João do Paraíso, Brazil 123 E3
São João do Piauí, Brazil 122 C3
São Joaquim da Barra, Brazil 123 F2
São Jorge, Pta. de, Madeira 36 D3
São José, B. de, Brazil ... 122 B3
São José da Laje, Brazil . 122 C4
São José de Mipibu, Brazil 122 C4
São José do Peixe, Brazil 122 C3
São José do Rio Prêto, Brazil 127 A6
São José dos Campos, Brazil 127 A6
São Leopoldo, Brazil 127 B5
São Lourenço, Brazil 123 F2
São Lourenço →, Brazil . 125 D6
São Lourenço, Pantanal do, Brazil 125 D6
São Lourenço, Pta. de, Madeira 36 D3
São Luís, Brazil 122 B3
São Luís do Curu, Brazil . 122 B4
São Luís Gonzaga, Brazil 127 B5
São Marcos →, Brazil ... 123 E2
São Marcos, B. de, Brazil 122 B3
São Martinho, Portugal ... 30 E2
São Mateus, Brazil 123 E4
São Mateus →, Brazil ... 123 E4
São Miguel do Araguaia, Brazil 123 D1
São Miguel dos Campos, Brazil 122 C4
São Nicolau →, Brazil ... 122 C4
São Paulo, Brazil 127 A6
São Paulo □, Brazil 127 A6
São Paulo, I., Atl. Oc. ... 2 D8
São Paulo de Olivença, Brazil 120 D4
São Pedro do Sul, Portugal 30 E2
São Rafael, Brazil 122 C4
São Raimundo das Mangabeiras, Brazil 122 C2
São Raimundo Nonato, Brazil 122 C3
São Romão, Brazil 123 E2
São Roque, Madeira 36 D3
São Roque, C. de, Brazil . 122 C4
São Sebastião, I. de, Brazil 127 A6
São Sebastião do Paraíso, Brazil 127 A6
São Simão, Brazil 123 E1

São Teotónio, Portugal ... 31 H2
São Tomé, Atl. Oc. 70 F4
São Tomé, Brazil 122 C4
São Tomé, C. de, Brazil .. 123 F3
São Tomé & Principe ■, Africa 71 F4
São Vicente, Brazil 127 A6
São Vicente, Madeira 36 D2
São Vicente, C. de, Portugal 31 H2
Saona, I., Dom. Rep. 117 C6
Saône →, France 27 C8
Saône-et-Loire □, France . 25 F11
Saonek, Indonesia 57 E8
Saoura, O. →, Algeria ... 75 C4
Sapanca, Turkey 66 B4
Sapão →, Brazil 122 D2
Saparua, Indonesia 57 E7
Sapé, Brazil 122 C4
Sapele, Nigeria 79 D6
Sapelo I., U.S.A. 105 K5
Sapiéntza, Greece 39 N4
Sapone, Burkina Faso ... 79 C4
Saposoa, Peru 124 B2
Sapozhok, Russia 42 D5
Sappemeer, Neths. 16 B9
Sappho, U.S.A. 112 B2
Sapporo, Japan 48 C10
Sapri, Italy 35 B8
Sapudi, Indonesia 57 G16
Sapulpa, U.S.A. 109 G7
Saqqez, Iran 67 D12
Sar Dasht, Iran 65 C6
Sar Gachīneh, Iran 65 D6
Sar Planina, Macedonia .. 38 G4
Sara, Burkina Faso 78 C4
Sara, Phil. 55 F5
Sarāb, Iran 67 D12
Sarabadi, Iraq 64 C5
Sarada →, India 61 F12
Saragossa = Zaragoza, Spain 28 D4
Saraguro, Ecuador 120 D2
Sarajevo, Bos.-H. 21 M8
Saramacca □, Surinam .. 121 C6
Saramacca →, Surinam . 121 B6
Saran, G., Indonesia 56 E4
Saranac Lake, U.S.A. ... 107 B10
Saranda, Tanzania 82 D3
Sarandí del Yi, Uruguay . 127 C4
Sarandí Grande, Uruguay . 126 C4
Sarangani B., Phil. 55 J6
Sarangani Is., Phil. 55 J6
Sarangarh, India 61 J13
Saransk, Russia 42 C7
Sarapul, Russia 44 D6
Sarasota, U.S.A. 105 M4
Saratoga, Calif., U.S.A. . 112 H4
Saratoga, Wyo., U.S.A. .. 110 F10
Saratoga Springs, U.S.A. . 107 C11
Saratov, Russia 42 E7
Saravane, Laos 58 E6
Sarawak □, Malaysia 56 D4
Saray, Tekirdağ, Turkey . 66 B2
Saray, Van, Turkey 67 C11
Saraya, Senegal 78 C2
Sarayköy, Turkey 66 D3
Sarayönü, Turkey 66 C5
Sarbāz, Iran 65 E9
Sarbīsheh, Iran 65 C8
Sarca →, Italy 32 C7
Sarda = Sarada →, India 61 F12
Sardalas, Libya 75 C7
Sardarshahr, India 62 E6
Sardegna □, Italy 34 B2
Sardhana, India 62 E7
Sardina, Pta., Canary Is. . 36 F4
Sardinata, Colombia 120 B3
Sardinia = Sardegna □, Italy 34 B2
Sardis, Turkey 66 C2
Sārdūīyeh = Dar Mazār, Iran 65 D8
Saréyamou, Mali 78 B4
Sargent, U.S.A. 108 E5
Sargodha, Pakistan 62 C5
Sarh, Chad 73 G8
Sarhro, Djebel, Morocco . 74 B3
Sārī, Iran 65 B7
Sária, Greece 39 P10
Sarıgöl, Turkey 66 C3
Sarikamiş, Turkey 67 B10
Sarıkaya, Turkey 66 C6
Sarikei, Malaysia 56 D4
Sarina, Australia 90 C4
Sariñena, Spain 28 D4
Sarita, U.S.A. 109 M6
Sariwŏn, N. Korea 51 E13
Sariyar Baraji, Turkey ... 66 B4
Sark, U.K. 13 H5
Sarkad, Hungary 21 J11
Şarköy, Turkey 66 B2
Şarkışla, Turkey 66 C7
Sarlat-la-Canéda, France .. 26 D5
Sarles, U.S.A. 108 A5
Sărmaşu, Romania 38 C7
Sarmi, Indonesia 57 E9
Sarmiento, Argentina 128 C3
Särna, Sweden 10 C7
Sarnano, Italy 33 E10
Sarnen, Switz. 22 C6
Sarnia, Canada 98 D3
Sarno, Italy 35 B7
Sarny, Ukraine 44 D3
Särö, Sweden 11 G5
Sarolangun, Indonesia ... 56 E2

Saronikós Kólpos, Greece . 39 M6
Saronno, Italy 32 C6
Saros Körfezi, Turkey 66 B2
Sárospatak, Hungary 21 G11
Sarpsborg, Norway 10 E5
Sarracín, Spain 28 C1
Sarralbe, France 25 D14
Sarre = Saar →, Europe . 25 C13
Sarre-Union, France 25 D14
Sarrebourg, France 25 D14
Sarreguemines, France ... 25 C14
Sarriá, Spain 30 C3
Sarrión, Spain 28 E4
Sarro, Mali 78 C3
Sarstedt, Germany 18 C5
Sartène, France 27 G12
Sarthe □, France 24 E7
Sarthe →, France 24 E6
Sartilly, France 24 D5
Sartynya, Russia 44 C7
Sárvár, Hungary 21 H6
Sarvestān, Iran 65 D7
Sárviz →, Hungary 21 J8
Sary-Tash, Kyrgyzstan .. 44 F8
Sarych, Mys, Ukraine ... 41 K7
Saryshagan, Kazakhstan . 44 E8
Sarzana, Italy 32 D6
Sarzeau, France 24 E4
Sas van Gent, Neths. 17 F3
Sasabeneh, Ethiopia 68 F3
Sasaram, India 63 G11
Sasebo, Japan 49 H4
Saser, India 63 B7
Saskatchewan □, Canada . 101 C7
Saskatchewan →, Canada 101 C8
Saskatoon, Canada 101 C7
Saskylakh, Russia 45 B12
Sasolburg, S. Africa 85 D4
Sasovo, Russia 42 C5
Sassandra, Ivory C. 78 E3
Sassandra →, Ivory C. .. 78 E3
Sássari, Italy 34 B1
Sassenheim, Neths. 16 D5
Sassnitz, Germany 18 A9
Sasso Marconi, Italy 32 D8
Sassocorvaro, Italy 33 E9
Sassoferrato, Italy 33 E9
Sassuolo, Italy 32 D7
Sástago, Spain 28 D4
Sastown, Liberia 78 E3
Sasumua Dam, Kenya ... 82 C4
Sasyk, Ozero, Ukraine ... 41 K5
Sata-Misaki, Japan 49 J5
Satadougou, Mali 78 C2
Satakunta, Finland 9 F20
Satanta, U.S.A. 109 G4
Satara, India 60 L8
Satilla →, U.S.A. 105 K5
Satipo, Peru 124 C3
Satmala Hills, India 60 J9
Satna, India 63 G9
Šátor, Bos.-H. 33 D13
Sátoraljaújhely, Hungary . 21 G11
Satpura Ra., India 62 J7
Satrup, Germany 18 A5
Satsuna-Shotō, Japan ... 49 K5
Sattahip, Thailand 58 F3
Satu Mare, Romania 38 B5
Satui, Indonesia 56 E5
Satun, Thailand 59 J3
Saturnina →, Brazil 125 C6
Sauce, Argentina 126 C4
Sauceda, Mexico 114 B4
Saucillo, Mexico 114 B3
Sauda, Norway 9 G12
Saúde, Brazil 122 D3
Saudi Arabia ■, Asia ... 68 B3
Sauer →, Germany 17 J9
Saugeen →, Canada 106 B3
Saugerties, U.S.A. 107 D11
Saugues, France 26 D7
Sauherad, Norway 10 E3
Saujon, France 26 C3
Sauk Centre, U.S.A. 108 C7
Sauk Rapids, U.S.A. 108 C7
Saül, Fr. Guiana 121 C7
Saulgau, Germany 19 G5
Saulieu, France 25 E11
Sault, France 27 D9
Sault Ste. Marie, Canada . 98 C3
Sault Ste. Marie, U.S.A. .. 104 B3
Saumlaki, Indonesia 57 F8
Saumur, France 24 E6
Saunders, C., N.Z. 87 L3
Saunders I., Antarctica .. 5 B1
Saunders Point, Australia . 89 E4
Sauri, Nigeria 79 C6
Saurimo, Angola 80 F4
Sausalito, U.S.A. 112 H4
Sautatá, Colombia 120 B2
Sauveterre-de-Béarn, France 26 E3
Sauzé-Vaussais, France ... 26 B4
Savá, Honduras 116 C2
Sava →, Serbia, Yug. ... 21 L10
Savage, U.S.A. 108 B2
Savage I. = Niue, Cook Is. 93 J11
Savai'i, W. Samoa 87 A12
Savalou, Benin 79 D5
Savane, Mozam. 83 F4
Savanna, U.S.A. 108 D9
Savanna la Mar, Jamaica . 116 C4
Savannah, Ga., U.S.A. .. 105 J5
Savannah, Mo., U.S.A. .. 108 F7
Savannah, Tenn., U.S.A. . 105 H1

Savannah →, U.S.A. 105 J5
Savannakhet, Laos 58 D5
Savant L., Canada 98 B1
Savant Lake, Canada 98 B1
Savanur, India 60 M9
Savé, Benin 79 D5
Save →, France 26 E5
Save →, Mozam. 85 C5
Sāveh, Iran 65 C6
Savelugu, Ghana 79 D4
Savenay, France 24 E5
Saverdun, France 26 E5
Saverne, France 25 D14
Savièse, Switz. 22 D4
Savigliano, Italy 32 D4
Savigny-sur-Braye, France 24 E7
Saviñao, Spain 30 C3
Savio →, Italy 33 D9
Savo, Finland 8 E22
Savognin, Switz. 23 C9
Savoie □, France 27 C10
Savona, Italy 32 D5
Savonlinna, Finland 40 B5
Savşat, Turkey 67 B10
Sawahlunto, Indonesia .. 56 E2
Sawai, Indonesia 57 E7
Sawai Madhopur, India . 62 F7
Sawang Daen Din, Thailand 58 D4
Sawankhalok, Thailand .. 58 D2
Sawara, Japan 49 G10
Sawatch Mts., U.S.A. ... 111 G10
Sawel Mt., U.K. 15 B4
Sawi, Thailand 59 G2
Sawmills, Zimbabwe 83 F2
Sawu, Indonesia 57 F6
Sawu Sea, Indonesia 57 F6
Saxby →, Australia 90 B3
Saxon, Switz. 22 D4
Saxony, Lower = Niedersachsen □, Germany 18 C5
Saxton, U.S.A. 106 F6
Say, Niger 79 C5
Saya, Nigeria 79 D5
Sayabec, Canada 99 C6
Sayaboury, Laos 58 C3
Sayán, Peru 124 C2
Sayan, Vostochnyy, Russia 45 D10
Sayan, Zapadnyy, Russia . 45 D10
Saydā, Lebanon 69 B4
Sayhan-Ovoo, Mongolia . 50 B2
Sayhandulaan, Mongolia . 50 B5
Sayhūt, Yemen 68 D5
Saykhin, Kazakhstan 43 F8
Saynshand, Mongolia ... 50 B6
Sayre, Okla., U.S.A. 109 H5
Sayre, Pa., U.S.A. 107 E8
Sayula, Mexico 114 D4
Sazin, Pakistan 63 B5
Sazlika →, Bulgaria 39 H8
Sbeïtla, Tunisia 75 A6
Scaër, France 24 D3
Scafell Pike, U.K. 12 C4
Scalea, Italy 35 C8
Scalpay, U.K. 14 D2
Scandia, Canada 100 C6
Scandiano, Italy 32 D7
Scandinavia, Europe 6 C8
Scansano, Italy 33 F8
Scapa Flow, U.K. 14 C5
Scappoose, U.S.A. 112 E4
Scarborough, Trin. & Tob. 117 D7
Scarborough, U.K. 12 C7
Scebeli, Wabi →, Somali Rep. 68 G3
Ščedro, Croatia 33 E13
Scenic, U.S.A. 108 D3
Schaalsee, Germany 18 B6
Schaan, Liech. 23 B9
Schaesberg, Neths. 17 G8
Schaffen, Belgium 17 G6
Schaffhausen, Switz. 23 A7
Schaffhausen □, Switz. .. 23 A7
Schagen, Neths. 16 C5
Schaijk, Neths. 16 E7
Schalkhaar, Neths. 16 D8
Schalkwijk, Neths. 16 E6
Schangnau, Switz. 22 C5
Schänis, Switz. 23 B8
Schärding, Austria 20 G3
Scharhörn, Germany 18 B4
Scharnitz, Austria 19 H7
Scheessel, Germany 18 B5
Schefferville, Canada ... 99 B6
Schelde →, Belgium 17 F4
Schell Creek Ra., U.S.A. . 110 G6
Schenectady, U.S.A. 107 D11
Scherfede, Germany 18 D5
Scherpenheuvel, Belgium . 17 G5
Scherpenzeel, Neths. ... 16 D7
Schesaplana, Switz. 23 B9
Schesslitz, Germany 19 F7
Scheveningen, Neths. ... 16 D4
Schiedam, Neths. 16 E4
Schiermonnikoog, Neths. . 16 B8
Schiers, Switz. 23 C9
Schifferstadt, Germany .. 19 F4
Schifflange, Lux. 17 K8
Schijndel, Neths. 17 E6
Schiltigheim, France 25 D14
Schio, Italy 32 C8
Schipbeek, Neths. 16 D8
Schipluiden, Neths. 16 E4
Schirmeck, France 25 D14
Schlanders = Silandro, Italy 32 B7

Schlei →, Germany 18 A5
Schleiden, Germany 18 E2
Schleiz, Germany 18 E7
Schleswig, Germany 18 A5
Schleswig-Holstein □, Germany 18 A5
Schlieren, Switz. 23 B6
Schlüchtern, Germany ... 19 E5
Schmalkalden, Germany . 18 E6
Schmölln, Brandenburg, Germany 18 B10
Schmölln, Thüringen, Germany 18 E8
Schneeberg, Austria 21 H5
Schneeberg, Germany ... 18 E8
Schoenberg, Belgium ... 17 H8
Schofield, U.S.A. 108 C10
Scholls, U.S.A. 112 E4
Schönberg, Mecklenburg-Vorpommern, Germany 18 B6
Schönberg, Schleswig-Holstein, Germany 18 A6
Schönebeck, Germany ... 18 C7
Schönenwerd, Switz. ... 22 B5
Schongau, Germany 19 H6
Schöningen, Germany ... 18 C6
Schoondijke, Neths. 17 F3
Schoonebeek, Neths. ... 16 C9
Schoonhoven, Neths. ... 16 E5
Schoorl, Neths. 16 C5
Schortens, Germany 18 B3
Schoten, Belgium 17 F5
Schouten I., Australia ... 90 G4
Schouten Is. = Supiori, Indonesia 57 E9
Schouwen, Neths. 17 E3
Schramberg, Germany ... 19 G4
Schrankogl, Austria 19 H7
Schreckhorn, Switz. 22 C6
Schreiber, Canada 98 C2
Schrobenhausen, Germany 19 G7
Schruns, Austria 19 H5
Schuler, Canada 101 C6
Schuls, Switz. 23 C10
Schumacher, Canada 98 C3
Schüpfen, Switz. 22 B4
Schüpfheim, Switz. 22 C6
Schurz, U.S.A. 110 G4
Schuyler, U.S.A. 108 E6
Schuylkill Haven, U.S.A. . 107 F8
Schwabach, Germany ... 19 F7
Schwäbisch Gmünd, Germany 19 G5
Schwäbisch Hall, Germany 19 F5
Schwäbische Alb, Germany 19 G5
Schwabmünchen, Germany 19 G6
Schwanden, Switz. 23 C8
Schwandorf, Germany ... 19 F8
Schwaner, Pegunungan, Indonesia 56 E4
Schwarmstedt, Germany . 18 C5
Schwärze, Germany 18 C9
Schwarze Elster →, Germany 18 D8
Schwarzenberg, Germany 18 E8
Schwarzenburg, Switz. .. 22 C4
Schwarzwald, Germany .. 19 H4
Schwaz, Austria 19 H7
Schwedt, Germany 18 B10
Schweinfurt, Germany .. 19 E6
Schweizer Mittelland, Switz. 22 C4
Schweizer-Reneke, S. Africa 84 D4
Schwenningen = Villingen-Schwenningen, Germany 19 G4
Schwerin, Germany 18 B7
Schweriner See, Germany 18 B7
Schwetzingen, Germany . 19 F4
Schwyz, Switz. 23 B7
Schwyz □, Switz. 23 B7
Sciacca, Italy 35 E6
Scicli, Italy 35 F7
Scilla, Italy 35 D8
Scilly, Isles of, U.K. 13 H1
Ścinawa, Poland 20 D6
Scioto →, U.S.A. 104 F4
Scobey, U.S.A. 108 A2
Scone, Australia 91 E5
Scórdia, Italy 35 E7
Scoresbysund, Greenland . 4 B6
Scorno, Punta dello, Italy . 34 A1
Scotia, Calif., U.S.A. 110 F1
Scotia, N.Y., U.S.A. 107 D11
Scotia Sea, Antarctica ... 5 B18
Scotland, U.S.A. 108 D6
Scotland □, U.K. 14 E5
Scotland Neck, U.S.A. .. 105 G7
Scott, C., Australia 88 B4
Scott City, U.S.A. 108 F4
Scott Glacier, Antarctica . 5 C8
Scott I., Antarctica 5 C11
Scott Inlet, Canada 97 A12
Scott Is., Canada 100 C3
Scott L., Canada 101 B7
Scott Reef, Australia ... 88 B3
Scottburgh, S. Africa ... 85 E5
Scottdale, U.S.A. 106 F5
Scottsbluff, U.S.A. 108 E3
Scottsboro, U.S.A. 105 H2
Scottsburg, U.S.A. 104 F3
Scottsdale, Australia ... 90 G4
Scottsville, Ky., U.S.A. . 105 G2
Scottsville, N.Y., U.S.A. . 106 C7
Scottville, U.S.A. 104 D2

Scranton, *U.S.A.* 107 E9
Scugog, L., *Canada* 106 B6
Scunthorpe, *U.K.* 12 D7
Scuol, *Switz.* 23 C10
Scusciuban, *Somali Rep.* .. 68 E5
Scutari = Üsküdar, *Turkey* 39 H11
Seabra, *Brazil* 123 D3
Seabrook, L., *Australia* .. 89 F2
Seaford, *U.S.A.* 104 F8
Seaforth, *Canada* 98 D3
Seagraves, *U.S.A.* 109 J3
Seal →, *Canada* 101 B10
Seal Cove, *Canada* 99 C8
Seal L., *Canada* 99 B7
Sealy, *U.S.A.* 109 L6
Searchlight, *U.S.A.* 113 K12
Searcy, *U.S.A.* 109 H9
Searles L., *U.S.A.* 113 K9
Seaside, *Calif., U.S.A.* .. 112 J5
Seaside, *Oreg., U.S.A.* .. 112 E3
Seaspray, *Australia* 91 F4
Seattle, *U.S.A.* 112 C4
Seaview Ra., *Australia* .. 90 B4
Sebastián Vizcaíno, B.,
  Mexico 114 B2
Sebastopol = Sevastopol,
  Ukraine 41 K7
Sebastopol, *U.S.A.* 112 G4
Sebderat, *Eritrea* 77 D4
Sebdou, *Algeria* 75 B4
Seben, *Turkey* 66 B4
Sebewaing, *U.S.A.* 104 D4
Sebezh, *Russia* 40 D5
Sebha = Sabhah, *Libya* .. 73 C7
Sébi, *Mali* 78 B4
Şebinkarahisar, *Turkey* .. 67 B8
Sebiş, *Romania* 38 C5
Sebkhet Te-n-Dghâmcha,
  Mauritania 78 B1
Sebkra Azzel Mati, *Algeria* 75 C5
Sebkra Mekerghene,
  Algeria 75 C5
Sebnitz, *Germany* 18 E10
Sebou, Oued →, *Morocco* 74 B3
Sebring, *Fla., U.S.A.* .. 105 M5
Sebring, *Ohio, U.S.A.* .. 106 F3
Sebringville, *Canada* 106 C3
Sebta = Ceuta, *N. Afr.* .. 74 A3
Sebuku, *Indonesia* 56 E5
Sebuku, Teluk, *Malaysia* .. 56 D5
Secchia →, *Italy* 32 C8
Sechelt, *Canada* 100 D4
Sechura, *Peru* 124 B1
Sechura, Desierto de, *Peru* 124 B1
Seclin, *France* 25 B10
Secondigny, *France* 24 F6
Secretary I., *N.Z.* 87 L1
Secunderabad, *India* 60 L11
Sécure →, *Bolivia* 125 D5
Sedalia, *U.S.A.* 108 F8
Sedan, *Australia* 91 E2
Sedan, *France* 25 C11
Sedan, *U.S.A.* 109 G6
Sedano, *Spain* 28 C1
Seddon, *N.Z.* 87 J5
Seddonville, *N.Z.* 87 J4
Sedeh, *Fārs, Iran* 65 D7
Sedeh, *Khorāsān, Iran* .. 65 C8
Sederot, *Israel* 69 D3
Sedgewick, *Canada* 100 C6
Sedhiou, *Senegal* 78 C1
Sedičany, *Czech.* 20 F4
Sedico, *Italy* 33 B9
Sedley, *Canada* 101 C8
Sedova, Pik, *Russia* 44 B6
Sedrata, *Algeria* 75 A6
Sedro-Woolley, *U.S.A.* .. 112 B4
Sedrun, *Switz.* 23 C7
Seebad Ahlbeck, *Germany* 18 B10
Seehausen, *Germany* 18 C7
Seeheim, *Namibia* 84 D2
Seekoei →, *S. Africa* 84 E4
Seelow, *Germany* 18 C10
Sées, *France* 24 D7
Seesen, *Germany* 18 D6
Sefadu, *S. Leone* 78 D2
Seferihisar, *Turkey* 66 C2
Séfeto, *Mali* 78 C3
Sefrou, *Morocco* 74 B4
Sefwi Bekwai, *Ghana* 78 D4
Segamat, *Malaysia* 59 L4
Segarcea, *Romania* 38 E6
Segbwema, *S. Leone* 78 D2
Seget, *Indonesia* 57 E8
Seggueur, O. →, *Algeria* 75 B5
Segonzac, *France* 26 C3
Segorbe, *Spain* 28 F4
Ségou, *Mali* 78 C3
Segovia = Coco →,
  Cent. Amer. 116 D3
Segovia, *Colombia* 120 B3
Segovia, *Spain* 30 E6
Segovia □, *Spain* 30 E6
Segré, *France* 24 E6
Segre →, *Spain* 28 D5
Séguéla, *Ivory C.* 78 D3
Seguin, *U.S.A.* 109 L6
Segundo →, *Argentina* .. 126 C3
Segura →, *Spain* 29 G4
Segura, Sierra de, *Spain* .. 29 G2
Seh Qal'eh, *Iran* 65 C8
Sehitwa, *Botswana* 84 C3
Sehore, *India* 62 H7
Sehwan, *Pakistan* 62 F2
Şeica Mare, *Romania* .. 38 C7
Seiland, *Norway* 8 A20
Seiling, *U.S.A.* 109 G5

Seille →, *Moselle, France* 25 C13
Seille →, *Saône-et-Loire,*
  France 27 B8
Seilles, *Belgium* 17 G6
Sein, I. de, *France* 24 D2
Seinäjoki, *Finland* 9 E20
Seine →, *France* 24 C7
Seine, B. de la, *France* .. 24 C6
Seine-et-Marne □, *France* 25 D9
Seine-Maritime □, *France* 24 C7
Seine-St.-Denis □, *France* 25 D9
Seistan, *Iran* 65 D9
Sejerø, *Denmark* 11 J5
Sejerø Bugt, *Denmark* .. 11 J5
Seka, *Ethiopia* 77 F4
Sekayu, *Indonesia* 56 E2
Seke, *Tanzania* 82 C3
Sekenke, *Tanzania* 82 C3
Sekondi-Takoradi, *Ghana* 78 E4
Seksna, *Russia* 40 C10
Sekuma, *Botswana* 84 C3
Selah, *U.S.A.* 110 C3
Selama, *Malaysia* 59 K3
Selárgius, *Italy* 34 C2
Selaru, *Indonesia* 57 F8
Selb, *Germany* 19 E8
Selby, *U.K.* 12 D6
Selby, *U.S.A.* 108 C4
Selca, *Croatia* 33 E13
Selçuk, *Turkey* 66 D2
Selden, *U.S.A.* 108 F4
Sele →, *Italy* 35 B7
Selemdzha →, *Russia* .. 45 D13
Selenga = Selenge
  Mörön →, *Asia* 54 A5
Selenge Mörön →, *Asia* .. 54 A5
Selenica, *Albania* 39 J2
Selenter See, *Germany* .. 18 A6
Sélestat, *France* 25 D14
Seletan, Tg., *Indonesia* .. 56 E4
Selfridge, *U.S.A.* 108 B4
Sélibabi, *Mauritania* 78 B2
Seliger, Ozero, *Russia* .. 42 B1
Seligman, *U.S.A.* 111 J7
Selîma, El Wâhât el, *Sudan* 76 C2
Selinda Spillway, *Botswana* 84 B3
Selinoús, *Greece* 39 M4
Selizharovo, *Russia* 42 B1
Seljord, *Norway* 10 E2
Selkirk, *Canada* 101 C9
Selkirk, *U.K.* 14 F6
Selkirk I., *Canada* 101 C9
Selkirk Mts., *Canada* .. 100 C5
Selles-sur-Cher, *France* .. 25 E8
Selliá, *Greece* 37 D6
Sellières, *France* 25 F12
Sells, *U.S.A.* 111 L8
Sellye, *Hungary* 21 K7
Selma, *Ala., U.S.A.* 105 J2
Selma, *Calif., U.S.A.* .. 111 H4
Selma, *N.C., U.S.A.* 105 H6
Selmer, *U.S.A.* 105 H1
Selongey, *France* 25 E12
Selowandoma Falls,
  Zimbabwe 83 G3
Selpele, *Indonesia* 57 E8
Selsey Bill, *U.K.* 13 G7
Seltso, *Russia* 42 D2
Seltz, *France* 25 D15
Selu, *Indonesia* 57 F8
Sélune →, *France* 24 D5
Selva, *Argentina* 126 B3
Selva, *Italy* 33 B8
Selva, *Spain* 28 D6
Selvas, *Brazil* 124 B4
Selwyn, *Australia* 90 C3
Selwyn L., *Canada* 101 A8
Selwyn Ra., *Australia* .. 90 C3
Selyatyn, *Ukraine* 38 B8
Semani →, *Albania* 39 J2
Semara, *W. Sahara* 74 C2
Semarang, *Indonesia* .. 57 G14
Semau, *Indonesia* 57 F6
Sembabule, *Uganda* 82 C3
Şemdinli, *Turkey* 67 D11
Sémé, *Senegal* 78 B2
Semeih, *Sudan* 77 E3
Semenov, *Russia* 42 B7
Semenovka, *Ukraine* 41 H7
Semenovka, *Ukraine* 41 F7
Semeru, *Indonesia* 57 H15
Semey, *Kazakhstan* 44 D9
Semikarakorskiy, *Russia* .. 43 G5
Semiluki, *Russia* 42 E4
Seminoe Reservoir, *U.S.A.* 110 E10
Seminole, *Okla., U.S.A.* .. 109 H6
Seminole, *Tex., U.S.A.* .. 109 J3
Semiozernoye, *Kazakhstan* 44 D7
Semipalatinsk = Semey,
  Kazakhstan 44 D9
Semirara Is., *Phil.* 55 F4
Semisopochnoi I., *U.S.A.* 96 C2
Semitau, *Indonesia* 56 D4
Semiyarka, *Kazakhstan* .. 44 D8
Semiyarskoye = Semiyarka,
  Kazakhstan 44 D8
Semmering P., *Austria* .. 21 H5
Semnān, *Iran* 65 C7
Semnān □, *Iran* 65 C7
Semois →, *Europe* 17 J5
Semporna, *Malaysia* 57 D5
Semuda, *Indonesia* 56 E4
Semur-en-Auxois, *France* 25 E11
Sena, *Bolivia* 124 C4
Senā, *Iran* 65 D6
Sena, *Mozam.* 83 F3

Sena →, *Bolivia* 124 C4
Sena Madureira, *Brazil* .. 124 B4
Senador Pompeu, *Brazil* .. 122 C4
Senaja, *Malaysia* 56 C5
Senanga, *Zambia* 84 B3
Senatobia, *U.S.A.* 109 H10
Sendafa, *Ethiopia* 77 F4
Sendai, *Kagoshima, Japan* 49 J5
Sendai, *Miyagi, Japan* .. 48 E10
Sendai-Wan, *Japan* 48 E10
Sendenhorst, *Germany* .. 18 D3
Seneca, *Oreg., U.S.A.* .. 110 D4
Seneca, *S.C., U.S.A.* .. 105 H4
Seneca Falls, *U.S.A.* .. 107 D8
Seneca L., *U.S.A.* 106 D8
Seneffe, *Belgium* 17 G4
Senegal ■, *W. Afr.* 78 C2
Senegal →, *W. Afr.* 78 B1
Senegambia, *Africa* 70 E2
Senekal, *S. Africa* 85 D4
Senftenberg, *Germany* .. 18 D10
Senga Hill, *Zambia* 83 D3
Senge Khambab =
  Indus →, *Pakistan* .. 62 G2
Sengerema □, *Tanzania* .. 82 C3
Sengiley, *Russia* 42 D9
Sengkang, *Indonesia* .. 57 E6
Sengua →, *Zimbabwe* .. 83 F2
Senguerr →, *Argentina* .. 128 C3
Senhor-do-Bonfim, *Brazil* 122 D3
Senica, *Slovak Rep.* 20 G7
Senigállia, *Italy* 33 E10
Senio →, *Italy* 33 D9
Senise, *Italy* 35 B9
Senj, *Croatia* 33 D11
Senja, *Norway* 8 B17
Senlis, *France* 25 C9
Senmonorom, *Cambodia* .. 58 F6
Sennâr, *Sudan* 77 E3
Senneterre, *Canada* 98 C4
Senniquelle, *Liberia* .. 78 D3
Senno, *Belarus* 40 E5
Sennori, *Italy* 34 B1
Seno, *Laos* 58 D5
Senonches, *France* 24 D8
Senorbì, *Italy* 34 C2
Senožeče, *Slovenia* 33 C11
Sens, *France* 25 D10
Senta, *Serbia, Yug.* 21 K10
Sentani, *Indonesia* 57 E10
Sentery, *Zaïre* 82 D2
Sentinel, *U.S.A.* 111 K7
Sentolo, *Indonesia* 57 G14
Senya Beraku, *Ghana* .. 79 D4
Seo de Urgel, *Spain* 28 C6
Seohara, *India* 63 E8
Seoni, *India* 63 H8
Seoul = Sŏul, *S. Korea* .. 51 F14
Separation Point, *Canada* 99 B8
Sepīdān, *Iran* 65 D7
Sepo-ri, *N. Korea* 51 E14
Sepone, *Laos* 58 D6
Sept-Îles, *Canada* 99 B6
Septemvri, *Bulgaria* .. 38 G7
Sepúlveda, *Spain* 30 D7
Sequeros, *Spain* 30 E4
Sequim, *U.S.A.* 112 B3
Sequoia National Park,
  U.S.A. 111 H4
Serafimovich, *Russia* .. 42 F6
Seraing, *Belgium* 17 G7
Seraja, *Indonesia* 59 L7
Serakhis →, *Cyprus* 37 D11
Seram, *Indonesia* 57 E7
Seram Laut, Kepulauan,
  Indonesia 57 E8
Seram Sea, *Indonesia* .. 57 E7
Serang, *Indonesia* 57 G12
Serasan, *Indonesia* 59 L7
Seravezza, *Italy* 32 E7
Serbia □, *Yugoslavia* .. 21 M11
Serdo, *Ethiopia* 77 E5
Serdobsk, *Russia* 42 D7
Seredka, *Russia* 40 C5
Şereflikoçhisar, *Turkey* .. 66 C5
Seregno, *Italy* 32 C6
Seremban, *Malaysia* 59 L3
Serengeti □, *Tanzania* .. 82 C3
Serengeti Plain, *Tanzania* 82 C3
Serenje, *Zambia* 83 E3
Sereth = Siret →,
  Romania 38 D11
Sergach, *Russia* 42 C7
Serge →, *Spain* 28 D5
Sergino, *Russia* 44 C7
Sergipe □, *Brazil* 122 D4
Sergiyev Posad, *Russia* .. 42 B4
Seria, *Brunei* 56 D4
Serian, *Malaysia* 56 D4
Seriate, *Italy* 32 C6
Seribu, Kepulauan,
  Indonesia 56 F3
Sérifontaine, *France* .. 25 C8
Sérifos, *Greece* 39 M7
Sérignan, *France* 26 E7
Serik, *Turkey* 66 D4
Seringapatam Reef,
  Australia 88 B3
Sermaize-les-Bains, *France* 25 D11
Sérmide, *Italy* 33 C8
Sernovodsk, *Russia* 42 D10
Sernur, *Russia* 42 B9
Serny Zavod, *Turkmenistan* 44 F6

Serón, *Spain* 29 H2
Serós, *Spain* 28 D5
Serov, *Russia* 44 D7
Serowe, *Botswana* 84 C4
Serpa, *Portugal* 31 H3
Serpeddi, Punta, *Italy* .. 34 C2
Serpentara, Isola, *Italy* .. 34 C2
Serpentine, *Australia* .. 89 F2
Serpentine Lakes, *Australia* 89 E4
Serpis →, *Spain* 29 G4
Serpukhov, *Russia* 42 C3
Serra do Navio, *Brazil* .. 121 C7
Serra San Bruno, *Italy* .. 35 D9
Serra Talhada, *Brazil* .. 122 C4
Serracapriola, *Italy* 35 A8
Serradilla, *Spain* 30 F4
Sérrai, *Greece* 39 H6
Serramanna, *Italy* 34 C1
Serrat, C., *Tunisia* 75 A6
Serre-Ponçon, L. de,
  France 27 D10
Serres, *France* 27 D9
Serrezuela, *Argentina* .. 126 C2
Serrinha, *Brazil* 123 D4
Serrita, *Brazil* 122 C4
Sersale, *Italy* 35 C9
Sertã, *Portugal* 30 F2
Sertânia, *Brazil* 122 C4
Sertanópolis, *Brazil* .. 127 A5
Sêrtar, *China* 52 A3
Sertig, *Switz.* 23 C9
Serua, *Indonesia* 57 F8
Serui, *Indonesia* 57 E9
Serule, *Botswana* 84 C4
Sérvia, *Greece* 39 J4
Sese Is., *Uganda* 82 C3
Sesepe, *Indonesia* 57 E7
Sesfontein, *Namibia* 84 B1
Sesheke, *Zambia* 84 B3
Sesia →, *Italy* 32 C5
Sesimbra, *Portugal* 31 G1
Sessa Aurunca, *Italy* .. 34 A6
Sesto San Giovanni, *Italy* . 32 C6
Sestri Levante, *Italy* .. 32 D6
Sestriere, *Italy* 32 D3
Sestroretsk, *Russia* 40 B6
Sestrunj, *Croatia* 33 D12
Sestu, *Italy* 34 C2
Sesvenna, *Switz.* 23 C10
Setana, *Japan* 48 C9
Sète, *France* 26 E7
Sete Lagôas, *Brazil* 123 E3
Sétif, *Algeria* 75 A6
Seto, *Japan* 49 G8
Setonaikai, *Japan* 49 G6
Settat, *Morocco* 74 B3
Setté-Cama, *Gabon* 80 E1
Séttimo Tor., *Italy* 32 C4
Setting L., *Canada* 101 B9
Settle, *U.K.* 12 C5
Settlement Pt., *Bahamas* .. 105 M6
Setto Calende, *Italy* .. 32 C5
Setúbal, *Portugal* 31 G2
Setúbal □, *Portugal* 31 G2
Setúbal, B. de, *Portugal* .. 31 G2
Seugne →, *France* 26 C3
Seulimeum, *Indonesia* .. 56 C1
Seuzach, *Switz.* 23 A7
Sevan, *Armenia* 43 K7
Sevan, Ozero = Sevana
  Lich, *Armenia* 43 K7
Sevana Lich, *Armenia* .. 43 K7
Sevastopol, *Ukraine* 41 K7
Sevelen, *Switz.* 23 B8
Seven Emu, *Australia* .. 90 B2
Seven Sisters, *Canada* .. 100 C3
Sevenum, *Neths.* 17 F8
Sever →, *Spain* 31 F3
Sévérac-le-Château, *France* 26 D7
Severn →, *Canada* 98 A2
Severn →, *U.K.* 13 F5
Severn L., *Canada* 98 B1
Severnaya Zemlya, *Russia* 45 B10
Severo-Kurilsk, *Russia* .. 45 D16
Severo-Yeniseyskiy, *Russia* 45 C10
Severodonetsk =
  Syeverodonetsk, *Ukraine* 41 H10
Severodvinsk, *Russia* .. 44 C4
Sevier →, *U.S.A.* 111 G7
Sevier, *U.S.A.* 111 G7
Sevier L., *U.S.A.* 110 G7
Sevilla, *Colombia* 120 C2
Sevilla, *Spain* 31 H5
Sevilla □, *Spain* 31 H5
Seville = Sevilla, *Spain* .. 31 H5
Sevnica, *Slovenia* 33 B12
Sèvre-Nantaise →, *France* 24 E5
Sèvre-Niortaise →, *France* 26 B3
Sevsk, *Russia* 42 D2
Seward, *Alaska, U.S.A.* .. 96 B5
Seward, *Nebr., U.S.A.* .. 108 E6
Seward Pen., *U.S.A.* 96 B3
Sewell, *Chile* 126 C1
Sewer, *Indonesia* 57 F8
Sewickley, *U.S.A.* 106 F4
Sexbierum, *Neths.* 16 B6
Sexsmith, *Canada* 100 B5
Seychelles ■, *Ind. Oc.* .. 47 K9
Seyðisfjörður, *Iceland* .. 8 D6
Seydişehir, *Turkey* 66 D4
Seydvān, *Iran* 67 C11
Seyhan Baraji, *Turkey* .. 66 D6
Seyitgazi, *Turkey* 66 C4
Seym →, *Ukraine* 41 G7
Seymchan, *Russia* 45 C16
Seymour, *Australia* 91 F4

Seymour, *S. Africa* 85 E4
Seymour, *Conn., U.S.A.* . 107 E11
Seymour, *Ind., U.S.A.* .. 104 F3
Seymour, *Tex., U.S.A.* .. 109 J5
Seymour, *Wis., U.S.A.* .. 104 C1
Seyne, *France* 27 D10
Seyssel, *France* 27 C9
Sežana, *Slovenia* 33 C10
Sézanne, *France* 25 D10
Sezze, *Italy* 34 A6
Sfântu Gheorghe, *Romania* 38 D8
Sfîntu Gheorghe,
  Brațul →, *Romania* ... 38 E12
Sha Xi →, *China* 53 D12
Sha Xian, *China* 53 D11
Shaanxi □, *China* 50 G5
Shaba □, *Zaïre* 82 D2
Shabunda, *Zaïre* 82 C2
Shache, *China* 54 C2
Shackleton Ice Shelf,
  Antarctica 5 C8
Shackleton Inlet, *Antarctica* 5 E11
Shādegān, *Iran* 65 D6
Shadi, *China* 53 D10
Shadi, *India* 63 C7
Shadrinsk, *Russia* 44 D7
Shaffa, *Nigeria* 79 C7
Shafter, *Calif., U.S.A.* .. 113 K7
Shafter, *Tex., U.S.A.* .. 109 L2
Shaftesbury, *U.K.* 13 F5
Shagamu, *Nigeria* 79 D5
Shagram, *Pakistan* 63 A5
Shah Bunder, *Pakistan* .. 62 G2
Shahabad, *Punjab, India* .. 62 D7
Shahabad, *Raj., India* .. 62 G7
Shahabad, *Ut. P., India* .. 63 F8
Shahadpur, *Pakistan* .. 62 G3
Shahba, *Syria* 69 C5
Shahdād, *Iran* 65 D8
Shahdadkot, *Pakistan* .. 62 F2
Shahe, *China* 50 F8
Shahganj, *India* 63 F10
Shahgarh, *India* 60 F6
Shaḩḩāt, *Libya* 73 B9
Shahjahanpur, *India* .. 63 F8
Shahpur, *India* 62 H7
Shahpur, *Pakistan* 62 E3
Shahpura, *India* 63 H9
Shahr Kord, *Iran* 65 C6
Shāhrakht, *Iran* 65 C9
Shahrig, *Pakistan* 62 D2
Shahukou, *China* 50 D7
Shaikhabad, *Afghan.* .. 62 B3
Shajapur, *India* 62 H7
Shakargarh, *Pakistan* .. 62 C6
Shakawe, *Botswana* 84 B3
Shaker Heights, *U.S.A.* .. 106 E3
Shakhty, *Russia* 43 G5
Shakhunya, *Russia* 42 B8
Shaki, *Nigeria* 79 D5
Shakopee, *U.S.A.* 108 C8
Shala, L., *Ethiopia* 77 F4
Shali, *Russia* 43 J7
Shallow Lake, *Canada* .. 106 B3
Shalqar, *Kazakhstan* .. 44 E6
Shaluli Shan, *China* .. 52 B2
Shām, *Iran* 65 E8
Shamâl Dârfûr □, *Sudan* . 77 D2
Shamâl Kordofân □, *Sudan* 77 D2
Shamanovo, *Russia* 45 C15
Shamattawa, *Canada* .. 101 B10
Shamattawa →, *Canada* .. 98 A2
Shambe, *Sudan* 77 F3
Shambu, *Ethiopia* 77 F4
Shamīl, *Iran* 65 E8
Shamkhor = Şämkir,
  Azerbaijan 43 K8
Shāmkūh, *Iran* 65 C8
Shamli, *India* 62 E7
Shamo = Gobi, *Asia* 50 C5
Shamo, L., *Ethiopia* 77 F4
Shamokin, *U.S.A.* 107 F8
Shamrock, *U.S.A.* 109 H4
Shamva, *Zimbabwe* 83 F3
Shan □, *Burma* 61 J21
Shan Xian, *China* 50 G9
Shanan →, *Ethiopia* 77 F5
Shanchengzhen, *China* .. 51 C13
Shandak, *Iran* 65 D9
Shandon, *U.S.A.* 112 K6
Shandong □, *China* 51 F10
Shandong Bandao, *China* . 51 F11
Shang Xian, *China* 50 H5
Shangalowe, *Zaïre* 83 E2
Shangani →, *Zimbabwe* .. 83 F2
Shangbancheng, *China* .. 51 D10
Shangcai, *China* 53 A10
Shangcheng, *China* 53 B10
Shangchuan Dao, *China* .. 53 G9
Shangdu, *China* 50 D7
Shanggao, *China* 53 C10
Shanghai, *China* 53 B13
Shanghang, *China* 53 E11
Shanghe, *China* 51 F9
Shangjin, *China* 53 A8
Shanglin, *China* 52 F7
Shangnan, *China* 50 H6
Shangqiu, *China* 50 G8
Shangrao, *China* 53 C11
Shangshui, *China* 50 H8
Shangsi, *China* 52 F6
Shangyou, *China* 53 E10
Shangzhi, *China* 51 B14
Shanhetun, *China* 51 B14
Shani, *Nigeria* 79 C7

Simeulue

Shaniko, U.S.A. 110 D3
Shannon, N.Z. 87 J5
Shannon →, Ireland 15 D2
Shansi = Shanxi □, China 50 F7
Shantar, Ostrov Bolshoy, Russia 45 D14
Shantipur, India 63 H13
Shantou, China 53 F11
Shantung = Shandong □, China 51 F10
Shanxi □, China 50 F7
Shanyang, China 50 H5
Shanyin, China 50 E7
Shaoguan, China 53 E9
Shaowu, China 53 D11
Shaoxing, China 53 C13
Shaoyang, Hunan, China 53 D8
Shaoyang, Hunan, China 53 D8
Shapinsay, U.K. 14 B6
Shaqra', Si. Arabia 64 E5
Shaqrā', Yemen 68 E4
Sharafa, Sudan 77 E2
Sharafkhāneh, Iran 67 C11
Sharbot Lake, Canada 107 B8
Shari, Japan 48 C12
Sharjah = Ash Shāriqah, U.A.E. 65 E7
Shark B., Australia 89 E1
Sharm el Sheikh, Egypt 76 B3
Sharon, Mass., U.S.A. 107 D13
Sharon, Pa., U.S.A. 106 E4
Sharon Springs, U.S.A. 108 F4
Sharp Pt., Australia 90 A3
Sharpe L., Canada 101 C10
Sharpsville, U.S.A. 106 E4
Sharq el Istiwa'iya □, Sudan 77 F3
Sharya, Russia 42 A7
Shasha, Ethiopia 77 F4
Shashemene, Ethiopia 77 F4
Shashi, Botswana 85 C4
Shashi, China 53 B9
Shashi →, Africa 83 G2
Shasta, Mt., U.S.A. 110 F2
Shasta L., U.S.A. 110 F2
Shatsk, Russia 42 C5
Shatt al'Arab →, Iraq 65 D6
Shattuck, U.S.A. 109 G5
Shatura, Russia 42 C4
Shaumyani = Shulaveri, Georgia 43 K7
Shaunavon, Canada 101 D7
Shaver L., U.S.A. 112 H7
Shaw →, Australia 88 D2
Shaw I., Australia 90 C4
Shawan, China 54 B3
Shawanaga, Canada 106 A4
Shawano, U.S.A. 104 C1
Shawinigan, Canada 98 C5
Shawnee, U.S.A. 109 H6
Shaybārā, Si. Arabia 64 E3
Shayib el Banat, Gebel, Egypt 76 B3
Shaykh Sa'īd, Iraq 67 F12
Shchekino, Russia 42 C3
Shcherbakov = Rybinsk, Russia 42 A4
Shchigry, Russia 42 E3
Shchors, Ukraine 41 G6
Shchuchinsk, Kazakhstan 44 D8
She Xian, Anhui, China 53 C12
She Xian, Hebei, China 50 F7
Shea, Guyana 121 C6
Shebekino, Russia 42 E3
Shebele = Scebeli, Wabi →, Somali Rep. 68 G3
Sheboygan, U.S.A. 104 D2
Shediac, Canada 99 C7
Sheelin, L., Ireland 15 C4
Sheep Haven, Ireland 15 A4
Sheerness, U.K. 13 F8
Sheet Harbour, Canada 99 D7
Sheffield, U.K. 12 D6
Sheffield, Ala., U.S.A. 105 H2
Sheffield, Mass., U.S.A. 107 D11
Sheffield, Pa., U.S.A. 106 E5
Sheffield, Tex., U.S.A. 109 K4
Sheho, Canada 101 C8
Shehojele, Ethiopia 77 E4
Shehong, China 52 B5
Shehuen →, Argentina 128 C3
Sheikhpura, India 63 G11
Shek Hasan, Ethiopia 77 E4
Shekhupura, Pakistan 62 D5
Sheki = Şaki, Azerbaijan 43 K8
Shelburne, N.S., Canada 99 D6
Shelburne, Ont., Canada 98 D3
Shelburne, U.S.A. 107 B11
Shelburne B., Australia 90 A3
Shelburne Falls, U.S.A. 107 D12
Shelby, Mich., U.S.A. 104 D2
Shelby, Mont., U.S.A. 110 B8
Shelby, N.C., U.S.A. 105 H5
Shelby, Ohio, U.S.A. 106 F2
Shelbyville, Ill., U.S.A. 108 F10
Shelbyville, Ind., U.S.A. 104 F3
Shelbyville, Tenn., U.S.A. 105 H2
Sheldon, U.S.A. 108 D7
Sheldrake, Canada 99 B7
Shelikhova, Zaliv, Russia 45 D16
Shell Lake, Canada 101 C7
Shell Lakes, Australia 89 E4
Shellbrook, Canada 101 C7
Shellharbour, Australia 91 E5
Shelling Rocks, Ireland 15 E1
Shelon →, Russia 40 C6
Shelton, Conn., U.S.A. 107 E11
Shelton, Wash., U.S.A. 112 C3
Shemakha = Şamaxi, Azerbaijan 43 K9
Shen Xian, China 50 F8
Shenandoah, Iowa, U.S.A. 108 E7
Shenandoah, Pa., U.S.A. 107 F8
Shenandoah, Va., U.S.A. 104 F6
Shenandoah →, U.S.A. 104 F7
Shenchi, China 50 E7
Shendam, Nigeria 79 D6
Shendî, Sudan 77 D3
Sheng Xian, China 53 C13
Shengfang, China 50 E9
Shëngjergji, Albania 39 H3
Shëngjini, Albania 39 H2
Shenjingzi, China 51 B13
Shenmu, China 50 E6
Shennongjia, China 53 B8
Shenqiu, China 50 H8
Shenqiucheng, China 50 H8
Shensi = Shaanxi □, China 50 G5
Shenyang, China 51 D12
Shenzhen, China 53 F10
Sheopur Kalan, India 60 G10
Shepetivka, Ukraine 41 G4
Shepetovka = Shepetivka, Ukraine 41 G4
Shepparton, Australia 91 F4
Sheqi, China 50 H7
Sher Qila, Pakistan 63 A6
Sherborne, U.K. 13 G5
Sherbro I., S. Leone 78 D2
Sherbrooke, Canada 99 C5
Shereik, Sudan 76 D3
Sheridan, Ark., U.S.A. 109 H8
Sheridan, Wyo., U.S.A. 110 D10
Sherkot, India 63 E8
Sherman, U.S.A. 109 J6
Sherridon, Canada 101 B8
Sherwood, N. Dak., U.S.A. 108 A4
Sherwood, Tex., U.S.A. 109 K4
Sherwood Forest, U.K. 12 D6
Sheslay, Canada 100 B2
Sheslay →, Canada 100 B2
Shethanei L., Canada 101 B9
Shetland □, U.K. 14 A7
Shetland Is., U.K. 14 A7
Shewa □, Ethiopia 77 F4
Shewa Gimira, Ethiopia 77 F4
Sheyenne, U.S.A. 108 B5
Sheyenne →, U.S.A. 108 B6
Shibām, Yemen 68 D4
Shibata, Japan 48 F9
Shibecha, Japan 48 C12
Shibetsu, Japan 48 B11
Shibîn el Kôm, Egypt 76 H7
Shibîn el Qanâtir, Egypt 76 H7
Shibing, China 52 D7
Shibogama L., Canada 98 B2
Shibushi, Japan 49 J5
Shicheng, China 53 D11
Shickshock Mts. = Chic-Chocs, Mts., Canada 99 C6
Shidao, China 51 F12
Shidian, China 52 E2
Shido, Japan 49 G7
Shiel, L., U.K. 14 E3
Shield, C., Australia 90 A2
Shiga □, Japan 49 G8
Shigaib, Sudan 73 E9
Shigu, China 52 D2
Shiguaigou, China 50 D6
Shihchiachuangi = Shijiazhuang, China 50 E8
Shijiazhuang, China 50 E8
Shijiu Hu, China 53 B12
Shikarpur, India 62 E8
Shikarpur, Pakistan 62 F3
Shikoku □, Japan 49 H6
Shikoku-Sanchi, Japan 49 H6
Shilabo, Ethiopia 68 F3
Shiliguri, India 61 F16
Shilka, Russia 45 D12
Shilka →, Russia 45 D13
Shillelagh, Ireland 15 D5
Shillong, India 61 G17
Shilo, West Bank 69 C4
Shilong, China 53 F9
Shilou, China 50 F6
Shilovo, Russia 42 C5
Shimabara, Japan 49 H5
Shimada, Japan 49 G9
Shimane □, Japan 49 G6
Shimanovsk, Russia 45 D13
Shimen, China 53 C8
Shimenjie, China 53 C11
Shimian, China 52 C4
Shimizu, Japan 49 G9
Shimodate, Japan 49 F9
Shimoga, India 60 N9
Shimoni, Kenya 82 C4
Shimonoseki, Japan 49 H5
Shimpuru Rapids, Angola 84 B2
Shimsk, Russia 40 C6
Shin, L., U.K. 14 C4
Shin-Tone →, Japan 49 G10
Shinan, China 52 F7
Shinano →, Japan 49 F9
Shīndand, Afghan. 60 C3
Shingleton, U.S.A. 98 C2
Shingū, Japan 49 H7
Shinjō, Japan 48 E10
Shinkafe, Nigeria 79 C6
Shinshār, Syria 69 A5
Shinyanga, Tanzania 82 C3
Shinyanga □, Tanzania 82 C3
Shiogama, Japan 48 E10
Shiojiri, Japan 49 F8
Ship I., U.S.A. 109 K10
Shipehenski Prokhod, Bulgaria 38 G8
Shiping, China 52 F4
Shipki La, India 60 D11
Shippegan, Canada 99 C7
Shippensburg, U.S.A. 106 F7
Shiprock, U.S.A. 111 H9
Shiqian, China 52 D7
Shiqma, N. →, Israel 69 D3
Shiquan, China 50 H5
Shīr Kūh, Iran 65 D7
Shiragami-Misaki, Japan 48 D10
Shirakawa, Fukushima, Japan 49 F10
Shirakawa, Gifu, Japan 49 F8
Shirane-San, Gumma, Japan 49 F9
Shirane-San, Yamanashi, Japan 49 G9
Shiraoi, Japan 48 C10
Shīrāz, Iran 65 D7
Shirbin, Egypt 76 H7
Shire →, Africa 83 F4
Shiretoko-Misaki, Japan 48 B12
Shirinab →, Pakistan 62 D2
Shiriya-Zaki, Japan 48 D10
Shiroishi, Japan 48 E10
Shīrvān, Iran 65 B8
Shirwa, L. = Chilwa, L., Malawi 83 F4
Shishou, China 53 C9
Shitai, China 53 B11
Shivpuri, India 62 G7
Shixian, China 51 C15
Shixing, China 53 E10
Shiyan, China 53 A8
Shiyata, Egypt 76 B2
Shizhu, China 52 C7
Shizong, China 52 E5
Shizuishan, China 50 E4
Shizuoka, Japan 49 G9
Shizuoka □, Japan 49 G9
Shklov = Shklow, Belarus 40 E6
Shklow, Belarus 40 E6
Shkoder = Shkodra, Albania 38 G2
Shkodra, Albania 38 G2
Shkumbini →, Albania 39 H2
Shmidta, O., Russia 45 A10
Shō-Gawa →, Japan 49 F8
Shoal Lake, Canada 101 C8
Shōdo-Shima, Japan 49 G7
Shoeburyness, U.K. 13 F8
Sholapur = Solapur, India 60 L9
Shologontsy, Russia 45 C12
Shōmrōn, West Bank 69 C4
Shoshone, Calif., U.S.A. 113 K10
Shoshone, Idaho, U.S.A. 110 E6
Shoshone L., U.S.A. 110 D8
Shoshone Mts., U.S.A. 110 G5
Shoshong, Botswana 84 C4
Shoshoni, U.S.A. 110 E9
Shostka, Ukraine 41 G7
Shou Xian, China 53 A11
Shouchang, China 53 C12
Shouguang, China 51 F10
Shouning, China 53 D12
Shouyang, China 50 F7
Show Low, U.S.A. 111 J9
Shpola, Ukraine 41 H6
Shreveport, U.S.A. 109 J8
Shrewsbury, U.K. 12 E5
Shrirampur, India 63 H13
Shropshire □, U.K. 13 E5
Shu, Kazakhstan 44 E8
Shuangbai, China 52 E3
Shuangcheng, China 51 B14
Shuangfeng, China 53 D9
Shuanggou, China 51 G9
Shuangjiang, China 52 F2
Shuangliao, China 51 C12
Shuangshanzi, China 51 D10
Shuangyang, China 51 C13
Shuangyashan, China 54 B8
Shucheng, China 53 B11
Shugozero, Russia 40 C8
Shuguri Falls, Tanzania 83 D4
Shuiji, China 53 D12
Shuiye, China 50 F8
Shujalpur, India 62 H7
Shukpa Kunzang, India 63 B8
Shulan, China 51 B14
Shulaveri, Georgia 43 K7
Shule, China 54 C2
Shumagin Is., U.S.A. 96 C4
Shumerlya, Russia 42 C8
Shumikha, Russia 44 D7
Shunchang, China 53 D11
Shunde, China 53 F9
Shungay, Kazakhstan 43 F8
Shungnak, U.S.A. 96 B4
Shuo Xian, China 50 E7
Shūr →, Iran 65 D7
Shūr Āb, Iran 65 C6
Shūr Gaz, Iran 65 D8
Shūrāb, Iran 65 C8
Shūrjestān, Iran 65 D7
Shurugwi, Zimbabwe 83 F3
Shūsf, Iran 65 D9
Shūsh, Iran 67 F13
Shūshtar, Iran 65 D6
Shuswap L., Canada 100 C5
Shuya, Russia 42 B5
Shuyang, China 51 G10
Shūzū, Iran 65 D7
Shwebo, Burma 61 H19
Shwegu, Burma 61 G20
Shweli →, Burma 61 H20
Shymkent, Kazakhstan 44 E7
Shyok, India 63 B8
Shyok →, Pakistan 63 B6
Si Chon, Thailand 59 H2
Si Kiang = Xi Jiang →, China 53 F9
Si-ngan = Xi'an, China 50 G5
Si Prachan, Thailand 58 E3
Si Racha, Thailand 58 F3
Si Xian, China 51 H9
Siahan Range, Pakistan 60 F4
Siaksriindrapura, Indonesia 56 D2
Sialkot, Pakistan 62 C6
Siam = Thailand ■, Asia 58 E4
Siantan, P., Indonesia 59 L6
Siàpo →, Venezuela 120 C4
Sīāreh, Iran 65 D9
Siargao, Phil. 55 G7
Siari, Pakistan 63 B7
Siasi, Phil. 57 C6
Siasi I., Phil. 55 J4
Siátista, Greece 39 J4
Siau, Indonesia 57 D7
Šiauliai, Lithuania 9 J20
Siaya □, Kenya 82 B3
Siazan = Siyäzän, Azerbaijan 43 K9
Sibâi, Gebel el, Egypt 76 B3
Sibari, Italy 35 C9
Sibayi, L., S. Africa 85 D5
Šibenik, Croatia 33 E12
Siberia, Russia 4 D13
Siberut, Indonesia 56 E1
Sibi, Pakistan 62 E2
Sibil, Indonesia 57 E10
Sibiti, Congo 80 E2
Sibiu, Romania 38 D7
Sibley, Iowa, U.S.A. 108 D7
Sibley, La., U.S.A. 109 J8
Sibolga, Indonesia 56 D1
Sibret, Belgium 17 J7
Sibsagar, India 61 F19
Sibu, Malaysia 56 D4
Sibuco, Phil. 55 H5
Sibuguey B., Phil. 55 H5
Sibut, C.A.R. 73 G8
Sibutu, Phil. 57 D5
Sibutu Group, Phil. 55 J3
Sibutu Passage, E. Indies 57 D5
Sibuyan, Phil. 55 E5
Sibuyan Sea, Phil. 55 E5
Sicamous, Canada 100 C5
Sichuan □, China 52 B5
Sicilia, Italy 35 E7
Sicilia □, Italy 35 E7
Sicilia, Canale di, Italy 34 E5
Sicilian Channel = Sicilia, Canale di, Italy 34 E5
Sicily = Sicilia, Italy 35 E7
Sicuani, Peru 124 C3
Siculiana, Italy 34 E6
Sidamo □, Ethiopia 77 G4
Sidaouet, Niger 79 B6
Sidári, Greece 37 A3
Siddeburen, Neths. 16 B9
Siddhapur, India 62 H5
Siddipet, India 60 K11
Sidéradougou, Burkina Faso 78 C4
Siderno, Italy 35 D9
Sídheros, Ákra, Greece 37 D8
Sidhirókastron, Greece 39 H6
Sîdi Abd el Rahmân, Egypt 76 H6
Sîdi Barrâni, Egypt 76 A2
Sidi-bel-Abbès, Algeria 75 A4
Sidi Bennour, Morocco 74 B3
Sidi Haneish, Egypt 76 A2
Sidi Kacem, Morocco 74 B3
Sidi Omar, Egypt 76 A1
Sidi Slimane, Morocco 74 B3
Sidi Smaïl, Morocco 74 B3
Sidlaw Hills, U.K. 14 E5
Sidley, Mt., Antarctica 5 D14
Sidmouth, U.K. 13 G4
Sidmouth, C., Australia 90 A3
Sidney, Canada 100 D4
Sidney, Mont., U.S.A. 108 B2
Sidney, N.Y., U.S.A. 107 D9
Sidney, Nebr., U.S.A. 108 E3
Sidney, Ohio, U.S.A. 104 E3
Sidoarjo, Indonesia 57 G15
Sidon = Saydā, Lebanon 69 B4
Sidra, G. of = Surt, Khalīj, Libya 73 B8
Siedlce, Poland 20 C12
Sieg →, Germany 18 E3
Siegburg, Germany 18 E3
Siegen, Germany 18 E4
Siem Pang, Cambodia 58 E6
Siem Reap, Cambodia 58 F4
Siena, Italy 33 E8
Sieradz, Poland 20 D8
Sierck-les-Bains, France 25 C13
Sierpc, Poland 20 C9
Sierpe, Bocas de la, Venezuela 121 B5
Sierra Blanca, U.S.A. 111 L11
Sierra Blanca Peak, U.S.A. 111 K11
Sierra City, U.S.A. 112 F6
Sierra Colorada, Argentina 128 B3
Sierra de Yeguas, Spain 31 H6
Sierra Gorda, Chile 126 A2
Sierra Grande, Argentina 128 B3
Sierra Leone ■, W. Afr. 78 D2
Sierra Madre, Mexico 115 D6
Sierra Mojada, Mexico 114 B4
Sierraville, U.S.A. 112 F6
Sierre, Switz. 22 D5
Sífnos, Greece 39 N7
Sifton, Canada 101 C8
Sifton Pass, Canada 100 B3
Sig, Algeria 75 A4
Sigdal, Norway 10 D3
Sigean, France 26 E6
Sighetu-Marmatiei, Romania 38 B6
Sighişoara, Romania 38 C7
Sigli, Indonesia 56 C1
Siglufjörður, Iceland 8 C4
Sigmaringen, Germany 19 G5
Signakhi = Tsnori, Georgia 43 K7
Signal, U.S.A. 113 L13
Signal Pk., U.S.A. 113 M12
Signau, Switz. 22 C5
Signy-l'Abbaye, France 25 C11
Sigsig, Ecuador 120 D2
Sigtuna, Sweden 10 E11
Sigüenza, Spain 28 D2
Siguiri, Guinea 78 C3
Sigulda, Latvia 9 H21
Sigurd, U.S.A. 111 G8
Sihanoukville = Kompong Som, Cambodia 59 G4
Sihaus, Peru 124 B2
Sihui, China 53 F9
Siikajoki →, Finland 8 D21
Siilinjärvi, Finland 8 E22
Siirt, Turkey 67 D9
Sijarira Ra., Zimbabwe 83 F2
Sikao, Thailand 59 J2
Sikar, India 62 F6
Sikasso, Mali 78 C3
Sikeston, U.S.A. 109 G10
Sikhote Alin, Khrebet, Russia 45 E14
Sikhote Alin Ra. = Sikhote Alin, Khrebet, Russia 45 E14
Sikiá., Greece 39 J6
Síkinos, Greece 39 N8
Sikkani Chief →, Canada 100 B4
Sikkim □, India 61 F16
Sikotu-Ko, Japan 48 C10
Sil →, Spain 30 C3
Silacayoapan, Mexico 115 D5
Silandro, Italy 32 B7
Silay, Phil. 55 F5
Silba, Croatia 33 D11
Silchar, India 61 G18
Silcox, Canada 101 B10
Şile, Turkey 66 B3
Silenrieux, Belgium 17 H4
Siler City, U.S.A. 105 H6
Silesia = Śląsk, Poland 20 E6
Silet, Algeria 75 D5
Silgarhi Doti, Nepal 63 E9
Silghat, India 61 F18
Silifke, Turkey 66 D5
Siliguri = Shiliguri, India 61 F16
Siling Co, China 54 C3
Silíqua, Italy 34 C1
Silistra, Bulgaria 38 E10
Silivri, Turkey 66 B3
Siljan, Sweden 9 F16
Silkeborg, Denmark 11 H3
Sillajhuay, Cordillera, Chile 124 D4
Sillamäe, Estonia 9 G22
Sillé-le-Guillaume, France 24 D6
Sillustani, Peru 124 D3
Siloam Springs, U.S.A. 109 G7
Silopi, Turkey 67 D10
Silsbee, U.S.A. 109 K7
Šilute, Lithuania 9 J19
Silva Porto = Kuito, Angola 81 G3
Silvan, Turkey 67 C9
Silvaplana, Switz. 23 D9
Silver City, N. Mex., U.S.A. 111 K9
Silver City, Nev., U.S.A. 110 G4
Silver Cr. →, U.S.A. 110 E4
Silver Creek, U.S.A. 106 D5
Silver L., Calif., U.S.A. 112 G6
Silver L., Calif., U.S.A. 113 K10
Silver Lake, U.S.A. 110 E3
Silver Streams, S. Africa 84 D3
Silverton, Colo., U.S.A. 111 H10
Silverton, Tex., U.S.A. 109 H4
Silves, Portugal 31 H2
Silvi Marina, Italy 33 F11
Silvia, Colombia 120 C2
Silvies →, U.S.A. 110 E4
Silvolde, Neths. 16 E8
Silvretta-Gruppe, Switz. 23 C10
Silwa Bahari, Egypt 76 C3
Silz, Austria 19 H6
Sim, C., Morocco 74 B3
Simanggang, Malaysia 56 D4
Simao, China 52 F3
Simão Dias, Brazil 122 D4
Simard, L., Canada 98 C4
Şimareh →, Iran 67 F12
Simav, Turkey 66 C3
Simba, Tanzania 82 C4
Simbach, Germany 19 G9
Simbirsk, Russia 42 C9
Simbo, Tanzania 82 C2
Simcoe, Canada 98 D3
Simcoe, L., Canada 98 D4
Simenga, Russia 45 C11
Simeto →, Italy 35 E8
Simeulue, Indonesia 56 D1

Simferopol, *Ukraine* 41 K8
Sími, *Greece* 66 D2
Simi Valley, *U.S.A.* 113 L8
Simikot, *Nepal* 63 E9
Simití, *Colombia* 120 B3
Simla, *India* 62 D7
Şimleu-Silvaniei, *Romania* . . 38 B5
Simme →, *Switz.* 22 C4
Simmern, *Germany* 19 F3
Simmie, *Canada* 101 D7
Simmler, *U.S.A.* 113 K7
Simões, *Brazil* 122 C3
Simojoki, *Finland* 8 D21
Simojovel, *Mexico* 115 D6
Simonette →, *Canada* 100 B5
Simonstown, *S. Africa* 84 E2
Simplício Mendes, *Brazil* . . 122 C3
Simplon, *Switz.* 22 D6
Simplon P., *Switz.* 22 D6
Simplon Pass = Simplon
   P., *Switz.* 22 D6
Simplon Tunnel, *Switz.* . . . 22 D6
Simpson Desert, *Australia* . . 90 D2
Simpungdong, *N. Korea* . . . 51 D15
Simrishamn, *Sweden* 9 J16
Simunjan, *Malaysia* 56 D4
Simushir, Ostrov, *Russia* . . 45 E16
Sinabang, *Indonesia* 56 D1
Sinadogo, *Somali Rep.* . . . 68 F4
Sinai = Es Sînâ', *Egypt* . . . 76 J8
Sinai,Mt. = Gebel Mûsa,
   Egypt 76 J8
Sinai, Mt. = Mûsa, G.,
   Egypt 76 J8
Sinai Peninsula, *Egypt* 69 F2
Sinaia, *Romania* 38 D8
Sinaloa □, *Mexico* 114 C3
Sinaloa de Levya, *Mexico* . 114 B3
Sinalunga, *Italy* 33 E8
Sinan, *China* 52 D7
Sinarádhes, *Greece* 37 A3
Sînâwan, *Libya* 75 B7
Sincan, *Turkey* 66 B5
Sincé, *Colombia* 120 B2
Sincelejo, *Colombia* 120 B2
Sinchang, *N. Korea* 51 D15
Sinchang-ni, *N. Korea* 51 E14
Sinclair, *U.S.A.* 110 F10
Sinclair Mills, *Canada* . . . 100 C4
Sincorá, Serra do, *Brazil* . . 123 D3
Sind, *Pakistan* 62 G3
Sind □, *Pakistan* 62 F3
Sind →, *India* 63 B6
Sind Sagar Doab, *Pakistan* . 62 D4
Sindal, *Denmark* 11 G4
Sindangan, *Phil.* 55 G5
Sindangbarang, *Indonesia* . . 57 G12
Sinde, *Zambia* 83 F2
Sinegorskiy, *Russia* 43 G5
Sinelnikovo =
   Synelnykove, *Ukraine* . . 41 H8
Sines, *Portugal* 31 H2
Sines, C. de, *Portugal* 31 H2
Sineu, *Spain* 36 B10
Sinfra, *Ivory C.* 78 D3
Sing Buri, *Thailand* 58 E3
Singa, *Sudan* 77 E3
Singapore ■, *Asia* 59 M4
Singapore, Straits of, *Asia* . 59 M5
Singaraja, *Indonesia* 56 F5
Singen, *Germany* 19 H4
Singida, *Tanzania* 82 C3
Singida □, *Tanzania* 82 D3
Singitikós Kólpos, *Greece* . . 39 J6
Singkaling Hkamti, *Burma* . 61 G19
Singkawang, *Indonesia* . . . 56 D3
Singleton, *Australia* 91 E5
Singleton, Mt., *N. Terr.*,
   Australia 88 D5
Singleton, Mt., *W. Austral.*,
   Australia 89 E2
Singoli, *India* 62 G6
Singora = Songkhla,
   Thailand 59 J3
Singosan, *N. Korea* 51 E14
Sinhung, *N. Korea* 51 D14
Sînî □, *Egypt* 69 F2
Siniscóla, *Italy* 34 B2
Sinj, *Croatia* 33 E13
Sinjai, *Indonesia* 57 F6
Sinjār, *Iraq* 67 D9
Sinkat, *Sudan* 76 D4
Sinkiang Uighur = Xinjiang
   Uygur Zizhiqu □, *China* 54 B3
Sinmak, *N. Korea* 51 E14
Sínnai, *Italy* 34 C2
Sinni →, *Italy* 35 B9
Sinnuris, *Egypt* 76 J7
Sinoe, *Romania* 38 E11
Sinop, *Turkey* 66 A6
Sinpo, *N. Korea* 51 E15
Sins, *Switz.* 23 B6
Sinsk, *Russia* 45 C13
Sint-Amandsberg, *Belgium* . 17 F3
Sint Annaland, *Neths.* 17 E4
Sint Annaparoch, *Neths.* . . . 16 B7
Sint-Denijs, *Belgium* 17 G2
Sint Eustatius, I.,
   Neth. Ant. 117 C7
Sint-Genesius-Rode,
   Belgium 17 G4
Sint-Gillis-Waas, *Belgium* . 17 F4
Sint-Huibrechts-Lille,
   Belgium 17 F6
Sint-Katelijne-Waver,
   Belgium 17 F5
Sint-Kruis, *Belgium* 17 F2

Sint-Laureins, *Belgium* . . . 17 F3
Sint Maarten, I., *W. Indies* 117 C7
Sint-Michiels, *Belgium* . . . 17 F2
Sint Nicolaasga, *Neths.* . . . 16 C7
Sint Niklaas, *Belgium* 17 F4
Sint Oedenrode, *Neths.* . . . 17 E6
Sint Pancras, *Neths.* 16 C5
Sint Philipsland, *Neths.* . . . 17 E4
Sint Truiden, *Belgium* 17 G6
Sint Willebrord, *Neths.* . . . 17 E5
Sîntana, *Romania* 38 C4
Sintang, *Indonesia* 56 D4
Sintjohannesga, *Neths.* . . . 16 C7
Sinton, *U.S.A.* 109 L6
Sintra, *Portugal* 31 G1
Sinŭiju, *N. Korea* 51 D13
Siocon, *Phil.* 55 H5
Siófok, *Hungary* 21 J8
Sioma, *Zambia* 84 B3
Sion, *Switz.* 22 D4
Sioux City, *U.S.A.* 108 D6
Sioux Falls, *U.S.A.* 108 D6
Sioux Lookout, *Canada* . . . 98 B1
Sipalay, *Phil.* 55 G5
Siping, *China* 51 C13
Sipiwesk L., *Canada* 101 B9
Sipura, *Indonesia* 56 E1
Siquia →, *Nic.* 116 D3
Siquijor, *Phil.* 55 G5
Siquirres, *Costa Rica* 116 D3
Siquisique, *Venezuela* 120 A4
Sir Edward Pellew Group,
   Australia 90 B2
Sir Graham Moore Is.,
   Australia 88 B4
Sira →, *Norway* 9 G12
Siracusa, *Italy* 35 E8
Sirajganj, *Bangla.* 63 G13
Sirakoro, *Mali* 78 C3
Şiran, *Turkey* 67 B8
Sirasso, *Ivory C.* 78 D3
Sīrdān, *Iran* 67 D13
Sirdaryo = Syrdarya →,
   Kazakhstan 44 E7
Sirer, *Spain* 36 C7
Siret, *Romania* 38 B9
Siret →, *Romania* 38 D11
Şiria, *Romania* 38 C4
Sirino, Mte., *Italy* 35 B8
Sírna, *Greece* 39 N9
Şırnak, *Turkey* 67 D10
Sirohi, *India* 62 G5
Sironj, *India* 62 G7
Síros, *Greece* 39 M7
Sirretta Pk., *U.S.A.* 113 K8
Sirsa, *India* 62 E6
Siruela, *Spain* 31 G5
Sisak, *Croatia* 33 C13
Sisaket, *Thailand* 58 E5
Sisante, *Spain* 29 F2
Sisargas, Is., *Spain* 30 B2
Sishen, *S. Africa* 84 D3
Sishui, *Henan, China* 50 G7
Sishui, *Shandong, China* . . 51 G9
Sisipuk L., *Canada* 101 B8
Sisophon, *Cambodia* 58 F4
Sissach, *Switz.* 22 B5
Sisseton, *U.S.A.* 108 C6
Sissonne, *France* 25 C10
Sīstān va Balūchestān □,
   Iran 65 E9
Sisteron, *France* 27 D9
Sisters, *U.S.A.* 110 D3
Sitamarhi, *India* 63 F11
Sitapur, *India* 63 F9
Siteki, *Swaziland* 85 D5
Sitges, *Spain* 28 D6
Sitía, *Greece* 37 D8
Sítio da Abadia, *Brazil* . . . 123 D2
Sitka, *U.S.A.* 96 C6
Sitoti, *Botswana* 84 C3
Sitra, *Egypt* 76 B2
Sittang Myit →, *Burma* . . 61 L20
Sittard, *Neths.* 17 G7
Sittensen, *Germany* 18 B5
Sittona, *Eritrea* 77 E4
Sittwe, *Burma* 61 J18
Siuna, *Nic.* 116 D3
Siuri, *India* 63 H12
Sivana, *India* 62 E8
Sīvand, *Iran* 65 D7
Sivas, *Turkey* 66 C7
Siverek, *Turkey* 67 D8
Sivrihisar, *Turkey* 66 C4
Sivry, *Belgium* 17 H4
Sîwa, *Egypt* 76 B2
Sîwa, El Wâhât es, *Egypt* . 76 B2
Siwalik Range, *Nepal* 63 F10
Siwan, *India* 63 F11
Siyâl, Jazâ'ir, *Egypt* 76 C4
Siyäzän, *Azerbaijan* 43 K9
Sizewell, *U.K.* 13 E9
Siziwang Qi, *China* 50 D6
Sjælland, *Denmark* 11 J5
Sjællands Odde, *Denmark* . 11 J5
Själevad, *Sweden* 10 A12
Sjenica, *Serbia, Yug.* 21 M10
Sjoa, *Norway* 10 C3
Sjöbo, *Sweden* 11 J7
Sjösa, *Sweden* 11 F11
Sjumen = Šumen, *Bulgaria* 38 F9
Skadovsk, *Ukraine* 41 J7
Skaftafell, *Iceland* 8 D5
Skagafjörður, *Iceland* 8 D4
Skagastølstindane, *Norway* . 9 F12

Skagen, *Denmark* 11 G4
Skagerrak, *Denmark* 11 G3
Skagit →, *U.S.A.* 112 B4
Skagway, *U.S.A.* 100 B1
Skala-Podilska, *Ukraine* . . 41 H4
Skala Podilska = Skala-
   Podilska, *Ukraine* 41 H4
Skalat, *Ukraine* 41 H3
Skalni Dol = Kamenyak,
   Bulgaria 38 F9
Skals, *Denmark* 11 H3
Skanderborg, *Denmark* . . . 11 H3
Skåne, *Sweden* 9 J15
Skanör, *Sweden* 11 J6
Skara, *Sweden* 9 G15
Skardu, *Pakistan* 63 B6
Skarrild, *Denmark* 11 J2
Skarzysko-Kamienna,
   Poland 20 D10
Skebokvarn, *Sweden* 10 E10
Skeena →, *Canada* 100 C2
Skeena Mts., *Canada* 100 B3
Skegness, *U.K.* 12 D8
Skeldon, *Guyana* 121 B6
Skellefte älv →, *Sweden* . . 8 D19
Skellefteå, *Sweden* 8 D19
Skelleftehamn, *Sweden* . . . 8 D19
Skender Vakuf, *Bos.-H.* . . 21 L7
Skene, *Sweden* 11 G6
Skerries, The, *U.K.* 12 D3
Skhoinoúsa, *Greece* 39 N8
Ski, *Norway* 10 E4
Skíathos, *Greece* 39 K6
Skibbereen, *Ireland* 15 E2
Skiddaw, *U.K.* 12 C4
Skien, *Norway* 10 E3
Skierniewice, *Poland* 20 D10
Skikda, *Algeria* 75 A6
Skilloura, *Cyprus* 37 D12
Skinári, Ákra, *Greece* 39 M3
Skipton, *Australia* 91 F3
Skirmish Pt., *Australia* . . . 90 A1
Skíros, *Greece* 39 L7
Skivarp, *Sweden* 11 J7
Skive, *Denmark* 11 H3
Skjálfandafljót →, *Iceland* . 8 D5
Skjálfandi, *Iceland* 8 C5
Skjeberg, *Norway* 10 E5
Skjern, *Denmark* 11 J2
Škofja Loka, *Slovenia* 33 B11
Skoghall, *Sweden* 9 G15
Skole, *Ukraine* 41 H2
Skópelos, *Greece* 39 K6
Skopí, *Greece* 37 D8
Skopin, *Russia* 42 D4
Skopje, *Macedonia* 39 G4
Skórcz, *Poland* 20 B8
Skövde, *Sweden* 9 G15
Skovorodino, *Russia* 45 D13
Skowhegan, *U.S.A.* 99 D6
Skownan, *Canada* 101 C9
Skradin, *Croatia* 33 E12
Skreanäs, *Sweden* 11 H6
Skull, *Ireland* 15 E2
Skultorp, *Sweden* 11 F7
Skunk →, *U.S.A.* 108 E9
Skuodas, *Lithuania* 9 H19
Skurup, *Sweden* 11 J7
Skutskär, *Sweden* 10 D11
Skvyra, *Ukraine* 41 H5
Skye, *U.K.* 14 D2
Skykomish, *U.S.A.* 110 C3
Skyros = Skíros, *Greece* . . 39 L7
Slættaratindur, *Færoe Is.* . . 8 E9
Slagelse, *Denmark* 11 J5
Slagharen, *Neths.* 16 C9
Slamet, *Indonesia* 56 F3
Slaney →, *Ireland* 15 D5
Slangerup, *Denmark* 11 J6
Slano, *Croatia* 21 N7
Slantsy, *Russia* 40 C5
Śląsk, *Poland* 20 E6
Slate Is., *Canada* 98 C2
Slaton, *U.S.A.* 109 J4
Slave →, *Canada* 100 A6
Slave Coast, *W. Afr.* 79 D5
Slave Lake, *Canada* 100 B6
Slave Pt., *Canada* 100 A5
Slavgorod, *Russia* 44 D8
Slavonska Požega, *Croatia* . 21 K7
Slavonski Brod, *Croatia* . . 21 K8
Slavuta, *Ukraine* 41 G4
Slavyanka, *Russia* 48 C5
Slavyansk = Slovyansk,
   Ukraine 41 H9
Slavyansk-na-Kubani,
   Russia 43 H4
Sławharad, *Belarus* 40 F6
Sławno, *Poland* 20 A6
Sławoborze, *Poland* 20 B5
Sleaford, *U.K.* 12 E7
Sleaford B., *Australia* 91 E2
Sleat, Sd. of, *U.K.* 14 D3
Sleeper Is., *Canada* 97 C11
Sleepy Eye, *U.S.A.* 108 C7
Sleidinge, *Belgium* 17 F3
Sleman, *Indonesia* 57 G14
Slemon L., *Canada* 100 A5
Slidell, *U.S.A.* 109 K10
Sliedrecht, *Neths.* 16 E5
Sliema, *Malta* 37 D2
Slieve Aughty, *Ireland* . . . 15 C3
Slieve Bloom, *Ireland* 15 C4
Slieve Donard, *U.K.* 15 B6

Slieve Gullion, *U.K.* 15 B5
Slieve Mish, *Ireland* 15 D2
Slievenamon, *Ireland* 15 D4
Sligeach = Sligo, *Ireland* . . 15 B3
Sligo, *Ireland* 15 B3
Sligo □, *Ireland* 15 B3
Sligo B., *Ireland* 15 B3
Slijpe, *Belgium* 17 F1
Slikkerveer, *Neths.* 16 E5
Slite, *Sweden* 9 H18
Sliven, *Bulgaria* 38 G9
Slivnitsa, *Bulgaria* 38 G6
Sljeme, *Croatia* 33 C12
Sloan, *U.S.A.* 113 K11
Sloansville, *U.S.A.* 107 D10
Slobozia, *Romania* 38 E10
Slocan, *Canada* 100 D5
Slochteren, *Neths.* 16 B9
Slöinge, *Sweden* 11 H6
Slonim, *Belarus* 41 F3
Slotermeer, *Neths.* 16 C7
Slough, *U.K.* 13 F7
Sloughhouse, *U.S.A.* 112 G5
Slovak Rep. ■, *Europe* . . . 20 G9
Slovakia = Slovak Rep. ■,
   Europe 20 G9
Slovakian Ore Mts. =
   Slovenské Rudohorie,
   Slovak Rep. 20 G9
Slovenia ■, *Europe* 33 C11
Slovenija = Slovenia ■,
   Europe 33 C11
Slovenj Gradec, *Slovenia* . . 33 B12
Slovenska Bistrica, *Slovenia* 33 B12
Slovenská Republika =
   Slovak Rep. ■, *Europe* . 20 G9
Slovenské Rudohorie,
   Slovak Rep. 20 G9
Slovyansk, *Ukraine* 41 H9
Słubice, *Poland* 20 C4
Sluch →, *Ukraine* 41 G4
Sluis, *Neths.* 17 F2
Slunj, *Croatia* 33 C12
Słupca, *Poland* 20 C7
Słupsk, *Poland* 20 A7
Slurry, *S. Africa* 84 D4
Slutsk, *Belarus* 41 F4
Slyne Hd., *Ireland* 15 C1
Slyudyanka, *Russia* 45 D11
Småland, *Sweden* 9 H16
Smålandsfarvandet,
   Denmark 11 J5
Smålandsstenar, *Sweden* . . 11 G7
Smalltree L., *Canada* 101 A7
Smara, *Morocco* 72 B3
Smarhon, *Belarus* 40 E4
Smarje, *Slovenia* 33 B12
Smartt Syndicate Dam,
   S. Africa 84 E3
Smartville, *U.S.A.* 112 F5
Smeaton, *Canada* 101 C8
Smederevo, *Serbia, Yug.* . . 21 L10
Smederevska Palanka,
   Serbia, Yug. 21 L10
Smela = Smila, *Ukraine* . . 41 H6
Smethport, *U.S.A.* 106 E6
Smidovich, *Russia* 45 E14
Smila, *Ukraine* 41 H6
Smilde, *Neths.* 16 C8
Smiley, *Canada* 101 C7
Smith, *Canada* 100 B6
Smith →, *Canada* 100 B3
Smith Arm, *Canada* 96 B7
Smith Center, *U.S.A.* 108 F5
Smith Sund, *Greenland* . . . 4 B4
Smithburne →, *Australia* . . 90 B3
Smithers, *Canada* 100 C3
Smithfield, *S. Africa* 85 E4
Smithfield, *N.C., U.S.A.* . . 105 H6
Smithfield, *Utah, U.S.A.* . . 110 F8
Smiths Falls, *Canada* 98 D4
Smithton, *Australia* 90 G4
Smithtown, *Australia* 91 E5
Smithville, *Canada* 106 C5
Smithville, *U.S.A.* 109 K6
Smoky →, *Canada* 100 B5
Smoky Bay, *Australia* 91 E1
Smoky Falls, *Canada* 98 B3
Smoky Hill →, *U.S.A.* . . . 108 F6
Smoky Lake, *Canada* 100 C6
Smøla, *Norway* 10 A2
Smolensk, *Russia* 40 E7
Smolikas, Óros, *Greece* . . . 39 J3
Smolník, *Slovak Rep.* 20 G10
Smolyan, *Bulgaria* 39 H7
Smooth Rock Falls, *Canada* 98 C3
Smoothstone L., *Canada* . . 101 C7
Smorgon = Smarhon,
   Belarus 40 E4
Smyadovo, *Bulgaria* 38 F10
Smyrna = İzmir, *Turkey* . . 66 C2
Snæfell, *Iceland* 8 D6
Snaefell, *U.K.* 12 C3
Snæfellsjökull, *Iceland* 8 D2
Snake →, *U.S.A.* 110 C4
Snake I., *Australia* 91 F4
Snake L., *Canada* 101 B7
Snake Range, *U.S.A.* 110 G6
Snake River Plain, *U.S.A.* . 110 E7
Snarum, *Norway* 10 D3
Snåsavatnet, *Norway* 8 D14
Snedsted, *Denmark* 11 H2
Sneek, *Neths.* 16 B7
Sneeker-meer, *Neths.* 16 B7
Sneeuberge, *S. Africa* 84 E3
Snejbjerg, *Denmark* 11 H2
Snelling, *U.S.A.* 112 H6

Snezhnoye, *Ukraine* 41 J10
Snežnik, *Slovenia* 33 C11
Snigirevka = Snihurivka,
   Ukraine 41 J7
Snihurivka, *Ukraine* 41 J7
Snizort, L., *U.K.* 14 D2
Snøhetta, *Norway* 10 B3
Snohomish, *U.S.A.* 112 C4
Snoul, *Cambodia* 59 F6
Snow Hill, *U.S.A.* 104 F8
Snow Lake, *Canada* 101 C8
Snow Mt., *U.S.A.* 112 F4
Snowbird L., *Canada* 101 A8
Snowdon, *U.K.* 12 D3
Snowdrift, *Canada* 101 A6
Snowdrift →, *Canada* 101 A6
Snowflake, *U.S.A.* 111 J8
Snowshoe Pk., *U.S.A.* . . . 110 B6
Snowtown, *Australia* 91 E2
Snowville, *U.S.A.* 110 F7
Snowy →, *Australia* 91 F4
Snowy Mts., *Australia* . . . 91 F4
Snug Corner, *Bahamas* . . . 117 B5
Snyatyn, *Ukraine* 41 H3
Snyder, *Okla., U.S.A.* . . . 109 H5
Snyder, *Tex., U.S.A.* 109 J4
Soacha, *Colombia* 120 C3
Soahanina, *Madag.* 85 B7
Soalala, *Madag.* 85 B8
Soan →, *Pakistan* 62 C4
Soanierana-Ivongo, *Madag.* 85 B8
Soap Lake, *U.S.A.* 110 C4
Sobat, Nahr →, *Sudan* . . . 77 F3
Sobhapur, *India* 62 H8
Sobinka, *Russia* 42 C5
Sobolevo, *Russia* 45 D16
Sobótka, *Poland* 20 E6
Sobradinho, Reprêsa de,
   Brazil 122 C3
Sobrado, *Spain* 30 B2
Sobral, *Brazil* 122 B3
Sobreira Formosa, *Portugal* 31 F3
Soc Giang, *Vietnam* 58 A6
Soc Trang, *Vietnam* 59 H5
Soča →, *Europe* 33 B10
Sochaczew, *Poland* 20 C10
Soch'e = Shache, *China* . . 54 C2
Sochi, *Russia* 43 J4
Société, Is. de la, *Pac. Oc.* 93 J12
Society Is. = Société, Is. de
   la, *Pac. Oc.* 93 J12
Socompa, Portezuelo de,
   Chile 126 A2
Socorro, *Colombia* 120 B3
Socorro, *U.S.A.* 111 J10
Socorro, I., *Mexico* 114 D2
Socotra, *Ind. Oc.* 68 E5
Socuéllmos, *Spain* 29 F2
Soda L., *U.S.A.* 111 J5
Soda Plains, *India* 63 B8
Soda Springs, *U.S.A.* 110 E8
Sodankylä, *Finland* 8 C22
Söderhamn, *Sweden* 9 F17
Söderköping, *Sweden* 9 G17
Södermanland, *Sweden* . . . 9 G17
Södermanlands län □,
   Sweden 10 E10
Södertälje, *Sweden* 10 E11
Sodiri, *Sudan* 77 E2
Sodo, *Ethiopia* 77 F4
Sodražica, *Slovenia* 33 C11
Sodus, *U.S.A.* 106 C7
Soekmekaar, *S. Africa* . . . 85 C4
Soest, *Germany* 18 D4
Soest, *Neths.* 16 D6
Soestdijk, *Neths.* 16 D6
Sofádhes, *Greece* 39 K5
Sofara, *Mali* 78 C4
Sofia = Sofiya, *Bulgaria* . . 38 G6
Sofia →, *Madag.* 85 B8
Sofievka, *Ukraine* 41 H7
Sofikón, *Greece* 39 M6
Sofiya, *Bulgaria* 38 G6
Sofiysk, *Russia* 45 D14
Sōfu-Gan, *Japan* 49 K10
Sogakofe, *Ghana* 79 D5
Sogamoso, *Colombia* 120 B3
Sogār, *Iran* 65 E8
Sögel, *Germany* 18 C3
Sogndalsfjøra, *Norway* . . . 9 F12
Søgne, *Norway* 9 G12
Sognefjorden, *Norway* 9 F11
Söğüt, *Turkey* 66 B4
Sŏgwi-po, *S. Korea* 51 H14
Soh, *Iran* 65 C6
Sohâg, *Egypt* 76 B3
Sŏhori, *N. Korea* 51 D15
Soignies, *Belgium* 17 G4
Soira, *Eritrea* 77 E4
Soissons, *France* 25 C10
Sōja, *Japan* 49 G6
Sojat, *India* 62 G5
Sok →, *Russia* 42 D10
Sokal, *Ukraine* 41 G3
Söke, *Turkey* 66 D2
Sokelo, *Zaïre* 83 D1
Sokhumi, *Georgia* 43 J5
Sokki, Oued In →, *Algeria* 75 C5
Sokna, *Norway* 10 D3
Soknedal, *Norway* 10 B4
Soko Banja, *Serbia, Yug.* . 21 M11
Sokodé, *Togo* 79 D5
Sokol, *Russia* 40 C11
Sokółka, *Poland* 20 B13
Sokolo, *Mali* 78 C3
Sokółów Małopolski, *Poland* 20 E12
Sokołów Podlaski, *Poland* . 20 C12

Staffordshire

Sokoto, *Nigeria* 79 C6
Sokoto □, *Nigeria* 79 C6
Sokoto →, *Nigeria* 79 C5
Sol Iletsk, *Russia* 44 D6
Solai, *Kenya* 82 B4
Solano, *Phil.* 55 C4
Solapur, *India* 60 L9
Solares, *Spain* 30 B7
Soléa □, *Cyprus* 37 D12
Solec Kujawski, *Poland* 20 B8
Soledad, *Colombia* 120 A3
Soledad, *U.S.A.* 111 H3
Soledad, *Venezuela* 121 B5
Solent, The, *U.K.* 13 G6
Solenzara, *France* 27 G13
Solesmes, *France* 25 B10
Solfonn, *Norway* 9 F12
Solhan, *Turkey* 67 C9
Soligorsk = Salihorsk, *Belarus* 41 F4
Solikamsk, *Russia* 44 D6
Solila, *Madag.* 85 C8
Solimões = Amazonas →, *S. Amer.* 121 D7
Solingen, *Germany* 17 F10
Sollebrunn, *Sweden* 11 F6
Sollefteå, *Sweden* 10 A11
Sollentuna, *Sweden* 10 E11
Sóller, *Spain* 36 B9
Solling, *Germany* 18 D5
Solna, *Sweden* 10 E12
Solnechnogorsk, *Russia* 42 B3
Sologne, *France* 25 E8
Solok, *Indonesia* 56 E2
Sololá, *Guatemala* 116 D1
Solomon, N. Fork →, *U.S.A.* 108 F5
Solomon, S. Fork →, *U.S.A.* 108 F5
Solomon Is. ■, *Pac. Oc.* 92 H7
Solon, *China* 54 B7
Solon Springs, *U.S.A.* 108 B9
Solonópole, *Brazil* 122 C4
Solor, *Indonesia* 57 F6
Solotcha, *Russia* 42 C4
Solothurn, *Switz.* 22 B5
Solothurn □, *Switz.* 22 B5
Solsona, *Spain* 28 D6
Šolta, *Croatia* 33 E13
Solṭānābād, *Khorāsān, Iran* 65 C8
Solṭānābād, *Khorāsān, Iran* 65 B8
Solṭānābād, *Markazī, Iran* 65 C6
Soltau, *Germany* 18 C5
Soltsy, *Russia* 40 C6
Solunska Glava, *Macedonia* 39 H4
Solvang, *U.S.A.* 113 L6
Solvay, *U.S.A.* 107 C8
Sölvesborg, *Sweden* 9 H16
Solway Firth, *U.K.* 12 C4
Solwezi, *Zambia* 83 E2
Sōma, *Japan* 48 F10
Soma, *Turkey* 66 C2
Somali Rep. ■, *Africa* 68 F4
Somalia = Somali Rep. ■, *Africa* 68 F4
Sombernon, *France* 25 E11
Sombor, *Serbia, Yug.* 21 K9
Sombra, *Canada* 106 D2
Sombrerete, *Mexico* 114 C4
Sombrero, *Anguilla* 117 C7
Someren, *Neths.* 17 F7
Somers, *U.S.A.* 110 B6
Somerset, *Canada* 101 D9
Somerset, *Colo., U.S.A.* 111 G10
Somerset, *Ky., U.S.A.* 104 G3
Somerset, *Mass., U.S.A.* 107 E13
Somerset, *Pa., U.S.A.* 106 F5
Somerset □, *U.K.* 13 F5
Somerset East, *S. Africa* 84 E4
Somerset I., *Canada* 96 A10
Somerset West, *S. Africa* 84 E2
Somerton, *U.S.A.* 111 K6
Somerville, *U.S.A.* 107 F10
Someş →, *Romania* 38 B5
Someşul Mare →, *Romania* 38 B7
Somma Lombardo, *Italy* 32 C5
Somma Vesuviana, *Italy* 35 B7
Sommariva, *Australia* 91 D4
Sommatino, *Italy* 34 E6
Somme □, *France* 25 C9
Somme →, *France* 25 B8
Somme, B. de la, *France* 24 B8
Sommelsdijk, *Neths.* 16 E4
Sommepy-Tahure, *France* 25 C11
Sömmerda, *Germany* 18 D7
Sommesous, *France* 25 D11
Sommières, *France* 27 E8
Somoto, *Nic.* 116 D2
Sompolno, *Poland* 20 C8
Somport, Paso, *Spain* 28 C4
Somport, Puerto de, *Spain* 28 C4
Somuncurá, Meseta de, *Argentina* 128 B3
Son, *Neths.* 17 E6
Son, *Norway* 10 E4
Son, *Spain* 30 C2
Son Ha, *Vietnam* 58 E7
Son Hoa, *Vietnam* 58 F7
Son La, *Vietnam* 58 B4
Son Tay, *Vietnam* 58 B5
Soná, *Panama* 116 E3
Sonamarg, *India* 63 B6
Sonamukhi, *India* 63 H12
Sŏnchŏn, *N. Korea* 51 E13
Soncino, *Italy* 32 C6
Sondags →, *S. Africa* 84 E4
Sóndalo, *Italy* 32 B7
Sondar, *India* 63 C6
Sønder Omme, *Denmark* 11 J2
Sønder Tornby, *Denmark* 11 G3
Sønderborg, *Denmark* 11 K3
Sønderjyllands Amtskommune □, *Denmark* 11 J3
Sondershausen, *Germany* 18 D6
Søndre Strømfjord, *Greenland* 97 B14
Sóndrio, *Italy* 32 B6
Sone, *Mozam.* 83 F3
Sonepur, *India* 61 J13
Song, *Thailand* 58 C3
Song Cau, *Vietnam* 58 F7
Song Xian, *China* 50 G7
Songchŏn, *N. Korea* 51 E14
Songea, *Tanzania* 83 E4
Songea □, *Tanzania* 83 E4
Songeons, *France* 25 C8
Songhua Hu, *China* 51 C14
Songhua Jiang →, *China* 54 B8
Songjiang, *China* 53 B13
Songjin, *N. Korea* 51 D15
Songjŏng-ni, *S. Korea* 51 G14
Songkan, *China* 52 C6
Songkhla, *Thailand* 59 J3
Songming, *China* 52 E4
Songnim, *N. Korea* 51 E13
Songpan, *China* 52 A4
Songtao, *China* 52 C7
Songwe, *Zaïre* 82 C2
Songwe →, *Africa* 83 D3
Songxi, *China* 53 D12
Songzi, *China* 53 B8
Sonid Youqi, *China* 50 C7
Sonipat, *India* 62 E7
Sonkovo, *Russia* 42 B3
Sonmiani, *Pakistan* 62 G2
Sonnino, *Italy* 34 A6
Sono →, *Minas Gerais, Brazil* 123 E2
Sono →, *Tocantins, Brazil* 122 C2
Sonogno, *Switz.* 23 D7
Sonora, *Calif., U.S.A.* 111 H3
Sonora, *Tex., U.S.A.* 109 K4
Sonora □, *Mexico* 114 B2
Sonora →, *Mexico* 114 B2
Sonora Desert, *U.S.A.* 113 L12
Sonoyta, *Mexico* 114 A2
Sonqor, *Iran* 67 E12
Sŏnsan, *S. Korea* 51 F15
Sonsonate, *El Salv.* 116 D2
Sonthofen, *Germany* 19 H6
Soochow = Suzhou, *China* 53 B13
Sop Hao, *Laos* 58 B5
Sop Prap, *Thailand* 58 D2
Sopachuy, *Bolivia* 125 D5
Sopi, *Indonesia* 57 D7
Sopo, Nahr →, *Sudan* 77 F2
Sopot, *Poland* 20 A8
Sopotnica, *Macedonia* 39 H4
Sopron, *Hungary* 21 H6
Sop's Arm, *Canada* 99 C8
Sopur, *India* 63 B6
Sør-Rondane, *Antarctica* 5 D4
Sør-Trøndelag fylke □, *Norway* 10 B3
Sora, *Italy* 34 A6
Sorah, *Pakistan* 62 F3
Söråker, *Sweden* 10 B11
Sorano, *Italy* 33 F8
Sorata, *Bolivia* 124 D4
Sorbas, *Spain* 29 H2
Sorel, *Canada* 98 C5
Sörenberg, *Switz.* 22 C6
Soreq, N. →, *Israel* 69 D3
Soresina, *Italy* 32 C6
Sorgono, *Italy* 34 B2
Sorgues, *France* 27 D8
Sorgun, *Turkey* 66 C6
Soria, *Spain* 28 D2
Soria □, *Spain* 28 D2
Soriano, *Uruguay* 126 C4
Soriano nel Cimino, *Italy* 33 F9
Sorkh, Kuh-e, *Iran* 65 C8
Sorø, *Denmark* 11 J5
Soro, *Guinea* 78 C3
Soroca, *Moldova* 41 H5
Sorocaba, *Brazil* 127 A6
Soroki = Soroca, *Moldova* 41 H5
Soron, *India* 63 F8
Sorong, *Indonesia* 57 E8
Soroní, *Greece* 37 C10
Soroti, *Uganda* 82 B3
Sørøya, *Norway* 8 A20
Sørøysundet, *Norway* 8 A20
Sorraia →, *Portugal* 31 G2
Sorrento, *Australia* 91 F3
Sorrento, *Italy* 35 B7
Sorsele, *Sweden* 8 D17
Sorso, *Italy* 34 B1
Sorsogon, *Phil.* 55 E6
Sortavala, *Russia* 40 B6
Sortino, *Italy* 35 E8
Sortland, *Norway* 8 B16
Sorvizhi, *Russia* 42 B9
Sos, *Spain* 28 C3
Sŏsan, *S. Korea* 51 F14
Soscumica, L., *Canada* 98 B4
Sosna →, *Russia* 42 D4
Sosnovka, *Russia* 42 B10
Sosnovka, *Russia* 42 D5
Sosnovka, *Russia* 45 D11
Sosnovyy Bor, *Russia* 40 C5
Sosnowiec, *Poland* 20 E9
Sospel, *France* 27 E11
Sostanj, *Slovenia* 33 B12
Sŏsura, *N. Korea* 51 C16
Sotkamo, *Finland* 8 D23
Soto la Marina →, *Mexico* 115 C5
Soto y Amío, *Spain* 30 C5
Sotteville-lès-Rouen, *France* 24 C8
Sotuta, *Mexico* 115 C7
Souanké, *Congo* 80 D2
Soúdha, *Greece* 37 D6
Soúdhas, Kólpos, *Greece* 37 D6
Sougne-Remouchamps, *Belgium* 17 H7
Souillac, *France* 26 D5
Souk-Ahras, *Algeria* 75 A6
Souk el Arba du Rharb, *Morocco* 74 B3
Soukhouma, *Laos* 58 E5
Sŏul, *S. Korea* 51 F14
Soulac-sur-Mer, *France* 26 C2
Soultz-sous-Forêts, *France* 25 D14
Soumagne, *Belgium* 17 G7
Sound, The = Øresund, *Europe* 11 J6
Sound, The, *U.K.* 13 G3
Soúnion, Ákra, *Greece* 39 M7
Sour el Ghozlane, *Algeria* 75 A5
Sources, Mt. aux, *Lesotho* 85 D4
Sourdeval, *France* 24 D6
Soure, *Brazil* 122 B2
Soure, *Portugal* 30 E2
Souris, *Man., Canada* 101 D8
Souris, *P.E.I., Canada* 99 C7
Souris →, *Canada* 108 A5
Sousa, *Brazil* 122 C4
Sousel, *Brazil* 122 B1
Sousel, *Portugal* 31 G3
Souss, O. →, *Morocco* 74 B3
Sousse, *Tunisia* 75 A7
Soustons, *France* 26 E2
South Africa ■, *Africa* 84 E3
South Aulatsivik I., *Canada* 99 A7
South Australia □, *Australia* 91 E2
South Baldy, *U.S.A.* 111 J10
South Bend, *Ind., U.S.A.* 104 E2
South Bend, *Wash., U.S.A.* 112 D3
South Boston, *U.S.A.* 105 G6
South Branch, *Canada* 99 C8
South Brook, *Canada* 99 C8
South Carolina □, *U.S.A.* 105 J5
South Charleston, *U.S.A.* 104 F5
South China Sea, *Asia* 56 C4
South Dakota □, *U.S.A.* 108 C5
South Downs, *U.K.* 13 G7
South East C., *Australia* 90 G4
South East Is., *Australia* 89 F3
South Esk →, *U.K.* 14 E5
South Foreland, *U.K.* 13 F9
South Fork →, *U.S.A.* 110 C7
South Fork, American →, *U.S.A.* 112 G5
South Fork, Feather →, *U.S.A.* 112 F5
South Georgia, *Antarctica* 5 B1
South Glamorgan □, *U.K.* 13 F4
South Haven, *U.S.A.* 104 D2
South Henik, L., *Canada* 101 A9
South Honshu Ridge, *Pac. Oc.* 92 E6
South Horr, *Kenya* 82 B4
South I., *Kenya* 82 B4
South I., *N.Z.* 87 L3
South Invercargill, *N.Z.* 87 M2
South Knife →, *Canada* 101 B10
South Korea ■, *Asia* 51 F15
South Lake Tahoe, *U.S.A.* 112 G6
South Loup →, *U.S.A.* 108 E5
South Magnetic Pole, *Antarctica* 5 C9
South Milwaukee, *U.S.A.* 104 D2
South Molton, *U.K.* 13 F4
South Nahanni →, *Canada* 100 A4
South Natuna Is. = Natuna Selatan, Kepulauan, *Indonesia* 59 L7
South Negril Pt., *Jamaica* 116 C4
South Orkney Is., *Antarctica* 5 C18
South Ossetia □, *Georgia* 43 J7
South Pagai, I. = Pagai Selatan, P., *Indonesia* 56 E2
South Pass, *U.S.A.* 110 E9
South Pittsburg, *U.S.A.* 105 H3
South Platte →, *U.S.A.* 108 E4
South Pole, *Antarctica* 5 E
South Porcupine, *Canada* 98 C3
South River, *Canada* 98 C4
South River, *U.S.A.* 107 F10
South Ronaldsay, *U.K.* 14 C6
South Sandwich Is., *Antarctica* 5 B1
South Saskatchewan →, *Canada* 101 C7
South Seal →, *Canada* 101 B9
South Shetland Is., *Antarctica* 5 C18
South Shields, *U.K.* 12 C6
South Sioux City, *U.S.A.* 108 D6
South Taranaki Bight, *N.Z.* 87 H5
South Thompson →, *Canada* 100 C4
South Twin I., *Canada* 98 B4
South Tyne →, *U.K.* 12 C5
South Uist, *U.K.* 14 D1
South West Africa = Namibia ■, *Africa* 84 C2
South West C., *Australia* 90 G4
South Yorkshire □, *U.K.* 12 D6
Southampton, *Canada* 98 D3
Southampton, *U.K.* 13 G6
Southampton, *U.S.A.* 107 F12
Southampton I., *Canada* 97 B11
Southbridge, *N.Z.* 87 K4
Southbridge, *U.S.A.* 107 D12
Southend, *Canada* 101 B8
Southend-on-Sea, *U.K.* 13 F8
Southern □, *Malawi* 83 F4
Southern □, *S. Leone* 78 D2
Southern □, *Uganda* 82 C3
Southern □, *Zambia* 83 F2
Southern Alps, *N.Z.* 87 K3
Southern Cross, *Australia* 89 F2
Southern Hills, *Australia* 89 F3
Southern Indian L., *Canada* 101 B9
Southern Ocean, *Antarctica* 5 C6
Southern Pines, *U.S.A.* 105 H6
Southern Uplands, *U.K.* 14 F5
Southington, *U.S.A.* 107 E12
Southold, *U.S.A.* 107 E12
Southport, *Australia* 91 D5
Southport, *U.K.* 12 D4
Southport, *U.S.A.* 105 J6
Southwest C., *N.Z.* 87 M1
Southwold, *U.K.* 13 E9
Soutpansberg, *S. Africa* 85 C4
Souvigny, *France* 26 B7
Sovetsk, *Kaliningd., Russia* 9 J19
Sovetsk, *Kirov, Russia* 42 B9
Sovetskaya Gavan, *Russia* 45 E15
Sovicille, *Italy* 33 E8
Sovra, *Croatia* 21 N7
Soweto, *S. Africa* 85 D4
Sōya-Kaikyō = La Perouse Str., *Asia* 48 B11
Sōya-Misaki, *Japan* 48 B10
Soyo, *Angola* 80 F2
Sozh →, *Belarus* 41 F6
Sozopol, *Bulgaria* 38 G10
Spa, *Belgium* 17 H7
Spain ■, *Europe* 7 H5
Spakenburg, *Neths.* 16 D6
Spalding, *Australia* 91 E2
Spalding, *U.K.* 12 E7
Spalding, *U.S.A.* 108 E5
Spangler, *U.S.A.* 106 F6
Spaniard's Bay, *Canada* 99 C9
Spanish, *Canada* 98 C3
Spanish Fork, *U.S.A.* 110 F8
Spanish Town, *Jamaica* 116 C4
Sparks, *U.S.A.* 112 F7
Sparta = Spárti, *Greece* 39 M5
Sparta, *Ga., U.S.A.* 105 J4
Sparta, *Wis., U.S.A.* 108 D9
Spartanburg, *U.S.A.* 105 H4
Spartansburg, *U.S.A.* 106 E5
Spartel, C., *Morocco* 74 A3
Spárti, *Greece* 39 M5
Spartivento, C., *Calabria, Italy* 35 E9
Spartivento, C., *Sard., Italy* 34 D1
Spas-Demensk, *Russia* 42 C2
Spas-Klepiki, *Russia* 42 C5
Spassk Dalniy, *Russia* 45 E14
Spassk-Ryazanskiy, *Russia* 42 C5
Spátha, Ákra, *Greece* 37 D5
Spatsizi →, *Canada* 100 B3
Spearfish, *U.S.A.* 108 C3
Spearman, *U.S.A.* 109 G4
Speer, *Switz.* 23 B8
Speers, *Canada* 101 C7
Speightstown, *Barbados* 117 D8
Speke Gulf, *Tanzania* 82 C3
Spekholzerheide, *Neths.* 17 G8
Spence Bay, *Canada* 96 B10
Spencer, *Idaho, U.S.A.* 110 D7
Spencer, *Iowa, U.S.A.* 108 D7
Spencer, *N.Y., U.S.A.* 107 D8
Spencer, *Nebr., U.S.A.* 108 D5
Spencer, *W. Va., U.S.A.* 104 F5
Spencer, C., *Australia* 91 F2
Spencer B., *Namibia* 84 D1
Spencer G., *Australia* 91 E2
Spencerville, *Canada* 107 B9
Spences Bridge, *Canada* 100 C4
Spenser Mts., *N.Z.* 87 K4
Sperkhiós →, *Greece* 39 L5
Sperrin Mts., *U.K.* 15 B5
Spessart, *Germany* 19 E5
Spétsai, *Greece* 39 M6
Spey →, *U.K.* 14 D5
Speyer, *Germany* 19 F4
Speyer →, *Germany* 19 F4
Spezzano Albanese, *Italy* 35 C9
Spiekeroog, *Germany* 18 B3
Spielfeld, *Austria* 33 B12
Spiez, *Switz.* 22 C5
Spijk, *Neths.* 16 B9
Spijkenisse, *Neths.* 16 E4
Spíli, *Greece* 37 D6
Spilimbergo, *Italy* 33 B9
Spin Baldak = Qala-i-Jadid, *Afghan.* 62 D2
Spinalónga, *Greece* 37 D7
Spinazzola, *Italy* 35 B9
Spirit Lake, *Idaho, U.S.A.* 110 C5
Spirit Lake, *Wash., U.S.A.* 112 D4
Spirit River, *Canada* 100 B5
Spiritwood, *Canada* 101 C7
Spišská Nová Ves, *Slovak Rep.* 20 G10
Spithead, *U.K.* 13 G6
Spittal, *Austria* 21 J3
Spitzbergen = Svalbard, *Arctic* 4 B8
Spjelkavik, *Norway* 9 E12
Split, *Croatia* 33 E13
Split L., *Canada* 101 B9
Splitski Kanal, *Croatia* 33 E13
Splügen, *Switz.* 23 C8
Splügenpass, *Switz.* 23 C8
Spofford, *U.S.A.* 109 L4
Spokane, *U.S.A.* 110 C5
Spoleto, *Italy* 33 F9
Spooner, *U.S.A.* 108 C9
Sporyy Navolok, Mys, *Russia* 44 B7
Spragge, *Canada* 98 C3
Sprague, *U.S.A.* 110 C5
Sprague River, *U.S.A.* 110 E3
Spratly I., *S. China Sea* 56 C4
Spray, *U.S.A.* 110 D4
Spree →, *Germany* 18 C9
Spremberg, *Germany* 18 D10
Sprengisandur, *Iceland* 8 D5
Sprimont, *Belgium* 17 G7
Spring City, *U.S.A.* 110 G8
Spring Garden, *U.S.A.* 112 F6
Spring Mts., *U.S.A.* 111 H6
Spring Valley, *Calif., U.S.A.* 113 N10
Spring Valley, *Minn., U.S.A.* 108 D8
Springbok, *S. Africa* 84 D2
Springdale, *Canada* 99 C8
Springdale, *Ark., U.S.A.* 109 G7
Springdale, *Wash., U.S.A.* 110 B5
Springe, *Germany* 18 C5
Springer, *U.S.A.* 109 G2
Springerville, *U.S.A.* 111 J9
Springfield, *Canada* 106 D4
Springfield, *N.Z.* 87 K3
Springfield, *Colo., U.S.A.* 109 G3
Springfield, *Ill., U.S.A.* 108 F10
Springfield, *Mass., U.S.A.* 107 D12
Springfield, *Mo., U.S.A.* 109 G8
Springfield, *Ohio, U.S.A.* 104 F4
Springfield, *Oreg., U.S.A.* 110 D2
Springfield, *Tenn., U.S.A.* 105 G2
Springfield, *Vt., U.S.A.* 107 C12
Springfontein, *S. Africa* 84 E4
Springhill, *Canada* 99 C7
Springhouse, *Canada* 100 C4
Springhurst, *Australia* 91 F4
Springs, *S. Africa* 85 D4
Springsure, *Australia* 90 C4
Springvale, *Queens., Australia* 90 C3
Springvale, *W. Austral., Australia* 88 C4
Springvale, *U.S.A.* 107 C14
Springville, *Calif., U.S.A.* 112 J8
Springville, *N.Y., U.S.A.* 106 D6
Springville, *Utah, U.S.A.* 110 F8
Springwater, *Canada* 101 C7
Spruce-Creek, *U.S.A.* 106 F6
Spur, *U.S.A.* 109 J4
Spurn Hd., *U.K.* 12 D8
Spuž, *Montenegro, Yug.* 21 N9
Spuzzum, *Canada* 100 D4
Squam L., *U.S.A.* 107 C13
Squamish, *Canada* 100 D4
Square Islands, *Canada* 99 B8
Squillace, G. di, *Italy* 35 D9
Squinzano, *Italy* 35 B11
Squires, Mt., *Australia* 89 E4
Sragen, *Indonesia* 57 G14
Srbac, *Bos.-H.* 21 K7
Srbija = Serbia □, *Yugoslavia* 21 M11
Srbobran, *Serbia, Yug.* 21 K9
Sre Khtum, *Cambodia* 59 F6
Sre Umbell, *Cambodia* 59 G4
Srebrnica, *Bos.-H.* 21 L9
Sredinny Ra. = Sredinnyy Khrebet, *Russia* 45 D16
Sredinnyy Khrebet, *Russia* 45 D16
Središče, *Slovenia* 33 B13
Sredna Gora, *Bulgaria* 38 G7
Sredne Tambovskoye, *Russia* 45 D14
Srednekolymsk, *Russia* 45 C16
Srednevilyuysk, *Russia* 45 C13
Śrem, *Poland* 20 C7
Sremska Mitrovica, *Serbia, Yug.* 21 L9
Srepok →, *Cambodia* 58 F6
Sretensk, *Russia* 45 D12
Sri Lanka ■, *Asia* 60 R12
Srikakulam, *India* 61 K13
Srinagar, *India* 63 B6
Środa Wielkopolski, *Poland* 20 C7
Srpska Itabej, *Serbia, Yug.* 21 K10
Staaten →, *Australia* 90 B3
Staberhuk, *Germany* 18 A7
Stabroek, *Belgium* 17 F4
Stad Delden, *Neths.* 16 D9
Stade, *Germany* 18 B5
Staden, *Belgium* 17 G2
Städjan, *Sweden* 10 C6
Stadskanaal, *Neths.* 16 B9
Stadthagen, *Germany* 18 C5
Stadtlohn, *Germany* 18 D2
Stadtroda, *Germany* 18 E7
Stäfa, *Switz.* 23 B7
Staffa, *U.K.* 14 E2
Stafford, *U.K.* 12 E5
Stafford, *U.S.A.* 109 G5
Stafford Springs, *U.S.A.* 107 E12
Staffordshire □, *U.K.* 12 E5

Stagnone, Isole dello, *Italy* 34 E5
Staines, *U.K.* 13 F7
Stakhanov, *Ukraine* 41 H10
Stalden, *Switz.* 22 D5
Stalingrad = Volgograd, *Russia* 43 F7
Staliniri = Tskhinvali, *Georgia* 43 J7
Stalino = Donetsk, *Ukraine* 41 J9
Stalinogorsk = Novomoskovsk, *Russia* 42 C4
Stalis, *Greece* 37 D7
Stalowa Wola, *Poland* 20 E12
Stalybridge, *U.K.* 12 D5
Stamford, *Australia* 90 C3
Stamford, *U.K.* 13 E7
Stamford, *Conn., U.S.A.* 107 E11
Stamford, *Tex., U.S.A.* 109 J5
Stamps, *U.S.A.* 109 J8
Stanberry, *U.S.A.* 108 E7
Stančevo = Kalipetrovo, *Bulgaria* 38 E10
Standerton, *S. Africa* 85 D4
Standish, *U.S.A.* 104 D4
Stanford, *U.S.A.* 110 C8
Stange, *Norway* 10 D5
Stanger, *S. Africa* 85 D5
Stanislaus →, *U.S.A.* 112 H5
Stanislav = Ivano-Frankivsk, *Ukraine* 41 H3
Stanke Dimitrov, *Bulgaria* 38 G6
Stanley, *Australia* 90 G4
Stanley, *N.B., Canada* 99 C6
Stanley, *Sask., Canada* 101 B8
Stanley, *Falk. Is.* 128 D5
Stanley, *Idaho, U.S.A.* 110 D6
Stanley, *N. Dak., U.S.A.* 108 A3
Stanley, *N.Y., U.S.A.* 106 D7
Stanley, *Wis., U.S.A.* 108 C9
Stanovoy Khrebet, *Russia* 45 D13
Stanovoy Ra. = Stanovoy Khrebet, *Russia* 45 D13
Stans, *Switz.* 23 C6
Stansmore Ra., *Australia* 88 D4
Stanthorpe, *Australia* 91 D5
Stanton, *U.S.A.* 109 J4
Stanwood, *U.S.A.* 112 B4
Staphorst, *Neths.* 16 C8
Staples, *U.S.A.* 108 B7
Stapleton, *U.S.A.* 108 E4
Star City, *Canada* 101 C8
Stara Moravica, *Serbia, Yug.* 21 K9
Stara Planina, *Bulgaria* 38 F6
Stara Zagora, *Bulgaria* 38 G8
Starachowice, *Poland* 20 D11
Staraya Russa, *Russia* 40 D6
Starbuck I., *Kiribati* 93 H12
Stargard Szczeciński, *Poland* 20 B5
Stari Trg, *Slovenia* 33 C12
Staritsa, *Russia* 42 B2
Starke, *U.S.A.* 105 K4
Starkville, *Colo., U.S.A.* 109 G2
Starkville, *Miss., U.S.A.* 105 J1
Starnberg, *Germany* 19 G7
Starnberger See, *Germany* 19 H7
Starobilsk, *Ukraine* 41 H10
Starodub, *Russia* 41 F7
Starogard Gdański, *Poland* 20 B8
Starokonstantinov = Starokonstyantyniv, *Ukraine* 41 H4
Starokonstyantyniv, *Ukraine* 41 H4
Starominskaya, *Russia* 43 G4
Staroshcherbinovskaya, *Russia* 43 G4
Start Pt., *U.K.* 13 G4
Staryy Biryuzyak, *Russia* 43 H8
Staryy Chartoriysk, *Ukraine* 41 G3
Staryy Kheydzhan, *Russia* 45 C15
Staryy Krym, *Ukraine* 41 K8
Staryy Oskol, *Russia* 42 E3
Stassfurt, *Germany* 18 D7
State College, *U.S.A.* 106 F7
Stateline, *U.S.A.* 112 G7
Staten, I. = Estados, I. de Los, *Argentina* 128 D4
Staten I., *U.S.A.* 107 F10
Statesboro, *U.S.A.* 105 J5
Statesville, *U.S.A.* 105 H5
Stauffer, *U.S.A.* 113 L7
Staunton, *Ill., U.S.A.* 108 F10
Staunton, *Va., U.S.A.* 104 F6
Stavanger, *Norway* 9 G11
Staveley, *N.Z.* 87 K3
Stavelot, *Belgium* 17 H7
Stavenhagen, *Germany* 18 B8
Stavenisse, *Neths.* 17 E4
Staveren, *Neths.* 16 C6
Stavern, *Norway* 10 F4
Stavre, *Sweden* 10 B9
Stavropol, *Russia* 43 H6
Stavrós, *Cyprus* 37 D11
Stavrós, *Greece* 37 D6
Stavros, Ákra, *Greece* 37 D6
Stavroúpolis, *Greece* 39 H7
Stawell, *Australia* 91 F3
Stawell →, *Australia* 90 C3
Stawiszyn, *Poland* 20 D8
Stayner, *Canada* 106 B4
Steamboat Springs, *U.S.A.* 110 F10
Steckborn, *Switz.* 23 A7
Steele, *U.S.A.* 108 B5
Steelton, *U.S.A.* 106 F8
Steelville, *U.S.A.* 109 G9

Steen River, *Canada* 100 B5
Steenbergen, *Neths.* 17 E4
Steenkool = Bintuni, *Indonesia* 57 E8
Steenvoorde, *France* 25 B9
Steenwijk, *Neths.* 16 C8
Steep Pt., *Australia* 89 E1
Steep Rock, *Canada* 101 C9
Ştefăneşti, *Romania* 38 B10
Stefanie L. = Chew Bahir, *Ethiopia* 77 G4
Stefansson Bay, *Antarctica* 5 C5
Steffisburg, *Switz.* 22 C5
Stege, *Denmark* 11 K6
Steiermark □, *Austria* 21 H5
Steigerwald, *Germany* 19 F6
Steilacoom, *U.S.A.* 112 C4
Stein, *Neths.* 17 G7
Steinbach, *Canada* 101 D9
Steinfort, *Lux.* 17 J7
Steinfurt, *Germany* 18 C3
Steinheim, *Germany* 18 D5
Steinhuder Meer, *Germany* 18 C5
Steinkjer, *Norway* 8 D14
Steinkopf, *S. Africa* 84 D2
Stekene, *Belgium* 17 F4
Stellarton, *Canada* 99 C7
Stellenbosch, *S. Africa* 84 E2
Stellendam, *Neths.* 16 E4
Stelvio, Paso dello, *Italy* 32 B7
Stemshaug, *Norway* 10 A2
Stendal, *Germany* 18 C7
Stene, *Belgium* 17 F1
Stenstorp, *Sweden* 11 F7
Steornabhaigh = Stornoway, *U.K.* 14 C2
Stepanakert = Xankändi, *Azerbaijan* 67 C12
Stepanavan, *Armenia* 43 K7
Stephen, *U.S.A.* 108 A6
Stephens Creek, *Australia* 91 E3
Stephens I., *Canada* 100 C2
Stephenville, *Canada* 99 C8
Stephenville, *U.S.A.* 109 J5
Stepnica, *Poland* 20 B4
Stepnoi = Elista, *Russia* 43 G7
Stepnyak, *Kazakhstan* 44 D8
Steppe, *Asia* 46 E7
Sterkstroom, *S. Africa* 84 E4
Sterling, *Colo., U.S.A.* 108 E3
Sterling, *Ill., U.S.A.* 108 E10
Sterling, *Kans., U.S.A.* 108 F5
Sterling City, *U.S.A.* 109 K4
Sterling Run, *U.S.A.* 106 E6
Sterlitamak, *Russia* 44 D6
Sternberg, *Germany* 18 B7
Šternberk, *Czech.* 20 F7
Stérnes, *Greece* 37 D6
Sterzing = Vipiteno, *Italy* 33 B8
Stettin = Szczecin, *Poland* 20 B4
Stettiner Haff, *Germany* 18 B10
Stettler, *Canada* 100 C6
Steubenville, *U.S.A.* 106 F4
Stevens Point, *U.S.A.* 108 C10
Stevenson, *U.S.A.* 112 E5
Stevenson L., *Canada* 101 C9
Stevns Klint, *Denmark* 11 J6
Stewart, *B.C., Canada* 100 B3
Stewart, *N.W.T., Canada* 96 B6
Stewart →, *Canada* 112 F7
Stewart, C., *Australia* 90 A1
Stewart, I., *Chile* 128 D2
Stewart I., *N.Z.* 87 M1
Stewarts Point, *U.S.A.* 112 G3
Stewiacke, *Canada* 99 C7
Steynsburg, *S. Africa* 84 E4
Steyr, *Austria* 21 G4
Steytlerville, *S. Africa* 84 E3
Stia, *Italy* 33 E8
Stiens, *Neths.* 16 B7
Stigler, *U.S.A.* 109 H7
Stigliano, *Italy* 35 B9
Stigsnæs, *Denmark* 11 J5
Stigtomta, *Sweden* 11 F10
Stikine →, *Canada* 100 B2
Stilfontein, *S. Africa* 84 D4
Stilís, *Greece* 39 L5
Stillwater, *N.Z.* 87 K3
Stillwater, *Minn., U.S.A.* 108 C8
Stillwater, *N.Y., U.S.A.* 107 D11
Stillwater, *Okla., U.S.A.* 109 G6
Stillwater Range, *U.S.A.* 110 G4
Stilwell, *U.S.A.* 109 H7
Štip, *Macedonia* 39 H5
Stíra, *Greece* 39 L7
Stirling, *Australia* 90 B3
Stirling, *Canada* 100 D6
Stirling, *U.K.* 14 E5
Stirling Ra., *Australia* 89 F2
Stittsville, *Canada* 107 A9
Stjernøya, *Norway* 8 A20
Stjørdalshalsen, *Norway* 8 E14
Stockach, *Germany* 19 H5
Stockerau, *Austria* 21 G6
Stockett, *U.S.A.* 110 C8
Stockholm, *Sweden* 10 E12
Stockholms län □, *Sweden* 10 E12
Stockhorn, *Switz.* 22 C5
Stockport, *U.K.* 12 D5
Stockton, *Calif., U.S.A.* 111 H3
Stockton, *Kans., U.S.A.* 108 F5
Stockton, *Mo., U.S.A.* 109 G8
Stockton-on-Tees, *U.K.* 12 C6
Stockvik, *Sweden* 10 B11
Stöde, *Sweden* 10 B10
Stogovo, *Macedonia* 39 H3
Stoke on Trent, *U.K.* 12 D5

Stokes Bay, *Canada* 98 C3
Stokes Pt., *Australia* 90 G3
Stokes Ra., *Australia* 88 C5
Stokksnes, *Iceland* 8 D6
Stokmarknes, *Norway* 8 B16
Stolac, *Bos.-H.* 21 M7
Stolberg, *Germany* 18 E2
Stolbovaya, *Russia* 45 C16
Stolbovoy, Ostrov, *Russia* 45 D17
Stolbtsy = Stowbtsy, *Belarus* 40 F4
Stolin, *Belarus* 41 G4
Stolwijk, *Neths.* 16 E5
Stomíon, *Greece* 37 D5
Ston, *Croatia* 21 N7
Stonehaven, *U.K.* 14 E6
Stonehenge, *Australia* 90 C3
Stonewall, *Canada* 101 C9
Stony L., *Man., Canada* 101 B9
Stony L., *Ont., Canada* 106 B6
Stony Rapids, *Canada* 101 B7
Stony Tunguska = Podkamennaya Tunguska →, *Russia* 45 C10
Stonyford, *U.S.A.* 112 F4
Stopnica, *Poland* 20 E10
Stora Lulevatten, *Sweden* 8 C18
Storavan, *Sweden* 8 D18
Stord, *Norway* 9 G11
Store Bælt, *Denmark* 11 J5
Store Creek, *Australia* 91 E4
Store Heddinge, *Denmark* 11 J6
Støren, *Norway* 10 A4
Storm B., *Australia* 90 G4
Storm Lake, *U.S.A.* 108 D7
Stormberge, *S. Africa* 84 E4
Stormsrivier, *S. Africa* 84 E3
Stornoway, *U.K.* 14 C2
Storozhinets = Storozhynets, *Ukraine* 41 H3
Storozhynets, *Ukraine* 41 H3
Storsjö, *Sweden* 10 B7
Storsjøen, *Hedmark, Norway* 10 D5
Storsjøen, *Hedmark, Norway* 10 C5
Storsjön, *Sweden* 10 B7
Storstrøms Amt. □, *Denmark* 11 K5
Storuman, *Sweden* 8 D17
Storuman, sjö, *Sweden* 8 D17
Stoughton, *Canada* 101 D8
Stour →, *Dorset, U.K.* 13 G5
Stour →, *Here. & Worcs., U.K.* 13 E5
Stour →, *Kent, U.K.* 13 F9
Stour →, *Suffolk, U.K.* 13 F9
Stourbridge, *U.K.* 13 E5
Stout, L., *Canada* 101 C10
Stove Pipe Wells Village, *U.S.A.* 113 J9
Stowbtsy, *Belarus* 40 F4
Stowmarket, *U.K.* 13 E9
Strabane, *U.K.* 15 B4
Strabane □, *U.K.* 15 B4
Stracin, *Macedonia* 38 G5
Stradella, *Italy* 32 C6
Strahan, *Australia* 90 G4
Strakonice, *Czech.* 20 F3
Straldzha, *Bulgaria* 38 G9
Stralsund, *Germany* 18 A9
Strand, *S. Africa* 84 E2
Stranda, *Møre og Romsdal, Norway* 9 E12
Stranda, *Nord-Trøndelag, Norway* 8 E14
Strangford L., *U.K.* 15 B6
Strängnäs, *Sweden* 10 E11
Strangsville, *U.S.A.* 106 E3
Stranraer, *U.K.* 14 G3
Strasbourg, *Canada* 101 C8
Strasbourg, *France* 25 D14
Strasburg, *Germany* 18 B9
Strasburg, *U.S.A.* 108 B4
Strassen, *Lux.* 17 J8
Stratford, *Canada* 98 D3
Stratford, *N.Z.* 87 H5
Stratford, *Calif., U.S.A.* 111 H4
Stratford, *Conn., U.S.A.* 107 E11
Stratford, *Tex., U.S.A.* 109 G3
Stratford-upon-Avon, *U.K.* 13 E6
Strath Spey, *U.K.* 14 D5
Strathalbyn, *Australia* 91 F2
Strathclyde □, *U.K.* 14 F4
Strathcona Prov. Park, *Canada* 100 D3
Strathmore, *Australia* 90 B3
Strathmore, *Canada* 100 C6
Strathmore, *U.K.* 14 E5
Strathmore, *U.S.A.* 112 J7
Strathnaver, *Canada* 100 C4
Strathpeffer, *U.K.* 14 D4
Strathroy, *Canada* 98 D3
Strathy Pt., *U.K.* 14 C4
Stratton, *U.S.A.* 108 F3
Straubing, *Germany* 19 G8
Straumnes, *Iceland* 8 C2
Strausberg, *Germany* 18 C9
Strawberry Reservoir, *U.S.A.* 110 F8
Strawn, *U.S.A.* 109 J5
Strážnice, *Czech.* 20 G7
Streaky B., *Australia* 91 E1
Streaky Bay, *Australia* 91 E1
Streator, *U.S.A.* 108 E10
Streé, *Belgium* 17 H4
Streeter, *U.S.A.* 108 B5

Streetsville, *Canada* 106 C5
Strehaia, *Romania* 38 E6
Strelcha, *Bulgaria* 38 G7
Strelka, *Russia* 45 D10
Streng →, *Cambodia* 58 F4
Strésa, *Italy* 32 C5
Streymoy, *Færoe Is.* 8 E9
Strezhevoy, *Russia* 44 C8
Stříbro, *Czech.* 20 F3
Strijen, *Neths.* 16 E5
Strímon →, *Greece* 39 J6
Strimonikós Kólpos, *Greece* 39 J6
Stroeder, *Argentina* 128 B4
Strofádhes, *Greece* 39 M4
Strömbacka, *Sweden* 10 C10
Strómboli, *Italy* 35 D8
Stromeferry, *U.K.* 14 D3
Stromness, *U.K.* 14 C5
Stromsburg, *U.S.A.* 108 E6
Strömstad, *Sweden* 9 G14
Strömsund, *Sweden* 8 E16
Stróngoli, *Italy* 35 C10
Stronsay, *U.K.* 14 B6
Stroud, *U.K.* 13 F5
Stroud Road, *Australia* 91 E5
Stroudsburg, *U.S.A.* 107 F9
Stroumbi, *Cyprus* 37 E11
Struer, *Denmark* 11 H2
Struga, *Macedonia* 39 H3
Strugi Krasnyye, *Russia* 40 C5
Strumica, *Macedonia* 39 H5
Strumica →, *Europe* 39 H6
Struthers, *Canada* 98 C2
Struthers, *U.S.A.* 106 E4
Stryker, *U.S.A.* 110 B6
Stryy, *Ukraine* 41 H2
Strzegom, *Poland* 20 E6
Strzelce Krajeńskie, *Poland* 20 C5
Strzelecki Cr. →, *Australia* 91 D2
Strzelin, *Poland* 20 E7
Strzelno, *Poland* 20 C8
Strzyzów, *Poland* 20 F11
Stuart, *Fla., U.S.A.* 105 M5
Stuart, *Nebr., U.S.A.* 108 D5
Stuart →, *Canada* 100 C4
Stuart Bluff Ra., *Australia* 88 D5
Stuart L., *Canada* 100 C4
Stuart Ra., *Australia* 91 D1
Stubbekøbing, *Denmark* 11 K6
Stugun, *Sweden* 10 A9
Stull, L., *Canada* 98 B1
Stung Treng, *Cambodia* 58 F5
Stupart →, *Canada* 101 B10
Stupino, *Russia* 42 C4
Sturgeon B., *Canada* 101 C9
Sturgeon Bay, *U.S.A.* 104 C2
Sturgeon Falls, *Canada* 98 C4
Sturgeon L., *Alta., Canada* 100 B5
Sturgeon L., *Ont., Canada* 106 B6
Sturgeon L., *Ont., Canada* 98 B1
Sturgis, *Mich., U.S.A.* 104 E3
Sturgis, *S. Dak., U.S.A.* 108 C3
Sturt Cr. →, *Australia* 88 C4
Sturt Creek, *Australia* 88 C4
Stutterheim, *S. Africa* 84 E4
Stuttgart, *Germany* 19 G5
Stuttgart, *U.S.A.* 109 H9
Stuyvesant, *U.S.A.* 107 D11
Stykkishólmur, *Iceland* 8 D2
Styria = Steiermark □, *Austria* 21 H5
Su Xian, *China* 50 H9
Suakin, *Sudan* 76 D4
Suan, *N. Korea* 51 E14
Suapure →, *Venezuela* 120 B4
Suaqui, *Mexico* 114 B3
Suatá →, *Venezuela* 121 B4
Subang, *Indonesia* 57 G12
Subansiri →, *India* 61 F18
Subayhah, *Si. Arabia* 64 D3
Subi, *Indonesia* 59 L7
Subiaco, *Italy* 33 G10
Subotica, *Serbia, Yug.* 21 J9
Success, *Canada* 101 C7
Suceava, *Romania* 38 B9
Suceava →, *Romania* 38 B9
Sucha-Beskidzka, *Poland* 20 F9
Suchan, *Poland* 20 B5
Suchan, *Russia* 48 C6
Suchitoto, *El Salv.* 116 D2
Suchou = Suzhou, *China* 53 B13
Süchow = Xuzhou, *China* 51 G9
Suchowola, *Poland* 20 B13
Sucio →, *Colombia* 120 B2
Suck →, *Ireland* 15 C3
Sucre, *Bolivia* 125 D4
Sucre, *Colombia* 120 B3
Sucre □, *Colombia* 120 B2
Sucre □, *Venezuela* 121 A5
Sucuaro, *Colombia* 120 C4
Súčuraj, *Croatia* 33 E14
Sucuriú →, *Brazil* 122 A2
Sucurú →, *Brazil* 125 C7
Sud, Pte., *Canada* 99 C7
Sud-Ouest, Pte. du, *Canada* 99 C7
Suda →, *Russia* 40 C9
Sudak, *Ukraine* 41 K8
Sudan ■, *Africa* 77 E3
Sudan, *U.S.A.* 109 H3
Sudbury, *Canada* 98 C3
Sudbury, *U.K.* 13 E8
Súdd, *Sudan* 77 F2
Suddie, *Guyana* 121 B6
Süderbrarup, *Germany* 18 A5
Süderlügum, *Germany* 18 A4
Süderoogsand, *Germany* 18 A4

Sudeten Mts. = Sudety, *Europe* 20 E6
Sudety, *Europe* 20 E6
Suðuroy, *Færoe Is.* 8 F9
Sudi, *Tanzania* 83 E4
Sudirman, Pegunungan, *Indonesia* 57 E9
Sudogda, *Russia* 42 C5
Sudr, *Egypt* 76 J8
Sudzha, *Russia* 42 E2
Sueca, *Spain* 29 F4
Suedala, *Sweden* 11 J7
Suez = El Suweis, *Egypt* 76 J8
Suez, G. of = Suweis, Khalîg el, *Egypt* 76 J8
Suez Canal = Suweis, Qanâ es, *Egypt* 76 H8
Suffield, *Canada* 101 C6
Suffolk, *U.S.A.* 104 G7
Suffolk □, *U.K.* 13 E9
Sugar City, *U.S.A.* 108 F3
Suğla Gölü, *Turkey* 66 D5
Sugluk = Salluit, *Canada* 97 B12
Sugny, *Belgium* 17 J5
Suhaia, L., *Romania* 38 F8
Suhār, *Oman* 65 E8
Suhbaatar, *Mongolia* 54 A5
Sühbaatar □, *Mongolia* 50 B8
Suhl, *Germany* 18 E6
Suhr, *Switz.* 22 B6
Suhut, *Turkey* 66 C4
Sui Xian, *Henan, China* 50 G8
Sui Xian, *Henan, China* 53 B9
Suiá Missu →, *Brazil* 125 C7
Suichang, *China* 53 C12
Suichuan, *China* 53 D10
Suide, *China* 50 F6
Suifenhe, *China* 51 B16
Suihua, *China* 54 B7
Suijiang, *China* 52 C4
Suining, *Hunan, China* 53 D8
Suining, *Jiangsu, China* 51 H9
Suining, *Sichuan, China* 52 B5
Suiping, *China* 50 H7
Suippes, *France* 25 C11
Suir →, *Ireland* 15 D4
Suixi, *China* 53 G8
Suiyang, *Guizhou, China* 52 D6
Suiyang, *Heilongjiang, China* 51 B16
Suizhong, *China* 51 D11
Sujangarh, *India* 62 F6
Sukabumi, *Indonesia* 57 G12
Sukadana, *Kalimantan, Indonesia* 56 E3
Sukadana, *Sumatera, Indonesia* 56 F3
Sukagawa, *Japan* 49 F10
Sukaraja, *Indonesia* 56 E4
Sukarnapura = Jayapura, *Indonesia* 57 E10
Sukchŏn, *N. Korea* 51 E13
Sukhinichi, *Russia* 42 C2
Sukhona →, *Russia* 44 C4
Sukhothai, *Thailand* 58 D2
Sukhumi = Sokhumi, *Georgia* 43 J5
Sukkur, *Pakistan* 62 F3
Sukkur Barrage, *Pakistan* 62 F3
Sukumo, *Japan* 49 H6
Sukunka →, *Canada* 100 B4
Sul, Canal do, *Brazil* 122 B2
Sula →, *Ukraine* 41 H7
Sula, Kepulauan, *Indonesia* 57 E7
Sulaco →, *Honduras* 116 C2
Sulaiman Range, *Pakistan* 62 D3
Sulak →, *Russia* 43 J8
Sülār, *Iran* 65 D6
Sulawesi □, *Indonesia* 57 E6
Sulawesi Sea = Celebes Sea, *Indonesia* 57 D6
Sulechów, *Poland* 20 C5
Sulejów, *Poland* 20 D9
Sulgen, *Switz.* 23 A8
Sulima, *S. Leone* 78 D2
Sulina, *Romania* 38 D12
Sulina, Braţul →, *Romania* 38 D12
Sulingen, *Germany* 18 C4
Sulitjelma, *Norway* 8 C17
Sullana, *Peru* 124 A1
Sullivan, *Ill., U.S.A.* 108 F10
Sullivan, *Ind., U.S.A.* 104 F2
Sullivan, *Mo., U.S.A.* 108 F9
Sullivan Bay, *Canada* 100 C3
Sully-sur-Loire, *France* 25 E9
Sulmona, *Italy* 33 F10
Sulphur, *La., U.S.A.* 109 K8
Sulphur, *Okla., U.S.A.* 109 H6
Sulphur Pt., *Canada* 100 A6
Sulphur Springs, *U.S.A.* 109 J7
Sulphur Springs Draw →, *U.S.A.* 109 J4
Sultan, *Canada* 98 C3
Sultan, *U.S.A.* 112 C5
Sultan Dağları, *Turkey* 66 C4
Sultanpur, *India* 63 F10
Sulu Arch., *Phil.* 55 J4
Sulu Sea, *E. Indies* 55 G4
Sülüklü, *Turkey* 66 C5
Sululta, *Ethiopia* 77 F4
Suluova, *Turkey* 66 B6
Suluq, *Libya* 73 B9
Sulzbach, *Germany* 19 F3
Sulzbach-Rosenberg, *Germany* 19 F7
Sulzberger Ice Shelf, *Antarctica* 5 D10

Takla Landing

Sumalata, Indonesia 57 D6
Sumampa, Argentina 126 B3
Sumatera □, Indonesia 56 D2
Sumatra = Sumatera □, Indonesia 56 D2
Sumatra, U.S.A. 110 C10
Sumba, Indonesia 57 F5
Sumba, Selat, Indonesia 57 F5
Sumbawa, Indonesia 56 F5
Sumbawa Besar, Indonesia 56 F5
Sumbawanga □, Tanzania 82 D3
Sumbe, Angola 80 G2
Sumburgh Hd., U.K. 14 B7
Sumdo, India 63 B8
Sumé, Brazil 122 C4
Sumedang, Indonesia 57 G12
Šumen, Bulgaria 38 F9
Sumenep, Indonesia 57 G15
Sumgait = Sumqayıt, Azerbaijan 43 K9
Sumiswald, Switz. 22 B5
Summer L., U.S.A. 110 E3
Summerland, Canada 100 D5
Summerside, Canada 99 C7
Summerville, Ga., U.S.A. 105 H3
Summerville, S.C., U.S.A. 105 J5
Summit Lake, Canada 100 C4
Summit Peak, U.S.A. 111 H10
Sumner, Iowa, U.S.A. 108 D8
Sumner, Wash., U.S.A. 112 C4
Sumoto, Japan 49 G7
Sumqayıt, Azerbaijan 43 K9
Sumter, U.S.A. 105 J5
Sumy, Ukraine 41 G8
Sun City, Ariz., U.S.A. 111 K7
Sun City, Calif., U.S.A. 113 M9
Sunagawa, Japan 48 C10
Sunan, N. Korea 51 E13
Sunart, L., U.K. 14 E3
Sunburst, U.S.A. 110 B8
Sunbury, Australia 91 F3
Sunbury, U.S.A. 107 F8
Sunchales, Argentina 126 C3
Suncho Corral, Argentina 126 B3
Sunchon, S. Korea 51 G14
Suncook, U.S.A. 107 C13
Sunda, Selat, Indonesia 56 F3
Sunda Is., Indonesia 46 K13
Sunda Str. = Sunda, Selat, Indonesia 56 F3
Sundance, U.S.A. 108 C2
Sundarbans, The, Asia 61 J16
Sundargarh, India 61 H14
Sundays = Sondags →, S. Africa 84 E4
Sundbyberg, Sweden 10 E11
Sunderland, Canada 106 B5
Sunderland, U.K. 12 C6
Sundre, Canada 100 C6
Sundridge, Canada 98 C4
Sunds, Denmark 11 H3
Sundsjö, Sweden 10 B9
Sundsvall, Sweden 10 B11
Sung Hei, Vietnam 59 G6
Sungai Kolok, Thailand 59 J3
Sungai Lembing, Malaysia 59 L4
Sungai Patani, Malaysia 59 K3
Sungaigerong, Indonesia 56 E2
Sungailiat, Indonesia 56 E3
Sungaipakning, Indonesia 56 D2
Sungaipenuh, Indonesia 56 E2
Sungaitiram, Indonesia 56 E5
Sungari = Songhua Jiang →, China 54 B8
Sungguminasa, Indonesia 57 F5
Sunghua Chiang = Songhua Jiang →, China 54 B8
Sungikai, Sudan 77 E2
Sungurlu, Turkey 66 B6
Sunja, Croatia 33 C13
Sunndalsøra, Norway 9 E13
Sunnyside, Utah, U.S.A. 110 G8
Sunnyside, Wash., U.S.A. 110 C3
Sunnyvale, U.S.A. 111 H2
Sunray, U.S.A. 109 G4
Suntar, Russia 45 C12
Sunyani, Ghana 78 D4
Suomenselkä, Finland 8 E21
Suomussalmi, Finland 8 D23
Suoyarvi, Russia 40 A7
Supai, U.S.A. 111 H7
Supamo →, Venezuela 121 B5
Supaul, India 63 F12
Supe, Peru 124 C2
Superior, Ariz., U.S.A. 111 K8
Superior, Mont., U.S.A. 110 C6
Superior, Nebr., U.S.A. 108 E5
Superior, Wis., U.S.A. 108 B8
Superior, L., U.S.A. 98 C2
Supetar, Croatia 33 E13
Suphan Buri, Thailand 58 E3
Suphan Dağı, Turkey 67 C10
Supiori, Indonesia 57 E9
Supung Sk., China 51 D13
Sūq Suwayq, Si. Arabia 64 E3
Suqian, China 51 H10
Sūr, Lebanon 69 B4
Sur, Pt., U.S.A. 111 H3
Sura →, Russia 42 C8
Surab, Pakistan 62 E2
Surabaja = Surabaya, Indonesia 57 G15
Surabaya, Indonesia 57 G15
Suraia, Romania 38 D10
Surakarta, Indonesia 57 G14
Surakhany, Azerbaijan 43 K10
Surat, Australia 91 D4
Surat, India 60 J8
Surat Thani, Thailand 59 H2
Suratgarh, India 62 E5
Surazh, Belarus 40 E6
Surazh, Russia 41 F7
Surduc Pasul, Romania 38 D6
Surdulica, Serbia, Yug. 21 N12
Sûre = Sauer →, Germany 17 J9
Surendranagar, India 62 H4
Surf, U.S.A. 113 L6
Surgères, France 26 B3
Surgut, Russia 44 C8
Surhuisterveen, Neths. 16 B8
Suriapet, India 60 L11
Surigao, Phil. 55 G6
Surigao Strait, Phil. 55 F6
Surin, Thailand 58 E4
Surin Nua, Ko, Thailand 59 H1
Surinam ■, S. Amer. 121 C6
Suriname □, Surinam 121 B6
Suriname = Surinam ■, S. Amer. 121 C6
Suriname →, Surinam 121 B6
Sürmaq, Iran 65 D7
Sürmene, Turkey 67 B9
Surovikino, Russia 43 F6
Surprise L., Canada 100 B2
Surrey □, U.K. 13 F7
Sursee, Switz. 22 B6
Sursk, Russia 42 D7
Surskoye, Russia 42 C8
Surt, Libya 73 B8
Surt, Khalīj, Libya 73 B8
Surtsey, Iceland 8 E3
Surubim, Brazil 122 C4
Sürüç, Turkey 67 D8
Suruga-Wan, Japan 49 G9
Surumu →, Brazil 121 C5
Susa, Italy 32 C4
Suså →, Denmark 11 J5
Sušac, Croatia 33 F13
Susak, Croatia 33 D11
Susaki, Japan 49 H6
Süsangerd, Iran 67 G13
Susanino, Russia 45 D15
Susanville, U.S.A. 110 F3
Susch, Switz. 23 C10
Suşehri, Turkey 67 B8
Susong, China 53 B11
Susquehanna →, U.S.A. 107 G8
Susquehanna Depot, U.S.A. 107 E9
Susques, Argentina 126 A2
Sussex, Canada 99 C6
Sussex, U.S.A. 107 E10
Sussex, E. □, U.K. 13 G8
Sussex, W. □, U.K. 13 G7
Susteren, Neths. 17 F7
Sustut →, Canada 100 B3
Susuman, Russia 45 C15
Susunu, Indonesia 57 E8
Susurluk, Turkey 66 C3
Susuz, Turkey 67 B10
Sütçüler, Turkey 66 D4
Sutherland, S. Africa 84 E3
Sutherland, U.S.A. 108 E4
Sutherland Falls, N.Z. 87 L1
Sutherlin, U.S.A. 110 E2
Sutivan, Croatia 33 E13
Sutlej →, Pakistan 62 E4
Sutter, U.S.A. 112 F5
Sutter Creek, U.S.A. 112 G6
Sutton, Canada 107 A12
Sutton, U.S.A. 108 E6
Sutton →, Canada 98 A3
Sutton in Ashfield, U.K. 12 D6
Suttor →, Australia 90 C4
Suttsu, Japan 48 C10
Suva, Fiji 87 D8
Suva Reka, Serbia, Yug. 21 N10
Suvo Rudište, Serbia, Yug. 21 M10
Suvorov, Russia 42 C3
Suvorov Is. = Suwarrow Is., Cook Is. 93 J11
Suwałki, Poland 20 A12
Suwannaphum, Thailand 58 E4
Suwannee →, U.S.A. 105 L4
Suwanose-Jima, Japan 49 K4
Suwarrow Is., Cook Is. 93 J11
Suwayq aş Şuqban, Iraq 64 D5
Suweis, Khalîg el, Egypt 76 J8
Suweis, Qanâ es, Egypt 76 H8
Suwŏn, S. Korea 51 F14
Suzdal, Russia 42 B5
Suzhou, China 53 B13
Suzu, Japan 49 F8
Suzu-Misaki, Japan 49 F8
Suzuka, Japan 49 G8
Suzzara, Italy 32 C7
Svalbard, Arctic 4 B8
Svalöv, Sweden 11 J7
Svappavaara, Sweden 8 C19
Svarstad, Norway 10 E3
Svartisen, Norway 8 C15
Svartvik, Sweden 10 B11
Svatove, Ukraine 41 H10
Svatovo = Svatove, Ukraine 41 H10
Svay Chek, Cambodia 58 F4
Svay Rieng, Cambodia 59 G5
Svealand □, Sweden 9 G16
Sveg, Sweden 9 E16
Svendborg, Denmark 11 J4
Svene, Norway 10 E3
Svenljunga, Sweden 11 G7
Svenstrup, Denmark 11 H3
Sverdlovsk = Yekaterinburg, Russia 44 D7
Sverdlovsk, Ukraine 41 H10
Sverdrup Is., Canada 4 B3
Svetac, Croatia 33 E12
Sveti Ivan Zelina, Croatia 33 C13
Sveti Jurij, Slovenia 33 B12
Sveti Lenart, Slovenia 33 B12
Sveti Nikole, Macedonia 39 H4
Sveti Trojica, Slovenia 33 B12
Svetlaya, Russia 48 A9
Svetlogorsk = Svyetlahorsk, Belarus 41 F5
Svetlograd, Russia 43 H6
Svetlovodsk = Svitlovodsk, Ukraine 41 H7
Svetozarevo, Serbia, Yug. 21 L11
Svidník, Slovak Rep. 20 F11
Svilaja Planina, Croatia 33 E13
Svilengrad, Bulgaria 39 H9
Svir →, Russia 40 B7
Sviritsa, Russia 40 B7
Svishtov, Bulgaria 38 F8
Svislach, Belarus 41 F3
Svitava →, Czech. 20 F6
Svitavy, Czech. 20 F6
Svitlovodsk, Ukraine 41 H7
Svobodnyy, Russia 45 D13
Svolvær, Norway 8 B16
Svratka →, Czech. 20 F6
Svrljig, Serbia, Yug. 21 M12
Svyetlahorsk, Belarus 41 F5
Swabian Alps = Schwäbische Alb, Germany 19 G5
Swainsboro, U.S.A. 105 J4
Swakopmund, Namibia 84 C1
Swale →, U.K. 12 C6
Swalmen, Neths. 17 F8
Swan Hill, Australia 91 F3
Swan Hills, Canada 100 C5
Swan Is., W. Indies 116 C3
Swan L., Canada 101 C8
Swan River, Canada 101 C8
Swanage, U.K. 13 G6
Swansea, Australia 91 E5
Swansea, U.K. 13 F4
Swar →, Pakistan 63 B5
Swartberge, S. Africa 84 E3
Swartmodder, S. Africa 84 D3
Swartruggens, S. Africa 84 D4
Swarzędz, Poland 20 C7
Swastika, Canada 98 C3
Swatow = Shantou, China 53 F11
Swaziland ■, Africa 85 D5
Sweden ■, Europe 9 G16
Swedru, Ghana 79 D4
Sweet Home, U.S.A. 110 D2
Sweetwater, Nev., U.S.A. 112 G7
Sweetwater, Tex., U.S.A. 109 J4
Sweetwater →, U.S.A. 110 E10
Swellendam, S. Africa 84 E3
Świdnica, Poland 20 E6
Świdnik, Poland 20 D12
Świdwin, Poland 20 B5
Świebodzin, Poland 20 C5
Świecie, Poland 20 B8
Świętokrzyskie, Góry, Poland 20 E10
Swift Current, Canada 101 C7
Swiftcurrent →, Canada 101 C7
Swilly, L., Ireland 15 A4
Swindle, I., Canada 100 C3
Swindon, U.K. 13 F6
Swinemünde = Świnoujście, Poland 20 B4
Świnoujście, Poland 20 B4
Switzerland ■, Europe 22 D6
Swords, Ireland 15 C5
Syasstroy, Russia 40 B7
Sychevka, Russia 42 C2
Sydney, Australia 91 E5
Sydney, Canada 99 C7
Sydney Mines, Canada 99 C7
Sydprøven, Greenland 4 C5
Sydra, G. of = Surt, Khalīj, Libya 73 B8
Syeverodonetsk, Ukraine 41 H10
Syke, Germany 18 C4
Syktyvkar, Russia 44 C6
Sylacauga, U.S.A. 105 J2
Sylarna, Sweden 8 E15
Sylhet, Bangla. 61 G17
Sylt, Germany 18 A4
Sylvan Lake, Canada 100 C6
Sylvania, U.S.A. 105 J5
Sylvester, U.S.A. 105 K4
Sym, Russia 44 C9
Symón, Mexico 114 C4
Synelnykove, Ukraine 41 H8
Synnott Ra., Australia 88 C4
Syracuse, Kans., U.S.A. 109 F4
Syracuse, N.Y., U.S.A. 107 C8
Syrdarya →, Kazakhstan 44 E7
Syria ■, Asia 67 E8
Syul'dzhyukyor, Russia 45 C12
Syzran, Russia 42 D9
Szaraz →, Hungary 21 J10
Szarvas, Hungary 21 J10
Szczebrzeszyn, Poland 20 E12
Szczecin, Poland 20 B4
Szczecinek, Poland 20 B6
Szczekocimy, Poland 20 E9
Szczytno, Poland 20 B11
Szechwan = Sichuan □, China 52 B5
Szeged, Hungary 21 J10
Szeghalom, Hungary 21 H11
Székesfehérvár, Hungary 21 H8
Szekszárd, Hungary 21 J8
Szendrö, Hungary 21 G10
Szentendre, Hungary 21 H9
Szentes, Hungary 21 J10
Szentgotthárd, Hungary 21 J6
Szentlörinc, Hungary 21 J8
Szigetvár, Hungary 21 J7
Szolnok, Hungary 21 H10
Szombathely, Hungary 21 H6
Szprotawa, Poland 20 D5
Szydłowiec, Poland 20 D10
Szypliszki, Poland 20 A13

T

't Harde, Neths. 16 D7
't Zandt, Neths. 16 B9
Ta Khli Khok, Thailand 58 E3
Ta Lai, Vietnam 59 G6
Tabacal, Argentina 126 A3
Tabaco, Phil. 55 E5
Tabagné, Ivory C. 78 D4
Ţabāh, Si. Arabia 64 E4
Tabajara, Brazil 125 B5
Tabalos, Peru 124 B2
Tabarca, I. de, Spain 29 G4
Tabarka, Tunisia 75 A6
Ţabas, Khorāsān, Iran 65 C9
Ţabas, Khorāsān, Iran 65 C8
Tabasará, Serranía de, Panama 116 E3
Tabasco □, Mexico 115 D6
Tabatinga, Serra da, Brazil 122 D3
Tabāzīn, Iran 65 D8
Tabelbala, Kahal de, Algeria 75 C4
Taber, Canada 100 D6
Tabernas, Spain 29 H2
Tabernes de Valldigna, Spain 29 F4
Tabira, Brazil 122 C4
Tablas, Phil. 55 E5
Tablas Strait, Phil. 55 E4
Table B. = Tafelbaai, S. Africa 84 E2
Table B., Canada 99 B8
Table Mt., S. Africa 84 E2
Tableland, Australia 88 C4
Tabletop, Mt., Australia 90 C4
Tábor, Czech. 20 F4
Tabora, Tanzania 82 D3
Tabora □, Tanzania 82 D3
Tabou, Ivory C. 78 E3
Tabrīz, Iran 67 C12
Tabuaeran, Pac. Oc. 93 G12
Tabuelan, Phil. 55 F5
Tabuenca, Spain 28 D3
Tabūk, Si. Arabia 64 D3
Tacámbaro de Codallos, Mexico 114 D4
Tacheng, China 54 B3
Tach'ing Shan = Daqing Shan, China 50 D6
Táchira □, Venezuela 120 B3
Tácina →, Italy 35 D9
Tacloban, Phil. 55 F6
Tacna, Peru 124 D3
Tacna □, Peru 124 D3
Tacoma, U.S.A. 112 C4
Tacuarembó, Uruguay 127 C4
Tacutu →, Brazil 121 C5
Tademaït, Plateau du, Algeria 75 C5
Tadent, O. →, Algeria 75 D6
Tadjerdjeri, O. →, Algeria 75 C6
Tadjerouna, Algeria 75 B5
Tadjettaret, O. →, Algeria 75 D6
Tadjmout, Oasis, Algeria 75 B5
Tadjmout, Saoura, Algeria 75 C5
Tadjoura, Djibouti 68 E3
Tadjoura, Golfe de, Djibouti 77 E5
Tadmor, N.Z. 87 J4
Tadoule, L., Canada 101 B9
Tadoussac, Canada 99 C6
Tadzhikistan = Tajikistan ■, Asia 44 F8
Taechŏn-ni, S. Korea 51 F14
Taegu, S. Korea 51 G15
Taegwan, N. Korea 51 D13
Taejŏn, S. Korea 51 F14
Tafalla, Spain 28 C3
Tafar, Sudan 77 F2
Tafassasset, O. →, Algeria 75 D6
Tafelbaai, S. Africa 84 E2
Tafelney, C., Morocco 74 B3
Tafermaar, Indonesia 57 F8
Taffermit, Morocco 74 C3
Tafí Viejo, Argentina 126 B2
Tafīhān, Iran 65 D7
Tafiré, Ivory C. 78 D3
Tafnidilt, Morocco 74 C2
Tafraoute, Morocco 74 C3
Taft, Iran 65 D7
Taft, Phil. 55 F6
Taft, Calif., U.S.A. 113 K7
Taft, Tex., U.S.A. 109 M6
Taga Dzong, Bhutan 61 F16
Taganrog, Russia 43 G4
Taganrogskiy Zaliv, Russia 43 G4
Tagânt, Mauritania 78 B2
Tagatay, Phil. 55 D4
Tagbilaran, Phil. 55 G5
Tággia, Italy 32 E4
Taghzout, Morocco 74 B4
Tagish, Canada 100 A2
Tagish L., Canada 100 A2
Tagliacozzo, Italy 33 F10
Tagliamento →, Italy 33 C10
Táglio di Po, Italy 33 D9
Tagna, Colombia 120 D3
Tago, Phil. 55 G7
Tagomago, I. de, Spain 36 B8
Taguatinga, Brazil 123 D3
Tagudin, Phil. 55 C4
Tagum, Phil. 55 H6
Tagus = Tejo →, Europe 31 G1
Tahakopa, N.Z. 87 M2
Tahala, Morocco 74 B4
Tahan, Gunong, Malaysia 59 K4
Tahat, Algeria 75 D6
Tāherī, Iran 65 E7
Tahiti, Pac. Oc. 93 J13
Tahoe, L., U.S.A. 112 G6
Tahoe City, U.S.A. 112 F6
Taholah, U.S.A. 112 C2
Tahoua, Niger 79 C6
Tahta, Egypt 76 B3
Tahtalı Dağları, Turkey 66 C7
Tahuamanu →, Bolivia 124 C4
Tahulandang, Indonesia 57 D7
Tahuna, Indonesia 57 D7
Taï, Ivory C. 78 D3
Tai Hu, China 54 C7
Tai Shan, China 51 F9
Tai Xian, China 53 A13
Tai'an, China 51 F9
Taibei, Taiwan 53 E13
Taibique, Canary Is. 36 G2
Taibus Qi, China 50 D8
T'aichung = Taizhong, Taiwan 53 E13
Taidong, Taiwan 53 F13
Taieri →, N.Z. 87 M3
Taigu, China 50 F7
Taihang Shan, China 50 G7
Taihape, N.Z. 87 H5
Taihe, Anhui, China 50 H8
Taihe, Jiangxi, China 53 D10
Taihu, China 53 B11
Taijiang, China 52 D7
Taikang, China 50 G8
Tailem Bend, Australia 91 F2
Tailfingen, Germany 19 G5
Taimyr Peninsula = Taymyr, Poluostrov, Russia 45 B11
Tain, U.K. 14 D4
Tainan, Taiwan 53 F13
Taínaron, Ákra, Greece 39 N5
Taining, China 53 D11
Taintignies, Belgium 17 G2
Taiobeiras, Brazil 123 E3
T'aipei = Taibei, Taiwan 53 E13
Taiping, China 53 B12
Taiping, Malaysia 59 K3
Taipingzhen, China 50 H6
Taipu, Brazil 122 C4
Tairbeart = Tarbert, U.K. 14 D2
Taishan, China 53 F9
Taishun, China 53 D12
Taita □, Kenya 82 C4
Taita Hills, Kenya 82 C4
Taitao, C., Chile 128 C1
Taitao, Pen. de, Chile 128 C2
Taivalkoski, Finland 8 D23
Taiwan ■, Asia 53 F13
Taiwan Shan, Taiwan 53 F13
Taixing, China 53 A13
Taïyetos Óros, Greece 39 N5
Taiyiba, Israel 69 C4
Taiyuan, China 50 F7
Taizhong, Taiwan 53 E13
Taizhou, China 53 A12
Taizhou Liedao, China 53 C13
Ta'izz, Yemen 68 E3
Tājābād, Iran 65 D7
Tajapuru, Furo do, Brazil 122 B1
Tajikistan ■, Asia 44 F8
Tajima, Japan 49 F9
Tajo = Tejo →, Europe 31 G1
Tajrīsh, Iran 65 C6
Tājūrā, Libya 73 B7
Tak, Thailand 58 D2
Takāb, Iran 67 D12
Takachiho, Japan 49 H5
Takada, Japan 49 F9
Takahagi, Japan 49 F10
Takaka, N.Z. 87 J4
Takamatsu, Japan 49 G7
Takaoka, Japan 49 F8
Takapuna, N.Z. 87 G5
Takasaki, Japan 49 F9
Takatsuki, Japan 49 G7
Takaungu, Kenya 82 C4
Takayama, Japan 49 F8
Take-Shima, Japan 49 J5
Takefu, Japan 49 G8
Takengon, Indonesia 56 D1
Takeo, Cambodia 59 G5
Takeo, Japan 49 H5
Tåkern, Sweden 11 F8
Tākestān, Iran 65 C6
Taketa, Japan 49 H5
Takh, India 63 C7
Takhman, Cambodia 59 G5
Takikawa, Japan 48 C10
Takla L., Canada 100 B3
Takla Landing, Canada 100 B3

Takla Makan

Takla Makan =
  Taklamakan Shamo,
  China ... 46 F12
Taklamakan Shamo, *China* .. 46 F12
Taku →, *Canada* ... 100 B2
Takum, *Nigeria* ... 79 D6
Takutu →, *Guyana* ... 121 C5
Tal Halāl, *Iran* ... 65 D7
Tala, *Uruguay* ... 127 C4
Talachyn, *Belarus* ... 40 E5
Talacogan, *Phil.* ... 55 G6
Talagante, *Chile* ... 126 C1
Talaïnt, *Morocco* ... 74 C3
Talak, *Niger* ... 79 B6
Talamanca, Cordillera de,
  Cent. Amer. ... 116 E3
Talara, *Peru* ... 124 A1
Talas, *Kyrgyzstan* ... 44 E8
Talas, *Turkey* ... 66 C6
Talâta, *Egypt* ... 69 E1
Talata Mafara, *Nigeria* ... 79 C6
Talaud, Kepulauan,
  Indonesia ... 57 D7
Talaud Is. = Talaud,
  Kepulauan, *Indonesia* .. 57 D7
Talavera de la Reina, *Spain* 30 F6
Talawana, *Australia* ... 88 D3
Talayan, *Phil.* ... 55 H6
Talbert, Sillon de, *France* .. 24 D3
Talbot, C., *Australia* ... 88 B4
Talbragar →, *Australia* ... 91 E4
Talca, *Chile* ... 126 D1
Talca □, *Chile* ... 126 D1
Talcahuano, *Chile* ... 126 D1
Talcher, *India* ... 61 J14
Talcho, *Niger* ... 79 C5
Taldy Kurgan =
  Taldyqorghan,
  Kazakhstan ... 44 E8
Taldyqorghan, *Kazakhstan* 44 E8
Tālesh, *Iran* ... 67 D13
Tālesh, Kūhhā-ye, *Iran* ... 67 D13
Talguharai, *Sudan* ... 76 D4
Tali Post, *Sudan* ... 77 F3
Talibon, *Phil.* ... 57 B6
Talibong, Ko, *Thailand* ... 59 J2
Talihina, *U.S.A.* ... 109 H7
Talisayan, *Phil.* ... 55 G6
Taliwang, *Indonesia* ... 56 F5
Tall 'Afar, *Iraq* ... 67 D10
Tall 'Asūr, *West Bank* ... 69 D4
Tall Kalakh, *Syria* ... 69 A5
Talla, *Egypt* ... 76 J7
Talladega, *U.S.A.* ... 105 J2
Tallahassee, *U.S.A.* ... 105 K3
Tallangatta, *Australia* ... 91 F4
Tallarook, *Australia* ... 91 F4
Tallering Pk., *Australia* ... 89 E2
Tallinn, *Estonia* ... 9 G21
Tallulah, *U.S.A.* ... 109 J9
Talmest, *Morocco* ... 74 B3
Talmont, *France* ... 26 B2
Talne, *Ukraine* ... 41 H6
Talnoye = Talne, *Ukraine* .. 41 H6
Talodi, *Sudan* ... 77 E3
Talovaya, *Russia* ... 42 E5
Talpa de Allende, *Mexico* .. 114 C4
Talsi, *Latvia* ... 9 H20
Talsinnt, *Morocco* ... 75 B4
Taltal, *Chile* ... 126 B1
Taltson →, *Canada* ... 100 A6
Talwood, *Australia* ... 91 D4
Talyawalka Cr. →,
  Australia ... 91 E3
Tam Chau, *Vietnam* ... 59 G5
Tam Ky, *Vietnam* ... 58 E7
Tam Quan, *Vietnam* ... 58 E7
Tama, *U.S.A.* ... 108 E8
Tamala, *Australia* ... 89 E1
Tamalameque, *Colombia* .. 120 B3
Tamale, *Ghana* ... 79 D4
Taman, *Russia* ... 43 H3
Tamanar, *Morocco* ... 74 B3
Tamano, *Japan* ... 49 G6
Tamanrasset, *Algeria* ... 75 D6
Tamanrasset, O. →,
  Algeria ... 75 D5
Tamaqua, *U.S.A.* ... 107 F9
Tamar →, *U.K.* ... 13 G3
Támara, *Colombia* ... 120 B3
Tamarang, *Australia* ... 91 E5
Tamarinda, *Spain* ... 36 B10
Tamarite de Litera, *Spain* . 28 D5
Tamashima, *Japan* ... 49 G6
Tamaské, *Niger* ... 79 C6
Tamaulipas □, *Mexico* ... 115 C5
Tamaulipas, Sierra de,
  Mexico ... 115 C5
Tamazula, *Mexico* ... 114 C3
Tamazunchale, *Mexico* ... 115 C5
Tamba-Dabatou, *Guinea* .. 78 C2
Tambacounda, *Senegal* .. 78 C2
Tambelan, Kepulauan,
  Indonesia ... 56 D3
Tambellup, *Australia* ... 89 F2
Tambo, *Australia* ... 90 C4
Tambo, *Peru* ... 124 C3
Tambo →, *Peru* ... 124 C3
Tambo de Mora, *Peru* ... 124 C2
Tambobamba, *Peru* ... 124 C3
Tambohorano, *Madag.* ... 85 B7
Tambopata →, *Peru* ... 124 C4
Tambora, *Indonesia* ... 56 F5
Tambov, *Russia* ... 42 D5
Tambre →, *Spain* ... 30 C2
Tambuku, *Indonesia* ... 57 G15
Tamburâ, *Sudan* ... 77 F2

Tâmchekket, *Mauritania* .. 78 B2
Tame, *Colombia* ... 120 B3
Tamega →, *Portugal* ... 30 D2
Tamelelt, *Morocco* ... 74 B3
Tamenglong, *India* ... 61 G18
Tamerza, *Tunisia* ... 75 B6
Tamgak, Mts., *Niger* ... 72 E6
Tamiahua, L. de, *Mexico* .. 115 C5
Tamil Nadu □, *India* ... 60 P10
Tamines, *Belgium* ... 17 H5
Tamis →, *Serbia, Yug.* ... 38 E3
Tamluk, *India* ... 63 H12
Tammerfors = Tampere,
  Finland ... 9 F20
Tammisaari, *Finland* ... 9 F20
Tamo Abu, Pegunungan,
  Malaysia ... 56 D5
Tampa, *U.S.A.* ... 105 M4
Tampa B., *U.S.A.* ... 105 M4
Tampere, *Finland* ... 9 F20
Tampico, *Mexico* ... 115 C5
Tampin, *Malaysia* ... 59 L4
Tamri, *Morocco* ... 74 B3
Tamrida = Qādib, *Yemen* .. 68 E5
Tamsagbulag, *Mongolia* .. 54 B6
Tamu, *Burma* ... 61 G19
Tamuja →, *Spain* ... 31 F4
Tamworth, *Australia* ... 91 E5
Tamworth, *U.K.* ... 13 E6
Tamyang, *S. Korea* ... 51 G14
Tan An, *Vietnam* ... 59 G6
Tan-tan, *Morocco* ... 74 C2
Tana →, *Kenya* ... 82 C5
Tana →, *Norway* ... 8 A23
Tana, L., *Ethiopia* ... 77 E4
Tana River, *Kenya* ... 82 C4
Tanabe, *Japan* ... 49 H7
Tanabi, *Brazil* ... 123 F2
Tanafjorden, *Norway* ... 8 A23
Tanaga, Pta., *Canary Is.* .. 36 G1
Tanagro →, *Italy* ... 35 B8
Tanahbala, *Indonesia* ... 56 E1
Tanahgrogot, *Indonesia* .. 56 E5
Tanahjampea, *Indonesia* .. 57 F6
Tanahmasa, *Indonesia* ... 56 E1
Tanahmerah, *Indonesia* ... 57 F10
Tanakura, *Japan* ... 49 F10
Tanami, *Australia* ... 88 C4
Tanami Desert, *Australia* .. 88 C5
Tanana, *U.S.A.* ... 96 B4
Tanana →, *U.S.A.* ... 96 B4
Tananarive =
  Antananarivo, *Madag.* .. 85 B8
Tanannt, *Morocco* ... 74 B3
Tánaro →, *Italy* ... 32 C5
Tanaunella, *Italy* ... 34 B2
Tanbar, *Australia* ... 90 D3
Tancarville, *France* ... 24 C7
Tancheng, *China* ... 51 G10
Tanchŏn, *N. Korea* ... 51 D15
Tanda, Ut. P., *India* ... 63 F10
Tanda, Ut. P., *India* ... 63 E8
Tanda, *Ivory C.* ... 78 D4
Tandag, *Phil.* ... 55 G7
Tandaia, *Tanzania* ... 83 D3
Tăndărei, *Romania* ... 38 E10
Tandaué, *Angola* ... 84 B2
Tandil, *Argentina* ... 126 D4
Tandil, Sa. del, *Argentina* . 126 D4
Tandlianwala, *Pakistan* ... 62 D5
Tando Adam, *Pakistan* ... 62 G3
Tandou L., *Australia* ... 91 E3
Tandsbyn, *Sweden* ... 10 A8
Tane-ga-Shima, *Japan* ... 49 J5
Taneatua, *N.Z.* ... 87 H6
Tanen Tong Dan, *Burma* . 58 D2
Tanezrouft, *Algeria* ... 75 D5
Tang, Koh, *Cambodia* ... 59 G4
Tang Krasang, *Cambodia* . 58 F5
Tanga, *Tanzania* ... 82 D4
Tanga □, *Tanzania* ... 82 D4
Tanganyika, L., *Africa* ... 82 D2
Tanger, *Morocco* ... 74 A3
Tangerang, *Indonesia* ... 57 G12
Tangerhütte, *Germany* ... 18 C7
Tangermünde, *Germany* .. 18 C7
Tanggu, *China* ... 51 E9
Tanggula Shan, *China* ... 54 C4
Tanghe, *China* ... 50 H7
Tangier = Tanger,
  Morocco ... 74 A3
Tangorin P.O., *Australia* .. 90 C3
Tangshan, *China* ... 51 E10
Tangtou, *China* ... 51 G10
Tanguiéta, *Benin* ... 79 C5
Tangxi, *China* ... 53 C12
Tangyan He →, *China* ... 52 C7
Tanimbar, Kepulauan,
  Indonesia ... 57 F8
Tanimbar Is. = Tanimbar,
  Kepulauan, *Indonesia* .. 57 F8
Taninges, *France* ... 27 B10
Tanjay, *Phil.* ... 55 G5
Tanjong Malim, *Malaysia* . 59 L3
Tanjore = Thanjavur, *India* 60 P11
Tanjung, *Indonesia* ... 56 E5
Tanjungbalai, *Indonesia* .. 56 D1
Tanjungbatu, *Indonesia* .. 56 D5
Tanjungkarang
  Telukbetung, *Indonesia* . 56 F3
Tanjungpandan, *Indonesia* . 56 E3
Tanjungpinang, *Indonesia* . 56 D2
Tanjungpriok, *Indonesia* .. 57 G12
Tanjungredeb, *Indonesia* . 56 D5
Tanjungselor, *Indonesia* .. 56 D5
Tank, *Pakistan* ... 62 C4
Tännäs, *Sweden* ... 10 B6

Tannis Bugt, *Denmark* ... 11 G4
Tannu-Ola, *Russia* ... 45 D10
Tano →, *Ghana* ... 78 D4
Tanon Str., *Phil.* ... 55 F5
Tanout, *Niger* ... 79 C6
Tanquinho, *Brazil* ... 123 D4
Tanta, *Egypt* ... 76 H7
Tantoyuca, *Mexico* ... 115 C5
Tantung = Dandong, *China* 51 D13
Tanumshede, *Sweden* ... 11 F5
Tanunda, *Australia* ... 91 E2
Tanus, *France* ... 26 D6
Tanzania ■, *Africa* ... 82 D3
Tanzilla →, *Canada* ... 100 B2
Tao Ko, *Thailand* ... 59 G2
Tao'an, *China* ... 51 B12
Tao'er He →, *China* ... 51 B13
Taohua Dao, *China* ... 53 C14
Taolanaro, *Madag.* ... 85 D8
Taole, *China* ... 50 E4
Taormina, *Italy* ... 35 E8
Taos, *U.S.A.* ... 111 H11
Taoudenni, *Mali* ... 74 D4
Taoudrart, Adrar, *Algeria* . 75 D5
Taounate, *Morocco* ... 74 B4
Taourirt, *Algeria* ... 75 C5
Taourirt, *Morocco* ... 75 B4
Taouz, *Morocco* ... 74 B4
Taoyuan, *China* ... 53 C8
Taoyuan, *Taiwan* ... 53 E13
Tapa, *Estonia* ... 9 G21
Tapa Shan = Daba Shan,
  China ... 52 B7
Tapachula, *Mexico* ... 115 E6
Tapah, *Malaysia* ... 59 K3
Tapajós →, *Brazil* ... 121 D7
Tapaktuan, *Indonesia* ... 56 D1
Tapanahoni →, *Surinam* .. 121 C7
Tapanui, *N.Z.* ... 87 L2
Tapauá, *Brazil* ... 125 B5
Tapauá →, *Brazil* ... 125 B5
Tapeta, *Liberia* ... 78 D3
Taphan Hin, *Thailand* ... 58 D3
Tapi →, *India* ... 60 J8
Tapia, *Spain* ... 30 B4
Tápiószele, *Hungary* ... 21 H9
Tapiraí, *Brazil* ... 123 E2
Tapirapé →, *Brazil* ... 122 D1
Tapirapecó, Serra,
  Venezuela ... 121 C5
Tapirapuã, *Brazil* ... 125 C6
Tapoeripa, *Surinam* ... 121 B6
Tapolca, *Hungary* ... 21 J7
Tappahannock, *U.S.A.* ... 104 G7
Tapuaenuku, Mt., *N.Z.* .. 87 J4
Tapul Group, *Phil.* ... 55 J4
Tapurucuará, *Brazil* ... 121 D4
Taqiābād, *Iran* ... 65 C8
Ţaqţaq, *Iraq* ... 67 E11
Taquara, *Brazil* ... 127 B5
Taquari →, *Brazil* ... 125 D6
Taquaritinga, *Brazil* ... 123 F2
Tara, *Australia* ... 91 D5
Tara, *Canada* ... 106 B3
Tara, *Russia* ... 44 D8
Tara, *Zambia* ... 83 F2
Tara →, *Russia* ... 44 D8
Taraba →, *Nigeria* ... 79 D7
Tarabagatay, Khrebet,
  Kazakhstan ... 44 E9
Tarabuco, *Bolivia* ... 125 D5
Tarābulus, *Lebanon* ... 69 A4
Tarābulus, *Libya* ... 75 B7
Tarahouahout, *Algeria* ... 75 D6
Tarajalejo, *Canary Is.* ... 36 F5
Tarakan, *Indonesia* ... 56 D5
Tarakit, Mt., *Kenya* ... 82 B4
Taralga, *Australia* ... 91 E4
Tarama-Jima, *Japan* ... 49 M2
Taran, Mys, *Russia* ... 9 J18
Taranagar, *India* ... 62 E6
Taranaki □, *N.Z.* ... 87 H5
Tarancón, *Spain* ... 28 E1
Taranga, *India* ... 62 H5
Taranga Hill, *India* ... 62 H5
Táranto, *Italy* ... 35 B10
Táranto, G. di, *Italy* ... 35 B10
Tarapacá, *Colombia* ... 120 D4
Tarapacá □, *Chile* ... 126 A2
Tarapoto, *Peru* ... 124 B2
Taraquá, *Brazil* ... 120 C4
Tarare, *France* ... 27 C8
Tararua Ra., *N.Z.* ... 87 J5
Tarascon, *France* ... 27 E8
Tarascon-sur-Ariège,
  France ... 26 F5
Tarashcha, *Ukraine* ... 41 H6
Tarata, *Peru* ... 124 D3
Tarauacá, *Brazil* ... 124 B3
Tarauacá →, *Brazil* ... 124 B4
Taravo →, *France* ... 27 G12
Tarawera, *N.Z.* ... 87 H6
Tarawera L., *N.Z.* ... 87 H6
Tarazona, *Spain* ... 28 D3
Tarazona de la Mancha,
  Spain ... 29 F3
Tarbat Ness, *U.K.* ... 14 D5
Tarbela Dam, *Pakistan* ... 62 B5
Tarbert, *Strath., U.K.* ... 14 F3
Tarbert, *W. Isles, U.K.* ... 14 D2
Tarbes, *France* ... 26 E4
Tarboro, *U.S.A.* ... 105 H7
Tarbrax, *Australia* ... 90 C3
Tarcento, *Italy* ... 33 B10
Tarcoola, *Australia* ... 91 E1
Tarcoon, *Australia* ... 91 E4
Tardets-Sorholus, *France* . 26 E3

Tardoire →, *France* ... 26 C4
Taree, *Australia* ... 91 E5
Tarentaise, *France* ... 27 C10
Tarf, Ras, *Morocco* ... 74 A3
Tarfa, W. el →, *Egypt* ... 76 J7
Tarfaya, *Morocco* ... 74 C2
Targon, *France* ... 26 D3
Targuist, *Morocco* ... 74 B4
Tarhbalt, *Morocco* ... 74 B3
Tarhit, *Algeria* ... 75 B4
Tariba, *Venezuela* ... 120 B3
Tarija, *Bolivia* ... 126 A3
Tarija □, *Bolivia* ... 126 A3
Tariku →, *Indonesia* ... 57 E9
Tarim Basin = Tarim
  Pendi, *China* ... 54 C3
Tarim He →, *China* ... 54 C3
Tarim Pendi, *China* ... 54 C3
Tarime □, *Tanzania* ... 82 C3
Taritatu →, *Indonesia* ... 57 E9
Tarka →, *S. Africa* ... 84 E4
Tarkastad, *S. Africa* ... 84 E4
Tarkhankut, Mys, *Ukraine* . 41 K7
Tarko Sale, *Russia* ... 44 C8
Tarkwa, *Ghana* ... 78 D4
Tarlac, *Phil.* ... 55 D4
Tarlton Downs, *Australia* . 90 C2
Tarm, *Denmark* ... 11 J2
Tarma, *Peru* ... 124 C2
Tarn □, *France* ... 26 E6
Tarn →, *France* ... 26 D5
Tarn-et-Garonne □, *France* 26 D5
Tarna →, *Hungary* ... 21 H9
Tårnby, *Denmark* ... 11 J6
Tarnobrzeg, *Poland* ... 20 E11
Tarnów, *Poland* ... 20 F11
Táro →, *Italy* ... 32 D7
Taroom, *Australia* ... 91 D4
Taroudannt, *Morocco* ... 74 B3
Tarp, *Germany* ... 18 A5
Tarpon Springs, *U.S.A.* .. 105 L4
Tarquínia, *Italy* ... 33 F8
Tarragona, *Spain* ... 28 D6
Tarragona □, *Spain* ... 28 D6
Tarrasa, *Spain* ... 28 D7
Tárrega, *Spain* ... 28 D6
Tarrytown, *U.S.A.* ... 107 E11
Tarshiha = Me'ona, *Israel* . 69 B4
Tarso Emissi, *Chad* ... 73 D8
Tarsus, *Turkey* ... 66 D6
Tartagal, *Argentina* ... 126 A3
Tártár, *Azerbaijan* ... 43 K8
Tártär →, *Azerbaijan* ... 43 K8
Tartas, *France* ... 26 E3
Tartu, *Estonia* ... 9 G22
Tarţūs, *Syria* ... 66 E6
Tarumirim, *Brazil* ... 123 E3
Tarumizu, *Japan* ... 49 J5
Tarussa, *Russia* ... 42 C3
Tarutao, Ko, *Thailand* ... 59 J2
Tarutung, *Indonesia* ... 56 D1
Tarvísio, *Italy* ... 33 B10
Tarz Ulli, *Libya* ... 75 C7
Tasawāh, *Libya* ... 73 C7
Taschereau, *Canada* ... 98 C4
Taseko →, *Canada* ... 100 C4
Tash-Kömür, *Kyrgyzstan* . 44 E8
Tash-Kumyr = Tash-
  Kömür, *Kyrgyzstan* ... 44 E8
Tashauz = Dashhowuz,
  Turkmenistan ... 44 E6
Tashi Chho Dzong =
  Thimphu, *Bhutan* ... 61 F16
Tashkent = Toshkent,
  Uzbekistan ... 44 E7
Tashtagol, *Russia* ... 44 D9
Tasikmalaya, *Indonesia* .. 57 G13
Taskan, *Russia* ... 45 C16
Tasman B., *N.Z.* ... 87 J4
Tasman Mts., *N.Z.* ... 87 J4
Tasman Pen., *Australia* .. 90 G4
Tasman Sea, *Pac. Oc.* ... 92 L8
Tasmania □, *Australia* ... 90 G4
Tăşnad, *Romania* ... 38 B5
Tassil Tin-Rerhoh, *Algeria* 75 D5
Tassili n-Ajjer, *Algeria* ... 75 C6
Tassili-Oua-n-Ahaggar,
  Algeria ... 75 D6
Tasu Sd., *Canada* ... 100 C2
Tata, *Morocco* ... 74 C3
Tata, *Hungary* ... 21 H8
Tatabánya, *Hungary* ... 21 H8
Tatahouine, *Tunisia* ... 75 B7
Tatar Republic =
  Tatarstan □, *Russia* ... 42 C10
Tatarbunary, *Ukraine* ... 41 K5
Tatarsk, *Russia* ... 44 D8
Tatarstan □, *Russia* ... 42 C10
Tateyama, *Japan* ... 49 G9
Tathlina L., *Canada* ... 100 A5
Tathra, *Australia* ... 91 F4
Tatinnai L., *Canada* ... 101 A9
Tatnam, C., *Canada* ... 101 B10
Tatra = Tatry, *Slovak Rep.* 20 F9
Tatry, *Slovak Rep.* ... 20 F9
Tatsuno, *Japan* ... 49 G7
Tatta, *Pakistan* ... 62 G2
Tatuí, *Brazil* ... 127 A6
Tatum, *U.S.A.* ... 109 J3
Tat'ung = Datong, *China* . 50 D7
Tatvan, *Turkey* ... 67 C10
Tauá, *Brazil* ... 122 C3
Taubaté, *Brazil* ... 127 A6
Tauberbischofsheim,
  Germany ... 19 F5

Taucha, *Germany* ... 18 D8
Taufikia, *Sudan* ... 77 F3
Taumarunui, *N.Z.* ... 87 H5
Taumaturgo, *Brazil* ... 124 B3
Taung, *S. Africa* ... 84 D3
Taungdwingyi, *Burma* ... 61 J19
Taunggyi, *Burma* ... 61 J20
Taungup, *Burma* ... 61 K19
Taungup Pass, *Burma* ... 61 K19
Taungup Taunggya, *Burma* 61 K18
Taunsa Barrage, *Pakistan* . 62 D4
Taunton, *U.K.* ... 13 F4
Taunton, *U.S.A.* ... 107 E13
Taunus, *Germany* ... 19 E4
Taupo, *N.Z.* ... 87 H6
Taupo, L., *N.Z.* ... 87 H5
Tauragè, *Lithuania* ... 9 J20
Tauranga, *N.Z.* ... 87 G6
Tauranga Harb., *N.Z.* ... 87 G6
Taurianova, *Italy* ... 35 D9
Taurus Mts. = Toros
  Dağları, *Turkey* ... 66 D5
Tauste, *Spain* ... 28 D3
Tauz = Tovuz, *Azerbaijan* . 43 K7
Tavannes, *Switz.* ... 22 B4
Tavas, *Turkey* ... 66 D3
Tavda, *Russia* ... 44 D7
Tavda →, *Russia* ... 44 D7
Taverny, *France* ... 25 C9
Taveta, *Tanzania* ... 82 C4
Taveuni, *Fiji* ... 87 C9
Tavignano →, *France* ... 27 F13
Tavira, *Portugal* ... 31 H3
Tavistock, *Canada* ... 106 C4
Tavistock, *U.K.* ... 13 G3
Tavolara, *Italy* ... 34 B2
Távora →, *Portugal* ... 30 D3
Tavoy, *Burma* ... 58 E2
Tavşanlı, *Turkey* ... 66 C3
Taw →, *U.K.* ... 13 F3
Tawas City, *U.S.A.* ... 104 C4
Tawau, *Malaysia* ... 56 D5
Tawitawi, *Phil.* ... 55 J4
Taxila, *Pakistan* ... 62 C5
Tay →, *U.K.* ... 14 E5
Tay, Firth of, *U.K.* ... 14 E5
Tay, L., *Australia* ... 89 F3
Tay, L., *U.K.* ... 14 E4
Tay Ninh, *Vietnam* ... 59 G6
Tayabamba, *Peru* ... 124 B2
Tayabas Bay, *Phil.* ... 55 E4
Taylakovy = Taylakova,
  Russia ... 44 D8
Taylor, *Canada* ... 100 B4
Taylor, *Nebr., U.S.A.* ... 108 E5
Taylor, *Pa., U.S.A.* ... 107 E9
Taylor, *Tex., U.S.A.* ... 109 K6
Taylor, Mt., *U.S.A.* ... 111 J10
Taylorville, *U.S.A.* ... 108 F10
Taymā, *Si. Arabia* ... 64 E3
Taymyr, Oz., *Russia* ... 45 B11
Taymyr, Poluostrov, *Russia* 45 B11
Tayport, *U.K.* ... 14 E6
Tayshet, *Russia* ... 45 D10
Tayside □, *U.K.* ... 14 E5
Taytay, *Phil.* ... 55 F3
Taz →, *Russia* ... 44 C8
Taza, *Morocco* ... 74 B4
Tazawa-Ko, *Japan* ... 48 E10
Tazenakht, *Morocco* ... 74 B3
Tazin L., *Canada* ... 101 B7
Tazoult, *Algeria* ... 75 A6
Tazovskiy, *Russia* ... 44 C8
Tbilisi, *Georgia* ... 43 K7
Tchad = Chad ■, *Africa* . 73 E8
Tchad, L., *Chad* ... 73 F7
Tchaourou, *Benin* ... 79 D5
Tch'eng-tou = Chengdu,
  China ... 52 B5
Tchentlo L., *Canada* ... 100 B4
Tchibanga, *Gabon* ... 80 E2
Tchien, *Liberia* ... 78 D3
Tchin Tabaraden, *Niger* .. 79 B6
Tch'ong-k'ing =
  Chongqing, *China* ... 52 C6
Tczew, *Poland* ... 20 A8
Te Anau, L., *N.Z.* ... 87 L1
Te Aroha, *N.Z.* ... 87 G5
Te Awamutu, *N.Z.* ... 87 H5
Te Kuiti, *N.Z.* ... 87 H5
Te Puke, *N.Z.* ... 87 G6
Te Waewae B., *N.Z.* ... 87 M1
Tea →, *Brazil* ... 120 D4
Tea Tree, *Australia* ... 90 C1
Teague, *U.S.A.* ... 109 K6
Teano, *Italy* ... 35 A7
Teapa, *Mexico* ... 115 D6
Teba, *Spain* ... 31 J6
Tebakang, *Malaysia* ... 56 D4
Teberda, *Russia* ... 43 J5
Tébessa, *Algeria* ... 75 A6
Tebicuary →, *Paraguay* .. 126 B4
Tebingtinggi, *Indonesia* .. 56 D1
Tébourba, *Tunisia* ... 75 A6
Téboursouk, *Tunisia* ... 75 A6
Tebulos, *Georgia* ... 43 J7
Tecate, *Mexico* ... 113 N10
Tecer Dağları, *Turkey* ... 66 C7
Tech →, *France* ... 26 F7
Techiman, *Ghana* ... 78 D4
Tecka, *Argentina* ... 128 B2
Tecomán, *Mexico* ... 114 D4
Tecopa, *U.S.A.* ... 113 K10
Tecoripa, *Mexico* ... 114 B3
Tecuala, *Mexico* ... 114 C3

Tecuci, *Romania* 38 D10
Tecumseh, *U.S.A.* 104 D4
Tedzhen = Tejen,
  Turkmenistan 44 F7
Tees →, *U.K.* 12 C6
Teesside, *U.K.* 12 C6
Teeswater, *Canada* 106 C3
Tefé, *Brazil* 121 D5
Tefé →, *Brazil* 121 D5
Tefenni, *Turkey* 66 D3
Tegal, *Indonesia* 57 G13
Tegelen, *Neths.* 17 F8
Teggiano, *Italy* 35 B8
Teghra, *India* 63 G11
Tegid, L. = Bala, L., *U.K.* . . 12 E4
Tegina, *Nigeria* 79 C6
Tegucigalpa, *Honduras* 116 D2
Tehachapi, *U.S.A.* 113 K8
Tehachapi Mts., *U.S.A.* 113 L8
Tehamiyam, *Sudan* 76 D4
Tehilla, *Sudan* 76 D4
Téhini, *Ivory C.* 78 D4
Tehrān, *Iran* 65 C6
Tehuacán, *Mexico* 115 D5
Tehuantepec, *Mexico* 115 D5
Tehuantepec, G. de,
  Mexico 115 D5
Tehuantepec, Istmo de,
  Mexico 115 D6
Teide, *Canary Is.* 36 F3
Teifi →, *U.K.* 13 E3
Teign →, *U.K.* 13 G4
Teignmouth, *U.K.* 13 G4
Teixeira, *Brazil* 122 C4
Teixeira Pinto,
  Guinea-Biss. 78 C1
Tejen, *Turkmenistan* 44 F7
Tejo →, *Europe* 31 G1
Tejon Pass, *U.S.A.* 113 L8
Tekamah, *U.S.A.* 108 E6
Tekapo, L., *N.Z.* 87 K3
Tekax, *Mexico* 115 C7
Tekeli, *Kazakhstan* 44 E8
Tekeze →, *Ethiopia* 77 E4
Tekija, *Serbia, Yug.* 21 L12
Tekirdağ, *Turkey* 66 B2
Tekkali, *India* 61 K14
Tekke, *Turkey* 66 B7
Tekman, *Turkey* 67 C9
Tekoa, *U.S.A.* 110 C5
Tekouiât, O., *Algeria* 75 D5
Tel Aviv-Yafo, *Israel* 69 C3
Tel Lakhish, *Israel* 69 D3
Tel Megiddo, *Israel* 69 C4
Tela, *Honduras* 116 C2
Télagh, *Algeria* 75 B4
Telanaipura = Jambi,
  Indonesia 56 E2
Telavi, *Georgia* 43 J7
Telde, *Canary Is.* 36 G4
Telegraph Creek, *Canada* . . . 100 B2
Telekhany = Tsyelyakhany,
  Belarus 41 F3
Telemark, *Norway* 9 G12
Telemark fylke □, *Norway* . . 10 E2
Telén, *Argentina* 126 D2
Teleng, *Iran* 65 E9
Teleño, *Spain* 30 C4
Teleorman →, *Romania* 38 E8
Teles Pires →, *Brazil* 125 B6
Telescope Pk., *U.S.A.* 113 J9
Teletaye, *Mali* 79 B5
Telford, *U.K.* 12 E5
Telkwa, *Canada* 100 C3
Tell City, *U.S.A.* 104 G2
Tellicherry, *India* 60 P9
Tellin, *Belgium* 17 H6
Telluride, *U.S.A.* 111 H10
Teloloapán, *Mexico* 115 D5
Telpos Iz, *Russia* 6 C17
Telsen, *Argentina* 128 B3
Telšiai, *Lithuania* 9 H20
Teltow, *Germany* 18 C9
Teluk Anson, *Malaysia* 59 K3
Teluk Betung =
  Tanjungkarang
  Telukbetung, *Indonesia* . 56 F3
Teluk Intan = Teluk
  Anson, *Malaysia* 59 K3
Telukbutun, *Indonesia* 59 K7
Telukdalem, *Indonesia* 56 D1
Tema, *Ghana* 79 D5
Temanggung, *Indonesia* 57 G14
Temapache, *Mexico* 115 C5
Temax, *Mexico* 115 C7
Temba, *S. Africa* 85 D4
Tembe, *Zaïre* 82 C2
Temblador, *Venezuela* 121 B5
Tembleque, *Spain* 28 F1
Temblor Range, *U.S.A.* 113 K7
Teme →, *U.K.* 13 E5
Temecula, *U.S.A.* 113 M9
Temerloh, *Malaysia* 59 L4
Temir, *Kazakhstan* 44 E6
Temirtau, *Kazakhstan* 44 D8
Temirtau, *Russia* 44 D9
Témiscaming, *Canada* 98 C4
Temma, *Australia* 90 G3
Temnikov, *Russia* 42 C6
Temo →, *Italy* 34 B1
Temora, *Australia* 91 E4
Temósachic, *Mexico* 114 B3
Tempe, *U.S.A.* 111 K8
Tempe Downs, *Australia* . . . 88 D5

Témpio Pausánia, *Italy* . . . 34 B2
Tempiute, *U.S.A.* 112 H11
Temple, *U.S.A.* 109 K6
Temple B., *Australia* 90 A3
Templemore, *Ireland* 15 D4
Templeton, *U.S.A.* 112 K6
Templeton →, *Australia* . . . 90 C2
Templeuve, *Belgium* 17 G2
Templin, *Germany* 18 B9
Tempoal, *Mexico* 115 C5
Temryuk, *Russia* 43 H3
Temse, *Belgium* 17 F4
Temska →, *Serbia, Yug.* . . . 21 M12
Temuco, *Chile* 128 A2
Temuka, *N.Z.* 87 L3
Ten Boer, *Neths.* 16 B9
Tena, *Ecuador* 120 D2
Tenabo, *Mexico* 115 C6
Tenaha, *U.S.A.* 109 K7
Tenali, *India* 60 L12
Tenancingo, *Mexico* 115 D5
Tenango, *Mexico* 115 D5
Tenasserim, *Burma* 59 F2
Tenasserim □, *Burma* 58 F2
Tenay, *France* 27 C9
Tenby, *U.K.* 13 F3
Tenda, Col di, *France* 27 D11
Tendaho, *Ethiopia* 68 E3
Tende, *France* 27 D11
Tendelti, *Sudan* 77 E3
Tendjedi, Adrar, *Algeria* . . . 75 D6
Tendrara, *Morocco* 75 B4
Tendre, Mt., *Switz.* 22 C2
Tendrovskaya Kosa,
  Ukraine 41 J6
Teneida, *Egypt* 76 B2
Tenente Marques →,
  Brazil 125 C6
Ténéré, *Niger* 79 B7
Tenerife, *Canary Is.* 36 F3
Tenerife, Pico, *Canary Is.* . . . 36 G1
Ténès, *Algeria* 75 A5
Teng Xian,
  Guangxi Zhuangzu,
  China 53 F8
Teng Xian, *Shandong,*
  China 51 G9
Tengah □, *Indonesia* 57 E6
Tengah Kepulauan,
  Indonesia 56 F5
Tengchong, *China* 52 E2
Tengchowfu = Penglai,
  China 51 F11
Tenggara □, *Indonesia* 57 E6
Tenggarong, *Indonesia* 56 E5
Tenggol, P., *Malaysia* 59 K4
Tengiz, Ozero, *Kazakhstan* . . 44 D7
Tenigerbad, *Switz.* 23 C7
Tenino, *U.S.A.* 112 D4
Tenkasi, *India* 60 Q10
Tenke, *Shaba, Zaïre* 83 E2
Tenke, *Shaba, Zaïre* 83 E2
Tenkodogo, *Burkina Faso* . . 79 C4
Tenna →, *Italy* 33 E10
Tennant Creek, *Australia* . . . 90 B1
Tennessee □, *U.S.A.* 105 H2
Tennessee →, *U.S.A.* 104 G1
Tenneville, *Belgium* 17 H7
Tennille, *U.S.A.* 105 J4
Tennsift, Oued →,
  Morocco 74 B3
Teno, Pta. de, *Canary Is.* . . 36 F3
Tenom, *Malaysia* 56 C5
Tenosique, *Mexico* 115 D6
Tenryū-Gawa →, *Japan* . . . 49 G8
Tent L., *Canada* 101 A7
Tenterfield, *Australia* 91 D5
Teófilo Otoni, *Brazil* 123 E3
Teotihuacán, *Mexico* 115 D5
Tepa, *Indonesia* 57 F7
Tepalcatepec →, *Mexico* . . . 114 D4
Tepehuanes, *Mexico* 114 B3
Tepic, *Mexico* 114 C4
Tepoca, C., *Mexico* 114 A2
Tequila, *Mexico* 114 C4
Ter →, *Spain* 28 C8
Ter Apel, *Neths.* 16 C10
Téra, *Niger* 79 C5
Tera →, *Spain* 30 D5
Teraina, *Kiribati* 93 G11
Téramo, *Italy* 33 F10
Terang, *Australia* 91 F3
Terborg, *Neths.* 16 E8
Tercan, *Turkey* 67 C9
Tercero →, *Argentina* 126 C3
Terebovlya, *Ukraine* 41 H3
Terek →, *Russia* 43 J8
Terenos, *Brazil* 125 E7
Tereshka →, *Russia* 42 E8
Teresina, *Brazil* 122 C3
Teresinha, *Brazil* 121 C7
Terewah, L., *Australia* 91 D4
Terges →, *Portugal* 31 H3
Tergnier, *France* 25 C10
Terhazza, *Mali* 74 D3
Terheijden, *Neths.* 17 E5
Teridgerie Cr. →,
  Australia 91 E4
Terlizzi, *Italy* 35 A9
Terme, *Turkey* 66 B7
Termez = Termiz,
  Uzbekistan 44 F7
Términi Imerese, *Italy* 34 E6
Términos, L. de, *Mexico* . . . 115 D6
Termiz, *Uzbekistan* 44 F7

Térmoli, *Italy* 33 F12
Ternate, *Indonesia* 57 D7
Terneuzen, *Neths.* 17 F3
Terney, *Russia* 45 E14
Terni, *Italy* 33 F9
Ternitz, *Austria* 21 H6
Ternopil, *Ukraine* 41 H3
Ternopol = Ternopil,
  Ukraine 41 H3
Terowie, *N.S.W., Australia* . . 91 E4
Terowie, *S. Austral.,*
  Australia 91 E2
Terra Bella, *U.S.A.* 113 K7
Terrace, *Canada* 100 C3
Terrace Bay, *Canada* 98 C2
Terracina, *Italy* 34 A6
Terralba, *Italy* 34 C1
Terranova = Ólbia, *Italy* . . . 34 B2
Terranuova Bracciolini,
  Italy 33 E8
Terrasini Favarotta, *Italy* . . . 34 D6
Terrassa = Tarrasa, *Spain* . . 28 D7
Terrasson-la-Villedieu,
  France 26 C5
Terre Haute, *U.S.A.* 104 F2
Terrebonne B., *U.S.A.* 109 L9
Terrecht, *Mali* 75 D4
Terrell, *U.S.A.* 109 J6
Terrenceville, *Canada* 99 C9
Terrick Terrick, *Australia* . . . 90 C4
Terry, *U.S.A.* 108 B2
Terschelling, *Neths.* 16 B6
Tersko-Kumskiy Kanal →,
  Russia 43 H7
Terter = Tärtär →,
  Azerbaijan 43 K8
Teruel, *Spain* 28 E3
Teruel □, *Spain* 28 E4
Tervel, *Bulgaria* 38 F10
Tervola, *Finland* 8 C21
Teryaweyna L., *Australia* . . . 91 E3
Tesanj, *Bos.-H.* 21 L7
Teseney, *Eritrea* 77 D4
Tesha →, *Russia* 42 C6
Teshio, *Japan* 48 B10
Teshio-Gawa →, *Japan* 48 B10
Tesiyn Gol →, *Mongolia* . . . 54 A4
Teslin, *Canada* 100 A2
Teslin →, *Canada* 100 A2
Teslin L., *Canada* 100 A2
Tesouro, *Brazil* 125 D7
Tessalit, *Mali* 79 A5
Tessaoua, *Niger* 79 C6
Tessenderlo, *Belgium* 17 F6
Tessin, *Germany* 18 A8
Tessit, *Mali* 79 B5
Test →, *U.K.* 13 F6
Testa del Gargano, *Italy* . . . 35 A9
Têt →, *France* 26 F7
Tetachuck L., *Canada* 100 C3
Tetas, Pta., *Chile* 126 A1
Tete, *Mozam.* 83 F3
Tete □, *Mozam.* 83 F3
Teterev →, *Ukraine* 41 G6
Teteringen, *Neths.* 17 E5
Teterow, *Germany* 18 B8
Teteven, *Bulgaria* 38 G7
Tethul →, *Canada* 100 A6
Tetiyev, *Ukraine* 41 H5
Teton →, *U.S.A.* 110 C8
Tétouan, *Morocco* 74 A3
Tetovo, *Macedonia* 38 G4
Tetuán = Tétouan,
  Morocco 74 A3
Tetyukhe Pristan, *Russia* . . . 48 B7
Tetyushi, *Russia* 42 C9
Teuco →, *Argentina* 126 B3
Teufen, *Switz.* 23 B8
Teulada, *Italy* 34 D1
Teulon, *Canada* 101 C9
Teun, *Indonesia* 57 F7
Teutoburger Wald,
  Germany 18 C4
Tévere →, *Italy* 33 G9
Teverya, *Israel* 69 C4
Teviot →, *U.K.* 14 F6
Tewantin, *Australia* 91 D5
Tewkesbury, *U.K.* 13 F5
Texada I., *Canada* 100 D4
Texarkana, *Ark., U.S.A.* . . . 109 J8
Texarkana, *Tex., U.S.A.* . . . 109 J7
Texas, *Australia* 91 D5
Texas □, *U.S.A.* 109 K5
Texas City, *U.S.A.* 109 L7
Texel, *Neths.* 16 B5
Texhoma, *U.S.A.* 109 G4
Texline, *U.S.A.* 109 G3
Texoma, L., *U.S.A.* 109 J6
Teykovo, *Russia* 42 B5
Teza →, *Russia* 42 B5
Tezin, *Afghan.* 62 B3
Tezpur, *India* 61 F18
Tezzeron L., *Canada* 100 C4
Teziutlán, *Mexico* 115 D5
Tha-anne →, *Canada* 101 A10
Tha Deua, *Laos* 58 D4
Tha Deua, *Laos* 58 C3
Tha Pla, *Thailand* 58 D3
Tha Rua, *Thailand* 58 E3
Tha Sala, *Thailand* 59 H2
Tha Song Yang, *Thailand* . . 58 D1
Thaba Putsoa, *Lesotho* 85 D4
Thabana Ntlenyana,
  Lesotho 85 D4
Thabazimbi, *S. Africa* 85 C4
Thai Binh, *Vietnam* 58 B6
Thai Hoa, *Vietnam* 58 C5

Thai Muang, *Thailand* 59 H2
Thai Nguyen, *Vietnam* 58 B5
Thailand ■, *Asia* 58 E4
Thailand, G. of, *Asia* 59 G3
Thakhek, *Laos* 58 D5
Thal, *Pakistan* 62 C4
Thal Desert, *Pakistan* 62 D4
Thala, *Tunisia* 75 A6
Thala La, *Burma* 61 E20
Thalabarivat, *Cambodia* 58 F5
Thallon, *Australia* 91 D4
Thalkirch, *Switz.* 23 C8
Thalwil, *Switz.* 23 B7
Thame →, *U.K.* 13 F6
Thames, *N.Z.* 87 G5
Thames →, *Canada* 98 D3
Thames →, *U.K.* 13 F8
Thames →, *U.S.A.* 107 E12
Thamesford, *Canada* 106 C3
Thamesville, *Canada* 106 D3
Than Uyen, *Vietnam* 58 B4
Thane, *India* 60 K8
Thanesar, *India* 62 D7
Thanet, I. of, *U.K.* 13 F9
Thangoo, *Australia* 88 C3
Thangool, *Australia* 90 C5
Thanh Hoa, *Vietnam* 58 C5
Thanh Hung, *Vietnam* 59 H5
Thanh Pho Ho Chi Minh =
  Phanh Bho Ho Chi
  Minh, *Vietnam* 59 G6
Thanh Thuy, *Vietnam* 58 A5
Thanjavur, *India* 60 P11
Thann, *France* 25 E14
Thaon-les-Vosges, *France* . . . 25 D13
Thap Sakae, *Thailand* 59 G2
Thap Than, *Thailand* 58 E2
Thar Desert, *India* 62 F4
Tharad, *India* 62 G4
Thargomindah, *Australia* . . . 91 D3
Tharrawaddy, *Burma* 61 L19
Tharthār, Mileh, *Iraq* 67 E10
Tharthār, W. ath →, *Iraq* . . . 67 E10
Thásos, *Greece* 39 J7
That Khe, *Vietnam* 58 A6
Thatcher, *Ariz., U.S.A.* 111 K9
Thatcher, *Colo., U.S.A.* 109 G2
Thaton, *Burma* 61 L20
Thau, Bassin de, *France* . . . 26 E7
Thaungdut, *Burma* 61 G19
Thayer, *U.S.A.* 109 G9
Thayetmyo, *Burma* 61 K19
Thaynes, *Switz.* 23 A7
Thazi, *Burma* 61 J20
The Alberga →, *Australia* . . . 91 D2
The Bight, *Bahamas* 117 B4
The Coorong, *Australia* . . . 91 F2
The Dalles, *U.S.A.* 110 D3
The English Company's Is.,
  Australia 90 A2
The Frome →, *Australia* . . . 91 D2
The Grampians, *Australia* . . 91 F3
The Great Divide = Great
  Dividing Ra., *Australia* . . 90 C4
The Hague = 's-
  Gravenhage, *Neths.* 16 D4
The Hamilton →, *Australia* . . 91 D2
The Macumba →,
  Australia 91 D2
The Neales →, *Australia* . . . 91 D2
The Officer →, *Australia* . . . 89 E5
The Pas, *Canada* 101 C8
The Range, *Zimbabwe* 83 F3
The Rock, *Australia* 91 F4
The Salt L., *Australia* 91 E3
The Stevenson →,
  Australia 91 D2
The Warburton →,
  Australia 91 D2
Thebes = Thívai, *Greece* . . . 39 L6
Thebes, *Egypt* 76 B3
Thedford, *Canada* 106 C3
Thedford, *U.S.A.* 108 E4
Theebine, *Australia* 91 D5
Thekulthili L., *Canada* 101 A7
Thelon →, *Canada* 101 A8
Thénezay, *France* 24 F6
Thenia, *Algeria* 75 A5
Thenon, *France* 26 C5
Theodore, *Australia* 90 C5
Thepha, *Thailand* 59 J3
Thérain →, *France* 25 C9
Theresa, *U.S.A.* 107 B9
Thermaïkós Kólpos, *Greece* . . 39 J5
Thermopolis, *U.S.A.* 110 E9
Thermopylae P., *Greece* 39 L5
Thessalía □, *Greece* 39 L4
Thessalon, *Canada* 98 C3
Thessaloníki, *Greece* 39 J5
Thessaloníki, Gulf of =
  Thermaïkós Kólpos,
  Greece 39 J5
Thessaly = Thessalía □,
  Greece 39 L4
Thetford, *U.K.* 13 E8
Thetford Mines, *Canada* . . . 99 C5
Theun →, *Laos* 58 C5
Theunissen, *S. Africa* 84 D4
Theux, *Belgium* 17 G7
Thevenard, *Australia* 91 E1
Thiámis →, *Greece* 39 K3
Thiberville, *France* 24 C7
Thibodaux, *U.S.A.* 109 L9
Thicket Portage, *Canada* . . . 101 B9
Thief River Falls, *U.S.A.* . . . 108 A6
Thiel Mts., *Antarctica* 5 E16
Thiene, *Italy* 33 C8

Thiérache, *France* 25 C10
Thiers, *France* 26 C7
Thies, *Senegal* 78 C1
Thiet, *Sudan* 77 F2
Thika, *Kenya* 82 C4
Thikombia, *Fiji* 87 B9
Thille-Boubacar, *Senegal* . . 78 B1
Thimphu, *Bhutan* 61 F16
þingvallavatn, *Iceland* 8 D3
Thionville, *France* 25 C13
Thíra, *Greece* 39 N8
Thirasía, *Greece* 39 N8
Thirsk, *U.K.* 12 C6
Thistle I., *Australia* 91 F2
Thívai, *Greece* 39 L6
Thiviers, *France* 26 C4
Thizy, *France* 27 B8
þjórsá →, *Iceland* 8 E3
Thlewiaza →, *Man.,*
  Canada 101 B8
Thlewiaza →, *N.W.T.,*
  Canada 101 A10
Thmar Puok, *Cambodia* . . . 58 F4
Tho Vinh, *Vietnam* 58 C5
Thoa →, *Canada* 101 A7
Thoen, *Thailand* 58 D2
Thoeng, *Thailand* 58 C3
Thoissey, *France* 27 B8
Tholdi, *Pakistan* 63 B7
Tholen, *Neths.* 17 E4
Thomas, *Okla., U.S.A.* 109 H5
Thomas, *W. Va., U.S.A.* . . . 104 F6
Thomas, L., *Australia* 91 D2
Thomaston, *U.S.A.* 105 J3
Thomasville, *Ala., U.S.A.* . . 105 K2
Thomasville, *Ga., U.S.A.* . . . 105 K3
Thomasville, *N.C., U.S.A.* . . 105 H5
Thommen, *Belgium* 17 H8
Thompson, *Canada* 101 B9
Thompson, *U.S.A.* 111 G9
Thompson →, *Canada* 100 C4
Thompson →, *U.S.A.* 108 F8
Thompson Falls, *U.S.A.* . . . 110 C6
Thompson Landing,
  Canada 101 A6
Thompson Pk., *U.S.A.* 110 F2
Thomson's Falls =
  Nyahururu, *Kenya* 82 B4
Thon Buri, *Thailand* 59 F3
Thônes, *France* 27 C10
Thonon-les-Bains, *France* . . . 27 B10
Thorez, *Ukraine* 41 H10
þórisvatn, *Iceland* 8 D4
Thornaby on Tees, *U.K.* . . . 12 C6
Thornbury, *Canada* 106 B4
Thorold, *Canada* 106 C5
þórshöfn, *Iceland* 8 C6
Thouarcé, *France* 24 E6
Thouars, *France* 24 F6
Thouet →, *France* 24 E6
Thouin, C., *Australia* 88 D2
Thousand Oaks, *U.S.A.* . . . 113 L8
Thrace, *Turkey* 66 B2
Thrakikón Pélagos, *Greece* . . 39 J8
Three Forks, *U.S.A.* 110 D8
Three Hills, *Canada* 100 C6
Three Hummock I.,
  Australia 90 G3
Three Points, C., *Ghana* . . . 78 E4
Three Rivers, *Australia* . . . 89 E2
Three Rivers, *Calif.,*
  U.S.A. 112 J8
Three Rivers, *Tex., U.S.A.* . . 109 L5
Three Sisters, *U.S.A.* 110 D3
Throssell, L., *Australia* 89 E3
Throssell Ra., *Australia* 88 D3
Thuan Hoa, *Vietnam* 59 H5
Thubun Lakes, *Canada* 101 A6
Thueyts, *France* 27 D8
Thuillies, *Belgium* 17 H4
Thuin, *Belgium* 17 H4
Thuir, *France* 26 F6
Thule, *Greenland* 4 B4
Thun, *Switz.* 22 C5
Thundelarra, *Australia* 89 E2
Thunder B., *U.S.A.* 106 B1
Thunder Bay, *Canada* 98 C2
Thunersee, *Switz.* 22 C5
Thung Song, *Thailand* 59 H2
Thunkar, *Bhutan* 61 F17
Thuong Tra, *Vietnam* 58 D6
Thur →, *Switz.* 23 A8
Thurgau □, *Switz.* 23 A8
Thüringen □, *Germany* 18 E7
Thüringer Wald, *Germany* . . 18 E7
Thurles, *Ireland* 15 D4
Thurloo Downs, *Australia* . . 91 D3
Thurn P., *Austria* 19 H8
Thursday I., *Australia* 90 A3
Thurso, *Canada* 98 C4
Thurso, *U.K.* 14 C5
Thurston I., *Antarctica* 5 D16
Thury-Harcourt, *France* 24 D6
Thusis, *Switz.* 23 C8
Thutade L., *Canada* 100 B3
Thyborøn, *Denmark* 9 H2
Thylungra, *Australia* 91 D3
Thyolo, *Malawi* 83 F4
Thysville = Mbanza
  Ngungu, *Zaïre* 80 F2
Ti-n-Barraouene, O. →,
  Africa 79 B5
Ti-n-Medjerdam, O. →,
  Algeria 75 C5

Ti-n-Tarabine, O.

Ti-n-Tarabine, O. →, *Algeria* 75 D6
Ti-n-Zaouaténe, *Algeria* 75 E5
Tia, *Australia* 91 E5
Tiahuanacu, *Bolivia* 124 D4
Tian Shan, *China* 54 B3
Tianchang, *China* 53 A12
Tiandong, *China* 52 F6
Tian'e, *China* 52 E6
Tianguá, *Brazil* 122 B3
Tianhe, *China* 52 E7
Tianjin, *China* 51 E9
Tiankoura, *Burkina Faso* 78 C4
Tianlin, *China* 52 E6
Tianmen, *China* 53 B9
Tianquan, *China* 52 B4
Tianshui, *China* 50 G3
Tiantai, *China* 53 C13
Tianyang, *China* 52 F6
Tianzhen, *China* 50 D8
Tianzhu, *China* 52 D7
Tianzhuangtai, *China* 51 D12
Tiaret, *Algeria* 75 A5
Tiassalé, *Ivory C.* 78 D4
Tibagi, *Brazil* 127 A5
Tibagi →, *Brazil* 127 A5
Tibati, *Cameroon* 79 D7
Tiber = Tévere →, *Italy* 33 G9
Tiber Reservoir, *U.S.A.* 110 B8
Tiberias = Teverya, *Israel* 69 C4
Tiberias, L. = Yam Kinneret, *Israel* 69 C4
Tibesti, *Chad* 73 D8
Tibet = Xizang □, *China* 54 C3
Tibiao, *Phil.* 55 F5
Tibiri, *Niger* 79 C6
Ţibleş, *Romania* 38 B7
Tibnī, *Syria* 67 E8
Tibooburra, *Australia* 91 D3
Tibro, *Sweden* 11 F8
Tibugá, G. de, *Colombia* 120 B2
Tiburón, *Mexico* 114 B2
Ticao I., *Phil.* 55 E5
Tîchît, *Mauritania* 78 B3
Tichla, *Mauritania* 74 D2
Ticho, *Ethiopia* 77 F4
Ticino □, *Switz.* 23 D7
Ticino →, *Italy* 32 C6
Ticonderoga, *U.S.A.* 107 C11
Ticul, *Mexico* 115 C7
Tidaholm, *Sweden* 11 F7
Tiddim, *Burma* 61 H18
Tideridjaouine, Adrar, *Algeria* 75 D5
Tidikelt, *Algeria* 75 C5
Tidjikja, *Mauritania* 78 B2
Tidore, *Indonesia* 57 D7
Tiébissou, *Ivory C.* 78 D3
Tiefencastel, *Switz.* 23 C9
Tiel, *Neths.* 16 E6
Tiel, *Senegal* 78 C1
Tieling, *China* 51 C12
Tielt, *Belgium* 17 F2
Tien Shan, *Asia* 46 E11
Tien-tsin = Tianjin, *China* 51 E9
Tien Yen, *Vietnam* 58 B6
T'ienching = Tianjin, *China* 51 E9
Tienen, *Belgium* 17 G5
Tiénigbé, *Ivory C.* 78 D3
Tientsin = Tianjin, *China* 51 E9
Tierra Amarilla, *Chile* 126 B1
Tierra Amarilla, *U.S.A.* 111 H10
Tierra Colorada, *Mexico* 115 D5
Tierra de Barros, *Spain* 31 G4
Tierra de Campos, *Spain* 30 C6
Tierra del Fuego □, *Argentina* 128 D3
Tierra del Fuego, I. Gr. de, *Argentina* 128 D3
Tierralta, *Colombia* 120 B2
Tiétar →, *Spain* 30 F4
Tieté →, *Brazil* 127 A5
Tieyon, *Australia* 91 D1
Tifarati, *W. Sahara* 74 C2
Tiffin, *U.S.A.* 104 E4
Tiflèt, *Morocco* 74 B3
Tiflis = Tbilisi, *Georgia* 43 K7
Tifton, *U.S.A.* 105 K4
Tifu, *Indonesia* 57 E7
Tighina, *Moldova* 41 J5
Tigil, *Russia* 45 D16
Tignish, *Canada* 99 C7
Tigray □, *Ethiopia* 77 E4
Tigre →, *Peru* 120 D3
Tigre →, *Venezuela* 121 B5
Tigris = Dijlah, Nahr →, *Asia* 64 D5
Tiguentourine, *Algeria* 75 C6
Tigyaing, *Burma* 61 H20
Tigzerte, O. →, *Morocco* 74 C3
Tîh, Gebel el, *Egypt* 76 J8
Tihodaine, Dunes de, *Algeria* 75 C6
Tijesno, *Croatia* 33 E12
Tījī, *Libya* 75 B7
Tijuana, *Mexico* 113 N9
Tikal, *Guatemala* 116 C2
Tikamgarh, *India* 63 G8
Tikhoretsk, *Russia* 43 H5
Tikhvin, *Russia* 40 C7
Tikkadouine, Adrar, *Algeria* 75 D5
Tiko, *Cameroon* 79 E6
Tikrīt, *Iraq* 67 E10
Tiksi, *Russia* 45 B13
Tilamuta, *Indonesia* 57 D6
Tilburg, *Neths.* 17 E6
Tilbury, *Canada* 98 D3
Tilbury, *U.K.* 13 F8
Tilcara, *Argentina* 126 A2
Tilden, *Nebr., U.S.A.* 108 D6
Tilden, *Tex., U.S.A.* 109 L5
Tilemses, *Niger* 79 B5
Tilemsi, Vallée du, *Mali* 79 B5
Tilhar, *India* 63 F8
Tilia, O. →, *Algeria* 75 C5
Tilichiki, *Russia* 45 C17
Tililane, *Algeria* 75 C4
Tílissos, *Greece* 37 D7
Till →, *U.K.* 12 B5
Tillabéri, *Niger* 79 C5
Tillamook, *U.S.A.* 110 D2
Tillberga, *Sweden* 10 E10
Tillia, *Niger* 79 B5
Tillsonburg, *Canada* 98 D3
Tillyeria □, *Cyprus* 37 D11
Tîlos, *Greece* 39 N10
Tilpa, *Australia* 91 E3
Tilrhemt, *Algeria* 75 B5
Tilsit = Sovetsk, *Russia* 9 J19
Tilt →, *U.K.* 14 E5
Tilton, *U.S.A.* 107 C13
Timagami L., *Canada* 98 C3
Timaru, *N.Z.* 87 L3
Timashevo, *Russia* 42 D10
Timashevsk, *Russia* 43 H4
Timau, *Italy* 33 B10
Timau, *Kenya* 82 B4
Timbákion, *Greece* 37 D6
Timbaúba, *Brazil* 122 C4
Timbedgha, *Mauritania* 78 B3
Timber Lake, *U.S.A.* 108 C4
Timber Mt., *U.S.A.* 112 H10
Timbío, *Colombia* 120 C2
Timbiqui, *Colombia* 120 C2
Timboon, *Australia* 91 F3
Timbuktu = Tombouctou, *Mali* 78 B4
Timellouline, *Algeria* 75 C6
Timétrine Montagnes, *Mali* 79 B4
Timfristós, Óros, *Greece* 39 L4
Timhadit, *Morocco* 74 B3
Timi, *Cyprus* 37 E11
Timia, *Niger* 79 B6
Timimoun, *Algeria* 75 C5
Timiş = Tamis →, *Serbia, Yug.* 38 E3
Timişoara, *Romania* 38 D4
Timmins, *Canada* 98 C3
Timok →, *Serbia, Yug.* 21 L12
Timon, *Brazil* 122 C3
Timor, *Indonesia* 57 F7
Timor □, *Indonesia* 57 F7
Timor Sea, *Ind. Oc.* 88 B4
Tin Alkoum, *Algeria* 75 D7
Tin Gornai, *Mali* 79 B4
Tin Mt., *U.S.A.* 112 J9
Tîna, Khalîg el, *Egypt* 76 H8
Tinaca Pt., *Phil.* 55 J6
Tinaco, *Venezuela* 120 B4
Tinafak, O. →, *Algeria* 75 C6
Tinajo, *Canary Is.* 36 E6
Tinaquillo, *Venezuela* 120 B4
Tinca, *Romania* 38 C4
Tinchebray, *France* 24 D6
Tindouf, *Algeria* 74 C3
Tinée →, *France* 27 E11
Tineo, *Spain* 30 B4
Tinerhir, *Morocco* 74 B3
Tinfouchi, *Algeria* 74 C3
Ting Jiang →, *China* 53 E11
Tinggi, Pulau, *Malaysia* 59 L5
Tinglev, *Denmark* 11 K3
Tingo Maria, *Peru* 124 B2
Tinh Bien, *Vietnam* 59 G5
Tinharé, I. de, *Brazil* 123 D4
Tinjoub, *Algeria* 72 C3
Tinkurrin, *Australia* 89 F2
Tinnevelly = Tirunelveli, *India* 60 Q10
Tinnoset, *Norway* 10 E3
Tinnsjø, *Norway* 10 E2
Tinogasta, *Argentina* 126 B2
Tínos, *Greece* 39 M8
Tiñoso, C., *Spain* 29 H3
Tinta, *Peru* 124 C3
Tintigny, *Belgium* 17 J7
Tintina, *Argentina* 126 B3
Tintinara, *Australia* 91 F3
Tinto →, *Spain* 31 H4
Tioga, *U.S.A.* 106 E7
Tioman, Pulau, *Malaysia* 59 L5
Tione di Trento, *Italy* 32 B7
Tionesta, *U.S.A.* 106 E5
Tior, *Sudan* 77 F3
Tioulilin, *Algeria* 75 C4
Tipongpani, *India* 61 F19
Tipperary, *Ireland* 15 D3
Tipperary □, *Ireland* 15 D4
Tipton, *U.K.* 13 E5
Tipton, *Calif., U.S.A.* 111 H4
Tipton, *Ind., U.S.A.* 104 E2
Tipton, *Iowa, U.S.A.* 108 E9
Tipton Mt., *U.S.A.* 113 K12
Tiptonville, *U.S.A.* 109 G10
Tiquié →, *Brazil* 120 C4
Tiracambu, Serra do, *Brazil* 122 B2
Tīrān, *Iran* 65 C6
Tīrān, *Si. Arabia* 76 B3
Tirana, *Albania* 39 H2
Tiranë = Tirana, *Albania* 39 H2
Tirano, *Italy* 32 B7
Tiraspol, *Moldova* 41 J5
Tirat Karmel, *Israel* 69 C3
Tiratimine, *Algeria* 75 C5
Tirdout, *Mali* 79 B4
Tire, *Turkey* 66 C2
Tirebolu, *Turkey* 67 B8
Tiree, *U.K.* 14 E2
Tîrgovişte, *Romania* 38 E8
Tîrgu Frumos, *Romania* 38 B10
Tîrgu-Jiu, *Romania* 38 D6
Tîrgu Mureş, *Romania* 38 C7
Tîrgu Neamţ, *Romania* 38 B9
Tîrgu Ocna, *Romania* 38 C9
Tîrgu Secuiesc, *Romania* 38 D9
Tirich Mir, *Pakistan* 60 A7
Tiriolo, *Italy* 35 D9
Tiririca, Serra da, *Brazil* 123 E2
Tiris, *W. Sahara* 74 D2
Tîrnava Mare →, *Romania* 38 C7
Tîrnava Mică →, *Romania* 38 C7
Tîrnăveni, *Romania* 38 C7
Tírnavos, *Greece* 39 K5
Tirodi, *India* 60 J11
Tiros, *Brazil* 123 E2
Tirschenreuth, *Germany* 19 F8
Tirso →, *Italy* 34 C1
Tirso, L. del, *Italy* 34 B1
Tiruchchirappalli, *India* 60 P11
Tirunelveli, *India* 60 Q10
Tirupati, *India* 60 N11
Tiruppur, *India* 60 P10
Tiruvannamalai, *India* 60 N11
Tisa →, *Serbia, Yug.* 21 J10
Tisdale, *Canada* 101 C8
Tishomingo, *U.S.A.* 109 H6
Tisnaren, *Sweden* 10 F9
Tisovec, *Slovak Rep.* 20 G9
Tissemsilt, *Algeria* 75 A5
Tissint, *Morocco* 74 C3
Tissø, *Denmark* 11 J5
Tisza = Tisa →, *Serbia, Yug.* 21 J10
Tiszafüred, *Hungary* 21 H10
Tiszavasvári, *Hungary* 21 H11
Tit, *Ahaggar, Algeria* 75 D6
Tit, *Tademait, Algeria* 75 C5
Tit-Ary, *Russia* 45 B13
Titaguas, *Spain* 28 F3
Titel, *Serbia, Yug.* 21 K10
Tithwal, *Pakistan* 63 B5
Titicaca, L., *S. Amer.* 124 D4
Titiwa, *Nigeria* 79 C7
Titlis, *Switz.* 23 C6
Titograd = Podgorica, *Montenegro, Yug.* 21 N9
Titov Veles, *Macedonia* 39 H4
Titova Korenica, *Croatia* 33 D12
Titova-Mitrovica, *Serbia, Yug.* 21 N10
Titovo Užice, *Serbia, Yug.* 21 M9
Titule, *Zaïre* 82 B2
Titumate, *Colombia* 120 B2
Titusville, *Fla., U.S.A.* 105 L5
Titusville, *Pa., U.S.A.* 106 E5
Tivaouane, *Senegal* 78 C1
Tiveden, *Sweden* 11 F8
Tiverton, *U.K.* 13 G4
Tívoli, *Italy* 33 G9
Tiyo, *Eritrea* 77 E5
Tizga, *Morocco* 74 B3
Ti'zi N'Isli, *Morocco* 74 B3
Tizi-Ouzou, *Algeria* 75 A5
Tizimín, *Mexico* 115 C7
Tiznados →, *Venezuela* 120 B4
Tiznit, *Morocco* 74 C3
Tjeggelvas, *Sweden* 8 C17
Tjeukemeer, *Neths.* 16 C7
Tjirebon = Cirebon, *Indonesia* 57 G13
Tjøme, *Norway* 10 E4
Tjonger Kanaal, *Neths.* 16 C7
Tjörn, *Sweden* 11 G5
Tkibuli = Tqibuli, *Georgia* 43 J6
Tkvarcheli = Tqvarcheli, *Georgia* 43 J5
Tlacotalpan, *Mexico* 115 D5
Tlahualilo, *Mexico* 114 B4
Tlaquepaque, *Mexico* 114 C4
Tlaxcala, *Mexico* 115 D5
Tlaxcala □, *Mexico* 115 D5
Tlaxiaco, *Mexico* 115 D5
Tlell, *Canada* 100 C2
Tlemcen, *Algeria* 75 B4
Tleta Sidi Bouguedra, *Morocco* 74 B3
Tlyarata, *Russia* 43 J8
Tmassah, *Libya* 73 C8
Tnine d'Anglou, *Morocco* 74 C3
To Bong, *Vietnam* 58 F7
Toad →, *Canada* 100 B4
Toamasina, *Madag.* 85 B8
Toamasina □, *Madag.* 85 B8
Toay, *Argentina* 126 D3
Toba, *Japan* 49 G8
Toba Kakar, *Pakistan* 62 D3
Toba Tek Singh, *Pakistan* 62 D5
Tobago, *W. Indies* 117 D7
Tobarra, *Spain* 29 G3
Tobelo, *Indonesia* 57 D7
Tobermorey, *Australia* 90 C2
Tobermory, *Canada* 98 C3
Tobermory, *U.K.* 14 E2
Tobin, *U.S.A.* 112 F5
Tobin, L., *Australia* 88 D4
Tobin L., *Canada* 101 C8
Toblach = Dobbiaco, *Italy* 33 B9
Toboali, *Indonesia* 56 E3
Tobol, *Kazakhstan* 44 D7
Tobol →, *Russia* 44 D7
Toboli, *Indonesia* 57 E6
Tobolsk, *Russia* 44 D7
Tobruk = Tubruq, *Libya* 73 B9
Tobyhanna, *U.S.A.* 107 E9
Tobyl = Tobol →, *Russia* 44 D7
Tocache Nuevo, *Peru* 124 B2
Tocantínia, *Brazil* 122 C2
Tocantinópolis, *Brazil* 122 C2
Tocantins □, *Brazil* 122 D2
Tocantins →, *Brazil* 122 B2
Toccoa, *U.S.A.* 105 H4
Toce →, *Italy* 32 C5
Tochigi, *Japan* 49 F9
Tochigi □, *Japan* 49 F9
Tocina, *Spain* 31 H5
Tocopilla, *Chile* 126 A1
Tocumwal, *Australia* 91 F4
Tocuyo →, *Venezuela* 120 A4
Tocuyo de la Costa, *Venezuela* 120 A4
Todd →, *Australia* 90 C2
Todeli, *Indonesia* 57 E6
Todenyang, *Kenya* 82 B4
Todi, *Italy* 33 F9
Tödi, *Switz.* 23 C7
Todos os Santos, B. de, *Brazil* 123 D4
Todos Santos, *Mexico* 114 C2
Todtnau, *Germany* 19 H3
Toecé, *Burkina Faso* 79 C4
Tofield, *Canada* 100 C6
Tofino, *Canada* 100 D3
Töfsingdalens nationalpark, *Sweden* 10 B6
Toftlund, *Denmark* 11 J3
Tofua, *Tonga* 87 D11
Tōgane, *Japan* 49 G10
Togba, *Mauritania* 78 B2
Toggenburg, *Switz.* 23 B8
Togian, Kepulauan, *Indonesia* 57 E6
Togliatti, *Russia* 42 D9
Togo ■, *W. Afr.* 79 D5
Togtoh, *China* 50 D6
Tohma →, *Turkey* 66 C7
Tōhoku □, *Japan* 48 E10
Toinya, *Sudan* 77 F2
Tojikiston = Tajikistan ■, *Asia* 44 F8
Tojo, *Indonesia* 57 E6
Tōjō, *Japan* 49 G6
Toka, *Guyana* 121 C6
Tokachi-Dake, *Japan* 48 C11
Tokachi-Gawa →, *Japan* 48 C11
Tokaj, *Hungary* 21 G11
Tokala, *Indonesia* 57 E6
Tōkamachi, *Japan* 49 F9
Tokanui, *N.Z.* 87 M2
Tokar, *Sudan* 76 D4
Tokara-Rettō, *Japan* 49 K4
Tokarahi, *N.Z.* 87 L3
Tokashiki-Shima, *Japan* 49 L3
Tokat, *Turkey* 66 B7
Tŏkchŏn, *N. Korea* 51 E14
Tokeland, *U.S.A.* 112 D3
Tokelau Is., *Pac. Oc.* 92 H10
Tokmak, *Kyrgyzstan* 44 E8
Tokmak, *Ukraine* 41 J8
Toko Ra., *Australia* 90 C2
Tokoro-Gawa →, *Japan* 48 B12
Tokuno-Shima, *Japan* 49 L4
Tokushima, *Japan* 49 G7
Tokushima □, *Japan* 49 H7
Tokuyama, *Japan* 49 G5
Tōkyō, *Japan* 49 G9
Tolaga Bay, *N.Z.* 87 H7
Tolbukhin = Dobrich, *Bulgaria* 38 F10
Toledo, *Spain* 30 F6
Toledo, *Ohio, U.S.A.* 104 E4
Toledo, *Oreg., U.S.A.* 110 D2
Toledo, *Wash., U.S.A.* 110 C2
Toledo, Montes de, *Spain* 31 F6
Tolentino, *Italy* 33 E10
Tolga, *Algeria* 75 B6
Tolga, *Norway* 10 B5
Toliara, *Madag.* 85 C7
Toliara □, *Madag.* 85 C8
Tolima, *Colombia* 120 C2
Tolima □, *Colombia* 120 C2
Tolitoli, *Indonesia* 57 D6
Tolkamer, *Neths.* 16 E8
Tolleson, *U.S.A.* 111 K7
Tollhouse, *U.S.A.* 112 H7
Tolmachevo, *Russia* 40 C5
Tolmezzo, *Italy* 33 B10
Tolmin, *Slovenia* 33 B10
Tolo, *Zaïre* 80 E3
Tolo, Teluk, *Indonesia* 57 E6
Tolochin = Talachyn, *Belarus* 40 E5
Tolosa, *Spain* 28 B2
Tolox, *Spain* 31 J6
Toltén, *Chile* 128 A2
Toluca, *Mexico* 115 D5
Tom Burke, *S. Africa* 85 C4
Tom Price, *Australia* 88 D2
Tomah, *U.S.A.* 108 D9
Tomahawk, *U.S.A.* 108 C10
Tomakomai, *Japan* 48 C10
Tomales, *U.S.A.* 112 G4
Tomales B., *U.S.A.* 112 G3
Tomar, *Portugal* 31 F2
Tomarza, *Turkey* 66 C6
Tomás Barrón, *Bolivia* 124 D4
Tomaszów Mazowiecki, *Poland* 20 D9
Tomatlán, *Mexico* 114 D3
Tombador, Serra do, *Brazil* 125 C6
Tombé, *Sudan* 77 F3
Tombigbee →, *U.S.A.* 105 K2
Tombouctou, *Mali* 78 B4
Tombstone, *U.S.A.* 111 L8
Tombua, *Angola* 84 B1
Tomé, *Chile* 126 D1
Tomé-Açu, *Brazil* 122 B2
Tomelilla, *Sweden* 11 J7
Tomelloso, *Spain* 29 F1
Tomingley, *Australia* 91 E4
Tomini, *Indonesia* 57 D6
Tomini, Teluk, *Indonesia* 57 E6
Tominian, *Mali* 78 C4
Tomiño, *Spain* 30 D2
Tomkinson Ras., *Australia* 89 E4
Tommot, *Russia* 45 D13
Tomnavoulin, *U.K.* 14 D5
Tomnop Ta Suos, *Cambodia* 59 G5
Tomo, *Colombia* 120 C4
Tomo →, *Colombia* 120 B4
Tomorit, *Albania* 39 J3
Toms Place, *U.S.A.* 112 H8
Toms River, *U.S.A.* 107 G10
Tomsk, *Russia* 44 D9
Tonalá, *Mexico* 115 D6
Tonale, Passo del, *Italy* 32 B7
Tonalea, *U.S.A.* 111 H8
Tonantins, *Brazil* 120 D4
Tonasket, *U.S.A.* 110 B4
Tonate, *Fr. Guiana* 121 C7
Tonawanda, *U.S.A.* 106 D6
Tonbridge, *U.K.* 13 F8
Tondano, *Indonesia* 57 D6
Tondela, *Portugal* 30 E2
Tønder, *Denmark* 11 K2
Tondi Kiwindi, *Niger* 79 C5
Tondibi, *Mali* 79 B4
Tonekābon, *Iran* 65 B6
Tong Xian, *China* 50 E9
Tonga ■, *Pac. Oc.* 87 D11
Tonga Trench, *Pac. Oc.* 92 J10
Tongaat, *S. Africa* 85 D5
Tong'an, *China* 53 E12
Tongareva, *Cook Is.* 93 H12
Tongatapu, *Tonga* 87 E11
Tongbai, *China* 53 A9
Tongcheng, *Anhui, China* 53 B11
Tongcheng, *Hubei, China* 53 C9
Tongchŏn-ni, *N. Korea* 51 E14
Tongchuan, *China* 50 G5
Tongdao, *China* 52 D7
Tongeren, *Belgium* 17 G6
Tonggu, *China* 53 C10
Tongguan, *China* 50 G6
Tonghai, *China* 52 E4
Tonghua, *China* 51 D13
Tongjiang, *Heilongjiang, China* 54 B8
Tongjiang, *Sichuan, China* 52 B6
Tongjosŏn Man, *N. Korea* 51 E14
Tongking, G. of = Tonkin, G. of, *Asia* 58 B7
Tongliang, *China* 52 C6
Tongliao, *China* 51 C12
Tongling, *China* 53 B11
Tonglu, *China* 53 C12
Tongnae, *S. Korea* 51 G15
Tongnan, *China* 52 B5
Tongobory, *Madag.* 85 C7
Tongoy, *Chile* 126 C1
Tongren, *China* 52 D7
Tongres = Tongeren, *Belgium* 17 G6
Tongsa Dzong, *Bhutan* 61 F17
Tongue, *U.K.* 14 C4
Tongue →, *U.S.A.* 108 B2
Tongwei, *China* 50 G3
Tongxin, *China* 50 F3
Tongyang, *N. Korea* 51 E14
Tongyu, *China* 51 B12
Tongzi, *China* 52 C6
Tonj, *Sudan* 77 F2
Tonk, *India* 62 F6
Tonkawa, *U.S.A.* 109 G6
Tonkin = Bac Phan, *Vietnam* 58 B5
Tonkin, G. of, *Asia* 58 B7
Tonlé Sap, *Cambodia* 58 F4
Tonnay-Charente, *France* 26 C3
Tonneins, *France* 26 D4
Tonnerre, *France* 25 E10
Tönning, *Germany* 18 A4
Tono, *Japan* 48 E10
Tonopah, *U.S.A.* 111 G5
Tonosí, *Panama* 116 E3
Tønsberg, *Norway* 10 E4
Tonya, *Turkey* 67 B8
Tooele, *U.S.A.* 110 F7
Toompine, *Australia* 91 D3
Toonpan, *Australia* 90 B4
Toora, *Australia* 91 F4
Toora-Khem, *Russia* 45 D10
Toowoomba, *Australia* 91 D5
Topalu, *Romania* 38 E11
Topaz, *U.S.A.* 112 G7
Topeka, *U.S.A.* 108 F7
Topki, *Russia* 44 D9
Topl'a →, *Slovak Rep.* 20 G11
Topley, *Canada* 100 C3
Toplica →, *Serbia, Yug.* 21 M11
Topliţa, *Romania* 38 C8
Topocalma, Pta., *Chile* 126 C1
Topock, *U.S.A.* 113 L12
Topola, *Serbia, Yug.* 21 L10

Tuatapere

Topol'čany, *Slovak Rep.* 20 G8
Topolnitsa →, *Bulgaria* 38 G7
Topolobampo, *Mexico* 114 B3
Topolovgrad, *Bulgaria* 38 G9
Toppenish, *U.S.A.* 110 C3
Topusko, *Croatia* 33 C12
Toquepala, *Peru* 124 D3
Torá, *Spain* 28 D6
Tora Kit, *Sudan* 77 E3
Toraka Vestale, *Madag.* 85 B7
Torata, *Peru* 124 D3
Torbalı, *Turkey* 66 C2
Torbay, *Canada* 99 C9
Torbay, *U.K.* 13 G4
Tørdal, *Norway* 10 E2
Tordesillas, *Spain* 30 D6
Tordoya, *Spain* 30 B2
Töreboda, *Sweden* 11 F8
Torgau, *Germany* 18 D8
Torgelow, *Germany* 18 B9
Torhout, *Belgium* 17 F2
Tori, *Ethiopia* 77 F3
Tori-Shima, *Japan* 49 J10
Torigni-sur-Vire, *France* 24 C6
Torija, *Spain* 28 E1
Torin, *Mexico* 114 B2
Toriñana, C., *Spain* 30 B1
Torino, *Italy* 32 C4
Torit, *Sudan* 77 G3
Torkamān, *Iran* 67 D12
Torkovichi, *Russia* 40 C6
Tormes →, *Spain* 30 D4
Tornado Mt., *Canada* 100 D6
Torne älv →, *Sweden* 8 D21
Torneå = Tornio, *Finland* 8 D21
Torneträsk, *Sweden* 8 B18
Tornio, *Finland* 8 D21
Tornionjoki →, *Finland* 8 D21
Tornquist, *Argentina* 126 D3
Toro, *Baleares, Spain* 36 B11
Toro, *Zamora, Spain* 30 D5
Torö, *Sweden* 11 F11
Toro, Cerro del, *Chile* 126 B2
Toro Pk., *U.S.A.* 113 M10
Törökszentmiklós, *Hungary* 21 H10
Toroníos Kólpos, *Greece* 39 J6
Toronto, *Australia* 91 E5
Toronto, *Canada* 98 D4
Toronto, *U.S.A.* 106 F4
Toropets, *Russia* 40 D6
Tororo, *Uganda* 82 B3
Toros Dağları, *Turkey* 66 D5
Torotoro, *Bolivia* 125 D4
Torpshammar, *Sweden* 10 B10
Torquay, *Canada* 101 D8
Torquay, *U.K.* 13 G4
Torquemada, *Spain* 30 C6
Torralba de Calatrava, *Spain* 31 F7
Torrance, *U.S.A.* 113 M8
Torrão, *Portugal* 31 G2
Torre Annunziata, *Italy* 35 B7
Tôrre de Moncorvo, *Portugal* 30 D3
Torre del Greco, *Italy* 35 B7
Torre del Mar, *Spain* 31 J6
Torre-Pacheco, *Spain* 29 H4
Torre Péllice, *Italy* 32 D4
Torreblanca, *Spain* 28 E5
Torrecampo, *Spain* 31 G6
Torrecilla en Cameros, *Spain* 28 C2
Torredembarra, *Spain* 28 D6
Torredonjimeno, *Spain* 31 H7
Torrejoncillo, *Spain* 30 F4
Torrelaguna, *Spain* 28 E1
Torrelavega, *Spain* 30 B6
Torremaggiore, *Italy* 35 A8
Torremolinos, *Spain* 31 J6
Torrens, L., *Australia* 91 E2
Torrens Cr. →, *Australia* 90 C4
Torrens Creek, *Australia* 90 C4
Torrente, *Spain* 29 F4
Torrenueva, *Spain* 29 G1
Torreón, *Mexico* 114 B4
Torreperogil, *Spain* 29 G1
Torres, *Mexico* 114 B2
Torres Novas, *Portugal* 31 F2
Torres Strait, *Australia* 92 H6
Torres Vedras, *Portugal* 31 F1
Torrevieja, *Spain* 29 H4
Torrey, *U.S.A.* 111 G8
Torridge →, *U.K.* 13 G3
Torridon, L., *U.K.* 14 D3
Torrijos, *Spain* 30 F6
Torrington, *Conn., U.S.A.* 107 E11
Torrington, *Wyo., U.S.A.* 108 D2
Torroella de Montgri, *Spain* 28 C8
Torrox, *Spain* 31 J7
Tórshavn, *Færoe Is.* 8 E9
Torsö, *Sweden* 11 F7
Tortola, *Virgin Is.* 117 C7
Tórtoles de Esgueva, *Spain* 30 D6
Tortona, *Italy* 32 D5
Tortoreto, *Italy* 33 F10
Tortorici, *Italy* 35 D7
Tortosa, *Spain* 28 E5
Tortosa, C. de, *Spain* 28 E5
Tortosendo, *Portugal* 30 E3
Tortue, I. de la, *Haiti* 117 B5
Tortum, *Turkey* 67 B9
Ţorūd, *Iran* 65 C7
Torul, *Turkey* 67 B8
Toruń, *Poland* 20 B8
Torup, *Denmark* 11 G3
Torup, *Sweden* 11 H7
Tory I., *Ireland* 15 A3
Torysa →, *Slovak Rep.* 20 G11
Torzhok, *Russia* 42 B2
Tosa, *Japan* 49 H6
Tosa-Shimizu, *Japan* 49 H6
Tosa-Wan, *Japan* 49 H6
Toscana □, *Italy* 32 E8
Toscano, Arcipelago, *Italy* 32 F7
Toshkent, *Uzbekistan* 44 E7
Tosno, *Russia* 40 C6
Tossa, *Spain* 28 D7
Tostado, *Argentina* 126 B3
Tostedt, *Germany* 18 B5
Tostón, Pta. de, *Canary Is.* 36 F5
Tosu, *Japan* 49 H5
Tosya, *Turkey* 66 B6
Totana, *Spain* 29 H3
Toten, *Norway* 10 D4
Toteng, *Botswana* 84 C3
Tôtes, *France* 24 C8
Tótkomlós, *Hungary* 21 J10
Totma, *Russia* 44 C5
Totnes, *U.K.* 13 G4
Totness, *Surinam* 121 B6
Totonicapán, *Guatemala* 116 D1
Totora, *Bolivia* 125 D4
Totten Glacier, *Antarctica* 5 C8
Tottenham, *Australia* 91 E4
Tottenham, *Canada* 106 B5
Tottori, *Japan* 49 G7
Tottori □, *Japan* 49 G7
Touat, *Algeria* 75 C5
Touba, *Ivory C.* 78 D3
Toubkal, Djebel, *Morocco* 74 B3
Toucy, *France* 25 E10
Tougan, *Burkina Faso* 78 C4
Touggourt, *Algeria* 75 B6
Tougué, *Guinea* 78 C2
Toukmatine, *Algeria* 75 D6
Toul, *France* 25 D12
Toulepleu, *Ivory C.* 78 D3
Toulon, *France* 27 E9
Toulouse, *France* 26 E5
Toummo, *Niger* 73 D7
Toumodi, *Ivory C.* 78 D3
Tounassine, Hamada, *Algeria* 74 C3
Toungoo, *Burma* 61 K20
Touques →, *France* 24 C7
Touraine, *France* 24 E7
Tourane = Da Nang, *Vietnam* 58 D7
Tourcoing, *France* 25 B10
Tourine, *Mauritania* 74 D2
Tournai, *Belgium* 17 G2
Tournan-en-Brie, *France* 25 D9
Tournay, *France* 26 E4
Tournon, *France* 27 C8
Tournon-St.-Martin, *France* 24 F7
Tournus, *France* 27 B8
Touros, *Brazil* 122 C4
Tours, *France* 24 E7
Touwsrivier, *S. Africa* 84 E3
Tovar, *Venezuela* 120 B3
Tovarkovskiy, *Russia* 42 D4
Tovdal, *Norway* 11 F2
Tovdalselva →, *Norway* 11 F2
Tovuz, *Azerbaijan* 43 K7
Towada, *Japan* 48 D10
Towada-Ko, *Japan* 48 D10
Towamba, *Australia* 91 F4
Towanda, *U.S.A.* 107 E8
Towang, *India* 61 F17
Tower, *U.S.A.* 108 B8
Towerhill Cr. →, *Australia* 90 C3
Towner, *U.S.A.* 108 A4
Townsend, *U.S.A.* 110 C8
Townshend I., *Australia* 90 C5
Townsville, *Australia* 90 B4
Towson, *U.S.A.* 104 F7
Toya-Ko, *Japan* 48 C10
Toyah, *U.S.A.* 109 K3
Toyahvale, *U.S.A.* 109 K3
Toyama, *Japan* 49 F8
Toyama □, *Japan* 49 F8
Toyama-Wan, *Japan* 49 F8
Toyohashi, *Japan* 49 G8
Toyokawa, *Japan* 49 G8
Toyonaka, *Japan* 49 G7
Toyooka, *Japan* 49 G7
Toyota, *Japan* 49 G8
Tozeur, *Tunisia* 75 B6
Tqibuli, *Georgia* 43 J6
Tqvarcheli, *Georgia* 43 J5
Trá Li = Tralee, *Ireland* 15 D2
Tra On, *Vietnam* 59 H5
Trabancos →, *Spain* 30 D5
Traben-Trarbach, *Germany* 19 F3
Trabzon, *Turkey* 67 B8
Tracadie, *Canada* 99 C7
Tracy, *Calif., U.S.A.* 111 H3
Tracy, *Minn., U.S.A.* 108 C7
Tradate, *Italy* 32 C5
Trafalgar, C., *Spain* 31 J4
Traiguén, *Chile* 128 A2
Trail, *Canada* 100 D5
Trainor L., *Canada* 100 A4
Traíra →, *Brazil* 120 D4
Trákhonas, *Cyprus* 37 D12
Tralee, *Ireland* 15 D2
Tralee B., *Ireland* 15 D2
Tramelan, *Switz.* 22 B4
Tramore, *Ireland* 15 D4
Tran Ninh, Cao Nguyen, *Laos* 58 C4
Tranås, *Sweden* 9 G16
Trancas, *Argentina* 126 B2
Trancoso, *Portugal* 30 E3
Tranebjerg, *Denmark* 11 J4
Tranemo, *Sweden* 11 G7
Trang, *Thailand* 59 J2
Trangahy, *Madag.* 85 B7
Trangan, *Indonesia* 57 F8
Trangie, *Australia* 91 E4
Trångsviken, *Sweden* 10 A8
Trani, *Italy* 35 A9
Tranoroa, *Madag.* 85 C8
Tranqueras, *Uruguay* 127 C4
Trans Nzoia □, *Kenya* 82 B3
Transantarctic Mts., *Antarctica* 5 E12
Transcona, *Canada* 101 D9
Transilvania, *Romania* 38 D8
Transilvanian Alps = Carpaţii Meridionali, *Romania* 38 D8
Transylvania = Transilvania, *Romania* 38 D8
Transylvanian Alps, *Romania* 6 F10
Trápani, *Italy* 34 D5
Trapper Pk., *U.S.A.* 110 D6
Traralgon, *Australia* 91 F4
Trarza, *Mauritania* 78 B2
Trasacco, *Italy* 33 G10
Trăscău, Munţii, *Romania* 38 C6
Trasimeno, L., *Italy* 33 E9
Trat, *Thailand* 59 F4
Traun, *Austria* 21 G4
Traunstein, *Germany* 19 H8
Tråvad, *Sweden* 11 F7
Traveller's L., *Australia* 91 E3
Travemünde, *Germany* 18 B6
Travers, Mt., *N.Z.* 87 K4
Traverse City, *U.S.A.* 104 C3
Travnik, *Bos.-H.* 21 L7
Trayning, *Australia* 89 F2
Trazo, *Spain* 30 B2
Trbovlje, *Slovenia* 33 B12
Trébbia →, *Italy* 32 C6
Trebel →, *Germany* 18 B9
Trebinje, *Bos.-H.* 21 N8
Trebisacce, *Italy* 35 C9
Trebišnica →, *Bos.-H.* 21 N8
Trebišov, *Slovak Rep.* 20 G11
Trebižat →, *Bos.-H.* 21 M7
Trebnje, *Slovenia* 33 C12
Třeboň, *Czech.* 20 G4
Trebujena, *Spain* 31 J4
Trecate, *Italy* 32 C5
Trece Martires, *Phil.* 55 D4
Tredegar, *U.K.* 13 F4
Tregaron, *U.K.* 13 E4
Trégastel-Plage, *France* 24 D3
Tregnago, *Italy* 33 C8
Tregrosse Is., *Australia* 90 B5
Tréguier, *France* 24 D3
Trégunc, *France* 24 E3
Treherne, *Canada* 101 D9
Tréia, *Italy* 33 E10
Treignac, *France* 26 C5
Treinta y Tres, *Uruguay* 127 C5
Treis, *Germany* 19 E3
Trelde Næs, *Denmark* 11 J3
Trelew, *Argentina* 128 B3
Trélissac, *France* 26 C4
Trelleborg, *Sweden* 11 J7
Trélon, *France* 25 B11
Tremiti, *Italy* 33 F12
Tremonton, *U.S.A.* 110 F7
Tremp, *Spain* 28 C5
Trenche →, *Canada* 98 C5
Trenčín, *Slovak Rep.* 20 G8
Trenggalek, *Indonesia* 57 H14
Trenque Lauquen, *Argentina* 126 D3
Trent →, *U.K.* 12 D7
Trentino-Alto Adige □, *Italy* 32 B8
Trento, *Italy* 32 B8
Trenton, *Canada* 98 D4
Trenton, *Mo., U.S.A.* 108 E8
Trenton, *N.J., U.S.A.* 107 F10
Trenton, *Nebr., U.S.A.* 108 E4
Trenton, *Tenn., U.S.A.* 109 H10
Trepassey, *Canada* 99 C9
Trepuzzi, *Italy* 35 B11
Tres Arroyos, *Argentina* 126 D3
Três Corações, *Brazil* 123 F2
Três Lagoas, *Brazil* 123 F1
Tres Lagos →, *Argentina* 128 C2
Tres Marías, *Mexico* 114 C3
Três Marias, Represa, *Brazil* 123 E2
Tres Montes, C., *Chile* 128 C1
Tres Pinos, *U.S.A.* 112 J5
Três Pontas, *Brazil* 123 F2
Tres Puentes, *Chile* 126 B1
Tres Puntas, C., *Argentina* 128 C3
Três Rios, *Brazil* 123 F3
Tres Valles, *Mexico* 115 D5
Treska →, *Macedonia* 39 H4
Trespaderne, *Spain* 28 C1
Trets, *France* 27 E9
Treuchtlingen, *Germany* 19 G6
Treuenbrietzen, *Germany* 18 C8
Trevíglio, *Italy* 32 C6
Trevínca, Peña, *Spain* 30 C4
Treviso, *Italy* 33 C9
Trévoux, *France* 27 C8
Treysa, *Germany* 18 E5
Trgovište, *Serbia, Yug.* 21 N12
Triabunna, *Australia* 90 G4
Triánda, *Greece* 37 C10
Triang, *Malaysia* 59 L4
Triaucourt-en-Argonne, *France* 25 D12
Tribsees, *Germany* 18 A8
Tribulation, C., *Australia* 90 B4
Tribune, *U.S.A.* 108 F4
Tricárico, *Italy* 35 B9
Tricase, *Italy* 35 C11
Trichinopoly = Tiruchchirappalli, *India* 60 P11
Trichur, *India* 60 P10
Trida, *Australia* 91 E4
Trier, *Germany* 19 F2
Trieste, *Italy* 33 C10
Trieste, G. di, *Italy* 33 C10
Trieux →, *France* 24 D3
Triggiano, *Italy* 35 A9
Triglav, *Slovenia* 33 B10
Trigno →, *Italy* 33 F11
Trigueros, *Spain* 31 H4
Trikhonis, Límni, *Greece* 39 L4
Tríkkala, *Greece* 39 K4
Trikomo, *Cyprus* 37 D12
Trikora, Puncak, *Indonesia* 57 E9
Trilj, *Croatia* 33 E13
Trillo, *Spain* 28 E2
Trim, *Ireland* 15 C5
Trincomalee, *Sri Lanka* 60 Q12
Trindade, *Brazil* 123 E2
Trindade, I., *Atl. Oc.* 2 F8
Trinidad, *Bolivia* 125 C5
Trinidad, *Colombia* 120 B3
Trinidad, *Cuba* 116 B3
Trinidad, *Uruguay* 126 C4
Trinidad, *U.S.A.* 109 G2
Trinidad, *W. Indies* 117 D7
Trinidad →, *Mexico* 115 D5
Trinidad, G., *Chile* 128 C1
Trinidad, I., *Argentina* 128 A4
Trinidad & Tobago ■, *W. Indies* 117 D7
Trinitápoli, *Italy* 35 A9
Trinity, *Canada* 99 C9
Trinity, *U.S.A.* 109 K7
Trinity →, *Calif., U.S.A.* 110 F2
Trinity →, *Tex., U.S.A.* 109 L7
Trinity B., *Canada* 99 C9
Trinity Range, *U.S.A.* 110 F4
Trinkitat, *Sudan* 76 D4
Trino, *Italy* 32 C5
Trion, *U.S.A.* 105 H3
Trionto, C., *Italy* 35 C9
Triora, *Italy* 32 E4
Tripoli = Tarābulus, *Lebanon* 69 A4
Tripoli = Tarābulus, *Libya* 75 B7
Tripp, *U.S.A.* 108 D6
Tripura □, *India* 61 H17
Tripylos, *Cyprus* 37 E11
Trischen, *Germany* 18 A4
Tristan da Cunha, *Atl. Oc.* 2 F9
Trivandrum, *India* 60 Q10
Trivento, *Italy* 35 A7
Trnava, *Slovak Rep.* 21 G7
Trochu, *Canada* 100 C6
Trodely I., *Canada* 98 B4
Trogir, *Croatia* 33 E13
Troglav, *Croatia* 33 E13
Trøgstad, *Norway* 10 E5
Tróia, *Italy* 35 A8
Troilus, L., *Canada* 98 B5
Troina, *Italy* 35 E7
Trois Fourches, Cap des, *Morocco* 75 A4
Trois-Pistoles, *Canada* 99 C6
Trois-Rivières, *Canada* 98 C5
Troisvierges, *Belgium* 17 H8
Troitsk, *Russia* 44 D7
Troitsko Pechorsk, *Russia* 44 C6
Trölladyngja, *Iceland* 8 D5
Trollhättan, *Sweden* 11 F6
Trollheimen, *Norway* 10 B3
Trombetas →, *Brazil* 121 D6
Tromsø, *Norway* 8 B18
Trona, *U.S.A.* 113 K9
Tronador, *Argentina* 128 B2
Trøndelag, *Norway* 8 D14
Trondheim, *Norway* 10 A4
Trondheimsfjorden, *Norway* 8 E14
Trönninge, *Sweden* 11 H6
Trönö, *Sweden* 10 C10
Tronto →, *Italy* 33 F10
Troodos, *Cyprus* 66 E5
Troon, *U.K.* 14 F4
Tropea, *Italy* 35 D8
Tropic, *U.S.A.* 111 H7
Tropoja, *Albania* 38 G3
Trossachs, The, *U.K.* 14 E4
Trostan, *U.K.* 15 A5
Trostberg, *Germany* 19 G8
Trostyanets, *Ukraine* 41 G8
Trotternish, *U.K.* 14 D2
Troup, *U.S.A.* 109 J7
Trout →, *Canada* 100 A5
Trout L., *N.W.T., Canada* 100 A4
Trout L., *Ont., Canada* 101 C10
Trout Lake, *Mich., U.S.A.* 98 C2
Trout Lake, *Wash., U.S.A.* 112 E5
Trout River, *Canada* 99 C8
Trouville-sur-Mer, *France* 24 C7
Trowbridge, *U.K.* 13 F5
Troy, *Turkey* 66 C2
Troy, *Ala., U.S.A.* 105 K3
Troy, *Idaho, U.S.A.* 110 C5
Troy, *Kans., U.S.A.* 108 F7
Troy, *Mo., U.S.A.* 108 F9
Troy, *Mont., U.S.A.* 110 B6
Troy, *N.Y., U.S.A.* 107 D11
Troy, *Ohio, U.S.A.* 104 E3
Troyan, *Bulgaria* 38 G7
Troyes, *France* 25 D11
Trpanj, *Croatia* 21 M7
Trstena, *Slovak Rep.* 20 F9
Trstenik, *Serbia, Yug.* 21 M10
Trubchevsk, *Russia* 41 F7
Trucial States = United Arab Emirates ■, *Asia* 65 F7
Truckee, *U.S.A.* 112 F6
Trudfront, *Russia* 43 H8
Trudovoye, *Russia* 48 C6
Trujillo, *Colombia* 120 C2
Trujillo, *Honduras* 116 C2
Trujillo, *Peru* 124 B2
Trujillo, *Spain* 31 F5
Trujillo, *U.S.A.* 109 H2
Trujillo, *Venezuela* 120 B3
Trujillo □, *Venezuela* 120 B3
Truk, *Pac. Oc.* 92 G7
Trumann, *U.S.A.* 109 H9
Trumbull, Mt., *U.S.A.* 111 H7
Trun, *France* 24 D7
Trun, *Switz.* 23 C7
Trundle, *Australia* 91 E4
Trung-Phan, *Vietnam* 58 E7
Truro, *Canada* 99 C7
Truro, *U.K.* 13 G2
Truskavets, *Ukraine* 41 H2
Truslove, *Australia* 89 F3
Trustrup, *Denmark* 11 H4
Truth or Consequences, *U.S.A.* 111 K10
Trutnov, *Czech.* 20 E5
Truyère →, *France* 26 D6
Tryavna, *Bulgaria* 38 G8
Tryon, *U.S.A.* 105 H4
Tryonville, *U.S.A.* 106 E5
Trzcianka, *Poland* 20 B6
Trzebiatów, *Poland* 20 A5
Trzebiez, *Poland* 20 B4
Trzebinia-Siersza, *Poland* 20 E9
Trzebnica, *Poland* 20 D7
Tržič, *Slovenia* 33 B11
Tsagan Aman, *Russia* 43 G8
Tsaratanana, *Madag.* 85 B8
Tsaratanana, Mt. de, *Madag.* 85 A8
Tsarevo = Michurin, *Bulgaria* 38 G10
Tsau, *Botswana* 84 C3
Tsebrykove, *Ukraine* 41 J6
Tselinograd = Aqmola, *Kazakhstan* 44 D8
Tsetserleg, *Mongolia* 54 B5
Tshabong, *Botswana* 84 D3
Tshane, *Botswana* 84 C3
Tshela, *Zaïre* 80 E2
Tshesebe, *Botswana* 85 C4
Tshibeke, *Zaïre* 82 C2
Tshibinda, *Zaïre* 82 C2
Tshikapa, *Zaïre* 80 F4
Tshilenge, *Zaïre* 82 D1
Tshinsenda, *Zaïre* 83 E2
Tshofa, *Zaïre* 82 D2
Tshwane, *Botswana* 84 C3
Tsigara, *Botswana* 84 C4
Tsihombe, *Madag.* 85 D8
Tsimlyansk, *Russia* 43 G6
Tsimlyansk Res. = Tsimlyanskoye Vdkhr., *Russia* 43 F6
Tsimlyanskoye Vdkhr., *Russia* 43 F6
Tsinan = Jinan, *China* 50 F9
Tsineng, *S. Africa* 84 D3
Tsinghai = Qinghai □, *China* 54 C4
Tsingtao = Qingdao, *China* 51 F11
Tsinjomitondraka, *Madag.* 85 B8
Tsiroanomandidy, *Madag.* 85 B8
Tsiteli-Tskaro, *Georgia* 43 K8
Tsivilsk, *Russia* 42 C8
Tsivory, *Madag.* 85 C8
Tskhinvali, *Georgia* 43 J7
Tsna →, *Russia* 42 C6
Tsnori, *Georgia* 43 K7
Tso Moriri, L., *India* 63 C8
Tsodilo Hill, *Botswana* 84 B3
Tsogttsetsiy, *Mongolia* 50 C3
Tsolo, *S. Africa* 85 E4
Tsomo, *S. Africa* 85 E4
Tsu, *Japan* 49 G8
Tsu L., *Canada* 100 A6
Tsuchiura, *Japan* 49 F10
Tsugaru-Kaikyō, *Japan* 48 D10
Tsumeb, *Namibia* 84 B2
Tsumis, *Namibia* 84 C2
Tsuruga, *Japan* 49 G8
Tsurugi-San, *Japan* 49 H7
Tsuruoka, *Japan* 48 E9
Tsushima, *Gifu, Japan* 49 G8
Tsushima, *Nagasaki, Japan* 49 G4
Tsvetkovo, *Ukraine* 41 H6
Tsyelyakhany, *Belarus* 41 F3
Tua →, *Portugal* 30 D3
Tual, *Indonesia* 57 F8
Tuam, *Ireland* 15 C3
Tuamotu Arch. = Tuamotu Is., *Pac. Oc.* 93 J13
Tuamotu Is., *Pac. Oc.* 93 J13
Tuamotu Ridge, *Pac. Oc.* 93 K14
Tuanfeng, *China* 53 B10
Tuanxi, *China* 52 D6
Tuao, *Phil.* 55 C4
Tuapse, *Russia* 43 H4
Tuatapere, *N.Z.* 87 M1

Tuba City

Tuba City, *U.S.A.* 111 H8
Tuban, *Indonesia* 57 G15
Tubarão, *Brazil* 127 B6
Tūbās, *West Bank* 69 C4
Tubau, *Malaysia* 56 D4
Tubbergen, *Neths.* 16 D9
Tübingen, *Germany* 19 G5
Tubize, *Belgium* 17 G4
Tubruq, *Libya* 73 B9
Tubuai Is., *Pac. Oc.* 93 K12
Tuc Trung, *Vietnam* 59 G6
Tucacas, *Venezuela* 120 A4
Tucano, *Brazil* 122 D4
Tuchang, *Taiwan* 53 E13
Tuchodi →, *Canada* 100 B4
Tuchola, *Poland* 20 B7
Tucson, *U.S.A.* 111 K8
Tucumán □, *Argentina* 126 B2
Tucumcari, *U.S.A.* 109 H3
Tucunaré, *Brazil* 125 B6
Tucupido, *Venezuela* 120 B4
Tucupita, *Venezuela* 121 B5
Tucuruí, *Brazil* 122 B2
Tucuruí, Reprêsa de, *Brazil* 122 B2
Tudela, *Spain* 28 C3
Tudela de Duero, *Spain* 30 D6
Tudmur, *Syria* 67 E8
Tudor, L., *Canada* 99 A6
Tudora, *Romania* 38 B9
Tuella →, *Portugal* 30 D3
Tuen, *Australia* 91 D4
Tueré →, *Brazil* 122 B1
Tugela →, *S. Africa* 85 D5
Tuguegarao, *Phil.* 55 C4
Tugur, *Russia* 45 D14
Tuineje, *Canary Is.* 36 F5
Tukangbesi, Kepulauan, *Indonesia* 57 F6
Tukarak I., *Canada* 98 A4
Tukayyid, *Iraq* 64 D5
Tûkh, *Egypt* 76 H7
Tukobo, *Ghana* 78 D4
Tūkrah, *Libya* 73 B9
Tuktoyaktuk, *Canada* 96 B6
Tukums, *Latvia* 9 H20
Tukuyu, *Tanzania* 83 D3
Tula, *Hidalgo, Mexico* 115 C5
Tula, *Tamaulipas, Mexico* 115 C5
Tula, *Nigeria* 79 D7
Tula, *Russia* 42 C3
Tulancingo, *Mexico* 115 C5
Tulare, *U.S.A.* 111 H4
Tulare Lake Bed, *U.S.A.* 111 J4
Tularosa, *U.S.A.* 111 K10
Tulbagh, *S. Africa* 84 E2
Tulcán, *Ecuador* 120 C2
Tulcea, *Romania* 38 D11
Tulchyn, *Ukraine* 41 H5
Tūleh, *Iran* 65 C7
Tulemalu L., *Canada* 101 A9
Tuli, *Indonesia* 57 E6
Tuli, *Zimbabwe* 83 G2
Tulia, *U.S.A.* 109 H4
Ţulkarm, *West Bank* 69 C4
Tullahoma, *U.S.A.* 105 H2
Tullamore, *Australia* 91 E4
Tullamore, *Ireland* 15 C4
Tulle, *France* 26 C5
Tullibigeal, *Australia* 91 E4
Tullins, *France* 27 C9
Tulln, *Austria* 21 G6
Tullow, *Ireland* 15 D4
Tullus, *Sudan* 77 E1
Tully, *Australia* 90 B4
Ţulmaythah, *Libya* 73 B9
Tulmur, *Australia* 90 C3
Tulnici, *Romania* 38 D9
Tulovo, *Bulgaria* 38 G8
Tulsa, *U.S.A.* 109 G7
Tulsequah, *Canada* 100 B2
Tulu Milki, *Ethiopia* 77 F4
Tulu Welel, *Ethiopia* 77 F3
Tulua, *Colombia* 120 C2
Tulun, *Russia* 45 D11
Tulungagung, *Indonesia* 56 F4
Tum, *Indonesia* 57 E8
Tuma, *Russia* 42 C5
Tuma →, *Nic.* 116 D3
Tumaco, *Colombia* 120 C2
Tumaco, Ensenada, *Colombia* 120 C2
Tumatumari, *Guyana* 121 B6
Tumba, *Sweden* 10 E11
Tumba, L., *Zaïre* 80 E3
Tumbarumba, *Australia* 91 F4
Tumbaya, *Argentina* 126 A2
Túmbes, *Peru* 124 A1
Tumbes □, *Peru* 124 A1
Tumbwe, *Zaïre* 83 E2
Tumby Bay, *Australia* 91 E2
Tumd Youqi, *China* 50 D6
Tumen, *China* 51 C15
Tumen Jiang →, *China* 51 C16
Tumeremo, *Venezuela* 121 B5
Tumiritinga, *Brazil* 123 E3
Tumkur, *India* 60 N10
Tummel, L., *U.K.* 14 E5
Tump, *Pakistan* 60 F3
Tumpat, *Malaysia* 59 J4
Tumu, *Ghana* 78 C4
Tumucumaque, Serra, *Brazil* 121 C7
Tumupasa, *Bolivia* 124 C4
Tumut, *Australia* 91 F4
Tumwater, *U.S.A.* 110 C2
Tunas de Zaza, *Cuba* 116 B4
Tunbridge Wells = Royal Tunbridge Wells, *U.K.* 13 F8
Tunceli, *Turkey* 67 C8
Tuncurry, *Australia* 91 E5
Tunduru, *Tanzania* 83 E4
Tunduru □, *Tanzania* 83 E4
Tundzha →, *Bulgaria* 39 H9
Tunga Pass, *India* 61 E19
Tungabhadra →, *India* 60 M11
Tungaru, *Sudan* 77 E3
Tungla, *Nic.* 116 D3
Tungsten, *Canada* 100 A3
Tungurahua □, *Ecuador* 120 D2
Tunguska, Nizhnyaya →, *Russia* 45 C9
Tunia, *Colombia* 120 C2
Tunica, *U.S.A.* 109 H9
Tunis, *Tunisia* 75 A7
Tunis, Golfe de, *Tunisia* 75 A7
Tunisia ■, *Africa* 75 B6
Tunja, *Colombia* 120 B3
Tunkhannock, *U.S.A.* 107 E9
Tunliu, *China* 50 F7
Tunnsjøen, *Norway* 8 D15
Tunungayualok I., *Canada* 99 A7
Tunuyán, *Argentina* 126 C2
Tunuyán →, *Argentina* 126 C2
Tunxi, *China* 53 C12
Tuo Jiang →, *China* 52 C5
Tuolumne, *U.S.A.* 111 H3
Tuolumne →, *U.S.A.* 112 H5
Tuoy-Khaya, *Russia* 45 C12
Tūp Āghāj, *Iran* 67 D12
Tupã, *Brazil* 127 A5
Tupaciguara, *Brazil* 123 E2
Tupelo, *U.S.A.* 105 H1
Tupik, *Russia* 42 C1
Tupik, *Russia* 45 D12
Tupinambaranas, *Brazil* 121 D6
Tupirama, *Brazil* 122 C2
Tupiratins, *Brazil* 122 C2
Tupiza, *Bolivia* 126 A2
Tupman, *U.S.A.* 113 K7
Tupper, *Canada* 100 B4
Tupper Lake, *U.S.A.* 107 B10
Tupungato, Cerro, *S. Amer.* 126 C2
Tuquan, *China* 51 B11
Túquerres, *Colombia* 120 C2
Tura, *Russia* 45 C11
Turabah, *Si. Arabia* 64 D4
Turagua, Serranía, *Venezuela* 121 B5
Tūrān, *Iran* 65 C8
Turan, *Russia* 45 D10
Turayf, *Si. Arabia* 64 D3
Turbenthal, *Switz.* 23 B7
Turégano, *Spain* 30 D6
Turek, *Poland* 20 C8
Turen, *Venezuela* 120 B4
Turfan = Turpan, *China* 54 B3
Turfan Depression = Turpan Hami, *China* 54 B3
Tŭrgovishte, *Bulgaria* 38 F9
Turgutlu, *Turkey* 66 C2
Turhal, *Turkey* 66 B7
Turia →, *Spain* 29 F4
Turiaçu, *Brazil* 122 B2
Turiaçu →, *Brazil* 122 B2
Turin = Torino, *Italy* 32 C4
Turin, *Canada* 100 D6
Turkana □, *Kenya* 82 B4
Turkana, L., *Africa* 82 B4
Turkestan = Türkistan, *Kazakhstan* 44 E7
Túrkeve, *Hungary* 21 H10
Turkey ■, *Eurasia* 66 C7
Turkey Creek, *Australia* 88 C4
Turki, *Russia* 42 D6
Türkistan, *Kazakhstan* 44 E7
Turkmenistan ■, *Asia* 44 F6
Türkoğlu, *Turkey* 66 D7
Turks & Caicos Is. ■, *W. Indies* 117 B5
Turks Island Passage, *W. Indies* 117 B5
Turku, *Finland* 9 F20
Turkwe →, *Kenya* 82 B4
Turlock, *U.S.A.* 111 H3
Turnagain →, *Canada* 100 B3
Turnagain, C., *N.Z.* 87 J6
Turneffe Is., *Belize* 115 D7
Turner, *Australia* 88 C4
Turner, *U.S.A.* 110 B9
Turner Pt., *Australia* 90 A1
Turner Valley, *Canada* 100 C6
Turners Falls, *U.S.A.* 107 D12
Turnhout, *Belgium* 17 F5
Turnor L., *Canada* 101 B7
Tŭrnovo = Veliko Tŭrnovo, *Bulgaria* 38 F8
Turnu Măgurele, *Romania* 38 F7
Turnu Roşu, P., *Romania* 38 D7
Turon, *U.S.A.* 109 G5
Turpan, *China* 54 B3
Turpan Hami, *China* 54 B3
Turriff, *U.K.* 14 D6
Tursāq, *Iraq* 67 F11
Tursi, *Italy* 35 B9
Turtle Head I., *Australia* 90 A3
Turtle L., *Canada* 101 C7
Turtle Lake, *N. Dak., U.S.A.* 108 B4
Turtle Lake, *Wis., U.S.A.* 108 C8
Turtleford, *Canada* 101 C7
Turukhansk, *Russia* 45 C9
Turzovka, *Slovak Rep.* 20 F8
Tuscaloosa, *U.S.A.* 105 J2
Tuscánia, *Italy* 33 F8
Tuscany = Toscana □, *Italy* 32 E8
Tuscola, *Ill., U.S.A.* 104 F1
Tuscola, *Tex., U.S.A.* 109 J5
Tuscumbia, *U.S.A.* 105 H2
Tuskar Rock, *Ireland* 15 D5
Tuskegee, *U.S.A.* 105 J3
Tustna, *Norway* 10 A2
Tutak, *Turkey* 67 C10
Tutayev, *Russia* 42 B4
Tuticorin, *India* 60 Q11
Tutin, *Serbia, Yug.* 21 N10
Tutóia, *Brazil* 122 B3
Tutong, *Brunei* 56 D4
Tutova →, *Romania* 38 C10
Tutrakan, *Bulgaria* 38 E9
Tutshi L., *Canada* 100 B2
Tuttle, *U.S.A.* 108 B5
Tuttlingen, *Germany* 19 H4
Tutuala, *Indonesia* 57 F7
Tutuila, *Amer. Samoa* 87 B13
Tututepec, *Mexico* 115 D5
Tuva □, *Russia* 45 D10
Tuvalu ■, *Pac. Oc.* 92 H9
Tuxpan, *Mexico* 115 C5
Tuxtla Gutiérrez, *Mexico* 115 D6
Tuy, *Spain* 30 C2
Tuy An, *Vietnam* 58 F7
Tuy Duc, *Vietnam* 59 F6
Tuy Hoa, *Vietnam* 58 F7
Tuy Phong, *Vietnam* 59 G7
Tuya L., *Canada* 100 B2
Tuyen Hoa, *Vietnam* 58 D6
Tuyen Quang, *Vietnam* 58 B5
Tūysarkān, *Iran* 67 E13
Tuz Gölü, *Turkey* 66 C5
Ţūz Khurmātū, *Iraq* 67 E11
Tuzla, *Bos.-H.* 21 L8
Tuzlov →, *Russia* 43 G4
Tuzluca, *Turkey* 67 B10
Tvååker, *Sweden* 11 G6
Tvedestrand, *Norway* 11 F2
Tver, *Russia* 42 B2
Tvŭrditsa, *Bulgaria* 38 G8
Twain, *U.S.A.* 112 E5
Twain Harte, *U.S.A.* 112 G6
Tweed, *Canada* 106 B7
Tweed →, *U.K.* 14 F7
Tweed Heads, *Australia* 91 D5
Tweedsmuir Prov. Park, *Canada* 100 C3
Twello, *Neths.* 16 D8
Twentynine Palms, *U.S.A.* 113 L10
Twillingate, *Canada* 99 C9
Twin Bridges, *U.S.A.* 110 D7
Twin Falls, *U.S.A.* 110 E6
Twin Valley, *U.S.A.* 108 B6
Twisp, *U.S.A.* 110 B3
Twistringen, *Germany* 18 C4
Two Harbors, *U.S.A.* 108 B9
Two Hills, *Canada* 100 C6
Two Rivers, *U.S.A.* 104 C2
Twofold B., *Australia* 91 F4
Tyachiv, *Ukraine* 41 H2
Tychy, *Poland* 20 E8
Tykocin, *Poland* 20 B12
Tyler, *U.S.A.* 103 D7
Tyler, *Minn., U.S.A.* 108 C6
Tyler, *Tex., U.S.A.* 109 J7
Tyligul →, *Ukraine* 41 J6
Tylldal, *Norway* 10 B4
Týn nad Vltavou, *Czech.* 20 F4
Tynda, *Russia* 45 D13
Tyne →, *U.K.* 12 C6
Tyne & Wear □, *U.K.* 12 C6
Tynemouth, *U.K.* 12 B6
Tynset, *Norway* 10 B4
Tyre = Sūr, *Lebanon* 69 B4
Tyrifjorden, *Norway* 10 D4
Tyringe, *Sweden* 11 H7
Tyristrand, *Norway* 10 D4
Tyrnyauz, *Russia* 43 J6
Tyrone, *U.S.A.* 106 F6
Tyrrell →, *Australia* 91 F3
Tyrrell, L., *Australia* 91 F3
Tyrrell Arm, *Canada* 101 A9
Tyrrell L., *Canada* 101 A7
Tyrrhenian Sea, *Medit. S.* 34 B5
Tysfjorden, *Norway* 8 B17
Tystberga, *Sweden* 11 F11
Tyub Karagan, Mys, *Kazakhstan* 43 H10
Tyuleni, Ostrova, *Kazakhstan* 43 H10
Tyuleniy, *Russia* 43 H8
Tyuleniy, Mys, *Azerbaijan* 43 K10
Tyumen, *Russia* 44 D7
Tywi →, *U.K.* 13 F3
Tywyn, *U.K.* 13 E3
Tzaneen, *S. Africa* 85 C5
Tzermiádhes, *Greece* 37 D7
Tzermiádhes Neápolis, *Greece* 39 P8
Tzoumérka, Óros, *Greece* 39 K4
Tzukong = Zigong, *China* 52 C5
Tzummarum, *Neths.* 16 B7

U

U Taphao, *Thailand* 58 F3
U.S.A. = United States of America ■, *N. Amer.* 102 C7
Uachadi, Sierra, *Venezuela* 121 C4
Uainambi, *Colombia* 120 C4
Uanda, *Australia* 90 C3
Uarsciek, *Somali Rep.* 68 G4
Uasin □, *Kenya* 82 B4
Uato-Udo, *Indonesia* 57 F7
Uatumã →, *Brazil* 121 D6
Uauá, *Brazil* 122 C4
Uaupés, *Brazil* 120 D4
Uaupés →, *Brazil* 120 C4
Uaxactún, *Guatemala* 116 C2
Ubá, *Brazil* 123 F3
Ubaitaba, *Brazil* 123 D4
Ubangi = Oubangi →, *Zaïre* 80 E3
Ubaté, *Colombia* 120 B3
Ubauro, *Pakistan* 62 E3
Ubaye →, *France* 27 D10
Ubayyiḍ, W. al →, *Iraq* 67 F10
Ube, *Japan* 49 H5
Ubeda, *Spain* 29 G1
Uberaba, *Brazil* 123 E2
Uberaba, L., *Brazil* 125 D6
Uberlândia, *Brazil* 123 E2
Überlingen, *Germany* 19 H5
Ubiaja, *Nigeria* 79 D6
Ubolratna Res., *Thailand* 58 D4
Ubombo, *S. Africa* 85 D5
Ubon Ratchathani, *Thailand* 58 E5
Ubondo, *Zaïre* 82 C2
Ubort →, *Belarus* 41 F5
Ubrique, *Spain* 31 J5
Ubundu, *Zaïre* 82 C2
Ucayali →, *Peru* 124 A3
Uccle, *Belgium* 17 G4
Uchi Lake, *Canada* 101 C10
Uchiura-Wan, *Japan* 48 C10
Uchiza, *Peru* 124 B2
Uchte, *Germany* 18 C4
Uchur →, *Russia* 45 D14
Ucluelet, *Canada* 100 D3
Ucuriş, *Romania* 38 C4
Uda →, *Russia* 45 D14
Udaipur, *India* 62 G5
Udaipur Garhi, *Nepal* 63 F12
Udbina, *Croatia* 33 D12
Uddel, *Neths.* 16 D7
Uddevalla, *Sweden* 11 F5
Uddjaur, *Sweden* 8 D17
Uden, *Neths.* 17 E7
Udgir, *India* 60 K10
Udhampur, *India* 63 C6
Udi, *Nigeria* 79 D6
Údine, *Italy* 33 B10
Udmurtia □, *Russia* 44 D6
Udon Thani, *Thailand* 58 D4
Udupi, *India* 60 N9
Udvoy Balkan, *Bulgaria* 38 G9
Udzungwa Range, *Tanzania* 83 D4
Ueckermünde, *Germany* 18 B10
Ueda, *Japan* 49 F9
Uedineniya, Os., *Russia* 4 B12
Uele →, *Zaïre* 80 D4
Uelen, *Russia* 45 C19
Uelzen, *Germany* 18 C6
Uetendorf, *Switz.* 22 C5
Ufa, *Russia* 44 D6
Uffenheim, *Germany* 19 F6
Ugab →, *Namibia* 84 C1
Ugalla →, *Tanzania* 82 D3
Uganda ■, *Africa* 82 B3
Ugchelen, *Neths.* 16 D7
Ugento, *Italy* 35 C11
Ugep, *Nigeria* 79 D6
Ugie, *S. Africa* 85 E4
Ugijar, *Spain* 29 J1
Ugine, *France* 27 C10
Uglegorsk, *Russia* 45 E15
Uglich, *Russia* 42 B4
Ugljane, *Croatia* 33 E13
Ugolyak, *Russia* 45 C13
Ugra →, *Russia* 42 C3
Ugûn Mûsa, *Egypt* 69 F1
Ugŭrchin, *Bulgaria* 38 F7
Uh →, *Slovak Rep.* 21 G11
Uherske Hradiště, *Czech.* 20 F7
Uhrichsville, *U.S.A.* 106 F3
Uibhist a Deas = South Uist, *U.K.* 14 D1
Uibhist a Tuath = North Uist, *U.K.* 14 D1
Uíge, *Angola* 80 F2
Uijŏngbu, *S. Korea* 51 F14
Ŭiju, *N. Korea* 51 D13
Uinta Mts., *U.S.A.* 110 F8
Uitenhage, *S. Africa* 84 E4
Uitgeest, *Neths.* 16 C5
Uithoorn, *Neths.* 16 D5
Uithuizen, *Neths.* 16 B9
Uitkerke, *Belgium* 17 F2
Újfehértó, *Hungary* 21 H11
Ujhani, *India* 63 F8
Uji-guntō, *Japan* 49 J4
Ujjain, *India* 62 H6
Újpest, *Hungary* 21 H9
Újszász, *Hungary* 21 H10
Ujung Pandang, *Indonesia* 57 F5
Uka, *Russia* 45 D17
Ukara I., *Tanzania* 82 C3
Uke-Shima, *Japan* 49 K4
Ukerewe □, *Tanzania* 82 C3
Ukerewe I., *Tanzania* 82 C3
Ukholovo, *Russia* 42 D5
Ukhrul, *India* 61 G19
Ukhta, *Russia* 44 C6
Ukiah, *U.S.A.* 112 F3
Ukki Fort, *India* 63 C7
Ukmerge, *Lithuania* 9 J21
Ukraine ■, *Europe* 41 H7
Ukwi, *Botswana* 84 C3
Ulaanbaatar, *Mongolia* 45 E11
Ulaangom, *Mongolia* 54 A4
Ulamba, *Zaïre* 83 D1
Ulan Bator = Ulaanbaatar, *Mongolia* 45 E11
Ulan Erge, *Russia* 43 G7
Ulan Khol, *Russia* 43 H8
Ulan Ude, *Russia* 45 D11
Ulanga □, *Tanzania* 83 D4
Ulanów, *Poland* 20 E12
Ulaş, *Turkey* 66 C7
Ulaya, *Morogoro, Tanzania* 82 D4
Ulaya, *Tabora, Tanzania* 82 C3
Ulcinj, *Montenegro, Yug.* 39 H2
Ulco, *S. Africa* 84 D3
Ulefoss, *Norway* 9 G13
Ulfborg, *Denmark* 11 H2
Ulft, *Neths.* 16 E8
Ulhasnagar, *India* 60 K8
Uljma, *Serbia, Yug.* 21 K11
Ulla →, *Spain* 30 C2
Ulladulla, *Australia* 91 F5
Ullånger, *Sweden* 10 B12
Ullapool, *U.K.* 14 D3
Ullared, *Sweden* 11 G6
Ulldecona, *Spain* 28 E5
Ullswater, *U.K.* 12 C5
Ullung-do, *S. Korea* 51 F16
Ulm, *Germany* 19 G5
Ulmarra, *Australia* 91 D5
Ulmeni, *Romania* 38 D9
Ulonguè, *Mozam.* 83 E3
Ulricehamn, *Sweden* 9 H15
Ulrum, *Neths.* 16 B8
Ulsan, *S. Korea* 51 G15
Ulsberg, *Norway* 10 B3
Ulster □, *U.K.* 15 B5
Ulubaria, *India* 63 H13
Ulubat Gölü, *Turkey* 66 B3
Ulubey, *Turkey* 66 C3
Uluborlu, *Turkey* 66 C4
Uluçinar, *Turkey* 66 D6
Uludağ, *Turkey* 66 B3
Uludere, *Turkey* 67 D10
Uluguru Mts., *Tanzania* 82 D4
Ulukışla, *Turkey* 66 D6
Ulungur He →, *China* 54 B3
Uluru = Ayers Rock, *Australia* 89 E5
Ulutau, *Kazakhstan* 44 E7
Ulvenhout, *Neths.* 17 E5
Ulverston, *U.K.* 12 C4
Ulverstone, *Australia* 90 G4
Ulya, *Russia* 45 D15
Ulyanovsk = Simbirsk, *Russia* 42 C9
Ulyasutay, *Mongolia* 54 B4
Ulysses, *U.S.A.* 109 G4
Umag, *Croatia* 33 C10
Umala, *Bolivia* 124 D4
Uman, *Ukraine* 41 H6
Umaria, *India* 61 H12
Umarkot, *Pakistan* 60 G6
Umatilla, *U.S.A.* 110 D4
Umba, *Russia* 44 C4
Umbértide, *Italy* 33 E9
Umbrella Mts., *N.Z.* 87 L2
Umbria □, *Italy* 33 F9
Ume älv →, *Sweden* 8 E19
Umeå, *Sweden* 8 E19
Umera, *Indonesia* 57 E7
Umfuli →, *Zimbabwe* 83 F2
Umgusa, *Zimbabwe* 83 F2
Umka, *Serbia, Yug.* 21 L10
Umkomaas, *S. Africa* 85 E5
Umm ad Daraj, J., *Jordan* 69 C4
Umm al Qaywayn, *U.A.E.* 65 E7
Umm al Qittayn, *Jordan* 69 C5
Umm Arda, *Sudan* 77 D3
Umm Bāb, *Qatar* 65 E6
Umm Bel, *Sudan* 77 E2
Umm Dubban, *Sudan* 77 D3
Umm el Fahm, *Israel* 69 C4
Umm Koweika, *Sudan* 77 E3
Umm Lajj, *Si. Arabia* 64 E3
Umm Merwa, *Sudan* 76 D3
Umm Ruwaba, *Sudan* 77 E3
Umm Sidr, *Sudan* 77 E2
Ummanz, *Germany* 18 A9
Umnak I., *U.S.A.* 96 C3
Umniati →, *Zimbabwe* 83 F2
Umpqua →, *U.S.A.* 110 E1
Umreth, *India* 62 H5
Umtata, *S. Africa* 85 E4
Umuahia, *Nigeria* 79 D6
Umuarama, *Brazil* 127 A5
Umvukwe Ra., *Zimbabwe* 83 F3
Umzimvubu = Port St. Johns, *S. Africa* 85 E4
Umzingwane →, *Zimbabwe* 83 G2
Umzinto, *S. Africa* 85 E5
Una, *India* 62 J4
Una →, *Bos.-H.* 33 C13
Unac →, *Bos.-H.* 33 D13
Unadilla, *U.S.A.* 107 D9
Unalaska, *U.S.A.* 96 C3
'Unāzah, J., *Asia* 67 F8
Uncastillo, *Spain* 28 C3
Uncía, *Bolivia* 124 D4
Uncompahgre Peak, *U.S.A.* 111 G10
Unden, *Sweden* 11 F8
Underbool, *Australia* 91 F3
Undersaker, *Sweden* 10 A7
Undersvik, *Sweden* 10 C10

Varese

Unecha, Russia 41 F7
Uneiuxi →, Brazil 120 D4
Ungarie, Australia 91 E4
Ungarra, Australia 91 E2
Ungava B., Canada 97 C13
Ungava Pen., Canada 97 C12
Ungeny = Ungheni, Moldova 41 J4
Unggi, N. Korea 51 C16
Ungheni, Moldova 41 J4
Ungwatiri, Sudan 77 D4
Uni, Russia 42 B10
União da Vitória, Brazil 127 B5
União dos Palmares, Brazil 122 C4
Unije, Croatia 33 D11
Unimak I., U.S.A. 96 C3
Unini →, Brazil 121 D5
Union, Miss., U.S.A. 109 J10
Union, Mo., U.S.A. 108 F9
Union, S.C., U.S.A. 105 H5
Union, Mt., U.S.A. 111 J7
Union City, Calif., U.S.A. 112 H4
Union City, N.J., U.S.A. 107 F10
Union City, Pa., U.S.A. 106 E5
Union City, Tenn., U.S.A. 109 G10
Union Gap, U.S.A. 110 C3
Union Springs, U.S.A. 105 J3
Uniondale, S. Africa 84 E3
Uniontown, U.S.A. 104 F6
Unionville, U.S.A. 108 E8
United Arab Emirates ■, Asia 65 F7
United Kingdom ■, Europe 7 E5
United States of America ■, N. Amer. 102 C7
Unity, Canada 101 C7
Universales, Mtes., Spain 28 E3
Unjha, India 62 H5
Unnao, India 63 F9
Uno, Ilha, Guinea-Biss. 78 C1
Unst, U.K. 14 A8
Unstrut →, Germany 18 D7
Unter-engadin, Switz. 23 C10
Unterägeri, Switz. 23 B7
Unterkulm, Switz. 22 B6
Unterseen, Switz. 22 C5
Unterwaldner Alpen, Switz. 23 C6
Unuk →, Canada 100 B2
Ünye, Turkey 66 B7
Unzha, Russia 42 A7
Unzha →, Russia 42 B6
Uors, Switz. 23 C8
Uozu, Japan 49 F8
Upa →, Czech. 20 E6
Upata, Venezuela 121 B5
Upemba, L., Zaïre 83 D2
Upernavik, Greenland 4 B5
Upington, S. Africa 84 D3
Upleta, India 62 J4
Upolu, W. Samoa 87 A13
Upper Alkali Lake, U.S.A. 110 F3
Upper Arrow L., Canada 100 C5
Upper Foster L., Canada 101 B7
Upper Hutt, N.Z. 87 J5
Upper Klamath L., U.S.A. 110 E3
Upper Lake, U.S.A. 112 F4
Upper Musquodoboit, Canada 99 C7
Upper Red L., U.S.A. 108 A7
Upper Sandusky, U.S.A. 104 E4
Upper Volta = Burkina Faso ■, Africa 78 C4
Upphärad, Sweden 11 F6
Uppland, Sweden 9 F17
Uppsala, Sweden 10 E11
Upshi, India 63 C7
Upstart, C., Australia 90 B4
Upton, U.S.A. 108 C2
Ur, Iraq 64 D5
Urabá, G. de, Colombia 120 B2
Uracara, Brazil 121 D6
Urad Qianqi, China 50 D5
Urakawa, Japan 48 C11
Ural = Zhayyq →, Kazakhstan 44 E6
Ural, Australia 91 E4
Ural Mts. = Uralskie Gory, Eurasia 44 D6
Uralla, Australia 91 E5
Uralsk = Oral, Kazakhstan 42 E10
Uralskie Gory, Eurasia 44 D6
Urambo, Tanzania 82 D3
Urambo □, Tanzania 82 D3
Urandangi, Australia 90 C2
Uranium City, Canada 101 B7
Uranquinty, Australia 91 F4
Uraricaá →, Brazil 121 C5
Uraricoera →, Brazil 121 C5
Urawa, Japan 49 G9
Uray, Russia 44 C7
'Uray'irah, Si. Arabia 65 E6
Urbana, Ill., U.S.A. 104 E1
Urbana, Ohio, U.S.A. 104 E4
Urbánia, Italy 33 E9
Urbano Santos, Brazil 122 B3
Urbel →, Spain 28 C1
Urbino, Italy 33 E9
Urbión, Picos de, Spain 28 C2
Urcos, Peru 124 C3
Urda, Spain 31 F7
Urdinarrain, Argentina 126 C4
Urdos, France 26 F3
Urdzhar, Kazakhstan 44 E9
Ure →, U.K. 12 C6
Uren, Russia 42 B7
Ures, Mexico 114 B2
Urfa = Sanliurfa, Turkey 67 D8
Urfahr, Austria 21 G4
Urganch, Uzbekistan 44 E7
Urgench = Urganch, Uzbekistan 44 E7
Uri, India 63 B6
Uri □, Switz. 23 C7
Uribante →, Venezuela 120 B3
Uribe, Colombia 120 C3
Uribia, Colombia 120 A3
Uriondo, Bolivia 126 A3
Urique, Mexico 114 B3
Urique →, Mexico 114 B3
Urirotstock, Switz. 23 C7
Urk, Neths. 16 C7
Urla, Turkey 66 C2
Urlati, Romania 38 E9
Urmia = Orūmīyeh, Iran 67 D11
Urmia, L. = Orūmīyeh, Daryācheh-ye, Iran 67 D11
Urner Alpen, Switz. 23 C7
Uroševac, Serbia, Yug. 21 N11
Urrao, Colombia 120 B2
Ursus, Poland 20 C10
Uruaçu, Brazil 123 D2
Uruana, Brazil 123 E2
Uruapan, Mexico 114 D4
Uruará →, Brazil 121 D7
Urubamba, Peru 124 C3
Urubamba →, Peru 124 C3
Urubaxi →, Brazil 121 D5
Urubu →, Brazil 121 D6
Uruçara, Brazil 121 D6
Uruçuí, Brazil 122 C3
Uruçuí, Serra do, Brazil 122 C3
Uruçuí Prêto →, Brazil 122 C3
Urucuia →, Brazil 123 E2
Urucurituba, Brazil 121 D6
Uruguai →, Brazil 127 B5
Uruguaiana, Brazil 126 B4
Uruguay ■, S. Amer. 126 C4
Uruguay →, S. Amer. 126 C4
Urumchi = Ürümqi, China 44 E9
Ürümqi, China 44 E9
Urup →, Russia 43 H5
Urup, Os., Russia 45 E16
Urutaí, Brazil 123 E2
Uryupinsk, Russia 42 E5
Urzhum, Russia 42 B9
Urziceni, Romania 38 E9
Uşak, Turkey 66 C3
Usakos, Namibia 84 C2
Usborne, Mt., Falk. Is. 128 D5
Ušće, Serbia, Yug. 21 M10
Usedom, Germany 18 B9
'Usfān, Si. Arabia 76 C4
Ush-Tobe, Kazakhstan 44 E8
Ushakova, Os., Russia 4 A12
Ushant = Ouessant, I. d', France 24 D1
Ushashi, Tanzania 82 C3
Ushat, Sudan 77 F2
Ushibuka, Japan 49 H5
Ushuaia, Argentina 128 D3
Ushumun, Russia 45 D13
Usk →, U.K. 13 F5
Üsküdar, Turkey 39 H11
Uslar, Germany 18 D5
Usman, Russia 42 D4
Usoke, Tanzania 82 D3
Usolye Sibirskoye, Russia 45 D11
Usoro, Nigeria 79 D6
Uspallata, P. de, Argentina 126 C2
Uspenskiy, Kazakhstan 44 E8
Usquert, Neths. 16 B9
Ussel, France 26 C6
Ussuri →, Asia 48 A7
Ussuriysk, Russia 45 E14
Ussurka, Russia 48 B6
Ust-Aldan = Batamay, Russia 45 C13
Ust Amginskoye = Khandyga, Russia 45 C14
Ust-Bolsheretsk, Russia 45 D16
Ust Buzulukskaya, Russia 42 E6
Ust Chaun, Russia 45 C18
Ust-Donetskiy, Russia 43 G5
Ust'-Ilga, Russia 45 D11
Ust Ilimpeya = Yukti, Russia 45 C11
Ust-Ilimsk, Russia 45 D11
Ust Ishim, Russia 44 D8
Ust-Kamchatsk, Russia 45 D17
Ust-Kamenogorsk = Öskemen, Kazakhstan 44 E9
Ust-Karenga, Russia 45 D12
Ust Khayryuzovo, Russia 45 D16
Ust-Kut, Russia 45 D11
Ust Kuyga, Russia 45 B14
Ust-Labinsk, Russia 43 H4
Ust Luga, Russia 40 C5
Ust Maya, Russia 45 C14
Ust-Mil, Russia 45 D14
Ust Muya, Russia 45 D12
Ust-Nera, Russia 45 C15
Ust-Nyukzha, Russia 45 D13
Ust Olenek, Russia 45 B12
Ust-Omchug, Russia 45 C15
Ust Port, Russia 44 C9
Ust Tsilma, Russia 44 C6
Ust-Tungir, Russia 45 D13
Ust Urt = Ustyurt, Plateau, Asia 44 E6
Ust Vorkuta, Russia 44 C7
Ustaoset, Norway 10 D2
Ustaritz, France 26 E2
Uster, Switz. 23 B7
Ústí nad Labem, Czech. 20 E4
Ústí nad Orlicí, Czech. 20 F6
Ustica, Italy 34 D6
Ustinov = Izhevsk, Russia 44 D6
Ustka, Poland 20 A6
Ustrzyki Dolne, Poland 20 F12
Ustye, Russia 45 D10
Ustyurt, Plateau, Asia 44 E6
Ustyuzhna, Russia 40 C9
Usu, China 54 B3
Usuki, Japan 49 H5
Usulután, El Salv. 116 D2
Usumacinta →, Mexico 115 D6
Usumbura = Bujumbura, Burundi 82 C2
Usure, Tanzania 82 C3
Uta, Indonesia 57 E9
Utah □, U.S.A. 110 G8
Utah, L., U.S.A. 110 F8
Ute Creek →, U.S.A. 109 H3
Utena, Lithuania 9 J21
Ütersen, Germany 18 B5
Utete, Tanzania 82 D4
Uthai Thani, Thailand 58 E3
Uthal, Pakistan 62 G2
Utiariti, Brazil 125 C6
Utica, N.Y., U.S.A. 107 C9
Utica, Ohio, U.S.A. 106 F2
Utiel, Spain 28 F3
Utik L., Canada 101 B9
Utikuma L., Canada 100 B5
Utinga, Brazil 123 D3
Utrecht, Neths. 16 D6
Utrecht, S. Africa 85 D5
Utrecht □, Neths. 16 D6
Utrera, Spain 31 H5
Utsjoki, Finland 8 B22
Utsunomiya, Japan 49 F9
Uttar Pradesh □, India 63 F9
Uttaradit, Thailand 58 D3
Uttoxeter, U.K. 12 E6
Ütze, Germany 18 C6
Uummannarsuaq = Farvel, Kap, Greenland 4 D5
Uusikaarlepyy, Finland 8 E20
Uusikaupunki, Finland 9 F19
Uva, Russia 42 B11
Uvá →, Colombia 120 C3
Uvalde, U.S.A. 109 L5
Uvarovo, Russia 42 E6
Uvat, Russia 44 D7
Uvinza, Tanzania 82 D3
Uvira, Zaïre 82 C2
Uvs Nuur, Mongolia 54 A4
Uwajima, Japan 49 H6
Uweinat, Jebel, Sudan 76 C1
Uxbridge, Canada 106 B5
Uxin Qi, China 50 E5
Uxmal, Mexico 115 C7
Uyandi, Russia 45 C15
Uyo, Nigeria 79 D6
Uyuni, Bolivia 124 E4
Uzbekistan ■, Asia 44 E7
Uzen, Bolshoi →, Kazakhstan 43 F9
Uzen, Mal →, Kazakhstan 43 F9
Uzerche, France 26 C5
Uzès, France 27 D8
Uzh →, Ukraine 41 G6
Uzhgorod = Uzhhorod, Ukraine 41 H2
Uzhhorod, Ukraine 41 H2
Uzlovaya, Russia 42 D4
Uzunköprü, Turkey 66 B2
Uzwil, Switz. 23 B8

V

Vaal →, S. Africa 84 D3
Vaal Dam, S. Africa 85 D4
Vaals, Neths. 17 G8
Vaalwater, S. Africa 85 C4
Vaasa, Finland 8 E19
Vaassen, Neths. 16 D7
Vabre, France 26 E6
Vác, Hungary 21 H9
Vacaria, Brazil 127 B5
Vacaville, U.S.A. 112 G5
Vaccarès, Étang de, France 27 E8
Vach = Vakh →, Russia 44 C8
Vache, I.-à-, Haiti 117 C5
Vadnagar, India 62 H5
Vado Lígure, Italy 32 D5
Vadodara, India 62 H5
Vadsø, Norway 8 A23
Vadstena, Sweden 11 F8
Vaduz, Liech. 23 B9
Værøy, Norway 8 C15
Vágar, Færoe Is. 8 E9
Vagney, France 25 E13
Vagnhärad, Sweden 10 F11
Vagos, Portugal 30 E2
Vågsfjorden, Norway 8 B17
Váh →, Slovak Rep. 21 H8
Vahsel B., Antarctica 5 D1
Váï, Greece 37 D8
Vaigach, Russia 44 B6
Vaiges, France 24 D6
Vaihingen, Germany 19 G4
Vailly-sur-Aisne, France 25 C10
Vaison-la-Romaine, France 27 D9
Vakfikebir, Turkey 67 B8
Vakh →, Russia 44 C8
Vakhtan, Russia 42 B8
Val-de-Marne □, France 25 D9
Val-d'Oise □, France 25 C9
Val d'Or, Canada 98 C4
Val Marie, Canada 101 D7
Valaam, Russia 40 B6
Valadares, Portugal 30 D2
Valahia, Romania 38 E8
Valais □, Switz. 22 D5
Valais, Alpes du, Switz. 22 D5
Valandovo, Macedonia 39 H5
Valcheta, Argentina 128 B3
Valdagno, Italy 33 C8
Valdahon, France 25 E13
Valday, Russia 42 B1
Valdayskaya Vozvyshennost, Russia 42 B1
Valdeazogues →, Spain 31 G6
Valdemarsvik, Sweden 11 F10
Valdepeñas, Ciudad Real, Spain 31 G7
Valdepeñas, Jaén, Spain 31 H7
Valderaduey →, Spain 30 D5
Valderrobres, Spain 28 E5
Valdés, Pen., Argentina 128 B4
Valdez, Ecuador 120 C2
Valdez, U.S.A. 96 B5
Valdivia, Chile 128 A2
Valdivia, Colombia 120 B2
Valdivia □, Chile 128 B2
Valdobbiádene, Italy 33 C9
Valdosta, U.S.A. 105 K4
Valdoviño, Spain 30 B2
Valdres, Norway 10 D3
Vale, Georgia 43 K6
Vale, U.S.A. 110 E5
Valea lui Mihai, Romania 38 B5
Valença, Brazil 123 D4
Valença, Portugal 30 C2
Valença do Piauí, Brazil 122 C3
Valençay, France 25 E8
Valence, Drôme, France 27 D8
Valence, Tarn-et-Garonne, France 26 D4
Valencia, Spain 29 F4
Valencia, Venezuela 120 A4
Valencia □, Spain 29 F4
Valencia, G. de, Spain 29 F5
Valencia de Alcántara, Spain 31 F3
Valencia de Don Juan, Spain 30 C5
Valencia del Ventoso, Spain 31 G4
Valencia Harbour, Ireland 15 E1
Valencia I., Ireland 15 E1
Valenciennes, France 25 B10
Valensole, France 27 E9
Valentim, Sa. do, Brazil 122 C3
Valentin, Russia 48 C7
Valentine, Nebr., U.S.A. 108 D4
Valentine, Tex., U.S.A. 109 K2
Valenza, Italy 32 C5
Valera, Venezuela 120 B3
Valga, Estonia 9 H22
Valguarnera Caropepe, Italy 35 E7
Valier, U.S.A. 110 B7
Valinco, G. de, France 27 G12
Valjevo, Serbia, Yug. 21 L9
Valka, Latvia 9 H21
Valkeakoski, Finland 9 F20
Valkenburg, Neths. 17 G7
Valkenswaard, Neths. 17 F6
Vall de Uxó, Spain 28 F4
Valla, Sweden 10 E10
Valladolid, Mexico 115 C7
Valladolid, Spain 30 D6
Valladolid □, Spain 30 D6
Vallata, Italy 35 A8
Valldemosa, Spain 36 B9
Valle d'Aosta □, Italy 32 C4
Valle de Arán, Spain 28 C5
Valle de Cabuérniga, Spain 30 B6
Valle de la Pascua, Venezuela 120 B4
Valle de las Palmas, Mexico 113 N10
Valle de Santiago, Mexico 114 C4
Valle de Suchil, Mexico 114 C4
Valle de Zaragoza, Mexico 114 B3
Valle del Cauca □, Colombia 120 C2
Valle Fértil, Sierra del, Argentina 126 C2
Valle Hermoso, Mexico 115 B5
Vallecas, Spain 30 E7
Valledupar, Colombia 120 A3
Vallehermoso, Canary Is. 36 F2
Vallejo, U.S.A. 112 G4
Vallenar, Chile 126 B1
Valleraugue, France 26 D7
Vallet, France 24 E5
Valletta, Malta 37 D2
Valley Center, U.S.A. 113 M9
Valley City, U.S.A. 108 B6
Valley Falls, U.S.A. 110 E3
Valley Springs, U.S.A. 112 G6
Valley Wells, U.S.A. 113 K11
Valleyview, Canada 100 B5
Valli di Comácchio, Italy 33 D9
Vallimanca, Arroyo, Argentina 126 D4
Vallo della Lucánia, Italy 35 B8
Vallon-Pont-d'Arc, France 27 D8
Vallorbe, Switz. 22 C2
Valls, Spain 28 D6
Vallsta, Sweden 10 C10
Valmaseda, Spain 28 B1
Valmiera, Latvia 9 H21
Valmont, France 24 C7
Valmontone, Italy 34 A5
Valmy, France 25 C11
Valnera, Mte., Spain 28 B1
Valognes, France 24 C5
Valona = Vlóra, Albania 39 J2
Valongo, Portugal 30 D2
Valozhyn, Belarus 40 E4
Valpaços, Portugal 30 D3
Valparaíso, Chile 126 C1
Valparaíso, Mexico 114 C4
Valparaiso, U.S.A. 104 E2
Valparaíso □, Chile 126 C1
Valpovo, Croatia 21 K8
Valréas, France 27 D8
Vals, Switz. 23 C8
Vals →, S. Africa 84 D4
Vals, Tanjung, Indonesia 57 F9
Vals-les-Bains, France 27 D8
Valsad, India 60 J8
Valskog, Sweden 10 E9
Válta, Greece 39 J6
Valtellina, Italy 32 B6
Valuyki, Russia 42 E4
Valverde, Canary Is. 36 G2
Valverde del Camino, Spain 31 H4
Valverde del Fresno, Spain 30 E4
Vama, Romania 38 B8
Vammala, Finland 9 F20
Vámos, Greece 37 D6
Van, Turkey 67 C10
Van, L. = Van Gölü, Turkey 67 C10
Van Alstyne, U.S.A. 109 J6
Van Bruyssel, Canada 99 C5
Van Buren, Canada 99 C6
Van Buren, Ark., U.S.A. 109 H7
Van Buren, Maine, U.S.A. 105 B11
Van Buren, Mo., U.S.A. 109 G9
Van Canh, Vietnam 58 F7
Van Diemen, C., N. Terr., Australia 88 B5
Van Diemen, C., Queens., Australia 90 B2
Van Diemen G., Australia 88 B5
Van Gölü, Turkey 67 C10
Van Horn, U.S.A. 109 K2
Van Ninh, Vietnam 58 F7
Van Rees, Pegunungan, Indonesia 57 E9
Van Tassell, U.S.A. 108 D2
Van Wert, U.S.A. 104 E3
Van Yen, Vietnam 58 B5
Vanadzor, Armenia 43 K7
Vanavara, Russia 45 C11
Vancouver, Canada 100 D4
Vancouver, U.S.A. 112 E4
Vancouver, C., Australia 89 G2
Vancouver I., Canada 100 D3
Vandalia, Ill., U.S.A. 108 F10
Vandalia, Mo., U.S.A. 108 F9
Vandenburg, U.S.A. 113 L6
Vanderbijlpark, S. Africa 85 D4
Vandergrift, U.S.A. 106 F5
Vanderhoof, Canada 100 C4
Vanderkloof Dam, S. Africa 84 E3
Vanderlin I., Australia 90 B2
Vandyke, Australia 90 C4
Vänern, Sweden 11 F7
Vänersborg, Sweden 11 F6
Vang Vieng, Laos 58 C4
Vanga, Kenya 82 C4
Vangaindrano, Madag. 85 C8
Vanguard, Canada 101 D7
Vanier, Canada 98 C4
Vankleek Hill, Canada 98 C5
Vanna, Norway 8 A18
Vännäs, Sweden 8 E18
Vannes, France 24 E4
Vanoise, Massif de la, France 27 C10
Vanrhynsdorp, S. Africa 84 E2
Vanrook, Australia 90 B3
Vansbro, Sweden 9 F16
Vansittart B., Australia 88 B4
Vantaa, Finland 9 F21
Vanthli, India 62 J4
Vanua Levu, Fiji 87 C8
Vanua Mbalavu, Fiji 87 C9
Vanuatu ■, Pac. Oc. 92 J8
Vanwyksvlei, S. Africa 84 E3
Vanzylsrus, S. Africa 84 D3
Vapnyarka, Ukraine 41 H5
Var □, France 27 E10
Var →, France 27 E11
Vara, Sweden 11 F6
Varades, France 24 E5
Varáita →, Italy 32 D4
Varallo, Italy 32 C5
Varanasi, India 63 G10
Varanger-halvøya, Norway 8 A23
Varangerfjorden, Norway 8 A23
Varaždin, Croatia 33 B13
Varazze, Italy 32 D5
Varberg, Sweden 11 G6
Vardar = Axiós →, Greece 39 J5
Varde, Denmark 11 J2
Varde Å →, Denmark 11 J2
Vardø, Norway 8 A24
Varel, Germany 18 B4
Varella, Mui, Vietnam 58 F7
Varėna, Lithuania 9 J21
Varennes-sur-Allier, France 26 B7
Vareš, Bos.-H. 21 L8
Varese, Italy 32 C5

Varese Lígure

Varese Lígure, *Italy*	32	D6
Vårgårda, *Sweden*	11	F6
Vargem Bonita, *Brazil*	123	F2
Vargem Grande, *Brazil*	122	B3
Varginha, *Brazil*	127	A6
Vargön, *Sweden*	11	F6
Variadero, *U.S.A.*	109	H2
Varillas, *Chile*	126	A1
Väring, *Sweden*	11	F8
Varkaus, *Finland*	9	E22
Varkaus, *Neths.*	16	E8
Varna, *Bulgaria*	38	F10
Värnamo, *Sweden*	9	H16
Värö, *Sweden*	11	G6
Vars, *Canada*	107	A9
Varsseveld, *Neths.*	16	E8
Varto, *Turkey*	67	C9
Varvarin, *Serbia, Yug.*	21	M11
Varzaneh, *Iran*	65	C7
Várzea Alegre, *Brazil*	122	C4
Várzea da Palma, *Brazil*	123	E3
Várzea Grande, *Brazil*	125	D6
Varzi, *Italy*	32	D6
Varzo, *Italy*	32	B5
Varzy, *France*	25	E10
Vasa Barris →, *Brazil*	122	D4
Vascão →, *Portugal*	31	H3
Vaşcău, *Romania*	38	C5
Vascongadas = País Vasco □, *Spain*	28	C2
Vasht = Khāsh, *Iran*	60	E2
Vasilevichi, *Belarus*	41	F5
Vasilikón, *Greece*	39	L6
Vasilkov = Vasylkiv, *Ukraine*	41	G6
Vaslui, *Romania*	38	C10
Vassar, *Canada*	101	D9
Vassar, *U.S.A.*	104	D4
Västerås, *Sweden*	10	E10
Västerbotten, *Sweden*	8	D18
Västerdalälven →, *Sweden*	9	F16
Västernorrlands län □, *Sweden*	10	A11
Västervik, *Sweden*	9	H17
Västmanland, *Sweden*	9	G16
Vasto, *Italy*	33	F11
Vasvár, *Hungary*	21	H6
Vasylkiv, *Ukraine*	41	G6
Vatan, *France*	25	E8
Vathí, *Greece*	39	M10
Váthia, *Greece*	39	N5
Vatican City ■, *Europe*	33	G9
Vaticano, C., *Italy*	35	D8
Vatili, *Cyprus*	37	D12
Vatnajökull, *Iceland*	8	D5
Vatnås, *Norway*	10	E3
Vatoa, *Fiji*	87	D9
Vatólakkos, *Greece*	37	D5
Vatoloha, *Madag.*	85	B8
Vatomandry, *Madag.*	85	B8
Vatra-Dornei, *Romania*	38	B8
Vättern, *Sweden*	11	F8
Vättis, *Switz.*	23	C8
Vaucluse □, *France*	27	E9
Vaucouleurs, *France*	25	D12
Vaud □, *Switz.*	22	C2
Vaughn, Mont., *U.S.A.*	110	C8
Vaughn, N. Mex., *U.S.A.*	111	J11
Vaulruz, *Switz.*	22	C3
Vaupés = Uaupés →, *Brazil*	120	C4
Vaupes □, *Colombia*	120	C3
Vauvert, *France*	27	E8
Vauxhall, *Canada*	100	C6
Vava'u, *Tonga*	87	D11
Vavoua, *Ivory C.*	78	D3
Vawkavysk, *Belarus*	41	F3
Vaxholm, *Sweden*	10	E12
Växjö, *Sweden*	9	H16
Vaygach, Ostrov, *Russia*	44	C6
Váyia, Akra, *Greece*	37	C10
Veadeiros, *Brazil*	123	D2
Vechta, *Germany*	18	C4
Vechte →, *Neths.*	16	C8
Vecsés, *Hungary*	21	H9
Veddige, *Sweden*	11	G6
Vedea →, *Romania*	38	F8
Vedia, *Argentina*	126	C3
Vedra, I. del, *Spain*	36	C7
Vedrin, *Belgium*	17	G5
Veendam, *Neths.*	16	B9
Veenendaal, *Neths.*	16	D7
Veerle, *Belgium*	17	F5
Vefsna →, *Norway*	8	D15
Vega, *Norway*	8	D14
Vega, *U.S.A.*	109	H3
Vegadeo, *Spain*	30	B3
Veghel, *Neths.*	17	E7
Vegreville, *Canada*	100	C6
Vegusdal, *Norway*	11	F2
Veii, *Italy*	33	F9
Vejen, *Denmark*	11	J3
Vejer de la Frontera, *Spain*	31	J5
Vejle, *Denmark*	11	J3
Vejle Fjord, *Denmark*	11	J3
Vela Luka, *Croatia*	33	F13
Velas, C., *Costa Rica*	116	D2
Velasco, Sierra de, *Argentina*	126	B2
Velay, Mts. du, *France*	26	D7
Velddrif, *S. Africa*	84	E2
Veldegem, *Belgium*	17	F2
Velden, *Neths.*	17	F8
Veldhoven, *Neths.*	17	F6
Velebit Planina, *Croatia*	33	D12
Velebitski Kanal, *Croatia*	33	D11
Veleka →, *Bulgaria*	38	G10
Velenje, *Slovenia*	33	B12
Velestínon, *Greece*	39	K5
Vélez, *Colombia*	120	B3
Vélez Blanco, *Spain*	29	H2
Vélez Málaga, *Spain*	31	J6
Vélez Rubio, *Spain*	29	H2
Velhas →, *Brazil*	123	E3
Velika, *Croatia*	21	K7
Velika Gorica, *Croatia*	33	C13
Velika Kapela, *Croatia*	33	C12
Velika Kladuša, *Bos.-H.*	33	C12
Velika Morava →, *Serbia, Yug.*	21	L11
Velikaya →, *Russia*	40	D5
Velikaya Kema, *Russia*	48	B8
Velikaya Lepetikha, *Ukraine*	41	J7
Velike Lašče, *Slovenia*	33	C11
Velikiye Luki, *Russia*	40	D6
Veliko Tŭrnovo, *Bulgaria*	38	F8
Velikonda Range, *India*	60	M11
Velingrad, *Bulgaria*	39	G6
Velino, Mte., *Italy*	33	F10
Velizh, *Russia*	40	E6
Velke Meziřiči, *Czech.*	20	F6
Velletri, *Italy*	34	A5
Vellinge, *Sweden*	11	J7
Vellore, *India*	60	N11
Velp, *Neths.*	16	D7
Velsen-Noord, *Neths.*	16	D5
Velsk, *Russia*	40	B11
Velten, *Germany*	18	C9
Veluwe Meer, *Neths.*	16	D7
Velva, *U.S.A.*	108	A4
Veme, *Norway*	10	D4
Ven, *Sweden*	11	J6
Venaco, *France*	27	F13
Venado Tuerto, *Argentina*	126	C3
Venafro, *Italy*	35	A7
Venarey-les-Laumes, *France*	25	E11
Venaria, *Italy*	32	C4
Venčane, *Serbia, Yug.*	21	L10
Vence, *France*	27	E11
Vendas Novas, *Portugal*	31	G2
Vendée □, *France*	24	F5
Vendée →, *France*	24	F5
Vendéen, Bocage, *France*	26	B2
Vendeuvre-sur-Barse, *France*	25	D11
Vendôme, *France*	24	E8
Vendrell, *Spain*	28	D6
Vendsyssel, *Denmark*	11	G4
Véneta, L., *Italy*	33	C9
Véneto □, *Italy*	33	C8
Venev, *Russia*	42	C4
Venézia, *Italy*	33	C9
Venézia, G. di, *Italy*	33	C10
Venezuela ■, *S. Amer.*	120	B4
Venezuela, G. de, *Venezuela*	120	A3
Vengurla, *India*	60	M8
Venice = Venézia, *Italy*	33	C9
Venkatapuram, *India*	61	K12
Venlo, *Neths.*	17	F8
Vennesla, *Norway*	9	G12
Venraij, *Neths.*	17	E7
Venta de Cardeña, *Spain*	31	G6
Venta de San Rafael, *Spain*	30	E6
Ventana, Punta de la, *Mexico*	114	C3
Ventana, Sa. de la, *Argentina*	126	D3
Ventersburg, *S. Africa*	84	D4
Venterstad, *S. Africa*	84	E4
Ventimíglia, *Italy*	32	E4
Ventnor, *U.K.*	13	G6
Ventotene, *Italy*	34	B6
Ventoux, Mt., *France*	27	D9
Ventspils, *Latvia*	9	H19
Ventuarí →, *Venezuela*	120	C4
Ventucopa, *U.S.A.*	113	L7
Ventura, *U.S.A.*	113	L7
Venus B., *Australia*	91	F4
Veøy, *Norway*	10	B1
Vera, *Argentina*	126	B3
Vera, *Spain*	29	H3
Veracruz, *Mexico*	115	D5
Veracruz □, *Mexico*	115	D5
Veraval, *India*	62	J4
Verbánia, *Italy*	32	C5
Verbicaro, *Italy*	35	C8
Verbier, *Switz.*	22	D4
Vercelli, *Italy*	32	C5
Verchovchevo, *Ukraine*	41	H8
Verdalsøra, *Norway*	8	E14
Verde →, *Argentina*	128	B3
Verde →, Goiás, *Brazil*	123	E1
Verde →, Goiás, *Brazil*	123	E1
Verde →, Mato Grosso, *Brazil*	125	C6
Verde →, Mato Grosso do Sul, *Brazil*	125	E7
Verde →, Chihuahua, *Mexico*	114	B3
Verde →, Oaxaca, *Mexico*	115	D5
Verde →, Veracruz, *Mexico*	114	C4
Verde →, *Paraguay*	126	A4
Verde, Cay, *Bahamas*	116	B4
Verde Grande →, *Brazil*	123	E3
Verde Island Pass, *Phil.*	55	E4
Verde Pequeno →, *Brazil*	123	D3
Verden, *Germany*	18	C5
Verdi, *U.S.A.*	112	F7
Verdigre, *U.S.A.*	108	D5
Verdon →, *France*	27	E9
Verdun, *France*	25	C12
Verdun-sur-le-Doubs, *France*	25	F12
Vereeniging, *S. Africa*	85	D4
Vérendrye, Parc Prov. de la, *Canada*	98	C4
Verga, C., *Guinea*	78	C2
Vergato, *Italy*	32	D8
Vergemont, *Australia*	90	C3
Vergemont Cr. →, *Australia*	90	C3
Vergennes, *U.S.A.*	107	B11
Vergt, *France*	26	C4
Verín, *Spain*	30	D3
Veriña, *Spain*	30	B5
Verkhnedvinsk = Vyerkhnyadzvinsk, *Belarus*	40	E4
Verkhnevilyuysk, *Russia*	45	C13
Verkhneye Kalinino, *Russia*	45	D11
Verkhniy Baskunchak, *Russia*	43	F8
Verkhnyaya Amga, *Russia*	45	D13
Verkhovye, *Russia*	42	D3
Verkhoyansk, *Russia*	45	C14
Verkhoyansk Ra. = Verkhoyanskiy Khrebet, *Russia*	45	C13
Verkhoyanskiy Khrebet, *Russia*	45	C13
Verlo, *Canada*	101	C7
Verma, *Norway*	10	B2
Vermenton, *France*	25	E10
Vermilion, *Canada*	101	C6
Vermilion →, Alta., *Canada*	101	C6
Vermilion →, Qué., *Canada*	98	C5
Vermilion, B., *U.S.A.*	109	L9
Vermilion Bay, *Canada*	101	D10
Vermilion Chutes, *Canada*	100	B6
Vermilion L., *U.S.A.*	108	B8
Vermillion, *U.S.A.*	108	D6
Vermont □, *U.S.A.*	107	C12
Vernal, *U.S.A.*	110	F9
Vernalis, *U.S.A.*	112	H5
Vernayaz, *Switz.*	22	D4
Verner, *Canada*	98	C3
Verneuil-sur-Avre, *France*	24	D7
Verneukpan, *S. Africa*	84	D3
Vernier, *Switz.*	22	D2
Vernon, *Canada*	100	C5
Vernon, *France*	24	C8
Vernon, *U.S.A.*	109	H5
Vernonia, *U.S.A.*	112	E3
Vero Beach, *U.S.A.*	105	M5
Véroia, *Greece*	39	J5
Verolanuova, *Italy*	32	C7
Véroli, *Italy*	34	A6
Verona, *Italy*	32	C8
Versailles, *France*	25	D9
Versalles, *Bolivia*	125	C5
Versoix, *Switz.*	22	D2
Vert, C., *Senegal*	78	C1
Vertou, *France*	24	E5
Vertus, *France*	25	D11
Verulam, *S. Africa*	85	D5
Verviers, *Belgium*	17	G7
Vervins, *France*	25	C10
Verzej, *Slovenia*	33	B13
Vescavato, *France*	27	F13
Vesdre →, *Belgium*	17	G7
Veselí nad Lužnicí, *Czech.*	20	F4
Veselovskoye Vdkhr., *Russia*	43	G5
Veshenskaya, *Russia*	42	F5
Vesle →, *France*	25	C10
Vesoul, *France*	25	E13
Vessigebro, *Sweden*	11	H6
Vesterålen, *Norway*	8	B16
Vestersche Veld, *Neths.*	16	C8
Vestfjorden, *Norway*	8	C15
Vestmannaeyjar, *Iceland*	8	E3
Vestmarka, *Norway*	10	E5
Vestsjællands Amtskommune □, *Denmark*	11	J5
Vestspitsbergen, *Svalbard*	4	B8
Vestvågøy, *Norway*	8	B15
Vesuvio, *Italy*	35	B7
Vesuvius, Mte. = Vesuvio, *Italy*	35	B7
Vesyegonsk, *Russia*	40	C9
Veszprém, *Hungary*	21	H7
Vésztő, *Hungary*	21	J11
Vetlanda, *Sweden*	9	H16
Vetluga, *Russia*	42	B8
Vetlugu →, *Russia*	42	B8
Vetluzhskiy, *Russia*	42	B7
Vetluzhskiy, *Russia*	42	A7
Vetovo, *Bulgaria*	38	F9
Vetralia, *Italy*	33	F9
Vettore, Mte., *Italy*	33	F10
Veurne, *Belgium*	17	F1
Vevey, *Switz.*	22	D3
Veynes, *France*	27	D9
Veys, *Iran*	65	D6
Vézelise, *France*	25	D13
Vézère →, *France*	26	D4
Vezirköprü, *Turkey*	66	B6
Vi Thanh, *Vietnam*	59	H5
Viacha, *Bolivia*	124	D4
Viadana, *Italy*	32	D7
Viamão, *Brazil*	127	C5
Viana, *Brazil*	122	B3
Viana, *Spain*	28	C2
Viana del Bollo, *Spain*	30	C3
Viana do Alentejo, *Portugal*	31	G3
Viana do Castelo, *Portugal*	30	D2
Vianden, *Belgium*	17	J8
Vianen, *Neths.*	16	E6
Vianna do Castelo □, *Portugal*	30	D2
Vianópolis, *Brazil*	123	E2
Viar →, *Spain*	31	H5
Viaréggio, *Italy*	32	E7
Viaur →, *France*	26	D5
Vibank, *Canada*	101	C8
Vibo Valéntia, *Italy*	35	D9
Viborg, *Denmark*	11	H3
Vibraye, *France*	24	D7
Vic, Étang de, *France*	26	E7
Vic-en-Bigorre, *France*	26	E4
Vic-Fézensac, *France*	26	E4
Vic-sur-Cère, *France*	26	D6
Vicenza, *Italy*	33	C8
Vich, *Spain*	28	D7
Vichada □, *Colombia*	120	C4
Vichada →, *Colombia*	120	C4
Vichuga, *Russia*	42	B5
Vichy, *France*	26	B7
Vicksburg, Ariz., *U.S.A.*	113	M13
Vicksburg, Mich., *U.S.A.*	104	D3
Vicksburg, Miss., *U.S.A.*	109	J9
Vico, L., di, *Italy*	33	F9
Vico del Gargano, *Italy*	35	A8
Viçosa, *Brazil*	122	C4
Viçosa do Ceará, *Brazil*	122	B3
Vicosoprano, *Switz.*	23	D9
Victor, *India*	62	J4
Victor, Colo., *U.S.A.*	108	F2
Victor, N.Y., *U.S.A.*	106	D7
Victor Harbor, *Australia*	91	F2
Victoria, *Argentina*	126	C3
Victoria, *Canada*	100	D4
Victoria, *Chile*	128	A2
Victoria, *Guinea*	78	C2
Victoria, *Malaysia*	56	C5
Victoria, *Malta*	37	C1
Victoria, *Phil.*	55	D4
Victoria, Kans., *U.S.A.*	108	F5
Victoria, Tex., *U.S.A.*	109	L6
Victoria →, *Australia*	88	C4
Victoria □, *Australia*	91	F3
Victoria, Grand L., *Canada*	98	C4
Victoria, L., *Africa*	82	C3
Victoria, L., *Australia*	91	E3
Victoria Beach, *Canada*	101	C9
Victoria de Durango, *Mexico*	114	C4
Victoria de las Tunas, *Cuba*	116	B4
Victoria Falls, *Zimbabwe*	83	F2
Victoria Harbour, *Canada*	98	D4
Victoria I., *Canada*	96	A8
Victoria Ld., *Antarctica*	5	D11
Victoria Nile →, *Uganda*	82	B3
Victoria Res., *Canada*	99	C8
Victoria River Downs, *Australia*	88	C5
Victoria Taungdeik, *Burma*	61	J18
Victoria West, *S. Africa*	84	E3
Victorias, *Phil.*	55	F5
Victoriaville, *Canada*	99	C5
Victorica, *Argentina*	126	D2
Victorville, *U.S.A.*	113	L9
Vicuña, *Chile*	126	C1
Vicuña Mackenna, *Argentina*	126	C3
Vidal, *U.S.A.*	113	L12
Vidal Junction, *U.S.A.*	113	L12
Vidalia, *U.S.A.*	105	J4
Vidauban, *France*	27	E10
Vídho, *Greece*	37	A3
Vidigueira, *Portugal*	31	G3
Vidin, *Bulgaria*	38	F5
Vidio, C., *Spain*	30	B4
Vidisha, *India*	62	H7
Vidzy, *Belarus*	9	J22
Viechtach, *Germany*	19	F8
Viedma, *Argentina*	128	B4
Viedma, L., *Argentina*	128	C2
Vieira, *Portugal*	30	D2
Viella, *Spain*	28	C5
Vielsalm, *Belgium*	17	H7
Vienenburg, *Germany*	18	D6
Vieng Pou Kha, *Laos*	58	B3
Vienna = Wien, *Austria*	19	D9
Vienna, *U.S.A.*	109	G10
Vienne, *France*	27	C8
Vienne □, *France*	26	B4
Vienne →, *France*	24	E7
Vientiane, *Laos*	58	D4
Vientos, Paso de los, *Caribbean*	117	C5
Vierlingsbeek, *Neths.*	17	E8
Viersen, *Germany*	18	D2
Vierwaldstättersee, *Switz.*	23	C7
Vierzon, *France*	25	E9
Vieste, *Italy*	35	A9
Vietnam ■, *Asia*	58	C5
Vieux-Boucau-les-Bains, *France*	26	E2
Vif, *France*	27	C9
Vigan, *Phil.*	55	C4
Vigévano, *Italy*	32	C5
Vigia, *Brazil*	122	B2
Vigía Chico, *Mexico*	115	D7
Víglas, Ákra, *Greece*	37	D9
Vignemale, Pic du, *France*	26	F3
Vigneulles-lès-Hattonchâtel, *France*	25	D12
Vignola, *Italy*	32	D8
Vigo, *Spain*	30	C2
Vigo, Ría de, *Spain*	30	C2
Vihiers, *France*	24	E6
Vijayawada, *India*	61	L12
Vijfhuizen, *Neths.*	16	D5
Vík, *Iceland*	8	E4
Vikeke, *Indonesia*	57	F7
Viken, *Sweden*	11	F8
Viking, *Canada*	100	C6
Vikna, *Norway*	8	D14
Viksjö, *Sweden*	10	B11
Vikulovo, *Russia*	44	D8
Vila da Maganja, *Mozam.*	83	F4
Vila de João Belo = Xai-Xai, *Mozam.*	85	D5
Vila de Rei, *Portugal*	31	F2
Vila do Bispo, *Portugal*	31	H2
Vila do Chibuto, *Mozam.*	85	C5
Vila do Conde, *Portugal*	30	D2
Vila Franca de Xira, *Portugal*	31	G2
Vila Gamito, *Mozam.*	83	E3
Vila Gomes da Costa, *Mozam.*	85	C5
Vila Machado, *Mozam.*	83	F3
Vila Mouzinho, *Mozam.*	83	E3
Vila Nova de Foscôa, *Portugal*	30	D3
Vila Nova de Ourém, *Portugal*	31	F2
Vila Novo de Gaia, *Portugal*	30	D2
Vila Pouca de Aguiar, *Portugal*	30	D3
Vila Real, *Portugal*	30	D3
Vila Real de Santo António, *Portugal*	31	H3
Vila Vasco da Gama, *Mozam.*	83	E3
Vila Velha, Amapá, *Brazil*	121	C7
Vila Velha, Espírito Santo, *Brazil*	123	F3
Vila Viçosa, *Portugal*	31	G3
Vilaboa, *Spain*	30	C2
Vilaine →, *France*	24	E4
Vilanandro, Tanjona, *Madag.*	85	B7
Vilanculos, *Mozam.*	85	C6
Vilar Formoso, *Portugal*	30	E4
Vilareal □, *Portugal*	30	D3
Vilaseca-Salou, *Spain*	28	D6
Vilcabamba, Cordillera, *Peru*	124	C3
Vilcanchos, *Peru*	124	C3
Vileyka, *Belarus*	40	E4
Vilhelmina, *Sweden*	8	D17
Vilhena, *Brazil*	125	C5
Viliga, *Russia*	45	C16
Viliya →, *Lithuania*	9	J21
Viljandi, *Estonia*	9	G21
Vilkovo = Vylkove, *Ukraine*	41	K5
Villa Abecia, *Bolivia*	126	A2
Villa Ahumada, *Mexico*	114	A3
Villa Ana, *Argentina*	126	B4
Villa Ángela, *Argentina*	126	B3
Villa Bella, *Bolivia*	125	C4
Villa Bens = Tarfaya, *Morocco*	74	C2
Villa Cañás, *Argentina*	126	C3
Villa Carlos, *Spain*	36	B11
Villa Cisneros = Dakhla, *W. Sahara*	74	D1
Villa Colón, *Argentina*	126	C2
Villa Constitución, *Argentina*	126	C3
Villa de Cura, *Venezuela*	120	A4
Villa de María, *Argentina*	126	B3
Villa del Rosario, *Venezuela*	120	A3
Villa Dolores, *Argentina*	126	C2
Villa Frontera, *Mexico*	114	B4
Villa Guillermina, *Argentina*	126	B4
Villa Hayes, *Paraguay*	126	B4
Villa Iris, *Argentina*	126	D3
Villa Juárez, *Mexico*	114	B4
Villa María, *Argentina*	126	C3
Villa Mazán, *Argentina*	126	B2
Villa Minozzo, *Italy*	32	D7
Villa Montes, *Bolivia*	126	A3
Villa Ocampo, *Argentina*	126	B4
Villa Ocampo, *Mexico*	114	B3
Villa Ojo de Agua, *Argentina*	126	B3
Villa San Giovanni, *Italy*	35	D8
Villa San José, *Argentina*	126	C4
Villa San Martín, *Argentina*	126	B3
Villa Santina, *Italy*	33	B9
Villa Unión, *Mexico*	114	C3
Villablino, *Spain*	30	C4
Villacañas, *Spain*	28	F1
Villacarriedo, *Spain*	28	B1
Villacarrillo, *Spain*	29	G1
Villacastín, *Spain*	30	E6
Villach, *Austria*	21	J3
Villacidro, *Italy*	34	C1
Villada, *Spain*	30	C6
Villadóssola, *Italy*	32	B5
Villafeliche, *Spain*	28	D3
Villafranca, *Spain*	28	C3
Villafranca de los Barros, *Spain*	31	G4

Villafranca de los Caballeros, *Baleares, Spain* 36 B10
Villafranca de los Caballeros, *Toledo, Spain* 29 F1
Villafranca del Bierzo, *Spain* 30 C4
Villafranca del Cid, *Spain* . 28 E4
Villafranca del Panadés, *Spain* 28 D6
Villafranca di Verona, *Italy* 32 C7
Villagarcía de Arosa, *Spain* 30 C2
Villagrán, *Mexico* 115 C5
Villaguay, *Argentina* 126 C4
Villaharta, *Spain* 31 G6
Villahermosa, *Mexico* 115 D6
Villahermosa, *Spain* 29 G2
Villaines-la-Juhel, *France* . 24 D6
Villajoyosa, *Spain* 29 G4
Villalba, *Spain* 30 B3
Villalba de Guardo, *Spain* 30 C6
Villalcampo, Pantano de, *Spain* 30 D4
Villalón de Campos, *Spain* 30 C5
Villalpando, *Spain* 30 D5
Villaluenga, *Spain* 30 E7
Villamanán, *Spain* 30 C5
Villamartín, *Spain* 31 J5
Villamayor, *Spain* 28 F2
Villamblard, *France* 26 C4
Villanova Monteleone, *Italy* 34 B1
Villanueva, *Colombia* 120 A3
Villanueva, *U.S.A.* 111 J11
Villanueva de Castellón, *Spain* 29 F4
Villanueva de Córdoba, *Spain* 31 G6
Villanueva de la Fuente, *Spain* 29 G2
Villanueva de la Serena, *Spain* 31 G5
Villanueva de la Sierra, *Spain* 30 E4
Villanueva de los Castillejos, *Spain* 31 H3
Villanueva del Arzobispo, *Spain* 29 G1
Villanueva del Duque, *Spain* 31 G5
Villanueva del Fresno, *Spain* 31 G3
Villanueva y Geltrú, *Spain* 28 D6
Villaodrid, *Spain* 30 B3
Villaputzu, *Italy* 34 C2
Villar del Arzobispo, *Spain* 28 F4
Villar del Rey, *Spain* 31 F4
Villarcayo, *Spain* 28 C1
Villard-Bonnot, *France* ... 27 C9
Villard-de-Lans, *France* ... 27 C9
Villarino de los Aires, *Spain* 30 D4
Villarosa, *Italy* 35 E7
Villarramiel, *Spain* 30 C6
Villarreal, *Spain* 28 F4
Villarrica, *Chile* 128 A2
Villarrica, *Paraguay* 126 B4
Villarrobledo, *Spain* 29 F2
Villarroya de la Sierra, *Spain* 28 D3
Villarrubia de los Ojos, *Spain* 29 F1
Villars-les-Dombes, *France* 27 B9
Villarta de San Juan, *Spain* 29 F1
Villasayas, *Spain* 28 D2
Villaseca de los Gamitos, *Spain* 30 D4
Villastar, *Spain* 28 E3
Villatobas, *Spain* 28 F1
Villavicencio, *Argentina* . 126 C2
Villavicencio, *Colombia* . 120 C3
Villaviciosa, *Spain* 30 B5
Villazón, *Bolivia* 126 A2
Ville-Marie, *Canada* 98 C4
Ville Platte, *U.S.A.* 109 K8
Villedieu-les-Poêlles, *France* 24 D5
Villefort, *France* 26 D7
Villefranche-de-Lauragais, *France* 26 E5
Villefranche-de-Rouergue, *France* 26 D6
Villefranche-du-Périgord, *France* 26 D5
Villefranche-sur-Cher, *France* 25 E8
Villefranche-sur-Saône, *France* 27 C8
Villegrande, *Bolivia* 125 D5
Villel, *Spain* 28 E3
Villemur-sur-Vanne, *France* 25 D10
Villemur-sur-Tarn, *France* 26 E5
Villena, *Spain* 29 G4
Villenauxe-la-Grande, *France* 25 D10
Villenave-d'Ornon, *France* 26 D3
Villeneuve, *Italy* 32 C4
Villeneuve, *Switz.* 22 D3
Villeneuve-l'Archevêque, *France* 25 D10
Villeneuve-lès-Avignon, *France* 27 E8
Villeneuve-St.-Georges, *France* 25 D9
Villeneuve-sur-Allier, *France* 26 B7
Villeneuve-sur-Lot, *France* 26 D4

Villeréal, *France* 26 D4
Villers-Bocage, *France* ... 24 C6
Villers-Bretonneux, *France* 25 C9
Villers-Cotterêts, *France* .. 25 C10
Villers-le-Bouillet, *Belgium* 17 G6
Villers-le-Gambon, *Belgium* 17 H5
Villers-sur-Mer, *France* ... 24 C6
Villersexel, *France* 25 E13
Villerupt, *France* 25 C12
Villerville, *France* 24 C7
Villiers, *S. Africa* 85 D4
Villingen-Schwenningen, *Germany* 19 G4
Villisca, *U.S.A.* 108 E7
Vilna, *Canada* 100 C6
Vilnius, *Lithuania* 9 J21
Vils →, *Germany* 19 G9
Vilsbiburg, *Germany* 19 G8
Vilshofen, *Germany* 19 G9
Vilusi, *Montenegro, Yug.* . 21 N8
Vilvoorde, *Belgium* 17 G4
Vilyuy →, *Russia* 45 C13
Vilyuysk, *Russia* 45 C13
Vimercate, *Italy* 32 C6
Vimiosa, *Portugal* 30 D4
Vimoutiers, *France* 24 D7
Vimperk, *Czech.* 20 F3
Viña del Mar, *Chile* 126 C1
Vinaroz, *Spain* 28 E5
Vincennes, *U.S.A.* 104 F2
Vincent, *U.S.A.* 113 L8
Vinces, *Ecuador* 120 D2
Vinchina, *Argentina* 126 B2
Vindelälven →, *Sweden* .. 8 E18
Vindeln, *Sweden* 8 D18
Vinderup, *Denmark* 11 H2
Vindhya Ra., *India* 62 H7
Vineland, *U.S.A.* 104 F8
Vinga, *Romania* 38 D4
Vingnes, *Norway* 10 C4
Vinh, *Vietnam* 58 C5
Vinh Linh, *Vietnam* 58 D6
Vinh Long, *Vietnam* 59 G5
Vinh Yen, *Vietnam* 58 B5
Vinhais, *Portugal* 30 D3
Vinica, *Croatia* 33 B13
Vinica, *Slovenia* 33 C12
Vinita, *U.S.A.* 109 G7
Vinkeveen, *Neths.* 16 D5
Vinkovci, *Croatia* 21 K8
Vinnitsa = Vinnytsya, *Ukraine* 41 H5
Vinnytsya, *Ukraine* 41 H5
Vinstra, *Norway* 10 C3
Vinton, *Calif., U.S.A.* ... 112 F6
Vinton, *Iowa, U.S.A.* 108 D8
Vinton, *La., U.S.A.* 109 K8
Vințu de Jos, *Romania* ... 38 D6
Viöl, *Germany* 18 A5
Vipava, *Slovenia* 33 C10
Vipiteno, *Italy* 33 B8
Vir, *Croatia* 33 D12
Virac, *Phil.* 55 E6
Virachei, *Cambodia* 58 F6
Virago Sd., *Canada* 100 C2
Viramgam, *India* 62 H5
Virananşehir, *Turkey* ... 67 D8
Virden, *Canada* 101 D8
Vire, *France* 24 D6
Vire →, *France* 24 C5
Virgem da Lapa, *Brazil* .. 123 E3
Vírgenes, C., *Argentina* .. 128 D3
Virgin →, *Canada* 101 B7
Virgin →, *U.S.A.* 111 H6
Virgin Gorda, *Virgin Is.* . 117 C7
Virgin Is. (British) ■, *W. Indies* 117 C7
Virgin Is. (U.S.) ■, *W. Indies* 117 C7
Virginia, *S. Africa* 84 D4
Virginia, *U.S.A.* 108 B8
Virginia □, *U.S.A.* 104 G7
Virginia Beach, *U.S.A.* ... 104 G8
Virginia City, *Mont., U.S.A.* 110 D8
Virginia City, *Nev., U.S.A.* 112 F7
Virginia Falls, *Canada* ... 100 A3
Virginiatown, *Canada* 98 C4
Virieu-le-Grand, *France* .. 27 C9
Viroqua, *U.S.A.* 108 D9
Virovitica, *Croatia* 21 K7
Virton, *Belgium* 17 J7
Virú, *Peru* 124 B2
Virudunagar, *India* 60 Q10
Vis, *Croatia* 33 E13
Vis Kanal, *Croatia* 33 E13
Visalia, *U.S.A.* 111 H4
Visayan Sea, *Phil.* 55 F5
Visby, *Sweden* 9 H18
Viscount Melville Sd., *Canada* 4 B2
Visé, *Belgium* 17 G7
Višegrad, *Bos.-H.* 21 M9
Viseu, *Brazil* 122 B2
Viseu, *Portugal* 30 E3
Viseu □, *Portugal* 30 E3
Vișeu de Sus, *Romania* ... 38 B7
Vishakhapatnam, *India* .. 61 L13
Viskafors, *Sweden* 11 G6
Visnagar, *India* 62 H5
Višnja Gora, *Slovenia* ... 33 C11
Viso, Mte., *Italy* 32 D4
Viso del Marqués, *Spain* . 29 G1
Visoko, *Bos.-H.* 21 M8
Visokoi I., *Antarctica* ... 5 B1
Visp, *Switz.* 22 D5
Vispa →, *Switz.* 22 D5

Visselhövede, *Germany* ... 18 C5
Vissoie, *Switz.* 22 D5
Vista, *U.S.A.* 113 M9
Vistula = Wisła →, *Poland* 20 A8
Vit →, *Bulgaria* 38 F7
Vitanje, *Slovenia* 33 B12
Vitebsk = Vitsyebsk, *Belarus* 40 E6
Viterbo, *Italy* 33 F9
Viti Levu, *Fiji* 87 C7
Vitigudino, *Spain* 30 D4
Vitim, *Russia* 45 D12
Vitim →, *Russia* 45 D12
Vitória, *Brazil* 123 F3
Vitoria, *Spain* 28 C2
Vitória da Conquista, *Brazil* 123 D3
Vitória de São Antão, *Brazil* 122 C4
Vitorino Friere, *Brazil* ... 122 B2
Vitré, *France* 24 D5
Vitry-le-François, *France* . 25 D11
Vitsi, Óros, *Greece* 39 J4
Vitsyebsk, *Belarus* 40 E6
Vitteaux, *France* 25 E11
Vittel, *France* 25 D12
Vittória, *Italy* 35 F7
Vittório Véneto, *Italy* ... 33 C9
Vivario, *France* 27 F13
Vivegnis, *Belgium* 17 G7
Viver, *Spain* 28 F4
Vivero, *Spain* 30 B3
Viviers, *France* 27 D8
Vivonne, *France* 26 B4
Vizcaíno, Desierto de, *Mexico* 114 B2
Vizcaíno, Sierra, *Mexico* . 114 B2
Vizcaya □, *Spain* 28 B2
Vize, *Turkey* 66 B2
Vizianagaram, *India* 61 K13
Vizille, *France* 27 C9
Viziñada, *Croatia* 33 C10
Viziru, *Romania* 38 E10
Vizovice, *Czech.* 20 F7
Vizzini, *Italy* 35 E7
Vlaardingen, *Neths.* 16 E4
Vlădeasa, *Romania* 38 C5
Vladikavkaz, *Russia* 43 J7
Vladimir, *Russia* 42 B5
Vladimir Volynskiy = Volodymyr-Volynskyy, *Ukraine* 41 G3
Vladimirovac, *Serbia, Yug.* 21 K10
Vladimirovka, *Russia* 43 F8
Vladimovka, *Kazakhstan* . 42 E10
Vladislavovka, *Ukraine* .. 41 K8
Vladivostok, *Russia* 45 E14
Vlamertinge, *Belgium* 17 G1
Vlasenica, *Bos.-H.* 21 L8
Vlasinsko Jezero, *Serbia, Yug.* 21 N12
Vleuten, *Neths.* 16 D6
Vlieland, *Neths.* 16 B5
Vliestroom, *Neths.* 16 B6
Vlijmen, *Neths.* 17 E6
Vlissingen, *Neths.* 17 F3
Vlóra, *Albania* 39 J2
Vlorës, Gjiri i, *Albania* .. 39 J2
Vltava →, *Czech.* 20 E4
Vo Dat, *Vietnam* 59 G6
Vobarno, *Italy* 32 C7
Voćin, *Croatia* 21 K7
Vodice, *Croatia* 33 E12
Vodnjan, *Croatia* 33 D10
Vogelkop = Doberai, Jazirah, *Indonesia* .. 57 E8
Vogelsberg, *Germany* 18 E5
Voghera, *Italy* 32 D6
Vohibinany, *Madag.* 85 B8
Vohimarina, *Madag.* 85 A9
Vohimena, Tanjon' i, *Madag.* 85 D8
Vohipeno, *Madag.* 85 C8
Voi, *Kenya* 82 C4
Void, *France* 25 D12
Voiron, *France* 27 C9
Voisey B., *Canada* 99 A7
Voitsberg, *Austria* 21 H5
Voivis Límni, *Greece* 39 K5
Vojens, *Denmark* 11 J3
Vojmsjön, *Sweden* 8 D17
Vojnić, *Croatia* 33 C12
Vojnik, *Italy* 33 B12
Vokhtoga, *Russia* 40 C11
Volborg, *U.S.A.* 108 C2
Volcano Is. = Kazan-Rettō, *Pac. Oc.* 92 E6
Volchansk = Vovchansk, *Ukraine* 41 G9
Volchayevka, *Russia* 45 E14
Volchya →, *Ukraine* 41 H8
Volda, *Norway* 9 E12
Volendam, *Neths.* 16 D6
Volga, *Russia* 42 A4
Volga →, *Russia* 43 G9
Volga Hts. = Privolzhskaya Vozvyshennost, *Russia* 42 E7
Volgo-Baltiyskiy Kanal, *Russia* 40 B9
Volgo-Donskoy Kanal, *Russia* 43 F7
Volgodonsk, *Russia* 43 G6
Volgograd, *Russia* 43 F7
Volgogradskoye Vdkhr., *Russia* 42 E8
Volgorechensk, *Russia* ... 42 B5
Volkach, *Germany* 19 F6

Volkerak, *Neths.* 17 E4
Volkhov, *Russia* 40 C7
Volkhov →, *Russia* 40 B7
Völklingen, *Germany* 19 F2
Volkovysk = Vawkavysk, *Belarus* 41 F3
Volksrust, *S. Africa* 85 D4
Vollenhove, *Neths.* 16 C7
Volnansk, *Ukraine* 41 H8
Volnovakha, *Ukraine* 41 J9
Volochanka, *Russia* 45 B10
Volodarsk, *Russia* 42 B6
Volodymyr-Volynskyy, *Ukraine* 41 G3
Vologda, *Russia* 40 C10
Volokolamsk, *Russia* 42 B2
Volokonovka, *Russia* 42 E3
Vólos, *Greece* 39 K5
Volosovo, *Russia* 40 C5
Volovets, *Ukraine* 41 H2
Volovo, *Russia* 42 D4
Volozhin = Valozhyn, *Belarus* 40 E4
Volsk, *Russia* 42 D8
Volta →, *Ghana* 79 D5
Volta, L., *Ghana* 79 D5
Volta Blanche = White Volta →, *Ghana* 79 D4
Volta Redonda, *Brazil* ... 123 F3
Volterra, *Italy* 32 E7
Voltri, *Italy* 32 D5
Volturara Appula, *Italy* .. 35 A8
Volturno →, *Italy* 34 A6
Volubilis, *Morocco* 74 B3
Volvo, *Australia* 91 E3
Volzhsk, *Russia* 42 C9
Volzhskiy, *Russia* 43 F7
Vondrozo, *Madag.* 85 C8
Voorburg, *Neths.* 16 D4
Voorne Putten, *Neths.* ... 16 E4
Voorst, *Neths.* 16 D8
Voorthuizen, *Neths.* 16 D7
Vopnafjörður, *Iceland* ... 8 D6
Vóras Óros, *Greece* 39 J4
Vorbasse, *Denmark* 11 J3
Vorden, *Neths.* 16 D8
Vorderrhein →, *Switz.* .. 23 C8
Vordingborg, *Denmark* ... 11 K5
Voreppe, *France* 27 C9
Voríai Sporádhes, *Greece* 39 K6
Vórios Evvoïkos Kólpos, *Greece* 39 L6
Vorkuta, *Russia* 44 C7
Vorma →, *Norway* 10 D5
Vormsi, *Estonia* 9 G20
Vorona →, *Russia* 42 E6
Voronezh, *Russia* 42 E4
Voronezh, *Ukraine* 41 G7
Voronezh →, *Russia* 42 E4
Vorontsovo-Aleksandrovskoye = Zelenokumsk, *Russia* . 43 H6
Voroshilovgrad = Luhansk, *Ukraine* 41 H10
Voroshilovsk = Alchevsk, *Ukraine* 41 H10
Vorovskoye, *Russia* 45 D16
Vorselaar, *Belgium* 17 F5
Vorskla →, *Ukraine* 41 H8
Voskopoja, *Albania* 39 J3
Voskresensk, *Russia* 42 C4
Voskresenskoye, *Russia* . 42 B7
Voss, *Norway* 9 F12
Vosselaar, *Belgium* 17 F5
Vostok I., *Kiribati* 93 J12
Vouga →, *Portugal* 30 E2
Vouillé, *France* 24 F7
Vouvray, *France* 24 E7
Vouvry, *Switz.* 22 D3
Voúxa, Ákra, *Greece* 37 D5
Vouziers, *France* 25 C11
Vovchansk, *Ukraine* 41 G9
Voves, *France* 25 D8
Vozhe Ozero, *Russia* 40 B10
Voznesenka, *Russia* 45 D10
Voznesensk, *Ukraine* 41 J6
Voznesenye, *Russia* 40 B8
Vráble, *Norway* 10 E2
Vrakhnéïka, *Greece* 39 L4
Vrancei, Munții, *Romania* 38 D9
Vrangelya, Ostrov, *Russia* 45 B19
Vranica, *Bos.-H.* 21 M7
Vranje, *Serbia, Yug.* 21 N11
Vransko, *Slovenia* 33 B11
Vratsa, *Bulgaria* 38 F6
Vrbas, *Serbia, Yug.* 21 K9
Vrbas →, *Bos.-H.* 21 K7
Vrbnik, *Croatia* 33 C11
Vrbovec, *Croatia* 33 C13
Vrbovsko, *Croatia* 33 C12
Vrchlabí, *Czech.* 20 E5
Vrede, *S. Africa* 85 D4
Vredefort, *S. Africa* 84 D4
Vredenburg, *S. Africa* 84 E2
Vredendal, *S. Africa* 84 E2
Vreeswijk, *Neths.* 16 D6
Vrena, *Sweden* 11 F10
Vrgorac, *Croatia* 21 M7

Vrhnika, *Slovenia* 33 C11
Vrídi, *Ivory C.* 78 D4
Vries, *Neths.* 16 B9
Vriezenveen, *Neths.* 16 D9
Vrindavan, *India* 62 F7
Vríses, *Greece* 37 D6
Vrnograč, *Bos.-H.* 33 C12
Vroomshoop, *Neths.* 16 D9
Vršac, *Serbia, Yug.* 21 K11
Vrsacki Kanal, *Serbia, Yug.* 21 K11
Vryburg, *S. Africa* 84 D3
Vryheid, *S. Africa* 85 D5
Vsetín, *Czech.* 20 F8
Vu Liet, *Vietnam* 58 C5
Vucha →, *Bulgaria* 39 G7
Vught, *Neths.* 17 E6
Vukovar, *Croatia* 21 K8
Vulcan, *Canada* 100 C6
Vulcan, *U.S.A.* 104 C2
Vulcăneşti, *Moldova* 41 K5
Vulcano, *Italy* 35 D7
Vůlchedruma, *Bulgaria* .. 38 F6
Vulci, *Italy* 33 F8
Vulkaneshty = Vulcăneşti, *Moldova* 41 K5
Vunduzi →, *Mozam.* 83 F3
Vung Tau, *Vietnam* 59 G6
Vŭrbitsa, *Bulgaria* 38 G9
Vyartsilya, *Russia* 40 A6
Vyatka = Kirov, *Russia* .. 44 D5
Vyatka →, *Russia* 42 C10
Vyatskiye Polyany, *Russia* 42 B10
Vyazemskiy, *Russia* 45 E14
Vyazma, *Russia* 42 C2
Vyazniki, *Russia* 42 B6
Vyborg, *Russia* 40 B5
Vychegda →, *Russia* 44 C5
Vychodné Beskydy, *Europe* 41 H2
Vyerkhnyadzvinsk, *Belarus* 40 E4
Vyksa, *Russia* 42 C6
Vylkove, *Ukraine* 41 K5
Vynohradiv, *Ukraine* 41 H2
Vyrnwy, L., *U.K.* 12 E4
Vyshniy Volochek, *Russia* 42 B2
Vyškov, *Czech.* 20 F6
Vysoké Mýto, *Czech.* 20 F6
Vysokovsk, *Russia* 42 B3
Vytegra, *Russia* 40 B9

W

W.A.C. Bennett Dam, *Canada* 100 B4
Wa, *Ghana* 78 C4
Waal →, *Neths.* 16 E6
Waalwijk, *Neths.* 17 E6
Waarschoot, *Belgium* 17 F3
Waasmunster, *Belgium* ... 17 F4
Wabakimi L., *Canada* 98 B2
Wabana, *Canada* 99 C9
Wabasca, *Canada* 100 B6
Wabash, *U.S.A.* 104 E3
Wabash →, *U.S.A.* 104 G1
Wabeno, *U.S.A.* 104 C1
Wabi →, *Ethiopia* 77 F5
Wabigoon L., *Canada* ... 101 D10
Wabowden, *Canada* 101 C9
Wąbrzeźno, *Poland* 20 B8
Wabu Hu, *China* 53 A11
Wabuk Pt., *Canada* 98 A2
Wabush, *Canada* 99 B6
Wabuska, *U.S.A.* 110 G4
Wachtebeke, *Belgium* 17 F3
Wächtersbach, *Germany* . 19 E5
Waco, *U.S.A.* 109 K6
Waconichi, L., *Canada* ... 98 B5
Wad Ban Naqa, *Sudan* ... 77 D3
Wad Banda, *Sudan* 77 E2
Wad el Haddad, *Sudan* .. 77 E3
Wad en Nau, *Sudan* 77 E3
Wad Hamid, *Sudan* 77 D3
Wâd Medanî, *Sudan* 77 E3
Wad Thana, *Pakistan* ... 62 F2
Wadayama, *Japan* 49 G7
Waddeneilanden, *Neths.* . 16 B6
Waddenzee, *Neths.* 16 B6
Wadderin Hill, *Australia* . 89 F2
Waddington, *U.S.A.* 107 B9
Waddington, Mt., *Canada* 100 C3
Waddinxveen, *Neths.* 16 D5
Waddy Pt., *Australia* 91 C5
Wadena, *Canada* 101 C8
Wadena, *U.S.A.* 108 B7
Wädenswil, *Switz.* 23 B7
Wadesboro, *U.S.A.* 105 H5
Wadhams, *Canada* 100 C3
Wâdī as Sîr, *Jordan* 69 D4
Wadi Gemâl, *Egypt* 76 C4
Wadian, *China* 53 A9
Wadowice, *Poland* 20 F9
Wadsworth, *U.S.A.* 110 G4
Waegwan, *S. Korea* 51 G15
Wafrah, *Si. Arabia* 64 D5
Wagenberg, *Neths.* 17 E5
Wageningen, *Neths.* 16 E7
Wageningen, *Surinam* ... 121 B6
Wager B., *Canada* 97 B11
Wager Bay, *Canada* 97 B10
Wagga Wagga, *Australia* . 91 F4
Waghete, *Indonesia* 57 E9
Wagin, *Australia* 89 F2
Wagon Mound, *U.S.A.* ... 109 G2
Wagoner, *U.S.A.* 109 G7

Wagrowiec

Wagrowiec, *Poland* 20 C7
Wah, *Pakistan* 62 C5
Wahai, *Indonesia* 57 E7
Wahiawa, *U.S.A.* 102 H15
Wâḥid, *Egypt* 69 E1
Wahnai, *Afghan.* 62 C1
Wahoo, *U.S.A.* 108 E6
Wahpeton, *U.S.A.* 108 B6
Wai, Koh, *Cambodia* 59 H4
Waiau →, *N.Z.* 87 K4
Waibeem, *Indonesia* 57 E8
Waiblingen, *Germany* 19 G5
Waidhofen, *Niederösterreich, Austria* 20 G5
Waidhofen, *Niederösterreich, Austria* 21 H4
Waigeo, *Indonesia* 57 E8
Waihi, *N.Z.* 87 G5
Waihou →, *N.Z.* 87 G5
Waika, *Zaïre* 82 C2
Waikabubak, *Indonesia* 57 F5
Waikari, *N.Z.* 87 K4
Waikato →, *N.Z.* 87 G5
Waikerie, *Australia* 91 E2
Waikokopu, *N.Z.* 87 H6
Waikouaiti, *N.Z.* 87 L3
Waimakariri →, *N.Z.* 87 K4
Waimate, *N.Z.* 87 L3
Waimes, *Belgium* 17 H8
Wainganga →, *India* 60 K11
Waingapu, *Indonesia* 57 F6
Waini →, *Guyana* 121 B6
Wainwright, *Canada* 101 C6
Wainwright, *U.S.A.* 96 A3
Waiouru, *N.Z.* 87 H5
Waipara, *N.Z.* 87 K4
Waipawa, *N.Z.* 87 H6
Waipiro, *N.Z.* 87 H7
Waipu, *N.Z.* 87 F5
Waipukurau, *N.Z.* 87 J6
Wairakei, *N.Z.* 87 H6
Wairarapa, L., *N.Z.* 87 J5
Wairoa, *N.Z.* 87 H6
Waitaki →, *N.Z.* 87 L3
Waitara, *N.Z.* 87 H5
Waitsburg, *U.S.A.* 110 C5
Waiuku, *N.Z.* 87 G5
Wajima, *Japan* 49 F8
Wajir, *Kenya* 82 B5
Wajir □, *Kenya* 82 B5
Wakasa, *Japan* 49 G7
Wakasa-Wan, *Japan* 49 G7
Wakatipu, L., *N.Z.* 87 L2
Wakaw, *Canada* 101 C7
Wakayama, *Japan* 49 G7
Wakayama-ken □, *Japan* 49 H7
Wake Forest, *U.S.A.* 105 H6
Wake I., *Pac. Oc.* 92 F8
Wakefield, *N.Z.* 87 J4
Wakefield, *U.K.* 12 D6
Wakefield, *Mass., U.S.A.* 107 D13
Wakefield, *Mich., U.S.A.* 108 B10
Wakeham Bay = Maricourt, *Canada* 97 C12
Wakema, *Burma* 61 L19
Wakkanai, *Japan* 48 B10
Wakkerstroom, *S. Africa* 85 D5
Wakool, *Australia* 91 F3
Wakool →, *Australia* 91 F3
Wakre, *Indonesia* 57 E8
Wakuach L., *Canada* 99 A6
Walamba, *Zambia* 83 E2
Wałbrzych, *Poland* 20 E6
Walbury Hill, *U.K.* 13 F6
Walcha, *Australia* 91 E5
Walcheren, *Neths.* 17 E3
Walcott, *U.S.A.* 110 F10
Wałcz, *Poland* 20 B6
Wald, *Switz.* 23 B7
Waldbröl, *Germany* 18 E3
Waldburg Ra., *Australia* 88 D2
Waldeck, *Germany* 18 D5
Walden, *Colo., U.S.A.* 110 F10
Walden, *N.Y., U.S.A.* 107 E10
Waldenburg, *Switz.* 22 B5
Waldport, *U.S.A.* 110 D1
Waldron, *U.S.A.* 109 H7
Waldshut, *Germany* 19 H4
Walembele, *Ghana* 78 C4
Walensee, *Switz.* 23 B8
Walenstadt, *Switz.* 23 B8
Wales □, *U.K.* 13 E4
Walewale, *Ghana* 79 C4
Walgett, *Australia* 91 E4
Walgreen Coast, *Antarctica* 5 D15
Walhalla, *Australia* 91 F4
Walhalla, *U.S.A.* 101 D9
Walker, *U.S.A.* 108 B7
Walker L., *Man., Canada* 101 C9
Walker L., *Qué., Canada* 99 B6
Walker L., *U.S.A.* 110 G4
Walkerston, *Australia* 90 C4
Walkerton, *Canada* 106 B3
Wall, *U.S.A.* 108 C3
Walla Walla, *U.S.A.* 110 C4
Wallabadah, *Australia* 90 B3
Wallace, *Idaho, U.S.A.* 110 C6
Wallace, *N.C., U.S.A.* 105 H7
Wallace, *Nebr., U.S.A.* 108 E4
Wallaceburg, *Canada* 98 D3
Wallachia = Valahia, *Romania* 38 E8
Wallal, *Australia* 91 D4
Wallal Downs, *Australia* 88 C3
Wallambin, L., *Australia* 89 F2
Wallaroo, *Australia* 91 E2
Wallasey, *U.K.* 12 D4
Walldürn, *Germany* 19 F5
Wallerawang, *Australia* 91 E5
Wallhallow, *Australia* 90 B2
Wallingford, *U.S.A.* 107 E12
Wallis & Futuna, Is., *Pac. Oc.* 92 J10
Wallisellen, *Switz.* 23 B7
Wallowa, *U.S.A.* 110 D5
Wallowa Mts., *U.S.A.* 110 D5
Wallsend, *Australia* 91 E5
Wallsend, *U.K.* 12 C6
Wallula, *U.S.A.* 110 C4
Wallumbilla, *Australia* 91 D4
Walmsley, L., *Canada* 101 A7
Walney, I. of, *U.K.* 12 C4
Walnut Creek, *U.S.A.* 112 H4
Walnut Ridge, *U.S.A.* 109 G9
Walsall, *U.K.* 13 E6
Walsenburg, *U.S.A.* 109 G2
Walsh, *U.S.A.* 109 G3
Walsh →, *Australia* 90 B3
Walsh P.O., *Australia* 90 B3
Walshoutem, *Belgium* 17 G6
Walsrode, *Germany* 18 C5
Walterboro, *U.S.A.* 105 J5
Walters, *U.S.A.* 109 H5
Waltershausen, *Germany* 18 E6
Waltham, *U.S.A.* 107 D13
Waltham Station, *Canada* 98 C4
Waltman, *U.S.A.* 110 E10
Walton, *U.S.A.* 107 D9
Walvisbaai, *Namibia* 84 C1
Wamba, *Kenya* 82 B4
Wamba, *Zaïre* 82 B2
Wamego, *U.S.A.* 108 F6
Wamena, *Indonesia* 57 E9
Wamulan, *Indonesia* 57 E7
Wan Xian, *China* 50 E8
Wana, *Pakistan* 62 C3
Wanaaring, *Australia* 91 D3
Wanaka, *N.Z.* 87 L2
Wanaka L., *N.Z.* 87 L2
Wan'an, *China* 53 D10
Wanapiri, *Indonesia* 57 E9
Wanapitei L., *Canada* 98 C3
Wanbi, *Australia* 91 E3
Wandaik, *Guyana* 121 C6
Wandarrie, *Australia* 89 E2
Wandel Sea = McKinley Sea, *Arctic* 4 A7
Wanderer, *Zimbabwe* 83 F3
Wandoan, *Australia* 91 D4
Wandre, *Belgium* 17 G7
Wanfercée-Baulet, *Belgium* 17 H5
Wanfu, *China* 51 D12
Wang →, *Thailand* 58 D2
Wang Kai, *Sudan* 77 F2
Wang Noi, *Thailand* 58 E3
Wang Saphung, *Thailand* 58 D3
Wang Thong, *Thailand* 58 D3
Wanga, *Zaïre* 82 B2
Wangal, *Indonesia* 57 F8
Wanganella, *Australia* 91 F3
Wanganui, *N.Z.* 87 H5
Wangaratta, *Australia* 91 F4
Wangary, *Australia* 91 E2
Wangcang, *China* 52 A6
Wangdu, *China* 50 E8
Wangerooge, *Germany* 18 B3
Wangi, *Kenya* 82 C5
Wangiwangi, *Indonesia* 57 F6
Wangjiang, *China* 53 B11
Wangmo, *China* 52 E6
Wangqing, *China* 51 C15
Wankaner, *India* 62 H4
Wanless, *Canada* 101 C8
Wannian, *China* 53 C11
Wanon Niwat, *Thailand* 58 D4
Wanquan, *China* 50 D8
Wanrong, *China* 50 G6
Wanshan, *China* 52 D7
Wanshengchang, *China* 52 C6
Wanssum, *Neths.* 17 E8
Wanxian, *China* 52 B7
Wanyuan, *China* 52 A7
Wanzai, *China* 53 C10
Wanze, *Belgium* 17 G6
Wapakoneta, *U.S.A.* 104 E3
Wapato, *U.S.A.* 110 C3
Wapawekka L., *Canada* 101 C8
Wapikopa L., *Canada* 98 B2
Wappingers Falls, *U.S.A.* 107 E11
Wapsipinicon →, *U.S.A.* 108 E9
Warangal, *India* 60 L11
Waratah, *Australia* 90 G4
Waratah B., *Australia* 91 F4
Warburg, *Germany* 18 D5
Warburton, *Vic., Australia* 91 F4
Warburton, *W. Austral., Australia* 89 E4
Warburton Ra., *Australia* 89 E4
Ward, *N.Z.* 87 J5
Ward →, *Australia* 91 D4
Ward Cove, *U.S.A.* 100 B2
Ward Mt., *U.S.A.* 112 H8
Warden, *S. Africa* 85 D4
Wardha, *India* 60 J11
Wardha →, *India* 60 K11
Wardlow, *Canada* 100 C6
Ware, *Canada* 100 B3
Ware, *U.S.A.* 107 D12
Waregem, *Belgium* 17 G2
Wareham, *U.S.A.* 107 E14
Waremme, *Belgium* 17 G6
Waren, *Germany* 18 B8
Warendorf, *Germany* 18 D3
Warialda, *Australia* 91 D5
Wariap, *Indonesia* 57 E8
Warin Chamrap, *Thailand* 58 E5
Warkopi, *Indonesia* 57 E8
Warley, *U.K.* 13 E6
Warm Springs, *U.S.A.* 111 G5
Warman, *Canada* 101 C7
Warmbad, *Namibia* 84 D2
Warmbad, *S. Africa* 85 C4
Warmenhuizen, *Neths.* 16 C5
Warmeriville, *France* 25 C11
Warmond, *Neths.* 16 D5
Warnambool Downs, *Australia* 90 C3
Warnemünde, *Germany* 18 A8
Warner, *Canada* 100 D6
Warner Mts., *U.S.A.* 110 F3
Warner Robins, *U.S.A.* 105 J4
Warnes, *Bolivia* 125 D5
Warneton, *Belgium* 17 G1
Warnow →, *Germany* 18 A8
Warnsveld, *Neths.* 16 D8
Waroona, *Australia* 89 F2
Warracknabeal, *Australia* 91 F3
Warragul, *Australia* 91 F4
Warrawagine, *Australia* 88 D3
Warrego →, *Australia* 91 E4
Warrego Ra., *Australia* 90 C4
Warren, *Australia* 91 E4
Warren, *Ark., U.S.A.* 109 J8
Warren, *Mich., U.S.A.* 104 D4
Warren, *Minn., U.S.A.* 108 A6
Warren, *Ohio, U.S.A.* 106 E4
Warren, *Pa., U.S.A.* 106 E5
Warrenpoint, *U.K.* 15 B5
Warrensburg, *U.S.A.* 108 F8
Warrenton, *S. Africa* 84 D3
Warrenton, *U.S.A.* 112 D3
Warrenville, *Australia* 91 D4
Warri, *Nigeria* 79 D6
Warrina, *Australia* 91 D2
Warrington, *U.K.* 12 D5
Warrington, *U.S.A.* 105 K2
Warrnambool, *Australia* 91 F3
Warroad, *U.S.A.* 108 A7
Warsa, *Indonesia* 57 E9
Warsaw = Warszawa, *Poland* 20 C11
Warsaw, *Ind., U.S.A.* 104 E3
Warsaw, *N.Y., U.S.A.* 106 D6
Warsaw, *Ohio, U.S.A.* 106 F2
Warstein, *Germany* 18 D4
Warszawa, *Poland* 20 C11
Warta →, *Poland* 20 C4
Warthe = Warta →, *Poland* 20 C4
Waru, *Indonesia* 57 E8
Warwick, *Australia* 91 D5
Warwick, *U.K.* 13 E6
Warwick, *U.S.A.* 107 E13
Warwickshire □, *U.K.* 13 E6
Wasaga Beach, *Canada* 106 B4
Wasatch Ra., *U.S.A.* 110 F8
Wasbank, *S. Africa* 85 D5
Wasco, *Calif., U.S.A.* 113 K7
Wasco, *Oreg., U.S.A.* 110 D3
Waseca, *U.S.A.* 108 C8
Wasekamio L., *Canada* 101 B7
Wash, The, *U.K.* 12 E8
Washago, *Canada* 106 B5
Washburn, *N. Dak., U.S.A.* 108 B4
Washburn, *Wis., U.S.A.* 108 B9
Washim, *India* 60 J10
Washington, *D.C., U.S.A.* 104 F7
Washington, *Ga., U.S.A.* 105 J4
Washington, *Ind., U.S.A.* 104 F2
Washington, *Iowa, U.S.A.* 108 E9
Washington, *Mo., U.S.A.* 108 F9
Washington, *N.C., U.S.A.* 105 H7
Washington, *N.J., U.S.A.* 107 F10
Washington, *Pa., U.S.A.* 106 F4
Washington, *Utah, U.S.A.* 111 H7
Washington □, *U.S.A.* 110 C3
Washington, Mt., *U.S.A.* 107 B13
Washington I., *U.S.A.* 104 C2
Washougal, *U.S.A.* 112 E4
Wasian, *Indonesia* 57 E8
Wasior, *Indonesia* 57 E8
Waskaganish, *Canada* 98 B4
Waskaiowaka, L., *Canada* 101 B9
Waskesiu Lake, *Canada* 101 C7
Wasmes, *Belgium* 17 H3
Waspik, *Neths.* 17 E5
Wassen, *Switz.* 23 C7
Wassenaar, *Neths.* 16 D4
Wasserburg, *Germany* 19 G8
Wasserkuppe, *Germany* 18 E5
Wassy, *France* 25 D11
Waswanipi, *Canada* 98 C4
Waswanipi, L., *Canada* 98 C4
Watangpone, *Indonesia* 57 E6
Water Park Pt., *Australia* 90 C5
Water Valley, *U.S.A.* 109 H10
Waterberge, *S. Africa* 85 C4
Waterbury, *Conn., U.S.A.* 107 E11
Waterbury, *Vt., U.S.A.* 107 B12
Waterbury L., *Canada* 101 B8
Waterdown, *Canada* 106 C5
Waterford, *Canada* 106 D4
Waterford, *Ireland* 15 D4
Waterford, *U.S.A.* 112 H6
Waterford □, *Ireland* 15 D4
Waterford Harbour, *Ireland* 15 D5
Waterhen L., *Man., Canada* 101 C9
Waterhen L., *Sask., Canada* 101 C7
Wateringen, *Neths.* 16 D4
Waterloo, *Belgium* 17 G4
Waterloo, *Ont., Canada* 98 D3
Waterloo, *Qué., Canada* 107 A12
Waterloo, *S. Leone* 78 D2
Waterloo, *Ill., U.S.A.* 108 F9
Waterloo, *Iowa, U.S.A.* 108 D8
Waterloo, *N.Y., U.S.A.* 106 D8
Watermeal-Boitsford, *Belgium* 17 G4
Watersmeet, *U.S.A.* 108 B10
Waterton-Glacier International Peace Park, *U.S.A.* 110 B7
Watertown, *Conn., U.S.A.* 107 E11
Watertown, *N.Y., U.S.A.* 107 C9
Watertown, *S. Dak., U.S.A.* 108 C6
Watertown, *Wis., U.S.A.* 108 D10
Waterval-Boven, *S. Africa* 85 D5
Waterville, *Canada* 107 A13
Waterville, *Maine, U.S.A.* 99 D6
Waterville, *N.Y., U.S.A.* 107 D9
Waterville, *Pa., U.S.A.* 106 E7
Waterville, *Wash., U.S.A.* 110 C3
Watervliet, *Belgium* 17 F3
Watervliet, *U.S.A.* 107 D11
Wates, *Indonesia* 57 G14
Watford, *Canada* 106 D3
Watford, *U.K.* 13 F7
Watford City, *U.S.A.* 108 B3
Wathaman →, *Canada* 101 B8
Watheroo, *Australia* 89 F2
Wating, *China* 50 G4
Watkins Glen, *U.S.A.* 106 D8
Watling I. = San Salvador, *Bahamas* 117 B5
Watonga, *U.S.A.* 109 H5
Watou, *Belgium* 17 G1
Watrous, *Canada* 101 C7
Watrous, *U.S.A.* 109 H2
Watsa, *Zaïre* 82 B2
Watseka, *U.S.A.* 104 E2
Watson, *Australia* 89 F5
Watson, *Canada* 101 C8
Watson Lake, *Canada* 100 A3
Watsonville, *U.S.A.* 111 H3
Wattenwil, *Switz.* 22 C5
Wattiwarriganna Cr. →, *Australia* 91 D2
Wattwil, *Switz.* 23 B8
Watuata = Batuata, *Indonesia* 57 F6
Watubela, Kepulauan, *Indonesia* 57 E8
Watubela Is. = Watubela, Kepulauan, *Indonesia* 57 E8
Waubach, *Neths.* 17 G8
Waubamik, *Canada* 106 A4
Waubay, *U.S.A.* 108 C6
Waubra, *Australia* 91 F3
Wauchope, *Australia* 91 E5
Wauchula, *U.S.A.* 105 M5
Waugh, *Canada* 101 D9
Waukarlycarly, L., *Australia* 88 D3
Waukegan, *U.S.A.* 104 D2
Waukesha, *U.S.A.* 104 D1
Waukon, *U.S.A.* 108 D9
Wauneta, *U.S.A.* 108 E4
Waupaca, *U.S.A.* 108 C10
Waupun, *U.S.A.* 108 D10
Waurika, *U.S.A.* 109 H6
Wausau, *U.S.A.* 108 C10
Wautoma, *U.S.A.* 108 C10
Wauwatosa, *U.S.A.* 104 D2
Wave Hill, *Australia* 88 C5
Waveney →, *U.K.* 13 E9
Waverley, *N.Z.* 87 H5
Waverly, *Iowa, U.S.A.* 108 D8
Waverly, *N.Y., U.S.A.* 107 D8
Wavre, *Belgium* 17 G5
Wavreille, *Belgium* 17 H6
Wâw, *Sudan* 77 F2
Wāw al Kabīr, *Libya* 73 C8
Wawa, *Canada* 98 C3
Wawa, *Nigeria* 79 D5
Wawa, *Sudan* 76 C3
Wawanesa, *Canada* 101 D9
Wawona, *U.S.A.* 112 H7
Waxahachie, *U.S.A.* 109 J6
Way, L., *Australia* 89 E3
Wayabula Rau, *Indonesia* 57 D7
Wayatinah, *Australia* 90 G4
Waycross, *U.S.A.* 105 K4
Wayi, *Sudan* 77 F3
Wayne, *Nebr., U.S.A.* 108 D6
Wayne, *W. Va., U.S.A.* 104 F4
Waynesboro, *Ga., U.S.A.* 105 J4
Waynesboro, *Miss., U.S.A.* 105 K1
Waynesboro, *Pa., U.S.A.* 104 F7
Waynesboro, *Va., U.S.A.* 104 F6
Waynesburg, *U.S.A.* 104 F5
Waynesville, *U.S.A.* 105 H4
Waynoka, *U.S.A.* 109 G5
Wāzin, *Libya* 75 B7
Wazirabad, *Pakistan* 62 C6
We, *Indonesia* 56 C1
Weald, The, *U.K.* 13 F8
Wear →, *U.K.* 12 C6
Weatherford, *Okla., U.S.A.* 109 H5
Weatherford, *Tex., U.S.A.* 109 J6
Weaverville, *U.S.A.* 110 F2
Webb City, *U.S.A.* 109 G7
Webo = Nyaake, *Liberia* 78 E3
Webster, *Mass., U.S.A.* 107 D13
Webster, *N.Y., U.S.A.* 106 C7
Webster, *S. Dak., U.S.A.* 108 C6
Webster, *Wis., U.S.A.* 108 C8
Webster City, *U.S.A.* 108 D8
Webster Green, *U.S.A.* 108 F9
Webster Springs, *U.S.A.* 104 F5
Weda, *Indonesia* 57 D7
Weda, Teluk, *Indonesia* 57 D7
Weddell I., *Falk. Is.* 128 D4
Weddell Sea, *Antarctica* 5 D1
Wedderburn, *Australia* 91 F3
Wedel, *Germany* 18 B5
Wedgeport, *Canada* 99 D6
Wedza, *Zimbabwe* 83 F3
Wee Waa, *Australia* 91 E4
Weed, *U.S.A.* 110 F2
Weed Heights, *U.S.A.* 112 G7
Weedsport, *U.S.A.* 107 C8
Weedville, *U.S.A.* 106 E6
Weemelah, *Australia* 91 D4
Weenen, *S. Africa* 85 D5
Weener, *Germany* 18 B3
Weert, *Neths.* 17 F7
Weesp, *Neths.* 16 D6
Weggis, *Switz.* 23 B6
Węgliniec, *Poland* 20 D5
Węgorzewo, *Poland* 20 A11
Węgrów, *Poland* 20 C12
Wehl, *Neths.* 16 E8
Wei He →, *Hebei, China* 50 F8
Wei He →, *Shaanxi, China* 50 G6
Weichang, *China* 51 D9
Weichuan, *China* 50 G7
Weida, *Germany* 18 E8
Weiden, *Germany* 19 F8
Weifang, *China* 51 F10
Weihai, *China* 51 F12
Weilburg, *Germany* 18 E4
Weilheim, *Germany* 19 H7
Weimar, *Germany* 18 E7
Weinan, *China* 50 G5
Weinfelden, *Switz.* 23 A8
Weingarten, *Germany* 19 H5
Weinheim, *Germany* 19 F4
Weining, *China* 52 D5
Weipa, *Australia* 90 A3
Weir →, *Australia* 91 D4
Weir →, *Canada* 101 B10
Weir River, *Canada* 101 B10
Weirton, *U.S.A.* 106 F4
Weisen, *Switz.* 23 C9
Weiser, *U.S.A.* 110 D5
Weishan, *Shandong, China* 51 G9
Weishan, *Yunnan, China* 52 E3
Weissenburg, *Germany* 19 F6
Weissenfels, *Germany* 18 D8
Weisshorn, *Switz.* 22 D5
Weissmies, *Switz.* 22 D6
Weisstannen, *Switz.* 23 C8
Weisswasser, *Germany* 18 D10
Weiswampach, *Belgium* 17 H8
Weixi, *China* 52 D2
Weixin, *China* 52 D5
Weiyuan, *China* 50 G3
Weiz, *Austria* 21 H5
Weizhou Dao, *China* 52 G7
Wejherowo, *Poland* 20 A8
Wekusko L., *Canada* 101 C9
Welbourn Hill, *Australia* 91 D1
Welch, *U.S.A.* 104 G5
Weldya, *Ethiopia* 77 E4
Welega □, *Ethiopia* 77 F3
Welkenraedt, *Belgium* 17 G7
Welkite, *Ethiopia* 77 F4
Welkom, *S. Africa* 84 D4
Welland, *Canada* 98 D4
Welland →, *U.K.* 12 E7
Wellen, *Belgium* 17 G6
Wellesley Is., *Australia* 90 B2
Wellin, *Belgium* 17 H6
Wellingborough, *U.K.* 13 E7
Wellington, *Australia* 91 E4
Wellington, *Canada* 98 D4
Wellington, *N.Z.* 87 J5
Wellington, *S. Africa* 84 E2
Wellington, *Shrops., U.K.* 12 E5
Wellington, *Somst., U.K.* 13 G4
Wellington, *Colo., U.S.A.* 108 E2
Wellington, *Kans., U.S.A.* 109 G6
Wellington, *Nev., U.S.A.* 112 G7
Wellington, *Ohio, U.S.A.* 106 E2
Wellington, *Tex., U.S.A.* 109 H4
Wellington, I., *Chile* 128 C2
Wellington, L., *Australia* 91 F4
Wells, *U.K.* 13 F5
Wells, *Maine, U.S.A.* 107 C14
Wells, *Minn., U.S.A.* 108 D8
Wells, *Nev., U.S.A.* 110 F6
Wells, L., *Australia* 89 E3
Wells Gray Prov. Park, *Canada* 100 C4
Wells-next-the-Sea, *U.K.* 12 E8
Wells River, *U.S.A.* 107 B12
Wellsboro, *U.S.A.* 106 E7
Wellsburg, *U.S.A.* 106 F4
Wellsville, *Mo., U.S.A.* 108 F9
Wellsville, *N.Y., U.S.A.* 106 D7
Wellsville, *Ohio, U.S.A.* 106 F4
Wellsville, *Utah, U.S.A.* 110 F8
Wellton, *U.S.A.* 111 K6
Welmel, Wabi →, *Ethiopia* 77 F5
Welo □, *Ethiopia* 77 E4
Wels, *Austria* 21 G4
Welshpool, *U.K.* 13 E4
Wem, *U.K.* 12 E5
Wembere →, *Tanzania* 82 C3
Wemindji, *Canada* 98 B4

Wemmel, *Belgium* 17 G4
Wen Xian, *Gansu, China* . 50 H3
Wen Xian, *Henan, China* . 50 G7
Wenatchee, *U.S.A.* 110 C3
Wenchang, *China* 58 C8
Wencheng, *China* 53 D13
Wenchi, *Ghana* 78 D4
Wenchow = Wenzhou,
  China 53 C13
Wenchuan, *China* 52 B4
Wendell, *U.S.A.* 110 E6
Wenden, *U.S.A.* 113 M13
Wendeng, *China* 51 F12
Wendesi, *Indonesia* 57 E8
Wendo, *Ethiopia* 77 F4
Wendover, *U.S.A.* 110 F6
Wenduine, *Belgium* 17 F2
Weng'an, *China* 52 D6
Wengcheng, *China* 53 E9
Wengen, *Switz.* 22 C5
Wengyuan, *China* 53 E10
Wenjiang, *China* 52 B4
Wenling, *China* 53 C13
Wenlock →, *Australia* ... 90 A3
Wenshan, *China* 52 F5
Wenshang, *China* 50 G9
Wenshui, *Guizhou, China* 52 C6
Wenshui, *Shanxi, China* . 50 F7
Wensu, *China* 54 B3
Wentworth, *Australia* 91 E3
Wenut, *Indonesia* 57 E8
Wenxi, *China* 50 G6
Wenzhou, *China* 53 C13
Weott, *U.S.A.* 110 F2
Wepener, *S. Africa* 84 D4
Werbomont, *Belgium* 17 H7
Werda, *Botswana* 84 D3
Werdau, *Germany* 18 E8
Werder, *Ethiopia* 68 F4
Werder, *Germany* 18 C8
Werdohl, *Germany* 18 D3
Wereilu, *Ethiopia* 77 E4
Weri, *Indonesia* 57 E8
Werkendam, *Neths.* 16 E5
Werne, *Germany* 18 D3
Werneck, *Germany* 19 F6
Wernigerode, *Germany* .. 18 D6
Werra →, *Germany* 18 D5
Werribee, *Australia* 91 F3
Werrimull, *Australia* 91 E3
Werris Creek, *Australia* . 91 E5
Wersar, *Indonesia* 57 E8
Wertach →, *Germany* ... 19 G6
Wertheim, *Germany* 19 F5
Wertingen, *Germany* 19 G6
Wervershoof, *Neths.* 16 C6
Wervik, *Belgium* 17 G2
Wesel, *Germany* 18 D2
Weser →, *Germany* 18 B4
Wesiri, *Indonesia* 57 F7
Wesley Vale, *U.S.A.* 111 J10
Wesleyville, *Canada* 99 C9
Wesleyville, *U.S.A.* 106 D4
Wessel, C., *Australia* 90 A2
Wessel Is., *Australia* 90 A2
Wesselburen, *Germany* .. 18 A4
Wessem, *Neths.* 17 F7
Wessington, *U.S.A.* 108 C5
Wessington Springs, *U.S.A.* 108 C5
West, *U.S.A.* 109 K6
West B., *U.S.A.* 109 L10
West Baines →, *Australia* 88 C4
West Bank □, *Asia* 69 C4
West Bend, *U.S.A.* 104 D1
West Bengal □, *India* ... 63 H12
West Beskids = Západné
  Beskydy, *Europe* 20 F9
West Branch, *U.S.A.* 104 C3
West Bromwich, *U.K.* ... 13 E5
West Bromwich Howe, *Australia* 89 G2
West Chazy, *U.S.A.* 107 B11
West Chester, *U.S.A.* 104 F8
West Columbia, *U.S.A.* . 109 L7
West Covina, *U.S.A.* 113 L9
West Des Moines, *U.S.A.* 108 E8
West End, *Bahamas* 116 A4
West Falkland, *Falk. Is.* . 128 D4
West Fjord = Vestfjorden,
  Norway 8 C15
West Frankfort, *U.S.A.* .. 108 G10
West Glamorgan □, *U.K.* 13 F4
West Hartford, *U.S.A.* .. 107 E12
West Haven, *U.S.A.* 107 E12
West Helena, *U.S.A.* 109 H9
West Ice Shelf, *Antarctica* 5 C7
West Indies, *Cent. Amer.* 117 C7
West Lorne, *Canada* 106 D3
West Lunga →, *Zambia* . 83 E1
West Memphis, *U.S.A.* .. 109 H9
West Midlands □, *U.K.* . 13 E6
West Mifflin, *U.S.A.* 106 F5
West Monroe, *U.S.A.* ... 109 J8
West Newton, *U.S.A.* ... 106 F5
West Nicholson, *Zimbabwe* 83 G2
West Palm Beach, *U.S.A.* 105 M5
West Plains, *U.S.A.* 109 G9
West Point, *Ga., U.S.A.* . 105 J3
West Point, *Miss., U.S.A.* 105 J1
West Point, *Nebr., U.S.A.* 108 E6
West Point, *Va., U.S.A.* . 104 G7
West Pokot □, *Kenya* ... 82 B4
West Pt. = Ouest, Pte.,
  Canada 99 C7
West Pt., *Australia* 91 E2
West Road →, *Canada* . 100 C4
West Rutland, *U.S.A.* ... 107 C11

West Schelde =
  Westerschelde →, *Neths.* 17 F2
West Seneca, *U.S.A.* 106 D6
West Siberian Plain, *Russia* 46 C11
West Sussex □, *U.K.* 13 G7
West-Terschelling, *Neths.* 16 B6
West Virginia □, *U.S.A.* . 104 F5
West-Vlaanderen □,
  Belgium 17 G2
West Walker →, *U.S.A.* . 112 G7
West Wyalong, *Australia* 91 E4
West Yellowstone, *U.S.A.* 110 D8
West Yorkshire □, *U.K.* . 12 D6
Westall Pt., *Australia* ... 91 E1
Westbrook, *Maine, U.S.A.* 105 D10
Westbrook, *Tex., U.S.A.* 109 J4
Westbury, *Australia* 90 G4
Westby, *U.S.A.* 108 A2
Westend, *U.S.A.* 113 K9
Westerbork, *Neths.* 16 C9
Westerland, *Germany* ... 9 J13
Western □, *Kenya* 82 B3
Western □, *Uganda* 82 B3
Western □, *Zambia* 83 F1
Western Australia □,
  Australia 89 E2
Western Cape □, *S. Africa* 84 E3
Western Ghats, *India* 60 N9
Western Isles □, *U.K.* ... 14 D1
Western Sahara ■, *Africa* 74 D2
Western Samoa ■,
  Pac. Oc. 87 A13
Westernport, *U.S.A.* 104 F6
Westerschelde →, *Neths.* 17 F2
Westerstede, *Germany* ... 18 B3
Westervoort, *Neths.* 16 E7
Westerwald, *Germany* ... 18 E4
Westfield, *Mass., U.S.A.* 107 D12
Westfield, *N.Y., U.S.A.* . 106 D5
Westfield, *Pa., U.S.A.* .. 106 E7
Westgat, *Neths.* 17 E3
Westhope, *U.S.A.* 108 A4
Westkapelle, *Belgium* ... 17 F2
Westkapelle, *Neths.* 17 E2
Westland Bight, *N.Z.* ... 87 K3
Westlock, *Canada* 100 C6
Westmalle, *Belgium* 17 F5
Westmeath □, *Ireland* ... 15 C4
Westminster, *U.S.A.* 104 F7
Westmorland, *U.S.A.* ... 111 K6
Weston, *Malaysia* 56 C5
Weston, *Oreg., U.S.A.* .. 110 D4
Weston, *W. Va., U.S.A.* . 104 F5
Weston I., *Canada* 98 B4
Weston-super-Mare, *U.K.* 13 F5
Westport, *Canada* 107 B8
Westport, *Ireland* 15 C2
Westport, *N.Z.* 87 J3
Westport, *Oreg., U.S.A.* . 112 D3
Westport, *Wash., U.S.A.* 110 C1
Westray, *Canada* 101 C8
Westray, *U.K.* 14 B6
Westree, *Canada* 98 C3
Westville, *Calif., U.S.A.* . 112 F6
Westville, *Ill., U.S.A.* ... 104 E2
Westville, *Okla., U.S.A.* . 109 G7
Westwood, *U.S.A.* 110 F3
Wetar, *Indonesia* 57 F7
Wetaskiwin, *Canada* 100 C6
Wethersfield, *U.S.A.* 107 E12
Wetteren, *Belgium* 17 G3
Wettingen, *Switz.* 23 B6
Wetzikon, *Switz.* 23 B7
Wetzlar, *Germany* 18 E4
Wevelgem, *Belgium* 17 G2
Wewoka, *U.S.A.* 109 H6
Wexford, *Ireland* 15 D5
Wexford □, *Ireland* 15 D5
Wexford Harbour, *Ireland* 15 D5
Weyburn, *Canada* 101 D8
Weyburn L., *Canada* 100 A5
Weyer, *Austria* 21 H4
Weyib →, *Ethiopia* 77 F5
Weymouth, *Canada* 99 D6
Weymouth, *U.K.* 13 G5
Weymouth, *U.S.A.* 107 D14
Weymouth, C., *Australia* 90 A3
Wezemaal, *Belgium* 17 G5
Wezep, *Neths.* 16 D7
Whakatane, *N.Z.* 87 G6
Whale →, *Canada* 99 A6
Whale Cove, *Canada* 101 A10
Whales, B. of, *Antarctica* 5 D12
Whalsay, *U.K.* 14 A7
Whangamomona, *N.Z.* .. 87 H5
Whangarei, *N.Z.* 87 F5
Whangarei Harb., *N.Z.* . 87 F5
Wharfe →, *U.K.* 12 D6
Wharfedale, *U.K.* 12 C5
Wharton, *N.J., U.S.A.* .. 107 F10
Wharton, *Pa., U.S.A.* ... 106 E6
Wharton, *Tex., U.S.A.* .. 109 L6
Wheatland, *Calif., U.S.A.* 112 F5
Wheatland, *Wyo., U.S.A.* 108 D2
Wheatley, *Canada* 106 D2
Wheaton, *U.S.A.* 108 C6
Wheelbarrow Pk., *U.S.A.* 112 H10
Wheeler, *Oreg., U.S.A.* . 110 D2
Wheeler, *Tex., U.S.A.* .. 109 H4
Wheeler →, *Canada* 101 B7
Wheeler Pk., *N. Mex.,
  U.S.A.* 111 H11
Wheeler Pk., *Nev., U.S.A.* 111 G6
Wheeler Ridge, *U.S.A.* .. 113 L8
Wheeling, *U.S.A.* 106 F4
Whernside, *U.K.* 12 C5
Whidbey I., *U.S.A.* 100 D4

Whiskey Gap, *Canada* ... 100 D6
Whiskey Jack L., *Canada* . 101 B8
Whistleduck Cr. →,
  Australia 90 C2
Whitby, *Canada* 106 C6
Whitby, *U.K.* 12 C7
White →, *Ark., U.S.A.* . 109 J9
White →, *Ind., U.S.A.* . 104 F2
White →, *S. Dak., U.S.A.* 108 D5
White →, *Utah, U.S.A.* . 110 F9
White →, *Wash., U.S.A.* 112 C4
White, L., *Australia* 88 D4
White B., *Canada* 99 B8
White Bear Res., *Canada* 99 C8
White Bird, *U.S.A.* 110 D5
White Butte, *U.S.A.* 108 B3
White City, *U.S.A.* 108 F6
White Cliffs, *Australia* .. 91 E3
White Deer, *U.S.A.* 109 H4
White Hall, *U.S.A.* 108 F9
White Haven, *U.S.A.* 107 E9
White Horse, Vale of, *U.K.* 13 F6
White I., *N.Z.* 87 G6
White L., *Canada* 107 A8
White L., *U.S.A.* 109 L8
White Mts., *Calif., U.S.A.* 111 H4
White Mts., *N.H., U.S.A.* 107 B13
White Nile = Nîl el
  Abyad →, *Sudan* 77 D3
White Nile Dam =
  Khazzân Jabal el Awliyâ,
  Sudan 77 D3
White Otter L., *Canada* . 98 C1
White Pass, *Canada* 100 B1
White Pass, *U.S.A.* 112 D5
White Plains, *U.S.A.* 107 E11
White River, *Canada* 98 C2
White River, *S. Africa* ... 85 D5
White River, *U.S.A.* 108 D4
White Russia = Belarus ■,
  Europe 40 F4
White Sea = Beloye More,
  Russia 44 C4
White Sulphur Springs,
  Mont., U.S.A. 110 C8
White Sulphur Springs,
  W. Va., U.S.A. 104 G5
White Swan, *U.S.A.* 112 D6
White Volta →, *Ghana* . 79 D4
Whitecliffs, *N.Z.* 87 K3
Whitecourt, *Canada* 100 C5
Whiteface, *U.S.A.* 109 J3
Whitefield, *U.S.A.* 107 B13
Whitefish, *Canada* 110 B6
Whitefish L., *Canada* 101 A7
Whitefish Point, *U.S.A.* . 104 B3
Whitegull, L., *Canada* ... 99 A7
Whitehall, *Mich., U.S.A.* 104 D2
Whitehall, *Mont., U.S.A.* 110 D7
Whitehall, *N.Y., U.S.A.* . 107 C11
Whitehall, *Wis., U.S.A.* . 108 C9
Whitehaven, *U.K.* 12 C4
Whitehorse, *Canada* 100 A1
Whitemark, *Australia* ... 90 G4
Whitemouth, *Canada* 101 D9
Whiteplains, *Liberia* 78 D2
Whitesboro, *N.Y., U.S.A.* 107 C9
Whitesboro, *Tex., U.S.A.* 109 J6
Whiteshell Prov. Park,
  Canada 101 C9
Whiteside, Canal, *Chile* . 128 D2
Whitetail, *U.S.A.* 108 A2
Whiteville, *U.S.A.* 105 H6
Whitewater, *U.S.A.* 104 D1
Whitewater Baldy, *U.S.A.* 111 K9
Whitewater L., *Canada* .. 98 B2
Whitewood, *Australia* ... 90 C3
Whitewood, *Canada* 101 C8
Whitfield, *Australia* 91 F4
Whithorn, *U.K.* 14 G4
Whitianga, *N.Z.* 87 G5
Whitman, *U.S.A.* 107 D14
Whitmire, *U.S.A.* 105 H5
Whitney, *Canada* 98 C4
Whitney, Mt., *U.S.A.* ... 111 H4
Whitney Point, *U.S.A.* .. 107 D9
Whitstable, *U.K.* 13 F9
Whitsunday I., *Australia* . 90 C4
Whittier, *U.S.A.* 113 M8
Whittlesea, *Australia* 91 F4
Whitwell, *U.S.A.* 105 H3
Wholdaia L., *Canada* 101 A8
Whyalla, *Australia* 91 E2
Whyjonta, *Australia* 91 D3
Wiarton, *Canada* 98 D3
Wiawso, *Ghana* 78 D4
Wibaux, *U.S.A.* 108 B2
Wichabai, *Guyana* 121 C6
Wichian Buri, *Thailand* . 58 E3
Wichita, *U.S.A.* 109 G6
Wichita Falls, *U.S.A.* ... 109 J5
Wick, *U.K.* 14 C5
Wickenburg, *U.S.A.* 111 K7
Wickepin, *Australia* 89 F2
Wickham, C., *Australia* . 90 F3
Wickliffe, *U.S.A.* 106 E3
Wicklow, *Ireland* 15 D5
Wicklow □, *Ireland* 15 D5
Wicklow Hd., *Ireland* ... 15 D5
Widgiemooltha, *Australia* 89 F3
Widnes, *U.K.* 12 D5
Wiedenbrück, *Germany* . 18 D4
Wiehl, *Germany* 18 E3
Wiek, *Germany* 18 A9
Wielbark, *Poland* 20 B10
Wieliczka, *Poland* 20 F10
Wieluń, *Poland* 20 D8

Wien, *Austria* 21 G6
Wiener Neustadt, *Austria* 21 H6
Wieprz →, *Koszalin,
  Poland* 20 A6
Wieprz →, *Lublin, Poland* 20 D11
Wierden, *Neths.* 16 D9
Wiers, *Belgium* 17 H3
Wiesbaden, *Germany* ... 19 E4
Wiesental, *Germany* 19 F4
Wight, I. of □, *U.K.* 13 G6
Wigston, *U.S.A.* 106 F5
Wigtown, *U.K.* 14 G4
Wigtown B., *U.K.* 14 G4
Wijchen, *Neths.* 16 E7
Wijhe, *Neths.* 16 D8
Wijk bij Duurstede, *Neths.* 16 E6
Wil, *Switz.* 23 B8
Wilber, *U.S.A.* 108 E6
Wilberforce, *Canada* 106 A6
Wilberforce, C., *Australia* 90 A2
Wilburton, *U.S.A.* 109 H7
Wilcannia, *Australia* 91 E3
Wilcox, *U.S.A.* 106 E6
Wildbad, *Germany* 19 G4
Wildervank, *Neths.* 16 B9
Wildeshausen, *Germany* . 18 C4
Wildhorn, *Switz.* 22 D4
Wildrose, *Calif., U.S.A.* . 113 J9
Wildrose, *N. Dak., U.S.A.* 108 A3
Wildspitze, *Austria* 19 J6
Wildstrubel, *Switz.* 22 D5
Wildwood, *U.S.A.* 104 F8
Wilge →, *S. Africa* 85 D4
Wilhelm II Coast,
  Antarctica 5 C7
Wilhelm-Pieck-Stadt-
  Guben, *Germany* 18 D10
Wilhelmina, Geb., *Surinam* 121 C6
Wilhelmsburg, *Austria* .. 21 G5
Wilhelmshaven, *Germany* 18 B4
Wilhelmstal, *Namibia* ... 84 C2
Wilkes-Barre, *U.S.A.* 107 E9
Wilkesboro, *U.S.A.* 105 G5
Wilkie, *Canada* 101 C7
Wilkinsburg, *U.S.A.* 106 F5
Wilkinson Lakes, *Australia* 89 E5
Willamina, *U.S.A.* 110 D2
Willandra Billabong
  Creek →, *Australia* .. 91 E4
Willapa B., *U.S.A.* 110 C2
Willapa Hills, *U.S.A.* ... 112 D3
Willard, *N. Mex., U.S.A.* 111 J10
Willard, *Utah, U.S.A.* ... 110 F7
Willcox, *U.S.A.* 111 K9
Willebroek, *Belgium* 17 F4
Willemstad, *Neth. Ant.* . 117 D6
Willeroo, *Australia* 88 C5
William →, *Canada* 101 B7
William Creek, *Australia* . 91 D2
Williambury, *Australia* .. 89 D2
Williams, *Australia* 89 F2
Williams, *Ariz., U.S.A.* . 111 J7
Williams, *Calif., U.S.A.* . 112 F4
Williams Lake, *Canada* .. 100 C4
Williamsburg, *Ky., U.S.A.* 105 G3
Williamsburg, *Pa., U.S.A.* 106 F6
Williamsburg, *Va., U.S.A.* 104 G7
Williamson, *N.Y., U.S.A.* 106 C7
Williamson, *W. Va.,
  U.S.A.* 104 G4
Williamsport, *U.S.A.* 106 E7
Williamston, *U.S.A.* 105 H7
Williamstown, *Australia* . 91 F3
Williamstown, *Mass.,
  U.S.A.* 107 D11
Williamstown, *N.Y.,
  U.S.A.* 107 C9
Williamsville, *U.S.A.* 109 G9
Willis Group, *Australia* . 90 B5
Willisau, *Switz.* 22 B6
Williston, *S. Africa* 84 E3
Williston, *Fla., U.S.A.* .. 105 L4
Williston, *N. Dak., U.S.A.* 108 A3
Williston L., *Canada* 100 B4
Willits, *U.S.A.* 110 G2
Willmar, *U.S.A.* 108 C7
Willoughby, *U.S.A.* 106 E3
Willow Bunch, *Canada* .. 101 D7
Willow L., *Canada* 100 A5
Willow Lake, *U.S.A.* 108 C6
Willow Springs, *U.S.A.* . 109 G8
Willow Wall, The, *China* 51 C12
Willowlake →, *Canada* . 100 A4
Willowmore, *S. Africa* .. 84 E3
Willows, *Australia* 90 C4
Willows, *U.S.A.* 112 F4
Willowvale = Gatyana,
  S. Africa 85 E4
Wills, L., *Australia* 88 D4
Wills Cr. →, *Australia* .. 90 C3
Wills Point, *U.S.A.* 109 J7
Willunga, *Australia* 91 F2
Wilmette, *U.S.A.* 104 D2
Wilmington, *Australia* .. 91 E2
Wilmington, *Del., U.S.A.* 104 F8
Wilmington, *Ill., U.S.A.* . 104 E1
Wilmington, *N.C., U.S.A.* 105 H7
Wilmington, *Ohio, U.S.A.* 104 F4
Wilpena Cr. →, *Australia* 91 E2
Wilrijk, *Belgium* 17 F4
Wilsall, *U.S.A.* 110 D8
Wilson, *U.S.A.* 105 H7

Wilson →, *Queens.,
  Australia* 91 D3
Wilson →, *W. Austral.,
  Australia* 88 C4
Wilson Bluff, *Australia* .. 89 F4
Wilsons Promontory,
  Australia 91 F4
Wilster, *Germany* 18 B5
Wilton, *U.K.* 13 F6
Wilton, *U.S.A.* 108 B4
Wilton →, *Australia* 90 A1
Wiltshire □, *U.K.* 13 F6
Wiltz, *Lux.* 17 J7
Wiluna, *Australia* 89 E3
Wimereux, *France* 25 B8
Wimmera →, *Australia* . 91 F3
Winam G., *Kenya* 82 C3
Winburg, *S. Africa* 84 D4
Winchendon, *U.S.A.* 107 D12
Winchester, *U.K.* 13 F6
Winchester, *Conn., U.S.A.* 107 E11
Winchester, *Idaho, U.S.A.* 110 C5
Winchester, *Ind., U.S.A.* 104 E3
Winchester, *Ky., U.S.A.* . 104 G3
Winchester, *N.H., U.S.A.* 107 D12
Winchester, *Nev., U.S.A.* 113 J11
Winchester, *Tenn., U.S.A.* 105 H2
Winchester, *Va., U.S.A.* . 104 F6
Wind →, *U.S.A.* 110 E9
Wind River Range, *U.S.A.* 110 E9
Windau = Ventspils, *Latvia* 9 H19
Windber, *U.S.A.* 106 F6
Windermere, L., *U.K.* ... 12 C5
Windfall, *Canada* 100 C5
Windflower L., *Canada* .. 100 A5
Windhoek, *Namibia* 84 C2
Windom, *U.S.A.* 108 D7
Windorah, *Australia* 90 D3
Window Rock, *U.S.A.* ... 111 J9
Windrush →, *U.K.* 13 F6
Windsor, *Australia* 91 E5
Windsor, *N.S., Canada* . 99 D7
Windsor, *Nfld., Canada* . 99 C8
Windsor, *Ont., Canada* . 98 D3
Windsor, *U.K.* 13 F7
Windsor, *Colo., U.S.A.* . 108 E2
Windsor, *Conn., U.S.A.* . 107 E12
Windsor, *Mo., U.S.A.* ... 108 F8
Windsor, *N.Y., U.S.A.* .. 107 D9
Windsor, *Vt., U.S.A.* ... 107 C12
Windsorton, *S. Africa* ... 84 D3
Windward Is., *W. Indies* . 117 D7
Windward Passage =
  Vientos, Paso de los,
  Caribbean 117 C5
Windy L., *Canada* 101 A8
Winefred L., *Canada* 101 B6
Winejok, *Sudan* 77 F2
Winfield, *U.S.A.* 109 G6
Wingate Mts., *Australia* . 88 B5
Wingen, *Australia* 91 E5
Wingene, *Belgium* 17 F2
Wingham, *Australia* 91 E5
Wingham, *Canada* 98 D3
Winifred, *U.S.A.* 110 C9
Winisk, *Canada* 98 A2
Winisk →, *Canada* 98 A2
Winisk L., *Canada* 98 B2
Wink, *U.S.A.* 109 K3
Winkler, *Canada* 101 D9
Winlock, *U.S.A.* 112 D4
Winneba, *Ghana* 79 D4
Winnebago, *U.S.A.* 108 D7
Winnebago, L., *U.S.A.* .. 104 D1
Winnecke Cr. →, *Australia* 88 C5
Winnemucca, *U.S.A.* 110 F5
Winnemucca L., *U.S.A.* . 110 F4
Winner, *U.S.A.* 108 D5
Winnett, *U.S.A.* 110 C9
Winnfield, *U.S.A.* 109 K8
Winnibigoshish, L., *U.S.A.* 108 B7
Winning, *Australia* 88 D1
Winnipeg, *Canada* 101 D9
Winnipeg →, *Canada* ... 101 C9
Winnipeg, L., *Canada* ... 101 C9
Winnipeg Beach, *Canada* 101 C9
Winnipegosis, *Canada* ... 101 C9
Winnipegosis L., *Canada* 101 C9
Winnipesaukee, L., *U.S.A.* 107 C13
Winnsboro, *La., U.S.A.* . 109 J9
Winnsboro, *S.C., U.S.A.* 105 H5
Winnsboro, *Tex., U.S.A.* 109 J7
Winokapau, L., *Canada* . 99 B7
Winona, *Minn., U.S.A.* . 108 C9
Winona, *Miss., U.S.A.* .. 109 J10
Winooski, *U.S.A.* 107 B11
Winschoten, *Neths.* 16 B10
Winsen, *Germany* 18 B6
Winslow, *Ariz., U.S.A.* . 111 J8
Winslow, *Wash., U.S.A.* 112 C4
Winsted, *U.S.A.* 107 E11
Winston-Salem, *U.S.A.* . 105 G5
Winsum, *Neths.* 16 B9
Winter Garden, *U.S.A.* . 105 L5
Winter Haven, *U.S.A.* .. 105 M5
Winter Park, *U.S.A.* 105 L5
Winterberg, *Germany* ... 18 D4
Winterhaven, *U.S.A.* 113 N12
Winters, *Calif., U.S.A.* .. 112 G5
Winters, *Tex., U.S.A.* ... 109 K5
Winterset, *U.S.A.* 108 E7
Wintersville, *U.S.A.* 106 F4
Winterswijk, *Neths.* 16 E9
Winterthur, *Switz.* 23 B7
Winthrop, *Minn., U.S.A.* 108 C7
Winthrop, *Wash., U.S.A.* 110 B3
Winton, *Australia* 90 C3

Winton, *N.Z.* 87 M2
Winton, *U.S.A.* 105 G7
Wintzenheim, *France* 25 D14
Wipper →, *Germany* 18 D7
Wirral, *U.K.* 12 D4
Wirrulla, *Australia* 91 E1
Wisbech, *U.K.* 12 E8
Wisconsin □, *U.S.A.* 108 C10
Wisconsin →, *U.S.A.* 108 D9
Wisconsin Dells, *U.S.A.* . 108 D10
Wisconsin Rapids, *U.S.A.* 108 C10
Wisdom, *U.S.A.* 110 D7
Wishaw, *U.K.* 14 F5
Wishek, *U.S.A.* 108 B5
Wisła, *Poland* 20 F8
Wisła →, *Poland* 20 A8
Wisłok →, *Poland* 20 E12
Wisłoka →, *Poland* 20 E11
Wismar, *Germany* 18 B7
Wismar, *Guyana* 121 B6
Wisner, *U.S.A.* 108 E6
Wissant, *France* 25 B8
Wissembourg, *France* 25 C14
Wissenkerke, *Neths.* 17 E3
Witbank, *S. Africa* 85 D4
Witdraai, *S. Africa* 84 D3
Witham, *U.K.* 13 F8
Withernsea, *U.K.* 12 D8
Witmarsum, *Neths.* 16 B6
Witney, *U.K.* 13 F6
Witnossob →, *Namibia* ... 84 D3
Wittdün, *Germany* 18 A4
Witten, *Germany* 17 F10
Wittenberg, *Germany* 18 D8
Wittenberge, *Germany* ... 18 B7
Wittenburg, *Germany* 18 B7
Wittenoom, *Australia* 88 D2
Wittingen, *Germany* 18 C6
Wittlich, *Germany* 19 F2
Wittmund, *Germany* 18 B3
Wittow, *Germany* 18 A9
Wittstock, *Germany* 18 B8
Witzenhausen, *Germany* .. 18 D5
Wlingi, *Indonesia* 57 H15
Włocławek, *Poland* 20 C9
Włodawa, *Poland* 20 D13
Włoszczowa, *Poland* 20 E9
Woburn, *U.S.A.* 107 D13
Wodian, *China* 50 H7
Wodonga, *Australia* 91 F4
Woerden, *Neths.* 16 D5
Woerth, *France* 25 D14
Woëvre, *France* 25 C12
Wognum, *Neths.* 16 C6
Wohlen, *Switz.* 23 B6
Woinbogoin, *China* 52 A2
Wokam, *Indonesia* 57 F8
Wolbrom, *Poland* 20 E9
Woldegk, *Germany* 18 B9
Wolf →, *Canada* 100 A2
Wolf Creek, *U.S.A.* 110 C7
Wolf L., *Canada* 100 A2
Wolf Point, *U.S.A.* 108 A2
Wolfe I., *Canada* 98 D4
Wolfenbüttel, *Germany* .. 18 C6
Wolfheze, *Neths.* 16 D7
Wolfsberg, *Austria* 21 J4
Wolfsburg, *Germany* 18 C6
Wolgast, *Germany* 18 A9
Wolhusen, *Switz.* 22 B6
Wolin, *Poland* 20 B4
Wollaston, Is., *Chile* 128 E3
Wollaston, L., *Canada* ... 101 B8
Wollaston Pen., *Canada* . 96 B8
Wollogorang, *Australia* .. 90 B2
Wollongong, *Australia* ... 91 E5
Wolmaransstad, *S. Africa* 84 D4
Wolmirstedt, *Germany* ... 18 C7
Wolseley, *Australia* 91 F3
Wolseley, *Canada* 101 C8
Wolseley, *S. Africa* 84 E2
Wolstenholme, C., *Canada* 94 C12
Wolsztyn, *Poland* 20 C6
Wolvega, *Neths.* 16 C7
Wolverhampton, *U.K.* ... 13 E5
Wommels, *Neths.* 16 B7
Wonarah, *Australia* 90 B2
Wonck, *Belgium* 17 G7
Wondai, *Australia* 91 D5
Wondelgem, *Belgium* 17 F3
Wongalarroo L., *Australia* 91 E3
Wongan Hills, *Australia* . 89 F2
Wongawol, *Australia* 89 E3
Wŏnju, *S. Korea* 51 F14
Wonosari, *Indonesia* 57 G14
Wŏnsan, *N. Korea* 51 E14
Wonthaggi, *Australia* 91 F4
Woocalla, *Australia* 91 E2
Wood Buffalo Nat. Park,
  Canada 100 B6
Wood Is., *Australia* 88 C3
Wood L., *Canada* 101 B8
Wood Lake, *U.S.A.* 108 D4
Woodah I., *Australia* 90 A2
Woodanilling, *Australia* . 89 F2
Woodbridge, *Canada* 106 C5
Woodburn, *Australia* 91 D5
Woodenbong, *Australia* .. 91 D5
Woodend, *Australia* 91 F3
Woodfords, *U.S.A.* 112 G7
Woodgreen, *Australia* ... 90 C1
Woodlake, *U.S.A.* 112 J7
Woodland, *U.S.A.* 112 G5
Woodlands, *Australia* 88 D2
Woodpecker, *Canada* 100 C4
Woodridge, *Canada* 101 D9
Woodroffe, Mt., *Australia* 89 E5

Woodruff, *Ariz., U.S.A.* . 111 J8
Woodruff, *Utah, U.S.A.* . 110 F8
Woods, L., *Australia* 90 B1
Woods, L., *Canada* 99 B6
Woods, L. of the, *Canada* 101 D10
Woodstock, *Queens.,
  Australia* 90 B4
Woodstock, *W. Austral.,
  Australia* 88 D2
Woodstock, *N.B., Canada* 99 C6
Woodstock, *Ont., Canada* 98 D3
Woodstock, *U.K.* 13 F6
Woodstock, *Ill., U.S.A.* . 108 D10
Woodstock, *Vt., U.S.A.* . 107 C12
Woodsville, *U.S.A.* 107 B13
Woodville, *N.Z.* 87 J5
Woodville, *U.S.A.* 109 K7
Woodward, *U.S.A.* 109 G5
Woody, *U.S.A.* 113 K8
Woolamai, C., *Australia* . 91 F4
Woolgoolga, *Australia* ... 91 E5
Woombye, *Australia* 91 D5
Woomera, *Australia* 91 E2
Woonsocket, *R.I., U.S.A.* 107 D13
Woonsocket, *S. Dak.,
  U.S.A.* 108 C5
Wooramel, *Australia* 89 E1
Wooramel →, *Australia* . 89 E1
Wooroloo, *Australia* 89 F2
Wooster, *U.S.A.* 106 F3
Worb, *Switz.* 22 C5
Worcester, *S. Africa* 84 E2
Worcester, *U.K.* 13 E5
Worcester, *Mass., U.S.A.* 107 D13
Worcester, *N.Y., U.S.A.* . 107 D10
Wörgl, *Austria* 19 H8
Workington, *U.K.* 12 C4
Worksop, *U.K.* 12 D6
Workum, *Neths.* 16 C6
Worland, *U.S.A.* 110 D10
Wormerveer, *Neths.* 16 D5
Wormhoudt, *France* 25 B9
Worms, *Germany* 19 F4
Wörth, *Germany* 19 F8
Wortham, *U.S.A.* 109 K6
Wörther See, *Austria* 21 J4
Worthing, *U.K.* 13 G7
Worthington, *U.S.A.* 108 D7
Wosi, *Indonesia* 57 E7
Wou-han = Wuhan, *China* 53 B10
Woubrugge, *Neths.* 16 D5
Woudenberg, *Neths.* 16 D6
Woudsend, *Neths.* 16 C7
Wour, *Chad* 73 D8
Wousi = Wuxi, *China* 53 B13
Wouw, *Neths.* 17 E4
Wowoni, *Indonesia* 57 E6
Woy Woy, *Australia* 91 E5
Wrangel I. = Vrangelya,
  Ostrov, *Russia* 45 B19
Wrangell, *U.S.A.* 96 C6
Wrangell I., *U.S.A.* 100 B2
Wrangell Mts., *U.S.A.* ... 96 B5
Wrath, C., *U.K.* 14 C3
Wray, *U.S.A.* 108 E3
Wrekin, The, *U.K.* 12 E5
Wrens, *U.S.A.* 105 J4
Wrexham, *U.K.* 12 D4
Wriezen, *Germany* 18 C10
Wright, *Canada* 100 C4
Wright, *Phil.* 55 F6
Wrightson Mt., *U.S.A.* .. 111 L8
Wrightwood, *U.S.A.* 113 L9
Wrigley, *Canada* 96 B7
Wrocław, *Poland* 20 D7
Września, *Poland* 20 C6
Wschowa, *Poland* 20 D6
Wu Jiang →, *China* 52 C6
Wu'an, *China* 50 F8
Wubin, *Australia* 89 F2
Wubu, *China* 50 F6
Wuchang, *China* 51 B14
Wucheng, *China* 50 F9
Wuchuan, *Guangdong,
  China* 53 G8
Wuchuan, *Guizhou, China* 52 C7
Wuchuan,
  *Nei Mongol Zizhiqu,
  China* 50 D6
Wudi, *China* 51 F9
Wuding, *China* 52 E4
Wuding He →, *China* 50 F6
Wudu, *China* 50 H3
Wufeng, *China* 53 B8
Wugang, *China* 53 D8
Wugong Shan, *China* 53 D9
Wuhan, *China* 53 B10
Wuhe, *China* 51 H9
Wuhsi = Wuxi, *China* ... 53 B13
Wuhu, *China* 53 B12
Wujiang, *China* 53 B13
Wukari, *Nigeria* 79 D6
Wulajie, *China* 51 B14
Wulanbulang, *China* 50 D6
Wulehe, *Ghana* 79 D5
Wulian, *China* 51 G10
Wuliang Shan, *China* 52 E3
Wuliaru, *Indonesia* 57 F8
Wulumuchi = Ürümqi,
  China 44 B3
Wum, *Cameroon* 79 D7
Wuming, *China* 52 F7
Wuning, *China* 53 C10
Wunnummin L., *Canada* . 98 B2
Wunsiedel, *Germany* 19 E8
Wunstorf, *Germany* 18 C5
Wuntho, *Burma* 61 H19

Wuping, *China* 53 E11
Wuppertal, *Germany* 18 D3
Wuppertal, *S. Africa* 84 E2
Wuqing, *China* 51 E9
Würenlingen, *Switz.* 23 A6
Wurung, *Australia* 90 B3
Würzburg, *Germany* 19 F5
Wurzen, *Germany* 18 D8
Wushan, *Gansu, China* .. 50 G3
Wushan, *Sichuan, China* . 52 B7
Wusuli Jiang = Ussuri →,
  Asia 48 A7
Wutach →, *Germany* 19 H4
Wutai, *China* 50 E7
Wuting = Huimin, *China* 51 F9
Wutong, *China* 53 E8
Wutonghaolai, *China* 51 C11
Wutongqiao, *China* 52 C4
Wuustwezel, *Belgium* 17 F5
Wuwei, *Anhui, China* 53 B11
Wuwei, *Gansu, China* 54 C5
Wuxi, *Jiangsu, China* 53 B13
Wuxi, *Sichuan, China* ... 52 B7
Wuxiang, *China* 50 F7
Wuxing, *China* 53 B13
Wuxuan, *China* 52 F7
Wuyang, *China* 50 H7
Wuyi, *Hebei, China* 50 F8
Wuyi, *Zhejiang, China* .. 53 C12
Wuyi Shan, *China* 53 D11
Wuyo, *Nigeria* 79 C7
Wuyuan, *Jiangxi, China* . 53 C11
Wuyuan,
  *Nei Mongol Zizhiqu,
  China* 50 D5
Wuzhai, *China* 50 E6
Wuzhi Shan, *China* 54 E5
Wuzhong, *China* 50 E4
Wuzhou, *China* 53 F8
Wyaaba Cr. →, *Australia* 90 B3
Wyalkatchem, *Australia* . 89 F2
Wyalusing, *U.S.A.* 107 E8
Wyandotte, *U.S.A.* 104 D4
Wyandra, *Australia* 91 D4
Wyangala Res., *Australia* 91 E4
Wyara, L., *Australia* 91 D3
Wycheproof, *Australia* ... 91 F3
Wye →, *U.K.* 13 F5
Wyemandoo, *Australia* .. 89 E2
Wyk, *Germany* 18 A4
Wymondham, *U.K.* 13 E7
Wymore, *U.S.A.* 108 E6
Wynbring, *Australia* 91 E1
Wyndham, *Australia* 88 C4
Wyndham, *N.Z.* 87 M2
Wyndmere, *U.S.A.* 108 B6
Wynne, *U.S.A.* 109 H9
Wynnum, *Australia* 91 D5
Wynyard, *Australia* 90 G4
Wynyard, *Canada* 101 C8
Wyola, L., *Australia* 89 E5
Wyoming □, *U.S.A.* 110 E10
Wyong, *Australia* 91 E5
Wyszków, *Poland* 20 C11
Wyszogród, *Poland* 20 C10
Wytheville, *U.S.A.* 104 G5

X

Xaçmaz, *Azerbaijan* 43 K9
Xai-Xai, *Mozam.* 85 D5
Xainza, *China* 54 C3
Xambioá, *Brazil* 122 C2
Xangongo, *Angola* 84 B2
Xankändi, *Azerbaijan* ... 67 C12
Xanlar, *Azerbaijan* 43 K8
Xanten, *Germany* 18 D2
Xánthi, *Greece* 39 H7
Xanthos, *Turkey* 66 D3
Xapuri, *Brazil* 124 C4
Xar Moron He →, *China* 51 C11
Xau, L., *Botswana* 84 C3
Xavantina, *Brazil* 127 A5
Xenia, *U.S.A.* 104 F4
Xeropotamos →, *Cyprus* 37 E11
Xhora, *S. Africa* 85 E4
Xhumo, *Botswana* 84 C3
Xi Jiang →, *China* 53 F9
Xi Xian, *Henan, China* .. 53 A10
Xi Xian, *Shanxi, China* . 50 F6
Xia Xian, *China* 50 G6
Xiachengzi, *China* 51 B16
Xiachuan Dao, *China* 53 G9
Xiaguan, *China* 52 E3
Xiajiang, *China* 53 D10
Xiajin, *China* 50 F8
Xiamen, *China* 53 E12
Xi'an, *China* 50 G5
Xi'an Xian, *China* 50 E9
Xianfeng, *China* 52 C7
Xiang Jiang →, *China* ... 53 C9
Xiangcheng, *Henan, China* 50 H8
Xiangcheng, *Henan, China* 50 H7
Xiangcheng, *Sichuan,
  China* 52 C2
Xiangdu, *China* 52 F6
Xiangfan, *China* 53 A9
Xianghuang Qi, *China* ... 50 C7
Xiangning, *China* 50 G6
Xiangquan, *China* 50 F7
Xiangshan, *China* 53 C13
Xiangshui, *China* 51 G10
Xiangtan, *China* 53 D9
Xiangxiang, *China* 53 D9

Xiangyin, *China* 53 C9
Xiangyun, *China* 52 E3
Xiangzhou, *China* 52 F7
Xianju, *China* 53 C13
Xianning, *China* 53 C10
Xianshui He →, *China* ... 52 B3
Xianyang, *China* 50 G5
Xianyou, *China* 53 E12
Xiao Hinggan Ling, *China* 54 B7
Xiao Xian, *China* 50 G9
Xiaofeng, *China* 53 B12
Xiaogan, *China* 53 B9
Xiaojin, *China* 52 B4
Xiaolan, *China* 53 F9
Xiaoshan, *China* 53 B13
Xiaoyi, *China* 50 F6
Xiapu, *China* 53 D12
Xiawa, *China* 51 C11
Xiayi, *China* 50 G9
Xichang, *China* 52 D4
Xichong, *China* 52 B5
Xichuan, *China* 50 H6
Xiemahe, *China* 53 B8
Xieng Khouang, *Laos* 58 C4
Xifei He →, *China* 50 H9
Xifeng, *Guizhou, China* . 52 D6
Xifeng, *Liaoning, China* . 51 C13
Xifengzhen, *China* 50 G4
Xigazê, *China* 54 D3
Xihe, *China* 50 G3
Xihua, *China* 50 H8
Xiliao He →, *China* 51 C12
Xilin, *China* 52 E5
Xilókastron, *Greece* 39 L5
Xin Jiang →, *China* 53 C11
Xin Xian, *China* 50 E7
Xinavane, *Mozam.* 85 D5
Xinbin, *China* 51 D13
Xincai, *China* 53 A10
Xinchang, *China* 53 C13
Xincheng,
  *Guangxi Zhuangzu,
  China* 52 E7
Xincheng, *Jiangxi, China* 53 D10
Xinfeng, *Guangdong,
  China* 53 E10
Xinfeng, *Jiangxi, China* . 53 D11
Xinfeng, *Jiangxi, China* . 53 E10
Xing Xian, *China* 50 E6
Xing'an,
  *Guangxi Zhuangzu,
  China* 53 E8
Xingan, *Jiangxi, China* .. 53 D10
Xingcheng, *China* 51 D11
Xingguo, *China* 53 D10
Xinghe, *China* 50 D7
Xinghua, *China* 51 H10
Xinghua Wan, *China* 53 E12
Xinglong, *China* 51 D9
Xingning, *China* 53 E10
Xingping, *China* 50 G5
Xingren, *China* 52 E5
Xingshan, *China* 53 B8
Xingtai, *China* 50 F8
Xingu →, *Brazil* 121 D7
Xingyang, *China* 50 G7
Xinhe, *China* 50 F8
Xinhua, *China* 53 D8
Xinhuang, *China* 52 D7
Xinhui, *China* 53 F9
Xining, *China* 54 C5
Xinjiang, *China* 50 G6
Xinjiang Uygur Zizhiqu □,
  China 54 B3
Xinjie, *China* 52 D3
Xinjin, *Liaoning, China* . 51 E11
Xinjin, *Sichuan, China* .. 52 B4
Xinkai He →, *China* 51 C12
Xinle, *China* 50 E8
Xinlitun, *China* 51 D12
Xinlong, *China* 52 B3
Xinmin, *China* 51 D12
Xinning, *China* 53 D8
Xinping, *China* 52 E3
Xinshao, *China* 53 D8
Xintai, *China* 51 G9
Xintian, *China* 53 E9
Xinxiang, *China* 50 G7
Xinxing, *China* 53 F9
Xinyang, *China* 53 A10
Xinye, *China* 53 A9
Xinyi, *China* 53 D10
Xinyu, *China* 53 D10
Xinzhan, *China* 51 C14
Xinzheng, *China* 50 G7
Xinzhou, *China* 53 B10
Xinzhu, *Taiwan* 53 E13
Xiong Xian, *China* 50 E9
Xiongyuecheng, *China* .. 51 D12
Xiping, *Henan, China* ... 50 H8
Xiping, *Henan, China* ... 50 H6
Xiping, *Zhejiang, China* . 53 C12
Xique-Xique, *Brazil* 122 D3
Xiruá →, *Brazil* 124 B4
Xisha Qundao = Hsisha
  Chuntao, *Pac. Oc.* 56 A4
Xishui, *China* 53 B10
Xituozhen, *China* 52 B7
Xiuning, *China* 53 C12
Xiuren, *China* 53 E8
Xiushan, *China* 52 C7
Xiushui, *China* 53 C10
Xiuwen, *China* 52 D6
Xiuyan, *China* 51 D12
Xixabangma Feng, *China* 61 E14
Xixia, *China* 50 H6
Xixiang, *China* 50 H4

Xiyang, *China* 50 F7
Xizang □, *China* 54 C3
Xlendi, *Malta* 37 C1
Xu Jiang →, *China* 53 D11
Xuan Loc, *Vietnam* 59 G6
Xuancheng, *China* 53 B12
Xuan'en, *China* 52 C7
Xuanhan, *China* 52 B6
Xuanhua, *China* 50 D8
Xuchang, *China* 50 G7
Xudat, *Azerbaijan* 43 K9
Xuefeng Shan, *China* 53 D8
Xuejiaping, *China* 53 B8
Xun Jiang →, *China* 53 F8
Xun Xian, *China* 50 G8
Xundian, *China* 52 E4
Xunwu, *China* 53 E10
Xunyang, *China* 50 H5
Xunyi, *China* 50 G5
Xupu, *China* 53 D8
Xushui, *China* 50 E8
Xuwen, *China* 53 G8
Xuyen Moc, *Vietnam* 59 G6
Xuyong, *China* 52 C5
Xuzhou, *China* 51 G9
Xylophagou, *Cyprus* 37 E12

Y

Ya Xian, *China* 58 C7
Yaamba, *Australia* 90 C5
Ya'an, *China* 52 C4
Yaapeet, *Australia* 91 F3
Yabassi, *Cameroon* 79 E6
Yabelo, *Ethiopia* 77 G4
Yablonovy Ra. =
  Yablonovyy Khrebet,
  Russia 45 D12
Yablonovyy Khrebet,
  Russia 45 D12
Yabrai Shan, *China* 50 E2
Yabrūd, *Syria* 69 B5
Yacuiba, *Bolivia* 126 A3
Yacuma →, *Bolivia* 125 C4
Yadgir, *India* 60 L10
Yadkin →, *U.S.A.* 105 H5
Yadrin, *Russia* 42 C8
Yagaba, *Ghana* 79 C4
Yagodnoye, *Russia* 45 C15
Yagoua, *Cameroon* 80 B3
Yaguas →, *Peru* 120 D3
Yaha, *Thailand* 59 J3
Yahila, *Zaïre* 82 B1
Yahk, *Canada* 100 D5
Yahotyn, *Ukraine* 41 G6
Yahuma, *Zaïre* 80 D4
Yahyalı, *Turkey* 66 C6
Yaita, *Japan* 49 F9
Yaiza, *Canary Is.* 36 F6
Yajiang, *China* 52 B3
Yajua, *Nigeria* 79 C7
Yakima, *U.S.A.* 110 C3
Yakima →, *U.S.A.* 110 C3
Yako, *Burkina Faso* 78 C4
Yakoruda, *Bulgaria* 39 G6
Yakovlevka, *Russia* 48 B6
Yaku-Shima, *Japan* 49 J5
Yakutat, *U.S.A.* 96 C6
Yakutia = Sakha □, *Russia* 45 C13
Yakutsk, *Russia* 45 C13
Yala, *Thailand* 59 J3
Yalbalgo, *Australia* 89 E1
Yalboroo, *Australia* 90 C4
Yale, *U.S.A.* 106 C2
Yalgoo, *Australia* 89 E2
Yalinga, *C.A.R.* 73 G9
Yalkubul, Punta, *Mexico* 115 C7
Yalleroi, *Australia* 90 C4
Yalobusha →, *U.S.A.* ... 109 J9
Yalong Jiang →, *China* .. 52 D3
Yalova, *Turkey* 66 B3
Yalpuh, Ozero, *Ukraine* . 38 D11
Yalta, *Ukraine* 41 K8
Yalu Jiang →, *China* 51 E13
Yalutorovsk, *Russia* 44 D7
Yalvaç, *Turkey* 66 C4
Yam Ha Melah = Dead
  Sea, *Asia* 69 D4
Yam Kinneret, *Israel* 69 C4
Yamada, *Japan* 49 H5
Yamagata, *Japan* 48 E10
Yamagata □, *Japan* 48 E10
Yamaguchi, *Japan* 49 G5
Yamaguchi □, *Japan* 49 G5
Yamal, Poluostrov, *Russia* 44 B8
Yamal Pen. = Yamal,
  Poluostrov, *Russia* ... 44 B8
Yamanashi □, *Japan* 49 G9
Yamantau, Gora, *Russia* . 44 D6
Yamba, N.S.W., *Australia* 91 D5
Yamba, S. Austral.,
  Australia 91 E3
Yambah, *Australia* 90 C1
Yambarran Ra., *Australia* 88 C5
Yâmbiô, *Sudan* 81 G3
Yambol, *Bulgaria* 38 G9
Yamdena, *Indonesia* 57 F8
Yame, *Japan* 49 H5
Yamethin, *Burma* 61 J20
Yamil, *Nigeria* 79 C6
Yamma-Yamma, L.,
  Australia 91 D3
Yamoussoukro, *Ivory C.* . 78 D3
Yampa →, *U.S.A.* 110 F9

Name	Page	Ref
Yampi Sd., *Australia*	88	C3
Yampil, *Moldova*	41	H5
Yampol = Yampil, *Moldova*	41	H5
Yamrat, *Nigeria*	79	C6
Yamrukchal, *Bulgaria*	38	G7
Yamuna →, *India*	63	G9
Yamzho Yumco, *China*	54	D4
Yan, *Nigeria*	79	C7
Yana →, *Russia*	45	B14
Yanac, *Australia*	91	F3
Yanagawa, *Japan*	49	H5
Yanai, *Japan*	49	H6
Yan'an, *China*	50	F5
Yanbian, *China*	52	D3
Yanbu 'al Baḥr, *Si. Arabia*	64	F3
Yancannia, *Australia*	91	E3
Yanchang, *China*	50	F6
Yancheng, *Henan, China*	50	H7
Yancheng, *Jiangsu, China*	51	H11
Yanchi, *China*	50	F4
Yanchuan, *China*	50	F6
Yanco Cr. →, *Australia*	91	F4
Yandal, *Australia*	89	E3
Yandanooka, *Australia*	89	E2
Yandaran, *Australia*	90	C5
Yandoon, *Burma*	61	L19
Yanfeng, *China*	52	E3
Yanfolila, *Mali*	78	C3
Yang Xian, *China*	50	H4
Yangambi, *Zaïre*	82	B1
Yangbi, *China*	52	E2
Yangcheng, *China*	50	G7
Yangch'ü = Taiyuan, *China*	50	F7
Yangchun, *China*	53	F8
Yanggao, *China*	50	D7
Yanggu, *China*	50	F8
Yangjiang, *China*	53	G8
Yangliuqing, *China*	51	E9
Yangon = Rangoon, *Burma*	61	L20
Yangping, *China*	53	B8
Yangpingguan, *China*	50	H4
Yangquan, *China*	50	F7
Yangshan, *China*	53	E9
Yangshuo, *China*	53	E8
Yangtze Kiang = Chang Jiang →, *China*	53	B13
Yangxin, *China*	53	C10
Yangyang, *S. Korea*	51	E15
Yangyuan, *China*	50	D8
Yangzhou, *China*	53	A12
Yanhe, *China*	52	C7
Yanji, *China*	51	C15
Yanjin, *China*	52	C5
Yanjing, *China*	52	C2
Yankton, *U.S.A.*	108	D6
Yanna, *Australia*	91	D4
Yanonge, *Zaïre*	82	B1
Yanqi, *China*	54	B3
Yanqing, *China*	50	D8
Yanshan, *Hebei, China*	51	E9
Yanshan, *Jiangxi, China*	53	C11
Yanshan, *Yunnan, China*	52	F5
Yanshou, *China*	51	B15
Yantabulla, *Australia*	91	D4
Yantai, *China*	51	F11
Yanting, *China*	52	B5
Yantra →, *Bulgaria*	38	F8
Yanwa, *China*	52	D2
Yanykurgan, *Kazakhstan*	44	E7
Yanyuan, *China*	52	D3
Yanzhou, *China*	50	G9
Yao, *Chad*	73	F8
Yao Xian, *China*	50	G5
Yao Yai, Ko, *Thailand*	59	J2
Yao'an, *China*	52	E3
Yaodu, *China*	52	A5
Yaoundé, *Cameroon*	79	E7
Yaowan, *China*	51	G10
Yap I., *Pac. Oc.*	92	G5
Yapen, *Indonesia*	57	E9
Yapen, Selat, *Indonesia*	57	E9
Yappar →, *Australia*	90	B3
Yaqui →, *Mexico*	114	B2
Yar-Sale, *Russia*	44	C8
Yaracuy □, *Venezuela*	120	A4
Yaracuy →, *Venezuela*	120	A4
Yaraka, *Australia*	90	C3
Yaransk, *Russia*	42	B8
Yardea P.O., *Australia*	91	E2
Yare →, *U.K.*	13	E9
Yaremcha, *Ukraine*	41	H3
Yarensk, *Russia*	44	C5
Yarí →, *Colombia*	120	D3
Yaritagua, *Venezuela*	120	A4
Yarkand = Shache, *China*	54	C2
Yarker, *Canada*	107	B8
Yarkhun →, *Pakistan*	63	A5
Yarmouth, *Canada*	99	D6
Yarmük →, *Syria*	69	C4
Yaroslavl, *Russia*	42	B4
Yarqa, W. →, *Egypt*	69	F2
Yarra Yarra Lakes, *Australia*	89	E2
Yarraden, *Australia*	90	A3
Yarraloola, *Australia*	88	D2
Yarram, *Australia*	91	F4
Yarraman, *Australia*	91	D5
Yarranvale, *Australia*	91	D4
Yarras, *Australia*	91	E5
Yarrowmere, *Australia*	90	C4
Yartsevo, *Russia*	40	E7
Yartsevo, *Russia*	45	C10
Yarumal, *Colombia*	120	B2
Yasawa Group, *Fiji*	87	C7
Yaselda, *Belarus*	41	F4
Yashi, *Nigeria*	79	C6
Yashkul, *Russia*	43	G7
Yasin, *Pakistan*	63	A5
Yasinovataya, *Ukraine*	41	H9
Yasinski, L., *Canada*	98	B4
Yasinya, *Ukraine*	41	H3
Yasothon, *Thailand*	58	E5
Yass, *Australia*	91	E4
Yata →, *Bolivia*	125	C4
Yatağan, *Turkey*	66	D3
Yates Center, *U.S.A.*	109	G7
Yathkyed L., *Canada*	101	A9
Yatsushiro, *Japan*	49	H5
Yatta Plateau, *Kenya*	82	C4
Yauca, *Peru*	124	D3
Yauya, *Peru*	124	B2
Yauyos, *Peru*	124	C2
Yavari →, *Peru*	124	A3
Yavatmal, *India*	60	J11
Yavne, *Israel*	69	D3
Yavoriv, *Ukraine*	41	H2
Yavorov = Yavoriv, *Ukraine*	41	H2
Yavuzeli, *Turkey*	66	D7
Yawatahama, *Japan*	49	H6
Yawri B., *S. Leone*	78	D2
Yaxi, *China*	52	D6
Yayama-Rettō, *Japan*	49	M1
Yazd, *Iran*	65	D7
Yazd □, *Iran*	65	D7
Yazoo →, *U.S.A.*	109	J9
Yazoo City, *U.S.A.*	109	J9
Yding Skovhøj, *Denmark*	9	J13
Ye Xian, *Henan, China*	50	H7
Ye Xian, *Shandong, China*	51	F10
Yealering, *Australia*	89	F2
Yebyu, *Burma*	61	M21
Yechŏn, *S. Korea*	51	F15
Yecla, *Spain*	29	G3
Yécora, *Mexico*	114	B3
Yedintsy = Edineţa, *Moldova*	41	H4
Yeeda, *Australia*	88	C3
Yeelanna, *Australia*	91	E2
Yefremov, *Russia*	42	D4
Yegorlyk →, *Russia*	43	G5
Yegorlykskaya, *Russia*	43	G5
Yegoryevsk, *Russia*	42	C4
Yegros, *Paraguay*	126	B4
Yehuda, Midbar, *Israel*	69	D4
Yei, *Sudan*	77	G3
Yei, Nahr →, *Sudan*	77	F3
Yejmiadzin, *Armenia*	43	K7
Yekaterinburg, *Russia*	44	D7
Yekaterinodar = Krasnodar, *Russia*	43	H4
Yekhegnadzor, *Armenia*	67	C11
Yelabuga, *Russia*	42	C11
Yelan, *Russia*	42	E6
Yelanskoye, *Russia*	45	C13
Yelarbon, *Australia*	91	D5
Yelatma, *Russia*	42	C5
Yelcho, L., *Chile*	128	B2
Yelets, *Russia*	42	D4
Yélimané, *Mali*	78	B2
Yelizavetgrad = Kirovohrad, *Ukraine*	41	H7
Yell, *U.K.*	14	A7
Yell Sd., *U.K.*	14	A7
Yellow Sea, *China*	51	G12
Yellowhead Pass, *Canada*	100	C5
Yellowknife, *Canada*	100	A6
Yellowknife →, *Canada*	100	A6
Yellowstone →, *U.S.A.*	108	B3
Yellowstone L., *U.S.A.*	110	D8
Yellowstone National Park, *U.S.A.*	110	D8
Yellowtail Res., *U.S.A.*	110	D9
Yelnya, *Russia*	40	E7
Yelsk, *Belarus*	41	G5
Yelvertoft, *Australia*	90	C2
Yelwa, *Nigeria*	79	C5
Yemen ■, *Asia*	68	E3
Yen Bai, *Vietnam*	58	B5
Yenakiyeve, *Ukraine*	41	H10
Yenakiyevo = Yenakiyeve, *Ukraine*	41	H10
Yenangyaung, *Burma*	61	J19
Yenbo = Yanbu 'al Baḥr, *Si. Arabia*	64	F3
Yenda, *Australia*	91	E4
Yendéré, *Ivory C.*	78	C4
Yendi, *Ghana*	79	D4
Yenice, *Ankara, Turkey*	66	C5
Yenice, *Çanakkale, Turkey*	66	C2
Yenice →, *Turkey*	66	D6
Yenisaía, *Greece*	39	H7
Yenişehir, *Turkey*	66	B3
Yenisey →, *Russia*	44	B9
Yeniseysk, *Russia*	45	D10
Yeniseyskiy Zaliv, *Russia*	44	B9
Yennádhi, *Greece*	37	C9
Yenne, *France*	27	C9
Yenotayevka, *Russia*	43	G8
Yenyuka, *Russia*	45	D13
Yeo →, *Australia*	89	E3
Yeola, *India*	60	J9
Yeoryioúpolis, *Greece*	37	D6
Yeovil, *U.K.*	13	G5
Yeppoon, *Australia*	90	C5
Yeráki, *Greece*	39	N4
Yerbent, *Turkmenistan*	44	F6
Yerbogachen, *Russia*	45	C11
Yerevan, *Armenia*	43	K7
Yerilla, *Australia*	89	E3
Yerköy, *Turkey*	66	C6
Yermak, *Kazakhstan*	44	D8
Yermakovo, *Russia*	45	D13
Yermo, *U.S.A.*	113	L10
Yerofey Pavlovich, *Russia*	45	D13
Yerólakkos, *Cyprus*	37	D12
Yeropol, *Russia*	45	C17
Yeropótamos →, *Greece*	37	D6
Yeroskipos, *Cyprus*	37	E11
Yersake, *Neths.*	17	F4
Yershov, *Russia*	42	E9
Yerunaja, Cerro, *Peru*	124	C2
Yerushalayim = Jerusalem, *Israel*	69	D4
Yerville, *France*	24	C7
Yes Tor, *U.K.*	13	G4
Yesan, *S. Korea*	51	F14
Yeşilhisar, *Turkey*	66	C6
Yeşilırmak →, *Turkey*	66	B7
Yeşilkent, *Turkey*	66	D7
Yesnogorsk, *Russia*	42	C3
Yeso, *U.S.A.*	109	H2
Yessentuki, *Russia*	43	H6
Yessey, *Russia*	45	C11
Yeste, *Spain*	29	G2
Yeu, I. d', *France*	24	F4
Yevlakh = Yevlax, *Azerbaijan*	43	K8
Yevlax, *Azerbaijan*	43	K8
Yevpatoriya, *Ukraine*	41	K7
Yeya →, *Russia*	43	G4
Yeysk, *Russia*	43	G4
Yezd = Yazd, *Iran*	65	D7
Yezerishche, *Belarus*	40	E5
Yhati, *Paraguay*	126	B4
Yhú, *Paraguay*	127	B4
Yi →, *Uruguay*	126	C4
Yi 'Allaq, G., *Egypt*	69	E2
Yi He →, *China*	51	G10
Yi Xian, *Anhui, China*	53	C11
Yi Xian, *Hebei, China*	50	E8
Yi Xian, *Liaoning, China*	51	D11
Yialí, *Greece*	39	N10
Yialiás →, *Cyprus*	37	D12
Yi'allaq, G., *Egypt*	76	H8
Yialousa, *Cyprus*	37	D13
Yiáltra, *Greece*	39	L5
Yianisádhes, *Greece*	37	D8
Yiannitsa, *Greece*	39	J5
Yibin, *China*	52	C5
Yichang, *China*	53	B8
Yicheng, *Henan, China*	53	B9
Yicheng, *Shanxi, China*	50	G6
Yichuan, *China*	50	F6
Yichun, *Heilongjiang, China*	54	B7
Yichun, *Jiangxi, China*	53	D10
Yidu, *Hubei, China*	53	B8
Yidu, *Shandong, China*	51	F10
Yidun, *China*	52	B2
Yihuang, *China*	53	D11
Yijun, *China*	50	G5
Yilan, *Taiwan*	53	E13
Yıldızeli, *Turkey*	66	C7
Yiliang, *Yunnan, China*	52	D5
Yiliang, *Yunnan, China*	52	E4
Yilong, *China*	52	B6
Yimen, *China*	52	E4
Yimianpo, *China*	51	B15
Yinchuan, *China*	50	E4
Yindarlgooda, L., *Australia*	89	F3
Ying He →, *China*	50	H9
Ying Xian, *China*	50	E7
Yingcheng, *China*	53	B9
Yingde, *China*	53	E9
Yingjiang, *China*	52	E1
Yingjing, *China*	52	C4
Yingkou, *China*	51	D12
Yingshan, *Henan, China*	50	H8
Yingshan, *Hubei, China*	53	B10
Yingshan, *Sichuan, China*	52	B6
Yingshang, *China*	53	A11
Yingtan, *China*	54	D6
Yining, *China*	44	E9
Yinjiang, *China*	52	C7
Yinmabin, *Burma*	61	H19
Yinnietharra, *Australia*	88	D2
Yiofiros →, *Greece*	37	D7
Yioúra, *Greece*	39	K7
Yipinglang, *China*	52	E3
Yirga Alem, *Ethiopia*	77	F4
Yishan, *China*	52	E7
Yishui, *China*	51	G10
Yitiaoshan, *China*	50	F3
Yitong, *China*	51	C13
Yiwu, *China*	53	C13
Yixing, *China*	53	B12
Yiyang, *Henan, China*	50	G7
Yiyang, *Hunan, China*	53	C9
Yiyang, *Jiangxi, China*	53	C11
Yizhang, *China*	53	E9
Yizheng, *China*	53	A12
Yli-Kitka, *Finland*	8	C23
Ylitornio, *Finland*	8	C20
Ylivieska, *Finland*	8	D21
Yngaren, *Sweden*	11	F10
Ynykchanskiy, *Russia*	45	C14
Yoakum, *U.S.A.*	109	L6
Yobe □, *Nigeria*	79	C7
Yog Pt., *Phil.*	57	B6
Yogan, *Togo*	79	D5
Yogyakarta, *Indonesia*	57	G14
Yoho Nat. Park, *Canada*	100	C5
Yojoa, L. de, *Honduras*	116	D2
Yŏju, *S. Korea*	51	F14
Yokadouma, *Cameroon*	80	D2
Yokkaichi, *Japan*	49	G8
Yoko, *Cameroon*	79	D7
Yokohama, *Japan*	49	G9
Yokosuka, *Japan*	49	G9
Yokote, *Japan*	48	E10
Yola, *Nigeria*	79	D7
Yolaina, Cordillera de, *Nic.*	116	D3
Yonago, *Japan*	49	G6
Yonaguni-Jima, *Japan*	49	M1
Yŏnan, *N. Korea*	51	F14
Yonezawa, *Japan*	48	F10
Yong Peng, *Malaysia*	59	L4
Yong Sata, *Thailand*	59	J2
Yongampo, *N. Korea*	51	E13
Yong'an, *China*	53	E11
Yongcheng, *China*	50	H9
Yongchuan, *China*	52	C5
Yongchun, *China*	53	E12
Yongdeng, *China*	50	F2
Yongding, *China*	53	E11
Yongfeng, *China*	53	D10
Yongfu, *China*	52	E7
Yonghe, *China*	50	F6
Yŏnghŭng, *N. Korea*	51	E14
Yongji, *China*	50	G6
Yŏngju, *S. Korea*	51	F15
Yongkang, *Yunnan, China*	52	E2
Yongkang, *Zhejiang, China*	53	C13
Yongnian, *China*	50	F8
Yongning, *Guangxi Zhuangzu, China*	52	F7
Yongning, *Ningxia Huizu, China*	50	E4
Yongping, *China*	52	E2
Yongqing, *China*	50	E9
Yongren, *China*	52	D3
Yongshan, *China*	52	C4
Yongsheng, *China*	52	D3
Yongshun, *China*	52	C7
Yongtai, *China*	53	E12
Yŏngwŏl, *S. Korea*	51	F15
Yongxin, *China*	53	D10
Yongxing, *China*	53	D9
Yongxiu, *China*	53	C10
Yonibana, *S. Leone*	78	D2
Yonkers, *U.S.A.*	107	F11
Yonne □, *France*	25	E10
Yonne →, *France*	25	D9
York, *Australia*	89	F2
York, *U.K.*	12	D6
York, *Ala., U.S.A.*	105	J1
York, *Nebr., U.S.A.*	108	E6
York, *Pa., U.S.A.*	104	F7
York, C., *Australia*	90	A3
York, Kap, *Greenland*	4	B4
York Sd., *Australia*	88	B4
Yorke Pen., *Australia*	91	E2
Yorkshire Wolds, *U.K.*	12	D7
Yorkton, *Canada*	101	C8
Yorktown, *U.S.A.*	109	L6
Yorkville, *U.S.A.*	112	G3
Yornup, *Australia*	89	F2
Yoro, *Honduras*	116	C2
Yoron-Jima, *Japan*	49	L4
Yos Sudarso, Pulau, *Indonesia*	57	F9
Yosemite National Park, *U.S.A.*	111	H4
Yosemite Village, *U.S.A.*	112	H7
Yoshkar Ola, *Russia*	42	B8
Yŏsu, *S. Korea*	51	G14
Yotala, *Bolivia*	125	D4
Yotvata, *Israel*	69	F4
You Xian, *China*	53	D9
Youbou, *Canada*	100	D4
Youghal, *Ireland*	15	E4
Youghal B., *Ireland*	15	E4
Youkounkoun, *Guinea*	78	C2
Young, *Australia*	91	E4
Young, *Canada*	101	C7
Young, *Uruguay*	126	C4
Younghusband, L., *Australia*	91	E2
Younghusband Pen., *Australia*	91	F2
Youngstown, *Canada*	101	C6
Youngstown, *N.Y., U.S.A.*	106	C5
Youngstown, *Ohio, U.S.A.*	106	E4
Youngsville, *U.S.A.*	106	E5
Youssoufia, *Morocco*	74	B3
Youxi, *China*	53	D12
Youyang, *China*	52	C7
Youyu, *China*	50	D7
Yoweragabbie, *Australia*	89	E2
Yozgat, *Turkey*	66	C6
Ypané →, *Paraguay*	126	A4
Yport, *France*	24	C7
Ypres = Ieper, *Belgium*	17	G1
Ypsilanti, *U.S.A.*	104	D4
Yreka, *U.S.A.*	110	F2
Ysleta, *U.S.A.*	111	L10
Yssingeaux, *France*	27	C8
Ystad, *Sweden*	11	J7
Ysyk-Köl, Ozero, *Kyrgyzstan*	44	E8
Ythan →, *U.K.*	14	D7
Ytterhogdal, *Sweden*	10	B8
Ytyk Kyuyel, *Russia*	45	C14
Yu Jiang →, *China*	54	D6
Yu Shan, *Taiwan*	53	F13
Yu Xian, *Hebei, China*	50	E8
Yu Xian, *Henan, China*	50	G7
Yu Xian, *Shanxi, China*	50	E7
Yuan Jiang →, *Hunan, China*	53	C8
Yuan Jiang →, *Yunnan, China*	52	F4
Yuan'an, *China*	53	B8
Yuanjiang, *Hunan, China*	53	C9
Yuanjiang, *Yunnan, China*	52	F4
Yuanli, *Taiwan*	53	E13
Yuanlin, *Taiwan*	53	F13
Yuanling, *China*	53	C8
Yuanmou, *China*	52	E3
Yuanqu, *China*	50	G6
Yuanyang, *Henan, China*	50	G7
Yuanyang, *Yunnan, China*	52	F4
Yuba →, *U.S.A.*	112	F5
Yuba City, *U.S.A.*	112	F5
Yūbari, *Japan*	48	C10
Yūbetsu, *Japan*	48	B11
Yucatán □, *Mexico*	115	C7
Yucatán, Canal de, *Caribbean*	116	B2
Yucatan Str. = Yucatán, Canal de, *Caribbean*	116	B2
Yucca, *U.S.A.*	113	L12
Yucca Valley, *U.S.A.*	113	L10
Yucheng, *China*	50	F9
Yuci, *China*	50	F7
Yudino, *Russia*	44	D7
Yudu, *China*	53	E10
Yuendumu, *Australia*	88	D5
Yueqing, *China*	53	C13
Yueqing Wan, *China*	53	C13
Yuexi, *Anhui, China*	53	B11
Yuexi, *Sichuan, China*	52	C4
Yueyang, *China*	53	C9
Yugan, *China*	53	C11
Yugoslavia ■, *Europe*	21	M10
Yuhuan, *China*	53	C13
Yujiang, *China*	53	C11
Yukhnov, *Russia*	42	C2
Yukon →, *U.S.A.*	96	B3
Yukon Territory □, *Canada*	96	B6
Yüksekova, *Turkey*	67	D11
Yukti, *Russia*	45	C11
Yukuhashi, *Japan*	49	H5
Yule →, *Australia*	88	D2
Yuli, *Nigeria*	79	D7
Yulin, *Guangxi Zhuangzu, China*	53	F8
Yulin, *Shaanxi, China*	50	E5
Yuma, *Ariz., U.S.A.*	113	N12
Yuma, *Colo., U.S.A.*	108	E3
Yuma, B. de, *Dom. Rep.*	117	C6
Yumbe, *Uganda*	82	B3
Yumbi, *Zaïre*	82	C2
Yumbo, *Colombia*	120	C2
Yumen, *China*	54	C4
Yumurtalık, *Turkey*	66	D6
Yun Ho →, *China*	51	E9
Yun Xian, *Hubei, China*	53	A8
Yun Xian, *Yunnan, China*	52	E3
Yunak, *Turkey*	66	C4
Yunan, *China*	53	F8
Yuncheng, *Henan, China*	50	G8
Yuncheng, *Shanxi, China*	50	G6
Yunfu, *China*	53	F9
Yungas, *Bolivia*	125	D4
Yungay, *Chile*	126	D1
Yungay, *Peru*	124	B2
Yunhe, *China*	53	C12
Yunlin, *Taiwan*	53	F13
Yunling, *China*	52	D2
Yunlong, *China*	52	E2
Yunmeng, *China*	53	B9
Yunnan □, *China*	52	E4
Yunquera de Henares, *Spain*	28	E1
Yunta, *Australia*	91	E2
Yunxi, *China*	50	H6
Yunxiao, *China*	53	F11
Yunyang, *China*	52	B7
Yuping, *China*	52	D7
Yupukarri, *Guyana*	121	C6
Yupyongdong, *N. Korea*	51	D15
Yuqing, *China*	52	D6
Yur, *Russia*	45	D14
Yurgao, *Russia*	44	D9
Yuribei, *Russia*	44	B8
Yurimaguas, *Peru*	124	B2
Yuryev-Polskiy, *Russia*	42	B4
Yuryevets, *Russia*	42	B6
Yuryung Kaya, *Russia*	45	B12
Yuscarán, *Honduras*	116	D2
Yushanzhen, *China*	52	C7
Yushe, *China*	50	F7
Yushu, *Jilin, China*	51	B14
Yushu, *Qinghai, China*	54	C4
Yusufeli, *Turkey*	67	B9
Yutai, *China*	50	G9
Yutian, *China*	51	E9
Yuxarı Qarabağ = Nagorno-Karabakh, *Azerbaijan*	67	C12
Yuxi, *China*	52	E4
Yuyao, *China*	53	B13
Yuzawa, *Japan*	48	E10
Yuzha, *Russia*	42	B6
Yuzhno-Sakhalinsk, *Russia*	45	E15
Yvelines □, *France*	25	D8
Yverdon, *Switz.*	22	C3
Yvetot, *France*	24	C7
Yvonand, *Switz.*	22	C3

Zaamslag

Z

Name	Region	Page	Grid
Zaamslag, *Neths.*		17	F3
Zaan →, *Neths.*		16	D5
Zaandam, *Neths.*		16	D5
Zab, Monts du, *Algeria*		75	B6
Žabalj, *Serbia, Yug.*		21	K10
Žabari, *Serbia, Yug.*		21	L11
Zabarjad, *Egypt*		76	C4
Zabaykalsk, *Russia*		45	E12
Ząbkowice Śląskie, *Poland*		20	E6
Zabłudów, *Poland*		20	B13
Zābol, *Iran*		65	D9
Zābolī, *Iran*		65	E9
Zabré, *Burkina Faso*		79	C4
Zabrze, *Poland*		20	E8
Zacapa, *Guatemala*		116	D2
Zacapu, *Mexico*		114	D4
Zacatecas, *Mexico*		114	C4
Zacatecas □, *Mexico*		114	C4
Zacatecoluca, *El Salv.*		116	D2
Zacoalco, *Mexico*		114	C4
Zacualtipán, *Mexico*		115	C5
Zadar, *Croatia*		33	D12
Zadawa, *Nigeria*		79	C7
Zadetkyi Kyun, *Burma*		59	H2
Zadonsk, *Russia*		42	D4
Zafarqand, *Iran*		65	C7
Zafra, *Spain*		31	G4
Żagań, *Poland*		20	D5
Zagazig, *Egypt*		76	H7
Zāgheh, *Iran*		65	C6
Zaghouan, *Tunisia*		75	A7
Zaglou, *Algeria*		75	C4
Zagnanado, *Benin*		79	D5
Zagorá, *Greece*		39	K6
Zagora, *Morocco*		74	B3
Zagorsk = Sergiyev Posad, *Russia*		42	B4
Zagreb, *Croatia*		33	C12
Zāgros, Kūhhā-ye, *Iran*		65	C6
Zagros Mts. = Zāgros, Kūhhā-ye, *Iran*		65	C6
Zaguinaso, *Ivory C.*		78	C3
Zāhedān, *Fārs, Iran*		65	D7
Zāhedān, *Sīstān va Balūchestān, Iran*		65	D9
Zahlah, *Lebanon*		69	B4
Zahna, *Germany*		18	D8
Zahrez Chergui, *Algeria*		75	A5
Zahrez Rharbi, *Algeria*		75	B5
Zainsk, *Russia*		42	C11
Zaïre ■, *Africa*		80	E4
Zaïre →, *Africa*		80	F2
Zaječar, *Serbia, Yug.*		21	M12
Zakamensk, *Russia*		45	D11
Zakataly = Zaqatala, *Azerbaijan*		43	K8
Zakhodnaya Dzvina = Daugava →, *Latvia*		9	H21
Zākhū, *Iraq*		67	D10
Zákinthos, *Greece*		39	M3
Zakopane, *Poland*		20	F9
Zákros, *Greece*		37	D8
Zala □, *Hungary*		21	J7
Zalaegerszeg, *Hungary*		21	J6
Zalalövö, *Hungary*		21	J6
Zalamea de la Serena, *Spain*		31	G5
Zalamea la Real, *Spain*		31	H4
Žalec, *Slovenia*		33	B12
Zaleshchiki = Zalishchyky, *Ukraine*		41	H3
Zalingei, *Sudan*		73	F9
Zalishchyky, *Ukraine*		41	H3
Zaltbommel, *Neths.*		16	E6
Zambeke, *Zaïre*		82	B2
Zambeze →, *Africa*		83	F4
Zambezi = Zambeze →, *Africa*		83	F4
Zambezi, *Zambia*		81	G4
Zambezia □, *Mozam.*		83	F4
Zambia ■, *Africa*		83	E2
Zamboanga, *Phil.*		55	H5
Zamboanguita, *Phil.*		55	G5
Zambrano, *Colombia*		120	B3
Zambrów, *Poland*		20	C12
Zametchino, *Russia*		42	D6
Zamora, *Ecuador*		120	D2
Zamora, *Mexico*		114	C4
Zamora, *Spain*		30	D5
Zamora □, *Spain*		30	D5
Zamora-Chinchipe □, *Ecuador*		120	D2
Zamość, *Poland*		20	E13
Zamuro, Sierra del, *Venezuela*		121	C5
Zan, *Ghana*		79	D4
Zanaga, *Congo*		80	E2
Záncara →, *Spain*		29	F1
Zandijk, *Neths.*		16	D5
Zandvoort, *Neths.*		16	D5
Zanesville, *U.S.A.*		106	C4
Zangābād, *Iran*		64	B5
Zangue →, *Mozam.*		83	F4
Zanjān, *Iran*		67	D13
Zanjān □, *Iran*		65	B6
Zannone, *Italy*		34	A6
Zante = Zákinthos, *Greece*		39	M3
Zanthus, *Australia*		89	F3
Zanzibar, *Tanzania*		82	D4
Zanzūr, *Libya*		75	B7
Zaouiet El-Kala = Bordj Omar Driss, *Algeria*		75	C6
Zaouiet Reggane, *Algeria*		75	C5
Zaoyang, *China*		53	A9
Zaozhuang, *China*		51	G9
Zap Suyu = Kabīr, Zab al →, *Iraq*		67	D10
Zapadna Morava →, *Serbia, Yug.*		21	M11
Zapadnaya Dvina, *Russia*		40	D7
Zapadnaya Dvina = Daugava →, *Latvia*		9	H21
Západné Beskydy, *Europe*		20	F9
Zapala, *Argentina*		128	A2
Zapaleri, Cerro, *Bolivia*		126	A2
Zapata, *U.S.A.*		109	M5
Zapatón →, *Spain*		31	G4
Zapiga, *Chile*		124	D4
Zaporizhzhya, *Ukraine*		41	J8
Zaporozhye = Žaporizhzhya, *Ukraine*		41	J8
Zapponeta, *Italy*		35	A8
Zaqatala, *Azerbaijan*		43	K8
Zara, *Turkey*		66	C7
Zaragoza, *Colombia*		120	B3
Zaragoza, *Coahuila, Mexico*		114	B4
Zaragoza, *Nuevo León, Mexico*		115	C5
Zaragoza, *Spain*		28	D4
Zaragoza □, *Spain*		28	D4
Zarand, *Kermān, Iran*		65	D8
Zarand, *Markazī, Iran*		65	C6
Zărandului, Munţii, *Romania*		38	C5
Zaranj, *Afghan.*		60	D2
Zarasai, *Lithuania*		9	J22
Zarate, *Argentina*		126	C4
Zaraysk, *Russia*		42	C4
Zaraza, *Venezuela*		121	B4
Zāreh, *Iran*		65	C6
Zarembo I., *U.S.A.*		100	B2
Zaria, *Nigeria*		79	C6
Zarneh, *Iran*		64	C5
Zarós, *Greece*		37	D6
Zarqā', *Jordan*		69	C4
Zarrīn, *Iran*		65	C7
Zaruma, *Ecuador*		120	D2
Zary, *Poland*		20	D5
Zarza de Alange, *Spain*		31	G4
Zarza de Granadilla, *Spain*		30	E4
Zarzaïtine, *Algeria*		75	C6
Zarzal, *Colombia*		120	C2
Zarzis, *Tunisia*		75	B7
Zas, *Spain*		30	B2
Zashiversk, *Russia*		45	C15
Zaskar →, *India*		63	B7
Zaskar Mts., *India*		63	C7
Zastron, *S. Africa*		84	E4
Zaterechnyy, *Russia*		43	H7
Zavāreh, *Iran*		65	C7
Zaventem, *Belgium*		17	G4
Zavetnoye, *Russia*		43	G6
Zavidovići, *Bos.-H.*		21	L8
Zavitinsk, *Russia*		45	D13
Zavodovski, I., *Antarctica*		5	B1
Zavolzhsk, *Russia*		42	B6
Zavolzhye, *Russia*		42	B6
Zawiercie, *Poland*		20	E9
Zawyet Shammâs, *Egypt*		76	A2
Zâwyet Um el Rakham, *Egypt*		76	A2
Zâwyet Ungeîla, *Egypt*		76	A2
Zāyā, *Iraq*		64	C5
Zayarsk, *Russia*		45	D11
Zaysan, *Kazakhstan*		44	E9
Zaysan, Oz., *Kazakhstan*		44	E9
Zayü, *China*		52	C1
Zazir, O. →, *Algeria*		75	D6
Zbarazh, *Ukraine*		41	H3
Zbąszyń, *Poland*		20	C5
Zblewo, *Poland*		20	B8
Zdolbuniv, *Ukraine*		41	G4
Ždrelo, *Serbia, Yug.*		21	L11
Zduńska Wola, *Poland*		20	D8
Zeballos, *Canada*		100	D3
Zebediela, *S. Africa*		85	C4
Zedelgem, *Belgium*		17	F2
Zeebrugge, *Belgium*		17	F2
Zeehan, *Australia*		90	G4
Zeeland, *Neths.*		17	E7
Zeeland □, *Neths.*		17	F3
Zeelst, *Neths.*		17	F6
Zeerust, *S. Africa*		84	D4
Zefat, *Israel*		69	C4
Zegdou, *Algeria*		75	C4
Zege, *Ethiopia*		77	E4
Zegelsem, *Belgium*		17	G3
Zégoua, *Mali*		78	C3
Zehdenick, *Germany*		18	C9
Zeil, Mt., *Australia*		88	D5
Zeila, *Somali Rep.*		68	E3
Zeist, *Neths.*		16	D6
Zeitz, *Germany*		18	D8
Zele, *Belgium*		17	F4
Zelenodolsk, *Russia*		42	C9
Zelenogorsk, *Russia*		40	B5
Zelenograd, *Russia*		42	B3
Zelenogradsk, *Russia*		9	J19
Zelenokumsk, *Russia*		43	H6
Zelhem, *Neths.*		16	D8
Zell, *Baden-W., Germany*		19	H3
Zell, *Rhld-Pfz., Germany*		19	E3
Zell am See, *Austria*		21	H2
Zella-Mehlis, *Germany*		18	E6
Zelzate, *Belgium*		17	F3
Zembra, I., *Tunisia*		75	A7
Zémio, *C.A.R.*		82	A2
Zemmora, *Algeria*		75	A5
Zemmur, *W. Sahara*		74	C2
Zemoul, O. →, *Algeria*		74	C3
Zemst, *Belgium*		17	G4
Zemun, *Serbia, Yug.*		21	L10
Zengbe, *Cameroon*		79	D7
Zengcheng, *China*		53	F9
Zenica, *Bos.-H.*		21	L7
Žepce, *Bos.-H.*		21	L8
Zerbst, *Germany*		18	D8
Zeraf, Bahr ez →, *Sudan*		77	F3
Zermatt, *Switz.*		22	D5
Zernez, *Switz.*		23	C10
Zernograd, *Russia*		43	G5
Zerqani, *Albania*		39	H3
Zestaponi, *Georgia*		43	J6
Zetel, *Germany*		18	B3
Zetten, *Neths.*		16	E7
Zeulenroda, *Germany*		18	E7
Zeven, *Germany*		18	B5
Zevenaar, *Neths.*		16	E8
Zevenbergen, *Neths.*		17	E5
Zévio, *Italy*		32	C8
Zeya, *Russia*		45	D13
Zeya →, *Russia*		45	D13
Zêzere →, *Portugal*		31	F2
Zghartā, *Lebanon*		69	A4
Zgierz, *Poland*		20	D9
Zgorzelec, *Poland*		20	D5
Zhabinka, *Belarus*		41	F3
Zhailma, *Kazakhstan*		44	D7
Zhambyl, *Kazakhstan*		44	E8
Zhangaly, *Kazakhstan*		43	G10
Zhangaqazaly, *Kazakhstan*		44	E7
Zhangbei, *China*		50	D8
Zhangguangcai Ling, *China*		51	B15
Zhanghua, *Taiwan*		53	E13
Zhangjiakou, *China*		50	D8
Zhangping, *China*		53	E11
Zhangpu, *China*		53	E11
Zhangwu, *China*		51	C12
Zhangye, *China*		54	C5
Zhangzhou, *China*		53	E11
Zhanhua, *China*		51	F10
Zhanjiang, *China*		53	G8
Zhanyi, *China*		52	E4
Zhanyu, *China*		51	B12
Zhao Xian, *China*		50	F8
Zhao'an, *China*		53	F11
Zhaocheng, *China*		50	F6
Zhaojue, *China*		52	C4
Zhaoping, *China*		53	E8
Zhaoqing, *China*		53	F9
Zhaotong, *China*		52	D4
Zhaoyuan, *Heilongjiang, China*		51	B13
Zhaoyuan, *Shandong, China*		51	F11
Zharkovskiy, *Russia*		40	E7
Zhashkiv, *Ukraine*		41	H6
Zhashui, *China*		50	H5
Zhayyq →, *Kazakhstan*		44	E6
Zhdanov = Mariupol, *Ukraine*		41	J9
Zhecheng, *China*		50	G8
Zhegao, *China*		53	B11
Zhejiang □, *China*		53	C13
Zheleznogorsk, *Russia*		42	D2
Zheleznogorsk-Ilimskiy, *Russia*		45	D11
Zheltyye Vody = Zhovti Vody, *Ukraine*		41	H7
Zhen'an, *China*		50	H5
Zhenfeng, *China*		52	E5
Zheng'an, *China*		52	C6
Zhengding, *China*		50	E8
Zhenghe, *China*		53	D12
Zhengyang, *China*		53	A10
Zhengyangguan, *China*		53	A11
Zhengzhou, *China*		50	G7
Zhenhai, *China*		53	C13
Zhenjiang, *China*		53	A12
Zhenlai, *China*		51	B12
Zhenning, *China*		52	D5
Zhenping, *Henan, China*		50	H7
Zhenping, *Shaanxi, China*		52	B7
Zhenxiong, *China*		52	D5
Zhenyuan, *Gansu, China*		50	G4
Zhenyuan, *Guizhou, China*		52	D7
Zherdevka, *Russia*		42	E5
Zherong, *China*		53	D12
Zhetiqara, *Kazakhstan*		44	D7
Zhezqazghan, *Kazakhstan*		44	E7
Zhidan, *China*		50	F5
Zhigansk, *Russia*		45	C13
Zhigulevsk, *Russia*		42	D9
Zhijiang, *Hubei, China*		53	B8
Zhijiang, *Hunan, China*		52	D7
Zhijin, *China*		52	D5
Zhilinda, *Russia*		45	C12
Zhirnovsk, *Russia*		42	E7
Zhitomir = Zhytomyr, *Ukraine*		41	G5
Zhizdra, *Russia*		42	D3
Zhlobin, *Belarus*		41	F6
Zhmerinka = Zhmerynka, *Ukraine*		41	H5
Zhmerynka, *Ukraine*		41	H5
Zhodino = Zhodzina, *Belarus*		40	E5
Zhodzina, *Belarus*		40	E5
Zhokhova, Ostrov, *Russia*		45	B16
Zhong Xian, *China*		52	B7
Zhongdian, *China*		52	D2
Zhongdong, *China*		52	F6
Zhongdu, *China*		52	E7
Zhongning, *China*		50	F3
Zhongshan, *Guangdong, China*		53	F9
Zhongshan, *Guangxi Zhuangzu, China*		53	E8
Zhongtiao Shan, *China*		50	G6
Zhongwei, *China*		50	F3
Zhongxiang, *China*		53	B9
Zhongyang, *China*		50	F6
Zhoucun, *China*		51	F9
Zhouning, *China*		53	D12
Zhoushan Dao, *China*		53	C14
Zhouzhi, *China*		50	G5
Zhovti Vody, *Ukraine*		41	H7
Zhovtneve, *Ukraine*		41	J7
Zhovtnevoye = Zhovtneve, *Ukraine*		41	J7
Zhuanghe, *China*		51	E12
Zhucheng, *China*		51	G10
Zhugqu, *China*		50	H3
Zhuhai, *China*		53	F9
Zhuji, *China*		53	C13
Zhukovka, *Russia*		42	D1
Zhumadian, *China*		50	H8
Zhuo Xian, *China*		50	E8
Zhuolu, *China*		50	D8
Zhuozi, *China*		50	D7
Zhupanovo, *Russia*		45	D16
Zhushan, *China*		53	A8
Zhuxi, *China*		52	A7
Zhuzhou, *China*		53	D9
Zhytomyr, *Ukraine*		41	G5
Zi Shui →, *China*		53	C9
Zīārān, *Iran*		65	B6
Ziarat, *Pakistan*		62	D2
Zibo, *China*		51	F10
Zichang, *China*		50	F5
Zichem, *Belgium*		17	F5
Zielona Góra, *Poland*		20	D5
Zierikzee, *Neths.*		17	E3
Ziesar, *Germany*		18	C8
Zifta, *Egypt*		76	H7
Zigey, *Chad*		73	F8
Zigong, *China*		52	C5
Zigui, *China*		53	B8
Ziguinchor, *Senegal*		78	C1
Zihuatanejo, *Mexico*		114	D4
Zijin, *China*		53	F10
Zile, *Turkey*		66	B6
Žilina, *Slovak Rep.*		20	F8
Zillah, *Libya*		73	C8
Zillertaler Alpen, *Austria*		19	H7
Zima, *Russia*		45	D11
Zimane, Adrar in, *Algeria*		75	D5
Zimapán, *Mexico*		115	C5
Zimba, *Zambia*		83	F2
Zimbabwe, *Zimbabwe*		83	G3
Zimbabwe ■, *Africa*		83	F2
Zimovniki, *Russia*		43	G6
Zinal, *Switz.*		22	D5
Zinder, *Niger*		79	C6
Zinga, *Tanzania*		83	D4
Zingem, *Belgium*		17	G3
Zingst, *Germany*		18	A8
Ziniaré, *Burkina Faso*		79	C4
Zinkgruvan, *Sweden*		11	F9
Zinnowitz, *Germany*		18	A9
Zion National Park, *U.S.A.*		111	H7
Zipaquirá, *Colombia*		120	C3
Zirc, *Hungary*		21	H7
Žiri, *Slovenia*		33	B11
Žirje, *Croatia*		33	E12
Zirl, *Austria*		19	H7
Ziros, *Greece*		37	D8
Zitácuaro, *Mexico*		114	D4
Zitava →, *Slovak Rep.*		21	G8
Zittau, *Germany*		18	E10
Zitundo, *Mozam.*		85	D5
Živinice, *Bos.-H.*		21	L8
Ziway, L., *Ethiopia*		77	F4
Zixi, *China*		53	D11
Zixing, *China*		53	E9
Ziyang, *Shaanxi, China*		50	H5
Ziyang, *Sichuan, China*		52	B5
Ziyun, *China*		52	E6
Ziz, Oued →, *Morocco*		74	B4
Zizhixian, *China*		53	E8
Zizhong, *China*		52	C5
Zlarin, *Croatia*		33	E12
Zlatar, *Croatia*		33	B13
Zlataritsa, *Bulgaria*		38	F8
Zlatitsa, *Bulgaria*		38	G7
Zlatograd, *Bulgaria*		39	H8
Zlatoust, *Russia*		44	D6
Zletovo, *Macedonia*		39	H5
Zlín, *Czech.*		20	F7
Zlītan, *Libya*		73	B7
Złocieniec, *Poland*		20	B6
Złoczew, *Poland*		20	D8
Złotoryja, *Poland*		20	D5
Złotów, *Poland*		20	B7
Zmeinogorsk, *Kazakhstan*		44	D9
Żmigród, *Poland*		20	D6
Zmiyev, *Ukraine*		41	H9
Znamenka = Znamyanka, *Ukraine*		41	H7
Znamyanka, *Ukraine*		41	H7
Żnin, *Poland*		20	C7
Znojmo, *Czech.*		20	G6
Zobeyrī, *Iran*		64	C5
Zobia, *Zaïre*		82	B2
Zoetermeer, *Neths.*		16	D5
Zofingen, *Switz.*		22	B5
Zogang, *China*		52	C1
Zogno, *Italy*		32	C6
Zogqên, *China*		52	A2
Zolder, *Belgium*		17	F6
Zollikofen, *Switz.*		22	C4
Zollikon, *Switz.*		23	B7
Zolochiv = Zolochiv, *Ukraine*		41	H3
Zolochiv, *Ukraine*		41	H3
Zolotonosha, *Ukraine*		41	H7
Zomba, *Malawi*		83	F4
Zomergem, *Belgium*		17	F3
Zongo, *Zaïre*		80	D3
Zonguldak, *Turkey*		66	B4
Zonhoven, *Belgium*		17	G6
Zonqor Pt., *Malta*		37	D2
Zonza, *France*		27	G13
Zorgo, *Burkina Faso*		79	C4
Zorita, *Spain*		31	F5
Zorritos, *Peru*		124	A1
Zorzor, *Liberia*		78	D3
Zossen, *Germany*		18	C9
Zottegem, *Belgium*		17	G3
Zou Xiang, *China*		50	G9
Zouar, *Chad*		73	D8
Zouérate, *Mauritania*		74	D2
Zousfana, O. →, *Algeria*		75	B4
Zoushan Dao, *China*		53	B14
Zoutkamp, *Neths.*		16	B9
Zrenjanin, *Serbia, Yug.*		21	K10
Zuarungu, *Ghana*		79	C4
Zuba, *Nigeria*		79	D6
Zubayr, *Yemen*		77	D5
Zubia, *Spain*		31	H7
Zubtsov, *Russia*		42	B2
Zudáñez, *Bolivia*		125	D5
Zuénoula, *Ivory C.*		78	D3
Zuera, *Spain*		28	D4
Zuetina = Az Zuwaytīnah, *Libya*		73	B9
Zufar, *Oman*		68	D5
Zug, *Switz.*		23	B7
Zug □, *Switz.*		23	B7
Zugdidi, *Georgia*		43	J5
Zugersee, *Switz.*		23	B7
Zugspitze, *Germany*		19	H6
Zuid-Holland □, *Neths.*		16	E5
Zuidbeveland, *Neths.*		17	F3
Zuidbroek, *Neths.*		16	B9
Zuidelijk-Flevoland, *Neths.*		16	D6
Zuidhorn, *Neths.*		16	B9
Zuidlaarder meer, *Neths.*		16	B9
Zuidlaren, *Neths.*		16	B9
Zuidwolde, *Neths.*		16	C8
Zújar, *Spain*		29	H2
Zújar →, *Spain*		31	G5
Zújar, Pantano del, *Spain*		31	G5
Zula, *Eritrea*		77	D4
Zulia □, *Venezuela*		120	B3
Zülpich, *Germany*		18	E2
Zumaia, *Spain*		28	B2
Zumbo, *Mozam.*		83	F3
Zummo, *Nigeria*		79	D7
Zumpango, *Mexico*		115	D5
Zundert, *Neths.*		17	F5
Zungeru, *Nigeria*		79	D6
Zunhua, *China*		51	D9
Zuni, *U.S.A.*		111	J9
Zunyi, *China*		52	D6
Zuoquan, *China*		50	F7
Zuozhou, *China*		52	F6
Županja, *Croatia*		21	K8
Zurbātīyah, *Iraq*		67	F12
Zürich, *Switz.*		23	B7
Zürich □, *Switz.*		23	B7
Zürichsee, *Switz.*		23	B7
Zuromin, *Poland*		20	B9
Zuru, *Nigeria*		79	C6
Zurzach, *Switz.*		23	A6
Žut, *Croatia*		33	E12
Zutendaal, *Belgium*		17	G7
Zutphen, *Neths.*		16	D8
Zuwārah, *Libya*		75	B7
Zūzan, *Iran*		65	C8
Žužemberk, *Slovenia*		33	C11
Zvenigorodka = Zvenyhorodka, *Ukraine*		41	H6
Zvenyhorodka, *Ukraine*		41	H6
Zverinogolovskoye, *Russia*		44	D7
Zvezdets, *Bulgaria*		38	G10
Zvishavane, *Zimbabwe*		83	G3
Zvolen, *Slovak Rep.*		20	G9
Zvonce, *Serbia, Yug.*		21	N12
Zvornik, *Bos.-H.*		21	L8
Zwaag, *Neths.*		16	C6
Zwanenburg, *Neths.*		16	D5
Zwarte Meer, *Neths.*		16	C7
Zwarte Waler, *Neths.*		16	C8
Zwartemeer, *Neths.*		16	C10
Zwartsluis, *Neths.*		16	C8
Zwedru = Tchien, *Liberia*		78	D3
Zweibrücken, *Germany*		19	F3
Zwenkau, *Germany*		18	D8
Zwevegem, *Belgium*		17	G2
Zwickau, *Germany*		18	E8
Zwiesel, *Germany*		19	F9
Zwijndrecht, *Belgium*		17	F3
Zwijndrecht, *Neths.*		16	E5
Zwischenahn, *Germany*		18	B4
Zwolle, *Neths.*		16	C8
Zwolle, *U.S.A.*		109	K8
Zymoetz →, *Canada*		100	C3
Zyrardów, *Poland*		20	C10
Zyryan, *Kazakhstan*		44	E9
Zyryanka, *Russia*		45	C16
Zyryanovsk = Zyryan, *Kazakhstan*		44	E9
Zyyi, *Cyprus*		37	E12